THE OFFICIAL® PRICE GUIDE TO ANTIQUE AND MODERN FIREARMS

THE OFFICIAL® PRICE GUIDE TO
ANTIQUE AND MODERN FIREARMS

EDITED BY
ROBERT H. BALDERSON

SEVENTH EDITION
House of Collectibles • New York

Important Notice. All of the information, including valuations, in this book has been compiled from the most reliable sources, and every effort has been made to eliminate errors and questionable data. Nevertheless, the possibility of error, in a work of such immense scope, always exists. The publisher will not be held responsible for losses that may occur in the purchase, sale, or other transaction of items because of information contained herein. Readers who feel they have discovered errors are invited to *write* and inform us, so they may be corrected in subsequent editions. Those seeking further information on the topics covered in this book are advised to refer to the complete line of *Official Price Guides* published by the House of Collectibles.

Copyright © 1994 by Random House, Inc.

All rights reserved under International and Pan-American Copyright Conventions.

HC This is a registered trademark of Random House, Inc.

Published by: House of Collectibles
201 East 50th Street
New York, NY 10022

Distributed by Ballantine Books, a division of Random House, Inc., New York, and simultaneously in Canada by Random House of Canada Limited, Toronto.

Manufactured in the United States of America

ISSN: 0743-9776

ISBN: 0-876-37908-0

Text design by Holly Johnson

Cover design by Kristine Mills

On the cover: Winchester M101 Over-under Double-Barrel Field Shotgun; Colt Combat Commander 9mm; Kentucky Flintlock Pistol; Remington .32 Rimfire Over-under Derringer. Cover photo by George Kerrigan.

Seventh Edition: October 1994

10 9 8 7 6 5 4 3 2 1

CONTENTS

Contents

ACKNOWLEDGMENTS

The prices listed in this guide were gathered from dealers, collectors, auctions, and ads in collectors' publications. They were then computer sorted and double-checkered to ensure maximum reliability.

Michael Forte
Larry Carpenter
Mitchell Luksich
Mike Clark
Victor Juskauskus
Peter Hischier
Bob Burton
Del Denny
Nick Todd
Stan Lukowicz
Jerry Johnson
Sterling Fligge
Kurt Jones
James L. Hanschu, Esq.
Vic Estacio
George Giumarra
Sherry Rich of Browning
Bill Mrock & Chuck Lanham of the
   B.A.T.F.
Tim Pancurak of Thompson-Center
Nadine Ljutic of Ljutic Industries
Jim Casillo and Fred Paddock of Navy
   Arms
Vicky Barton of Universal
Fred Karp of Sears, Roebuck & Co.
Brian Herrick of Hi Standard
Charley Gara of Charter Arms
Nolen Jackson of Wichita
   Engineering & Supply
Sharon Cunningham of Dixie Gun
   Works
Pat Bogush of Colt
Chris Graziano of Ruger
Judy Schroepfer of Kreighoff
Jinny Sundius of Marlin
Bob Greenleaf of Savage
Fred Hill of Dan Wesson

Bob Magee of Interarms
Ron Vogel of F.I.E.
Allen Fire Arms Co.
Boyd Davis of E.M.F.
V. Fresi & A. Seidel of Mauser-Werke
C. Ledoux of ManuFrance
Jennings Firearms
Beeman, Inc.
Rick Kenny of Stoeger Industries
J.P. Sauer & Sohn GmbH
John Hanson of Magnum Research,
   Inc.
Dynamit Nobel of America
Peter Hoffman of Carl Walther GmbH
Bob Saunders of American Derringer
   Corp.
Astra-Unceta y Cia.
Vincenzo Bernardelli
Dan Coonan of Coonan Arms, Inc.
Charles Meyers and Gary Rathman of
   the Florida Regional Crime Lab
Linda Lassotta of Heckler & Koch
Dot Ferreira of Remington
Jan Herriott of Detonics
Tol Cherry of Cherry's
Nancy Damone of Mossberg
Deanna McDermott of U.S. Repeating
   Arms
Frederich Hege of Hege Waffen
Bruce Hacker of Ventura Imports
Debbie Dean of Weatherby's
I.W. Walentiny of Tradewinds
Marian Partridge of Ithaca
Sy Wiley of Randall Firearms
John Hill of Webley & Scott
Tom Barness of Manurhin
John Leek of Sterling Arms Corp.

Ilan Shalev of I.M.I.
Marc Bauer of Action Arms Ltd.
Ira Trast of Auto Ordnance
George Numrich of Numrich Arms
Sig Himmelmann of United Sporting
  Arms
Bill Clede & June Sears of Smith &
  Wesson

Iver Johnson
Raven Arms
R.G. Industries
Guy Lepeintre
Peter Potter
Col. Mel Pfankuche
Bill Drollinger

MARKET REVIEW

The major development in the firearms market since publication of our last edition was U.S. relaxation of import restrictions. This occurred in October 1984. Some noticeable changes in values have taken place. The greater ease with which firearms can now be imported into the U.S. will create, in the coming months, abundant supplies of guns that were previously difficult to get in this country. Military models from Germany, Italy, South America, and elsewhere are now being imported in large numbers, with a corresponding decline in market value. It is believed the military models will continue to comprise the largest category of imports, at least for the next several years. This could mean an eventual decline in price to a virtual fraction of the pre-October 1984 levels.

The rewritten laws apply exclusively to arms manufactured at least twenty-five years ago. Hence the value of currently or recently produced foreign guns are not likely to change. The laws were designed to cover secondhand and obsolete models that are not in direct competition against guns made by U.S. companies. In a sense it could be termed a "collector law(s)," but collectors are far from universally enthusiastic about it. The beginning gun collector will certainly appreciate the lower prices, as will veteran hobbyists who want to add specific foreign models to their collections. However, the collectors who already own foreign guns for which they paid pre-October 1984 prices are now in a position of watching their investments decline. Nor can this be regarded as a temporary decline, such as occurs during times of economic slumps. It is likely to be permanent, as the quantities of guns imported into the country are not apt to be exported. They will always be with us, and for all practical purposes one must assume that the old price levels will not return.

At this point it is too early to say how low the prices will go. In the final analysis some models, and possibly all the models of some manufacturers, may be hit much harder than others. This all depends on the stockpiles that exist in foreign countries and the eagerness of foreign dealers to export them. At first, of course, the situation greatly favored foreign exporters. They could ship their guns to this country and receive a much higher price for them than at home. With prices then declining in the U.S., the margin of profit became smaller. If prices dip really low, it is probable that many foreign dealers will have nothing to gain by exportation, and a stabilization will be brought about.

Various intangibles are involved which make predictions impossible. For one thing, the reduced prices on so many foreign arms may encourage their purchase by persons who would not otherwise have bought them. If the number of buyers increases, this in itself could provide some measure of price stabilization. For another, the very strong hobbyist interest in certain foreign military guns, such as those of Nazi Germany, could be sufficient to prevent a drastic price decline. There are undoubtedly many collectors who will rush to buy Nazi guns at a 20% or 25% savings. Then again, the foreign dealers have a healthy market for guns of that type in their homeland, and may not export them in wholesale numbers.

The basically common guns of World Wars I and II are likely to suffer the greatest value declines. Guns classified as antiques should not be hurt in the least, but many of the "curio" graded guns will be. Collectors should keep in mind that the model year for a gun is not necessarily the year of manufacture. During World War I, a number of foreign countries were using rifles with model years in the 1880s and 1890s, even though the war was fought from 1914 to 1918. They were not using "old" guns but guns that had remained in production for several decades. This was also true, though to a lesser degree, in World War II.

Elsewhere in the firearms market, commemoratives had a generally off year, most of them slipping in value from 5% to around 15%. Non-commemorative limited editions did considerably better on the whole, either holding steady or even gaining. This development seems to vindicate those who had long warned of a saturation of commemorative guns on the market. Commemoratives have been issued in increasing numbers since the mid 1970s, sparked by the success of the many Bicentennial models. With the secondary market on commemoratives going soft, a decrease in the number issued may follow. This could, however, be merely a temporary situation. Even with their value declines, it should be noted, most commemoratives did no worse than return to their late 1982/early 1983 value levels. They simply lost the increases gained thereafter. Most commemoratives are still selling for more than their original factory prices.

FACTORS THAT DETERMINE VALUE

CONDITION

With the passage of time everything deteriorates and guns are no exception. Use, abuse, wear, and aging all adversely affect the price of guns to a varying degree, and in the case of collectible guns the difference in price can be very significant. Because of the importance of describing the condition of a gun, the N.R.A. devised a set of guidelines to standardize firearms grading. The prices listed in this guide are for guns in N.R.A. Very Good and N.R.A. Excellent condition *(Antiques are N.R.A. Antique Very Good to Antique Fine)*, and you can easily adjust those prices to determine the value of your gun if it does not fall into either of those categories. But strict grading of condition following N.R.A. guidelines is essential.

Antique firearms in excellent to new condition add 25% to 100% to the "excellent" price depending on scarcity and demand. For antiques in good condition, deduct 30% to 35% from "very good."

Modern firearms in good condition deduct 20% to 25% from "very good"; fair condition, deduct 45% to 55%. Arms in "perfect" to "new" add 30% to 75% depending on collectibility.

Any collectible firearm, no matter how poor the condition (so long as it hasn't been crushed or melted), should fetch 20% to 30% of the "very good" price. As the saying goes, "old guns never die, they just get reblued."

N.R.A. CONDITION GUIDELINES

NEW: not previously sold at retail, in same condition as current factory production.
NEW-DISCONTINUED: Same as New, but discontinued model.

The following definitions will apply to all secondhand articles:
PERFECT: In new condition in every respect.
EXCELLENT: New condition, used but little, no noticeable marring of wood or metal, bluing perfect (except at muzzle or sharp edges).
VERY GOOD: In perfect working condition, no appreciable wear on working surfaces, no corrosion or pitting, only minor surface dents or scratches.
GOOD: In safe working condition, minor wear on working surfaces, no broken parts, no corrosion or pitting that will interfere with proper functioning.
FAIR: In safe working condition, but well worn, perhaps requiring replacement of minor parts or adjustments, which should be indicated in advertisement, no rust, but may have corrosion pits which do not render article unsafe or inoperable.

Another set of standards applies to "antique" arms as follows:

FACTORY NEW: 100% original finish and parts, everything perfect.

EXCELLENT: All parts and 80%–100% finish original; all letters, numerals, designs sharp; unmarred wood, fine bore.

FINE: All parts and over 30% finish original; all letters, numerals, designs sharp; only minor wood marks, good bore.

VERY GOOD: Up to 30% original finish, all original parts; metal surfaces smooth, with all edges sharp; clear letters, numerals, designs, wood slightly scratched or bruised; bore on collector items disregarded.

GOOD: Only minor replacement parts; metal smoothly rusted or lightly pitted in places; cleaned or reblued; principal letters, numerals, designs legible; wood refinished, scratched, bruised, or with minor cracks repaired; mechanism in good working order.

FAIR: Some major parts replaced; minor replacements; metal may be lightly pitted all over, vigorously cleaned or reblued, edges partly rounded; wood scratched, bruised, cracked or repaired; mechanism in working order.

ORNAMENTATION

Engraving

It's hard to generalize about art, and that is what engraving is. You must examine a number of examples to learn to judge the quality of the work.

Crude engraving: sparse, add about 25%; medium coverage, add 50% to 75%; full coverage add 100% to 125%.

High quality engraving: sparse, add 50% to 100%; medium coverage, add 150% to 200%; full coverage, add 300% up.

Ornate, high quality work with gold inlays, etc., add 400% up.

Wood carving and marquetry (stock inlays)

This is also in the realm of art, and you should try to look at as many specimens as possible to compare craftsmanship.

Carvings: simple, add $10 to $40 each depending on the quality of execution; complex, add $60 to $150. Full coverage, good quality, add $125 up. Remember that a poor carving (such as crude initials) will detract from the value.

Inlays: simple, add $10 to $25 each; ornate, add $50 up. Exotic materials, such as ivory or mother-of-pearl, can double the value of the inlay. The value of wire inlays depends as much on the coverage as the execution. Simple wire inlays using brass or German silver should start at $40 each, tripling if silver is used, and multiplying by 10 if gold is used. Initial shields that are unmarked and not standard equipment on the gun add $15; $25 for sterling silver; $100 for 14k gold.

Heat carving, stampings, and woodburnings are becoming increasingly common and should not be confused with real carving. These should add about $25 if done well.

Note: N.R.A. Grading Standards reprinted with the permission of the N.R.A.

Custom checkering

As with carving, craftsmanship is paramount. A poorly done checkering job will lower the value of a gun. Nicely executed patterns on a long gun, add $35 to $50. Fine, complex patterns with wide coverage, add $60 up.

Gold damascening:

This is the art of applying gold leaf or gold plate in a fancy pattern, usually in conjunction with engraving, and should not be confused with gold inlay. Simple patterns, add $60 to $85; fancy patterns, add $265 to $395.

LOCATION OF SALE

As this guide lists average national prices, several regional factors must be considered.

Antiques: If a particular arm was made in your area, or saw wide service there, there should be more interest in it. This increased market demand will run prices 10% to 15% higher than listed. The reverse is also true.

Modern: Much depends on the type of area you live in. In wide-open places where long-range shooting is possible, high-powered rifles may bring 10% over value listed, whereas shotguns will be 15% less. In wooded areas the reverse will occur. In high crime areas, handguns for home protection will bring premiums. Trap and skeet generally stay constant. Wherever you are, judge the type of hobby shooting most prevalent, and the types of guns used for it will follow the above pattern.

SPECIAL MARKINGS AND COMMEMORATIVES

Standard firearms of most all companies have at some time been ordered or issued with special markings, special features, or as commemoratives. The important consideration in this section is that all deviations from the norm be factory original.

Special markings

Governments, law enforcement agencies, and stores have ordered the factory to put special marks on guns, and the main requirement in adding value to a gun with these marks is that the gun itself be collectible. The percentage additions shown reflect "common" variations. Rare marks on already very scarce guns may run five to ten times that percentage; however, caution is advisable since this particular market is limited and highly specialized, and as always with rare items, when you get out of your field it's best to consult an expert.

Police or agency markings in lieu of regular marks (not overstamps or extra stamps), add 25% to 50%; trademarks of stores in exotic locales (Zimbabwe, etc.), add 50% to 75%; foreign military marks, add 50% to 75%.

Mismarked guns: No stamps, upside-down stamps, wrong markings, etc., add 100% up depending on the collectibility of the gun itself.

Special features: This section applies to custom modifications done by the factory and not listed under a particular manufacturer elsewhere in this guide.

Special sights, add 10% to 15%; special metal finish (nickel, etc.), add 10% to 15%; extra-fancy wood on long guns, add 15% to 25%; special barrel lengths, add 20% to 30%.

Commemoratives

One very important question to ask yourself: Is this gun a standard mass-produced item with just an extra stamp or applied token, or is it actually from a limited production and different from standard in style and embellishment? If your gun falls into the first category, appreciation will be quite slow; if the latter, then the value will rise sharply for the first two or three years, thereafter leveling off to a little better than the inflation rate.

HISTORIC RELICS

Documentation is the key word in connecting an old gun with a historic event or famous person. Saying "it used to belong to grandpa and he was so and so" just isn't enough. To be absolutely certain of a weapon's ownership or use, records contemporary with its use must be available. They can be factory records showing the gun's disposition, wills, diaries, etc. Lacking that, if there is strong evidence of ownership such as a name engraved and some documentation showing that the person could have owned it, then it should be labeled "probably." "Grandpa" testimony without supporting evidence can be labeled "possibly." The value of a historic relic transcends the worth of the gun, and depends on the fame (or infamy) of the owner, the artistic value, the location of the sale, and the intangible "mood" of the public as to what period of history is "in."

LEGAL CLASSIFICATIONS OF FIREARMS

There are four classifications of firearms used by the Bureau of Alcohol, Tobacco, and Firearms of the Treasury Department.

Antique: Any firearm manufactured in or before 1898, and replicas that do not fire rim-fire or center-fire cartridges readily available in commercial trade. Antiques are exempt from federal regulation.

Modern: Firearms manufactured after 1898, excluding Replica Antiques, and with special regulations for Class III arms.

Curios and Relics: Certain modern firearms that can be sent interstate to licensed collectors.

Class III Arms: This includes machine guns, silencers, short (under 18") shotguns, short (under 16") rifles, modern smoothbore handguns, and modern arms with a rifled bore diameter greater than .50".

All of the above may be legally owned, notwithstanding federal regulations and local restrictions in a few areas. For further information, contact your local office of the Bureau of Alcohol, Tobacco, and Firearms.

A special note about legal classifications

Curios: This is a subdivision of "modern" and pertains to arms that may be sent interstate to licensed collectors. However, there is a great deal of confusion as to what constitutes a "curio." The B.A.T.F. issues a yearly list of arms so classified, which is constantly changing and, by virtue of time and space limitations, is incomplete.

Since this guide followed the curio list in force at the time of writing, far more arms are "curios" than are described as such.

The following is the federal guideline to use to determine if a specific firearm or cartridge is a "curio." It must:

1. have been manufactured at least 50 years prior to the current date, but not including replicas there of, or

2. be certified by the curator of a municipal, state, or federal museum that exhibits firearms to be curios or relics of museum interest; or

3. derive a substantial part of its monetary value from the fact that it is novel, rare, or bizarre, or from the fact of its association with some historical figure, period, or event.

Collectors wishing to obtain a curio or relic determination from ATF on a specific firearm or round of ammunition should submit a letter to the Chief of the Firearms Technology Branch, Bureau of Alcohol, Tobacco, and Firearms, Washington, D.C. 20226. The letter should include a complete physical description of the firearm or ammunition, stating the reasons that the collector believes that the firearm or ammunition in question merits such classification, and supporting data concerning the history of the firearm or ammunition, including production figures, if available, and market value.

Antiques: Many arms listed in this guide were produced between dates overlapping the "antique" determination date. In cases where experts have given a recognized serial number cutoff for "antiques" I have tried to include it. In other instances where arms have no numbers, or where no number is generally recognized as the magic one, I have classified them as modern and leave it to a specialist to make an individual determination.

How to Buy and Sell Firearms

BUYING COLLECTOR GUNS

Where to buy

Reliable estimates place the number of guns in private hands in the U.S. at over 100 million! Quite a lot, but if you've picked out the special items you wish to collect and started looking you've probably noticed that you can generally find everything but what you need. So where do you go to find them? There are several sources.

Mail Order. Even though the Gun Control Act of 1968 prohibited the mailing of firearms to individuals, the mail order gun business is alive and well. However, the method is a little different because of the laws and the nature of the business. According to U.S. law only federally licensed gun dealers may ship and receive modern firearms, but many dealers for a small fee will be happy to receive the gun you've ordered and transfer it to you. Another alternative for the collector is to apply for a collector's license from the Bureau of Alcohol, Tobacco and Firearms. This license allows the collector to receive and send interstate shipments of modern firearms that are classified as curios to another licensee. For more information about licenses contact your local office of the B.A.T.F.

Mail order done properly is legal and fairly simple and, most importantly, an excellent way to build your collection and to take advantage of prices that may be more competitive than in your local area. Most specialist mail order dealers are very reputable, and many offer an inspection period so that you may return the gun in the same condition as it arrived if you're not satisfied. Almost all of the dealers of collectible guns advertise, and many have regular lists of guns offered for sale that you can subscribe to for a nominal rate. Many gun magazines and collector newsletters have classified sections that provide good leads, but an excellent starting point would be Shotgun News (P.O. Box 669, Hastings, Nebr. 68901).

Gun Shows. There are a great many gun shows held in all parts of the U.S. with good frequency. They provide an opportunity to examine a large number of collectible guns at one place, and a chance to bargain with the owners for a better price. Gun show listings can be found in magazines such as *Gun Report* (P.O. Box 111, Aledo, Ill. 61231).

Gun Shops. Gun stores and pawn shops offer an exciting chance to find a collector's item at a good price because they may not have a market to sell some of the more interesting items. As a result they sometimes buy low and sell low in order to turn their inventory.

Private Individuals. This category includes non-gun shops as well as individuals, and this is the area where real caution must be exercised. Although bargains may be found, many times people have an inflated idea of the value of their gun, and very often the article for sale is misidentified. Remember, knowledge is power!

Pitfalls

Refinished Guns. A refinished gun can be beautiful. Unfortunately it also drastically reduces the value of a collector's item, so it's valuable to know how to spot refinishing. Most of the time when a gun is reblued or replated it must be heavily polished to remove small pits. A good craftsman will keep all of the edges sharp, will preserve the lettering, and will avoid "ripple" (waves polished into the gun in places where the metal should be flat). Poor craftsmen will remove lettering, round edges, and in general remove too much metal. The finish on a good job will be even and bright, on a poor job it will look splotchy and uneven. If you suspect that a gun has been refinished look for these signs: the lettering will have "drag-out marks" (one edge of the letter will be furrowed from polishing); the quality of finish doesn't match the original factory job; parts have been finished to a different color than original. Remember, most factories did an excellent job of finishing.

Upgrades. Upgrading is taking a normal gun that is in decent condition and engraving or otherwise embellishing it so that it is more valuable. In many cases a good upgrade comes within 60% to 70% of the value of the factory original if the job is well done. But beware of guns that people try to pass off as original. The best defense is education. If you're interested in high grade guns try to examine as many known originals as you can to get a feel for that factory's style and quality, or enlist the aid of an expert to help you.

Fakes. Counterfeits, it seems, have always been with us, and as with any item of value, low cost reproductions have been made and passed along as the real thing. There are all kinds of reproductions, from the crude kitchen table conversion with the uneven lettering stamps to the ultra-sophisticated copy made with some original parts. Fakes include complete reproductions of antique guns to $1/8$" police stamps on World War II German pistols. Once again knowledge is everything. Learn all you can before buying, and on valuable items buy from someone you can trust. Most dealers of collectable guns are extremely honest, and it's very rare to hear of a dealer intentionally trying to sell a fake.

Condition Descriptions. The N.R.A. guidelines are not always used by dealers and collectors when describing their guns. Many times there will be descriptions such as "95% blue" or "near mint," which, while they sound good, sometimes mask a multitude of sins. Just because someone uses either vague descriptions or their own grading does not necessarily mean that they're trying to hide something. Sometimes people get entrenched in their ways and you have to learn their system. But it does pay to ask a few questions to make sure that everything is functioning as it should be, and that all of the parts are there. Accurate percentage descriptions are an acquired skill and when used in conjunction with a good description can give an accurate picture, but be sure that you have complete information.

SELLING COLLECTOR GUNS

As important as buying is the ability to sell what you have, and there are many ways to do this. The major things to consider when you sell is how fast do you want to sell your guns and how much do you want for them. The two are not necessarily mutually exclusive, but usually if you want top price you have to compete with the dealer and it takes time. Always remember that guns are cashable items and the choice of what you are willing to take for them is yours and will be based on your salesmanship.

Where to sell

Gun Stores. The local gun dealer generally cannot pay you a top price on a collectable gun unless he has a good market for it. Even then he must make a profit. But this is a good source to sell your guns quickly.

Specialist and Mail Order Dealers. Many times these dealers will pay somewhat higher prices and work on a slimmer margin because they have built up customer lists over the years and may have a guaranteed resale of your gun.

Your Own Ad. This may be the way to get the most for your guns, but it also takes the longest and requires the cooperation of a gun licensee for shipping. There is usually a four to eight week time lag between the time you place an ad and the time it is in print and the publication distributed. Additionally, you also have the cost of the ad to consider as well as the cost of packaging and shipping.

Gun Shows. This can provide not only a place to sell your guns but a great meeting ground for fellow collectors. Of course your salesmanship is of prime importance to get your best price, but you will meet people with similar interests who may be very interested in buying what you have.

Auctions. This can sometimes be a risky venture. In an unreserved auction the highest bid wins, and if there is a bad crowd your guns could go for very little, and to add insult to injury you will have to pay a commission. In a reserved auction you are allowed to set a reasonable bottom figure, and if the gun does not reach that amount you get it back. However, you will generally have to pay a small commission to have it returned on reserve. But the other side of the coin is that people sometimes get carried away at an auction, and many times guns fetch a much higher price than what is expected. With auctions you have to be lucky.

Recordkeeping

U.S. law is very specific about a firearms licensee's recordkeeping responsibilities, but although the private individual is not required to, he should also keep records. Suggested information to keep for your own use would include the name and address of the person you acquired the gun from and the date, the make, model, caliber, type, and serial number of your gun, and when you sell it the name and address of the buyer and the date you sold it. It would also be handy to keep a record of the price you paid.

THE NATIONAL RIFLE ASSOCIATION OF AMERICA

The right to private ownership of firearms, a right so obviously vital to gun collectors as well as sportsmen, has been the primary cause championed by the National Rifle Association of Washington, D.C. This historic organization, now more than a century old and numbering well over 3 million members, has also made vast contributions toward the study, technology, history, and safe use of firearms. Nearly all U.S. gun dealers, and a large proportion of collectors, are members of the NRA, and have derived numerous benefits from membership.

Most readers of this book are, undoubtedly, already familiar with the NRA. But a work on firearms collecting could hardly be complete without a few words on the organization, and (at the end of this brief article) information on becoming a member.

While the firearms hobbyist has his choice of many organizations to join, membership in the nationwide NRA seems almost basic for anyone interested in gun collecting. The NRA's strength, supplied by its ever-increasing roster of members, insures a strong voice for the hobby. Whether the collector cares to realize it or not, there are individuals, including some in government—who would strangle the hobby by outlawing the possession, sale, or trade of ALL firearms ... or who would support such stringent restrictions on firearms ownership that gun collection would, for all practical purposes, come to an end. This is a battle that is never officially over. The tide can be kept in the collector's favor ONLY by interested parties making themselves known and counted. And the fact that the NRA membership has increased more dramatically in recent years, than ever in the past, is solid evidence that the future will be bright for gun enthusiasts.

The National Rifle Association has many goals and serves multitudes of purposes. The public hears, occasionally of its activities in lobbying against gun control legislation. Seldom does the news media report the numerous other NRA functions. Among these is its continuing efforts to promote better understanding of the safe use and care of all types of firearms, in conjunction with this goal, the NRA holds many seminars on gun-use instruction, as well as field meets and other training activities for firearms owners. It believes—and the belief is an historic one, a long tradition of the organization—that citizens well-trained in the use of firearms will be better citizens, and will be more capable of contributing to the defense of themselves, their community, and the nation. The NRA is also very active in conservation programs, to preserve endangered species and to encourage hunting only when and where the hunter presents no danger to the ecology.

THE HISTORY

The NRA is now more than 114 years old, having been chartered (originally by the State of New York) in 1871. It was born as a direct outgrowth of the Civil War. Of the many lessons that came from the war's battlefields, one was imprinted indelibly on the minds of officers; the majority of infantry soldiers were simply unskilled in the use of firearms. Even the rudimentary rules of gun use were foreign to them. In part the military was to blame. It devoted more attention to parade marching and drills than to firearms instruction. If Uncle Sam could not be counted on to do the job, it was then the responsibility of concerned citizens to promote firearms training. In 1871, the New York National Guard comprised a number of such concerned citizens. They were all ex-Union veterans and had seen at first hand, the severity of the problem in combat. So in September of that year an ambitious group of 15 of them collected to establish an organization—the first of its kind in the country. It would strive to instill pride in proper gun handling, and marksmanship, to increase the level of firearms knowledge among U.S. citizens, and in this way, better prepare Americans for military service in the event of war. It was a lofty ideal, but history showed it was unachievable. A hundred years earlier, the American colonists were highly skilled in firearms use because the necessity to hunt and protect one's property left little choice in the matter. There was no doubt that proper education could once again hone the shooting skills of the average citizen.

It was decided to model the organization after Britain's National Rifle Association, so the name National Rifle Association of America was chosen. A leader with military background and national recognition was a necessity; one was found in the person of General Ambrose Burnside who had served in the Civil War. On November 17, 1871, the charter was formally granted. But the new organization faced stiff challenges. The "media" of that time consisted almost wholly of newspapers, and newspaper accounts of the young NRA brought no groundswell of membership. There were the inevitable difficulties with funding, which limited the number of tournaments and other activities; and the hazards faced by changes in the government's administration, since some Presidents were more supportive of the NRA than others.

Though times occasionally looked bleak, the organization pushed forward, spread its message, and succeeded in surviving. Finally the country was awakened to the truth of the NRA's warnings about ill-prepared soldiers, when the Spanish-American War broke out in the late 1890s. This conflict brought immediate attention to the NRA, and when the war ended things began changing. In 1903 the government established its National Board for the Promotion of Rifle Practice, and NRA training activities were greatly increased. Thanks to the NRA, which grew impressively in the years from 1903 to 1916, the country was far better prepared for entry into World War I than it could otherwise have been. Many of the enlisted men had received NRA training. This was doubly so 25 years later, when America went into World War II. In the meantime, the NRA was also at work with law enforcement agencies, on federal and local levels, to promote more efficient firearms use by police officers. The firearms collector, if he takes an interest in memorabilia, has certainly seen and perhaps owned some of the NRA award medals. These handsome medals took the place of large-size trophies of earlier years, and were eagerly competed for in NRA-sanctioned events. A number of types exist, for competition among civilians and law enforcement agents.

After World War II, the NRA inaugurated the first hunter safety program, designed to eliminate hunting accidents arising from ignorance of firearms use and/or poor marksmanship. Then in 1975 came the epochal establishment of the NRA Institute for Legislative Action, to protect the right of law-abiding citizens to own firearms.

The three millionth member was added to the NRA membership rolls in 1985—a striking record of growth for an organization that began with little more than guts, hope and 15 far-sighted members 114 years earlier.

THE NRA INSTITUTE FOR LEGISLATIVE ACTION

The NRA's Institute for Legislative Action performs many functions. It monitors all gun-related bills put before Congress, to study their fairness and seek change when necessary. It likewise keeps careful watch on court rulings in all parts of the country, in cases involving the right to own and bear arms or similar questions. When rulings are made contrary to the NRA's position, it often assigns an attorney and allocates funds for the preparation of appeals, and to date has been very successful in this phase of its operations.

NRA FIELD SERVICES

The NRA Field Services are designed primarily for furthering the goals of the organization's founders and promoting a better understanding of firearms use among private citizens. Officers of the Field Services work closely with those of the Institute for Legislative Action in a number of interrelated areas. One of the primary arms of the NRA Field Services is its Volunteer Resources Department, which recruits and trains volunteer members. The Range Development Department, also a branch of Field Services, is active in inspecting target-shooting ranges at various firearms clubs. One of the goals of the NRA, through its Field Services, is to arrive at a level of standardization in rifle and pistol tournaments so that each tournament is held under similar conditions and with corresponding rules and regulations. This, of course, is an aid to the shooter and a springboard to developing increased skill, rather than having to adapt to different rules and conditions at each tournament. Shooting tournaments are growing at such a rapid rate that the NRA has had to greatly expand its staff to keep pace with the demand for skilled range and tournament supervision. The Field Services are also involved with selection of suitable sites for tournament and practice ranges; design of ranges for maximum efficiency and safety; and legal assistance on all aspects of range establishment and operation. This is vital because the laws of individual states sometimes differ and a range operator must be fully informed of the local applicable laws.

In 1981, the NRA reached an all-time high in the number of its affiliated range clubs, with 12,560. Also, in 1981, the Field Services appointed separate State Association Coordinators for the range clubs in each State, thereby providing an individual with local knowledge to work directly with the clubs in his state and act as a kind of liason between them and the NRA.

One of the chief aspects of Field Services is the NRA Range Loan Program, which has so far supplied more than $400,000 to local clubs for the establishment or renovation of their range shooting facilities.

NRA PUBLIC EDUCATION

The NRA Public Education department is the link between the NRA and the general public—"general public" meaning persons who are not members of the NRA nor who are even gun owners or hunting enthusiasts. Its purpose is to explain the position of NRA members and sportsmen in general, on various affairs, to the public. This is of course of great significance because the general public elects the country's legislators and, in a roundabout way, makes its laws. Whenever an issue arises involving the ownership of firearms or anything to concern hunters and gun hobbyists, the Public Education branch of the NRA prepares its view and disseminates it to the news media. Usually, the matters involved in legal questions or other complex subjects need to be put into plain language for the public to better understand. This is seldom done by the news media itself, which contains many elements opposed to the principles of the NRA. Unfortunately some segments of the public have formed very false conclusions about gun owners and hunters, and about the motives of the NRA. They assume that hunters are automatically bad for the ecology and that firearms ownership among private citizens breeds criminal activity. One project of the NRA Public Education department has been an advertising campaign in various national magazines, picturing the hunter and gun hobbyist as he really is; just an average citizen like the "general public" and not someone to be feared or shunned.

But the Public Education activities go deeper than this. They involve the development of such tools as the Shooting Sports Library Kit, designed to be placed into public and school libraries and containing various publications on the positive aspects of hunting, shooting, and gun ownership. The NRA strongly believes that gun education, like other forms of education, is most effective when begun early, and that the rudiments of gun knowledge should be taught to even very young children.

NRA'S OTHER OPERATIONS

The other operations of the National Rifle Association comprise: Membership Services; Competitions; Hunter Services; Junior Programs; Education and Training; Law Enforcement Services, and NRA Publications. All of these interrelated activities bring the NRA's activities and purposes close to the public. Among the Membership Benefits are of course the well-known *American Rifleman* and *American Hunter* magazines which are sent automatically to NRA members. The most widely read and authorative publications of their kind, they carry articles on all aspects of hunting, shooting, gun care, and related topics, authored by experts in their fields; and also the latest reports on news of interest to hunters and gun hobbyists in the way of pending legislation, improvements in gun design, inauguration of new clubs, and so on.

One of the highlights of the NRA is its sponsorship of shooting tournaments, which has been a vital function of the organization since its earliest pioneer days. The number of events and the total of competitors has constantly increased over the years, reaching unprecedented heights in 1984 (the most recent year for which statistics are available). In 1984 the NRA's famous National Matches were participated in by 3,838 contestants, and attended by more than 6,000 spectators. They were held at Camp Perry, Ohio. The NRA is likewise active in sponsoring collegiate shooting competitions, and in 1981 organized the first National Collegiate Pistol Championships at Massachusetts Institute of Technology.

The NRA's Youth Programs include National Junior Olympic Shooting Camps, State Junior Olympic Shooting Camps, National Junior Smallbore Camp, Junior Rifle and Pistol Clubs, Junior Gun Collecting Activities, 4-H State Shooting Sports Programs, and a variety of programs in partnership with the Boy Scouts of America. In addition to rifle and pistol shooting for youth, the NRA also sponsors air-gun shooting matches.

MEMBERSHIP

Membership in the NRA is both inexpensive and rewarding for anyone interested in firearms. Membership places one in league with all the leading sportsmen and gun hobbyists of the country, and adds further weight to the NRA's ability to carry out its programs and objectives.

NRA		NRA SENIOR	
		(65 and over)	
1 Year	$ 15	1 Year	$ 10
3 Years	$ 40	Life	$150
5 Years	$ 60		
Life	$300		

NRA ASSOCIATE		NRA JUNIOR	
(spouse)		(Under 20)	
(WITHOUT MAGAZINE)		1 Year	$5
1 Year	$10	(WITHOUT MAGAZINE)	
Life	$100	1 Year	$12
		Life	$150

Foreign: Canada add $2.00; Other countries add $3.00 postage per year.

GLOSSARY

ACP. Abbreviation for Automatic Colt Pistol, applied to ammunition designed originally or adopted by Colt.

ACTION. That part of a firearm made up of the breech and the parts designed to fire and cycle cartridges.

ADJUSTABLE CHOKE. Device attached to the muzzle of a shotgun enabling a change of choke by a rotational adjustment or by changing tubes.

ANTIQUE. A legal classification that in the U.S. is applied to weapons manufactured in or before 1898, and replicas that don't fire fixed ammunition.

ARSENAL. Military installation that stores and usually upgrades and modifies military weapons, and sometimes also applies to governmental weapon manufacturing facilities.

AUTOMATIC. Action type that ejects a spent cartridge and brings a fresh cartridge into firing position without manual intervention and has the capability of firing more than one shot with each pull of the trigger.

AUTOMATIC EJECTOR. Cases are ejected from the firearm when the action is opened without any manual intervention.

AUTOMATIC REVOLVER. Firearm action which resembles a conventional revolver except that on firing the cylinder is rotated and the hammer recocked by the recoil energy of the firing cartridge.

AUTOMATIC SAFETY. A block that prevents firing which is applied by the gun every time the action is cycled.

AYDT ACTION. A singleshot action utilizing a curved breechblock and a hinged section below the forward part of the chamber. The breechblock moves downward in an arc when pressure is applied to the finger lever.

BACKSTRAP. Rearmost part of the grip portion of a handgun frame.

BACK LOCK. Self-contained hammer, sear, and spring mounted on a single plate with the exposed hammer on the forward part of the plate, set into the side of a gun.

BARREL. Tube through which the bullet or shot passes on firing.

BARREL BAND. Metal band that secures the barrel to the forend.

BARRELED ACTION. The assembled barrel and complete action.

BARREL LINER. Thin steel tube usually permanently inserted into the barrel to either change the caliber, restore the gun, or to make the gun more functional when the barrel is formed from softer material.

BAYONET LUG. Metal projection at the end of the barrel for attaching a bayonet.

BAYONET. A knife or spike designed to be attached to a firearm.

BEAD SIGHT. Usually a round bead on the forward top of the barrel to aid in aiming (pointing) without the aid of a rear sight.

BEAVERTAIL FOREND. A wide, hand-filling forestock on long guns.

BENCHREST RIFLE. A heavy rifle designed for accurate shooting supported on a bench.

BIPOD. A two legged support attached to the forend of a rifle.

BLOWBACK ACTION. Automatic and semi-automatic action in which the breechblock is held forward only by spring pressure and cycles from the rearward gas thrust of the fired cartridge.

BLOW FORWARD ACTION. Automatic and semi-automatic action which has a fixed breechblock and in which spring pressure secures a barrel that reciprocates and cycles the action from the pressure of expanding gasses when a cartridge is fired.

BLUE. An artificial oxidation process that yields some rust protection and leaves steel surfaces with a blue-black color.

BLUNDERBUSS. A smoothbore weapon with a very flared muzzle.

BOLT ACTION. A manual action cycled by moving a reciprocating breechbolt.

BORE. The inside of a barrel; the diameter of a barrel.

BOX LOCK. Generally a break top action which contains the hammer, sear, springs and trigger in an integral unit directly behind the breech.

BREAK TOP. Action which exposes the breech by unlocking and the barrel(s) tipping downward, rotating on a point just forward of the breech.

BREECH. Rear end of the barrel; that part of the action that contacts the rear of the cartridge.

BREECHBOLT. The part of the action that secures the cartridge in the chamber.

BULL BARREL. A heavy barrel, usually with no taper.

BUTT. The rearmost portion of a stock.

BUTT PLATE. A plate fastened to the rear of the butt.

CALIBER. Bore diameter usually measured land to land in decimals of an inch or in millimeters.

CARBINE. A short, lightweight rifle.

CARTRIDGE. A self contained unit of ammunition.

CASE HARDENED. A surface hardening on that firearms is usually done so as to leave a broad spectrum of colors on the metal.

CENTER FIRE. Cartridge that contains a primer in the center of the base of the case.

CHAMBER. Portion of the gun in which the cartridge is placed.

CHECKERING. Geometric carving in the shape of parallel lines that cross to form diamonds, and used for both beauty and to provide a better handgrip.

CHEEKPIECE. A raised portion of the stock where the shooter's cheek touches the butt.

CHOKE. A muzzle constriction on shotguns which is used to control the pattern of shot.

CLIP. A detachable box that holds feeds ammunition into the gun by spring pressure.

COMBINATION GUN. A multi-barreled weapon that has a rifle barrel and a shotgun barrel.

CONDITION. The state of newness or wear of a gun. See the introduction for a complete description.

CONVERSION. The rebuilding of a military arm into a sporting arm; converting the arm to use a different cartridge; changing the general configuration of a gun.

CURIO. Curios and Relics are a legal subclassification of modern arms. See the complete definition in the introduction.

CUT-OFF. A device that can stop the flow of ammunition from the magazine.

CYLINDER. The rotating container with cartridge chambers in a revolver.

DAMASCENE. An overlay of metal, usually gold leaf, sometimes combined with light engraving and used for decoration.

DAMASCENING. Also called Engine Turning or Jeweling, this is an ornamental polishing consisting of repeated and overlapping circles.

DAMASCUS. A metal formed usually by twisting strands of iron and steel and repeatedly hammer-welding them.

DERINGER. A small percussion pistol developed by Henry Deringer.

DERRINGER. A copy of the Deringer, now meaning any very small manually operated pistol.

DOUBLE ACTION. The ability to both cock and fire a gun by the single pull of a trigger.

DOUBLE-BARREL. A gun having two barrels.

DOUBLE TRIGGER. A gun having two triggers, each usually firing a different trigger.

DRILLING. A three-barreled gun usually consisting of two shotgun barrels and one rifle barrel.

DUMMY SIDEPLATES. Metal plates usually used for decorative purposes and on the sides of boxlock actions to simulate sidelocks.

DUST COVER. Usually a sliding or turning piece of sheet metal used to keep foreign matter out of the action.

EJECTOR. Metal stud or rod that forcibly knocks cases out of the chamber.

ENGRAVING. Metal carving for decoration.

EXPRESS SIGHTS. The rear open rifle sight that has folding leafs for different elevations.

EXTRACTOR. The metal part that lifts the case out of the chamber.

FALLING BLOCK. Singleshot action type in which the breechblock moves vertically, propelled by a finger lever.

FIELD GRADE. Usually the standard grade of gun with little or no embellishment.

FINGER GROOVE. A groove cut into the forend of a long gun to aid in gripping.

FINISH. Materials used to coat the wood or the treatment of the metal parts.

FIXED SIGHTS. Non-adjustable sights.

FLASH HIDER. A device that reduces the amount of muzzle flash.

FLINTLOCK. Muzzle-loading action type that utilizes a hammer holding a flint that strikes a spring-loaded frizzen/pan cover to produce ignition.

FLOBERT. Singleshot action for low power cartridges employing a hammer and rotating breechblock.

FLUTED BARREL. A barrel with longitudinal grooves cut into it for decoration and for strength.

FOLDING GUN. Usually a break-top shotgun that pivots until folded in half.

FOREND. The forward part of a long gun's stock forward of the breech and under the barrel.

FRAME. The metal part of the gun that contains the action.

FREE PISTOL. A handgun designed for certain types of target shooting.

FREE RIFLE. A rifle designed for certain types of target shooting.

FRIZZEN. The part of the flintlock or snaphaunce lock that is hit by the flint to produce sparks.

FURNITURE. Metal parts except for the action and barrel.

GALLERY GUN. A gun designed to fire .22 Shorts for use in shooting galleries.

GAS OPERATED. Automatic or semi-automatic action type using vented gasses from the fired cartridge to cycle the action.

GAUGE. A unit of shotgun bore measurement derived from the number of lead balls of that diameter to a pound.

GERMAN SILVER. Also known as nickel silver, consisting of copper, nickel and zinc, used for gun decorations.

GRIP. The portion of the gun to the rear of the trigger that is held by the firing hand.

GRIPFRAME. On handguns that portion of the frame that is held by the hand.

GRIPS. On handguns the stocks.

GRIP SAFETY. A mechanical block that is released when the gun is held by hand in the firing position.

GRIPSTRAP. The exposed metal portion of the gripframe to the front or rear of the grips.

HAMMER. The part of the mechanism that hits and imparts thrust to the firing pin.

HAMMERLESS. A term applied to both striker-actuated guns and guns with hammers hidden within the action.

HAMMER SHROUD. A device that covers the sides of a hammer, while leaving the top exposed.

HANDGUARD. On rifles the forestock above the barrel and forward of the breech.

HANDGUN. A firearm designed to be held and fired with one hand.

HEAT CARVING. Decorative patterns in wood formed either by heat or the combination of heat and pressure.

HOLSTER STOCK. A holster usually made of wood, or wood and leather, that attaches to a handgun for use as a shoulderstock.

HOODED SIGHT. A front sight with a protective cover over it.

INLAY. Decoration made by inlaying patterns on metal or wood.

IRON SIGHTS. Open sights, usually with a rear sight adjustable for elevation, and a front sight adjustable for windage by drifting it.

KENTUCKY RIFLE. A style of gun developed around 1770 in Pennsylvania, and produced first in flintlock and later in percussion varieties.

KNURLING. Checkering on metal.

LANYARD RING. A ring used to secure the gun by a lanyard to the shooter so it won't be lost if dropped.

LEVER ACTION. Usually a repeating type of action with a reciprocating breechblock powered by a finger lever.

LIP-FIRE. An early type of rimfire cartridge.

LOCK. The part of the action that carries the firing mechanism.

LONG GUN. A term used to describe rifles and shotguns.

MAGAZINE. In repeating arms a storage device that feeds cartridges into the breech.

MAGNUM. Usually refers to arms or cartridges that more powerful than normal, or of higher pressure.

MANNLICHER. In common usage does not refer to the man or his guns but to a type of rifle stock in which the forestock extends to the end of the muzzle.

MANUAL SAFETY. A block which prevents discharge that must be engaged and disengaged manually.

MARTINI ACTION. A singleshot action that utilizes a rear pivoting breechblock with a striker operated by finger lever.

MATCH RIFLE. A rifle specifically designed for target shooting.

MATCHLOCK. A muzzle loading arm that uses "Slow Match" to ignite a priming charge.

MATTE FINISH. A dull finish that does not reflect light.

MAUSER ACTION. A type of reciprocating turn-bolt action.

MIQUELET LOCK. A flintlock action that has an exposed sear on the outside of the lockplate.

MODERN. A legal term applied to cartridge firearms manufactured after 1898. Also see the introduction.

MONTE CARLO. A raised portion on the top of the buttstock that elevates the cheek over the level of the buttplate.

MUSKET. A long military style gun with a long forend.

MUZZLE. The most forward end of the barrel.

MUZZLE BRAKE. A device to capture powder gasses at the end of the muzzle to reduce recoil and barrel climb.

MUZZLE LOADER. A black powder arm that is loaded through the muzzle.

NIPPLE. The hollow projection that the percussion cap is fitted to.

OCTAGON BARREL. A barrel with the outside ground into an octagonal shape.

OFF-HAND RIFLE. A target rifle designed to be held, not rested.

OPEN SIGHTS. Iron Sights.

OVER-UNDER. Barrel mounting on double barreled guns with the barrels superposed over one another.

PALM REST. Hand support on the forend of an off-hand match rifle.

PAN. The place on flintlock and earlier arms in which the priming powder is placed.

PARKERIZED. A matte, phosphated finish that is highly rust resistant and usually placed on military arms.

PATCH BOX. A container inletted into the butt of a muzzle loading long gun.

PEEP SIGHT. A circular rear sight with a small hole in the center to aim through.

PEPPERBOX. A revolving pistol with multiple rotating barrels.

PERCUSSION ARM. A muzzle loader that uses a percussion cap placed over a nipple to ignite the powder charge.

PERCUSSION CAP. A small disc that contains a fulminating chemical to ignite a powder charge.

PINFIRE. A type of cartridge with an exposed side pin that detonates the primer when struck.

PISTOL. A non-revolving handgun.

PISTOL GRIP. The grip on a pistol.

PLAINS RIFLE. Percussion rifle design of the mid-1800s developed in St. Louis.

POCKET REVOLVER. A small revolver.

PORT. An opening into the action for ejected cases to pass through; an opening for gasses to flow through.

PROOF. The testing of a gun to see if it stands the stress of firing.

PUMP ACTION. Slide Action.

RAMP SIGHT. A front sight mounted on a ramp.

RAMROD. A rod used to push the charge down the barrel of a muzzle loader.

RECEIVER. The part of the frame that houses the bolt or breechblock.

RECOIL. The rearward push of the gun when fired.

RECOIL OPERATED. An automatic or semi-automatic action that is cycled by the recoil from the fired cartridge.

RECOIL PAD. A rubber pad at the end of the butt to absorb recoil.

REPEATER. Capable of firing more that one round of ammunition; having a magazine.

REVOLVER. A firearm with a revolving cylinder containing multiple chambers.

RIFLE. A long gun with a rifled barrel.

RIFLING. Grooves cut into the bore to impart a spin to a bullet.

RIMFIRE. Cartridges containing the priming compound in the rim.

ROLLING BLOCK. Action with a pivoting breechblock that rotates ahead of the hammer, and which is locked by the hammer.

SADDLE RING. A ring on the side of rifles to attach a lanyard to.

SAFETY. A mechanical block that prevents the gun from firing.

SAWED-OFF SHOTGUN. A legal term describing a shotgun with barrels shorter than 16"; a Class 3 weapon.

SCHNABEL FOREND. A downcurving projection at the end of a forestock.

SCHUETZEN RIFLE. A type of fancy singleshot target rifle used for off-hand matches.

SCOPE. Telescopic sights.

SCOPE BASES. The mounts that attach scopes to guns.

SEAR. That part of the action that engages the striker or hammer, and allows them to fall when released by the trigger.

SEMI-AUTOMATIC. Action type that ejects the spent case and cycles a new round into the chamber with the energy of the fired round, and only fires one shot with each pull of the trigger.

SET TRIGGER. A trigger that can be "cocked" so that the final pull is very light.

SHOTGUN. A smoothbore gun designed to fire small shot pellets.

SIDE-BY-SIDE. A double barreled gun with the barrels mounted next to each other.

SIDEHAMMER. A gun having the hammer mounted on the side rather than in the center.

SIDE LEVER. A gun with the action operating lever on the side of the action.

SIDEPLATE. A plate that covers the action, or that the action is mounted on.

SIDELOCK. An action that is contained on the inside of a plate mounted directly behind the breech.

SIGHT. A device that allows precise aim.

SIGHT COVER. Protective covering placed around a sight to prevent damage from jarring.

SIGHT RADIUS. The distance between the front and rear sight.

SILENCER. A devise that reduces the noise of firing.

SINGLE ACTION. An action type that requires manual cocking for each shot.

SINGLESHOT. A gun capable of firing only one shot; having no magazine.

SKELETON BUTTPLATE. A buttplate with the center section removed to let the wood show through.

SLEEVE. Either a barrel liner or a tube placed on the outside of target barrel to stiffen it.

SKELETON STOCK. A buttstock, generally of wood or plastic, with the center removed to lighten the weight.

SLIDE. The reciprocating part of a semi-automatic pistol containing the breechblock.

SLIDE ACTION. A repeating action with a reciprocating forestock connected to the breechbolt.

SLING. A carrying strap on a long gun.

SLUG GUN. A shotgun designed to shoot lead slugs rather than pellets.

SNAPHAUNCE. An early form of flintlock with a manual frizzen.

SOLID FRAME. A non-takedown gun; a revolver that does not have a hinged frame.

SOLID RIB. A raised sighting plane on a barrel.

SPLINTER FOREND. A small wood forend under the barrel.

SPORTERIZED. A conversion of military arms to sporting type.

SPUR TRIGGER. A trigger with no guard, but protected by a sheath.

STIPPLING. An area roughened by center-punching for improved grip.

STOCK. The non-metal portion of the gun which is actually held.

STRIKER. A spring activated firing pin held in place by a sear which when released has enough energy to fire a primer.

SWIVELS. The metal loop that the sling is attached to.

TAKEDOWN. Capable of coming apart easily.

TARGET. Designed for target shooting.

TARGET STOCK. A stock designed for target shooting.

THUMBHOLE STOCK. A stock with a hole for the thumb to wrap around in the pistol grip.

THUMB REST. A ledge on the side of target grips for the thumb to rest on.

TIP-UP. A revolver with a frame hinged at the upper rear portion; a single shot pistol that has a break-top action.

TOE. The area on the bottom of the buttplate and the bottom rear of the stock.

TOGGLE ACTION. A semi-automatic action with a toggle joint that locks the breechblock.

TOP BREAK. Another term for tip-up, meaning that the barrel assembly swivels down on a hinge pin to expose the action.

TOP LEVER. An action actuated or opened with a lever on top.

TOP STRAP. The portion of a revolver above the cylinder.

TOUCH HOLE. The hole into the chamber area on muzzle loaders through which the priming flash ignites the charge.

TRIGGER. The exterior sear release.

TRIGGER, DOUBLE PULL. Two stage trigger in which the slack must be taken up before the sear can be released.

TRIGGER GUARD. A band usually of metal that encircles the trigger preventing accidental discharge.

TRIGGER PULL. The amount of force required to release the sear.

TRIGGER SHOE. An accessory fitted to the trigger to provide a wide gripping surface.

TRIGGER STOP. A device to prevent trigger overtravel.

TRY-GUN. A long gun with a completely adjustable stock for measuring the proper fit of a custom gun.

TUBE FEED. A magazine with cartridges loaded behind one another instead of stacked.

TWIST BARREL. A gun with superposed barrels that are manually turned to bring a fresh charge into play; damascus steel barrel.

UNDER LEVER. An action actuated or opened by a lever underneath the action.

UNDERHAMMER. An action with the hammer on the bottom of the frame.

VARMINT RIFLE. A heavy barreled small caliber hunting rifle designed for accuracy.

VENT RIB. A raised sighting plane on barrels with air vents between it and the barrel.

VIERLING. A combination weapon with four barrels.

WATER TABLE. The flat part of the action forward of the standing breech on break open actions.

WHEEL-LOCK. A muzzle loading action that used a spring operated spinning wheel to ignite sparks.

WITNESS MARK. A line place on assembled parts to show proper line-up between the two.

WILDCAT. A non-standard cartridge.

ZWILLING. A double-barrel long gun with one smooth bore barrel and one rifled barrel.

Shotgun Gauges

The gauge of a shotgun or any smoothbore was standardized in the last half of the nineteenth century in England by the Gun Barrel Proof Act of 1868. Until that time the general rule of thumb among gunmakers was the formula that gauge was the number of round lead balls of a given bore diameter in a pound. This still holds true with the exception of the obsolete letter gauges, and .410 gauge which is the actual bore diameter.

Gauge	Diameter	Gauge	Diameter
A	2.000"	21	.605"
B	1.938"	22	.596"
C	1.875"	23	.587"
D	1.813"	24	.579"
E	1.750"	25	.571"
F	1.688"	26	.563"
1	1.669"	27	.556"
H	1.625"	28	.550"
J	1.563"	29	.543"
K	1.500"	30	.537"
L	1.438"	31	.531"
M	1.375"	32	.526"
2	1.325"	33	.520"
O	1.313"	34	.515"
P	1.250"	35	.510"
3	1.157"	36	.506"
4	1.052"	37	.501"
5	.976"	38	.497"
6	.919"	39	.492"
7	.873"	40	.488"
8	.835"	41	.484"
9	.803"	42	.480"
10	.775"	43	.476"
11	.751"	44	.473"
12	.729"	45	.469"
13	.710"	46	.466"
14	.693"	47	.463"
15	.677"	48	.459"
16	.662"	49	.456"
17	.649"	50	.453"
18	.637"		
19	.626"		
20	.615"	.410	.410"

AMMUNITION INTERCHANGEABILITY

Many calibers (or cartridges) are known by more than one name and there are some that, while having different case sizes, can fit in an arm chambered for another caliber. Other cartridges may have a one-way interchangeability because of power. Caution must always be used when interchanging ammunition for gaps as small as several thousandths of an inch between the cartridge case and the limits of the chamber can destroy a gun and injure the shooter.

.22 W.R.F.
.22 Remington Special
.22 Win. M-1890

.25 Stevens Short R.F. in
.25 Stevens, but not the reverse

.25-20 Marlin
.25-20 Remington
.25-20 W.C.F.
.25-20 Win.

.25 Automatic
.25 A.C.P.
6.35mm Browning
6.35mm Automatic Pistol

.30-30 Marlin
.30-30 Savage
.30-30 W.C.F.
.30-30 Win.

.32 Short R.F. in
.32 Long R.F., but not the reverse

.32 Short Colt in
.32 Long Colt, but not the reverse
   (not to be used in .32 S&W or
   .32 S&W Long)

.32 A.C.P.
.32 Colt Automatic
7.65mm Automatic Pistol
7.65mm Browning

.32 S&W in
.32 S&W Long, but not the reverse

.32 Colt New Police
.32 Colt Police Positive
.32 S&W Long

.32-20 Colt
.32-20 Marlin
.32-20 Win.
.32-20 W.C.F.
.32-20 Win. & Marlin
.32 Marlin
.32 Rem.
.32 Win.
.32 W.C.F.
(Hi Speed are for rifles only)

.38 S&W
.38 Colt New Police

.38 Short Colt in
.38 Long Colt, but not the reverse. Both can
   be used in .38 Special.

.38 Colt Special

.38 S&W Special

.38 Targetmaster

.38-44 Special

(Hi Speed or Plus P cartridges are not to be used in light frame guns. Check with the manufacturer.)

.38 Marlin

.38 Rem.

.38 W.C.F.

.38 Win.

.38-40 Win.

.38 Automatic (A.C.P.) in

.38 Super but not the reverse

.380 Automatic

.380 A.C.P.

9mm Browning Short

9mm Corto

9mm Kurz

.380 Automatic

.380 A.C.P.

9mm Browning Short

9mm Corto

9mm Kurz

9mm Luger

9mm Parabellum

(9×19mm is Plus P)

.44 S&W Russian in

.44 Special, but not the reverse

.44 S&W Special in

.44 Magnum, but not the reverse

.44 Marlin

.44 Rem.

.44 Win.

.44 W.C.F.

.44-40 Win.

.45-70 Government

.45-70 Marlin

.45-70 Win.

.45-70-405

How to Use This Guide

There are three price columns found next to each listing. The first two columns show the retail selling price for each piece in very good to excellent condition. The third column is last edition's value in excellent condition. It shows which items have decreased or increased in value over the previous year. The prices reflect the geographical differences in the market and were determined by averaging the prices of actual sales across the country. They should be used only as a guideline.

For the sake of simplicity the following organization has been adopted for this book:
1. Manufacturer, importer, or brand name
2. Type of gun
3. Type of action
4. Model
5. Caliber or gauge

To find your gun in this guide first look under the name of the manufacturer, importer, or brand name, then look under the subdivision "type of gun" (i.e., rifle, handgun, etc.). For instance if you want to find a "General Hood Centennial" Colt Scout .22 l.r.r.f. single action revolver, look for:

COLT; Handgun, Revolver; General Hood Centennial, .22 l.r.r.f.

If nothing is known about the origin of a particular gun, an approximation of the value can be determined by checking the categories of: "type of action" (wheel lock, percussion, cartridge weapon, etc.), "Unknown Maker." To further aid in evaluating guns of unknown origin look under "Firearms, Custom Made," "Plains Rifles," "Scheutzen Rifles," and "Kentucky Rifles and Pistols."

In some cases there is a general listing for a manufacturer or a specific model of gun with the instructions "add" a given value. These additions should be made for all guns in the listed category that have the modification mentioned.

A

	V.G.	Exc.	Prior Edition Exc. Value

A & R SALES South El Monte, Calif. Current.

HANDGUN, SEMI-AUTOMATIC

| Government, .45 ACP, Lightweight, Clip Fed "Parts Gun" *Modern*.... | $175 | $225 | $275 |

RIFLE, SEMI-AUTOMATIC

| Mark IV Sporter, .308 Win., Clip Fed, Version of M-14, Adjustable Sights, *Modern* | 225 | 295 | 475 |

ABBEY, GEORGE T. Chicago, Ill. 1858–1875.

RIFLE, PERCUSSION

| .44, Octagon Barrel, Brass Furniture, *Antique* | 400 | 575 | 575 |
| .44, Double Barrel, Over-Under, Brass Furniture, *Antique* | 700 | 1,050 | 1,050 |

ABBEY, J.F. & CO. Chicago, Ill. 1871–1875. Also made by Abbey & Foster.

RIFLE, PERCUSSION

| Various Calibers, *Antique* | 300 | 450 | 450 |

SHOTGUN, PERCUSSION

| Various Gauges, *Antique* | 350 | 500 | 500 |

ABILENE See Mossberg.

ACHA Domingo Acha y Cia., Ermua, Spain 1927–1937.

HANDGUN, SEMI-AUTOMATIC

| Ruby M1916, .32 ACP, Clip Fed, *Curio* | 95 | 150 | 145 |

ACME Made by Hopkins & Allen, Sold by Merwin & Hulbert, c. 1880.

HANDGUN, REVOLVER

| .22 Short R.F., 7 Shot, Spur Trigger, Solid Frame, Single Action, *Antique* | 95 | 150 | 165 |
| .32 Short R.F., 5 Shot, Spur Trigger, Solid Frame, Single Action, *Antique* | 95 | 165 | 175 |

	V.G.	Exc.	Prior Edition Exc. Value

ACME ARMS Maker unknown, sold by J. Stevens Arms Co., c. 1880.

HANDGUN, REVOLVER

	V.G.	Exc.	Prior
.22 Short R.F., 7 Shot, Spur Trigger, Solid Frame, Single Action, *Antique*	$95	$160	$160
.32 Short R.F., 5 Shot, Spur Trigger, Solid Frame, Single Action, *Antique*	95	175	175

SHOTGUN, DOUBLE BARREL, SIDE-BY-SIDE

	V.G.	Exc.	Prior
12 Gauge, Damascus Barrel, *Antique*	95	195	190

ACME HAMMERLESS Made by Hopkins & Allen for Hulbert Bros. 1893.

HANDGUN, REVOLVER

	V.G.	Exc.	Prior
.32 S & W, 5 Shot, Top Break, Hammerless, Double Action, 2½" Barrel, *Antique*	75	145	135
.38 S & W, 5 Shot, Top Break, Hammerless, Double Action, 3" Barrel, *Antique*	75	145	135

ACRA Tradename used by Reinhard Fajen of Warsaw, Mo., c. 1970.

RIFLE, BOLT ACTION

	V.G.	Exc.	Prior
RA, Various Calibers, Santa Barbara Barreled Action, Checkered Stock, *Modern*	125	200	225
S24, Various Calibers, Santa Barbara Barreled Action, Fancy Checkering, *Modern*	150	225	245
M18, Various Calibers, Santa Barbara Barreled Action, Mannlicher Checkered Stock, *Modern*	175	275	300

ACTION Modesto Santos; Eibar, Spain.

HANDGUN, SEMI-AUTOMATIC

	V.G.	Exc.	Prior
Model 1920, .25 ACP, Clip Fed, *Curio*	75	150	175
#2, .32 ACP, Clip Fed, *Curio*	125	225	235

ADAMS Made by Deane, Adams, & Deane, London, England.

HANDGUN, PERCUSSION

	V.G.	Exc.	Prior
.38 M1851, Revolver, Double Action, 4½" Barrel, *Antique*	600	1,000	975
.38 M1851, Revolver, Double Action, 4½" Barrel, Cased with Accessories, *Antique*	800	1,200	1,200
.44 M1851, Revolver, Double Action, 6" Barrel, *Antique*	400	775	750
.44 M1851, Revolver, Double Action, 6" Barrel, Cased with Accessories, *Antique*	450	800	775
.500 M1851, Dragoon, Revolver, Double Action, 8" Barrel, *Antique*	450	825	800

	V.G.	Exc.	Prior Edition Exc. Value
.500 M1851 Dragoon, Revolver, Double Action, 8" Barrel, Cased with Accessories, *Antique*	$675	$1,150	$1,100
.54 Beaumont-Adams, Revolver, Double Action, 5½" Barrel, *Antique*	550	850	825
.54 Beaumont-Adams, Revolver, Double Action, 5½" Barrel, *Antique*	650	1200	1400

RIFLE, PERCUSSION
.50 Sporting Rifle, Revolver, Double Action, 20" Barrel, *Antique*	500	800	800

ADAMS, JOSEPH Birmingham, England 1767–1813.

RIFLE, FLINTLOCK
.65 Officers Model Brown Bess, Musket, Military, *Antique*	1,000	1,750	1,600

ADAMY GEBRUDER Suhl, Germany 1921–1939.

SHOTGUN, DOUBLE BARREL, OVER-UNDER
16 Ga., Automatic Ejector, Double Trigger, Engraved, Cased, *Modern*	1,450	2,100	1,900

ADIRONDACK ARMS CO. Plattsburg, N.Y. 1870–1874. Purchased by Winchester 1874.

RIFLE, LEVER ACTION
Robinson 1875 Patent, Various Rimfires, Octagon Barrel, Open Rear Sight, *Antique*	600	1,250	1,425
Robinson Patent, Various Calibers, Octagon Barrel, *Antique*	700	1,300	1,325

ADLER Engelbrecht & Wolff; Zella St. Blasii, Germany 1904–1906.

HANDGUN, SEMI-AUTOMATIC
7.25 Adler, Clip Fed, *Curio*	1,500	2,000	2,500

AERTS, JAN Maastricht, Holland, c. 1650.

HANDGUN, FLINTLOCK
Ornate Pair, Very Long Ebony Full Stock, Silver Inlay, High Quality, *Antique*		RARE	

AETNA Made by Harrington & Richardson, c. 1876.

HANDGUN, REVOLVER
.22 Short R.F., 7 Shot, Spur Trigger, Solid Frame, Single Action, *Antique*	75	100	150
Aetna, .32 Short R.F., 5 Shot, Spur Trigger, Solid Frame, Single Action, *Antique*	75	150	165

	V.G.	Exc.	Prior Edition Exc. Value
Aetna 2, .32 Short R.F., 5 Shot, Spur Trigger, Solid Frame, Single Action, *Antique*	$75	$150	$165
Aetna 2½, .32 Short R.F., 5 Shot, Spur Trigger, Solid Frame, Single Action, *Antique*	75	150	165

AETNA ARMS CO. N.Y.C., c. 1880.

HANDGUN, REVOLVER

	V.G.	Exc.	Prior
.22 Short R.F., 7 Shot, Spur Trigger, Tip-Up Barrel, *Antique*	225	350	375
.32 Short R.F., 5 Shot, Spur Trigger, Tip-Up Barrel, *Antique*	250	375	400

AFFERBACH, WILLIAM Philadelphia, Pa. 1860–1866.

HANDGUN, PERCUSSION

.40 Derringer, Full Stock, *Antique*	450	650	675

AGAWAM ARMS Agawam, Mass., c. 1970.

RIFLE, SINGLESHOT

Model M-68, .22 L.R.R.F., Lever Action, Open Sights, *Modern*	35	65	55
Model M-68M, .22 W.M.R., Lever Action, Open Sights, *Modern*	45	75	70

AJAX ARMY Maker Unknown, Sold by E.C. Meacham Co., c. 1880.

HANDGUN, REVOLVER

.44 Short R.F., 5 Shot, Spur Trigger, Solid Frame, Single Action, *Antique*	150	250	275

AKRILL, E. Probably St. Etienne, France, c. 1810.

RIFLE, FLINTLOCK

.69, Smoothbore, Octagon Barrel, Damascus Barrel, Breech Loader, Plain, *Antique*	1,000	2,500	2,100

ALAMO Tradename used by Stoeger Arms, c. 1958.

HANDGUN, REVOLVER

Alamo, .22 L.R.R.F., Double Action, Ribbed Barrel, *Modern*	25	50	35

ALASKA Made by Hood Firearms, Sold by E. C. Meacham Co. 1880.

HANDGUN, REVOLVER

.22 Short R.F., 7 Shot, Spur Trigger, Solid Frame, Single Action, *Antique*	75	150	160

	V.G.	Exc.	Prior Edition Exc. Value

ALASKAN Skinner's Sportsman's Supply, Juneau, Alaska, C. 1970.
RIFLE, BOLT ACTION
Standard, Various Calibers, Checkered Stock, Sling Swivels, *Modern* ... $195 $295 $285

Magnum, Various Calibers, Checkered Stock, Recoil Pad, Sling Swivels, *Modern* ... 225 300 300

Carbine, Various Calibers, Checkered Stock, Sling Swivels, *Modern* ... 225 300 300

ALBRECHT, ANDREW Lancaster, Pa. 1779–1782. See Kentucky Rifles and Pistols.

ALBRIGHT, HENRY Lancaster, Pa. 1740–1745. See Kentucky Rifles and Pistols.

ALDENDERFER, M. Lancaster, Pa. 1763–1784. See Kentucky Rifles and Pistols.

ALERT Made by Hood Firearms Co., C. 1874.
HANDGUN, REVOLVER
.22 Short R.F., 7 Shot, Spur Trigger, Solid Frame, Single Action, *Antique* ... 175 200 160

ALEXIA Made by Hopkins & Allen, c. 1880.
HANDGUN, REVOLVER
.22 Short R.F., 7 Shot, Spur Trigger, Solid Frame, Single Action, *Antique* ... 150 175 160

.32 Short R.F., 5 Shot, Spur Trigger, Solid Frame, Single Action, *Antique* ... 150 175 170

.38 Short R.F., 5 Shot, Spur Trigger, Solid Frame, Single Action, *Antique* ... 150 175 180

.41 Short R.F., 5 Shot, Spur Trigger, Solid Frame, Single Action, *Antique* ... 150 225 250

ALEXIS Made by Hood Firearms Co., Sold by Turner & Ross Co. Boston, Mass.
HANDGUN, REVOLVER
.22 Short R.F., 7 Shot, Spur Trigger, Solid Frame, Single Action, *Antique* ... 100 150 160

	V.G.	Exc.	Prior Edition Exc. Value

ALFA Armero Especialistas Reunidas, Eibar, Spain, c. 1920.

HANDGUN, REVOLVER

	V.G.	Exc.	Prior Edition Exc. Value
Colt Police Positive Type, .38, Double Action, Blue, *Curio*	$85	$125	$125
S. & W. M & P Type, .38, Double Action, 6 Shot, Blue, *Curio*	85	125	125
S. & W. #2 Type, Various Calibers, Double Action, Blue, Break-Top, *Curio*	100	150	150

ALFA Adolf Frank, Hamburg, Germany, c. 1900.

HANDGUN, MANUAL REPEATER

	V.G.	Exc.	Prior Edition Exc. Value
"Reform" Type, .230 C.F., Four-barreled Repeater, Engraved, *Curio*	150	250	240

HANDGUN, SEMI-AUTOMATIC

	V.G.	Exc.	Prior Edition Exc. Value
Pocket, .25 ACP, Clip Fed, Blue, *Curio*	100	150	140

RIFLE, PERCUSSION

	V.G.	Exc.	Prior Edition Exc. Value
Back-lock, Various Calibers, Imitation Damascus Barrel, *Antique*	75	100	90
Back-lock, Various Calibers, Carved, Inlaid Stock, Imitation Damascus Barrel, *Antique*	95	150	150

SHOTGUN, PERCUSSION

	V.G.	Exc.	Prior Edition Exc. Value
Double Barrel, Various Gauges, Back-lock, Double Triggers, Damascus Barrels, *Antique*	75	125	120
Double Barrel, Various Gauges, Back-lock, Double Triggers, Damascus Barrels, Carved Stock, Engraved, *Antique*	125	175	200

SHOTGUN, DOUBLE BARREL, SIDE-BY-SIDE

	V.G.	Exc.	Prior Edition Exc. Value
Greener Boxlock, Various Gauges, Checkered Stock, Double Triggers, *Curio*	150	200	200
Greener Boxlock, Various Gauges, Checkered Stock, Double Triggers, Engraved, *Curio*	175	265	260

SHOTGUN, SINGLESHOT

	V.G.	Exc.	Prior Edition Exc. Value
Roux Underlever, Various Gauges, Tip-Down Barrel, No Forestock, *Curio*	50	55	55
Nuss Underlever, Various Gauges, Tip-Down Barrel, No Forestock, *Curio*	50	65	55
Sidebutton, Various Gauges, Tip-Down Barrel, No Forestock, *Curio*	50	60	50

ALKARTASUNA Spain Made by Alkartasuna Fabrica De Armas 1910–1922.

HANDGUN, SEMI-AUTOMATIC

	V.G.	Exc.	Prior Edition Exc. Value
Alkar 1924, .25 ACP, Cartridge Counter, Grips, Clip Fed, *Curio*	225	350	400
Pocket, .32 ACP, Clip Fed, Long Grip, *Curio*	125	175	190

	V.G.	Exc.	Prior Edition Exc. Value
Pocket, .32 ACP, Clip Fed, Short Grip, *Curio*	*$125*	*$175*	*$170*
Vest Pocket, .25 ACP, Clip Fed, Cartridge Counter, *Modern*	*125*	*200*	*195*
Vest Pocket, .25 ACP, Clip Fed, *Modern*	*95*	*155*	*165*

ALLEGHENY WORKS Allegheny, Pa. 1836–1875. See Kentucky Rifles and Pistols.

ALLEN Made by Hopkins & Allen, c. 1880.

HANDGUN, REVOLVER

22 Short R.F., 7 Shot, Spur Trigger, Solid Frame, Single Action, *Antique*	75	165	160

ALLEN Tradename used by McKeown's Guns of Pekin, Ill., c. 1970.

SHOTGUN, DOUBLE BARREL, OVER-UNDER

MCK 68, 12 Ga., Vent Rib, Double Triggers, Plain, *Modern*	175	275	300
Olympic 68, 12 Ga., Vent Rib, Single Selective Trigger, Automatic Ejectors, Checkered Stock, Engraved, *Modern* ......:........................	250	425	450
S201, Various Gauges, Vent Rib, Double Triggers, Checkered Stock, Light Engraving, *Modern*..	225	375	395
S201 Deluxe, Various Gauges, Vent Rib, Single Trigger, Automatic Ejectors, Checkered Stock, Engraved, *Modern*	300	450	475

ALLEN & THURBER Grafton, Mass. 1837–1842, Norwich, Conn. 1842–1847.

HANDGUN, PERCUSSION

.28 (Grafton) Pepperbox, 6 Shot, 3" Barrel, *Antique*	700	1,700	1,300
.28 (Norwich) Pepperbox, 6 Shot, Bar Hammer, 3" Barrel, *Antique*..	295	600	600
.28 (Norwich) Pepperbox, 6 Shot, Hammerless, 3" Barrel, *Antique*..	325	675	695
.28, Singleshot, Bar Hammer, Various Barrel Lengths, Half-Octagon Barrel, *Antique*...	150	285	275
.31 (Grafton) Pepperbox, 6 Shot, 3" Barrel, *Antique*	495	1,000	975
.31 (Norwich) Pepperbox, 6 Shot, Bar Hammer, 3" Barrel, *Antique*..	295	650	625
.31 (Norwich) Pepperbox, 6 Shot, Hammerless, 3" Barrel, *Antique*..	375	775	750
.31, Singleshot, Tube Hammer, Various Barrel Lengths, Half-Octagon Barrel, *Antique*...	550	1,000	995
.31, Singleshot, Under Hammer, Various Barrel Lengths, Half-Octagon Barrel, *Antique*...	295	650	675

	V.G.	Exc.	Prior Edition Exc. Value
.31, Singleshot, Under Hammer, Various Barrel Lengths, Saw-Handle Grip, Half-Octagon Barrel, *Antique*	$250	$475	$490
.31, "In-Line" Singleshot, Center Hammer, Various Barrel Lengths, Half-Octagon Barrel, *Antique*	175	325	300
.34, Singleshot, Side Hammer, Various Barrel Lengths, Half-Octagon Barrel, *Antique*	195	500	495
.36 (Grafton) Pepperbox, 6" Barrel, *Antique*	750	1,250	1,350
.36 (Norwich) Pepperbox, 6 Shot, Bar Hammer, 6" Barrel, *Antique*	450	800	775
.36 (Norwich) Pepperbox, 6 Shot, Ring Trigger, 6" Barrel, *Antique*	575	1,100	1,125
.36, Singleshot, Bar Hammer, Various Barrel Lengths, Half-Octagon Barrel, *Antique*	125	275	300
.36, Singleshot, Center Hammer, Various Barrel Lengths, Half-Octagon Barrel, *Antique*	150	300	320
.41, Singleshot, Side Hammer, Various Barrel Lengths, Half-Octagon Barrel, *Antique*	175	450	475

ALLEN & THURBER Worcester, Mass. 1855–1856.

COMBINATION WEAPON, PERCUSSION

Over-Under, Various Calibers, Rifle and Shotgun Barrels, *Antique*	657	1,600	1,600

HANDGUN, PERCUSSION

.28, Pepperbox, Bar Hammer, Various Barrel Lengths, 5 Shot, *Antique*	250	475	450
.30, Pepperbox, Ring Hammerless, 6 Shot, *Antique*	400	600	775
.31, Pepperbox, Bar Hammer, 5 Shot, Various Barrel Lengths, *Antique*	325	400	495

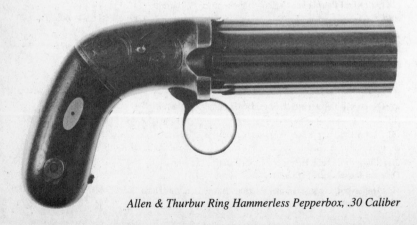

Allen & Thurbur Ring Hammerless Pepperbox, .30 Caliber

	V.G.	Exc.	Prior Edition Exc. Value
.31, Pepperbox, Thumb Hammer, 5 Shot, Various Barrel Lengths, *Antique*	$300	$550	$600
.34, Pepperbox, Bar Hammer, Various Barrel Lengths, 4 Shot, *Antique*	250	550	550
.36, Target Pistol, 12" Octagon Barrel, Adjustable Sights, Detachable Shoulder Stock, *Antique*	800	1,750	2,100

RIFLE, PERCUSSION
| **.43, Singleshot**, Sporting Rifle, *Antique* | 475 | 725 | 775 |

ALLEN & WHEELOCK Worcester, Mass. 1856–1865.
HANDGUN, PERCUSSION
.25, Pepperbox, 4" Barrel, 5 Shot, *Antique*	225	450	475
.36, Pepperbox, 6" Barrel, 6 Shot, *Antique*	425	750	900
.28, Revolver, Side Hammer, Octagon Barrel, 3" Barrel, 5 Shot, *Antique*	150	375	425
.31, Revolver, Bar Hammer, Octagon Barrel, 2¼" Barrel, 5 Shot, *Antique*	150	300	310
.34, Revolver, Bar Hammer, Octagon Barrel, 4" Barrel, 5 Shot, *Antique*	225	400	420
.34, Revolver, Bar Hammer, Octagon Barrel, 4" Barrel, 5 Shot, *Antique*	225	400	420
.31, Revolver, Side Hammer, Octagon Barrel, 3" Barrel, 5 Shot, *Antique*	150	400	400
.36, Revolver, Center Hammer, Octagon Barrel, 3" Barrel, 6 Shot, Spur Trigger, *Antique*	175	450	465
.36, Revolver, Side Hammer, Octagon Barrel, 6" Barrel, 6 Shot, *Antique*	400	800	900
.36, Revolver, Center Hammer, Octagon Barrel, 7½" Barrel, 6 Shot, *Antique*	400	900	1,100
.44, Revolver, Center Hammer, Half Octagon Barrel, 7½" Barrel, 6 Shot, *Antique*	425	950	975

HANDGUN, REVOLVER
.22 Short R.F., 7 Shot, Side Hammer, Solid Frame, *Antique*	125	275	290
.25 L.F., 7 Shot, Side Hammer, Solid Frame, *Antique*	325	475	475
.32 L.F., 6 Shot, Side Hammer, Solid Frame, *Antique*	325	600	625
.32 Short R.F., 6 Shot, Side Hammer, Solid Frame, *Antique*	125	275	290
.36 L.F., 6 Shot, Side Hammer, Solid Frame, *Antique*	400	650	675
.38 Short R.F., 6 Shot, Side Hammer, Solid Frame, *Antique*	125	300	310
.44 L.F., 6 Shot, Side Hammer, Solid Frame, *Antique*	600	1,100	1,100
.44 Short R.F., 6 Shot, Side Hammer, Solid Frame, *Antique*	175	350	375

HANDGUN, SINGLESHOT
| **.22 Short R.F.**, Derringer, Spur Trigger, *Antique* | 150 | 175 | 300 |
| **.22 Short R.F.**, Large Frame, Spur Trigger, *Antique* | 150 | 250 | 265 |

	V.G.	Exc.	Prior Edition Exc. Value
.32 Short R.F., Derringer, Spur Trigger, *Antique*	$300	$550	$600
.32 Short R.F., Large Frame, Spur Trigger, *Antique*	125	250	260
.41 Short R.F., Derringer, Spur Trigger, *Antique*	250	450	500

RIFLE, PERCUSSION

	V.G.	Exc.	Prior Edition Exc. Value
.36 Allen Patent, Carbine, Tap Breech Loader, *Antique*	450	850	850
.36 Allen Patent, Tap Breech Loader, Sporting Rifle, *Antique*	400	850	835
.38 Sidehammer, Plains Rifle, Iron Mounted, Walnut Stock, *Antique*	300	525	535
.44 Center Hammer, Octagon Barrel, Iron Frame, *Antique*	300	600	630
.44 Revolver, Carbine, 6 Shot, *Antique*	4,000	9,900	10,250

RIFLE, REVOLVING

	V.G.	Exc.	Prior Edition Exc. Value
.44 L.F., Walnut Stock, 6 Shot, *Antique*	4,000	7,000	7,175

RIFLE, SINGLESHOT

	V.G.	Exc.	Prior Edition Exc. Value
.22 R.F., Falling Block, Sporting Rifle, *Antique*	300	500	520
.38 R.F., Falling Block, Sporting Rifle, *Antique*	285	400	410
.62 Allen R.F., Falling Block, Sporting Rifle, *Antique*	275	450	450
.64 Allen R.F., Falling Block, Sporting Rifle, *Antique*	275	450	450

SHOTGUN, PERCUSSION

	V.G.	Exc.	Prior Edition Exc. Value
12 Ga. Double, Hammers, Light Engraving, *Antique*	275	425	450

SHOTGUN, DOUBLE BARREL, SIDE-BY-SIDE

	V.G.	Exc.	Prior Edition Exc. Value
12 Ga., Checkered Stock, Hammers, Double Triggers, *Antique*	225	425	425

ALLEN, C.B. Springfield, Mass. 1836–1841. Also See U.S. Military.

HANDGUN, PERCUSSION

	V.G.	Exc.	Prior Edition Exc. Value
.36 Cochran Turret, 7 Shot, 4³/₄" Barrel, *Antique*	6,000	8,500	9,000
.40 Cochran Turret, 7 Shot, 5" Barrel, *Antique*	7,500	9,800	9,950
.35 Elgin Cutlass, Octagon Barrel, with Built-in Knife, Smoothbore, *Antique*	3,850	5,000	5,500
.54 Elgin Cutlass, Octagon Barrel, with Built-in Knife, Smoothbore, *Antique*	6,500	12,000	13,000

RIFLE, PERCUSSION

	V.G.	Exc.	Prior Edition Exc. Value
.40 Cochran Turret, 7 Shot, Octagon Barrel, *Antique*	5,500	8,000	8,500
.40 Cochran Turret, 9 Shot, Octagon Barrel, *Antique*	5,800	8,000	8,500

ALLEN, ETHAN Grafton, Mass. 1835–1837, E. Allen & Co. Worcester, Mass. 1865–1871.

HANDGUN, PERCUSSION

	V.G.	Exc.	Prior Edition Exc. Value
Various Calibers, Various Barrel Lengths, Under Hammer, Singleshot, Saw Handle Grip, *Antique*	250	450	475
.31, Singleshot, Under Hammer, Half-Octagon Barrel, *Antique*	275	600	625

	V.G.	Exc.	Prior Edition Exc. Value
.31, Pepperbox, 6 Shot, 3" Barrel, *Antique*	$475	$900	$950
.36, Pepperbox, 6 Shot, 5" Barrel, *Antique*	650	1,000	1,200

HANDGUN, REVOLVER

	V.G.	Exc.	Prior
.22 Short R.F., 7 Shot, Side Hammer, Sheath Trigger, *Antique*	100	250	250
.32 Short R.F., 6 Shot, Side Hammer, Sheath Trigger, *Antique*	100	250	250

HANDGUN, SINGLESHOT

	V.G.	Exc.	Prior
Derringer, .32 Short R.F., Side-Swing Barrel, Round Barrel, *Antique*	350	650	600
Derringer, .32 Short R.F., Side-Swing Barrel, Half-Octagon Barrel, *Antique*	175	250	240
Derringer, .41 Short R.F., Side-Swing Barrel, Half-Octagon Barrel, *Antique*	275	475	485
Derringer, .41 Short R.F., Side-Swing Barrel, Round Barrel, *Antique*	175	325	295
Derringer, .41 Short R.F., Side-Swing Barrel, Octagon Barrel, *Antique*	175	325	295

RIFLE, SINGLESHOT

	V.G.	Exc.	Prior
Various Rimfires, Sporting Rifle, *Antique*	375	475	500

ALLEN, SILAS Shrewsbury, Mass. 1796–1843. See Kentucky Rifles and Pistols.

ALLIES Berasaluze Areitio-Arutena y Cia., Eibar, Spain, c. 1920.

HANDGUN, SEMI-AUTOMATIC

	V.G.	Exc.	Prior
Model 1924, .25 ACP, Clip Fed, *Curio*	75	175	175
Pocket, .32 ACP, Clip Fed, *Curio*	75	175	180
Vest Pocket, .25 ACP, Clip Fed, *Curio*	75	150	150
Vest Pocket, .32 ACP, Clip Fed, Short Grip, *Curio*	75	150	165

ALL RIGHT FIREARMS CO. Lawrence, Mass., c. 1876.

HANDGUN, REVOLVER

	V.G.	Exc.	Prior
Little All Right Palm Pistol, .22 Short R.F., Squeeze Trigger, 5 Shot, *Antique*	450	775	775

ALPINE INDUSTRIES Los Angeles, Calif. 1962–1965.

RIFLE, SEMI-AUTOMATIC

	V.G.	Exc.	Prior
M-1 Carbine, .30 Carbine, Clip Fed, Military Style, *Modern*	150	250	275

	V.G.	Exc.	Prior Edition Exc. Value

ALSOP, C.R. Middleton, Conn. 1858–1866.

HANDGUN, PERCUSSION

.36 Navy, 5 Shot, Octagon Barrel, Spur Trigger, Top Hammer, Safety, *Antique* ... $1,150 $1,750 $1,850

.36 Navy, 5 Shot, Octagon Barrel, Spur Trigger, Top Hammer, No Safety, *Antique* ... 895 1,400 1,350

.36 Pocket, 5 Shot, Octagon Barrel, Spur Trigger, *Antique* ... 575 750 675

AMERICA Made by Bliss & Goodyear, c. 1878.

HANDGUN, REVOLVER

.22 Short R.F., 7 Shot, Spur Trigger, Solid Frame, Single Action, *Antique* ... 95 175 160

AMERICA Made by Norwich Falls Pistol Co., c. 1880.

HANDGUN, REVOLVER

.32 Long R.F., Double Action, Solid Frame, *Modern* ... 75 125 120

AMERICAN ARMS CO. Boston, Mass. 1861–1897, Milwaukee, Wisc. 1897–1901. Purchased by Marlin 1901.

HANDGUN, DOUBLE BARREL, OVER-UNDER

Wheeler Pat., .22 Short R.F., 32 Short R.F., Brass Frame, Spur Trigger, *Antique* ... 425 500 725

Wheeler Pat, .32 Short R.F., Brass Frame, Spur Trigger, *Antique* ... 450 500 525

Wheeler Pat, .41 Short R.F., Brass Frame, Spur Trigger, *Antique* ... 600 650 725

HANDGUN, REVOLVER

.38 S & W, 5 Shot, Double Action, Top Break, *Antique* ... 100 125 140

.38 S & W, 5 Shot, Single Action, Top Break, Spur Trigger, *Antique* ... 125 150 150

.32 S & W, 5 Shot, Double Action, Top Break, Hammerless, *Antique* ... 125 175 175

SHOTGUN, DOUBLE BARREL, SIDE-BY-SIDE

12 Ga., Semi-Hammerless, Checkered Stock, *Antique* ... 550 600 475

Whitmore Patent, 10 Ga., 2⅞", Hammerless, Checkered Stock, *Antique* ... 550 625 475

Whitmore Patent, 12 Ga., Hammerless, Checkered Stock, *Antique* ... 450 675 550

SHOTGUN, SINGLESHOT

12 Ga., Semi-Hammerless, Checkered Stock, *Antique* ... 200 250 260

	V.G.	Exc.	Prior Edition Exc. Value

AMERICAN ARMS & AMMUNITION CO. Miami,
Florida, c. 1979. Successors to Norton Armament Corp. (Norarmco).

HANDGUN, SEMI-AUTOMATIC

TP-70, .22 L.R.R.F., Double Action, Stainless, Clip Fed, *Modern*...	$175	$275	$275
TP-70, .25 ACP, Double Action, Stainless, Clip Fed, *Modern*	150	250	235

AMERICAN ARMS INTERNATIONAL Salt Lake City,
Utah, Current.

AUTOMATIC WEAPON, SUBMACHINE GUN

American 180, .22 L.R.R.F., 177 Round Drum Magazine, Peep Sights, *Class 3*	500	600	400

Laser-Lok Sight System, *Add* **$350.00–$450.00**
Extra Magazine, *Add* **$50.00–$75.00**

RIFLE, SEMI-AUTOMATIC

American 180, .22 L.R.R.F., 177 Round Drum Magazine, Peep Sights, *Modern*	500	600	400

Laser-Lok Sight System, *Add* **$350–$450**
Extra Magazine, *Add* **$50–$75**

AMERICAN BARLOCK WONDER Made by Crescent for
Sears-Roebuck & Co.

SHOTGUN, DOUBLE BARREL, SIDE-BY-SIDE

Various Gauges, Outside Hammers, Damascus Barrel, *Modern*	150	225	185
Various Gauges, Hammerless, Steel Barrel, *Modern*	240	275	220
Various Gauges, Hammerless, Damascus Barrel, *Modern*	150	225	185
Various Gauges, Outside Hammers, Steel Barrel, *Modern*	175	250	195

SHOTGUN, SINGLESHOT

Various Gauges, Hammer, Steel Barrel, *Modern*	125	150	90

AMERICAN BOY Made by Bliss & Goodyear for Townley Hdw. Co.

HANDGUN, REVOLVER

.32 Short R.F., Single Action, Solid Frame, Spur Trigger, 7 Shot, *Antique*	100	125	150

AMERICAN BULLDOG Made by Johnson, Bye & Co., Worcester,
Mass. 1882–1900.

HANDGUN, REVOLVER

.22 Short R.F., 7 Shot, Spur Trigger, Solid Frame, Single Action, *Antique*	100	175	175

	V.G.	Exc.	Prior Edition Exc. Value
.32 S & W, 5 Shot, Spur Trigger, Solid Frame, Single Action, *Modern*	$100	$150	$150
.32 Short R.F., 5 Shot, Spur Trigger, Solid Frame, Single Action, *Antique*	100	175	175
.38 S & W, 5 Shot, Spur Trigger, Solid Frame, Single Action, *Modern*	100	150	155
.38 Short R.F., 5 Shot, Spur Trigger, Solid Frame, Single Action, *Antique*	100	175	180
.41 Short C.F., 5 Shot, Spur Trigger, Solid Frame, Single Action, *Antique*	100	200	195

AMERICAN CHAMPION
SHOTGUN, SINGLESHOT

M1899, 12 Gauge, Plain, *Modern*	75	100	125

AMERICAN DERRINGER CORP. Waco, Texas 1979 to date.

HANDGUN, DOUBLE BARREL, OVER-UNDER

Model AD, .32 S & W Long, Remington Style Derringer, Stainless Steel, Spur Trigger, Hammer, *Modern*	150	175	145
Model AD, .38 Spec., Remington Style Derringer, Stainless Steel, Spur Trigger, Hammer, *Modern*	150	175	150
Model AD, .357 Mag., Remington Style Derringer, Stainless Steel, Spur Trigger, Hammer, *Modern*	150	175	155
Model AD, .41 Mag., Remington Style Derringer, Stainless Steel, Spur Trigger, Hammer, *Modern*	175	275	275
Model AD, .44 Mag., Remington Style Derringer, Stainless Steel, Spur Trigger, Hammer, *Modern*	200	275	275
Model AD, .45 A.C.P., Remington Style Derringer, Stainless Steel, Spur Trigger, Hammer, *Modern*	150	200	185
Model AD, .45 Win. Mag., Remington Style Derringer, Stainless Steel, Spur Trigger, Hammer, *Modern*	225	350	350
Model ADL, Various Calibers, Remington Style Derringer, Stainless Steel, Lightweight, Spur Trigger, Hammer, *Modern*	125	150	140

HANDGUN, SINGLESHOT

Model ADS, Various Calibers, Remington Style Derringer, Stainless Steel, Spur Trigger, Hammer, *Modern*	125	150	160

HANDGUN, SEMI-AUTOMATIC

Model ADSS, .25 ACP, Clip Fed, Stainless Steel, *Modern*	50	75	85
Model ADBS, .25 ACP, Clip Fed, Blue, *Modern*	50	75	65
Model ADM, .250 Mag., Clip Fed, Stainless Steel, *Modern*	75	125	115
Model ADMB, .250 Mag., Clip Fed, Blue, *Modern*	50	75	95

American Derringer ADSS, .25 Auto

American Derringer AD, .44 Magnum

American Derringer Corp. Model ADL

	V.G.	Exc.	Prior Edition Exc. Value

AMERICAN FIREARMS CO. San Antonion, Texas 1966–1974.

HANDGUN, SEMI-AUTOMATIC

	V.G.	Exc.	Prior Edition Exc. Value
.22 L.R.R.F., Clip Fed, Stainless Steel, *Modern*	$75	$150	$130
.25 ACP, Clip Fed, Blue, *Modern*	125	150	100
.25 ACP, Clip Fed, Stainless Steel, *Modern*	150	175	120
.32 ACP, Clip Fed, Stainless Steel, *Modern*	75	150	145
.380 ACP, Clip Fed, Stainless Steel, *Modern*	250	300	195

AMERICAN EAGLE Made by Hopkins & Allen 1870–1898.

HANDGUN, REVOLVER

	V.G.	Exc.	
.22 Short R.F., 7 Shot, Spur Trigger, Solid Frame, Single Action, *Antique*	125	175	175
.32 Short R.F., 5 Shot, Spur Trigger, Solid Frame, Single Action, *Antique*	150	200	195

AMERICAN GUN CO. Made by Crescent Firearms Co. Sold by H. & D. Folsom Co.

HANDGUN, REVOLVER

.32 S & W, 5 Shot, Double Action, Top Break, *Modern*	150	175	125

SHOTGUN, DOUBLE BARREL, SIDE-BY-SIDE

Various Gauges, Outside Hammers, Damascus Barrel, *Modern*	150	200	175
Various Gauges, Hammerless, Steel Barrel, *Modern*	225	250	220
Various Gauges, Hammerless, Damascus Barrel, *Modern*	150	200	175
Various Gauges, Outside Hammers, Steel Barrel, *Modern*	200	250	200

SHOTGUN, SINGLESHOT

Various Gauges, Hammer, Steel Barrel, *Modern*	55	85	85

AMERICAN STANDARD TOOL CO. Newark, N.J. 1865–1870, Successor to Manhattan Firearms Co.

HANDGUN, PERCUSSION

Hero, .34, Screw Barrel, Center Hammer, Spur Trigger, *Antique*	100	200	190

HANDGUN, REVOLVER

.22 Short R.F., 7 Shot, Spur Trigger, Tip-Up, *Antique*	250	375	375

AMERICUS Made by Hopkins & Allen 1870–1900.

HANDGUN, REVOLVER

.22 Short R.F., 7 Shot, Spur Trigger, Solid Frame, Single Action, *Antique*	100	150	170
.32 Short R.F., 5 Shot, Spur Trigger, Solid Frame, Single Action, *Antique*	100	175	180

	V.G.	Exc.	Prior Edition Exc. Value

AMSDEN, B.W. Saratoga Springs, N.Y. 1852.
COMBINATION WEAPON, PERCUSSION

	V.G.	Exc.	Prior Edition Exc. Value
.40-16 Ga., Double Barrel, Rifled, *Antique*	$650	$900	$995

RIFLE, PERCUSSION

.40, Octagon Barrel, Set Trigger, Rifled, *Antique*	400	600	700

AMT Arcadia Machine & Tool, since 1976 in Arcadia, Calif.
HANDGUN, SEMI-AUTOMATIC

	V.G.	Exc.	Prior Ed.
Back Up, .22 L.R.R.F., Stainless Steel, Clip Fed, *Modern*	225	250	250
Back Up, .380 ACP, AMT, Stainless Steel, Clip Fed, *Modern*	225	250	250
Back Up, .380 ACP, TDE, Stainless Steel, Clip Fed, *Modern*	175	250	250
Back Up, .380 ACP, OMC, Stainless Steel, Clip Fed, *Modern*	150	175	180
Combat Skipper, .45 ACP, Stainless Steel, Clip Fed, Fixed Sights, *Modern*	325	375	350
Government, .45 ACP, Stainless Steel, Clip Fed, Fixed Sights, *Modern*	215	310	300
Hardballer, .45 ACP, Stainless Steel, Clip Fed, Adjustable Sights, *Modern*	325	425	400
Lightning, .22 L.R., Stainless Steel, 5" Bull Barrel, Adjustable Sights	262	280	280
As Above, Fixed Sights	230	250	250
As Above, 6½" Bull Barrel, Adjustable Sights	262	280	280

AMT Skipper .45

AMT Back-Up .380

	V.G.	Exc.	Prior Edition Exc. Value
As Above, Fixed Sights	$230	$250	$250
Lightning, .22 L.R., Stainless Steel, 6½" Tapered Barrel, Adjustable Sights	262	280	280
As Above, Fixed Sights	230	250	250
Longslide, .45 ACP, Stainless Steel, Clip Fed, Adjustable Sights, *Modern*	350	450	500
Skipper, .45 ACP, Stainless Steel, Clip Fed, Adjustable Sights, *Modern*	275	350	375

ANDRUS & OSBORNE Canton, Conn. 1847–1850, moved to
Southbridge, Mass. 1850–1851.

HANDGUN, PERCUSSION
.36 Underhammer, Boot Pistol, Half-Octagon Barrel, *Antique*	150	250	275

ANGSTADT, A. & J. Berks County, Pa. 1792–1808. See Kentucky
Rifles and U.S. Military.

ANGSTADT, PETER Lancaster County, Pa. 1770–1777. See Kentucky Rifles and Pistols.

ANGUSH, JAMES Lancaster County, Pa. 1771. See Kentucky Rifles
and Pistols.

ANNELY, L. London, England 1650–1700.
HANDGUN, FLINTLOCK
.62, Holster Pistol, Brass Mounting, *Antique*	450	950	995

ANSCHUTZ, E. Philadelphia, Pa., c. 1860.
RIFLE, PERCUSSION
.36 Schutzen Rifle, Octagon Barrel, Target, *Antique*	1,250	2,000	2,250

ANSCHUTZ, J.G. Zella Mehlis, Germany 1922–1938, 1945 to date in
Ulm, West Germany. Also see Savage Arms Co. for rifle listings.
HANDGUN, REVOLVER
J.G.A., 7mm C.F., Folding Trigger, Pocket Revolver, *Curio*	125	200	195

ANSCHUTZ, UDO Zella Mehlis, Germany 1927–1939.
HANDGUN, SINGLESHOT
Record-Match M1933, .22 L.R.R.F., Free Pistol, Martini Action, Fancy Stocks, Target Sights, *Modern*	450	650	700

Anschutz, J.G. Revolver

	V.G.	Exc.	Prior Edition Exc. Value
Record-Match M210, .22 L.R.R.F., Free Pistol, Martini Action, Fancy Stocks, Target Sights, Light Engraving, *Modern*....................	*$550*	*$800*	*$900*

ANSTADT, JACOB Kurztown, Pa. 1815–1817. See Kentucky Rifles and Pistols.

APACHE Fab. de Armas Garantazadas, Spain, c. 1920.
HANDGUN, REVOLVER
| **Colt Police Positive Type**, .38, Double Action, 6 Shots, *Curio* .... | *75* | *100* | *120* |

APACHE Tempe, Ariz., c. 1970.
RIFLE, SEMI-AUTOMATIC
| **Thompson Replica**, .45 ACP, Clip Fed, *Class 3* .... | *100* | *150* | *165* |

APACHE Made by Ojanguren y Vidosa; Eibar, Spain.
HANDGUN, SEMI-AUTOMATIC
| **.25 ACP**, Clip Fed, *Modern*... | *150* | *175* | *135* |

APAOLOZO HERMANOS Zumorraga, Spain, c. 1925.
HANDGUN, REVOLVER
| **Colt Police Positive Type**, .38 Spec., Double Action, *Curio* .... | *75* | *125* | *120* |

APEX RIFLE CO. Sun Valley, Calif., c. 1952.
RIFLE, BOLT ACTION
Bantam Light Sporter, Various Calibers, 7 Lbs., Monte Kennedy Stock, Standard Grade, No Sights, *Modern*......................................	*250*	*400*	*495*
Apex Eight, Various Calibers, 8 Lbs., Monte Kennedy Stock, Standard Grade, No Sights, *Modern*..	*200*	*350*	*450*
Reliable Nine, Various Calibers, 9 Lbs., Monte Kennedy Stock, Standard Grade, No Sights, *Modern*..	*200*	*350*	*450*
Varmint & Target, Various Calibers, Monte Kennedy Target Stock, Heavy Barrel, No Sights, *Modern*...	*250*	*425*	*525*

	V.G.	Exc.	Prior Edition Exc. Value
Bench Rester, Various Calibers, Monte Kennedy Laminated Stock with Rails, Bull Barrel, Canjar Trigger, *Modern*	$250	$475	$675

ARAMBERRI Spain

SHOTGUN, DOUBLE BARREL, SIDE-BY-SIDE

Boxlock, 12 Gauge, Single Trigger, Checkered Stock, Vent Rib, *Modern*	125	150	195

ARGENTINE MILITARY

AUTOMATIC WEAPON, SUBMACHINE GUN

C-3, .45 ACP, *Class 3*	250	395	395
C-4 Hafdasa, .45 ACP, *Class 3*	200	375	375
M E M S, 9mm Luger, *Class 3*	475	675	675
M1943, .45 ACP, *Class 3*	225	375	375
M1946, .45 ACP, *Class 3*	225	375	375
P A M, 9mm Luger, *Class 3*	350	675	675
Star M D, 9mm Luger, *Class 3*	475	775	775

HANDGUN, REVOLVER

Colt M 1985, Double Trigger, Solid Frame, Swing-Out Cylinder, Military, *Modern*	125	175	180

HANDGUN, SEMI-AUTOMATIC

Ballester-Molina, .45 ACP, Clip Fed, *Modern*	225	295	295
Ballester-Rigaud, .45 ACP, Clip Fed, *Modern*	225	325	335
Mannlicher M1905, 7.63 Mannlicher, *Curio*	150	250	260
Modelo 1916 (Colt 1911), .45 ACP, Clip Fed, *Modern*	200	375	380
Modelo 1927 (Colt 1911A1), .45 ACP, Clip Fed, *Modern*	225	400	420

Argentine M1905

	V.G.	Exc.	Prior Edition Exc. Value

RIFLE, BOLT ACTION

M 1908/09, 7.65 Argentine, Carbine, Open Rear Sight, Full-Stocked Military, *Modern* — $100 $150 $160

M 1891, 7.65 Argentine, Rifle, Full Stocked Military, *Modern* — 50 75 90

M 1891, 7.65 Argentine, Carbine, Open Rear Sight, Full Stocked Military, *Modern* — 50 100 100

M 1909, 7.65 Argentine, Rifle, Full Stocked Military, *Modern* — 75 100 105

RIFLE, SINGLESHOT

M 1879, .43 Mauser, Rolling Block, *Antique* — 275 400 375

ARISTOCRAT Made by Hopkins & Allen for Suplee Biddle Hardware 1870–1900.

HANDGUN, REVOLVER

.22 Short R.F., 7 Shot, Spur Trigger, Solid Frame, Single Action, *Antique* — 75 150 160

.32 Short R.F., 5 Shot, Spur Trigger, Solid Frame, Single Action, *Antique* — 75 175 175

ARISTOCRAT Made by Stevens Arms.

SHOTGUN, DOUBLE BARREL, SIDE-BY-SIDE

M 315, Various Gauges, Hammerless, Steel Barrel, *Modern* — 75 150 165

ARIZAGA, GASPAR Eibar, Spain.

HANDGUN, SEMI-AUTOMATIC

.32 ACP, Clip Fed, *Modern* — 75 125 150

ARMALITE Costa Mesa, Calif.

RIFLE, SEMI-AUTOMATIC

AR-180 .223 Rem., Clip Fed, Folding Stock, *Modern* — 750 875 450

AR-7 Explorer, .22 L.R.R.F., Clip Fed, *Modern* — 75 100 80

AR-7 Explorer Custom, .22 L.R.R.F., Checkered Stock, Clip Fed, *Modern* — 100 150 100

SHOTGUN, SEMI-AUTOMATIC

AR-17, 12 Ga., Lightweight, *Modern* — 475 575 650

ARMI JAGER Turin, Italy. Imported by E.M.F.

HANDGUN, REVOLVER

Dakota, .22 L.R.R.F., Single Action, Western Style, Various Barrel Lengths, *Modern* — 100 150 140

	V.G.	Exc.	Prior Edition Exc. Value
Dakota, .22 L.R.R.F. and .22 W.M.R. Single Action, Western Style, Various Barrel Lengths, *Modern*	*$125*	*$175*	*$170*
Dakota, Various Calibers, Single Action, Western Style, Various Barrel Lengths, *Modern*	*125*	*175*	*170*
Dakota, Various Calibers, Single Action, Western Style, Buntline Barrel Lengths, *Modern*	*125*	*175*	*195*
Dakota, Various Calibers, Single Action, Western Style, Engraved, Various Barrel Lengths, *Modern*	*225*	*325*	*300*
Dakota Sheriff, Various Calibers, Single Action, Western Style, 3½" Barrel, *Modern*..................................	*125*	*200*	*180*
Dakota Target, Various Calibers, Single Action, Western Style, Adjustable Sights, Various Barrel Lengths, *Modern*.........................	*150*	*200*	*200*

RIFLE, SEMI-AUTOMATIC

	V.G.	Exc.	Prior Edition Exc. Value
AP-74 Standard, .22 L.R.R.F., Military Style, Plastic Stock, *Modern*..................................	*50*	*100*	*100*
AP-74 Standard, .32 ACP, Military Style, Plastic Stock, *Modern*..................................	*75*	*125*	*110*
AP-74, .22 L.R.R.F., Military Style, Wood Stock, *Modern*.............	*75*	*100*	*100*
AP-74, .31 ACP, Military Style, Wood Stock, *Modern*....................	*75*	*125*	*120*
AP-74 Commando, .22 L.R.R.F., Military Style, Wood Stock, *Modern*..................................	*75*	*125*	*120*

ARMINEX LTD. Scottsdale, Ariz. since 1982.

HANDGUN, SEMI-AUTOMATIC

	V.G.	Exc.	Prior Edition Exc. Value
Trifire, .45 A.C.P., 9mm Luger, or .38 Super, Blue or Nickel, Clip Fed, Hammer, Adjustable Sights, *Modern*...	*350*	*400*	*300*
Trifire Presentation, .45 A.C.P., 9mm Luger, or .38 Super, Cased, Blue or Nickel, Clip Fed, Hammer, Adjustable Sights, *Modern*.......	*400*	*450*	*335*

ARMINIUS Herman Weihrauch Sportwaffenfabrik, Mellrichstadt/Bayern, West Germany before 1968; for Current Models, See F.I.E.

HANDGUN, REVOLVER

	V.G.	Exc.	Prior Edition Exc. Value
HW-3, .22 L.R.R.F., *Modern*	*25*	*50*	*35*
HW-3, .32 S & W Long, *Modern*..................................	*25*	*50*	*45*
HW-5, .22 L.R.R.F., *Modern*	*25*	*25*	*35*
HW-5, .32 S & W Long, *Modern*..................................	*25*	*50*	*40*
HW-7, .22 L.R.R.F., *Modern*	*25*	*50*	*35*
HW-9, .22 L.R.R.F., Adjustable Sights, *Modern*.............................	*50*	*75*	*55*

ARMINIUS Friederich Pickert, Zella-Mehlis, Germany 1922–1939.

HANDGUN, REVOLVER

	V.G.	Exc.	Prior Edition Exc. Value
Model 1, .22 L.R.R.F., Hammerless, *Modern*..................................	*200*	*250*	*140*

Arminex - Trifire Standard

Arminex - Trifire Target

	V.G.	Exc.	Prior Edition Exc. Value
Model 2, .22 L.R.R.F., Hammer, *Modern*	$250	$300	$140
Model 3, .25 ACP, Hammerless, Folding Trigger, *Modern*	125	175	140
Model 4, 5.5 Velo Dog, Hammerless, Folding Trigger, *Modern*	75	150	140
Model 5/1, 7.5mm Swiss, Hammer, *Modern*	100	175	165
Model 5/2, 7.62 Nagant, Hammer, *Modern*	100	175	155
Model 7, .320 Revolver, Hammer, *Modern*	75	125	130
Model 8, .320 Revolver, Hammerless, Folding Trigger, *Modern*	125	150	130
Model 9, .32 ACP, Hammer, *Modern*	125	175	140
Model 10, .32 ACP, Hammerless, Folding Trigger, *Modern*	100	150	140
Model 13, .380 Revolver, Hammer, *Modern*	100	150	140
Model 14, .380 Revolver, Hammerless, *Modern*	100	150	140

HANDGUN, SINGLESHOT

	V.G.	Exc.	
TP 1, .22 L.R.R.F., Target Pistol, Hammer, *Modern*	150	300	375
TP 2, .22 L.R.R.F., Hammerless, Set Triggers, *Modern*	150	300	375

ARMSPORT Current Importers, Miami, Fla.

HANDGUN, FLINTLOCK

	V.G.	Exc.	
Kentucky, .45, Reproduction, *Antique*	50	85	80

HANDGUN, PERCUSSION

	V.G.	Exc.	
New Remington Army, .44, Stainless Steel, Brass Trigger Guard, Reproduction, *Antique*	75	125	125
New Remington Army, .44, Blue, Brass Trigger Guard, Reproduction, *Antique*	75	100	95
Whitney, .36, Solid Frame, Brass Trigger Guard, Reproduction, *Antique*	75	100	95
Spiller & Burr, .36, Solid Frame, Brass Frame, Reproduction, *Antique*	50	75	70
1851 Colt Navy, .36, Brass Frame, Reproduction, *Antique*	50	75	75
1851 Colt Navy, .44, Brass Frame, Reproduction, *Antique*	50	75	75
1851 Colt Navy, .36, Steel Frame, Reproduction, *Antique*	50	100	90
1851 Colt Navy, .44, Steel Frame, Reproduction, *Antique*	50	100	90
1860 Colt Army, .44, Brass Frame, Reproduction, *Antique*	50	75	85
1860 Colt Army, .44, Steel Frame, Reproduction, *Antique*	50	100	95
New Hartford Police, .36, Reproduction, *Antique*	50	100	85
1847 Colt Walker, .44, Reproduction, *Antique*	75	125	120
Corsair, .44, Double Barrel, Reproduction, *Antique*	50	75	85
Kentucky, .45 or .50, Reproduction, *Antique*	50	75	75
Patriot, .45, Target Sights, Set Triggers, Reproduction, *Antique*	75	100	100

RIFLE, BOLT ACTION

	V.G.	Exc.	
Tikka, Various Calibers, Open Sights, Checkered Stock, Clip Fed, *Modern*	275	400	395

	V.G.	Exc.	Prior Edition Exc. Value

RIFLE, LEVER ACTION

Premier 1873 Winchester, Various Calibers, Rifle, Engraved, Reproduction, *Modern* .... $750 | $1,000 | $950

Premier 1873 Winchester, Various Calibers, Carbine, Engraved, Reproduction, *Modern* .... 650 | 850 | 800

RIFLE, FLINTLOCK

Kentucky, .45, Reproduction, *Antique* .... 125 | 150 | 145

Deluxe Kentucky, .45, Reproduction, *Antique* .... 150 | 200 | 200

Hawkin, .45, Reproduction, *Antique* .... 125 | 175 | 160

Deluxe Hawkin, .50, Reproduction, *Antique* .... 125 | 175 | 170

RIFLE, PERCUSSION

Kentucky, .45 or .50, Reproduction, *Antique* .... 100 | 150 | 140

Deluxe Kentucky, .45, Reproduction, *Antique* .... 150 | 200 | 185

Hawkin, Various Calibers, Reproduction, *Antique* .... 125 | 150 | 150

Deluxe Hawkin, Various Calibers, Reproduction, *Antique* .... 150 | 175 | 160

COMBINATION WEAPON, OVER-UNDER

Tikka Turkey Gun, 12 Ga. and .222 Rem., Vent Rib, Sling Swivels, Muzzle Break, Checkered Stock, *Modern* .... 450 | 625 | 600

RIFLE, DOUBLE BARREL, SIDE-BY-SIDE

Emperor, Various Calibers, Holland and Holland Type Sidelock, Engraved, Checkered Stock, Extra Barrels, Cased, *Modern* .... 12,225 | 16,250 | 9,950

Emperor Deluxe, Various Calibers, Holland and Holland Sidelock, Fancy Engraving, Checkered Stock, Extra Barrels, *Modern* .... 20,000 | 25,000 | 15,000

RIFLE, DOUBLE BARREL, OVER-UNDER

Emperor, Various Calibers, Checkered Stock, Engraved, Extra Barrels, Cased, *Modern* .... 12,000 | 15,000 | 7,750

Express, Various Calibers, Checkered Stock, Engraved, *Modern* .... 3,000 | 3,500 | 2,350

SHOTGUN, PERCUSSION

Hook Breech, Double Barrel, Side-by-Side, 10 and 12 Gauges, Reproduction, *Antique* .... 175 | 250 | 225

SHOTGUN, DOUBLE BARREL, SIDE-BY-SIDE

Goose Gun, 10 Ga. 3½" Mag., Checkered Stock, *Modern* .... 375 | 475 | 465

Side-by-Side, 12 and 20 Gauges, Checkered Stock, *Modern* .... 325 | 425 | 420

Express, 12 and 20 Gauges, Holland and Holland Type Sidelock, Engraved, Checkered Stock, *Modern* .... 3,000 | 3,500 | 2,850

Western Double, 12 Ga. Mag. 3", Outside Hammers Double Trigger, *Modern* .... 300 | 400 | 395

SHOTGUN, DOUBLE BARREL, OVER-UNDER

Premier, 12 Ga., Skeet Grade, Checkered Stock, Engraved, *Modern* .... 900 | 1,200 | 1,400

Model 2500, 12 and 20 Ga., Checkered Stock, Adjustable Choke, Single Selective Trigger, *Modern* .... 450 | 650 | 550

	V.G.	Exc.	Prior Edition Exc. Value
SHOTGUN, SINGLESHOT			
Monotrap, 12 Ga., Two Barrel Set, Checkered Stock, *Modern*	*$1,600*	*$2,300*	*$2,100*
Monotrap, 12 Ga., Checkered Stock, *Modern*..................................	*1,200*	*1,550*	*1,450*

ARMSTRONG, JOHN Gettysburg, Pa. 1813–1817. Also See Kentucky Rifles and Pistols.

ARRIOLA HERMANOS Eibar, Spain, c. 1930.

HANDGUN, REVOLVER

Colt Police Positive Copy, .38 Spec., Double Action, *Modern*	*50*	*100*	*115*

ARRIZABALAGA, HIJOS DE CALIXTO Eibar, Spain, c. 1915.

HANDGUN, SEMI-AUTOMATIC

Ruby Type, .32 ACP, Clip Fed, Blue, *Curio*.....................................	*125*	*150*	*150*

ASCASO, FRANCISCO Tarassa, Spain, c. 1937.

HANDGUN, SEMI-AUTOMATIC

Astra 400 Copy, 9mm, Clip Fed, Military Type, *Curio*...................	*900*	*1,000*	*975*

ASHEVILLE ARMORY Asheville, N.C. 1861–1864.

RIFLE, PERCUSSION

.58 Enfield Type, Rifled, Brass Furniture, Military, *Antique*............	*2,500*	*3,500*	*2,150*

ASTRA Founded in 1908 as Unceta y Esperanza in Eibar, Spain. In 1913 moved to Guernica, Spain and the name was reversed to Esperanza y Unceta; name changed again in 1926 to Unceta y Cia.; name changed again in 1953 to Astra-Unceta y Cia.

HANDGUN, REVOLVER

Model 41, .41 Magnum, Blue, *Modern*..	*250*	*275*	*350*
Model 45, .45 Colt, Blue, *Modern*..	*300*	*350*	*350*
250, .22 L.R.R.F., Double Action, Small Frame, *Modern*.................	*100*	*150*	*140*
250, .22 W.M.R., Double Action, Small Frame, *Modern*..................	*100*	*150*	*140*
250, .32 S & W Long, Double Action, Small Frame, *Modern*..........	*100*	*150*	*140*
250, .38 Special, Double Action, Small Frame, *Modern*...................	*125*	*175*	*150*
357 Magnum, .357 Magnum, Double Action, Adjustable Sights, *Modern*...	*200*	*275*	*250*
357 Magnum, .357 Magnum, Double Action, Adjustable Sights, Stainless Steel, *Modern*..	*250*	*300*	*285*

Astra Model 900

Astra M1911 .32

Astra Club

Astra Model 200 with Long Clip

	V.G.	Exc.	Prior Edition Exc. Value
44 Magnum, .44 Magnum, Double Action, Adjustable Sights, *Modern*	$300	$350	$335
960, .38 Special, Double Action, Adjustable Sights, *Modern*	100	175	165
Cadix, .22 L.R.R.F., Double Action, Adjustable Sights, *Modern*	75	150	140
Cadix, .22 W.M.R., Double Action, Adjustable Sights, *Modern*	100	150	150
Cadix, .32 S & W Long, Double Action, Adjustable Sights, *Modern*	100	150	130
Cadix, .38 Special, Double Action, Adjustable Sights, *Modern*	150	175	160
Inox, .38 Special, Stainless Steel, Double Action, Small Frame, *Modern*	150	200	190
Match, .38 Special, Double Action, Adjustable Sights, *Modern*	100	175	165

HANDGUN, SEMI-AUTOMATIC

Chrome Plating, *Add* $25.00–$45.00

Light Engraving, *Add* $60.00–$110.00

	V.G.	Exc.	Prior Edition Exc. Value
A-50, Various Calibers, Blue, Single Action, *Modern*	150	225	220
A-80, Various Calibers, Double Action, Blue, Large Magazine, *Modern*	300	375	385
A-80, Various Calibers, Double Action, Chrome, Large Magazine, *Modern*	300	400	400
Constable, Various Calibers, Blue, *Modern*	250	300	250
Constable Pocket, Various Calibers, Blue, *Modern*	250	300	250
Constable Sport, Various Calibers, Blue, *Modern*	250	300	270
Constable Target, .22 L.R.R.F., Blue, *Modern*	300	350	325
Model 100, .32 ACP, *Curio*	225	275	165
Model 100 Special, .32 ACP, 9 Shot, *Curio*	250	300	185
Model 1000, .32 ACP, 12 Shot, *Modern*	400	500	200
Model 1911, .32 ACP, *Curio*	250	300	225
Model 1915, .32 ACP, *Curio*	200	275	170
Model 1916, .32 ACP, *Curio*	200	300	190
Model 1924, .25 ACP, *Curio*	175	225	165
Model 200 Firecat, .25 ACP, Early Model, Concave Indicator Cut, *Modern*	200	250	165
Model 200 Firecat, .25 ACP, Late Model, Rear Indicator, *Modern*	100	150	145
Model 200 Firecat, .25 ACP, Late Model, Long Clip, *Modern*	125	175	150
Model 2000 Camper, .22 Short R.F., *Modern*	250	300	170
Model 2000 Cub, .22 Short R.F., *Modern*	150	175	150
Model 2000 Cub, .25 ACP, *Modern*	150	175	145
Model 2000 Camper or Cub, Conversion Kit Only,	75	100	90
Model 300, .32 ACP, Clip Fed, *Modern*	200	300	220
Model 300, .32 ACP, Nazi-Proofed, Clip Fed, *Curio*	375	475	475
Model 300, .380 ACP, Clip Fed, *Modern*	225	325	235
Model 300, .380 ACP, Nazi-Proofed, Clip Fed, *Curio*	400	500	475

	V.G.	Exc.	Prior Edition Exc. Value
Model 3000 (Late), .380 ACP, Clip Fed, *Modern*............................	*$200*	*$250*	*$155*
Model 400, .32 ACP, *Modern*..	*500*	*600*	*695*
Model 400, 9mm Bayard Long, Nazi-Proofed, Clip Fed, *Curio*.......	*700*	*750*	*650*
Model 400, 9mm Bayard Long, *Modern*...	*300*	*375*	*345*
Model 4000 Falcon, Conversion Unit Only....................................	*75*	*100*	*100*
Model 4000 Falcon, .22 L.R.R.F., Clip Fed, *Modern*.......................	*400*	*500*	*220*
Model 4000 Falcon, .32 ACP, Clip Fed, *Modern*.............................	*250*	*300*	*200*
Model 4000 Falcon, .380 ACP, Clip Fed, *Modern*...........................	*250*	*300*	*200*
Model 600, .32 ACP, Clip Fed, *Modern*	*200*	*300*	*250*
Model 600, 9mm Luger, Nazi-Proofed, Clip Fed, *Curio*	*400*	*500*	*400*
Model 600, 9mm Luger, Clip Fed, *Modern*	*200*	*300*	*270*
Model 700, .32 ACP, Clip Fed, *Curio*...	*450*	*500*	*675*
Model 700 Special, .32 ACP, 12 Shots, Clip Fed, *Modern*	*500*	*600*	*625*

Astra A-80

Astra Constable

Astra TS-22

Astra 44 Magnum

Astra 7000

Astra Model 960

	V.G.	Exc.	Prior Edition Exc. Value
Model 7000, .22 L.R.R.F., Clip Fed, *Modern*	$125	$175	$165
Model 800 Condor, .380 ACP, Clip Fed, *Modern*	850	1,000	185
Model 900, 7.63 Mauser, Holster Stock, *Modern*	1,750	2,000	1,475
Model 5000 Sport (Constable), .22 L.R.R.F. Target Pistol, Clip Fed, *Modern*	250	300	275
Model TS-22, .22 L.R.R.F. Target Pistol, Single Action, Clip Fed, *Modern*	225	325	325

RIFLE, SEMI-AUTOMATIC

Model 1000, .32 ACP, Clip Fed, *Modern*	325	450	435
Model 3000 (Early), .32 ACP, *Modern*	125	175	170
Model 3000 (Late), .22 L.R.R.F., *Modern*	100	150	150
Model 3000 (Late), .32 ACP, *Modern*	100	175	160
Model 800 Condor, 9mm Luger, *Curio*	450	650	625
Model 902, 7.63 Mauser, *Modern*	1,000	1,600	1,700

SHOTGUN, DOUBLE BARREL, OVER-UNDER

Model 650, 12 Gauge, Checkered Stock, Double Triggers, Vent Rib, *Modern*	200	275	285
Model 650E, 12 Gauge, Checkered Stock, Double Triggers, Vent Rib, Selective Ejectors, *Modern*	225	375	385
Model 750, 12 Gauge, Checkered Stock, Double Triggers, Vent Rib, *Modern*	225	375	385
Model 750E, 12 Gauge, Checkered Stock, Single Trigger, Vent Rib, Selective Ejectors, *Modern*	350	525	490
Model 750 Skeet, 12 Gauge, Checkered Stock, Single Trigger, Vent Rib, Selective Ejectors, *Modern*	350	500	525
Model 750 Trap, 12 Gauge, Checkered Stock, Single Trigger, Vent Rib, Selective Ejectors, *Modern*	350	500	525
Model ID-13, 12 Gauge, Checkered Stock, Single Trigger, Selective Ejectors, Vent Rib, *Modern*	325	475	465

SHOTGUN, DOUBLE BARREL, SIDE-BY-SIDE

Model 811, 10 Gauge Magnum, Checkered Stock, Double Triggers, *Modern*	195	275	300
Model 805, Various Gauges, Checkered Stock, Double Triggers, *Modern*	150	250	265

SHOTGUN, SINGLESHOT

Cyclops, Various Gauges, Checkered Stock, *Modern*	75	100	90

ATIS Ponte S. Marco, Italy.

SHOTGUN, SEMI-AUTOMATIC

12 Ga., Lightweight, Vent Rib, *Modern*	150	225	240
12 Ga., Lightweight, Vent Rib, Left-Hand, *Modern*	200	275	290

	V.G.	Exc.	Prior Edition Exc. Value

ATLAS Domingo Acha y Cia., Ermua, Spain, c. 1920.

HANDGUN, SEMI-AUTOMATIC

	V.G.	Exc.	Prior Edition Exc. Value
Vest Pocket, .25 ACP, Clip Fed, *Modern*	$100	$125	$130

ATLAS ARMS Chicago, Ill. from about 1962 to 1972.

HANDGUN, DOUBLE BARREL, OVER-UNDER

	V.G.	Exc.	Prior Edition Exc. Value
Derringer, .22 L.R.R.F., Remington Style, *Modern*	50	75	55
Derringer, .38 Spec., Remington Style, *Modern*	50	75	65

SHOTGUN, DOUBLE BARREL, SIDE-BY-SIDE

	V.G.	Exc.	Prior Edition Exc. Value
Model 145, Various Gauges, Boxlock, Vent Rib, Engraved, Hammerless, Checkered Stock, *Modern*	300	425	440
Model 200, Various Gauges, Boxlock, Double Triggers, Hammerless, Checkered Stock, *Modern*	175	275	260
Model 204, Various Gauges, Boxlock, Single Trigger, Hammerless, Checkered Stock, *Modern*	225	275	300
Model 206, Various Gauges, Boxlock, Single Trigger, Automatic Ejector, Hammerless, Checkered Stock, *Modern*	275	350	335
Model 208, Various Gauges, Boxlock, Double Triggers, Vent Rib, Recoil Pad, *Modern*	250	325	300
Model 500, Various Gauges, Boxlock, Double Triggers, Vent Rib, Recoil Pad, *Modern*	250	325	300

SHOTGUN, SINGLESHOT

	V.G.	Exc.	Prior Edition Exc. Value
Trap Gun, 12 Gauge, Automatic Ejector, Engraved, Checkered Stock, *Modern*	425	525	490
Insuperable 101, Various Gauges, Vent Rib, Engraved, Checkered Stock, *Modern*	75	100	90

SHOTGUN, DOUBLE BARREL, OVER-UNDER

	V.G.	Exc.	Prior Edition Exc. Value
Model 65, Various Gauges, Boxlock, Double Triggers, Vent Rib, *Modern*	250	350	340
Model 65-ST, Various Gauges, Boxlock, Single Trigger, Vent Rib, *Modern*	250	400	375
Model 87, Various Gauges, Merkel Type Sidelock, Single Trigger, Vent Rib, Engraved, *Modern*	350	450	435
Model 150, Various Gauges, Boxlock, Single Trigger, Vent Rib, *Modern*	250	400	375
Model 150, Various Gauges, Boxlock, Single Trigger, Vent Rib, Automatic Ejectors, *Modern*	300	425	400
Model 160, Various Gauges, Boxlock, Single Trigger, Vent Rib, Automatic Ejectors, *Modern*	350	450	435
Model 180, Various Gauges, Boxlock, Single Trigger, Vent Rib, Automatic Ejectors, Light Engraving, *Modern*	375	500	490
Model 750, Various Gauges, Merkel Type Sidelock, Single Trigger, Vent Rib, Engraved, *Modern*	350	450	435

	V.G.	Exc.	Prior Edition Exc. Value
Model 750, Various Gauges, Merkel Type Sidelock, Single Trigger, Vent Rib, Engraved, Automatic Ejectors, *Modern*	$375	$550	$525
Grand Prix, 12 or 20 Gauge, Merkel Type Sidelock, Single Selective Trigger, Fancy Engraving, Automatic Ejectors, *Modern*	850	1,200	1,150

ATKIN, HENRY E. & CO. London, England 1874–1900.

SHOTGUN, DOUBLE BARREL, SIDE-BY-SIDE

	V.G.	Exc.	Prior Edition
Raleigh, 12 Gauge, Sidelock, Double Triggers, Checkered Stock, Engraved, Automatic Ejectors, "Purdey" Barrels, *Modern*	5,500	8,750	8,500

AUBREY Made by Meridan Arms Co., sold by Sears-Roebuck 1900–1930.

HANDGUN, REVOLVER

	V.G.	Exc.	Prior Edition
.32 S & W, 5 Shot, Double Action, Top Break, *Modern*	75	95	95
.38 S & W, 5 Shot, Double Action, Top Break, *Modern*	75	95	95

AUDAX Trade name of Manufacture D'Armes Des Pyrenees, Hendaye, France, marketed by La Cartoucherie Francaise, Paris 1931–1939.

HANDGUN, SEMI-AUTOMATIC

	V.G.	Exc.	Prior Edition
.25 ACP, Clip Fed, Magazine Disconnect, Grip Safety, *Modern*	75	95	140
.32 ACP, Clip Fed, Magazine Disconnect, Blue, *Modern*	75	95	150

AUSTRALIAN MILITARY

RIFLE BOLT ACTION

	V.G.	Exc.	Prior Edition
Mk. III, .303 British, Clip Fed, WW I Issue, *Curio*	100	175	165
Mk. III, .303 British, Clip Fed, WW II Issue, *Curio*	75	150	150

RIFLE, SINGLESHOT

	V.G.	Exc.	Prior Edition
Martini, .32/40, Small Action, *Curio*	125	225	210

AUSTRIAN MILITARY

HANDGUN, FLINTLOCK

	V.G.	Exc.	Prior Edition
.64 Dragoon, with Shoulder Stock, Singleshot, *Antique*	525	825	800

HANDGUN, PERCUSSION

	V.G.	Exc.	Prior Edition
.64 Dragoon, with Shoulder Stock, Singleshot, *Antique*	350	550	600

HANDGUN, REVOLVER

	V.G.	Exc.	Prior Edition
M1898 Rast Gasser, 8mm Rast-Gasser, *Curio*	150	250	260

HANDGUN, SEMI-AUTOMATIC

	V.G.	Exc.	Prior Edition
M1907 Roth Steyr, 8mm Roth-Steyr, *Curio*	175	275	280
M1908 Steyr, 8mm Roth-Steyr, *Curio*	125	250	240

	V.G.	Exc.	Prior Edition Exc. Value
M1911 Steyr Hahn, 9mm Steyr, *Curio*	$175	$275	$290
M1912 Steyr Hahn, 9mm Steyr, *Curio*	125	225	235
Mannlicher 1901, 7.63 Mannlicher, *Curio*	150	250	260
Mannlicher 1905, 7.63 Mannlicher, *Curio*	150	250	250

HANDGUN, SINGLESHOT

	V.G.	Exc.	Prior Edition Exc. Value
Werder Lightning, 11mm, *Antique*	375	575	550

RIFLE, BOLT ACTION

	V.G.	Exc.	Prior Edition Exc. Value
M1883 Schulhof, 11.15 × 58R Werndl, 8 Shot, *Antique*	375	575	550
M1885 Steyr, 11.15 × 58R Werndl, Straight-Pull, *Antique*	275	450	425
M1886 Steyr, 11.15 × 58R Werndl, Straight Pull Bolt, *Antique*	75	150	150
M1888, 8 × 50R Mannlicher, *Antique*	75	150	150
M1888/90, 8 × 50R Mannlicher, *Antique*	75	150	125
M1890, 8 × 50R Mannlicher, Carbine, *Antique*	100	150	125
M1895, 8 × 50R Mannlicher, Carbine, *Modern*	75	100	85
M1895, 8 × 50R Mannlicher, *Curio*	50	100	80
M1895 Stutzen, 8 × 50R Mannlicher, *Curio*	75	125	120

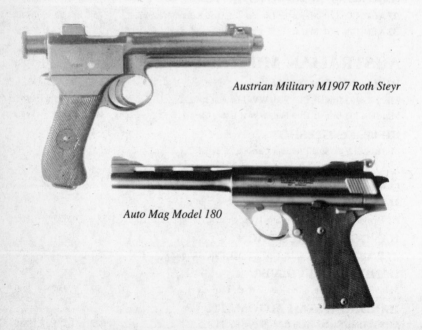

Austrian Military M1907 Roth Steyr

Auto Mag Model 180

AUTO MAG Started in Pasadena, Calif. about 1968, and moved to North Hollywood, Calif. when purchased by T D E in 1971. Marketed by T D E, Jurras Associates, and High Standard.

HANDGUN, SEMI-AUTOMATIC

	V.G.	Exc.	Prior Edition Exc. Value
First Model (Pasadena), .44 AMP, Clip Fed, Stainless Steel, Hammer, Adjustable Sights, Cased, *Modern*	*$1,900*	*$2,000*	*$1,450*
Model 160, .357 AMP, Clip Fed, Stainless Steel, Hammer, Adjustable Sights, Cased, *Modern*	*1,700*	*1,800*	*1,250*
Model 170, .41 JMP, Clip Fed, Stainless Steel, Hammer, Adjustable Sights, Cased, *Modern*	*1,400*	*1,500*	*1,400*
Model 180, .44 AMP, Clip Fed, Stainless Steel, Hammer, Adjustable Sights, Cased, *Modern*	*1,750*	*1,850*	*1,050*
Model 260, .357 AMP, Clip Fed, Stainless Steel, Hammer, Adjustable Sights, Cased, *Modern*	*1,250*	*1,350*	*1,100*
Model 280, .44 AMP, Clip Fed, Stainless Steel, Hammer, Adjustable Sights, Cased, *Modern*	*1,100*	*1,200*	*995*
Alaskan Model, .44 AMP, Clip Fed, Stainless Steel, Hammer, Adjustable Sights, Cased, *Modern*	*1,600*	*1,950*	*2,500*
High Standard, .44 AMP, Clip Fed, Stainless Steel, Hammer, Adjustable Sights, Cased, *Modern*	*1,500*	*1,800*	*1,250*
Jurras Custom Model 200, .44 AMP, Clip Fed, Stainless Steel, Hammer, Adjustable Sights, Cased, *Modern*	*2,350*	*2,500*	*3,875*

AUTOMATIC Made by Hopkins & Allen, c. 1900.

HANDGUN, REVOLVER

	V.G.	Exc.	Prior Edition Exc. Value
.32 S & W, 5 Shot, Top Break, Hammerless, Double Action, *Modern*	*75*	*100*	*95*
.38 S & W, 5 Shot, Top Break, Hammerless, Double Action, *Modern*	*75*	*100*	*95*

AUTOMATIC HAMMERLESS Made by Iver Johnson, c. 1900.

HANDGUN, REVOLVER

	V.G.	Exc.	Prior Edition Exc. Value
.22 L.R.R.F., 7 Shot, Double Action, Top Break, Hammerless, *Modern*	*75*	*100*	*90*
.32 S & W, 5 Shot, Top Break, Hammerless, Double Action, *Modern*	*50*	*75*	*100*
.38 S & W, 5 Shot, Top Break, Hammerless, Double Action, *Modern*	*50*	*75*	*100*

AUTOMATIC PISTOL Spain, Maker Unknown.

HANDGUN, SEMI-AUTOMATIC

	V.G.	Exc.	Prior Edition Exc. Value
Pocket, .32 ACP, Clip Fed, *Modern*	*50*	*75*	*100*

	V.G.	Exc.	Prior Edition Exc. Value

AUTOMATIC POLICE See Forehand & Wadsworth.

AUTO-ORDNANCE CORP. See Thompson.

AUTO-POINTER Made by Yamamoto Mfg. Co., Imported by Sloans.
SHOTGUN, SEMI-AUTOMATIC

	V.G.	Exc.	Prior Ed.
12 and 20 Gauges, Tube Feed, Checkered Stock, *Modern*...............	$175	$275	$295

AUTOSTAND Made for ManuFrance by Mre. d'Armes des Pyrenees.
HANDGUN, SINGLESHOT

	V.G.	Exc.	Prior Ed.
E-1 (Unique), .22 L.R.R.F., Target Pistol, Adjustable Sights, *Modern*..	50	75	95

AVENGER
HANDGUN, REVOLVER

	V.G.	Exc.	Prior Ed.
.32 Long R.F., 5 Shot, Single Action, Spur Trigger, *Antique*...........	75	125	140

AVION Azpiri y. Cia., Eibar, Spain, c. 1915.
HANDGUN, SEMI-AUTOMATIC

	V.G.	Exc.	Prior Ed.
Vest Pocket, .25 ACP, Clip Fed, *Curio*	75	125	120

A Y A Aguirre y Aranzabal, Spain. Now Imported by Ventura.
SHOTGUN, DOUBLE BARREL, OVER-UNDER

	V.G.	Exc.	Prior Ed.
Model 37 Super, Various Gauges, Single Selective Trigger, Automatic Ejector, Fancy Engraving, Sidelock, *Modern*..................	1,450	2,100	1,850

SHOTGUN, DOUBLE BARREL, SIDE-BY-SIDE

	V.G.	Exc.	Prior Ed.
Bolero, Various Gauges, Single Trigger, Checkered Stock, *Modern*..	325	350	250
Matador, Various Gauges, Single Selective Trigger, Checkered Stock, Selective Ejector, *Modern*...	325	375	350
Matador II, Various Gauges, Single Selective Trigger, Checkered Stock, Selective Ejector, Vent Rib, *Modern*.....................................	350	425	425
Model 1, Various Gauges, Automatic Ejector, Sidelock, Fancy Checkering, Engraved, Lightweight, *Modern*....................................	2,250	2,750	1,700
Model 117, 12 Gauge, Sidelock, Single Selective Trigger, Engraved, Checkered Stock, *Modern*..	650	725	725
Model 2, Various Gauges, Automatic Ejector, Sidelock, Engraved, Checkered Stock, Double Trigger, *Modern*.....................................	950	1,250	725
Model 53E, 12 and 20 Gauges, Sidelock, Single Selective Trigger, Fancy Checkering, Fancy Engraving, *Modern*	1,500	1,950	1,400

	V.G.	Exc.	Prior Edition Exc. Value
Model 56, 12 and 20 Gauges, Sidelock, Raised Matted Rib, Fancy Checkering, Fancy Engraving, *Modern*	$2,500	$3,000	$1,850
Model 76, 12 and 20 Gauges, Automatic Ejector, Single Selective Trigger, Engraved, Checkered Stock, *Modern*	375	650	440
Model 76, .410 Gauge, Double Triggers, Engraved, Checkered Stock, *Modern*	375	550	325
Model 400, Various Gauges, Single Trigger, Checkered Stock, *Modern*	325	575	250
Model 400E, Various Gauges, Single Selective Trigger, Checkered Stock, Selective Ejector, *Modern*	375	450	350
Model XXV/SL, 12 Ga., Sidelock, Automatic Ejector, Engraved Checkered Stock, *Modern*	1,250	1,600	800

AZANZA Y ARRIZABALAGA Eibar, Spain, c. 1916.
HANDGUN, SEMI-AUTOMATIC

	V.G.	Exc.	Prior
M1916, .32 ACP, Clip Fed, Long Grip, *Modern*	100	150	145

AZUL Eulegio Aristegui, Eibar, Spain, c. 1930.
HANDGUN, SEMI-AUTOMATIC

	V.G.	Exc.	Prior
Azul, 7.63mm Mauser, Copy of Broomhandle Mauser, *Modern*	550	950	875
Azul, .25 ACP, Clip Fed, Hammerless, *Modern*	75	125	125
Azul, .32 ACP, Clip Fed, Hammerless, *Modern*	75	125	135
Azul, .32 ACP, Clip Fed, Hammer, *Modern*	100	150	150

B

	V.G.	Exc.	Prior Edition Exc. Value

BABCOCK Maker Unknown c. 1880.

HANDGUN, REVOLVER

.32 Short R.F., 5 Shot, Spur Trigger, Solid Frame, Single Action,
Antique .... $75 | $150 | $160

BABY BULLDOG

HANDGUN, REVOLVER

.22 L.R.R.F., Double Action, Hammerless, Folding Trigger,
Modern.. 75 | 150 | 135

.32 Short R.F., Double Action, Hammerless, Folding Trigger,
Modern.. 75 | 125 | 125

BABY RUSSIAN Made by American Arms Co. c. 1890.

.38 S & W, 5 Shot, Single Action, Spur Trigger, Top Break,
Curio .... 125 | 225 | 200

BACKHOUSE, RICHARD Easton, Pa. 1774–1781. See Kentucky Rifles.

BACKUP See T D E, and A M T.

BACON ARMS CO. Norwich, Conn. 1858–1891. Also known as Bacon & Co. and Bacon Mfg. Co.

HANDGUN, PERCUSSION

.34, Boot Gun, Underhammer, Half-Octagon Barrel, *Antique* .... 200 | 350 | 325

6 Shot, Fluted Barrel, Pepperbox, Underhammer, Pocket Pistol,
Antique.. 625 | 850 | 800

HANDGUN, REVOLVER

.22 Short R.F., 7 Shot, Spur Trigger, Solid Frame, Single Action,
Antique.. 125 | 175 | 195

.32 Short R.F., 5 Shot, Spur Trigger, Solid Frame, Single Action,
Antique.. 125 | 175 | 190

Bacon Ring Trigger, Single Shot, .31 Caliber

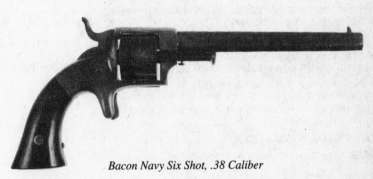

Bacon Navy Six Shot, .38 Caliber

	V.G.	Exc.	Prior Edition Exc. Value
.32 Short R.F., 6 Shot, Solid Frame, Spur Trigger, Single Action, *Antique*	$175	$300	$295
.32 Short R.F., 6 Shot, Solid Frame, Single Action with Trigger Guard, *Antique*	150	300	275
"Navy," .38 Long R.F., 6 Shot, 7½" Barrel, Solid Frame, Spur Trigger, Single Action, *Antique*	175	375	385

HANDGUN, SINGLESHOT

	V.G.	Exc.	Prior Edition Exc. Value
Derringer, .32 R.F., Spur Trigger, Side-Swing Barrel, *Antique*	175	350	345
SS Percussion, .31 Cal., Ring Trigger, *Antique*	175	275	270

	V.G.	Exc.	Prior Edition Exc. Value

BAIKAL Made in U.S.S.R., imported by Commercial Trading Imports.

SHOTGUN, DOUBLE BARREL, OVER-UNDER

MC-5-105, 20 Gauge, Boxlock, Engraved, Checkered Stock, Double Triggers, Solid Rib, Cased, *Modern* ..... $875 / $950 / $800

MC-6-105, 12 Gauge, Boxlock, Engraved, Checkered Stock, Double Triggers, Solid Rib, Cased, *Modern* ..... 950 / 1,500 / 1,275

MC-7-105, 12 or 20 Gauge, Boxlock, Engraved, Checkered Stock, Single Triggers, Selective Ejector, Solid Rib, Cased, *Modern* ..... 1,700 / 2,300 / 2,200

MC-8-105, 12 Gauge, Trap or Skeet, Boxlock, Engraved, Checkered Stock, Single Trigger, Solid Rib, Cased, *Modern* ..... 1,400 / 1,900 / 1,900

MC-109, 12 Gauge, Sidelock, Engraved, Checkered Stock, Single Selective Trigger, Selective Ejectors, Vent Rib, Cased, *Modern* ..... 2,500 / 3,000 / 4,000

IJ-27E1C, 12 or 20 Gauge, Boxlock, Engraved, Checkered Stock, Single Selective Trigger, Selective Ejectors, Vent Rib, *Modern* ..... 225 / 375 / 375

IJ-27E1C Silver, 12 or 20 Gauge, Boxlock, Engraved, Checkered Stock, Single Selective Trigger, Selective Ejectors, Vent Rib, *Modern* ..... 200 / 300 / 450

IJ-27E1C Super, 12 or 20 Gauge, Boxlock, Engraved, Checkered Stock, Single Selective Trigger, Selective Ejectors, Vent Rib, *Modern* ..... 350 / 550 / 595

TOZ-34E, 12 or 28 Gauge, Boxlock, Engraved, Checkered Stock, Double Triggers, Vent Rib, *Modern* ..... 325 / 450 / 495

SHOTGUN, DOUBLE BARREL, SIDE-BY-SIDE

MC-110, 12 or 20 Gauge, Boxlock, Engraved, Checkered Stock, Double Triggers, Solid Rib, Cased, *Modern* ..... 1,500 / 2,000 / 2,300

MC-111, 12 Gauge, Sidelock, Engraved, Checkered Stock, Single Selective Trigger, Selective Ejectors, Cased, *Modern* ..... 2,500 / 3,000 / 4,000

IJ-58MAE, 12 or 20 Gauge, Boxlock, Engraved, Checkered Stock, Double Triggers, *Modern* ..... 100 / 200 / 220

SHOTGUN, SINGLESHOT

IJ-18E, 12 or 20 Gauge, Checkered Stock, *Modern* ..... 50 / 75 / 55

BAKER GUN & FORGING CO. Batavia, N.Y. 1886–1919, Purchased by Folsom in 1919.

RIFLE, SEMI-AUTOMATIC

Batavia, .22 Short, Clip Fed, *Modern* ..... 275 / 450 / 425

SHOTGUN, DOUBLE BARREL, SIDE-BY-SIDE

Single Trigger, Add **$90.00–165.00**

Deduct **50%** for Damascus Barrels

Automatic Ejectors, Add **$110.00–225.00**

Batavia Leader, Various Gauges, Sidelock, Double Trigger, Checkered Stock, *Modern* ..... 425 / 500 / 450

Batavia Leader Special, Various Gauges, Sidelock, Double Trigger, Checkered Stock, Automatic Ejector, *Modern* ..... 425 / 625 / 560

	V.G.	Exc.	Prior Edition Exc. Value
Black Beauty, Various Gauges, Sidelock, Double Trigger, Checkered Stock, *Modern*	$450	$675	$645
Black Beauty Special, Various Gauges, Sidelock, Double Trigger, Checkered Stock, Automatic Ejector, *Modern*	750	850	725
Deluxe ($1,000 Grade), Various Gauges, Sidelock, Fancy Wood, Fancy Engraving, Fancy Checkering, Automatic Ejector, *Modern*	10,000	12,500	14,000
Deluxe ($300 Grade), Various Gauges, Sidelock, Fancy Wood, Fancy Engraving, Fancy Checkering, Automatic Ejector, *Modern*	2,950	3,250	4,450
Expert, Various Gauges, Sidelock, Fancy Wood, Fancy Engraving, Fancy Checkering, Automatic Ejector, *Modern*	1,850	2,100	3,150
Grade A, Various Gauges, Sidelock, Hammerless, Engraved, Damascus Barrel, *Modern*	200	350	325
Grade B, Various Gauges, Sidelock, Hammerless, Engraved, Damascus Barrels, *Modern*	175	310	310
Grade C Batavia, Various Gauges, Boxlock, Hammerless, Engraved, Damascus Barrels, *Modern*	175	250	245
Grade H Deluxe, Various Gauges, Sidelock, Fancy Engraving, *Modern*	2,850	3,650	3,600
Grade L Pigeon, Various Gauges, Sidelock, Fancy Engraving, *Modern*	1,550	2,150	2,100
Grade N Krupp Trap, 12 Ga., Sidelock, Engraved, *Modern*	950	1,400	1,350
Grade R, Various Gauges, Sidelock, Light Engraving, *Modern*	450	675	660
Grade S, Various Gauges, Sidelock, Light Engraving, *Modern*	425	575	560
Model 1896, 10 and 12 Gauges, Hammers, *Modern*	225	275	265
Model 1897, Various Gauges, Hammers, *Modern*	225	275	265
New Baker Model, 10 and 12 Gauges, Hammers, *Modern*	260	300	250
Paragon, Various Gauges, Sidelock, Double Trigger, Engraved, Fancy Checkering, *Modern*	1,350	1,450	1,150
Paragon, Various Gauges, Sidelock, Double Trigger, Engraved, Fancy Checkering, Automatic Ejector, *Modern*	1,475	1,575	1,475
Paragon Special, 12 Ga., Sidelock, Fancy Wood, Fancy Engraving, *Modern*	1,250	1,950	1,700

SHOTGUN, SINGLESHOT

	V.G.	Exc.	Prior
Elite, 12 Ga., Vent Rib, Fancy Engraving, *Modern*	775	1,250	1,200
Sterling, 12 Ga., Vent Rib, Light Engraving, *Modern*	550	775	750
Superba, 12 Ga., Trap Grade, Fancy Wood, Fancy Engraving, Fancy Checkering, Automatic Ejector, *Antique*	1,950	2,775	2,725

BAKER GUN CO. Made in Belgium for H & D Folsom Arms Co.
SHOTGUN, DOUBLE BARREL, SIDE-BY-SIDE

	V.G.	Exc.	Prior
Various Gauges, Outside Hammers, Damascus Barrel, *Antique*	75	175	160
Various Gauges, Hammerless, Steel Barrel, *Antique*	125	200	190
Various Gauges, Hammerless, Damascus Barrel, *Antique*	100	175	160
Various Gauges, Outside Hammers, Steel Barrel, *Antique*	100	200	185

	V.G.	Exc.	Prior Edition Exc. Value

SHOTGUN, SINGLESHOT
Various Gauges, Hammer, Steel Barrel, *Antique* .... $50 / $75 / $75

	V.G.	Exc.	Prior Edition Exc. Value
Various Gauges, Hammer, Steel Barrel, *Antique*	$50	$75	$75

BAKER, EZEKIEL London, England 1784–1825
HANDGUN, PERCUSSION

	V.G.	Exc.	Prior Edition Exc. Value
.58, Holster Pistol, Round Barrel, Light Ornamentation, *Antique*	550	750	675

BAKER, JOHN Providence, Pa. 1768–1775. See Kentucky Rifles.

BAKER, W.H. & CO. Marathon, N.Y. 1870, Syracuse, N.Y. 1878–1886.

COMBINATION WEAPON, DRILLING

	V.G.	Exc.	Prior Edition Exc. Value
Hammer Drilling, Various Gauges, Damascus Barrels, Front Trigger Break, *Antique*	450	725	675

RIFLE, PERCUSSION

	V.G.	Exc.	Prior Edition Exc. Value
.60, Brass Furniture, Scope Mounted, Target, Octagon Barrel, *Antique*	2,000	2,750	2,500

SHOTGUN, DOUBLE BARREL, SIDE-BY-SIDE

	V.G.	Exc.	Prior Edition Exc. Value
Hammer Double, 10 and 12 Gauges, Damascus Barrels, Front Trigger Break, *Antique*	275	375	350

BALL & WILLIAMS Worcester, Mass. 1861–1866.

RIFLE, SINGLESHOT

	V.G.	Exc.	Prior Edition Exc. Value
Ballard, .44 Long R.F., Military, Carbine, Falling Block, *Antique*	600	700	750
Ballard, .46 Long R.F., Kentucky Rifle, Falling Block, *Antique*	750	875	900
Ballard, Various Rimfires, Falling Block, Sporting Rifle, *Antique*	425	525	550
Ballard, Various Rimfires, Military, Falling Block, *Antique*	675	950	925
Merwin & Bray, .54 Ballard R.F., Military, Carbine, Falling Block, *Antique*	625	825	875
Merwin & Bray, Various Rimfires, Falling Block, Sporting Rifle, *Antique*	525	650	700

BALLARD RIFLE Made by Ball & Williams 1861–1866, Merrimack Arms & Mfg. Co. 1866–1869, Brown Mfg. Co. 1869–1873, J.M. Marlin from 1875.

RIFLE, SINGLESHOT

	V.G.	Exc.	Prior Edition Exc. Value
#1½ Hunter (Marlin), .40-65 Ballard Everlasting, Falling Block, Sporting Rifle, Open Rear Sight, *Antique*	600	1,250	825
#1 Hunter (Marlin), .44 Long R F/C F, Falling Block, Sporting Rifle, Recoil Pad, *Antique*	500	900	825
#2 (Marlin), .44-40 WCF, Falling Block, Sporting Rifle, Open Rear Sight, *Antique*	500	800	900

	V.G.	Exc.	Prior Edition Exc. Value
#2 (Marlin), Various Calibers, Falling Block, Sporting Rifle, Recoil Pad, Early Model, *Antique*	$400	$750	$825
#3¹/₂ (Marlin), .40-65 Ballard Everlasting, Falling Block, Target Rifle, Target Sights, Octagon Barrel, *Antique*	700	1,100	1,100
#3 Gallery (Marlin), .22 Short R.F., Falling Block, Target Rifle, Early Model, *Antique*	400	800	630
#4¹/₂ (Marlin), .40-65 Ballard Everlasting, Falling Block, Mid-Range Target Rifle, Checkered Stock, *Antique*	1,050	1,700	1,100
#4¹/₂ (Marlin), .45-70 Government, Falling Block, Sporting Rifle, *Antique*	875	1,250	1,050
#4¹/₂ (Marlin), Various Calibers, Falling Block, Sporting Rifle, *Antique*	950	1,150	935
#4¹/₂ (Marlin), Various Calibers, Falling Block, Mid-Range Target Rifle, Target Sights, Fancy Wood, *Antique*	1,500	2,500	1,600
#4 Perfection (Marlin), Various Calibers, Falling Block, Target Rifle, Target Sights, Set Trigger, Early Model, *Antique*	600	950	875
#5 Pacific (Marlin), .45-70 Government, Falling Block, Target Rifle, Open Rear Sight, Set Trigger, Octagon Barrel, *Antique*	700	1,500	1,000
#5 Pacific (Marlin), Various Calibers, Falling Block, Target Rifle, Open Rear Sight, Set Trigger, Octagon Barrel, *Antique*	650	1,250	850
#6¹/₂ (Marlin), .40-65 Ballard Everlasting, Falling Block, Off-Hand Target Rifle, Target Sights, Set Trigger, *Antique*	900	2,000	1,375
#6¹/₂ (Marlin), Various Calibers, Falling Block, Mid-Range Target Rifle, *Antique*	1,200	3,000	1,500
#6 Pacific (Marlin), Various Calibers, Falling Block, Schutzen Rifle, Target Sights, Fancy Wood, Set Trigger, *Antique*	1,700	3,000	2,150
#7 A-1 (Marlin), .44-75 Ballard Everlasting, Falling Block, Creedmore Long Range, Target Sights, Fancy Wood, Set Trigger, *Antique*	2,500	3,500	2,875
#7 A (Marlin), .44-100 Ballard Everlasting, Falling Block, Long Range Target Rifle, Target Sights, Set Trigger, *Antique*	2,200	3,200	1,375
#7 A-1 (Marlin), .44-100 Ballard Everlasting, Falling Block, Long Range Target Rifle, Target Sights, Set Trigger, Fancy Wood, *Antique*	2,000	4,000	1,950
#7 A-1 Extra Deluxe, .44-100 Ballard Everlasting, Falling Block, Long Range Target Rifle, Target Sights, Set Trigger, Fancy Wood, *Antique*	2,500	5,000	2,500
1¹/₂ Hunter (Marlin), .45-70 Government, Falling Block, Sporting Rifle, Open Rear Sight, *Antique*	700	1,200	925
1³/₄ Far West (Marlin), .40-65 Ballard Everlasting, Falling Block, Sporting Rifle, Open Rear Sight, Set Trigger, *Antique*	625	1,200	850
1³/₄ Far West (Marlin), .45-70 Government, Falling Block, Sporting Rifle, Open Rear Sight, Set Trigger, *Antique*	675	1,250	950
5¹/₂ Montana (Marlin), .45-100 Sharps, Falling Block, Sporting Rifle, Octagon Barrel, *Antique*	1,500	3,000	1,385
#8 (Marlin), .44-75 Ballard Everlasting, Falling Block, Creedmore Long Range, Target Sights, Pistol-Grip Stock, Set Trigger, *Antique*	800	1,500	800

	V.G.	Exc.	Prior Edition Exc. Value
#9 (Marlin), .44-75 Ballard Everlasting, Falling Block, Creedmore Long Range, Target Sights, Set Trigger, *Antique*	$700	$1,200	$930
(Ball & Williams), .44 Long R.F., Military, Carbine, Falling Block, *Antique*	675	850	780
(Ball & Williams), .46 Long R.F., Kentucky Rifle, Falling Block, *Antique*	850	1,025	950
(Ball & Williams), .54 Ballard R.F., Military, Carbine, Falling Block, *Antique*	675	950	875
(Ball & Williams), Various Rimfires, Falling Block, Sporting Rifle, *Antique*	475	675	590
(Ball & Williams), Various Rimfires, Military, Falling Block, *Antique*	750	1,050	975
Brown Mfg. Co., .44 Long R.F., Falling Block, Mid-Range Target Rifle, *Antique*	875	1,175	1,100
Hunter, .44 Long R F/C F, Falling Block, Sporting Rifle, Recoil Pad, *Antique*	675	750	675
Merrimack Arms, .44 Long R.F., Falling Block, Carbine, *Antique*	675	950	825
Merrimack Arms, .46 Long R.F., Falling Block, Military, *Antique*	775	1,025	930
Merrimack Arms, .56-52 Spencer R.F., Falling Block, Carbine, *Antique*	675	925	845
Merrimack Arms, Various Rimfires, Falling Block, Sporting Rifle, *Antique*	675	950	825
Merwin & Bray, Various Rimfires, Falling Block, Sporting Rifle, *Antique*	575	775	710

BALLARD & CO. Worcester, Mass 1861–1871. Also see U.S. Military.

RIFLE, SINGLESHOT

#2 (Marlin), Various Calibers, Falling Block, Sporting Rifle, *Antique*	700	750	875
#3 Gallery (Marlin), Various Calibers, Falling Block, Target Rifle, *Antique*	700	750	775
#3 Gallery (Marlin), Various Rimfires, Falling Block, Target Rifle, *Antique*	400	600	585
#3-F Gallery (Marlin), .22 Long R.F., Falling Block, Target Rifle, Fancy Wood, *Antique*	700	800	850
#4 Perfection (Marlin), Various Calibers, Falling Block, Target Rifle, Target Sights, Set Trigger, Octagon Barrel, *Antique*	750	650	850

BANG-UP Made by Hopkins & Allen, c. 1880.

HANDGUN, REVOLVER

.22 Short R.F., 7 Shot, Spur Trigger, Solid Frame, Single Action, *Antique*	100	150	160

	V.G.	Exc.	Prior Edition Exc. Value

BARKER, F.A. Fayettesville, N.C. 1860–1864. See Confederate Military.

BARKER, T. Made by Crescent; Also Made in Belgium.
SHOTGUN, DOUBLE BARREL, SIDE-BY-SIDE

	V.G.	Exc.	Prior
Various Gauges, Outside Hammers, Damascus Barrel, *Modern*	$100	$125	$150
Various Gauges, Hammerless, Steel Barrel, *Modern*	100	175	185
Various Gauges, Hammerless, Damascus Barrel, *Modern*	75	150	150
Various Gauges, Outside Hammers, Steel Barrel, *Modern*	75	175	185

SHOTGUN, SINGLESHOT

Various Gauges, Hammer, Steel Barrel, *Modern*	50	75	75

BARLOW, J. Moscow, Ind. 1836–1840. See Kentucky Rifles.

BARNETT & SON London, England 1750–1832.
RIFLE, FLINTLOCK

.75, 3rd. Model Brown Bess, Musket, Military, *Antique*	1,250	1,850	1,675

BARNETT, J. & SONS London, England 1835–1875.
RIFLE, PERCUSSION

.577, C.W. Enfield, Rifled, Musket, Military, *Antique*	500	750	700

BARRETT, J. Wythesville, Va. 1857–1865. See Confederate Military.

BAUER FIREARMS (FRASER ARMS CO.) Fraser, Mich.
COMBINATION WEAPON, OVER-UNDER

Rabbit, .22/.410, Metal Frame, Survival Gun, *Modern*	50	75	70

HANDGUN, SEMI-AUTOMATIC

25-Bicentennial, .25 ACP, Clip Fed, Pocket Pistol, Stainless Steel, Hammerless, Engraved, *Modern*	150	225	230
25-SS, .25 ACP, Clip Fed, Pocket Pistol, Stainless Steel, Hammerless, *Modern*	75	125	100

BAUER, GEORGE Lancaster, Pa. 1770–1781. See Kentucky Rifles.

BAY STATE ARMS CO. Uxbridge & Worcester, Mass. 1873–1874.
RIFLE, SINGLESHOT

.32 Long R.F., Dropping Block, *Antique*	125	175	190
Various Calibers, Target Rifle, *Antique*	600	875	850

	V.G.	Exc.	Prior Edition Exc. Value

SHOTGUN, SINGLESHOT
Davenport Patent, 12 Ga., *Antique* $200 $275 $285

BAYARD Belgium. Made by Anciens Etablissments Pieper, c. 1900. Also see Bergmann and Danish Military.

HANDGUN, SEMI-AUTOMATIC

	V.G.	Exc.	Prior Edition Exc. Value
Bergmann/Bayard 1910, 9mm Bayard, Clip Fed, Blue, Commercial, *Curio*	450	675	635
Bergmann/Bayard 1910, 9mm Bayard, Clip Fed, Blue, Commercial, with Holster/Stock, *Curio*	650	850	825
Model 1908 (1912) Pocket, .25 ACP, Blue, Clip Fed, *Modern*	150	195	190
Model 1908 (1912) Pocket, .25 ACP, Nickel, Clip Fed, *Modern*	150	225	200
Model 1908 (1910) Pocket, .32 ACP, Blue, Clip Fed, German Military, *Modern*	175	225	190
Model 1908 (1910) Pocket, .32 ACP, Blue, Clip Fed, *Modern*	150	225	210
Model 1908 (1910) Pocket, .32 ACP, Nickel, Clip Fed, *Modern*	150	225	215
Model 1908 (1911) Pocket, .380 ACP, Blue, Clip Fed, *Modern*	175	300	280
Model 1908 (1911) Pocket, .380 ACP, Nickel, Clip Fed, *Modern*	175	300	300
Model 1923 Pocket, Early, .25 ACP, Blue, Clip Fed, With Magazine Safety, *Modern*	150	200	200
Model 1923 Pocket, Standard, .25 ACP, Blue, Clip Fed, No Magazine Safety, *Modern*	125	195	170
Model 1923 Pocket, Early, .32 ACP, Blue, Clip Fed, With Magazine Safety, *Modern*	150	200	220
Model 1923 Pocket, Standard, .32 ACP, Blue, Clip Fed, No Magazine Safety, *Modern*	125	225	200

Bayard Model 1930

Bayard Model 1908 (1910) .32 ACP

	V.G.	Exc.	Prior Edition Exc. Value
Model 1923 Pocket, Early, .380 ACP, Blue, Clip Fed, With Magazine Safety, *Modern*	$175	$325	$260
Model 1923 Pocket, Standard, .380 ACP, Blue, Clip Fed, No Magazine Safety, *Modern*	150	225	225
Model 1930 Pocket, .25 ACP, Blue, Clip Fed, *Modern*	150	200	175
Model 1930 Pocket, .32 ACP, Blue, Clip Fed, *Modern*	150	200	180
Model 1930 Pocket, .380 ACP, Blue, Clip Fed, *Modern*	175	325	220

HANDGUN, REVOLVER

	V.G.	Exc.	Prior Edition Exc. Value
S & W Style, .32 S&W Long, Double Action, *Modern*	50	100	90
S & W Style, .38 S&W, Double Action, *Modern*	50	100	95

RIFLE, SINGLESHOT

	V.G.	Exc.	Prior Edition Exc. Value
Boy's Rifle, .22 L.R.R.F., Plain, Takedown, *Modern*	50	75	55
Half-Auto Carbine, .22 Short, Plain, *Curio*	50	75	60
Half-Auto Carbine, .22 Short, Checkered Stock, *Curio*	50	75	70

SHOTGUN, DOUBLE BARREL, SIDE-BY-SIDE

	V.G.	Exc.	Prior Edition Exc. Value
Hammerless, 12 Gauge, Double Triggers, Light Engraving, Boxlock, Steel Barrels, *Curio*	125	200	175
Hammer, 12 Gauge, Double Triggers, Light Engraving, Boxlock, Damascus Barrels, *Curio*	75	150	135
Hammer, 12 Gauge, Double Triggers, Light Engraving, Boxlock, Steel Barrels, *Curio*	75	150	145
Hammer, 12 Gauge, Double Triggers, Fancy Engraving, Boxlock, Steel Barrels, *Curio*	125	225	210

BECK, GIDEON Lancaster, Pa. 1780–1788. See Kentucky Rifles and Pistols.

BECK, JOHN Lancaster, Pa. 1772–1777. See Kentucky Rifles and Pistols.

BECK, ISAAC Miffinberg, Pa. 1830–1840.

RIFLE, PERCUSSION

	V.G.	Exc.	Prior Edition Exc. Value
.47, Octagon Barrel, Brass Furniture, *Antique*	1,200	1,500	1,275

BEEMAN PRECISION FIREARMS San Raphael, Calif., Importers.

HANDGUN, SEMI-AUTOMATIC

	V.G.	Exc.	Prior Edition Exc. Value
Agner M80, .22 L.R.R.F., Clip Fed, Bright or Black Chrome Plating, Adjustable Target Grips, Adjustable Trigger, *Modern*	575	800	800
FAS Model 601, .22 Short R.F., Clip Fed, Target Grip, Rapid Fire Target Pistol, *Modern*	525	600	600
FAS Model 602, .22 L.R.R.F., Clip Fed, Target Grip, Match Pistol, *Modern*	550	775	775

	V.G.	Exc.	Prior Edition Exc. Value
FAS Model 603, .32 S&W Wadcutter, Clip Fed, Target Grip, Match Pistol, *Modern*	*$500*	*$725*	*$725*
Unique Model 69, .22 L.R.R.F., Clip Fed, Adjustable Target Grips, Match Pistol, *Modern*	*400*	*550*	*550*
Unique Model 823-U, .22 Short R.F., Clip Fed, Adjustable Target Grips, Rapid Fire Match Pistol, *Modern*	*450*	*600*	*600*

HANDGUN, PERCUSSION

	V.G.	Exc.	Prior Edition Exc. Value
PB Aristocrat, .36 or .44, Single Set Trigger, Fluted Stock, Reproduction, *Antique*	*175*	*225*	*225*
Hege-Siber, French, .33, Checkered Stock, Engraved, Gold Inlays, Cased, Reproduction, *Antique*	*775*	*1,100*	*1,100*
Hege-Siber, English, .33, Checkered Stock, Light Engraving, Cased, Reproduction, *Antique*	*500*	*600*	*600*

RIFLE, BOLT ACTION

	V.G.	Exc.	Prior Edition Exc. Value
Feinwerkbau 2000 Match, .22 L.R.R.F., Single Shot, Adjustable Trigger, Adjustable Target Stock, *Modern*	*400*	*575*	*575*
Feinwerkbau 2000 Mini, .22 L.R.R.F., Single Shot, Adjustable Trigger, Adjustable Target Stock, *Modern*	*475*	*550*	*535*
Feinwerkbau 2000 Running Target, .22 L.R.R.F., Single Shot, Adjustable Trigger, Adjustable Target Stock, *Modern*	*475*	*650*	*650*
Feinwerkbau 2000 Universal, .22 L.R.R.F., Single Shot, Adjustable Trigger, Adjustable Target Stock, *Modern*	*500*	*600*	*600*
Feinwerkbau Free Rifle, .22 L.R.R.F., Single Shot, Adjustable Electric Trigger, Adjustable Target Stock, Counterweights, Hook Buttplate, *Modern*	*750*	*1,100*	*1,100*
Krico Model 302, .22 L.R.R.F., Clip Fed, Checkered Stock, Open Sights, *Modern*	*225*	*300*	*300*
Krico Model 304, .22 L.R.R.F., Clip Fed, Checkered Stock, Mannlicher Stock, Set Triggers, Open Sights, *Modern*	*275*	*375*	*375*
Krico Model 340, .22 L.R.R.F., Metallic Silhouette Match Rifle, Clip Fed, Checkered Stock, Target Stock, *Modern*	*375*	*450*	*430*
Krico Model 340, .22 L.R.R.F., Mini-Sniper Match Rifle, Clip Fed, Checkered Stock, Target Stock, *Modern*	*350*	*475*	*475*
Krico Model 400, .22 Hornet, Clip Fed, Checkered Stock, Open Sights, *Modern*	*325*	*425*	*425*
Krico Model 420, .22 Hornet, Clip Fed, Checkered Stock, Set Triggers, Mannlicher Stock, Open Sights, Sling Swivels, *Modern*	*350*	*475*	*465*
Krico Model 600, Various Calibers, Clip Fed, Checkered Stock, Open Sights, Sling Swivels, Recoil Pad, *Modern*	*450*	*650*	*635*
Krico Model 620, Various Calibers, Clip Fed, Checkered Stock, Set Triggers, Mannlicher Stock, Open Sights, Sling Swivels, *Modern*	*475*	*650*	*650*
Krico Model 640, Various Calibers, Deluxe Varmint Rifle, Clip Fed, Checkered Stock, Target Stock, *Modern*	*450*	*650*	*630*
Krico Model 650, Various Calibers, Sniper/Match Rifle, Clip Fed, Checkered Stock, Target Stock, *Modern*	*575*	*800*	*800*

Beeman FAS Model 601

Beeman Agner M80

Beeman Unique Model 69

Beeman Fabarm Gamma

Beeman Feinwerkbau 2000 Match

Beeman Krico Model 650

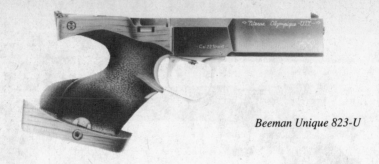

Beeman Unique 823-U

	V.G.	Exc.	Prior Edition Exc. Value
Krico Model 700, Various Calibers, Clip Fed, Checkered Stock, Open Sights, Sling Swivels, Recoil Pad, *Modern*	*$450*	*$650*	*$635*
Krico Model 720, Various Calibers, Clip Fed, Checkered Stock, Set Triggers, Mannlicher Stock, Open Sights, Sling Swivels, *Modern*	*525*	*650*	*650*
Weihrauch HW60, .22 L.R.R.F., Singleshot Target Rifle, Target Sights, Target Stock, Heavy Barrel, *Modern*	*325*	*400*	*390*

SHOTGUN, DOUBLE BARREL, OVER-UNDER

	V.G.	Exc.	Prior Edition Exc. Value
Fabarm Gamma, 12 Gauge, Trap/Field Model, Single Selective Trigger, Checkered Stock, Vent Rib, *Modern*	*325*	*450*	*450*
Fabarm Gamma, 12 Gauge, Skeet Model, Single Selective Trigger, Checkered Stock, Vent Rib, *Modern*	*325*	*450*	*450*
Fabarm Gamma, 12 Gauge, Trap/Skeet Combo, 2 Barrels, Single Selective Trigger, Checkered Stock, Vent Rib, *Modern*	*500*	*700*	*700*

BEERSTECHER, FREDERICK Lewisburg, Pa. 1849–1860.

HANDGUN, PERCUSSION

	V.G.	Exc.	Prior Edition Exc. Value
.40, Double Shot, Superimposed Loading, Derringer Style, *Antique*	*4,000*	*4,750*	*4,500*

BEHOLLA Made by Becker & Hollander, Suhl, Germany c. 1910. Also made under this patent were the Stenda, Leonhardt, and Menta.

HANDGUN, SEMI-AUTOMATIC

	V.G.	Exc.	Prior Edition Exc. Value
.32 ACP, Clip Fed, Commercial, Blue, Hard Rubber Grips, *Curio*	*150*	*200*	*265*
.32 ACP, Clip Fed, Military, Blue, Hard Rubber Grips, *Curio*	*125*	*150*	*160*
.32 ACP, Clip Fed, Commercial, Blue, Wood Grips, *Curio*	*125*	*150*	*250*
.32 ACP, Clip Fed, Military, Blue, Wood Grips, *Curio*	*125*	*150*	*145*

BELGIAN MILITARY Also see Browning, FN.

RIFLE, BOLT ACTION

	V.G.	Exc.	Prior Edition Exc. Value
M 1924, Various Calibers, Military, *Curio*	*100*	*150*	*115*

	V.G.	Exc.	Prior Edition Exc. Value
M 1930, Various Calibers, Military, *Curio*	*$100*	*$150*	*$115*
M 1934/30, Various Calibers, Military, *Curio*	*100*	*125*	*115*
M 1950, .30-06 Springfield, Military, *Modern*	*125*	*175*	*150*
M 1889 Mauser, Military, *Curio*	*75*	*100*	*75*
M 1889 Mauser, Carbine, Military, *Curio*	*100*	*125*	*80*
M 1935 Mauser, Military, *Modern*	*100*	*125*	*87*
M 1936 Mauser, Military, *Modern*	*75*	*100*	*80*

RIFLE, SEMI-AUTOMATIC

M 1949, .30-06 Springfield, Military, *Modern*	*300*	*450*	*375*
M 1949, Various Calibers, Military, *Modern*	*250*	*375*	*310*

BELL, JOHN Carlisle, Pa. c. 1800. See Kentucky Rifles and Pistols.

BELLMORE GUN CO. Made by Crescent, c. 1900.
SHOTGUN, DOUBLE BARREL, SIDE-BY-SIDE

Various Gauges, Outside Hammers, Damascus Barrel, *Modern*	75	150	150
Various Gauges, Hammerless, Steel Barrel, *Modern*	100	175	185
Various Gauges, Hammerless, Damascus Barrel, *Modern*	75	175	150
Various Gauges, Outside Hammers, Steel Barrel, *Modern*	100	200	185

SHOTGUN, SINGLESHOT

Various Gauges, Hammer, Steel Barrel, *Modern*	50	100	75

BENELLI Made in Italy, imported by H & K Inc. and Sile.
HANDGUN, SEMI-AUTOMATIC

B 76, 9mm Luger, Clip Fed, Blue, *Modern*	275	350	275

RIFLE, SEMI-AUTOMATIC

Model 940, .30-06 Springfield, Clip Fed, Open Sights, Recoil Pad, Sling Swivels, *Modern*	350	425	400

SHOTGUN, SEMI-AUTOMATIC

Model SL 121V, 12 Gauge, Slug Gun, Open Sights, Checkered Stock, Recoil Pad, *Modern*	200	275	375
Model SL 121MI, 12 Gauge, Police, Open Sights, Checkered Stock, Recoil Pad, *Modern*	275	325	380
Model SL 201, 20 Gauge, Checkered Stock, Plain Barrel, *Modern*	250	300	345
Model 123V, 12 Gauge, Standard Model, Checkered Stock, Vent Rib, *Modern*	275	325	345
Model 123V Deluxe, 12 Gauge, Engraved Model, Checkered Stock, Vent Rib, *Modern*	350	425	450
Special Trap, 12 Gauge, White Receiver, Checkered Stock, Vent Rib, *Modern*	375	450	550
Special Skeet, 12 Gauge, White Receiver, Checkered Stock, Vent Rib, *Modern*	400	475	575

		Prior Edition Exc.
V.G.	Exc.	Value

BENFER, AMOS Beaverstown, Pa. c. 1810. See Kentucky Rifles and Pistols.

BERETTA, GIOVANNI Brescia, Italy, c. 1700

HANDGUN, SNAPHAUNCE

Belt Pistol, Engraved, Carved, Light Ornamentation, *Antique* $3,000 $4,250 $3,900

BERETTA Pietro Beretta; Gardone V.T., Italy. Company history extends back to 1680.

HANDGUN, SEMI-AUTOMATIC

	V.G.	Exc.	Prior Edition Exc. Value
1915, .32 ACP, Clip Fed, Military, *Modern*	250	275	145
1915, .380 ACP, Clip Fed, Military, *Modern*	300	350	190
1915/1919, .32 ACP, Clip Fed, Military, *Modern*	225	275	150

Beretta Model 1935 .32 ACP

Beretta Bantam

Beretta Model 1915/19 .32 ACP

	V.G.	Exc.	Prior Edition Exc. Value
1919 V P, .25 ACP, Clip Fed, *Modern*	$225	$275	$175
Cougar, .380 ACP, Clip Fed, *Modern*	175	225	200
Jaguar, .22 L.R.R.F., Clip Fed, *Modern*	150	200	175
Jetfire, .25 ACP, Clip Fed, Blue, *Modern*	100	150	130
Jetfire, .25 ACP, Clip Fed, Nickel, *Modern*	100	150	135
Minx, .22 Short, Clip Fed, Blue, *Modern*	100	150	130
Minx, .22 Short, Clip Fed, Nickel, *Modern*	125	150	135
Model 100, .32 ACP, Clip Fed, *Modern*	125	175	165
Model 101, .22 L.R.R.F., Clip Fed, Adjustable Sights, *Modern*	125	175	175
Model 1923, 9mm Luger, Clip Fed, Military, *Modern*	175	225	225
Model 1923, 9mm Luger, Clip Fed, Military, with Detachable Shoulder Stock, *Curio*	400	550	550
Model 1931 Navy, .32 ACP, Clip Fed, Military, *Modern*	125	175	170
Model 1934, .380 ACP, Clip Fed, Military, *Modern*	75	125	105
Model 1934, .380 ACP, Clip Fed, Commercial, *Modern*	200	250	235
Model 1935, .32 ACP, Clip Fed, Commercial, *Modern*	150	200	200
Model 1935, .32 ACP, Clip Fed, Military, *Modern*	75	100	100
Model 318, .25 ACP, Clip Fed, *Modern*	125	200	180
Model 418, .25 ACP, Clip Fed, *Modern*	125	175	175
Model 420, .25 ACP, Clip Fed, Chrome, Light Engraving, *Modern*	250	300	285
Model 421, .25 ACP, Clip Fed, Gold Plated, Fancy Engraving, *Modern*	325	400	395
Model 70S, .380 ACP, Clip Fed, *Modern*	125	225	215
Model 70T, .32 ACP, Clip Fed, Adjustable Sights, *Modern*	125	200	195
Model 76, .22 L.R.R.F., Clip Fed, Adjustable Sights, *Modern*	200	275	275
Model 81, .32 ACP, Clip Fed, Double Action, *Modern*	200	325	320
Model 82, .32 ACP, Clip Fed, Double Action, *Modern*	200	300	300
Model 84, .380 ACP, Clip Fed, Double Action, *Modern*	200	300	300
Model 85, .380 ACP, Clip Fed, Double Action, *Modern*	250	325	315
Model 84 Tercentennial, .380 ACP, Clip Fed, Double Action, Engraved, Cased, *Modern*	750	1,250	1,250
Model 90, .32 ACP, Clip Fed, Double Trigger, *Modern*	200	275	275
Model 92, 9mm Luger, 13 Shot Clip Fed, Double Action, *Modern*	325	450	440
Model 92, 9mm Luger, 15 Shot Clip Fed, Double Action, *Modern*	375	450	450
Model 948, .22 L.R.R.F., Clip Fed, Lightweight *Modern*	100	150	140
Model 949 Olympic, .22 L.R.R.F., Clip Fed, Target Pistol, *Modern*	300	350	335
Model 949 Olympic, .22 Short R.F., Clip Fed, Target Pistol, *Modern*	300	350	330
Model 950 Minx, .22 Short R.F., Clip Fed, 2" Barrel, *Modern*	100	150	140
Model 950B Minx, .22 Short R.F., Clip Fed, 4" Barrel, *Modern*	100	150	140

	V.G.	Exc.	Prior Edition Exc. Value
Model 951 Brigadier, 9mm Luger, Clip Fed, Commercial, *Modern*	$275	$325	$315
Model 951 Egyptian, 9mm Luger, Clip Fed, Military, *Curio*	250	375	365
Model 951 Israeli, 9mm Luger, Clip Fed, Military, *Curio*	250	375	365
Puma, .32 ACP, Clip Fed, *Modern*	175	200	195

RIFLE, SEMI-AUTOMATIC

	V.G.	Exc.	Prior Edition Exc. Value
Olympia, .22 L.R.R.F., Clip Fed, Tangent Sights, Checkered Stock, *Modern*	150	200	200
Silver Gyrfalcon, .22 L.R.R.F., Checkered Stock, *Modern*	150	225	195
Super Sport, .22 L.R.R.F., Fancy Checkering, Clip Fed, *Modern*	150	225	220

SHOTGUN, DOUBLE BARREL, OVER-UNDER

	V.G.	Exc.	Prior Edition Exc. Value
Golden Snipe, 12 and 20 Gauges, Single Trigger, Automatic Ejector, Engraved, Fancy Checkering, *Modern*	550	600	460
Golden Snipe, 12 and 20 Gauges, Single Selective Trigger, Automatic Ejector, Engraved, Fancy Checkering, *Modern*	600	675	650
Golden Snipe Deluxe, 12 and 20 Gauges, Single Selective Trigger, Automatic Ejector, Fancy Engraving, Fancy Checkering, *Modern*	625	750	700
Model ASEL, 12 and 20 Gauges, Single Trigger, Checkered Stock, *Modern*	875	950	920
Model BL 1, 12 Ga., Field Grade, Double Trigger, Checkered Stock, *Modern*	275	350	375
Model BL 2, 12 Ga., Field Grade, Single Selective Trigger, Checkered Stock, *Modern*	325	375	450
Model BL 3, 12 Ga., Trap Grade, Single Selective Trigger, Checkered Stock, Light Engraving, Vent Rib, *Modern*	475	550	520
Model BL 3, Various Gauges, Skeet Grade, Single Selective Trigger, Checkered Stock, Light Engraving, Vent Rib, *Modern*	500	550	525
Model BL 3, Various Gauges, Field Grade, Single Selective Trigger, Checkered Stock, Light Engraving, Vent Rib, *Modern*	500	550	525
Model BL 4, 12 Ga., Trap Grade, Single Selective Trigger, Selective Ejector, Engraved, Vent Rib, *Modern*	600	650	720
Model BL 4, Various Gauges, Skeet Grade, Single Selective Trigger, Selective Ejector, Engraved, Vent Rib, *Modern*	625	700	720
Model BL 4, Various Gauges, Field Grade, Single Selective Trigger, Selective Ejector, Engraved, Vent Rib, *Modern*	575	625	650
Model BL 5, 12 Ga., Trap Grade, Single Selective Trigger, Selective Ejector, Fancy Engraving, Vent Rib, *Modern*	700	850	995
Model BL 5, Various Gauges, Skeet Grade, Single Selective Trigger, Selective Ejector, Fancy Engraving, Vent Rib, *Modern*	725	875	995
Model BL 5, Various Gauges, Field Grade, Single Selective Trigger, Selective Ejector, Fancy Engraving, Vent Rib, *Modern*	750	825	925
Model BL 6, 12 Ga., Trap Grade, Single Selective Trigger, Selective Ejector, Fancy Engraving, Vent Rib, *Modern*	925	1,000	1,400
Model BL 6, Various Gauges, Field Grade, Single Selective Trigger, Selective Ejector, Fancy Engraving, Vent Rib, *Modern*	1,000	1,100	1,350

	V.G.	Exc.	Prior Edition Exc. Value
Model BL 6, Various Gauges, Skeet Grade, Single Selective Trigger, Selective Ejector, Fancy Engraving, Vent Rib, *Modern*	$1,050	$1,125	$1,375
Model S02, 12 Ga., Sidelock, Selective Ejector, Single Trigger, Checkered Stock, Engraved, *Modern*	1,850	2,375	2,250
Model S03, 12 Ga., Sidelock, Automatic Ejector, Single Selective Trigger, Fancy Engraving, Fancy Wood, *Modern*	2,875	3,650	3,500
Model S03 EELL, 12 Ga., Sidelock, Automatic Ejector, Single Selective Trigger, Fancy Engraving, Fancy Wood, *Modern*	4,850	6,175	5,800
Model S03 EL, 12 Ga. Sidelock, Automatic Ejector, Single Selective Trigger, Fancy Engraving, Fancy Wood, *Modern*	3,625	4,150	4,000
Model S04, 12 Ga., Sidelock, Automatic Ejector, Single Trigger, Fancy Engraving, Fancy Wood, *Modern*	2,825	3,950	3,700
Model S05, 12 Ga., Sidelock, Selective Ejector, Single Trigger, Fancy Engraving, Fancy Checkering, *Modern*	4,650	5,475	5,200
Model S55B, 12 and 20 Gauges, Single Selective Trigger, Automatic Ejector, Vent Rib, Checkered Stock, *Modern*	450	625	575
Model S56E, 12 and 20 Gauges, Single Selective Trigger, Automatic Ejector, Engraved, Checkered Stock, *Modern*	475	625	600
Model S58, 12 Ga., Trap Grade, Automatic Ejector, Single Selective Trigger, Engraved, Checkered Stock, *Modern*	625	750	695
Model S58, 12 and 20 Gauges, Skeet Grade, Automatic Ejector, Single Selective Trigger, Engraved, Checkered Stock, Light Engraving, *Modern*	700	775	725
Silver Snipe, 12 and 20 Gauges, Single Trigger, Checkered Stock, Light Engraving, *Modern*	425	500	425
Silver Snipe, 12 and 20 Gauges, Single Selective Trigger, Checkered Stock, Light Engraving, *Modern*	350	400	450
Silver Snipe, 12 and 20 Gauges, Single Trigger, Checkered Stock, Light Engraving, Vent Rib, *Modern*	325	425	420
Silver Snipe, 12 and 20 Gauges, Single Selective Trigger, Light Engraving, Vent Rib, *Modern*	575	650	735
Model 680, 12 Gauge, Skeet Grade, Automatic Ejector, Single Selective Trigger, Engraved, Checkered Stock, Light Engraving, *Modern*	675	875	865
Model 680, 12 Gauge, Trap Grade, Automatic Ejector, Single Selective Trigger, Checkered Stock, Light Engraving, *Modern*	675	925	865
Model 680, 12 Gauge, Mono Trap Grade, Automatic Ejector, Single Trigger, Checkered Stock, Light Engraving, *Modern*	675	950	875
Model 686, 12 Gauge, Field Grade, Automatic Ejector, Single Selective Trigger, Checkered Stock, Light Engraving, *Modern*	550	675	650
Model 687EL, 12 Gauge, Skeet Grade, Automatic Ejector, Single Selective Trigger, Checkered Stock, Fancy Engraving, *Modern*	900	1,275	1,450

SHOTGUN, DOUBLE BARREL, SIDE-BY-SIDE

	V.G.	Exc.	Prior Value
Model 409PB, Various Gauges, Double Trigger, Light Engraving, Checkered Stock, *Modern*	600	675	465
Model 410 Early, 10 Ga. 3½", Double Trigger, Engraved, Checkered Stock, *Modern*	475	550	500

	V.G.	Exc.	Prior Edition Exc. Value
Model 410 Late, 10 Ga. 3½", *Modern*	$875	$975	$850
Model 410E, Various Gauges, Double Trigger, Engraved, Checkered Stock, Automatic Ejector, *Modern*	700	775	650
Model 411E, Various Gauges, Double Trigger, Engraved, Fancy Checkering, Automatic Ejector, *Modern*	1,050	1,125	960
Model 424, 12 and 20 Gauges, Double Trigger, Light Engraving, Checkered Stock, *Modern*	625	700	570
Model 426E, 12 and 20 Gauges, Single Selective Trigger, Automatic Ejector, Engraved, Checkered Stock, *Modern*	775	875	790
Model GR 2, 12 and 20 Gauges, Double Trigger, Checkered Stock, Light Engraving, *Modern*	475	600	450
Model GR 3, 12 and 20 Gauges, Single Selective Trigger, Checkered Stock, Light Engraving, *Modern*	575	675	525
Model GR 4, 12 Ga., Single Selective Trigger, Selective Ejector, Checkered Stock, Engraved, *Modern*	650	725	600
Silver Hawk, 10 Ga. 3½", Double Trigger, Magnum, *Modern*	425	475	575
Silver Hawk, 12 Ga., Mag. 3", Double Trigger, Magnum, *Modern*	325	375	475
Silver Hawk, 12 Ga. Mag. 3", Magnum, *Modern*	350	400	515
Silver Hawk, Various Gauges, Double Trigger, Lightweight, *Modern*	375	450	425
Silver Hawk, Various Gauges, Single Trigger, Lightweight, *Modern*	450	500	475

SHOTGUN, SEMI-AUTOMATIC

	V.G.	Exc.	Prior Edition Exc. Value
Gold Lark, 12 Ga., Vent Rib, Light Engraving, Checkered Stock, *Modern*	350	425	300
Model A301, 12 Ga., Slug, Open Rear Sight, *Modern*	275	400	365
Model A301, 12 Ga., Trap Grade, Vent Rib, *Modern*	375	425	400
Model A301, 12 and 20 Gauges, Field Grade, Vent Rib, *Modern*	275	375	375
Model A301, 12 and 20 Gauges, Skeet Grade, Vent Rib, *Modern*	275	400	375
Model A301, 12 Ga., Mag. 3", Field Grade, Vent Rib, *Modern*	325	450	400
Model A302, 12 Ga., Slug, Open Rear Sight, *Modern*	275	425	365
Model A302, 12 Ga., Trap Grade, Vent Rib, *Modern*	275	375	400
Model A302, 12 and 20 Gauges, Field Grade, Vent Rib, *Modern*	250	375	375
Model A302, 12 and 20 Gauges, Skeet Grade, Vent Rib, *Modern*	250	375	375
Model A302, 12 Ga., Mag. 3", Field Grade, Vent Rib, *Modern*	300	400	400
Model AL 1, 12 and 20 Gauges, Checkered Stock, *Modern*	300	350	290
Model AL 2, 12 Ga., Vent Rib, Trap Grade, Checkered Stock, *Modern*	300	350	310
Model AL 2, 12 and 20 Gauges, Vent Rib, Checkered Stock, *Modern*	275	300	275
Model AL 2, 12 and 20 Gauges, Vent Rib, Skeet Grade, Checkered Stock, *Modern*	325	350	310
Model AL 3, 12 Ga., Vent Rib, Checkered Stock, Light Engraving, Trap Grade, *Modern*	300	350	375

	V.G.	Exc.	Prior Edition Exc. Value
Model AL 3, 12 and 20 Gauges, Vent Rib, Checkered Stock, Light Engraving, *Modern*	$300	$375	$360
Model AL3, 12 and 20 Gauges, Vent Rib, Checkered Stock, Light Engraving, Skeet Grade, *Modern*	300	375	350
Model AL 3, 12 Ga. Mag. 3", Vent Rib, Checkered Stock, Light Engraving, *Modern*	325	400	385
Ruby Lark, 12 Ga., Vent Rib, Fancy Engraving, Fancy Checkering, *Modern*	450	525	395
Silver Lark, 12 Ga., Checkered Stock, *Modern*	200	275	220

SHOTGUN, SINGLESHOT

	V.G.	Exc.	
Companion FS 1, Various Gauges, Folding Gun, *Modern*	125	150	125
Model Mark II, 12 Ga., Trap Grade, Vent Rib, Light Engraving, Checkered Stock, Monte Carlo Stock, *Modern*	375	450	420
Model TR 1, 12 Ga., Trap Grade, Vent Rib, Light Engraving, Checkered Stock, Monte Carlo Stock, *Modern*	200	250	265

SHOTGUN, SLIDE ACTION

	V.G.	Exc.	
Gold Pigeon, 12 Ga., Vent Rib, Checkered Stock, Engraved, *Modern*	325	375	250
Gold Pigeon, 12 Ga., Vent Rib, Fancy Engraving, Fancy Checkering, *Modern*	425	475	385
Model SL 2, 12 Ga., Vent Rib, Checkered Stock, *Modern*	250	275	260
Ruby Pigeon, 12 Ga., Vent Rib, Fancy Engraving, Fancy Checkering, *Modern*	425	475	540
Silver Pigeon, 12 Ga., Light Engraving, Checkered Stock, *Modern*	150	200	210

BERGMANN Gaggenau, Germany 1892–1944; Company Renamed Bergmann Erben 1931.

HANDGUN, SEMI-AUTOMATIC

	V.G.	Exc.	
Model 1894, 5mm, Blow Back, Clip Fed, *Antique*	5,000	6,500	19,500
Model 1894, 8mm, Blow Back, Clip Fed, *Antique*	3,500	4,000	9,750
Model 1896 #2, 5mm, Small Frame, Clip Fed, *Curio*	1,500	1,800	1,500
Model 1896 #3, 6.5mm, Clip Fed, *Curio*	1,400	2,000	2,000
Model 1896 #4, 8mm, Military, Clip Fed, *Curio*	1,450	2,150	2,300
Model 1897 #5, 7.8mm, Clip Fed, *Curio*	2,150	2,400	2,400
Simplex, 8mm, Clip Fed, *Curio*	650	975	950
Bergmann Mars, 9mmB, Clip Fed, *Curio*	2,750	3,250	3,000
Bergmann/Bayard, Model 1908, 9mmB, Clip Fed, *Curio*	1,050	1,200	890
Bergmann/Bayard, Model 1910, 9mmB, Clip Fed, *Curio*	750	950	940
Bergmann/Bayard, Model 1910/21, 9mmB, Clip Fed, *Curio*	1,000	1,250	750
Model 2, .25 ACP, Clip Fed, *Modern*	250	350	300
Model 2A, .25 ACP, Einhand, Clip Fed, *Modern*	300	400	350
Model 3, .25 ACP, Long Grip, Clip Fed, *Modern*	250	300	300

Bergmann Model 1896 #3

Bergmann Model 2

	V.G.	Exc.	Prior Edition Exc. Value
Model 3A, .25 ACP, Einhand, Long Grip, Clip Fed, *Modern*	$250	$350	$360
Erben Special, .32 ACP, Clip Fed, *Modern*	225	325	335
Erben Model I, .25 ACP, Clip Fed, *Modern*....................................	175	275	270
Erben Model II, .25 ACP, Clip Fed, *Modern*..................................	200	300	320

RIFLE, SEMI-AUTOMATIC
Model 1897, Karabiner, 7.8mm, Long Barrel, Detachable Stock, *Modern*..	4,400	5,250	5,600

BERLIN, ABRAHAM Caston, Pa. 1773–1786. See Kentucky Rifles and Pistols.

BERNARDON-MARTIN St. Etienne, France 1906–1912.
HANDGUN, SEMI-AUTOMATIC
Automatique Francais, .32 ACP, Clip Fed, *Curio*	225	275	295

BERNARDELLI Vincenzo Bernardelli, Gardon V.T., Italy.
HANDGUN, SEMI-AUTOMATIC
M1956, 9mm Luger, Clip Fed, *Curio*...	975	1,250	1,450
Model 100, .22 L.R.R.F., Clip Fed, Blue, Target Pistol, *Modern*.....	250	300	280
Model 60, .22 L.R.R.F., Clip Fed, Blue, *Modern*.............................	125	175	160
Model 60, .22 L.R.R.F., Clip Fed, Blue, 8" Barrel, Detachable Front Sight, Adjustable Sights, *Modern*	275	350	325
Model 60, .32 ACP, Clip Fed, Blue, *Modern*..................................	150	200	170

	V.G.	Exc.	Prior Edition Exc. Value
Model 60, .380 ACP, Clip Fed, Blue, *Modern*	*$150*	*$200*	*$190*
Model 80, .22 L.R.R.F., Clip Fed, Blue, *Modern*	125	175	180
Model 80, .22 L.R.R.F., Clip Fed, Blue, 6" Barrel, *Modern*	125	200	190
Model 80, .32 ACP, Clip Fed, Blue, *Modern*	125	175	180
Model 80, .380 ACP, Clip Fed, Blue, *Modern*	125	200	190
Model V P, .22 L.R.R.F., Clip Fed, Blue, *Modern*	150	200	195
Model V P, .25 ACP, Clip Fed, Blue, *Modern*	100	175	170
Standard, .22 L.R.R.F., Clip Fed, Blue, *Modern*	100	175	170
Standard, .22 L.R.R.F., Clip Fed, Blue, 6" Barrel, Detachable Front Sight, *Modern*	150	225	215
Standard, .22 L.R.R.F., Clip Fed, Blue, 8" Barrel, Detachable Front Sight, *Modern*	150	275	265
Standard, .22 L.R.R.F., Clip Fed, Blue, 10" Barrel, Detachable Front Sight, *Modern*	225	350	375
Standard, .32 ACP, Original 17 Shot Clip only, Add **$35.00–$60.00**			
Standard, .32 ACP, Clip Fed, Blue, *Modern*	150	200	190
Standard, .32 ACP, Clip Fed, Blue, 6" Barrel, Detachable Front Sight, *Modern*	225	300	275
Standard, .32 ACP, Clip Fed, Blue, 8" Barrel, Detachable Front Sight, *Modern*	325	400	385
Standard, .32 ACP, Clip Fed, Blue, 10" Barrel, Detachable Front Sight, *Modern*	350	425	425
Standard, .380 ACP, Clip Fed, Blue, *Modern*	150	250	225
Standard, 9mm Luger, Clip Fed, Blue, *Modern*	325	450	425

HANDGUN, REVOLVER

	V.G.	Exc.	Prior Edition Exc. Value
Standard, .22 L.R.R.F. or .32 S&W Long, Double Action, Blue, *Modern*	200	275	260
Target, .22 L.R.R.F., Double Action, Blue, Target Sights, *Modern*	200	275	280
Target, .22 L.R.R.F., Double Action, Engraved, Chrome Plated, Target Sights, *Modern*	350	425	400

Bernardelli Standard .32, 8" Barrel

	V.G.	Exc.	Prior Edition Exc. Value

RIFLE, DOUBLE BARREL, OVER-UNDER

Various Calibers, Checkered Stock, Engraved, *Modern* .... $975 | $1,150 | $1,050

SHOTGUN, DOUBLE BARREL, SIDE-BY-SIDE

	V.G.	Exc.	Prior Edition Exc. Value
Brescia, 12 and 20 Gauges, Checkered Stock, Hammer, *Modern*........	1,200	1,650	600
Elio, 12 Ga., Checkered Stock, Light Engraving, Lightweight Selective Ejector, *Modern*....................................	775	950	775
Game Cock, 12 and 20 Gauges, Checkered Stock, Double Trigger, *Modern*..................	575	675	675
Game Cock Premier, 12 and 20 Gauges, Checkered Stock, Single Trigger, Selective Ejector, *Modern*.....................	700	850	845
Holland, Various Gauges, Sidelock, Engraved, Checkered Stock, Automatic Ejector, *Modern*	3,350	3,950	2,950
Holland Deluxe, Various Gauges, Sidelock, Fancy Engraving, Fancy Checkering, Automatic Ejector, *Modern*	3,850	4,250	3,650
Holland Presentation, Various Gauges, Sidelock, Fancy Engraving, Fancy Checkering, Automatic Ejector, *Modern*	5,250	6,150	4,100
Italia, 12 and 20 Gauges, Checkered Stock, Hammer, Light Engraving, *Modern*..................	725	875	725
Roma #3, Various Gauges, Engraved, Checkered Stock, Automatic Ejector, *Modern*	750	825	670
Roma #4, Various Gauges, Fancy Engraving, Fancy Checkering, Automatic Ejector, *Modern*	650	875	800
Roma #6, Various Gauges, Fancy Engraving, Fancy Checkering, Automatic Ejector, *Modern*	825	950	925
St. Uberto F.S., 12 and 16 Gauges, Checkered Stock, Double Trigger, Automatic Ejector, *Modern*	750	875	695
Wesley Richards, Various Gauges, Checkered Stock, Light Engraving, Double Trigger, *Modern*	1,650	2,150	1,800
Wesley Richards, Various Gauges, Fancy Checkering, Fancy Engraving, Single Trigger, Selective Ejector, Vent Rib, *Modern*	2,875	3,650	3,450

BERSA Baraldo S.A.C.I. Argentina.

HANDGUN, SEMI-AUTOMATIC

	V.G.	Exc.	Prior Edition Exc. Value
Model 62, .22 L.R.R.F., Clip Fed, Blue, *Modern*............................	100	125	100
Model 97, .380 A.C.P., Clip Fed, Blue, *Modern*............................	125	175	140
Model 622, .22 L.R.R.F., Clip Fed, Blue, *Modern*...........................	100	150	125
Model 644, .22 L.R.R.F., Clip Fed, Blue, *Modern*...........................	100	150	130

BERTUZZI Gardone V.T., Italy; Imported by Ventura.

SHOTGUN, DOUBLE BARREL, OVER-UNDER

	V.G.	Exc.	Prior Edition Exc. Value
Zeus, 12 Ga., Sidelock, Automatic Ejector, Single Selective Trigger, Fancy Checkering, Fancy Engraving, *Modern*	6,500	7,500	2,850
Zeus Extra Lusso, 12 Ga., Sidelock, Automatic Ejector, Single Selective Trigger, Fancy Checkering, Fancy Engraving, *Modern*	8,500	10,500	5,250

	V.G.	Exc.	Prior Edition Exc. Value

BICYCLE Bicycle by Harrington & Richardson c. 1895.
HANDGUN, REVOLVER
.22 L.R.R.F., Top Break, Double Action, *Modern* $100 $125 $100
.32 S & W, 5 Shot, Double Action, Top Break, *Modern* 75 100 95

BICYCLE French, Maker Unknown.
HANDGUN, SINGLESHOT
.22 L.R.R.F., Auto Styling, *Modern* 275 350 365

BIG BONANZA Made by Bacon Arms Co. c. 1880.
HANDGUN, REVOLVER
.22 Short R.F., 7 Shot, Spur Trigger, Solid Frame, Single Action,
Antique 125 175 160

BIG HORN ARMS CO. Watertown, S.D.
HANDGUN, SINGLESHOT
Target Pistol, .22 Short, Plastic Stock, Vent Rib, *Modern* $100 $150 $145

Big Horn .22 Pistol

	V.G.	Exc.	Prior Edition Exc. Value

SHOTGUN, SINGLESHOT

12 Ga. Short, Plastic Stock, *Modern* $75 $100 $100

BILLINGHURST, WILLIAM Rochester, N.Y. 1843–80
HANDGUN, PERCUSSION

Buggy Pistol, Various Calibers, Detachable Stock, Heavy Barrel,
Antique 750 1,500 1,300

RIFLE, PERCUSSION

.36, Revolver, 7 Shot, Octagon Barrel, *Antique*................. 2,150 2,750 2,650
.40, Revolver, 7 Shot, Octagon Barrel, *Antique*................. 1,875 2,400 2,350

RIFLE, PILL LOCK

.40, 7 Shot, Octagon Barrel, *Antique* 2,425 2,775 2,700
.40, Carbine, 7 Shot, Octagon Barrel, *Antique*.................. 2,275 2,775 2,750

BISBEE, D.H. Norway, Me. 1835–1860.
RIFLE, PERCUSSION

.44, Octagon Barrel, Silver Inlay, *Antique*........................ 1,750 2,175 2,150

BISON Imported from Germany by Jana International c. 1971.
HANDGUN, REVOLVER

.22 LR/.22 WMR Combo, Adjustable Sights, Western Style,
Single Action, *Modern*.. 25 50 45
.22 L.R.R.F., Adjustable Sights, Western Style, Single Action,
Modern.. 25 50 40

BITTERLICH, FRANK J. Nashville, Tenn. from about 1855 until about 1867.
HANDGUN, PERCUSSION

Derringer, .40, Plain, *Antique*.. 1,200 1,350 950

BITTNER, GUSTAV Vejprty, Bohemia, Austria-Hungary c. 1893.
HANDGUN, MANUAL REPEATER

Model 1893, 7.7mm Bittner, Box Magazine, Checkered Stocks,
Antique 2,500 2,800 2,600

BLAKE, ANN London, England c. 1812.
HANDGUN, FLINTLOCK

Holster Pistol, .62, Walnut Stock, *Antique*...................... 575 725 725

	V.G.	Exc.	Prior Edition Exc. Value

BLANCH, JOHN A. London, England 1809–1835.

HANDGUN, PERCUSSION

.68 Pair, Double Barrel, Side by Side, Officer's Belt Pistol,
Engraved, Silver Inlay, Steel Furniture, Cased with Accessories,
Antique $3,500 $4,250 $5,000

Pair, Pocket Pistol, Converted from Flintlock, High Quality, Cased
with Accessories, *Antique*... 2,500   3,000   2,900

BLAND, T. & SONS London & Birmingham, England from 1876.

SHOTGUN, DOUBLE BARREL, SIDE-BY-SIDE

12 Ga., Boxlock, Adjustable Choke, Color Case Hardened Frame,
Engraved, *Modern*.. 1,875   2,250   2,000

BLANGLE, JOSEPH Gratz, Styria, Austria, c. 1670.

RIFLE, WHEEL-LOCK

Brass Furniture, Engraved, Silver Inlay, Light Ornamentation,
Full-Stocked, *Antique* 5,800   6,500   7,100

BLEIBERG London, England c. 1690.

HANDGUN, FLINTLOCK

Holster Pistol, Engraved, Silver Inlay, High Quality, *Antique*......... 7,900   9,500   9,400

BLICKENSDOERFER & SCHILLING St. Louis, Mo. 1871–1875.

RIFLE, PERCUSSION

.48, Octagon Barrel, Fancy Wood, Brass Furniture, *Antique* 950   1,325   1,300

BLOODHOUND Made by Hopkins & Allen c. 1880.

HANDGUN, REVOLVER

.22 Short R.F., 7 Shot, Spur Trigger, Solid Frame, Single Action,
Antique 75   150   150

BLUE JACKET Made by Hopkins & Allen c. 1880.

HANDGUN, REVOLVER

Model 1, .22 Short R.F., 7 Shot, Spur Trigger, Solid Frame, Single
Action, *Antique* 100   150   150

Model 2, .32 Short R.F., 5 Shot, Spur Trigger, Solid Frame, Single
Action, *Antique* 100   175   160

	V.G.	Exc.	Prior Edition Exc. Value

BLUE WHISTLER Made by Hopkins & Allen c. 1880.
HANDGUN, REVOLVER
.32 Short R.F., 5 Shot, Spur Trigger, Solid Frame, Single Action,
Antique .... $100 | $175 | $160

BLUMENFELD Memphis, Tenn. c. 1970
SHOTGUN, SEMI-AUTOMATIC
Volunteer Pointer, 12 Gauge, Checkered Stock, Modern .... 125 | 225 | 200
SHOTGUN, DOUBLE BARREL, SIDE-BY-SIDE
Arizaga, 20 Gauge, Double Triggers, Checkered Stock, Modern .... 125 | 200 | 180

BLUNT, ORISON & SIMS N.Y.C. 1837–1865.
HANDGUN, PERCUSSION
Boot Pistol, Various Calibers, Bar Hammer, Antique .... 175 | 250 | 245
Boot Pistol, Various Calibers, Side Hammer, Antique .... 225 | 300 | 285
Boot Pistol, Various Calibers, Side Hammer, Ramrod, Antique .... 175 | 300 | 285
Boot Pistol, Various Calibers, Ring Trigger, Antique .... 175 | 275 | 265
Boot Pistol, Various Calibers, Underhammer, Antique .... 175 | 250 | 240
Pocket Pepperbox, Various Calibers, Ring Trigger, Antique .... 200 | 350 | 345
Belt Pepperbox, Various Calibers, Ring Trigger, Antique .... 225 | 350 | 335
Dragoon Pepperbox, Various Calibers, Ring Trigger, Antique .... 475 | 550 | 600
RIFLE, PERCUSSION
.37, Octagon Barrel, Brass Furniture, Antique .... 525 | 625 | 675

BOITO Brazil.
HANDGUN, SINGLESHOT
.44 C.F., Break-Open, Hammer, Blue, Modern .... 75 | 100 | 95
SHOTGUN, DOUBLE BARREL, OVER-UNDER
O/U, 12 or 20 Gauge, Checkered Stock, Modern .... 100 | 175 | 160
SHOTGUN, DOUBLE BARREL, SIDE-BY-SIDE
S/S, 12 or 20 Gauge, Checkered Stock, Modern .... 75 | 150 | 135
SHOTGUN, SINGLESHOT
SS, 12 or 20 Gauge, Checkered Stock, Modern .... 25 | 50 | 45

BONANZA Made by Bacon Arms Co.
HANDGUN, REVOLVER
Model 1½, .22 Short R.F., 7 Shot, Spur Trigger, Solid Frame,
Single Action, Antique .... 100 | 175 | 160

	V.G.	Exc.	Prior Edition Exc. Value

BOND, EDWARD London, England 1800–1830.

HANDGUN, FLINTLOCK

.68, Pair Officers' Type, Holster Pistol, Brass Furniture, Plain,
Antique $2,450 $2,950 $2,850

BOND, WM. London, England 1798–1812.

HANDGUN, FLINTLOCK

Pair, Folding Bayonet, Belt Pistol, Box Lock, Cannon Barrel,
Brass Frame and Barrel, Cased with Accessories, *Antique* 5,225 5,850 5,900

BONEHILL, C.G. Birmingham, England c. 1880.

SHOTGUN, DOUBLE BARREL, OVER-UNDER

.450 N.E. 3¹/⁴", Under-Lever, Recoil Pad, Plain, *Modern*................. 1,250 1,500 1,300

BONIWITZ, JAMES Lebanon, Pa. c. 1775. See Kentucky Rifles.

BOOWLES, R. London, England c. 1690.

HANDGUN, FLINTLOCK

Holster Pistol, Engraved, Iron Mounts, Medium Quality, *Antique* 975 1,425 1,375

BOSS & CO. LTD. London, England 1832 To Date.

SHOTGUN, DOUBLE BARREL, OVER-UNDER

12 Ga., Single Selective Trigger, Straight Grip, Vent Rib, Trap
Grade, Cased, *Modern* 18,750 24,225 17,000
16 Ga., Double Trigger, Plain, *Modern*... 8,275 7,950 6,250
20 Ga., Single Selective Trigger, Vent Rib, High Quality,
Modern... 22,500 27,500 20,000

SHOTGUN, DOUBLE BARREL, SIDE-BY-SIDE

12 Ga., Vent Rib, Fancy Wood, Fancy Checkering, Fancy
Engraving, *Modern* 6,500 7,750 5,750
Pair, 12 Ga., Straight Grip, Plain, Cased, *Modern*............................ 18,750 22,500 11,500

BOSTON BULLDOG Made by Iver Johnson, sold by J.P. Lovell & Sons, Boston, Mass.

HANDGUN, REVOLVER

.22 Short R.F., 7 Shot, Double Action, Solid Frame, *Modern* 75 100 85
.32 S & W, 5 Shot, Double Action, Solid Frame, *Modern*............... 75 100 85
.32 Short R.F., 5 Shot, Double Action, Solid Frame, *Modern* 75 100 75
.38 S & W, 5 Shot, Double Action, Solid Frame, *Modern*............... 75 100 85
.38 Short R.F., 5 Shot, Double Action, Solid Frame, *Modern* 50 100 80

	V.G.	Exc.	Prior Edition Exc. Value

BOSWORTH Lancaster, Pa. 1760–1775. See Kentucky Rifles.

BOYINGTON, JOHN S. Coventry, Conn. 1841–1847.
RIFLE, PERCUSSION

	V.G.	Exc.	Prior Ed.
.50, Octagon Barrel, Brass Furniture, *Antique*	$775	$925	$900

BOY'S CHOICE Made by Hood Firearms Co. c. 1875.
HANDGUN, REVOLVER

	V.G.	Exc.	Prior Ed.
.22 Short R.F., 7 Shot, Spur Trigger, Solid Frame, Single Action, *Antique*	100	175	165

BREDA Brescia, Italy, Diana Import Co., Current
SHOTGUN, DOUBLE BARREL, OVER-UNDER

	V.G.	Exc.	Prior Ed.
.410 Ga., Light Engraving, Checkered Stock, *Modern*	425	475	460

SHOTGUN, SEMI-AUTOMATIC

	V.G.	Exc.	Prior Ed.
"Magnum", 12 Ga., Mag. 3", Checkered Stock, Vent Rib, Lightweight, *Modern*	400	475	400
Grade 1, 12 Ga., Checkered Stock, Vent Rib, Lightweight, Engraved, *Modern*	425	500	465
Grade 2, 12 Ga., Fancy Checkering, Vent Rib, Lightweight, Fancy Engraving, *Modern*	575	650	585
Grade 3, 12 Ga., Fancy Checkering, Vent Rib, Lightweight, Fancy Engraving, *Modern*	750	825	675
Standard, 12 Ga., Checkered Stock, Plain Barrel, Lightweight, *Modern*	300	375	265
Standard, 12 Ga., Checkered Stock, Vent Rib, Lightweight *Modern*	250	325	275

B.R.F. Successor to Pretoria Arms Factory, South Africa, about 1957.
HANDGUN, SEMI-AUTOMATIC

	V.G.	Exc.	Prior Ed.
"Junior", .25 ACP, Clip Fed, Blue, *Modern*	225	300	325
"Junior", .25 ACP, Clip Fed, Blue, Rough Ground Slide, *Modern*	175	200	225
"Junior", .25 ACP, Clip Fed, Blue, Raised Sight Rib, *Modern*	225	275	325
"Junior", .25 ACP, Clip Fed, Blue, Low Slide, *Modern*	175	225	275
"Junior", .25 ACP, Clip Fed, Blue, PAF Logo on Slide, *Modern*	200	300	350
"Junior", .25 ACP, Clip Fed, Factory Chrome Plated, *Modern*	325	400	425
"Junior", for Cocking Indicator, Add **$75–$125**			

BRIGGS, WILLIAM Norristown, Pa. 1848–1875.
SHOTGUN, PERCUSSION

	V.G.	Exc.	Prior Ed.
12 Ga., Underhammer, *Antique*	275	350	345

	V.G.	Exc.	Prior Edition Exc. Value

BRITARMS Aylesbury, England
HANDGUN, SEMI-AUTOMATIC
M2000 Mk.II, .22 L.R.R.F., Clip Fed, Target Pistol, *Modern*.......... $650 | $775 | $825

BRITISH BULLDOG Made by Forehand & Wadsworth.
HANDGUN, REVOLVER

.32 S & W, 5 Shot, Double Action, Solid Frame, *Modern*...............	75	100	90
.38 S & W, 5 Shot, Double Action, Solid Frame, *Modern*...............	75	100	90
.44 S & W, 5 Shot, Double Action, Solid Frame, *Modern*...............	100	125	130

BRITISH MILITARY
HANDGUN, FLINTLOCK

.58, New Land M1796 Tower, Long Tapered Round Barrel, Belt Hook, Brass Furniture, *Antique*	1,750	2,250	2,100
.67, George III Tower, Calvary Pistol, Military, Tapered Round Barrel, Brass Furniture, *Antique*	1,250	1,550	1,500
.80, Modified M1796 Spooner, Holster Pistol, Plain Brass Furniture, *Antique*	1,450	1,950	1,900

HANDGUN, REVOLVER

#2 Mk I, .38 S & W, Military, Top Break, *Curio*	75	100	90
#2 Mk I R.A.F., .38 S & W, Military, Top Break, *Curio*	75	125	110

British Military #1 MK III

British Military Webley MK I No. 2 .455

	V.G.	Exc.	Prior Edition Exc. Value
S & W M38/200, .38 S & W, Solid Frame, Swing-Out Cylinder, Double Action, Military, *Curio*	$75	$125	$115
Webley Mk I, .455 Revolver Mk I, Top Break, Round Butt, Military, *Antique*	225	350	335
Webley Mk 1*, .455 Revolver Mk I, Top Break, Round Butt, Military, *Antique*	225	300	310
Webley Mk I**, .455 Revolver Mk I, Top Break, Round Butt, Military, *Curio*	100	150	—
Webley Mk II, .455 Revolver Mk I, Top Break, Round Butt, Military, *Curio*	125	200	185
Webley Mk II*, .455 Revolver Mk I, Top Break, Round Butt, Military, *Curio*	75	175	150
Webley Mk II**, .455 Revolver Mk I, Top Break, Round Butt, Military, *Curio*	100	150	140
Webley Mk III, .455 Revolver Mk I, Top Break, Round Butt, Military, *Curio*	150	225	200
Webley Mk IV, .455 Revolver MK I, Top Break, Round Butt, Military, *Curio*	100	175	170
Webley Mk V, .455 Revolver Mk I, Top Break, Round Butt, Military, *Curio*	150	200	195
Webley Mk VI, .455 Revolver Mk I, Top Break, Square Butt, Military, *Curio*	125	175	165

HANDGUN, SEMI-AUTOMATIC

	V.G.	Exc.	Prior Edition Exc. Value
Webley Mk.I, .455 Webley Auto, Clip Fed, *Curio*	550	650	230
Webley Mk.I No. 2 R.A.F., .455 Webley Auto, Clip Fed, Cut for Shoulder Stock, *Curio*	1,250	1,450	625
M1911A1 Colt, .455 Webley Auto, Clip Fed, Military, *Curio*	375	450	385

RIFLE, BOLT ACTION

	V.G.	Exc.	Prior Edition Exc. Value
Lee Metford Mk I, .303 British, Clip Fed, Carbine, *Curio*	125	175	150
Lee Metford Mk I, .303 British, Clip Fed, *Curio*	100	150	140
Lee Metford MK I*, .303 British, Clip Fed, Carbine, *Curio*	125	175	135
Lee Metford MK II, .303 British, Clip Fed, *Curio*	100	150	135
Lee Metford MK II*, .303 British, Clip Fed, *Curio*	125	175	145
M1896 Lee Metford, .303 British, Clip Fed, Military, Carbine, *Curio*	100	150	100
Pattern 14 (U.S.), .303 British, *Curio*	125	175	150
SMLE #1 MK I, .303 British, Military, *Curio*	125	150	145
SMLE #1 MK III, .303 British, Military, *Curio*	100	150	125
SMLE #1 Mk III*, .303 British, Tangent Sights, Military, Ishapore, *Curio*	75	125	90
SMLE #1 MK III*, .303 British, Military, *Curio*	75	125	95
SMLE #2 MK IV, .22 L.R.R.F., Singleshot, Training Rifle, *Curio*	125	150	120
SMLE #3 Mk I* (1914 Enfield), .303 British, Military, *Curio*	100	125	105
SMLE #4 MK I*, .303 British, Military, Lightweight, *Curio*	125	150	105
SMLE #4 Sniper, .303 British, Military, Scope Mounted, *Curio*	475	550	365

	V.G.	Exc.	Prior Edition Exc. Value
SMLE #4 MK I*, .303 British, Military, Canadian, Lightweight, *Curio*	$75	$125	$100
SMLE #4 MK I*, .303 British, Military, New Zealand, Lightweight, *Curio*	125	175	130
SMLE #4 MK I*, .303 British, Military, *Curio*	75	100	90
SMLE #MK V Jungle Carbine, .303 British, Peep Sights, Military, *Curio*	125	175	—
Santa Fe Jungle Carbine Mk.I MD12011, .303 British, Peep Sights, No Flash Hider, Commercial, *Modern*	75	125	95
SMLE #7, .22 L.R.R.F., Singleshot, Training Rifle, *Curio*	75	150	130
SMLE #8, .22 L.R.R.F., Singleshot, Training Rifle, *Curio*	100	150	130
SMLE #9, .22 L.R.R.F., Singleshot, Training Rifle, *Curio*	100	150	130

RIFLE, FLINTLOCK

	V.G.	Exc.	Prior Edition Exc. Value
.75, 1st Model Brown Bess, Musket, Brass Furniture, *Antique*	4,200	4,800	4,000
.75, 2nd Model Brown Bess, Musket, Military, *Antique*	2,800	3,300	2,450
.75, 3rd Model Brown Bess, Musket, Military, *Antique*	2,350	2,475	1,900

RIFLE, PERCUSSION

	V.G.	Exc.	Prior Edition Exc. Value
.58 Snider-Enfield, Military, Musket, *Antique*	525	675	600
.60 M1856 Tower, Military, Musket, *Antique*	350	550	500
.60 M1869 Enfield, Military, Musket, *Antique*	350	475	500

RIFLE, SINGLESHOT

	V.G.	Exc.	Prior Edition Exc. Value
Martini-Henry, .303 British, Carbine, *Antique*	175	275	250
Martini-Henry, .303 British, *Antique*	275	325	275
Martini-Henry, .577/.450 Martini-Henry, Carbine, *Antique*	175	250	230
Martini-Henry, .577/.450 Martini-Henry, *Antique*	225	275	265
Martini-Henry, .577/.450 Martini-Henry, Long Lever, *Antique*	200	250	210

SHOTGUN, SINGLESHOT

	V.G.	Exc.	Prior Edition Exc. Value
Martini-Henry, .12 Gauge Special, Long Lever, *Antique*	125	175	160

BRETTON St. Etienne, France.

SHOTGUN, DOUBLE BARREL, OVER-UNDER

	V.G.	Exc.	Prior Edition Exc. Value
Standard, 12 Gauge, Dural Frame, Double Triggers, Barrels Can Be Unscrewed, *Modern*	500	625	400
Deluxe, 12 Gauge, Engraved, Dural Frame, Double Triggers, Barrels Can Be Unscrewed, *Modern*	600	750	500

BORCHARDT Made by Ludwig Lowe, Berlin, Germany 1893–1897. In 1897 acquired by D.W.M., superseded by the Luger in 1900.

HANDGUN, SEMI-AUTOMATIC

	V.G.	Exc.	Prior Edition Exc. Value
Lowe, 7.65mm Borchardt, Clip Fed, Blue, Cased with Accessories, *Antique*	7,500	10,500	9,000

	V.G.	Exc.	Prior Edition Exc. Value
DWM, 7.65mm Borchardt, Clip Fed, Blue, Cased with Accessories, *Curio*	$6,500	$9,500	$7,750

BRNO Ceska Zbrojovka, Brno, Czechoslovakia since 1922.

RIFLE, BOLT ACTION

	V.G.	Exc.	Prior Ed. Exc. Value
21 H, Various Calibers, Sporting Rifle, Express Sights, Cheekpiece, Checkered Stock, Set Trigger, *Modern*	675	750	745
22 F, Various Calibers, Sporting Rifle, Express Sights, Mannlicher, Checkered Stock, Set Trigger, *Modern*	650	825	775
Model I, .22 L.R.R.F., Sporting Rifle, Express Sights, 5 Shot Clip, Checkered Stock, Set Trigger, *Modern*	350	400	400
Model II, .22 L.R.R.F., Sporting Rifle, Express Sights, 5 Shot Clip, Fancy Wood, Set Trigger, *Modern*	275	375	400
Z-B Mauser, .22 Hornet, Sporting Rifle, Express Sights, 5 Shot Clip, Checkered Stock, Set Trigger, *Modern*	575	800	775
ZKB 680 Fox, .222 Rem., Clip Fed, Checkered Stock, Sling Swivels, *Modern*	350	475	365
ZKM 452, .22 L.R.R.F., Clip Fed, Checkered Stock, Tangent Sights, *Modern*	100	150	135

RIFLE, DOUBLE BARREL, OVER-UNDER

	V.G.	Exc.	Prior Ed. Exc. Value
Super Express, Various Calibers, Fancy Checkering, Sidelock, Engraved, Double Triggers, *Modern*	1,600	2,250	695
Super Express Grade III, Various Calibers, Fancy Checkering, Sidelock, Fancy Engraving, Double Triggers, *Modern*	3,250	3,750	1,600
Super Express Grade IV, Various Calibers, Fancy Checkering, Sidelock, Fancy Engraving, Double Triggers, *Modern*	2,650	3,250	1,250

RIFLE, SEMI-AUTOMATIC

	V.G.	Exc.	Prior Ed. Exc. Value
ZKM 581, .22 L.R.R.F., Clip Fed, Checkered Stock, Tangent Sights, *Modern*	300	375	175

SHOTGUN, DOUBLE BARREL, OVER-UNDER

	V.G.	Exc.	Prior Ed. Exc. Value
Super, 12 Gauge, Fancy Checkering Sidelock, Plain, Ejectors, Double Triggers, *Modern*	475	725	695
Super Grade IV, 12 Gauge, Fancy Checkering, Sidelock, Engraved, Ejectors, Double Triggers, *Modern*	625	875	865
Super Grade I, 12 Gauge, Fancy Checkering, Sidelock, Fancy Engraving, Ejectors, Double Triggers, *Modern*	1,275	1,850	1,750
ZH 303 Field, 12 Gauge, Boxlock, Checkered Stock, *Modern*	400	500	450

SHOTGUN, DOUBLE BARREL, SIDE-BY-SIDE

	V.G.	Exc.	Prior Ed. Exc. Value
ZP 47, 12 Gauge, Sidelock, Double Triggers, Extractors, Checkered Stock, *Modern*	275	350	335
ZP 49, 12 Gauge, Sidelock, Double Triggers, Ejectors, Checkered Stock, *Modern*	450	525	465

	V.G.	Exc.	Prior Edition Exc. Value

BROCKWAY, NORMAN S. West Brookfield, Mass. 1861–1867, Bellows Falls, Vt. 1867–1900.

RIFLE, PERCUSSION
Various Calibers, Target Rifle, *Antique*............................ $1,750 $2,450 $—

BRONCO Imported by Garcia, c. 1970.

COMBINATION WEAPON, OVER-UNDER
.22/.410, Skeleton Stock, *Modern*...................... 75   100   75

RIFLE, SINGLESHOT
Skeleton Stock, *Modern*................................... 50   75   55

SHOTGUN, SINGLESHOT
.410 Ga., Skeleton Stock, *Modern*...................... 50   75   65

BRONCO Echave y Arizmendi, Eibar, Spain 1911–1974.

HANDGUN, SEMI—AUTOMATIC
1918 Vest Pocket, .32 ACP, Clip Fed, *Curio* 100   150   150
Vest Pocket, .25 ACP, Clip Fed, *Modern* 100   150   135
Vest Pocket, .25 ACP, Clip Fed, Light Engraving, *Modern*............ 125   200   185

BROOKLYN ARMS CO. Brooklyn, N.Y. 1863–1867.

HANDGUN, REVOLVER
Slocum Patent, .32 R.F., 5 Shot Cylinder with Sliding Chambers, Spur Trigger, Single Action, Engraved, *Antique*............................... 275   395   395

BROWN MFG. CO. Newburyport, Mass. 1869–73. Also see Ballard Rifles.

HANDGUN, SINGLESHOT
Southerner Derringer, .41 R.F., Side-Swing Barrel, Spur Trigger, Brass Frame, *Antique*.. 250   325   295

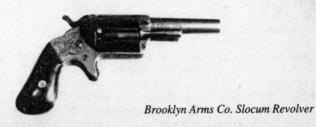

Brooklyn Arms Co. Slocum Revolver

	V.G.	Exc.	Prior Edition Exc. Value

RIFLE, BOLT ACTION

1853 Long Enfield, .58 U.S. Musket, Converted from Percussion, Brass Furniture, *Antique* .... | $325 | $500 | $625

U.S. M1861 Musket, .58 U.S. Musket, Converted from Percussion, Brass Furniture, *Antique* .... | 350 | 525 | 650

BROWN, JOHN & SONS Fremont, N.J. 1840–1871.

RIFLE, PERCUSSION

Various Calibers, Sporting Rifle, *Antique*.. | 850 | 1,275 | 1,200

.50, Target Rifle, Scope Mounted, Set Trigger, *Antique*.................. | 1,650 | 2,250 | 2,000

BROWN PRECISION CO. San Jose, Calif. since 1975.

RIFLE, BOLT ACTION

Sporter, Various Calibers, Fiberglass Stock, Rem. 700 Action, Sling Swivels, *Modern*.. | 525 | 750 | 310

BROWNING Established 1870 in St. Louis, Mo., now at Morgan, Utah. Also see F.N.

HANDGUN, SEMI-AUTOMATIC

Various Calibers, Baby-.380-Hi Power Set, Renaissance, Nickel Plated, Engraved, *Modern*.. | 2,750 | 3,500 | 5,250

380 Auto, .380 ACP, Clip Fed, Renaissance, Nickel Plated, Engraved, *Modern*.. | 850 | 1,050 | 1,650

380 Auto, .380 ACP, Clip Fed, Adjustable Sights, *Modern* .... | 250 | 300 | 330

380 Auto Standard, .380 ACP, Clip Fed, *Modern*............................ | 175 | 225 | 250

Baby, .25 ACP, Clip Fed, Lightweight, Nickel Plated, *Modern*....... | 350 | 395 | 475

Baby, .25 ACP, Clip Fed, Renaissance, Nickel Plated, Engraved, *Modern*.. | 725 | 875 | 1,500

Baby Standard, .25 ACP, Clip Fed, *Modern* .... | 225 | 275 | 290

BDA 380, .380 ACP, Clip Fed, Double Action, Fixed Sights, *Modern*.. | 325 | 375 | 310

BDA 380, .380 ACP, Clip Fed, Double Action, Fixed Sights, Nickel, *Modern*.. | 350 | 400 | 340

BDA 38 Super, .38 Super, Clip Fed, Double Action, Fixed Sights, *Modern*.. | 575 | 650 | 800

BDA 45, .45 ACP, Clip Fed, Double Action, 7 Shot, *Modern*.......... | 425 | 500 | 450

BDA 9, 9mm Luger, Clip Fed, Double Action, 9 Shot, *Modern*....... | 400 | 450 | 400

Challenger, .22 L.R.R.F., Clip Fed, Checkered Wood Grips, Adjustable Sights, *Modern*.. | 300 | 375 | 350

Challenger, .22 L.R.R.F., Clip Fed, Renaissance, Checkered Wood Grips, Fancy Engraving, Nickel Plated, *Modern*................................ | 975 | 1,100 | 1,775

Challenger, .22 L.R.R.F., Clip Fed, Checkered Wood Grips, Gold Inlays, Engraved, *Modern*.. | 1,250 | 1,400 | 1,450

Challenger II, .22 L.R.R.F., Clip Fed, Adjustable Sights, *Modern* ..... | 175 | 225 | 165

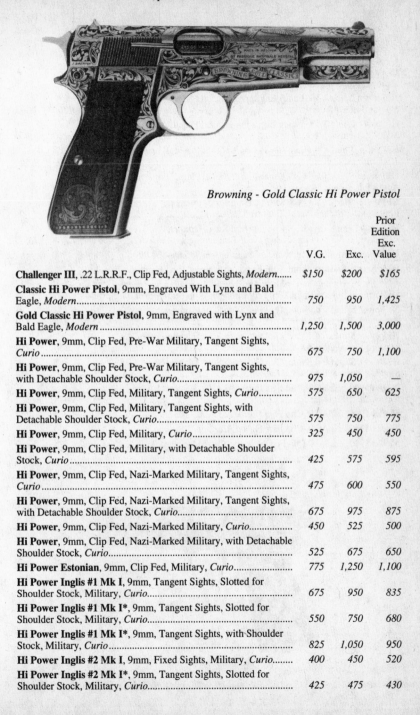

Browning - Gold Classic Hi Power Pistol

	V.G.	Exc.	Prior Edition Exc. Value
Challenger III, .22 L.R.R.F., Clip Fed, Adjustable Sights, *Modern*......	*$150*	*$200*	*$165*
Classic Hi Power Pistol, 9mm, Engraved With Lynx and Bald Eagle, *Modern*..	750	950	1,425
Gold Classic Hi Power Pistol, 9mm, Engraved with Lynx and Bald Eagle, *Modern*	1,250	1,500	3,000
Hi Power, 9mm, Clip Fed, Pre-War Military, Tangent Sights, *Curio*	675	750	1,100
Hi Power, 9mm, Clip Fed, Pre-War Military, Tangent Sights, with Detachable Shoulder Stock, *Curio*...	975	1,050	—
Hi Power, 9mm, Clip Fed, Military, Tangent Sights, *Curio*............	575	650	625
Hi Power, 9mm, Clip Fed, Military, Tangent Sights, with Detachable Shoulder Stock, *Curio*...	575	750	775
Hi Power, 9mm, Clip Fed, Military, *Curio*	325	450	450
Hi Power, 9mm, Clip Fed, Military, with Detachable Shoulder Stock, *Curio*	425	575	595
Hi Power, 9mm, Clip Fed, Nazi-Marked Military, Tangent Sights, *Curio*	475	600	550
Hi Power, 9mm, Clip Fed, Nazi-Marked Military, Tangent Sights, with Detachable Shoulder Stock, *Curio*...	675	975	875
Hi Power, 9mm, Clip Fed, Nazi-Marked Military, *Curio*................	450	525	500
Hi Power, 9mm, Clip Fed, Nazi-Marked Military, with Detachable Shoulder Stock, *Curio*..	525	675	650
Hi Power Estonian, 9mm, Clip Fed, Military, *Curio*......................	775	1,250	1,100
Hi Power Inglis #1 Mk I, 9mm, Tangent Sights, Slotted for Shoulder Stock, Military, *Curio*..	675	950	835
Hi Power Inglis #1 Mk I*, 9mm, Tangent Sights, Slotted for Shoulder Stock, Military, *Curio*..	550	750	680
Hi Power Inglis #1 Mk I*, 9mm, Tangent Sights, with Shoulder Stock, Military, *Curio*..	825	1,050	950
Hi Power Inglis #2 Mk I, 9mm, Fixed Sights, Military, *Curio*........	400	450	520
Hi Power Inglis #2 Mk I*, 9mm, Tangent Sights, Slotted for Shoulder Stock, Military, *Curio*..	425	475	430

	V.G.	Exc.	Prior Edition Exc. Value
Hi Power "FM" Argentine, 9mm, Clip Fed, Made Under License, Military, *Modern*	$425	$475	$450
Hi Power Louis XVI, Fancy Engraving, Nickel Plated, Fixed Sights, Cased, *Modern*	850	1,100	1,175
Hi Power Louis XVI, Fancy Engraving, Nickel Plated, Adjustable Sights, Cased, *Modern*	950	1,200	1,200
Hi Power, 9mm, Clip Fed, Renaissance, Nickel Plated, Engraved, *Modern*	725	1,100	1,500
Hi Power, 9mm, Clip Fed, Renaissance, Nickel Plated, Engraved, Adjustable Sights, *Modern*	850	1,200	1,550
Hi Power, 9mm, Clip Fed, with Lanyard Ring Hammer, Renaissance, Nickel Plated, Engraved, *Modern*	875	1,250	1,600
Hi Power, 9mm, Clip Fed, with Lanyard Ring Hammer, Renaissance, Nickel Plated, Engraved, Tangent Sights, *Modern*	950	1,350	1,650
Hi Power Standard, 9mm, Nickel Plating, *Add* **$35.00–$50.00**			
Hi Power Standard, 9mm, Clip Fed, with Lanyard Ring Hammer, *Modern*	400	450	425
Hi Power Standard, 9mm, Clip Fed, with Spur Hammer, *Modern*	375	400	380
Hi Power Standard, 9mm, Clip Fed, with Spur Hammer, Adjustable Sights, *Modern*	375	450	410
Hi Power Standard, 9mm, Clip Fed, with Spur Hammer, with Tangent Sights, *Modern*	575	650	750
Hi Power Standard, 9mm, Clip Fed, with Spur Tangent Sights, Slotted for Shoulder Stock, *Modern*	850	950	—
Model 1900, .32 ACP, Clip Fed, Early Type, No Lanyard Ring, *Curio*	325	425	395
Model 1900, .32 ACP, Clip Fed, *Curio*	200	275	250
Model 1900, .32 ACP, Clip Fed, Nickel, *Curio*	275	300	285
Model 1900, .32 ACP Clip Fed, Military, *Curio*	275	325	260

Browning High Power Standard, Adj. Sights

Browning M1922

Browning Hi Power 9mm Military

Browning Model 1900

Browning Challenger III

Browning M1903 9mmK

	V.G.	Exc.	Prior Edition Exc. Value
Model 1903, 9mm Browning Long, Clip Fed, *Curio*	$250	$300	$450
Model 1903, 9mm Browning Long, Clip Fed, Light Engraving, *Curio*	450	650	1,100
Model 1903, 9mm Browning Long, Clip Fed, Fancy Engraving, *Curio*	550	850	1,600
Model 1903, 9mm Browning Long, Clip Fed, Military, *Curio*	275	325	280
Model 1903, 9mm Browning Long, Clip Fed, Cut for Shoulder Stock, Military, *Modern*	400	450	490
Model 1903, 9mm Browning Long, Clip Fed, Cut for Shoulder Stock, with Holster Stock, Military, *Modern*	600	650	1,300
Model 1905, .25 ACP, Clip Fed, Grip Safety, *Modern*	200	275	260
Model 1905, .25 ACP, Clip Fed, Grip Safety, Nickel, *Modern*	200	325	420
Model 1905, .25 ACP, Clip Fed, Grip Safety, Russian Contract, Nickel, *Modern*	350	450	375
Model 1910, .32 ACP, Clip Fed, Japanese Military, *Curio*	225	325	325
Model 1910, .32 ACP, Clip Fed, Peruvian Military, *Curio*	275	325	400
Model 1910, .32 ACP, Clip Fed, Syrian Police, *Curio*	300	350	475
Model 1910, .32 ACP, Clip Fed, West German Police, *Modern*	200	275	295
Model 1910, .32 ACP, Clip Fed, Military, *Curio*	325	400	280
Model 1910, .32 ACP, Clip Fed, *Modern*	225	300	215
Model 1910, .380 ACP, Clip Fed, *Modern*	300	350	240
Model 1922, .32 ACP, Clip Fed, *Modern*	200	250	240
Model 1922, .32 ACP, Clip Fed, Nazi-Marked Military, *Modern*	250	275	235
Model 1922, .380 ACP, Clip Fed, Military, *Curio*	275	350	390
Model 1922, .380 ACP, Clip Fed, Dutch Military, *Curio*	200	275	260
Model 1922, .380 ACP, Clip Fed, Turkish Military, *Curio*	225	300	390
Model 1922, .380 ACP, Clip Fed, Yugoslavian Military, *Curio*	225	300	390
Model 1922, .380 ACP, Clip Fed, *Modern*	200	225	240
Medalist, .22 L.R.R.F., Clip Fed, Checkered Wood Target Grips, Wood Forestock, Target Sights, *Modern*	575	700	675
Medalist, .22 L.R.R.F., Clip Fed, Renaissance, Checkered Wood Target Grips, Fancy Engraving, Target Sights, *Modern*	1,500	2,500	3,200
Medalist, .22 L.R.R.F., Clip Fed, Checkered Wood Target Grips, Wood Forestock, Gold Inlays, Engraved, *Modern*	1,200	2,200	2,600
Medalist International, .22 L.R.R.F., Clip Fed, Checkered Wood Target Grips, Target Sights, *Modern*	450	600	550
Medalist International, .22 L.R.R.F., Clip Fed, Checkered Wood Target Grips, Gold Inlays, Engraved, Target Sights, *Modern*	750	1,000	2,400
Medalist International, .22 L.R.R.F., Clip Fed, Renaissance, Checkered Wood Target Grips, Fancy Engraving, Target Sights, *Modern*	950	1,200	3,000
Nomad, .22 L.R.R.F., Clip Fed, Plastic Grips, Adjustable Sights, *Modern*	250	300	375

RIFLE, BOLT ACTION

Model BBR, Various Calibers, Checkered Stock, *Modern*	400	450	395

	V.G.	Exc.	Prior Edition Exc. Value
Exhibition Olympian Grade, Various Calibers, Gold Inlays, Fancy Wood, Fancy Checkering, Engraved, *Modern*..................................	$6,750	$8,700	$8,700
Medallion Grade, .458 Win. Mag., Long Action, Fancy Wood, Fancy Checkering, Engraved, Open Rear Sight, *Modern*..................	1,250	1,500	1,575
Medallion Grade, Various Calibers, Short Action, Fancy Wood, Fancy Checkering, Engraved, *Modern*	1,150	1,400	1,475
Medallion Grade, Various Calibers, Long Action, Magnum, Fancy Wood, Fancy Checkering, Engraved, *Modern*....................................	1,250	1,600	1,680
Olympian Grade, .458 Win. Mag., Long Action, Fancy Wood, Fancy Checkering, Engraved, *Modern*	2,250	2,825	2,575

Browning B-92 .357

Browning BAR .22

Browning Model BBR

Browning Citori Superlight

Browning B-80

Browning BAR

	V.G.	Exc.	Prior Edition Exc. Value
Olympian Grade, Various Calibers, Short Action, Fancy Wood, Fancy Checkering, Fancy Engraving, *Modern*	$2,000	$2,250	$2,725
Olympian Grade, Various Calibers, Medium Action, Fancy Wood, Fancy Checkering, Fancy Engraving, *Modern*	2,000	2,250	2,300
Olympian Grade, Various Calibers, Long Action, Fancy Wood, Fancy Checkering, Fancy Engraving, *Modern*	2,000	2,250	2,500
Olympian Grade, Various Calibers, Long Action, Magnum, Fancy Wood, Fancy Checkering, Fancy Engraving, *Modern*	2,250	2,850	2,825
Safari Grade, Various Calibers, Short Action, Checkered Stock, *Modern*	675	800	650
Safari Grade, Various Calibers, Medium Action, Checkered Stock, *Modern*	700	825	710
Safari Grade, Various Calibers, Long Action, Checkered Stock, *Modern*	725	850	815
Safari Grade, Various Calibers, Long Action, Magnum, Checkered Stock, *Modern*	800	1,000	865
T-Bolt T-1, .22 L.R.R.F., 5 Shot Clip, Plain, Open Rear Sight, *Modern*	175	250	155
T-Bolt T-1, .22 L.R.R.F., 5 Shot Clip, Plain, Open Rear Sight, Left-Hand, *Modern*	275	300	190
T-Bolt T-2, .22 L.R.R.F., 5 Shot Clip, Checkered Stock, Fancy Wood, Open Rear Sight, *Modern*	325	400	250

RIFLE, LEVER ACTION

	V.G.	Exc.	Prior Edition Exc. Value
BL-22, Belgian Manufacture, *Add 15%–25%*			
BL-22 Grade 1, .22 L.R.R.F., Tube Feed, Checkered Stock, *Modern*	225	285	185
BL-22 Grade 2, .22 L.R.R.F., Tube Feed, Checkered Stock, Light Engraving, *Modern*	250	325	210
BLR, Various Calibers, Center-Fire, Plain, Clip Fed, Checkered Stock, *Modern*	250	325	260
Model 92, .357 Mag., Tube Feed, Open Sights, *Modern*	225	275	250
Model 92, .44 Mag., Tube Feed, Open Sights, *Modern*	275	300	255
Model 92 Centennial, Tube Feed, Open Sights, Commemorative, *Modern*	275	400	335

RIFLE, PERCUSSION

	V.G.	Exc.	Prior Edition Exc. Value
J. Browning Mountain Rifle, Various Calibers, Singleshot, Octagon Barrel, Open Rear Sight, Single Set Trigger, Brass Finish, Reproduction, *Antique*	250	375	350
J. Browning Mountain Rifle, Various Calibers, Singleshot, Octagon Barrel, Open Rear Sight, Single Set Trigger, Browned Finish, Reproduction, *Antique*	250	375	350

RIFLE, SEMI-AUTOMATIC

	V.G.	Exc.	Prior Edition Exc. Value
Auto-Rifle, Belgian Mfg., *Add 20%–30%*			
Auto-Rifle Grade I, .22 L.R.R.F., Tube Feed, Takedown, Open Rear Sight, Checkered Stock, *Modern*	175	225	195

	V.G.	Exc.	Prior Edition Exc. Value
Auto-Rifle Grade I, .22 Short, Tube Feed, Takedown, Open Rear Sight, Checkered Stock, *Modern*	$175	$225	$205
Auto-Rifle Grade II, .22 L.R.R.F., Tube Feed, Takedown, Open Rear Sight, Satin Chrome Receiver, Engraved, *Modern*	275	350	295
Auto-Rifle Grade III, .22 L.R.R.F., Takedown, Satin Chrome Receiver, Fancy Wood, Fancy Checkering, Fancy Engraving, Cased, *Modern*	550	650	635
BAR Grade I, .22 L.R.R.F., Checkered Stock, *Modern*	200	225	175
BAR Grade II, .22 L.R.R.F., Checkered Stock, *Modern*	250	275	250
BAR, Various Calibers, Center-Fire, Belgian Mfg., *Add 15%–25%*			
BAR, Various Calibers, Center-Fire, Magnum Calibers, *Add 10%*			
BAR Grade 1, Various Calibers, Center-Fire, Checkered Stock, Plain, *Modern*	400	450	400
BAR Grade 2, Various Calibers, Center-Fire, Checkered Stock, Light Engraving, *Modern*	425	500	485
BAR Grade 3, Various Calibers, Center-Fire, Fancy Wood, Fancy Checkering, Engraved, *Modern*	650	800	785
BAR Grade 4, Various Calibers, Center-Fire, Fancy Wood, Fancy Checkering, Fancy Engraving, *Modern*	1,125	1,300	1,375
BAR Grade 5, Various Calibers, Center-Fire, Fancy Wood, Fancy Checkering, Fancy Engraving, Gold Inlays, *Modern*	2,350	2,750	2,850
Classic Light, 12 Gauge, Engraved With Mallard Ducks, Labrador Retriever and Portrait of John M. Browning, *Modern*	1,275	1,450	1,275
Gold Classic Light, 12 Gauge, Engraved With Mallard Ducks, Labrador Retriever and Portrait of John M. Browning, *Modern*	3,525	4,275	6,700

RIFLE, SINGLESHOT

Model 78, Various Calibers, Various Barrel Styles, Checkered Stock, *Modern*	350	425	350
Model 78, 45-70 Govt., Bicentennial Commemorative, Checkered Stock, *Modern*	375	425	1,900

RIFLE, DOUBLE BARREL, OVER-UNDER

Superposed Continental, 20 Ga. and 30/06, Engraved, Fancy Wood, Fancy Checkering, *Modern*	2,725	2,950	3,550
Express Rifle, 30/06 or .270 Win., Engraved, Fancy Wood, Fancy Checkering, Cased, *Modern*	1,850	2,575	2,750
Centennial Superposed, 20 Ga. and 30/06, Engraved, Fancy Checkering, Fancy Wood, Cased, Commemorative, *Modern*	3,250	5,825	7,150

RIFLE, SLIDE ACTION

BPR, .22 L.R.R.F., Grade I, Checkered Stock, *Modern*	150	200	170
BPR, .22 Mag., Grade I, Checkered Stock, *Modern*	175	225	185
BPR, .22 Mag., Grade II, Checkered Stock, Engraved, *Modern*	300	350	240

SHOTGUN, DOUBLE BARREL, OVER—UNDER

Citori, 12 Ga., Trap Grade, Vent Rib, Checkered Stock, *Modern*	725	850	565
Citori, 12 and 20 Gauges, Standard Grade, Vent Rib, Checkered Stock, *Modern*	725	850	540

	V.G.	Exc.	Prior Edition Exc. Value
Citori, 12 and 20 Gauges, Skeet Grade, Vent Rib, Checkered Stock, *Modern*	$750	$925	$565
Citori International, 12 Ga., Trap Grade, Vent Rib, Checkered Stock, *Modern*	775	950	615
Citori International, 12 Ga., Skeet Grade, Vent Rib, Checkered Stock, *Modern*	750	925	615
Citori Grade II, Various Gauges, Hunting Model, Engraved, Checkered Stock, Single Selective Trigger, *Modern*	800	950	875
Citori Grade II, Trap and Skeet Models, *Add* **10%**			
Citori Grade V, Various Gauges, Fancy Engraving, Checkered Stock, Single Selective Trigger, *Modern*	1,250	1,400	1,380
Citori Grade V, Trap and Skeet Models, *Add* **10%**			
Classic, 20 Gauge, 26" Barrel, Engraved with Bird Dogs, Pheasant and Quail, *Modern*	2,000	2,250	2,500
Gold Classic, 20 Gauge, 26" Barrel, Engraved with Bird Dogs, Pheasant and Quail, *Modern*	7,000	7,500	8,500
Superposed, 12 Ga., Broadway Trap Model, Presentation Grade 4, Fancy Engraving, with Sideplates, Gold Inlays, Fancy Checkering, Fancy Wood, *Modern*	4,250	5,000	6,500
Superposed, 12 Ga., Lightning Trap Model, Presentation Grade 4, Fancy Engraving, with Sideplates, Gold Inlays, Fancy Checkering, Fancy Wood, *Modern*	4,200	5,750	—
Superposed, 12 Ga., Broadway Trap Model, Presentation Grade 4, Fancy Engraving, with Sideplates, Fancy Checkering, Fancy Wood, *Modern*	4,500	5,500	6,200
Superposed, 12 Ga., Lightning Trap Model, Presentation Grade 4, Fancy Engraving, with Sideplates, Fancy Checkering, Fancy Wood, *Modern*	4,625	5,250	5,925
Superposed, 12 Ga., Broadway Trap Model, Presentation Grade 3, Fancy Engraving, Gold Inlays, Fancy Checkering, Fancy Wood, *Modern*	3,850	4,675	5,450

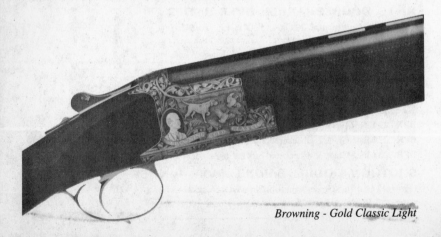

Browning - Gold Classic Light

	V.G.	Exc.	Prior Edition Exc. Value
Superposed, 12 Ga., Lightning Trap Model, Presentation Grade 3, Fancy Engraving, Gold Inlays, Fancy Checkering, Fancy Wood, *Modern*	$2,975	$4,225	$5,350
Superposed, 12 Ga., Broadway Trap Model, Presentation Grade 2, Fancy Engraving, Fancy Checkering, Fancy Wood, *Modern*	2,200	2,675	3,400
Superposed, 12 Ga., Lightning Trap Model, Presentation Grade 2, Fancy Engraving, Fancy Checkering, Fancy Wood, *Modern*	2,375	2,750	3,225
Superposed, 12 Ga., Broadway Trap Model, Presentation Grade 2, Fancy Engraving, Gold Inlays, Fancy Checkering, Fancy Wood, *Modern*	2,650	3,250	3,975
Superposed, 12 Ga., Lightning Trap Model, Presentation Grade 2, Fancy Engraving, Gold Inlays, Fancy Checkering, Fancy Wood, *Modern*	3,500	3,750	3,975
Superposed, 12 Ga., Broadway Trap Model, Presentation Grade 1, Engraved, Gold Inlays, Fancy Checkering, Fancy Wood, *Modern*	2,150	2,650	2,900
Superposed, 12 Ga., Lightning Trap Model, Presentation Grade 1, Engraved, Gold Inlays, Fancy Checkering, Fancy Wood, *Modern*	2,125	2,500	2,825
Superposed, 12 Ga., Broadway Trap Model, Presentation Grade 1, Engraved, Fancy Checkering, Fancy Wood, *Modern*	2,025	2,475	2,700
Superposed, 12 Ga., Lightning Trap Model, Presentation Grade 1, Engraved, Fancy Checkering, Fancy Wood, *Modern*	1,675	2,225	2,650
Superposed, 12 and 20 Gauges, Lightning Skeet Model, Presentation Grade 4, Fancy Engraving, with Sideplates, Gold Inlays, Fancy Checkering, Fancy Wood, *Modern*	5,250	5,675	6,900
Superposed, 12 and 20 Gauges, Super-Light Hunting Model, Presentation Grade 4, Extra Barrels, Fancy Engraving, with Sideplates, Gold Inlays, Fancy Checkering, Fancy Wood, *Modern*	4,750	5,825	7,500
Superposed, 12 and 20 Gauges, Lightning Hunting Model, Presentation Grade 4, Fancy Engraving, with Sideplates, Gold Inlays, Fancy Checkering, Fancy Wood, Extra Barrels, *Modern*	6,125	6,725	7,500
Superposed, 12 and 20 Gauges, Lightning Skeet Model, Presentation Grade 4, Fancy Engraving, with Sideplates, Fancy Checkering, Fancy Wood, Extra Barrels, *Modern*	4,000	6,475	7,250
Superposed, 12 and 20 Gauges, Super-Light Hunting Model, Presentation Grade 4, Fancy Engraving with Sideplates, Fancy Checkering, Fancy Wood, Extra Barrels, *Modern*	4,125	5,000	6,000
Superposed, 12 and 20 Gauges, Lightning Hunting Model, Presentation Grade 4, Fancy Engraving, with Sideplates, Fancy Checkering, Fancy Wood, Extra Barrels, *Modern*	5,250	5,500	6,000
Superposed, 12 and 20 Gauges, Lightning Skeet Model, Presentation Grade 3, Fancy Engraving, Gold Inlays, Fancy Checkering, Fancy Wood, *Modern*	3,000	3,250	3,700
Superposed, 12 and 20 Gauges, Super-Light Hunting Model, Presentation Grade 2, Fancy Engraving, Fancy Checkering, Fancy Wood, Extra Barrels, *Modern*	2,475	3,625	3,750
Superposed, 12 and 20 Gauges, Lightning Hunting Model, Presentation Grade 2, Fancy Engraving, Fancy Checkering, Fancy Wood, Extra Barrels, *Modern*	2,325	3,575	3,750

	V.G.	Exc.	Prior Edition Exc. Value
Superposed, 12 and 20 Gauges, Lightning Skeet Model, Presentation Grade 2, Fancy Engraving, Gold Inlays, Fancy Checkering, Fancy Wood, *Modern*	$2,550	$2,575	$3,600
Superposed, 12 and 20 Gauges, Super-Light Hunting Model, Presentation Grade 2, Fancy Engraving, Gold Inlays, Fancy Checkering, Fancy Wood, Extra Barrels, *Modern*	3,125	3,650	4,900
Superposed, 12 and 20 Gauges, Lightning Hunting Model, Presentation Grade 2, Fancy Engraving, Gold Inlays, Fancy Checkering, Fancy Wood, Extra Barrels, *Modern*	3,600	4,150	4,900
Superposed, 12 and 20 Gauges, Lightning Skeet Model, Presentation Grade 1, Engraved, Gold Inlays, Fancy Checkering, Fancy Wood, *Modern*	1,650	2,325	2,975
Superposed, 12 and 20 Gauges, Super-Light Hunting Model, Presentation Grade 1, Engraved, Gold Inlays, Fancy Checkering, Fancy Wood, *Modern*	1,750	2,350	2,900
Superposed, 12 and 20 Gauges, Lightning Hunting Model, Presentation Grade 1, Engraved, Gold Inlays, Fancy Checkering, Fancy Wood, *Modern*	2,225	2,450	2,850
Superposed, 12 and 20 Gauges, Lightning Skeet Model, Presentation Grade 1, Engraved, Fancy Checkering, Fancy Wood, *Modern*	1,675	2,350	2,700
Superposed, 12 and 20 Gauges, Super-Light Hunting Model, Presentation Grade 1, Engraved, Fancy Checkering, Fancy Wood, *Modern*	1,525	2,225	2,700
Superposed, 12 and 20 Gauges, Lightning Hunting Model, Presentation Grade 1, Engraved, Fancy Checkering, Fancy Wood, *Modern*	1,500	2,000	2,500
Superposed, 28 Ga. or .410 Ga., Lightning Skeet Model, Presentation Grade 4, Fancy Engraving, with Sideplates, Gold Inlays, Fancy Checkering, Fancy Wood, *Modern*	4,675	5,475	5,875
Superposed, 28 Ga. or .410 Ga., Lightning Hunting Model, Presentation Grade 4, Fancy Engraving, with Sideplates, Gold Inlays, Fancy Checkering, Fancy Wood, *Modern*	4,125	5,250	5,850
Superposed, 28 Ga. or .410 Ga., Lightning Skeet Model, Presentation Grade 4, Fancy Engraving, with Sideplates, Gold Inlays, Fancy Checkering, Fancy Wood, *Modern*	3,925	5,125	—
Superposed, 28 Ga. or .410 Ga., Lightning Hunting Model, Presentation Grade 4, Fancy Engraving, with Sideplates, Gold Inlays, Fancy Checkering, Fancy Wood, *Modern*	3,250	4,800	5,800
Superposed, 28 Ga. or .410 Ga., Lightning Skeet Model, Presentation Grade 4, Fancy Engraving, with Sideplates, Fancy Checkering, Fancy Wood, *Modern*	2,625	3,750	4,900
Superposed, 28 Ga. or .410 Ga., Lightning Hunting Model, Presentation Grade 4, Fancy Engraving, with Sideplates, Fancy Checkering, Fancy Wood, *Modern*	2,750	3,950	4,875
Superposed, 28 Ga. or .410 Ga., Lightning Skeet Model, Presentation Grade 3, Fancy Engraving, Gold Inlays, Fancy Checkering, Fancy Wood, *Modern*	2,025	3,125	4,350

	V.G.	Exc.	Prior Edition Exc. Value
Superposed, 28 Ga. or .410 Ga., Lightning Hunting Model, Presentation Grade 3, Fancy Engraving, Gold Inlays, Fancy Checkering, Fancy Wood, *Modern*	$2,275	$3,575	$4,350
Superposed, 28 Ga. or .410 Ga., Lightning Skeet Model, Presentation Grade 2, Fancy Engraving, Fancy Checkering, Fancy Wood, *Modern*	1,450	2,550	3,150
Superposed, 28 Ga. or .410 Ga., Lightning Hunting Model, Presentation Grade 2, Fancy Engraving, Fancy Checkering, Fancy Wood, *Modern*	1,750	2,850	3,175
Superposed, 28 Ga. or .410 Ga., Lightning Skeet Model, Presentation Grade 2, Fancy Engraving, Gold Inlays, Fancy Checkering, Fancy Wood, *Modern*	2,650	3,100	3,600
Superposed, 28 Ga. or .410 Ga., Lightning Hunting Model, Presentation Grade 2, Fancy Engraving, Gold Inlays, Fancy Checkering, Fancy Wood, *Modern*	1,850	2,875	3,550
Superposed, 28 Ga. or .410 Ga., Lightning Skeet Model, Presentation Grade 1, Engraved, Gold Inlays, Fancy Checkering, Fancy Wood, *Modern*	1,725	2,250	2,900
Superposed, 28 Ga. or .410 Ga., Lightning Hunting Model, Presentation Grade 1, Engraved, Gold Inlays, Fancy Checkering, Fancy Wood, *Modern*	1,250	2,250	2,825
Superposed, 28 Ga. or .410 Ga., Lightning Skeet Model, Presentation Grade 1, Engraved, Fancy Checkering, Fancy Wood, *Modern*	1,850	2,250	2,600
Superposed, 28 Ga. or .410 Ga., Lightning Hunting Model, Presentation Grade 1, Engraved, Fancy Checkering, Fancy Wood, *Modern*	1,250	1,975	2,425

Superposed, Various Gauges, Presentation Grade 4, Extra Sets of Barrels, *Add for each*: **$1200.00–$1700.00**

Superposed, Various Gauges, Presentation Grade 3, Extra Sets of Barrels, *Add for each*: **900.00–$1500.00**

Superposed, Various Gauges, Presentation Grade 2, Extra Sets of Barrels, *Add for each*: **$825.00–$1250.00**

Superposed, Various Gauges, Presentation Grade 1, Extra Sets of Barrels, *Add for each*: **$725.00–$1100.00**

Superposed, Pre-1977, Lightning Skeet, *Add* **5%–10%**

Superposed, Pre-1977, Extra Barrel, *Add* **$35%–40%**

Superposed, Pre-1977, 4-Barrel, Skeet Set, *Add* **275%–300%**

Superposed, Pre-War, Raised Solid Rib, *Add* **$60.00–$90.00**

Superposed, Pre-1977, Vent Rib, Pre-War, *Add* **10%–15%**

Superposed, Pre-1977, Super-Light Lightning, *Add* **15%–20%**

Superposed, Pre-1977, Lightning Trap Model, *Add* **5%–10%**

Superposed, Pre-1977, Broadway Trap Model, *Add* **8%–13%**

Superposed, For .410 or 28 Gauge, *Add* **15%–25%**

Superposed, For 20 Gauge, *Add* **10%–15%**

	V.G.	Exc.	Prior Edition Exc. Value
Superposed, Various Gauges, Pre-1977, Super Exhibition Grade, Fancy Wood, Fancy Checkering, Fancy Engraving, Gold Inlays, *Modern*	14,500	21,750	27,500

	V.G.	Exc.	Prior Edition Exc. Value
Superposed, Various Gauges, Pre-1977, Field Grade, Engraved, Checkered Stock, Vent Rib, Single Selective Trigger, *Modern*	$700	$950	$1,250
Superposed, Various Gauges, Pre-1977, Pointer Grade, Fancy Engraving, Fancy Checkering, Single Selective Trigger, *Modern*	1,625	2,150	2,500
Superposed, Various Gauges, Pre-1977, Pigeon Grade Hunting Model, Satin Nickel-Plated Frame, Fancy Engraving, Fancy Checkering, Fancy Wood, *Modern*	1,625	1,950	2,375
Superposed, Various Gauges, Pre-1977, Diana Grade Hunting Model, Satin Nickel-Plated Frame, Fancy Engraving, Fancy Checkering, Fancy Wood, *Modern*	1,825	2,350	2,875
Superposed, Various Gauges, Pre-1977, Midas Grade Hunting Model, Fancy Engraving, Fancy Checkering, Fancy Wood, Gold Inlays, *Modern*	2,575	3,250	4,000
Superposed, Various Gauges, Pre-1977, Exhibition Grade, Fancy Engraving, Fancy Checkering, Fancy Wood, Gold Inlays, *Modern*	5,250	7,500	9,200
Superposed Bicentennial, Fancy Engraving, Gold Inlays, Fancy Wood, Fancy Checkering, Cased, Commemorative, *Modern*	4,625	7,800	9,200
Grand Liege, 12 Ga., Engraved, Single Trigger, Checkered Stock, *Modern*	475	625	675
Liege, 12 Ga., Engraved, Single Trigger, Checkered Stock, *Modern*	275	350	475
ST-100, 12 Ga., Trap Special, Engraved, Checkered Stock, *Modern*	1,250	1,725	2,200

SHOTGUN, DOUBLE BARREL, SIDE-BY-SIDE

	V.G.	Exc.	Prior Edition Exc. Value
B-SS, 12 and 20 Gauges, Checkered Stock, Field Grade, *Modern*	450	500	435
B-SS, 12 and 20 Gauges, Checkered Stock, Sporter Grade, *Modern*	550	600	435
B-SS, 12 and 20 Gauges, Checkered Stock, Grade II, Engraved, *Modern*	775	975	675

SHOTGUN, SEMI-AUTOMATIC

	V.G.	Exc.	Prior Edition Exc. Value
Auto-5, For Belgian Make *Add* **15%–25%**			
Auto-5, 12 Ga., Trap Grade, Vent Rib, Checkered Stock, *Modern*	400	475	435
Auto-5, 12 and 20 Gauges, Magnum, Checkered Stock, Light Engraving, Plain Barrel, *Modern*	400	450	420
Auto-5, 12 and 20 Gauges, Skeet Grade, Checkered Stock, Light Engraving, Vent Rib, *Modern*	500	550	445
Auto-5, 16 Ga. 2⁹/₁₆", Pre-WW2, Checkered Stock, Light Engraving, Plain Barrel, *Modern*	400	525	510
Auto-5, 16 Gauge, Sweet Sixteen, Lightweight, Checkered Stock, Light Engraving, Plain Barrel, *Modern*	450	500	520
Auto-5, Various Gauges, Lightweight, Checkered Stock, Light Engraving, Plain Barrel, *Modern*	450	525	420
Auto-5, Various Gauges, Buck Special, Checkered Stock, Light Engraving, Plain Barrel, *Modern*	475	525	445
Auto-5, Various Gauges, Vent Rib, *Add* **$35.00–$50.00**			
Auto-5, Various Gauges, Raised Solid Rib, *Add* **$30.00–$50.00**			

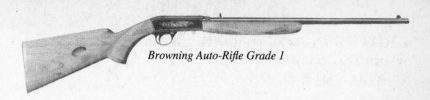

Browning Auto-Rifle Grade 1

	V.G.	Exc.	Prior Edition Exc. Value
Auto-5, Various Gauges, Diana Grade, Pre-WW2, Plain Barrel, Fancy Engraving, *Modern*	$750	$1,200	$1,000
Auto-5, Various Gauges, Midas Grade, Pre-WW2, Plain Barrel, Fancy Engraving, Gold Inlays, *Modern*	950	1,450	1,275
Auto-5, Various Gauges, Grade V, Plain Barrel, Fancy Engraving, *Modern*	1,875	2,650	2,500
B-80, 12 Gauge, Lightweight, Checkered Stock, Vent Rib, *Modern*	300	375	365
Double-Auto, 12 Ga., Trap Model, *Add* **10%–15%**			
Double-Auto, 12 Gauge, Checkered Stock, Engraved, Plain Barrel, *Modern*	200	275	275
Double-Auto, 12 and 20 Gauges, Lightweight, Checkered Stock, Engraved, Plain Barrel, *Modern*	225	325	310
Double-Auto, Vent Rib, *Add* **$35.00–$50.00**			
Double-Auto, Skeet Model, *Add* **10%–15%**			
Model 2000, 12 Ga., Trap Grade, Vent Rib, Tube Feed, Checkered Stock, *Modern*	275	375	350
Model 2000, 12 and 20 Gauges, Vent Rib, Tube Feed, Checkered Stock, *Modern*	250	325	310
Model 2000, 12 and 20 Gauges, Buck Special, Open Rear Sight, Tube Feed, Checkered Stock, *Modern*	250	325	320
Model 2000, 12 and 20 Gauges, Skeet Grade, Vent Rib, Tube Feed, Checkered Stock, *Modern*	275	350	350
Model 2000 Montreal Olympic, 12 Ga., Trap Grade, Vent Rib, Engraved, Gold Inlays, Commemorative, Tube Feed, Checkered Stock, *Modern*	950	1,550	1,750

SHOTGUN, SINGLESHOT

	V.G.	Exc.	Prior Edition Exc. Value
BT-99, 12 Ga., Trap Grade, Vent Rib, with extra Single Trap Barrel, Checkered Stock, Engraved, *Modern*	675	850	550
BT-99, 12 Ga., Pigeon Grade, Checkered Stock, Engraved, Vent Rib, *Modern*	1,150	1,250	900
BT-99, 12 Ga., Trap Grade, Vent Rib, Checkered Stock, Engraved, *Modern*	325	450	410

SHOTGUN, SLIDE ACTION

	V.G.	Exc.	Prior Edition Exc. Value
BPS, 12 Ga., Checkered Stock, Vent Rib, *Modern*	300	375	240
BPS, 12 Ga., Invector Trap, Checkered Stock, Vent Rib, *Modern*	275	300	275
BPS, 12 Ga., Buck Special, Rifle Sights, *Modern*	300	375	260

	V.G.	Exc.	Prior Edition Exc. Value

BRUTUS Made by Hood Firearms Co. c. 1875–76.

HANDGUN, REVOLVER

.22 Short R.F., 7 Shot, Spur Trigger, Solid Frame, Single Action, *Antique* .... $100 | $175 | $160

	V.G.	Exc.	Prior Value
.22 Short R.F., 7 Shot, Spur Trigger, Solid Frame, Single Action, *Antique*	$100	$175	$160

BSA Birmingham Small Arms, Ltd., Birmingham, England. From 1885.

RIFLE, BOLT ACTION

	V.G.	Exc.	Prior Value
Model CF-2, Various Calibers, Sporting Rifle, Checkered Stock, Open Rear Sight, *Modern*	225	375	350
Model CF-2, Various Calibers, Sporting Rifle, Checkered Stock, Double Set Triggers, Open Rear Sight, *Modern*	275	400	400
Imperial, Various Calibers, Sporting Rifle, Muzzle Brake, Checkered Stock, Open Rear Sight, *Modern*	175	275	265
Imperial, Various Calibers, Sporting Rifle, Muzzle Brake, Checkered Stock, Open Rear Sight, Lightweight, *Modern*	300	275	275
Majestic Deluxe, .458 Win. Mag., Sporting Rifle, Muzzle Brake, Lightweight, Checkered Stock, Open Rear Sight, *Modern*	225	325	320
Majestic Deluxe, Various Calibers, Sporting Rifle, Muzzle Brake, Lightweight, Checkered Stock, Open Rear Sight, *Modern*	175	275	270
Majestic Deluxe, Various Calibers, Sporting Rifle, Checkered Stock, Open Rear Sight, *Modern*	175	275	270
Monarch Deluxe, Various Calibers, Sporting Rifle, Checkered Stock, Open Rear Sight, *Modern*	200	300	295
Monarch Deluxe, Various Calibers, Varmint, Heavy Barrel, Checkered Stock, Open Rear Sight, *Modern*	225	300	295

RIFLE, SINGLESHOT

	V.G.	Exc.	Prior Value
#12 Martini, .22 L.R.R.F., Target, Target Sights, Checkered Stock, *Modern*	200	300	295
#12/15 Martini, .22 L.R.R.F., Target, Target Sights, Target Stock, *Modern*	250	350	340
#12/15 Martini, .22 L.R.R.F., Target, Target Sights, Target Stock, Heavy Barrel, *Modern*	250	375	375
#13 Martini, .22 Hornet, Sporting Rifle, Checkered Stock, *Modern*	275	375	360
#13 Martini, .22 L.R.R.F., Target, Target Sights, Checkered Stock, *Modern*	200	275	265
#13 Martini, .22 L.R.R.F., Sporting Rifle, Checkered Stock, *Modern*	200	275	255
#15 Martini, .22 L.R.R.F., Target, Target Sights, Target Stock, *Modern*	350	450	430
Centurian Martini, .22 L.R.R.F., Target, Target Sights, Target Stock, Target Barrel, *Modern*	250	375	365
International Martini, .22 L.R.R.F., Target, Target Sights, Heavy Barrel, Target Stock, *Modern*	250	400	380
International MK 2 Martini, .22 L.R.R.F., Target, Target Sights, Target Stock, *Modern*	275	400	400

	V.G.	Exc.	Prior Edition Exc. Value
International MK 2 Martini, .22 L.R.R.F., Target, Target Sights, Target Stock, Heavy Barrel, *Modern*	$250	$375	$370
International MK 3 Martini, .22 L.R.R.F., Target, Target Sights, Target Stock, Heavy Barrel, *Modern*	325	400	395
Mark V, .22 L.R.R.F., Heavy Barrel, Target Rifle, Target Sights, Target Stock, *Modern*	350	475	475
Martini I S U, .22 L.R.R.F., Target Rifle, Target Sights, Target Stock, *Modern*	250	475	475

RIFLE, SLIDE ACTION

.22 L.R.R.F., Clip Fed, Takedown, *Modern*	75	150	135
.22 L.R.R.F., Tube Feed, Takedown, *Modern*	100	150	150

BUDDY ARMS Fort Worth, Tex. during the early 1960's.

HANDGUN, DOUBLE BARREL, OVER-UNDER

Double Deuce, .22 L.R.R.F., Remington Derringer Copy, *Modern*	50	75	60

BUDISCHOWSKY Made by Norton Armament (Norarmco), Mt. Clemens, Mich. 1973–1977.

HANDGUN, SEMI-AUTOMATIC

TP-70, .22 L.R.R.F., Clip Fed, Double Action, Pocket Pistol, Stainless Steel, Hammer, *Modern*	350	425	375
TP-70, .25 ACP, Clip Fed, Double Action, Pocket Pistol, Stainless Steel, Hammer, Presentation, Custom Serial Number, *Curio*	750	950	1,500
TP-70, .25 ACP, Clip Fed, Double Action, Pocket Pistol, Stainless Steel, Hammer, *Modern*	250	325	325

Budischowski TP-70 .25

	V.G.	Exc.	Prior Edition Exc. Value

BUFALO Gabilondo y Cia., Elgoibar, Spain.

HANDGUN, SEMI-AUTOMATIC

Model 1920, .25 ACP, Clip Fed, *Modern*	$100	$150	$130
Pocket, .32 ACP, Clip Fed, *Modern*	100	150	135

BUFFALO ARMS Tonawanda, N.Y.

HANDGUN, DOUBLE BARREL, OVER-UNDER

Model 1, .357 Mag., Hammer, Blue or Nickel, *Modern*	75	100	100

BUFFALO BILL Maker Unknown, Sold by Homer Fisher Co.

HANDGUN, REVOLVER

.22 Short R.F., 7 Shot, Spur Trigger, Solid Frame, Single Action, *Antique*	100	150	160

BUFFALO STAND Tradename used by ManuFrance.

HANDGUN, SINGLESHOT

Bolt Action, .22 L.R.R.F., Target Pistol, Modern	50	100	120

BUCHEL, ERNST FRIEDRICH Zella Mehlis, Germany, 1919–1926.

HANDGUN, SINGLESHOT

Luna, .22 L.R.R.F., Rotary Breech, Free Pistol, Set Triggers, Light Engraving, *Curio*	650	750	1,000
Practice, .22 Short R.F., Warnant Action, Hammer, Target Pistol, *Curio*	225	300	295
Model W.B., .22 L.R.R.F., Roux Action, Target Pistol, Hammerless, Tip-Down Barrel, *Curio*	350	475	495
Tell I, .22 L.R.R.F., Rotary Breech, Free Pistol, Set Triggers, Light Engraving, *Curio*	700	850	1,000
Tell II, .22 L.R.R.F., Rotary Breech, Free Pistol, Set Triggers, Light Engraving, *Curio*	700	850	1,000

BUHAG Buchsenmacher-Handwerkgenossenschaft M.B.H. of Suhl, East Germany.

HANDGUN, SEMI-AUTOMATIC

Olympia, .22 Short R.F., Clip Fed, Target Pistol, *Modern*	375	550	545

BULL DOZER Made by Norwich Pistol Co., Sold by J. McBride & Co. c. 1875–1883.

HANDGUN, REVOLVER

.22 Short R.F., 7 Shot, Spur Trigger, Solid Frame, Single Action, *Antique*	100	175	165

	V.G.	Exc.	Prior Edition Exc. Value
.38 Short R.F., 5 Shot, Spur Trigger, Solid Frame, Single Action, *Antique*	$100	$200	$180
.41 Short R.F., 5 Shot, Spur Trigger, Solid Frame, Single Action, *Antique*	125	200	200
.44 Short R.F., 5 Shot, Spur Trigger, Solid Frame, Single Action, *Antique*	175	275	260

BULLARD REPEATING ARMS CO. Springfield, Mass.
1887–1889.

RIFLE, LEVER ACTION

	V.G.	Exc.	Prior Ed.
Military, Full Stocked, with Bayonet, Open Rear Sight, *Antique*	2,750	3,800	2,800
Military, Full Stocked, with Bayonet, Open Rear Sight, Carbine, *Antique*	900	1,500	2,800
Various Calibers, Small Frame, Tube Feed, Round Barrel, Plain, Open Rear Sight, Sporting Rifle, *Antique*	750	900	725
Various Calibers, Tube Feed, Round Barrel, Plain, Open Rear Sight, Sporting Rifle, *Antique*	650	1,050	900
Various Calibers, Light Engraving, *Add* $55.00–$160.00			
Various Calibers, Medium Engraving, *Add* $220.00–$435.00			
Various Calibers, Ornate Engraving, *Add* $775.00–$1,150.00			
Various Calibers, Full Nickel Plating, $55.00–$80.00			
Various Calibers, for Fancy Wood, *Add* $30.00–$50.00			
Various Calibers, for Standard Checkering, *Add* $35.00–$50.00			
Various Calibers, Fancy Checkering, *Add* $75.00–$110.00			
Various Calibers, Octagon Barrel, *Add* $30.00–$55.00			
Various Calibers, Half-Octagon Barrel, *Add* $35.00–$65.00			
Various Calibers, Target Sights, *Add* $125.00–$185.00			
Various Calibers, for Lyman Sights, *Add* $45.00–$75.00			
Various Calibers, for Express Sights, *Add* $110.00–$160.00			

RIFLE, SINGLESHOT

	V.G.	Exc.	Prior Ed.
Military, Full-Stocked, with Bayonet, Open Rear Sight, *Antique*	1,450	2,500	1,550
Military, Full-Stocked, with Bayonet, Open Rear Sight, Carbine, *Antique*	1,500	2,750	1,550
Various Calibers, Schuetzen Target Rifle, Octagon Barrel, Target Sights, Swiss Buttplate, Checkered Stock, *Antique*	1,150	2,500	1,975
Various Calibers, Sporting Rifle, Octagon Barrel, Open Rear Sight, *Antique*	450	950	845
Various Rimfires, Target Rifle, Octagon Barrel, Target Sights, Swiss Buttplate, Checkered Stock, *Antique*	750	1,750	975
Various Rimfires, Sporting Rifle, Octagon Barrel, Open Rear Sight, *Antique*	575	975	925

	V.G.	Exc.	Prior Edition Exc. Value

BULLDOG   Made by Forehand & Wadsworth.

HANDGUN, REVOLVER

.32 S & W, 7 Shot, Double Action, Solid Frame, *Modern*	$75	$100	$100
.38 S & W, 6 Shot, Double Action, Solid Frame, *Modern*	75	100	100
.44 S & W, 5 Shot, Double Action, Solid Frame, *Modern*	75	125	130

BULLS EYE   Maker Unknown c. 1875.

HANDGUN, REVOLVER

.22 Short R.F., 7 Shot, Spur Trigger, Solid Frame, Single Action, *Antique*	100	150	155

BULWARK   Beistegui Hermanos, Eibar, Spain.

HANDGUN, SEMI-AUTOMATIC

.25 ACP, External Hammer, Clip Fed, Blue, *Curio*	225	325	335
.25 ACP, Hammerless, Clip Fed, Blue, *Curio*	100	150	150
.32 ACP, External Hammer, Clip Fed, Blue, *Curio*	175	300	295
.32 ACP, Hammerless, Clip Fed, Blue, *Curio*	100	150	150

BUMFORD   London, England 1730–1760.

HANDGUN, FLINTLOCK

.38, Pocket Pistol, Boxlock, Queen Anne Style, Screw Barrel, Silver Inlay, *Antique*	550	775	775

BURGESS, ANDREW   Oswego, N.Y. 1874–1887.

RIFLE, LEVER ACTION

Model 1876, .45-70 Government, Tube Feed, Octagon Barrel, *Antique*	950	1,750	1,700

RIFLE, SLIDE ACTION

Various Calibers, Folding Gun, With Case, *Antique*	850	1,475	1,375

SHOTGUN, SLIDE ACTION

12 Ga., Takedown, Solid Rib, Light Engraving, *Antique*	325	475	395
12 Ga., Folding Gun, With Case, *Antique*	475	750	725

BUSHMASTER   Gwinn Arms Co., Winston-Salem, N.C.

HANDGUN, SEMI-AUTOMATIC

Bushmaster, .223 Rem., Clip Fed, *Modern*	250	325	330

RIFLE, SEMI-AUTOMATIC

.223 Rem., Clip Fed, Wood Stock, *Modern*	250	300	300
.223 Rem., Clip Fed, Folding Stock, *Modern*	275	350	335

	V.G.	Exc.	Prior Edition Exc. Value

BUSOMS Spain c. 1780.

HANDGUN, MIQUELET-LOCK

.70 Pair, Belt Pistol, Belt Hook, Engraved, Brass Furniture,
Antique .... $2,150 $2,475 $—

BUSTINDUI, AUGUSTIN Toledo, Spain c. 1765.

HANDGUN, MIQUELET-LOCK

Pair, Locks by Guisasola, Half-Octagon Barrel, *Antique*   4,175   5,275   5,250

BUSTINDIU, JUAN ESTEBAN Eibar, Spain c. 1775.

HANDGUN, MIQUELET-LOCK

Pair, Half-Octagon Barrel, Silver Inlay, Light Decoration,
Antique   2,950   4,000   4,000

C

C.A.C. Made by A.I.G. Corp., North Haven, Conn. Distributed by Mossberg.

HANDGUN, SEMI-AUTOMATIC

	V.G.	Exc.	Prior Edition Exc. Value
Combat, .45 ACP, Clip Fed, Stainless Steel, *Modern*	$375	$450	$440

CADET Sold by Maltby-Curtis Co.

HANDGUN, REVOLVER

	V.G.	Exc.	Value
.22 Long R.F., 7 Shot, Single Action, Solid Frame, Spur Trigger, *Antique*	100	150	145

CALDERWOOD, WILLIAM Phila., Pa. 1808–1816. See Kentucky Rifles and Pistols and U.S. Military.

CANADIAN MILITARY

HANDGUN, SEMI-AUTOMATIC

	V.G.	Exc.	Value
Hi Power Inglis #1 Mk I, 9mm, Tangent Sights, Slotted for Shoulder Stock, Military, *Modern*	675	950	1,075
Hi Power Inglis #1 Mk I* 9mm, Tangent Sights, Slotted for Shoulder Stock, Military, *Modern*	550	750	965
Hi Power Inglis #2 Mk I, 9mm, Fixed Sights, Military, *Modern*	400	450	800
Hi Power Inglis #2 Mk I*, 9mm, Tangent Sights, Slotted for Shoulder Stock, Military, *Modern*	425	475	625

RIFLE, BOLT ACTION

	V.G.	Exc.	Value
SMLE #4 Mk.1*, .303 British, Clip Fed, *Curio*	75	150	125
1907 MK 2 Ross, .303 British, Full-Stocked, Military, *Modern*	100	175	170
1910 MK 3 Ross, .303 British, Full-Stocked, Military, *Modern*	100	175	185

CAPT. JACK Made by Hopkins & Allen 1871–1875.

HANDGUN, REVOLVER

	V.G.	Exc.	Value
.22 Short R.F., 7 Shot, Spur Trigger, Solid Frame, Single Action, *Antique*	75	150	155

	V.G.	Exc.	Prior Edition Exc. Value

CAROLINE ARMS Made by Crescent Firearms Co. 1892–1900.

SHOTGUN, DOUBLE BARREL, SIDE-BY-SIDE

	V.G.	Exc.	Prior Edition Exc. Value
Various Gauges, Outside Hammers, Damascus Barrel, *Modern*	$75	$150	$155
Various Gauges, Hammerless, Steel Barrel, *Modern*	100	175	180
Various Gauges, Hammerless, Damascus Barrel, *Modern*	75	175	155
Various Gauges, Outside Hammers, Steel Barrel, *Modern*	75	175	180

SHOTGUN, SINGLESHOT

	V.G.	Exc.	Prior Edition Exc. Value
Various Gauges, Hammer, Steel Barrel, *Modern*	50	75	75

CARPENTER, JOHN Lancaster, Pa. 1771–1790. See Kentucky Rifles.

CARROLL, LAWRENCE Philadelphia, Pa. 1786–1790. See Kentucky Rifles.

CARTRIDGE FIREARMS Unknown Makers.

HANDGUN, REVOLVER

	V.G.	Exc.	Prior Edition Exc. Value
11mm Pinfire, Lefaucheux Military Style, *Antique*	150	225	235
11mm Pinfire, Lefaucheux Military Style, Engraved, *Antique*	225	375	395
7mm Pinfire, Pocket Pistol, Folding Trigger, Engraved, *Antique*	75	125	135
.22 Short, Small Pocket Pistol, Folding Trigger, *Modern*.................	50	125	120
.22 Short, Small Pocket Pistol, Double Action, *Modern*	50	75	90
.25 A.C.P., Small Pocket Pistol, Folding Trigger, *Modern*..............	50	100	120
.25 A.C.P., Small Pocket Pistol, Double Action, *Modern*................	25	75	90
Belgian Proofs, Various Calibers, Top Break, Double Action, Medium Quality, *Modern*	50	75	95
Belgian Proofs, Various Calibers, Top Break, Double Action, Engraved, Medium Quality, *Modern*	75	125	125
Belgian Proofs, Various Calibers, Top Break, Double Action, Folding Trigger, Medium Quality, *Modern*..	75	100	95
Chinese Copy of Colt Police Positive, .38 Special, Double Action, Solid Frame, Swing-Out Cylinder, Low Quality, *Modern*	50	75	95
Chinese Copy of Police Positive, 9mm Luger, Double Action, Solid Frame, Swing-Out Cylinder, Low Quality, *Modern*	50	75	80
Copy of Colt SAA, Various Calibers, Western Style, Single Action, Low Quality, *Modern*..	50	100	100
Copy of Colt SAA, Various Calibers, Western Style, Single Action, Medium Quality, *Modern*	75	125	130
Chinese Copy of S&W M-10, .38 Special, Double Action, Solid Frame, Swing-Out Cylinder, Low Quality, *Modern*..........................	50	75	95
Spanish Copy of S&W M-10, .38 Special, Double Action, Solid Frame, Swing-Out Cylinder, Low Quality, *Modern*..........................	50	75	95
Copy of S&W Russian Model, Various Calibers, Break, Single Action, Low Quality, *Antique*...	75	150	140

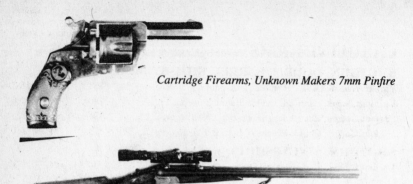

Cartridge Firearms, Unknown Makers 7mm Pinfire

Cartridge Firearms, Unknown Makers Drilling

	V.G.	Exc.	Prior Edition Exc. Value
Copy of S&W Russian Model, Various Calibers, Top Break, Single Action, Medium Quality, *Antique*	*$150*	*$250*	*$245*
Copy of S&W Russian Model, Various Calibers, Top Break, Single Action, High Quality, *Antique*..	*350*	*500*	*525*
Spanish Copy of S&W M-10, .32-20 WCF, Double Action, Solid Frame, Swing-Out Cylinder, Low Quality, *Modern*..........................	*50*	*75*	*85*
Spanish Copy of S&W M-10, .38 Special, Double Action, Solid Frame, Swing-Out Cylinder, Low Quality, *Modern*..........................	*50*	*75*	*75*
Various Centerfire Calibers, Folding Trigger, Open Top Frame, *Modern*...	*75*	*100*	*100*
Various Centerfire Calibers, Bulldog Style, Double Action, Solid Frame, *Modern*..	*50*	*75*	*90*
Various Centerfire Calibers, Small Pocket Pistol, Hammerless, Folding Trigger, with Safety, *Modern*...	*75*	*100*	*100*
7.62mm Nagent, Nagent Style Gas Seal, Solid Frame, Double Action, Modern	*75*	*150*	*165*
Various Centerfire Calibers, European Military Style, Double Action, Solid Frame, Modern	*75*	*150*	*155*
Various Centerfire Calibers, Warnant Style, Top Break, Double Action, *Modern*...	*75*	*150*	*155*
Various Centerfire Calibers, Gasser Style, Solid Frame, Double Action, *Modern*...	*75*	*150*	*100*

HANDGUN, SEMI-AUTOMATIC

Chinese Broomhandle, 7.63 Mauser, Low Quality, Modern.............	*100*	*175*	*175*
Chinese Copy of FN 1900, Various Calibers, Clip Fed, Low Quality, Modern..	*75*	*100*	*95*

	V.G.	Exc.	Prior Edition Exc. Value
Chinese Pocket Pistols, Various Calibers, Clip Fed, Low Quality, Modern	$75	$100	$100
Copy of Colt M1911, .45 ACP, Clip Fed, Military, High Quality, *Modern*	175	250	275
Spanish Pocket Pistols, .25 ACP, Clip Fed, Low Quality, *Modern*	75	100	100
Spanish Pocket Pistols, .32 ACP, Clip Fed, Low Quality, *Modern*	75	125	125
Spanish Pocket Pistols, .32 ACP, Clip Fed, Low Quality, Ruby Style, *Modern*	75	125	125

HANDGUN, SINGLESHOT

	V.G.	Exc.	Prior Edition Exc. Value
Flobert Style, Various Configurations, *Modern*	50	100	90
.22 Short, Target Pistol, Tip-Up Barrel, Plain, *Modern*	75	125	135
.22 Short, Fancy German Target Pistol, Tip-Up Barrel, Engraved, Set Triggers, *Modern*	350	450	550
.22 R.F., Fancy Target Pistol, Hammerless, Set Triggers, *Modern*	275	425	425

RIFLE, BOLT ACTION

	V.G.	Exc.	Prior Edition Exc. Value
Various Rimfire Calibers, Singleshot, Checkered Stock, European, *Modern*	25	50	55
Various Centerfire Calibers, Commercial Sporting Rifle, Low Quality, *Modern*	75	125	130
Arabian Copies, Various Calibers, Military, Reproduction, Low Quality, *Modern*	50	75	95

RIFLE, SINGLESHOT

	V.G.	Exc.	Prior Edition Exc. Value
Various Calibers, Flobert Style, Checkered Stock, *Modern*	75	100	100
Various Calibers, Warnant Style, Checkered Stock, *Modern*	75	125	130
Belgian Proofs, .22 Long R.F., Tip-Up, Octagon Barrel, Medium Quality, *Antique*	75	100	100

SHOTGUN, DOUBLE BARREL, SIDE-BY-SIDE

	V.G.	Exc.	Prior Edition Exc. Value
Belgian Proofs, Various Gauges, Damascus Barrel, Low Quality, Outside Hammers, *Modern*	75	100	125
English Proofs, Various Gauges, Damascus Barrel, Low Quality, Outside Hammers, *Modern*	75	125	125
No Proofs, Various Gauges, Damascus Barrel, Low Quality, Outside Hammers, *Modern*	50	100	100
Various Gauges, American, Outside Hammers, Damascus Barrel, *Modern*	75	150	155
Various Gauges, American, Hammerless, Steel Barrel, *Modern*	100	175	180
Various Gauges, American, Hammerless, Damascus Barrel, *Modern*	75	150	155
Various Gauges, American, Outside Hammers, Steel Barrel, *Modern*	75	175	180

SHOTGUN, SINGLESHOT

	V.G.	Exc.	Prior Edition Exc. Value
Various Gauges, American, Hammer, Steel Barrel, *Modern*	50	75	80
Various Gauges, Warnant Style, Checkered Stock, *Modern*	50	75	75
"Zulu", 12 Ga., Converted from Perc. Musket, Trap Door Action, *Antique*	75	125	130

	V.G.	Exc.	Prior Edition Exc. Value

COMBINATION WEAPON, DRILLING
German, Various Calibers, Light Engraving, *Modern* .... $500 | $850 | $800

CEBRA Arizmendi, Zulaika y Cia., Eibar, Spain.
HANDGUN, SEMI-AUTOMATIC
Pocket, .25 ACP, Clip Fed, Curio .... 75 | 125 | 135

CELTA Tomas de Urizar y Cia., Eibar, Spain c. 1935.
HANDGUN, SEMI-AUTOMATIC
Pocket, .25 ACP, Clip Fed, Curio .... 75 | 125 | 135

CENTENNIAL Made by Derringer Rifle & Pistol Works 1876.
HANDGUN, REVOLVER

	V.G.	Exc.	Prior Ed.
.22 Short R.F., 7 Shot, Spur Trigger, Tip-Up, *Antique*	250	350	390
.32 Short R.F., 5 Shot, Spur Trigger, Solid Frame, Single Action, *Antique*	100	175	180
.38 Short R.F., 5 Shot, Spur Trigger, Solid Frame, Single Action, *Antique*	100	175	185
Centennial '76, .38 Long R.F., 5 Shot, Single Action, Spur Trigger, Tip-Up, *Antique*	250	350	365
Model 2, .32 R.F., 5 Shot, Single Action, Spur Trigger, Tip-Up, *Antique*	250	350	350

CENTRAL Made by Stevens Arms.
SHOTGUN, DOUBLE BARREL, SIDE-BY-SIDE

	V.G.	Exc.	Prior Ed.
Model 315, Various Gauges, Hammerless, Steel Barrel, *Modern*	100	175	170
Model 215, 12 and 16 Gauges, Outside Hammers, Steel Barrel, *Modern*	100	175	175
Model 311, Various Gauges, Hammerless, Steel Barrel, *Modern*	100	175	185

SHOTGUN, SINGLESHOT

	V.G.	Exc.	Prior Ed.
Model 94, Various Gauges, Takedown, Automatic Ejector, Plain Hammer, *Modern*	50	75	70

CENTRAL ARMS CO. Made by Crescent, For Shapleigh Hardware Co., c. 1900.
SHOTGUN, DOUBLE BARREL, SIDE-BY-SIDE

	V.G.	Exc.	Prior Ed.
Various Gauges, Outside Hammers, Damascus Barrel, *Modern*	75	150	155
Various Gauges, Hammerless, Steel Barrel, *Modern*	100	175	180
Various Gauges, Hammerless, Damascus Barrel, *Modern*	75	150	155
Various Gauges, Outside Hammers, Steel Barrel, *Modern*	100	175	180

			Prior Edition Exc.
	V.G.	Exc.	Value

SHOTGUN, SINGLESHOT

Various Gauges, Hammer, Steel Barrel, *Modern*............................ $50 | $75 | $80

CHALLENGE Made by Bliss & Goodyear, c. 1878.

HANDGUN, REVOLVER

.32 Short R.F., 5 Shot, Spur Trigger, Solid Frame, Single Action,
Antique.. 100 | 150 | 160

CHAMPION Unknown Maker c. 1870.

HANDGUN, REVOLVER

.22 Short R.F., 7 Shot, Spur Trigger, Solid Frame, Single Action,
Antique.. 100 | 150 | 160

CHAMPLIN FIREARMS Enid, Oklahoma.

RIFLE, BOLT ACTION

Basic Rifle, with Quarter Rib, Express Sights,
Add **$185.00–$270.00**

Basic Rifle, Fancy Wood, *Add* **$55.00–$90.00**

Basic Rifle, Fancy Checkering, *Add* **$30.00–$45.00**

Basic Rifle, Various Calibers, Adjustable Trigger, Round or
Octagon Tapered Barrel, Checkered Stock, *Modern*......................... 2,750 | 3,500 | 2,525

SHOTGUN, DOUBLE BARREL, OVER-UNDER

12 Ga., Extra Barrels, *Add* **$175.00–$250.00**

Model 100, 12 Ga., Field Grade, Checkered Stock, Vent Rib,
Single Selective Trigger, Engraved, *Modern*..................................... 525 | 850 | 850

Model 100, 12 Ga., Trap Grade, Checkered Stock, Vent Rib,
Single Selective Trigger, Engraved, *Modern*..................................... 575 | 925 | 925

Model 100, 12 Ga., Skeet Grade, Checkered Stock, Vent Rib,
Single Selective Trigger, Engraved, *Modern*..................................... 575 | 925 | 925

Model 500, 12 Ga., Field Grade, Checkered Stock, Vent Rib,
Single Selective Trigger, Engraved, *Modern*..................................... 850 | 1,375 | 1,375

Model 500, 12 Ga., Skeet Grade, Checkered Stock, Vent Rib,
Single Selective Trigger, Engraved, *Modern*..................................... 900 | 1,500 | 1,500

Model 500, 12 Ga., Trap Grade, Checkered Stock, Vent Rib,
Single Selective Trigger, Engraved, *Modern*..................................... 975 | 1,600 | 1,600

SHOTGUN, SINGLESHOT

Model SB 100, 12 Ga., Trap Grade, Checkered Stock, Vent Rib,
Single Selective Trigger, Engraved, *Modern*..................................... 575 | 875 | 875

Model SB 500, 12 Ga., Trap Grade, Checkered Stock, Vent Rib,
Single Selective Trigger, Engraved, *Modern*..................................... 875 | 1,350 | 1,350

	V.G.	Exc.	Prior Edition Exc. Value

CHAPUIS St. Bonnet-le-Chateau, France.
SHOTGUN, DOUBLE BARREL, SIDE-BY-SIDE

Progress RBV, R20, 12 or 20 Gauge, Automatic Ejectors, Sideplates, Double Triggers, Checkered Stock, *Modern* .... $1,275 / $1,450 / $1,200

Progress RG, 12 or 20 Gauge, Automatic Ejectors, Double Triggers, Checkered Stock, *Modern* .... 1,800 / 2,000 / 675

Progress Slug, 12 or 20 Gauge, Automatic Ejectors, Slug Barrel, Double Triggers, Checkered Stock, *Modern* .... 1,975 / 2,200 / 850

CHARLES DALY Tradename on guns made in Suhl, Germany prior to WWII, and by Miroku and Breda after WWII.
COMBINATION WEAPON, DRILLING

Diamond, Various Calibers, Fancy Engraving, Fancy Checkering, *Modern* .... 6,000 / 6,700 / 4,800

Regent Diamond, Various Calibers, Fancy Engraving, Fancy Checkering, Fancy Wood, *Modern* .... 4,400 / 4,800 / 7,000

Superior, Various Calibers, Engraved, *Modern* .... 2,300 / 2,600 / 3,500

RIFLE, BOLT ACTION

.22 Hornet, 5 Shot Clip, Checkered Stock, *Modern* .... 550 / 625 / 995

SHOTGUN, DOUBLE BARREL, OVER-UNDER
For 28 Ga., *Add 10%–15%*

12 Ga., for Wide Vent Rib, *Add $25.00–$45.00*

Various Gauges, Field Grade, Light Engraving, Single Selective Trigger, Automatic Ejector, Post-War, *Modern* .... 300 / 425 / 400

Commander 100, Various Gauges, Automatic Ejector, Checkered Stock, Double Trigger, *Modern* .... 325 / 450 / 425

Commander 100, Various Gauges, Automatic Ejector, Checkered Stock, Single Trigger, *Modern* .... 375 / 500 / 475

Commander 200, Various Gauges, Double Trigger, *Modern* .... 475 / 650 / 600

Commander 200, Various Gauges, Automatic Ejector, Checkered Stock, Engraved, Single Trigger, *Modern* .... 550 / 725 / 625

Diamond, 12 Ga., Trap Grade, Selective Ejector, Single Selective Trigger, Post-War, *Modern* .... 500 / 700 / 750

Diamond, 12 and 20 Gauges, Field Grade, Trap Grade, Selective Ejector, Single Selective Trigger, Post-War, *Modern* .... 500 / 750 / 800

Diamond, 12 and 20 Gauges, Skeet Grade, Trap Grade, Selective Ejector, Single Selective Trigger, Post-War, *Modern* .... 500 / 750 / 800

Diamond, Various Gauges, Double Trigger, Automatic Ejector, Fancy Engraving, Fancy Checkering, *Modern* .... 2,500 / 4,575 / 5,250

Empire, Various Gauges, Double Trigger, Automatic Ejector, Checkered Stock, Engraved, *Modern* .... 1,875 / 3,650 / 4,275

Superior, 12 Ga., Trap Grade, Automatic Ejector, Single Selective Trigger, Post-War, *Modern* .... 350 / 475 / 465

Superior, Various Gauges, Field Grade, Trap Grade, Automatic Ejector, Single Selective Trigger, Post-War, *Modern* .... 350 / 475 / 465

	V.G.	Exc.	Prior Edition Exc. Value
Superior, Various Gauges, Skeet Grade, Trap Grade, Automatic Ejector, Single Selective Trigger, Post-War, *Modern*	$350	$475	$465
Venture, 12 Ga., Trap Grade, Single Trigger, Monte Carlo Stock, Post-War, *Modern*	250	375	375
Venture, 12 and 20 Gauges, Field Grade, Single Trigger, Trap Grade, Post-War, *Modern*	250	375	365
Venture, 12 and 20 Gauges, Skeet Grade, Single Trigger, Trap Grade, Post-War, *Modern*	275	375	375

SHOTGUN, DOUBLE BARREL, SIDE-BY-SIDE

	V.G.	Exc.	Prior Edition Exc. Value
Diamond, Various Gauges, Double Trigger, Fancy Engraving, Fancy Checkering, Fancy Wood, Automatic Ejector, *Modern*	3,275	3,950	4,250
Empire, Various Gauges, Double Trigger, Engraved, Checkered Stock, Automatic Ejector, *Modern*	1,825	2,525	2,700
Empire, Various Gauges, Vent Rib, Single Trigger, Checkered Stock, Engraved, Post-War, *Modern*	250	350	340
Regent Diamond, Various Gauges, Double Trigger, Fancy Engraving, Fancy Checkering, Fancy Wood, Automatic Ejector, *Modern*	2,875	5,250	5,500
Superior, Various Gauges, Double Trigger, Light Engraving, Checkered Stock, *Modern*	850	1,275	1,700

SHOTGUN, SEMI-AUTOMATIC

	V.G.	Exc.	Prior Edition Exc. Value
Novamatic, 12 Ga., Takedown, Trap Grade, Vent Rib, Checkered Stock, Monte Carlo Stock, *Modern*	275	325	240
Novamatic, 12 and 20 Gauges, Takedown, Plain Barrel, Checkered Stock, Lightweight, *Modern*	225	275	190
Novamatic, 12 and 20 Gauges, Takedown, Vent Rib, Checkered Stock, Lightweight, *Modern*	200	250	200
Novamatic, 12 and 20 Gauges, Takedown, Plain Barrel, Checkered Stock, Lightweight, Interchangeable Choke Tubes, *Modern*	225	275	200
Novamatic, 12 and 20 Gauges, Takedown, Vent Rib, Checkered Stock, Lightweight, Interchangeable Choke Tubes, *Modern*	250	275	225
Novamatic, 12 Ga. Mag. 3", Takedown, Vent Rib, Checkered Stock, Magnum, *Modern*	275	300	230
Novamatic, 20 Ga., Takedown, Checkered Stock, Magnum, Lightweight, *Modern*	250	300	215
Novamatic Super Light, 12 and 20 Gauges, Takedown, Plain Barrel, Checkered Stock, *Modern*	200	275	200
Novamatic Super Light, 12 and 20 Gauges, Takedown, Plain Barrel, Checkered Stock, Interchangeable Choke Tubes, *Modern*	175	250	220
Novamatic Super Light, 12 and 20 Gauges, Takedown, Vent Rib, Checkered Stock, *Modern*	150	325	235

SHOTGUN, SINGLESHOT

	V.G.	Exc.	Prior Edition Exc. Value
Empire, 12 Ga., Trap Grade, Fancy Engraving, Fancy Wood, Automatic Ejector, *Modern*	3,450	4,750	4,975

Charola y Anitua, Spanish

	V.G.	Exc.	Prior Edition Exc. Value
Sextuple Empire, 12 Ga., Trap Grade, Fancy Checkering, Fancy Engraving, Fancy Wood, Automatic Ejector, *Modern*	$3,675	$4,975	$5,400
Sextuple Regent Diamond, 12 Ga., Trap Grade, Fancy Checkering, Fancy Engraving, Fancy Wood, Automatic Ejector, *Modern*	4,625	6,675	6,950
Superior, 12 Ga., Trap Grade, Monte Carlo Stock, Selective Ejector, Engraved, Post-War, *Modern*	275	375	385

CHAROLA Y ANITUA Garate, Anitua y Cia., Eibar, Spain, c. 1898.

HANDGUN, SEMI-AUTOMATIC

	V.G.	Exc.	Prior Edition Exc. Value
Charola, 5mm Clement, Locked Breech, Box Magazine, Belgian Made, *Curio*	450	625	600
Charola, 5mm Clement, Locked Breech, Box Magazine, Spanish Made, *Curio*	575	875	845

CHARTER ARMS Stratford, Conn. since 1965.

HANDGUN, REVOLVER

	V.G.	Exc.	Prior Edition Exc. Value
Milestone Limited Edition, .44 Special, Bulldog, Engraved, Silver Plated, Cased with Accessories, *Modern*	775	995	1,175
Bulldog Tracker, .357 Magnum, Double Action, Blue, Adjustable Sights, *Modern*	200	225	160
Bulldog, .44 Special, Double Action, Blue, *Modern*	175	200	155
Bulldog, .44 Special, Double Action, Nickel Plated, *Modern*	200	225	165
Bulldog, .44 Special, Double Action, Stainless, *Modern*	225	250	180
Off-Duty, .38 SPL, 5 Shot, 2" Barrel, Steel Frame, *Modern*	150	175	160
Off-Duty, .38 SPL, 5 Shot, 2" Barrel, Stainless, *Modern*	225	275	250
Pathfinder, .22 L.R.R.F., Adjustable Sights, Bulldog Grips, Double Action, *Modern*	175	200	155
Pathfinder, .22 L.R.R.F., Adjustable Sights, Bulldog Grips, Double Action, Stainless Steel, *Modern*	225	275	195
Pathfinder, .22 L.R.R.F., Adjustable Sights, Square-Butt, Double-Action, *Modern*	125	175	145

	V.G.	Exc.	Prior Edition Exc. Value
Pathfinder, .22 WMR, Adjustable Sights, Double Action, Bulldog Grips, *Modern*	*$125*	*$175*	*$150*
Pathfinder, .22 WMR, Adjustable Sights, Double Action, Square-Butt, *Modern*	*125*	*175*	*145*
Police Bulldog, .38 Special, Double Action, Blue, Adjustable Sights, *Modern*	*125*	*200*	*140*
Police Bulldog, .32 H&R Magnum, 4" Bull Barrel, Checkered Grips, Blue, *Modern*	*175*	*225*	*250*
Police Bulldog, .38 Special, 4" Tapered Barrel, Square Grips, Stainless, *Modern*	*175*	*250*	*275*
Police Bulldog, .38 Special, 1" Bull Barrel, Stainless, *Modern*	*250*	*275*	*275*
Police Bulldog Tracker, .357 Magnum, 2½" Barrel, Blue, *Modern*	*200*	*250*	*250*
Police Bulldog Tracker, .357 Magnum, 4" Barrel, Bulldog Grips, Blue, *Modern*	*200*	*250*	*260*
Police Undercover, .32 H&R Magnum, 2" Barrel, Checkered Panel Grips, Blue, *Modern*	*175*	*200*	*220*
Police Undercover, .38 Special, 2" Barrel, Blue, Pocket Hammer, *Modern*	*175*	*200*	*220*

Charter Arms Police Bulldog

Charter Arms Bulldog "Tracker" .357 Magnum 5-Shot, 4" Barrel

Charter Arms M40, Double Action Pistol

Charter Arms M79K, .380 Caliber

	V.G.	Exc.	Prior Edition Exc. Value
Police Undercover, Law Enforcement Version, .38 Special, Five Shot, Neoprene Grips, *Modern*	*$250*	*$275*	*$280*
Target Bulldog, .357 Magnum, Double Action, Blue, Adjustable Sights, *Modern*	*150*	*175*	*170*
Target Bulldog, .44 Special, Double Action, Blue, Adjustable Sights, *Modern*	*150*	*200*	*175*
Undercover, .38 Special, Double Action, Blue, *Modern*	*125*	*175*	*145*
Undercover, .38 Special, Double Action, Stainless Steel, *Modern*	*175*	*225*	*185*
Undercover, .38 Special, Double Action, Blue, Bulldog Grips, *Modern*	*125*	*175*	*155*
Undercover, .38 Special, Double Action, Nickel Plated, *Modern*	*125*	*175*	*145*
Undercoverette, .32 S & W Long, Double Action, Blue, Bulldog Grips, *Modern*	*100*	*150*	*135*

HANDGUN, SEMI-AUTOMATIC

	V.G.	Exc.	Prior Edition Exc. Value
Model 40, .22 L.R., 8 Shot Mag, Checkered Walnut Gripstock, Stainless, *Modern*	*200*	*225*	*325*
Model 79K, .380 Autoloader, 7 Shot Mag, Checkered Gripstock, Stainless, *Modern*	*250*	*300*	*400*
Model 79K32, .32 Caliber Autoloader, 7 Shot Mag, Stainless, *Modern*	*350*	*400*	*450*
Explorer II, .22 L.R.R.F., Clip Fed, Takedown, *Modern*	*75*	*100*	*75*
Explorer SII, .22 L.R.R.F., Clip Fed, Takedown, 6" and 10" Optional Barrels, *Modern*	*100*	*125*	*130*

RIFLE, SEMI-AUTOMATIC

	V.G.	Exc.	Prior Edition Exc. Value
Explorer, .22 L.R.R.F., Clip Fed, Takedown, *Modern*	*100*	*125*	*80*

CHASE, WILLIAM Pandora, Ohio 1854–1860.
COMBINATION WEAPON, PERCUSSION

	V.G.	Exc.	Prior Edition Exc. Value
Various Calibers, Double Barrel, *Antique*	*850*	*1,250*	*1,275*

CHEROKEE ARMS CO. Made by Crescent, C.M. McClung & Co. Tennessee, c. 1900.
SHOTGUN, DOUBLE BARREL, SIDE-BY-SIDE

	V.G.	Exc.	Prior Edition Exc. Value
Various Gauges, Outside Hammers, Damascus Barrel, *Modern*	*75*	*150*	*155*
Various Gauges, Hammerless, Steel Barrel, *Modern*	*100*	*175*	*180*
Various Gauges, Hammerless, Damascus Barrel, *Modern*	*75*	*150*	*155*
Various Gauges, Outside Hammers, Steel Barrel, *Modern*	*75*	*175*	*180*

RIFLE, SINGLESHOT

	V.G.	Exc.	Prior Edition Exc. Value
Various Gauges, Hammer, Steel Barrel, *Modern*	*50*	*75*	*80*

CHERRINGTON, THOMAS P. Cattawissa, Pa. 1847–1858.
RIFLE, PILL LOCK

	V.G.	Exc.	Prior Edition Exc. Value
.40, Revolver, Octagon Barrel, *Antique*	*2,000*	*2,500*	*2,675*

Chicago Fire Arms Co. Palm Pistol

		Prior Edition Exc.
	V.G.	Exc.	Value

CHICAGO ARMS CO. Sold by Fred Bifflar Co. Made by Meriden Firearms Co. 1870–1890.

HANDGUN, REVOLVER

	V.G.	Exc.	Value
.32 S & W, 5 Shot, Double Action, Top Break, *Modern*	$50	$100	$100
.38 S & W, 5 Shot, Double Action, Top Break, *Modern*	50	100	100
.38 S & W, Top Break, Hammerless, Double Action, Grip Safety, *Modern*	75	125	130

CHICAGO FIRE ARMS CO. Chicago, Ill. 1883–1894.

HANDGUN, PALM PISTOL

	V.G.	Exc.	Value
.32 Extra Short R.F., Engraved, *Antique*	650	850	800

CHESAPEAKE GUN CO. Made by Crescent c. 1900.

SHOTGUN, DOUBLE BARREL, SIDE-BY-SIDE

	V.G.	Exc.	Value
Various Gauges, Outside Hammers, Damascus Barrel, *Modern*	75	150	155
Various Gauges, Hammerless, Steel Barrel, *Modern*	100	175	180
Various Gauges, Hammerless, Damascus Barrel, *Modern*	75	150	155
Various Gauges, Outside Hammers, Steel Barrel, *Modern*	100	175	180

SHOTGUN, SINGLESHOT

	V.G.	Exc.	Value
Various Gauges, Hammer, Steel Barrel, *Modern*	50	75	80

CHICNESTER Made by Hopkins & Allen, c. 1880.

HANDGUN, REVOLVER

	V.G.	Exc.	Value
.38 Short R.F., 5 Shot, Spur Trigger, Solid Frame, Single Action, *Antique*	100	175	175

CHIEFTAIN Made by Norwich Pistol Co., c. 1880.

HANDGUN, REVOLVER

	V.G.	Exc.	Value
.32 Short R.F., 5 Shot, Spur Trigger, Solid Frame, Single Action, *Antique*	100	150	160

	V.G.	Exc.	Prior Edition Exc. Value

CHILEAN MILITARY
RIFLE, BOLT ACTION

	V.G.	Exc.	Prior Edition Exc. Value
M1895 Rifle, 7mm Mauser, Military, *Curio*	$50	$100	$90
M1895 Short Rifle, 7mm Mauser, Military, *Curio*	50	100	95
M1895 Carbine, 7mm Mauser, Military, *Curio*	50	100	92

CHINESE MILITARY
HANDGUN, SEMI-AUTOMATIC

	V.G.	Exc.	Prior
Makarov, 9mm Mak., Clip Fed, *Modern*	575	775	875
Tokarev, 7.62mm Tokarev, Clip Fed, *Modern*	175	275	275
Walther PPk Type, .32 A.C.P., Double Action, Blue, Clip Fed, Military, *Modern*	750	950	1,700

RIFLE, BOLT ACTION

Type 53 (Nagent), 7.62 × 54R Russian, *Modern*	75	175	155

RIFLE, SEMI-AUTOMATIC

SKS, 7.62 × 39 Russian, Folding Bayonet, Military, *Modern*	250	375	375

CHINESE NATIONALIST MILITARY
HANDGUN, SEMI-AUTOMATIC

Hi Power, 9mm Luger, Clip Fed, Military, Tangent Sights, *Curio*	375	575	620
Hi Power, 9mm Luger, Clip Fed, Military, Tangent Sight, with Detachable Shoulder Stock, *Curio*	525	675	750

RIFLE, BOLT ACTION

Kar 98k Type 79, 8mm Mauser, *Modern*	75	150	145
M1871 Mauser, .43 Mauser, Carbine, *Antique*	100	175	165
M1888 Hanyang, 8mm Mauser, 5 Shot, *Curio*	75	125	120
M98 Mukden, 8mm Mauser, *Modern*	100	175	180

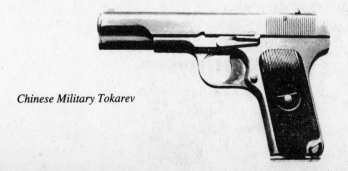

Chinese Military Tokarev

	V.G.	Exc.	Prior Edition Exc. Value

CHIPMUNK Medford, Ore. since 1982.
RIFLE, BOLT ACTION
.22 L.R.R.F., Single Shot, Manual Cocking, Modern...................... $75 | $100 | $80

CHURCHILL, E.J. & ROBERT London, England 1892 to Date.
RIFLE, BOLT ACTION
One of 1,000, Various Calibers, Checkered Stock, Recoil Pad,
Express Sights, Cartridge Trap, *Modern*.. 1,000 | 1,250 | 900

One of 1,000, Various Calibers, Fancy Checkering, Engraved
Express Sights, Cartridge Trap, Cased With Accessories, *Modern*....... 1,850 | 2,575 | 2,375

SHOTGUN, DOUBLE BARREL, SIDE-BY-SIDE
Utility Model, Various Gauges, Boxlock, Double Triggers, Color
Case Hardened Frame, Engraved, *Modern*...................................... 3,500 | 4,500 | 3,450

Hercules Model XXV, Various Gauges, Hammerless Sidelock,
Engraved, Fancy Checkering, Fancy Wood, Cased, *Modern*............ 6,000 | 7,000 | 5,400

Field Model, Various Gauges, Hammerless Sidelock, Fancy
Checkering, Automatic Ejectors, Engraved, *Modern*........................ 6,000 | 7,000 | 8,150

Imperial Model XXV, Various Gauges, Hammerless Sidelock,
Fancy Checkering, Automatic Ejectors, Engraved, *Modern*............ 7,500 | 9,500 | 8,000

Premier Quality, Various Gauges, Hammerless Sidelock, Fancy
Checkering, Automatic Ejectors, Engraved, *Modern*........................ 10,000 | 12,000 | 9,100

Regal Model XXV, Various Gauges, Hammerless Sidelock, Fancy
Checkering, Automatic Ejectors, Engraved, *Modern*........................ 3,750 | 4,300 | 4,450

For Single Selective Trigger *Add* $375.00–$535.00

SHOTGUN, DOUBLE BARREL, OVER-UNDER
Premier Quality, Various Gauges, Hammerless Sidelock, Fancy
Checkering, Automatic Ejectors, Engraved, *Modern*........................ 12,000 | 15,000 | 14,000

Premier Quality, for Single Selective Trigger, *Add* $400.00–$535.00

Premier Quality, for Raised Vent Rib, *Add* $350.00–$520.00

CHYLEWSKI, WITOLD Austria, 1910–1918. Pistols made by S.I.G.
HANDGUN, SEMI-AUTOMATIC
Einhand, .25 ACP, Clip Fed, Blue, With Locking Screw, *Curio*..... 675 | 750 | 700
Einhand, .25 ACP, Clip Fed, Blue, No Locking Screw, *Curio*........ 650 | 875 | 850

Chylewski .25 With Locking Screw

	V.G.	Exc.	Prior Edition Exc. Value

CLARK, F.H. Memphis, Tenn., c. 1860.

HANDGUN, PERCUSSION

	V.G.	Exc.	Prior Edition Exc. Value
Deringer, .41, German Silver Mountings, *Antique*	$750	$1,100	$750
Deringer Copy, .41, German Silver Mountings, *Antique*	950	1,250	850

CLARKSON, J. London, England 1680–1740.

HANDGUN, FLINTLOCK

	V.G.	Exc.	Prior Edition Exc. Value
.32, Pocket Pistol, Queen Anne Style, Box Lock, Screw Barrel, Silver Furniture, *Antique*	475	700	700

CLASSIC ARMS Palmer, Mass.

HANDGUN, PERCUSSION

	V.G.	Exc.	Prior Edition Exc. Value
.36 Duckfoot, 3 Shot, Brass Frame, Reproduction, *Antique*	25	50	40
.36 Twister, 2 Shot, Brass Frame, Reproduction, *Antique*	25	50	40
.36 Ethan Allen, Pepperbox, 4 Shot, Brass Frame, Reproduction, *Antique*	25	50	40
.36 Snake-Eyes, Double Barrel, Side by Side, Brass Frame, Reproduction, *Antique*	25	50	35
.44 Ace, Rifled, Brass Frame, Reproduction, *Antique*	25	25	25

CLEMENT, CHARLES Liege, Belgium 1886–1914.

HANDGUN, SEMI-AUTOMATIC

	V.G.	Exc.	Prior Edition Exc. Value
M1903, 5mm Clement, Clip Fed, Blue, *Curio*	375	500	500

Clement M1903 5mm

Clement M1909 .25

	V.G.	Exc.	Prior Edition Exc. Value
M1907, .25 ACP, Clip Fed, Blue, *Curio*	$250	$325	$320
M1907, .32 ACP, Clip Fed, Blue, *Curio*	275	375	395
M1908, .25 ACP, Clip Fed, Blue, *Curio*	325	400	395
M1909, .25 ACP, Clip Fed, Blue, *Curio*	225	325	320
M1909, .32 ACP, Clip Fed, Blue, *Curio*	275	375	410
M1912 Fulgor, .32 ACP, Clip Fed, Blue, *Curio*	450	650	700

RIFLE, SEMI-AUTOMATIC

Clement-Neumann, .401 Win., Clip Fed, Checkered Stock, Matted Rib, *Curio*	450	650	650

SHOTGUN, DOUBLE BARREL, SIDE-BY-SIDE

Various Gauges, Outside Hammers, Damascus Barrel, *Curio*	125	200	185
Various Gauges, Hammerless, Steel Barrel, *Curio*	150	225	220
Various Gauges, Hammerless, Damascus Barrel, *Curio*	125	200	185

CLEMENT, J.B. Belgium.
SHOTGUN, DOUBLE BARREL, SIDE-BY-SIDE

Various Gauges, Hammerless, Steel Barrel, *Modern*	150	225	210
Various Gauges, Outside Hammers, Steel Barrel, *Modern*	150	200	200

CLERKE Santa Monica, Calif.
HANDGUN, REVOLVER

32-200, .32 S & W, Nickel Plated, *Modern*	25	50	25
CF200, .22 L.R.R.F., Nickel Plated, *Modern*	25	50	25

RIFLE, SINGLESHOT

Hi-Wall, Various Calibers, Fancy Wood, *Modern*	200	250	325
Hi-Wall Deluxe, Various Calibers, Octagon Barrel, Fancy Wood, *Modern*	250	300	425
Hi-Wall Deluxe, Various Calibers, Octagon Barrel, Set Trigger, Fancy Wood, *Modern*	275	325	465

CLIMAS Made by Stevens Arms.
SHOTGUN, SINGLESHOT

Model 90, Various Gauges, Takedown, Automatic Ejector, Plain Hammer, *Modern*	50	75	65

CLIPPER Maker unknown, c. 1880.
HANDGUN, REVOLVER

.22 Short R.F., 7 Shot, Spur Trigger, Solid Frame, Single Action, *Antique*	100	150	155

	V.G.	Exc.	Prior Edition Exc. Value

CODY MANUFACTURING CO. Chicopee, Mass. 1957–1959.
HANDGUN, REVOLVER
Thunderbird, .22 R.F., 6 Shot, Double Action, Aluminum with Steel Liners, *Modern*.. $125 $175 $180

COGSWELL & HARRISON London, England 1770 to Date; Branch in Paris 1924–1938.
HANDGUN, REVOLVER
S & W Victory, .38 Special, Double Action, Swing-Out Cylinder, Refinished and Customized. Rebored from .38 S & W and may be unsafe with .38 Spec., *Modern*.. 75 150 140

RIFLE, BOLT ACTION
BSA-Lee Speed, .303 British, Sporting Rifle, Express Sights, Engraved, Checkered Stock, Commercial, *Modern*........................... 550 825 825

SHOTGUN, DOUBLE BARREL, SIDE-BY-SIDE
Avant Tout (Konor), Various Gauges, Box Lock, Automatic Ejector, Fancy Checkering, Fancy Engraving, Double Trigger, *Modern*.. 2,025 2,375 3,000

Avant Tout (Konor), Various Gauges, Box Lock, Automatic Ejector, Fancy Checkering, Fancy Engraving, Single Trigger, *Modern*.. 2,350 2,750 3,350

Avant Tout (Konor), Various Gauges, Box Lock, Automatic Ejector, Fancy Checkering, Fancy Engraving, Single Selective Trigger, *Modern*.. 2,775 2,925 3,550

Avant Tout (Rex), Various Gauges, Box Lock, Automatic Ejector, Checkered Stock, Light Engraving, Double Trigger, *Modern*........... 1,450 1,750 2,250

Avant Tout (Rex), Various Gauges, Box Lock, Automatic Ejector, Checkered Stock, Light Engraving, Single Trigger, *Modern*............ 1,275 1,750 2,450

Avant Tout (Rex), Various Gauges, Box Lock, Automatic Ejector, Checkered Stock, Light Engraving, Single Selective Trigger, *Modern*.. 1,700 1,925 2,675

Avant Tout (Sandhurst), Various Gauges, Box Lock, Automatic Ejector, Fancy Checkering, Engraved, Double Trigger, *Modern*...... 1,875 2,450 2,900

Avant Tout (Sandhurst), Various Gauges, Box Lock, Automatic Ejector, Fancy Checkering, Engraved, Single Trigger, *Modern*........ 1,850 2,675 3,100

Avant Tout (Sandhurst), Various Gauges, Box Lock, Automatic Ejector, Fancy Checkering, Engraved, Single Selective Trigger, *Modern*.. 2,275 2,850 3,300

Cogswell & Harrison Lee Speed

	V.G.	Exc.	Prior Edition Exc. Value
Huntic, Various Gauges, Sidelock, Automatic Ejector, Checkered Stock, Double Trigger, *Modern*	$3,000	$3,200	$3,600
Huntic, Various Gauges, Sidelock, Automatic Ejector, Checkered Stock, Single Trigger, *Modern*	2,675	3,350	3,800
Huntic, Various Gauges, Sidelock, Automatic Ejector, Checkered Stock, Single Selective Trigger, *Modern*	2,875	3,325	3,900
Markor, Various Gauges, Box Lock, Automatic Ejector, Checkered Stock, Double Trigger, *Modern*	1,350	1,500	2,300
Markor, Various Gauges, Box Lock, Checkered Stock, Double Trigger, *Modern*	1,200	1,350	1,925
Primic, Various Gauges, Sidelock, Automatic Ejector, Fancy Engraving, Fancy Checkering, Double Trigger, *Modern*	2,750	3,850	4,575
Primic, Various Gauges, Sidelock, Automatic Ejector, Fancy Engraving, Fancy Checkering, Single Trigger, *Modern*	3,375	4,150	4,775
Primic, Various Gauges, Sidelock, Automatic Ejector, Fancy Engraving, Fancy Checkering, Single Selective Trigger, *Modern*	3,150	4,275	4,800
Victor, Various Gauges, Sidelock, Automatic Ejector, Engraved, Checkered Stock, Double Trigger, *Modern*	4,450	5,125	6,700
Victor, Various Gauges, Sidelock, Automatic Ejector, Engraved, Checkered Stock, Single Trigger, *Modern*	5,225	5,875	7,000
Victor, Various Gauges, Sidelock, Automatic Ejector, Engraved, Checkered Stock, Single Selective Trigger, *Modern*	4,675	6,150	7,000

COLON Antonio Azpiri y Cia. Eibar, Spain 1914–1918.

HANDGUN, SEMI-AUTOMATIC

Pocket, .25 ACP, Clip Fed, *Curio*	100	125	125

COLON Made by Orbea Hermanos Eibar, Spain c. 1925.

HANDGUN, REVOLVER

Colt Police Positive Copy, .32/20, Double Action, Blue, *Curio*	100	125	140

COLONIAL Fabrique d'Armes de Guerre de Grand Precision, Eibar, Spain.

HANDGUN, SEMI-AUTOMATIC

.25 ACP, Clip Fed, Blue, *Modern*	75	125	125
.32 ACP, Clip Fed, Blue, *Modern*	100	150	150

COLT Patterson, N.J. 1836–1841. Whitneyville, Conn. 1847–1848. Hartford, Conn. 1848 to Date; London, England 1853–1864. Also see U.S. Military.

HANDGUN, PERCUSSION

.28 Model 1855 Root, Full Fluted Cylinder, Side Hammer, Spur Trigger, Revolver, Octagon Barrel, *Antique*	750	1,000	770
.28 Model 1855 Root, Full Fluted Cylinder, Side Hammer, Spur Trigger, Revolver, Round Barrel, *Antique*	850	1,250	775

	V.G.	Exc.	Prior Edition Exc. Value
.28 Model 1855 Root, Round Cylinder, Side Hammer, Spur Trigger, Revolver, Octagon Barrel, *Antique*	*$650*	*$850*	*$725*
.28 Model 1855 Root, Round Cylinder, Side Hammer, Spur Trigger, Revolver, Round Barrel, *Antique*	*1,500*	*2,000*	*775*
.28 Model Patterson (Baby), 5 Shot, Various Barrel Lengths, Octagon Barrel, no Loading Lever, *Antique*	*21,000*	*24,000*	*3,850*
.28 Model Patterson (Baby), 5 Shot, Various Barrel Lengths, Octagon Barrel, with Factory Loading Lever, *Antique*	*22,000*	*26,000*	*4,350*
.31 Model 1848 Revolver, Baby Dragoon, 5 Shot, Various Barrel Lengths, no Loading Lever, no Capping Groove, *Antique*	*8,550*	*9,225*	*3,175*
.31 Model 1848 Revolver, Baby Dragoon, 5 Shot, Various Barrel Lengths, no Loading Lever, Stagecoach Cylinder, *Antique*	*7,200*	*8,250*	*2,450*
.31 Model 1848 Revolver, Baby Dragoon, 5 Shot, Various Barrel Lengths, no Loading Lever, *Antique*	*7,650*	*8,450*	*2,850*
.31 Model 1848 Revolver, Baby Dragoon, 5 Shot, Various Barrel Lengths, with Loading Lever, *Antique*	*7,550*	*8,675*	*3,100*
.31 Model 1849 Revolver, Wells Fargo, 5 Shot, no Loading Lever, Pocket Pistol, *Antique*	*3,500*	*5,500*	*2,025*
.31 Model 1849 Revolver, Pocket Pistol, with Loading Lever, 5 Shot, Round-Backed Trigger Guard, Large, 1-Line N.Y. Address, Brass Frame, *Antique*	*2,200*	*2,800*	*680*
.31 Model 1849 Revolver, Pocket Pistol, with Loading Lever, 5 Shot, Large Round-Backed Trigger Guard, 1-Line Hartford Address, Brass Frame, *Antique*	*2,400*	*3,000*	*800*
.31 Model 1849 Revolver, Pocket Pistol, with Loading Lever, 5 Shot, Round-Backed Trigger Guard, Large, 1-Line Hartford Address, Iron Frame, *Antique*	*2,200*	*3,200*	*845*
.31 Model 1849 Revolver, Pocket Pistol, with Loading Lever, 5 Shot, Large Round-backed Trigger Guard, 1-Line London Address, Iron Frame, *Antique*	*800*	*1,250*	*1,050*
.31 Model 1849 Revolver, Pocket Pistol, with Loading Lever, 5 Shot, Round-Backed Trigger Guard, Small, 2-Line N.Y. Address, Iron Frame, *Antique*	*600*	*850*	*625*
.31 Model 1849 Revolver, Pocket Pistol, with Loading Lever, 5 Shot, Round-Backed Trigger Guard, Small, 2-Line N.Y. Address, Brass Frame, *Antique*	*600*	*850*	*625*
.31 Model 1849 Revolver, Pocket Pistol, with Loading Lever, 5 Shot, Square-Backed Trigger Guard, Small, 2-Line N.Y. Address, *Antique*	*1,250*	*1,850*	*1,725*
.31 Model 1849, For 5" Barrel, *Add 10%–15%*			
.31 Model 1849, For 6" Barrel, *Add 15%–25%*			
.31 Model 1849, 6 Shot (Model 1850), *Add 15%–25%*			
.31 Baby Dragoon, Late, Unfluted Cylinder, Reproduction, *Antique*	*150*	*225*	*210*
.31 Model 1855 Root, Full Fluted Cylinder, Side Hammer, Spur Trigger, Revolver, Octagon Barrel, *Antique*	*950*	*1,350*	*875*
.31 Model 1855 Root, Full Fluted Cylinder, Side Hammer, Spur Trigger, Revolver, Round Barrel, *Antique*	*1,350*	*2,100*	*875*

	V.G.	Exc.	Prior Edition Exc. Value
.31 Model 1855 Root, Round Fluted Cylinder, Side Hammer, Spur Trigger, Revolver, Octagon Barrel, *Antique*	$950	$1,350	$875
.31 Model 1855 Root, Round Fluted Cylinder, Side Hammer, Spur Trigger, Revolver, Round Barrel, *Antique*	1,025	1,450	1,025
.31 Model 1855, For 4½" Barrel, *Add* **10%–15%**			
.31, .28 Model 1855, London Markings, *Add* **50%–75%**			
.31 Model Patterson (Baby), 5 Shot, Octagon Barrel, Various Barrel Lengths, no Loading Lever, no Capping Groove, *Antique*	5,000	7,000	3,925
.31 Model Patterson (Baby), 5 Shot, Octagon Barrel, Various Barrel Lengths, with Factory Loading Lever, *Antique*	5,500	7,500	4,350
.31, .34 Model Patterson (Pocket), 5 Shot, Octagon Barrel, Various Barrel Lengths, no Loading Lever, no Capping Groove, *Antique*	6,000	8,000	4,375
.31 Model Patterson (Pocket), 5 Shot, Octagon Barrel, Various Barrel Lengths, with Factory Loading Lever, *Antique*	7,000	9,000	5,075
.31 Model Patterson (Belt), 5 Shot, Octagon Barrel, Various Barrel Lengths, no Loading Lever, no Capping Groove, Straight Grip, *Antique*	6,500	8,500	4,750
.31 Model Patterson (Belt), 5 Shot, Octagon Barrel, Various Barrel Lengths, no Loading Lever, no Capping Groove, Flared Grip, *Antique*	7,500	9,500	5,250
.36 M1851 Grant-Lee Set, Revolver, Commemorative, Cased Reproduction, *Antique*	600	1,250	1,100
.36 M1851 Late, Revolver, 6 Shot, Reproduction, *Antique*	130	230	230
.36 M1851 R.E. Lee, Revolver, Commemorative, Cased Reproduction, *Antique*	300	550	380
.36 M1851 U.S. Grant, Revolver, Commemorative, Cased Reproduction, *Antique*	300	550	380
.36 Model 1851, Half-Fluted, Rebated Cylinder, *Add* **25%–40%**			
.36 Model 1851 Navy, Revolver, with Loading Lever, Square-Backed Trigger Guard, 1st Type, Under #1250, 6 Shot, *Antique*	3,800	6,500	4,250
.36 Model 1851 Navy, Revolver, with Loading Lever, Square-Backed Trigger Guard, 2nd Type, #1250 to #3500, 6 Shot, *Antique*	3,200	4,500	2,400
.36 Model 1851 Navy, Revolver, with Loading Lever, 6 Shot, Small Round-Backed Guard, Small Loading Cut, *Antique*	1,600	2,400	1,500
.36 Model 1851 Navy, Revolver, with Loading Lever, 6 Shot, Small Round-Backed Guard, Large Loading Cut, *Antique*	1,450	2,250	1,500
.36 Model 1851 Navy, Revolver, with Loading Lever, 6 Shot, Round-Backed Trigger Guard, Large Loading Cut, London Address, Iron Frame, *Antique*	1,800	3,000	1,600
.36 Model 1851 Navy, Revolver, with Loading Lever, 6 Shot, Round-Backed Trigger Guard, Small Loading Cut, London Address, Iron Frame, *Antique*	1,950	3,500	1,900
.36 Model 1851 Navy, Revolver, with Loading Lever, 6 Shot, Large Round-Backed Guard, Large Loading Cut, N.Y. Address, *Antique*	850	1,650	1,050

	V.G.	Exc.	Prior Edition Exc. Value
.36 Model 1851 Navy, Revolver, with Loading Lever, 6 Shot, Large Round-Backed Guard, Large Loading Cut, Hartford Address, *Antique*	*$1,200*	*$2,000*	*$1,250*
.36 Model 1851 Navy, Revolver, with Loading Lever, 6 Shot, Large Round-Backed Guard, Cut for Shoulder Stock, Iron Backstrap, *Antique*	2,000	3,500	3,350
.36 Model 1851 Navy, Revolver, with Loading Lever, 6 Shot, Large Round-Backed Guard, with Detachable Shoulder Stock, Iron Backstrap, *Antique*	6,000	7,500	6,100
.36 Model 1862 Navy, Revolver, New Navy Pocket Pistol 4½" Barrel, Rebated Cylinder, *Antique*	850	1,250	960
.36 Model 1862 Navy, Revolver, New Navy Pocket Pistol 5½" Barrel, Rebated Cylinder, *Antique*	1,100	1,650	1,020
.36 Model 1862 Navy, Revolver, New Navy Pocket Pistol 1861, 6½" Barrel, Rebated Cylinder, *Antique*	950	1,475	975
.36 Model 1862 Navy, Revolver, Late New Navy Pocket Pistol 5½" Barrel, Rebated Cylinder, Reproduction, *Antique*	150	225	215
.36 Model 1861 Navy, Revolver, Round Barrel, Military Model, no Cuts for Shoulder Stock, *Antique*	3,200	4,500	3,300
.36 Model 1861 Navy, Revolver, Round Barrel, Civilian Model, no Cuts for Shoulder Stock, *Antique*	1,900	3,250	1,500
.36 Model 1861 Navy, Revolver, Round Barrel, Military, Cut for Shoulder Stock, *Antique*	4,200	5,500	4,225
.36 Model 1861 Navy, Revolver, Round Barrel, Military, With Shoulder Stock, *Antique*	5,750	8,500	6,850
.36 Model 1861 Navy, Revolver, Late, Round Barrel, Civilian Model, no Cuts for Shoulder Stock, Reproduction, *Antique*	150	250	225
.36 Model 1862 Police, Revolver, Half-Fluted Rebated Cylinder, *Antique*	600	1,000	950
.36 Model 1862 Police, Revolver, Late, Half-Fluted Rebated Cylinder, Reproduction, *Antique*	150	225	210
.36 Model 1862 Police, for Hartford Marks, *Add 10%–20%*			
.36 Model 1862 Police, for London Marks, *Add 10%–20%*			
.36 Model Patterson (Holster), 5 Shot, Octagon Barrel, Various Barrel Lengths, no Loading Lever, no Capping Groove, *Antique*	8,500	12,500	10,250
.36 Model Patterson (Holster), 5 Shot, Octagon Barrel, Various Barrel Lengths, with Factory Loading Lever, *Antique*	10,000	15,000	18,000
.44 Model 1847, Revolver, Whitneyville Walker (U.S.M.R.), Square-Backed Trigger Guard, 6 Shot, *Antique*	25,000	35,000	28,500
.44 Model 1847 Revolver, Dragoon, (Hartford) Horizontal Loading Lever Latch, 6 Shot, *Antique*	12,000	20,000	10,000
.44 Model 1847, Revolver, Dragoon, (Hartford) Vertical Loading Lever Latch, Square-Backed Trigger Guard, 6 Shot, *Antique*	8,000	10,000	5,275
.44 Dragoon 1st Model, Revolver, 6 Shot, Civilian, *Antique*	8,000	10,000	4,175
.44 Dragoon 1st Model, Revolver, 6 Shot, Military, *Antique*	10,000	12,000	4,700
.44 Dragoon 1st Model, Revolver, 6 Shot, Reproduction, *Antique*	175	250	235

	V.G.	Exc.	Prior Edition Exc. Value
.44 Dragoon 1st Model, Revolver, 6 Shot, Fluck Variation, *Antique*	$3,700	$8,500	$4,900
.44 Dragoon 2nd Model, Revolver, 6 Shot, Civilian, *Antique*	4,500	7,500	3,800
.44 Dragoon 2nd Model, Revolver, 6 Shot, Military, *Antique*	5,500	8,500	3,975
.44 Dragoon 2nd Model, Revolver, 6 Shot, Militia, *Antique*	10,000	12,000	4,800
.44 Dragoon 3rd Model, Revolver, 6 Shot, Civilian, *Antique*	3,000	6,000	3,025
.44 Dragoon 3rd Model, Revolver, 6 Shot, Military, *Antique*	3,500	8,000	3,250
.44 Dragoon 3rd Model, Revolver, 6 Shot, Military, Cut for Shoulder Stock, *Antique*	4,500	10,000	4,000
.44 Dragoon 3rd Model, Revolver, 6 Shot, Military, With Shoulder Stock, *Antique*	6,500	14,000	6,100
.44 Model 1860 Army, Revolver, Cut for Shoulder Stock, *Antique*	950	2,500	1,250
.44 Model 1860 Army, Revolver, Cut for Shoulder Stock, Four-Screw Frame, *Antique*	1,250	2,800	1,550
.44 Model 1860 Army, Revolver, Cut for Shoulder Stock, Four-Screw Frame, with Shoulder Stock, *Antique*	3,700	5,000	3,925
.44 Model 1860 Army, Revolver, Cut for Shoulder Stock, Four-Screw Frame, Fluted Cylinder, *Antique*	2,200	4,500	2,050
.44 Model 1860 Army, Revolver, Cut for Shoulder Stock, Four-Screw Frame, Fluted Cylinder, Hartford Address, *Antique*	1,950	4,800	2,550
.44 Model 1860 Army, Revolver, Cut for Shoulder Stock, Four-Screw Frame, Fluted Cylinder, Hartford Address, with Shoulder Stock, *Antique*	2,500	5,500	4,785
.44 Model 1860 Army, Revolver, Cut for Shoulder Stock, Civilian Model, *Antique*	1,200	3,000	1,300
.44 Model 1860 Army, Revolver, Cut for Shoulder Stock, London Markings, *Add 50%–75%*			
.44 Model 1860 Army, Revolver, Fluted Cylinder, Reproduction, *Antique*	200	275	260
.44 Model 1860 Army, Revolver, Butterfield Overland Express Commemorative, Two Cylinders, Reproduction, *Antique*	400	700	690

HANDGUN, CARTRIDGE CONVERSIONS

	V.G.	Exc.	Prior Edition Exc. Value
Model 1851 Navy, .38 R.F. or C.F., Richards-Mason, *Antique*	1,500	2,500	765
Model 1851 Navy, .36 Thuer, Thuer Style, *Antique*	2,500	4,500	3,600
Model 1860 Army, .44 Thuer, Thuer Style, *Antique*	2,500	4,500	3,600
Model 1860 Army, .44 Colt, Richards, *Antique*	700	2,000	900
Model 1860 Army, .44 Colt, Richards-Mason, *Antique*	3,000	6,000	1,275
Model 1861 Navy, .36 Thuer, Thuer Style, *Antique*	2,500	5,500	4,800
Model 1862 Pocket Navy, .36 Thuer, Thuer Style, *Antique*	2,600	5,500	3,925
Model 1862 Pocket Navy, .38 R.F., no Ejector, Octagon Barrel, *Antique*	600	1,250	650
Model 1862 Pocket Navy, .38 R.F., no Ejector, Round Barrel, *Antique*	450	1,000	610
Model 1862 Pocket Navy, .38 R.F., with Ejector, Round Barrel, *Antique*	650	1,500	—

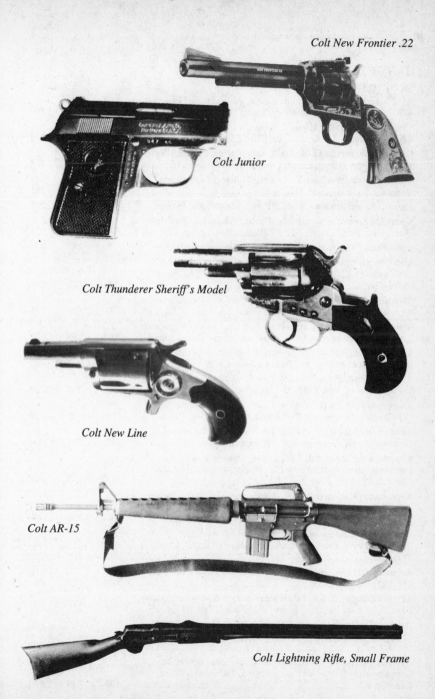

Colt New Frontier .22

Colt Junior

Colt Thunderer Sheriff's Model

Colt New Line

Colt AR-15

Colt Lightning Rifle, Small Frame

	V.G.	Exc.	Prior Edition Exc. Value

HANDGUN, REVOLVER

For Nickel Plating, *Add* **$20.00–$30.00**

".357 Magnum", .357 Magnum, 6 Shot, Various Barrel Lengths, Adjustable Sights, Target Hammer, Target Grips, *Modern*	$325	$475	$460
".357 Magnum", .357 Magnum, 6 Shot, Various Barrel Lengths, Adjustable Sights, *Modern*	275	400	390
125th Anniversary, .45 Colt, Single Action Army, Commemorative, Blue, with Gold Plating, Cased, *Curio*	500	900	715
Agent, .38 Special, 6 Shot, Parkerized, 2" Barrel, Lightweight, *Modern*	150	250	155
Agent, .38 Special, 6 Shot, Blue, 2" Barrel, Lightweight, *Modern*	150	225	205
Agent, .38 Special, 6 Shot, Nickel Plated, 2" Barrel, Lightweight, *Modern*	150	250	225
Agent Early, .38 Special, 6 Shot, 2" Barrel, Lightweight, *Modern*	175	250	230
Alabama Sesquicentennial, .22 L.R.R.F., Frontier Scout S.A., Commemorative, Gold Plated, with Nickel Plating, 4³/₄" Barrel, Cased, *Curio*	200	325	295
Alamo Model, .22 L.R.R.F., Frontier Scout S.A., Commemorative, Blue, with Gold Plating, 4³/₄" Barrel, Cased, *Curio*	200	325	275
Alamo Model, .22 L.R.R.F., and .45 Colt Set, Frontier Scout and S.A.A., Commemorative, Blue, with Gold Plating, Cased, *Curio*	700	1,250	1,075
Alamo Model, .45 Colt, Single Action Army, Commemorative, Blue, with Gold Plating, 5¹/₂" Barrel, Cased, *Curio*	500	1,000	775
Abercrombie & Fitch, .45 Colt, Trailblazer New Frontier S.A., Commemorative, New York, 7¹/₂" Barrel, Cased, *Curio*	750	1,200	1,900
Abercrombie & Fitch, .45 Colt, Trailblazer New Frontier S.A., Commemorative, Chicago, 7¹/₂" Barrel, Cased, *Curio*	750	1,200	1,900
Abercrombie & Fitch, .45 Colt, Trailblazer New Frontier S.A., Commemorative, San Francisco, 7¹/₂" Barrel, Cased, *Curio*	750	1,200	1,900
Appomattox Centennial, .22 L.R.R.F., Frontier Scout S.A., Commemorative, Blue, With Nickel Plating, 4³/₄" Barrel, Cased, *Curio*	225	325	305
Appomattox Centennial, .22 L.R.R.F., and .45 Colt Set, Frontier Scout and S.A.A., Commemorative, Blue, with Nickel Plating, Cased, *Curio*	700	1,250	1,025
Appomattox Centennial, .45 Colt, Single Action Army, Commemorative, Blue, with Nickel Plating, 5¹/₂" Barrel, Cased, *Curio*	500	875	775
Argentine M1895, .38, Double Action, Solid Frame, Swing-Out Cylinder, Military, *Curio*	125	175	180
Arizona Ranger, .22 L.R.R.F., Frontier Scout S.A., Commemorative, Blue, Color Case Hardened Frame, 4³/₄" Barrel, Cased, *Curio*	200	325	295
Arizona Territorial Centennial, .22 L.R.R.F., Frontier Scout S.A., Commemorative, Blue, with Gold Plating, 4³/₄" Barrel, Cased, *Curio*	200	350	305
Arizona Territorial Centennial, .45 Colt, Single Action Army, Commemorative, Blue, with Gold Plating, 4³/₄" Barrel, Cased, *Curio*	500	950	810

	V.G.	Exc.	Prior Edition Exc. Value
Arkansas Territorial Sesquicentennial, .22 L.R.R.F., Frontier Scout S.A., Commemorative, Blue, 4¾" Barrel, Cased, *Curio*	$200	$350	$230
Army Special, .32-20 WCF, 6 Shot, Various Barrel Lengths, *Curio*	200	350	360
Army Special, .38 Special, 6 Shot, Various Barrel Lengths, *Curio*	200	350	310
Army Special, .41 Long Colt, 6 Shot, Various Barrel Lengths, *Curio*	200	350	250
Banker's Special, .22 L.R.R.F., 6 Shot, 2" Barrel, *Modern*	550	850	790
Banker's Special, Fitzgerald Trigger Guard, *Add* **$150.00–$250.00**			
Banker's Special, .38 S & W, 6 Shot, 2" Barrel, *Modern*	350	525	465
Battle of Gettysburg Centennial, .22 L.R.R.F., Frontier Scout S.A., Nickel Plated, Blue, with Gold Plating, 4¾" Barrel, Cased, *Curio*	225	325	315
Bicentennial Set, Python, SAA, Dragoon, Commemorative, Cased, *Curio*	1,500	2,000	2,300
California Bicentennial, .22 L.R.R.F., Frontier Scout S.A., Commemorative, Gold Plated, with Nickel Plating, 6" Barrel, Cased, *Curio*	200	350	300
California Gold Rush, .22 L.R.R.F., Frontier Scout S.A., Commemorative, Gold Plated, 4¾" Barrel, Cased, *Curio*	225	375	320
California Gold Rush, .45 Colt, Single Action Army, Commemorative, Gold Plated, 5½" Barrel, Cased, *Curio*	800	1,075	1025
Carolina Charter Tercentennial, .22 L.R.R.F., Frontier Scout S.A., Commemorative, Blue, with Gold Plating, 4¾" Barrel, Cased, *Curio*	275	400	375
Carolina Charter Tercentennial, .22 L.R.R.F., and .45 Colt Set, Frontier Scout & S.A.A., Commemorative, Blue, with Gold Plating, 4¾" Barrel, Cased, *Curio*	700	1,200	1,025
Chamizal Treaty, .22 L.R.R.F., Frontier Scout S.A., Commemorative, Blue, with Gold Plating, 4¾" Barrel, Cased, *Curio*	225	375	290
Chamizal Treaty, .22 L.R.R.F., and .45 Colt Set, Frontier Scout and S.A.A., Commemorative, Blue, with Gold Plating, Cased, *Curio*	1,200	1,950	1,850
Chamizal Treaty, .45 Colt, Single Action Army, Commemorative, Blue, with Gold Plating, 5½" Barrel, Cased, *Curio*	775	1,250	1,100
Cherry's 35th Anniversary, .22 L.R.R.F., and .45 Colt Set, Frontier Scout and S.A.A., Nickel Plated, Gold Plated, 4¾" Barrel, Cased, *Curio*	900	1,550	1,400
Cobra, .38 Special, Blue, 2" Barrel, 6 Shot, Lightweight, *Modern*	175	250	230
Cobra, .38 Special, Nickel Plated, 2" Barrel, 6 Shot, Lightweight, *Modern*	175	275	245
Cobra, .38 Special, 6 Shot, 5" Barrel, Military, Lightweight, *Modern*	150	225	205
Cobra Early, .38 Special, 6 Shot, 2" Barrel, Lightweight, *Modern*	200	275	235
Cobra Early, .38 Special, 6 Shot, 4" Barrel, Lightweight, *Modern*	200	300	245

	V.G.	Exc.	Prior Edition Exc. Value
Cobra Early, .38 Special, 6 Shot, 2" Barrel, Lightweight, Hammer Shroud, *Modern*	$275	$375	$255
Cobra Early, .38 Special, 6 Shot, 4" Barrel, Lightweight, Hammer Shroud, *Modern*	250	350	265
Col. Sam Colt Sesquicentennial, .45 Colt, Single Action Army, Commemorative, Blue, Silver-Plated Gripframe, 7½" Barrel, Cased, *Curio*	650	950	870
Col. Sam Colt Sesquicentennial, .45 Colt, Single Action Army, Commemorative, Deluxe, Blue, Silver-Plated Gripframe, 7½" Barrel, Cased, *Curio*	1,275	1,975	1,825
Col. Sam Colt Sesquicentennial, .45 Colt, Single Action Army, Commemorative, Special Deluxe, Blue, Silver-Plated Gripframe, 7½" Barrel, Cased, *Curio*	2,200	3,000	2,850
Colorado Gold Rush, .22 L.R.R.F., Frontier Scout S.A., Commemorative, Gold Plated, with Nickel Plating, 4¾" Barrel, Cased, *Curio*	200	375	295
Columbus Sesquicentennial, .22 L.R.R.F., Frontier Scout S.A., Commemorative, Gold Plated, 4¾" Barrel, Cased, *Curio*	400	550	535
Commando, .38 Special, 6 Shot, Military, *Curio*	200	250	195
Commando Special, .38 Caliber, Snub Nose, Similar To Banker's Special, Matt Finish, *Modern*	200	250	295
Courier, .22 L.R.R.F., 6 Shot, 2" Barrel, Lightweight, *Modern*	400	675	735
Courier, .32 S & W Long, 6 Shot, 2" Barrel, Lightweight, *Modern*	450	725	700
Dakota Territory, .22 L.R.R.F., Frontier Scout S.A., Commemorative, Blue, with Gold Plating, 4¾" Barrel Cased, *Curio*	250	325	300
Detective Special, .38 Special, 6 Shot, 4" Barrel, Heavy Barrel, *Modern*	275	425	305
Detective Special Early, .32 S & W, 6 Shot, 2" Barrel, *Modern*	175	325	195
Detective Special Early, .38 S & W, 6 Shot, 2" Barrel, *Modern*	175	350	200
Detective Special Early, .38 Special, 6 Shot, 2" Barrel, *Modern*	200	400	235

Colt - Commando Special .38 Caliber

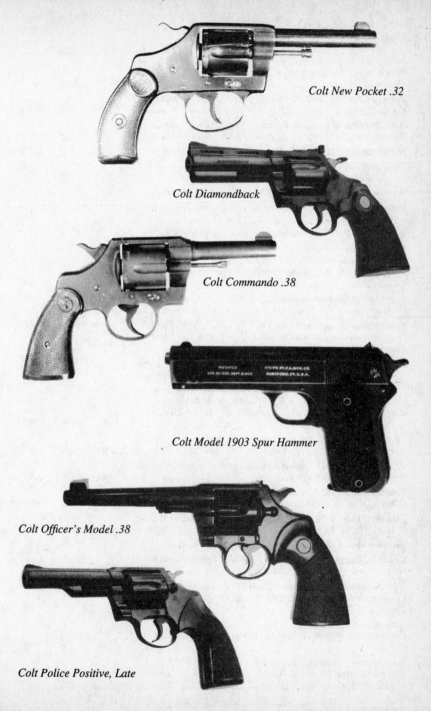

Colt New Pocket .32

Colt Diamondback

Colt Commando .38

Colt Model 1903 Spur Hammer

Colt Officer's Model .38

Colt Police Positive, Late

	V.G.	Exc.	Prior Edition Exc. Value
Detective Special Late, .38 Special, 6 Shot, 2" Barrel, Blue, *Modern*	*$175*	*$250*	*$250*
Detective Special Late, .38 Special, 6 Shot, 2" Barrel, Nickel Plated, *Modern*	225	400	280
Detective Special Late, .38 Special, 6 Shot, 2" Barrel, Electroless Nickel Plated, *Modern*	225	425	315
Diamondback, .22 L.R.R.F., Blue, Vent Rib, 6 Shot, *Modern*	225	300	295
Diamondback, .22 L.R.R.F., Electroless Nickel Plated, Vent Rib, 6 Shot, *Modern*	250	350	335
Diamondback, .38 Special, Blue, Vent Rib, 6 Shot, *Modern*	200	275	270
Diamondback, .38 Special, Electroless Nickel Plated, Vent Rib, 6 Shot, *Modern*	250	375	350
Diamondback, .38 Special, Nickel Plated, Vent Rib, 6 Shot, *Modern*	250	325	295
Florida Sesquicentennial, .22 L.R.R.F., Frontier Scout S.A., Commemorative, Blue, Color Case, Hardened Frame, 4³/₄" Barrel, Cased, *Curio*	225	350	265
Fort Findlay Sesquicentennial, .22 L.R.R.F., Frontier Scout S.A., Commemorative, Gold Plated, 4³/₄" Barrel, Cased, *Curio*	400	625	500
Fort Findlay Sesquicentennial Pair, .22 LR/.22 WMR Combo, Frontier Scout S.A., Commemorative, Gold Plated, 4³/₄" Barrel, Cased, *Curio*	1,800	2,700	2,200
Fort Stephenson Sesquicentennial, .22 L.R.R.F., Frontier Scout S.A., Nickel Plated, Blue, with Nickel Plating, 4³/₄" Barrel, Cased, *Curio*	400	525	520
Forty-Niner Miner, .22 L.R.R.F., Frontier Scout S.A., Commemorative, Blue with Gold Plating, 4³/₄" Barrel, Cased, *Curio*	225	350	275
Frontier Scout, .22 L.R.R.F., Single Action, Western Style, 6 Shot, Various Barrel Lengths, *Modern*	250	350	190
Frontier Model 1878 Double Action, Various Calibers, Various Barrel Lengths, with Ejector, *Curio*	750	950	550
Frontier Model 1878 Double Action, Sheriff's Model, Various Calibers, Various Barrel Lengths, no Ejector, *Curio*	450	975	570
Frontier Model 1878 Double Action, Phillipine Model, .45 Colt, 6" Barrel, Large Trigger Guard, *Curio*	600	1,250	725
Frontier Model 1878, Serial #'s under 39,000 are *Antique*.			
Gen. J.H. Morgan Indian Raid, .22 L.R.R.F., Frontier Scout S.A., Nickel Plated, Blue, with Gold Plating, 4³/₄" Barrel, Cased, *Curio*	300	675	710
Gen. Nathan Bedford Forrest, .22 L.R.R.F., Frontier Scout S.A., Commemorative, Blue, with Gold Plating, 4³/₄" Barrel, Cased, *Curio*	250	375	300
Gen. Hood Centennial, .22 L.R.R.F., Frontier Scout S.A., Commemorative, Blue, with Gold Plating, 4³/₄" Barrel, Cased, *Curio*	200	325	300
Gen. Meade Campaign, .22 L.R.R.F., Frontier Scout S.A., Commemorative, Blue, with Gold Plating, 4³/₄" Barrel, Cased, *Curio*	225	325	280

	V.G.	Exc.	Prior Edition Exc. Value
Gen. Meade Campaign, .45 Colt, Single Action Army, Commemorative, Blue, with Gold Plating, 5¹/₂" Barrel, Cased, *Curio*	$600	$975	$850
Golden Spike, .22 L.R.R.F., Frontier Scout S.A., Commemorative, Blue, with Gold Plating, 6" Barrel, Cased, *Curio*	225	350	280
H. Cook 1 of 100, .22 L.R.R.F., and .45 Colt Set, Commemorative, Nickel Plated, Blue Frame, Cased, *Curio*	700	1,000	1,100
House Pistol, .41 Short R.F., Cloverleaf-Cylinder Model 1871, 4 Shot, 3" Barrel, Round Barrel, Spur Trigger, *Antique*	400	650	480
House Pistol, .41 Short R.F., Cloverleaf-Cylinder Model 1871, 4 Shot, 1¹/₂" Barrel, Round Barrel, Spur Trigger, *Antique*	550	950	690
House Pistol, .41 Short R.F., Cloverleaf-Cylinder Model 1871, 4 Shot, 1¹/₂" Barrel, Octagon Barrel, Spur Trigger, *Antique*	800	1,500	925
House Pistol, .41 Short R.F., Round Cylinder Model of 1871, 5 Shot, 2⁵/₈" Barrel, Round Barrel, Spur Trigger, *Antique*	400	550	515
Idaho Territorial Centennial, .22 L.R.R.F., Frontier Scout S.A., Nickel Plated, Blue, with Nickel Plating, 4³/₄" Barrel, Cased, *Curio*	250	375	400
Indiana Sesquicentennial, .22 L.R.R.F., Frontier Scout S.A., Commemorative, Blue, with Gold Plating, 4³/₄" Barrel, Cased, *Curio*	225	350	270
Joaquin Murietta, .22 L.R.R.F., and .45 Colt Set, Frontier Scout and S.A.A., Commemorative, Blue, with Gold Plating, Cased, *Curio*	950	1,575	1,375
Kansas Centennial, .22 L.R.R.F., Frontier Scout S.A., Commemorative, Gold Plated, Walnut Grips, Cased, *Curio*	225	350	270
Kansas Cowtown: Abilene, .22 L.R.R.F., Frontier Scout S.A., Commemorative, Gold Plated, 4³/₄" Barrel, Cased, *Curio*	225	350	285
Kansas Cowtown: Coffyville, .22 L.R.R.F., Frontier Scout S.A., Commemorative, Blue, with Gold Plating, 4³/₄" Barrel, Cased, *Curio*	225	350	285
Kansas Cowtown: Dodge City, .22 L.R.R.F., Frontier Scout S.A., Commemorative, Blue, with Gold Plating, 4³/₄" Barrel, Cased, *Curio*	225	350	285
Kansas Cowtown: Wichita, .22 L.R.R.F., Frontier Scout S.A., Commemorative, Gold Plated, 4³/₄" Barrel, Cased, *Curio*	225	350	285
Kansas Fort Hays, .22 L.R.R.F., Frontier Scout S.A., Commemorative, Blue, with Nickel Plating, 4³/₄" Barrel, Cased, *Curio*	225	350	285
Kansas Fort Learned, .22 L.R.R.F., Frontier Scout S.A., Commemorative, Blue, with Nickel Plating, Cased, *Curio*	225	350	280
Kansas Fort Riley, .22 L.R.R.F., Frontier Scout S.A., Commemorative, Blue, with Nickel Plating, 4³/₄" Barrel, Cased, *Curio*	225	350	280
Kansas Fort Scott, .22 L.R.R.F., Frontier Scout S.A., Commemorative, Blue, with Nickel Plating, 4³/₄" Barrel, Cased, *Curio*	225	350	305
Kansas: Chisholm Trail, .22 L.R.R.F., Frontier Scout S.A., Commemorative, Blue, with Nickel Plating, 4³/₄" Barrel, Cased, *Curio*	225	350	280

	V.G.	Exc.	Prior Edition Exc. Value
Kansas: Pawnee Trail, .22 L.R.R.F., Frontier Scout S.A., Commemorative, Blue, with Nickel Plating, 4³/₄" Barrel, Cased, *Curio*	$225	$350	$280
Kansas: Santa Fe Trail, .22 L.R.R.F., Frontier Scout S.A., Commemorative, Blue, with Nickel Plating, 4³/₄" Barrel, Cased, *Curio*	225	350	280
Kansas: Shawnee Trail, .22 L.R.R.F., Frontier Scout S.A., Commemorative, Blue, with Nickel Plating, 4³/₄" Barrel, Cased, *Curio*	250	350	280
Lawman MK III, .357 Magnum, Various Barrel Lengths, Blue, 6 Shot, *Modern*	150	200	185
Lawman MK III, .357 Magnum, Various Barrel Lengths, Nickel Plated, 6 Shot, *Modern*	150	225	190
Lawman MK V, .357 Magnum, Various Barrel Lengths, Blue, 6 Shot, *Modern*	150	200	240
Lawman MK V, .357 Magnum, Various Barrel Lengths, Nickel Plated, 6 Shot, *Modern*	150	225	260
Lawman: Bat Masterson, .22 L.R.R.F., Frontier Scout S.A., Commemorative, Nickel Plated, 4³/₄" Barrel, Cased, *Curio*	250	350	335
Lawman: Bat Masterson, .45 Colt, Single Action Army, Commemorative, Nickel Plated, 4³/₄" Barrel, Cased, *Curio*	600	1,250	865
Lawman: Pat Garrett, .22 L.R.R.F., Frontier Scout S.A., Commemorative, Gold Plated, with Nickel Plating, 4³/₄" Barrel, Cased, *Curio*	225	350	335
Lawman: Pat Garrett, .45 Colt, Single Action Army, Commemorative, Gold Plated, with Nickel Plating, 5¹/₂" Barrel, Cased, *Curio*	500	1,000	865
Lawman: Wild Bill Hickock, .22 L.R.R.F., Frontier Scout S.A., Commemorative, Blue, with Nickel Plating, 6" Barrel, Cased, *Curio*	225	350	335
Lawman: Wild Bill Hickock, .45 Colt, Single Action Army, Commemorative, Blue, with Nickel Plating, 7¹/₂" Barrel, Cased, *Curio*	500	975	865

Colt - Lawman MK V

	V.G.	Exc.	Prior Edition Exc. Value
Lawman: Wyatt Earp, .22 L.R.R.F., Frontier Scout S.A., Commemorative, Blue, with Nickel Plating, Cased, *Curio*	$300	$425	$410
Lawman: Wyatt Earp, .45 Colt, Single Action Army, Commemorative, Blue, with Nickel Plating, 16⅛" Barrel, Cased, *Curio*	800	1,600	1,365
Lightning Model 1877, .38 Colt, 6 Shot, Double Action, Standard Model, *Curio*	400	550	445
Lightning Model 1877, .38 Colt, 6 Shot, Double Action, Sheriff's Model, *Curio*	500	650	490
Lightning Model 1877, Serial Numbers under 105, 123 are *Antique*.			
Maine Sesquicentennial, .22 L.R.R.F., Frontier Scout S.A., Commemorative, Gold Plated, with Nickel Plating, 4¾" Barrel, Cased, *Curio*	225	350	290
Marshal, .38 Special, 6 Shot, Round Butt, *Modern*	350	425	300
Metropolitan MK III, .38 Special, 4" Barrel, 6 Shot, *Modern*	150	225	240
Missouri Sesquicentennial, .22 L.R.R.F., Frontier Scout S.A., Commemorative, Blue, with Gold Plating, 4¾" Barrel, Cased, *Curio*	225	350	285
Missouri Sesquicentennial, .45 Colt, Single Action Army, Commemorative, Blue, with Gold Plating, 5½" Barrel, Cased, *Curio*	400	775	650
Model 1872 Army, .44 Henry R.F., Open-Top Frontier Single Action, Army Style Gripframe, *Antique*	2,500	4,500	2,800
Model 1872 Army, .44 Henry R.F., Open-Top Frontier Single Action, Navy Style Gripframe, *Antique*	3,000	5,000	2,950
Model 1889, .38 Long Colt, 6 Shot, Commercial, Various Barrel Lengths, Double Action, Swing-Out Cylinder, *Antique*	375	550	395
Model 1889, .41 Long Colt, 6 Shot, Commercial, Various Barrel Lengths, Double Action, Swing-Out Cylinder, *Antique*	400	575	385
Model 1889 Navy, .38 Long Colt, 6 Shot, Military, 6" Barrel, Double Action, Swing-Out Cylinder, *Antique*	550	775	510
Model 1892 New Army, .38 Long Colt, 6 Shot, Military, 6" Barrel, Double Action, Swing-Out Cylinder, *Antique*	300	500	300
Model 1892 New Navy, .38 Long Colt, 6 Shot, Military, 6" Barrel, Double Action, Swing-Out Cylinder, *Antique*	400	600	360
Model 1892 New Navy, .38 Long Colt, 6 Shot, Commercial, Various Barrel Lengths, Double Action, Swing-Out Cylinder, *Antique*	175	275	240
Model 1892 New Navy, .41 Long Colt, 6 Shot, Commercial, Various Barrel Lengths, Double Action, Swing-Out Cylinder, *Antique*	175	275	245
Model 1894 New Army, .38 Long Colt, 6 Shot, Military, 6" Barrel, Double Action, Swing-Out Cylinder, *Antique*	250	325	285
Model 1894 New Navy, .38 Long Colt, 6 Shot, Military, 6" Barrel, Double Action, Swing-Out Cylinder, *Antique*	250	350	310
Model 1895 New Army, .38 Long Colt, 6 Shot, Military, 6" Barrel, Double Action, Swing-Out Cylinder, *Antique*	225	300	270
Model 1895 New Navy, .38 Long Colt, 6 Shot, Military, 6" Barrel, Double Action, Swing-Out Cylinder, *Antique*	300	375	355

	V.G.	Exc.	Prior Edition Exc. Value
Model 1896 New Army, .38 Long Colt, 6 Shot, Military, 6" Barrel, Double Action, Swing-Out Cylinder, *Curio*	$275	$325	$285
Model 1896 New Navy, .38 Long Colt, 6 Shot, Military, 6" Barrel, Double Action, Swing-Out Cylinder, *Curio*	175	325	285
Model 1901 New Army, .38 Long Colt, 6 Shot, Military, 6" Barrel, Double Action, Swing-Out Cylinder, *Curio*	200	250	245
Model 1902 Army, .45 Colt, 6 Shot, Military, 6" Barrel, Double Action, *Curio*	450	550	515
Model 1903 New Army, .38 Long Colt, 6 Shot, Military, 6" Barrel, Double Action, Swing-Out Cylinder, *Curio*	200	275	245
Model 1903 New Navy, .32-20 WCF, 6 Shot Commercial, Various Barrel Lengths, Double Action, Swing-Out Cylinder, *Curio*	275	350	360
Model 1903 New Navy, .38 Long Colt, 6 Shot, Commercial, Various Barrel Lengths, Double Action, Swing-Out Cylinder, *Curio*	275	350	305
Model 1903 New Navy, .38 Long Colt, 6 Shot, Commercial, Various Barrel Lengths, Double Action, Swing-Out Cylinder, *Curio*	250	325	300
Model 1905 U.S.M.C., .38 Long Colt, 6 Shot, Military, 6" Barrel, Swing-Out Cylinder, *Curio*	1,500	2,250	1,350
Model 1905 U.S.M.C., .38 Long Colt, 6 Shot, Commercial, 6" Barrel, Swing-Out Cylinder, *Curio*	1,250	1,750	1,450
Model 1909 Army, .45 Colt, 6 Shot, Military, 5½" Barrel, *Curio*	725	950	530
Model 1909 U.S.M.C., .45 Colt, 6 Shot, 5½" Barrel, *Modern*	950	1,450	900
Model 1909 U.S.N., .45 Colt, 6 Shot, Military, 5½" Barrel, *Modern*	1,250	1,750	610
Model 1917 Army, .45 Auto-Rim, 6 Shot, Military, 5½" Barrel, *Modern*	500	650	415
Montana Territory Centennial, .22 L.R.R.F., Frontier Scout S.A., Commemorative, Blue, with Gold Plating, 4¼" Barrel, Cased, *Curio*	225	375	305
Montana Territory Centennial, .45 Colt, Single Action Army, Commemorative, Blue, with Gold Plating, 7½" Barrel, Cased, *Curio*	600	975	815
Nebraska Centennial, .22 L.R.R.F., Frontier Scout S.A., Commemorative, Gold Plated, 4¾" Barrel, Cased, *Curio*	200	300	285
Ned Buntline, .45 Colt, New Frontier Single Action Army, 12" Barrel, Commemorative, *Modern*	800	950	965
Nevada Battle Born, .22 L.R.R.F., Frontier Scout S.A., Commemorative, Blue, with Nickel Plating, 4¾" Barrel, Cased, *Curio*	225	350	330
Nevada Battle Born, .22 L.R.R.F. and .45 Colt Set, Frontier Scout and S.A.A., Commemorative, Blue, with Nickel Plating, Cased, *Curio*	1,250	2,750	2,400
Nevada Battle Born, .45 Colt, Single Action Army, Commemorative, Blue, with Nickel Plating, 5½" Barrel, Cased, *Curio*	750	1,300	1,250

Colt Old Line .22

Colt Woodsman Huntsman

Colt .22 Banker's Special

Colt Model 1855 Root Revolver

Colt Model 1903 Pocket Military

Colt Model 1855 Root Fluted Cylinder

	V.G.	Exc.	Prior Edition Exc. Value
Nevada Centennial, .22 L.R.R.F., Frontier Scout S.A., Commemorative, Blue, with Nickel Plating, 4¾" Barrel, Cased, *Curio*	$225	$350	$285
Nevada Centennial, .22 L.R.R.F. and .45 Colt Set, Frontier Scout and S.A.A., Nickel Plated, Blue, with Nickel Plating, Cased, *Curio*	800	1,275	800
Nevada Centennial, .22 L.R.R.F. and .45 Colt Set, Frontier Scout and S.A.A., Commemorative, Blue, with Nickel Plating, with Extra Engraved Cylinder, Cased, *Curio*	850	1,400	1,315
Nevada Centennial, .45 Colt, Single Action Army, Nickel Plated, Blue, with Nickel Plating, 5½" Barrel, Cased, *Curio*	650	1,000	1,125
New Frontier, .22 L.R.R.F., Various Barrel Lengths, Blue, 6 Shot, Adjustable Sights, *Modern*	150	200	190
New Frontier, .22 L.R.R.F., 7½" Barrel, Blue, 6 Shot, Adjustable Sights, *Modern*	150	225	200
New Frontier, .22LR/.22WMR Combo, Various Barrel Lengths, Blue, 6 Shot, Adjustable Sights, *Modern*	175	250	240
New Frontier, .22R/.22 WRM Combo, 7½" Barrel, Blue, 6 Shot, Adjustable Sights, *Modern*	200	275	235
New Jersey Tercentenary, .22 L.R.R.F., Frontier Scout S.A., Commemorative, Blue, with Nickel Plating, 4¾" Barrel, Cased, *Curio*	225	350	295
New Jersey Tercentenary, .45 Colt, Single Action Army, Commemorative, Blue, with Nickel Plating, 5½" Barrel, Cased, *Curio*	600	975	880
New Line, .38 Long Colt, Police and Thug Model, with Ejector, 5 Shot, Spur Trigger, Standard, *Antique*	850	1,200	725
New Line, .32 or .41 C.F., Police and Thug Model, with Ejector, 5 Shot, Spur Trigger, *Antique*	950	1,400	985
New Line, .38 Long Colt, House Civilian Model, with Ejector, 5 Shot, Spur Trigger, *Antique*	350	425	410
New Line, .38 Long Colt, House Civilian Model, no Ejector, 5 Shot, Spur Trigger, *Antique*	350	425	405
New Line, .41 Short C.F., House Civilian Model, with Ejector, 5 Shot, Spur Trigger, *Antique*	375	475	475
New Line, .41 Short C.F., House Civilian Model, no Ejector, 5 Shot, Spur Trigger, *Antique*	375	450	410
New Line Pocket, Locking Notches on Cylinder Periphery, *Add 20%-30%*			
New Line Pocket, .22 Long R.F., "the Little Colt," 7 Shot, Spur Trigger, *Antique*	250	375	350
New Line Pocket, .30 Long R.F., "the Pony Colt," 5 Shot, Spur Trigger, *Antique*	275	375	360
New Line Pocket, .32 Long R.F. or .32 Long Colt, for 4" Barrel, *Add 100%-150%*			
New Line Pocket, .32 Long Colt, "the Ladies Colt," 5 Shot, Spur Trigger, *Antique*	275	350	325
New Line Pocket, .32 Long R.F., "the Ladies Colt," 5 Shot, Spur Trigger, *Antique*	225	325	315

	V.G.	Exc.	Prior Edition Exc. Value
New Line Pocket, .38 Long Colt, "the Pet Colt," 5 Shot, Spur Trigger, *Antique*	$300	$375	$370
New Line Pocket, .38 Long R.F., "the Pet Colt," 5 Shot, Spur Trigger, *Antique*	275	325	315
New Line Pocket, .41 Long R.F., "the Big Colt," 5 Shot, Spur Trigger, *Antique*	350	425	405
New Line Pocket, .41 Short C.F., "the Big Colt," 5 Shot, Spur Trigger, *Antique*	350	425	420
New Mexico Golden Anniv., .22 L.R.R.F., Frontier Scout S.A., Commemorative, Blue, with Gold Plating, 4³/₄" Barrel, Cased, *Curio*	250	400	340
New Pocket, .32 Long Colt, 6 Shot, Various Barrel Lengths, *Curio*	250	325	310
New Pocket, .32 S & W Long, 6 Shot, Various Barrel Lengths, *Curio*	275	350	325
New Police, .32 Long Colt, 6 Shot, Various Barrel Lengths, *Curio*	350	425	300
New Police, Serial Numbers under 7,300 are Antique.			
New Police, .32 S & W Long, 6 Shot, Various Barrel Lengths, *Curio*	300	375	270
New Police Target, .32 Long Colt, 6 Shot, 6" Barrel, Adjustable, *Modern*	400	500	400
New Police Target, .32 S & W Long, 6 Shot, 6" Barrel, Adjustable Sights, *Modern*	500	525	400
New Service, .357 Magnum, 6 Shot, Commercial, Various Barrel Lengths, *Modern*	1,000	1,225	575
New Service, .38 Special, 6 Shot, Commercial, Various Barrel Lengths, *Modern*	950	1,075	410
New Service, .38-40 WCF, 6 Shot, Commercial, Various Barrel Lengths, *Modern*	1,025	1,150	490
New Service, .38-44, 6 Shot, Commercial, Various Barrel Lengths, *Modern*	975	1,200	525
New Service, .44 Special, 6 Shot, Commercial, Various Barrel Lengths, *Modern*	1,000	1,250	600
New Service, .44-40 WCF, 6 Shot, Commercial, Various Barrel Lengths, *Modern*	1,025	1,225	535
New Service, .45 Auto-Rim, 6 Shot, Commercial, Various Barrel Lengths, *Modern*	800	1,100	425
New Service, .45 Colt, 6 Shot, Commercial, Various Barrel Lengths, *Modern*	975	1,175	510
New Service, .455 Colt, 6 Shot, Commercial, Various Barrel Lengths, *Modern*	900	1,125	485
New Service Target, .44 Special, 6 Shot, Commercial, 7¹/₂" Barrel, Adjustable Sights, *Modern*	1,000	1,375	830
New Service Target, .45 Auto-Rim, 6 Shot, Commercial, 7¹/₂" Barrel, Adjustable Sights, *Modern*	1,200	1,400	765

	V.G.	Exc.	Prior Edition Exc. Value
New Service Target, .45 Colt, 6 Shot, Commercial, 7½" Barrel, Adjustable Sights, *Modern*................	$1,350	$1,425	$875
New Service Target, .455 Colt, 6 Shot, Commercial, 7½" Barrel, Adjustable Sights, *Modern*................	1,375	1,450	860
NRA Centennial, .357 Mag. or .45 Colt, Single Action Army, Commemorative, Blue, Color Case, Hardened Frame, Various Barrel Lengths, Cased, *Curio*................	400	775	715
Officer's Model, .38 Special, 6 Shot, Adjustable Sights, with Detachable Shoulder Stock, *Curio*................	750	1,650	1,600
Officer's Model Match, .22 L.R.R.F., 6 Shot, Adjustable Sights, 6" Barrel, Target Grips, Target Hammer, *Modern*	350	475	410
Officer's Model Match, .22 W.M.R., 6 Shot, Adjustable Sights, 6" Barrel, Target Grips, Target Hammer, *Modern*	675	775	715
Officer's Model Match, .32 S&W Long, 6 Shot, Adjustable Sights, 6" Barrel, Target Grips, Target Hammer, *Modern*	650	750	700
Officer's Model Match, .38 Special, 6 Shot, Adjustable Sights, 6" Barrel, Target Grips, Target Hammer, *Modern*	300	375	340
Officer's Model Special, .22 L.R.R.F., 6 Shot, Adjustable Sights, 6" Barrel, Heavy Barrel, *Modern*................	250	350	345
Officer's Model Special, .38 Special, 6 Shot, Adjustable Sights, 6" Barrel, Heavy Barrel, *Modern*................	275	375	350
Officer's Model Target, .22 L.R.R.F., 6 Shot, Adjustable Sights, 6" Barrel, Second Issue, *Modern*	400	475	450
Officer's Model Target, .32 S & W Long, 6 Shot, Adjustable Sights, 6" Barrel, Second Issue, *Modern*	425	500	475
Officer's Model Target, .38 Special, 6 Shot, Adjustable Sights, 6" Barrel, *Modern*	375	450	425
Officer's Model Target, .38 Special, 6 Shot, Adjustable Sights, 6" Barrel, Second Issue, *Modern*	425	500	470
Official Police, .22 L.R.R.F., 6 Shot, Various Barrel Lengths, *Modern*................	275	325	275
Official Police, .32-30 WCF, 6 Shot, *Modern*................	275	325	380
Official Police, .38 Special, 6 Shot, *Modern*................	250	300	215
Official Police, .41 Long Colt, 6 Shot, *Modern*	200	250	250
Official Police Mk.III, .38 Special, 6 Shot, *Modern*	175	225	240
Oklahoma Territory, .22 L.R.R.F., Frontier Scout S.A., Commemorative, Blue, with Gold Plating, 4¾" Barrel, Cased, *Curio*	225	350	320
Old Fort Des Moines, .22 L.R.R.F., Frontier Scout S.A., Commemorative, Gold Plated, 4¾" Barrel, Cased, *Curio*................	250	375	360
Old Fort Des Moines, .22 L.R.R.F. and .45 Colt Set, Frontier Scout S.A. and S.A.A., Commemorative, Gold Plated, Cased, *Curio*	900	1,550	1,275
Old Fort Des Moines, .45 Colt, Single Action Army, Commemorative, Gold Plated, 5½" Barrel, Cased, *Curio*................	500	1,050	875
Old Line Pocket, .22 Short R.F., Open Top, First Model with Ejector, 7 Shot, Spur Trigger, *Antique*................	775	875	825

	V.G.	Exc.	Prior Edition Exc. Value
Old Line Pocket, .22 Short R.F., Open Top, Second Model, No Ejector, 7 Shot, Spur Trigger, *Antique*	$375	$425	$375
Oregon Trail, .22 L.R.R.F., Frontier Scout S.A., Commemorative, Blue, with Gold Plating, 4³/₄" Barrel, Cased, *Curio*	225	350	275
Peacemaker, .22LR/.22 WMR Combo, Various Barrel Lengths, Blue, 6 Shot, *Modern*	225	350	200
Peacemaker, .22 LR/.22 WMR Combo, 7¹/₂" Barrel, Blue, 6 Shot, *Modern*	250	375	205
Peacemaker Centennial, .44-40 WCF, Single Action Army, Commemorative, Blue, Color Case, Hardened Frame, 7¹/₂" Barrel, Cased, *Curio*	450	975	780
Peacemaker Centennial, .44-40 and .45 Colt Set, Single Action Army, Commemorative, Blue, Color Case, Hardened Frame, 7¹/₂" Barrel, Cased, *Curio*	1,400	2,000	1,500
Peacemaker Centennial, .45 Colt, Single Action Army, Commemorative, Blue, Color Case, Hardened Frame, 7¹/₂" Barrel, Cased, *Curio*	400	975	780
Pocket Positive, .32 Long Colt, 6 Shot, Various Barrel Lengths, *Modern*	300	375	280
Pocket Positive, .32 S & W Long, 6 Shot, Various Barrel Lengths, *Modern*	325	400	310
Police Positive, .22 L.R.R.F., 6 Shot, Various Barrel Lengths, *Modern*	275	325	235
Police Positive, .22 WRF, 6 Shot, Various Barrel Lengths, *Modern*	300	350	280
Police Positive, .32 Long Colt, 6 Shot, Various Barrel Lengths, *Modern*	200	250	185
Police Positive, .32 S & W Long, 6 Shot, Various Barrel Lengths, *Modern*	225	275	190
Police Positive, .38 S & W, 6 Shot, Various Barrel Lengths, *Modern*	250	300	195
Police Positive Late, .38 Special, Blue, 4" Barrel, *Modern*	175	225	205
Police Positive Late, .38 Special, Nickel Plated, 4" Barrel, 6 Shot, *Modern*	200	250	230
Police Positive Special, .32 S & W Long, 6 Shot, Various Barrel Lengths, *Modern*	200	250	195
Police Positive Special, .32-20 WCF, 6 Shot, Various Barrel Lengths, *Modern*	250	300	300
Police Positive Special, .38 S & W, 6 Shot, Various Barrel Lengths, *Modern*	175	225	185
Police Positive Special, .38 Special, Shot, Various Barrel Lengths, *Modern*	225	275	205
Police Positive Target, .22 L.R.R.F., 6 Shot, 6" Barrel, Adjustable Sights, *Modern*	475	525	410
Police Positive Target, .22 WRF, 6 Shot, 6" Barrel, Adjustable Sights, *Modern*	500	550	445
Police Positive Target, .32 Long Colt, 6 Shot, 6" Barrel, Adjustable Sights, *Modern*	450	500	360

	V.G.	Exc.	Prior Edition Exc. Value
Police Positive Target, .32 S & W Long, 6 Shot, 6" Barrel, Adjustable Sights, *Modern*	$450	$500	$360
Police Positive Target, .38 S & W Long, 6 Shot, 6" Barrel, Adjustable Sights, *Modern*	425	475	350
Pony Express Centennial, .22 L.R.R.F., Frontier Scout S.A., Commemorative, 4³/₄" Barrel, Gold Plated, Cased, *Curio*	250	475	490
Pony Express Presentation, .45 Colt, Single Action Army, Commemorative, Nickel Plated, 7¹/₂" Barrel, Cased, *Curio*	725	1,100	975
Pony Express Presentation 4 Gun Set, .45 Colt, Single Action Army, Commemorative, Nickel Plated, 7¹/₂" Barrel, Cased, *Curio*	2,500	4,500	3,500
Python, .357 Magnum, 2" Barrel, Blue, Vent Rib, Adjustable Sights, 6 Shot, *Modern*	400	500	395
Python, .357 Magnum, 4" Barrel, Blue, Vent Rib, 6 Shot, Adjustable Sights, *Modern*	425	500	380
Python, .357 Magnum, 4" Barrel, Nickel, Vent Rib, 6 Shot, Adjustable Sights, *Modern*	450	525	400
Python, .357 Magnum, 6" Barrel, Blue, Vent Rib, 6 Shot, Adjustable Sights, *Modern*	475	550	400
Python, .357 Magnum, 6" Barrel, Nickel, Vent Rib, 6 Shot, Adjustable Sights, *Modern*	500	575	425
Python, .357 Magnum, 8" Barrel, Blue, Vent Rib, 6 Shot, Adjustable Sights, *Modern*	525	600	410
Python, .357 Magnum, 8" Barrel, Nickel, Vent Rib, 6 Shot, Adjustable Sights, *Modern*	575	650	445
Sheriff's Model, .45 Colt, Single Action Army, Commemorative, Blue, Color Case, Hardened Frame, 3" Barrel, *Curio*	950	1,850	1,325
Sheriff's Model, .45 Colt, Single Action Army, Commemorative, Nickel Plated, 3" Barrel, *Curio*	2,500	4,750	3,100
Shooting Master, .357 Magnum, 6 Shot, Commercial, 6" Barrel, Adjustable Sights, *Modern*	825	900	725
Shooting Master, .38 Special, 6 Shot, Commercial, 6" Barrel, Adjustable Sights, *Modern*	750	825	635
Shooting Master, .44 Special, 6 Shot, Commercial, 6" Barrel, Adjustable Sights, *Modern*	800	875	700
Shooting Master, .45 Auto-Rim, 6 Shot, Commercial, 6" Barrel, Adjustable Sights, *Modern*	725	800	600
Shooting Master, .45 Colt, 6 Shot, Commercial, 6" Barrel, Adjustable Sights, *Modern*	775	850	690
Single Action Army Late, .357 Magnum, Various Barrel Lengths, Blue, 6 Shot, *Modern*	575	650	445
Single Action Army Late, .357 Magnum, 7¹/₂" Barrel, Blue, 6 Shot, *Modern*	550	625	405
Single Action Army Late, .44 Special, 7¹/₂" Barrel, Blue, 6 Shot, *Modern*	550	625	415
Single Action Army Late, .45 Colt, 7¹/₂" Barrel, Blue, 6 Shot, *Modern*	625	700	400
Single Action Army Late, .45 Colt, Various Barrel Lengths, Blue, 6 Shot, *Modern*	675	750	405

	V.G.	Exc.	Prior Edition Exc. Value
Single Action Army Buntline Late, .45 Colt, 12" Barrel, Blue, 6 Shot, *Modern*..........	*$550*	*$625*	*$515*
Single Action Army Late, .45 Colt, 7½" Barrel, Nickel Plated, 6 Shot, *Modern*..........	*650*	*725*	*415*
Single Action Army New Frontier, .357 Magnum, Various Barrel Lengths, Blue, 6 Shot, Adjustable Sights, *Modern*............	*400*	*475*	*450*
Single Action Army New Frontier, .44 Special, 7½" Barrel, Blue, 6 Shot, Adjustable Sights, *Modern*	*425*	*500*	*460*
Single Action Army New Frontier, .45 Colt, Various Barrel Lengths, Blue, 6 Shot, Adjustable Sights, *Modern*............	*425*	*500*	*460*
Single Action Army Buntline New Frontier, .45 Colt, 12" Barrel, Blue, 6 Shot, Adjustable Sights, *Modern*............	*600*	*675*	*615*
Single Action Army, .45 Colt, Standard Cavalry Model # Under 15,000, Screw-Retained Cylinder Pin, Blue, Military, 7½" Barrel, *Antique*............	*7,000*	*8,500*	*3,175*
Single Action Army, .45 Colt, Artillery Model, Screw-Retained Cylinder Pin, Military, 5½" Barrel, *Antique*............	*2,500*	*3,000*	*2,100*
Single Action Army, Various Calibers, Storekeeper's Model, No Ejector, Short Barrel, Commercial, *Antique*	*10,000*	*12,000*	*3,250*
Single Action Army, Various Calibers, Standard Peacemaker, Calibers: .45 Colt, .44-40, .38-40, .41, .32-20, Commercial, *Antique*............	*6,000*	*7,500*	*1,250*
Single Action Army, for Rare Calibers, *Add* **50%–200%**			
Single Action Army, Folding Rear Sight, Long Barrel, *Add* **$1975.00–$3000.00**			
Single Action Army, Target Model (Flat-Top), *Add* **$975.00–$1900.00**			
Single Action Army, 8" or 9" Barrel, *Add* **$375.00–$600.00**			
Single Action Army, for 12" Barrel, *Add* **$445.00–$700.00**			
Single Action Army, for 16" Barrel, *Add* **$580.00–$995.00**			
Single Action Army, Shoulder Stock, *Add* **$995.00–$1850.00**			
Single Action Army, #'s over 182,000 are *Modern*, #'s under 165,000 are Black Powder Only			
Single Action Army, Nickel Plating, *Add* **15%–25%**			
Single Action Army, Rimfire Calibers, *Add* **100%–125%**			
Single Action Army, Long-Fluted Cylinder #'s 330,000 to 331,379, Commercial, *Curio*	*1,800*	*2,500*	*1,700*
Single Action Bisley, Various Calibers, Standard Model, Calibers: 32-20, 38-40, 41, 41-40, 45, Target Trigger, *Modern*........	*5,500*	*6,500*	*1,000*
Single Action Bisley, Various Calibers, Target Model, (Flat-Top), *Modern*............	*6,500*	*7,500*	*2,050*
Single Action Bisley, other than Standard Calibers, *Add* **50%–100%**			
Single Action Bisley, Non-Standard Barrel Lengths, *Add* **20%–30%**			
Single Action Bisley, No Ejector Housing, *Add* **25%–35%**			
Second Amendment, .22 L.R.R.F., Frontier Scout, Cased, *Curio*	*200*	*325*	*330*

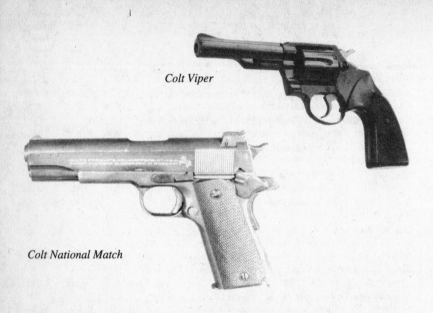

Colt Viper

Colt National Match

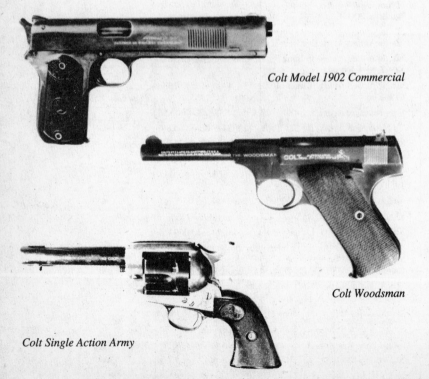

Colt Model 1902 Commercial

Colt Woodsman

Colt Single Action Army

	V.G.	Exc.	Prior Edition Exc. Value
St. Augustine Quadricentennial, .22 L.R.R.F., Frontier Scout S.A., Commemorative, Blue, with Gold Plating, 4³/₄" Barrel, Cased, *Curio*	$250	$350	$330
St. Louis Bicentennial, .22 L.R.R.F., Frontier Scout S.A., Commemorative, Blue, with Gold Plating, 4³/₄" Barrel, Cased, *Curio*	250	350	—
St. Louis Scout, .22 L.R.R.F. and .45 Colt Set, Frontier Scout and S.A.A., Commemorative, Blue, with Gold Plating, Cased, *Curio*	750	1,250	1,050
St. Louis Bicentennial, .45 Colt, Single Action Army, Commemorative, Blue, with Gold Plating, 5¹/₂" Barrel, Cased, *Curio*	525	975	775
Texas Ranger, Standard, .45 Colt, Single Action Army, Commemorative, Blue, Color Case Hardened Frame, Cased, *Curio*	950	1,750	1,400
Thunderer Model 1877, .41 Colt, 6 Shots, Double Action, Standard Model, *Modern*	900	1,500	460
Thunderer Model 1877, .41 Colt, 6 Shots, Double Action, Sheriff's Model, *Modern*	1,200	1,700	470
Trooper, .22 L.R.R.F., 6 Shot, Adjustable Sights, Target Grips, Target Hammer, *Modern*	275	325	310
Trooper, .357 Magnum, 6 Shot, 4" Barrel, Adjustable Sights, *Modern*	250	300	305
Trooper, .357 Magnum, 6 Shot, Adjustable Sights, Target Grips, Target Hammer, *Modern*	275	325	305
Trooper, .38 Special, 6 Shot, 4" Barrel, Adjustable Sights, *Modern*	250	300	295
Trooper, .38 Special, 6 Shot, Adjustable Sights, Target Grips, Target Hammer, *Modern*	250	300	295
Trooper MK III, .22 L.R.R.F., 4" Barrel, Blue, 6 Shot, Adjustable Sights, *Modern*	175	225	190
Trooper MK III, .22 L.R.R.F., 8" Barrel, Blue, 6 Shot, Adjustable Sights, *Modern*	225	275	260
Trooper MK III, .22 L.R.R.F., 6" Barrel, 6 Shot, Adjustable Sights, *Modern*	175	225	185
Trooper MK III, .357 Magnum, 4" Barrel, Blue, 6 Shot, Adjustable Sights, *Modern*	175	225	180
Trooper MK III, .357 Magnum, 4" Barrel, Nickel Plated, 6 Shot, Adjustable Sights, *Modern*	175	225	185
Trooper MK III, .357 Magnum, 6" Barrel, 6 Shot, Adjustable Sights, *Modern*	175	225	200
Trooper MK III, .357 Magnum, 6" Barrel, Nickel Plated, 6 Shot, Adjustable Sights, *Modern*	200	250	210
Trooper MK III, .357 Magnum, 8" Barrel, 6 Shot, Adjustable Sights, *Modern*	200	250	210
Trooper MK III, .357 Magnum, 8" Barrel, Nickel Plated, 6 Shot, Adjustable Sights, *Modern*	175	225	215
Trooper MK IV, .22 W.M.R., 4" Barrel, Blue, 6 Shot, Adjustable Sights, *Modern*	200	250	220

	V.G.	Exc.	Prior Edition Exc. Value
Trooper MK IV, .22 W.M.R., 6" Barrel, 6 Shot, Adjustable Sights, *Modern*	$200	$250	$220
Trooper MK IV, .357 Magnum, 6" Barrel, 6 Shot, Adjustable Sights, *Modern*	200	250	235
Trooper MK V, .357 Magnum, 4" Barrel, Blue, 6 Shot, Adjustable Sights, *Modern*	225	275	225
Trooper MK V, .357 Magnum, 6" Barrel, Blue, 6 Shot, Adjustable Sights, *Modern*	225	275	225
Trooper MK V, .357 Magnum, 4" Barrel, Nickel, 6 Shot, Adjustable Sights, *Modern*	250	300	240
Trooper MK V, .357 Magnum, 6" Barrel, Nickel, 6 Shot, Adjustable Sights, *Modern*	250	300	245
Viper, .38 Special, Blue, 4" Barrel, 6 Shot, Lightweight, *Modern*	225	275	230
West Virginia Centennial, .22 L.R.R.F., Frontier Scout S.A., Commemorative, Blue, with Gold Plating, 4¾" Barrel, Cased, *Curio*	250	350	295
West Virginia Centennial, .45 Colt, Single Action Army, Commemorative, Blue, with Gold Plating, 4¾" Barrel, Cased, *Curio*	600	950	750
Wyatt Earp Buntline, .45 Colt, Single Action Army, Commemorative, Gold Plated, 12" Barrel, Cased, *Curio*	1,200	1,800	1,725
Wyoming Diamond Jubilee, .22 L.R.R.F., Frontier Scout S.A., Commemorative, Blue, with Nickel Plating, 4¾" Barrel, Cased, *Curio*	250	350	300

HANDGUN, SEMI-AUTOMATIC

	V.G.	Exc.	Prior Edition Exc. Value
Ace, .22 L.R.R.F., Clip Fed, Adjustable Sights, Target Pistol, Blue, *Curio*	800	1,250	800
Ace, Mk. IV, .22 L.R.R.F., Clip Fed, Adjustable Sights, Target Pistol, Blue, *Modern*	425	500	350
Ace, Mk. IV, .22 L.R.R.F., Clip Fed, Adjustable Sights, Target Pistol, Nickel Plated, *Modern*	450	550	410
Ace Signature, .22 L.R.R.F., Clip Fed, Adjustable Sights, Target Pistol, Etched and Gold Plated, *Modern*	500	750	700
Ace Service Model, .22 L.R.R.F., Clip Fed, Adjustable Sights, Target Pistol, *Curio*	950	1,350	1,075
Conversion Unit, .22 L.R.R.F., Clip Fed, Blue, Adjustable Sights, *Modern*	225	250	195
Conversion Unit, Service Ace, .22 L.R.R.F., Clip Fed, Blue, Adjustable Sights, *Modern*	750	950	1,650
Ace 45-22 Conversion Unit, .45 ACP, Clip Fed, Adjustable Sights, Target Pistol, *Curio*	250	300	295
Challenger, .22 L.R.R.F., Clip Fed, *Modern*	225	275	245
Combat Commander, .38 Super, Clip Fed, Blue, *Modern*	350	425	305
Combat Commander, .45 ACP, Clip Fed, Blue, *Modern*	300	375	305
Combat Commander, .45 ACP, Clip Fed, Satin Nickel, *Modern*	325	400	340
Combat Commander, 9mm Luger, Clip Fed, Blue, *Modern*	325	400	305
Commander, .45 ACP, Clip Fed, Blue, Lightweight, *Modern*	350	425	315

	V.G.	Exc.	Prior Edition Exc. Value
Gold Cup, .45 ACP, Clip Fed, Adjustable Sights, Target Pistol, Military Style Stock, *Modern*	$475	$550	$475
Gold Cup MK III, .38 Special, Clip Fed, Adjustable Sights, Target Pistol, Military Style Stock, *Modern*	600	675	530
Gold Cup MK IV, .45 ACP, Clip Fed, Blue, Target Trigger, *Modern*	450	525	450
Gold Cup Camp Perry, .45 ACP, Commemorative, Target Pistol, Light Engraving, Cased, *Modern*	520	730	730
Gold Cup NRA Centennial, .45 ACP, Commemorative, Target Pistol, Light Engraving, Cased, *Curio*	450	725	580
Gold Cup D.E.A. Commemorative, .45 ACP, Clip Fed, Adjustable Sights, Commemorative, Cased, *Modern*	750	1,075	1,125
Government, .45 ACP, Clip Fed, Commercial, *Modern*	650	750	390

Colt Model 1892 New Navy

Colt Police Positive

Colt Agent

Colt Model 1902 Military

	V.G.	Exc.	Prior Edition Exc. Value
Government John Browning M1911, .45 ACP, Commemorative, Light Engraving, Cased, *Modern*	$600	$775	$1,025
Government 1911 English, .455 Webley Auto., Clip Fed, Military, *Curio*	950	1,075	760
Government 1911 English, .455 Webley Auto., Clip Fed, Military, R.A.F. Markings, *Curio*	775	875	1,000
Government BB 1911A1, .45 ACP, Clip Fed, *Curio*	450	550	500
Government M1911, M1911A1, .45 ACP, *Also See U.S. Military.*			
Government M1911, .45 ACP, Clip Fed, Commercial, *Curio*	1,125	1,400	865
Government M1911, .45 ACP, Clip Fed, Military, *Curio*	750	975	900
Government M1911A1, .45 ACP, Clip Fed, Military, *Modern*	450	625	600
Government MK IV, .38 Super, Clip Fed, Blue, *Modern*	275	500	350
Government MK IV, .45 ACP, Clip Fed, Blue, *Modern*	350	425	345
Government MK IV, .45 ACP, Clip Fed, Nickel Plated, *Modern*	325	450	365
Government MK IV, 9mm Luger, Clip Fed, Blue, *Modern*	325	400	350
Government MK IV U.S.M.C. Limited Edition, .45 ACP, Clip Fed, Cased, Commemorative, *Modern*	350	650	715
GM Mark IV/80 380 Auto, .380 Caliber ACP, 7 Round Mag, Composition Gripstock, Blue, *Modern*	225	275	330
As Above, Nickel	300	350	370
As Above, Satin Nickel In Blue	275	325	350
GM Mark IV/Series 80, Various Calibers, Checkered Walnut Gripstock, Blue, *Modern*	375	450	500
GM Mark IV/Series 80 Combat, Various Calibers, Checkered Walnut Gripstock, Blue, *Modern*	400	475	500
As Above, Satin Nickel	425	500	—
As Above, Light Weight	425	500	500
As Above, Stainless Steel	475	550	532
Mark IV/80 Combat Commander, Various Calibers, O Frame, Checkered Walnut Gripstock, Blue, *Modern*	450	525	500
Mark IV/80 Gold Cup National Match, .45 ACP, 7 Round Mag, 5" Barrel, Blue, *Modern*	600	675	660
Officer's ACP MK IV/80, .45 ACP, 6 Round Clip, Checkered Walnut Gripstock, Matt Finish, *Modern*	450	525	500
As Above, Satin Nickel	350	500	525
M 1911A1 (British), .455 Webley Auto., Clip Fed, Military, *Modern*	500	725	775
Junior, .22 Short R.F., Clip Fed, *Modern*	175	250	205
Junior, .25 ACP, Clip Fed, *Modern*	150	225	200
Model 1900, .38 ACP, Clip Fed, 6" Barrel, Commercial, Safety Sight, *Curio*	3,500	5,000	1,350
Model 1900, .38 ACP, Clip Fed, 6" Barrel, Commercial, Forward Slide Serrations, *Curio*	3,000	3,800	950
Model 1900, .38 ACP, Clip Fed, 6" Barrel, Commercial, *Curio*	2,700	3,500	700
Model 1900 U.S. Army, .38 ACP, Clip Fed, 6" Barrel, Military, *Curio*	4,500	6,000	1,550

	V.G.	Exc.	Prior Edition Exc. Value
Model 1900 U.S. Navy, .38 ACP, Clip Fed, 6" Barrel, Military, *Curio*	$5,800	$6,500	$1,325
Model 1902, .38 ACP, Clip Fed, 6" Barrel, Forward Slide Serrations, Sporting, *Curio*	1,500	2,000	575
Model 1902, .38 ACP, Clip Fed, 6" Barrel, Commercial, *Curio*	1,450	1,950	675
Model 1902 Military, .38 ACP, Clip Fed, 6" Barrel, Forward Slide Serrations, *Curio*	1,250	1,750	650
Model 1902 Military, .38 ACP, Clip Fed, 6" Barrel, *Curio*	1,150	1,650	575
Model 1902 Military U.S. Army, .38 ACP, Clip Fed, 6" Barrel, *Curio*	3,800	5,000	1,500
Model 1903 Round Hammer, .38 ACP, Clip Fed, *Curio*	450	775	425
Model 1903 Spur Hammer, .38 ACP, Clip Fed, *Curio*	475	750	395
Model 1903 Hammerless Pocket 1st Type, .32 ACP, Clip Fed, Barrel Bushing, Commercial, *Curio*	300	525	360
Model 1903 Hammerless Pocket 2nd Type, .32 ACP, Clip Fed, Commercial, *Curio*	275	500	285
Model 1903 Hammerless Pocket 3rd Type, .32 ACP, Clip Fed, Commercial, Magazine Disconnect, *Modern*	275	500	290
Model 1903 Hammerless U.S., .32 ACP, Clip Fed, Military, Magazine Disconnect, *Curio*	550	650	—
Model 1905, .45 ACP, Clip Fed, *Curio*	1,500	2,500	1,250
Model 1905, .45 ACP, Clip Fed, Adjustable Sights, with Detachable Shoulder Stock, *Curio*	3,000	5,000	4,150
Model 1905/07 U.S., .45 ACP, Clip Fed, Blue, Military, *Curio*	4,500	7,500	2,250
Model 1908 Hammerless Pocket 1st Type, .380 ACP, Clip Fed, Barrel Bushing, Commercial, *Curio*	575	625	365
Model 1908 Hammerless Pocket 2nd Type, .380 ACP, Clip Fed, Commercial, *Curio*	525	600	320
Model 1908 Hammerless Pocket 3rd Type, .380 ACP, Clip Fed, Commercial, Magazine Disconnect, *Modern*	525	600	330
Model 1908 Hammerless U.S., .380 ACP, Clip Fed, Military, Magazine Disconnect, *Curio*	725	850	625
Model 1908 Pocket, .25 ACP, Clip Fed, Hammerless, *Curio*	275	350	285
Model 1908 Pocket, .25 ACP, Clip Fed, Hammerless, Magazine Disconnect, *Modern*	250	325	255
Model 1908 Pocket, .25 ACP, Clip Fed, Hammerless, Magazine Disconnect, Military, *Curio*	500	750	430
National Match, .45 ACP, Clip Fed, Target Pistol, Adjustable Sights, *Modern*	1,150	1,450	860
National Match, .45 ACP, Clip Fed, Target Pistol, *Modern*	1,450	1,850	745
Pony, .380 ACP, Clip Fed, Hammer, *Modern*	875	1,425	1,425
Super, .38 Super, Clip Fed, Commercial, *Modern*	750	1,500	460
Super Match, .38 Super, Clip Fed, Adjustable Sights, Target Pistol, *Modern*	2,800	3,500	740
Super Match, .38 Super, Clip Fed, Target Pistol, *Modern*	2,950	3,750	580
Super Mexican Police, .38 Super, Clip Fed, Military, *Modern*	600	750	565

Colt - Python .357 Magnum

Colt - Trooper MK V

Colt.- Mark IV/80 Gold Cup National Match

Colt - GM Mark IV/80 380 Auto

	V.G.	Exc.	Prior Edition Exc. Value
WWI Battle of 2nd Marne, .45 ACP, Commemorative, M1911, Light Engraving, Cased, *Curio*	$400	$550	$475
WWI Battle of 2nd Marne Deluxe, .45 ACP, Commemorative, M1911, Engraved, Cased, *Curio*	950	1,250	1,275
WWI Battle of 2nd Marne Special Deluxe, .45 ACP, Commemorative, M1911, Fancy Engraving, Cased, *Curio*	1,750	2,500	2,275
WWI Belleau Wood, .45 ACP, Commemorative, M1911, Light Engraving, Cased, *Curio*	400	550	510
WWI Belleau Wood Special Deluxe, .45 ACP, Commemorative, M1911, Fancy Engraving, Cased, *Curio*	1,750	2,500	2,275
WWI Belleau Wood Deluxe, .45 ACP, Commemorative, M1911, Engraved, Cased, *Curio*	950	1,250	1,300
WWI Chateau Thierry, .45 ACP, Commemorative, M1911, Light Engraving, Cased, *Curio*	400	550	475
WWI Chateau Thierry Deluxe, .45 ACP, Commemorative, M1911, Engraved, Cased, *Curio*	950	1,250	1,325
WWI Chateau Thierry Special Deluxe, .45 ACP, Commemorative, M1911, Fancy Engraving, Cased, *Curio*	1,750	2,500	2,125
WWI Meuse-Argonne, .45 ACP, Commemorative, M1911, Light Engraving, Cased, *Curio*	400	550	470
WWI Meuse-Argonne Deluxe, .45 ACP, Commemorative, M1911, Engraved, Cased, *Curio*	950	1,250	1,275
WWI Meuse-Argonne Special Deluxe, .45 ACP, Commemorative, M1911, Fancy Engraving, Cased, *Curio*	1,750	2,500	2,175
WWII E.T.O., .45 ACP, Commemorative, M1911A1, Light Engraving, Cased, *Curio*	400	600	510
WWII P.T.O., .45 ACP, Commemorative, M1911A1, Light Engraving, Cased, *Curio*	400	600	510
Woodsman Huntsman, .22 L.R.R.F., Clip Fed, Blue, Adjustable Sights, *Modern*	250	300	280
Woodsman Match Target 1st Type, .22 L.R.R.F., Clip Fed, Extended Target Grips, *Modern*	700	950	700
Woodsman Match Target 2nd Type, .22 L.R.R.F., Clip Fed, Blue, Adjustable Sights, *Modern*	425	475	340
Woodsman Sport 1st. Type, .22 L.R.R.F., Clip Fed, Adjustable Sights, *Modern*	500	550	430
Woodsman Sport, .22 L.R.R.F., Clip Fed, Blue, Adjustable Sights, *Modern*	375	450	350
Woodsman Target 1st Type, .22 L.R.R.F., Clip Fed, Adjustable Sights, *Modern*	400	475	335
Woodsman Target 1st. Type, .22 L.R.R.F., Clip Fed, Adjustable Sights, with Extra Mainspring Housing, *Modern*	325	500	490
Woodsman Target 2nd. Type, .22 L.R.R.F., Clip Fed, Adjustable Sights, *Modern*	325	400	380
Woodsman Target 3rd. Type, .22 L.R.R.F., Clip Fed, Blue, Adjustable Sights, *Modern*	275	350	390
Woodsman Targetsman, .22 L.R.R.F., Clip Fed, Blue, Adjustable Sights, *Modern*	225	300	275

	V.G.	Exc.	Prior Edition Exc. Value

HANDGUN, SINGLESHOT

	V.G.	Exc.	Prior Edition Exc. Value
#1 Deringer, .41 Short R.F., all Metal, Spur Trigger, Light Engraving, *Antique*	$650	$950	$850
#2 Deringer, .41 Short R.F., "Address Col. Colt," Wood Grips, Spur Trigger, Light Engraving, *Antique*	950	1,250	1,000
#2 Deringer, .41 Short R.F., Wood Grips, Spur Trigger, Light Engraving, *Antique*	600	750	610
#3 Deringer Thuer, .41 Short R.F., Wood Grips, Spur Trigger, 1st Issue, Contoured Swell at Pivot, High-Angled Hammer, *Antique*	1,250	1,850	1,025
#3 Deringer Thuer, .41 Short R.F., Wood Grips, Spur Trigger, 2nd Issue, Angled Frame, no Swell, High Angled Hammer, *Antique*	850	1,250	550
#3 Deringer Thuer, .41 Short R.F., Wood Grips, Spur Trigger, 3rd Issue, Straight Thick Frame, High-Angled Hammer, *Antique*	400	550	450
#3 Deringer Thuer, .41 Short R.F., Wood Grips, Spur Trigger, London Marked, *Antique*	500	650	860
#4 Deringer, .22 Short R.F., Geneseo Anniversary Commemorative, Spur Trigger, *Curio*	350	600	490
#4 Deringer, .22 Short R.F., Fort McPherson Commemorative, Spur Trigger, *Curio*	275	375	310
#4 Deringer, .22 Short R.F., Spur Trigger, *Modern*	75	100	85
#4 Deringer, .22 Short R.F., Spur Trigger, Cased Pair, *Modern*	150	225	170
#4 Lord Deringer, .22 Short R.F., Spur Trigger, Cased Pair, *Modern*	100	150	160
#4 Lady Deringer, .22 Short R.F., Spur Trigger, Cased Pair, *Modern*	100	150	165
#4 Lord and Lady Deringers, .22 Short R.F., Spur Trigger, Cased Pair, *Modern*	150	275	160
Camp Perry 1st Issue, .22 L.R.R.F., Adjustable Sights, Target Pistol, *Modern*	750	975	935
Camp Perry 2nd Issue, .22 L.R.R.F., Adjustable Sights, Target Pistol, *Modern*	850	1,250	1,300
Civil War Centennial, .22 Short R.F., ⅞ Scale 1860 Army Replica, Commemorative, 6" Barrel, Blue, Cased, *Curio*	75	150	85

RIFLE, BOLT ACTION

	V.G.	Exc.	Prior Edition Exc. Value
Colteer 1-22, .22 L.R.R.F., Singleshot, Plain, *Modern*	100	150	65
Colteer 1-22, .22 WMR, Singleshot, Plain, *Modern*	125	175	75
Coltsman Custom (FN), Various Calibers, Sporting Rifle, Fancy Wood, Light Engraving, Checkered Stock, Monte Carlo Stock, *Modern*	425	550	435
Coltsman Custom (Sako), Various Calibers, Sporting Rifle, Fancy Wood, Checkered Stock, Monte Carlo Stock, *Modern*	450	600	480
Coltsman Deluxe (FN), Various Calibers, Sporting Rifle, Checkered Stock, Monte Carlo Stock, *Modern*	350	425	385
Coltsman Deluxe (Sako), Various Calibers, Sporting Rifle, Checkered Stock, Monte Carlo Stock, *Modern*	400	475	450

Colt - Mark IV/80 Combat Commander

Colt - GM Mark IV/Series 80 Combat

Colt - Detective Special

Colt - GM Mark IV/Series 80

	V.G.	Exc.	Prior Edition Exc. Value
Coltsman Standard (FN), Various Calibers, Sporting Rifle, Checkered Stock, *Modern*	$275	$350	$330
Coltsman Standard (Sako), Various Calibers, Sporting Rifle, Checkered Stock, *Modern*	300	375	390
Sauer, Various Calibers, Clip Fed, Checkered Stock, Short Action, *Modern*	575	875	815
Sauer, Various Calibers, Clip Fed, Checkered Stock, Magnum, *Modern*	675	975	895
Sauer, Various Calibers, Clip Fed, Checkered Stock, *Modern*	625	925	850
Sauer Grand African, .458 Win. Mag., Clip Fed, Fancy Wood, *Modern*	775	1,075	985
Sauer Grand Alaskan, .375 H & H Mag., Clip Fed, Checkered Stock, Magnum, *Modern*	725	1,025	925

RIFLE, SEMI-AUTOMATIC

	V.G.	Exc.	Prior Edition Exc. Value
AR-15, .223 Rem., Clip Fed, *Modern*	700	850	435
AR-15, .223 Rem., Clip Fed, Collapsible Stock, *Modern*	800	950	465
AR-15 A2 Sporter II, .223 Rem., Pistol Grip, 20" Barrel, *Modern*	725	850	720
Colteer 22 Autoloader, .22 L.R.R.F., Tube Feed, Plain, *Modern*	100	175	140
Colteer Stagecoach, .22 L.R.R.F., Tube Feed, Light Engraving, *Modern*	125	225	150

RIFLE, PERCUSSION

	V.G.	Exc.	Prior Edition Exc. Value
1st Model Ring Lever, Various Calibers, 8 or 10 Shot Revolving Cylinder, with Topstrap, *Antique*	8,500	10,500	7,250
2nd Model Ring Lever, .44, 8 or 10 Shot Revolving Cylinder, no Topstrap, *Antique*	7,250	8,500	6,700
Model 1839, 6 Shot Cylinder, with Hammer, *Antique*	6,250	7,300	4,950
Model 1855 Sporting Rifle, .36, 6 Shot Revolving Cylinder, Sidehammer, no Forestock, Spur Triggerguard, *Antique*	3,650	5,200	3,400
Model 1855 Sporting Rifle, Various Calibers, 6 Shot Revolving Cylinder, Sidehammer, Halfstock, Scroll Triggerguard, *Antique*	2,875	4,400	2,850
Model 1855 Sporting Rifle, Various Calibers, 6 Shot Revolving Cylinder, Sidehammer, Full Stock, Scroll Triggerguard, *Antique*	3,100	4,200	2,850
Model 1855 Carbine, Various Calibers, 6 Shot Revolving Cylinder, Sidehammer, no Forestock, *Antique*	4,250	7,500	2,850
Model 1855 Military Rifle, Various Calibers, 6 Shot Revolving Cylinder, Sidehammer, Full Stock, U.S. Military, *Antique*	8,500	12,000	4,600
Model 1861 Musket, .58, Military Contract Musket, *Antique*	1,250	1,750	900

RIFLE, SINGLESHOT

	V.G.	Exc.	Prior Edition Exc. Value
Sharps, Various Calibers, Fancy Wood, Fancy Checkering, Cased with Accessories, *Modern*	1,550	1,850	2,050

RIFLE, SLIDE ACTION

	V.G.	Exc.	Prior Edition Exc. Value
Lightning, .22 R.F., Small Frame (Numbers over 35,300 are Modern), *Antique*	850	1,050	500

	V.G.	Exc.	Prior Edition Exc. Value
Lightning, Various Calibers, Medium Frame (Numbers over 84,000 are Modern), *Antique*	$1,500	$2,000	$510
Lightning Carbine, Various Calibers, Medium Frame (Numbers over 84,000 are Modern), *Antique*	2,000	3,500	875
Lightning Baby Carbine, Various Calibers, Medium Frame (Numbers over 84,000 are Modern), *Antique*	2,750	5,000	950
Lightning, Various Calibers, Large Frame, *Antique*	3,500	4,250	690
Lightning Carbine, Various Calibers, Large Frame, *Antique*	4,500	6,500	1,450
Lightning Baby Carbine, Various Calibers, Large Frame, *Antique*	7,500	9,000	1,850

SHOTGUN, DOUBLE BARREL, SIDE-BY-SIDE

	V.G.	Exc.	
Custom, 12 and 16 Gauges, Double Trigger, Automatic Ejector, Checkered Stock, Beavertail Forend, Hammerless, *Modern*	1,650	2,250	400
Model 1878 Standard, Various Gauges, Outside Hammers, Damascus Barrel, *Antique*	1,850	2,750	600
Model 1883 Standard, Various Gauges, Hammerless, Damascus Barrel, *Antique*	2,250	3,250	700

SHOTGUN, SEMI-AUTOMATIC

Various Gauges, for Solid Rib, *Add* **$15.00–$25.00**
Various Gauges, for Vent Rib, *Add* **$25.00–$35.00**

	V.G.	Exc.	
Ultra-Light, 12 and 20 Gauges, Checkered Stock, Takedown, *Modern*	275	350	235
Ultra-Light Custom, 12 and 20 Gauges, Checkered Stock, Light Engraving, Takedown, *Modern*	300	375	260
Ultra-Light Magnum, 12 and 20 Gauges 3", Checkered Stock, Takedown, *Modern*	300	375	260
Ultra-Light Magnum Custom, 12 and 20 Gauges 3", Checkered Stock, Light Engraving, Takedown, *Modern*	325	400	280

SHOTGUN, SLIDE ACTION

	V.G.	Exc.	
Coltsman Custom, Various Gauges, Takedown, Checkered Stock, Vent Rib, *Modern*	275	350	245
Coltsman Standard, Various Gauges, Takedown, Plain, *Modern*	225	300	195

COLUMBIA ARMORY Tenn., Maltby & Henley Distributors, c. 1890.

HANDGUN, REVOLVER

	V.G.	Exc.	
New Safety, .22 L.R.R.F., 7 Shot, Double Action, Solid Frame, Grip Safety, *Modern*	100	125	120
New Safety, .32 S & W, 5 Shot, Double Action, Solid Frame, Grip Safety, *Modern*	100	125	135
New Safety, .38 S & W, 5 Shot, Double Action, Solid Frame, Grip Safety, *Modern*	125	150	145

	V.G.	Exc.	Prior Edition Exc. Value

COLUMBIAN Made by Foehl & Weeks, Philadelphia, Pa. c. 1890.
HANDGUN, REVOLVER
.32 S & W, 5 Shot, Double Action, Solid Frame, *Modern*............... $75 | $100 | $95
.38 S & W, 5 Shot, Double Action, Solid Frame, *Modern*............... 75 | 100 | 95

COMET
HANDGUN, REVOLVER
.32 Long R.F., 7 Shot, Single Action, Spur Trigger, Solid Frame, *Antique* .... 75 | 150 | 150

COMINAZZO OR COMINAZZI Family of armorers in Brescia, Italy from about 1593 to about 1875.
HANDGUN, FLINTLOCK
.54, Mid-1600's, Belt Pistol, Brass Furniture, Ornate *Antique*.......... 4,150 | 5,750 | 5,500
HANDGUN, WHEEL-LOCK
Ebony Full Stock, Ivory Pom, Holster Pistol, German Style, Military, Engraved, *Antique*................ 4,250 | 5,950 | 5,700

COMMANDO ARMS Made by Volunteer Enterprises in Knoxville, Tenn. since 1969.
RIFLE, SEMI-AUTOMATIC
Commando MK III, .45 ACP, Clip Fed, Horizontal Forend, with Compensator, Carbine, *Modern*.............. 150 | 250 | 145
Commando MK III, .45 ACP, Clip Fed, Vertical Forend, with Compensator, Carbine, *Modern*.............. 175 | 275 | 155
Commando MK 9, 9mm Luger, Clip Fed, Horizontal Forend, with Compensator, Carbine, *Modern*.............. 150 | 250 | 155
Commando MK 9, 9mm Luger, Clip Fed, Vertical Forend, with Compensator, Carbine, *Modern*.............. 175 | 275 | 160
Commando MK 45, .45 ACP, Clip Fed, Horizontal Forend, with Compensator, Carbine, *Modern*.............. 150 | 250 | 155
Commando MK 45, .45 ACP, Clip Fed, Vertical Forend, with Compensator, Carbine, *Modern*.............. 175 | 275 | 160

COMMANDER
HANDGUN, REVOLVER
.32 Long R.F., 7 Shot, Single Action, Spur Trigger, Solid Frame, *Antique* .... 100 | 150

COMMERCIAL See Smith, Otis A.

	V.G.	Exc.	Prior Edition Exc. Value

COMPEER Made by Crescent for Van Camp Hardware c. 1900.

SHOTGUN, DOUBLE BARREL, SIDE-BY-SIDE

Various Gauges, Outside Hammers, Damascus Barrel, *Modern*	$150	$175	$155
Various Gauges, Hammerless, Steel Barrel, *Modern*	150	175	180
Various Gauges, Hammerless, Damascus Barrel, *Modern*	150	175	155
Various Gauges, Outside Hammers, Steel Barrel, *Modern*	125	200	180

SHOTGUN, SINGLESHOT

Various Gauges, Hammer, Steel Barrel, *Modern*	75	100	80

CONE, D.D. Washington, D.C. c. 1865.

HANDGUN, REVOLVER

.22 Long R.F., 7 Shot, Single Action, Spur Trigger, Solid Frame, *Antique*	125	200	180
.32 Long R.F., 6 Shot, Single Action, Spur Trigger, Solid Frame, *Antique*	150	225	215

CONFEDERATE MILITARY

HANDGUN, PERCUSSION

.36 Columbus, Revolver, Brass Trigger Guard, 6 Shot, *Antique*	14,500	18,500	10,250
.36 Dance Bros., Revolver, Iron Frame, 6 Shot, *Antique*	10,500	12,500	8,200
.36 Griswald & Gunnison, Revolver, Brass Frame, 6 Shot, Serial No. is the Only Marking, *Antique*	4,500	5,000	4,500
.36 Leech & Co., Revolver, Brass Grip Frame, 6 Shot, *Antique*	6,400	7,250	4,900
.36 Leech & Rigdon, Revolver, Brass Grip Frame, 6 Shot, *Antique*	5,500	6,500	3,500
.36 Rigdon & Ansley, Revolver, Brass Grip Frame, 6 Shot, *Antique*	5,500	6,500	4,100
.36 Shawk & McLanahan, Revolver, Brass Frame, 6 Shot, *Antique*	8,400	9,750	8,950
.36 Spiller & Burr, Revolver, Brass Frame, 6 Shot, *Antique*	6,000	7,500	4,075
.36 T.W. Cofer, Revolver, Brass Frame, 6 Shot, *Antique*	25,000	35,000	17,500
.44 Dance Bros., Revolver, Brass Grip Frame, 6 Shot, *Antique*	8,000	9,500	5,075
.44 Tucker & Sherrod, Revolver, Copy of Colt Dragoon, Serial Number is the Only Marking, *Antique*	19,000	22,500	9,900
.54 Palmetto, Singleshot, Brass Furniture, *Antique*	2,900	3,750	1,900
.58 Fayetteville, Singleshot, Rifled, *Antique*	3,150	3,950	—
.58 Fayetteville, Singleshot, Rifled, with Shoulder Stock, *Antique*	1,950	3,250	2,850
.60 Sutherland, Singleshot, Brass Barrel, Converted from Flintlock, *Antique*	1,450	2,500	1,025

RIFLE, PERCUSSION

.52, "P," Tallahassee, Breech Loader, Carbine, *Antique*	5,500	17,000	4,450
.52, Tarpley, Breech Loader, Carbine, Brass Breech, *Antique*	12,750	29,500	8,600

	V.G.	Exc.	Prior Edition Exc. Value
.54, L.G. Sturdivant, Brass Furniture, Rifled, Serial No. is the Only Marking, *Antique*	$1,225	$2,100	$2,100
.54, Wytheville-Hall, Muzzle Loader, Rifled, Brass Frame, *Antique*	3,250	6,500	2,375
.57, Texas Enfield, Brass Furniture, *Antique*	6,500	12,500	4,600
.58, Musketoon, Brass Furniture, Military, Cook & Brother, *Antique*	3,500	7,000	3,100
.58, Military, Carbine, Dickson, Nelson & Co., *Antique*	5,500	8,500	4,700
.58, Military, Dickson, Nelson & Co., *Antique*	3,000	7,500	2,900
.58, Artillery, Brass Furniture, Military, Cook & Brother, *Antique*	3,000	6,500	3,675
.58, D.C. Hodgkins & Co., Iron Mounts, Rifled, Carbine, *Antique*	4,000	7,500	4,100
.58, Enfield Type, Brass Furniture, Military, Cook & Brother, *Antique*	3,250	6,500	2,850
.58, Fayetteville, Brass Furniture, 2 Bands, Rifled, *Antique*	3,000	5,250	3,150
.58, Georgia, Brass Furniture, Rifled, *Antique*	2,800	3,500	2,800
.58, H.C. Lamb & Co., Brass Furniture, 2 Bands, Rifled, *Antique*	5,000	8,500	4,450
.58, Palmetto, Musket, *Antique*	2,500	4,750	2,300
.58, Richmond, Carbine, *Antique*	2,250	4,500	1,950
.58, Richmond, Musket, Rifled, *Antique*	1,850	4,500	1,750
.58, Tallahassee, Carbine, Brass Furniture, 2 Bands, *Antique*	5,000	14,000	4,900
.58, Whitney, Rifled, Musket, *Antique*	750	950	700
.61, Whitney Enfield, Rifled, Brass Furniture, *Antique*	900	1,200	800
.62, Richmond Navy, Musketoon, Smoothbore, *Antique*	3,625	5,750	2,350
.69, Prussian Musket, Brass Furniture, Military, *Antique*	600	750	600

RIFLE, SINGLESHOT

	V.G.	Exc.	Prior Edition Exc. Value
.50, S.C. Robinson, Brass Furniture, Breech Loader, Carbine, Imitation Sharps, *Antique*	2,800	3,500	2,300
.69, Morse, Smoothbore, Carbine, Breech Loader, *Antique*	4,650	6,000	2,850
.69, Morse, Smoothbore, Breech Loader, *Antique*	4,250	5,500	2,250

CONN. ARMS CO. Norfolk, Conn. 1862–1869.

HANDGUN, REVOLVER

	V.G.	Exc.	Prior Edition Exc. Value
Wood's Patent, .28 T.F., Tip-Up Barrel, 6 Shot, Spur Trigger, *Antique*	175	325	310

CONN. ARMS & MFG. CO. Naubuc, Conn. 1863–1869.

HANDGUN, SINGLESHOT

	V.G.	Exc.	Prior Edition Exc. Value
Hammond Patent Bulldog, .44 R.F., Pivoting Breechblock, Hammer, Spur Trigger, *Antique*	200	325	300
Hammond Patent Bulldog, .44 R.F., Pivoting Breechblock, Hammer, Spur Trigger, Very Long Barrel, *Antique*	300	450	445

	V.G.	Exc.	Prior Edition Exc. Value
Hammond Patent Bull-Dozer, .44 R.F., Pivoting Breechblock, Hammer, Spur Trigger, *Antique*...............	$225	$325	$315

CONQUERER Made by Bacon Arms Co., c. 1880.

HANDGUN, REVOLVER

	V.G.	Exc.	Prior Edition Exc. Value
.22 Short R.F., 7 Shot, Spur Trigger, Solid Frame, Single Action, *Antique*...............	100	175	160
.32 Short R.F., 5 Shot, Spur Trigger, Solid Frame, Single Action, *Antique*...............	100	175	160

CONSTABLE, RICHARD Philadelphia, Pa. 1817–1851.

HANDGUN, PERCUSSION

	V.G.	Exc.	Prior Edition Exc. Value
Dueling Pistols, Cased Pair, with Accessories, *Antique*...............	1,800	3,500	3,500

RIFLE, PERCUSSION

	V.G.	Exc.	Prior Edition Exc. Value
.44, Octagon Barrel, Brass Furniture, *Antique*...............	950	1,800	1,800

CONTENTO See Ventura Imports.

CONTINENTAL Made by Jules Bertrand, Liege, Belgium c. 1910.

HANDGUN, SEMI-AUTOMATIC

	V.G.	Exc.	Prior Edition Exc. Value
Pocket, .25 ACP, Clip Fed, *Curio*...............	175	250	240

CONTINENTAL Rheinische Waffen u. Munitionsfabrik. Possibly a tradename used by Arizmendi, c. 1910.

HANDGUN, SEMI-AUTOMATIC

	V.G.	Exc.	Prior Edition Exc. Value
.25 ACP, Clip Fed, Blue, *Curio*...............	100	150	135
.32 ACP, Clip Fed, Webley Copy, Blue, *Curio*...............	150	200	180

CONTINENTAL Made by Stevens Arms.

RIFLE, BOLT ACTION

	V.G.	Exc.	Prior Edition Exc. Value
Model 52, .22 L.R.R.F., Singleshot, Takedown, *Modern*...............	50	75	55

SHOTGUN, DOUBLE BARREL, SIDE-BY-SIDE

	V.G.	Exc.	Prior Edition Exc. Value
Model 315, Various Gauges, Hammerless, Steel Barrel, *Modern*....	125	175	185
Model 215, 12 and 16 Gauges, Outside Hammers, Steel Barrel, *Modern*...............	100	175	175
Model 311, Various Gauges, Hammerless, Steel Barrel, *Modern*....	125	200	210

SHOTGUN, SINGLESHOT

	V.G.	Exc.	Prior Edition Exc. Value
Model 90, Various Gauges, Takedown, Automatic Ejector, Plain Hammer, *Modern*...............	50	75	65

Continental Arms Co. Pepperbox

	V.G.	Exc.	Prior Edition Exc. Value

CONTINENTAL Made by Hood Firearms Co., Successors to Continental Arms Co.; Sold by Marshall Wells Co., Duluth, Minn., c. 1870.

HANDGUN, REVOLVER

.22 Short R.F., 7 Shot, Spur Trigger, Solid Frame, Single Action, *Antique*	$100	$175	$165
.32 Short R.F., 5 Shot, Spur Trigger, Solid Frame, Single Action, *Antique*	100	175	175

CONTINENTAL ARMS CO. Norwich, Conn. 1866–1867.

HANDGUN, PEPPERBOX

Continental 1, .22 R.F., 7 Shot, Spur Trigger, Solid Frame, *Antique*	450	575	465
Continental 2, .32 R.F., 5 Shot, Spur Trigger, Solid Frame, *Antique*	525	600	570

COONAN ARMS, INC. St. Paul, Minn. since 1982.

HANDGUN, SEMI-AUTOMATIC

Model A, .357 Magnum, Single Action, Stainless, *Modern*	375	600	615
Model 357, .357 Magnum, Pre-Production Model, Serial Numbers Under 1000, Stainless Steel, Clip Fed, Adjustable Sights, *Modern*	350	675	650
Model 357, .357 Magnum, Standard Production Model, Stainless Steel, Clip Fed, Adjustable Sights, *Modern*	450	650	425

COOPER FIREARMS MFG. CO. Philadelphia, Pa. 1851–1869.

HANDGUN, PERCUSSION

Pocket, .31, 5 or 6 Shots, Double Action, *Antique*	425	500	475
Navy, .31, 5 Shots, Double Action, *Antique*	475	550	585

C.O.P. M & N Distributers, Torrance, Calif.

HANDGUN, REPEATER

Model SS-1, .357 Mag., Four Barrels, Stainless Steel, Hammerless, Double Action, *Modern*	200	275	190

	V.G.	Exc.	Prior Edition Exc. Value
Model Mini, .22 W.M.R., Four Barrels, Stainless Steel, Hammerless, Double Action, *Modern*	$175	$250	$225
Model Mini, .22 L.R.R.F., Four Barrels, Aluminum Frame, Hammerless, Double Action, *Modern*	125	175	155

HANDGUN, SEMI-AUTOMATIC

	V.G.	Exc.	Prior Edition Exc. Value
TP-70 AAI, .22 L.R.R.F., Double Action, Clip Fed, Stainless Steel, Hammer, *Modern*	125	175	170
TP-70 AAI, .25 A.C.P., Double Action, Clip Fed, Stainless Steel, Hammer, *Modern*	125	175	165

COPELAND, F. Made by Frank Copeland, Worcester, Mass. 1868–1874.

HANDGUN, REVOLVER

	V.G.	Exc.	Prior Edition Exc. Value
.22 Short R.F., 7 Shot, Spur Trigger, Solid Frame, Single Action, *Antique*	125	200	200
.32 Short R.F., 5 Shot, Spur Trigger, Solid Frame, Single Action, *Antique*	150	225	225

COQ Spain, unknown maker, c. 1900.

HANDGUN, SEMI-AUTOMATIC

	V.G.	Exc.	Prior Edition Exc. Value
K-25, .25 ACP, Clip Fed, *Modern*	75	125	125

CORNFORTH London, England 1725–1760.

HANDGUN, FLINTLOCK

	V.G.	Exc.	Prior Edition Exc. Value
Pair, Belt Pistol, Brass Barrel, Brass Furniture, Plain, *Antique*	2,700	4,000	4,000

COSENS, JAMES Gunmaker in Ordinary to Charles II England, Late 1600's.

HANDGUN, FLINTLOCK

	V.G.	Exc.	Prior Edition Exc. Value
Pair, Holster Pistol, Silver Furniture, Engraved Silver Inlay, High Quality, *Antique*	9,350	16,000	16,000

COSMI Made for Abercrombie & Fitch c. 1960.

SHOTGUN, SEMI-AUTOMATIC

	V.G.	Exc.	Prior Edition Exc. Value
12 or 20 Gauge, Top Break, Engraved, Checkered Stock, Vent Rib, *Modern*	2,200	2,850	1,950

COSMOPOLITAN ARMS CO. Hamilton, Ohio 1860–1865. Also see U.S. Military.

RIFLE, PERCUSSION

	V.G.	Exc.	Prior Edition Exc. Value
.45, Sporting Rifle, *Antique*	1,200	1,400	1,175
.50, Carbine, *Antique*	850	1,200	985

	V.G.	Exc.	Prior Edition Exc. Value

COWLES & SON Cowles & Smith, 1866–1871, Cowles & Son 1871–1876 in Chicopee Falls, Mass.

HANDGUN, SINGLESHOT

.22 Short R.F., Brass Frame, Side Swing Barrel, *Antique*.............. $175 $250 $240

CRAFT PRODUCTS
HANDGUN, SEMI-AUTOMATIC
.25 ACP, Clip Fed, *Modern*.. 75 125 115

COWELS & SMITH Chicopee Falls, Mass. 1863–1876. Became Cowels & Son in 1871.

HANDGUN, SINGLESHOT

.22 R.F., Side-Swing Barrel, Hammer, Spur Trigger, *Antique*.......... 150 225 220
.30 R.F., Side-Swing Barrel, Hammer, Spur Trigger, *Antique*.......... 150 250 245

CRESCENT Made by Norwich Falls Pistol Co., c. 1880.

HANDGUN, REVOLVER

.32 Short R.F., 5 Shot, Spur Trigger, Solid Frame, Single Action,
Antique.. 100 175 165

CRESCENT FIRE ARMS CO. Norwich, Conn., 1892; Purchased by H & D Folsom in 1893, and Absorbed by Stevens Arms & Tool 1926.

SHOTGUN, DOUBLE BARREL, SIDE-BY-SIDE

Various Gauges, Outside Hammers, Damascus Barrel, *Modern* 175 225 155
Various Gauges, Hammerless, Steel Barrel, *Modern*....................... 225 300 185
Various Gauges, Hammerless, Damascus Barrel, *Modern* 175 225 155
Various Gauges, Outside Hammers, Steel Barrel, *Modern*.............. 200 275 180

SHOTGUN, SINGLESHOT

Various Gauges, Hammer, Steel Barrel, *Modern*............................ 75 100 80

CREEDMORE Made by Hopkins & Allen, c. 1870.

HANDGUN, REVOLVER

#1, .22 Short R.F., 7 Shot, Spur Trigger, Solid Frame, Single
Action, *Antique* 100 175 160

CRIOLLA Hispano Argentine Automoviles, Buenos Aires, Argentina, c. 1935.

HANDGUN, SEMI-AUTOMATIC

La Criolla, .22 L.R.R.F., Colt M1911 Ace Copy, Clip Fed, Blue,
Modern.. 250 325 350

			Prior Edition Exc.
	V.G.	Exc.	Value

CROWN JEWEL Made by Norwich Falls Pistol Co., c. 1880.

HANDGUN, REVOLVER

.32 Short R.F., 5 Shot, Spur Trigger, Solid Frame, Single Action,
Antique $100 $175 $165

CRUCELEGUI Spain, Imported by Mandall Shooting Supplies, Scotsdale, Ariz.

SHOTGUN, DOUBLE BARREL, SIDE-BY-SIDE

Model 150, 12 and 20 Gauges, Outside Hammers, Double Trigger,
Modern.. 150 200 190

CRUSO Made by Stevens Arms.

RIFLE, BOLT ACTION

Model 53, .22 L.R.R.F., Singleshot, Takedown, *Modern* 50 75 55

SHOTGUN, SINGLESHOT

Model 90, Various Gauges, Takedown, Automatic Ejector, Plain
Hammer, *Modern*.. 50 75 65

CUMBERLAND ARMS CO. Made by Crescent for Hibbard-Spencer Bartlett Co., c. 1900.

SHOTGUN, DOUBLE BARREL, SIDE-BY-SIDE

Various Gauges, Outside Hammers, Damascus Barrel, *Modern* 125 200 185
Various Gauges, Hammerless, Steel Barrel, *Modern*........................ 150 225 220
Various Gauges, Hammerless, Damascus Barrel, *Modern* 125 200 180
Various Gauges, Outside Hammers, Steel Barrel, *Modern*.............. 150 200 195

SHOTGUN, SINGLESHOT

Various Gauges, Hammer, Steel Barrel, *Modern*............................. 50 100 85

C.V.A. (CONNECTICUT VALLEY ARMS) Norcross, GA Current (Prices reflect Factory Assembled Guns, not Kits).

HANDGUN, FLINTLOCK

.50 Hawken, Brass Furniture, Reproduction, *Antique* $75 $125 $80
.45 Kentucky, Brass Furniture, Reproduction, *Antique, Out of
Production, Kit Available* 50 75 60

HANDGUN, PERCUSSION

.50 Hawken, Brass Furniture, Set Triggers, Reproduction, *Antique*..... 50 100 75
.45 or .50 Mountain Pistol, Brass Furniture, Reproduction,
Antique, Out of Production, Kit Available... 50 100 80
.45 Kentucky, Brass Furniture, Reproduction, *Antique*..................... 50 75 55
.45 Tower Pistol, Brass Furniture, Reproduction, *Antique*.............. 25 75 55

	V.G.	Exc.	Prior Edition Exc. Value
45 Colonial Pistol, Brass Furniture, Reproduction, *Antique*.............	25	50	45
.45 Philadelphia Derringer, Reproduction, *Antique*........................	25	75	40
PP258, Pioneer, .32 Caliber, Octagonal Barrel, Reproduction, *Antique*	75	100	90
PP640, Prospector, .44 Caliber, Single Shot, Reproduction, *Antique*	75	100	100

HANDGUN, REVOLVER

	V.G.	Exc.	Prior Edition Exc. Value
RV600, 1851 Colt Navy, .36 Caliber, Six Shot, Brass Frame, Reproduction, *Antique*	75	125	125
RV610, 1860 Colt Army, .44 Caliber, Six Shot, Reproduction, *Antique*..	150	200	180
RV620, 1861 Colt Navy, .44 Caliber, Steel Frame, Reproduction, *Antique*..	125	175	178
RV622, 1861 Colt Navy, .44 Caliber, Brass Frame, Reproduction, *Antique*..	75	125	125
RV630, 1858 Remington Army, .44 Caliber, One Piece Frame, Reproduction, *Antique*	150	200	200
RV632, 1858 Remington Army, .44 Caliber, Brass Frame, Reproduction, *Antique*	125	150	150
RV650. New Model Pocket Remington, .31 Caliber, Spur Trigger, Reproduction, *Antique*	75	100	100

RIFLE, FLINTLOCK

	V.G.	Exc.	Prior Edition Exc. Value
.50 Frontier Rifle, Brass Furniture, Reproduction, *Antique*	100	150	145
.50 or .54 Hawken Rifle, Brass Furniture, Reproduction, *Antique*.......	125	175	170
.45 or .50 Mountain Rifle, German Silver Furniture, Reproduction, *Antique*, *.45 Out of Production*..	125	200	180
.45 Kentucky Rifle, Brass Furniture, Reproduction, *Antique*...........	100	150	130
FR503, Squirrel Rifle, .32 Caliber, Double Set Triggers, Reproduction, *Antique*	200	250	250
FR504, Pennsylvania Long Rifle, .50 Caliber, Brass Butt Plate, Reproduction, *Antique*	300	375	365

CVA Kentucky Pistol

Antique and Modern Firearms   181

CVA Mountain Pistol

CVA Pioneer Pistol

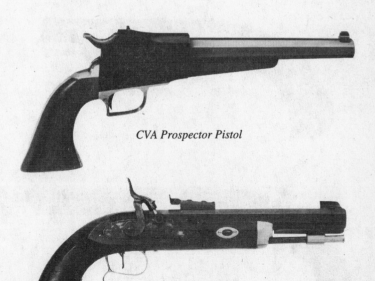

CVA Prospector Pistol

CVA Hawken Pistol

CVA Tower Pistol

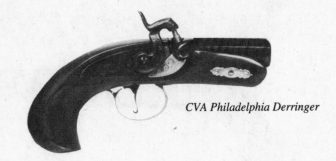

CVA Philadelphia Derringer

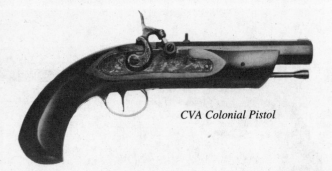

CVA Colonial Pistol

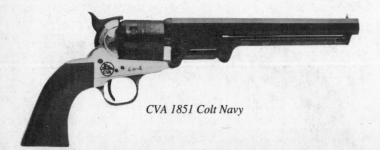

CVA 1851 Colt Navy

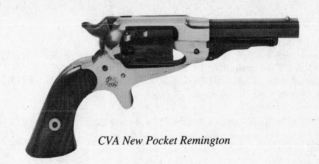

CVA New Pocket Remington

CVA Squirrel Rifle

CVA Pennsylvania Long Rifle

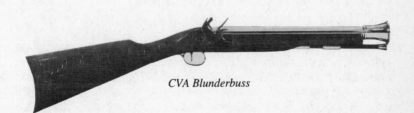

CVA Blunderbuss

	V.G.	Exc.	Prior Edition Exc. Value

.RIFLE, PERCUSSION

.50 or .54 Hawken Rifle, Brass Furniture, Reproduction, *Antique* ... $125 $175 $165

.45, .50, .54, or .58 Mountain Rifle, German Silver Furniture, Reproduction, *Antique, .58 Available in Kit Only* ... 125 175 180

.45 or .50 Frontier Rifle, Brass Furniture, Reproduction, *Antique, .45 Available in Kit Only* ... 100 150 140

.45 Kentucky Rifle, Brass Furniture, Reproduction, *Antique* ... 75 125 130

.58 Zouave, Brass Furniture, Reproduction, *Antique, Out of Production* ... 100 150 155

PR403, Squirrel Rifle, .32 Caliber, Right Handed Model, Reproduction, *Antique* ... 175 225 220

PR404, Pennsylvania Long Rifle, .50 Caliber, Brass Butt Plate, Reproduction, *Antique* ... 300 375 335

PR407, Big Bore Mountain Rifle, .54 Caliber, Undecorated Stock, Beavertail Cheekpiece, Reproduction, *Antique* ... 300 350 345

PR456, Squirrel Rifle, .32 Caliber, Left Handed Model, Reproduction, *Antique* ... 175 225 230

SHOTGUN, SINGLE BARREL

FB557, Blunderbuss, .69 Caliber, Flintlock, Brass Trigger, Reproduction, *Antique* ... 225 275 275

SHOTGUN, DOUBLE BARREL, SIDE-BY-SIDE

PS409..12 Gauge, Percussion, Muzzleloading, Reproduction, *Antique* ... $225 $275 $290

CZ Czechoslovakia from 1918 to date. This listing includes both Ceska Zbrojovka Brno and Ceskslovenska Zbrojovka. Also see BRNO.

HANDGUN, REVOLVER

Grand, .38 Spec., Double Action, Swing-Out Cylinder, *Modern* ... 125 175 165

Grand, .357 Mag., Double Action, Swing-Out Cylinder, *Modern* ... 125 175 180

ZKR 551, .38 Spec., Single Action, Swing-Out Cylinder, Target Pistol, *Modern* ... 175 250 250

HANDGUN, SEMI-AUTOMATIC

CZ1922, .25 ACP, Clip Fed, *Curio* ... 300 375 410

CZ1924, .380 ACP, Clip Fed, *Curio* ... 300 350 265

CZ1936, .25 ACP, Clip Fed, *Curio* ... 225 250 180

CZ 70, .32 ACP, Clip Fed, Blue, Double Action, *Modern* ... 250 300 200

CZ 75, 9mm P, Clip Fed, Double Action, Blue, *Modern* ... 300 350 500

Duo, .25 ACP, Clip Fed, *Modern* ... 125 175 180

Fox, .25 ACP, Clip Fed, *Curio* ... 275 325 365

M1938, .380 ACP, Clip Fed, Double Action, *Curio* ... 175 250 220

Niva, .25 ACP, Clip Fed, *Curio* ... 275 325 310

PZK, .25 ACP, Clip Fed, *Modern* ... 250 300 300

	V.G.	Exc.	Prior Edition Exc. Value
Vest Pocket CZ 1945, .25 ACP, Clip Fed, *Modern*............................	150	175	200
CZ NB 50 Police, .32 ACP, Clip Fed, Double Action, *Curio*...........	275	350	365
CZ1922, .380 ACP, Clip Fed, *Curio*..	250	325	255
CZ1924, .380 ACP, Clip Fed, *Curio*..	250	325	215
CZ1924, .380 ACP, 10 Shot, Long Grip, Clip Fed, *Curio*................	450	600	600
CZ1924 Navy, .380 ACP, Clip Fed, Nazi-Proofed, *Curio*................	225	375	295
CZ1938, .380 ACP, Clip Fed, Double Action, Nazi-Proofed, *Curio*	1,300	1,350	295
CZ1938, .380 ACP, Clip Fed, Double Action, With Safety, *Curio*	750	950	650
CZ1938, .380 ACP, Clip Fed, Double Action, *Curio*	250	300	275
CZ27, .22 L.R.R.F., Clip Fed, Nazi-Proofed, *Curio*	600	750	750
CZ27 Postwar, .32 ACP, Clip Fed, Commercial, *Curio*	175	200	240
CZ27 Pre-War, .32 ACP, Clip Fed, Commercial, *Curio*	200	250	225
CZ27 Communist, .32 ACP, Clip Fed, *Curio*....................................	225	300	260
CZ27 Early Luftwaffe, .32 ACP, Clip Fed, Nazi-Proofed, *Curio*.......	225	300	250
CZ27 Late Luftwaffe, .32 ACP, Clip Fed, Nazi-Proofed, *Curio*.........	250	275	235
CZ27 Navy, .32 ACP, Clip Fed, Nazi-Proofed, *Curio*......................	300	350	295
CZ27 Police, .32 ACP, Clip Fed, Nazi-Proofed, *Curio*	325	375	325
CZ50, .32 ACP, Clip Fed, Double Action, Military, *Modern*...........	125	150	245
CZ52, 7.62mm Tokarev, Clip Fed, Single Action, *Curio*	100	135	995

CZ VZ 27

CZ VZ 38

	V.G.	Exc.	Prior Edition Exc. Value

HANDGUN, SINGLESHOT

Drulov, .22 L.R.R.F., Top Break, Target Pistol, Target Sights, *Modern* .... | $175 | $200 | $425

Model P, .22 L.R.R.F., Top Break, Target Pistol, *Modern* .... | 175 | 250 | 265

Model P, 6mm Flobert, Top Break, Target Pistol, *Modern* .... | 150 | 225 | 235

RIFLE, BOLT ACTION

ZKK 602, Various Magnum Calibers, Checkered Stock, Express Sights, *Modern* .... | 300 | 450 | 465

ZKK 600, Various Calibers, Checkered Stock, Express Sights, *Modern* .... | 250 | 350 | 360

SHOTGUN, DOUBLE BARREL, OVER-UNDER

Model 581, 12 Gauge, Checkered Stock with Cheekpiece, *Modern* .... | 275 | 400 | 420

CZAR Made by Hood Firearms, c. 1876.

HANDGUN, REVOLVER

.22 Short R.F., 7 Shot, Spur Trigger, Solid Frame, Single Action, *Antique* .... | 100 | 175 | 165

CZAR Made by Hopkins & Allen, c. 1880.

HANDGUN, REVOLVER

.22 Short R.F., 7 Shot, Spur Trigger, Solid Frame, Single Action, *Antique* .... | 100 | 150 | 165

.32 Short R.F., 5 Shot, Spur Trigger, Solid Frame, Single Action, *Antique* .... | 125 | 175 | 170

CZECHOSLAVAKIAN MILITARY Also see German Military, CZ.

RIFLE, BOLT ACTION

GEW 33/40, 8mm Mauser, Military, Nazi-Proofed, Carbine, *Modern* .... | 225 | 250 | 215

Gewehr 24 T, 8mm Mauser, Military, Nazi-Proofed, *Curio* .... | 150 | 200 | 200

VZ 24, 8mm Mauser, Military, *Modern* .... | 125 | 175 | 160

VZ 33, 8mm Mauser, Military, Carbine, *Modern* .... | 100 | 150 | 160

D

	V.G.	Exc.	Prior Edition Exc. Value

DAISY Made by Bacon Arms Co., c. 1880.

HANDGUN, REVOLVER

.22 Short R.F. 7 Shot, Spur Trigger, Solid Frame, Single Action, *Antique* .... | $75 | $150 | $160 |

DAKIN GUN CO. San Francisco, Calif., c. 1960.

SHOTGUN, DOUBLE BARREL, OVER-UNDER

Model 170, Various Gauges, Light Engraving, Checkered Stock, Double Triggers, Vent Rib, *Modern* .... | 400 | 650 | 440 |

SHOTGUN, DOUBLE BARREL, SIDE-BY-SIDE

Model 100, 12 or 20 Gauges, Boxlock, Light Engraving, Double Triggers, *Modern* .... | 300 | 350 | 240 |

Model 147, Various Magnum Gauges, Boxlock, Light Engraving, Double Triggers, Vent Rib, *Modern* .... | 350 | 400 | 290 |

Model 215, 12 or 20 Gauges, Sidelock, Fancy Engraving, Fancy Wood, Ejectors, Single Selective Trigger, Vent Rib, *Modern* .... | 800 | 950 | 745 |

DALBY, DAVID Lincolnshire, England, c. 1835.

HANDGUN, FLINTLOCK

.50. Pocket Pistol, Box Lock, Screw Barrel, Folding Trigger, Silver Inlay, *Antique* .... | 600 | 850 | 835 |

DALY ARMS CO. N.Y.C., c. 1890.

HANDGUN, REVOLVER

.22 Long R.F., 6 Shot, Double Action, Ring Trigger, Solid Frame, *Antique* .... | 175 | 250 | 250 |

Peacemaker, .32 Short R.F., 5 Shot Spur Trigger, Solid Frame, Single Action, *Antique* .... | 100 | 175 | 170 |

DAN WESSON ARMS Monson, Mass. since 1970.

HANDGUN, REVOLVER

Model 11, .357 Magnum, Double Action, 3-Barrel Set, Satin Blue, *Modern* .... | 175 | 200 | 220 |

	V.G.	Exc.	Prior Edition Exc. Value
Model 11, .357 Magnum, Double Action, 3-Barrel Set, Nickel Plated, *Modern*	$175	$225	$240
Model 11, .357 Magnum, Various Barrel Lengths, Satin Blue, Double Action, *Modern*	100	150	145
Model 11, .357 Magnum, Various Barrel Lengths, Nickel Plated, Double Action, *Modern*	100	175	160
Model 11, .38 Special, Various Barrel Lengths, Satin Blue, Double Action, *Modern*	100	125	135
Model 11, .38 Special, Various Barrel Lengths, Nickel Plated, Double Action, *Modern*	100	125	130
Model 12, .357 Magnum, Double Action, 3-Barrel Set, Satin Blue, Adjustable Sights, *Modern*	200	250	240
Model 12, .357 Magnum, Various Barrel Lengths, Double Action, Blue, Adjustable Sight, *Modern*	175	275	350
Model 12, .357 Magnum, Various Barrel Lengths, Double Action, Blue, Adjustable Sights, *Modern*	125	150	145
Model 12, .357 Magnum, Various Barrel Lengths, Double Action, Nickel Plated, Adjustable Sights, *Modern*	125	175	155
Model 12, .38 Special, Various Barrel Lengths, Double Action, Blue, Adjustable Sights, *Modern*	100	125	135
Model 12, .38 Special, Various Barrel Lengths, Double Action, Nickel Plated, Adjustable Sights, *Modern*	100	150	150
Model 14, .357 Magnum, Double Action, 3-Barrel Set, Satin Blue, *Modern*	225	275	310
Model 14, .357 Magnum, Double Action, 3-Barrel Set, Nickel Plated, *Modern*	225	300	340
Model 14, .357 Magnum, Various Barrel Lengths, Double Action, Satin Blue, *Modern*	125	150	145
Model 14, .357 Magnum, Various Barrel Lengths, Double Action, Nickel Plated, *Modern*	125	175	165
Model 14, .38 Special, Various Barrel Lengths, Double Action, Satin Blue, *Modern*	100	150	140
Model 14, .38 Special, Various Barrel Lengths, Double Action, Nickel Plated, *Modern*	100	150	160
Model 14-2, .357 Magnum, Various Barrel Lengths, Double Action, Satin Blue, *Modern*	125	150	145
Model 14-2, .357 Magnum, Double Action, 4-Barrel Set, Blue, *Modern*	250	325	350
Model 14-2B, .357 Magnum, Various Barrel Lengths, Double Action, Brite Blue, *Modern*	100	150	155
Model 14-2B, .357 Magnum, Double Action, 4-Barrel Set, Brite Blue, *Modern*	275	350	375
Model 15, .357 Magnum, Various Barrel Lengths, Double Action, Nickel Plated, Adjustable Sights, *Modern*	125	175	165
Model 15, .357 Magnum, Double Action, 3-Barrel Set, Satin Blue, Adjustable Sights, *Modern*	250	325	315
Model 15, .357 Magnum, Double Action, 3-Barrel Set, Blue, Adjustable Sights, *Modern*	250	350	360

	V.G.	Exc.	Prior Edition Exc. Value
Model 15, .357 Magnum, Double Action, 3-Barrel Set, Blue, Adjustable Sights, *Modern*	$250	$325	$320
Model 15, .357 Magnum, Various Barrel Lengths, Double Action, Satin Blue, Adjustable Sights, *Modern*	125	175	—
Model 15, .357 Magnum, Various Barrel Lengths, Double Action, Blue, Adjustable Sights, *Modern*	125	175	175
Model 15, .38 Special, Various Barrel Lengths, Double Action, Nickel Plated, Adjustable Sights, *Modern*	125	175	170
Model 15, .38 Special, Various Barrel Lengths, Double Action, Satin Blue, Adjustable Sights, *Modern*	100	150	150
Model 15, .38 Special, Various Barrel Lengths, Double Action, Blue, Adjustable Sights, *Modern*	100	150	155
Model 15-2, .357 Magnum or .22 L.R.R.F., Various Barrel Lengths, Double Action, Blue, Adjustable Sights, *Modern*	150	200	195
Model 15-2, .357 Magnum or .22 L.R.R.F., Double Action, 4-Barrel Set, Blue, Adjustable Sights, *Modern*	275	350	350
Model 15-2H, .357 Magnum or .22 L.R.R.F., Various Barrel Lengths, Double Action, Blue, Adjustable Sights, Heavy Barrel, *Modern*	150	225	215
Model 15-2H, .357 Magnum or .22 L.R.R.F., Double Action, 4-Barrel Set, Blue, Adjustable Sights, Heavy Barrel, *Modern*	275	350	400
Model 15-2V, .357 Magnum or .22 L.R.R.F., Various Barrel Lengths, Double Action, Blue, Adjustable Sights, Vent Rib, *Modern*	150	225	225
Model 15-2V, .357 Magnum or .22 L.R.R.F., Double Action, 4-Barrel Set, Blue, Adjustable Sights, Vent Rib, *Modern*	325	400	435
Model 15-2VH, .357 Magnum or .22 L.R.R.F., Various Barrel Lengths, Double Action, Adjustable Sights, Heavy Barrel, Vent Rib, *Modern*	150	225	240
Model 15-2VH,. 357 Magnum or .22 L.R.R.F., Double Action, 4-Barrel, Vent Rib, *Modern*	300	375	490
Model 714-2, .357 Magnum, Various Barrel Lengths, Double Action, Stainless Steel, Fixed Sights, *Modern*	125	175	190
Model 714-2, .357 Magnum, Double Action, 4-Barrel Set, Stainless Steel, Fixed Sights, *Modern*	225	300	325
Model 715-2, .357 Magnum, Various Barrel Lengths, Double Action, Stainless Steel, Adjustable Sights, *Modern*	175	250	240
Model 715-2, .357 Magnum, Double Action, 4-Barrel Set, Stainless Steel, Adjustable Sights, *Modern*	325	400	440
Model 715-2V, .357 Magnum, Various Barrel Lengths, Double Action, Stainless Steel, Adjustable Sights, Vent Rib, *Modern*	200	275	270
Model 715-2V, .357 Magnum, Double Action, 4-Barrel Set, Stainless Steel, Adjustable Sights, Vent Rib, *Modern*	400	475	510
Model 715-2VH, .357 Magnum, Double Action, 4-Barrel Set, Stainless Steel, Adjustable Sights, Vent Rib, Heavy Barrel, *Modern*	400	500	550
Model 44-V, .44 Magnum, Various Barrel Lengths, Double Action, Blue, Adjustable Sights, Vent Rib, *Modern*	225	350	300

	V.G.	Exc.	Prior Edition Exc. Value
Model 44-V, .44 Magnum, Double Action, 4-Barrel Set, Blue, Adjustable Sights, Vent Rib, *Modern*	*$350*	*$450*	*$465*
Model 44-VH, .44 Magnum, Various Barrel Lengths, Double Action, Adjustable Sights, Heavy Barrel, Vent Rib, *Modern*	225	350	335
Model 44-VH, .44 Magnum, Double Action, 4-Barrel Set, Blue, Adjustable Sights, Heavy Barrel, Vent Rib, *Modern*	350	450	500
Model 744-V, .44 Magnum, Various Barrel Lengths, Double Action, Stainless, Adjustable Sights, Vent Rib, *Modern*	225	325	330
Model 744-V .44 Magnum, Double Action, 4-Barrel Set, Stainless, Adjustable Sights, Vent Rib, *Modern*	350	450	490
Model 744-VH, .44 Magnum, Various Barrel Lengths, Double Action, Adjustable Sights, Stainless, Heavy Barrel, Vent Rib, *Modern*	250	350	365
Model 744-VH, .44 Magnum, Various Barrel Lengths, Double Action, Adjustable Sights, Stainless, Heavy Barrel, Vent Rib, *Modern*	400	525	530

Extra Barrel Assemblies, Add:

15"   15-2 **$75.00–$110.00**; 15-2H **$95.00–$135.00**; 15-2V **$95.00–$135.00**; 15-2VH **$120.00–$160.00**; 715 **$80.00–120.00**; 715V **$95.00–$140.00**; 715VH **$100.00–$155.00**

12"   15-2 **$50.00–$80.00**; 15-2H **$75.00–$110.00**; 15-2V **$75.00–$110.00**; 15-2VH **$80.00–$120.00**; 715 **$60.00–$90.00**; 715V **$80.00–$120.00**; 715VH **$95.00–$140.00**

10"   15-2 **$45.00–$70.00**; 15-2H **$55.00–$85.00**; 15-2V **$55.00–$85.00**; 15-2VH **$70.00–$100.00**; 44-V **$80.00–$100.00**; 44-VH **$80.00–$120.00**; 715 **$45.00–$70.00**; 715V **$65.00–$95.00**; 715VH **$75.00–$110.00**; 744-V **$70.00–$115.00**; 744-VH **$90.00–$135.00**

Others   15-2 **$20.00–$40.00**; 15-2H **$35.00–$55.00**; 15-2V **$35.00–$55.00**; 15-2VH **$40.00–$70.00**; 44-V **$55.00–$85.00**; 44-VH; 715 **$35.00–$55.00**; 715V **$45.00–$65.00**; 715VH **$50.00–$80.00**; 744-V **$60.00–$100.00**; 44-VH **$70.00–$110.00**

DANISH MILITARY

HANDGUN, REVOLVER

	V.G.	Exc.	Prior
9.1mm Ronge 1891, Military, Top Break, Hammer-Like Latch, *Antique*	300	375	350

HANDGUN, SEMI-AUTOMATIC

M1910, 9mm B, Made By Pieper, Clip Fed, *Curio*	475	650	620
M1910/21, 9mm B, Converted From M1910, Clip Fed, *Curio*	375	525	520
M1910/21, 9mm B, Made By Danish Army Arsenal, Clip Fed, *Curio*	550	725	710
S.I.G. SG/8 9mm Luger, Clip Fed, Military, *Modern*	1,250	1,375	1,375

RIFLE, BOLT ACTION

M98 Mauser, 6.5 x 57, Haerens Vabenarsenal, *Curio*	250	350	310
M1889 Krag, 8 x 54 Krag-Jorgensen, Carbine, *Antique*	425	575	575

	V.G.	Exc.	Prior Edition Exc. Value

RIFLE, SINGLESHOT

M1867, Remington Rolling Block, Full Stock, *Antique* $475 $650 $650

DANIELS, HENRY & CHARLES Chester, Conn., 1835–1850.

RIFLE, PERCUSSION

Turret Rifle, .40, Underhammer, 8 Shot, Manual Repeater,
Octagon Barrel, *Antique*.. 6,500 7,500 6,900

DANTON Made By Gabilondo y Cia., Elgoibar, Spain, 1925–1933.

HANDGUN, SEMI-AUTOMATIC

Pocket, .25 ACP, Clip Fed, *Modern*.. 100 150 155
Pocket, .32 ACP, Clip Fed, *Modern*.. 100 175 165
Pocket, .25 ACP, Grip Safety, Clip Fed, *Modern*............................. 125 175 170
Pocket, .32 ACP, Grip Safety, Clip Fed, *Modern*............................. 125 175 175

DARDICK Hamden, Conn., 1954–1962.

HANDGUN, REVOLVER

Series 1100, .38 Dardick Tround, Double Action, Clip Fed,
3" Barrel, 11 Shot, *Modern*.. 550 750 580
Series 1500, .30, Double Action, Clip Fed, 4³/₄" Barrel, *Modern* 750 950 890
Series 1500, .38 Dardick Tround, Double Action, Clip Fed,
6" Barrel, 15 Shot, *Modern*.. 450 650 580
Series 1500, .22, Double Action, Clip Fed, 2" and 11" Barrels,
Modern... 750 950 940

For Carbine Conversion Unit .38, Add **$215.00–$325.00**
For Carbine Conversion Unit .22, Add **$25.00–$395.00**

DARNE St. Etienne, France.

SHOTGUN, DOUBLE BARREL, SIDE-BY-SIDE

Bird Hunter, Various Gauges, Sliding Breech, Ejectors, Double
Triggers, Checkered Stock, *Modern*... 800 1,000 790

Danton .25

	V.G.	Exc.	Prior Edition Exc. Value
Hors Serie #1, Various Gauges, Sliding Breech, Ejectors, Fancy Engraving, Checkered Stock, *Modern*	$3,200	$4,500	$4,475
Magnum, 12 or 20 Gauges 3", Sliding Breech, Ejectors, Double Triggers, Checkered Stock, *Modern*	2,250	3,250	1,450
Pheasant Hunter, Various Gauges, Sliding Breech, Ejectors, Light Engraving, Checkered Stock, *Modern*	2,000	2,500	1,200
Quail Hunter, Various Gauges, Sliding Breech, Ejectors, Engraved, Checkered Stock, *Modern*	2,750	3,750	1,865

DAVENPORT, W.H. Providence, R.I. 1880–1883, Norwich, Conn. 1890–1900.

SHOTGUN, DOUBLE BARREL, SIDE-BY-SIDE

8 Ga., *Modern*	250	300	545

SHOTGUN, SINGLESHOT

Various Gauges, Hammer, Steel Barrel, *Modern*	150	200	75

DAVIDSON Spain Mfg. by Fabrica de Armas, Imported by Davidson Firearms Co., Greensboro, N.C.

SHOTGUN, DOUBLE BARREL, SIDE-BY-SIDE

73 Stagecoach, 12 or 20 Gauges, Magnum, Checkered Stock, *Modern*	225	275	175
Model 673B, 10 Ga. 3½", Magnum, Engraved, Nickel Plated, Checkered Stock, *Modern*	200	275	210
Model 63B, 12 and 20 Gauges, Magnum, Engraved, Nickel Plated, Checkered Stock, *Modern*	175	250	185
Model 63B, Various Gauges, Engraved, Nickel Plated, Checkered Stock, *Modern*	125	200	180
Model 69 SL, 12 and 20 Gauges, Sidelock, Light Engraving, Checkered Stock, *Modern*	325	400	225

DAVIS, N.R. & CO. Freetown Mass. 1853–1917. Merged with Warner Co. of Norwich, Conn. and became Davis-Warner Arms Co. It was not active between 1920–1922, but in 1930 started again as Crescent-Davis Arms Co., Norwich. This included Crescent Firearms Co. They relocated in Springfield, Mass. 1931–1932 and were taken over in 1932 by Stevens Arms.

RIFLE, PERCUSSION

.45, Octagon Barrel, *Antique*	400	675	650

SHOTGUN, PERCUSSION

#1 Various Gauges, Double Barrel, Side by Side, Damascus Barrel, Outside Hammers, *Antique*	325	475	475
#3, Various Gauges, Double Barrel, Side by Side, Damascus Barrel, Outside Hammers, *Antique*	275	400	380

	V.G.	Exc.	Prior Edition Exc. Value
SHOTGUN, DOUBLE BARREL, SIDE-BY-SIDE			
Various Gauges, Outside Hammers, Damascus Barrel, *Modern*.........	$100	$175	$155
Various Gauges, Hammerless, Steel Barrel, *Modern*.......................	125	200	180
Various Gauges, Hammerless, Damascus Barrel, *Modern*	100	175	155
Various Gauges, Outside Hammers, Steel Barrel, *Modern*..............	100	200	180
SHOTGUN, SINGLESHOT			
Various Gauges, Hammer, Steel Barrel, *Modern*............................	50	100	80

DAVIS INDUSTRIES Current manufacturer in Chino, Calif.

HANDGUN, DOUBLE BARREL, OVER-UNDER

	V.G.	Exc.	Prior Ed.
Model D-22, .22 L.R.R.F., Remington Derringer Style, Chrome, *Modern*..	25	50	40
Model D-22, .22 L.R.R.F., Remington, Derringer Style, Black Teflon, *Modern*	25	50	40
Model D-22, .25 ACP, Remington Derringer Style, Chrome, *Modern*..	25	50	40
Model D-22, .25 ACP, Remington Derringer Style, Black Teflon, *Modern*..	25	50	40

DEANE, ADAMS & DEANE See Adams.

DAY ARMS CO. San Antonio, Tex.

HANDGUN, SEMI-AUTOMATIC

	V.G.	Exc.	Prior Ed.
Conversion Unit Only, .22 L.R.R.F., For Colt M1911, Clip Fed, *Modern*..	125	150	150

DEAD SHOT L.W. Pond Co.

HANDGUN, REVOLVER

	V.G.	Exc.	Prior Ed.
.22 Long R.F., 6 Shot, Single Action, Solid Frame, Spur Trigger, *Antique*	225	275	265

DEBATIR

HANDGUN, SEMI-AUTOMATIC

	V.G.	Exc.	Prior Ed.
.25 ACP, Clip Fed, *Modern*...	150	225	220
.32 ACP, Clip Fed, *Modern*...	175	250	255

Debatir .25

	V.G.	Exc.	Prior Edition Exc. Value

DEBERIERE, HENRY Phila., Pa. 1769–1774, See Kentucky Rifles & Pistols.

DECKER, WILHELM Zella St. Blasii, Germany, c. 1913.

HANDGUN, REVOLVER

Decker, .25 ACP, Hammerless, 6 Shot, *Curio*	$650	$875	$875
Mueller Special, .25 ACP, Hammerless, 6 Shot, *Curio*	675	975	975

DEFENDER Made by Iver-Johnson, Sold by J.P. Lovell Arms 1875–1895.

HANDGUN, REVOLVER

.22 Short R.F., 7 Shot, Spur Trigger, Solid Frame, Single Action, *Antique*	100	175	165
.32 Short R.F., 5 Shot, Spur Trigger, Solid Frame, Single Action, *Antique*	125	175	170
#89, .22 Short R.F., 7 Shot, Spur Trigger, Solid Frame, Single Action, *Antique*	100	150	160
#89, .32 Short R.F., 5 Shot, Spur Trigger, Solid Frame, Single Action, *Antique*	125	175	170

DEFENDER N. Shore & Co., Chicago, Ill., c. 1922.

HANDGUN, KNIFE PISTOL

#215, .22 R.F., 3" Over All Length, 1 Blade, *Class 3*	100	175	150

DEFIANCE Made By Norwich Falls Pistol Co., c. 1880.

HANDGUN, REVOLVER

.22 Short R.F., 7 Shot, Spur Trigger, Solid Frame, Single Action, *Antique*	100	175	155

DEHUFF, ABRAHAM Lancaster, Pa., c. 1779. See Kentucky rifles & pistols.

DEK-DU Tomas de Urizar y Cia., Eibar, Spain, c. 1910.

HANDGUN, REVOLVER

Velo Dog, 5.5mm Velo Dog, 12 Shots, Folding Trigger, *Curio*	100	150	155
Velo Dog, .25 ACP, 12 Shots, Folding Trigger, *Curio*	125	175	165

DELPHIAN Made by Stevens Arms.

SHOTGUN, SINGLESHOT

Model 90, Various Gauges, Takedown, Automatic Ejector, Plain Hammer, *Modern*	50	75	65

	V.G.	Exc.	Prior Edition Exc. Value

DELU Fab. d'Armes Delu & Co.

HANDGUN, SEMI-AUTOMATIC

	V.G.	Exc.	Prior Ed.
.25 ACP, Clip Fed, *Curio*	$150	$175	$200

DEMRO Manchester, Conn.

HANDGUN, SEMI-AUTOMATIC

	V.G.	Exc.	Prior Ed.
T.A.C. XF-7 Wasp, .45 ACP or 9mm Luger, Clip Fed, *Modern*	300	350	375

RIFLE, SEMI-AUTOMATIC

	V.G.	Exc.	Prior Ed.
T.A.C. Model 1, .45 ACP or 9mm Luger, Clip Fed, *Modern*	225	350	340
T.A.C. XF-7 Wasp, .45 ACP or 9mm Luger, Clip Fed, Folding Stock, *Modern*	350	400	390

DERR, JOHN Lancaster, Pa. 1810–1844. See Kentucky Rifles & Pistols.

DERINGER, HENRY, SR. Richmond, Va. & Philadelphia, Pa. 1768–1814. See Kentucky Rifles & Pistols; U.S. Military.

DERINGER, HENRY, JR. Philadelphia, Pa. 1806–1868. Also see U.S. Military.

HANDGUN, PERCUSSION

	V.G.	Exc.	Prior Ed.
Pocket, .41, Back Lock, German Silver Mounts, *Antique*	750	1,250	750
Medium Pocket, .41, Back Lock, German Silver Mounts, *Antique*	1,000	1,500	795
Dueller, .41, Back Lock, German Silver Mounts, *Antique*	2,000	2,500	1,500

DERINGER RIFLE AND PISTOL WORKS

Philadelphia, Pa. 1870–1880.

HANDGUN, REVOLVER

	V.G.	Exc.	Prior Ed.
Centennial '76, .38 Long R.F., 5 Shot, Single Action, Spur Trigger, Tip-up, *Antique*	350	400	365
Model 1, .22 Short R.F., 7 Shot, Spur Trigger, Tip-up, *Antique*	350	400	340
Model 2, .22 Short R.F., 7 Shot, Spur Trigger, Tip-up, *Antique*	325	375	310
Model 2, .32 Long R.F., 5 shot, Single Action, Spur Trigger, Tip-up, *Antique*	325	375	310

DESPATCH Made by Hopkins & Allen, c. 1875.

HANDGUN, REVOLVER

	V.G.	Exc.	Prior Ed.
.22 Short R.F., 7 Shot, Spur Trigger, Solid Frame, Single Action, *Antique*	125	175	165

Destroyer .25

Destroyer .32

	V.G.	Exc.	Prior Edition Exc. Value

DESTROYER Made in Spain by Isidro Gaztanaga 1914–1933, reorganized as Gaztanaga, Trocaola y Ibarzabal 1933–1936.

HANDGUN, SEMI-AUTOMATIC

	V.G.	Exc.	Value
Model 1913, .25 ACP, Clip Fed, *Modern*	$125	$175	$165
Destroyer, .25 ACP, Clip Fed, *Curio*	125	175	170
Model 1919, .32 ACP, Clip Fed, *Modern*	125	175	170
Destroyer, .32 ACP, Clip Fed, Long Grip, *Curio*	150	200	185
Super Destroyer, .32 ACP, Clip Fed, *Modern*	175	225	235

DESTRUCTOR Iraola Salaverria, Eibar, Spain.

HANDGUN, SEMI-AUTOMATIC

.25 ACP, Clip Fed, *Modern*	100	150	150
.32 ACP, Clip Fed, *Modern*	125	175	165

DETONICS Seattle, Washington.

Combat MC-1, .45 ACP, Combat Modifications, Clip Fed, Pocket Pistol, Matt Blue, *Modern*	450	575	400
Combat MC-1, 9mm P., Combat Modifications, Clip Fed, Pocket Pistol, Matt Blue, *Modern*	550	675	440
Combat MC-1, .38 Super, Combat Modifications, Clip Fed, Pocket Pistol, Matt Blue, *Modern*	550	675	440
Combat Master Mk.I, .45 ACP, Combat Modifications, Clip Fed, Pocket Pistol, Matt Blue, *Modern*	500	600	425
Combat Master Mk.IV, .45 ACP, Combat Modifications, Clip Fed, Pocket Pistol, Matt Blue, Adjustable Sights, *Modern*	450	550	410
Combat Master Mk.V, .45 ACP, Combat Modifications, Clip Fed, Pocket Pistol, Matt Stainless, *Modern*	600	750	425
Combat Master Mk.V, 9mm P., Combat Modifications, Clip Fed, Pocket Pistol, Matt Stainless, *Modern*	700	775	445
Combat Master Mk.V., .38 Super, Combat Modifications, Clip Fed, Pocket Pistol, Matt Stainless, *Modern*	700	775	445

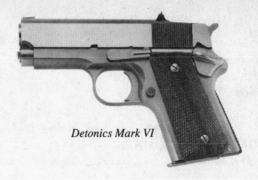

Detonics Mark VI

	V.G.	Exc.	Prior Edition Exc. Value
Combat Master Mk.VI, .45 ACP, Combat Modifications, Clip Fed, Pocket Pistol, Polished Stainless, Adjustable Sights, *Modern*.......	$725	$800	$475
Combat Master Mk.VI, 9mm P., Combat Modifications, Clip Fed, Pocket Pistol, Polished Stainless, Adjustable Sights, *Modern*...........	750	825	500
Combat Master MK.VI, .451 Mag., Combat Modifications, Clip Fed, Pocket Pistol, Polished Stainless, Adjustable Sights, *Modern*.......	775	875	700
Combat Master Mk.VII, .45 ACP, Combat Modifications, Clip Fed, Pocket Pistol, Matt Stainless, No Sights, Lightweight, *Modern*........	825	900	490
Combat Master Mk.VII, 9mm P., Combat Modifications, Clip Fed, Pocket Pistol, Matt Stainless, No Sights, Lightweight, *Modern*........	850	925	525
Combat Master Mk.VII, .38 Super, Combat Modifications, Clip Fed, Pocket Pistol, Matt Stainless, No Sights, Lightweight, *Modern*....	850	925	525
Combat Master Mk.VII, .451 Mag., Combat Modifications, Clip Fed, Pocket Pistol, Matt Stainless, No Sights, Lightweight, *Modern*....	900	1,200	700
Military Combat OM-3, .45 ACP, Clip Fed, Pocket Pistol, Matt Stainless, *Modern*..	575	625	455
Military Combat OM-3, 9mm P., Clip Fed, Pocket Pistol, Matt Stainless, *Modern*..	600	650	485
Military Combat OM-3, .38 Super, Clip Fed, Pocket Pistol, Matt Stainless, *Modern*..	600	650	485
Scoremaster, .45 ACP, I.P.S.C. Target Pistol, Target Sights, Stainless Steel, *Modern*..	1,000	1,150	695
Scoremaster, .451 Mag., I.P.S.C. Target Pistol, Target Sights, Stainless Steel, *Modern*..	1,000	1,150	695

DIAMOND Made by Stevens Arms.

SHOTGUN, SINGLESHOT

Model 89 Dreadnaught, Various Gauges, Hammer, *Modern*..........	75	100	70
Model 90, Various Gauges, Takedown, Automatic Ejector, Plain Hammer, *Modern*..	50	75	65
Model 95, 12 and 16 Gauge, Takedown, *Modern*..............................	50	75	60

	V.G.	Exc.	Prior Edition Exc. Value

DIANE Made by Wilkinson Arms, Covina, Calif.
HANDGUN, SEMI-AUTOMATIC

	V.G.	Exc.	Prior Edition Exc. Value
Standard Model, .25 ACP, Clip Fed, *Modern*	$100	$125	$275

DIANE Erquiaga, Muguruzu, y Cia., Eibar, Spain, c. 1923.
HANDGUN, SEMI-AUTOMATIC

.25 ACP, Clip Fed, Blue, *Curio*..	225	275	275

DICKINSON, J. & L. Also E. L. & J. Dickinson, Springfield, Mass. 1863–1880.
HANDGUN, SINGLESHOT

.22 R.F., Brass Frame, Pivoting Barrel, Rack Ejector, *Antique*	350	400	390
.32 R.F., Brass Frame, Pivoting Barrel, Rack Ejector, *Antique*	250	300	290

DICKSON Made in Italy for American Import Co. until 1968.
HANDGUN, SEMI-AUTOMATIC

Detective, .25 ACP, Clip Fed, *Modern*	100	125	125

DICTATOR Made by Hopkins & Allen, c. 1880.
HANDGUN, REVOLVER

.22 Short R.F., 7 Shot, Spur Trigger, Solid Frame, Single Action, *Antique*	125	175	165
.32 Short R.F., 5 Shot, Spur Trigger, Solid Frame, Single Action, *Antique*	125	175	165
#2, .32 Short R.F., 5 Shot, Spur Trigger, Solid Frame, Single Action, *Antique*	150	200	175

DIXIE GUN WORKS Union City, Tenn.
HANDGUN, FLINTLOCK

Tower, .67, Brass Furniture, Reproduction, *Antique*	25	50	30

HANDGUN, PERCUSSION

Army, .44 Revolver, Buntline, Reproduction, *Antique*......................	125	150	75
Navy, .36, Revolver, Buntline, Brass Frame, Reproduction, *Antique*..	150	200	40
Navy, .36, Revolver, Buntline, Brass Frame, Engraved, Reproduction, *Antique*	175	225	45
Spiller & Burr, .36, Revolver, Buntline, Brass Frame, Reproduction, *Antique*	75	100	60
Wyatt Earp, .44 Revolver, Buntline, Brass Frame, Reproduction, *Antique*..	$75	$100	$55

	V.G.	Exc.	Prior Edition Exc. Value

Wyatt Earp, .44 Revolver, Buntline, Brass Frame, With Shoulder Stock, Reproduction, *Antique* *150* *175* *85*

RIFLE, FLINTLOCK

1st. Model Brown Bess, .75, Military, Reproduction, *Antique* *325* *400* *365*

2nd. Model Brown Bess, .74, Military, Reproduction, *Antique* *425* *500* *215*

Coach Guard, .95, Blunderbuss, Brass Furniture, Reproduction, *Antique* *100* *150* *125*

Day Rifle, .45, Double Barrel, Over-under, Swivel Breech, Brass Furniture, Reproduction, *Antique* *300* *375* *360*

Deluxe Pennsylvania, .45, Kentucky Rifle, Full-Stocked, Brass Furniture, Light Engraving, Reproduction, *Antique* *275* *350* *265*

Deluxe Pennsylvania, .45, Kentucky Rifle, Full-Stocked, Brass Furniture, Reproduction, *Antique* *250* *325* *275*

Kentuckian, .45, Kentucky Rifle, Full-Stocked, Brass Furniture, Reproduction, *Antique* *100* *150* *125*

Kentuckian, .45, Kentucky Rifle, Full-Stocked, Brass Furniture, Reproduction, Carbine, *Antique* *150* *225* *125*

Musket, .67 Smoothbore, Reproduction, Carbine, *Antique* *75* *125* *85*

Squirel Rifle, .45, Kentucky Rifles, Full-Stocked, Brass Furniture, Reproduction, *Antique* *275* *375* *215*

York County, .45, Kentucky Rifle, Full-Stocked, Brass Furniture, Reproduction, *Antique* *150* *175* *135*

RIFLE, LEVER ACTION

Win. 73 (Italian), .44-40 WCF, Tube Feed, Octagon Barrel, Carbine, *Modern* *475* *600* *285*

Win 73 (Italian), .44-40 WCF, Tube Feed, Octagon Barrel, Color Cased Hardened Frame, Engraved, *Modern* *475* *600* *320*

RIFLE, PERCUSSION

Day Rifle,. 45, Double Barrel, Over-under, Swivel Breech, Brass Furniture, Reproduction, *Antique* *225* *275* *245*

Deluxe Pennsylvania, .45, Kentucky Rifle, Full-Stocked, Brass Furniture, Reproduction, *Antique* *275* *325* *240*

Deluxe Pensylvania, .45, Kentucky Rifle, Full-Stocked, Brass Furniture, Light Engraving, Reproduction, *Antique* *275* *350* *260*

Dixie Hawkin, .45, Half-Stocked, Octagon Barrel, Set Trigger, Brass Furniture, Reproduction, *Antique* *150* *200* *155*

Dixie Hawkin, .50, Half-Stocked, Octagon Barrel, Set Trigger, Brass Furniture, Reproduction, *Antique* *150* *200* *155*

Enfield Two-Band, .577, Musketoon, Military, Reproduction, *Antique* *125* *200* *150*

Kentuckian, .45, Kentucky Rifle, Full-Stocked, Brass Furniture, Reproduction, *Antique* *125* *175* *125*

Kentuckian, .45, Kentucky Rifle, Full-Stocked, Brass Furniture, Reproduction, Carbine, *Antique* *200* *250* *125*

	V.G.	Exc.	Prior Edition Exc. Value
Musket, .66, Smoothbore, Reproduction, *Antique*	$125	$175	$75
Plainsman, .45, Half-Stocked, Octagon Barrel, Reproduction, *Antique*	200	250	145
Plainsman, .50, Half-Stocked, Octagon Barrel, Reproduction, *Antique*	150	275	145
Squirrel Rifle, .45, Kentucky Rifle, Full-Stocked, Brass Furniture, Reproduction, *Antique*	300	375	200
Target, .45, Half-Stocked, Octagon Barrel, Reproduction, *Antique*	75	125	75
York County, .45, Kentucky Rifle, Full-Stocked, Brass Furniture, Reproduction, *Antique*	125	175	125
Zouave M 1863, .58, Military, Reproduction, *Antique*	175	250	125

SHOTGUN, FLINTLOCK

	V.G.	Exc.	Prior Edition Exc. Value
Fowling Piece, 14 Gauge, Single Barrel, Reproduction, *Antique*	100	105	85

SHOTGUN, PERCUSSION

	V.G.	Exc.	Prior Edition Exc. Value
12 Gauge, Double Barrel, Side by Side, Double Trigger, Reproduction, *Antique*	150	225	135
28 Gauge, Single Barrel, Reproduction, *Antique*	75	100	45

DOBSON T. London, England, c. 1780.

HANDGUN, FLINTLOCK

	V.G.	Exc.	Prior Edition Exc. Value
.64, Presentation, Holster Pistol, Gold Inlays, Engraved, Half-Octagon Barrel, High Quality, *Antique*	2,500	4,000	3,800

DOMINO Made in Italy, Imported by Mandell Shooting Sports. Also see Beeman.

HANDGUN, SEMI-AUTOMATIC

	V.G.	Exc.	Prior Edition Exc. Value
Model O.P. 601, .22 Short, Target Pistol, Adjustable Sights, Target Grips, *Modern*	625	725	675
Model O.P. 602, 22 Short, Target Pistol, Adjustable Sights, Target Grips, *Modern*	700	800	675

DREADNAUGHT Made by Hopkins & Allen c. 1880.

HANDGUN, REVOLVER

	V.G.	Exc.	Prior Edition Exc. Value
.22 Short R.F., 7 Shot, Spur Trigger, Solid Frame, Single Action, *Antique*	100	150	155
.32 Short R.F., 5 Shot, Spur Trigger, Solid Frame, Single Action, *Antique*	125	175	170

DREYSE Dreyse Rheinische Metallwaren Machinenfabrik, Sommerda, Germany since 1889. In 1936 merged and became Rheinmetall-Borsig, Dusseldorf, Germany.

Dreyse Model 2

Dreyse Model 1907 Late

	V.G.	Exc.	Prior Edition Exc. Value
HANDGUN, SEMI-AUTOMATIC			
M1907, .32 ACP, Clip Fed, Early Model, *Modern*	$150	$200	$300
M1907, .32 ACP, Clip Fed, *Modern*	125	175	200
M1910, 9mm Luger, Clip Fed, *Curio*	475	575	840
Rheinmetall, .32 ACP, Clip Fed, *Modern*	225	275	325
Vest Pocket, .25 ACP, Clip Fed, Early, *Modern*	175	225	230
Vest Pocket, .25 ACP, Clip Fed, *Modern*	150	200	200
RIFLE, SEMI-AUTOMATIC			
Carbine, .32 ACP, Clip Fed, Checkered Stock, *Curio*	375	450	435

DRIPPARD, F. Lancaster, Pa., 1767–1773, See Kentucky Rifles & Pistols.

DRISCOLL, J.B. Springfield, Mass., c. 1870.
HANDGUN, SINGLESHOT

	V.G.	Exc.	
.22 R.F., Brass Frame, Spur Trigger, *Antique*	300	350	295

DUMARESD, B. Marseille, France, probably c. 1730.
HANDGUN, FLINTLOCK

	V.G.	Exc.	
Holster Pistol, Engraved, Horn Inlays, Ornate, Silver Furniture, *Antique*	1,500	2,000	1,975

DUBIEL ARMS CO. Sherman, Tex. since 1975.
RIFLE, BOLT ACTION

	V.G.	Exc.	
Custom Rifle, Various Calibers, Various Styles, Fancy Wood, *Modern*	2,000	2,250	1,750

	V.G.	Exc.	Prior Edition Exc. Value

DUMOULIN FRERES ET CIE Milmort, Belgium since 1849.

RIFLE, BOLT ACTION

Grade I, Various Calibers, Fancy Checkering, Engraved, *Modern* $1,500 $1,750 $1,450

Grade II, Various Calibers, Fancy Checkering, Engraved, Fancy Wood, *Modern* 1,750 2,000 1,975

Grade III, Various Calibers, Fancy Checkering, Fancy Engraving, Fancy Wood, *Modern* 3,250 3,750 2,550

RIFLE, DOUBLE BARREL, SIDE-BY-SIDE

Various Calibers, Fancy Checkering, Engraved, Fancy Wood, *Modern* 3,500 3,800 2,250

DUO Frantisek Dusek, Opocno, Czechoslovakia 1926–1948. Ceska Zbrojovka from 1948 to date.

HANDGUN, SEMI-AUTOMATIC

.25 ACP, Clip Fed, *Modern* 125 175 175

DUTCH MILITARY

HANDGUN, REVOLVER

Model 1871 Hemberg, 9.4 mm, Military, *Antique* 125 175 165

RIFLE, BOLT ACTION

Model 95, 6.5mm Mannlicher, Full Stock, *Curio* 75 100 70

Model 95, 6.5mm Mannlicher, Carbine, Full Stock, *Curio* 50 75 70

Beaumont-Vitale M1871/88, Military, *Antique* 150 200 185

RIFLE, FLINTLOCK

.70, Officers Type, Musket, Brass Furniture, *Antique* 900 1,500 1,300

DUTTON, JOHN S. Jaffrey, N.H. 1855–1870.

RIFLE PERCUSSION

.36, Target Rifle, Swiss Buttplate, Octagon Barrel, Target Sights, *Antique* 900 1,600 1,500

DWM Deutche Waffen und Munitionsfabrik, Berlin, Germany 1896–1945. Also see Luger and Borchardt.

HANDGUN, SEMI-AUTOMATIC

Pocket, .32 ACP, Clip Fed, *Curio* 250 350 400

E

E.A. Echave y Arizmendi, Eibar, Spain 1911–1975. Also see Echasa and MAB.

HANDGUN, SEMI-AUTOMATIC

	V.G.	Exc.	Prior Edition Exc. Value
1916 Model, .25 ACP, Clip Fed, *Curio*	$75	$125	$125

E.A. Eulogio Arostegui, Eibar, Spain, c. 1930.

HANDGUN, SEMI-AUTOMATIC

	V.G.	Exc.	
.25 ACP, Clip Fed, Blue, Dog Logo on Grips, *Modern*	75	125	120

EAGLE Made by Iver-Johnson, c. 1879–1886.

HANDGUN, REVOLVER

	V.G.	Exc.	
.22 Short F.F., 7 Shot, Spur Trigger, Solid Frame, Single Action, *Antique*	100	150	155
.32 Short R.F., 5 Shot, Spur Trigger, Solid Frame, Single Action, *Antique*	100	150	155
.38 Short R.F., 5 Shot, Spur Trigger, Solid Frame, Single Action, *Antique*	125	175	175
.44 Short R.F., 5 Shot, Spur Trigger, Solid Frame, Single Action, *Antique*	200	275	260

EAGLE ARMS CO. N.Y.C., c. 1865.

HANDGUN, REVOLVER

	V.G.	Exc.	
.30 Cup Primed Cartridge, 5 Shot, Single Action, Spur Trigger, *Antique*	250	325	200

Eagle Arms Plants Patent, .30 Caliber Revolver

	V.G.	Exc.	Prior Edition Exc. Value
.30 Cup Primed Cartridge, 6 Shot, Single Action, Spur Trigger, Solid Frame, *Antique*	$400	$500	$320
.30 Cup Primed Cartridge, 6 Shot, Single Action, Spur Trigger, Tip-up, *Antique*	525	650	365
.42 Cup Primed Cartridge, 6 Shot, Single Action, Spur Trigger, Solid Frame, *Antique*	850	950	295
.42 Cup Primed Cartridge, 6 Shot, Single Action, Spur Trigger, Tip-up, *Antique*	950	1,150	425

EARLHOOD   Made by E.L. Dickinson Co. Springfield, Mass. 1870–1880.

HANDGUN, REVOLVER

	V.G.	Exc.	Prior Edition Exc. Value
.32 Short R.F., 5 Shot, Spur Trigger, Solid Frame, Single Action, *Antique*	125	175	165

EARLY, AMOS   Dauphin Co. Pa. See Kentucky Rifles.

EARLY, JACOB   Dauphin Co. Pa. See Kentucky Rifles.

EARTHQUAKE   Made by E.L. Dickinson Co. Springfield, Mass. 1870–1880.

HANDGUN, REVOLVER

	V.G.	Exc.	Prior Edition Exc. Value
.32 Short R.F., 5 Shot, Spur Trigger, Solid Frame, Single Action, *Antique*	100	175	175

EASTERN ARMS CO.   Made by Meriden Firearms and sold by Sears-Roebuck.

HANDGUN, REVOLVER

	V.G.	Exc.	Prior Edition Exc. Value
.32 S & W, 5 Shot, Double Action, Top Break, *Modern*	75	100	100
.38 S & W, 5 Shot, Double Action, Top Break, *Modern*	100	125	110

EASTFIELD   See Smith & Wesson.

EASTERN   Made by Stevens Arms.

SHOTGUN, DOUBLE BARREL, SIDE-BY-SIDE

	V.G.	Exc.	Prior Edition Exc. Value
Model 311, Various Gauges, Hammerless, Steel Barrel, *Modern*	150	175	185

SHOTGUN, SINGLESHOT

	V.G.	Exc.	Prior Edition Exc. Value
Model 94, Various Gauges, Takedown, Automatic Ejector, Plain Hammer, *Modern*	50	75	55

Echasa GZ-MAB

	V.G.	Exc.	Prior Edition Exc. Value

ECHASA Tradename used in the 1950's by Echave, Arizmendi y Cia., Eibar, Spain.

HANDGUN, SEMI-AUTOMATIC
	V.G.	Exc.	Prior Ed.
Model GZ MAB, .22 L.R.R.F., Clip Fed, Hammer, *Modern*	$100	$150	$140
Model GZ MAB, .25 ACP, Clip Fed, Hammer, *Modern*	125	150	150
Model GZ MAB, .32 ACP, Clip Fed, Hammer, *Modern*	125	175	160

ECHABERRIA, ARTURA Spain, c. 1790.

HANDGUN, MIQUELET-LOCK
	V.G.	Exc.	Prior Ed.
Pair, Holster Pistol, Plain, Brass Furniture, *Antique*	3,500	4,500	4,350

ECLIPSE Made by Johnson, Bye & Co., c. 1875.

HANDGUN, SINGLESHOT
	V.G.	Exc.	Prior Ed.
.25 Short R.F., Derringer, Spur Trigger, Antique	75	125	125

EDGESON Lincolnshire, England, 1810–1830.

HANDGUN, FLINTLOCK
	V.G.	Exc.	Prior Ed.
.45, Pair, Box Lock, Screw Barrel, Pocket Pistol, Folding Trigger, Plain, *Antique*	1,000	1,800	1,700

EDMONDS, J. See Kentucky Rifles.

EGG, CHARLES London, England, c. 1850.

HANDGUN, PERCUSSION
	V.G.	Exc.	Prior Ed.
Pepperbox, .36, 6 Shot, 3½" Barrels, *Antique*	300	400	395

EGG, DURS London, England 1770–1840. Also see British Military.

HANDGUN, FLINTLOCK
	V.G.	Exc.	Prior Ed.
.50, Duelling Type, Holster Pistol, Octagon Barrel, Steel Furniture, Light Ornamentation, *Antique*	1,000	1,800	1,650

	V.G.	Exc.	Prior Edition Exc. Value

HANDGUN, PERCUSSION

6 Shot, Pepperbox, Fluted Barrel, Pocket Pistol, Engraved, *Antique*.... $1,500 $2,000 $1,750

EGYPTIAN MILITARY
HANDGUN, SEMI-AUTOMATIC
Tokagypt M-58, 9mm Luger, Clip Fed, *Curio*................................. 225 350 345

RIFLE, SEMI-AUTOMATIC
Hakim, .22 L.R.R.F., Training Rifle, Military, *Modern* 225 375 345
Hakim, 8mm Mauser, Military, *Modern*.. 500 650 635

84 GUN CO. Eighty Four, Pa., c. 1973.
RIFLE, BOLT ACTION
Classic Rifle, Various Calibers, Checkered Stock, Standard Grade, *Modern*.................. 200 250 315
Classic Rifle, Various Calibers, Checkered Stock, Grade 1, *Modern*.................. 275 325 400
Classic Rifle, Various Calibers, Checkered Stock, Grade 2, *Modern*.................. 400 600 600
Classic Rifle, Various Calibers, Checkered Stock, Grade 3, *Modern*.................. 550 675 1,300
Classic Rifle, Various Calibers, Checkered Stock, Grade 4, *Modern*.................. 950 1,200 2,000
Lobo Rifle, Various Calibers, Checkered Stock, Grade 1, *Modern*.................. 200 275 320
Lobo Rifle, Various Calibers, Checkered Stock, Grade 2, *Modern*.................. 400 525 600
Lobo Rifle, Various Calibers, Checkered Stock, Grade 3, *Modern*.................. 900 1,050 1,300
Lobo Rifle, Various Calibers, Checkered Stock, Grade 4, *Modern*.................. 1,250 1,550 2,000
Pennsy Rifle, Various Calibers, Checkered Stock, Standard Grade, *Modern*.................. 250 325 325
Pennsy Rifle, Various Calibers, Checkered Stock, Grade 1, *Modern*.................. 350 400 420
Pennsy Rifle, Various Calibers, Checkered Stock, Grade 2, *Modern*.................. 450 600 600
Pennsy Rifle, Various Calibers, Checkered Stock, Grade 3, *Modern*.................. 950 1,250 1,325
Pennsy Rifle, Various Calibers, Checkered Stock, Grade 4, *Modern*.................. 1,250 1,750 2,000

ELECTOR Made by Hopkins & Allen, c. 1880.
HANDGUN, REVOLVER
.22 Short R.F., 7 Shot, Spur Trigger, Solid Frame, Single Action, *Antique* 100 150 160

	V.G.	Exc.	Prior Edition Exc. Value

.32 Short R.F., 5 Shot, Spur Trigger, Solid Frame, Single Action, *Antique* $125 $175 $170

ELECTRIC Made by Forehand & Wadsworth 1871–1880.
HANDGUN, REVOLVER
.32 Short R.F., 5 Shot, Spur Trigger, Solid Frame, Single Action, *Antique* 125 175 160

EL FAISAN
SHOTGUN, DOUBLE BARREL, SIDE-BY-SIDE
El Faisan, .410 Gauge, Folding Gun, Double Trigger, Outside Hammers, *Modern* 75 100 110

ELGIN ARMS CO. Made by Crescent for Fred Bifflar & Co., Chicago, Ill.
SHOTGUN, DOUBLE BARREL, SIDE-BY-SIDE
Various Gauges, Outside Hammers, Damascus Barrel, *Modern* 100 175 155
Various Gauges, Hammerless, Steel Barrel, *Modern* 125 175 185
Various Gauges, Hammerless, Damascus Barrel, *Modern* 100 150 155
Various Gauges, Outside Hammers, Steel Barrel, *Modern* 150 200 180
SHOTGUN, SINGLESHOT
Various Gauges, Hammer, Steel Barrel, *Modern* 50 75 75

ELLIS, REUBEN Albany, N.Y. 1808–1829.
RIFLE, FLINTLOCK
Ellis-Jennings, .69, Sliding Lock for Multiple Loadings, 4 shot, *Antique* 15,000 20,000 9,200
Ellis-Jennings, .69, Sliding Lock for Multiple Loadings, 10 shot, *Antique* 25,000 30,000 16,250

EL TIGRE
RIFLE, LEVER ACTION
Copy of Winchester M1892, 44–40 WCF, Tube Feed, *Modern* 200 275 270

Elgin Cutlass Pistol, .54 Caliber

	V.G.	Exc.	Prior Edition Exc. Value

E.M.F. (Early and Modern Firearms Co., Inc) Studio City, Calif.

HANDGUN, REVOLVER

	V.G.	Exc.	Prior Edition Exc. Value
California Dragoon, .44 Magnum, Single Action, Western Style, Engraved, *Modern*	$225	$275	$235
Dakota, Various Calibers, Single Action, Western Style, *Modern*	175	225	175
Dakota, Various Calibers, Single Action, Western Style, Engraved, *Modern*	250	325	275
Dakota, Various Calibers, Single Action, Western Style, Nickel Plated, *Modern*	200	275	210
Dakota, Various Calibers, Single Action, Western Style, Nickel Plated, Engraved, *Modern*	275	350	295
Dakota Buntline, Various Calibers, 12" Barrel, Single Action, Western Style, *Modern*	200	250	190
Dakota Buckhorn, Various Calibers, 16¼" Barrel, Single Action, Western Style, *Modern*	200	275	225
Dakota Buckhorn, Various Calibers, 16¼" Barrel, Single Action, Western Style, with Shoulder Stock, *Modern*	200	300	255
Dakota Sheriff, Various Calibers, Single Action, Western Style, *Modern*	225	275	225
Super Dakota, Various Calibers, Single Action, Western Style, Magnum, *Modern*	225	300	235
Outlaw 1875, Various Calibers, Single Action, Remington Style, Engraved, *Modern*	175	250	190
Outlaw 1875, Various Calibers, Single Action, Remington Style, Engraved, *Modern*	225	325	275
Thermodynamics, .357 Magnum, Solid Frame, Swing-out Cylinder, Vent Rib, Stainless Steel, *Modern*	150	225	180

HANDGUN, SINGLESHOT

	V.G.	Exc.	Prior Edition Exc. Value
Baron, .22 Short R.F., Derringer, Gold Frame, Blue Barrel, Wood Grips, *Modern*	50	75	45
Baron, Count, Etc., Derringer, if Cased Add **$10.00–$15.00**			
Baroness, .22 Short R.F., Derringer, Gold Plated, Pearl Grips, *Modern*	50	75	55
Count, .22 Short R.F., Derringer, Blue, Wood Grips, *Modern*	25	50	45
Rolling Block, .357 Magnum, Remington Copy, *Modern*	100	150	135

E.M.F. Dakota Buntline

	V.G.	Exc.	Prior Edition Exc. Value

RIFLE, LEVER ACTION

1866 Yellowboy, Various Calibers, Brass Frame, Winchester Copy, *Modern* $325 $400 $245

1866 Yellowboy, Various Calibers, Brass Frame, Winchester Copy, Engraved, *Modern* 375 450 325

1873 Carbine, Various Calibers, Winchester Copy, *Modern* 375 450 365

1873 Rifle, Various Calibers, Winchester Copy, *Modern* 350 475 400

1873 Rifle, Various Calibers, Winchester Copy, Engraved, *Modern* 475 550 500

EM-GE Gerstenberger & Eberwein, Gussenstadt, West Germany.

HANDGUN, REVOLVER

Model 220 KS, .22 L.R.R.F., Double Action, *Modern* 25 50 35

Model 223, .22 W.M.R., Double Action, *Modern* 25 50 55

Target Model 200, .22 L.R.R.F., Double Action, Target Sights, Vent Rib, *Modern* 50 75 60

EMPIRE Made by Jacob Rupertus 1858–1888.

HANDGUN, REVOLVER

.22 Short R.F., 7 Shot, Spur Trigger, Solid Frame, Single Action, *Antique* 100 175 160

.38 Short R.F., 5 Shot, Spur Trigger, Solid Frame, Single Action, *Antique* 150 200 195

.41 Short R.F., 5 Shot, Spur Trigger, Solid Frame, Single Action, *Antique* 175 225 225

EMPIRE ARMS Made by Meriden, and distributed by H. & D. Folsom.

HANDGUN, REVOLVER

.32 S & W, 5 Shot, Double Action, Top Break, *Modern* 75 125 100

.38 S & W, 5 Shot, Double Action, Top Break, *Modern* 75 125 100

EMPIRE ARMS CO. Made by Crescent for Sears Roebuck & Co., c. 1900.

SHOTGUN, DOUBLE BARREL, SIDE-BY-SIDE

Various Gauges, Outside Hammers, Damascus Barrel, *Modern* 100 150 155

Various Gauges, Hammerless, Steel Barrel, *Modern* 125 175 185

Various Gauges, Hammerless, Damascus Barrel, *Modern* 100 150 155

Various Gauges, Outside Hammers, Steel Barrel, *Modern* 125 175 180

SHOTGUN, SINGLESHOT

Various Gauges, Hammer, Steel Barrel, *Modern* 50 75 75

	V.G.	Exc.	Prior Edition Exc. Value

EMPIRE STATE Made by Meriden Firearms, and distributed by H & D Folsom.

HANDGUN, REVOLVER

.32 S & W, 5 Shot, Double Action, Top Break, *Modern*	$75	$100	$95
.38 S & W, 5 Shot, Double Action, Top Break, *Modern*	75	100	100

EMPRESS Made by Jacob Rupertus 1858–1888.

HANDGUN, REVOLVER

.32 Short R.F., 5 Shot, Spur Trigger, Solid Frame, Single Action, *Antique*	125	150	175

ENCORE Made by Johnson-Bye, also by Hopkins & Allen 1847–1887.

HANDGUN, REVOLVER

.22 Short R.F., 7 Shot, Spur Trigger, Solid Frame, Single Action, *Antique*	100	150	160
.32 Short R.F., 5 Shot, Spur Trigger, Solid Frame, Single Action, *Antique*	125	175	175
.38 R.F., 5 Shot, Spur Trigger, Solid Frame, Single Action, *Antique*	150	200	195

ENDERS OAKLEAF Made by Crescent for Shapleigh Hardware Co., St. Louis, Mo.

SHOTGUN, DOUBLE BARREL, SIDE-BY-SIDE

Various Gauges, Outside Hammers, Damascus Barrel, *Modern*	100	150	155
Various Gauges, Hammerless, Steel Barrel, *Modern*	125	175	185
Various Gauges, Hammerless, Damascus Barrel, *Modern*	100	150	155
Various Gauges, Outside Hammers, Steel Barrel, *Modern*	125	175	180

SHOTGUN, SINGLESHOT

Various Gauges, Hammer, Steel Barrel, *Modern*	50	75	75

ENDERS ROYAL SERVICE Made by Crescent for Shapleigh Hardware Co., St. Louis, Mo.

SHOTGUN, DOUBLE BARREL, SIDE-BY-SIDE

Various Gauges, Outside Hammers, Damascus Barrel, *Modern*	100	150	155
Various Gauges, Hammerless, Steel Barrel, *Modern*	125	175	185
Various Gauges, Hammerless, Damascus Barrel, *Modern*	100	150	155
Various Gauges, Outside Hammers, Steel Barrel, *Modern*	100	175	180

SHOTGUN, SINGLESHOT

Various Gauges, Hammer, Steel Barrel, *Modern*	50	75	75

	V.G.	Exc.	Prior Edition Exc. Value

ENTERPRISE Made by Enterprise Gun Works, Pittsburgh, PA., c. 1875.

	V.G.	Exc.	Prior
#1, .22 Short R.F., 7 Shot, Spur Trigger, Solid Frame, Single Action, *Antique*	$125	$175	$175
#2, .32 Short R.F., 5 Shot, Spur Trigger, Solid Frame, Single Action, *Antique*	150	200	190
#3, .38 Short R.F., 5 Shot, Spur Trigger, Solid Frame, Single Action, *Antique*	175	225	215
#4, .41 Short R.F., 5 Shot, Spur Trigger, Solid Frame, Single Action, *Antique*	200	250	250

ERBI
SHOTGUN, DOUBLE BARREL, SIDE-BY-SIDE

	V.G.	Exc.	Prior
Deluxe Ejector Grade, 12 and 20 Gauge, Raised Matted Rib, Double Trigger, Checkered Stock, Beavertail Forend, Automatic Ejector, *Modern*	175	250	240
Field Grade, 12 and 20 Gauge, Raised Matted Rib, Double Trigger, Checkered Stock, *Modern*	150	200	195

ERIKA Francois Pfannl, Krems, Austria 1913–1926.
HANDGUN, SEMI-AUTOMATIC

	V.G.	Exc.	Prior
4.25mm, Clip Fed, Blue, *Curio*	450	650	650

ERMA Erfurter Maschinen u. Werkzeugfabrik, Erfurt, Germany prior to WW-II, and after the war became Erma-Werke, Munich-Dachau, West Germany. Imported by Excam, Miami, Fla.
HANDGUN, SEMI-AUTOMATIC

	V.G.	Exc.	Prior
EP-22, .22 L.R.R.F., Clip Fed, *Modern*	150	275	150
EP-25, .25 ACP, Clip Fed, *Modern*	175	250	145
ET-22 Navy, .22 L.R.R.F., Clip Fed, *Modern*	275	350	235
ET-22 Navy, .22 L.R.R.F., Clip Fed, With Conversion Kit, Cased with Accessories, *Modern*	350	425	335
FB-1, .25 ACP, Clip, *Modern*	75	125	75
KGP-68 (Baby), .32 ACP, Clip Fed, *Modern*	250	325	165
KGP-68 (Baby), .380 ACP, Clip Fed, *Modern*	275	350	175
KGP-69, .22 L.R.R.F., Clip Fed, *Modern*	275	350	150
LA-22 PO 8, .22 L.R.R.F., Clip Fed, *Modern*	200	275	160
RX-22, .22 L.R.R.F., Double Action, Clip Fed, *Modern*	175	200	145
Old Model Target, .22 L.R.R.F., Clip Fed, *Modern*	225	250	225
New Model Target, .22 L.R.R.F., Clip Fed, *Modern*	250	275	250

	V.G.	Exc.	Prior Edition Exc. Value

HANDGUN, REVOLVER

Model 442, .22 L.R.R.F., Double Action, Swing-Out Cylinder, Blue, *Modern* ... $125 $175 $145

Model 443, .22 W.M.R., Double Action, Swing-Out Cylinder, Blue, *Modern* ... 125 175 145

Model 440, .38 Spec., Double Action, Swing-Out Cylinder, Stainless, *Modern* ... 175 225 195

RIFLE, BOLT ACTION

M98 Conversation Unit, .22 L.R.R.F., Clip Fed, Cased, *Modern* ... 250 325 285

EG-61, .22 L.R.R.F., Singleshot, Open Sights, *Modern* ... 75 100 75

M1957 KK, .22 L.R.R.F., Military Style Training Rifle, *Modern* ... 75 100 90

Master Target, .22 L.R.R.F., Checkered Stock, Peep Sights, *Modern* ... 125 175 150

RIFLE, LEVER ACTION

EG-71, .22 L.R.R.F., Tube Feed, *Modern* ... 100 150 145

EG-712, .22 L.R.R.F., Tube Feed, *Modern* ... 125 175 155

EG-712 L, .22 L.R.R.F., Tube Feed, Octagon Barrel, Nickel Silver Receiver, *Modern* ... 200 275 240

EG-73, .22 W.M.R., Tube Feed, *Modern* ... 150 200 160

RIFLE, SEMI-AUTOMATIC

EM-1, .22 L.R.R.R., Clip Fed, *Modern* ... 125 150 140

EGM-1, .22 L.R.R.F., Clip Fed, *Modern* ... 125 150 140

ESG22, .22 L.R.R.F., Clip Fed, *Modern* ... 125 150 150

ESG22, .22 W.M.R., Clip Fed, *Modern* ... 175 250 240

ESSEX Made by Crescent for Belknap Hardware Co. Louisville, Ky.

SHOTGUN, DOUBLE BARREL, SIDE-BY-SIDE

Various Gauges, Outside Hammers, Damascus Barrel, *Modern* ... 100 150 155

Various Gauges, Hammerless, Steel Barrel, *Modern* ... 125 175 185

Various Gauges, Hammerless, Damascus Barrel, *Modern* ... 100 150 155

Various Gauges, Outside Hammers, Steel Barrel, *Modern* ... 125 175 180

SHOTGUN, SINGLESHOT

Various Gauges, Hammer, Steel Barrel, *Modern* ... 50 75 75

ESSEX Made by Stevens Arms.

RIFLE, BOLT ACTION

Model 50, .22 L.R.R.F., Singleshot, Takedown, *Modern* ... 25 50 45

Model 53, .22 L.R.R.F., Singleshot, Takedown, *Modern* ... 25 50 45

Model 56 Buckhorn, .22 L.R.R.F., 5 Shot Clip, Open Rear Sight, *Modern* ... 25 50 55

	V.G.	Exc.	Prior Edition Exc. Value

SHOTGUN, DOUBLE BARREL, SIDE-BY-SIDE

	V.G.	Exc.	Prior Edition Exc. Value
Model 515, Various Gauges, Hammerless, *Modern*	$100	$150	$160

ESSEX Makers of pistol frames in Island Pond, Vt.
HANDGUN, SEMI-AUTOMATIC

Colt M1911 Copy, .45 ACP, Parts Gun, *Modern*	200	275	260

ESTEVA, PEDRO Spain, c. 1740.
HANDGUN, FLINTLOCK

Pair, Belt Pistol, Silver Inlay, Silver Furniture, Engraved, Half-Octagon Barrel, *Antique*	7,500	9,000	9,000

EVANS RIFLE MFG. CO. Mechanic Falls, Maine 1868–1880.
RIFLE, LEVER ACTION

Old Model, .44 C.F., Upper Buttstock Only, Tube Feed, Sporting Rifle, *Antique*	950	1,100	1,050
New Model, .44 C.F., Tube Feed, Dust Cover, Sporting Rifle, *Antique*	500	600	800
New Model, .44 C.F., Tube Feed, Dust Cover, Military Style, *Antique*	900	1,100	1,000
New Model, .44 C.F., Tube Feed, Dust Cover, Carbine, *Antique*	750	900	850

EVANS, STEPHEN Valley Forge, Pa. 1742–1797. See Kentucky Rifles and U. S. Military.

EVANS, WILLIAM London, England 1883–1900.
SHOTGUN, DOUBLE BARREL, SIDE-BY-SIDE

Pair, 12 Gauge, Double Trigger, Plain, Cased *Modern*	5,000	6,000	5,700
Pair, 12 Gauge, Double Trigger, Straight Grip, Cased, *Modern*	6,000	7,000	6,700

EXCAM Importers, Hialeah, Fla. Also see Erma and Tanarmi.
HANDGUN, DOUBLE BARREL, OVER-UNDER

TA-38, .38 Special, 2 Shot, Derringer, *Modern*	50	75	55

HANDGUN, REVOLVER

Buffalo Scout TA-76, .22 LR/.22 WMR Combo, Western Style, Single Action, *Modern*	50	75	55
Buffalo Scout TA-76, .22 L.R.R.F., Western Style, Single Action, *Modern*	50	75	45
Buffalo Scout TA-22, .22LR/.22 WMR Combo, Western Style, Single Action, Brass Backstrap, *Modern*	50	75	65

	V.G.	Exc.	Prior Edition Exc. Value
Buffalo Scout TA-22, .22LR/.22 WMR Combo, Western Style, Single Action, Brass Backstrap, Target Sights, *Modern*	$50	$75	$75
Buffalo Scout TA-22, .22 L.R.R.F., Western Style, Single Action, Brass Backstrap, *Modern*	25	50	50
Warrior, .22 L.R.R.F., Double Action, Blue, Vent Rib, *Modern*	50	75	75
Warrior, .22LR/.22 WMR Combo, Double Action, Blue, Vent Rib, *Modern*	100	125	110
Warrior, .38 Spec., Double Action, Blue, Vent Rib, Target Sights, *Modern*	75	100	100
Warrior, .357 Mag., Double Action, Blue, Vent Rib, Target Sights, *Modern*	100	150	140

HANDGUN, SEMI-AUTOMATIC

	V.G.	Exc.	Prior
GT-22, .22 L.R.R.F., Clip Fed, *Modern*	75	150	100
GT-26, .25 ACP, Clip Fed, Steel Frame, *Modern*	25	50	55
GT-27, .25 ACP, Clip Fed, *Modern*	25	50	45
GT-27, .25 ACP, Clip Fed, Steel Frame, *Modern*	50	75	110
GT-32, .32 ACP, Clip Fed, *Modern*	125	150	110
GT-380, .380 ACP, Clip Fed, *Modern*	100	125	120
GT-380, .25 ACP, Clip Fed, Engraved, *Modern*	125	150	145
GT-32, .32 ACP, Clip Fed, 12 Shot, *Modern*	125	150	140
GT-380, .380 ACP, Clip Fed, 11 Short, *Modern*	125	150	155
RX-22, .22 L.R.R.F., Clip Fed, *Modern*	100	125	110

EXCELSIOR Made by Norwich Pistol Co., c. 1880.

HANDGUN, REVOLVER

	V.G.	Exc.	Prior
.32 Short R.F., 5 Shot, Spur Trigger, Solid Frame, Single Action, *Antique*	125	175	165

EXCELSIOR Made in Italy.

SHOTGUN, DOUBLE BARREL, SIDE-BY-SIDE

	V.G.	Exc.	Prior
Super 88, 12 Ga. Mag. 3", Boxlock, Checkered Stock, *Modern*	275	350	335

EXPRESS Made by Bacon Arms Co., c. 1880.

HANDGUN, REVOLVER

	V.G.	Exc.	Prior
.22 Short R.F., 7 Shot, Spur Trigger, Solid Frame, Single Action, *Antique*	125	175	165

EXPRESS Tomas de Urizar y Cia., Eibar, Spain, c. 1905–1921

HANDGUN, SEMI-AUTOMATIC

	V.G.	Exc.	Prior
Type 1, .25 ACP, Clip Fed, Fixed Ribbed Barrel, *Curio*	200	250	245
Type 1, .32 ACP, Clip Fed, 4" Fixed Barrel, *Curio*	175	225	235

	V.G.	Exc.	Prior Edition Exc. Value
Type 2, .25 ACP, Clip Fed, Hammerless, Eibar Style, *Curio*............	$100	$125	$135
Type 2, .32 ACP, Clip Fed, Hammerless, Eibar Style, *Curio*...........	100	150	140
Type 3, .25 ACP, Clip Fed, Hammer, Eibar Style, *Curio*................	100	150	145
Type 3, .32 ACP, Clip Fed, Hammer, Eibar Style, *Curio*................	100	150	150

F

	V.G.	Exc.	Prior Edition Exc. Value

FABRIQUE D'ARMES DE GUERRE Spain, unknown maker, c. 1900.

HANDGUN, SEMI-AUTOMATIC

	V.G.	Exc.	Prior Edition Exc. Value
Paramount, .25 ACP, Clip Fed, *Curio*	$125	$150	$135

FABRIQUE D'ARMES DE GUERRE DE GRAND PRECISION
Tradename used by Etxezagarra & Abitua, Eibar, Spain, c. 1920.

HANDGUN, SEMI-AUTOMATIC

	V.G.	Exc.	Prior Edition Exc. Value
Bulwak, .25 ACP, Clip Fed, *Modern*	125	150	145
Colonial, .25 ACP, Clip Fed, *Modern*	150	175	155
Colonial, .32 ACP, Clip Fed, *Modern*	175	200	190
Helvece, .25 ACP, Clip Fed, *Modern*	125	150	135
Jupiter, .32 ACP, Clip Fed, *Modern*	125	150	150
Libia, .32 ACP, Clip Fed, *Modern*	150	175	175
Looking Glass, .32 ACP, Clip Fed, *Modern*	150	175	155
Looking Glass, .32 ACP, Clip Fed, Grip Safety, *Modern*	175	200	185
Trust, .25 ACP, Clip Fed, *Modern*	125	150	145

FALCON

HANDGUN, SEMI-AUTOMATIC

	V.G.	Exc.	Prior Edition Exc. Value
.25 ACP, Clip Fed, Blue, *Modern*	50	75	80

FAMARS Brescia, Italy.

SHOTGUN, DOUBLE BARREL, SIDE-BY-SIDE

	V.G.	Exc.	Prior Edition Exc. Value
Hammer Gun, Various Gauges, Automatic Ejector, Fancy Wood, Fancy Engraving, Double Trigger, *Modern*	7,000	7,500	6,750
Sidelock Gun, Various Gauges, Automatic Ejector, Double Trigger, Fancy Engraving, Fancy Wood, *Modern*	8,500	10,000	9,975

FARNOT, FRANK Lancaster, Pa. 1779–1783. See Kentucky Rifles and Pistols.

FARNOT, FREDERICK Lancaster, Pa. 1779–1782. See Kentucky Rifles and Pistols.

FARROW ARMS CO. Holyoke, Mass. Established by William Farrow 1878–1885. Became Farrow Arms Co. About 1885 and moved to Mason, Tenn. in 1904, then to Washington, D.C. in 1904 and remained in business until 1917.

RIFLE, SINGLESHOT

	V.G.	Exc.	Value
#1, .30 Long R.F., Target Rifle, Octagon Barrel, Target Sights, Fancy Wood, *Antique*	$2,500	$3,500	$3,000
#2, .30 Long R.F., Target Rifle, Octagon Barrel, Target Sights, *Antique*	2,000	2,500	2,100

FAST Echave, Arizmendi y Cia, Eibar, Spain.

HANDGUN, SEMI-AUTOMATIC

	V.G.	Exc.	Value
Model 221, .22 L.R.R.F., Clip Fed, Blue, *Modern*	95	150	150
Model 221, .22 L.R.R.F., Clip Fed, Chrome, *Modern*	150	175	160
Model 631, .25 ACP, Clip Fed, Blue, *Modern*	125	150	140
Model 631, .25 ACP, Clip Fed, Chrome, *Modern*	125	150	145
Model 761, .32 ACP, Clip Fed, Blue, *Modern*	150	175	160
Model 761, .32 ACP, Clip Fed, Chrome, *Modern*	150	175	170
Model 901, .380 ACP, Clip Fed, Blue, *Modern*	150	175	165
Model 901, .380 ACP, Clip Fed, Chrome, *Modern*	150	175	185

FAULTLESS GOOSE GUN Made by Crescent for John M. Smythe Hdw. Co., Chicago, Ill.

SHOTGUN, DOUBLE BARREL, SIDE-BY-SIDE

	V.G.	Exc.	Value
Various Gauges, Outside Hammers, Damascus Barrel, *Modern*	125	175	155
Various Gauges, Hammerless, Steel Barrel, *Modern*	150	200	185
Various Gauges, Hammerless, Damascus Barrel, *Modern*	125	175	155
Various Gauges, Outside Hammers, Steel Barrel, *Modern*	150	200	180

SHOTGUN, SINGLESHOT

	V.G.	Exc.	Value
Various Gauges, Hammer, Steel Barrel, *Modern*	75	100	75

FAVORITE Made by Johnson-Bye Co., c. 1874–1884.

HANDGUN, REVOLVER

	V.G.	Exc.	Value
#1, .22 Short R.F., 7 Shot, Spur Trigger, Solid Frame, Single Action, *Antique*	125	175	165

	V.G.	Exc.	Prior Edition Exc. Value
#2, .32 Short R.F., 5 Shot, Spur Trigger, Solid Frame, Single Action, *Antique*	$125	$175	$170
#3, .38 Short R.F., 5 Shot, Spur Trigger, Solid Frame, Single Action, *Antique*	150	200	190
#4, .41 Short R.F., 5 Shot, Spur Trigger, Solid Frame, Single Action, *Antique*	175	225	210

FAVORITE NAVY Made by Johnson-Bye Co., c. 1874–1884.

HANDGUN, REVOLVER

	V.G.	Exc.	Prior Edition Exc. Value
.44 Short R.F., 5 Shot, Spur Trigger, Solid Frame, Single Action, *Antique*	250	300	290

FAY, HENRY C. Lancaster, Mass., c. 1837.

RIFLE, PERCUSSION

	V.G.	Exc.	Prior Edition Exc. Value
.58, Military, *Antique*	2,750	3,500	2,875

FECHT, G. VAN DER Berlin, Germany, c. 1733.

RIFLE, FLINTLOCK

	V.G.	Exc.	Prior Edition Exc. Value
Yaeger, Half-Octagon Barrel, Brass Furniture, Engraved, Carved, *Antique*	4,500	5,000	4,875

FEDERAL ARMS Made by Meriden Firearms, sold by Sears-Roebuck.

HANDGUN, REVOLVER

	V.G.	Exc.	Prior Edition Exc. Value
.32 S & W, 5 Shot, Double Action, Top Break, *Modern*	75	100	95
.38 S & W, 5 Shot, Double Action, Top Break, *Modern*	75	100	100

FEMARU Made by Femaru Fegyver es Gepgyar (Fegyvergyar) Pre-War; Post War Made by Femaru es Szerszamgepgyar, N.V., Budapest, Hungary. Also see Frommer, Hungarian Military.

HANDGUN, SEMI-AUTOMATIC

	V.G.	Exc.	Prior Edition Exc. Value
M 29, .380 ACP, Clip Fed, Military, *Curio*	175	225	220
M 37, .380 ACP, Clip Fed, Military, *Modern*	200	250	235
M 37, .32 ACP, Clip Fed, Nazi-Proofed, *Modern*	200	250	230
M 37, .380 ACP, Clip Fed, Nazi-Proofed, *Modern*	225	275	270

FENNO Lancaster Pa. 1790–1800. See Kentucky Rifles and Pistols.

FERLACH Genossenschaft der Buchsenmachermeister, Ferlach, Austria.

RIFLE, DOUBLE BARREL, SIDE-BY-SIDE

	V.G.	Exc.	Prior Edition Exc. Value
Standard Grade, Various Calibers, Boxlock, Engraved, Checkered Stock, Fancy Wood, *Modern*	3,000	3,500	3,000

	V.G.	Exc.	Prior Edition Exc. Value

Standard Grade, Various Calibers, Sidelock, Engraved, Checkered Stock, Fancy Wood, *Modern* $4,500 $5,000 $4,500

FERREE, JACOB Lancaster, Pa. 1774–1784, see Kentucky Rifles and U.S. Military.

FESIG, CONRAD Reading, Pa. 1779–1790, see Kentucky Rifles and Pistols.

FIALA Made for Fiala Arms & Equipment Co. by Blakslee Forging Co., New Haven, Conn.

HANDGUN, MANUAL REPEATER

	V.G.	Exc.	Prior
.22 L.R.R.F., Clip Fed, Target Pistol, *Curio*	350	400	395
.22 L.R.R.F., Clip Fed, Target Pistol, With Shoulder Stock, 20" Barrel, 3" Barrel, Cased, *Curio*	850	1,000	665

F.I.E. Firearms Import & Export Corp., Miami, Fla.

HANDGUN, DOUBLE BARREL, OVER-UNDER

	V.G.	Exc.	Prior
.38 S & W, Derringer, *Modern*	50	50	50
.38 Special, Derringer, *Modern*	50	75	55

HANDGUN, FLINTLOCK

	V.G.	Exc.	Prior
Kentucky, .44, Belt Pistol, Reproduction, *Antique*	25	50	50
Kentucky, .44, Belt Pistol, Engraved, Reproduction, *Antique*	25	50	55
Tower, .69, *Antique*	25	25	30

HANDGUN, PERCUSSION

	V.G.	Exc.	Prior
Baby Dragoon, .31, Revolver, Reproduction, *Antique*	25	50	40
Baby Dragoon, .31, Revolver, Engraved, Reproduction, *Antique*	25	50	45
Kentucky, .44, Belt Pistol, Reproduction, *Antique*	25	50	45
Kentucky, .44, Belt Pistol, Engraved, Reproduction, *Antique*	25	50	50
Navy, .36, Revolver, Reproduction, *Antique*	25	25	35
Navy, .36, Revolver, Engraved, Reproduction, *Antique*	25	50	40
Navy, .44, Revolver, Reproduction, *Antique*	25	50	40
Navy, .44, Revolver, Engraved, Reproduction, *Antique*	25	50	45
Remington, .36, Revolver, Reproduction, *Antique*	25	50	45
Remington, .36, Revolver, Engraved, Reproduction, *Antique*	25	50	55
Remington, .44, Revolver, Reproduction, *Antique*	25	50	45
Remington, .44, Revolver, Engraved, Reproduction, *Antique*	25	50	55

HANDGUN, REVOLVER

	V.G.	Exc.	Prior
Arminius, .22 L.R.R.F., Double Action, Swing-out Cylinder, Fixed Sights, Chrome, *Modern*	50	75	70

	V.G.	Exc.	Prior Edition Exc. Value
Arminius, .22 LR/.22 WMR Combo, Double Action, Swing-out Cylinder, Fixed Sights, Chrome, *Modern*	$75	$100	$90
Arminius, .22 LR/.22 WMR Combo, Double Action, Swing-out Cylinder, Adjustable Sights, Chrome, *Modern*	75	100	95
Arminius, .22 LR/.22 WMR Combo, Double Action, Swing-out Cylinder, Adjustable Sights, Blue, *Modern*	75	100	90
Arminius, .22 LR/.22 WMR Combo, Double Action, Swing-out Cylinder, Adjustable Sights, Blue, Target, *Modern*	50	75	75
Arminius, .22 L.R.R.F., Double Action, Swing-out Cylinder, Adjustable Sights, Blue, *Modern*	50	75	70
Arminius, .22 L.R.R.F., Double Action, Swing-out Cylinder, Adjustable Sights, Chrome, *Modern*	75	100	80
Arminius, .22 L.R.R.F., Double Action, Swing-out Cylinder, Adjustable Sights, Blue, Target, *Modern*	75	100	80
Arminius, .22 L.R.R.F., Double Action, Swing-out Cylinder, Adjustable Sights, Chrome, Target, *Modern*	75	100	80
Arminius, .32 S & W, Double Action, Swing-out Cylinder, Adjustable Sights, Blue, Target, *Modern*	75	100	80
Arminius, .32 S & W, Double Action, Swing-out Cylinder, Adjustable Sights, Chrome, Target, *Modern*	75	100	80
Arminius, .357 Magnum, Double Action, Swing-out Cylinder, Adjustable Sights, Chrome, Target, *Modern*	100	125	115
Arminius, .357 Magnum, Double Action, Swing-out Cylinder, Adjustable Sights, Blue, Target, *Modern*	100	125	115
Arminius, .38 Special, Double Action, Swing-out Cylinder, Adjustable Sights, Blue, Target, *Modern*	75	100	80
Arminius, .38 Special, Double Action, Swing-out Cylinder, Adjustable Sights, Chrome Target, *Modern*	75	100	80
Arminius, .38 Special, Double Action, Swing-out Cylinder, Blue, *Modern*	50	75	65
Arminius, .38 Special, Double Action, Swing-out Cylinder, Chrome, *Modern*	50	75	65
Buffalo Scout, .22LR/.22 WMR Combo, Single Action, Western Style, *Modern*	25	50	55
Buffalo, .22 L.R.R.F., Single Action, Western Style, *Modern*	25	50	45
Guardian, .22 L.R.R.F., Double Action, Swing-out Cylinder, *Modern*	25	50	40
Guardian, .22 L.R.R.F., Double Action, Swing-out Cylinder, Chrome, *Modern*	25	50	45
Guardian, .32 S & W, Double Action, Swing-out Cylinder, *Modern*	25	50	40
Guardian, .32 S & W, Double Action, Swing-out Cylinder, Chrome, *Modern*	25	50	45
Hombre, .357 Mag, Single Action, Western Style, Steel Frame, *Modern*	100	125	115

	V.G.	Exc.	Prior Edition Exc. Value
Hombre, .44 Mag, Single Action, Western Style, Steel Frame, *Modern*	$125	$150	$135
Hombre, .45 L.C., Single Action, Western Style, Steel Frame, *Modern*	100	125	115
Legend, .22LR/.22 WMR Combo, Single Action, Western Style, Steel Frame, *Modern*	50	75	70
Legend, .22 L.R.R.F., Single Action, Western Style, Steel Frame, *Modern*	50	75	50
Texas Ranger, .22LR/.22 WMR Combo, Single Action, Western Style, Steel Frame, *Modern*	25	50	45
Titan Tiger, .38 Spec., Double Action, Blue, *Modern*	50	75	75

HANDGUN, SEMI-AUTOMATIC

	V.G.	Exc.	Prior Edition Exc. Value
Best, .25 ACP, Hammer, Steel Frame, Blue, *Modern*	75	100	100
Best, .32 ACP, Hammer, Steel Frame, Blue, *Modern*	100	125	110
Guardian, .25 ACP, Hammer, Blue, *Modern*	25	50	35
Guardian, .25 ACP, Hammer, Chrome, *Modern*	25	50	35
Guardian, .25 ACP, Hammer, Gold Plated, *Modern*	25	50	40
Interdynamics KG-9, 9mm Luger, Clip Fed, *Modern*	325	350	325
Interdynamics Mini-99, 9mm Luger, Clip Fed, *Modern*	200	225	200
Titan, .25 ACP, Hammer, Blue, *Modern*	25	50	35
Titan, .25 ACP, Hammer, Chrome, *Modern*	25	50	40
Super Titan II, .32 ACP, Hammer, Steel Frame, Blue, 13 Shot, *Modern*	100	125	130
Titan, .32 ACP, Hammer, Steel Frame, Blue, *Modern*	75	100	80
Titan, .32 ACP, Hammer, Steel Frame, Chrome, *Modern*	75	100	85
Titan, .32 ACP, Hammer, Steel Frame, Engraved, Chrome, *Modern*	75	100	95
Titan, .32 ACP, Hammer, Steel Frame, Engraved, Blue, *Modern*	75	100	90
Super Titan II, .380 ACP, Hammer, Steel Frame, Blue, 12 Shot, *Modern*	125	150	140
Titan, .380 ACP, Hammer, Steel Frame Blue, *Modern*	75	100	100
Titan, .380 ACP, Hammer, Steel Frame, Chrome, *Modern*	100	125	115
Titan, .380 ACP, Hammer, Steel Frame, Engraved, Blue, *Modern*	125	150	135
Titan, .380 ACP, Hammer, Steel Frame, Engraved, Chrome, *Modern*	125	150	140
TZ-75, 9mm Luger, Clip Fed, Double Action, Hammer, Adjustable Sights, Wood Grips, *Modern*	225	250	235

RIFLE, FLINTLOCK

	V.G.	Exc.	Prior Edition Exc. Value
Kentucky, .45, Reproduction, *Antique*	50	75	85
Kentucky, .45, Engraved, Reproduction, *Antique*	50	75	85

RIFLE, PERCUSSION

	V.G.	Exc.	Prior Edition Exc. Value
Berdan, .45, Reproduction, *Antique*	50	75	80

	V.G.	Exc.	Prior Edition Exc. Value
Kentucky, .45 Reproduction, *Antique*	$50	$75	$80
Kentucky, .45, Engraved, Reproduction, *Antique*	50	75	80
Zoave, .58, Reproduction, *Antique*	75	100	95

COMBINATION WEAPON, OVER-UNDER

Combo, 30/30–20 Ga., *Modern*	75	100	75

SHOTGUN, DOUBLE BARREL, OVER-UNDER

OU, 12 and 20 Ga., Field Grade, Vent Rib, *Modern*	150	175	165
OU 12 T, 12 Ga., Trap Grade, Vent Rib, *Modern*	150	175	175
OU-S, 12 and 20 Ga., Skeet Grade, Vent Rib, *Modern*	150	175	175

SHOTGUN, DOUBLE BARREL, SIDE-BY-SIDE

DB, Various Gauges, Hammerless, *Modern*	75	125	125
DB Riot, Various Gauges, Hammerless, *Modern*	75	150	125
Brute, Various Gauges, Short Barrels, Short Stock, *Modern*	100	175	155

SHOTGUN, SINGLESHOT

SB 40, 12 Ga., Hammer, Button Break, *Modern*	25	50	45
SB 41, 20 Ga., Hammer, Button Break, *Modern*	25	50	45
SB 42, .410 Ga., Hammer, Button Break, *Modern*	25	50	45
SB Youth, Various Gauges, Hammer, *Modern*	25	50	35
SB 12 16 20 .410, Various Gauges, Hammer, *Modern*	25	50	40
S.O.B., 12 and 20 Gauges, Short Barrel, Short Stock, *Modern*	25	50	55

FIEHL & WEEKS FIRE ARMS MFG. CO. Philadelphia, Pa., c. 1895.

HANDGUN, REVOLVER

.32 S & W, 5 Shot, Top Break, Hammerless, Double Action, *Modern*	75	100	100

FIEL Erquiaga, Muguruzu y Cia., Eibar, Spain, c., 1920.

HANDGUN, SEMI-AUTOMATIC

Fiel #1, .25 ACP, Clip Fed, Eibar Style, *Curio*	125	150	135
Fiel #1, .32 ACP, Clip Fed, Eibar Style, *Curio*	125	150	145
Fiel #2, .25 ACP, Clip Fed, Breech Bolt, *Curio*	175	225	210

FIGTHORN, ANDREW Reading, Pa. 1779–1790, see Kentucky Rifles.

FINNISH LION Made by Valmet, Jyvaskyla, Finland.

RIFLE, BOLT ACTION

Standard, .22 L.R.R.F., Singleshot, Target Rifle, Target Stock, Target Sights, U.I.T. Rifle, *Modern*	225	275	450

	V.G.	Exc.	Prior Edition Exc. Value
Match, .22 L.R.R.F., Singleshot, Target Rifle, Thumbhole Stock, Target Sights, *Modern*	$350	$400	$540
Champion, .22 L.R.R.F., Singleshot, Free Rifle, Thumbhole Stock, Target Sights, Heavy Barrel, *Modern*..	450	500	625

FIREARMS, CUSTOM MADE
This category covers some of the myriad special firearms that are built to an individual's specifications by a competent gunsmith, and not by the original factory. Most firearms in this class will appeal only to a person who happens to want the same special features, and because of this many of these guns will sell for less than the cost of the conversion.

HANDGUN, REVOLVER

P.P.C. Conversion, .38 Special, Heavy Barrel, Rib with Target Sights, Target Trigger, Target Grips, *Modern*	400	300
"F.B.I." Conversion, .38 Special, Cut Trigger Guard, Spurless Hammer, Short Barrel, *Modern*	350	240
Recoil Compensation Devices or Ports, Add **$25.00–$45.00**		

HANDGUN, SEMI-AUTOMATIC

M1911A1, Double Action Conversion, Add **$95.00–$175.00**		
M1911A1, I.P.S.C. Conversion, Extended Trigger Guard, Ambidextrous Safety, Special Slide Release, Ported, Target Sights, Extended Grip Safety, *Modern*..	500	460
M1911A1, Combat Conversion, Extended Trigger Guard, Ambidextrous Safety, Special Slide Release, Ported, Combat Sights, *Modern*..	450	425

HANDGUN, SINGLESHOT

Silhouette Pistol, Various Calibers, Bolt Action, Thumbhole Stock, Target Sights, Target Trigger, *Modern*...	450	400

HANDGUN, PERCUSSION

Target Revolver, Various Calibers, Tuned, Target Sights, Reproduction, *Antique*	200	150

RIFLE, BOLT ACTION

Sporting Rifle, Various Calibers, Checkered Stock, Recoil Pad, Simple Military Conversion, *Modern*..	175	145
Sporting Rifle, Various Calibers, Fancy Wood, Recoil Pad, Fancy Military Conversion, *Modern*	450	400
Sporting Rifle, Various Calibers, Plain Stock, Commercial Parts, *Modern*..	200	165
Sporting Rifle, Various Calibers, Fancy Stock, High Quality Commercial Parts, Fancy Checkering, Stock Inlays, *Modern*...........	1,100	975
Sporting Rifle, Various Calibers, Fancy Stock, High Quality Commercial Parts, Fancy Checkering, Stock Inlays, Engraved, *Modern*..	1,750	1,500
Sporting Rifle, Various Calibers, Fancy Stock, High Quality Commercial Parts, Fancy Checkering, Stock Inlays, Engraved, Gold Inlays, *Modern*..	3,000	2,500

	V.G.	Exc.	Prior Edition Exc. Value
Sporting Rifle, Various Calibers, Mauser 1871 Action, Checkered Stock, *Antique*		$300	$265

RIFLE, SINGLESHOT

	V.G.	Exc.	Prior Edition Exc. Value
Target Rifle, Centerfire Calibers, Plain, Target Sights, Built on Various Bolt Actions, *Modern*		500	390
Target Rifle, Centerfire Calibers, Plain, Target Sights, Built on Various Moving Block Actions, *Modern*		350	290
Target Rifle, Centerfire Calibers, Fancy, Target Sights, Built on Various Moving Block Actions, *Modern*		500	425
Target Rifle, Rimfire Calibers, Plain, Target Sights, Built on Various Moving Block Actions, *Modern*		300	265

SHOTGUN, SLIDE ACTION

	V.G.	Exc.	Prior Edition Exc. Value
Combat Conversion, 12 Ga., Short Barrel, Extended Magazine Tube, Folding Stock, Rifle Sights, *Modern*		350	275
Competition Conversion, Various Gauges, High Rib, Recoil Reducer in Stock, Fancy Wood, *Modern*		450	375

SHOTGUN, DOUBLE BARREL, OVER-UNDER

Trap Conversion, 12 Ga., Recoil Reducer in Stock, Release Triggers, Throated Chambers, Trap Pad, Add **$275.00–$400.00**

FIREARMS CO. LTD. Made in England for Mandall Shooting Supplies.

RIFLE, BOLT ACTION

	V.G.	Exc.	Prior Edition Exc. Value
Alpine Standard, Various Calibers, Checkered Stock, Recoil Pad, Open Rear Sight, *Modern*	250	300	285
Alpine Custom, Various Calibers, Checkered Stock, Recoil Pad, Open Rear Sight *Modern*	275	325	320

FIREARMS INTERNATIONAL Washington, D.C.

HANDGUN, REVOLVER

	V.G.	Exc.	Prior Edition Exc. Value
Regent, .22 L.R.R.F., 8 Shot, Various Barrel Lengths, Blue, *Modern*	75	100	60
Regent, .22 L.R.R.F., 7 Shot, Various Barrel Lengths, Blue, *Modern*	75	100	65

HANDGUN, SEMI-AUTOMATIC

	V.G.	Exc.	Prior Edition Exc. Value
Combo, .22 L.R.R.F., Unique Model L Pistol with Conversion Kit for Stocked Rifle, *Modern*	125	150	140
Model D, .380 ACP, Clip Fed. Adjustable Sights, Blue, *Modern*	125	175	145
Model D, .380 ACP, Clip Fed, Adjustable Sights, Chrome, *Modern*	150	175	155
Model D, .380 ACP, Clip Fed, Adjustable Sights, Matt Blue, *Modern*	125	175	145

	V.G.	Exc.	Prior Edition Exc. Value

SHOTGUN, DOUBLE BARREL, SIDE-BY-SIDE

Model 400, Various Gauges, Single Trigger, Checkered Stock, *Modern* ... $175 / $225 / $215

Model 400E, Various Gauges, Single Selective Trigger, Checkered Stock, Selective Ejector, Vent Rib, *Modern* ... 225 / 275 / 265

Model 400E, Various Gauges, Single Selective Trigger, Selective Ejector, *Modern* ... 200 / 250 / 240

FIREARMS SPECIALTIES Owosso, Mich., c. 1972.

HANDGUN, REVOLVER

.45/70 Custom Revolver, Brass Frame, Single Action, Western Style, *Modern* ... 500 / 550 / 575

FIREBIRD Made by Femaru for German exporter for U.S. sales.

HANDGUN, SEMI-AUTOMATIC

Tokagypt Type, 9mm Luger, Clip Fed, Blue, *Modern* ... 400 / 600 / 600

FITCH & WALDO New York City, c. 1862–67.

HANDGUN, REVOLVER

Pocket Model, .31, 5 Shot, *Antique* ... 225 / 275 / 250

FLINTLOCK, UNKNOWN MAKER Also see Miquelet-Lock, Unknown Maker and Snaphaunce, Unknown Maker.

HANDGUN, FLINTLOCK

.28, English, Pocket Pistol, Queen Anne Style, Box Lock, Screw Barrel, Plain, *Antique* ... 550 / 450

.40, India Herdsman Pistol, Long Tapered Round Barrel, Silver Furniture, *Antique* ... 650 / 635

Fitch & Waldo Pocket Revolver, .31 Caliber

	V.G.	Exc.	Prior Edition Exc. Value
.45, French, Mid-1700's, Screw Barrel, Long Cannon Barrel, Silver Furniture, *Antique*		$1,500	$1,250
.60, Continental, Early 1700's, Holster Pistol, Half-Octagon Barrel, Engraved, High Quality, *Antique*		2,500	2,300
.60, Oval Bore, Box Lock, Pocket Pistol, Steel Furniture, *Antique*		950	795
.62, Crantham English, Holster Pistol, Brass Furniture, Plain, *Antique*		650	420
.63, Spanish, Mid-1600's, Holster Pistol, Silver Inlay, Engraved, *Antique*		4,500	3,500
.68, Tower, Continental, Plain, *Antique*		400	325
.65, Arabian, Holster Pistol, Flared, Round Barrel, Low Quality, *Antique*		400	250
English Lock, mid-1600's, Military, Holster Pistol, Iron Mounts, Plain, *Antique*		5,000	—
English, Early 1700's, Pocket Pistol, Queen Anne Style, Box Lock, Screw Barrel, All Metal, *Antique*		750	550
English, Early 1700's, Pocket Pistol, Box Lock, Double Barrel, Screw Barrel, Low Quality, *Antique*		700	525
English, Mid-1600's, Button Triger, Brass Barrel, Octagon Fishtail Butt, *Antique*		3,000	2,500
French Officer's Type, c. 1650, Steel Furniture, Rifled, *Antique*		2,500	2,300
French Sedan Mid-1600's, Long Screw Barrel, Rifled, Plain, *Antique*		3,000	2,500

RIFLE, FLINTLOCK

	V.G.	Exc.	Prior Edition Exc. Value
.64, Continental, Carbine, Musket, Brass Furniture, *Antique*		650	495
.72, Continental, 1650, Musket, Brass Furniture, Plain, *Antique*		1,200	975

SHOTGUN, FLINTLOCK

	V.G.	Exc.	Prior Edition Exc. Value
.65, American Hudson Valley, *Antique*		1,500	1,250

F.N. Fabrique Nationale, Herstal, Belgium from 1889. Also see Browning, Belgian Military.

RIFLE, BOLT ACTION

	V.G.	Exc.	Prior Edition Exc. Value
Model 1925, .22 L.R.R.F., Singleshot, *Modern*	50	75	50
Model 1925 Deluxe, .22 L.R.R.F., Singleshot, Checkered Stock, *Modern*	75	100	75
Mauser 98 Military Style, 30/06, Military Finish, Military Stock, Commercial, *Modern*	200	250	210
Mauser 98 Military Style, Various Military Calibers, Military Finish, Military Stock, Commercial, *Modern*	125	150	140
Mauser Deluxe, Various Calibers, Sporting Rifle, Checkered Stock, *Modern*	400	450	410
Mauser Deluxe Presentation, Various Calibers, Sporting Rifle, Fancy Wood, Engraved, *Modern*	650	850	750
Mauser Supreme, Various Calibers, Sporting Rifle, Checkered Stock, *Modern*	475	525	475

	V.G.	Exc.	Prior Edition Exc. Value
Mauser Supreme, Various Calibers, Sporting Rifle, Checkered Stock, Magnum, *Modern*	*$500*	*$500*	*$525*

RIFLE, SEMI-AUTOMATIC

	V.G.	Exc.	Prior Edition Exc. Value
FN FAL, .308 Win., Clip Fed, Commercial, *Modern*	750	950	1,100
FN LAR Competition, .308 Win., Clip Fed, Commercial, Flash Hider, *Modern*	1,250	1,600	1,200
FN LAR Paratrooper, .308 Win., Clip Fed, Commercial, Folding Stock, *Modern*	750	850	1,250
FN LAR Heavy Barrel, .308 Win., Clip Fed, Commercial, Synthetic Stock, Bipod, *Modern*	1,650	1,850	1,425
FN LAR Heavy Barrel, .308 Win., Clip Fed, Commercial, Wood Stock, Bipod, *Modern*	1,750	1,950	1,550
FNC Competition, .223 Rem., Clip Fed, Commercial, Flash Hider, *Modern*	750	825	625
FNC Paratrooper, .223 Rem., Clip Fed, Commercial, Folding Stock, *Modern*	850	925	1,000
Model 1949, 30/06, Clip Fed, Military, *Modern*	350	400	375
Model 1949, 7mm or 8mm Mauser, Clip Fed, Military, *Modern*	250	300	270
M-49 Egyptian, 8mm Mauser, Clip Fed, Military, *Modern*	275	325	285

SHOTGUN, BOLT ACTION

	V.G.	Exc.	Prior
9mm Shotshell, *Modern*	125	150	125

FOLGER, WILLIAM H. Barnsville, Ohio 1830–1854, also See Kentucky Rifles.

FOLK'S GUN WORKS Bryan, Ohio 1860–1891.
RIFLE, SINGLESHOT

	V.G.	Exc.	Prior
.32 L.R.R.F., Side Lever, Octagon Barrel, *Antique*	325	375	365

FONDERSMITH, JOHN Strasburg, Pa. 1749–1801. See Kentucky Rifles, U.S. Military.

FORBES, F.F. Made by Crescent, c. 1900.
SHOTGUN, DOUBLE BARREL, SIDE-BY-SIDE

	V.G.	Exc.	Prior
Various Gauges, Outside Hammers, Damascus Barrel, *Modern*	125	150	155
Various Gauges, Hammerless, Steel Barrel, *Modern*	150	175	185
Various Gauges, Hammerless, Damascus Barrel, *Modern*	125	150	155
Various Gauges, Outside Hammers, Steel Barrel, *Modern*	125	175	180

SHOTGUN, SINGLESHOT

	V.G.	Exc.	Prior
Various Gauges, Hammer, Steel Barrel, *Modern*	50	75	75

Forehand Arms Co., .32 S&W

	V.G.	Exc.	Prior Edition Exc. Value

FOREHAND ARMS CO.

HANDGUN, REVOLVER

	V.G.	Exc.	Prior Edition Exc. Value
.32 S & W, 5 Shot, Double Action, Solid Frame, 2" Barrel, *Antique*	$75	$100	$95
.38 S & W, 5 Shot, Double Action, Solid frame, 2" Barrel, *Antique*	75	100	95
Perfection Automatic, .32 S & W, 5 Shot, Double Action, Top Break, Hammerless, *Antique*	125	150	130
Perfection Automatic, .32 S & W, 5 Shot, Double Action, Top Break, *Antique*	100	125	110

FOREHAND & WADSWORTH Worcester, Mass. Successors and sons-in-law to Ethan Allen 1871–1902. In 1872 the name was changed to Forehand & Wadsworth, in 1890 to Forehand Arms Co.

HANDGUN, REVOLVER

	V.G.	Exc.	Prior Edition Exc. Value
.22 Short R.F., Single Action, Spur Trigger, Solid Frame, Side Hammer, *Antique*	250	300	190
.22 Short R.F., 7 Shot, Single Action, Solid Frame, *Antique*	225	275	150
.30 Short R.F., Single Action, Spur Trigger, Solid Frame, Side Hammer, *Antique*	175	225	175
.32 Short R.F., Single Action, Spur Trigger Solid Frame, Side Hammer, *Antique*	200	250	190
.44 Short R.F., Single Action, Spur Trigger, Solid Frame, Side Hammer, *Antique*	400	550	225
Army, .38 Long R.F., 6 Shot, Single Action, Solid Frame, *Antique*	550	650	525
British Bulldog, .32 S & W, 7 Shot, Double Action, Solid Frame, *Antique*	225	250	95
British Bulldog, .38 S & W, 6 Shot, Double Action, Solid Frame, *Antique*	225	250	95
British Bulldog, .44 S & W, 5 Shot, Double Action, Solid Frame, *Antique*	250	275	120
Bulldog, .38 Long R.F., 5 Shot, Single Action, Solid Frame, 2" Barrel, *Antique*	150	175	150

Forehand & Wadsworth Old Army Model, .44 Caliber

	V.G.	Exc.	Prior Edition Exc. Value
Bulldog, .44 S & W, 5 Shot, Double Action, Solid Frame, 2" Barrel, *Antique*	$125	$200	$120
New Navy, .44 Russian, 6 Shot, Double Action, Solid Frame, 6" Barrel, *Antique*	575	625	525
Old Army, .44 Russian, 6 Shot, Single Action, Solid Frame, 7" Barrel, *Antique*	650	750	420
Pocket Model, .32 S & W Long, 6 Shot, Double Action, Top Break, *Antique*	75	100	95
Russian Model, .32 Short R.F., 5 Shot, Single Action, Solid Frame, Spur Trigger, *Antique*	150	200	195
Swamp Angel, .41 Short R.F., 5 Shot, Single Action, Solid Frame, Spur Trigger, *Antique*	175	200	200
Terror, .32 Short R.F., 5 Shot, Single Action, Solid Frame, Spur Trigger, *Antique*	125	175	165

HANDGUN, SINGLESHOT

	V.G.	Exc.	Prior Edition Exc. Value
.22 Short R.F., Spur Trigger, Side-swing Barrel, *Antique*	250	300	260
.41 Short R.F., Spur Trigger, Side-swing Barrel, *Antique*	400	450	365

FOREVER YOURS Flaig's Lodge, Millvale, Pa.

SHOTGUN, DOUBLE BARREL, OVER-UNDER

	V.G.	Exc.	Prior Edition Exc. Value
Various Gauges, Automatic Ejector, Checkered Stock, Vent Rib, Double Trigger, *Modern*	550	650	640
Various Gauges, Automatic Ejector, Checkered Stock, Vent Rib, Single Trigger, *Modern*	550	700	690

FOULKES, ADAM Easton & Allentown, Pa. 1773–1794. See Kentucky Rifles and U.S. Military.

FOUR ACE CO. Brownsville, Texas.

HANDGUN, SINGLESHOT

Four Ace, Derringer, Presentation Case Add **$10.00–$15.00**

	V.G.	Exc.	Prior Edition Exc. Value
Four Ace Model 200, .22 Short R.F., Derringer, 4 Shot, Spur Trigger, *Modern*	25	50	45

	V.G.	Exc.	Prior Edition Exc. Value
Four Ace Model 200, .22 Short R.F., Derringer, 4 Shot, Spur Trigger, Nickel Plated, Gold Plated, *Modern*	$25	$50	$55
Four Ace Model 202, .22 L.R.R.F., Derringer, 4 Shot, Spur Trigger, Nickel Plated, Gold Plated, *Modern*	50	75	60
Four Ace Model, 202, .22 L.R.R.F., Derringer, 4 Shot, Spur Trigger, *Modern*	25	50	50
Four Ace Model 204, .22 L.R.R.F., Derringer, 4 Shot, Spur Trigger, Stainless Steel, *Modern*	50	75	65
Little Ace Model 300, .22 Short R.F., Derringer, Side-swing Barrel, Spur Trigger, *Modern*	25	50	40

FOX, A.H. GUN CO. Philadelphia, Pa. Formerly Philadelphia Arms Co., now a subsidiary of Savage Arms Co., 1930 to date. Also see Savage Arms Co.

SHOTGUN, DOUBLE BARREL, SIDE-BY-SIDE

Various Gauges, Single Selective Trigger Add $175.00–$295.00

Various Gauges, For Vent Rib Add $175.00–$295.00

Various Gauges, Beavertail Forend Add 10%–15%

Various Gauges, For Single Trigger Add $125.00–$200.00

Various Grades, for 20 Ga. Add 50%–75%

	V.G.	Exc.	Prior
A Grade, Various Gauges, Box Lock, Light Engraving, Checkered Stock, *Modern*	1,150	1,400	750
AE Grade, Various Gauges, Box Lock, Light Engraving, Checkered Stock, Automatic Ejector, *Modern*	1,500	1,700	975
BE Grade, Various Gauges, Box Lock, Engraved, Checkered Stock, Automatic Ejector, *Modern*	2,000	2,500	1,275
CE Grade, Various Gauges, Box Lock, Engraved, Fancy Checkering, Automatic Ejector, *Modern*	2,500	3,000	1,725
DE Grade, Various Gauges, Box Lock, Fancy Engraving, Fancy Checkering, Fancy Wood, Automatic Ejector, *Modern*	7,000	8,000	5,775
FE Grade, Various Gauges, Box Lock, Fancy Engraving, Fancy Checkering, Fancy Wood, Automatic Ejector, *Modern*	14,000	20,000	9,575
HE Grade, 12 and 20 Gauge, Box Lock, Light Engraving, Checkered Stock, Automatic Ejector, *Modern*	2,200	2,500	965
SP Grade, Various Gauges, Box Lock, Checkered Stock, *Modern*	800	1,000	525
SP Grade, Various Gauges, Box Lock, Checkered Stock, Automatic Ejector, *Modern*	900	1,200	575
SP Grade, Various Gauges, Box Lock, Skeet Grade, Checkered Stock, *Modern*	775	875	575
SP Grade, Various Gauges, Box Lock, Skeet Grade, Automatic Ejector, Checkered Stock, *Modern*	750	950	650
Sterlingworth, Various Gauges, Box Lock, Checkered Stock, Hammerless, *Modern*	1,000	1,200	500
Sterlingworth, Various Gauges, Box Lock, Checkered Stock, Hammerless, Automatic Ejector, *Modern*	875	925	650

	V.G.	Exc.	Prior Edition Exc. Value
Sterlingworth, Various Gauges, Box Lock, Skeet Grade, Checkered Stock, *Modern*	$675	$850	$575
Sterlingworth, Various Gauges, Box Lock, Skeet Grade, Checkered Stock, Automatic Ejector, *Modern*	1,250	1,450	820
Sterlingworth Deluxe, Various Gauges, Box Lock, Checkered Stock, Hammerless, Recoil Pad, *Modern*	1,400	1,600	600
Sterlingworth Deluxe, Various Gauges, Box Lock, Checkered Stock, Hammerless, Recoil Pad, Automatic Ejector, *Modern*	1,650	1,850	835
XE Grade, Various Gauges, Box Lock, Fancy Engraving, Fancy Checkering, Fancy Wood, Automatic Ejector, *Modern*	4,500	5,000	2,925

SHOTGUN, SINGLESHOT

	V.G.	Exc.	Prior Edition Exc. Value
JE Grade, 12 Gauge, Trap Grade, Vent Rib, Automatic Ejector, Engraved, Fancy Checkering, *Modern*	1,475	1,775	1,725
KE Grade, 12 Gauge, Trap Grade, Vent Rib, Automatic Ejector, Engraved, Fancy Checkering, *Modern*	2,250	2,550	2,350
LE Grade, 12 Gauge, Trap Grade, Vent Rib, Automatic Ejector, Fancy Engraving, Fancy Checkering, *Modern*	3,000	3,475	3,300
ME Grade, 12 Gauge, Trap Grade, Vent Rib, Automatic Ejector, Fancy Engraving, Fancy Checkering, *Modern*	6,500	7,500	6,900

FOX Foxco Products, Inc. Manchester, Conn. Also see Demro, T.A.C.

RIFLE, SEMI-AUTOMATIC

	V.G.	Exc.	Prior Edition Exc. Value
9mm Luger or .45 ACP, Clip Fed, *Modern*	175	275	250

FRANCAIS France, Made by Manufacture D'Armes Automatiques Francaise.

HANDGUN, SEMI-AUTOMATIC

	V.G.	Exc.	Prior Edition Exc. Value
Prima, .25 ACP, Clip Fed, *Modern*	100	125	145

FRANCHI Brescia, Italy, now imported by F.I.E.

RIFLE, SEMI-AUTOMATIC

	V.G.	Exc.	Prior Edition Exc. Value
Centennial, .22 L.R.R.F., Checkered Stock, Tube Feed, Takedown, *Modern*	225	250	225
Centennial Deluxe, .22 L.R.R.F., Checkered Stock, Tube Feed, Takedown, Light Engraving, *Modern*	300	350	335
Centennial Gallery, .22 Short R.F., Checkered Stock, Tube Feed, Takedown, *Modern*	150	200	210

SHOTGUN, DOUBLE BARREL, OVER-UNDER

	V.G.	Exc.	Prior Edition Exc. Value
Alcione Super, 12, Vent Rib, Single Selective Trigger, Automatic Ejector, Engraved, *Modern*	450	525	500
Alcione Super Deluxe, 12, Vent Rib, Single Selective Trigger, Automatic Ejector, Engraved, *Modern*	857	975	775
Aristocrat, 12 Ga., Field Grade, Automatic Ejectors, Single Selective Trigger, Vent Rib, *Modern*	400	500	600

	V.G.	Exc.	Prior Edition Exc. Value
Aristocrat, 12 Ga., Imperial Grade, Automatic Ejectors, Single Selection Trigger, Vent Rib, *Modern*	$1,800	$2,100	$1,850
Aristocrat, 12 Ga., Monte Carlo Grade, Automatic Ejectors, Single Selective Trigger, Vent Rib, *Modern*	2,500	3,000	2,675
Barrage Skeet, 12 Ga., Vent Rib, Single Selective Trigger, Automatic Ejector, Recoil Pad, *Modern*	900	1,100	945
Barrage Trap, 12 Ga., Vent Rib, Single Selective Trigger, Automatic Ejector, Recoil Pad, *Modern*	900	1,100	945
Dragon Skeet, 12 Ga., Vent Rib, Single Selective Trigger, Automatic Ejector, Recoil Pad, *Modern*	800	950	650
Dragon Trap, 12 Ga., Vent Rib, Single Selective Trigger, Automatic Ejector, Recoil Pad, *Modern*	800	950	650
Falconet Buckskin, 12 and 20 Ga., Vent Rib, Single Selective Trigger, Automatic Ejector, *Modern*	475	550	460
Falconet Ebony, 12 and 20 Ga., Vent Rib, Single Selective Trigger, Automatic Ejector, *Modern*	425	500	435
Falconet Peregrine 400, 12 and 20 Ga., Vent Rib, Single Selective Trigger, Automatic Ejector, *Modern*	575	650	435
Falconet Peregrine 451, 12 and 20 Ga., Vent Rib, Single Selective Trigger, Automatic Ejector, *Modern*	500	600	475
Falconet Pigeon, 12 Ga. Vent Rib, Single Selective Trigger, Automatic Ejector, Fancy Engraving, Fancy Checkering, *Modern*	1,000	1,200	1,400
Falconet Silver, 12 Ga., Vent Rib, Single Selective Trigger, Automatic Ejector, *Modern*	550	625	490
Falconet Super, 12 Ga., Vent Rib, Single Selective Trigger, Automatic Ejector, *Modern*	650	725	515
Falconet Super Deluxe, 12 Ga., Vent Rib, Single Selective Trigger, Automatic Ejector, *Modern*	750	950	700
Model 255, 12 Ga., Vent Rib, Single Selective Trigger, Automatic Ejector, *Modern*	500	525	435
Model 2003, 12 Ga. Trap Grade, Vent Rib, Single Selective Trigger, Automatic Ejector, *Modern*	1,075	1,250	1,100
Model 2005/2, 12 Ga., Trap Grade, Vent Rib, Single Selective Trigger, Automatic Ejector, Extra Shotgun Barrel, *Modern*	2,000	2,250	1,800
Model 2005/3, 12 Ga., Trap Grade, Vent Rib, Single Selective Trigger, Automatic Ejector, Extra Shotgun Barrel, Custom Choke, *Modern*	2,250	2,500	2,150

SHOTGUN, DOUBLE BARREL, SIDE-BY-SIDE

	V.G.	Exc.	Prior Edition Exc. Value
Airone, 12 Ga., Box Lock, Hammerless, Checkered Stock, Automatic Ejector, *Modern*	800	1,000	775
Astore, 12 Ga. Box Lock, Hammerless, Checkered Stock, *Modern*	700	800	600
Astore 5, 12 Ga., Box Lock, Hammerless, Checkered Stock, Light Engraving, *Modern*	1,500	1,700	1,400
Condor, Various Gauges, Sidelock, Engraved, Checkered Stock, Automatic Ejector, *Modern*	5,000	6,000	3,300

	V.G.	Exc.	Prior Edition Exc. Value
Imperial, Various Gauges, Sidelock, Engraved, Checkered Stock, Automatic Ejector, *Modern*	$8,000	$9,000	$4,625
Imperial Monte Carlo #11, Various Gauges, Sidelock, Fancy Engraving, Fancy Checkering, Automatic Ejector, *Modern*	10,000	13,000	9,650
Imperial Monte Carlo Extra, Various Gauges, Sidelock, Fancy Engraving, Fancy Checkering, Automatic Ejector, *Modern*	14,000	16,000	12,250
Imperial Monte Carlo #5, Various Gauges, Sidelock, Fancy Engraving, Fancy Checkering, Automatic Ejector, *Modern*	11,500	12,000	9,950
Imperiales, Various Gauges, Sidelock, Engraved, Checkered Stock, Automatic Ejector, *Modern*	8,000	9,000	4,675

SHOTGUN, SEMI-AUTOMATIC

	V.G.	Exc.	Prior Edition Exc. Value
Dynamic (Heavy), 12 Ga., Plain Barrel, *Modern*	250	325	250
Dynamic (Heavy), 12 Ga., Vent Rib, *Modern*	300	350	255
Dynamic (Heavy), 12 Ga., Skeet Grade, Vent Rib, Checkered Stock, *Modern*	275	375	275
Dynamic (Heavy), 12 Ga., Checkered Stock, Slug, Open Rear Sight, *Modern*	275	375	285
Eldorado, 12 and 20 Ga., Vent Rib, Engraved, Fancy Checkering, Lightweight, *Modern*	350	450	385
Hunter, 12 and 20 Ga., Vent Rib, Engraved, Checkered Stock, Lightweight, *Modern*	400	500	340
Model 500, 12 Ga., Vent Rib, Checkered Stock, Engraved, *Modern*	350	450	325
Model 500, 12 Ga., Vent Rib, Checkered Stock, *Modern*	250	350	250
Slug Gun, 12 and 20 Ga., Open Rear Sight, Sling Swivels, *Modern*	350	450	295
SPAS 12, 12 Gauge, Combat Shotgun, Folding Stock, Rifle Sights, Lightweight, *Modern*	400	500	425
Standard, 12 and 20 Ga., Plain Barrel, Lightweight, Checkered Stock, *Modern*	325	425	275
Standard, 12 and 20 Ga., Solid Rib, Lightweight, Checkered Stock, *Modern*	350	450	270
Standard, 12 and 20 Ga., Vent Rib, Lightweight, Checkered Stock, *Modern*	375	475	295
Standard Magnum, 12 and 20 Gauges, Vent Rib, Lightweight, Checkered Stock, *Modern*	250	350	315
Superange (Heavy), 12 and 20 Gauges, Magnum, Plain Barrel, Checkered Stock, *Modern*	250	350	255
Superange (Heavy), 12 and 20 Gauges, Magnum, Vent Rib, Checkered Stock, *Modern*	375	425	290
Wildfowler (Heavy), 12 and 20 Gauges, Magnum, Vent Rib, Checkered Stock, Engraved, *Modern*	375	450	340

SHOTGUN, SINGLESHOT

	V.G.	Exc.	Prior Edition Exc. Value
Model 2004, 12 Ga., Trap Grade, Vent Rib, Automatic Ejector, *Modern*	1,500	1,800	1,100
Model 3000/2, 12 Ga., Trap Grade, Vent Rib, Automatic Ejector, with Choke Tubes, *Modern*	2,000	2,600	2,050

	V.G.	Exc.	Prior Edition Exc. Value

FRANCI, PIERO INZI Brescia, Italy, c. 1640.

HANDGUN, WHEEL-LOCK

Octagon-Barrel, Dagger Handle Butt, *Antique*	$4,000	$5,000	$3,700

FRANCOTTE, AUGUST Liege, Belgium 1844 to date, also London, England 1877–1893.

HANDGUN, REVOLVER

| Military Style, Various Calibers, Double Action, *Antique* | 100 | 150 | — |
| Bulldog, Various Calibers, Double Action, Solid Frame, *Curio* | 100 | 150 | 125 |

HANDGUN, SEMI-AUTOMATIC

| Vest Pocket, .25 ACP, Clip Fed, *Curio* | 275 | 350 | 325 |

HANDGUN, SINGLESHOT

| Target Pistol, .22 L.R.R.F., Toggle Breech, *Modern* | 300 | 375 | 375 |

RIFLE, DOUBLE BARREL, SIDE-BY-SIDE

| Luxury Double, .458 Win., Sidelock, Hammerless, Double Triggers, Fancy Engraving, *Modern* | 17,500 | 20,000 | 15,000 |

SHOTGUN, DOUBLE BARREL, SIDE-BY-SIDE

A & F #14, Various Gauges, Box Lock, Automatic Ejector, Checkered Stock, Engraved, Hammerless, *Modern*	1,750	2,000	2,975
A & F #20, Various Gauges, Box Lock, Automatic Ejector, Checkered Stock, Engraved, Hammerless, *Modern*	2,700	3,000	3,475
A & F #25, Various Gauges, Box Lock, Automatic Ejector, Checkered Stock, Engraved, Hammerless, *Modern*	3,200	3,500	4,000
A & F #30, Various Gauges, Box Lock, Automatic Ejector, Checkered Stock, Fancy Engraving, Hammerless, *Modern*	3,800	4,500	4,500
A & F #45, Various Gauges, Box Lock, Automatic Ejector, Checkered Stock, Fancy Engraving, Hammerless, *Modern*	4,000	4,500	5,250

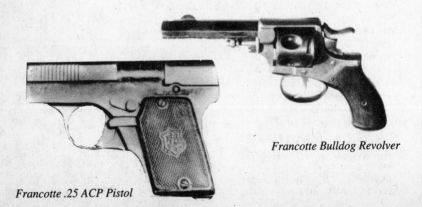

Francotte Bulldog Revolver

Francotte .25 ACP Pistol

	V.G.	Exc.	Prior Edition Exc. Value
A & F Jubilee, Various Gauges, Box Lock, Automatic Ejector, Checkered Stock, Light Engraving, Hammerless, *Modern*	$1,250	$1,500	$3,000
A & F Knockabout, Various Gauges, Box Lock, Automatic Ejector, Checkered Stock, Hammerless, *Modern*	1,000	1,250	2,250
Francotte Original, Various Gauges, Box Lock, Automatic Ejector, Checkered Stock, Hammerless, Engraved, *Modern*	2,000	3,000	2,900
Francotte Special, Various Gauges, Box Lock, Automatic Ejector, Checkered Stock, Hammerless, Light Engraving, *Modern*	1,500	2,500	2,400
Model 10/18E/628, Various Gauges, Box Lock, Automatic Ejector, Checkered Stock, Hammerless, Light Engraving, *Modern*	3,000	4,000	3,750
Model 10594, Various Gauges, Box Lock, Automatic Ejector, Checkered Stock, Hammerless, Engraved, *Modern*	2,500	3,000	3,100
Model11/18E, Various Gauges, Box Lock, Automatic Ejector, Checkered Stock, Hammerless, Engraved, *Modern*	2,500	3,000	3,100
Model 120.HE/328, Various Gauges, Sidelock, Automatic Ejector, Checkered Stock, Hammerless, Fancy Engraving, *Modern*	7,000	8,500	8,500
Model 4996, Various Gauges, Box Lock, Automatic Ejector, Checkered Stock, Hammerless, Light Engraving, *Modern*	1,500	2,500	2,475
Model 6886, Various Gauges, Box Lock, Automatic Ejector, Checkered Stock, Hammerless, *Modern*	1,500	2,500	2,300
Model 6930, Various Gauges, Box Lock, Automatic Ejector, Checkered Stock, Hammerless, Light Engraving, *Modern*	1,500	2,500	2,400
Model 6982, Various Gauges, Box Lock, Automatic Ejector, Checkered Stock, Hammerless, Engraved, *Modern*	2,500	3,500	3,300
Model 8455, Various Gauges, Box Lock, Automatic Ejector, Checkered Stock, Hammerless, *Modern*	2,000	3,500	3,500
Model 8457, Various Gauges, Box Lock, Automatic Ejector, Checkered Stock, Hammerless, Engraved, *Modern*	2,500	3,000	3,000
Model 9/40.SE, Various Gauges, Box Lock, Automatic Ejector, Checkered Stock, Hammerless, Fancy Engraving, *Modern*	7,000	9,500	9,750
Model 9/40E/38321, Various Gauges, Box Lock, Automatic Ejector, Checkered Stock, Hammerless, Engraved, *Modern*	3,000	4,000	4,000
Model SOB.E/11082, Various Gauges, Box Lock, Automatic Ejector, Checkered Stock, Hammerless, Engraved, *Modern*	5,000	6,000	5,900

FRANKLIN, C.W. Belgium, c. 1900.
SHOTGUN, DOUBLE BARREL, SIDE-BY-SIDE

	V.G.	Exc.	
Various Gauges, Outside Hammers, Damascus Barrel, *Modern*	125	175	155
Various Gauges, Hammerless, Steel Barrel, *Modern*	150	200	185
Various Gauges, Hammerless, Damascus Barrel, *Modern*	125	175	155
Various Gauges, Outside Hammers, Steel Barrel, *Modern*	125	175	180

SHOTGUN, SINGLESHOT
Various Gauges, Hammer, Steel Barrel, *Modern*	75	100	75

	V.G.	Exc.	Prior Edition Exc. Value

FRANKONIA Franconia Jagd, arms dealers and manufacturers in West Germany.

RIFLE, SINGLESHOT

Heeren Rifle, Various Calibers, Fancy Engraving, Fancy wood Octagon Barrel, *Modern* $2,700 $3,000 $2,600

Heeren Rifle, Various Calibers, Fancy Engraving, Fancy wood, Round Barrel, *Modern* 2,200 2,500 1,950

RIFLE, BOLT ACTION

Favorit, Various Calibers, Set Triggers, Checkered Stock, *Modern* 275 325 270

Favorit Deluxe, Various Calibers, Set Triggers, Checkered Stock, *Modern* 425 475 290

Favorit Leichtmodell, Various Calibers, Lightweight, Set Triggers, Checkered Stock, *Modern* 400 450 395

Safari, Various Calibers, Target Trigger, Checkered Stock, *Modern* 425 475 410

Stutzen, Various Calibers, Carbine, Set Triggers, Full Stock, *Modern* 400 450 290

FRASER (FORMERLY BAUER FIREARMS) Fraser, Mich.

HANDGUN, SEMI-AUTOMATIC

.25 ACP, Stainless Steel, Clip Fed, Hammerless, Browning Baby Style, *Modern* 100 125 90

FRASER, D. & J. Edinburgh, Scotland 1870–1900.

RIFLE, DOUBLE BARREL, SIDE-BY-SIDE

.360 N.E. #2, Automatic Ejector, Express Sights, Engraved, Extra Set of Barrels, Cased with Accessories, *Modern* 7,500 8,500 8,500

FRAZIER, CLARK K. Rawson, Ohio.

RIFLE, PERCUSSION

Matchmate Offhand, Various Calibers, Under-Hammer, Thumbhole Stock, Heavy Barrel, Reproduction, *Antique* 450 650 640

FRAZIER, JAY Tyler, Wash. c. 1974.

RIFLE, SINGLESHOT

Creedmore Rifle, Various Calibers, Single Set Trigger, Vernier Sights, Skeleton Buttplate, Pistol Grip Stock, *Modern* 600 800 775

Schuetzen Rifle, Various Calibers, Single Set Trigger, Vernier Sights, Helm Buttplate, Palm Rest, False Muzzle, *Modern* 600 800 775

	V.G.	Exc.	Prior Edition Exc. Value

FREEDOM ARMS Freedom, Wyo.

HANDGUN, REVOLVER

	V.G.	Exc.	Prior Edition Exc. Value
FA-S, .22 L.R.R.F., Stainless Steel, Matt Finish, Spur Trigger, 1" Barrel, Single Action, *Modern*	*$100*	*$125*	*$85*
FA-L, .22 L.R.R.F., Stainless Steel, Matt Finish, Spur Trigger, 1¾" Barrel, Single Action, *Modern*	*100*	*125*	*90*
FA-S, .22 W.M.R., Stainless Steel, Matt Finish, Spur Trigger, 1" Barrel, Single Action, *Modern*	*125*	*150*	*105*
FA-L, .22 W.M.R., Stainless Steel, Matt Finish, Spur Trigger, 1¾" Barrel, Single Action, *Modern*	*150*	*175*	*110*
FA-BG, .22 L.R.R.F., Stainless Steel, Spur Trigger, 3" Barrel, Single Action, *Modern*	*175*	*200*	*110*
FA-BG, .22 W.M.R., Stainless Steel, Spur Trigger, 3" Barrel, Single Action, *Modern*	*200*	*225*	*120*
For High Gloss Finish Add **$5.00–$10.00**			

FRENCH MILITARY

HANDGUN, FLINTLOCK

	V.G.	Exc.	Prior Edition Exc. Value
.69 Charleville 1810, Cavalry Pistol, Brass Furniture, Plain, *Antique*	*800*	*900*	*900*
.69 Charleville 1777, Cavalry Pistol, Brass Frame, Belt Hook, *Antique*	*1,050*	*1,200*	*1,075*
.69, Model 1763, Belt Pistol, Military, *Antique*	*1,000*	*1,250*	*1,650*

HANDGUN, PERCUSSION

	V.G.	Exc.	Prior Edition Exc. Value
.69 AN XIII, Officer's Pistol, Made in France, *Antique*	*450*	*575*	*490*
.69 AN XIII, Officer's Pistol, Made in Occupied Country, *Antique*	*500*	*650*	*600*
.69 Charleville 1810 Cavalry Pistol, Brass Furniture, Converted from Flintlock, Plain, *Antique*	*400*	*550*	*530*

HANDGUN, REVOLVER

	V.G.	Exc.	Prior Edition Exc. Value
Model 1873, 11mm French Ordnance, Double Action, Solid Frame, *Antique*	*200*	*275*	*260*
Model 1873 Officer's, 11mm French Ordnance, Double Action, Solid Frame, *Antique*	*225*	*300*	*290*
Model 1892, 8mm Lebel Revolver, Double Action, Solid Frame, *Curio*	*125*	*175*	*165*
Model 1915, 8mm Lebel Revolver, Double Action, Solid Frame, Spanish Contract, *Curio*	*100*	*150*	*125*

HANDGUN, SEMI-AUTOMATIC

	V.G.	Exc.	Prior Edition Exc. Value
Model 1935-A, 7.65 MAS, Clip Fed, Blued, *Curio*	*100*	*150*	*100*
Model 1935-A, 7.65 MAS, Clip Fed, Black Paint, *Curio*	*75*	*125*	*100*
Model 1935-A, 7.65 MAS, Clip Fed, Nazi Proofed, *Curio*	*175*	*225*	*170*
Model 1935-S, 7.65 MAS, M.A.C., Clip Fed, *Curio*	*150*	*175*	*95*

French Military M1777 Charleville

French Military AN XIII

French Military M1935A

French Military M1950

French Military M1873 Revolver

	V.G.	Exc.	Prior Edition Exc. Value
Model 1935-S, 7.65 MAS, M.A.C., Clip Fed, Nazi Proofed, *Curio*	$150	$200	$135
Model 1935-S, 7.65 MAS, M.A.S., Clip Fed, *Curio*	75	125	95
Model 1935-S, 7.65 MAS, M.A.C. M-1, Clip Fed, *Curio*	75	125	95
Model 1935-S, 7.65 MAS, M.A.S., Clip Fed, Nazi Proofed, *Curio*	125	175	160
Model 1935-S, 7.65 MAS, M.A.T., Clip Fed, *Curio*	100	150	130
Model 1935-S, 7.65 MAS, M.A.T., Clip Fed, Nazi Proofed, *Curio*	150	200	165
Model 1935-S, 7.65 MAS, SAGEM M-1, Clip Fed, *Curio*	100	150	110
Model 1935-S, 7.65 MAS, SAGEM M-1, Clip Fed, Nazi Proofed, *Curio*	150	200	150
Model 1935-S, 7.65 MAS, SACM, Clip Fed, *Curio*	125	150	105
Model 1935-S, 7.65 MAS, SAGEM M-1, Clip Fed, Nazi Proofed, *Curio*	150	200	145
Model 1950, 9mm Luger, M.A.S., Clip Fed, *Modern*	350	475	465

RIFLE, BOLT ACTION

6.5 X 53.5 Daudetau, Carbine, *Curio*	100	150	130
Model 1874, 11 X 59R Gras, *Antique*	125	175	170
Model 1874, 11 X 59R Gras, Carbine, *Antique*	150	200	200
Model 1886/93 Lebel, 8 X 50R Lebel, *Curio*	75	100	100
Model 1907/15 Remington, 8 X 50R Lebel, *Curio*	100	125	105
Model 1916 St. Etienne, 8 X 50R Lebel, Carbine, *Curio*	125	150	115
Model 1936 MAS, 7.5 X 54 MAS, with Bayonet, *Curio*	125	175	145

RIFLE, FLINTLOCK

.69, Model 1763 Charleville 1st. Type, Musket, *Antique*	1,500	1,850	1,700
.69, Model 1763/66 Charleville, Musket, *Antique*	850	1,200	1,200

RIFLE, PERCUSSION

Model 1840, Short Rifle, *Antique*	700	850	825

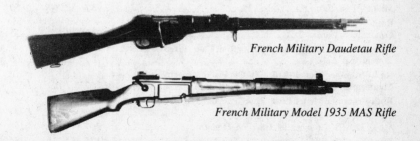

French Military Daudetau Rifle

French Military Model 1935 MAS Rifle

Frommer Liliput

Frommer Roth Frommer 1910

	V.G.	Exc.	Prior Edition Exc. Value

FROMMER Made by Femaru-Fegyver-Es Gepgyar R.T., (Fegyvergyar) Budapest, Hungary. All see Femaru.

HANDGUN, SEMI-AUTOMATIC

	V.G.	Exc.	Prior Edition Exc. Value
Baby Stop, .32 ACP, Clip Fed, *Modern*	$125	$150	$205
Baby Stop, .380 ACP, Clip Fed, *Modern*	150	175	270
Liliput, .22 L.R.R.F., Clip Fed, *Modern*	300	350	400
Liliput, .25 ACP, Clip Fed, *Modern*	175	200	270
Roth-Frommer Model 1901, 8mm Roth Sauer, Fixed Magazine, Commercial, *Curio*	1,500	1,750	1,700
Roth-Frommer Model 1901, 8mm Roth Sauer, Fixed Magazine, Military Test, *Curio*	1,750	2,000	2,050
Roth-Frommer Model 1906, 7.65mm Roth Sauer, Clip Fed, Commercial, *Curio*	1,250	1,500	1,425
Roth-Frommer Model 1906, 7.65mm Roth Sauer, Fixed Magazine, Commercial, *Curio*	1,100	1,300	1,300
Roth-Frommer Model 1910, .32 ACP, Fixed Magazine, Commercial, *Curio*	1,200	1,400	1,250
Roth-Frommer Model 1910, .32 ACP, Fixed Magazine, Police, *Curio*	1,400	1,600	1,475
Stop, .32 ACP, Commercial, Clip Fed, *Modern*	200	250	165
Stop, .32 ACP, WW-1 Military, Clip Fed, *Modern*	175	225	135
Stop, .32 ACP, M-19 Military, Clip Fed, *Modern*	175	225	145

	V.G.	Exc.	Prior Edition Exc. Value
Stop, .32 ACP, Police, Clip Fed, *Modern*	$200	$250	$170
Stop, .380 ACP, Military, Clip Fed, *Modern*	275	325	210
Stop, .32 ACP, Commercial, Clip Fed, *Modern*	225	275	200

FRONTIER Made by Norwich Falls Pistol Co., c. 1880.
HANDGUN, REVOLVER

	V.G.	Exc.	Prior Edition Exc. Value
.32 Short R.F., 5 Shot, Spur Trigger, Solid Frame, Single Action, *Antique*	100	175	170

FRYBERG, ANDREW Hopkintown, Mass., c. 1905.
HANDGUN, REVOLVER

	V.G.	Exc.	Prior Edition Exc. Value
.32 S & W, 5 Shot, Top Break, Hammerless, Double Action, *Modern*	75	100	100
.32 S & W, 5 Shot, Top Break, Double Action, *Modern*	75	100	100
.38 S & W., 5 Shot, Top Break, Double Action, Hammerless, *Modern*	75	100	100
.38 S & W, 5 Shot, Top Break, Double Action, *Modern*	75	100	100

FTL Covina, Calif.
HANDGUN, SEMI-AUTOMATIC

	V.G.	Exc.	Prior Edition Exc. Value
.22 L.R.R.F., Clip Fed, Chrome Plated, *Modern*	100	150	135

G

GALAND, CHARLES FRANCOIS From 1865 until about 1910 with plants in London, England, Paris, France, and Liege, Belgium.

HANDGUN, REVOLVER

	V.G.	Exc.	Prior Edition Exc. Value
Galand, Various Calibers, Double Action, Underlever Extraction, *Curio*	$275	$325	$295
Galand-Perrin, Various Calibers, Double Action, Underlever Extraction, *Curio*	250	300	285
Galand & Sommerville, .38 C.F., Double Action, Underlevel Extraction, *Curio*	275	325	295
Galand & Sommerville, .450 C.F., Double Action, Underlever Extraction, *Curio*	300	350	325
Le Novo, .25 ACP, Double Action, Folding Trigger, *Curio*	150	200	135

SHOTGUN, PERCUSSION

	V.G.	Exc.	Prior Edition Exc. Value
Various Gauges, Checkered Stock, Double Barrel, Plain, *Antique*	200	250	210

SHOTGUN, DOUBLE BARREL, SIDE-BY-SIDE

	V.G.	Exc.	Prior Edition Exc. Value
Various Gauges, Checkered Stock, Plain, Hammers, *Curio*	125	175	155

GALEF Importers in N.Y.C.

HANDGUN, REVOLVER

	V.G.	Exc.	Prior Edition Exc. Value
Stallion, 22LR/.22 WMR Combo, Western Style, Single Action, *Modern*	75	100	95

HANDGUN, SEMI-AUTOMATIC

	V.G.	Exc.	Prior Edition Exc. Value
Brigadier, 9mm Luger, Beretta, Clip Fed, *Modern*	200	300	225
Cougar, .380 ACP, Beretta, Clip Fed., *Modern*	175	225	210
Jaguar, .22 L.R.R.F., Beretta, Clip Fed, *Modern*	150	200	185
Puma, .32 ACP, Beretta, Clip Fed, *Modern*	150	200	180
Sable, .22 L.R.R.F., Beretta, Clip Fed, Adjustable Sights, *Modern*	150	225	215

RIFLE, BOLT ACTION

	V.G.	Exc.	Prior Edition Exc. Value
BSA Monarch, Various Calibers, Checkered Stock, *Modern*	200	250	250
BSA Monarch, Various Calibers, Checkered Stock Magnum Action, *Modern*	225	275	275
BSA Monarch Varmint, Various Calibers, Checkered Stock, Heavy Barrel, *Modern*	250	300	290

	V.G.	Exc.	Prior Edition Exc. Value

SHOTGUN, DOUBLE BARREL, OVER-UNDER

Golden Snipe, 12 Ga., Trap Grade, Single Trigger, Automatic Ejector, Engraved, Checkered Stock, *Modern*.................................... $450 $500 $490

Golden Snipe, 12 and 20 Gauges, Beretta, Single Trigger, Automatic Ejector, Engraved, Fancy Checkering, *Modern*.............. 350 400 400

Golden Snipe, 12 and 20 Gauges, Beretta, Single Selective Trigger, Automatic Ejector, Engraved, Fancy Checkering, *Modern*.............. 425 475 475

Golden Snipe, 12 and 20 Gauges, Skeet Grade, Single Trigger, Automatic Ejector, Engraved, Checkered Stock, *Modern*................. 450 500 490

Golden Snipe Deluxe, 12 and 20 Gauges, Beretta, Single Selective Trigger, Automatic Ejector, Fancy Engraving, Fancy Checkering, *Modern*.. 475 525 525

Silver Snipe, 12 Ga., Trap Grade, Single Trigger, Vent Rib, Engraved, Checkered Stock, *Modern* 375 425 435

Silver Snipe, 12 and 20 Gauges, Skeet Grade, Single Trigger, Vent Rib, Engraved, Checkered Stock, *Modern*... 375 425 430

Silver Snipe, 12 and 20 Gauges, Beretta, Single Trigger, Checkered Stock, *Modern*... 300 350 340

Silver Snipe, 12 and 20 Gauges, Beretta, Single Selective Trigger, Checkered Stock, Light Engraving, *Modern* 325 375 380

Zoli Golden Snipe, 12 and 20 Gauges, Vent Rib, Single Trigger, Adjustable Choke, Engraved, Checkered Stock, *Modern*................. 400 450 460

Zoli Silver Snipe, 12 and 20 Gauges, Vent Rib, Single Trigger, Engraved, Checkered Stock, *Modern* 350 400 385

SHOTGUN, DOUBLE BARREL, SIDE-BY-SIDE

M213CH, 10 Ga. 3½", Double Trigger, Checkered Stock, Light Engraving, Recoil Pad, *Modern*.. 200 250 250

M213CH, Various Gauges, Double Trigger, Checkered Stock, Light Engraving, Recoil Pad, *Modern* 125 175 175

Silver Hawk, 10 Ga. 3½", Beretta, Double Trigger, Magnum, *Modern*.. 450 500 490

Silver Hawk, 12 and 20 Gauges, Double Trigger, Engraved, Checkered Stock, *Modern*.. 325 375 375

Silver Hawk, 12 Ga. Mag. 3", Beretta, Double Trigger, Magnum, *Modern*.. 325 375 375

Silver Hawk, 12 Ga. Mag. 3", Beretta, Single Trigger, Magnum, *Modern*.. 375 425 435

Silver Hawk, Various Gauges, Beretta, Double Trigger, Lightweight, *Modern* 275 325 325

Silver Hawk, Various Gauges, Beretta, Double Trigger, Lightweight, *Modern* 350 400 385

Zabala 213, 10 GA 3½", Double Trigger, *Modern*........................... 150 200 200

Zabala 213, 12 and 20 Gauges, Double Trigger, *Modern* 125 175 165

Zabala 213, 12 and 20 Gauges, Double Trigger, Vent Rib, *Modern*.. 125 175 175

Zabala Police, 12 and 20 Gauges, Double Trigger, *Modern*............ 125 175 180

	V.G.	Exc.	Prior Edition Exc. Value

SHOTGUN, SEMI-AUTOMATIC

	V.G.	Exc.	Prior Edition Exc. Value
Gold Lark, 12 Ga., Beretta, Vent Rib, Light Engraving, Checkered Stock, *Modern*	$200	$250	$235
Ruby Lark, 12 Ga., Beretta, Vent Rib, Fancy Engraving, Fancy Checkering, *Modern*	300	350	350
Silver Gyrfalcon, 12 Ga., Beretta, Checkered Stock, *Modern*	100	125	125
Silver Lark, 12 Ga., Beretta, Checkered Stock, *Modern*	125	150	165

SHOTGUN, SINGLESHOT

Companion, Various Gauges, Folding Gun, Checkered Stock, *Modern*	50	75	55
Companion, Various Gauges, Folding Gun, Checkered Stock, Vent Rib, *Modern*	50	75	65
Monte Carlo, 12 Ga., Trap Grade, Vent Rib, Engraved, Checkered Stock, *Modern*	175	225	210

SHOTGUN, SLIDE ACTION

Gold Pigeon, 12 Ga., Beretta, Vent Rib, Fancy Engraving, Fancy Checkering, *Modern*	300	350	350
Ruby Pigeon, 12 Ga., Beretta, Vent Rib, Fancy Engraving, Fancy Checkering, *Modern*	400	450	450
Silver Pigeon, 12 Ga., Beretta, Light Engraving, Checkered Stock, *Modern*	125	150	140

GALESI Industria Armi Galesi, Brescia, Italy since 1910.

HANDGUN, SEMI-AUTOMATIC

Model 506, .22 L.R.R.F., Clip Fed, *Modern*	100	125	125
Model 6, .22 Long R.F., Clip Fed, *Modern*	100	125	100
Model 6, .25 ACP, Clip Fed, *Modern*	100	125	95

Galesi Model 9 Pistol

Galesi Revolver

	V.G.	Exc.	Prior Edition Exc. Value
Model 9, .22 L.R.R.F., Clip Fed, *Modern*	$125	$150	$130
Model 9, .32 ACP, Clip Fed, *Modern*	150	175	140
Model 9, .380 ACP, Clip Fed, *Modern*	125	150	155

GALLATIN, ALBERT See Kentucky Rifles and Pistols.

GALLUS Retoloza Hermanos, Eibar, Spain, c. 1920.

HANDGUN, SEMI-AUTOMATIC

.25 ACP, Clip Fed, Blue, *Modern*	100	125	130

GAMBA Renato Gamba, Brescia, Italy.

RIFLE, SINGLESHOT

Mustang, Various Calibers, Holland Type Sidelock Action, Set Triggers, Checkered Stock, Engraved, Zeiss Scope, *Modern*	7,000	10,000	6,250

RIFLE, DOUBLE BARREL, OVER-UNDER

Safari, Various Calibers, Boxlock, Checkered Stock, Engraved, Double Triggers, *Modern*	3,000	4,000	5,750

SHOTGUN, DOUBLE BARREL, SIDE-BY-SIDE

London, 12 or 20 Ga., Sidelock,Checkered Stock, Engraved, *Modern*	3,500	4,500	2,500
Oxford, 12 or 20 Ga., Boxlock, Checkered Stock, Engraved, *Modern*	1,500	1,700	1,100

GANDER, PETER Lancaster, Pa. 1779–1782, see Kentucky Rifles.

GARATE, ANITUA Eibar, Spain, c. 1915.

HANDGUN, REVOLVER

Pistol O.P. # Mk.I, .455 Webley, British Military, *Curio*	250	275	265

HANDGUN, SEMI-AUTOMATIC

.32 ACP, Clip Fed, Long Grip, *Modern*	125	150	195

GARBI Amas Garbi, Eibar, Spain.

SHOTGUN, DOUBLE BARREL, SIDE-BY-SIDE

Model 51, Various Gauges, Boxlock, Checkered Stock, Engraved, *Modern*	300	350	390
Model 60, Various Gauges, Sidelock, Checkered Stock, Engraved, *Modern*	475	525	565
Model 60, Various Gauges, Sidelock, Checkered Stock, Engraved, Automatic Ejectors, *Modern*	700	800	775

	V.G.	Exc.	Prior Edition Exc. Value

GARRISON Made by Hopkins & Allen, c. 1880–1890.

HANDGUN, REVOLVER

| .22 Short R.F., 7 Shot, Spur Trigger, Solid Frame, Single Action, Antique | $125 | $175 | $175 |

GARRUCHA Made by Amadeo Rossi, Sao Leopoldo, Brazil.

HANDGUN, DOUBLE BARREL, SIDE-BY-SIDE

| .22 L.R.R.F., Double Triggers, Outside Hammers, Modern | 50 | 75 | 55 |

GASSER Leopold Gasser, Vienna, Austria.

HANDGUN, REVOLVER

| Montenegrin Gasser, 11mm Montenegrin, Double Action, Break Top, Ring Extractor, Antique | 325 | 400 | 290 |
| Rast & Gasser, 8mm R&G, Double Action, Solid Frame, Curio | 225 | 275 | 235 |

GASTINE RENETTE Paris, France since 1812.

RIFLE, DOUBLE BARREL, SIDE-BY-SIDE

Chapuis Standard, Various Calibers, Boxlock Action, Engraved, Checkered Stock, Double Trigger, Open Sights, Modern	2,000	2,200	1,750
Chapuis de Luxe, Various Calibers, Boxlock Action with Sideplates, Fancy Engraving, Checkered Stock, Double Trigger, Open Sights, Modern	2,250	2,600	2,100
Chapuis President, Various Calibers, Boxlock Action With Sideplates, Engraved, Gold Inlays, Checkered Stock, Double Trigger, Open Sights, Modern	2,500	3,200	2,350
Chapuis, For Claw Mounts Add $100.00–$150.00			
Chapuis, With 20 Gauge Barrels Add $325.00–$550.00			

SHOTGUN, DOUBLE BARREL, SIDE-BY-SIDE

Model 353, 12 or 20 Gauge, Sidelock Action, Fancy Engraving, Fancy Wood, Checkered Stock, Double Trigger, Modern	10,000	14,000	7,000
Model 202, 12 or 20 Gauge, Boxlock Action With Sideplates, Fancy Engraving, Fancy Wood, Checkered Stock, Double Trigger, Modern	3,500	4,000	2,450
Model 98, 12 or 20 Gauge, Boxlock Action, Engraved, Fancy Wood, Checkered Stock, Double Trigger, Modern	1,800	2,000	1,850
Model 105, 12 or 20 Gauge, Boxlock Action, Engraved, Fancy Wood, Checkered Stock, Double Trigger, Modern	1,200	1,400	1,400

SHOTGUN, DOUBLE BARREL, OVER-UNDER

| Bretton Baby Standard, Lightweight, Double Trigger, Checkered Stock, Modern | 350 | 400 | 350 |
| Bretton Baby-Elite, Lightweight, Double Trigger, Checkered Stock, Modern | 375 | 425 | 360 |

	V.G.	Exc.	Prior Edition Exc. Value
Bretton Baby Luxe, Lightweight, Double Trigger, Checkered Stock, Engraved, Chrome Frame, *Modern*	*$400*	*$450*	*$385*

GATLING ARMS & AMMUNITION CO. Birmingham, England, c. 1890.

HANDGUN, REVOLVER

Dimancea, .450 C.F., Hammerless, Twist Opening, Double Action, *Antique*	*800*	*900*	*750*

GAULOIS Tradename used by Mrs. Francaise de Armes et Cycles de St. Etienne, France 1897–1910.

HANDGUN, MANUAL REPEATER

Palm Pistol, 8mm, Engraved, *Curio*	*500*	*650*	*525*

GAUTEC, PETER Lancaster, Pa. c. 1780 Kentucky Rifles & Pistols.

GAVAGE Fab. d'Armes de Guerre de Haute Precision Armand Gavage, Leige, Belgium, c. 1940.

HANDGUN, SEMI-AUTOMATIC

.32 ACP, Clip Fed, Blue, *Modern*	*300*	*350*	*275*
.32 ACP, Clip Fed, Blue, Nazi-Proofed, *Modern*	*400*	*450*	*350*

GECADO Suhl, Germany, by G.C. Dornheim.

HANDGUN, SEMI-AUTOMATIC

Model 11, .25 ACP, Clip Fed, *Modern*	*100*	*125*	*125*

Gavage .32 Pistol

Gaulois Palm Pistol

	V.G.	Exc.	Prior Edition Exc. Value

GECO Tradename used by Gustav Genschow, Hamburg, Germany.

HANDGUN, REVOLVER

	V.G.	Exc.	Prior Ed.
Velo Dog, .25 ACP, Double Action, *Modern*	$100	$125	$110
Bulldog, .32 ACP, Double Action, *Modern*	100	125	110

SHOTGUN, DOUBLE BARREL, SIDE-BY-SIDE

12 Gauge, Checkered Stock, Double Triggers, Plain, *Modern*	125	175	155

GEM Made by Bacon Arms Co., c. 1880.

HANDGUN, REVOLVER

.22 Short R.F., 7 Shot, Spur Trigger, Solid Frame, Single Action, *Antique*	175	225	200

GEM Made by J. Stevens Arms & Tool, Chicopee Falls, Mass.

HANDGUN, SINGLESHOT

.22 or .30 R.F., Side-Swing Barrel, Spur Trigger, *Antique*	125	175	185

GERMAN MILITARY Also See: Walther, Mauser, Luger.

HANDGUN, FLINTLOCK

Model 1830, .63, Military, *Antique*	550	650	600

HANDGUN, PERCUSSION

Model 1860, .63, Military, *Antique*	350	425	390

HANDGUN, REVOLVER

Model 1879 Troopers Model, 11mm German Service, Solid Frame, Single Action, Safety, 7" Barrel, 6 Shot, *Antique*	375	425	400
Model 1883 Officers' Model, 11mm Germany Service, Solid Frame, Single Action, Safety, 5" Barrel, 6 Shot, *Antique*	300	375	350

RIFLE, BOLT ACTION

GEW 88 Commission, 8 x 57 JRS, Clip Fed, *Antique*	75	125	90
GEW 98 (Average), 8mm Mauser Military, *Curio*	175	250	145
GEW 98 Sniper, 8mm Mauser, Scope Mounted, Military, *Curio*	650	750	690
K98K Sniper, 8mm Mauser, Scope Mounted, Military, *Curio*	475	550	450
KAR 98 (Average), 8mm Mauser, Military, Carbine, *Curio*	150	175	160
KAR 98A (Average), 8mm Mauser, Military, Carbine, *Curio*	150	175	160
M-95, 8mm Mauser, Steyr-Mannlicher, German Military, Nazi-Proofed, *Curio*	125	150	125
M-95, 8mm Mauser, Steyr-Mannlicher, German Military, Carbine, Nazi-Proofed, *Curio*	100	125	115
Model 1871 Mauser, .43 Mauser, Singleshot, Military, *Antique*	300	350	325
Model 1871 Mauser, .43 Mauser, Carbine, Singleshot, Military, *Antique*	400	475	425
Model 71/84 Mauser, .43 Mauser, Tube Feed, Military, *Antique*	325	375	350

	V.G.	Exc.	Prior Edition Exc. Value
Model 45 Mauser, .22 L.R.R.F., Training Rifle, Military, *Curio*.....	*$150*	*$175*	*$170*
Model 1936 Falke KK, .22 L.R.R.F., Training Rifle, Military, *Curio*	*75*	*100*	*70*
Model 29/40, 8mm Mauser, Nazi-Proofed, Military, *Curio*	*100*	*150*	*120*
Model 33/40, 8mm Mauser, Nazi-Proofed, Military, *Curio*	*125*	*175*	*150*
VK-98, 8mm Mauser, Nazi-Proofed, Military, *Curio*	*175*	*200*	*190*
VZ-24 BRNO, 8mm Mauser, Nazi-Proofed, Military, *Curio*	*125*	*150*	*145*
Needle Gun, 11mm, Singleshot, Military, *Antique*	*525*	*600*	

RIFLE, PERCUSSION

	V.G.	Exc.	Prior Edition Exc. Value
M1839, .69, Musket, Brass Furniture, Military, *Antique*	*400*	*450*	*430*
M1842, .75, Musket, Brass Furniture, Military, *Antique*	*325*	*375*	*350*

German Military Model 1879 Revolver

German Military Model 1883 Revolver

German Military Model 1871 Rifle

German Military Model 1871/84 Rifle

	V.G.	Exc.	Prior Edition Exc. Value

RIFLE, SEMI-AUTOMATIC

G43, 8mm Mauser, Clip Fed, 10 Shot, Military, *Curio*	$275	$325	$265
GEW 41, 8mm Mauser, 10 Shot, Military, *Curio*	425	475	420
GEW 41(W), 8mm Mauser, 10 Shot, Military, *Curio*	375	450	385
KAR 43 Sniper, 8mm Mauser, Scope Mounted, Clip Fed, 10 Shot, Military, *Curio*	675	750	650
VG 2, 8mm Mauser, Clip Fed, 10 Shot, Military, *Curio*	300	375	315

RIFLE, SINGLESHOT

Model 1869 Werder, 11.5mm, Bavarian, *Antique*	700	850	725

GESSCER, GEORG Saxony, 1591–1611.

HANDGUN, WHEEL-LOCK

Pair, Military, Inlays, Pear Pommel, Medium Ornamentation, *Antique*	15,000	20,000	20,000

GEVARM Gevelot, St. Etienne, France.

RIFLE, SEMI-AUTOMATIC

Model A3, .22 L.R.R.F., Target Sights, Clip Fed, *Modern*	100	150	160
Model A6, .22 L.R.R.F., Open Sights, Clip Fed, *Modern*	100	125	125
Model A7, .22 L.R.R.F., Target Sights, Clip Fed, *Modern*	150	175	190
.32 S & W, 5 Shot, Double Action, Top Break, *Modern*	75	100	100
.38 S & W, 5 Shot, Double Action, Top Break, *Modern*	75	100	100

GIBRALTER Made by Stevens Arms.

SHOTGUN, SINGLESHOT

Model 116, Various Gauges, Hammer, Automatic Ejector, Raised Matted Rib, *Modern*	50	75	65

GILL, THOMAS London, England 1770–1812.

HANDGUN, FLINTLOCK

.68, Pocket Pistol, Octagon Barrel, Plain, High Quality, *Antique*	800	1,000	975

GLASER WAFFEN Zurich, Switzerland.

HANDGUN, SINGLESHOT

Target Pistol, .22 L.R.R.F., Toggle Breech, Francotte, *Modern*	350	400	375

RIFLE, BOLT ACTION

Custom Rifle, Various Calibers, Fancy Wood, *Modern*	1,000	1,200	1,050

RIFLE, SINGLESHOT

Heeren Rifle, Various Calibers, Engraved, Fancy Wood, *Modern*	2,000	2,500	2,500

	V.G.	Exc.	Prior Edition Exc. Value

GLASSBRENNER, DAVID Lancaster, Pa., c. 1800. See Kentucky Rifles.

GLAZIER, JOHN Belleville, Ind., c. 1820. See Kentucky Rifles.

GLENFIELD See Marlin.

GLENN, ROBERT Edinburgh, Scotland, c. 1860. Made fine copies of Highland Pistols.

HANDGUN, SNAPHAUNCE

	V.G.	Exc.	Prior
Replica Highland, All Brass, Engraved, Ovoid Pommel, *Antique*... $2,500	$3,000	$3,000

GLISENTI Soc. Siderugica Glisenti, Turin, Italy, c. 1889–1930.

HANDGUN, REVOLVER

	V.G.	Exc.	Prior
M1889, 10.4mm Glisenti, Double Action, Folding Trigger, Military, *Curio*	125	150	145
M1889, 10.4mm Glisenti, Double Action, Trigger Guard, Military, *Curio*	125	150	135

HANDGUN, SEMI-AUTOMATIC

	V.G.	Exc.	Prior
Brixia, 9mm Glisenti, Clip Fed, Hard Rubber Grips, *Modern*	375	425	400
M910 Army, 9mm Glisenti, Clip Fed, Wood Grips, *Modern*	500	550	425
M910 Navy, 9mm Glisenti, Clip Fed, Hard Rubber Grips, *Modern*	575	650	400
M906, 7.63 Mauser, Clip Fed, Military, *Modern*	475	550	500

GOLDEN EAGLE Nikko Arms Co. Ltd., Japan.

RIFLE, BOLT ACTION

	V.G.	Exc.	Prior
Model 7000, Various Calibers, Grade 1, Checkered Stock, *Modern*	425	500	395
Model 7000, Various African Calibers, Grade 1, Checkered Stock, *Modern*	475	550	420
Model 7000, Various Calibers, Grade 2, Checkered Stock, *Modern*	575	650	420
Model 7000, Various African Calibers, Grade 2, Checkered Stock, *Modern*	625	700	475

SHOTGUN, DOUBLE BARREL, OVER-UNDER

	V.G.	Exc.	Prior
Model 5000, 12 and 20 Gauges, Field Grade, Vent Rib, Checkered Stock, Light Engraving, Gold Overlay, *Modern*	725	850	595
Model 5000, 12 and 20 Gauges, Skeet Grade, Vent Rib, Checkered Stock, Light Engraving, Gold Overlay, *Modern*	875	950	695
Model 5000, 12 and 20 Gauges, Trap Grade, Vent Rib, Checkered Stock, Light Engraving, Gold Overlay, *Modern*	875	950	695
Model 5000, 12 and 20 Gauges, Field Grade 2, Vent Rib, Checkered Stock, Light Engraving, Gold Overlay, *Modern*	850	1,000	695

	V.G.	Exc.	Prior Edition Exc. Value
Model 5000, 12 and 20 Gauges, Skeet Grade 2, Vent Rib, Checkered Stock, Light Engraving, Gold Overlay, *Modern*	$950	$1,100	$775
Model 5000, 12 and 20 Gauges, Trap Grade 2, Vent Rib, Checkered Stock, Light Engraving, Gold Overlay, *Modern*	950	1,050	730
Model 5000 Grandee, 12 and 20 Gauges, Field Grade 3, Vent Rib, Checkered Stock, Fancy Engraving, Gold Overlay, *Modern*	2,000	2,250	2,550
Model 5000 Grandee, 12 and 20 Gauges, Skeet Grade 3, Vent Rib, Checkered Stock, Fancy Engraving, Gold Overlay, *Modern*	2,250	2,500	2,800
Model 5000 Grandee, 12 Ga., Trap Grade 3, Vent Rib, Checkered Stock, Fancy Engraving, Gold Overlay, *Modern*	2,250	2,500	2,800

GONTER, PETER Lancaster, Pa. 1770–1778. See Kentucky Rifles.

GOFF, DANIEL London, England 1779–1810.
HANDGUN, FLINTLOCK
Duelling Pistols, .50, Cased pair, with Accessories, *Antique* ... 2,000   2,500   2,400

GOLCHER, JAMES Philadelphia, Pa. 1820–1833.

GOLCHER, JOHN Easton, Pa., c. 1775.

GOLCHER, JOSEPH Philadelphia, Pa., c. 1800.

GOOSE GUN Made by Stevens Arms.
SHOTGUN, SINGLESHOT
Model 89 Dreadnaught, Various Gauges, Hammer, *Modern* ... 50   75   65

GOVERNOR Made by Bacon Arms Co.
HANDGUN, REVOLVER
.22 Short R.F., 7 Shot, Spur Trigger, Solid Frame, Single Action, *Antique* ... 125   175   165

GOVERNOR Various makers, c. 1880.
HANDGUN, REVOLVER
.32 S & W, 5 Shot, Double Action, Top Break, *Modern* ... 75   100   95
.38 S & W, 5 Shot, Double Action, Top Break, *Modern* ... 75   125   100

GRAEFF, WM. Reading, Pa. 1751–1784. See Kentucky Rifles.

GRANT HAMMOND New Haven, Conn. 1915–1917.
HANDGUN, SEMI-AUTOMATIC
U.S. Test, .45 ACP, Clip Fed, Hammer, *Curio* ... 7,000   8,000   7,650

	V.G.	Exc.	Prior Edition Exc. Value

GRANT, W.L.

HANDGUN, REVOLVER

.22 Long R.F., 6 Shot, Single Action, Solid Frame, Spur Trigger, Antique $200 $250 $230

.32 Short R.F., 6 Shot, Single Action, Solid Frame, Spur Trigger, Antique 200 250 250

GRAVE, JOHN Lancaster, Pa. 1769–1773. See Kentucky Rifles.

GREAT WESTERN Venice, Calif. 1954–1962. Moved to North Hollywood, Calif. in 1959.

HANDGUN, REVOLVER

Frontier, .22 L.R.R.F., Single Action, Western Style, *Modern* 275 325 50

Frontier, Various Calibers, Single Action, Western Style, *Modern* 300 350 65

Deputy, .22 L.R.R.F., Single Action, Western Style, *Modern* 250 300 50

Deputy, .22 L.R.R.F., Single Action, Western Style, *Modern* 250 300 50

Buntline, Various Calibers, Single Action, Western Style, *Modern* 350 400 75

HANDGUN, DOUBLE BARREL, OVER-UNDER

Double Derringer, .38 Spec., Remington Copy, *Modern* 225 275 45

GREAT WESTERN GUN WORKS Pittsburg, Pa., 1860 to about 1923.

HANDGUN, REVOLVER

.22 Short R.F., 7 Shot, Spur Trigger, Solid Frame, Single Action, Antique 125 175 165

RIFLE, PERCUSSION

No. 5, Various Calibers, Various Barrel Lengths, Plains Rifle, Octagon Barrel, Brass Fittings, *Antique* 575 650 575

GREEK MILITARY

RIFLE, BOLT ACTION

M 1903 Mannlicher Schoenauer, 6.5mm M.S., Military, *Curio* 75 100 90

M 1903 Mannlicher Schoenauer, 8mm Mauser, Military, *Curio* 75 100 95

M 1930 Greek, 8mm Mauser, Military, *Curio* 100 125 100

GREENER, W.W. Established in 1829 in Northumberland, England as W. Greener, moved to Birmingham, England in 1844; name changed to W.W. Greener in 1860, and to W.W. Greener & Son in 1879.

SHOTGUN, DOUBLE BARREL, SIDE-BY-SIDE

Various Gauges, Single Non-Selective Trigger Add **$185.00–$280.00**

	V.G.	Exc.	Prior Edition Exc. Value
Various Gauges, Single Selective Trigger Add **$265.00–$385.00**			
Crown DH-55, Various Gauges, Box Lock, Automatic Ejector, Checkered Stock, Fancy Engraving, *Modern*	$3,250	$3,500	$2,700
Empire, 12 Ga. Mag. 3", Box Lock, Hammerless, Light Engraving, Checkered Stock, *Modern*	1,550	1,750	1,395
Empire, 12 Ga. Mag. 3", Box Lock, Hammerless, Light Engraving, Checkered Stock, Automatic Ejector, *Modern*	2,000	2,250	1,800
Empire Deluxe, 12 Ga. Mag. 3", Box Lock, Hammerless, Engraved, Checkered Stock, *Modern*	2,000	2,250	1,800
Empire Deluxe, 12 Ga. Mag. 3", Box Lock, Hammerless, Engraved, Checkered Stock, Automatic Ejector, *Modern*	2,100	2,300	2,000
Far-Killer F35, 10 Ga. 3¹/₂", Box Lock, Hammerless, Engraved, Checkered Stock, *Modern*	2,250	2,500	1,950
Far-Killer F35, 10 Ga. 3¹/₂", Box Lock, Hammerless, Engraved, Checkered Stock, Automatic Ejector, *Modern*	2,750	3,000	2,825
Far-Killer F35, 12 Ga. Mag. 3", Box Lock, Hammerless, Engraved, Checkered Stock, *Modern*	2,500	2,750	2,300
Far-Killer F35, 12 Ga. Mag. 3", Box Lock, Hammerless, Engraved, Checkered Stock, Automatic Ejector, *Modern*	2,600	2,900	2,800
Far-Killer F35, 8 Ga., Box Lock, Hammerless, Engraved, Checkered Stock, *Modern*	2,500	2,750	2,300
Far-Killer F35, 8 Ga. Box Lock, Hammerless, Engraved, Checkered Stock, Automatic Ejector, *Modern*	3,000	3,200	3,000
Jubilee DH-35, Various Gauges, Box Lock, Automatic Ejector, Checkered Stock, Engraved, *Modern*	2,350	2,500	2,000
Royal DH-75, Various Gauges, Box Lock, Automatic Ejector, Checkered Stock, Fancy Engraving, *Modern*	3,700	3,950	3,525
Sovereign DH-40, Various Gauges, Box Lock, Automatic Ejector, Checkered Stock, Engraved, *Modern*	2,650	2,800	2,575

SHOTGUN, SINGLESHOT

G. P. Martini, 12 Ga., Checkered Stock, Takedown, *Modern*	300	350	295

GREGORY Mt. Vernon, Ohio 1837–1842. See Kentucky Rifles.

GREIFELT & CO. Suhl, Germany from 1885.

COMBINATION WEAPON, OVER-UNDER

Various Calibers, Solid Rib, Engraved, Checkered Stock, *Modern*	4,500	5,000	4,000
Various Calibers, Solid Rib, Engraved, Checkered Stock, Automatic Ejector, *Modern*	5,000	5,500	5,025

COMBINATION WEAPON, DRILLING

Various Calibers, Fancy Wood, Fancy Checkering, Engraved, *Modern*	4,000	4,500	4,750
Various Calibers, Engraved, Checkered Stock, *Modern*	3,500	3,500	3,700

RIFLE, BOLT ACTION

Sport, .22 Hornet, Checkered Stock, Express Sights, *Modern*	850	950	800

	V.G.	Exc.	Prior Edition Exc. Value

SHOTGUN, DOUBLE BARREL, OVER-UNDER

Various Gauges, Single Trigger, Add **$245.00–$350.00**

Various Gauges, For Vent Rib **Add $195.00–$300.00**

	V.G.	Exc.	Prior Edition Exc. Value
#1, .410 Ga., Automatic Ejector, Fancy Engraving, Checkered Stock, Fancy Wood, Solid Rib, *Modern*	$5,000	$5,500	$5,625
#1, Various Gauges, Automatic Ejector, Fancy Engraving, Checkered Stock, Fancy Wood, Solid Rib, *Modern*	3,000	3,500	3,875
#3, .410 Ga., Automatic Ejector, Engraved, Checkered Stock, Solid Rib, *Modern*	3,000	3,500	3,900
#3, Various Gauges, Automatic Ejector, Engraved, Checkered Stock, Solid Rib, *Modern*	2,250	2,750	2,500
Model 143E, Various Gauges, Automatic Ejector, Engraved, Checkered Stock, Solid Rib, Double Trigger, *Modern*	2,000	2,250	2,000
Model 143E, Various Gauges, Automatic Ejector, Engraved, Checkered Stock, Vent Rib, Single Selective Trigger, *Modern*	2,250	2,500	2,300

SHOTGUN, DOUBLE BARREL, SIDE-BY-SIDE

	V.G.	Exc.	Prior Edition Exc. Value
Model 103, 12 and 16 Gauges, Box Lock, Double Trigger, Checkered Stock, Light Engraving, *Modern*	1,750	2,000	1,100
Model 103E, 12 and 16 Gauges, Box Lock, Double Trigger, Checkered Stock, Light Engraving, Automatic Ejector, *Modern*	2,000	2,250	1,400
Model 22, 12 and 16 Gauges, Box Lock, Double Trigger, Checkered Stock, Engraved, *Modern*	1,650	1,850	1,050
Model 22E, 12 and 16 Gauges, Box Lock, Double Trigger, Checkered Stock, Engraved, Automatic Ejector, *Modern*	2,000	2,250	1,500

GREYHAWK ARMS CORP. South El Monte, Calif., c. 1975.

RIFLE, SINGLESHOT

	V.G.	Exc.	Prior Edition Exc. Value
Model 74, Various Calibers, Rolling Block, Octagon Barrel, Open Rear Sight, Reproduction, *Modern*	100	125	125

GRIFFEN & HOWE N.Y.C. 1923, absorbed by Abercrombie & Fitch 1930.

RIFLE, BOLT ACTION

	V.G.	Exc.	Prior Edition Exc. Value
Mauser 98, .30/06, Sporterized, Engraved, Fancy Wood, Fancy Checkering, *Modern*	2,000	2,250	1,800
Mauser 98, .30/06, Sporterized, Fancy Engraving, Fancy Wood, Fancy Checkering, Gold Inlays, *Modern*	5,000	5,500	4,500
Springfield, .30/06, Sporterized, Engraved, Fancy Wood, Fancy Checkering, *Modern*	1,500	1,800	1,775
Springfield, .30/06, Sporterized, Fancy Engraving, Fancy Wood, Fancy Checkering, *Modern*	3,000	3,500	3,250
Winchester M70, .30/06, Sporterized, Engraved, Fancy Wood, Fancy Checkering, *Modern*	3,000	3,500	1,975

	V.G.	Exc.	Prior Edition Exc. Value

GROOM, RICHARD London, England, c. 1855.
HANDGUN, FLINTLOCK
.68, East India Company, Calvary Pistol, Military, Tapered Round Barrel, Brass Furniture, *Antique* $1,800 $2,000 $1,850

GROSS ARMS CO. Tiffin, Ohio 1862–1865.
HANDGUN, REVOLVER
.22 Short R.F., 7 Shot, Spur Trigger, Tip-Up, *Antique* 650   725   625
.25 Short R.F., 6 Shot, Single Action, Spur Trigger, Tip-Up, *Antique* 600   750   650
.32 Short R.F., 5 Shot, Spur Trigger, Tip-Up, *Antique* 650   725   625

GRUENEL Gruenig & Elmiger, Malters, Switzerland.
RIFLE, BOLT ACTION
Model K 31, .308 Win., U.I.T. Target Rifle, Target Sights, Ventilated Forestock, *Modern* 750   900   875
Match 300m, Various Calibers, Offhand Target Rifle, Target Sights, Ventilated Forestock, Palm Rest, Hook Buttplate, *Modern*... 1,000   1,200   1,125
U.I.T. Standard, .308 Win., Target Rifle, Target Sights, Ventilated Forestock, *Modern* 700   800   750

GUARDIAN Made by Bacon Arms Co., c. 1880.
HANDGUN, REVOLVER
.22 Short R.F., 7 Shot, Spur Trigger, Solid Frame, Single Action, *Antique* 125   175   165
.32 Short R.F., 5 Shot, Spur Trigger, Solid Frame, Single Action, *Antique* 150   200   175

GUMPH, CHRISTOPHER Lancaster, Pa. 1779–1803. See Kentucky Rifles and Pistols.

GUSTAF, CARL See Husqvarna.

GUSTLOFF WERKE Suhl, Germany.
HANDGUN, SEMI-AUTOMATIC
.32 ACP, Clip Fed, Hammer, Single Action, *Modern* 1,200   1,500   1,800
.380 ACP, Clip Fed, Hammer, Single Action, *Modern* 2,500   3,000   3,100
RIFLE, BOLT ACTION
Mauser M98, 8mm Mauser, Military, *Curio* 75   100   95
Model KKW, .22 L.R.R.F., Pre-WW2, Singleshot, Tangent Sights, Military Style Stock, *Modern* 350   400   410

Gustloff Werke .32 Pistol

			Prior Edition Exc.
	V.G.	Exc.	Value

SHOTGUN, DOUBLE BARREL, SIDE-BY-SIDE
16 Ga., Engraved, Color Case Hardened Frame, *Modern*................. $400 $500 $490

GYROJET See M.B. Associates.

H

HACKETT, EDWIN AND GEORGE London, England, c. 1870.

SHOTGUN, DOUBLE BARREL, SIDE-BY-SIDE

10 Ga. 2⅞", Damascus Barrel, Plain, *Antique* *$150*   *$200*   *$200*

HADDEN, JAMES Philadelphia, PA, c. 1769. See Kentucky Rifles and Pistols.

HAEFFER, JOHN Lancaster, Pa., c. 1800. See Kentucky Rifles and Pistols.

HAENEL, C.G. C.G. Haenel Waffen und Fahrradfabrik, Suhl, Germany 1840–1945.

HANDGUN, SEMI-AUTOMATIC

Schmiesser Model 1, .25 ACP, Clip Fed, *Modern*	225	275	245
Schmiesser Model 2, .25 ACP, Clip Fed, *Modern*	250	300	290

Hafdasa

Haenel Schmeisser Model 1

	V.G.	Exc.	Prior Edition Exc. Value

RIFLE, BOLT ACTION

Model 88, Various Calibers, Sporting Rifle, Half-Octagon Barrel, Open Rear Sight, *Modern* ... 300 350 345

Model 88 Sporter, Various Calibers, 5 Shot Clip, Half-Octagon Barrel, Open Rear Sight, *Modern* ... 350 400 385

HAFDASA Hispano Argentina Fab. de Automoviles, Buenos Aires, Argentina, c. 1935.

HANDGUN, SEMI-AUTOMATIC

.22 L.R.R.F., Blowback, *Modern* ... $375 $450 $325

HALF-BREED Made by Hopkins & Allen, c. 1880.

HANDGUN, REVOLVER

.32 Short R.F., 5 Shot, Spur Trigger, Solid Frame, Single Action, *Antique* ... 125 175 170

HAMMERLI Lenzburg, Switzerland.

HANDGUN, REVOLVER

Virginian, .357 Magnum, Single Action, Western Style, *Modern* ... 225 250 200

Virginian, .45 Colt, Single Action, Western Style, *Modern* ... 250 275 225

HANDGUN, SEMI-AUTOMATIC

Model 200 Walther Olympia, .22 L.R.R.F., Target Pistol, *Modern* ... 600 625 520

Model 200 Walther Olympia, .22 L.R.R.F., Target Pistol, Muzzle Brake, *Modern* ... 650 675 570

Model 201 Walther Olympia, .22 L.R.R.F., Target Pistol, Adjustable Grips, *Modern* ... 600 625 520

Model 202 Walther Olympia, .22 L.R.R.F., Target Pistol, Adjustable Grips, *Modern* ... 700 750 570

Model 203 Walther Olympia, .22 L.R.R.F., Target Pistol, Adjustable Grips, *Modern* ... 650 700 625

Model 203 Walther Olympia, .22 L.R.R.F., Target Pistol, Adjustable Grips, Muzzle Brake, *Modern* ... 725 775 695

Model 204 Walther Olympia, .22 L.R.R.F., Target Pistol, *Modern* ... 700 750 695

Model 204 Walther Olympia, .22 L.R.R.F., Target Pistol, Muzzle Brake, *Modern* ... 750 800 750

Model 205 Walther Olympia, .22 L.R.R.F., Target Pistol, Fancy Wood, *Modern* ... 775 850 750

Model 205 Walther Olympia, .22 L.R.R.F., Target Pistol, Fancy Wood, Muzzle Brake, *Modern* ... 900 950 800

	V.G.	Exc.	Prior Edition Exc. Value
Model 206, .22 L.R.R.F., Target Pistol, *Modern*	$650	$700	$595
Model 207, .22 L.R.R.F., Target Pistol, Adjustable Grips, *Modern*	700	725	675
Model 208, .22 L.R.R.F., Target Pistol, Clip Fed, Adjustable Grips, *Modern*	1,600	1,675	800
Model 208, .22 L.R.R.F., Target Pistol, Clip Fed, Adjustable Grips, Left-Hand, *Modern*	1,650	1,725	810
Model 209, .22 Short R.F., Target Pistol, 5 Shot Clip, Muzzle Brake, *Modern*	700	775	670
Model 210, .22 L.R.R.F., Target Pistol, *Modern*	800	850	645
Model 210, .22 L.R.R.F., Target Pistol, Adjustable Grips, *Modern*	800	875	670
Model 211, .22 L.R.R.F., Target Pistol, Clip Fed, *Modern*	1,500	1,800	775
Model 212 SIG, .22 L.R.R.F., Target Pistol, Clip Fed, *Modern*	1,500	1,600	825
Model 215, .22 L.R.R.F., Target Pistol, Clip Fed, *Modern*	850	900	690
Model 230-1, .22 Short R.F., Target Pistol, 5 Shot Clip, *Modern*	575	650	725
Model 230-2, .22 Short R.F., Target Pistol, 5 Shot Clip, Adjustable Grips, *Modern*	625	675	795
Model 230-2, .22 Short R.F., Target Pistol, 5 Shot Clip, Adjustable Grips, Left-Hand, *Modern*	600	675	810
Model P-240 SIG, .22 L.R.R.F., Target Pistol, Clip Fed, Conversion Unit Only, *Modern*	525	600	545
Model P-240 SIG, .32 S & W Long, Clip Fed, Target Pistol, Cased with Accessories, *Modern*	800	850	795
Model P-240 SIG, .38 Special, Clip Fed, Target Pistol, Cased with Accessories, *Modern*	825	875	845

HANDGUN, SINGLESHOT

Model 100, .22 L.R.R.F., Target Pistol, *Modern*	750	800	585
Model 100 Deluxe, .22 L.R.R.F., Target Pistol, *Modern*	800	850	665
Model 101, .22 L.R.R.F., Target Pistol, *Modern*	775	825	635
Model 102, .22 L.R.R.F., Target Pistol, *Modern*	800	850	620
Model 102 Deluxe, .22 L.R.R.F., Target Pistol, *Modern*	825	875	685
Model 103, .22 L.R.R.F., Target Pistol, Carved, Inlays, *Modern*	825	900	740
Model 103, .22 L.R.R.F., Target Pistol, Carved, *Modern*	850	925	665
Model 104, .22 L.R.R.F., Target Pistol, Round Barrel, *Modern*	875	950	615
Model 105, .22 L.R.R.F., Target Pistol, Octagon Barrel, *Modern*	875	950	665
Model 106, .22 L.R.R.F., Target Pistol, Round Barrel, *Modern*	875	950	640
Model 107, .22 L.R.R.F., Target Pistol, Octagon Barrel, *Modern*	975	1,075	735
Model 107 Deluxe, .22 L.R.R.F., Target Pistol, Octagon Barrel, Engraved, *Modern*	1,150	1,250	950
Model 110, .22 L.R.R.F., Target Pistol, *Modern*	850	925	615
Model 120, .22 L.R.R.F., Target Pistol, Heavy Barrel, *Modern*	400	450	510
Model 120, .22 L.R.R.F., Target Pistol, Heavy Barrel, Adjustable Grips, *Modern*	400	475	535

	V.G.	Exc.	Prior Edition Exc. Value
Model 120, .22 L.R.R.F., Target Pistol, Heavy Barrel, Left-Hand, Adjustable Grips, *Modern*	$550	$500	$540
Model 120-1, .22 L.R.R.F., Target Pistol, *Modern*	450	450	500
Model 120-2, .22 L.R.R.F., Target Pistol, Adjustable Grips, *Modern*	400	475	525
Model 120-2, .22 L.R.R.F., Target Pistol, Adjustable Grips, Left-Hand, *Modern*	425	475	540
Model 150, .22 L.R.R.F., Target Pistol, *Modern*	1,250	1,500	900
Model 152 Electronic, .22 L.R.R.F., Target Pistol, *Modern*	1,250	1,600	865

RIFLE, BOLT ACTION

	V.G.	Exc.	Prior Edition Exc. Value
Model 45, .22 L.R.R.F., Singleshot, Thumbhole Stock, Target Sights, with Accessories, *Modern*	500	550	585
Model 54, .22 L.R.R.F., Singleshot, Thumbhole Stock, Target Sights, with Accessories, *Modern*	525	575	585
Model 503, .22 L.R.R.F., Singleshot, Thumbhole Stock, Target Sights, with Accessories, *Modern*	500	550	585
Model 506, .22 L.R.R.F., Singleshot, Thumbhole Stock, Target Sights, with Accessories, *Modern*	550	600	625
Olympia 300 Meter, Various Calibers, Singleshot, Thumbhole Stock, Target Sights, with Accessories, *Modern*	675	750	720
Tanner, Various Calibers, Singleshot, Thumbhole Stock, Target Sights, with Accessories, *Modern*	750	825	845
Sporting Rifle, Various Calibers, Set Triggers, Fancy Wood, Checkered Stock, Open Sights, *Modern*	525	600	590

HAMPTON, JOHN Dauphin County, Pa. See Kentucky Rifles and Pistols.

HARD PAN Made by Hood Firearms, c. 1875.

HANDGUN, REVOLVER

	V.G.	Exc.	Prior Edition Exc. Value
.22 Short R.F., 7 Shot, Spur Trigger, Solid Frame, Single Action, *Antique*	100	150	165
.32 Short R.F., 5 Shot, Spur Trigger, Solid Frame, Single Action, *Antique*	125	175	170

HARPERS FERRY ARMS CO.

RIFLE, FLINTLOCK

	V.G.	Exc.	Prior Edition Exc. Value
.72 Lafayette, Musket, Reproduction, *Antique*	250	300	280

RIFLE, PERCUSSION

	V.G.	Exc.	Prior Edition Exc. Value
.51 Maynard, Carbine, Breech Loader, Reproduction, *Antique*	150	200	190
.58, 1861 Springfield, Rifled, Musket, Reproduction, *Antique*	150	200	190

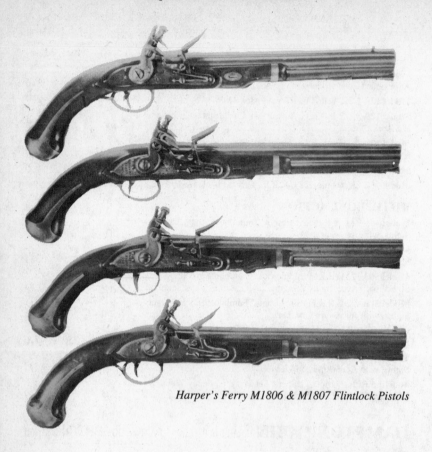

Harper's Ferry M1806 & M1807 Flintlock Pistols

	V.G.	Exc.	Prior Edition Exc. Value

HARRINGTON & RICHARDSON ARMS CO.

Worcester, Mass. Successors to Wesson & Harrington, 1874 to Date.

HANDGUN, REVOLVER

	V.G.	Exc.	Prior Edition Exc. Value
Abilene Anniversary, .22 L.R.R.F., Commemorative, *Curio*	$75	$100	$100
American, Various Calibers, Double Action, Solid Frame, *Modern*	50	75	85
Auto Ejecting, Various Calibers, Top Break, Hammer, Double Action, *Modern*	100	125	120
Bobby, Various Calibers, 6 Shot, Top Break, Double Action, *Modern*	100	100	100
Bulldog, Various Calibers, Double Action, Solid Frame, *Modern*	75	100	85
Defender, .38 S & W, Top Break, 6 Shot, Double Action, Adjustable Sights, *Modern*	100	125	110

	V.G.	Exc.	Prior Edition Exc. Value
Expert, .22 L.R.R.F., Top Break, 9 Shot, Double Action, Wood Grips, *Modern*	$125	$150	$140
Expert, .22 W.R.F., Top Break, 9 Shot, Double Action, Wood Grips, *Modern*	125	150	150
Hammerless, Various Calibers, Double Action, Solid Frame, *Modern*	75	100	100
Hunter (Early), .22 L.R.R.F., 7 Shot, Solid Frame, Wood Grips, Double Action, *Modern*	75	100	100
Hunter (Later), .22 L.R.R.F., 9 Shot, Solid Frame, Wood Grips, Double Action, *Modern*	75	100	95
Model 199, .22 L.R.R.F., Single Action, 9 Shot, Top Break, Adjustable Sights, *Modern*	75	100	95
Model 4, Various Calibers, Double Action, Solid Frame, *Modern*	75	100	95
Model 40, Various Calibers, Top Break, Hammerless, Double Action, *Modern*	100	125	115
Model 5, .32 S & W Double Action, 5 Shot, Solid Frame, *Modern*	75	100	90
Model 6, .22 L.R.R.F., Double Action, 7 Shot, Solid Frame, *Modern*	75	100	90

H & R .32 Pistol

H & R American .44

H & R Auto Ejecting

	V.G.	Exc.	Prior Edition Exc. Value
Model 603, .22 W.M.R., 9 Shot, Solid Frame, Double Action, Swing-Out Cylinder, Adjustable Sights, *Modern*	*$100*	*$125*	*$105*
Model 604, .22 W.M.R., 9 Shot, Solid Frame, Double Action, Swing-Out Cylinder, Adjustable Sights, *Modern*	75	100	100
Model 622, .22 L.R.R.F., Solid Frame, 6 Shot, Double Action, *Modern*	50	75	60
Model 632, .32 S & W Long, Solid Frame, 6 Shot, Double Action, *Modern*	50	75	60
Model 633, .32 S & W Long, Solid Frame, 6 Shot, Chrome, Double Action, *Modern*	50	75	70
Model 649, .22LR/.22 W.M.R. Combo, Western Style, 9 Shot, Double Action, Adjustable Sights, *Modern*	50	75	70
Model 650, .22LR/.22 W.M.R. Combo, Western Style, 9 Shot, Double Action, Adjustable Sights, *Modern*	50	75	75
Model 666, .22LR/.22 W.M.R. Combo, Solid Frame, 9 Shot, Double Action, *Modern*	50	75	70
Model 676, .22 LR/.22 W.M.R. Combo, Western Style, 9 Shot, Double Action, Adjustable Sights, *Modern*	75	100	95
Model 676-12", .22 LR/.22 W.M.R. Combo, Western Style, 9 Shot, Double Action, Adjustable Sights, *Modern*	75	100	85
Model 686, .22 LR/.22 W.M.R. Combo, Western Style, 9 Shot, Double Action, Adjustable Sights, *Modern*	75	100	100
Model 732, .32 S & W Long, Solid Frame, 6 Shot, Double Action, Swing-Out Cylinder, *Modern*	50	75	65
Model 733, .32 S & W Long, Solid Frame, 6 Shot, Double Action, Swing-Out Cylinder, *Modern*	50	75	75
Model 766, .22 L.R.R.F., Top Break, 7 Shot, Double Action, Wood Grips, *Modern*	100	150	135
Model 766, .22 W.R.F., Top Break, 7 Shot, Double Action, Wood Grips, *Modern*	125	150	150
Model 826, .22 W.M.R., 6 Shot, Double Action, Adjustable Sights, Swing-Out Cylinder, *Modern*	75	100	100
Model 829, .22 L.R.R.F., 9 Shot, Double Action, Adjustable Sights, Swing-Out Cylinder, *Modern*	75	100	100
Model 832, .32 S & W, 6 Shot, Double Action, Adjustable Sights, Swing-Out Cylinder, *Modern*	75	100	100
Model 900, .22 L.R.R.F., Solid Frame, 9 Shot, Double Action, *Modern*	75	75	55
Model 901, .22 L.R.R.F., Solid Frame, 9 Shot, Double Action, *Modern*	75	75	55
Model 922 (Early), .22 L.R.R.F., 9 Shot, Solid Frame, Wood Grips, Octagon Barrel, Double Action, *Modern*	75	100	95
Model 922 (Early), .22 L.R.R.F., 9 Shot, Solid Frame, Double Action, *Modern*	75	100	90
Model 922 (Early), .22 L.R.R.F., 9 Shot, Solid Frame, Pocket Pistol, Double Action, *Modern*	75	100	90
Model 922 (Late), .22 L.R.R.F., 9 Shot, Solid Frame, Swing-Out Cylinder, Double Action, *Modern*	50	75	55

Harrington & Richardson, M649, .22 Caliber

Harrington & Richardson M900, .22 Caliber

Harrington & Richardson M929, .22 Caliber

Harrington & Richardson M970, .22 Caliber

	V.G.	Exc.	Prior Edition Exc. Value
Model 925, .22 L.R.R.F., 9 Shot, Solid Frame, Double Action, Swing-Out Cylinder, *Modern*	$50	$75	$70
Model 925, .38 S & W, Solid Frame, 5 Shot, Adjustable Sights, *Modern*	75	100	80
Model 926, .22 L.R.R.F., 5 Shot, Solid Frame, Adjustable Sights, *Modern*	75	100	80
Model 926, .38 S & W, Solid Frame, 5 Shot, Adjustable Sights, *Modern*	75	100	80
Model 929, .22 L.R.R.F., 9 Shot, Solid Frame, Double Action, Swing-Out Cylinder, *Modern*	50	75	55
Model 930, .22 L.R.R.F., 9 Shot, Solid Frame, Double Action, Swing-Out Cylinder, Adjustable Sights, *Modern*	50	75	65
Model 939, .22 L.R.R.F., 9 Shot, Solid Frame, Double Action, Swing-Out Cylinder, Adjustable *Modern*	50	75	70
Model 940, .22 L.R.R.F., 9 Shot, Solid Frame, Double Action, Swing-Out Cylinder, *Modern*	50	75	70
Model 949, .22 L.R.R.F., 9 Shot, Western Style, Double Action, Adjustable Sights, *Modern*	50	75	60
Model 950, .22 L.R.R.F., 9 Shot, Western Style, Double Action, Adjustable Sights, *Modern*	50	75	60
Model 970, .22 Checkered Grip, *Modern*	50	75	75
Model 999 (Early), .22 L.R.R.F., 9 Shot, Top Break, Double Action, Adjustable Sights, *Modern*	75	100	85
Model 999 (Early), .22 W.R.F., Top Break, 9 Shot, Double Action, Adjustable Sights, *Modern*	125	150	135
Model 999 (Late), .22 L.R.R.F., Top Break, 9 Shot, Double Action, Adjustable Sights, *Modern*	50	75	70
New Defender, .22 L.R.R.F., Top Break, 9 Shot, Double Action, Wood Grips, Adjustable Sights, *Modern*	100	125	125
Special, .22 L.R.R.F., Top Break; 9 Shot, Double Action, Wood Grips, *Modern*	100	125	135
Special, .22 W.R.F., Top Break, 9 Shot, Double Action, Wood Grips, *Modern*	125	150	150
Target (Early), .22 L.R.R.F., Top Break, 9 Shot, Double Action, Wood Grips, *Modern*	100	125	125
Target (Early), .22 W.R.F., Top Break, 9 Shot, Double Action, Wood Grips, *Modern*	125	150	135
Target (Hi Speed), .22 W.R.F., Top Break, 9 Shot, Double Action, Wood Grips, *Modern*	125	150	140
Target (Hi Speed), .22 L.R.R.F., Top Break, 9 Shot, Double Action, Wood Grips, *Modern*	125	150	130
Trapper, .22 L.R.R.F., 7 Shot, Solid Frame, Wood Grips, Double Action, *Modern*	75	100	100
Vest Pocket, Various Calibers, Double Action, Solid Frame, Spurless Hammer, *Modern*	75	100	90
Young America, Various Calibers, Double Action, Solid Frame, *Modern*	75	100	90

	V.G.	Exc.	Prior Edition Exc. Value

HANDGUN, SEMI-AUTOMATIC

Self-Loading, .25 ACP, Clip Fed, *Modern*	$275	$325	$300
Self-Loading, .32 ACP, Clip Fed, *Modern*	225	275	250

HANDGUN, SINGLESHOT

U.S.R.A. Target, .22 L.R.R.F., Top Break, Adjustable Sights, Wood Grips, *Modern*	325	375	375

RIFLE, BOLT ACTION

Model 250 Sportster, .22 L.R.R.F., 5 Shot Clip, Open Rear Sight, *Modern*	50	75	53
Model 251 Sportster, .22 L.R.R.F., 5 Shot Clip, Open Rear Sight, *Modern*	50	75	65
Model 265 Reg'lar, .22 L.R.R.F., Clip Fed, Peep Sights, *Modern*	50	75	58
Model 300, Various Calibers, Cheekpiece, Monte Carlo Stock, Checkered Stock, *Modern*	300	350	330
Model 301, Various Calibers, Checkered Stock, Mannlicher, *Modern*	350	400	380
Model 317, Various Calibers, Checkered Stock, Monte Carlo Stock, *Modern*	275	325	310
Model 317P, .223 Rem., Fancy Checkering, Monte Carlo Stock, Fancy Wood, *Modern*	450	500	485
Model 330, Various Calibers, Checkered Stock, Monte Carlo Stock, *Modern*	225	275	260
Model 333, Various Calibers, Monte Carlo Stock, *Modern*	225	275	260
Model 340, Various Calibers, Monte Carlo Stock, Recoil Pad, *Modern*	250	300	280
Model 365 ACE, .22 L.R.R.F., Singleshot, Peep Sights, *Modern*	50	50	48
Model 370, Various Calibers, Target Stock, Heavy Barrel, *Modern*	300	350	345
Model 450 Medalist, .22 L.R.R.F., 5 Shot Clip, No Sights, Target Stock, *Modern*	125	150	140
Model 451 Medalist, .22 L.R.R.F., 5 Shot Clip, Lyman Sights, Target Stock, *Modern*	125	175	170
Model 465 Targeteer, .22 L.R.R.F., Clip Fed, Peep Sights, *Modern*	75	100	85
Model 465 Targeteer Jr., .22 L.R.R.F., Clip Fed, Peep Sights, *Modern*	75	100	85
Model 750 Pioneer, .22 L.R.R.F., Singleshot, Open Rear Sight, *Modern*	50	50	50
Model 751 Pioneer, .22 L.R.R.F., Singleshot, Open Rear Sight, Mannlicher, *Modern*	50	75	60
Model 765 Pioneer, .22 L.R.R.F., Singleshot, Open Rear Sight, *Modern*	50	50	38
Model 852 Fieldsman, .22 L.R.R.F., Tube Feed, Open Rear Sight, *Modern*	50	75	65
Model 865 Plainsman, .22 L.R.R.F., 5 Shot Clip, Open Rear Sights, *Modern*	50	75	65

	V.G.	Exc.	Prior Edition Exc. Value
Model 866 Plainsman, .22 L.R.R.F., 5 Shot Clip, Open Rear Sight, Mannlicher, *Modern*	$50	$75	$70
Model 5200 Match, .22 L.R.R.F., Target Rifle, Single Shot, Heavy Barrel, No Sights, *Modern*	225	275	270
Model 5200 Sporter, .22 L.R.R.F., Target Rifle, Clip Fed, Target Sights, Checkered Stock, *Modern*	225	275	270

RIFLE, PERCUSSION

	V.G.	Exc.	Prior Edition Exc. Value
Huntsman .45, Top Break, Side Lever, Rifled, Reproduction, *Antique*	75	100	90
Huntsman. 50, Top Break, Side Lever, Rifled, Reproduction, *Antique*	75	100	80
Model 175, .45 or .58 Caliber, Springfield Style, Open Sights, Reproduction, *Antique*	125	175	165
Model 175 Deluxe, .45 or .58 Caliber, Springfield Style, Open Sights, Checkered Stock, Reproduction, *Antique*	225	275	260

RIFLE, SEMI-AUTOMATIC

	V.G.	Exc.	Prior Edition Exc. Value
Model 150 Leatherneck, .22 L.R.R.F., 5 shot Clip, Open Rear Sight, *Modern*	75	100	75
Model 151 Leatherneck, .22 L.R.R.F., 5 Shot Clip, Peep Sights, *Modern*	75	100	85
Model 165 Leatherneck, .22 L.R.R.F., Clip Fed, Heavy Barrel, Peep Sights, *Modern*	100	125	115
Model 308, Various Calibers, Checkered Stock, Monte Carlo Stock, *Modern*	275	325	300
Model 360, Various Calibers, Checkered Stock, Monte Carlo Stock, *Modern*	250	300	285
Model 361, Various Calibers, Checkered Stock, Monte Carlo Stock, *Modern*	275	325	310
Model 60 Reising, .45 ACP, Clip Fed, Carbine, Open Rear Sight, *Modern*	350	400	390
Model 65 General, .22 L.R.R.F., Clip Fed, Heavy Barrel, Peep Sights, *Modern*	200	250	235
Model 700, .22 W.M.R., Monte Carlo Stock, 5 Shot Clip, *Modern*	125	150	135
Model 700 Deluxe, .22 W.M.R., Monte Carlo Stock, 5 Shot Clip, *Modern*	200	225	210
Model 800 Lynx, .22 L.R.R.F., Clip Fed, Open Rear Sight, *Modern*	75	100	70

RIFLE, SINGLESHOT

	V.G.	Exc.	Prior Edition Exc. Value
1871 Springfield Deluxe, .45–70 Government, Trap Door Action, Carbine, Light Engraving, *Modern*	225	250	230
1871 Springfield Officers', .45–70 Government, Commemorative, Trap Door Action, *Curio*	275	350	330
1871 Springfield Standard, .45–70 Government, Trap Door Action, Carbine, *Modern*	175	200	190
1873 Springfield Officers', .45–70 Government, Trap Door Action, Light Engraving, Peep Sights, *Modern*	250	300	280

	V.G.	Exc.	Prior Edition Exc. Value
1873 Springfield Standard, .45–70 Government, Trap Door Action, Commemorative, *Modern*	$200	$225	$210
Custer Memorial Enlisted Model, .45–70 Government, Commemorative, Trap Door Action, Carbine, Fancy Engraving, Fancy Wood, *Curio*	1,000	1,500	2,175
Custer Memorial Officers' Model, .45–70 Government, Commemorative, Trap Door Action, Carbine, Fancy Engraving, Fancy Wood, *Curio*	2,000	2,750	3,350
Little Big Horn Springfield Standard, .45–70 Government, Commemorative, Trap Door Action, Carbine, *Curio*	300	350	200
Model 172 Springfield, .45–70 Government, Trap Door Action, Carbine, Engraved, Silver Plated, Tang Sights, Checkered Stock, *Modern*	350	400	850
Model 157, Various Calibers, Top Break, Side Lever, Automatic Ejector, Open Rear Sight, Mannlicher, *Modern*	50	75	68
Model 158 Topper, Various Calibers, Top Break, Side Lever, Automatic Ejector, Open Rear Sight, *Modern*	50	75	60
Model 158 Topper, Various Calibers, Top Break, Side Lever, Automatic Ejector, Open Rear Sight, Extra Set of Rifle Barrels, *Modern*	75	100	80
Model 158 Topper, Various Calibers, Top Break, Side Lever, Automatic Ejector, Open Rear Sight, Extra Shotgun Barrel, *Modern*	75	100	75
Model 163, Various Calibers, Top Break, Side Lever, Automatic Ejector, Open Rear Sight, *Modern*	50	75	63
Model 755 Sahara, .22 L.R.R.F., Singleshot, Open Rear Sight, Mannlicher, *Modern*	50	75	48
Model 760 Sahara, .22 L.R.R.F., Singleshot, Open Rear Sight, *Modern*	50	50	43
Shikari, .44 Magnum, Top Break, Side Lever, Automatic Ejector, *Modern*	50	75	70
Shikari, .45–70 Government, Top Break, Side Lever, Automatic Ejector, *Modern*	75	100	80

RIFLE, SLIDE ACTION

	V.G.	Exc.	Prior Edition Exc. Value
Model 422, .22 L.R.R.F., Tube Feed, Open Rear Sight, *Modern*	100	125	100

SHOTGUN, BOLT ACTION

	V.G.	Exc.	Prior Edition Exc. Value
Model 348 Gamemaster, 12 and 16 Gauges, Tube Feed, Takedown, *Modern*	50	75	60
Model 349 Deluxe, 12 and 16 Gauges, Tube Feed, Takedown, Adjustable Choke, *Modern*	50	75	70
Model 351 Huntsman, 12 and 16 Gauges, Tube Feed, Takedown, Monte Carlo Stock, Adjustable Choke, *Modern*	50	75	70

SHOTGUN, DOUBLE BARREL, OVER-UNDER

	V.G.	Exc.	Prior Edition Exc. Value
Model 1212, 12 Ga., Field Grade, Vent Rib, Single Selective Trigger, *Modern*	325	375	360
Model 1212 Waterfowl, Ga. Mag. 3", Field Grade, Vent Rib, Single Selective Trigger, *Modern*	350	400	380

	V.G.	Exc.	Prior Edition Exc. Value

SHOTGUN, DOUBLE BARREL, SIDE-BY-SIDE

Model 404, Various Gauges, Hammerless, *Modern* .... $150 / $175 / $175

Model 404C, Various Gauges, Hammerless, Checkered Stock, *Modern*.. 125 / 175 / 175

SHOTGUN, PERCUSSION

Huntsman 12 Ga., Top Break, Side Lever, Reproduction, *Antique*..... 75 / 100 / 85

SHOTGUN, SEMI-AUTOMATIC

Model 403, .410 Ga., Takedown, *Modern* .... 150 / 200 / 180

SHOTGUN, SINGLESHOT

Folding Gun, Various Gauges, Top Break, Hammer, Automatic Ejector, *Modern* .... 50 / 75 / 65

Model #1 Harrich, 12 Ga., Vent Rib, Engraved, Fancy Checkering, *Modern* .... 1,200 / 1,550 / 1,600

Model 148, Various Gauges, Top Break, Side Lever, Automatic Ejector, *Modern* .... 50 / 75 / 53

Model 158, Various Gauges, Top Break, Side Lever, Automatic Ejector, *Modern* .... 50 / 75 / 53

Model 159, Various Gauges, Top Break, Side Lever, Automatic Ejector, *Modern* .... 50 / 75 / 63

Model 162 Buck, 12 Ga., Top Break, Side Lever, Automatic Ejector, Peep Sights, *Modern*.. 50 / 75 / 63

Model 176, 10 Ga. 3½", Top Break, Side Lever, Automatic Ejector, *Modern* .... 50 / 75 / 63

Model 188 Deluxe, Various Gauges, Top Break, Side Lever, Automatic Ejector, *Modern* .... 25 / 50 / 47

Model 198 Deluxe, Various Gauges, Top Break, Side Lever, Automatic Ejector, *Modern* .... 25 / 50 / 47

Model 3, Various Gauges, Top Break, Hammerless, Automatic Ejector, *Modern* .... 50 / 75 / 62

Model 459 Youth, Various Gauges, Top Break, Side Lever, Automatic Ejector, *Modern* .... 50 / 75 / 53

Model 48, Various Gauges, Top Break, Hammer, Automatic Ejector, *Modern* .... 50 / 50 / 47

Model 480 Youth, Various Gauges, Top Break, Side Lever, Automatic Ejector, *Modern* .... 50 / 50 / 47

Model 488 Deluxe, Various Gauges, Top Break, Hammer, Automatic Ejector, *Modern* .... 50 / 75 / 53

Model 490 Youth, Various Gauges, Top Break, Side Lever, Automatic Ejector, *Modern* .... 50 / 50 / 47

Model 5, Various Gauges, Top Break, Lightweight, Automatic Ejector, *Modern* .... 75 / 100 / 75

Model 6, Various Gauges, Top Break, Heavyweight, Automatic Ejector, *Modern* .... 75 / 100 / 80

Model 7, Various Gauges, Top Break, Automatic Ejector, *Modern*..... 50 / 75 / 60

Model 8 Standard, Various Gauges, Top Break, Automatic Ejector, *Modern* .... 50 / 75 / 60

	V.G.	Exc.	Prior Edition Exc. Value
Model 9, Various Gauges, Top Break, Automatic Ejector, *Modern*	$50	$75	$60
Model 98, Various Gauges, Top Break, Side Lever, Automatic Ejector, *Modern*	50	75	55

SHOTGUN, SLIDE ACTION

	V.G.	Exc.	Prior
Model 400, Various Gauges, Solid Frame, *Modern*	150	175	155
Model 401, Various Gauges, Solid Frame, Adjustable Choke, *Modern*	150	175	160
Model 402, .410 Ga., Solid Frame, *Modern*	150	175	155
Model 440, Various Gauges, Solid Frame, *Modern*	150	175	160
Model 400, Various Gauges, Solid Frame, Vent Rib, *Modern*	150	175	170

HARRIS, HENRY Payton, Pa. 1779–1783. See Kentucky Rifles.

HARRISON ARMS CO. Made in Belgium for Sickles & Preston, Davenport, Iowa.

SHOTGUN, DOUBLE BARREL, SIDE-BY-SIDE

	V.G.	Exc.	Prior
Various Gauges, Outside Hammers, Damascus Barrel, *Modern*	100	150	155
Various Gauges, Hammerless, Steel Barrel, *Modern*	125	200	185
Various Gauges, Hammerless, Damascus Barrel, *Modern*	100	150	155
Various Gauges, Outside Hammers, Steel Barrel, *Modern*	125	200	180

SHOTGUN, SINGLESHOT

	V.G.	Exc.	Prior
Various Gauges, Hammer, Steel Barrel, *Modern*	50	75	75

HARTFORD ARMS & EQUIPMENT CO. Hartford, Conn. 1929–1930.

HANDGUN, MANUAL REPEATER

	V.G.	Exc.	Prior
.22 L.R.R.F., Clip Fed, Target Pistol, *Curio*	475	550	475

HANDGUN, SEMI-AUTOMATIC

	V.G.	Exc.	Prior
Model 1928, .22 L.R.R.F., Clip Fed, Target Pistol, *Curio*	425	500	415

HANDGUN, SINGLESHOT

	V.G.	Exc.	Prior
.22 L.R.R.F., Target Pistol, *Curio*	450	525	500

HARTFORD ARMS CO. Made by Norwich Falls Pistol Co., c. 1880.

HANDGUN, REVOLVER

	V.G.	Exc.	Prior
.32 Short R.F., 5 Shot, Spur Trigger, Solid Frame, Single Action, *Antique*	125	175	165

	V.G.	Exc.	Prior Edition Exc. Value

HARTFORD ARMS CO. Made by Crescent for Simmons Hardware Co., St. Louis, Mo.

SHOTGUN, DOUBLE BARREL, SIDE-BY-SIDE

	V.G.	Exc.	Prior Edition Exc. Value
Various Gauges, Outside Hammers, Damascus Barrel, *Modern*	$125	$175	$155
Various Gauges, Hammerless, Steel Barrel, *Modern*	150	200	185
Various Gauges, Hammerless, Damascus Barrel, *Modern*	100	150	155
Various Gauges, Outside Hammers, Steel Barrel, *Modern*	150	200	180

SHOTGUN, SINGLESHOT

	V.G.	Exc.	Prior Edition Exc. Value
Various Gauges, Hammer, Steel Barrel, *Modern*	50	75	75

HARVARD Made by Crescent, c. 1900.

SHOTGUN, DOUBLE BARREL, SIDE-BY-SIDE

	V.G.	Exc.	Prior Edition Exc. Value
Various Gauges, Outside Hammers, Damascus Barrel, *Modern*	125	175	155
Various Gauges, Hammerless, Steel Barrel, *Modern*	150	200	185
Various Gauges, Hammerless, Damascus Barrel, *Modern*	100	150	155
Various Gauges, Outside Hammers, Steel Barrel, *Modern*	150	200	180

SHOTGUN, SINGLESHOT

	V.G.	Exc.	Prior Edition Exc. Value
Various Gauges, Hammer, Steel Barrel, *Modern*	50	75	75

HAUCK, WILBUR West Arlington, Vt., c. 1950.

RIFLE, SINGLESHOT

	V.G.	Exc.	Prior Edition Exc. Value
Target Rifle, Various Calibers, Target Sights, Target Stock, Adjustable Trigger, *Modern*	475	525	485

HAWES FIREARMS Van Nuys, Calif.

HANDGUN, REVOLVER

	V.G.	Exc.	Prior Edition Exc. Value
Montana Marshall, .22 L.R.R.F./.22 W.M.R. Combo, Western Style, Single Action, Brass Grip Frame, *Modern*	100	125	80
Montana Marshall, .22 L.R.R.F., Western Style, Single Action, Brass Grip Frame, *Modern*	75	100	75
Montana Marshall, .357 Magnum/9mm Combo, Western Style, Single Action, Brass Grip Frame, *Modern*	175	225	165
Montana Marshall, .44 Magnum, Western Style, Single Action, Brass Grip Frame, *Modern*	150	200	145
Montana Marshall, .44 Magnum/.44–40 Combo, Western Style, Single Action, Brass Grip Frame, *Modern*	175	225	180
Montana Marshall, .45 Colt, Western Style, Single Action, Brass Grip Frame, *Modern*	150	200	150
Montana Marshall, .45 Colt/.45 ACP Combo, Western Style, Single Action, Brass Grip Frame, *Modern*	175	250	200
Silver City Marshall, .22 L.R.R.F./.22 W.M.R. Western Style, Single Action, Brass Grip Frame, *Modern*	100	150	90

	V.G.	Exc.	Prior Edition Exc. Value
Silver City Marshall, .22 L.R.R.F., Western Style, Single Action, Brass Grip Frame, *Modern*	$75	$100	$75
Silver City Marshall, .357 Magnum/9mm Combo, Western Style, Single Action, Brass Grip Frame, *Modern*	150	225	175
Silver City Marshall, .44 Magnum, Western Style, Single Action, Brass Grip Frame, *Modern*	150	225	165
Silver City Marshall, .44 Magnum/.44–40 Combo, Western Style, Single Action, Brass Grip Frame, *Modern*	150	225	185
Silver City Marshall, .45 Colt, Western Style, Single Action, Brass Grip Frame, *Modern*	125	200	160
Silver City Marshall, .45 Colt/.45 ACP Combo, Western Style, Single Action, Brass Grip Frame, *Modern*	150	250	200
Texas Marshall, .22 L.R.R.F./.22 W.M.R. Combo, Western Style, Single Action, Nickel Plated, *Modern*	125	150	90
Texas Marshall, .22 L.R.R.F., Western Style, Single Action, Nickel Plated, *Modern*	75	100	75
Texas Marshall, .357 Magnum, Western Style, Single Action, Nickel Plated, *Modern*	125	200	155
Texas Marshall, .357 Magnum/9mm Combo, Western Style, Single Action, Nickel Plated, *Modern*	150	225	185
Texas Marshall, .44 Magnum, Western Style, Single Action, Nickel Plated, *Modern*	125	200	170
Texas Marshall, .44 Magnum/.44–40 Combo, Western Style, Single Action, Nickel Plated, *Modern*	175	250	195
Texas Marshall, .45 Colt, Western Style, Single Action, Nickel Plated, *Modern*	125	200	155
Texas Marshall, .45 Colt/.45 ACP Combo, Western Style, Single Action, Nickel Plated, *Modern*	175	250	200
Denver Marshall, .22 L.R.R.F./.22 W.M.R. Combo, Western Style, Single Action, Adjustable Sights, *Modern*	125	150	90
Denver Marshall, .22 L.R.R.F., Western Style, Single Action, Brass Grip Frame, Adjustable Sights, *Modern*	75	100	75
Chief Marshall, .357 Magnum, Western Style, Single Action, Brass Grip Frame, Adjustable Sights, *Modern*	125	200	150
Chief Marshall, .44 Magnum, Western Style, Single Action, Brass Grip Frame, Adjustable Sights, *Modern*	125	200	160
Chief City Marshall, .25 Colt, Western Style, Single Action, Brass Grip Frame, Adjustable Sights, *Modern*	125	200	155

HANDGUN SINGLESHOT

	V.G.	Exc.	Prior Edition Exc. Value
Stevens Favorite Copy, .22 L.R.R.F., Tip-Up, Rosewood Grips, *Modern*	100	125	80
Stevens Favorite Copy, 22 L.R.R.F., Tip-Up, Plastic Grips, *Modern*	100	125	80
Stevens Favorite Copy, .22 L.R.R.F., Tip-Up, Plastic Grips, Target Sights, *Modern*	100	125	85

HANDGUN, SEMI-AUTOMATIC

	V.G.	Exc.	Prior Edition Exc. Value
.25 ACP, Clip Fed, *Modern*	100	125	100

	V.G.	Exc.	Prior Edition Exc. Value

HAWKIN, J. & S. Jacob and Samuel Hawkin, St. Louis, Mo. 1822–1862. John Gemmer purchased the business and continued it until 1890.

RIFLE, PERCUSSION

	V.G.	Exc.	Prior Edition Exc. Value
Hawkin Plains Rifle, Various Calibers, Hawkin Style, *Antique*	$5,500	$8,500	$6,500
Gemmer Plains Rifle, Various Calibers, Hawkin Style, *Antique*	4,500	6,500	4,500

HAWKINS, HENRY Schenectady, N.Y. 1769–1775. See Kentucky Rifles.

H & D Henrion & Dassy, Liege, Belgium, c. 1900.

HANDGUN, SEMI-AUTOMATIC

	V.G.	Exc.	Prior Edition Exc. Value
H & D Patent, .25 ACP, Clip Fed, *Curio*	450	625	600

H.D.H. Mre. D'Armes HDH, Liege, Belgium, c. 1910.

HANDGUN, REVOLVER

	V.G.	Exc.	Prior Edition Exc. Value
20 Shot, Various Calibers, Over-Under Barrels, Two Row Cylinder, Double Action, *Curio*	225	275	250
10 Shot, Various Calibers, Double Action, *Curio*	125	200	170
Ordnance Type, Various Calibers, Double Action *Curio*	150	175	170
Constabulary Type, Various Calibers, Double Action, *Curio*	125	150	135
Velo-Dog, Various Calibers, Folding Trigger, Double Action, *Curio*	100	125	110
Velo-Dog, Various Calibers, Folding Trigger, Double Action, Hammerless, *Curio*	100	125	110

HECKERT, PHILIP York, Pa. 1769–1779. See Kentucky Rifles and Pistols.

HECKLER & KOCH Oberndorf/Neckar, Germany.

HANDGUN, SEMI-AUTOMATIC

	V.G.	Exc.	Prior Edition Exc. Value
HK-4, .22 L.R.R.F., Clip Fed, Double Action, *Modern*	275	325	285
HK-4, .25 ACP, Clip Fed, Double Action, *Modern*	225	300	280
HK-4, .32 ACP, Clip Fed, Double Action, German Police, *Modern*	225	275	170
HK-4, .32 AcP, Clip Fed, Double Action, French Made, *Modern*	200	275	200
HK-4, .32 ACP, Clip Fed, Double Action, *Modern*	200	250	285
HK-4, .380 ACP, Clip Fed, Double Action, *Modern*	250	325	300
HK, Various Calibers, Clip Fed, Conversion Kit Only, *Each*	50	75	70
HK-4, Various Calibers, Clip Fed, Double Action, with Conversion Kits All 4 Calibers, *Modern*	375	450	450
HK P-7(PSP), 9mm Luger, Squeeze Cocking, *Modern*	475	550	425
HK P-9S, .45 ACP, Clip Fed, Double Action, *Modern*	325	400	400
HK P-9S, .45 ACP, Target Model, Clip Fed, Double Action, *Modern*	525	600	475

Heckler & Koch HK 93 A-3

Heckler & Koch HK Model 940

Heckler & Koch HK SL 7

Heckler & Koch HK 94 A-2

Heckler & Koch HK P9S Competition

	V.G.	Exc.	Prior Edition Exc. Value
HK P-9S, .45 ACP, with Extra 8" Barrel, Clip Fed, Double Action, *Modern*	$650	$725	$525
P-9S Competition Kit, 9mm Luger, Clip Fed, Double Action, Extra Barrel, Target Sights, Target Grips, *Modern*	725	850	770
P-9S Target, 9mm Luger, Clip Fed, Double Action 5½" Barrel, Target Sights, *Modern*	725	825	475
P-9S Combat, 9mm Luger, Clip Fed, Double Action, 4" Barrel, *Modern*	475	550	400
P-9S Combat, 9mm Luger, Clip Fed, Double Action 4" Barrel with .30 Luger Conversion Kit, *Modern*	675	750	625
VP-70Z, 9mm Luger, Clip Fed, Double Action, 18 Shot Clip, *Modern*	225	275	300

RIFLE, SEMI-AUTOMATIC

	V.G.	Exc.	Prior Edition Exc. Value
HK 91, 22 L.R.R.F., Clip Fed, Conversion Unit Only	300	350	225
HK 91 A-2, .308 Win., Clip Fed, Sporting Version of Military Rifle, with Compensator, *Modern*	850	950	500
HK 91 A-3, .308 Win., Clip Fed, Sporting Version of Military Rifle, Folding Stock with Compensator, *Modern*	1,200	1,400	560
HK 91 A-4, .308 Win., Clip Fed, Sporting Version of Military Rifle, with Compensator, Polygonal Rifling, *Modern*	675	750	675
HK 91 A-5, .308 Win., Clip Fed, Sporting Version of Military Rifle, Folding Stock with Compensator, Polygonal Rifling, *Modern*	750	900	825
HK 91/93, Light Bipod, Add **$40.00–$60.00**			
HK 91/93, For Scope Mount Add **$75.00–$120.00**			
HK 93 A-2, .223 Rem., Clip Fed, Sporting Version of Military Rifle, with Compensator, *Modern*	725	950	500
HK 93 A-3, .223 Rem., Clip Fed, Sporting Version of Military Rifle, Folding Stock, with Compensator, *Modern*	850	1,000	550
HK 94 A-2, 9mm Luger, Clip Fed, Sporting Version of MP5 S.M.G., Standard Stock, *Modern*	925	1,100	500
HK 94 A-3, 9mm Luger, Clip Fed, Sporting Version of MP5 S.M.G., Folding Stock, *Modern*	1,000	1,200	560
Model 270, .22 L.R.R.F., Clip Fed, Checkered Stock, Open Rear Sight, *Modern*	300	325	200
Model 300, .22 WMR, Clip Fed, Checkered Stock, Open Rear Sight, *Modern*	375	425	275
Model 630, .223 Rem., Clip Fed, Checkered Stock, Open Rear Sight, *Modern*	450	500	450
HK 770, .308 Win., Sporting Rifle, Checkered Stock, Monte Carlo Stock, *Modern*	500	575	450
Model 940, .30/06, Clip Fed, Checkered Stock, Open Rear Sight, *Modern*	525	600	460
Model SL 6, .223 Rem., Clip Fed. Military Style Carbine, Open Rear Sight, *Modern*	450	525	400
Model SL 7, .308 Win., Clip Fed, Military Style Carbine, Open Rear Sight, *Modern*	450	525	400

Hege AP-66 .32

	V.G.	Exc.	Prior Edition Exc. Value

HEGE Tradename of Hebsacker Gesellschaft and Hege GmbH, established in 1959 in Schwabisch Halle, West Germany. Now in Uberlingen/Bodensee, West Germany. Also see Beeman's.

COMBINATION WEAPON, OVER-UNDER
President, Various Calibers, Box Lock, Solid Rib, Double Trigger, Checkered Stock, *Modern*....................	$675	$725	$695

HANDGUN, PERCUSSION
Silber Pistol, .33 Caliber, French Style, Engraved, Gold Inlays, Cased, Reproduction, *Antique*....................	600	650	600
Silber Pistol, .33 Caliber, British Style, Engraved, Cased, Reproduction, *Antique*	375	425	400

HANDGUN, SEMI-AUTOMATIC
AP-63, .32 ACP, Clip Fed, Double Action, *Modern*....................	275	325	295
AP-66, .32 ACP, Clip Fed, Double Action, *Modern*....................	225	275	235
AP-66, .380 ACP, Clip Fed, Double Action, *Modern*....................	250	300	250

RIFLE, MATCHLOCK
Zeughaus Musket, .63 Caliber, Heavy Swiss Style, Plain, Reproduction, *Antique*	250	300	250

HEINZELMANN, C.E. Plochingen, Germany 1921–1928.

HANDGUN, SEMI-AUTOMATIC
Heim, .25 ACP, Clip Fed, Blue, *Curio*....................	650	725	575

HELFRICHT Alfred Krauser Waffenfabrik, Zella Mehlis, Germany 1921–1929.

HANDGUN, SEMI-AUTOMATIC
Model 1, .25 ACP, Clip Fed, *Curio*....................	425	475	450
Model 2, .25 ACP, Clip Fed, *Curio*....................	400	450	425
Model 3, .25 ACP, Clip Fed, *Curio*....................	400	450	425
Model 4, .25 ACP, Clip Fed, *Curio*....................	350	400	395

	V.G.	Exc.	Prior Edition Exc. Value

HELVICE Fab. D'Armes de Guerre de Grand Precision, Eibar Spain.

HANDGUN, SEMI-AUTOMATIC

.25 ACP, Clip Fed, *Modern*	$125	$150	$135

HENNCH, PETER Lancaster, Pa. 1770–1774. See Kentucky Rifles.

HENRY, ALEXANDER Edinburgh, Scotland 1869–1895.

RIFLE, DOUBLE BARREL, SIDE-BY-SIDE

.500/450 Mag. BPE, Damascus Barrel, Engraved, Fancy Checkering, Ornate, Cased with Accessories, Hammerless, *Antique*	4,500	5,000	4,650

HENRY GUN CO. Belgium, c. 1900.

SHOTGUN, DOUBLE BARREL, SIDE-BY-SIDE

Various Gauges, Outside Hammers, Damascus Barrel, *Modern*	150	200	180
Various Gauges, Hammerless, Steel Barrel, *Modern*	175	225	200
Various Gauges, Hammerless, Damascus Barrel, *Modern*	150	200	180
Various Gauges, Outside Hammers, Steel Barrel, *Modern*	150	200	190

SHOTGUN, SINGLESHOT

Various Gauges, Hammer, Steel Barrel, *Modern*	75	100	85

HERCULES Made by Stevens Arms.

SHOTGUN, DOUBLE BARREL, SIDE-BY-SIDE

M 315, Various Gauges, Hammerless, Steel Barrel, *Modern*	150	175	175
Model 215, 12 and 16 Gauges, Outside Hammers, Steel Barrel, *Modern*	150	175	165
Model 311, Various Gauges, Hammerless, Steel Barrel, *Modern*	175	200	185
Model 3151, Various Gauges, Hammerless, Recoil Pad, Front & Rear Bead Sights, *Modern*	175	200	190
Model 5151, Various Gauges, Hammerless, Steel Barrel, *Modern*	175	200	180

SHOTGUN, SINGLESHOT

Model 94, Various Gauges, Takedown, Automatic Ejector, Plain Hammer, *Modern*	50	75	65

HERMETIC Tradename used by Bernadon-Martin, St. Etienne, France, c. 1912.

HANDGUN, SEMI-AUTOMATIC

B.M., .32 ACP, Clip Fed, *Curio*	275	325	320

	V.G.	Exc.	Prior Edition Exc. Value

HERMITAGE Made by Stevens Arms.

SHOTGUN, SINGLESHOT

	V.G.	Exc.	Prior Ed.
Model 90, Various Gauges, Takedown, Automatic Ejector, Plain Hammer, *Modern*	$50	$75	$65

HERMITAGE ARMS CO. Made by Crescent for Grey & Dudley Hdw. Co., Nashville, Tenn.

SHOTGUN, DOUBLE BARREL, SIDE-BY-SIDE

	V.G.	Exc.	Prior Ed.
Various Gauges, Outside Hammers, Damascus Barrel, *Modern*	150	175	155
Various Gauges, Hammerless, Steel Barrel, *Modern*	175	200	185
Various Gauges, Hammerless, Damascus Barrel, *Modern*	150	175	155
Various Gauges, Outside Hammers, Steel Barrel, *Modern*	175	200	180

SHOTGUN, SINGLESHOT

	V.G.	Exc.	Prior Ed.
Various Gauges, Hammer, Steel Barrel, *Modern*	50	75	75

HERO Made by Rupertus Arms for Tryon Bros. Co., c. 1880.

HANDGUN, REVOLVER

	V.G.	Exc.	Prior Ed.
.22 Short R.F., 7 Shot, Spur Trigger, Solid Frame, Single Action, *Antique*	125	175	165
.32 Short R.F., 5 Shot, Spur Trigger, Solid Frame, Single Action, *Antique*	150	175	170
.38 Short R.F., 5 Shot, Spur Trigger, Solid Frame, Single Action, *Antique*	100	200	180
.41 Short R.F., 5 Shot, Spur Trigger, Solid Frame, Single Action, *Antique*	175	225	200

HEROLD Tradename of Franz Jager & Co., Suhl, Germany 1923–1939.

	V.G.	Exc.	Prior Ed.
Herold Repetierbuchse, .22 Hornet, Set Triggers, Checkered Stock, *Modern*	750	800	765

HERTERS Distributer & Importer in Waseca, Minn.

HANDGUN, REVOLVER

	V.G.	Exc.	Prior Ed.
Guide, .22 L.R.R.F., Swing-Out Cylinder, Double Action, *Modern*	75	100	50
Power-Mag, .357 Magnum, Western Style, Single Action, *Modern*	100	125	85
Power-Mag, .401 Herter Mag., Western Style, Single Action, *Modern*	100	125	85
Power-Mag, .44 Magnum, Western Style, Single Action, *Modern*	125	150	100
Western, .22 L.R.R.F., Single Action, Western Style, *Modern*	50	75	50

	V.G.	Exc.	Prior Edition Exc. Value

RIFLE, BOLT ACTION

Model J-9 Hunter, Various Calibers, Plain, Monte Carlo Stock, *Modern*.. $200 $225 $200

Model J-9 Presentation, Various Calibers, Checkered Stock, Monte Carlo Stock, Sling Swivels, *Modern* 225 250 225

Model J-9 Supreme, Various Calibers, Checkered Stock, Monte Carlo Stock, Sling Swivels, *Modern*.. 200 250 225

Model U-9 Hunter, Various Calibers, Plain, Monte Carlo Stock, *Modern*.. 200 225 190

Model U-9 Presentation, Various Calibers, Checkered Stock, Sling Swivels, Monte Carlo Stock, *Modern* 225 250 225

Model U-9 Supreme, Various Calibers, Checkered Stock, Sling Swivels, Monte Carlo Stock, *Modern*.................................. 175 225 195

SHOTGUN, SINGLESHOT

Model 151, Various Gauges, Hammer, *Modern* 50 75 45

SHOTGUN, SEMI-AUTOMATIC

Model SL-18, 12 Ga. 3", Checkered Stock, *Modern* 225 275 255

HESS, JACOB Stark Co., Ohio 1842–1860. See Kentucky Rifles.

HESS, SAMUEL Lancaster, Pa., c. 1771. See Kentucky Rifles.

HEYM Franz W. Heym, 1934–1945 in Suhl, Germany, now in Munnerstadt, West Germany.

COMBINATION WEAPON, DRILLING

Model 33, Various Calibers, Hammerless, Double Triggers, Engraved, Checkered Stock, Express Sights, *Modern*...................... 4,500 5,500 3,600

Model 37, Various Calibers, Hammerless, Sidelock, Engraved, Checkered Stock, *Modern*.. 7,500 8,500 4,000

Model 37, Various Calibers, Hammerless, Sidelock, Double Rifle Barrels, Engraved, Checkered Stock, *Modern*.................................... 8,500 9,500 5,500

Model 37 Deluxe, Various Calibers, Hammerless, Sidelock, Double Rifle Barrels, Engraved, Checkered Stock, *Modern* 8,700 9,700 5,900

COMBINATION WEAPON, OVER-UNDER

Model 22S, Various Calibers, Single Set Trigger, Checkered Stock, Light Engraving, *Modern* 1,850 2,250 1,200

Model 55BF (77BF), Various Calibers, Boxlock, Double Triggers, Checkered Stock, Engraved, *Modern* 3,800 4,500 2,550

Model 55BFSS (77BFSS), Various Calibers, Sidelock, Double Triggers, Checkered Stock, *Modern*... 8,250 9,000 4,300

RIFLE, DOUBLE BARREL, OVER-UNDER

Model 55B (77B), Various Calibers, Boxlock, Engraved, Checkered Stock, *Modern*.. 5,500 6,500 2,750

Model 55BSS(77BSS), Various Calibers, Sidelock, Engraved, Checkered Stock, *Modern*.. 6,500 7,500 4,350

	V.G.	Exc.	Prior Edition Exc. Value

SHOTGUN, DOUBLE BARREL, OVER-UNDER

Model 55F (77F), Various Gauges, Boxlock, Engraved, Checkered Stock, Double Triggers, *Modern* $3,250 $3,750 $2,550

Model 55FSS (77FSS), Various Gauges, Sidelock, Engraved, Checkered Stock, Double Triggers, *Modern* 3,000 3,500 3,575

RIFLE, BOLT ACTION

Model SR-20, Various Calibers, Fancy Wood, Double Set Triggers, *Modern* 800 1,000 600

Model SR-20, Various Calibers, Fancy Wood, Double Set Triggers, Left Hand, *Modern* 950 1,200 725

RIFLE, SINGLESHOT

Model HR-30, Various Calibers, Fancy Wood, Engraved, Single Set Trigger, Ruger Action, Round Barrel, *Modern* 2,000 2,500 1,575

Model HR-38, Various Calibers, Fancy Wood, Engraved, Single Set Trigger, Ruger Action, Octagon Barrel, *Modern* 2,500 3,000 1,750

HIGGINS, J.C. Trade Name used by Sears-Roebuck.

HANDGUN, REVOLVER

Model 88, .22 L.R.R.F., *Modern* 50 75 70
Model 88 Fisherman, .22 L.R.R.F., *Modern* 50 75 70
Ranger, .22 L.R.R.F., *Modern* 50 75 70

HANDGUN, SEMI-AUTOMATIC

Model 80, .22 L.R.R.F., Clip Fed, Hammerless, *Modern* 75 100 105
Model 85, .22 L.R.R.F., Clip Fed, Hammer, *Modern* 100 125 125

RIFLE, BOLT ACTION

Model 228, .22 L.R.R.F., Clip Fed, *Modern* 25 50 50
Model 229, .22 L.R.R.F., Tube Feed, *Modern* 25 50 55
Model 245, .22 L.R.R.F., Singleshot, *Modern* 25 50 40
Model 51, Various Calibers, Checkered Stock, *Modern* 175 225 225
Model 51 Special, Various Calibers, Checkered Stock, Light Engraving, *Modern* 225 275 300

RIFLE, LEVER ACTION

.22 WMR, *Modern* 50 75 85
Model 45, Various Calibers, Tube Feed, Carbine, *Modern* 50 75 80

RIFLE, SEMI-AUTOMATIC

Model 25, .22 LR.R.F., Clip Feed, *Modern* 25 50 55
Model 31, .22 L.R.R.F., Tube Feed, *Modern* 50 75 65

RIFLE, SLIDE ACTION

Model 33, .22 LR.R.F., Tube Feed, *Modern* 50 75 65

SHOTGUN, BOLT ACTION

Model 10, Various Gauges, Tube Feed, 5 Shot, *Modern* 50 75 65

	V.G.	Exc.	Prior Edition Exc. Value
Model 11, Various Gauges, Tube Feed, 3 Shot, *Modern*	$50	$50	$55

SHOTGUN, DOUBLE BARREL, SIDE-BY-SIDE

	V.G.	Exc.	Prior
Various Calibers, Plain, Takedown, Hammerless, *Modern*	150	175	170

SHOTGUN, SEMI-AUTOMATIC

Model 66, 12 Ga., Plain Barrel, *Modern*	125	175	160
Model 66, 12 Ga., Plain Barrel, Adjustable Choke, *Modern*	150	175	170
Model 66, 12 Ga., Vent Rib, Adjustable Choke, *Modern*	150	175	170
Model 66 Deluxe, 12 Ga., *Modern*	150	175	175

SHOTGUN, SINGLESHOT

Various Calibers, Takedown, Adjustable Choke, Plain, Hammer, *Modern*	50	75	55

SHOTGUN, SLIDE ACTION

Model 20 Deluxe, 12 Ga., *Modern*	125	150	145
Model 20 Deluxe, 12 Ga., Vent Rib, Adjustable Choke, *Modern*	125	150	155
Model 20 Special, 12 Ga., Vent Rib, Adjustable Choke, *Modern*	150	200	190
Model 20 Standard, 12 Ga., *Modern*	100	150	135

HIGH STANDARD   High Standard Mfg. Co. 1926 to the present, first
in New Haven, Conn., then as High Standard Sporting Firearms in Hamden, Conn.,
now as High Standard, Inc. in East Hartford, Conn. All High Standard machinery
was sold at auction October 5, 1984.

HANDGUN, DOUBLE BARREL, OVER-UNDER

Derringer, 22 L.R.R.F., Double Action, 2 Shot, *Modern*	125	150	115
Derringer, .22 WMR, Double Action, 2 Shot, *Modern*	150	175	120
Derringer, .22 L.R.R.F., Double Action, Top Break, Nickel Plated, Hammerless, Cased, *Modern*	150	175	120
Derringer, .22 WMR, Double Action, Top Break, Nickel Plated, Hammerless, Cased, *Modern*	175	200	130
Derringer, .22 L.R.R.F., Double Action, Top Break, Electroless Nickel Plated, Hammerless, Walnut Grips, Cased, *Modern*	150	175	120
Derringer, .22 WMR, Double Action, Top Break, Electroless Nickel Plated, Hammerless, Walnut Grips, Cased, *Modern*	175	200	130
Gold Derringer, .22 WMR, Double Action, 2 Shot, *Modern*	300	350	175
Presidential Derringer, .22 WMR, Double Action, Top Break, Gold Plated, Hammerless, Cased, *Modern*	200	225	225

HANDGUN, PERCUSSION

.36, Griswald & Gunnison, Revolver, Commemorative, Cased, Reproduction, *Antique*	200	225	215
.36 Leech & Rigdon, Revolver, Commemorative, Cased, Reproduction, *Antique*	200	225	215
.36 Schneider & Glassick, Revolver, Commemorative, Cased, Reproduction, *Antique*	250	275	320

	V.G.	Exc.	Prior Edition Exc. Value

HANDGUN, REVOLVER
For Nickel Plating, Add $7.50–$12.50

Camp Gun, .22 L.R.R.F., Double Action, Swing-Out Cylinder, Adjustable Sights, *Modern*.. | $125 | $175 | $100 |

	V.G.	Exc.	Prior Edition Exc. Value
Camp Gun, .22 L.R.R.F., Double Action, Swing-Out Cylinder, Adjustable Sights, *Modern*	$125	$175	$100
Camp Gun, .22 WMR, Double Action, Swing-Out Cylinder, Adjustable Sight, *Modern*	175	200	115
Crusader, Deluxe Pair, .44 Mag. & .45 Colt, Commemorative, Double Action, Swing-Out Cylinder, Gold Inlays, Engraved, *Modern*	2,500	3,000	2,600
Double-Nine, .22LR/.22 WMR Combo, Double Action, Western Style, Alloy Frame, *Modern*	150	175	95
Double-Nine, .22LR/.22 WMR Combo, Double Action, Western Style, *Modern*	150	200	130
Double-Nine, .22 L.R.R.F., Double Action, Western Style, *Modern*	125	150	105
Double-Nine Deluxe, .22LR/.22 WMR Combo, Double Action, Western Style, Adjustable Sights, *Modern*	200	225	145
Durango, .22 L.R.R.F., Double Action, Western Style, *Modern*	100	125	105
High Sierra, .22LR/.22 WMR Combo, Double Action, Western Style, Octagon Barrel, *Modern*	125	150	140
High Sierra Deluxe, .22Lr/.22 WMR Combo, Double Action, Western Style, Octagon Barrel, Adjustable Sights, *Modern*	150	175	165
Longhorn, .22LR/.22 WMR Combo, Double Action, Western Style, Alloy Frame, *Modern*	100	125	100
Longhorn, .22LR/.22 WMR Combo, Double Action, Western Style, *Modern*	125	150	140
Longhorn, .22LR/.22 WMR Combo, Double Action, Adjustable Sights, Western Style, *Modern*	150	175	165
Natchez, .22LR/.22 WMR Combo, Double Action, Western Style, Birdshead Grip, Allow Frame, *Modern*	75	100	100
Posse, .22LR/.22 WMR Combo, Double Action, Western Style, Brass Gripframe, *Modern*	75	100	130
Sentinel, .22 L.R.R.F., Double Action, Swing-Out Cylinder, *Modern*	75	100	95
Sentinel Deluxe, .22 L.R.R.F., Double Action, Swing-Out Cylinder, *Modern*	100	125	95
Sentinel Imperial, .22 L.R.R.F., Double Action, Swing-Out Cylinder, *Modern*	100	125	95
Sentinel Mk III, .357 Magnum, Double Action, Swing-Out Cylinder, Adjustable Sights, *Modern*	150	175	170
Sentinel Mk II, .357 Magnum, Double Action, Swing-Out Cylinder, *Modern*	125	150	150
Sentinel Mk. I, .22 L.R.R.F., Double Action, Swing-Out Cylinder, *Modern*	75	100	105
Sentinel Mk. I, .22 L.R.R.F., Double Action, Swing-Out Cylinder, Adjustable Sights, *Modern*	100	125	120
Sentinel Mk. IV, .22 L.R.R.F., Double Action, Swing-Out Cylinder, Adjustable Sights, *Modern*	150	175	160

	V.G.	Exc.	Prior Edition Exc. Value
Sentinel Mk. IV, .22 WMR, Double Action, Swing-Out Cylinder, Adjustable Sights, *Modern*	$150	$175	$165
Sentinel Mk. IV, .22 WMR, Double Action, Swing-Out Cylinder, *Modern*	100	125	130
Sentinel Snub, .22 L.R.R.F., Double Action, Swing-Out Cylinder, *Modern*	75	100	95

HANDGUN, SEMI-AUTOMATIC

For Nickel Plating, Add $20.00–$35.00

	V.G.	Exc.	Prior Edition Exc. Value
"Benner Olympic," .22 L.R.R.F., Supermatic, Military, Engraved, *Curio*	650	750	850
Citation (Early), .22 L.R.R.F., Supermatic, Clip Fed, Hammerless, Tapered Barrel, *Modern*	375	455	190
Citation (Early), .22 L.R.R.F., Supermatic, Clip Fed, Hammerless, Heavy Barrel, *Modern*	350	400	185
Citation (Late), .22 L.R.R.F., Supermatic, Military, Hammerless, Frame-Mounted Rear Sight, Fluted Barrel, *Modern*	400	475	245
Citation (Late), .22 L.R.R.F., Supermatic, Military, Hammerless, Frame-Mounted Rear Sight, Heavy Barrel, *Modern*	375	425	225
Citation (Late), .22 L.R.R.F., Supermatic, Clip Fed, Hammerless, Frame-Mounted Rear Sight, Heavy Barrel, *Modern*	375	425	225
Dura-Matic, .22 L.R.R.F., Clip Fed, Hammerless, *Modern*	250	300	145
Field King, .22 L.R.R.F., Clip Fed, Hammerless, Heavy Barrel, *Modern*	300	350	160
Flight King, .22 Short R.F., Clip Fed, Hammerless, Lightweight, Modern	275	325	150
Flight King, .22 Short R.F., Clip Fed, Hammerless, Lightweight, Extra Barrel, *Modern*	300	350	195
Flight King, .22 Short R.F., Clip Fed, Hammerless, *Modern*	275	325	165
Flight King, .22 Short R.F., Clip Fed, Hammerless, Extra Barrel, *Modern*	300	350	190
Model A, .22 L.R.R.F., Clip Fed, Hammerless, *Curio*	400	450	250
Model B, .22 L.R.R.F., Clip Fed, Hammerless, *Curio*	350	400	265
Model B, .22 L.R.R.F., Navy, Clip Fed, Hammerless, *Curio*	475	550	525
Model C, .22 Short R.F., Clip Fed, Hammerless, *Curio*	450	525	275
Model D, .22 L.R.R.F., Clip Fed, Hammerless, Heavy Barrel, *Curio*	500	550	280
Model E, .22 L.R.R.F., Clip Fed, Hammerless, Heavy Barrel, Target Grips, *Curio*	650	750	360
Model G-380, .380 ACP, Clip Fed, Hammer, Takedown, *Curio*	425	500	390
Model G-B, .22 L.R.R.F., Clip Fed, Hammerless, Takedown, *Curio*	400	450	240
Model G-B, .22 L.R.R.F., Clip Fed, Hammerless, Takedown, Extra Barrel, *Curio*	450	525	280
Model G-D, .22 L.R.R.F., Clip Fed, Hammerless, Takedown, *Curio*	500	550	290
Model G-D, .22 L.R.R.F., Clip Fed, Hammerless, Takedown, Extra Barrel, *Curio*	500	575	315

	Prior Edition Exc.		
	V.G.	Exc.	Value
Model G-E, .22 L.R.R.F., Clip Fed, Hammerless, Takedown, Extra Barrel, *Curio*	$650	$850	$400
Model G-E, .22 L.R.R.F., Clip Fed, Hammerless, Takedown, *Curio*	600	800	305
Model G-O, .22 Short R.F., Clip Fed, Hammerless, Takedown, Extra Barrel, *Curio*	650	825	400
Model G-O, .22 Short R.F., Clip Fed, Hammerless, Takedown, *Curio*	675	775	350
Model H-A, .22 L.R.R.F., Clip Fed, Hammer, *Curio*	475	550	250
Model H-B, .22 L.R.R.F., Clip Fed, Hammer, *Curio*	500	525	250
Model H-D, .22 L.R.R.F., Clip Fed, Hammer, Heavy Barrel, *Curio*	500	600	265
Model H-D Military, .22 L.R.R.F., Clip Fed, Hammer, Heavy Barrel, Thumb Safety, *Curio*	375	425	310
Model H-E, .22 L.R.R.F., Clip Fed, Hammer, Heavy Barrel, Target Grips, *Curio*	850	1,110	325
Model SB, .22 L.R.R.F., Clip Fed, Hammerless, Smoothbore, Class 3	400	475	210
Olympic, .22 Short R.F., Clip Fed, Hammerless, *Modern*	425	500	250
Olympic, .22 Short R.F., Clip Fed, Hammerless, Extra Barrel, *Modern*	450	525	280
Olympic I.S.U., .22 Short R.F., Supermatic, Clip Fed, Hammerless, Military, *Modern*	500	600	260
Olympic I.S.U., .22 Short R.F., Supermatic, Clip Fed, Hammerless, *Modern*	475	575	245
Olympic I.S.U., .22 Short R.F., Clip Fed, Hammerless, Military, Frame-Mounted Rear Sight, *Modern*	500	600	260
Olympic I.S.U., .22 Short R.F., Clip Fed, Hammerless, Frame-Mounted Rear Sight, *Modern*	525	600	265
Plinker, .22 L.R.R.F., Clip Fed, Hammer, *Modern*	300	350	155
Sharpshooter, .22 L.R.R.F., Clip Fed, Hammerless, *Modern*	250	300	175
Sharpshooter (Late), .22 L.R.R.F., Military Grip, Clip Fed, Hammerless, *Modern*	300	350	230
Sport King, .22 L.R.R.F., Clip Fed, Hammerless, Lightweight, *Modern*	225	275	140
Sport King, .22 L.R.R.F., Clip Fed, Hammerless, Lightweight, Extra Barrel, *Modern*	225	300	170
Sport King, .22 L.R.R.F., Clip Fed, Hammerless, *Modern*	200	300	170
Sport King, .22 L.R.R.F., Clip Fed, Hammerless, Extra Barrel, *Modern*	225	300	170
Sport King (Late), .22 L.R.R.F., Military Grip, Clip Fed, Hammerless, *Modern*	275	350	195
Supermatic, .22 L.R.R.F., Clip Fed, Hammerless, *Modern*	450	525	190
Supermatic, .22 L.R.R.F., Clip Fed, Hammerless, Extra Barrel, *Modern*	450	550	235
Survival Pack, .22 L.R.R.F., Sharpshooter (Late), Electroless Nickel Plated, Cased with Accessories, *Modern*	375	450	250

High Standard Sentinel

High Standard Olympic O.S.U.   *High Standard Sharpshooter*

High Standard Victor   *High Standard Longhorn*

High Standard Trophy   *High Standard Sport King*

	V.G.	Exc.	Prior Edition Exc. Value
Tournament, .22 L.R.R.F., Supermatic, Clip Fed, Hammerless, *Modern*	$375	$425	$195
Tournament, .22 L.R.R.F., Supermatic, Clip Fed, Hammerless, Military, *Modern*	350	400	215
Trophy (Early), .22 L.R.R.F., Supermatic, Clip Fed, Hammerless, *Modern*	475	525	235
Trophy (Late), .22 L.R.R.F., Supermatic, Military, Hammerless, Frame-Mounted Rear Sight, Fluted Barrel, *Modern*	400	500	230
Trophy (Late), .22 L.R.R.F., Supermatic, Military, Hammerless, Frame-Mounted Rear Sight, Heavy Barrel, *Modern*	500	575	260
Victor, .22 L.R.R.F., Heavy Barrel, Military Grip, Solid Rib, Target Sights, *Modern*	450	550	300
Victor, .22 L.R.R.F., Heavy Barrel, Military Grip, Vent Rib, Target Sights, *Modern*	500	575	315
10-X Custom, .22 L.R.R.F., Heavy Barrel, Military Grip, Target Sights, *Modern*	750	950	470

RIFLE, BOLT ACTION

	V.G.	Exc.	Prior Edition Exc. Value
High Power, Various Calibers, Field Grade, *Modern*	175	225	205
Hi Power Deluxe, Various Calibers, Monte Carlo Stock, Checkered Stock, *Modern*	200	250	240

RIFLE, SLIDE ACTION

	V.G.	Exc.	Prior Edition Exc. Value
.22 L.R.R.F., Flight-King, Tube Feed, Monte Carlo Stock, *Modern*	75	100	115

RIFLE, SEMI-AUTOMATIC

	V.G.	Exc.	Prior Edition Exc. Value
Sport King, .22 L.R.R.F., Field Grade, Tube Feed, *Modern*	50	75	100
Sport King, .22 L.R.R.F., Field Grade, Carbine, Tube Feed, *Modern*	75	100	110
Sport King Deluxe, .22 L.R.R.F., Tube Feed, Monte Carlo Stock, Checkered Stock, *Modern*	100	125	110
Sport King Special, .22 L.R.R.F., Tube Feed, Monte Carlo Stock, *Modern*	75	100	95

SHOTGUN, SEMI-AUTOMATIC

	V.G.	Exc.	Prior Edition Exc. Value
Trap Grade, Vent Rib, Recoil Pad, *Modern*	200	225	200
Skeet Grade, Vent Rib, Recoil Pad, *Modern*	225	250	200
12 Ga., Supermatic, Field Grade, *Modern*	150	175	165
20 Ga. Mag., Supermatic, Field Grade, *Modern*	150	175	160
20 Ga., Mag., Supermatic, Skeet Grade, Vent Rib, *Modern*	145	225	190
Deer Gun, 12 Ga., Supermatic, Open Rear Sight, Recoil Pad, *Modern*	175	200	195
Deluxe, Recoil Pad, *Modern*	150	175	165
Deluxe, Recoil Pad, Vent Rib, *Modern*	175	200	190
Deluxe, 20 Ga. Mag., Supermatic, Recoil Pad, *Modern*	150	175	170
Deluxe, 20 Ga. Mag., Supermatic, Recoil Pad, Vent Rib, *Modern*	175	200	195
Duck Gun, 12 Ga. Mag. 3", Supermatic, Recoil Pad, Field Grade, *Modern*	175	200	200

	V.G.	Exc.	Prior Edition Exc. Value
Duck Gun, 12 Ga. Mag. 3", Supermatic, Vent Rib, Recoil Pad, *Modern*	$175	$200	$200
Model 10, 12 Ga., Riot Gun, *Modern*	350	375	365
Special, 12 Ga., Field Grade, Adjustable Choke, *Modern*	175	200	190
Special, 20 Ga. Mag., Supermatic, Field Grade, Adjustable Choke, *Modern*	175	200	190
Trophy, Recoil Pad, Vent Rib, Adjustable Choke, *Modern*	200	225	220
Trophy, 20 Ga. Mag., Supermatic, Recoil Pad, Vent Rib, Adjustable Choke, *Modern*	200	225	225

SHOTGUN, SLIDE ACTION

	V.G.	Exc.	Prior Edition Exc. Value
.410 Ga. 3", Flight-King, Field Grade, *Modern*	125	150	145
.410 Ga. 3", Flight-King, Skeet Grade, *Modern*	150	175	170
12 Ga., Flight King, Trap Grade, Vent Rib, Recoil Pad, *Modern*	150	175	170
12 Ga., Flight-King, Skeet Grade, Vent Rib, Recoil Pad, *Modern*	150	175	160
12 and 20 Gauges, Flight-King, Field Grade, *Modern*	125	150	150
28 Fa., Flight-King, Field Grade, *Modern*	150	175	160
28 Ga., Flight-King, Skeet Grade, Vent Rib, *Modern*	150	175	165
Brush Gun, 12 Ga., Flight-King, Open Rear Sight, *Modern*	125	150	145
Deluxe, .410 Ga. 3", Flight-King, Vent Rib, *Modern*	150	175	150
Deluxe, 12 and 20 Gauges, Flight-King, Recoil Pad, *Modern*	125	150	130
Deluxe, 12 and 20 Gauges, Flight-King, Recoil Pad, Vent Rib, *Modern*	150	175	150
Deluxe, .28 Ga., Flight-King, Vent Rib, *Modern*	150	175	160
Deluxe Brush Gun, 12 Ga., Flight-King, Peep Sights, Sling Swivels, *Modern*	175	200	165
Riot, 12 Ga., Flight-King, Plain Barrel, *Modern*	150	175	155
Riot, 12 Ga., Flight-King, Open Rear Sight, *Modern*	150	175	170
Special, 12 and 20 Gauges, Flight-King, Field Grade, Adjustable Choke, *Modern*	150	175	145
Trophy, 12 and 20 Gauges, Flight-King, Recoil Pad, Vent Rib, Adjustable Choke, *Modern*	150	175	175

SHOTGUN, DOUBLE BARREL, OVER-UNDER

	V.G.	Exc.	Prior Edition Exc. Value
Shadow Indy, 12 Ga., Single Selective Trigger, Selective Ejectors, Checkered Stock, Engraved, *Modern*	650	750	585
Shadow Seven, 12 Ga., Single Selective Trigger, Selective Ejectors, Checkered Stock, Light Engraving, *Modern*	550	650	495

HIJO Tradename used by Sloan's of N.Y.C.

HANDGUN, SEMI-AUTOMATIC

	V.G.	Exc.	Prior Edition Exc. Value
Hijo, .25 ACP, Clip Fed, *Modern*	75	100	100
Hijo Military, .22 L.R.R.F., Clip Fed, *Modern*	100	125	110

HILL, S.W. See Kentucky Rifles and Pistols.

HILLEGAS, J. Pottsville, Pa. 1810–1830. See Kentucky Rifles.

HILLIARD, D.H. & GEORGE C. D. H. Hilliard, Cornish, New
Hampshire, 1842–1877, taken over by George C. Hilliard and operated 1877–1880.

HANDGUN, PERCUSSION
.34, Underhammer Target Pistol, *Antique* $400 $450 $325

HINO-KOMORO Kumaso Hino and Tomisiro Komoro, Tokyo, Japan,
c. 1910.

HANDGUN, SEMI-AUTOMATIC
Blow-Forward, .32 ACP, Clip Fed, *Curio* 3,000   3,250   2,700

HOCKLEY, JAMES Chester County, Pa. 1769–1771. See Kentucky
Rifles.

HOLDEN, CYRUS B. Worcester, Mass, c. 1861–1880.

RIFLE, SINGLESHOT
Model 1862, .44 Henry, Octagon Barrel, *Antique*............................. 550   775   550
Tip-Up, .22 R.F., Nickel Plated Frame, Blued Barrel, *Antique* 450   600   450

HOLLAND & HOLLAND London, England since 1835.

RIFLE, BOLT ACTION
Best Quality, Various Calibers, Express Sights, Fancy Checkering,
Engraved, *Modern*.. 8,000   9,500   2,900
Best Quality, Various Calibers, Express Sights, Checkered Stock,
Modern... 6,000   7,500   2,000

RIFLE, DOUBLE BARREL, SIDE-BY-SIDE
#2, Various Calibers, Sidelock, Checkered Stock, Engraved,
Hammerless, *Modern*.. 12,000   14,500   9,000
Deluxe, Various Calibers, Sidelock, Automatic Ejector, Fancy
Engraving, Fancy Checkering, Double Trigger, *Modern* 42,500   45,000   16,000
Royal, Various Calibers, Sidelock, Automatic Ejector, Fancy
Engraving, Fancy Checkering, Double Trigger, *Modern* 52,500   55,000   10,000

SHOTGUN, DOUBLE BARREL, OVER-UNDER
Deluxe Royal, 12 Ga., Sidelock, Automatic Ejector, Fancy
Engraving, Fancy Checkering, Double Triggers, *Modern*................. 35,000   40,000   16,500
Deluxe Royal, 12 Ga., Sidelock Automatic Ejector, Fancy
Engraving, Fancy Checkering, Single Trigger, *Modern*.................... 45,000   50,000   19,000
Royal Model (Late), 12 Ga., Sidelock, Automatic Ejector, Fancy
Engraving, Fancy Checkering, Double Triggers, *Modern*................ 22,500   25,000   14,000
Royal Model (Late), 12 Ga., Sidelock, Automatic Ejector, Fancy
Engraving, Fancy Checkering, Single Trigger, *Modern*................... 25,000   27,500   15,000

	V.G.	Exc.	Prior Edition Exc. Value

Royal Model (Old), 12 Ga., Sidelock, Automatic Ejector, Fancy
Engraving, Fancy Checkering, Double Triggers, *Modern*.................$17500 $20,000 $11,000

Royal Model (Old), 12 Ga., Sidelock, Automatic Ejector, Fancy
Engraving, Fancy Checkering, Single Trigger, *Modern*....................20,000 22,000 13,000

SHOTGUN, DOUBLE BARREL, SIDE-BY-SIDE

Badminton, Various Gauges, Sidelock, Automatic Ejector, Fancy
Engraving, Fancy Checkering, Double Triggers, *Modern*.................8,500 10,000 7,500

Badminton, Various Gauges, Sidelock, Automatic Ejector, Fancy
Engraving, Fancy Checkering, Single Trigger, *Modern*....................10,000 12,000 8,000

Centenary Badminton, 12 Ga. 2", Sidelock. Automatic Ejector,
Fancy Engraving, Fancy Checkering, Double Triggers, *Modern*......7,500 9,000 7,000

Centenary Deluxe, 12 Ga. 2", Sidelock, Automatic Ejector, Fancy
Engraving, Fancy Checkering, Double Triggers, *Modern*.................8,500 11,000 13,000

Centenary Dominion, 12 Ga. 2", Sidelock, Automatic Ejector,
Engraved, Checkered Stock, Double Triggers, *Modern*....................6,000 7,500 4,500

Centenary Royal, 12 Ga. 2", Sidelock, Automatic Ejector, Fancy
Engraving, Fancy Checkering, Double Triggers, *Modern*.................12,500 15,000 11,500

Deluxe, Various Gauges, Sidelock, Automatic Ejector, Fancy
Engraving, Fancy Checkering, Double Triggers, *Modern*.................35,000 40,000 13,000

Deluxe, Various Gauges, Sidelock, Automatic Ejector, Fancy
Engraving, Fancy Checkering, Single Trigger, *Modern*....................40,000 45,000 13,500

Dominion, Various Gauges, Sidelock, Automatic Ejector,
Engraved, Checkered Stock, Double Triggers, *Modern*....................2,800 10,000 4,750

Northwood, Various Gauges, Boxlock, Automatic Ejector,
Checkered Stock, Engraved, *Modern* 1,750 2,700 2,700

Riviera, Various Gauges, Extra Shotgun Barrel, Automatic
Ejector, Fancy Engraving, Fancy Checkering, Double Triggers,
Modern..12,000 14,000 9,500

Royal, Various Gauges, Sidelock, Automatic Ejector, Fancy
Engraving, Fancy Checkering, Double Triggers, *Modern*.................12,500 14,000 12,000

Royal, Various Gauges, Sidelock, Automatic Ejector, Fancy
Engraving, Fancy Checkering, Single Trigger, *Modern*....................14,500 16,000 14,000

Royal Ejector Grade, 12 Ga. Mag. 3", Single Selective Trigger,
Vent Rib, Pistol-Grip Stock, Cased with Accessories, *Modern* 10,000 12,500 16,000

SHOTGUN, SINGLESHOT

Standard Super Trap, 12 Ga., Boxlock, Automatic Ejector,
Vent Rib, Fancy Engraving, Checkered Stock, *Modern*....................5,000 6,000 8,500

Deluxe Super Trap, 12 Ga., Boxlock, Automatic Ejector, Vent
Rib, Fancy Engraving, Checkered Stock, *Modern* 6,000 7,500 9,250

Exhibition Super Trap, 12 Ga., Boxlock, Automatic Ejector,
Vent Rip, Fancy Engraving, Checkered Stock, *Modern*....................7,500 9,000 12,000

HOLLIS, CHAS. & SONS London, England.

SHOTGUN, DOUBLE BARREL, SIDE-BY-SIDE

12 Ga., Hammerless, Engraved, Fancy Checkering, Fancy Wood,
Modern...2,500 3,000 2,900

	V.G.	Exc.	Prior Edition Exc. Value

HOLLIS, RICHARD London, England 1800–1850.

HANDGUN, FLINTLOCK

.68, Holster Pistol, Round Barrel, Brass Furniture, Plain, *Antique* .... | $550 | $775 | $765

SHOTGUN, PERCUSSION

12 Ga., Double Barrels, Double Triggers, Hook Breech, Light Engraving, Checkered Stock, *Antique* .... | 450 | 550 | 500

HOLMES, BILL Fayetteville, Ark.

SHOTGUN, SINGLESHOT

Supertrap, 12 Ga., Various Action Types, Checkered Stock, *Modern*.. | 1,650 | 1,800 | 1,750

HOOD FIRE ARMS CO. Norwich, Conn., c. 1875.

HANDGUN, REVOLVER

.32 Short R.F., 5 Shot, Spur Trigger, Solid Frame, Single Action, *Antique* .... | 125 | 175 | 165

HOPKINS & ALLEN Norwich, Conn. 1868–1917, taken over by Marlin-Rockwell in 1917. Later purchased by Numrich Arms Corp., West Hurley, N.Y., and now in Hawthorne, N.J.

HANDGUN, PERCUSSION

"Boot Pistol," .36, Under-Hammer, Octagon Barrel, Reproduction, (Numrich), *Antique* .... | 25 | 50 | 50

HANDGUN, REVOLVER

Model 1876 Army, .44–40 WCF, Solid Frame, Single Action, 6 Shot, Finger-Rest Trigger Guard, *Antique*...................................... | 550 | 650 | 600

Safety Police, .22 L.R.R.F., Top Break, Double Action, Various Barrel Lengths, *Modern*.. | 125 | 150 | 125

Safety Police, .32 S & W, Top Break, Double Action, Various Barrel Lengths, *Modern*.. | 125 | 150 | 125

Safety Police, .38 S & W, Top Break, Double Action, Various Barrel Lengths, *Modern*.. | 125 | 150 | 125

XL .30 Long, .30 Long R.F., Solid Frame, Spur Trigger, Single Action, 5 Shot, *Antique*.. | 150 | 175 | 165

XL 1 Double Action, .22 Short R.F., Solid Frame, Folding Hammer, *Modern*... | 100 | 125 | 105

XL 3 Double Action, .32 S & W, Solid Frame, Folding Hammer, *Modern*... | 75 | 100 | 105

XL Bulldog, .32 S & W, Solid Frame, Folding Hammer, *Modern*....... | 100 | 125 | 105

XL Bulldog, .32 Short R.F., Solid Frame, Folding Hammer, *Modern*... | 75 | 100 | 95

XL Bulldog, .38 S & W, Solid Frame, Folding Hammer, *Modern*....... | 75 | 100 | 105

	V.G.	Exc.	Prior Edition Exc. Value
XL CR .22 Short R.F., Solid Frame, Spur Trigger, Single Action, 7 Shot, *Antique*	$150	$175	$160
XL Double Action, .32 S & W, Solid Frame, Folding Hammer, *Modern*	75	100	105
XL Double Action, .38 S & W, Solid Frame, Folding Hammer, *Modern*	75	100	105
XL Navy, .38 Short R.F., Solid Frame, Single Action, 6 shot, *Antique*	425	500	475
XL No. 1, .22 Short R.F., Solid Frame, Spur Trigger, Single Action, 7 Shot, *Antique*	150	175	185
XL No. 2, .30 Short R.F., Solid Frame, Spur Trigger, Single Action, 5 Shot, *Antique*	175	200	190
XL No. 3, .32 Short R.F., Solid Frame, Spur Trigger, Single Action, 5 Shot, Safety Cylinder, *Antique*	175	200	200
XL No. 4, .38 Short R.F., Solid Frame, Spur Trigger, Single Action, 5 Shot, *Antique*	175	200	200
XL No. 5, .38 S&W, Solid Frame, Spur Trigger, Single Action, 5 Shot, *Antique*	350	400	380
XL No. 5, .38 Short R.F., Solid Frame, Spur Trigger, Single Action, 5 Shot, Safety Cylinder, Engraved, *Antique*	300	350	350
XL No. 6, .41 Short R.F., Solid Frame, Spur Trigger, Single Action, 5 Shot, *Antique*	175	225	230
XL No. 7, .41 Short R.F., Solid Frame, Spur Trigger, Single Action, 5 Shot, Swing-Out Cylinder, *Antique*	225	275	275
XL No. 8 (Army), .44 R.F., Solid Frame, Single Action, 6 Shot, *Antique*	500	550	560
XL Police, .38 Short R.F., Solid Frame, Single Action, 6 Shot, *Antique*	150	175	180

HANDGUN, SINGLESHOT

	V.G.	Exc.	Prior Edition Exc. Value
Ladies Garter Pistol, .22 Short R.F., Tip-Up, Folding Trigger, Single Action, *Antique*	125	150	140
New Model Target, .22 L.R.R.F., Top Break, 10" Barrel, Adjustable Sights, Target Grips, *Modern*	300	350	360
XL Derringer, .41 Short R.F., Spur Trigger, Single Action, *Antique*	475	550	600

RIFLE, BOLT ACTION

	V.G.	Exc.	Prior Edition Exc. Value
American Military, .22 L.R.R.F., Singleshot, Takedown, Open Rear Sight, Round Barrel, *Modern*	150	200	200

RIFLE, FLINTLOCK

	V.G.	Exc.	Prior Edition Exc. Value
"Kentucky," .31, Octagon Barrel, Full-Stocked, Brass Furniture, Reproduction, (Numrich), *Antique*	175	200	185
"Kentucky," .36, Octagon Barrel, Full-Stocked, Brass Furniture, Reproduction, (Numrich), *Antique*	150	200	185
"Kentucky," .45, Octagon Barrel, Full-Stocked, Brass Furniture, Reproduction, (Numrich), *Antique*	175	200	195
"Minuteman Brush," .45, Octagon Barrel, Full-Stocked, Carbine, Reproduction, (Numrich), *Antique*	175	200	195

	V.G.	Exc.	Prior Edition Exc. Value
"Minute Brush," .50, Octagon Barrel, Full-Stocked, Carbine, Reproduction (Numrich), *Antique*	$175	$200	$195
"Minuteman," .31, Octagon Barrel, Full-Stocked, Brass Furniture, Reproduction, (Numrich), *Antique*	150	200	185
"Minuteman," .36, Octagon Barrel, Full-Stocked, Brass Furniture, Reproduction, (Numrich), *Antique*	150	175	185
"Minuteman," .45, Octagon Barrel, Full-Stocked, Brass Furniture, Reproduction, (Numrich), *Antique*	175	200	195
"Minuteman," .50, Octagon Barrel, Full-Stocked, Brass Furniture, Reproduction, (Numrich), *Antique*	175	200	195
"Pennsylvania," .31, Octagon Barrel, Half-Stocked, Brass Furniture, Reproduction, (Numrich), *Antique*	150	175	180
"Pennsylvania," .36, Octagon Barrel, Half-Stocked, Brass Furniture, Reproduction, (Numrich), *Antique*	150	175	180
"Pennsylvania," .45, Octagon Barrel, Half-Stocked, Brass Furniture, Reproduction, (Numrich), *Antique*	175	200	190
"Pennsylvania," .50, Octagon Barrel, Half-Stocked, Brass Furniture, Reproduction, (Numrich), *Antique*	150	175	190

RIFLE, PERCUSSION

	V.G.	Exc.	Prior
"Buggy Deluxe," .36, Under-Hammer, Octagon Barrel, Carbine, Reproduction, (Numrich), *Antique*	75	100	105
"Buggy Deluxe," .45, Under-Hammer, Octagon Barrel, Carbine, Reproduction, (Numrich), *Antique*	100	125	115
"Deer Stalker," .58, Under-Hammer, Octagon Barrel, Reproduction, (Numrich), *Antique*	75	100	105
"Heritage," .36, Under-Hammer, Octagon Barrel, Brass Furniture, Reproduction, (Numrich), *Antique*	100	125	115
"Heritage," .45, Under-Hammer, Octagon Barrel, Brass Furniture, Reproduction, (Numrich), *Antique*	100	125	120
"Kentucky," .31, Full-Stocked, Octagon Barrel, Brass Furniture, Reproduction, (Numrich), *Antique*	150	175	180
"Kentucky," .36, Full-Stocked, Octagon Barrel, Brass Furniture, Reproduction, (Numrich), *Antique*	150	175	180
"Kentucky," .45, Full-Stocked, Octagon Barrel, Brass Furniture, Reproduction, (Numrich), *Antique*	150	175	185
"Minuteman Brush," .45, Full-Stocked, Octagon Barrel, Carbine, Reproduction, (Numrich), *Antique*	150	175	185
"Minuteman Brush," .50, Full-Stocked, Octagon Barrel, Carbine, Reproduction, (Numrich), *Antique*	175	200	185
"Minuteman," .31, Full-Stocked, Octagon Barrel, Brass Furniture, Reproduction, (Numrich), *Antique*	150	175	180
"Minuteman," .36, Full-Stocked, Octagon Barrel, Brass Furniture, Reproduction, (Numrich), *Antique*	150	175	180

Hopkins & Allen Heritage Rifle

	V.G.	Exc.	Prior Edition Exc. Value
"Minuteman," .45, Full-Stocked, Octagon Barrel, Brass Furniture, Reproduction, (Numrich), *Antique*	*$150*	*$175*	*$185*
"Minuteman," .50, Full-Stocked, Octagon Barrel, Brass Furniture, Reproduction, (Numrich), *Antique*	*125*	*175*	*185*
"Offhand Deluxe," .36, Under-Hammer, Octagon Barrel, Reproduction, (Numrich), *Antique*	*75*	*100*	*105*
"Offhand Deluxe," .45, Under-Hammer, Octagon Barrel, Reproduction, (Numrich), *Antique*	*75*	*100*	*105*
"Offhand Deluxe," .45, Under-Hammer, Octagon Barrel, Reproduction, (Numrich), *Antique*	*75*	*100*	*105*
"Pennsylvania," .31, Half-Stocked, Octagon Barrel, Brass Furniture, Reproduction, (Numrich), *Antique*	*125*	*150*	*170*
"Pennsylvania," .36, Half-Stocked, Octagon Barrel, Brass Furniture, Reproduction, (Numrich), *Antique*	*150*	*175*	*170*
"Pennsylvania," .45, Half-Stocked, Octagon Barrel, Brass Furniture, Reproduction, (Numrich), *Antique*	*150*	*175*	*175*
"Pennsylvania," .50, Half-Stocked, Octagon Barrel, Brass Furniture, Reproduction, (Numrich), *Antique*	*150*	*175*	*175*
"Target," .45, Under-Hammer, Octagon Barrel, Reproduction, (Numrich), *Antique*	*75*	*100*	*100*
.45, Double Barrel, Over-Under, Swivel Breech, Brass Furniture, Reproduction, (Numrich), *Antique*	*100*	*125*	*125*

RIFLE, SINGLESHOT

	V.G.	Exc.	Prior Edition Exc. Value
Model 1881 (XL), Various Calibers, Falling Block, Takedown, Lever Action, Round Barrel, Open Rear Sight, *Antique*	*325*	*375*	*375*
Model 1881 Junior, .22 L.R.R.F., Falling Block, Takedown, Lever Action, Round Barrel, Open Rear Sight, *Antique*	*125*	*150*	*160*
No. 1922 New Model Junior, .22 L.R.R.F., Falling Block, Takedown, Lever Action, Octagon Barrel, Open Rear Sight, *Modern*	*200*	*225*	*235*
No. 1925 New Model Junior, .25 Short R.F., Falling Block, Takedown, Lever Action, Octagon Barrel, Open Rear Sight, *Modern*	*250*	*275*	*265*
No. 1932 New Model Junior, .32 Long R.F., Falling Block, Takedown, Lever Action, Octagon Barrel, Open Rear Sight, *Modern*	*225*	*250*	*255*
No. 1938 New Model Junior, .38 S & W, Falling Block, Takedown, Lever Action, Octagon Barrel, Open Rear Sight, *Modern*	*250*	*275*	*275*
No. 2922 New Model Junior, .22 L.R.R.F., Falling Block, Takedown, Lever Action, Octagon Barrel, Checkered Stock, Open Rear Sight, *Modern*	*225*	*250*	*260*
No. 2925 New Model Junior, .25 Short R.F., Falling Block, Takedown, Lever Action, Octagon Barrel, Checkered Stock, Open Rear Sight, *Modern*	*250*	*275*	*275*
No. 2932 New Model Junior, .32 Long R.F., Falling Block, Takedown, Lever Action, Octagon Barrel, Checkered Stock, Open Rear Sight, *Modern*	*250*	*275*	*275*

	V.G.	Exc.	Prior Edition Exc. Value
No. 2938 New Model Junior, .38 S & W, Falling Block, Takedown, Lever Action, Octagon Barrel, Checkered Stock, Open Rear Sight, *Modern*	$275	$300	$310
No. 3922 Schuetzen Target, .22 L.R.R.F., Falling Block, Takedown, Lever Action, Octagon Barrel, Checkered Stock, Swiss Buttplate, *Modern*	600	650	660
No. 3925 Schuetzen Target, .25–20 WCF, Falling Block, Takedown, Lever Action, Octagon Barrel, Checkered Stock, Swiss Buttplate, *Modern*	700	750	750
No. 722, .22 L.R.R.F., Rolling Block, Takedown, Round Barrel, Open Rear Sight, *Modern*	100	125	135
No. 822, .22 L.R.R.F., Rolling Block, Takedown, Lever Action, Round Barrel, Open Rear Sight, *Modern*	125	150	160
No. 832, .32 Short R.F., Rolling Block, Takedown, Lever Action, Round Barrel, Open Rear Sight, *Modern*	150	175	170
No.922 New Model Junior, .22 L.R.R.F., Falling Block, Takedown, Lever Action, Round Barrel, Open Rear Sight, *Modern*	150	175	170
No. 925 New Model Junior, .25 Short R.F., Falling Block, Takedown, Lever Action, Round Barrel, Open Rear Sight, *Modern*	150	175	170
No. 932 New Model Junior, .32 Long R.F., Falling Block, Takedown, Lever Action, Round Barrel, Open Rear Sight, *Modern*	125	175	170
No. 938 New Model Junior, .38 S & W, Falling Block, Takedown, Lever Action, Round Barrel, Open Rear Sight, *Modern*	225	250	240
Noiseless, .22 L.R.R.F., Falling Block, Takedown, Lever Action, Round Barrel, Silencer, *Class 3*	400	450	450

SHOTGUN, DOUBLE BARREL, SIDE-BY-SIDE

	V.G.	Exc.	
No. 100, 12 and 16 Ga., Double Trigger, Outside Hammers, Checkered Stock, Steel Barrel, *Modern*	125	150	160
No. 110, 12 and 16 Ga., Double Trigger, Hammerless, Checkered Stock, Steel Barrel, *Modern*	150	175	175

SHOTGUN, SINGLESHOT

	V.G.	Exc.	
New Model, Various Gauges, Hammer, Top Break, Steel Barrel, *Modern*	50	75	65
New Model, Various Gauges, Hammer, Top Break, Steel Barrel, Automatic Ejector, Checkered Stock, *Modern*	50	75	85
New Model, Various Gauges, Hammer, Top Break, Damascus Barrel, Checkered Stock, *Modern*	50	75	70

HOPKINS, C.W. Made by Bacon Mfg. Co., Norwich, Conn.

HANDGUN, REVOLVER

	V.G.	Exc.	
.32 Short R.F., Single Action, Solid Frame, Swing-Out Cylinder, *Antique*	300	350	335
.38 Long R.F., Single Action, Solid Frame, Swing-Out Cylinder, *Antique*	575	625	625

	V.G.	Exc.	Prior Edition Exc. Value

HOROLT, LORENZ Nuremberg, Germany, c. 1600.
HANDGUN, WHEEL-LOCK
Long Barreled, Holster Pistol, Hexagonal Ball Pommel, Light
Ornamentation, *Antique* $7,500 $8,500 $7,950

HOWARD ARMS Made by Meriden Firearms Co.
HANDGUN, REVOLVER
.32 S & W, 5 Shot, Double Action, Top Break, *Modern* 75 100 100
.38 S & W, 5 Shot, Double Action, Top Break, *Modern* 75 100 100

HOWARD ARMS Made by Cresent for Fred Bifflar & Co.
SHOTGUN, DOUBLE BARREL, SIDE-BY-SIDE
Various Gauges, Outside Hammers, Damascus Barrel, *Modern*......... 150 175 170
Various Gauges, Hammerless, Steel Barrel, *Modern*...................... 175 200 185
Various Gauges, Hammerless, Damascus Barrel, *Modern* 150 175 165
Various Gauges, Outside Hammers, Steel Barrel, *Modern*.............. 150 175 180
SHOTGUN, SINGLESHOT
Various Gauges, Hammer, Steel Barrel, *Modern*........................... 50 75 75

HOWARD BROTHERS Detroit, Mich., c. 1868.
RIFLE, SINGLESHOT
.44 Henry R.F., **Round Barrel**, *Antique* 375 500 495

HOUILLER, BLANCHAR Paris, France, c. 1845.
HANDGUN, PERCUSSION
Pepperbox, .48, 6 Shot, *Antique* 375 500 490

HUMBERGER, PETER JR. Ohio 1791–1852. See Kentucky Rifles.

HUMBERGER, PETER SR. Pa. 1774–1791, then Ohio 1791–
1811. See Kentucky Rifles.

HUMMER Belgium, for Lee Hdw., Kansas.
SHOTGUN, DOUBLE BARREL, SIDE-BY-SIDE
Various Gauges, Outside Hammers, Damascus Barrel, *Modern*......... 150 175 170
Various Gauges, Hammerless, Steel Barrel, *Modern*...................... 175 200 190
Various Gauges, Outside Hammers, Steel Barrel, *Modern*.............. 150 175 180
SHOTGUN, SINGLESHOT
Various Gauges, Hammer, Steel Barrel, *Modern*........................... 50 75 80

Hungarian Military 37M Femaru

	V.G.	Exc.	Prior Edition Exc. Value
HUNGARIAN MILITARY			
HANDGUN, SEMI-AUTOMATIC			
19M Frommer Stop, .380 ACP, Clip Fed, Blue, Military, *Curio*	$200	$225	$200
29M Femaru, .380 ACP, Clip Fed, Blue, Military, *Curio*...............	150	175	160
37M Femaru, .380 ACP, Clip Fed, Blue, Military, *Curio*...............	125	150	145
RIFLE, BOLT ACTION			
1943M, 8mm Mauser, Mannlicher, Military, *Curio*..........................	125	150	125
8mm 1935M, Mannlicher, Military, *Curio*	75	100	75

HUNTER ARMS See L.C. Smith.

HUNTING WORLD N.Y.C.

	V.G.	Exc.	Prior Edition Exc. Value
SHOTGUN, DOUBLE BARREL, SIDE-BY-SIDE			
Royal Deluxe Game Gun, 12 or 20 Gauges, Sidelock, Fancy Wood, Engraved, *Modern*..	3,500	4,000	4,350

HUSQVARNA VAPENFABRIK AKITIEBOLAG
Husqvarna, Sweden.

	V.G.	Exc.	Prior Edition Exc. Value
HANDGUN, REVOLVER			
Model 1887 Swedish Nagent, 7.5mm, Double Action, Blue, Military, *Antique*...	225	250	250
HANDGUN, SEMI-AUTOMATIC			
Model 07, 9mm Browning Long, Clip Fed, Swedish Military, *Modern*..	300	350	190
Model 07, 9mm Browning Long, Clip Fed, Belgian Military, *Modern*..	325	375	200
RIFLE, BOLT ACTION			
Various Calibers, Sporting Rifle, Checkered Stock, *Modern*..........	250	300	290

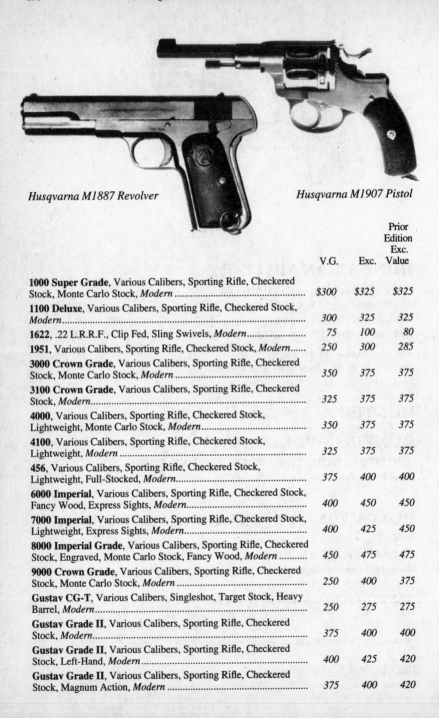

Husqvarna M1887 Revolver   *Husqvarna M1907 Pistol*

	V.G.	Exc.	Prior Edition Exc. Value
1000 Super Grade, Various Calibers, Sporting Rifle, Checkered Stock, Monte Carlo Stock, *Modern*	$300	$325	$325
1100 Deluxe, Various Calibers, Sporting Rifle, Checkered Stock, *Modern*..	300	325	325
1622, .22 L.R.R.F., Clip Fed, Sling Swivels, *Modern*......................	75	100	80
1951, Various Calibers, Sporting Rifle, Checkered Stock, *Modern*......	250	300	285
3000 Crown Grade, Various Calibers, Sporting Rifle, Checkered Stock, Monte Carlo Stock, *Modern*	350	375	375
3100 Crown Grade, Various Calibers, Sporting Rifle, Checkered Stock, *Modern*..	325	375	375
4000, Various Calibers, Sporting Rifle, Checkered Stock, Lightweight, Monte Carlo Stock, *Modern*...	350	375	375
4100, Various Calibers, Sporting Rifle, Checkered Stock, Lightweight, *Modern*...	325	375	375
456, Various Calibers, Sporting Rifle, Checkered Stock, Lightweight, Full-Stocked, *Modern*...	375	400	400
6000 Imperial, Various Calibers, Sporting Rifle, Checkered Stock, Fancy Wood, Express Sights, *Modern*..................................	400	450	450
7000 Imperial, Various Calibers, Sporting Rifle, Checkered Stock, Lightweight, Express Sights, *Modern*......................................	400	425	450
8000 Imperial Grade, Various Calibers, Sporting Rifle, Checkered Stock, Engraved, Monte Carlo Stock, Fancy Wood, *Modern*	450	475	475
9000 Crown Grade, Various Calibers, Sporting Rifle, Checkered Stock, Monte Carlo Stock, *Modern*	250	400	375
Gustav CG-T, Various Calibers, Singleshot, Target Stock, Heavy Barrel, *Modern*...	250	275	275
Gustav Grade II, Various Calibers, Sporting Rifle, Checkered Stock, *Modern*..	375	400	400
Gustav Grade II, Various Calibers, Sporting Rifle, Checkered Stock, Left-Hand, *Modern*...	400	425	420
Gustav Grade II, Various Calibers, Sporting Rifle, Checkered Stock, Magnum Action, *Modern*	375	400	420

	V.G.	Exc.	Prior Edition Exc. Value
Gustav Grade III, Various Calibers, Sporting Rifle, Checkered Stock, Magnum Action, Left-Hand, *Modern*	$400	$425	$425
Gustav Grade III, Various Calibers, Sporting Rifle, Checkered Stock, Magnum Action, Light Engraving, Left-Hand, *Modern*	400	475	475
Gustav Grade III, Various Calibers, Sporting Rifle, Checkered Stock, Magnum Action, Light Engraving, *Modern*	450	475	475
Gustav Grade III, Various Calibers, Sporting Rifle, Checkered Stock, Light Engraving, *Modern*	450	500	475
Gustav Grade III, Various Calibers, Sporting Rifle, Checkered Stock, Light Engraving, Left-Hand, *Modern*	425	475	475
Gustav Grade V, Various Calibers, Sporting Rifle, Checkered Stock, Engraved, *Modern*	600	650	670
Gustav Grade V, Various Calibers, Sporting Rifle, Checkered Stock, Engraved, Left-Hand, *Modern*	575	650	670
Gustav Grade V, Various Calibers, Sporting Rifle, Checkered Stock, Engraved, Magnum Action, *Modern*	600	675	670
Gustav Grade V, Various Calibers, Sporting Rifle, Checkered Stock, Engraved, Magnum Action, Left-Hand, *Modern*	625	675	675
Gustav Swede, Various Calibers, Sporting Rifle, Checkered Stock, *Modern*	300	325	320
Gustav Swede Deluxe, Various Calibers, Sporting Rifle, Checkered Stock, Light Engraving, *Modern*	300	350	345
Gustav V-T, Various Calibers, Varmint, Target Stock, Heavy Barrel, *Modern*	400	450	425
P 3000 Presentation, Various Calibers, Sporting Rifle, Checkered Stock, Engraved, Fancy Wood, *Modern*	625	650	670

HUTZ, BENJAMIN Lancaster, Pa. c. 1802. See Kentucky Rifles.

HVA See Husqvarna.

HY HUNTER Burbank, Calif.
HANDGUN, REVOLVER

	V.G.	Exc.	Prior Edition Exc. Value
Chicago Cub, .22 Short, 6 Shot, Folding Trigger, *Modern*	25	50	35
Detective, .22 L.R.R.F., Double Action, 6 Shot, *Modern*	50	75	45
Detective, .22 W.M.R., Double Action, 6 Shot, *Modern*	50	75	45
Frontier Six Shooter, .22 L.R.R.F., Single Action, Western Style, *Modern*	50	75	60
Frontier Six Shooter, .22 LR/.22 WRF Combo, Single Action, Western Style, *Modern*	50	75	60
Frontier Six Shooter, .357 Mag., Single Action, Western Style, *Modern*	75	100	95
Frontier Six Shooter, .44 Mag., Single Action, Western Style, *Modern*	125	150	140
Frontier Six Shooter, ".45 Mag.", Single Action, Western Style, *Modern*	100	125	125

	V.G.	Exc.	Prior Edition Exc. Value

HANDGUN, SEMI-AUTOMATIC

Maxim, .25 ACP, Clip Fed, *Modern* .... $50 / $75 / $75

	V.G.	Exc.	Value
Maxim, .25 ACP, Clip Fed, *Modern*	$50	$75	$75
Militar, .22 L.R.R.F., Double Action, Hammer, Clip Fed, Blue, *Modern*	50	100	85
Militar, .32 ACP, Double Action, Hammer, Clip Fed. Blue, *Modern*	75	100	95
Militar, .380 ACP, Double Action, Hammer, Clip Fed, Blue, *Modern*	75	100	100
Panzer, .22 L.R.R.F., Clip Fed, Blue, *Modern*	50	75	70
Stingray, .25 ACP, Clip Fed, Blue, *Modern*	50	75	65
Stuka, .22 Long, Clip Fed, Blue, *Modern*	50	75	70

HANDGUN, DOUBLE BARREL, OVER-UNDER

	V.G.	Exc.	Value
Automatic Derringer, .22 L.R.R.F., Blue, *Modern*	25	50	45

HANDGUN, SINGLESHOT

	V.G.	Exc.	Value
Accurate Ace, .22 Short, Flobert Type, Chrome Plated, *Modern*	25	50	45
Favorite, .22 L.R.R.F., Stevens Copy, *Modern*	50	75	60
Favorite, .22 W.M.R., Stevens Copy, *Modern*	50	75	70
Gold Rush Derringer, .22 L.R.R.F., Spur Trigger *Modern*	25	50	45
Target, .22 L.R.R.F., Bolt Action, *Modern*	25	50	50
Target, .22 W.M.R., Bolt Action, *Modern*	25	50	55

RIFLE, BOLT ACTION

	V.G.	Exc.	Value
Maharaja, Various Calibers, Various Actions, Custom Made, Fancy Engraving, Fancy Wood, Fancy Inlays, Gold Plates, *Modern*	4,500	5,500	5,750

HYPER Jenks, Okla.

RIFLE, SINGLESHOT

	V.G.	Exc.	Value
Hyper-Single Rifle, Various Calibers, Fancy Wood, No Sights, Falling Block, Fancy Checkering, *Modern*	1,750	2,000	1,000
Hyper-Single Rifle, Various Calibers, Fancy Wood, No Sights, Falling Block, Fancy Checkering, Stainless Steel Barrel, *Modern*	2,000	2,250	1,100

HY SCORE ARMS Brooklyn, N.Y.

HANDGUN, REVOLVER

	V.G.	Exc.	Value
.22 L.R.R.F., Double Action, *Modern*	25	50	35

I

	V.G.	Exc.	Prior Edition Exc. Value

IAB Puccinelli Co., San Anselmo, Calif.

SHOTGUN, DOUBLE BARREL, OVER-UNDER

	V.G.	Exc.	Prior Edition Exc. Value
C-3000 Combo, 12 Ga., Vent Rib, Single Selective Trigger, Checkered Stock, with 2 Extra Single Barrels, *Modern*	$1,500	$1,750	$2,500
C-300 Super Combo, 12 Ga. Vent Rib, Single Selective Trigger, Checkered Stock, with 2 Extra Single Barrels, *Modern*	2,250	2,750	3,025

SHOTGUN, SINGLESHOT

	V.G.	Exc.	Prior Edition Exc. Value
S-300, 12 Ga., Vent Rib, Checkered Stock, Trap Grade, *Modern*	850	950	1,325

I G Grey, of Dundee, c. 1630.

HANDGUN, SNAPHAUNCE

	V.G.	Exc.	Prior Edition Exc. Value
Belt Pistol, Engraved, Ovoid Pommel, All Metal, *Antique*	20,000	25,000	22,500

IMPERIAL Maker unknown, c. 1880.

HANDGUN, REVOLVER

	V.G.	Exc.	Prior Edition Exc. Value
.22 Short R.F., 7 Shot, Spur Trigger, Solid Frame, Single Action, *Antique*	125	150	165
.32 Short R.F., 5 Shot, Spur Trigger, Solid Frame, Single Action, *Antique*	150	175	170

IMPERIAL ARMS Made by Hopkins & Allen, c. 1880.

HANDGUN, REVOLVER

	V.G.	Exc.	Prior Edition Exc. Value
.32 Short R.F., 5 Shot, Spur Trigger, Solid Frame, Single Action, *Antique*	125	150	165
.38 Short R.F., 5 Shot, Spur Trigger, Solid Frame, Single Action, *Antique*	150	175	170

	V.G.	Exc.	Prior Edition Exc. Value

I.N.A. Industria Nacional de Armas, Sao Paulo, Brazil.

HANDGUN, REVOLVER

Tiger, .22 L.R.R.F., Single Action, Western Style, *Modern*	$50	$75	$65
Tiger, .32 S&W Long, Single Action, Western Style, *Modern*	50	75	70

INDIA MILITARY

AUTOMATIC WEAPON, HEAVY MACHINE GUN

Bira Gun, .450/.577 Martini-Henry, Drum Magazine, Carriage Mount, Twin Barrels, *Antique*	10,000	12,000	11,000

RIFLE, BOLT ACTION

S.M.L.E. No. 1 Mk.III, .303 British, Clip Fed, Ishapore, *Curio*	75	100	90

INDIAN ARMS Detroit, Mich., c. 1976.

HANDGUN, SEMI-AUTOMATIC

.380 ACP, Clip Fed, Stainless Steel, Vent Rib, Double Action, *Modern*	375	475	475

INDIAN SALES Cheyenne, Wyo.

HANDGUN, REVOLVER

HS-21, .22, L.R.R.F., Double Action, Blue, *Modern*	25	50	30

HANDGUN, SEMI-AUTOMATIC

Model 4, .25 ACP, Clip Fed, Blue, *Modern*	50	75	85

INGRAM Invented by Gordon Ingram. Made by Police Ordnance Co., Los Angeles, Calif. and Military Armament Corp., Georgia.

SEMI-AUTOMATIC WEAPON

M A C10, .45, ACP or 9mm, Clip Fed, Folding Stock, *Commercial,*	650	750	195
M A C10A1, 9mm Luger or .45 ACP, Clip Fed, Folding Stock, *Commercial,*	250	275	315
M A C11, .380 ACP, Clip Fed, Folding Stock, *Commercial,*	500	575	400

INGRAM, CHARLES Glasgow, Scotland, c. 1860.

SHOTGUN, DOUBLE BARREL, SIDE-BY-SIDE

Extra Set of Rifle Barrels, High Quality, Cased with Accessories, Engraved, Checkered Stock, *Antique*	6,500	7,500	7,250

INHOFF, BENEDICT Berks County, Pa. 1781–1783. See Kentucky Rifles.

	V.G.	Exc.	Prior Edition Exc. Value

INTERCHANGEABLE Belgium, Trade Name Schoverlin-Daley & Gales, c. 1880.

SHOTGUN, DOUBLE BARREL, SIDE-BY-SIDE
Various Gauges, Outside Hammers, Damascus Barrel, *Modern* ..... $100 | $150 | $155

INTERDYNAMIC Miami, Fla., c. 1979. Now made by F.I.E.
HANDGUN, SEMI-AUTOMATIC
KG-9, 9mm Luger, Clip Fed, SMG Styling, *Modern* ...... 600 | 650 | 300

INTERNATIONAL Made by Hood Firearms, c. 1875.
HANDGUN, REVOLVER
.22 Short R.F., 7 Shot, Spur Trigger, Solid Frame, Single Action, *Antique* ... 125 | 175 | 165
.32 Short R.F., 5 Shot, Spur Trigger, Solid Frame, Single Action, *Antique* ... 125 | 175 | 170

INTERNATIONAL DISTRIBUTERS Miami, Florida.
RIFLE, BOLT ACTION
Mauser Type, Various Calibers, Checkered Stock, Sling Swivels, Recoil Pad, *Modern* ... 150 | 200 | 200

INTERSTATE ARMS CO. Made by Crescent for Townley Metal & Hdw., Kansas City, Mo.
SHOTGUN, DOUBLE BARREL, SIDE-BY-SIDE
Various Gauges, Outside Hammers, Damascus Barrel, *Modern* ..... 150 | 175 | 180
Various Gauges, Hammerless, Steel Barrel, *Modern* ... 175 | 200 | 190
Various Gauges, Hammerless, Damascus Barrel, *Modern* ... 175 | 200 | 180
Various Gauges, Outside Hammers, Steel Barrel, *Modern* ... 150 | 175 | 185

SHOTGUN, SINGLESHOT
Various Gauges, Hammer, Steel Barrel, *Modern* ... 50 | 75 | 80

I P Probably German, 1580–1600.
RIFLE, WHEEL-LOCK
.60, German Style, Brass Furniture, Light Ornamentation, Horn Inlays, Set Trigger, *Antique* ... 4,000 | 4,500 | 4,450

ISRAELI MILITARY This list includes both military arms and the commercial arms made by Israeli Military Industries (I.M.I.). Also see Magnum Research, Inc. (M.R.I.).

	V.G.	Exc.	Prior Edition Exc. Value

HANDGUN, REVOLVER

	V.G.	Exc.	Prior Edition Exc. Value
S & W Model 10 Copy, 9mm Luger, Solid Frame, Swing-Out Cylinder, Double Action, Military, *Modern*	$500	$575	$595

RIFLE, SEMI-AUTOMATIC

	V.G.	Exc.	
Galil, .223 Rem., Clip Fed, Assault Rifle, Folding Stock, *Modern*	800	950	800
Galil, .308 Win., Clip Fed, Assault Rifle, Folding Stock, *Modern*	900	1,050	900
UZI, 9mm Luger, Clip Fed, Folding Stock, Commercial, *Modern*	750	850	430

ITALGUNS INTERNATIONAL Cusago, Italy

COMBINATION WEAPON, OVER-UNDER

	V.G.	Exc.	
Various Calibers, Checkered Stock, Double Triggers, *Modern*	275	325	315

HANDGUN, REVOLVER

	V.G.	Exc.	
Western Style, Various Calibers, Single Action, *Modern*	125	150	135
Western Style, Various Calibers, Single Action, Automatic Hammer Safety, *Modern*	125	150	140

SHOTGUN, DOUBLE BARREL, OVER-UNDER

	V.G.	Exc.	
Model 125, 12 Gauge, Checkered Stock, Vent Rib, Double Triggers, *Modern*	200	225	210
Model 150, 12 or 20 Gauges, Checkered Stock, Vent Rib, Single Trigger, *Modern*	225	250	235

ITALIAN MILITARY Also See Beretta.

HANDGUN, REVOLVER

	V.G.	Exc.	
Service Revolver, 10.4mm, Double Action, 6 Shot, Folding Trigger, *Curio*	100	125	110
Service Revolver, 10.4mm, Double Action, 6 Shot, Trigger Guard, *Curio*	100	125	110

HANDGUN, SEMI-AUTOMATIC

	V.G.	Exc.	
Brixia, 9mm Glisenti, Clip Fed, Military, *Curio*	250	300	285
M910 Army, 9mm Glisenti, Clip Fed, Military, *Curio*	275	300	285
M1934 Beretta, .380 ACP, Clip Fed, Military, *Modern*	150	175	285

RIFLE, BOLT ACTION

	V.G.	Exc.	
M1891, 6.5 × 52 Mannlicher-Carcano, Military, *Modern*	50	100	70
M38, 7.35mm Carcano, Military, *Modern*	50	75	70
M91 T.S., 6.5 × 52 Mannlicher-Carcano, Carbine, Folding Bayonet, Military, *Modern*	75	100	75
M91 T.S. (Late), 6.5 × 52 Mannlicher-Carcano, Carbine, Folding Bayonet, Military, *Modern*	50	75	55
M91/24, 6.5 × 52 Mannlicher-Carcano, Carbine, Military, *Modern*	50	75	55
M91/24, 6.5 × 52 Mannlicher-Carcano, Military, *Modern*	50	75	55

Italian Military M910

Italian Military Service Revolver Folding Trigger

Italian Military M91/24 Rifle

Italian Military M91 Rifle

	V.G.	Exc.	Prior Edition Exc. Value
Vetterli M1870/1887, 10.4 × 47R Italian Vetterli, *Antique*.............	$100	$125	$110
Vetterli M1870/87/15, 6.5 × 52 Mannlicher-Carcano, *Antique*.......	100	125	120

ITHACA GUN CO. Ithaca, N.Y. 1873 to Date. Absorbed Lefever Arms Co., Syracuse Arms Co., Union Firearms Co., and Wilkes Barre Gun Co.

COMBINATION WEAPON, OVER-UNDER

LSA 55 Turkey Gun, 12 Ga./.222, Open Rear Sight, Monte Carlo Stock, *Modern*...	425	475	385

RIFLE, BOLT ACTION

BSA CF 2, Various Calibers, Magnum Action, Monte Carlo Stock, Checkered Stock, *Modern*...	325	350	290
LSA 55, Various Calibers, Monte Carlo Stock, Cheekpiece, Heavy Barrel, *Modern*...	350	375	350
LSA-55, Various Calibers, Monte Carlo Stock, Open Rear Sight, *Modern*..	325	350	300
LSA-55 Deluxe, Various Calibers, Monte Carlo Stock, Cheekpiece, No Sights, Scope Mounts, *Modern*...	350	400	355

	V.G.	Exc.	Prior Edition Exc. Value
LSA-65, Various Calibers, Monte Carlo Stock, Open Rear Sight, *Modern*	$300	$350	$340
LSA-65 Deluxe, Various Calibers, Monte Carlo Stock, Cheekpiece, No Sights, Scope Mounts, *Modern*	325	375	350

RIFLE, LEVER ACTION

	V.G.	Exc.	
Model 49, .22 L.R.R.F., Singleshot, *Modern*	50	75	55
Model 49, .22 WMR, Singleshot, *Modern*	50	75	60
Model 49 Deluxe, .22 L.R.R.F., Singleshot, Fancy Wood, *Modern*	50	75	65
Model 49 Presentation, .22 L.R.R.F., Singleshot, Engraved, Fancy Checkering, *Modern*	125	150	175
Model 49 R, .22 L.R.R.F., Tube Feed, *Modern*	75	100	80
Model 49 St. Louis, .22 L.R.R.F., Bicentennial, Fancy Wood, Singleshot, *Curio*	125	150	155
Model 49 Youth, .22 L.R.R.F., Singleshot, *Modern*	25	50	53
Model 72, .22 L.R.R.F., Tube Feed, *Modern*	100	125	125
Model 72, .22 WMR, Tube Feed, *Modern*	125	150	145
Model 72 Deluxe, .22 L.R.R.F., Tube Feed, Octagon Barrel, *Modern*	125	175	170

RIFLE, SEMI-AUTOMATIC

	V.G.	Exc.	
X-15, Lightning, .22 L.R.R.F., Clip Fed, *Modern*	75	100	85
X5 C Lightning, .22 L.R.R.F., Clip Fed, *Modern*	75	100	90
X5 T Lightning, .22 L.R.R.F., Tube Feed, *Modern*	75	100	90

SHOTGUN, DOUBLE BARREL, OVER-UNDER

	V.G.	Exc.	
Model 500, 12 and 20 Gauges, Field Grade, Selective Ejector, Vent Rib, *Modern*	350	400	400
Model 500, 12 Ga. Mag. 3", Field Grade, Selective Ejector, Vent Rib, *Modern*	375	425	410
Model 600, 12 Ga., Trap Grade, Selective Ejector, Vent Rib, *Modern*	450	525	550
Model 600, 12 Ga., Trap Grade, Selective Ejector, Vent Rib, Monte Carlo Stock, *Modern*	475	550	550
Model 600, 12 and 20 Gauges, Field Grade, Selective Ejector, Vent Rib, *Modern*	400	475	520
Model 600, 12 and 20 Gauges, Skeet Grade, Selective Ejector, Vent Rib, *Modern*	475	525	550
Model 600, 28 and .410 Gauges, Skeet Grade, Selective Ejector, Vent Rib, *Modern*	575	650	560
Model 600 Combo Set, Various Gauges, Skeet Grade, Selective Ejector, Vent Rib, Cased, *Modern*	950	1,350	1,300
Model 680 English, 12 and 20 Gauges, Field Grade, Selective Ejector, Vent Rib, *Modern*	575	625	540
Model 700, 12 Ga., Trap Grade, Selective Ejector, Vent Rib, *Modern*	675	750	650

		V.G.	Exc.	Prior Edition Exc. Value
Model 700, 12 Ga., Trap Grade, Selective Ejector, Vent Rib, Monte Carlo Stock, *Modern*		$725	$775	$650
Model 700, 12 and 20 Gauges, Skeet Grade, Selective Ejector, Vent Rib, *Modern*		675	750	650
Model 700 Combo Set, Various Gauges, Skeet Grade, Selective Ejector, Vent Rib, Cased, *Modern*		1,500	1,750	1,725
Perazzi Light Game Model, 12 Ga., Automatic Ejector, Vent Rib, Single Trigger, *Modern*		3,000	3,500	1,400
Perazzi Competition 1, 12 Ga., Trap Grade, Automatic Ejector, Vent Rib, Single Trigger, Cased, *Modern*		2,850	3,250	1,400
Perazzi Competition 1, 12 Ga., Skeet Grade, Automatic Ejector, Vent Rib, Single Trigger, Cased, *Modern*		3,000	3,500	1,400
Perazzi Mirage, 12 Ga., Trap Grade, Automatic Ejector, Vent Rib, Cased, *Modern*		2,000	2,750	2,000
Perazzi Mirage 4-Barrel Set, Various Gauges, Skeet Grade, Automatic Ejector, Vent Rib, Cased, *Modern*		5,500	6,500	4,800
Perazzi MT-6, 12 Ga., Trap Grade, Automatic Ejector, Vent Rib, Cased, *Modern*		3,000	3,500	2,000
Perazzi MT-6, 12 Ga., Skeet Grade, Automatic Ejector, Vent Rib, Cased, *Modern*		3,250	3,750	2,650
Perazzi MX-8, 12 Ga., Trap Grade, Automatic Ejector, Vent Rib, Cased, *Modern*		2,500	3,000	2,050
Perazzi MX-8 Combo, 12 Ga., Trap Grade, Automatic Ejector, Vent Rib, Cased, *Modern*		3,500	3,950	2,950

SHOTGUN, DOUBLE BARREL, SIDE-BY-SIDE

Early Model, Serial Numbers under 425,000, *Deduct* **50%**

Outside Hammers, *Deduct Another* **20%–30%**

	V.G.	Exc.	Prior
Various Gauges, Field Grade, Hammerless, Magnum, Beavertail Forend, *Modern*	650	725	825
Various Gauges, Field Grade, Hammerless, Beavertail Forend, Double Trigger, *Modern*	700	775	760
Various Gauges, Field Grade, Hammerless, Double Trigger, Checkered Stock, *Modern*	550	600	575
Various Gauges, Field Grade, Hammerless, Magnum, Double Trigger, *Modern*	575	650	620
#1 E Grade, Various Gauges, Hammerless, Automatic Ejector, Beavertail Forend, Double Trigger, *Modern*	925	1,075	1,050
#1 E Grade, Various Gauges, Hammerless, Automatic Ejector, Magnum, Beavertail Forend, Double Trigger, *Modern*	1,100	1,350	1,300
#1 E Grade, Various Gauges, Hammerless, Automatic Ejector, Magnum, Double Trigger, *Modern*	975	1,200	1,150
#1 E Grade, Various Gauges, Hammerless, Automatic Ejector, Light Engraving, Checkered Stock, Double Trigger, *Modern*	800	950	900
#1 Grade, Various Gauges, Hammerless, Magnum, Double Trigger, Light Engraving, Checkered Stock, *Modern*	700	850	800
#1 Grade, Various Gauges, Hammerless, Double Trigger, Checkered Stock, Light Engraving, *Modern*	575	725	690

	V.G.	Exc.	Prior Edition Exc. Value
#1 Grade, Various Gauges, Hammerless, Magnum, Beavertail Forend, Double Trigger, *Modern*	$875	$1,050	$975
#1 Grade, Various Gauges, Hammerless, Beavertail Forend, Light Engraving, Checkered Stock, Double Trigger, *Modern*	700	850	810
#2 E Grade, Various Gauges, Hammerless, Automatic Ejector, Magnum, Beavertail Forend, Double Trigger, *Modern*	1,200	1,500	1,400
#2 E Grade, Various Gauges, Hammerless, Automatic Ejector, Magnum, Double Trigger, *Modern*	1,000	1,250	1,150
#2 E Grade, Various Gauges, Hammerless, Automatic Ejector, Beavertail Forend, Double Trigger, *Modern*	1,100	1,375	1,250
#2 E Grade, Various Gauges, Hammerless, Automatic Ejector, Double Trigger, Engraved, Checkered Stock, *Modern*	950	1,150	1,075
#2 Grade, Various Gauges, Hammerless, Magnum, Beavertail Forend, Double Trigger, *Modern*	1,150	1,275	1,100
#2 Grade, Various Gauges, Hammerless, Magnum, Beavertail Forend, Double Trigger, *Modern*	975	1,225	1,100
#2 Grade, Various Gauges, Hammerless, Beavertail Forend, Double Trigger, Engraved, Checkered Stock, *Modern*	950	1,025	875
#2 Grade, Various Gauges, Hammerless, Magnum, Double Trigger, Engraved, Checkered Stock, *Modern*	1,000	1,150	900
#2 Grade, Various Gauges, Hammerless, Double Trigger, Engraved, Checkered Stock, *Modern*	875	925	700
#3 E Grade, Various Gauges, Hammerless, Magnum, Beavertail Forend, Automatic Ejector, Double Trigger, *Modern*	1,500	1,825	1,650
#3 E Grade, Various Gauges, Hammerless, Magnum, Double Trigger, Engraved, Checkered Stock, *Modern*	1,500	1,625	1,475
#3 E Grade, Various Gauges, Hammerless, Beavertail Forend, Automatic Ejector, Double Trigger, *Modern*	1,375	1,550	1,400
#3 E Grade, Various Gauges, Hammerless, Double Trigger, Engraved, Checkered Stock, Automatic Ejector, *Modern*	1,250	1,450	1,350
#3 Grade, Various Gauges, Hammerless, Magnum, Beavertail Forend, Double Trigger, *Modern*	1,350	1,475	1,350
#3 Grade, Various Gauges, Hammerless, Magnum, Double Trigger, Engraved, Checkered Stock, *Modern*	1,125	1,325	1,250
#3 Grade, Various Gauges, Hammerless, Beavertail Forend, Engraved, Checkered Stock, Double Trigger, *Modern*	1,050	1,250	1,150
#3 Grade, Various Gauges, Hammerless, Double Trigger, Engraved, Checkered Stock, *Modern*	1,225	1,550	1,200
#4 E Grade, Various Gauges, Hammerless, Automatic Ejector, Vent Rib, Beavertail Forend, *Modern*	3,000	3,500	3,250
#4 E Grade, Various Gauges, Hammerless, Automatic Ejector, Vent Rib, Fancy Checkering, Fancy Engraving, *Modern*	2,625	3,125	2,750
#4 E Grade, Various Gauges, Hammerless, Automatic Ejector, Beavertail Forend, Fancy Checkering, Fancy Engraving, *Modern*	2,250	2,875	2,400
#5 E Grade, Various Gauges, Hammerless, Automatic Ejector, Vent Rib, Beavertail Forend, *Modern*	6,250	7,000	4,150
#5 E Grade, Various Gauges, Hammerless, Automatic Ejector, Vent Rib, Fancy Checkering, Fancy Engraving, *Modern*	6,500	7,250	4,150

	V.G.	Exc.	Prior Edition Exc. Value
#5 E Grade, Various Gauges, Hammerless, Automatic Ejector, Beavertail Forend, Fancy Checkering, Fancy Engraving, *Modern*	$5,750	$6,500	$3,750
#5 E Grade, Various Gauges, Hammerless, Automatic Ejector, Fancy Checkering, Fancy Engraving, Double Trigger, *Modern*	5,500	6,250	3,600
#7 E Grade, Various Gauges, Hammerless, Automatic Ejector, Vent Rib, Beavertail Forend, *Modern*	6,500	7,250	8,700
#7 E Grade, Various Gauges, Hammerless, Automatic Ejector, Vent Rib, Fancy Checkering, Fancy Engraving, *Modern*	6,250	7,000	8,350
#7 E Grade, Various Gauges, Hammerless, Automatic Ejector, Beavertail Forend, Fancy Checkering, Fancy Engraving, *Modern*	6,000	6,800	8,100
#7 E Grade, Various Gauges, Hammerless, Automatic Ejector, Fancy Checkering, Fancy Engraving, Double Trigger, *Modern*	5,750	6,500	8,000
$2000 Grade, Various Gauges, Hammerless, Automatic Ejector, Single Selective Trigger, Ornate, *Modern*	8,500	9,500	11,000
$2000 Grade, Various Gauges, Hammerless, Automatic Ejector, Single Selective Trigger, Vent Rib, Ornate, *Modern*	7,500	10,000	12,000
$2000 Grade, Various Gauges, Hammerless, Automatic Ejector, Single Selective Trigger, Beavertail Forend, Ornate, *Modern*	8,000	9,500	11,000
$2000 Grade, Various Gauges, Hammerless, Automatic Ejector, Single Selective Trigger, Vent Rib, Beavertail Forend, *Modern*	8,500	10,250	12,500
Model 100, 12 and 20 Gauges, Hammerless, Field Grade, *Modern*	300	325	295
Model 200 E, 12 and 20 Gauges, Hammerless, Selective Ejector, Field Grade, *Modern*	350	400	385
Model 200 E, 12 and 20 Gauges, Hammerless, Selective Ejector, Skeet Grade, *Modern*	375	425	390
Model 280 English, 12 and 20 Gauges, Hammerless, Selective Ejector, Field Grade, *Modern*	400	450	440

SHOTGUN, LEVER ACTION

	V.G.	Exc.	Prior Edition Exc. Value
Model 66 Supersingle, Various Gauges, Singleshot, *Modern*	50	75	58
Model 66 Buck, Various Gauges, Singleshot, Open Rear Sight, *Modern*	50	75	65
Model 66 Youth, Various Gauges, Singleshot, *Modern*	50	75	58

SHOTGUN, PISTOL

	V.G.	Exc.	Prior Edition Exc. Value
Auto Burglar, Various Gauges, Double Barrel, Side by Side, Short Shotgun, *Curio*	650	850	620

SHOTGUN, SEMI-AUTOMATIC

	V.G.	Exc.	Prior Edition Exc. Value
300 Standard, 12 and 20 Gauges, *Modern*	175	200	190
300 Standard, 12 and 20 Gauges, Vent Rib, *Modern*	175	225	200
300 XL Standard, 12 and 20 Gauges, *Modern*	200	225	200
300 XL Standard, 12 and 20 Gauges, Vent Rib, *Modern*	200	250	230
900 Deluxe, 12 and 20 Gauges, Vent Rib, *Modern*	275	325	980
900 XL, 12 Ga., Trap Grade, *Modern*	225	275	260
900 XL, 12 Ga., Trap Grade, Monte Carlo Stock, *Modern*	250	275	260
900 XL, 12 and 20 Gauges, Skeet Grade, *Modern*	200	250	245

	V.G.	Exc.	Prior Edition Exc. Value
900 XL Deluxe, 12 and 20 Gauges, Vent Rib, *Modern*	$225	$250	$230
900 XL Slug, 12 and 20 Gauges, Open Rear Sight, *Modern*	225	250	230
Mag 10 Deluxe, 10 Ga. 3¹/₂", Takedown, Vent Rib, Fancy Wood, Checkered Stock, *Modern*	475	525	510
Mag 10 Standard, 10 Ga. 3¹/₂", Takedown, Vent Rib, Recoil Pad, Checkered Stock, Sling Swivels, *Modern*	450	500	405
Mag 10 Standard, 10 Ga. 3¹/₂", Takedown, Recoil Pad, Checkered Stock, Sling Swivels, *Modern*	375	425	360
Mag 10 Supreme, 10 Ga. 3¹/₂", Takedown, Vent Rib, Fancy Wood, Engraved, Checkered Stock, *Modern*	600	750	630
Model 51, 12 and 20 Gauges, Takedown, Vent Rib, Recoil Pad, Magnum, *Modern*	225	275	270
Model 51 Deerslayer, 12 Ga., Takedown, Open Rear Sight, Sling Swivels, *Modern*	250	275	260
Model 51 Deluxe, 12 Ga., Trap Grade, Takedown, Checkered Stock, Fancy Wood, Recoil Pad, *Modern*	300	350	330
Model 51 Deluxe, 12 Ga., Trap Grade, Monte Carlo Stock, Fancy Wood, Recoil Pad, *Modern*	325	350	345
Model 51 Deluxe, 12 and 20 Gauges, Skeet Grade, Takedown, Checkered Stock, Fancy Wood, Recoil Pad, *Modern*	250	300	295
Model 51 Standard, 12 and 20 Gauges, Takedown, Checkered Stock, *Modern*	200	225	230
Model 51 Standard, 12 and 20 Gauges, Takedown, Vent Rib, Checkered Stock, *Modern*	225	250	255

SHOTGUN, SINGLESHOT

	V.G.	Exc.	Prior Edition Exc. Value
$5000 Grade, 12 Ga., Trap Grade, Automatic Ejector, Ornate, *Modern*	7,500	8,500	5,050
4 E Grade, 12 Gauge, Trap Grade, Automatic Ejector, Engraved, Fancy Checkering, *Modern*	1,000	1,200	3,025
5 E Grade, 12 Gauge, Trap Grade, Automatic Ejector, Fancy Engraving, Fancy Checkering, *Modern*	1,800	2,200	3,950
7 E Grade, 12 Gauge, Trap Grade, Automatic Ejector, Fancy Engraving, Fancy Checkering, *Modern*	2,750	3,250	4,300

Ithaca Model 51

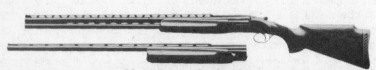

Ithaca Perazzi Combination

	V.G.	Exc.	Prior Edition Exc. Value
Century 12 Ga., Trap Grade, Automatic Ejector, Engraved, Checkered Stock, *Modern*	$425	$475	$450
Century II, 12 Ga., Trap Grade, Automatic Ejector, Engraved, Checkered Stock, *Modern*	450	500	485
Perazzi Competition 1, 12 Ga., Trap Grade, Automatic Ejector, Vent Rib, Cased, *Modern*	950	1,250	1,500
Victory Grade, 12 Ga., Automatic Ejector, Checkered Stock, Vent Rib, Trap Grade, *Modern*	675	750	1,200

SHOTGUN, SLIDE ACTION

	V.G.	Exc.	Prior Edition Exc. Value
Model 37, for Extra Barrel, *Add* **$50.00–$75.00**			
Model 37, Extra Vent Rib Barrel, *Add* **$60.00–$85.00**			
Model 37, 12 Ga., Takedown, Bicentennial, Engraved, Fancy Wood, Checkered Stock, *Modern*	325	350	580
Model 37, Various Gauges, Takedown, Plain, *Modern*	125	175	145
Model 37 Deerslayer, Various Gauges, Takedown, Checkered Stock, Recoil Pad, Open Rear Sight, *Modern*	200	225	195
Model 37 Deerslayer, Various Gauges, Takedown, Fancy Wood, Checkered Stock, Recoil Pad, Open Rear Sight, *Modern*	225	250	225
Model 37 DSPS, 12 Ga., Takedown, Checkered Stock, 8 Shot, Open Rear Sight, *Modern*	225	250	225
Model 37 DSPS, 12 Ga., Takedown, Checkered Stock, 5 Shot, Open Rear Sight, *Modern*	200	225	210
Model 37 M & P, 12 Ga., Takedown, Parkerized, 5 Shot, *Modern*	200	225	200
Model 37 M & P, Bayonet & Adapter, *Add* **$25.00–$45.00**			
Model 37-V Standard, Various Gauges, Takedown, Checkered Stock, Vent Rib, *Modern*	225	250	200
Model 37 Standard, Various Gauges, Takedown, Checkered Stock, *Modern*	200	225	175
Model 37 Supreme, Various Gauges, Takedown, Trap Grade, Fancy Wood, Checkered Stock, *Modern*	350	400	380
Model 37 Supreme, Various Gauges, Takedown, Skeet Grade, Fancy Wood, Checkered Stock, *Modern*	375	400	380
Model 37-$1000 Grade, Various Gauges, Takedown, Fancy Wood, Fancy Checkering, Fancy Engraving, Gold Inlays, *Modern*	4,000	5,000	4,000
Model 37-$5000 Grade, Various Gauges, Takedown, Fancy Wood, Fancy Checkering, Fancy Engraving, Gold Inlays, *Modern*	3,500	4,500	4,000
Model 37-D, Various Gauges, Takedown, Checkered Stock, Beavertail Forend, *Modern*	225	250	165
Model 37-Deluxe, Various Gauges, Takedown, Checkered Stock, Recoil Pad, *Modern*	175	200	175
Model 37-Deluxe, Various Gauges, Takedown, Checkered Stock, Recoil Pad, Vent Rib, *Modern*	200	225	215

	V.G.	Exc.	Prior Edition Exc. Value
Model 37-R, Various Gauges, Takedown, Solid Rib, Checkered Stock, *Modern*	$175	$200	$170
Model 37-R, Various Gauges, Takedown, Solid Rib, Plain, *Modern*	150	175	165
Model 37-R Deluxe, Various Gauges, Takedown, Solid Rib, Fancy Wood, Checkered Stock, *Modern*	225	250	215
Model 37-S, Various Gauges, Takedown, Skeet Grade, Checkered Stock, Fancy Wood, *Modern*	350	375	325
Model 37-T, Various Gauges, Takedown, Trap Grade, Checkered Stock, Fancy Wood, *Modern*	350	375	325

IVER JOHNSON Started as Johnson & Bye 1871 in Worcester, Mass. In 1883 became Iver Johnson's Arms & Cycle Works. 1891 to 1982 at Fitchburg, Mass., now located in Jacksonville, Ark.

HANDGUN, PERCUSSION

	V.G.	Exc.	Prior Edition Exc. Value
Prince, .30, Singleshot, Spur Trigger, Various Barrel Lengths, Screw Barrel, *Antique*	300	325	330
Uncle Sam 1871, .30, Singleshot, Spur Trigger, Various Barrel Lengths, *Antique*	250	300	300
.36 1861 Navy, Revolver, Reproduction, *Antique*	50	75	80
.36 New Model Navy, Revolver, Reproduction, *Antique*	50	75	68
.36 Pocket Model, Revolver, Reproduction, *Antique*	50	75	80
.36 Remington Army, Revolver, Reproduction, *Antique*	50	75	80
.44 1860 Army, Revolver, Reproduction, *Antique*	50	75	80
.44 Confederate Army, Revolver, Reproduction, *Antique*	50	75	60
.44 Remington Army, Revolver, Reproduction, *Antique*	75	100	80
.44 Remington Target, Revolver, Reproduction, *Antique*	75	100	100

HANDGUN, REVOLVER

	V.G.	Exc.	Prior Edition Exc. Value
.22 Supershot, .22 L.R.R.F., 7 Shot, Blue, Wood Grips, Top Break, Double Action, *Modern*	75	100	95
Armsworth M855, .22 L.R.R.F., 8 Shot, Single Action, Top Break, Adjustable Sights, Wood Grips, *Modern*	100	125	120
Cadet, .22 WMR, 8 Shot, Solid Frame, Double Action, Plastic Stock, Blue, *Modern*	50	75	75
Cadet, .32 S & W Long, 5 Shot, Solid Frame Double Action, Plastic Stock, Nickel Plated, *Modern*	50	75	70
Cadet, .32 S & W, 5 Shot, Solid Frame, Double Action, Plastic Stock, Blue, *Modern*	50	75	65
Cadet, .38 Special, 5 Shot, Solid Frame, Double Action, Plastic Stock, Blue, *Modern*	50	75	70
Cadet, .38 Special, 5 Shot, Solid Frame, Double Action, Plastic Stock, Nickel Plated, *Modern*	50	75	75
Cattleman, .357 Magnum, Single Action, Western Style, Color Case Hardened Frame, Various Barrel Lengths, *Modern*	125	150	150

	V.G.	Exc.	Prior Edition Exc. Value
Cattleman, .44 Magnum, Single Action, Western Style, Color Case Hardened Frame, Various Barrel Lengths, *Modern*	$150	$175	$175
Cattleman, .45 Colt, Single Action, Western Style, Color Case Hardened Frame, Various Barrel Lengths, *Modern*	125	150	155
Cattleman Buckhorn, .357 Magnum, Single Action, Western Style, Color Case Hardened Frame, Adjustable Sights, Various Barrel Lengths, *Modern*	125	150	150
Cattleman Buckhorn, .357 Magnum, Single Action, Western Style, Color Case Hardened Frame, Adjustable Sights, 12" Barrel, *Modern*	175	200	195
Cattleman Buckhorn, .44 Magnum, Single Action, Western Style, Color Case Hardened Frame, Adjustable Sights, Various Barrel Lengths, *Modern*	175	200	195
Cattleman Buckhorn, .44 Magnum, Single Action, Western Style, Color Case Hardened Frame, *Modern*	150	175	175
Cattleman Buckhorn, .45 Colt, Single Action, Western Style, Color Case Hardened Frame, Adjustable Sights, Various Barrel Lengths, *Modern*	150	175	170
Cattleman Buckhorn, .45 Colt, Single Action, Western Style, Color Case Hardened Frame, Adjustable Sights, 12" Barrel, *Modern*	175	200	200
Cattleman Buntline, .357 Magnum, Single Action, Western Style, with Detachable Shoulder Stock, Adjustable Sights, 18" Barrel, *Modern*	275	300	315
Cattleman Buntline, .44 Magnum, Single Action, Western Style, with Detachable Shoulder Stock, Adjustable Sights, 18" Barrel, *Modern*	300	325	320
Cattleman Buntline, .45 Colt, Single Action, Western Style, with Detachable Shoulder Stock, Adjustable Sights, 18" Barrel, *Modern*	275	300	310
Cattleman Trailblazer, .22LR/.22 WMR Combo, Single Action, Western Style, Color Case Hardened Frame, Adjustable Sights, *Modern*	125	150	145
Champion Target, .22 L.R.R.F., 8 Shot, Single Action, Top Break, Adjustable Sights, Wood Grips, *Modern*	100	125	130
Model 1900, .22 L.R.R.F., 7 Shot, Blue, Double Action, Solid Frame, *Modern*	75	100	100
Model 1900, .22 L.R.R.F., 7 Shot, Nickel Plated, Double Action, Solid Frame, *Modern*	75	100	100
Model 1900, .32 S & W Long, 6 Shot, Blue, Double Action, Solid Frame, *Modern*	75	100	100
Model 1900, .32 S & W Long, 6 Shot, Nickel Plated, Double Action, Solid Frame, *Modern*	75	100	100
Model 1900, .32 Short R.F., 6 Shot, Blue, Double Action, Solid Frame, *Modern*	75	100	100
Model 1900, .32 Short R.F., 6 Shot, Nickel Plated, Double Action, Solid Frame, *Modern*	100	125	105
Model 1900, .38 S & W, 5 Shot, Blue, Double Action, Solid Frame, *Modern*	100	125	105

	V.G.	Exc.	Prior Edition Exc. Value
Model 1900, .38 S & W, 5 Shot, Nickel Plated, Double Action, Solid Frame, *Modern*	$125	$150	$120
Model 1900 Target, .22 L.R.R.F., 7 Shot, Blue, Wood Grips, Solid Frame, Double Action, *Modern*	125	175	130
Model 50A Sidewinder, .22 L.R.R.F., 8 Shot, Solid Frame, Double Action, Plastic Stock, Western Style, *Modern*	50	75	70
Model 50A Sidewinder, .22 L.R.R.F., 8 Shot, Solid Frame, Double Action, Wood Grips, Western Style, *Modern*	50	75	75
Model 55, .22 L.R.R.F., 8 Shot, Solid Frame, Double Action, Wood Grips, Blue, *Modern*	50	75	70
Model 55-S Cadet, .32 S & W, 5 Shot, Solid Frame, Double Action, Plastic Stock, Blue, *Modern*	50	75	70
Model 55-S Cadet, .38 S & W, 5 Shot, Solid Frame, Double Action, Plastic Stock, Blue, *Modern*	50	75	70
Model 55-SA Cadet, .22 L.R.R.F., 8 Shot, Solid Frame, Double Action, Plastic, Blue, *Modern*	50	75	70
Model 55-SA Cadet, .32 S & W, 5 Shot, Solid Frame, Double Action, Plastic Stock, Blue, *Modern*	50	75	70
Model 55-SA Cadet, .38 S & W, 5 Shot, Solid Frame, Double Action, Plastic Stock, Blue, *Modern*	50	75	75
Model 55A, .22 L.R.R.F., 8 Shot, Solid Frame, Double Action, Wood Grips, Blue, *Modern*	75	100	70
Model 55A, .22 L.R.R.F., 8 Shot, Solid Frame, Double Action, Wood Grips, Blue, *Modern*	75	100	70
Model 55A, .22 L.R.R.F., 8 Shot, Solid Frame, Double Action, Plastic Stock, Blue, *Modern*	75	100	70
Model 55S, .22 L.R.R.F., 8 Shot, Solid Frame, Double Action, Plastic Stock, Blue, *Modern*	50	75	70
Model 57 Target, .22 L.R.R.F., 8 Shot, Solid Frame, Double Action, Plastic Stock, Adjustable Sights, *Modern*	75	100	75
Model 57 Target, .22 L.R.R.F., 8 Shot, Solid Frame, Double Action, Wood Grips, Adjustable Sights, *Modern*	75	100	75
Model 57-A Target, .22 L.R.R.F., 8 Shot, Solid Frame, Double Action, Plastic Stock, Adjustable Sights, *Modern*	75	100	80
Model 57-A Target, .22 L.R.R.F., 8 Shot, Solid Frame, Double Action, Wood Grips, Adjustable Sights, *Modern*	75	100	80
Model 66 Trailsman, .22 L.R.R.F., 8 Shot, Top Break, Double Action, Wood Grips, Adjustable Sights, *Modern*	75	100	80
Model 67 Viking, .22 L.R.R.F., 8 Shot, Top Break, Double Action, Plastic Stock, Adjustable Sights, *Modern*	75	100	75
Model 76S Viking, .22 L.R.R.F., 8 Shot, Top Break, Double Action, Plastic Stock, Adjustable Sights, *Modern*	75	100	70
Model 67S Viking, .32 S & W, 5 Shot, Top Break, Double Action, Plastic Stock, Adjustable Sights, *Modern*	75	100	75
Model 67S Viking, .38 S & W, 5 Shot, Top Break, Double Action, Plastic Stock, Adjustable Sights, *Modern*	50	75	65
Petite, .22 Short Nickel Plated, Folding Trigger, 5 Shot, "Baby" Style, *Antique*	200	250	330

	V.G.	Exc.	Prior Edition Exc. Value
Safety, .22 L.R.R.F., 7 Shot, Top Break, Double Action, Hammer, Blue, *Modern*	*$100*	*$125*	*$105*
Safety, .22 L.R.R.F., 7 Shot, Top Break, Double Action, Hammer, Nickel Plated, *Modern*	*125*	*150*	*130*
Safety, .22 L.R.R.F., 7 Shot, Top Break, Double Action, Hammerless, Blue, *Modern*	*125*	*150*	*130*
Safety, .22 L.R.R.F., 7 Shot, Top Break, Double Action, Hammerless, Nickel Plated, *Modern*	*125*	*150*	*135*
Safety, .32 S & W, 5 Shot, Top Break, Double Action, Hammer, Nickel Plated, *Modern*	*125*	*150*	*130*
Safety, .32 S & W, 5 Shot, Top Break, Double Action, Hammer, Blue, *Modern*	*100*	*125*	*105*
Safety, .32 S & W, 5 Shot, Top Break, Double Action, Hammerless, Blue, *Modern*	*125*	*150*	*130*
Safety, .32 S & W, 5 Shot, Top Break, Double Action, Hammerless, Nickel Plated, *Modern*	*125*	*150*	*135*
Safety, .32 S & W Long, 6 Shot, Top Break, Double Action, Hammer, Blue, *Modern*	*100*	*125*	*105*
Safety, .32 S & W Long, 6 Shot, Top Break, Double Action, Hammer, Nickel Plated, *Modern*	*100*	*125*	*120*
Safety, .32 S & W Long, 6 Shot, Top Break, Double Action, Hammerless, Blue, *Modern*	*100*	*125*	*115*
Safety, .38 S & W, 5 Shot, Top Break, Double Action, Hammerless, Nickel Plated, *Modern*	*125*	*150*	*130*
Sealed 8 Protector, .22 L.R.R.F., 8 Shot, Blue, Wood Grips, Top Break, Double Action, *Modern*	*125*	*150*	*125*
Sealed 8 Supershot, .22 L.R.R.F., Adjustable Sights, Blue, Wood Grips, Top Break, Double Action, *Modern*	*125*	*150*	*130*
Sealed 8 Target, .22 L.R.R.F., 8 Shot, Blue, Wood Grips, Solid Frame, Double Action, *Modern*	*100*	*125*	*115*
Sidewinder, .22LR/.22WMR Combo, Western Style, 4" Barrel, Adjustable Sights, *Modern*	*75*	*100*	*95*
Sidewinder, .22LR/.22 WMR Combo, Western Style, 6" Barrel, Adjustable Sights, *Modern*	*75*	*100*	*95*
Supershot 9, .22 L.R.R.F., 9 Shot, Adjustable Sights, Blue, Wood Grips, Top Break, *Modern*	*100*	*125*	*120*
Supershot M 844, .22 L.R.R.F., 8 Shot, Double Action, Top Break, Adjustable Sights, Wood Grips, *Modern*	*75*	*100*	*95*
Swing Out, .22 L.R.R.F., Swing-Out Cylinder, Various Barrel Lengths, Double Action, Wood Grips, Blue, *Modern*	*75*	*100*	*95*
Swing Out, .22 L.R.R.F., Swing-Out, Cylinder, 4" Barrel, Double Action, Wood Grips, Blue, *Modern*	*75*	*100*	*100*
Swing Out, .22 L.R.R.F., Swing-Out Cylinder, 4" Barrel, Double Action. Adjustable Sights, Blue, *Modern*	*125*	*150*	*135*
Swing Out, .22 L.R.R.F., Swing-Out Cylinder, 6" Barrel, Double Action, Adjustable Sights, Blue, *Modern*	*100*	*125*	*115*
Swing Out, .22 WMR, Swing-Out Cylinder, Various Barrel Lengths, Double Action, Wood Grips, Blue, *Modern*	*75*	*100*	*95*

	V.G.	Exc.	Prior Edition Exc. Value
Swing Out, .22 WMR, Swing-Out Cylinder, 4" Barrel, Double Action, Wood Grips, Blue, *Modern*	$75	$100	$100
Swing Out, .22 WMR, Swing-Out Cylinder, 4" Barrel, Double Action, Adjustable Sights, Blue, *Modern*	125	150	135
Swing Out, .22 WMR, Swing-Out Cylinder, 6" Barrel, Double Action, Adjustable Sights, Blue, *Modern*	100	125	115
Swing Out, .32 S & W Long, Swing-Out Cylinder, Various Barrel Lengths, Double Action, Wood Grips, Blue, *Modern*	75	100	90
Swing Out, .32 S & W Long, Swing-Out Cylinder, Various Barrel Lengths, Double Action, Wood Grips, Nickel Plated, *Modern*	100	125	100
Swing Out, .32 S & W Long, Swing-Out Cylinder, 4" Barrel, Double Action, Wood Grips, Blue, *Modern*	100	125	100
Swing Out, .32 S & W Long, Swing-Out Cylinder, 4" Barrel, Double Action, Adjustable Sights, Blue, *Modern*	125	150	135
Swing Out, .32 S & W Long, Swing-Out Cylinder, 6" Barrel, Double Action, Adjustable Sights, Blue, *Modern*	100	125	115
Swing Out, .38 Special, Swing-Out Cylinder, Various Barrel Lengths, Double Action, Wood Grips, Blue, *Modern*	100	125	100
Swing Out, .38 Special, Swing-Out Cylinder, Various Barrel Lengths, Double Action, Wood Grips, Nickel Plated, *Modern*	100	125	105
Swing Out, .38 Special, Swing-Out Cylinder, 4" Barrel, Double Action, Wood Grips, Blue, *Modern*	100	125	105
Swing Out, .38 Special, Swing-Out Cylinder, 4" Barrel, Double Action, Adjustable Sights, Blue, *Modern*	125	150	140
Swing Out, .38 Special, Swing-Out Cylinder, 6" Barrel, Double Action, Adjustable Sights, Blue, *Modern*	125	150	120
Swing Out Model 1879, .38 S & W, 5 Shot, Swing Right, Forward Hinge, Solid Frame, *Antique*	275	300	275
Target 9, .22 L.R.R.F., 9 Shot, Blue, Solid Frame, Wood Grips, Double Action, *Modern*	100	125	100
Trigger-Cocking, .22 L.R.R.F., 8 Shot, Single Action, Top Break, Adjustable Sights, Wood Grips, *Modern*	125	150	125

HANDGUN, SEMI-AUTOMATIC

	V.G.	Exc.	Prior Edition Exc. Value
Model TP-22, .22 L.R.R.F., Double Action, Hammer, Clip Fed, Blue, *Modern*	150	175	110
Model TP-25, .25 ACP, Double Action, Hammer, Clip Fed, Blue, *Modern*	150	175	110
PP30 Enforcer, .30 M1 Carbine, Clip Fed, Blue, *Modern*	200	225	195
PP30S Enforcer, .30 M1 Carbine, Clip Fed, Stainless, *Modern*	225	250	230
Trailsman, .22 L.R.R.F., Clip Fed, Blue, *Modern*	125	150	120
X-300 Pony, .380 ACP, Hammer, Clip Fed, Blue, *Modern*	200	225	155
X-300 Pony, .380 ACP, Hammer, Clip Fed, Nickel Plated, *Modern*	225	250	165
X-300 Pony, .380 ACP, Hammer, Clip Fed, Matt Blue, *Modern*	200	225	155

HANDGUN, SINGLESHOT

	V.G.	Exc.	Prior Edition Exc. Value
Eclipse 1872, .22 R.F., Spur Trigger, Side-Swing Barrel, Hammer, *Antique*	250	275	230

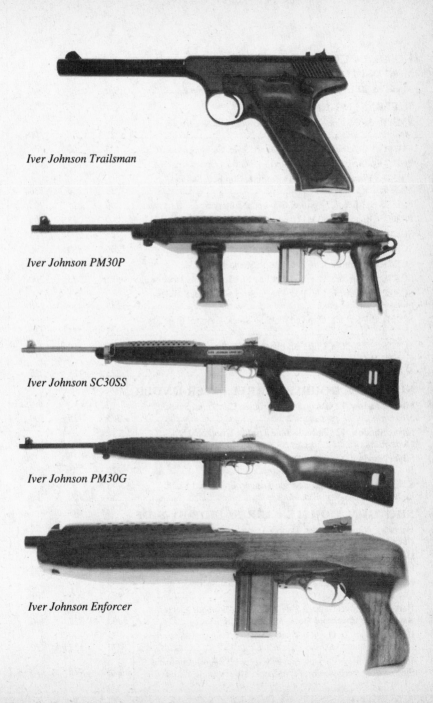

Iver Johnson Trailsman

Iver Johnson PM30P

Iver Johnson SC30SS

Iver Johnson PM30G

Iver Johnson Enforcer

	V.G.	Exc.	Prior Edition Exc. Value

RIFLE, BOLT ACTION

	V.G.	Exc.	Prior Edition Exc. Value
Model 2X, .22 L.R.R.F., Singleshot, Takedown, *Modern*	$50	$75	$60
Model X, .22 L.R.R.F., Singleshot, Takedown, *Modern*	50	75	60

RIFLE, SEMI-AUTOMATIC

	V.G.	Exc.	Prior Edition Exc. Value
PM30P, .30 Carbine, Clip Fed, Telescoping Stock, Carbine, *Modern*	225	250	190
PM30G, .30 Carbine, Clip Fed, Military Style, Carbine, *Modern*	175	200	165
PM5.7 Spitfire, 5.7 Spitfire, Clip Fed, Military Style, *Modern*	150	175	165
PM30PS Paratrooper, .30 M1 Carbine, Clip Fed, Stainless, *Modern*	225	250	230
PM5.7S Spitfire, 5.7 Spitfire, Clip Fed, Military Style, *Modern*	200	225	205
PP30GS Standard, .30 M1 Carbine, Clip Fed, Stainless, *Modern*	200	225	205
SC30S, .30 Carbine, Clip Fed, Plastic Stock, Carbine, *Modern*	175	200	175
SC30F, .30 Carbine, Clip Fed, Folding Stock, Carbine, *Modern*	200	250	200
SC5.7S, 5.7 Spitfire, Clip Fed, Plastic Stock, *Modern*	175	200	170
SC5.7S, 5.7 Spitfire, Clip Fed, Folding Stock, Carbine, *Modern*	175	225	200
SC30S, .30 Carbine, Clip Fed, Plastic Stock, Carbine, Stainless, *Modern*	225	250	210
SC30F, .30 Carbine, Clip Fed, Folding Stock, Carbine, Stainless, *Modern*	225	275	240
SC5.7S, 5.7 Spitfire, Clip Fed, Plastic Stock, Stainless, *Modern*	225	250	210
SC5.7S, 5.7 Spitfire, Clip Fed, Folding Stock, Carbine, Stainless, *Modern*	225	275	235

SHOTGUN, DOUBLE BARREL, OVER-UNDER

	V.G.	Exc.	Prior Edition Exc. Value
Silver Shadow, 12 Gauge, Single Trigger, Checkered Stock, *Modern*	275	325	300
Silver Shadow, 12 Gauge, Double Trigger, Checkered Stock, *Modern*	200	275	275
Silver Shadow, 12 Gauge, Double Trigger, Checkered Stock, Light Engraving, Vent Rib, *Modern*	225	275	260
Silver Shadow, 12 Gauge, Single Trigger, Checkered Stock, Light Engraving, Vent Rib, *Modern*	250	300	290

SHOTGUN, DOUBLE BARREL, SIDE-BY-SIDE

	V.G.	Exc.	Prior Edition Exc. Value
Hercules, Various Gauges, Double Trigger, Checkered Stock, Hammerless, *Modern*	375	450	300
Hercules, Various Gauges, Double Trigger, Automatic Ejector, Hammerless, Checkered Stock, *Modern*	400	475	360
Hercules, Various Gauges, Single Trigger, Hammerless, Checkered Stock, *Modern*	425	500	395
Hercules, Various Gauges, Single Trigger, Automatic Ejector, Hammerless, Checkered Stock, *Modern*	450	525	440
Hercules, Various Gauges, Single Selective Trigger, Hammerless, Checkered Stock, *Modern*	475	525	470
Hercules, Various Gauges, Single Selective Trigger, Automatic Ejector, Hammerless, Checkered Stock, *Modern*	450	550	510

	V.G.	Exc.	Prior Edition Exc. Value
Knox-All, Various Gauges, Double Trigger, Hammer, Checkered Stock, *Modern*..	$300	$350	$285
Skeeter, Various Gauges, Double Trigger, Hammerles, *Modern*	550	650	435
Skeeter, Various Gauges, Skeet Grade, Double Trigger, Automatic Ejector, Hammerless, *Modern*	575	675	540
Skeeter, Various Gauges, Skeet Grade, Single Trigger, Hammerless, *Modern*..	600	675	515
Skeeter, Various Gauges, Skeet Grade, Single Trigger, Automatic Ejector, Hammerless, *Modern*	650	700	550
Skeeter, Various Gauges, Skeet Grade, Single Selective Trigger, Hammerless, *Modern*..	650	700	565
Skeeter, Various Gauges, Skeet Grade, Single Selective Trigger, Automatic Ejector, Hammerless, *Modern*	625	675	530
Super, 12 Gauge, Trap Grade, Double Trigger, Hammerless, *Modern*..	600	650	575
Super, 12 Gauge, Trap Grade, Single Trigger, Hammerless, *Modern*..	650	700	650
Super, 12 Gauge, Trap Grade, Single Selective Trigger, Hammerless, *Modern*..	700	750	775

SHOTGUN, SINGLESHOT

	V.G.	Exc.	Prior Edition Exc. Value
Side Snap, 12 Gauge, Steel Barrel, Hammer, *Antique*.....................	75	100	80
Side Snap, 12 Gauge, Damascus Barrel, Hammer, *Antique*	50	75	70
Top Snap, 12 Gauge, Steel Barrel, Hammer, *Antique*	75	100	90
12 Gauge, Trap Grade, Vent Rib, Checkered Stock, *Modern*...........	150	175	150
Champion, Various Gauges, Automatic Ejector, *Modern*................	50	75	70
Mat Rib Grade, Various Gauges, Raised Matted Rib, Automatic Ejector, Checkered Stock, *Modern*...	75	100	90

IZARRA Made by Bonifacio Echeverra, Eibar, Spain, c. 1918.

HANDGUN, SEMI-AUTOMATIC

	V.G.	Exc.	Prior Edition Exc. Value
.32 ACP, Clip Fed, Long Grip, *Modern*..	150	175	175

J

J & R Burbank, Calif.

RIFLE, SEMI-AUTOMATIC

Model 68, 9mm Luger, Clip Fed, Flash Hider, Takedown,
Modern $150 $175 $175

JACKRABBIT Continental Arms Corp., N.Y.C., c. 1960.

RIFLE, SINGLESHOT

Handy Gun, .44 Magnum, Detachable Shoulder Stock, *Modern* 75 100 80

SHOTGUN, SINGLESHOT

Handy Gun, .410 3", Detachable Shoulder Stock, *Modern* 50 75 75

JACKSON ARMS CO. Made by Crescent for C.M. McClung & Co., Knoxville, Tenn.

SHOTGUN, DOUBLE BARREL, SIDE-BY-SIDE

Various Gauges, Outside Hammers, Damascus Barrel, *Modern* 150 175 170
Various Gauges, Hammerless, Steel Barrel, *Modern* 175 200 200
Various Gauges, Hammerless, Damascus Barrel, *Modern* 150 175 175
Various Gauges, Outside Hammers, Steel Barrel, *Modern* 175 200 195

SHOTGUN, SINGLESHOT

Various Gauges, Hammer, Steel Barrel, *Modern* 55 75 80

JACKSON HOLE RIFLE CO. Jackson Hole, Wyo., c. 1970.

RIFLE, BOLT ACTION

Sportsman, Various Calibers, with 3 Interchangable Barrels,
Checkered Stock, *Modern* 700 800 600
Custom, Various Calibers, with 3 Interchangable Barrels, Fancy
Checkering, Fancy Wood, *Modern* 800 900 865
Presentation, Various Calibers, with 3 Interchangable Barrels,
Fancy Checkering, Fancy Wood, Engraved, *Modern* 1,000 1,200 1,100

JAGA Frantisek Dusek, Opocno, Czechoslovakia, c. 1930.

HANDGUN, SEMI-AUTOMATIC

.25 ACP, Clip Fed, Blue, *Modern* 125 150 135

	V.G.	Exc.	Prior Edition Exc. Value

JAGER Suhl, Germany.
HANDGUN, SEMI-AUTOMATIC

.32 ACP, Clip Fed, Military, *Modern*	$400	$450	$450
.32 ACP, Clip Fed, Commercial, *Modern*	350	375	365

JAGER
HANDGUN, REVOLVER

Jager, .22LR/.22 WMR Combo, Single Action, Western Style, Adjustable Sights, *Modern*	100	125	100
Jager, .22LR/.22 WMR Combo, Single Action, Western Style, *Modern*	75	100	95
Jager Centerfire, Various Calibers, Single Action, Western Style, Adjustable Sights, *Modern*	125	150	125
Jager Centerfire, Various Calibers, Single Action, Western Style, *Modern*	100	125	115

JAGER, F. & CO. See Herold.

JANSSEN FRERES Liege, Belgium, c. 1925
SHOTGUN, DOUBLE BARREL, SIDE-BY-SIDE

Various Gauges, Hammerless, Steel Barrel, *Modern*	175	200	180

JAPANESE MILITARY
HANDGUN, REVOLVER

Model 26, 9mm, Military, *Curio*	250	275	225

HANDGUN, SEMI-AUTOMATIC

Baby Nambu, 7mm Nambu, Clip Fed, Military, *Curio*	2,250	2,500	1,725
Baby Nambu, 7mm Nambu, Presentation, Military, Clip Fed, Military, *Curio*	3,500	3,500	2,100
Type 14 Nambu, 8mm Nambu, Clip Fed, Small Trigger Guard, Military, *Curio*	425	475	450
Type 14 Nambu, 8mm Nambu, Clip Fed, Large Trigger Guard, Military, *Curio*	350	375	350
Type 1902 "Grandpa", 8mm Nambu, Tokyo Arsenal, Clip Fed, Military, *Curio*	2,500	3,000	1,100
Type 1904 "Papa", 8mm Nambu, TGE Navy, Clip Fed, Military, *Curio*	1,150	1,400	800
Type 1904 "Papa", 8mm Nambu, TGE Commercial, Clip Fed, *Curio*	1,250	1,500	875
Type 1904 "Papa", 8mm Nambu, Tokyo Arsenal, Clip Fed, Military, *Curio*	1,000	1,175	510

Japanese Military Type 14 Pistol

Japanese Military Type 26 Revolver

Japanese Military Type 99 Rifle

	V.G.	Exc.	Prior Edition Exc. Value
Type 1904 "Papa", 8mm Nambu, Thailand, Clip Fed, Military, *Curio*	$1,000	$1,150	$1,500
Type 94, 8mm Nambu, Clip Fed, Military, *Curio*	225	250	190

RIFLE, BOLT ACTION

The following World War I and World War II rifles were made by a few national armories: Nagoya, Tokyo, Kokura, Jinsen, and Inchon (located in occupied Korea) and the private plant of Chuo Kogyo Kabushiki.

In dealing with Japanese weapons, remember that when it says "Type 38 or Type 99" this is not the year of manufacture in the Roman calendar system but a Japanese calendar denoting the reign of their emperor. For example, Type 38 would mean it was adopted in 1905 and Type 99 would have been adopted in 1939.

Model 38 (1905), 6.5 × 50 Arisaka, Military, *Curio*	125	150	90
Model 38 (1905), 6.5 × 50 Arisaka, Military, Carbine, *Curio*	150	175	90
Model 44 (1911), 6.5 × 50 Arisaka, Military, Carbine, *Curio*	225	275	90
Model 99 (1939), 7.7 × 58 Arisaka, Military, Open Rear Sight, *Curio*	125	150	90
Type 30 (1897), 6.5 Arisaka, Bolt Action, 31-Inch Barrel, Often Referred To As The "Hook Safety Rifle," *Curio*	150	175	85
Type 38 Carbine, 6.5 Cal., Arisaka, 19-Inch Barrel, Modified For Paratroop Use By The Edition Of A Hinge To The Wrist Of The Stock For Folding, Somewhat Rare, *Curio*	150	175	95

	V.G.	Exc.	Prior Edition Exc. Value
Type 38, 6.5 × 50 Arisaka, Late Model, Military, *Curio*	$125	$150	$75
Type 44, 6.5 × 50 Arisaka, Folding Bayonet, Military, *Curio*	200	225	135
Type 97 Sniper Rifle, Arisaka, 31-Inch Barrel, Specially Selected For Extreme Accuracy And Then Fitted With Telescopic Sight, *Curio*	275	325	135
Type 99, 7.7 × 58 Arisaka, Aircraft Sights Dust Cover, Military, *Curio*	225	250	100
Type 99, 7.7 Cal., Arisaka, 31-Inch Barrel, Five Shot Mauser Type Magazine, Bolt Action, Long Barrel Infantry Model, Becoming Scarce, *Curio*	125	150	60
Type 99, Type 2 Take Down Rifle, 7.7 Cal., Arisaka, 25-Inch Barrel, A Standard Type 99 Rifle Modified To Break In Half For Compact Paratroop Use, Very Rare, *Curio*	250	275	150
Japanese "Siamese Mauser", 8 × 52R Cal., Made By Japan For The Government Of Siam In The Early 1920s. A Modified 98 Mauser, Bolt Action, 30-Inch Barrel, *Curio*	100	125	50

JENNINGS FIREARMS, INC. Chino, Calif., current.

HANDGUN, SEMI-AUTOMATIC

Model J-22, .22 L.R.R.F., Clip Fed, Black Teflon Plate, *Modern*	50	50	50
Model J-22, .22 L.R.R.F., Clip Fed, Satin Nickel Plate, *Modern*	50	50	50

JEWEL Made by Hood Firearms Co., c. 1876.

HANDGUN, REVOLVER

#1, .22 Short R.F., 7 Shot, Spur Trigger, Solid Frame, Single Action, *Antique*	150	175	165

JIEFFCO Mre. Liegoise d'Armes a Feu Robar et Cie, Liege, Belgium, c. 1912–1914.

HANDGUN, SEMI-AUTOMATIC

.25 ACP, Clip Fed, Blue, *Curio*	250	275	290
.32 ACP, Clip Fed, Blue, *Curio*	250	275	275

JIEFFCO Tradename used by Davis-Warner on pistols made by Robar et Cie., c. 1920.

HANDGUN, SEMI-AUTOMATIC

New Model Melior, .25 ACP, Clip Fed, *Curio*	150	175	170

J.G.L. Jos. G. Landmann, Holstein, W. Germany, c. 1968.

RIFLE, SEMI-AUTOMATIC

JGL-68 Model 1, .22 L.R.R.F., Clip Fed, Carbine Style, *Modern*	50	75	75

	V.G.	Exc.	Prior Edition Exc. Value
JGL-68 Model 2, .22 L.R.R.F., Clip Fed, Vertical Grip & Foregrip, *Modern*	$50	$75	$85
JGL-68 Model 3, .22 L.R.R.F., Clip Fed, Vertical Grip, *Modern*	50	75	80

JOFFRE Spain, Unknown Maker, c. 1900.

HANDGUN, SEMI-AUTOMATIC

M1916, .32 ACP, Clip Fed, *Modern*	100	125	130

JOHNSON AUTOMATICS Providence, R.I. Also see U.S. Military.

RIFLE, BOLT ACTION

Diamond Cherry Featherweight, Various Calibers, Engraved, Carved Cherry Stock, Muzzle Brake, *Modern*	1,000	1,250	1,200
Honey Featherweight, Various Calibers, Engraved, Carved Stock, Muzzle Brake, Gold and Silver Inlays, *Modern*	1,500	1,750	2,075
Laminar Sporter, Various Calibers, Laminated Stock, *Modern*	650	750	725

RIFLE, SEMI-AUTOMATIC

Model 1941, .30-06 Springfield, Military, *Curio*	700	775	700
Model 1941, 7mm Mauser, Military, *Modern*	775	850	800

JO-LO-AR Hijos de Arrizabalaga, Eibar, Spain, c. 1920.

HANDGUN, SEMI-AUTOMATIC

.380 ACP, Tip-up, Clip Fed, Hammer, Spur Trigger, Military, *Modern*	200	250	250
9mm Bergmann, Tip-up, Clip Fed, Hammer, Spur Trigger, Military, *Modern*	150	200	200

JONES, CHARLES Lancaster, Pa. 1780. See Kentucky Rifles.

JONES, J.N. & CO. London, England, c. 1760.

HANDGUN, FLINTLOCK

.60, George III, Navy Pistol, Brass Barrel, Brass Furniture, Military, *Antique*	1,250	1,500	1,000

HANDGUN, PERCUSSION

.58, Holster Pistol, Converted from Flintlock, Brass Furniture, Plain, *Antique*	750	1,000	715

JUPITER Fabrique d'Armes de Guerre de Grand Precision, Eibar, Spain.

HANDGUN, SEMI-AUTOMATIC

.32 ACP, Clip Fed, Blue, *Curio*	125	150	140

K

KABA SPEZIAL Made by August Menz, Suhl, Germany, for Karl Bauer & Co., Berlin, Germany, c. 1925.

HANDGUN, SEMI-AUTOMATIC

	V.G.	Exc.	Prior Edition Exc. Value
Liliput, .25 ACP, Clip Fed, Blue, *Modern*	$225	$250	$240
Liliput, .32 ACP, Clip Fed, Blue, *Modern*	250	275	265

KABA SPEZIAL Made by Francisco Arizmendi, Eibar, Spain.

HANDGUN, SEMI-AUTOMATIC

	V.G.	Exc.	Prior Edition Exc. Value
.25 ACP, Clip Fed, Blue, *Modern*	150	175	165

KART

HANDGUN, SEMI-AUTOMATIC

	V.G.	Exc.	Prior Edition Exc. Value
Target, .22 L.R.R.F., Clip Fed, M1911 Frame, 6" Barrel, *Modern*	575	650	625
For Colt Government Target, .22 L.R.R.F., Conversion Unit Only	150	175	190

KASSNAR IMPORTS Harrisburg, Pa.

RIFLE, BOLT ACTION

	V.G.	Exc.	Prior Edition Exc. Value
Model M-14S, .22 L.R.R.F., Clip Fed, Checkered Stock, *Modern*	50	75	65
Model M-15S, .22 WMR, Clip Fed, Checkered Stock, *Modern*	50	75	80
Model M-1400, .22 L.R.R.F., Clip Fed, Checkered Stock, *Modern*	50	75	70
Model M-1500, .22 WMR, Clip Fed, Checkered Stock, *Modern*	75	100	85
Parker Hale Midland, Various Calibers, Checkered Stock, Open Sights, *Modern*	200	225	220
Parker Hale Super, Various Calibers, Checkered Stock, Open Sights, Monte Carlo Stock, *Modern*	250	300	285
Parker Hale Varmint, Various Calibers, Checkered Stock, Open Sights, Varmint Stock, *Modern*	275	300	285

RIFLE, SEMI-AUTOMATIC

	V.G.	Exc.	Prior Edition Exc. Value
Model M-16, .22 L.R.R.F., Clip Fed, Military Style, *Modern*	50	75	80
Model M-20S, .22 L.R.R.F., *Modern*	50	75	65

	V.G.	Exc.	Prior Edition Exc. Value
SHOTGUN, DOUBLE BARREL, OVER-UNDER			
Fias SK-1, 12 and 20 Gauges, Double Trigger, Checkered Stock, *Modern*	$350	$375	$335
Fias SK-3, 12 and 20 Gauges, Single Selective Trigger, Checkered Stock, *Modern*	350	400	375
Fias SK-4, 12 and 20 Gauges, Single Selective Trigger, Checkered Stock, Automatic Ejector, *Modern*	375	450	435
Fias SK-4D, 12 and 20 Gauges, Single Selective Trigger, Fancy Checkering, Fancy Wood, Engraved, Automatic Ejector, *Modern*	400	475	455
Fias SK-4T, 12 Ga., Trap Grade, Single Selective Trigger, Automatic Ejector, Checkered Stock, Wide Vent Rib, *Modern*	425	475	455
SHOTGUN, DOUBLE BARREL, SIDE-BY-SIDE			
Zabala, Various Gauges, Checkered Stock, Double Triggers, *Modern*	325	375	260
SHOTGUN, SINGLESHOT			
Taiyojuki, Various Gauges, Top Break, Plain, *Modern*	25	50	45

KEFFER, JACOB Lancaster, Pa., c. 1802. See Kentucky Rifles and Pistols.

KEIM, JOHN Reading, Pa. 1820–1839. See Kentucky Rifles and Pistols.

KENTUCKY RIFLES AND PISTOLS The uniquely American "Kentucky" (or, as some prefer, "Pennsylvania") expressed in wood & metal the attitude of strength and independence that fostered our young nation. For the most part Kentuckys are custom guns, and, aside from general style similarities, virtually all are different, even those by the same maker. To add to the problem of price generalization, gunsmiths purchased parts from various makers and there may be three different names on a single gun or none at all. The main considerations in determining value are: 1. Type of ignition; 2. Quality of workmanship; 3. Decoration; 4. Originality; 5. Condition. Except for orginality this list also applies to contemporary makers.

RIFLES, FLINTLOCK

	V.G.	Exc.	Prior Edition Exc. Value
Moderate Quality, Plain, *Antique*	2,500	5,000	1,300
Moderate Quality, Medium Decoration, *Antique*	5,000	10,000	4,400
High Quality, Fancy Decoration, *Antique*	10,000	15,000	6,300
Over-Under, Swivel-Breech, Plain, *Antique*	5,000	7,500	1,700
Over-Under, Swivel-Breech, Medium Quality, *Antique*	7,500	10,000	5,750
Over-Under, Swivel-Breech, High Quality, *Antique*	12,500	20,000	8,650
Deduct 30%–40%, if Converted from Percussion			

RIFLES, PERCUSSION

	V.G.	Exc.	Prior Edition Exc. Value
Moderate Quality, Plain, *Antique*	500	1,500	1,300
Moderate Quality, Medium Decoration, *Antique*	2,000	5,000	1,800

	V.G.	Exc.	Prior Edition Exc. Value
High Quality, Fancy Decoration, *Antique*	$7,500	$10,000	$5,650
Over-Under, Medium Quality, Swivel Breech, Plain, *Antique*	2,000	2,500	1,200
Over-Under, Medium Quality, Swivel-Breech, *Antique*	5,000	8,500	2,650
Over-Under, High Quality, Swivel-Breech, *Antique*	10,000	12,500	4,200

Add 20%, if converted from Flintlock to Percussion

PISTOLS, FLINTLOCK

Moderate Quality, Medium Decoration, *Antique*	4,000	5,000	3,400
High Quality, Fancy Decoration, *Antique*	8,000	10,000	6,875

PISTOLS, PERCUSSION (ORIGINAL)

Moderate Quality, Medium Decoration, *Antique*	3,500	4,000	2,500
High Quality, Fancy Decoration, *Antique*	4,000	5,000	3,875

PISTOLS, PERCUSSION (CONVERTED FROM FLINTLOCK)

Moderate Quality, Medium Decoration, *Antique*	3,000	3,500	1,500
High Quality, Fancy Decoration, *Antique*	4,000	4,500	2,500

Arms with signatures are more desirable than those without markings. No name–deduct **10%–15%**. *If of recent vintage, and handmade, use this chart and deduct* **50%.**

KETLAND & CO. Birmingham & London, England 1760–1831. Also See Kentucky Rifles.

HANDGUN, FLINTLOCK

.58, Holster Pistol, Plain, Tapered Round Barrel, Brass Furniture, *Antique*	1,000	1,250	995
.62, Belt Pistol, Brass Barrel, Brass Furniture, Light Ornamentation, *Antique*	1,250	1,500	1,045

KETLAND, T. Birmingham, England 1750–1829.

HANDGUN, FLINTLOCK

.69, Pair, Belt Pistol, Brass Furniture, Plain, *Antique*	2,250	2,500	2,400

RIFLE, FLINTLOCK

.65, Officers Model Brown Bess, Musket, Military, *Antique*	3,000	3,500	3,400
.73, 2nd. Model Brown Bess, Musket, Military, *Antique*	2,250	2,500	2,250

KETLAND, WILLIAM & CO.

HANDGUN, FLINTLOCK

.63, Holster Pistol, Round Barrel, Plain, *Antique*	700	900	895

KETTNER, ED Suhl, Thuringia, Germany 1922–1939.

COMBINATION WEAPON, DRILLING

12 × 12 × 10.75 × 65R Collath, Engraved, Checkered Stock, Sling Swivels, *Modern*..	1,750	2,000	1,550

	V.G.	Exc.	Prior Edition Exc. Value

KIMBALL, J.M. ARMS CO. Detroit, Mich., c. 1955.

HANDGUN, SEMI-AUTOMATIC

	V.G.	Exc.	Prior Edition Exc. Value
Standard Model, .30 Carbine, Clip Fed, Blue, *Modern*	$750	$850	$750
Standard Model, .22 Hornet, Clip Fed, Blue, *Modern*	900	1,000	1,650
Target Model, .30 Carbine, Clip Fed, Blue, Adjustable Sights, *Modern*	800	900	850
Combat Model, .30 Carbine, Clip Fed, Blue, Short Barrel, *Modern*	800	900	725

KIMBER Clackamas, Ore.

RIFLE, BOLT ACTION

	V.G.	Exc.	Prior Edition Exc. Value
Model 82 Cascade, .22 L.R.R.F., Checkered Stock, Clip Fed, No Sights, Monte Carlo Stock, *Modern*	245	600	335
Model 82 Cascade, .22 W.M.R., Checkered Stock, Clip Fed, No Sights, Monte Carlo Stock, *Modern*	265	625	350
Model 82 Classic, .22 L.R.R.F., Checkered Stock, Clip Fed, No Sights, *Modern*	240	550	320
Model 82 Classic, .22 W.M.R., Checkered Stock, Clip Fed, No Sights, *Modern*	255	575	330

KIMEL INDUSTRIES Matthews, N.C.

HANDGUN, DOUBLE BARREL, OVER-UNDER

	V.G.	Exc.	Prior Edition Exc. Value
Twist, .22 Short R.F., Swivel Breech, Derringer, Spur Trigger, *Modern*	25	50	35

KING NITRO Made by Stevens Arms.

RIFLE, BOLT ACTION

	V.G.	Exc.	Prior Edition Exc. Value
Model 53, .22 L.R.R.F., Singleshot, Takedown, *Modern*	25	50	50

SHOTGUN, DOUBLE BARREL, SIDE-BY-SIDE

	V.G.	Exc.	Prior Edition Exc. Value
M 315 Various Gauges, Hammerless, Steel Barrel, *Modern*	150	175	175

KINGLAND SPECIAL Made by Crescent for Geller, Wards & Hasner St. Louis, Mo.

SHOTGUN, DOUBLE BARREL, SIDE-BY-SIDE

	V.G.	Exc.	Prior Edition Exc. Value
Various Gauges, Outside Hammers, Damascus Barrel, *Modern*	150	175	170
Various Gauges, Hammerless, Steel Barrel, *Modern*	175	200	190
Various Gauges, Hammerless, Damascus Barrel, *Modern*	150	175	170
Various Gauges, Outside Hammers, Steel Barrel, *Modern*	150	175	185

SHOTGUN, SINGLESHOT

	V.G.	Exc.	Prior Edition Exc. Value
Various Gauges, Hammer, Steel Barrel, *Modern*	50	75	85

	V.G.	Exc.	Prior Edition Exc. Value

KINGLAND 10-STAR Made by Crescent for Geller, Wards & Hasner St. Louis, Mo. See Kingsland Special.

KIRIKKALE Makina ve Kimya Endustrisi Kurumu Kirrikale, Ankara, Turkey.

HANDGUN, SEMI-AUTOMATIC

	V.G.	Exc.	Prior Value
MKE, .380 ACP, Clip Fed, Double Action, *Modern*	$300	$350	$200

KITTEMAUG Maker Unknown, c. 1800.

HANDGUN, REVOLVER

	V.G.	Exc.	Prior Value
.32 Short R.F., 5 Shot, Spur Trigger, Solid Frame, Single Action, *Antique*	150	175	165

KLEINGUENTHER'S Seguin, Texas.

HANDGUN, REVOLVER

	V.G.	Exc.	Prior Value
Reck R-18, .357 Magnum, Adjustable Sights, Western Style, Single Action, *Modern*	100	125	110

RIFLE, BOLT ACTION

	V.G.	Exc.	Prior Value
K-10, .22 L.R.R.F., Single Shot, Tangent Sights, *Modern*	50	50	50
K-12, .22 L.R.R.F., Clip Fed, Checkered Stock, *Modern*	50	75	75
K-13, .22 W.M.R., Clip Fed, Checkered Stock, *Modern*	100	125	120
K-14 Insta-fire, Various Calibers, Checkered Stock, No Sights, Recoil Pad, *Modern*	700	800	420
K-15 Insta-fire, Various Calibers, Checkered Stock, No Sights, Recoil Pad, *Modern*	800	1,000	595
K-15, .22 L.R.R.F., Clip Fed, Checkered Stock, *Modern*	100	125	110
V2130, Various Calibers, Checkered Stock, Recoil Pad, *Modern*	200	225	220

RIFLE, DOUBLE BARREL, OVER-UNDER

	V.G.	Exc.	Prior Value
Model 222, .22 WMR, Plain, *Modern*	125	150	130

SHOTGUN, DOUBLE BARREL, OVER-UNDER

	V.G.	Exc.	Prior Value
Condor, 12 Gauge, Skeet Grade, Single Selective Trigger, Automatic Ejector, Wide Vent Rib, *Modern*	400	450	450
Condor, 12 Gauge, Single Selective Trigger, Automatic Ejector, Vent Rib, *Modern*	375	425	425

SHOTGUN, DOUBLE BARREL, SIDE-BY-SIDE

	V.G.	Exc.	Prior Value
Brescia, 12 Gauge, Hammerless, Light Engraving, Double Trigger, *Modern*	200	250	240

SHOTGUN, SEMI-AUTOMATIC

	V.G.	Exc.	Prior Value
12 Ga., Checkered Stock, Vent Rib, Engraved, Right Hand, *Modern*	175	200	195
12 Ga., Checkered Stock, Vent Rib, Engraved, Left Hand, *Modern*	200	225	220

	V.G.	Exc.	Prior Edition Exc. Value

KLETT, SIMON Probably Leipzig, c. 1620.
RIFLE, WHEEL-LOCK
.54, Rifled, Octagon Barrel, Brass Furniture, Medium Ornamentation, Engraved, High Quality, *Antique* .... $10,000 | $12,000 | $9,750

KNICKERBOCKER Made by Crescent for H & D Folsom, c. 1900.
SHOTGUN, DOUBLE BARREL, SIDE-BY-SIDE
	V.G.	Exc.	Prior
Various Gauges, Hammerless, *Modern*	150	175	190
Various Gauges, Outside Hammers, *Modern*	175	200	185

KNICKERBOCKER Made by Stevens Arms.
SHOTGUN, DOUBLE BARREL, SIDE-BY-SIDE
Model 311, Various Gauges, Hammerless, Steel Barrel, *Modern*	150	175	180

KNOCKABOUT Made by Stevens Arms.
SHOTGUN, DOUBLE BARREL, SIDE-BY-SIDE
Model 311, Various Gauges, Hammerless, Steel Barrel, *Modern*	150	175	180

KNOXALL Made by Crescent, c. 1900.
SHOTGUN, DOUBLE BARREL, SIDE-BY-SIDE
Various Gauges, Hammerless, Steel Barrel, *Modern*	175	200	190
Various Gauges, Outside Hammers, Steel Barrel, *Modern*	150	175	185

KODIAK MFG. CO. North Haven, Conn., c. 1965.
RIFLE, BOLT ACTION
Model 98 Brush Carbine, Various Calibers, Checkered Stock, *Modern*	150	175	155
Model 99 Deluxe Brush Carbine, Various Calibers, Checkered Stock, *Modern*	150	175	165
Model 100 Deluxe Rifle, Various Calibers, Checkered Stock, *Modern*	175	200	175
Model 100M Deluxe Rifle, Various Magnum Calibers, Checkered Stock, *Modern*	175	200	185
Model 101 Ultra, Various Calibers, Monte Carlo Stock, *Modern*	175	200	185
Model 101M Ultra, Various Magnum Calibers, Monte Carlo Stock, *Modern*	200	225	200
Model 102 Ultra Varmint, Various Calibers, Heavy Barrel, *Modern*	200	225	200

RIFLE, SEMI-AUTOMATIC
Model 260 Autoloader, .22 L.R.R.F., Tube Feed, Open Sights, 22" Barrel, *Modern*	75	100	90

	V.G.	Exc.	Prior Edition Exc. Value
Model 260 Magnum, .22 W.M.R., Tube Feed, Open Sights, 22" Barrel, *Modern*	$125	$150	$130
Model 260 Autoloader Carbine, .22 L.R.R.F., Tube Feed, Open Sights, 20" Barrel, *Modern*	75	100	95
Model 260 Magnum Carbine, .22 W.M.R., Tube Feed, Open Sights, 20" Barrel, *Modern*	125	150	140

KOHOUT & SPOL Kdyne, Czechoslovakia.
HANDGUN, SEMI-AUTOMATIC

Mars, .25 ACP, Clip Fed, *Modern*	150	175	170
Mars, .32 ACP, Clip Fed, *Modern*	175	200	180

KOMMER, THEODOR Zella Mehlis, Germany, c. 1920.
HANDGUN, SEMI-AUTOMATIC

Model I, .25 ACP, Clip Fed, *Modern*	275	300	400
Model II, .25 ACP, Clip Fed, *Modern*	250	275	275

Kommer Model 1

Kommer Model 2

Kommer Model 4

	V.G.	Exc.	Prior Edition Exc. Value
Model III, .25 ACP, Clip Fed, *Modern*...	$225	$250	$390
Model IV, .32 ACP, Clip Fed, *Modern*...	300	325	410

KORTH Wilhelm Korth Waffenfabrik, Ratzburg, West Germany.
HANDGUN, REVOLVER

Target, .22 L.R.R.F., 6 Shot, *Modern*..	1,200	1,800	600

KRAFT, JACOB Lancaster, Pa. 1771–1782. See Kentucky Rifles and Pistols.

KRICO Stuttgart, West Germany. Also see Beeman's.
RIFLE, BOLT ACTION

.22 Rem. Rifle, Checkered Stock, Double Set Triggers, *Modern*.....	550	600	475
.22 Rem. Carbine, Checkered Stock, Double Set, Triggers, *Modern*..	575	625	500
Model DJV, .22 Various Calibers, Checkered Target Stock, Double Set Triggers, *Modern*	500	550	450
Special Varmint, .222 Rem., Checkered Stock, Heavy Barrel, Double Set Triggers, *Modern*	550	600	475
Krico Model 302, .22 L.R.R.F., Clip Fed, Checkered Stock, Open Sights, *Modern*..	625	675	300
Krico Model 304, .22 L.R.R.F., Clip Fed, Checkered Stock, Mannlicher Stock, Set Triggers, Open Sights, *Modern*....................	625	675	375
Model 311, .22 L.R.R.F., Checkered Stock, Double Set Trigger, *Modern*..	300	325	265
Krico Model 340, .22 L.R.R.F., Metallic Silhouette Match Rifle, Clip Fed, Checkered Stock, Target Stock, *Modern*	600	650	430
Krico Model 340, .22 L.R.R.F., Mini-Sniper Match Rifle, Clip Fed, Checkered Stock, Target Stock, *Modern*..	650	700	475
Model 351, .22 WMR, Checkered Stock, Double Set Triggers, *Modern*..	500	550	290
Model 354, .22 WMR, Checkered Stock, Double Set Triggers, *Modern*..	600	650	345
Krico Model 400, .22 Hornet, Clip Fed, Checkered Stock, Open Sights, *Modern*..	625	700	425
Krico Model 420, .22 Hornet, Clip Fed, Checkered Stock, Set Triggers, Mannlicher Stock, Open Sights, Sling Swivels, *Modern*.......	800	875	465
Krico Model 600, Various Calibers, Clip Fed, Checkered Stock, Open Sights, Sling Swivels, Recoil Pad, *Modern*.............................	800	1,000	635
Model 600 Export, Various Calibers, Checkered Stock, Double Set Triggers, *Modern*	400	450	310
Model 600 Luxus, Various Calibers, Checkered Stock, Double Set Triggers, *Modern*	475	525	360

	V.G.	Exc.	Prior Edition Exc. Value
Krico Model 620, Various Calibers, Clip Fed, Checkered Stock, Set Triggers, Mannlicher Stock, Open Sights, Sling Swivels, *Modern*	$900	$1,150	$650
Model 620 Luxus, Various Calibers, Checkered Stock, Double Set Triggers, *Modern*	550	625	450
Krico Model 640, Various Calibers, Deluxe Varmint Rifle, Clip Fed, Checkered Stock, Target Stock, *Modern*	1,025	1,175	630
Krico Model 650, Various Calibers, Sniper/Match Rifle, Clip Fed, Checkered Stock, Target Stock, *Modern*	950	1,200	800
Krico Model 700, Various Calibers, Clip Fed, Checkered Stock, Open Sights, Sling Swivels, Recoil Pad, *Modern*	750	900	635
Model 700 Export, Various Calibers, Checkered Stock, Double Set Triggers, *Modern*	550	650	400
Model 700 Luxus, Various Calibers, Checkered Stock, Double Set Triggers, *Modern*	600	675	450
Krico Model 720, Various Calibers, Clip Fed, Checkered Stock, Set Triggers, Mannlicher Stock, Open Sights, Sling Swivels, *Modern*	950	1,100	650
Model 720 Luxus, Various Calibers, Checkered Stock, Double Set Triggers, *Modern*	775	850	475

KRIEGHOFF GUN CO. Suhl, Germany 1929–1945, and from 1945 to date in Ulm, West Germany. Also see Shotguns of Ulm.

RIFLE, DOUBLE BARREL, OVER-UNDER

	V.G.	Exc.	Prior
Teck, Various Calibers, Hammerless, Engraved, Fancy Checkering, *Modern*	4,000	4,500	2,650
Teck Dural, Various Calibers, Hammerless, Engraved, Fancy Checkering, Lightweight, *Modern*	4,100	4,600	2,750
Ulm, Various Calibers, Hammerless, Engraved, Fancy Checkering, Sidelock, *Modern*	7,000	7,500	4,300
Ulm Dural, Various Calibers, Hammerless, Engraved, Fancy Checkering, Sidelock, *Modern*	7,200	7,700	4,300
Ulm Primus, Various Calibers, Hammerless, Engraved, Fancy Checkering, Sidelock, *Modern*	8,000	10,000	4,650
Ulm Primus Dural, Various Calibers, Hammerless, Engraved, Fancy Checkering, Sidelock, Lightweight, *Modern*	8,500	10,500	5,750

COMBINATION WEAPON, DRILLING

Neptun, Various Calibers, Hammerless, Engraved, Fancy Checkering, Sidelock, *Modern*	10,000	12,000	4,475
Neptun Dural, Various Calibers, Hammerless, Engraved, Fancy Checkering, Sidelock, *Modern*	10,500	12,500	4,500
Neptun Primus, Various Calibers, Hammerless, Fancy Checkering, Fancy Engraving, Sidelock, *Modern*	12,000	15,000	5,500
Neptun Primus Dural, Various Calibers, Hammerless, Fancy Checkering, Fancy Engraving, Sidelock, Lightweight, *Modern*	12,500	15,500	5,500
Trumpf, Various Calibers, Hammerless, Engraved, Fancy Checkering, *Modern*	6,000	6,500	3,100

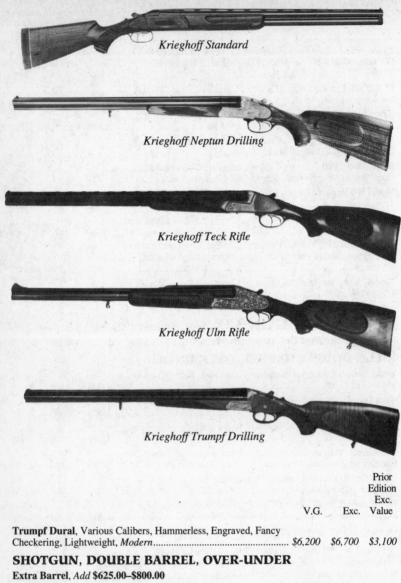

Krieghoff Standard

Krieghoff Neptun Drilling

Krieghoff Teck Rifle

Krieghoff Ulm Rifle

Krieghoff Trumpf Drilling

	V.G.	Exc.	Prior Edition Exc. Value
Trumpf Dural, Various Calibers, Hammerless, Engraved, Fancy Checkering, Lightweight, *Modern*	$6,200	$6,700	$3,100

SHOTGUN, DOUBLE BARREL, OVER-UNDER

Extra Barrel, *Add* $625.00–$800.00

	V.G.	Exc.	Prior Edition Exc. Value
Crown, 12 Gauge, Trap Grade, *Modern*	15,000	18,000	10,100
Exhibition, 12 Gauge, Trap Grade, *Modern*	25,000	30,000	26,250
Monte Carlo, 12 Gauge, Trap Grade, *Modern*	10,000	13,000	9,750
Munchen, Various Gauges, Skeet Grade, *Modern*	5,000	7,000	7,300
San Remo, 12 Gauge, Trap Grade, *Modern*	6,000	8,000	4,400
Standard, 12 Gauge, Trap Grade, *Modern*	4,500	5,000	2,050

	V.G.	Exc.	Prior Edition Exc. Value
Standard, 12 Gauge, Field Grade, *Modern*	$3,500	$4,000	$2,350
Standard, Various Gauges, Skeet Grade, *Modern*	3,500	4,000	2,350
Super Crown, 12 Gauge, Trap Grade, *Modern*	15,000	17,000	14,000

KRUSCHITZ Vienna, Austria.
RIFLE, BOLT ACTION
Mauser 98, .30/06, Checkered Stock, Double Set Triggers,
Modern ....

| 250 | 300 | 295 |

KROYDEN Tradename used by Savage Arms Corp.
RIFLE, SEMI-AUTOMATIC
.22 L.R.R.F., Tube Feed, Plain Stock, *Modern* ....

| 50 | 75 | 60 |

KYNOCH GUN FACTORY Birmingham, England.
HANDGUN, REVOLVER
Schlund, .476 Eley, Hammerless, Top Break, Double Trigger
Cocking, *Antique* ....

| 750 | 900 | 735 |

Kynoch Schlund Revolver

L

	V.G.	Exc.	Prior Edition Exc. Value

LAHTI Developed and made by Valtion Kivaarithedas, Jyvaskyla, Finland. Also made by Husqvarna in Sweden.

HANDGUN, SEMI-AUTOMATIC

	V.G.	Exc.	Prior Edition Exc. Value
L-35 Finnish, 9mm Luger, Clip Fed, Military, *Curio*	$950	$1,250	$620
M 40 Swedish, 9mm Luger, Clip Fed, Military, *Modern*	200	250	190

LAKESIDE Made by Crescent for Montgomery Ward & Co., c. 1900.

SHOTGUN, DOUBLE BARREL, SIDE-BY-SIDE

	V.G.	Exc.	Prior Edition Exc. Value
Various Gauges, Outside Hammers, Damascus Barrel, *Modern*	150	175	170
Various Gauges, Hammerless, Steel Barrel, *Modern*	150	200	190
Various Gauges, Hammerless, Damascus Barrel, *Modern*	125	150	170
Various Gauges, Outside Hammers, Steel Barrel, *Modern*	175	200	185

SHOTGUN, SINGLESHOT

	V.G.	Exc.	Prior Edition Exc. Value
Various Gauges, Hammer, Steel Barrel, *Modern*	50	75	85

LAMES Chiavari, Italy.

SHOTGUN, DOUBLE BARREL, OVER-UNDER

	V.G.	Exc.	Prior Edition Exc. Value
12 Gauge Mag. 3", Field Grade, Automatic Ejector, Single Selective Trigger, Vent Rib, Checkered Stock, *Modern*	350	400	365
12 Gauge Mag. 3", Skeet Grade, Automatic Ejector, Single Selective Trigger, Vent Rib, Checkered Stock, *Modern*	500	575	420
12 Gauge Mag. 3", Trap Grade, Automatic Ejector, Single Selective Trigger, Vent Rib, Checkered Stock, *Modern*	500	575	420
12 Gauge Mag. 3", Trap Grade, Automatic Ejector, Single Selective Trigger, Vent Rib, Monte Carlo Stock, *Modern*	625	600	475
California, 12 Gauge Mag. 3", Trap Grade, Automatic Ejector, Single Selective Trigger, Vent Rib, Checkered Stock, *Modern*	675	725	635

LANBER Lanber Armas, S.A., Vizcaya, Spain.

SHOTGUN, DOUBLE BARREL, OVER-UNDER

	V.G.	Exc.	Prior Edition Exc. Value
Model 844 ST, 12 Gauge, Double Triggers, Checkered Stock, Light Engraving, *Modern*	375	425	320

	V.G.	Exc.	Prior Edition Exc. Value
Model 844 MST, 12 Gauge 3", Double Triggers, Checkered Stock, Light Engraving, *Modern*	$375	$425	$330
Model 844 EST, 12 Gauge, Automatic Ejectors, Double Triggers, Checkered Stock, Light Engraving, *Modern*	400	475	390
Model 844 EST CHR, 12 Gauge, Automatic Ejectors, Double Triggers, Checkered Stock, Light Engraving, *Modern*	350	400	375
Model 2004 LCH, 12 Gauge, Automatic Ejector, Single Trigger, Checkered Stock, Light Engraving, Lanber Choke, *Modern*	600	725	450
Model 2008 LCH, 12 Gauge, Automatic Ejector, Single Trigger, Checkered Stock, Light Engraving, Lanber Choke, *Modern*	650	775	600
Model 2009 LCH, 12 Gauge, Trap Grade, Automatic Ejector, Single Trigger, Checkered Stock, Light Engraving, Lanber Choke, *Modern*	700	850	600

LANCASTER, CHARLES London, England 1889–1936.

RIFLE, BOLT ACTION

Various Calibers, Sporting Rifle, Checkered Stock, *Modern*	700	900	895

LANCELOT

HANDGUN, SEMI-AUTOMATIC

.25 ACP, Clip Fed, Blue, *Modern*	150	175	195

LANE & READ Boston, Mass. 1826–1835.

SHOTGUN, PERCUSSION

28 Gauge, Double Barrel, Side by Side, Light Engraving, Checkered Stock, *Antique*	400	475	465

LANG, JOSEPH London, England, established in 1821.

HANDGUN, PERCUSSION

Pair, Double Barrel, Over-Under, Officer's Belt Pistol, Light Engraving, Cased With Accessories, *Antique*	3,500	4,500	4,600

SHOTGUN, SINGLESHOT

12 Gauge, Plain, Trap Grade, *Modern*	1,200	1,500	1,400

LANGENHAN Friedrich Langenhan Gewehr u. Fahrradfabrik, Zella Mehlis, Germany.

HANDGUN, SEMI-AUTOMATIC

Model I, .32 ACP, Clip Fed, Military, *Modern*	225	250	235

Langenhan Model I

Langenhan Model III

	V.G.	Exc.	Prior Edition Exc. Value
Model II, .25 ACP, Clip Fed, *Modern*	$275	$300	$275
Model III, .25 ACP, Clip Fed, *Modern*	275	325	300

LA SALLE Tradename used by Manufrance.

SHOTGUN, SLIDE ACTION

	V.G.	Exc.	Prior
12 Gauge Mag. 3", Field Grade, Plain, *Modern*	225	250	140
12 Gauge Mag. 3", Checkered Stock, Fancy Wood, *Modern*	250	275	150
20 Gauge Mag., Field Grade, Plain, *Modern*	125	150	135

SHOTGUN, SEMI-AUTOMATIC

Custom, 12 Ga., Checkered Stock, *Modern*	250	300	175

LAURONA Spain.

SHOTGUN, DOUBLE BARREL, OVER-UNDER

Model 67-G, 12 Gauge 3", Checkered Stock, Vent Rib, Double Triggers, *Modern*	150	225	225

LE BARON

RIFLE, FLINTLOCK

.69 Presentation, Silver Furniture, Fancy Wood, Fancy Checkering, Fancy Engraving, *Antique*	4,000	4,500	4,300

Le Francaise Military

Le Francaise Policeman

	V.G.	Exc.	Prior Edition Exc. Value

LE BASQUE
HANDGUN, SEMI-AUTOMATIC
.32 ACP, Clip Fed, Blue, *Modern* .... *$150* | *$200* | *$200*

LE FRANCAISE Mre. Francaise de Armes et Cycles de St. Etienne, St. Etienne, France.

HANDGUN, SEMI-AUTOMATIC
	V.G.	Exc.	Prior
Champion, .25 ACP, Clip Fed, Long Grip, *Modern*	250	275	285
Le Francais, .32 ACP, Clip Fed, *Modern*	350	400	420
Military Model, 9mm French Long, Clip Fed, *Modern*	800	850	875
Pocket Model, .25 ACP, Clip Fed, *Modern*	175	200	210
Policeman, .25 ACP, Clip Fed, *Modern*	250	275	285
Staff Officer's, .25 ACP, Clip Fed, *Modern*	300	350	350

LE MARTINY
HANDGUN, SEMI-AUTOMATIC
.25 ACP, Clip Fed, Blue, *Modern* .... 100 | 125 | 140

LE MONOBLOC Jules Jacquemart, Liege, Belgium, c. 1910.
HANDGUN, SEMI-AUTOMATIC
.25 ACP, Clip Fed, *Modern* .... 325 | 375 | 385

	V.G.	Exc.	Prior Edition Exc. Value

LE SANS PARIEL Mre. d'Armes des Pyrenees.
HANDGUN, SEMI-AUTOMATIC
.25 ACP, Clip Fed, Blue, *Modern* .... | $125 | $150 | $140

LE TOUTACIER Mre. d'Armes des Pyrenees.
HANDGUN, SEMI-AUTOMATIC
.25 ACP, Clip Fed, Blue, *Modern* .... | 125 | 150 | 135

LEADER Possibly Hopkins & Allen, c. 1880.
HANDGUN, REVOLVER
.22 Short R.F., 7 Shot, Spur Trigger, Solid Frame, Single Action,
Antique .... | 150 | 175 | 165
.32 Short R.F., 5 Shot, Spur Trigger, Solid Frame, Single Action,
Antique .... | 150 | 175 | 170

LEADER GUN CO. Made by Crescent for Charles Willian Stores Inc., c. 1900.
SHOTGUN, DOUBLE BARREL, SIDE-BY-SIDE
Various Gauges, Outside Hammers, Damascus Barrel, *Modern* ..... | 150 | 175 | 170
Various Gauges, Hammerless, Steel Barrel, *Modern* .... | 175 | 200 | 190
Various Gauges, Hammerless, Damascus Barrel, *Modern* .... | 125 | 175 | 170
Various Gauges, Outside Hammers, Steel Barrel, *Modern* .... | 150 | 200 | 185
SHOTGUN, SINGLESHOT
Various Gauges, Hammer, Steel Barrel, *Modern* .... | 50 | 75 | 85

LEATHER, JACOB York, Pa. 1779–1802. See U.S. Military, Kentucky Rifles.

LEE ARMS CO. Wilkes-Barre, Pa. c. 1870. Also See Red Jacket.
HANDGUN, REVOLVER
.22 Short R.F., 7 Shot, Spur Trigger, Solid Frame, Single Action,
Antique .... | 150 | 175 | 165
.32 Short R.F., Spur Trigger, Nickel Plated, *Antique* .... | 125 | 150 | 145
.32 Short R.F., 5 Shot, Spur Trigger, Solid Frame, Single Action,
Antique .... | 150 | 175 | 165

LEBEAU-COURALLY Lebeau-Courally Continental Firearms, Liege, Belgium since 1865.
RIFLE, DOUBLE BARREL, SIDE-BY-SIDE
Ardennes, Various Calibers, Fancy Engraving, Double Triggers, Checkered Stock, Automatic Ejector, Boxlock, Fancy Wood,
Modern .... | 11,500 | 14,000 | 2,975

	V.G.	Exc.	Prior Edition Exc. Value

St. Hubert, Various Calibers, Fancy Engraving, Double Triggers, Checkered Stock, Automatic Ejector, Sidelocks, Fancy Wood, *Modern* $20,000 $25,000 $6,750

SHOTGUN, DOUBLE BARREL, SIDE-BY-SIDE

Grand Russe, 12 Gauge, Fancy Engraving, Double Triggers, Checkered Stock, Automatic Ejector, Boxlock, Fancy Wood, *Modern* 7,500 10,000 3,100

Sologne, 12 Gauge, Medium Engraving, Double Triggers, Checkered Stock, Automatic Ejector, Boxlock with Sideplates, Fancy Wood, *Modern* 9,500 12,000 3,100

LEE SPECIAL Made by Crescent for Lee Hardware, Salina, Kans. c. 1900.

SHOTGUN, DOUBLE BARREL, SIDE-BY-SIDE

Various Gauges, Outside Hammers, Damascus Barrel, *Modern* 150 175 170
Various Gauges, Hammerless, Steel Barrel, *Modern* 175 200 190
Various Gauges, Hammerless, Damascus Barrel, *Modern* 150 175 170
Various Gauges, Outside Hammers, Steel Barrel, *Modern* 150 175 185

SHOTGUN, SINGLESHOT

Various Gauges, Hammer, Steel Barrel, *Modern* 50 75 85

LEFAUCHEUX Paris, France.

HANDGUN, REVOLVER

9mm Pinfire, Double Action, Folding Trigger, Belgian, *Antique* 125 175 175
9mm Pinfire, Double Action, Paris, *Antique* 250 300 295
12mm Pinfire, Model 1863, Double Action, Finger Rest Trigger Guard, *Antique* 275 325 325

SHOTGUN, DOUBLE BARREL, SIDE-BY-SIDE

Various Pinfire Gauges, Double Triggers, Hammers, *Antique* 125 150 145

LEFEVER SONS & CO. Syracuse, N.Y. Nichols & Lefever, 1876–1878; D.M. Lefever, 1879–1889; Lefever Arms Co. 1889–1899; Lefever, Sons & Co. 1899–1926. Purchased by Ithaca Gun Co. 1926.

SHOTGUN, DOUBLE BARREL, SIDE-BY-SIDE

B, Various Gauges, Sidelock, Hammerless, Fancy Checkering, Fancy Engraving, Monte Carlo Stock, *Modern* 4,000 4,500 2,825

BE, Various Gauges, Sidelock, Hammerless, Fancy Checkering, Fancy Engraving, Monte Carlo Stock, Automatic Ejector, *Modern* 6,500 8,000 3,100

C, Various Gauges, Sidelock, Hammerless, Fancy Checkering, Fancy Engraving, Monte Carlo Stock, *Modern* 2,750 3,000 2,325

CE, Various Gauges, Sidelock, Hammerless, Fancy Checkering, Fancy Engraving, Monte Carlo Stock, Automatic Ejector, *Modern* 4,500 5,000 2,450

D, Various Gauges, Sidelock, Hammerless, Fancy Checkering, Engraved, Monte Carlo Stock, *Modern* 1,550 1,800 1,975

	V.G.	Exc.	Prior Edition Exc. Value
DE, Various Gauges, Sidelock, Hammerless, Fancy Checkering, Engraved, Monte Carlo Stock, Automatic Ejector, *Modern*	$2,100	$2,500	$2,250
D S, Various Gauges, Sidelock, Hammerless, Checkered Stock, *Modern*	750	900	600
D SE, Various Gauges, Sidelock, Hammerless, Checkered Stock, Automatic Ejector, *Modern*	1,000	1,200	795
E, Various Gauges, Sidelock, Hammerless, Fancy Checkering, Engraved, *Modern*	1,400	1,550	1,550
EE, Various Gauges, Sidelock, Hammerless, Fancy Checkering, Engraved, *Modern*	1,700	2,000	1,900
F, Various Gauges, Sidelock, Hammerless, Checkered Stock, Engraved, *Modern*	1,200	1,400	1,400
FE, Various Gauges, Sidelock, Hammerless, Checkered Stock, Engraved, Automatic Ejector, *Modern*	1,600	1,800	1,500
G, Various Gauges, Sidelock, Hammerless, Checkered Stock, Light Engraving, *Modern*	1,100	1,300	895
GE, Various Gauges, Sidelock, Hammerless, Checkered Stock, Light Engraving, Automatic Ejector, *Modern*	1,400	1,600	1,025
H, Various Gauges, Sidelock, Hammerless, Checkered Stock, Light Engraving, *Modern*	850	1,000	725
HE, Various Gauges, Sidelock, Hammerless, Checkered Stock, Light Engraving, Automatic Ejector, *Modern*	1,250	1,500	865
Nitro Special, Various Gauges, Box Lock, Double Trigger, Checkered Stock, *Modern*	325	375	425
Nitro Special, Various Gauges, Box Lock, Single Trigger, Checkered Stock, *Modern*	450	500	500

SHOTGUN, SINGLESHOT

	V.G.	Exc.	Prior Edition Exc. Value
12 Gauge, Trap Grade, Hammerless, Vent Rib, Checkered Stock, Automatic Ejector, *Modern*	500	550	325
D.M. Lefever, 12 Gauge, Trap Grade, Hammerless, Vent Rib, Checkered Stock, Automatic Ejector, *Modern*	600	675	650
Long Range, Various Gauges, Field Grade, Hammerless, Checkered Stock, *Modern*	300	350	160

LEFEVRE, PHILIP Beaver Valley, Pa. 1731–1756. See Kentucky Rifles.

LEFEVRE, SAMUEL Strasbourg, Pa. 1770–1771. See Kentucky Rifles and Pistols.

LEIGH, HENRY Belgium, c. 1890.
SHOTGUN, DOUBLE BARREL, SIDE-BY-SIDE

	V.G.	Exc.	Prior Edition Exc. Value
Various Gauges, Outside Hammers, Damascus Barrel, *Modern*	100	150	155

LEITNER, ADAM York Co, Pa. See Kentucky Rifles and Pistols.

LENNARD Lancaster, Pa. 1770–1772. See Kentucky Rifles and Pistols.

Leonhardt Gering

LePage

Lepco

	V.G.	Exc.	Prior Edition Exc. Value

LEONHARDT H.M. Gering & Co., Arnstadt, Germany, c. 1917.

HANDGUN, SEMI-AUTOMATIC

	V.G.	Exc.	Prior Edition Exc. Value
Army, .32 ACP, Clip Fed, *Modern*	$175	$200	$200
Gering, .32 ACP, Clip Fed, *Modern*	220	225	210

LEPAGE Made by Manufacture D'Armes Le Page, Liege, Belgium.

HANDGUN, SEMI-AUTOMATIC

	V.G.	Exc.	Prior Edition Exc. Value
.25 ACP, Clip Fed, *Modern*	225	250	250
.32 ACP, Clip Fed, *Modern*	375	400	390
.380 ACP, Clip Fed, Adjustable Sights, *Modern*	400	450	440
9mm Browning Long, Clip Fed, Adjustable Sights, *Modern*	450	600	600
9mm Browning Long, Clip Fed, Adjustable Sights, Detachable Shoulder Stock, *Class 3*	800	900	900

LEPCO

HANDGUN, SEMI-AUTOMATIC

	V.G.	Exc.	Prior Edition Exc. Value
.25 ACP, Clip Fed, Blue, *Modern*	100	125	130

	V.G.	Exc.	Prior Edition Exc. Value

L.E.S. Skokie, Ill.

HANDGUN, SEMI-AUTOMATIC

P-18, 9mm Luger, Matte Stainless Steel, Clip Fed, Hammer, Double Action, *Modern* $225 $275 $245

P-18 Deluxe, 9mm Luger, Polished Stainless Steel, Clip Fed, Hammer, Double Action, *Modern* 250 325 300

LESCHER Philadelphia, Pa., c. 1730. See Kentucky Rifles and Pistols.

LESCONNE, A. Maybe French, c. 1650.

HANDGUN, FLINTLOCK

Pair, Engraved, Silver Inlay, Long Screw Barrel, Rifled, Belt Hook, *Antique* 7,500 10,000 10,000

LIBERTY Made by Hood Firearms, 1880–1900.

HANDGUN, REVOLVER

.22 Short R.F., 7 Shot, Spur Trigger, Solid Frame, Single Action, *Antique* 150 175 165

.32 Short R.F., 5 Shot, Spur Trigger, Solid Frame, Single Action, *Antique* 150 175 170

LIBERTY Montrose, Calif.

HANDGUN, REVOLVER

Mustang, .22LR/.22 WMR Combo, Single Action, Western Style, Adjustable Sights, *Modern* 25 50 45

Mustang, .22 L.R.R.F., Single Action, Western Style, Adjustable Sights, *Modern* 25 50 40

Liberty M1924   *Liberty Long Grip*

	V.G.	Exc.	Prior Edition Exc. Value

LIBERTY Retolaza Hermanos, Eibar, Spain, c. 1920.

HANDGUN, SEMI-AUTOMATIC

	V.G.	Exc.	Prior Edition Exc. Value
M1924, .32 ACP, Clip Fed, *Modern*	$125	$150	$145
Model 1914, .32 ACP, Clip Fed, Blue, *Modern*	150	175	160
.25 ACP, Clip Fed, Blue, Long Grip, *Modern*	150	175	175

LIBERTY CHIEF Miroku Firearms, Kochi, Japan.

HANDGUN, REVOLVER

	V.G.	Exc.	Prior Edition Exc. Value
Model 6, .38 Spec., Double Action, Blue, *Modern*	125	150	130

LIBIA Made by Beistegui Hermanos, c. 1920.

HANDGUN, SEMI-AUTOMATIC

	V.G.	Exc.	Prior Edition Exc. Value
.25 ACP, Clip Fed, Blue, *Modern*	175	200	195
.32 ACP, Clip Fed, Blue, *Modern*	200	225	225

LIEGEOISE D'ARMES A FEU Robar et Cie., Liege, Belgium, c. 1920.

HANDGUN, SEMI-AUTOMATIC

	V.G.	Exc.	Prior Edition Exc. Value
Spanish Copy, .25 ACP, Blue, Clip Fed, *Curio*	100	125	130
Spanish Copy, .32 ACP, Blue, Clip Fed, *Curio*	125	150	140
New Model Melior, .25 ACP, Clip Fed, Blue, *Curio*	150	175	175

LIGHTNING Echave y Arizmendi, Eibar, Spain, c. 1920.

HANDGUN, SEMI-AUTOMATIC

	V.G.	Exc.	Prior Edition Exc. Value
.25 ACP, Clip Fed, Blue, *Modern*	125	150	135

LIGNITZ, I.H. Continental, c. 1650.

HANDGUN, WHEEL-LOCK

	V.G.	Exc.	Prior Edition Exc. Value
Brass Barrel, Holster Pistol, Medium Ornamentation, *Antique*	6,500	7,500	7,000

LIGNOSE Successors to Theodor Bergmann, Suhl, Germany, c. 1925.

HANDGUN, SEMI-AUTOMATIC

For Original Wood Grips *Add 10%–15%*

	V.G.	Exc.	Prior Edition Exc. Value
Model 2, .25 ACP, Clip Fed, *Modern*	150	200	295
Model 2A, .25 ACP, Clip Fed, Einhand, Steel Cocking Piece, *Modern*	200	250	265

Lignose 3A

	V.G.	Exc.	Prior Edition Exc. Value
Model 3A, .25 ACP, Clip Fed, Long Grip, Einhand, Brass Cocking Piece, *Modern*..	$200	$250	$300

LILIPUT August Menz, Suhl, Germany, c. 1920.

HANDGUN, SEMI-AUTOMATIC

4.25mm Liliput, Clip Fed, Blue, *Curio*	400	450	575
25 ACP, Clip Fed, Blue, *Modern*	125	150	285

LION Made by Johnson Bye & Co., c. 1870–1880. Sold by J.P. Lovell, Boston, Mass.

HANDGUN, REVOLVER

#1, .22 Short R.F., 7 Shot, Spur Trigger, Solid Frame, Single Action, *Antique*	150	175	165
#2, .32 Short R.F., 5 Shot Spur Trigger, Solid Frame, Single Action, *Antique*	150	175	170
#3, .38 Short R.F., 5 Shot, Spur Trigger, Solid Frame, Single Action, *Antique*	150	175	175
#4, .41 Short R.F., 5 Shot, Spur Trigger, Solid Frame, Single Action, *Antique*	175	200	185

LITTLE GIANT Made by Bacon Arms Co., c. 1880.

HANDGUN, REVOLVER

.22 Short R.F., 7 Shot, Spur Trigger, Solid Frame, Single Action, *Antique*	150	175	165

	V.G.	Exc.	Prior Edition Exc. Value

LITTLE JOHN Made by Hood Firearms., c. 1876.

HANDGUN, REVOLVER

.22 Short R.F., 7 Shot, Spur Trigger, Solid Frame, Single Action,
Antique *$150* *$175* *$165*

LITTLE JOKER Made by John M. Marlin, New Haven, Conn. 1873–1875.

HANDGUN, REVOLVER

.22 Short R.F., 7 Shot, Spur Trigger, Solid Frame, Single Action,
Antique *175* *200* *195*

LITTLE PET Made by Stevens Arms.

SHOTGUN, SINGLESHOT

Model 958, .410 Gauge, Automatic Ejector, Hammer, *Modern* *50* *75* *60*
Model 958, 32 Gauge, Automatic Ejector, Hammer, *Modern* *50* *75* *70*

LITTLE TOM Alois Tomiska, Pilsen, Czechoslovakia 1909–1918.

HANDGUN, SEMI-AUTOMATIC

.25 ACP, Clip Fed, Blue, Hammer, *Curio* *375* *425* *420*
.32 ACP, Clip Fed, Blue, Hammer, *Curio* *450* *500* *485*

LITTLE TOM Wiener Waffenfabrik, Vienna, Austria 1918–1925.

HANDGUN, SEMI-AUTOMATIC

.25 ACP, Clip Fed, Blue, Hammer, *Curio* *325* *375* *365*

LJUTIC INDUSTRIES, INC. Yakima, Wash.

SHOTGUN, DOUBLE BARREL, OVER-UNDER

Bi Gun, 12 Gauge, High Rib, Live Pigeon, Checkered Stock,
Choke Tubes, *Modern* *4,000* *4,500* *4,300*
Bi Gun, 12 Gauge, Vent Rib, Trap Grade, Checkered Stock,
Modern *3,800* *4,250* *4,100*
Bi Gun Set, Various Calibers, Vent Rib, Skeet Grade, Checkered
Stock, With 4 Sets of Barrels, *Modern* *7,000* *9,000* *8,900*

SHOTGUN, SEMI-AUTOMATIC

Bi Matic, 12 Gauge, Vent Rib, Trap Grade, Checkered Stock,
Modern *1,800* *2,000* *2,100*

SHOTGUN, SINGLESHOT

Dyn-A-Trap, 12 Gauge, Trap Grade, Checkered Stock, Vent Rib,
Modern *1,800* *2,000* *1,200*
Dyn-A-Trap, 12 Gauge, Release Trigger, *Add* **$95.00–$150.00**
Dyn-A-Trap, 12 Gauge, for Custom Stock *Add* **$115.00–$170.00**

	V.G.	Exc.	Prior Edition Exc. Value
Mono-Gun, 12 Gauge, Trap Grade, Checkered Stock, Vent Rib, *Modern*	$3,000	$3,500	$2,600
Mono-Gun, 12 Gauge, Trap Grade, Checkered Stock, Olympic Rib, *Modern*	4,000	5,000	3,100
Mono-Gun, 12 Gauge, For Extra Barrel *Add* **$350.00–$565.00**			
Mono-Gun, 12 Gauge, Release Trigger *Add* **$150.00–$220.00**			
Mono-Gun, 12 Gauge, Trap Grade, Checkered Stock, Vent Rib, Adjustable Pattern, *Modern*	3,800	4,500	3,100
X-73, 12 Gauge, Trap Grade, Checkered Stock, Vent Rib, *Modern*	2,000	2,500	1,200
X-73, 12 Gauge, For Extra Barrel *Add* **$300.00–$435.00**			
X-73, 12 Gauge, Release Trigger *Add* **$150.00–$220,00**			

LLAMA Gabilondo y Cia., Elgoibar, Spain from 1930 to date. Imported by Stoeger Arms.

HANDGUN, REVOLVER

Chrome Plate *Add* **20%–30%**

Engraving *Add* **25%–35%**

Gold Damascening *Add* **300%–400%**

	V.G.	Exc.	Prior Edition Exc. Value
Commanche I, .22 L.R.R.F., Swing-Out Cylinder, Double Action, Blue, *Modern*	150	175	175
Commanche II, .38 Special, Swing-Out Cylinder, Double Action, Blue, *Modern*	175	200	175
Commanche III, .357 Magnum, Swing-Out Cylinder, Double Action, Blue, *Modern*	200	225	200
Martial, .22 L.R.R.F., Swing-Out Cylinder, Double Action, Blue, *Modern*	150	175	145
Martial, .22 WMR, Swing-Out Cylinder, Double Action, Blue, *Modern*	150	200	160
Martial, .38 Special, Swing-Out Cylinder, Double Action, Blue, *Modern*	150	175	145
Super Commanche, .357 Magnum, Swing-Out Cylinder, Double Action, Blue, *Modern*	225	250	220
Super Commanche, .44 Magnum, Swing-Out Cylinder, Double Action, Blue, *Modern*	250	275	325

HANDGUN, SEMI-AUTOMATIC

Chrome Plate *Add* **20%–30%**

Engraving *Add* **25%–35%**

Gold Damascening *Add* **300%–400%**

	V.G.	Exc.	Prior Edition Exc. Value
Model I, .32 ACP, Clip Fed, Blue, *Modern*	175	200	165
Model II, .380 ACP, Clip Fed, Blue, *Modern*	200	225	185
Model III, .380 ACP, Clip Fed, Blue, *Modern*	175	200	175
Model IIIA, .380 ACP, Clip Fed, Grip Safety, Blue, *Modern*	200	225	190
Model IV, 9mm Bergmann, Clip Fed, Blue, *Modern*	175	200	170
Model IX, .45 ACP, Clip Fed, Blue, *Modern*	275	300	190

	V.G.	Exc.	Prior Edition Exc. Value
Model IXA, .45 ACP, Clip Fed, Blue, *Modern*	$275	$300	$225
Model V, .38 ACP, Clip Fed, Blue, *Modern*	175	200	190
Model VII, .38 ACP, Clip Fed, Blue, *Modern*	225	250	190
Model VIII, .38 ACP, Grip Safety, Blue, *Modern*	250	275	225
Model X, .32 ACP, Clip Fed, Blue, *Modern*	175	200	165
Model XA, .32 ACP, Clip Fed, Grip Safety, Blue, *Modern*	200	225	190
Model XI, 9mm Luger, Clip Fed, Blue, *Modern*	275	300	225
Model XV, .22 L.R.R.F., Clip Fed, Grip Safety, Blue, *Modern*	225	250	185
Omni, 9mm Luger or .45 ACP, Clip Fed, Double Action, Blue, Military, *Antique*	350	375	250

LOBINGER, JOHANN Vienna, Austria, c. 1780.

RIFLE, FLINTLOCK

	V.G.	Exc.	
Yaeger, Smoothbore, Half-Octagon Barrel, Silver Furniture, Carved, *Antique*	3,500	4,000	3,700

LONGINES Cooperative Orbea, Eibar, Spain, c. 1920.

HANDGUN, SEMI-AUTOMATIC

	V.G.	Exc.	
.32 ACP, Clip Fed, *Modern*	175	200	200

LONG RANGE WONDER Tradename used by Sears, Roebuck & Co.

SHOTGUN, SINGLESHOT

	V.G.	Exc.	
12 Ga., Hammer, Break-Open, *Modern*	50	75	60

LONG TOM Made by Stevens Arms.

SHOTGUN, SINGLESHOT

	V.G.	Exc.	
Model 90, Various Gauges, Takedown, Automatic Ejector, Plain, Hammer, *Modern*	50	75	60
Model 95, 12 and 16 Gauges, Hammer, Automatic Ejector, *Modern*	50	75	60

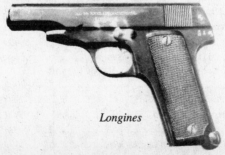

Longines

	V.G.	Exc.	Prior Edition Exc. Value

LOOKING GLASS Domingo Acha and Acha Hermanos, Ermua, Spain, c. 1920.

HANDGUN, SEMI-AUTOMATIC

	V.G.	Exc.	Prior Value
.25 ACP, Clip Fed, Hammer, *Modern*	$125	$150	$150
.25 ACP, Clip Fed, Hammerless, *Modern*	100	125	130
.32 ACP, Clip Fed, Long Grip, Hammerless, *Modern*	125	150	140
.32 ACP, Clip Fed, Long Grip, Hammer, *Modern*	150	175	160

LORD, J. Orwigsburg, Pa. 1842–55. See Kentucky Rifles.

LOWELL ARMS CO. Lowell, Mass. 1864–68.

HANDGUN, REVOLVER

	V.G.	Exc.	Prior Value
.22 Short R.F., 7 Shot, Spur Trigger, Tip-up, *Antique*	300	350	345
.32 Long R.F., 6 Shot, Spur Trigger, Tip-up, Single Action, *Antique*	250	275	265
.38 Long R.F., 6 Shot, Spur Trigger, Tip-up, Single Action, *Antique*	350	400	390

RIFLE, SINGLESHOT

	V.G.	Exc.	Prior Value
.38 Long R.F., *Antique*	350	375	365

LOWER, J.P. Philadelphia, Pa., c. 1875.

HANDGUN, REVOLVER

	V.G.	Exc.	Prior Value
.22 Long R.F., 7 Shot, Single Action, Solid Frame, Spur Trigger, *Antique*	150	175	185
.32 Long R.F., 7 Shot, Single Action, Solid Frame, Spur Trigger, *Antique*	175	200	200

LUGER Made by various companies for commercial and military use from 1900–45. Also see Mauser Parabellum.

HANDGUN, SEMI-AUTOMATIC

	V.G.	Exc.	Prior Value
1900 Commercial, .30 Luger, *Curio*	2,225	2,500	1,600
1900 Eagle, .30 Luger, *Curio*	2,000	2,250	1,400
1900 Swiss Commercial, .30 Luger, *Curio*	2,250	2,500	1,600
1900 Swiss Military, .30 Luger, *Curio*	2,000	2,250	1,500
1900 Swiss Military, .30 Luger, Wide Trigger, *Curio*	2,450	2,600	1,850
1902, .30 Luger and 9mm Luger, Carbine, Blue, *Curio Add* **50%** for Stock	4,000	5,000	4,000
1902, 9mm Luger, Cartridge Counter, *Curio*	12,500	15,000	5,300
1902 Commercial, 9mm Luger, *Curio*	4,000	4,500	4,300
1902 Eagle, 9mm Luger, *Curio*	5,000	5,500	3,500
1902 Prototype, .30 Luger and 9mm Luger, *Curio*		RARE	9,950

	V.G.	Exc.	Prior Edition Exc. Value
1902 Test, .30 Luger, and 9mm Luger, *Curio*	$3,500	$4,000	$3,000
1902–3 Presentation, .30 Luger, Carbine, *Curio*		*RARE*	28,000
1903 Commercial, .30 Luger, *Curio*	6,500	8,000	5,800
1904 Navy, 9mm Luger, *Curio*	10,000	12,500	6,700
1906 Brazilian, .30 Luger, *Curio*	1,200	1,500	1,125
1906 Bulgarian, .30 Luger, *Curio*	3,000	3,500	3,875
1906 Bulgarian, 9mm Luger, *Curio*	2,500	3,000	3,750
1906 Commercial, .30 Luger, *Curio*	1,250	1,500	1,175
1906 Commercial, 9mm Luger, *Curio*	1,750	2,000	1,800
1906 Dutch, 9mm Luger, *Curio*	1,350	1,600	1,175
1906 Eagle, .30 Luger, *Curio*	1,750	2,000	1,400
1906 Eagle, 9mm Luger, *Curio*	2,000	2,250	1,500
1906 French, .30 Luger, *Curio*	1,550	1,800	6,700
1906 Navy Commercial, 9mm Luger, *Curio*	2,500	3,000	3,675
1906 Navy Military, 9mm Luger, *Curio*	2,000	2,500	1,700
1906 Portuguese Army, .30 Luger, *Curio*	1,000	1,200	1,100
1906 Portuguese Navy Crown, .30 Luger and 9mm Luger, *Curio*	6,500	7,250	8,500
1906 Portuguese Navy, RP, .30 Luger, *Curio*	6,500	7,000	3,350
1906 Russian, 9mm Luger, *Curio*	7,500	9,500	6,750
1906 Swiss Commercial, .30 Luger, *Curio*	2,000	2,350	2,000
1906 Swiss Military, .30 Luger, *Curio*	1,900	2,250	975
1906 Swiss Police, .30 Luger, *Curio*	2,250	2,500	1,400
1908 Bolivian, 9mm Luger, *Curio*	2,500	2,750	6,000
1908 Bulgarian, 9mm Luger, *Curio*	1,500	1,750	1,450
1908 DWM Commercial, 9mm Luger, *Curio*	600	700	810
1908 Military, 9mm Luger, *Curio*	575	650	650
1908 Navy Commercial, .30 Luger, *Curio*	3,000	3,500	2,500
1908 Navy Military, 9mm Luger, *Curio*	1,750	2,000	1,380
1913 Commercial, 9mm Luger, *Curio*	1,400	1,650	1,100
1914 Commercial, 9mm Luger, *Curio*	750	900	1,100
1914 Artillery, 9mm Luger, *Curio*	1,250	1,500	1,100
1914 Military, 9mm Luger, *Curio*	800	1,000	550
1914 Navy, 9mm Luger, *Curio*	2,450	2,600	1,075
1918 Spandau, 9mm Luger, *Curio*		*RARE*	4,300
1920 Abercrombie & Fitch, .30 Luger and 9mm Luger, *Curio*	4,000	4,500	4,000
1920 Artillery, 9mm Luger, *Curio*	1,000	1,300	800
1920 Commercial, .30 Luger and 9mm Luger, *Curio*	550	600	550
1920 Navy, 9mm Luger, *Curio*	1,800	2,000	1,300
1920 Simson, 9mm Luger, *Curio*	700	800	625
1920 Swiss Commercial, .30 Luger and 9mm Luger, *Curio*	1,250	1,500	950
1920 Swiss Rework, .30 Luger and 9mm Luger, *Curio*	1,200	1,550	1,175
1920–21, .30 Luger and 9mm Luger, *Curio*	500	650	500

Luger 1906 Commercial

Luger 1940 42 with Snail Drum

Luger 1902 Commercial

Luger 1906 Navy

Luger VOPO

	V.G.	Exc.	Prior Edition Exc. Value
1921 Krieghoff, .30 Luger, *Curio*	$2,500	$2,800	$900
1923 Commercial, .30 Luger and 9mm Luger, *Curio*	650	750	550
1923 Commercial Krieghoff, 9mm Luger, *Curio*	1,250	1,500	800
1923 Commercial "Safe-Loaded", .30 Luger and 9mm Luger, *Curio*	1,000	1,250	810
1923 Dutch, 9mm Luger, *Curio*	1,200	1,450	770
1923 Simson Commercial, 9mm Luger, *Curio*	1,800	2,000	1,100
1923 Simson Military, 9mm Luger, *Curio*	2,000	2,250	1,300
1923 Stoeger, .30 Luger and 9mm Luger, *Curio*	2,000	2,250	3,275
1924–7 Simson, 9mm Luger, *Curio*	1,800	2,000	1,300
1929 Bern, .30 Luger and 9mm Luger, *Curio*	1,250	1,500	1,550
1930–33 Death Head, 9mm Luger, *Curio*	1,250	1,500	950
1923 Finnish Army, 9mm Luger, *Curio*	550	600	1,175
1933 K.I., 9mm Luger, *Curio*	850	1,000	1,150
1933–35 Dutch, 9mm Luger, *Curio*	1,450	1,650	1,450
1933–35 Mauser Commercial, 9mm Luger, *Curio*	1,250	1,500	1,175
1934 P Commercial Krieghoff, .30 Luger and 9mm Luger, *Curio*	2,250	2,500	1,750
1934 P Commercial, Krieghoff, 9mm Luger, *Curio*	2,000	2,250	1,600
1934 Sideframe, Krieghoff, 6" Barrel, 9mm Luger, *Curio*	2,500	3,000	5,300
1935 Portuguese, .30 Luger, *Curio*	1,750	2,000	850
1936 Persian, 9mm Luger, *Curio*	3,000	3,500	4,900
1936–37, 9mm Luger, Krieghoff, *Curio*	2,500	3,000	1,400
1936–39, .30 Luger and 9mm Luger, 4" Barrel, *Curio*	750	900	600
1936–40 Dutch Banner, 9mm Luger, *Curio*	1,250	1,500	950
1936–9 S/42, 9mm Luger, *Curio*	750	875	575
1937–39 Banner Commercial, .30 Luger, 4" Barrel, *Curio*	1,400	1,600	1,450
1938, 9mm Luger, Krieghoff, *Curio*	2,500	2,650	3,100
1939–40 42, 9mm Luger, *Curio*	625	750	410
1940, 9mm Luger, Krieghoff, *Curio*	2,250	2,500	1,350
1940 42/42 byf, 9mm Luger, *Curio*	600	750	1,175
1940 Mauser Banner, .30 Luger and 9mm Luger, *Curio*	1,250	1,500	910
1940–1 S/42, 9mm Luger, *Curio*	1,250	1,500	590
1941–2 byf, 9mm Luger, *Curio*	750	900	500
1941–4, 9mm Luger, Krieghoff, *Curio*	1,800	2,100	1,950
1945, 9mm Luger, Krieghoff, *Curio*	8,500	9,500	3,500
36, 9mm Luger, Krieghoff, *Curio*	2,250	2,500	1,200
41 & 42 Banner, 9mm Luger, *Curio*	850	1,200	635
42/41, 9mm Luger, *Curio*	800	950	650
Artillery, Stock Only, *Curio*	300	350	320
Austrian Banner, 9mm Luger, *Curio*	1,500	1,850	700
Banner Commercial, .30 Luger, 4" Barrel, *Curio*	1,200	1,450	1,675
Bulgarian, .30 Luger, *Curio*	3,500	4,000	5,400

	V.G.	Exc.	Prior Edition Exc. Value
Double Date, 9mm Luger, *Curio*	$550	$700	$670
G-S/42, 9mm Luger, *Curio*	650	800	875
G-S/42, DWM, 9mm Luger, *Curio*	750	900	950
G.L. Baby, 9mm Luger, *Curio*		RARE	30,000
Ideal, Holster Stock, *Curio*	1,000	1,250	460
K U, 9mm Luger, *Curio*	1,500	1,650	900
K-S/42, 9mm Luger, *Curio*	2,500	3,000	1,075
K-S/42 Navy, 9mm Luger, *Curio*	3,000	3,500	1,775
Mauser Banner Commercial, 9mm Luger, *Curio*	800	1,000	,925
Navy, Stock Only, *Curio*	500	650	550
Post War, 9mm Luger, Krieghoff, *Curio*	1,500	1,750	1,575
S/42 Navy, 9mm Luger, *Curio*	850	1,000	1,000
Snail Drum, Magazine, *Curio*	500	600	310
Stoeger (New) STLR, .22 L.R.R.F., Clip Fed, Alloy Frame, *Modern*	100	125	85
Stoeger (New) STLR, .22 L.R.R.F., Clip Fed, Alloy Frame, Checkered Wood Grips, Early, *Modern*	125	150	95
Stoeger (New) STLR, .22 L.R.R.F., Clip Fed, Steel Frame, *Modern*	125	150	98
Stoeger (New) TLR, .22 L.R.R.F., Clip Fed, Adjustable Sights, *Modern*	125	150	95
U.S. Test Eagle, .30 Luger, *Curio*	2,500	3,000	2,600
Vickers Commercial, 9mm Luger, *Curio*	3,000	3,500	2,600
Vickers Military, 9mm Luger, *Curio*	2,000	2,500	1,400
VOPO, 9mm Luger, Clip Fed, *Modern*	1,250	1,450	500

LUR-PANZER Echave y Arizmendi, Eibar, Spain.
HANDGUN, SEMI-AUTOMATIC

Luger Type, .22 L.R.R.F., Toggle Action, Clip Fed, *Modern*	125	150	155

LYMAN GUN SIGHT CORP. Middlefield, Conn.
HANDGUN, PERCUSSION

.36 1851 Navy, Color Case Hardened Frame, Engraved Cylinder, Reproduction, *Antique*	100	125	95
.36 New Model Navy, Brass Trigger Guard, Solid Frame, Reproduction, *Antique*	75	100	85
.44 1860 Army, Color Case Hardened Frame, Engraved Cylinder, Reproduction, *Antique*	100	125	95
.44 New Model Army, Brass Trigger Guard, Solid Frame, Reproduction, *Antique*	100	125	95

RIFLE, FLINTLOCK

Plains Rifle, Various Calibers, Brass Furniture, Set Trigger, Reproduction, *Antique*	200	225	210

	V.G.	Exc.	Prior Edition Exc. Value

RIFLE, PERCUSSION

Plains Rifle, Various Calibers, Brass Furniture, Set Trigger,
Reproduction, *Antique* $150 $175 $170

Trade Rifle, Various Calibers, Brass Furniture, Set Trigger,
Reproduction, *Antique* 125 150 150

RIFLE, SINGLESHOT

Centennial, 45/70 Government, Ruger #1, Commemorative,
Cased with Accessories, *Modern* 1,200 1,450 1,425

M

MAADI

RIFLE, SEMI-AUTOMATIC

Paratrooper AKM, 7.62 × 39mm, Clip Fed, Assault Rifle,
Modern.. $750 $1,050 $1,025

Standard AKM, 7.62 × 39mm, Clip Fed, Assault Rifle,
Modern.. 750 950 900

MAB Mre. d'Armes Automatiques Bayonne, Bayonne, France since 1921.

HANDGUN, SEMI-AUTOMATIC

Nazi Proofs *Add* **20%–30%**

Nazi Navy Proofs *Add* **40%–50%**

W.A.C. Markings, *Deduct* **5%–10%**

	V.G.	Exc.	Prior Ed.
Modele A, .25 ACP, Clip Fed, *Modern*...	125	150	145
Modele B, .25 ACP, Clip Fed, *Modern*...	225	250	220
Modele C, .32 ACP, Clip Fed, *Modern*...	200	225	175
Modele C, .380 ACP, Clip Fed, *Modern*...	225	250	210
Modele C/D, .32 ACP, Clip Fed, *Modern*...	150	175	155
Modele C/D, .380 ACP, Clip Fed, *Modern*.......................................	175	200	180
Modele D, .32 ACP, Clip Fed, *Modern*..	150	175	150
Modele D, .32 ACP, Clip Fed, French Military, *Modern*	225	250	225
Modele D, .380 ACP, Clip Fed, *Modern*...	200	225	160
Modele E, .25 ACP, Clip Fed, Long Grip, *Modern*	200	225	200
Modele F, .22 L.R.R.F., Clip Fed, Hammer, 3" Barrel, *Modern*	175	200	185
Modele F, .22 L.R.R.F., Clip Fed, Hammer, 5" Barrel, *Modern*	200	225	190
Modele G, .22 L.R.R.F., Clip Fed, *Modern*	125	150	140
Modele GZ, .22 L.R.R.F., Clip Fed, Blue, *Modern*...........................	175	200	155
Modele GZ, .22 L.R.R.F., Clip Fed, Green, *Modern*.........................	150	175	165
Modele GZ, .25 ACP, Clip Fed, *Modern*...	175	200	175
Modele Le Chasseur, .22 L.R.R.F., Clip Fed, Hammer, Target Grips, *Modern*...	200	225	200
Modele PA-15, 9mm Luger, Clip Fed, Hammer, *Modern*.................	350	375	325
Modele R Para, 9mm Luger, Clip Fed, Hammer, *Curio*.................	350	400	325
Modele R Court, .32 ACP, Clip Fed, Hammer, *Modern*	275	300	260
Modele R Longue, 7.65 MAS, Clip Fed, Hammer, *Modern*............	250	275	245

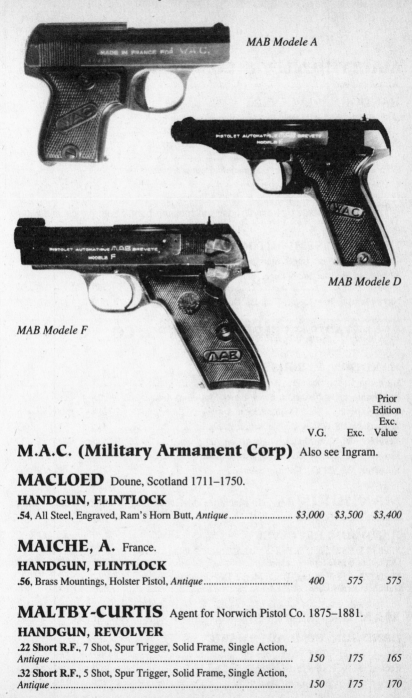

MAB Modele A

MAB Modele D

MAB Modele F

	V.G.	Exc.	Prior Edition Exc. Value

M.A.C. (Military Armament Corp) Also see Ingram.

MACLOED Doune, Scotland 1711–1750.
HANDGUN, FLINTLOCK

	V.G.	Exc.	Prior Edition Exc. Value
.54, All Steel, Engraved, Ram's Horn Butt, *Antique*	*$3,000*	*$3,500*	*$3,400*

MAICHE, A. France.
HANDGUN, FLINTLOCK

	V.G.	Exc.	Prior Edition Exc. Value
.56, Brass Mountings, Holster Pistol, *Antique*	*400*	*575*	*575*

MALTBY-CURTIS Agent for Norwich Pistol Co. 1875–1881.
HANDGUN, REVOLVER

	V.G.	Exc.	Prior Edition Exc. Value
.22 Short R.F., 7 Shot, Spur Trigger, Solid Frame, Single Action, *Antique*	*150*	*175*	*165*
.32 Short R.F., 5 Shot, Spur Trigger, Solid Frame, Single Action, *Antique*	*150*	*175*	*170*

	V.G.	Exc.	Prior Edition Exc. Value

MALTY-HENLEY & CO. N.Y.C. 1878–1889. Made by Columbia Armory, Tenn.

HANDGUN, REVOLVER

	V.G.	Exc.	Prior
.22 L.R.R.F., 7 Shot, Double Action, Hammerless, Top Break, Curio	$75	$100	$95
.32 S & W, 5 Shot, Top Break, Hammerless, Double Action, Curio	75	100	100
.38 S & W, 5 Shot, Top Break, Hammerless, Double Action, Curio	75	125	105

MAMBA Made by Relay Products in Johannesburg, South Africa, and Navy Arms in the U.S.

HANDGUN, SEMI-AUTOMATIC

	V.G.	Exc.	Prior
Relay Mamba, 9mm Luger, Stainless, Double Action, *Modern*	425	475	465
Rhodesian Mamba, 9mm, Luger, Stainless, Double Action, *Modern*	1,500	2,000	2,000
Navy Mamba, 9mm Luger, Stainless, Double Action, *Modern*	300	325	320

MANHATTAN FIREARMS MFG. CO. N.Y.C. & Newark, N.J. 1849–1864.

HANDGUN, PERCUSSION

	V.G.	Exc.	Prior
Hero, Singleshot, Derringer, *Antique*	225	250	210
Bar Hammer, Double Action, Screw Barrel, Singleshot, *Antique*	225	250	235
Pepperbox, .28, 3 Shot, Double Action, *Antique*	550	600	495
Pepperbox, .28, 6 Shot, Double Action, *Antique*	450	500	345
Revolver, .36, Navy Model, Single Action, *Antique*	625	700	550
Revolver, .36, Pocket Model, Single Action, *Antique*	400	450	345
Revolver, M2, .22 Cal. Cartridge, *Antique*	325	350	200

MANHURIN Mre. de Machines du Haut-Rhin, Mulhouse-Bourtzwiller, France. Also see Walther.

HANDGUN, REVOLVER

	V.G.	Exc.	Prior
Model 73, .357 Magnum, Police Model, Double Action, Swing-Out Cylinder, *Modern*	900	1,200	500
Model 73, .357 Magnum, Target Model, Double Action, Swing-Out Cylinder, *Modern*	1,000	1,300	600

MANN Fritz Mann Werkzeugfabrik, Suhl, Germany 1919–1924.

HANDGUN, SEMI-AUTOMATIC

	V.G.	Exc.	Prior
Model Wt, .25 ACP, Clip Fed, *Modern*	300	325	260
Pocket, .32 ACP, Clip Fed, *Modern*	300	350	300
Pocket, .380 ACP, Clip Fed, *Modern*	325	375	340

Manhattan Second Model, .22 Caliber

Manhattan Bar Hammer, .31 Caliber

Mann Pocket

	V.G.	Exc.	Prior Edition Exc. Value

MANN, MICHEL Uhlenberg, Germany, c. 1630.
HANDGUN, WHEEL-LOCK

	V.G.	Exc.	Prior Ed.
Miniature, All Metal, Gold Damascened, Ball Pommel, Antique	$3,500	$4,000	$3,650

MANNLICHER-SCHOENAUER Steyr-Daimler-Puch, Steyr, Austria.
RIFLE, DOUBLE BARREL, OVER-UNDER

	V.G.	Exc.	Prior Ed.
Safari 72, .375 H & H Mag., Checkered Stock, Engraved, Double Trigger, *Modern*	3,000	3,500	3,450
Safari 77, Various Calibers, Checkered Stock, Engraved, Double Trigger, Automatic Ejector, *Modern*	4,000	4,500	4,500

RIFLE, BOLT ACTION

	V.G.	Exc.	Prior Ed.
Alpine, Various Caliber, Sporting Rifle, Full-Stocked, *Modern*	425	475	475
Custom M-S, Various Calibers, Sporting Rifle, Scope Mounted, Carbine, *Modern*	650	700	690
Custom M-S, Various Calibers, Sporting Rifle, Scope Mounted, *Modern*	675	725	690
High Velocity, Various Calibers, Sporting Rifle, Set Trigger, *Modern*	750	825	825
High Velocity, Various Calibers, Sporting Rifle, Takedown, Set Trigger, *Modern*	775	875	875
M-72 LM, Various Calibers, Sporting Rifle, Full-Stocked, *Modern*	750	800	750
M-72 S, Various Calibers, Sporting Rifle, *Modern*	775	850	835
M-72 T, Various Calibers, Sporting Rifle, *Modern*	800	875	875
Magnum M-S, Various Calibers, Sporting Rifle, Monte Carlo Stock, Set Trigger, *Modern*	825	875	875
MCA, Various Calibers, Sporting Rifle, Carbine, Monte Carlo Stock, *Modern*	875	950	940
MCA, Various Calibers, Sporting Rifle, Monte Carlo Stock, *Modern*	850	950	935
Model 1903, Various Calibers, Sporting Rifle, Carbine, Set Trigger, Full-Stocked, *Modern*	900	950	830
Model 1905, 9 × 56 M.S., Sporting Rifle, Carbine, Set Trigger, Full-Stocked, *Modern*	900	1,200	750
Model 1908, Various Calibers, Sporting Rifle, Carbine, Set Trigger, Full-Stocked, *Modern*	925	975	725
Model 1910, 9.5 × 57 M.S., Sporting Rifle, Carbine, Set Trigger, Full-Stocked, *Modern*	950	1,025	750
Model 1924, .30-06 Springfield, Sporting Rifle, Carbine, Set Trigger, Full-Stocked, *Modern*	1,000	1,175	975
Model 1950, 6.5 × 54 M.S., Sporting Rifle, Carbine, Set Trigger, Full-Stocked, *Modern*	850	975	700

	V.G.	Exc.	Prior Edition Exc. Value
Model 1950, Various Calibers, Sporting Rifle, Set Trigger, *Modern*	$750	$825	$775
Model 1950, Various Calibers, Sporting Rifle, Carbine, Set Trigger, Full-Stocked, *Modern*	850	950	800
Model 1952, 6.5 × 54 M.S., Sporting Rifle, Carbine, Set Trigger, Full-Stocked, *Modern*	900	1,050	750
Model 1952, Various Calibers, Sporting Rifle, Carbine, Set Trigger, Full-Stocked, *Modern*	800	1,000	775
Model 1952, Various Calibers, Sporting Rifle, Set Trigger, *Modern*	650	800	775
Model 1956, Various Calibers, Sporting Rifle, Carbine, Set Trigger, Full-Stocked, *Modern*	750	800	775
Model 1956, Various Calibers, Sporting Rifle, Set Trigger, *Modern*	725	800	775
Premier, Various Calibers, Sporting Rifle, Magnum Action, Fancy Checkering, Engraved, *Modern*	1,250	1,400	1,250
Premier, Various Calibers, Sporting Rifle, Fancy Checkering, Engraved, *Modern*	575	650	625
Model SSG, .308 Win., Synthetic Target Stock, Set Triggers, *Modern*	450	500	495
Model SSG Match, .308 Win., Synthetic Target Stock, Set Triggers, Walther Peep Sights, *Modern*	575	650	625
Model ML 79, Various Calibers, Checkered Stock, Set Trigger, *Modern*	700	750	735
Model L Varmint, Various Calibers, Checkered Stock, Set Trigger, *Modern*	475	525	495
Model M, Various Calibers, Checkered Stock, Set Trigger, *Modern*	550	600	575
Model M Professional, Various Calibers, Checkered Stock, Set Trigger, *Modern*	375	425	395
Model S/T Magnum, Various Calibers, Checkered Stock, Set Trigger, *Modern*	650	675	650
Model S, Various Calibers, Checkered Stock, Set Trigger, *Modern*	625	675	650

RIFLE, DOUBLE BARREL, SIDE-BY-SIDE

	V.G.	Exc.	Prior Edition Exc. Value
Mustang, Various Calibers, Standard, Checkered Stock, Sidelock, *Modern*	5,000	6,000	5,850
Mustang, Various Calibers, Standard, Checkered Stock, Sidelock, Engraved, *Modern*	5,500	6,500	6,000

SHOTGUN, DOUBLE BARREL, OVER-UNDER

	V.G.	Exc.	Prior Edition Exc. Value
Edinbourgh, 12 Ga., Checkered Stock, Vent Rib, *Modern*	1,250	1,500	1,475

SHOTGUN, DOUBLE BARREL, SIDE-BY-SIDE

	V.G.	Exc.	Prior Edition Exc. Value
Ambassador English, 12 and 20 Gauges, Checkered Stock, Sidelock, Automatic Ejectors, Engraved, *Modern*	7,000	7,500	7,350
Ambassador Extra, 12 and 20 Gauges, Checkered Stock, Sidelock, Automatic Ejectors, Engraved, *Modern*	6,500	7,250	7,150

	V.G.	Exc.	Prior Edition Exc. Value
Ambassador Golden Black, 12 and 20 Gauges, Checkered Stock, Sidelock, Automatic Ejectors, Engraved, Gold Inlays, *Modern*	$8,500	$9,500	$9,250
Ambassador Executive, 12 and 20 Gauges, Checkered Stock, Sidelock, Automatic Ejectors, Fancy Engraving, *Modern*	12,000	15,000	15,000
Oxford Field, 12 and 20 Gauges, Checkered Stock, Automatic Ejectors, Engraved, *Modern*	1,000	1,300	1,250
London, 12 and 20 Gauges, Checkered Stock, Sidelock, Automatic Ejectors, Engraved, Cased, *Modern*	2,250	2,500	2,450

MANTON, J. & CO. Belgium, c. 1900.

SHOTGUN, DOUBLE BARREL, SIDE-BY-SIDE

Various Gauges, Outside Hammers, Damascus Barrel, *Modern*	150	175	170
Various Gauges, Hammerless, Steel Barrel, *Modern*	150	200	190
Various Gauges, Hammerless, Damascus Barrel, *Modern*	150	175	170
Various Gauges, Outside Hammers, Steel Barrel, *Modern*	150	175	185

SHOTGUN, SINGLESHOT

Various Gauges, Hammer, Steel Barrel, *Modern*	50	75	85

MANTON, JOSEPH London, England 1795–1835.

HANDGUN, FLINTLOCK

Pair, Octagon Barrel, Duelling Pistols, Gold Inlays, Light Engraving, Cased with Accessories, *Antique*	4,000	5,000	4,625

HANDGUN, PERCUSSION

.55, Pair, Duelling Pistols, Octagon Barrel, Light Ornamentation, Cased with Accessories, *Antique*	4,000	5,000	4,800

SHOTGUN, PERCUSSION

12 Ga. Double Barrel, Side by Side, Damascus Barrels, Light Engraving, Gold Inlays, *Antique*	500	650	630

MANUFRANCE Manufacture Francaise de Armes et Cycles de St. Etienne, St. Etienne, France. Also see Le Francaise.

HANDGUN, SEMI-AUTOMATIC

Model 1911 Astra-Manufrance, .32 ACP, CLip Fed, Blue, *Curio*	125	175	165

RIFLE, SEMI-AUTOMATIC

Reina, .22 L.R.R.F., Carbine, Clip Fed, *Modern*	90	150	145
Sniper, .22 W.M.R., Carbine, Clip Fed, *Modern*	150	200	190

RIFLE, BOLT ACTION

Mauser K98 Sporter, .270 Win., Sporterized, Plain, *Modern*	100	150	135
Mauser K98 Sporter, .270 Win., Sporterized, Checkered Stock, *Modern*	125	150	145

	V.G.	Exc.	Prior Edition Exc. Value
Club, .22 L.R.R.F., Singleshot, Carbine, *Modern*	$75	$100	$90
Club, .22 L.R.R.F., Singleshot, Carbine, Checkered Stock, *Modern*	100	125	100
Buffalo Match, .22 L.R.R.F., Target Rifle, *Modern*	150	175	160
Rival, 375 H & H Mag., Checkered Stock, *Modern*	250	300	285

SHOTGUN, DOUBLE BARREL, OVER-UNDER

	V.G.	Exc.	Prior Edition Exc. Value
Falcor Field, 12 Ga., Vent Rib, Automatic Ejector, Single Selective Trigger, Checkered Stock, *Modern*	575	650	600
Falcor Trap, 12 Ga., Vent Rib, Automatic Ejector, Single Selective Trigger, Checkered Stock, *Modern*	625	675	650
Falcor Sport, 12 Ga., Vent Rib, Automatic Ejector, Single Selective Trigger, Checkered Stock, Extra Barrels, *Modern*	725	775	750

SHOTGUN, DOUBLE BARREL, SIDE-BY-SIDE

	V.G.	Exc.	Prior Edition Exc. Value
Ideal DeLuxe, 12 Ga. 3", Fancy Engraving, Checkered Stock, Double Triggers, *Modern*	1,750	1,950	1,750
Ideal Prestige, 12 Ga. 3", Fancy Engraving, Checkered Stock, Double Triggers, *Modern*	2,500	2,750	2,500
Robust, 12 Ga. 3", Checkered Stock, Double Triggers, *Modern*	350	375	365
Robust Luxe, 12 Ga. 3", Engraved, Automatic Ejectors, Checkered Stock, Double Triggers, *Modern*	600	650	600

SHOTGUN, SEMI-AUTOMATIC

	V.G.	Exc.	Prior Edition Exc. Value
Perfex Special, 12 Ga. Mag. 3", Open Sights, Short Barrel, Checkered Stock, *Modern*	325	375	365
Perfex, 12 Ga. Mag. 3", Checkered Stock, *Modern*	300	350	335

SHOTGUN, SINGLESHOT

	V.G.	Exc.	Prior Edition Exc. Value
Simplex, 12 Gauge, Sling Swivels, *Modern*	125	150	125

SHOTGUN, SLIDE ACTION

	V.G.	Exc.	Prior Edition Exc. Value
Rapid, 12 or 16 Gauges, Plain, *Modern*	150	175	170

MARK X Made in Zestavia, Yugoslavia. Imported by Interarms.

RIFLE, BOLT ACTION

	V.G.	Exc.	Prior Edition Exc. Value
Alaskan, Various Calibers, Magnum, Open Rear Sight, Checkered Stock, Sling Swivels, *Modern*	250	300	285
Cavalier, Various Calibers, Cheekpiece, Checkered Stock, Open Rear Sight, Sling Swivels, *Modern*	225	275	265
Mannlicher, Various Calibers, Carbine, Full-Stocked, Checkered Stock, Open Rear Sight, Sling Swivels, *Modern*	250	300	285
Marquis, Various Calibers, Carbine, Mauser Action, *Modern*	425	475	460
Standard, Various Calibers, Checkered Stock, Open Rear Sight, Sling Swivels, *Modern*	225	250	235
Viscount, Various Calibers, Plain, Open Rear Sight, Checkered Stock, Sling Swivels, *Modern*	175	200	180

	V.G.	Exc.	Prior Edition Exc. Value

MARKWELL ARMS CO. Chicago, Ill.

HANDGUN, PERCUSSION

	V.G.	Exc.	Prior Ed.
.41 Derringer, Singleshot, Brass Furniture, Reproduction, *Antique*	$25	$50	$30
.44 C S A 1860, Revolver, 6 Shot, Brass Frame, Reproduction, *Antique*	50	75	65
.44 New Army, Revolver, 6 Shot, Brass Trigger Guard, Reproduction, *Antique*	50	75	65
.45 Colonial, Singleshot, Brass Furniture, Reproduction, *Antique*	25	50	35
.45 Kentucky, Singleshot, Brass Furniture, Reproduction, *Antique*	25	50	45
.45 Loyalist, Singleshot, Brass Furniture, Set Trigger, Adjustable Sights, Reproduction, *Antique*	50	75	65

RIFLE, PERCUSSION

	V.G.	Exc.	Prior Ed.
.45 Hawken, Brass Furniture, Reproduction, *Antique*	75	100	90
.45 Kentucky, Brass Furniture, Reproduction, *Antique*	50	75	75
.45 Super Kentucky, Brass Furniture, Set Trigger, Reproduction, *Antique*	100	125	110

MARLIN FIREARMS CO. New Haven, Conn. J.M. Marlin, from 1870–1881. Marlin Firearms from 1881–1915. Marlin-Rockwell Corp. 1915–1926. From 1926 to Date as Marlin Firearms Co. Also See Ballard.

HANDGUN, REVOLVER

	V.G.	Exc.	Prior Ed.
Standard 1875, .30 R.F., Tip Up, Spur Trigger, *Antique*	200	225	190
XX Standard 1873, .22 R.F., Tip Up, Spur Trigger, *Antique*	250	300	200

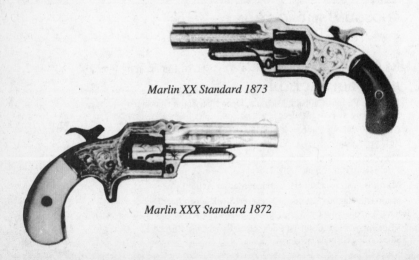

Marlin XX Standard 1873

Marlin XXX Standard 1872

	V.G.	Exc.	Prior Edition Exc. Value
XX Standard 1873, .22 R.F., Tip Up, Spur Trigger, Octagon Barrel, *Antique*	$325	$350	$210
XXX Standard 1872, .30 R.F., Tip Up, Spur Trigger, *Antique*	325	350	190
XXX Standard 1872, .30 R.F., Tip Up, Spur Trigger, Octagon Barrel, *Antique*	350	375	230
Model 1887, .32 and .38, Double Action, Top Break, *Antique*	300	350	195

RIFLE, BOLT ACTION

	V.G.	Exc.	Prior Edition Exc. Value
Glenfield M10, .22 L.R.R.F., Singleshot, *Modern*	25	50	42
Glenfield M20, .22 L.R.R.F., Clip Fed, *Modern*	50	75	55
Model 100, .22 L.R.R.F., Singleshot, Open Rear Sight, Takedown, *Modern*	25	50	43
Model 100-S, .22 L.R.R.F., Singleshot, Peep Sights, Takedown, *Modern*	75	100	75
Model 100-SB, .22 L.R.R.F., Singleshot, Smoothbore, Takedown, *Modern*	25	50	43
Model 101, .22 L.R.R.F., Singleshot, Open Rear Sight, Takedown, Beavertail Forend, *Modern*	50	75	50
Model 101-DL, .22 L.R.R.F., Singleshot, Takedown, Peep Sights, Beavertail Forend, *Modern*	50	75	50
Model 122, .22 L.R.R.F., Singleshot, Open Rear Sight, Monte Carlo Stock, *Modern*	50	75	50
Model 322 (Sako), .222 Rem., Clip Fed, Peep Sights, Checkered Stock, *Modern*	275	325	290
Model 455 (FN), Various Calibers, Peep Sights, Monte Carlo Stock, Checkered Stock, *Modern*	300	325	295
Model 65, .22 L.R.R.F., Singleshot, Open Rear Sight, *Modern*	50	75	50
Model 65E, .22 L.R.R.F., Singleshot, Peep Sights, *Modern*	50	75	50
Model 780, .22 L.R.R.F., Clip Fed, Open Rear Sight, *Modern*	75	100	70
Model 781, .22 L.R.R.F., Tube Feed, Open Rear Sight, *Modern*	75	100	75
Model 782, .22 WMR, Clip Fed, Open Rear Sight, *Modern*	75	100	80
Model 783, .22 WMR, Tube Feed, Open Rear Sight, *Modern*	100	125	80
Model 80, .22 L.R.R.F., Clip Fed, Open Rear Sight, Takedown, *Modern*	50	75	60
Model 80 DL, .22 L.R.R.F., Clip Fed, Beavertail Forend, Takedown, Peep Sights, *Modern*	50	75	70
Model 80C, .22 L.R.R.F., Clip Fed, Beavertail Forend, Takedown, Open Rear Sight, *Modern*	50	75	65
Model 80E, .22 L.R.R.F., Clip Fed, Peep Sights, Takedown, *Modern*	50	75	60
Model 81, .22 L.R.R.F., Tube Feed, Takedown, Open Rear Sight, *Modern*	50	75	70
Model 81C, .22 L.R.R.F., Tube Feed, Takedown, Open Rear Sight, Beavertail Forend, *Modern*	50	75	70
Model 81DL, .22 L.R.R.F., Tube Feed, Takedown, Peep Sights, Beavertail Forend, *Modern*	50	75	65

	V.G.	Exc.	Prior Edition Exc. Value
Model 81E, .22 L.R.R.F., Tube Feed, Takedown, Peep Sights, *Modern*	$50	$75	$65
Model 81G, .22 L.R.R.F., Tube Feed, Takedown, Open Rear Sight, Beavertail Forend, *Modern*	50	75	65
Model 980, .22 WMR, Clip Fed, Monte Carlo Stock, Open Rear Sight, *Modern*	75	100	80

RIFLE, LEVER ACTION

	V.G.	Exc.	Prior Edition Exc. Value
Centennial Set 336-39, Fancy Checkering, Fancy Wood, Engraved, Brass Furniture, *Modern*	1,000	1,250	1,200
Glenfield M 30 A, .30-30 Win., Tube Feed, *Modern*	125	175	145
M1894 (Late), .357 Magnum, Tube Feed, Open Rear Sight, *Modern*	200	225	195
M1894 (Late), .41 Magnum, Tube Feed, Open Rear Sight, *Modern*	175	200	180
M1894 (Late), .44 Magnum, Tube Feed, Open Rear Sight, *Modern*	175	200	180
M1895 (Late), .45-70 Government, Tube Feed, Open Rear Sight, *Modern*	200	225	190
Model 1881 Standard, Various Calibers, Tube Feed, Open Rear Sight, *Antique*	725	775	715
Model 1888, Various Calibers, Tube Feed, Open Rear Sight, *Antique*	800	950	875
Model 1889 Standard, Various Calibers, Tube Feed, Open Rear Sight, *Antique*	475	575	515
Model 1891, .22 L.R.R.F., Tube Feed, Open Rear Sight, *Antique*	400	450	410
Model 1892, Various Calibers, Tube Feed, Open Rear Sight, *Antique*	400	450	400
Model 1892 Over #177382, Various Calibers, Tube Feed, *Modern*	350	400	350
Model 1893, Various Calibers, Tube Feed, Solid Frame, Octagon Barrel, *Antique*	475	550	475
Model 1893, Various Calibers, Tube Feed, Solid Frame, Round Barrel, *Antique*	400	475	410
Model 1893, Various Calibers, Tube Feed, Solid Frame, Round Barrel, Carbine, *Antique*	575	650	575
Model 1893, Various Calibers, Tube Feed, Takedown, Octagon Barrel, *Antique*	600	675	600
Model 1893, Various Calibers, Tube Feed, Takedown, Round Barrel, *Antique*	525	575	500
Model 1893, Various Calibers, Tube Feed, Sporting Carbine, 5 Shot, *Antique*	700	750	670
Model 1893, Various Calibers, Tube Feed, Sporting Carbine, Takedown, 5 Shot, *Antique*	775	825	700
Model 1893, Various Calibers, Tube Feed, Full-Stocked, with Bayonet, *Antique*	2,500	3,250	2,850
Model 1893 over #177304, Various Calibers, Tube Feed, Solid Frame, Octagon Barrel, *Modern*	550	550	470

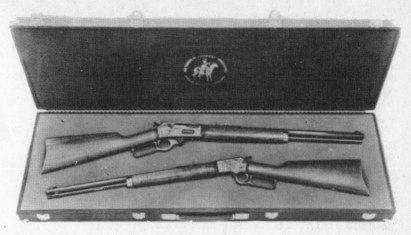

Marlin Cased Centennial Pair

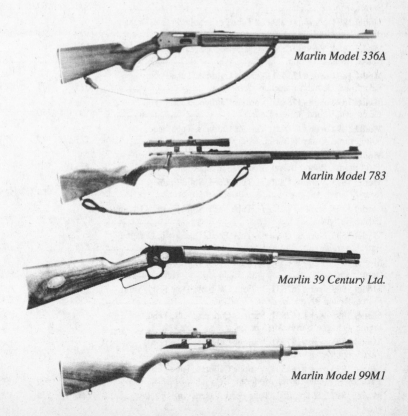

Marlin Model 336A

Marlin Model 783

Marlin 39 Century Ltd.

Marlin Model 99M1

	V.G.	Exc.	Prior Edition Exc. Value
Model 1893 over #177304, Various Calibers, Tube Feed, Solid Frame, Round Barrel, *Modern*	$400	$450	$400
Model 1893 over #177304, Various Calibers, Tube Feed, Solid Frame, Round Barrel, Carbine, *Modern*	500	550	515
Model 1893 over #177304, Various Calibers, Tube Feed, Takedown, Octagon Barrel, *Modern*	450	525	500
Model 1893 over #177304, Various Calibers, Tube Feed, Takedown, Round Barrel, *Modern*	400	450	400
Model 1893 over #177304, Various Calibers, Tube Feed, Sporting Carbine, 5 Shot, *Modern*	500	550	500
Model 1893 over #177304, Various Calibers, Tube Feed, Sporting Carbine, Takedown, 5 Shot, *Modern*	650	750	675
Model 1893 over #177304, Various Calibers, Tube Feed, Full-Stocked, with Bayonet, *Modern*	1,500	1,850	2,950
Model 1894, Various Calibers, Tube Feed, Takedown, Octagon Barrel, *Antique*	600	675	625
Model 1894, Various Calibers, Tube Feed, Takedown, Round Barrel, *Antique*	600	650	575
Model 1894, Various Calibers, Tube Feed, Solid Frame, Octagon Barrel, *Antique*	500	575	500
Model 1894, Various Calibers, Tube Feed, Solid Frame, Round Barrel, *Antique*	475	525	410
Model 1894 over #175431, Various Calibers, Tube Feed, Takedown, Octagon Barrel, *Modern*	625	700	625
Model 1894 over #175431, Various Calibers, Tube Feed, Takedown, Round Barrel, *Modern*	500	550	475
Model 1894 over #175431, Various Calibers, Tube Feed, Solid Frame, Octagon Barrel, *Modern*	525	575	475
Model 1894 over #175431, Various Calibers, Tube Feed, Solid Frame, Round Barrel, *Modern*	475	525	400
Model 1895, Various Calibers, Tube Feed, Solid Frame, Round Barrel, *Antique*	875	950	825
Model 1895, Various Calibers, Tube Feed, Solid Frame, Octagon Barrel, *Antique*	775	850	775
Model 1895, Various Calibers, Tube Feed, Takedown, Octagon Barrel, *Antique*	875	975	900
Model 1895, Various Calibers, Tube Feed, Takedown, Round Barrel, *Antique*	850	1,050	900
Model 1895 over #167531, Various Calibers, Tube Feed, Solid Frame, Round Barrel, *Modern*	750	825	700
Model 1895 over #167531, Various Calibers, Tube Feed, Solid Frame, Octagon Barrel, *Modern*	800	875	750
Model 1895 over #167531, Various Calibers, Tube Feed, Takedown, Octagon Barrel, *Modern*	850	950	825
Model 1895 over #167531, Various Calibers, Tube Feed, Takedown, Round Barrel, *Modern*	800	900	800
Model 1897, .22 L.R.R.F., Tube Feed, Takedown, *Antique*	500	525	400

	V.G.	Exc.	Prior Edition Exc. Value
Model 1897 over #177197, .22 L.R.R.F., Tube Feed, Takedown, *Modern*	$400	$475	$375
Model 336, .219 Zipper, Tube Feed, Sporting Carbine, Open Rear Sight, 5 Shot, *Modern*	400	475	350
Model 336, Various Calibers, Tube Feed, Sporting Carbine, Open Rear Sight, 5 Shot, *Modern*	225	275	165
Model 336 Marauder, Various Calibers, Tube Feed, Carbine, Open Rear Sight, Straight Grip, *Modern*	300	350	275
Model 336 Zane Grey, .30-.30 Win., Tube Feed, Octagon Barrel, Open Rear Sight, *Modern*	300	350	230
Model 336A, Various Calibers, Tube Feed, Sporting Rifle, Open Rear Sight, 5 Shot, *Modern*	225	275	165
Model 336A-DL, Various Calibers, Tube Feed, Sporting Rifle, Open Rear Sight, 5 Shot, Checkered Stock, *Modern*	175	225	170
Model 336C, Various Calibers, Tube Feed, Carbine, Open Rear Sight, *Modern*	175	225	165
Model 336T, .44 Magnum, Tube Feed, Carbine, Open Rear Sight, Straight Grip, *Modern*	175	225	180
Model 336T, Various Calibers, Tube Feed, Carbine, Open Rear Sight, Straight Grip, *Modern*	175	225	165
Model 36, Various Calibers, Tube Feed, Beavertail Forend, Open Rear Sight, Carbine, *Modern*	225	275	230
Model 36, Various Calibers, Tube Feed, Beavertail Forend, Open Rear Sight, Sporting Carbine, 5 Shot, *Modern*	250	300	235
Model 36A, Various Calibers, Tube Feed, Beavertail Forend, Open Rear Sight, 5 Shot, *Modern*	225	275	235
Model 36DL, Various Calibers, Tube Feed, Fancy Checkering, Open Rear Sight, 5 Shot, *Modern*	350	350	285
Model 39, .22 L.R.R.F., Takedown, Tube Feed, Hammer, Octagon Barrel, *Modern*	325	350	285
Model 39 Article II, .22 L.R.R.F., Takedown, Tube Feed, Hammer, Octagon Barrel, *Modern*	275	325	230
Model 39 Article II, .22 L.R.R.F., Takedown, Tube Feed, Hammer, Octagon Barrel, Carbine, *Modern*	325	350	235
Model 39 Century, .22 L.R.R.F., Takedown, Tube Feed, Hammer, Octagon Barrel, *Modern*	300	325	230
Model 39 M, .22 L.R.R.F., Takedown, Tube Feed, Hammer, Round Barrel, Carbine, *Modern*	275	250	140
Model 39A, .22 L.R.R.F., Takedown, Tube Feed, Hammer, Round Barrel, *Modern*	200	225	145
Model 39A Mountie, .22 L.R.R.F., Takedown, Tube Feed, Hammer, Round Barrel, *Modern*	175	200	150
Model 444, .444 Marlin, Tube Feed, Monte Carlo Stock, Open Rear Sight, Straight Grip, *Modern*	225	250	190
Model 56, .22 L.R.R.F., Clip Fed, Open Rear Sight, Monte Carlo Stock, *Modern*	125	150	100
Model 57, .22 L.R.R.F., Tube Feed, Open Rear Sight, Monte Carlo Stock, *Modern*	125	150	100

Marlin Model 49DL

Marlin Model 989M2

Marlin Model 39A

Marlin Model 55 Slug Gun

Marlin Model 1891

Marlin Model 780

	V.G.	Exc.	Prior Edition Exc. Value
Model 57M, .22 WMR, Tube Feed, Open Rear Sight, Monte Carlo Stock, *Modern*	$150	$175	$105
Model 62, Various Calibers, Clip Fed, Open Rear Sight, Monte Carlo Stock, *Modern*	200	225	155

RIFLE, SEMI-AUTOMATIC

	V.G.	Exc.	Prior Edition Exc. Value
Glenfield M40, .22 L.R.R.F., Tube Feed, *Modern*	100	125	65
Glenfield M60, .22 L.R.R.F., Tube Feed, *Modern*	50	75	53
Model 49 DL, .22 L.R.R.F., Tube Feed, Open Rear Sight, *Modern*	75	100	65
Model 50, .22 L.R.R.F., Clip Fed, Open Rear Sight, Takedown, *Modern*	75	100	65
Model 50E, .22 L.R.R.F., Clip Fed, Peep Sights, Takedown, *Modern*	75	100	65
Model 88C, .22 L.R.R.F., Tube Feed, Takedown, Open Rear Sight, *Modern*	75	100	65
Model 88DL, .22 L.R.R.F., Tube Feed, Takedown, Peep Sights, *Modern*	100	125	70
Model 89 DL, .22 L.R.R.F., Clip Fed, Takedown, Peep Sights, *Modern*	100	125	70
Model 89C, .22 L.R.R.F., Clip Fed, Takedown, Open Rear Sight, *Modern*	75	100	70
Model 98, .22 L.R.R.F., Tube Feed, Solid Frame, Open Rear Sight, Monte Carlo Stock, *Modern*	75	100	70
Model 989, .22 L.R.R.F., Clip Fed, Open Rear Sight, Monte Carlo Stock, *Modern*	50	75	63
Model 989 G, .22 L.R.R.F., Clip Fed, Open Rear Sight, Monte Carlo Stock, *Modern*	50	75	68
Model 990, .22 L.R.R.F., Tube Feed, Open Rear Sight, Monte Carlo Stock, *Modern*	50	75	68
Model 995, .22 L.R.R.F., Clip Fed, Open Rear Sight, *Modern*	50	75	63
Model 99, .22 L.R.R.F., Tube Feed, Open Rear Sight, *Modern*	50	75	63
Model 99 M-1, .22 L.R.R.F., Tube Feed, Open Rear Sight, Monte Carlo Stock, *Modern*	50	75	63
Model 99 M-2, .22 L.R.R.F., Clip Fed, Open Rear Sight, *Modern*	50	75	58
Model 99C, .22 L.R.R.F., Tube Feed, Open Rear Sight, Monte Carlo Stock, *Modern*	50	75	58
Model 99DL, .22 L.R.R.F., Tube Feed, Open Rear Sight, Monte Carlo Stock, *Modern*	50	75	58
Model A-1, .22 L.R.R.F., Clip Fed, Takedown, Open Rear Sight, *Modern*	50	75	58
Model A-1E, .22 L.R.R.F., Clip Fed, Takedown, Peep Sights, *Modern*	50	75	58

RIFLE, SLIDE ACTION

	V.G.	Exc.	Prior Edition Exc. Value
Model 18, .22 L.R.R.F., Solid Frame, Tube Feed, Hammer, *Modern*	250	275	250
Model 20, .22 L.R.R.F., Takedown, Tube Feed, Hammer, Octagon Barrel, *Modern*	225	250	225

	V.G.	Exc.	Prior Edition Exc. Value
Model 25, .22 Short R.F., Takedown, Tube Feed, Hammer, *Modern*	$325	$350	$300
Model 27, Various Calibers, Takedown, Tube Feed, Hammer, Octagon Barrel, *Modern*	275	300	275
Model 27-S, Various Calibers, Takedown, Tube Feed, Hammer, Round Barrel, *Modern*	250	300	270
Model 29, .22 L.R.R.F., Takedown, Tube Feed, Hammer, Round Barrel, *Modern*	225	275	245
Model 32, .22 L.R.R.F., Takedown, Tube Feed, Hammerless, Octagon Barrel, *Modern*	250	275	240
Model 38, .22 L.R.R.F., Takedown, Tube Feed, Hammerless, Octagon Barrel, *Modern*	250	275	235

SHOTGUN, LEVER ACTION

	V.G.	Exc.	
Four-Tenner, .410 Ga., Tube Feed, *Modern*	50	625	565

SHOTGUN, SLIDE ACTION

	V.G.	Exc.	
Model 1898 Field, 12 Ga., Hammer, Tube Feed, *Modern*	325	375	340
Model 1898 B, 12 Ga., Hammer, Tube Feed, Checkered Stock, *Modern*	375	425	390
Model 1898 C, 12 Ga., Hammer, Tube Feed, Checkered Stock, Fancy Wood, Light Engraving, *Modern*	775	800	750
Model 1898 D, 12 Ga., Hammer, Tube Feed, Checkered Stock, Fancy Wood, Engraved, *Modern*	1,500	1,750	1,525
Model 19 Field, 12 Ga., Hammer, Tube Feed, *Modern*	275	300	275
Model 19 B, 12 Ga., Hammer, Tube Feed, Checkered Stock, *Modern*	350	400	400
Model 19 C, 12 Ga., Hammer, Tube Feed, Checkered Stock, Fancy Wood, Light Engraving, *Modern*	450	500	550
Model 19 D, 12 Ga., Hammer, Tube Feed, Checkered Stock, Fancy Wood, Engraved, *Modern*	900	1,050	1,200
Model 21 Field, 12 Ga., Hammer, Tube Feed, *Modern*	250	275	270
Model 21 B, 12 Ga., Hammer, Tube Feed, Checkered Stock, *Modern*	350	400	385
Model 21 C, 12 Ga., Hammer, Tube Feed, Checkered Stock, Fancy Wood, Light Engraving, *Modern*	350	500	540
Model 21 D, 12 Ga., Hammer, Tube Feed, Checkered Stock, Fancy Wood, Engraved, *Modern*	875	1,050	1,175
Model 24 Field, 12 Ga., Hammer, Tube Feed, *Modern*	250	300	290
Model 24 B, 12 Ga., Hammer, Tube Feed, Checkered Stock, *Modern*	350	400	400
Model 24 C, 12 Ga., Hammer, Tube Feed, Checkered Stock, Fancy Wood, Light Engraving, *Modern*	500	550	550
Model 24 D, 12 Ga., Hammer, Tube Feed, Checkered Stock, Fancy Wood, Engraved, *Modern*	1,025	1,100	1,250
Model 16 Field, 12 Ga., Hammer, Tube Feed, *Modern*	250	275	295
Model 16 B, 12 Ga., Hammer, Tube Feed, Checkered Stock, *Modern*	350	400	400

	V.G.	Exc.	Prior Edition Exc. Value
Model 16 C, 12 Ga., Hammer, Tube Feed, Checkered Stock, Fancy Wood, Light Engraving, *Modern*	$450	$500	$560
Model 16D, 12 Ga., Hammer, Tube Feed, Checkered Stock, Fancy Wood, Engraved, *Modern*	850	1,000	1,250
Model 30 Field, 12 Ga., Hammer, Tube Feed, *Modern*	275	300	290
Model 30 B, 12 Ga., Hammer, Tube Feed, Checkered Stock, *Modern*	350	400	395
Model 30 C, 12 Ga., Hammer, Tube Feed, Checkered Stock, Fancy Wood, Light Engraving, *Modern*	450	500	550
Model 30 D, 12 Ga., Hammer, Tube Feed, Checkered Stock, Fancy Wood, Engraved, *Modern*	850	1,000	1,270
Model 28 Field, 12 Ga., Hammerless, Tube Feed, *Modern*	250	275	340
Model 28 B, 12 Ga., Hammerless, Tube Feed, Checkered Stock, *Modern*	350	400	500
Model 28 C, 12 Ga., Hammerless, Tube Feed, Checkered Stock, Fancy Wood, Light Engraving, *Modern*	425	500	675
Model 28 D, 12 Ga., Hammerless, Tube Feed, Checkered Stock, Fancy Wood, Engraved, *Modern*	850	1,000	1,450
Model 28 Trap, 12 Ga., Hammerless, Tube Feed, *Modern*	275	300	490
Model 31 Field, 12 Ga., Hammerless, Tube Feed, *Modern*	250	275	360
Model 31 B, 12 Ga., Hammerless, Tube Feed, Checkered Stock, *Modern*	350	400	490
Model 31 C, 12 Ga., Hammerless, Tube Feed, Checkered Stock, Fancy Wood, Light Engraving, *Modern*	450	500	675
Model 31 D, 12 Ga., Hammerless, Tube Feed, Checkered Stock, Fancy Wood, Engraved, *Modern*	1,000	1,200	1,450
Model 17 Field, 12 Ga., Hammer, Tube Feed, *Modern*	400	450	350
Model 26 Field, 12 Ga., Hammer, Tube Feed, *Modern*	225	275	300
Model 44 Field, 12 Ga., Hammerless, Tube Feed, *Modern*	350	375	340
Model 63 Field, 12 Ga., Hammerless, Tube Feed, *Modern*	325	350	285
Premier Mark I, 12 Ga., Hammerless, Tube Feed, *Modern*	200	225	—
Premier Mark II, 12 Ga., Hammerless, Tube Feed, *Modern*	225	250	185
Premier Mark IV, 12 Ga., Hammerless, Tube Feed, Vent Rib, *Modern*	250	300	290
Model 120, 12 Ga., 3", Hammerless, Tube Feed, *Modern*	250	300	165
Glenfield Model 778, 12 Ga., Hammerless, Tube Feed, *Modern*	175	225	145

SHOTGUN, DOUBLE BARREL, OVER-UNDER

	V.G.	Exc.	Prior Edition Exc. Value
Model 90, 12 and 16 Gauges, Checkered Stock, Double Triggers, *Modern*	350	400	375
Model 90, 20 and .410 Gauges, Checkered Stock, Double Triggers, *Modern*	425	475	450
Model 90, 12 and 16 Gauges, Checkered Stock, Single Triggers, *Modern*	400	450	435
Model 90, 20 and 16 Gauges, Checkered Stock, Single Triggers, *Modern*	475	525	510

	V.G.	Exc.	Prior Edition Exc. Value

SHOTGUN, BOLT ACTION

Model 55, Various Gauges, Clip Fed, *Modern*	$75	$100	$68
Model 55, Various Gauges, Clip Fed, Adjustable Choke, *Modern*	100	125	80
Model 55 Goose Gun, 12 Ga. 3", Clip Fed, *Modern*	150	175	80
Model 55, 12 Ga. 3", Clip Fed, Adjustable Choke, *Modern*	100	125	80
Model 55S, 12 Ga. 3", Clip Fed, *Modern*	125	150	80
Model Super Goose, 10 Ga. 3½", Clip Fed, *Modern*	175	200	150
Glenfield 50, 12 Ga. 3", Clip Fed, *Modern*	75	100	75

MAROCCINI Fabricca Fucili da Caccia di Luciano Maroccini, Gardone Val Trompia, Italy.

SHOTGUN, DOUBLE BARREL, OVER-UNDER

Mistral, Various Gauges, Checkered Stock, Sling Swivels, Double Triggers, Boxlock, *Modern*	150	175	165
Mistral Trap, Various Gauges, Checkered Stock, Single Trigger, Boxlock, Automatic Ejectors, *Modern*	225	250	200
Commander, 12 Gauge Magnum, Police Style, Detachable Buttstock, Double Triggers, Boxlock, *Modern*	175	200	180

SHOTGUN, DOUBLE BARREL, SIDE-BY-SIDE

| Mondial, 12 Gauge, Checkered Stock, Sling Swivels, Double Triggers, Boxlock, *Modern* | 175 | 200 | 195 |

MARQUIS OF LORNE Made by Hood Arms Co. Norwich, Conn., c. 1880.

HANDGUN, REVOLVER

| .22 Short R.F., 7 Shot, Spur Trigger, Solid Frame, Single Action, *Antique* | 150 | 175 | 165 |
| .32 Short R.F., 5 Shot, Spur Trigger, Solid Frame, Single Action, *Antique* | 175 | 200 | 170 |

MARS Unknown maker, Spain, c. 1920.

HANDGUN, SEMI-AUTOMATIC

| Automat Pistole Mars, .25 ACP, Clip Fed, *Modern* | 175 | 200 | 195 |

MARS Kohout & Spolecnost, Kydne, Czechoslovakia, c. 1925.

HANDGUN, SEMI-AUTOMATIC

| Mars, .25 ACP, Clip Fed, Blue, *Modern* | 200 | 250 | 245 |
| Mars, .32 ACP, Clip Fed, Blue, *Modern* | 250 | 300 | 275 |

	V.G.	Exc.	Prior Edition Exc. Value

MARS AUTOMATIC PISTOL SYNDICATE Distrib-
uters of the Gabbet-Fairfax pistol made by Webley & Scott, Birmingham, England, c. 1902.

HANDGUN, SEMI-AUTOMATIC
9mm, Clip Fed, Blue, Hammer, *Curio* $8,000 $10,000 $3,650
.45 Long, Clip Fed, Blue, Hammer, *Curio* 12,000 15,000 4,700

MARSHWOOD Made by Stevens Arms.
SHOTGUN, DOUBLE BARREL, SIDE-BY-SIDE
M 315, Various Gauges, Hammerless, Steel Barrel, *Modern* 150 175 165

MARSTON, STANHOPE N.Y.C., c. 1850.
HANDGUN, PERCUSSION
Swivel Breech, .31, Two Barrels, Ring Trigger, Bar Hammer, *Antique* 700 850 695

MARSTON, WILLIAM W. N.Y.C. 1850–1863
HANDGUN, PERCUSSION
Pepperbox, .31, Double Action, 6 Shot, Bar Hammer, *Antique* 500 600 400
Single Shot, .36, Bar Hammer, Double Action, Screw Barrel, *Antique* 300 375 235
Single Shot, .36, Bar Hammer, Single Action, Screw Barrel, *Antique* 350 425 245
Breech Loader, .36, Half Octagon Barrel, Engraved, *Antique* 1,800 2,100 1,325

MARTE Erquiaga, Muguruzu y Cia., Eibar, Spain, c. 1920.
HANDGUN, SEMI-AUTOMATIC
.25 ACP, Clip Fed, Blue, *Curio* 125 150 135

MARTIAN Martin A Bascaran, Eibar, Spain 1916–1927.

Martian

	V.G.	Exc.	Prior Edition Exc. Value

HANDGUN, SEMI-AUTOMATIC

	V.G.	Exc.	Prior Edition Exc. Value
.25 ACP, Clip Fed, Trigger Guard Takedown, *Curio*	$225	$250	$235
.32 ACP, Clip Fed, Trigger Guard Takedown, *Curio*	250	275	270
.25 ACP, Clip Fed, Eibar Type, *Modern*	125	150	135
.32 ACP, Clip Fed, Eibar Type, *Modern*	150	175	165

MARTIAN COMMERCIAL Martin A Bascaran, Eibar, Spain 1919–1927.

HANDGUN, SEMI-AUTOMATIC

	V.G.	Exc.	Prior
.25 ACP, Clip Fed, Eibar Type, *Modern*	125	150	135
.25 ACP, Clip Fed, Eibar Type, *Modern*	150	175	160

MARTIN, ALEXANDER Glasgow & Aberdeen, Scotland 1922–1928.

RIFLE, BOLT ACTION

	V.G.	Exc.	Prior
.303 British, Sporting Rifle, Express Sights, Engraved, Fancy Wood, Cased, *Modern*	950	1,350	1,300

MASSACHUSETTS ARMS Made by Stevens Arms.

SHOTGUN, DOUBLE BARREL, SIDE-BY-SIDE

	V.G.	Exc.	Prior
Model 311, Various Gauges, Hammerless, Steel Barrel, *Modern*	150	175	175

SHOTGUN, SINGLESHOT

	V.G.	Exc.	Prior
Model 90, Various Gauges, Takedown, Automatic Ejector, Plain, Hammer, *Modern*	50	75	65
Model 94, Various Gauges, Takedown, Automatic Ejector, Plain, Hammer, *Modern*	50	75	65

MASSACHUSETTS ARMS CO. Chicopee Falls, Mass. 1850–1866. Also see Adams.

HANDGUN, PERCUSSION

	V.G.	Exc.	Prior
Maynard Pocket Revolver, .28, 6 Shot, *Antique*	600	750	375
Maynard Belt Revolver, .31, 6 Shot, *Antique*	800	950	525
Wesson & Leavitt Belt Revolver, .31, 6 Shot, *Antique*	800	950	500
Wesson & Leavitt Dragoon Revolver, .40, 6 Shot, *Antique*	1,750	2,000	1,250

MATCHLOCK ARMS, UNKNOWN MAKER

RIFLE, MATCHLOCK

	V.G.	Exc.	Prior
.45, India Mid-1600's, 4 Shot, Revolving Cylinder, Light Ornamentation, Brass Furniture, *Antique*	1,750	2,000	1,700
.57, Japanese Full Stock Musket, Octagon Barrel, Silver Inlay, Brass Furniture, *Antique*	600	750	750

	V.G.	Exc.	Prior Edition Exc. Value

MATADOR Made in Spain for Firearms International, Washington, D.C.

SHOTGUN, DOUBLE BARREL, SIDE-BY-SIDE

	V.G.	Exc.	Prior Edition Exc. Value
Matador II, 12 or 20 Gauges, Checkered Stock, Single Trigger, Selective Ejectors, *Modern*	$200	$250	$235

MAUSER Germany Gebruder Mauser et Cie from 1864–1890. From 1890 to date is known as Mauser Werke. Also see German Military, Luger.

HANDGUN, REVOLVER

	V.G.	Exc.	Prior Edition Exc. Value
Colt Type, .38 Spec., Double Action, 6 Shot, 2" Barrel, *Modern*	125	175	170
M 78 Zig Zag, Tip-Up, Fancy Engraving, *Antique*	3,500	5,000	4,900
M 78 Zig Zag, 9mm Mauser, Tip-Up, *Antique*	2,500	3,000	2,700
M 78 Zig Zag, 10.6mm, Tip-Up, *Antique*	3,000	3,500	3,550
M 78 Zig Zag, 7.6mm, Tip-Up, *Antique*	2,500	3,000	2,900

HANDGUN, SEMI-AUTOMATIC

	V.G.	Exc.	Prior Edition Exc. Value
Chinese Shansei, .45 ACP, With Shoulder Stock, *Curio*	3,600	4,800	4,800
HSC, .32 ACP, Pre-War, Prototype, Commercial, *Modern*	300	325	900
HSC, .32 ACP, Post-War, Prototype, Commercial, *Modern*	275	300	490
HSC, .32 ACP, Pre-War, Nazi-Proofed, Commercial, *Modern*	300	325	260
HSC, .32 ACP, Post-War, Blue, *Modern*	225	250	200
HSC, .32 ACP, Nickel Plated, Post-War, *Modern*	225	275	215
HSC, .380 ACP, Blue, Post-War, *Modern*	225	250	210
HSC, .380 ACP, Nickel Plated, Post-War, *Modern*	225	275	225
HSC 1 of 5,000, .380 ACP, Blue, Post-War, Cased, *Modern*	200	300	205
HSC French, .32 ACP, Nazi-Proofed, *Curio*	325	375	240
HSC Navy, .32 ACP, Nazi-Proofed, *Curio*	500	575	450
HSC NSDAP SA, .32 ACP, Nazi-Proofed, *Curio*	600	750	490
HSC Police, .32 ACP, Nazi-Proofed, *Curio*	300	375	310
HSC Swiss, .32 ACP, Nazi-Proofed, *Curio*	950	1,200	700
M 1896, 7.63 Mauser, 10 Shot, Conehammer, *Curio*	4,000	4,500	1,800
M 1896, 7.63 Mauser, 10 Shot, with Loading Lever, *Curio*	3,500	4,000	1,400
M 1896, 7.63 Mauser, Conehammer, with Shoulder Stock, *Curio*	4,300	4,800	2,100
M 1896, 7.63 Mauser, with Loading Lever, with Shoulder Stock, *Curio*	3,700	4,300	1,750
M 1896, 7.63 Mauser, with Loading Lever, Transitional, *Curio*	2,250	2,500	1,600
M 1896, 7.63 Mauser, Slabside, *Curio*	2,000	2,200	1,300
M 1896 (Early), 7.63 Mauser, Small Ring, *Curio*	2,000	2,400	1,325
M 1896 (Italian), 7.63 Mauser, Slabside, *Curio*	2,400	2,800	1,925
M 1896 Shallow Mill, 7.63 Mauser, with Loading Lever, *Curio*	1,600	1,750	1,150
M 1896 Turkish, 7.63 Mauser, Conehammer, *Curio*	5,000	5,800	2,600
M 1921, 9mm Luger, *Clip Fed, Curio*	1,250	1,500	4,650
M 1895, 7.65 Borchardt, *Antique*	8,500	9,500	3,550
M 1896, 6-Shot Model Add **75%–100%**			

	V.G.	Exc.	Prior Edition Exc. Value
M 1896, 20-Shot Model Add **50%–80%**			
M 1896, 40-Shot Model Add **100%**			
M 1896, Factory Engraving Add **300%**			
M 1896, Original Holster Stock Add **20%–35%**			
M 1896, 7.63 Mauser, Pre-War, Commercial, *Curio*	$1,250	$1,400	$1,175
M 1896 1920 Police, 7.63 Mauser, *Curio*	1,050	1,250	1,075
M 1896 Banner, 7.63 Mauser, *Curio*	2,000	2,250	1,500
M 1896 Bolo, 7.63 Mauser, Post-War, *Curio*	1,600	1,750	1,525
M 1896 French Police, 7.63 Mauser, *Curio*	1,500	1,750	2,100
M 1896 Persian, 7.63 Mauser, *Curio*	1,750	1,950	2,450
M 1896 WW I, 7.63 Mauser, Commercial, *Curio*	1,000	1,200	720
M 1896 WW I, 7.63 Mauser, Military, *Curio*	950	1,150	720
M 1896 WW I, 9mm Luger, Military, *Curio*	1,200	1,450	790
M 1906/08, 7.63 Mauser, Clip Fed, *Curio*	25,000	30,000	3,650
M 1910, .25 ACP, Clip Fed, *Curio*	300	350	230
M 1910/14, .25 ACP, Clip Fed, *Curio*	300	350	240
M 1910/34, .25 ACP, Clip Fed, *Modern*	300	350	370
M 1912, 9mm Luger, Clip Fed, *Curio*	17,500	20,000	2,750
M 1914 Humpback, .32 ACP, Long Barrel, Clip Fed, *Curio*	2,500	2,700	2,500
M 1914 Transition Humpback, .32 ACP, Clip Fed, *Curio*	2,000	2,200	2,000
M 1914 Late Humpback, .32 ACP, Clip Fed, *Curio*	1,800	2,000	1,800
M 1914 Early, .32 ACP, Clip Fed, *Curio*	300	375	310
M 1914 War Commercial, .32 ACP, Clip Fed, *Curio*	350	400	325
M 1914 Post-War, .32 ACP, Clip Fed, *Modern*	325	375	310
M 1914 Army, .32 ACP, Clip Fed, *Curio*	400	450	180
M 1914 Navy, .32 ACP, Clip Fed, *Curio*	725	800	375
M 1914/34, .32 ACP, Clip Fed, *Modern*	250	300	240
M 1930, 7.63 Mauser, Commercial, *Curio*	1,000	1,250	750
M 1930, 9mm Luger, Commercial, *Curio*	950	1,200	700
M 1934, .32 ACP, Clip Fed, *Modern*	375	425	230
M 1934 Navy, .32 ACP, Clip Fed, *Curio*	825	900	300
M 1934 Police, .32 ACP, Clip Fed, *Curio*	675	750	290

Mauser M 1914

Mauser M 78 Zig Zag

Mauser M1910

Mauser WTP

Mauser 1896 Conehammer

Mauser M 1896 WW I with Holster Stock

	V.G.	Exc.	Prior Edition Exc. Value
Parabellum PO 8, .30 Luger, 6" Barrel, Grip Safety, *Modern*.........	$600	$650	$545
Parabellum Model Carbine, 9mm Luger, 12" Barrel, Grip Safety, *Modern*..	4,500	5,500	2,450
Parabellum PO 8, .30 Luger, 4" Barrel, Grip Safety, *Modern*.........	575	625	565
Parabellum PO 8, 9mm Luger, Various Barrel Lengths, Grip Safety, *Modern*..	500	600	520
Parabellum Swiss, .30 Luger, 6" Barrel, Grip Safety, *Modern*........	450	550	475
Parabellum Swiss, 9mm Luger, 4" Barrel, Grip Safety, *Modern*.....	450	550	475
Parabellum Bulgarian, .30 Luger, Grip Safety, Commemorative, *Modern*...	1,000	1,500	1,800
Parabellum Russian, .30 Luger, Grip Safety, Commemorative, *Modern*...	1,000	1,500	1,800
Parabellum Kriegsmarine, 9mm Luger, Grip Safety, Commemorative, *Modern*...	2,300	3,000	3,000
Parabellum Sport, .30 or 9mm Luger, Heavy Barrel, Target Sights, *Modern*	1,200	1,500	1,400
W T P, .25 ACP, Clip Fed, *Modern*	400	450	400
W T P 2, .25 ACP, Clip Fed, *Modern*	375	425	425

RIFLE, BOLT ACTION

	V.G.	Exc.	Prior Edition Exc. Value
Various Calibers, Sporting Rifle, Set Trigger, Pre-WWI, Short Action, *Modern*...	2,500	3,250	620
Various Calibers, Sporting Rifle, Set Trigger, Pre-WWI, Carbine, Full-Stocked, *Modern*..	1,750	2,250	620
Various Calibers, Sporting Rifle, Pre-WWI, Military, Commercial, *Modern*...	1,500	1,750	410
Model 10 Varminter, .22-250 Post-War, Heavy Barrel, Monte Carlo Stock, Checkered Stock, *Modern*...	1,400	1,550	390
Model 2000, Various Calibers, Post-War, Monte Carlo Stock, Checkered Stock, *Modern*..	300	350	370
Model 3000, Various Calibers, Post-War, Monte Carlo Stock, *Modern*...	325	375	420
Model 3000, Various Calibers, Post-War, Left-Hand, Monte Carlo Stock, Checkered Stock, *Modern*...	325	400	430
Model 3000, Various Calibers, Post-War, Magnum Action, Monte Carlo Stock, Checkered Stock, *Modern*...................................	375	425	430
Model 3000, Various Calibers, Post-War, Left-Hand, Magnum Action, Monte Carlo Stock, Checkered Stock, *Modern*	425	475	445
Model 4000, Various Calibers, Varmint, Fancy Checkering, Flared, *Modern*...	350	400	440
Model 66S, Various Calibers, Post-War, Takedown, Monte Carlo Stock, Checkered Stock, *Modern*...	1,000	1,200	850
Model 66S Safari, Various Calibers, Post-War, Takedown, Monte Carlo Stock, Checkered Stock, Magnum, *Modern*	1,250	1,500	975
Model 98, Various Calibers, Sporting Rifle, Full-Stocked, Pre-WW2, Military, Commercial, *Modern*	325	375	420
Model A, Various Calibers, Sporting Rifle, Pre-WW2, Short Action, *Modern*..	3,250	3,500	630

	V.G.	Exc.	Prior Edition Exc. Value
Model A, Various Calibers, Sporting Rifle, Pre-WW2, Magnum Action, *Modern*..	$2,000	$2,500	$645
Model A British, Various Calibers, Sporting Rifle, Express Sights, Pre-WW2, *Modern*...	3,000	4,000	435
Model A British, Various Calibers, Sporting Rifle, Peep Sights, Pre-WW2, Octagon Barrel, Set Trigger, *Modern*.............................	2,800	4,500	670
Model B, Various Calibers, Sporting Rifle, Pre-WW2, Set Trigger, Express Sights, *Modern*..	2,250	2,500	480
Model B, Various Calibers, Sporting Rifle, Pre-WW2, Octagon Barrel, Set Trigger, *Modern*...	2,500	3,000	545
Model DSM 34, .22 L.R.R.F., Pre-WW2, Singleshot, Tangent Sights, Military Style, Stock, *Modern*	275	325	310
Model EL 320, .22 L.R.R.F., Pre-WW2, Singleshot, Sporting Rifle, Adjustable Sights, *Modern*..	225	275	230
Model EN 310, .22 L.R.R.F., Pre-WW2, Singleshot, Open Rear Sight, *Modern*	200	250	195
Model ES 340, .22 L.R.R.F., Pre-WW2, Singleshot, Tangent Sights, Sporting Rifle, *Modern*..	250	300	205
Model ES 340B, .22 L.R.R.F., Pre-WW2, Singleshot, Tangent Sights, Sporting Rifle, *Modern*..	250	300	250
Model ES 350, .22 L.R.R.F., Pre-WW2, Singleshot, Target Sights, Target Stock, *Modern*	400	450	370
Model ES 350B, .22 L.R.R.F., Pre-WW2, Singleshot, Target Sights, Target Stock, *Modern*	350	400	340
Model K, Various Calibers, Sporting Rifle, Pre-WW2, Short Action, *Modern*...	425	500	480
Model KKW, .22 L.R.R.F., Pre-WW2, Singleshot, Tangent Sights, Military Style Stock, *Modern*	350	400	375
Model M, Various Calibers, Express Sights, Carbine, *Modern*........	550	700	690
Model M, Various Calibers, Sporting Rifle, Pre-WW2, Full-Stocked, Tangent Sights, Carbine, *Modern*	450	500	480
Model MM 410, .22 L.R.R.F., Pre-WW2, 5 Shot Clip, Tangent Sights, Sporting Rifle, *Modern*	250	300	285
Model MM 410B, .22 L.R.R.F., Pre-WW2, 5 Shot Clip, Tangent Sights, Sporting Rifle, *Modern*	325	375	370
Model MS 350B, .22 L.R.R.F., Pre-WW2, 5 Shot Clip, Target Sights, Target Stock, *Modern*	400	450	435
Model MS 420, .22 L.R.R.F., Pre-WW2, 5 Shot Clip, Tangent Sights, Sporting Rifle, *Modern*	225	275	270
Model MS 420B, .22 L.R.R.F., Pre-WW2, 5 Shot Clip, Tangent Sights, Target Stock, *Modern*	350	400	390
Model S, Various Calibers, Sporting Rifle, Pre-WW2, Full-Stocked, Set Trigger, Carbine, *Modern*..	425	475	465
Standard, Various Calibers, Sporting Rifle, Set Trigger, Pre-WW1, *Modern*..	450	500	495

	V.G.	Exc.	Prior Edition Exc. Value

RIFLE, DOUBLE BARREL, OVER-UNDER

Model Aristocrat, .375 H & H Magnum, Fancy Checkering, Engraved, Open Rear Sight, Cheekpiece, Double Trigger, *Modern* ... $1,750 $2,000 $2,000

Model Aristocrat, Various Calibers, Fancy Checkering, Engraved, Open Rear Sight, Checkpiece, Double Trigger, *Modern* ... 1,250 1,500 1,500

RIFLE, SEMI-AUTOMATIC

M 1896, 7.63 Mauser, Carbine, *Curio* ... 4,000 4,500 4,500

SHOTGUN, BOLT ACTION

16 Gauge, *Modern* ... 100 125 135

SHOTGUN, DOUBLE BARREL, OVER-UNDER

Model 610, 12 Gauge, Trap Grade, Vent Rib, Checkered Stock, *Modern* ... 750 900 890

Model 610, 12 Gauge, Skeet Grade, with Conversion Kit, Vent Rib, Checkered Stock, *Modern* ... 1,500 1,600 1,550

Model 620, 12 Gauge, Automatic Ejector, Single Selective Trigger, Vent Rib, Fancy Wood, *Modern* ... 850 1,000 950

Model 620, 12 Gauge, Automatic Ejector, Single Trigger, Vent Rib, Fancy Wood, *Modern* ... 700 950 900

Model 620, 12 Gauge, Automatic Ejector, Double Trigger, Vent Rib, Fancy Wood, *Modern* ... 800 875 850

Model 71E, 12 Gauge, Field Grade, Double Trigger, Checkered Stock, *Modern* ... 325 375 370

Model 72E, 12 Gauge, Trap Grade, Checkered Stock, Light Engraving, *Modern* ... 450 500 495

Model 72E, 12 Gauge, Skeet Grade, Checkered Stock, Light Engraving, *Modern* ... 450 500 490

SHOTGUN, DOUBLE BARREL, SIDE-BY-SIDE

Model 496, 12 Gauge, Trap Grade, Vent Rib, Single Trigger, Checkered Stock, Box Lock, *Modern* ... 500 575 525

Model 545, 12 and 20 Gauges, Single Trigger, Recoil Pad, Checkered Stock, Box Lock, *Modern* ... 450 500 465

Model 580, 12 Gauge, Engraved, Fancy Checkering, Fancy Wood, *Modern* ... 800 975 900

SHOTGUN, SINGLESHOT

Model 496, 12 Gauge, Trap Grade, Engraved, Checkered Stock, *Modern* ... 500 550 490

Model 496 Competition, 12 Gauge, Trap Grade, Engraved, Fancy Wood, Fancy Checkering, *Modern* ... 650 725 675

MAYESCH Lancaster, Pa. 1760–1770. See Kentucky Rifles and Pistols.

	V.G.	Exc.	Prior Edition Exc. Value

MAYER & SOEHNE Arnsberg, W. Germany.
HANDGUN, REVOLVER

	V.G.	Exc.	Prior Edition Exc. Value
Target, .22 L.R.R.F., Break Top, 5 Shot, Target Sights, Double Action, *Modern*	$100	$125	$120

MAYOR, FRANCOIS Lausanne, Switzerland.
HANDGUN, SEMI-AUTOMATIC

Rochat, .25 ACP, Clip Fed, *Modern*	500	650	625

M.B. ASSOCIATES San Ramon, Calif.
HANDGUN, ROCKET PISTOL

Gyrojet, For Nickel Plating, *Add* **10%–15%**			
Gyrojet, For U.S. Property Stamping *Add* **75%–100%**			
Gyrojet Mark I Model A, Clip Fed, *Modern*	625	700	900
Gyrojet Mark I Model A Exp., Clip Fed, *Modern*	1,225	1,350	1,475
Gyrojet Mark II Model B, Clip Fed, *Modern*	600	650	750
Gyrojet Mark II Model B Exp., Clip Fed, *Modern*	8,000	1,000	1,265
Gyrojet Mark II Model B Snub, Clip Fed, *Modern*	575	650	825
Gyrojet Mark II Model C, Clip Fed, *Modern*	450	500	590
Gyrojet Mark II B, Clip Fed, Presentation Cased with Accessories, *Modern*	1,500	1,850	1,500

MCCOY, ALEXANDER Philadelphia, Pa. 1779. See Kentucky Rifles.

MCCOY, KESTER Lancaster, Pa. See Kentucky Rifles and Pistols.

MCCULLOUGH, GEORGE Lancaster, Pa. 1770–1773. See Kentucky Rifles.

MEIER, ADOLPHUS St. Louis, Mo. 1845–1850.
RIFLE, PERCUSSION

.58 Plains Type, Double Barrel, Side by Side, Half-Octagon Barrel, Rifled, Plain, *Antique*	1,750	2,000	1,900

MELIOR Liege, Belgium, Made by Robar et Cie. 1900–1959.
HANDGUN, SEMI-AUTOMATIC

New Model Pocket, .22 L.R.R.F., Clip Fed, *Modern*	150	175	195
New Model Pocket, .32 ACP, Clip Fed, *Modern*	125	150	170
New Model Pocket, .380 ACP, Clip Fed, *Modern*	150	175	190
New Model Vest Pocket, .22 Long R.F., Clip Fed, *Modern*	125	150	170
New Model Vest Pocket, .25 ACP, Clip Fed, *Modern*	150	175	170

	V.G.	Exc.	Prior Edition Exc. Value
Old Model Pocket, .32 ACP, Clip Fed, *Modern*	$150	$175	$180
Old Model Vest Pocket, .25 ACP, Clip Fed, *Modern*......................	150	175	180
Target, .22 L.R.R.F., Clip Fed, Long Barrel, *Modern*......................	200	250	240

MENDOZA Mexico City, Mexico.
HANDGUN, SINGLESHOT
K-62, .22 L.R.R.F., *Modern*	100	125	120

RIFLE, BOLT ACTION
Modelo Conejo, .22 L.R.R.F., 2 Shot, *Modern*	125	175	165

MENTA Made by August Menz, Suhl, Germany, c. 1916.
.25 ACP, Clip Fed, *Modern*..	350	400	450
.32 ACP, Clip Fed, Military, *Modern*..	200	250	240
.32 ACP, Clip Fed, Commercial, *Modern*.......................................	200	225	215

Menta .25

Menta .32

Menz Model I

	V.G.	Exc.	Prior Edition Exc. Value

MENZ, AUGUST Suhl, Germany 1912–1924.

HANDGUN, SEMI-AUTOMATIC

	V.G.	Exc.	Prior Edition Exc. Value
Lilliput, .25 ACP, Clip Fed. *Curio*	$300	$350	$275
Model I, .32 ACP, Clip Fed, *Curio*	250	300	295
Model II, .32 ACP, Clip Fed, *Curio*	300	350	345
Model III, .32 ACP, Clip Fed, Hammer, *Curio*	325	400	355
P & B Special, .32 ACP, Clip Fed, Hammer, Double Action, *Curio*	500	575	550
P & B Special, .380 ACP, Clip Fed, Hammer, Double Action, *Curio*	725	825	800

MERCURY Made by Robar et Cie., Liege, Belgium for Tradewinds.

HANDGUN, SEMI-AUTOMATIC

	V.G.	Exc.	Prior Edition Exc. Value
M 622 VP, .22 L.R.R.F., Clip Fed, *Modern*	100	300	155

SHOTGUN, DOUBLE BARREL, SIDE-BY-SIDE

	V.G.	Exc.	Prior Edition Exc. Value
Mercury, 10 Gauge 3", Hammerless, Magnum, Checkered Stock, Double Trigger, *Modern*	170	350	265
Mercury, 12 and 20 Gauges, Hammerless, Magnum, Checkered Stock, Double Trigger, *Modern*	160	325	220

MERIDEN FIRE ARMS CO. Meriden, Conn. 1907–1909.

HANDGUN, REVOLVER

	V.G.	Exc.	Prior Edition Exc. Value
.38 S & W, 5 Shot, Top Break, Hammerless, Double Action, *Modern*	100	125	100

RIFLE, SINGLESHOT

	V.G.	Exc.	Prior Edition Exc. Value
Model 10, .22 L.R.R.F., *Modern*	50	75	70

RIFLE, SLIDE ACTION

	V.G.	Exc.	Prior Edition Exc. Value
Model 15, .22 L.R.R.F., Tube Feed, *Modern*	200	225	220

MERKEL Gebruder Merkel, Suhl, Germany, from 1920. After WW II, VEB Fahrzeug u. Jagdwaffenwerk Ernst Thalmann, Suhl, East Germany.

COMBINATION WEAPON, OVER-UNDER

	V.G.	Exc.	Prior Edition Exc. Value
Model 210, Various Calibers, Pre-WW2, Engraved, Checkered Stock, *Modern*	1,200	1,400	1,300
Model 210E, Various Calibers, Engraved, Checkered Stock, Automatic Ejector, *Modern*	1,400	1,650	1,450
Model 211, Various Calibers, Pre-WW2, Engraved, Checkered Stock, *Modern*	1,750	2,000	1,700
Model 211E, Various Calibers, Engraved, Checkered Stock, Automatic Ejector, *Modern*	2,000	2,250	1,800
Model 212, Various Calibers, Pre-WW2, Fancy Engraving, Fancy Checkering, *Modern*	2,000	2,200	1,800

	V.G.	Exc.	Prior Edition Exc. Value
Model 212E, Various Calibers, Pre-WW2, Fancy Engraving, Fancy Checkering, Automatic Ejector, *Modern*	$2,250	$2,500	$2,400
Model 213E, Various Calibers, Sidelock, Fancy Checkering, Fancy Engraving, Automatic Ejector, *Modern*	3,500	3,800	3,000
Model 214E, Various Calibers, Pre-WW2, Sidelock, Fancy Checkering, Fancy Engraving, Automatic Ejector, *Modern*	3,750	4,000	3,000
Model 310, Various Calibers, Pre-WW2, Engraved, Checkered Stock, *Modern*	2,100	2,400	1,850
Model 310E, Various Calibers, Pre-WW2, Engraved, Checkered Stock, Automatic Ejector, *Modern*	3,000	3,250	2,400
Model 311, Various Calibers, Pre-WW2, Fancy Engraving, Fancy Checkering, *Modern*	2,700	3,000	2,175
Model 311E, Various Calibers, Pre-WW2, Fancy Engraving, Fancy Checkering, Automatic Ejector, *Modern*	3,000	3,300	2,465
Model 312, Various Calibers, Pre-WW2, Fancy Engraving, Fancy Checkering, Automatic Ejector, *Modern*	3,200	3,600	2,800
Model 313, Various Calibers, Sidelock, Fancy Checkering, Fancy Engraving, Automatic Ejector, *Modern*	6,750	7,250	5,500
Model 314, Various Calibers, Sidelock, Fancy Checkering, Fancy Engraving, Automatic Ejector, *Modern*	9,500	10,750	7,375
Model 410, Various Calibers, Pre-WW2, Engraved, Checkered Stock, *Modern*	1,500	1,700	1,300
Model 410E, Various Calibers, Pre-WW2, Engraved, Checkered Stock, Automatic Ejector, *Modern*	1,750	2,000	1,400
Model 411, Various Calibers, Pre-WW2, Engraved, Checkered Stock, *Modern*	1,500	1,750	1,550
Model 411E, Various Calibers, Pre-WW2, Engraved, Checkered Stock, Automatic Ejector, *Modern*	1,800	2,100	1,700

COMBINATION WEAPON, DRILLING

	V.G.	Exc.	Prior
Model 142, Various Calibers, Pre-WW2, Double Trigger, Engraved, Checkered Stock, *Modern*	2,900	3,250	3,800
Model 144, Various Calibers, Pre-WW2, Double Trigger, Engraved, Checkered Stock, *Modern*	3,000	3,500	3,875
Model 145, Various Calibers, Pre-WW2, Double Trigger, Engraved, Checkered Stock, *Modern*	2,500	3,000	3,650

RIFLE, DOUBLE BARREL, OVER-UNDER

	V.G.	Exc.	Prior
Model 220, Various Calibers, Pre-WW2, Checkered Stock, Engraved, *Modern*	5,500	6,500	1,300
Model 220E, Various Calibers, Engraved, Checkered Stock, Automatic Ejector, *Modern*	7,000	8,000	1,400
Model 221, Various Calibers, Pre-WW2, Checkered Stock, Engraved, *Modern*	6,500	7,500	1,350
Model 221E, Various Calibers, Engraved, Checkered Stock, Automatic Ejector, *Modern*	7,500	9,000	1,925
Model 320, Various Calibers, Pre-WW2, Checkered Stock, Engraved, *Modern*	3,650	4,250	1,925

	V.G.	Exc.	Prior Edition Exc. Value
Model 320E, Various Calibers, Pre-WW2, Checkered Stock, Engraved, Automatic Ejector, *Modern*	$4,000	$4,500	$2,500
Model 321, Various Calibers, Pre-WW2, Fancy Engraving, Fancy Checkering, *Modern*	4,000	4,500	2,300
Model 321E, Various Calibers, Pre-WW2, Fancy Engraving, Fancy Checkering, Automatic Ejector, *Modern*	4,000	4,750	2,600
Model 322, Various Calibers, Pre-WW2, Fancy Engraving, Fancy Checkering, Automatic Ejector, *Modern*	5,000	5,650	2,775
Model 323, Various Calibers, Sidelock, Fancy Checkering, Fancy Engraving, Automatic Ejector, *Modern*	12,500	15,000	5,800
Model 324, Various Calibers, Sidelock, Fancy Checkering, Fancy Engraving, Automatic Ejector, *Modern*	15,000	20,000	7,500

SHOTGUN, DOUBLE BARREL, OVER-UNDER

	V.G.	Exc.	Prior Edition Exc. Value
Model 100, Various Gauges, Pre-WW2, Plain Barrel, Checkered Stock, *Modern*	900	1,100	750
Model 100, Various Gauges, Pre-WW2, Raised Matted Rib, Checkered Stock, *Modern*	1,000	1,200	800
Model 101, Various Gauges, Pre-WW2, Raised Matted Rib, Checkered Stock, Light Engraving, *Modern*	1,050	1,250	875
Model 101E, Various Gauges, Pre-WW2, Raised Matted Rib, Checkered Stock, Light Engraving, Automatic Ejector, *Modern*	1,100	1,350	975
Model 200, Various Gauges, Pre-WW2, Raised Matted Rib, Checkered Stock, Light Engraving, *Modern*	950	1,200	1,300
Model 200E, Various Gauges, Pre-WW2, Raised Matted Rib, Checkered Stock, Light Engraving, Automatic Ejector, *Modern*	1,300	1,600	1,700
Model 201, Various Gauges, Pre-WW2, Raised Matted Rib, Checkered Stock, Engraved, *Modern*	1,200	1,400	1,600
Model 201E, Various Gauges, Pre-WW2, Raised Matted Rib, Checkered Stock, Engraved, Automatic Ejector, *Modern*	1,250	1,500	1,875
Model 202, Various Gauges, Pre-WW2, Raised Matted Rib, Fancy Checkering, Fancy Engraving, *Modern*	1,950	2,200	1,900
Model 202E, Various Gauges, Pre-WW2, Raised Matted Rib, Fancy Checkering, Fancy Engraving, Automatic Ejector, *Modern*	2,250	2,600	2,500
Model 203E, Various Gauges, Sidelock, Fancy Checkering, Fancy Engraving, Automatic Ejector, *Modern*	2,650	3,000	3,300
Model 203E, Various Gauges, Sidelock, Single Selective Trigger, Automatic Ejector, Fancy Checkering, Fancy Engraving, *Modern*	3,150	3,500	4,700
Model 204E, Various Gauges, Pre-WW2, Sidelock, Fancy Checkering, Fancy Engraving, Automatic Ejector, *Modern*	4,250	4,700	3,500
Model 300, Various Gauges, Pre-WW2, Raised Matted Rib, Checkered Stock, Engraved, *Modern*	1,750	2,000	1,950
Model 300E, Various Gauges, Pre-WW2, Raised Matted Rib, Checkered Stock, Engraved, Automatic Ejector, *Modern*	1,950	2,200	2,500
Model 301, Various Gauges, Pre-WW2, Raised Matted Rib, Fancy Checkering, Engraved, *Modern*	3,500	4,000	2,400
Model 301E, Various Gauges, Pre-WW2, Raised Matted Rib, Fancy Checkering, Engraved, Automatic Ejector, *Modern*	4,500	5,000	2,600

	V.G.	Exc.	Prior Edition Exc. Value
Model 302, Various Gauges, Pre-WW2, Raised Matted Rib, Fancy Checkering, Fancy Engraving, Automatic Ejector, *Modern*..............	$7,250	$7,500	$3,150
Model 303E, Various Gauges, Sidelock, Single Selective Trigger, Automatic Ejector, Fancy Engraving, Fancy Checkering, *Modern*.......	9,500	11,000	5,700
Model 304E, Various Gauges, Sidelock, Single Selective Trigger, Automatic Ejector, Fancy Engraving, Fancy Checkering, *Modern*.......	9,000	12,000	7,500
Model 400, Various Gauges, Pre-WW2, Raised Matted Rib, Checkered Stock, Engraved, *Modern*	1,100	1,300	1,100
Model 400E, Various Gauges, Pre-WW2, Raised Matted Rib, Checkered Stock, Engraved, Automatic Ejector, *Modern*..................	1,200	1,400	1,350
Model 401, Various Gauges, Pre-WW2, Raised Matted Rib, Checkered Stock, Fancy Engraving, *Modern*	1,200	1,400	1,450
Model 401E, Various Gauges, Pre WW-2, Raised Matted Rib, Checkered Stock, Fancy Engraving, Automatic Ejector, *Modern*.....	1,250	1,550	1,650

SHOTGUN, DOUBLE BARREL, SIDE-BY-SIDE

	V.G.	Exc.	Prior Edition Exc. Value
Model 127, Various Gauges, Pre-WW2, Sidelock, Fancy Engraving, Fancy Checkering, Automatic Ejector, *Modern*..............	17,500	20,000	7,200
Model 130, Various Gauges, Pre-WW2, Fancy Engraving, Fancy Checkering, Automatic Ejector, *Modern*..	8,500	10,000	3,800
Model 147E, Various Gauges, Fancy Checkering, Fancy Engraving, *Modern*	1,250	1,400	1,150
Model 147E, Various Gauges, Fancy Checkering, Fancy Engraving, Single Selective Trigger, *Modern*	1,450	1,600	1,350
Model 147S, Various Gauges, Fancy Checkering, Fancy Engraving, Sidelock, *Modern*	3,250	3,600	2,550
Model 147S, Various Gauges, Fancy Checkering, Fancy Engraving, Sidelock, Single Selective Trigger, *Modern*	4,000	4,600	2,875
Model 47E, Various Gauges, Checkered Stock, Engraved, *Modern*...	850	1,000	875
Model 47E, Various Gauges, Single Selective Trigger, Checkered Stock, Engraved, *Modern*	950	1,100	1,025
Model 47S, Various Gauges, Sidelock, Checkered Stock, Engraved, *Modern*..	2,500	2,800	1,850
Model 47S, Various Gauges, Sidelock, Single Selective Trigger, Checkered Stock, Engraved, *Modern*	2,750	3,000	2,100

MERRILL CO. Formerly in Rockwell City, Iowa, now in Fullerton, Calif.

HANDGUN, SINGLESHOT

Sportsman, For Extra Barrel *Add* **$75.00–$110.00**

Sportsman, For Extra 14" Barrel and Dies *Add* $*125*.00–**$185.00**

Sportsman, Wrist Attachment *Add* **$15.00–$25.00**

	V.G.	Exc.	Prior Edition Exc. Value
Sportsman, Various Calibers, Target Pistol, Top Break, Adjustable Sights, Vent Rib, *Modern*...	350	450	270

	V.G.	Exc.	Prior Edition Exc. Value

MERRIMAC ARMS & MFG. CO. Newburyport, Mass. Absorbed by Brown Mfg. Co. Worcester, Mass. 1861–1866. Also see Ballard.

HANDGUN, SINGLESHOT

Southerner, .41 Short R.F., Derringer, Iron Frame, Light Engraving, *Antique*	$425	$475	$450

RIFLE, DOUBLE BARREL, SIDE-BY-SIDE

Various Calibers, Octagon Barrel, *Antique*	950	1,200	1,100

SHOTGUN, SINGLESHOT

20 Gauge, Falling Block, *Antique*	250	300	285

MERWIN & BRAY Worcester, Mass. 1864–1868. Became Merwin & Simpkins in 1868 and also Merwin-Taylor & Simpkins the same year, also within the same year became Merwin, Hulbert & Co. Also see Ballard, Merwin, Hulbert & Co.

HANDGUN, REVOLVER

.22 Short R.F., 7 Shot, Single Action, Solid Frame, Spur Trigger, *Antique*	150	200	185
.28 Cup Primed Cartridge, 6 Shot, Single Action, Spur Trigger, Solid Frame, *Antique*	150	200	190
.30 Cup Primed Cartridge, 6 Shot, Single Action, Spur Trigger, Solid Frame, *Antique*	175	225	200
.31 R.F., 6 Shot, Single Action, Solid Frame, Spur Trigger, *Antique*	125	175	170
.32 Short R.F., 6 Shot, Single Action, Solid Frame, Spur Trigger, *Antique*	125	175	180
.42 Cup Primed Cartridge, 6 Shot, Single Action, Spur Trigger, Solid Frame, *Antique*	200	250	240
.42 Cup Primed Cartridge, 6 Shot, Single Action, Spur Trigger, Solid Frame, 6" Barrel, *Antique*	375	425	400
"Navy", .32 Short R.F., 6 Shot, Single Action, Solid Frame, Finger-Rest Trigger Guard, *Antique*	400	475	450
"Navy", .38 Short R.F., 6 Shot, Single Action, Solid Frame, Finger-Rest Trigger Guard, *Antique*	475	550	500
"Original", .28 Cup Primed Cartridge, 6 Shot, Single Action, Spur Trigger, Tip-Up, *Antique*	600	675	665
"Original", .30 Cup Primed Cartridge, 6 Shot, Single Action, Spur Trigger, Tip-Up, *Antique*	650	725	700
"Original", .42 Cup Primed Cartridge, 6 Shot, Single Action, Spur Trigger, Tip-Up, *Antique*	700	775	765
"Original", Various Cup-Primed Calibers, Extra Cylinder, Percussion, *Add* **$95.00–$160.00**			
Reynolds, .25 Short R.F., 5 Shot, Single Action, Spur Trigger, 3" Barrel, *Antique*	175	200	185

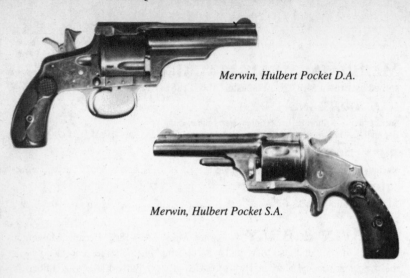

Merwin, Hulbert Pocket D.A.

Merwin, Hulbert Pocket S.A.

	V.G.	Exc.	Prior Edition Exc. Value

HANDGUN, SINGLESHOT

.32 Short R.F., Side-Swing Barrel, Brass Frame, 3" Barrel, Spur Trigger, *Antique* *$150* *$200* *$180*

MERWIN, HULBERT & CO. Successors to Merwin & Bray, et al. in 1868, and became Hulbert Bros. in 1892. Out of business in 1896.

HANDGUN, REVOLVER

Army Model, Extra Barrel, *Add* **$145.00–$200.00**

Army Model, "Safety Hammer", *Add* **$40.00–$65.00**

Army Model, .44-40 WCF, Belt Pistol, 7" Barrel, Double Action, Round Butt, 6 Shot, *Antique* 625 700 595

Army Model, .44-40 WCF, Belt Pistol, 7" Barrel, Single Action, Square Butt, 6 Shot, *Antique* 675 750 675

Army Model, .44-40 WCF, Pocket Pistol, 3¹/₂" Barrel, Double Action, Round Butt, 6 Shot, *Antique* 500 650 545

Army Model, .44-40 WCF, Pocket Pistol, 3¹/₂" Barrel, Single Action, Square-Butt, 6 Shot, *Antique* 600 675 565

Pocket Model, .32 S & W, 5 Shot, Double Action, *Antique* 225 250 275

Target Model, .32 S & W, 7 Shot, Double Action, *Antique* 225 275 325

MERVEILLEUX Rouchouse, Paris, France.

HANDGUN, MANUAL REPEATER

Palm Pistol, 6mm, Engraved, Nickel Plated, *Curio* 500 650 500

	V.G.	Exc.	Prior Edition Exc. Value

MESSERSMITH, JACOB Lancaster, Pa. 1779–1782. See Kentucky Rifles & Pistols.

METEOR Made by Stevens Arms.
RIFLE, BOLT ACTION
Model 52, .22 L.R.R.F., Singleshot, Takedown, *Modern* $25 $50 $50

METROPOLITAN Made by Crescent for Siegel Cooper Co., N.Y.C., c. 1900.
SHOTGUN, DOUBLE BARREL, SIDE-BY-SIDE
Various Gauges, Outside Hammers, Damascus Barrel, *Modern*	150	175	170
Various Gauges, Hammerless, Steel Barrel, *Modern*	175	200	190
Various Gauges, Hammerless, Damascus Barrel, *Modern*	150	175	170

SHOTGUN, SINGLESHOT
Various Gauges, Hammer, Steel Barrel, *Modern* 50 75 85

METROPOLITAN POLICE Made by Norwich Falls Pistol Co. Norwich, Conn., c. 1885.
HANDGUN, REVOLVER
.32 Short R.F., 5 Shot, Spur Trigger, Solid Frame, Single Action,
Antique 125 175 165

METZGER, J. Lancaster, Pa., c. 1728. See Kentucky Rifles.

MEUHIRTER, S. See Kentucky Rifles.

MEXICAN MILITARY
HANDGUN, SEMI-AUTOMATIC
Obregon, .45 ACP, Clip Fed, Military, *Modern* 325 375 375

RIFLE, BOLT ACTION
M1902 Mauser, 7mm, Military, *Modern*	150	175	180
M1936 Mauser, 7mm, Military, *Modern*	175	200	195

RIFLE, SEMI-AUTOMATIC
M1908 Mondragon, 7mm, Clip Fed, S.I.G., *Curio* 750 800 800

MIDLAND Imported from England by Jana International, c. 1973.
RIFLE, BOLT ACTION
Midland, Various Calibers, Checkered Stock, Open Sights,
Modern 225 275 265

	V.G.	Exc.	Prior Edition Exc. Value

MIIDA Tradename of Marubeni America Corp. on Japanese shotguns.

SHOTGUN, DOUBLE BARREL, OVER-UNDER

	V.G.	Exc.	Value
Model 2100, 12 Gauge, Skeet Grade, Checkered Stock, Engraved, Single Selective Trigger, Vent Rib, *Modern*	$800	$950	$495
Model 2200 S, 12 Gauge, Skeet Grade, Checkered Stock, Engraved, Single Selective Trigger, wide Vent Rib, *Modern*	900	1,050	585
Model 2200 T, 12 Gauge, Trap Grade, Checkered Stock, Engraved, Single Selective Trigger, Wide Vent Rib, *Modern*	1,000	1,150	650
Model 2300 S, 12 Gauge, Skeet Grade, Fancy Wood, Engraved, Single Selective Trigger, Vent Rib, *Modern*	1,100	1,300	650
Model 2300 T, 12 Gauge, Trap Grade, Fancy Wood, Engraved, Single Selective Trigger, Vent Rib, *Modern*	1,250	1,400	700
Model 612, 12 Gauge, Field Grade, Checkered Stock, Light Engraving, Single Selective Trigger, Vent Rib, *Modern*	700	850	500
Model Grandee, 12 Gauge, Fancy Engraving, Fancy Wood, Gold Inlays, Single Selective Trigger, Vent Rib, *Modern*	1,750	2,000	1,450

MIKROS Tradename of Manufacture D'Armes Des Pyrenees, Heydaye, France, 1934–1939, 1958 to date.

HANDGUN, SEMI-AUTOMATIC

	V.G.	Exc.	Value
.25 ACP, Clip Fed, Magazine Disconnect, *Modern*	150	175	170
.32 ACP, Clip Fed, Magazine Disconncet, *Modern*	150	175	170
KE, .22 Short R.F., Clip Fed, Hammer, Magazine Disconnect, 2" Barrel, *Modern*	125	150	140
KE, .22 Short R.F., Clip Fed, Hammer, Magazine Disconnect, 4" Barrel, *Modern*	125	150	145
KE, .22 Short R.F., Clip Fed, Hammer, Magazine Disconnect, 2" Barrel, Lightweight, *Modern*	100	125	130
KE, .22 Short R.F., Clip Fed, Hammer, Magazine Disconnect, 4" Barrel, Lightweight, *Modern*	100	125	125
KN, .25 ACP, Clip Fed, Hammer, Magazine Disconnect, 2" Barrel, *Modern*	100	125	125
KN, .25 ACP, Clip Fed, Hammer, Magazine Disconnect, 2" Barrel, Lightweight, *Modern*	100	125	130

MILITARY Retolaza Hermanos, Eibar, Spain, c. 1915

HANDGUN, SEMI-AUTOMATIC

	V.G.	Exc.	Value
Model 1914, .32 ACP, Clip Fed, *Modern*	125	150	145

MILLER, MATHIAS Easton, Pa. 1771–1788. See Kentucky Rifles.

MILLS, BENJAMIN Charlottesville, N.C. 1784–1790, 1790–1814 at Harrodsburg, Ky. See Kentucky Rifles, U.S. Military.

	V.G.	Exc.	Prior Edition Exc. Value

MINNEAPOLIS FIREARMS CO. Minneapolis, Minn., c. 1883.

HANDGUN, PALM PISTOL

	V.G.	Exc.	Prior Edition Value
The Protector, .32 Extra Short R.F., Nickel Plated, *Antique*	$675	$825	$600

MIQUELET-LOCK, UNKNOWN MAKER

HANDGUN, MIQUELET-LOCK

	V.G.	Exc.	Value
.52 Arabian, Holster Pistol, Tapered Round Barrel, Low Quality, *Antique*	300	350	350
.55, Russian Cossack Type, Tapered Round Barrel, Steel Furniture, Silver Furniture, *Antique*	600	850	825
Central Italian 1700's, Holster Pistol, Brass Furniture, Brass Overlay Stock, Medium Quality, *Antique*	2,250	2,500	2,400
Pair Late 1700's, Pocket Pistol, Medium Quality, Brass Furniture, Light Ornamentation, *Antique*	1,750	2,000	1,650
Pair Spanish Late 1600's, Belt Hook, Brass Overlay Stock, High Quality, *Antique*	17,500	20,000	20,000
Pair Cominazzo Early 1700's, Steel Inlay, Medium Quality, Holster Pistol, *Antique*	3,250	3,500	3,500
Ripoll Type Late 1600's, Blunderbuss, Brass Inlay, *Antique*	4,250	4,500	4,350
Ripoll Type Late 1600's, Blunderbuss, Silver Inlay, *Antique*..........	7,000	7,500	7,250

RIFLE, MIQUELET-LOCK

	V.G.	Exc.	Value
Mid-Eastern, Gold Inlays, Cannon Barrel, Front & Rear Bead Sights, Silver Overlay Stock, Silver Furniture, *Antique*	3,500	3,750	3,600
Mid-Eastern 1700's, Damascus Barrel, Gold Inlays, Many Semi-Precious Gem Inlays, Silver Furniture, Ornate, *Antique*	6,500	7,500	7,000

MIROKU Tokyo, Japan.

HANDGUN, REVOLVER

	V.G.	Exc.	Value
Model 6, .38 Spec., Double Action, Swing-Out Cylinder, *Modern*	125	150	130

RIFLE, LEVER ACTION

	V.G.	Exc.	Value
Center Fire, Various Calibers, Checkered Stock, Clip Fed, *Modern*	200	225	235
.22 L.R.R.F., Tube Feed, Plain, *Modern*	225	250	240

RIFLE, SEMI-AUTOMATIC

	V.G.	Exc.	Value
.22 L.R.R.F., Takedown, Tube Feed Through Butt, *Modern*	175	200	180

RIFLE, SINGLESHOT

	V.G.	Exc.	Value
Model 78, Various Calibers, Checkered Stock, Falling Block, *Modern*	325	350	325

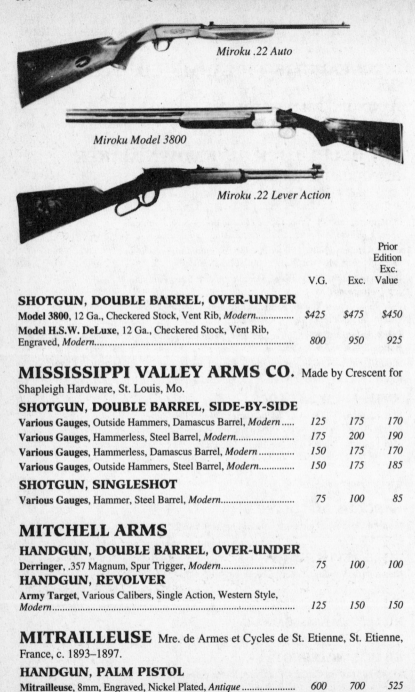

Miroku .22 Auto

Miroku Model 3800

Miroku .22 Lever Action

	V.G.	Exc.	Prior Edition Exc. Value
SHOTGUN, DOUBLE BARREL, OVER-UNDER			
Model 3800, 12 Ga., Checkered Stock, Vent Rib, *Modern*...............	$425	$475	$450
Model H.S.W. DeLuxe, 12 Ga., Checkered Stock, Vent Rib, Engraved, *Modern*..	800	950	925

MISSISSIPPI VALLEY ARMS CO. Made by Crescent for
Shapleigh Hardware, St. Louis, Mo.

SHOTGUN, DOUBLE BARREL, SIDE-BY-SIDE

	V.G.	Exc.	Prior Edition Exc. Value
Various Gauges, Outside Hammers, Damascus Barrel, *Modern*	125	175	170
Various Gauges, Hammerless, Steel Barrel, *Modern*.......................	175	200	190
Various Gauges, Hammerless, Damascus Barrel, *Modern*	150	175	170
Various Gauges, Outside Hammers, Steel Barrel, *Modern*..............	150	175	185

SHOTGUN, SINGLESHOT

	V.G.	Exc.	Prior Edition Exc. Value
Various Gauges, Hammer, Steel Barrel, *Modern*............................	75	100	85

MITCHELL ARMS

HANDGUN, DOUBLE BARREL, OVER-UNDER

	V.G.	Exc.	Prior Edition Exc. Value
Derringer, .357 Magnum, Spur Trigger, *Modern*............................	75	100	100

HANDGUN, REVOLVER

	V.G.	Exc.	Prior Edition Exc. Value
Army Target, Various Calibers, Single Action, Western Style, *Modern*..	125	150	150

MITRAILLEUSE Mre. de Armes et Cycles de St. Etienne, St. Etienne,
France, c. 1893–1897.

HANDGUN, PALM PISTOL

	V.G.	Exc.	Prior Edition Exc. Value
Mitrailleuse, 8mm, Engraved, Nickel Plated, *Antique*	600	700	525

	V.G.	Exc.	Prior Edition Exc. Value

MOHAWK Made by Crescent for Blish, Mize & Stillman, c. 1900.

SHOTGUN, DOUBLE BARREL, SIDE-BY-SIDE

	V.G.	Exc.	Prior
Various Gauges, Outside Hammers, Damascus Barrel, *Modern*	$150	$175	$170
Various Gauges, Hammerless, Steel Barrel, *Modern*	175	200	190
Various Gauges, Hammerless, Damascus Barrel, *Modern*	150	175	170
Various Gauges, Outside Hammers, Steel Barrel, *Modern*	150	175	185

SHOTGUN, SINGLESHOT

	V.G.	Exc.	Prior
Various Gauges, Hammer, Steel Barrel, *Modern*	75	100	85

MOLL, DAVID Hellerstown, Pa. 1814–1833. See Kentucky Rifles.

MOLL, JOHN Hellerstown, PA 1770–1794. See Kentucky Rifles.

MOLL, JOHN III Hellerstown, PA 1824–1863. See Kentucky Rifles.

MOLL, JOHN, JR. Hellerstown, Pa. 1794–1824. See Kentucky Rifles.

MOLL, PETER Hellerstown, Pa. 1804–1833 with Brother John Moll Jr. Made Some of the Finest Kentucky Rifles in Pa. See Kentucky Rifles.

MONARCH Maker Unknown c. 1880

HANDGUN, REVOLVER

	V.G.	Exc.	Prior
.32 Short R.F., 5 Shot, Spur Trigger, Solid Frame, Single Action, *Antique*	100	150	165

MONARCH Made by Hopkins & Allen, c. 1880.

HANDGUN, REVOLVER

	V.G.	Exc.	Prior
#1, .22 Short R.F., 7 Shot, Spur Trigger, Solid Frame, Single Action, *Antique*	100	150	165
#2, .32 Short R.F., 5 Shot, Spur Trigger, Solid Frame, Single Action, *Antique*	125	175	170
#3, .38 Short R.F., 5 Shot, Spur Trigger, Solid Frame, Single Action, *Antique*	125	175	175
#4, .41 Short R.F., 5 Shot, Spur Trigger, Solid Frame, Single Action, *Antique*	175	200	190

MONDIAL Gaspar Arrizaga, Eibar, Spain.

HANDGUN, SEMI-AUTOMATIC

	V.G.	Exc.	Prior
Model 1, .25 ACP, Clip Fed, Grip Safety, Magazine Disconnect, *Modern*	200	250	250
Model 2, .25 ACP, Clip Fed, Blue, *Modern*	150	200	190

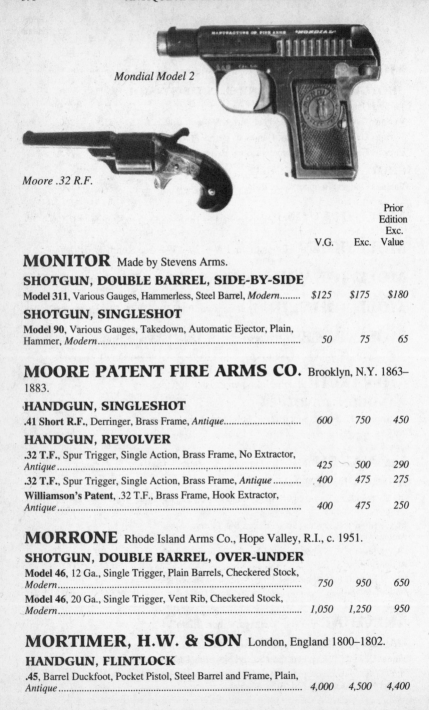

Mondial Model 2

Moore .32 R.F.

	V.G.	Exc.	Prior Edition Exc. Value
MONITOR Made by Stevens Arms.			
SHOTGUN, DOUBLE BARREL, SIDE-BY-SIDE			
Model 311, Various Gauges, Hammerless, Steel Barrel, *Modern*........	$125	$175	$180
SHOTGUN, SINGLESHOT			
Model 90, Various Gauges, Takedown, Automatic Ejector, Plain, Hammer, *Modern*.............	50	75	65
MOORE PATENT FIRE ARMS CO. Brooklyn, N.Y. 1863–1883.			
HANDGUN, SINGLESHOT			
.41 Short R.F., Derringer, Brass Frame, *Antique*.............	600	750	450
HANDGUN, REVOLVER			
.32 T.F., Spur Trigger, Single Action, Brass Frame, No Extractor, *Antique*.............	425	500	290
.32 T.F., Spur Trigger, Single Action, Brass Frame, *Antique*...........	400	475	275
Williamson's Patent, .32 T.F., Brass Frame, Hook Extractor, *Antique*.............	400	475	250
MORRONE Rhode Island Arms Co., Hope Valley, R.I., c. 1951.			
SHOTGUN, DOUBLE BARREL, OVER-UNDER			
Model 46, 12 Ga., Single Trigger, Plain Barrels, Checkered Stock, *Modern*.............	750	950	650
Model 46, 20 Ga., Single Trigger, Vent Rib, Checkered Stock, *Modern*.............	1,050	1,250	950
MORTIMER, H.W. & SON London, England 1800–1802.			
HANDGUN, FLINTLOCK			
.45, Barrel Duckfoot, Pocket Pistol, Steel Barrel and Frame, Plain, *Antique*.............	4,000	4,500	4,400

	V.G.	Exc.	Prior Edition Exc. Value

MOSSBERG, O.F. & SONS New Haven, Conn. 1919 to date.
Fitchburg & Chicopee Falls, Mass, 1892–1919 as Oscar F. Mossberg.

HANDGUN, MANUAL REPEATER

	V.G.	Exc.	Prior Edition Exc. Value
Brownie, .22 L.R.R.F., Top Break, Double Action, Rotating Firing Pin, 4 Barrels, 4 Shot, *Modern*........................	$160	$275	$245

HANDGUN, REVOLVER

	V.G.	Exc.	Prior Edition Exc. Value
Abilene, .357 Mag., Single Action, Western Style, Adjustable Sights, Various Barrel Lengths, *Modern*	175	225	220
Abilene, .44 Mag., Single Action, Western Style, Adjustable Sights, Various Barrel Lengths, *Modern*	200	250	230
Abilene Silhouette, .357 Mag., Single Action, Western Style, Adjustable Sights, 10" Barrel, *Modern*.............................	225	275	260

RIFLE, BOLT ACTION

	V.G.	Exc.	Prior Edition Exc. Value
Model 10, .22 L.R.R.F., Singleshot, Takedown, *Modern*	50	75	63
Model 14, .22 L.R.R.F., Singleshot, Takedown, Peep Sights, *Modern*...	50	75	68
Model 140B, .22 L.R.R.F., Clip Fed, Peep Sights, Monte Carlo Stock, *Modern*..	75	100	80
Model 140K, .22 L.R.R.F., Clip Fed, Open Rear Sight, Monte Carlo Stock, *Modern*..	75	100	75
Model 142A, .22 L.R.R.F., Clip Fed, Peep Sights, *Modern*	75	100	85
Model 142A, .22 L.R.R.F., Clip Fed, Carbine, Monte Carlo Stock, Peep Sights, *Modern*	75	100	85
Model 142K, .22 L.R.R.F., Clip Fed, Open Rear Sight, *Modern*	75	100	85
Model 142K, .22 L.R.R.F., Clip Fed, Carbine, Monte Carlo Stock, *Modern*...	50	75	68
Model 144, .22 L.R.R.F., Clip Fed, Heavy Barrel, Target Stock, Target Sights, *Modern*	100	125	125
Model 144LS, .22 L.R.R.F., Clip Fed, Heavy Barrel, Lyman Sights, Target Stock, *Modern*...	125	150	135
Model 146B, .22 L.R.R.F., Takedown, Tube Feed, Monte Carlo Stock, Peep Sights, *Modern*...	75	100	85
Model 20, .22 L.R.R.F., Singleshot, Takedown, *Modern*	50	75	68
Model 25, .22 L.R.R.F., Singleshot, Takedown, Peep Sights, *Modern*...	50	75	68
Model 25A, .22 L.R.R.F., Singleshot, Takedown, Peep Sights, *Modern*...	75	100	75
Model 26B, .22 L.R.R.F., Singleshot, Takedown, Peep Sights, *Modern*...	50	75	63
Model 26C, .22 L.R.R.F., Singleshot, Takedown, Open Rear Sight, *Modern*...	50	75	60
Model 30, .22 L.R.R.F., Singleshot, Takedown, Peep Sights, *Modern*...	50	75	68
Model 320B, .22 L.R.R.F., Singleshot, Peep Sights, *Modern*..........	75	100	75
Model 320K, .22 L.R.R.F., Singleshot, Open Rear Sight, Monte Carlo Stock, *Modern*...	50	75	60

Mossberg Abilene, .357 Magnum

Mossberg Abilene, .44 Magnum

Mossberg 395 K, 12 Gauge

	V.G.	Exc.	Prior Edition Exc. Value
Model 321K, .22 L.R.R.F., Singleshot, Open Rear Sight, *Modern*	$50	$75	$53
Model 340B, .22 L.R.R.F., Clip Fed, Peep Sights, *Modern*..............	75	100	80
Model 340K, .22 L.R.R.F., Clip Fed, Open Rear Sight, *Modern*	50	75	68
Model 340M, .22 L.R.R.F., Clip Fed, Full-Stocked, Carbine, *Modern*..	100	125	90
Model 341, .22 L.R.R.F., Clip Fed, Open Rear Sight, *Modern*	75	100	75
Model 342K, .22 L.R.R.F., Clip Fed, Open Rear Sight, *Modern*	50	75	68
Model 346B, .22 L.R.R.F., Tube Feed, Peep Sights, Monte Carlo Stock, *Modern*...	75	100	85
Model 346K, .22 L.R.R.F., Tube Feed, Monte Carlo Stock, Open Rear Sight, *Modern*..	75	100	75
Model 352K, .22 L.R.R.F., Clip Fed, Monte Carlo Stock, Open Rear Sight, Carbine, *Modern*..	75	100	85
Model 450, .22 L.R.R.F., Tube Feed, Monte Carlo Stock, Checkered Stock, Open Rear Sight, *Modern*....................................	75	100	90
Model 432, .22 L.R.R.F., Tube Feed, Western Style, Carbine, *Modern*...	75	100	85
Model 50, .22 L.R.R.F., Takedown, Tube Feed, Open Rear Sight, *Modern*...	75	100	85
Model 51, .22 L.R.R.F., Takedown, Tube Feed, Peep Sight, *Modern*...	75	100	90
Model 51M, .22 L.R.R.F., Takedown, Tube Feed, Peep Sight, Full-Stocked, *Modern*...	75	100	90

RIFLE, SINGLESHOT

	V.G.	Exc.	Prior Edition Exc. Value
Model L, .22 L.R.R.F., Lever Action, Falling Block, Takedown, *Modern*...	250	300	225

RIFLE, SLIDE ACTION

	V.G.	Exc.	Prior Edition Exc. Value
Model K, .22 L.R.R.F., Takedown, Tube Feed, Hammerless, *Modern*...	125	150	90
Model M, .22 L.R.R.F., Takedown, Tube Feed, Hammerless, Octagon Barrel, *Modern* ..../.....	125	175	120

RIFLE, LEVER ACTION

	V.G.	Exc.	Prior Edition Exc. Value
Model 400, .22 L.R.R.F., Tube Feed, Open Rear Sight, *Modern*	125	150	85
Model 402, .22 L.R.R.F., Tube Feed, Open Rear Sight, Monte Carlo Stock, *Modern*..	125	150	90
Model 472C, Various Calibers, Straight Grip, Tube Feed, Open Rear Sight, Carbine, *Modern*..	150	200	140
Model 472P, Various Calibers, Pistol-Grip Stock, Tube Feed, Open Rear Sight, Carbine, *Modern*...	125	175	135
RM-7, Various Calibers, Open Sights, *Modern*	175	225	190

RIFLE, SEMI-AUTOMATIC

	V.G.	Exc.	Prior Edition Exc. Value
Model 151K, .22 L.R.R.F., Takedown, Tube Feed, Open Rear Sight, *Modern*	100	125	90
Model 151M, .22 L.R.R.F., Takedown, Tube Feed, Peep Sights, Full-Stocked, *Modern*...	100	125	90

	V.G.	Exc.	Prior Edition Exc. Value
Model 152, .22 L.R.R.F., Clip Fed, Monte Carlo Stock, Peep Sights, Carbine, *Modern*	$100	$125	$90
Model 152K, .22 L.R.R.F., Clip Fed, Monte Carlo Stock, Open Rear Sight, Carbine, *Modern*	125	150	95
Model 350K, .22 L.R.R.F., Clip Fed, Monte Carlo Stock, Open Rear Sight, *Modern*	100	125	90
Model 351C, .22 L.R.R.F., Tube Feed, Monte Carlo Stock, Open Rear Sight, Carbine, *Modern*	100	125	90
Model 351K, .22 L.R.R.F., Tube Feed, Monte Carlo Stock, Open Rear Sight, *Modern*	100	100	80
Model 35, .22 L.R.R.F., Singleshot, Target Stock, Target Sights, *Modern*	175	225	130
Model 35A, .22 L.R.R.F., Singleshot, Target Stock, Target Sights, *Modern*	200	250	125
Model 35A-LS, .22 L.R.R.F., Singleshot, Target Stock, Lyman Sights, *Modern*	225	275	130
Model 35B, .22 L.R.R.F., Singleshot, Target Sights, Heavy Barrel, Target Stock, *Modern*	200	225	125
Model 40, .22 L.R.R.F., Takedown, Tube Feed, Open Rear Sight, *Modern*	75	100	73
Model 42, .22 L.R.R.F., Takedown, Clip Fed, Open Rear Sight, *Modern*	75	100	73
Model 42A, .22 L.R.R.F., Takedown, Clip Fed, Peep Sights, *Modern*	75	100	73
Model 42B, .22 L.R.R.F., Takedown, 5 Shot Clip, Peep Sights, *Modern*	75	100	73
Model 42C, .22 L.R.R.F., Takedown, 5 Shot Clip, Open Rear Sight, *Modern*	75	100	73
Model 42M, .22 L.R.R.F., Takedown, Clip Fed, Full-Stocked, Peep Sights, *Modern*	100	125	85
Model 42MB (British), .22 L.R.R.F., Takedown, Clip Fed, Full-Stocked, Peep Sights, *Modern*	125	150	110
Model 43, .22 L.R.R.F., Clip Fed, Heavy Barrel, Target Sights, Target Stock, *Modern*	200	225	115
Model 44, .22 L.R.R.F., Takedown, Tube Feed, Open Rear Sight, *Modern*	100	125	80
Model 44 US, .22 L.R.R.F., Clip Fed, Target Sights, Target Stock, Heavy Barrel, *Modern*	150	200	145
Model 44B, .22 L.R.R.F., Target Stock, Clip Fed, Target Sights, *Modern*	200	225	130
Model 45, .22 L.R.R.F., Takedown, Tube Feed, Peep Sights, *Modern*	125	150	75
Model 45A, .22 L.R.R.F., Takedown, Tube Feed, Peep Sights, *Modern*	125	150	75
Model 45AC, .22 L.R.R.F., Takedown, Tube Feed, Open Rear Sight, *Modern*	100	125	75
Model 45B, .22 L.R.R.F., Takedown, Tube Feed, Open Rear Sight, *Modern*	100	125	80

	V.G.	Exc.	Prior Edition Exc. Value
Model 45B, .22 L.R.R.F., Takedown, Tube Feed, Open Rear Sight, *Modern*	$100	$125	$85
Model 45C, .22 L.R.R.F., Takedown, Tube Feed, no Sights, *Modern*	100	125	80
Model 46, .22 L.R.R.F., Takedown, Tube Feed, Peep Sights, *Modern*	125	150	95
Model 46A-LS, .22 L.R.R.F., Takedown, Tube Feed, Lyman Sights, *Modern*	175	200	110
Model 46AC, .22 L.R.R.F., Takedown, Tube Feed, Open Rear Sight, *Modern*	100	125	80
Model 46B, .22 L.R.R.F., Takedown, Tube Feed, Peep Sights, *Modern*	100	125	80
Model 46M, .22 L.R.R.F., Takedown, Tube Feed, Full-Stocked, Peep Sights, *Modern*	125	150	105
Model 46T, .22 L.R.R.F., Takedown, Tube Feed, Heavy Barrel, Target Stock, Peep Sights, *Modern*	150	175	105
Model 83D, .410 Ga., Takedown, 3 Shot, *Modern*	75	100	68
Model 85D, .20 Ga. Takedown, 3 Shot, Adjustable Choke, *Modern*	75	100	68

SHOTGUN, BOLT ACTION

	V.G.	Exc.	Prior Edition Exc. Value
Model 173, .410 Ga. Takedown, Singleshot, *Modern*	50	75	65
Model 173Y, .410 Ga., Clip Fed, Singleshot, *Modern*	50	75	65
Model 183D, .410 Ga., Takedown, 3 Shot, *Modern*	50	75	70
Model 183K, .410 Ga., Takedown, Adjustable Choke, Clip Fed, *Modern*	50	75	70
Model 183T, .410 Ga., Clip Fed, *Modern*	50	75	75
Model 185D, 20 Ga., Takedown, 3 Shot, *Modern*	50	75	70
Model 185K, 20 Ga., Takedown, 3 Shot, Adjustable Choke, *Modern*	50	75	70
Model 190D, 16 Ga., Takedown, Clip Fed, *Modern*	50	75	70
Model 190K, 16 Ga., Takedown, Adjustable Choke, Clip Fed, *Modern*	50	75	70
Model 195D, 12 Ga., Takedown, Clip Fed, *Modern*	50	75	75
Model 195K, 12 Ga., Takedown, Adjustable Choke, Clip Fed, *Modern*	50	75	75
Model 385K, 20 Ga., Clip Fed, Adjustable Choke, *Modern*	50	75	80
Model 385T, 20 Ga., Clip Fed, *Modern*	50	75	75
Model 390K, 16 Ga., Clip Fed, Adjustable Choke, *Modern*	50	75	80
Model 390T, 16 Ga., Clip Fed, *Modern*	50	75	75
Model 395K, 12 Ga. Mag. 3", Clip Fed, Adjustable Choke, *Modern*	50	75	80
Model 395S, 12 Ga. Mag. 3", Clip Fed, Open Rear Sight, *Modern*	50	75	80
Model 395T, 12 Ga., Clip Fed, *Modern*	50	75	75
Model 73, .410 Ga., Takedown, Singleshot, *Modern*	50	75	60

	V.G.	Exc.	Prior Edition Exc. Value
Model 800, Various Calibers, Open Rear Sight, Monte Carlo Stock, *Modern*	$175	$200	$190
Model 800D, Various Calibers, Monte Carlo Stock, Cheekpiece, Checkered Stock, Open Rear Sight, *Modern*	200	225	200
Model 800M, Various Calibers, Open Rear Sight, Full-Stocked, *Modern*	200	225	200
Model 800SM, Various Calibers, Scope Mounted, Monte Carlo Stock, *Modern*	225	250	230
Model 800V, Various Calibers, no Sights, Monte Carlo Stock, Heavy Barrel, *Modern*	200	225	200
Model 810, Various Calibers, Magnum Action, Open Rear Sight, Monte Carlo Stock, *Modern*	200	225	205
Model 810, Various Calibers, Open Rear Sight, Long Action, Monte Carlo Stock, *Modern*	200	225	205
Model B, .22 L.R.R.F., Singleshot, Takedown, *Modern*	50	75	50
Model L42A, .22 L.R.R.F., Takedown, Clip Fed, Peep Sights, Left-Hand, *Modern*	75	100	90
Model L43, .22 L.R.R.F., Clip Fed, Heavy Barrel, Target Sights, Target Stock, Left-Hand, *Modern*	125	150	135
Model L45A, .22 L.R.R.F., Takedown, Tube Feed, Peep Sights, *Modern*	100	125	90
Model L46A-LS, .22 L.R.R.F., Takedown, Tube Feed, Lyman Sights, Left-Hand, *Modern*	125	150	125
Model R, .22 L.R.R.F., Takedown, Tube Feed, Open Rear Sight, *Modern*	50	75	63

SHOTGUN, SLIDE ACTION

	V.G.	Exc.	Prior Edition Exc. Value
Cruiser, 12 Ga., One-Hand Grip, Nickel Plated, *Modern*	200	250	200
Model 200D, 12 Ga., Clip Fed, Adjustable Choke, *Modern*	100	125	95
Model 200K, 12 Ga., Clip Fed, Adjustable Choke, *Modern*	125	150	100
Model 500 Super, Checkered Stock, Vent Rib, *Modern*	150	200	185
Model 500A, 12 Ga. Mag. 3", Field Grade, *Modern*	125	175	160
Model 500AA, 12 Ga. Mag. 3", Trap Grade, *Modern*	200	225	195
Model 500AK, Field Grade, Adjustable Choke, *Modern*	150	200	165
Model 500AKR, Field Grade, Adjustable Choke, Vent Rib, *Modern*	175	225	175
Model 500AM, Field Grade, Magnum, *Modern*	125	175	155
Model 500AMR, Field Grade, Magnum, Vent Rib, *Modern*	150	175	165
Model 500AR, Field Grade, Vent Rib, *Modern*	150	175	160
Model 500AS, Field Grade, Open Rear Sight, *Modern*	150	200	170
Model 500ATR, Trap Grade, Vent Rib, *Modern*	175	200	190
Model 500AHTD, Trap Grade, High Vent Rib, with Choke Tubes, *Modern*	300	350	315
Model 500B, 16 Ga., Field Grade, *Modern*	175	200	160
Model 500BK, 16 Ga., Adjustable Choke, *Modern*	125	175	150
Model 500BS, 16 Ga., Open Rear Sight, *Modern*	125	175	155

	V.G.	Exc.	Prior Edition Exc. Value
Model 500C, 20 Ga., Field Grade, *Modern*	*$150*	*$175*	*$155*
Model 500CK, 20 Ga., Field Grade, Adjustable Choke, *Modern*	*125*	*175*	*160*
Model 500CKR, 20 Ga., Field Grade, Vent Rib, Adjustable Choke, *Modern*	*150*	*175*	*165*
Model 500CR, 20 Ga., Field Grade, Vent Rib, *Modern*	*150*	*175*	*160*
Model 500CS, 20 Ga., Field Grade, Open Rear Sight, *Modern*	*175*	*200*	*160*
Model 500E, .410 Ga., Field Grade, *Modern*	*150*	*175*	*150*
Model 500EK, .410 Ga., Field Grade, Adjustable Choke, *Modern*	*150*	*200*	*155*
Model 500EKR, .410 Ga., Field Grade, Vent Rib, Adjustable Choke, *Modern*	*120*	*175*	*175*
Model 500ER, .410 Ga., Field Grade, Vent Rib, *Modern*	*150*	*175*	*165*

MOSTER, GEO. Lancaster, Pa. 1771–1779. See Kentucky Rifles and Pistols.

M.R.I. Magnum Research, Inc., Minneapolis, Minn. Also see Israeli Military.

HANDGUN, SEMI-AUTOMATIC

Eagle, .357 Magnum, Clip Fed, Interchangeable Barrels, Gas Operated, Blue, *Modern*	*500*	*550*	*495*

M.S. Modesto Santos, Eibar, Spain, c. 1920.

HANDGUN, SEMI-AUTOMATIC

Model 1920, .25 ACP, Clip Fed, Blue, *Curio*	*100*	*125*	*135*
Action, .32 ACP, Clip Fed, Blue, *Curio*	*125*	*150*	*145*

MT. VERNON ARMS Belgium, c. 1900.

SHOTGUN, DOUBLE BARREL, SIDE-BY-SIDE

Various Gauges, Outside Hammers, Damascus Barrel, *Modern*	*150*	*175*	*170*
Various Gauges, Hammerless, Steel Barrel, *Modern*	*175*	*200*	*190*

M.R.I. Eagle

	V.G.	Exc.	Prior Edition Exc. Value
Various Gauges, Hammerless, Damascus Barrel, *Modern*	$150	$175	$170
Various Gauges, Outside Hammers, Steel Barrel, *Modern*..............	150	175	185
SHOTGUN, SINGLESHOT			
Various Gauges, Hammer, Steel Barrel, *Modern*............................	50	75	85

MOUNTAIN EAGLE Made by Hopkins & Allen, c. 1880.

HANDGUN, REVOLVER

.32 Short R.F., 5 Shot, Spur Trigger, Solid Frame, Single Action, *Antique*	100	150	165

MUGICA Jose Mugica, Eibar, Spain, tradename on Llama pistols. See Llama for equivilent models.

MUSGRAVE South Africa.

RIFLE, BOLT ACTION

Mk. III, Various Calibers, Checkered Stock, *Modern*	275	325	240
Valiant NR6, Various Calibers, Checkered Stock, *Modern*	250	300	215
Premier NR5, Various Calibers, Checkered Stock, *Modern*............	300	350	285

MUSKETEER Tradename used by Firearms International, Washington, D.C., c. 1968.

RIFLE, BOLT ACTION

Carbine, Various Calibers, Monte Carlo Stock, Checkered Stock, Sling Swivels, *Modern*..	300	325	230
Deluxe, Various Calibers, Monte Carlo Stock, Checkered Stock, Sling Swivels, *Modern*..	325	350	260
Sporter, Various Calibers, Monte Carlo Stock, Checkered Stock, Sling Swivels, *Modern*..	275	300	240
Mannlicher, Various Calibers, Full Stock, *Modern*	275	325	245

MUTTI, GEROLIMO Brescia, c. 1680.

HANDGUN, SNAPHAUNCE

Pair, Belt Pistol, Brass Mounts, Engraved, Ornate, *Antique*.............	10,000	15,000	14,450

MUTTI, GIESU Brescia, c. 1790.

HANDGUN, SNAPHAUNCE

Pair, Engraved, Belt Hook, Medium Ornamentation, *Antique*	7,500	10,000	10,000

N

		V.G.	Exc.	Prior Edition Exc. Value

NAPOLEON Made by Thomas Ryan, Jr., Pistol Mfg. Co., c. 1870–1876.

HANDGUN, REVOLVER

	V.G.	Exc.	Prior
.22 Short R.F., 7 Shot, Spur Trigger, Solid Frame, Single Action, Antique	$125	$150	$165
.32 Short R.F., 5 Shot, Spur Trigger, Solid Frame, Single Action, Antique	150	175	170

NATIONAL Made by Norwich Falls Pistol Co., c. 1880.

HANDGUN, REVOLVER

.32 Short R.F., 5 Shot, Spur Trigger, Solid Frame, Single Action, Antique	150	175	165
.38 Short R.F., 5 Shot, Spur Trigger, Solid Frame, Single Action, Antique	150	175	175

HANDGUN, SINGLESHOT

.41 Short R.F., Derringer, all Metal, Light Engraving, Antique	225	275	265

NATIONAL ARMS CO. Made by Crescent, c. 1900.

SHOTGUN, DOUBLE BARREL, SIDE-BY-SIDE

Various Gauges, Outside Hammers, Damascus Barrel, Modern	150	175	170
Various Gauges, Hammerless, Steel Barrel, Modern	175	200	190
Various Gauges, Hammerless, Damascus Barrel, Modern	125	150	170
Various Gauges, Outside Hammers, Steel Barrel, Modern	150	175	185

SHOTGUN, SINGLESHOT

Various Gauges, Hammer, Steel Barrel, Modern	50	75	85

NATIONAL ORDNANCE South El Monte, Calif.

RIFLE, BOLT ACTION

1903A3, .30-06 Springfield, Reweld, Military, Modern	125	150	135

RIFLE, SEMI-AUTOMATIC

Garand, .30-06 Springfield, Reweld, Military, Modern	400	450	445
M-1 Carbine, .30 Carbine, Clip Fed, Reweld, Modern	125	150	150

	V.G.	Exc.	Prior Edition Exc. Value
M-1 Carbine, .30 Carbine, Clip Fed, Folding Stock, Reweld, *Modern*	$150	$175	$160
Tanker Garand, .308 Win., Reweld, Military, *Modern*	400	450	440

NAVY ARMS Ridgefield, N.J.

Presentation Case Only, *Add* $15.00–$25.00
A Engraving Pistol, *Add* $75.00–$115.00
B Engraving Pistol, *Add* $95.00–$140.00
C Engraving Pistol, *Add* $195.00–$265.00
A Engraving Rifle, *Add* $95.00–$145.00
B Engraving Rifle, *Add* $155.00–$215.00
C Engraving Rifle, *Add* $365.00–$495.00
Tiffany Grips Only, *Add* $95.00–$155.00
Silver Plating, *Add* $65.00–$95.00

HANDGUN, FLINTLOCK

	V.G.	Exc.	Prior
.44 "Kentucky", Belt Pistol, Reproduction, Brass Furniture, *Antique*	75	100	95
.44 "Kentucky", Belt Pistol, Reproduction, Brass Furniture, Brass Barrel, *Antique*	75	100	95
.577 Scotch Black Watch, Military, Reproduction, Belt Pistol, all Metal, *Antique*	100	125	100
.69 M1763 Charleville, Military, Reproduction, Belt Pistol, *Antique*	225	250	245
.69 M1763 Charleville, Military, Reproduction, Belt Pistol, *Antique*	100	125	100
.69 M1777 Charleville, Military, Reproduction, Belt Pistol, *Antique*	100	125	100
.69 Tower, Military, Reproduction, Belt Pistol, *Antique*	25	50	48

HANDGUN, PERCUSSION

	V.G.	Exc.	Prior
.36 M1851 New Navy, Revolver, Reproduction, Brass Grip Frame, *Antique*	75	100	95
.36 M1851 New Navy, Revolver, Reproduction, Silver-Plated Grip Frame, *Antique*	75	100	95
.36 M1853, Revolver, Reproduction, Pocket Pistol, 4¹/₂" Barrel, *Antique*	75	100	95
.36 M1853, Revolver, Reproduction, Pocket Pistol, 5¹/₂" Barrel, *Antique*	75	100	95
.36 M1853, Revolver, Reproduction, Pocket Pistol, 6¹/₂" Barrel, *Antique*	75	100	95
.36 M1860 Reb, Revolver, Reproduction, Brass Frame, *Antique*	75	100	63
.36 M1860 Sheriff, Revolver, Reproduction, Brass Frame, *Antique*	75	100	63
.36 M1861, Revolver, Reproduction, Sheriff's Model, with Short Barrel, *Antique*	75	100	95

	V.G.	Exc.	Prior Edition Exc. Value
.36 M1861 Navy, Revolver, Reproduction, Fluted Cylinder, *Antique*	$75	$100	$95
.36 M1861 Navy, Revolver, Reproduction, Engraved Cylinder, *Antique*	75	100	90
.36 M1862 Police, Revolver, Reproduction, 5 Shot, Brass Grip Frame, Cased with Accessories, *Antique*	125	150	135
.36 M1862 Police, Revolver, Reproduction, 5 Shot, Brass Grip Frame, 4¹/₂" Barrel, *Antique*	75	100	90
.36 M1862 Police, Revolver, Reproduction, 5 Shot, Brass Grip Frame, 5¹/₂" Barrel, *Antique*	75	100	90
.36 M1862 Police, Revolver, Reproduction, 5 Shot, Brass Grip Frame, 6¹/₂" Barrel, *Antique*	75	100	90
.36 M1862 Police, Revolver, Reproduction, Fancy Engraving, Silver Plated, Gold Plated, *Antique*	450	500	490
.36 M1863, Revolver, Reproduction, Sheriff's Model, with Short Barrel, *Antique*	75	100	95
.36 Remington, Revolver, Reproduction, Target Pistol, Adjustable Sights, *Antique*	100	125	115
.36 Spiller & Burr, Revolver, Reproduction, Solid Frame, *Antique*	75	100	75
.44 "Kentucky", Belt Pistol, Reproduction, Brass Furniture, *Antique*	75	100	90
.44 "Kentucky", Belt Pistol, Reproduction, Brass Furniture, Brass Barrel, *Antique*	100	125	105
.44 First Model Dragoon, Revolver, Reproduction, Brass Grip Frame, *Antique*	100	125	115
.44 M1847 Walker, Revolver, Reproduction, Brass Grip Frame, *Antique*	125	150	125
.44 M1847 Walker, Revolver, Reproduction, Brass Grip Frame, Engraved, Gold Inlays, *Antique*	225	275	255
.44 M1860, Revolver, Reproduction, Sheriff's Model, with Short Barrel, *Antique*	75	100	95
.44 M1860 Army, Revolver, Reproduction, Fluted Cylinder, *Antique*	75	100	95
.44 M1860 Army, Revolver, Reproduction, Engraved Cylinder, *Antique*	75	100	95
.44 M1860 Reb, Revolver, Reproduction, Shoulder Stock Only	25	50	48
.44 M1860 Sheriff, Revolver, Reproduction, Brass Frame, *Antique*	50	75	63
.44 Remington, Revolver, Reproduction, Target Pistol, Adjustable Sights, *Antique*	125	150	125
.44 Remington, Revolver, Reproduction, Solid Frame, *Antique*	75	100	95
.44 Remington, Revolver, Reproduction, Stainless Steel, *Antique*	125	150	145
.44 Remington Army, Revolver, Reproduction, Nickel Plated, *Antique*	125	150	125
.44 Second Model, Dragoon, Revolver, Reproduction, Brass Grip Frame, *Antique*	100	125	115

	V.G.	Exc.	Prior Edition Exc. Value
.44 Third Model Dragoon, Revolver, Reproduction, Buntline, with Detachable Shoulder Stock, *Antique*	$175	$200	$180
.44 Third Model Dragoon, Revolver, Reproduction, Brass Grip Frame, *Antique*	125	150	125
.44 Third Model Dragoon, Revolver, Reproduction, Brass Grip Frame, with Detachable Shoulder Stock, *Antique*	150	175	170
.58 M1806, Harper's Ferry, Reproduction, Brass Furniture, Military, Belt Pistol, *Antique*	75	100	90
.58 M1855, Harper's Ferry, Reproduction, Holster Pistol, Military, with Detachable Shoulder Stock, *Antique*	125	150	130
.58 M1855, Harper's Ferry, Shoulder Stock Only	25	50	43

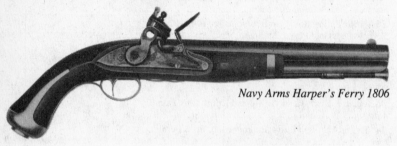

Navy Arms Harper's Ferry 1806

Navy Arms .44 Remington Target

Navy Arms .44 Remington Stainless

	V.G.	Exc.	Prior Edition Exc. Value

HANDGUN, REVOLVER

	V.G.	Exc.	Prior Edition Exc. Value
Frontier, Various Calibers, Color Case Hardened Frame, Single Action, Western Style, *Modern*	$150	$175	$155
Frontier Target, .357 Magnum, Color Case Hardened Frame, Single Action, Western Style, Adjustable Sights, with Detachable Shoulder Stock, *Modern*	200	225	210
Frontier Target, .45 Colt, Color Case Hardened Frame, Single Action, Western Style, Adjustable Sights, with Detachable Shoulder Stock, *Modern*	200	225	200
Frontier Target, Various Calibers, Color Case Hardened Frame, Single Action, Western Style, Adjustable Sights, *Modern*	150	175	155
M1875 Remington, .357 Magnum, Color Case Hardened Frame, Western Style, Single Action, *Modern*	150	175	160
M1875 Remington, .357 Magnum, Nickel Plated, Western Style, Single Action, *Modern*	175	200	185
M1875 Remington, .44-40 WCF, Color Case Hardened Frame, Western Style, Single Action, *Modern*	150	175	160
M1875 Remington, .44-40 WCF, Nickel Plated, Western Style, Single Action, *Modern*	150	175	165
M1875 Remington, .45 Colt, Color Case Hardened Frame, Western Style, Single Action, *Modern*	150	175	165
M1875 Remington, .45 Colt, Stainless Steel, Western Style, Single Action, *Modern*	175	200	180
M1875 Remington, .45 Colt, Nickel Plated, Western Style, Single Action, *Modern*	175	200	185

HANDGUN, SINGLESHOT

	V.G.	Exc.	Prior Edition Exc. Value
Rolling Block, .22 Hornet, Half-Octagon Barrel, Color Case Hardened Frame, Adjustable Sights, *Modern*	125	150	135
Rolling Block, .22 L.R.R.F., Half-Octagon Barrel, Color Case Hardened Frame, Adjustable Sights, *Modern*	100	125	105
Rolling Block, .357 Magnum, Half-Octagon Barrel, Color Case Hardened Frame, Adjustable Sights, *Modern*	125	150	130

RIFLE, BOLT ACTION

	V.G.	Exc.	Prior Edition Exc. Value
Mauser '98, .45-70 Government, Checkered Stock, *Modern*	125	150	145
Mauser '98, .45-70 Government, Carbine, Checkered Stock, *Modern*	125	150	145

RIFLE, FLINTLOCK

	V.G.	Exc.	Prior Edition Exc. Value
.45 "Kentucky", Long Rifle, Reproduction, Brass Furniture, *Antique*	150	175	170
.45 "Kentucky", Carbine, Reproduction, Brass Furniture, *Antique*	150	175	170
.58 M1803, Harper's Ferry, Reproduction, Brass Furniture, Military, *Antique*	175	200	180
.69 M1795 Springfield, Modern, Reproduction, Musket, *Antique*	200	250	240
.69 M1809 Springfield, Modern, Reproduction, Musket, *Antique*	225	250	240

	V.G.	Exc.	Prior Edition Exc. Value
.75 Brown Bess, Modern, Reproduction, Musket, *Antique*	$250	$300	$275
.75 Brown Bess, Modern, Reproduction, Carbine, *Antique*	250	300	275
.75 Brown Bess (Jap), Modern, Reproduction, Musket, *Antique*	225	250	200

RIFLE, LEVER ACTION

	V.G.	Exc.	Prior Edition Exc. Value
M1873 1 of 1000, .44-40 WCF, Blue Tube, Octagon Barrel, Steel Buttplate, Engraved, *Modern*	675	750	725
M1873-"101", .22 L.R.R.F., Color Case Hardened Frame, Tube Feed, Round Barrel, Steel Buttplate, Carbine, *Modern*	200	225	210
M1873-"101", .44-40 WCF, Color Case Hardened Frame, Tube Feed, Octagon Barrel, Steel Buttplate, *Modern*	225	250	235
M1873-"101", .44-40 WCF, Color Case Hardened Frame, Tube Feed, Round Barrel, Steel Buttplate, Carbine, *Modern*	200	225	210
M1873-"101", Trapper, .22 L.R.R.F., Color Case Hardened Frame, Tube Feed, Round Barrel, Steel Buttplate, *Modern*	200	225	210
M1873-"101", Trapper, .44-40 WCF, Color Case Hardened Frame, Tube Feed, Round Barrel, Steel Buttplate, *Modern*	200	225	210
Yellowboy, .22 L.R.R.F., Brass Frame, Tube Feed, Round Barrel, Brass Buttplate, Saddle-Ring Carbine, *Modern*	200	225	200
Yellowboy, .38 Special, Brass Frame, Tube Feed, Octagon Barrel, Brass Buttplate, *Modern*	200	225	210
Yellowboy, .38 Special, Brass Frame, Tube Feed, Round Barrel, Brass Buttplate, Saddle-Ring Carbine, *Modern*	175	200	200
Yellowboy, .44-40 WCF, Brass Frame, Tube Feed, Octagon Barrel, Brass Buttplate, *Modern*	200	225	210
Yellowboy, .44-40 WCF, Brass Frame, Tube Feed, Round Barrel, Brass Buttplate, Saddle-Ring Carbine, *Modern*	200	225	200
Yellowboy Trapper, .22 L.R.R.F., Brass Frame, Tube Feed, Round Barrel, Brass Buttplate, *Modern*	200	225	200
Yellowboy Trapper, .38 Special, Brass Frame, Tube Feed, Round Barrel, Brass Buttplate, *Modern*	200	225	200
Yellowboy Trapper, .44-40 WCF, Brass Frame, Tube Feed, Round Barrel, Brass Buttplate, *Modern*	200	225	200

RIFLE, PERCUSSION

	V.G.	Exc.	Prior Edition Exc. Value
.44 Remington, Revolver, Reproduction, Carbine, Brass Furniture, *Antique*	125	150	145
.45 "Kentucky", Long Rifle, Reproduction, Brass Furniture, *Antique*	150	175	160
.45 "Kentucky", Carbine, Reproduction, Brass Furniture, *Antique*	150	175	155
.45 "Kentucky", Carbine, Reproduction, Brass Furniture, *Antique*	150	175	160
.45 Hawken Hurricane, Octagon Barrel, Brass Furniture, Reproduction, *Antique*	150	200	175
.45 Morse, Octagon Barrel, Brass Frame, Reproduction, *Antique*	100	125	120
.50 Hawken Hurricane, Octagon Barrel, Brass Furniture, Reproduction, *Antique*	150	200	180

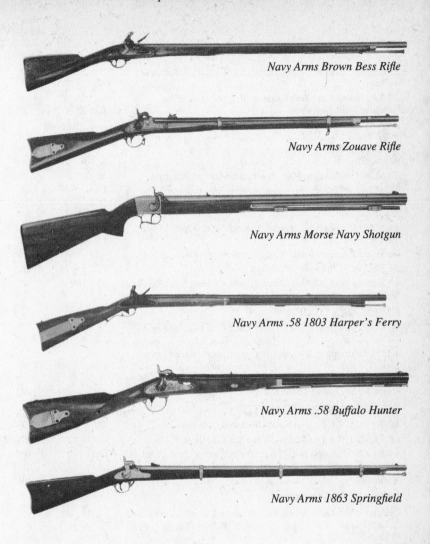

Navy Arms Brown Bess Rifle

Navy Arms Zouave Rifle

Navy Arms Morse Navy Shotgun

Navy Arms .58 1803 Harper's Ferry

Navy Arms .58 Buffalo Hunter

Navy Arms 1863 Springfield

	V.G.	Exc.	Prior Edition Exc. Value
.50 Morse, Octagon Barrel, Brass Frame, Reproduction, *Antique*	$125	$150	$125
.54 Gallagher, Carbine, Reproduction, Military, Steel Furniture, *Antique*	175	200	195
.577 M1853 3-Band, Military, Reproduction, Musket, (Parker-Hale) *Antique*	200	225	250
.577 M1858 2-Band, Military, Reproduction, Rifled, (Parker-Hale) *Antique*	175	200	190

	V.G.	Exc.	Prior Edition Exc. Value
.577 M1861, Military, Reproduction, Musketoon, (Parker-Hale) *Antique*	$175	$200	$190
.58 J.P. Murray Artillery Carbine, Reproduction, Brass Furniture, Military, *Antique*	150	175	145
.58 Buffalo Hunter, Round Barrel, Brass Furniture, Reproduction, *Antique*	150	175	160
.58 Hawken Hunter, Octagon Barrel, Brass Furniture, Reproduction, *Antique*	175	200	180
.58 M1841 Mississippi Rifle, Reproduction, Brass Furniture, Military, *Antique*	150	175	155
.58 M1863 Springfield, Military, Reproduction, Rifled, Musket, *Antique*	150	175	175
.58 M1864 Springfield, Military, Reproduction, Rifled, Musket, *Antique*	175	200	180
.58 Morse, Octagon Barrel, Brass Frame, Reproduction, *Antique*....	90	150	130
.58 Zouave, Military, Reproduction, *Antique*	150	175	150
.58 Zouave 1864, Military, Reproduction, Carbine, Brass Furniture, *Antique*	150	175	150

RIFLE, REVOLVER

	V.G.	Exc.	
M1875 Remington, .357 Magnum, Color Case Hardened Frame, Carbine, Single Action, Brass Furniture, *Modern*	175	200	190
M1875 Remington, .44-40 WCF, Color Case Hardened Frame, Carbine, Single Action, Brass Furniture, *Modern*	175	200	190
M1875 Remington, .45 Colt, Color Case Hardened Frame, Carbine, Single Action, Brass Furniture, *Modern*	175	200	190

RIFLE, SEMI-AUTOMATIC

AP-74, .22 L.R.R.F., Clip Fed, Plastic Stock, *Modern*	75	100	95
AP-74, .22 L.R.R.F., Clip Fed, Wood Stock, *Modern*	100	125	105
AP-74, .32 ACP, Clip Fed, Plastic Stock, *Modern*	100	125	105
AP-74 Commando, .22 L.R.R.F., Clip Fed, Wood Stock, *Modern*	75	100	105

RIFLE, SINGLESHOT

Buffalo, .45-70 Government, Rolling Block, Color Case Hardened Frame, Octagon Barrel, Open Rear Sight, Various Barrel Lengths, *Modern*	150	175	160
Buffalo, .45-70 Government, Rolling Block, Color Case Hardened Frame, Half-Octagon Barrel, Open Rear Sight, Various Barrel Lengths, *Modern*	150	175	155
Buffalo, .50 U.S. Carbine, Rolling Block, Color Case Hardened Frame, Octagon Barrel, Open Rear Sight, Various Barrel Lengths, *Modern*	150	175	150
Buffalo, .50 U.S. Carbine, Rolling Block, Color Case Hardened Frame, Half-Octagon Barrel, Open Rear Sight, Various Barrel Lengths, *Modern*	125	150	145
Creedmore, .45-70 Government, Rolling Block, Color Case Hardened Frame, Octagon Barrel, Vernier Sights, 30" Barrel, *Modern*	200	225	220

	V.G.	Exc.	Prior Edition Exc. Value
Creedmore, .45-70 Government, Rolling Block, Color Case Hardened Frame, Half-Octagon Barrel, Vernier Sights, 30" Barrel, *Modern*	$175	$200	$205
Creedmore, .50 U.S. Carbine, Rolling Block, Color Case Hardened Frame, Octagon Barrel, Vernier Sights, 30" Barrel, *Modern*	175	200	200
Creedmore, .50 U.S. Carbine, Rolling Block, Color Case Hardened Frame, Half-Octagon Barrel, Vernier Sights, 30" Barrel, *Modern*	175	200	195
Creedmore, .50-140 Sharps, Rolling Block, Color Case Hardened Frame, Octagon Barrel, Vernier Sights, 30" Barrel, *Modern*	200	225	200
Martini, .45-70 Government, Color Case Hardened Frame, Half-Octagon Barrel, Open Rear Sight, Checkered Stock, *Modern*	225	250	250
Martini, .45-70 Government, Color Case Hardened Frame, Octagon Barrel, Open Rear Sight, Checkered Stock, *Modern*	225	250	240
Rolling Block, .22 Hornet, Carbine, Color Case Hardened Frame, Adjustable Sights, *Modern*	150	175	150
Rolling Block, .22 L.R.R.F., Carbine, Color Case Hardened Frame, Adjustable Sights, *Modern*	125	150	145
Rolling Block, .357 Magnum, Carbine, Color Case Hardened Frame, Adjustable Sights, *Modern*	125	150	145

SHOTGUN, PERCUSSION

	V.G.	Exc.	Prior Edition Exc. Value
Magnum Deluxe, 12 Ga., Double Barrel, Side by Side, Reproduction, Outside Hammers, Checkered Stock, *Antique*	175	200	195
Morse/Navy, 12 Ga., Singleshot, Reproduction, Brass Frame, *Antique*	125	150	135
Upland Deluxe, .12 Ga., Double Barrel, Side by Side, Reproduction, Outside Hammers, Checkered Stock, *Antique*	125	150	135
Zouave, 12 Ga., Brass Furniture, Reproduction, *Antique*	125	150	140

NEIHARD, PETER Northhampton, Pa. 1785–1787. See Kentucky Rifles.

NERO Made by J. Rupertus Arms Co., c. 1880. Sold by E. Tryon Co.

HANDGUN, REVOLVER

	V.G.	Exc.	Prior Edition Exc. Value
.22 Short R.F., 7 Shot, Spur Trigger, Solid Frame, Single Action, *Antique*	150	175	170
.32 Short R.F., 5 Shot, Spur Trigger, Solid Frame, Single Action, *Antique*	175	200	175

NERO Made by Hopkins & Allen., c. 1880. Sold by C.L. Riker.

HANDGUN, REVOLVER

	V.G.	Exc.	Prior Edition Exc. Value
.22 Short R.F., 7 Shot, Spur Trigger, Solid Frame, Single Action, *Antique*	125	150	165
.32 Short R.F., 5 Shot, Spur Trigger, Solid Frame, Single Action, *Antique*	150	175	170

	V.G.	Exc.	Prior Edition Exc. Value

NEW CHIEFTAIN Made by Stevens Arms.

SHOTGUN, SINGLESHOT

Model 94, Various Gauges, Takedown, Automatic Ejector, Plain,
Hammer, *Modern* .... $50 | $75 | $65

NEW NAMBU Shin Chuo Kogyo, Tokyo, Japan, c. 1960.

HANDGUN, REVOLVER

Model 58, .38 Spec., Swing-Out Cylinder, Double Action,
Modern .... 100 | 125 | 120

HANDGUN, SEMI-AUTOMATIC

Model 57A, 9mm Luger, Clip Fed, Blue, *Modern* .... 175 | 200 | 210
Model 57B, .32 ACP, Clip Fed, Blue, *Modern* .... 150 | 175 | 185

NEW RIVAL Made by Crescent for Van Camp Hardware & Iron Co., Indianapolis, Ind.

SHOTGUN, DOUBLE BARREL, SIDE-BY-SIDE

Various Gauges, Outside Hammers, Damascus Barrel, *Modern* ..... 150 | 175 | 170
Various Gauges, Hammerless, Steel Barrel, *Modern* .... 175 | 200 | 190
Various Gauges, Hammerless, Damascus Barrel, *Modern* .... 150 | 175 | 170
Various Gauges, Outside Hammers, Steel Barrel, *Modern* .... 150 | 175 | 185

SHOTGUN, SINGLESHOT

Various Gauges, Hammer, Steel Barrel, *Modern* .... 50 | 75 | 85

NEW YORK ARMS CO. Made by Crescent for Garnet Carter Co. Tenn., c. 1900.

SHOTGUN, DOUBLE BARREL, SIDE-BY-SIDE

Various Gauges, Outside Hammers, Damascus Barrel, *Modern* ..... 150 | 175 | 170
Various Gauges, Hammerless, Steel Barrel, *Modern* .... 175 | 200 | 190
Various Gauges, Hammerless, Damascus Barrel, *Modern* .... 150 | 175 | 170
Various Gauges, Outside Hammers, Steel Barrel, *Modern* .... 175 | 200 | 185

SHOTGUN, SINGLESHOT

Various Gauges, Hammer, Steel Barrel, *Modern* .... 50 | 75 | 85

NEW YORK PISTOL CO. N.Y.C., c. 1870.

HANDGUN, REVOLVER

.22 Short R.F., 7 Shot, Spur Trigger, Solid Frame, Single Action,
Antique .... 150 | 175 | 165
.32 Short R.F., 5 Shot, Spur Trigger, Solid Frame, Single Action,
Antique .... 125 | 150 | 170

		Prior Edition Exc.
V.G.	Exc.	Value

NEWCOMER, JOHN Lancaster, Pa. 1770–1772. See Kentucky Rifles.

NEWHARDT, JACOB Allentown, Pa. 1770–1777. See Kentucky Rifles.

NEWPORT Made by Stevens Arms.

SHOTGUN, DOUBLE BARREL, SIDE-BY-SIDE
Model 311, Various Gauges, Hammerless, Steel Barrel,
Modern $150 $175 $180

NEWTON ARMS CO. Buffalo, N.Y. 1914–1918, reorganized 1918–1930 as Newton Rifle Corp.

RIFLE, BOLT ACTION
1st Type, Various Calibers, Sporting Rifle, Set Trigger, Checkered
Stock, Open Rear Sight, *Modern* 500   600   595
2nd Type, Various Calibers, Sporting Rifle, Set Trigger,
Checkered Stock, Open Rear Sight, *Modern* 550   650   650
Newton-Mauser, Various Calibers, Sporting Rifle, Set Trigger,
Checkered Stock, Open Rear Sight, *Modern* 450   525   500

NICHOLS, JOHN Oxford, England 1730–1775.

HANDGUN, FLINTLOCK
Holster Pistol, Engraved, Brass Furniture, High Quality, *Antique* 3,000   3,500   3,500

NIKKO SPORTING FIREARMS Japan Imported by Kanematsu-Gosho U.S.A. Inc., Arlington Heights, Ill.

RIFLE, BOLT ACTION
Model 7000, Various Calibers, Grade 1, Checkered Stock,
Modern 250   300   300
Model 7000, Various African Calibers, Grade 1, Checkered Stock,
Modern 300   350   350

SHOTGUN, DOUBLE BARREL, OVER-UNDER
Model 5000, 12 and 20 Gauges, Field Grade, Vent Rib, Checkered
Stock, Light Engraving, Gold Overlay, *Modern* 425   475   465
Model 5000, 12 and 20 Gauges, Skeet Grade, Vent Rib, Checkered
Stock, Light Engraving, Gold Overlay, *Modern* 500   575   560
Model 5000, 12 and 20 Gauges, Trap Grade, Vent Rib, Checkered
Stock, Light Engraving, Gold Overlay, *Modern* 525   575   560

Nikko Model 5000 Grandee

	V.G.	Exc.	Prior Edition Exc. Value
Model 5000, 12 and 20 Gauges, Field Grade 2, Vent Rib, Checkered Stock, Light Engraving, Gold Overlay, *Modern*	$525	$575	$560
Model 5000, 12 and 20 Gauges, Skeet Grade 2, Vent Rib, Checkered Stock, Light Engraving, Gold Overlay, *Modern*	550	600	600
Model 5000, 12 and 20 Gauges, Trap Grade 2, Vent Rib, Checkered Stock, Light Engraving, Gold Overlay, *Modern*	550	600	600
Model 5000 Grandee, 12 and 20 Gauges, Field Grade 3, Vent Rib, Checkered Stock, Fancy Engraving, Gold Overlay, *Modern*	1,750	2,000	2,000
Model 5000 Grandee, 12 and 20 Gauges, Skeet Grade 3, Vent Rib, Checkered Stock, Fancy Engraving, Gold Overlay, *Modern*	1,750	2,000	2,000
Model 5000 Grandee, 12 Ga., Trap Grade 3, Vent Rib, Checkered Stock, Fancy Engraving, Gold Overlay, *Modern*	1,750	2,000	2,000

NITRO PROOF Made by Stevens Arms.

SHOTGUN, SINGLESHOT

	V.G.	Exc.	Prior Edition Exc. Value
Model 115, Various Gauges, Hammer, Automatic Ejector, *Modern*	50	75	65

NIVA Kohout & Spolecnost, Kydne, Czechoslovakia.

HANDGUN, SEMI-AUTOMATIC

	V.G.	Exc.	Prior Edition Exc. Value
Niva, .25 ACP, Clip Fed, Blue, *Modern*..	175	200	200

NOBLE Haydenville, Mass. 1950–1971.

RIFLE, BOLT ACTION

	V.G.	Exc.	Prior Edition Exc. Value
.98 Mauser, .30-06 Springfield, Monte Carlo Stock, Open Rear Sight, *Modern*	100	125	145
Model 10, .22 L.R.R.F., Singleshot, *Modern*....................................	25	50	45
Model 20, .22 L.R.R.F., Singleshot, *Modern*....................................	25	50	45
Model 222, .22 L.R.R.F., Singleshot, *Modern*.................................	50	75	55

RIFLE, LEVER ACTION

	V.G.	Exc.	Prior Edition Exc. Value
Model 275, .22 L.R.R.F., Tube Fed, *Modern*....................................	50	75	80

RIFLE, SEMI-AUTOMATIC

	V.G.	Exc.	Prior Edition Exc. Value
Model 285, .22 L.R.R.F., Tube Fed, *Modern*....................................	75	100	85

RIFLE, SLIDE ACTION

	V.G.	Exc.	Prior Edition Exc. Value
Model 235, .22 L.R.R.F., Wood Stock, *Modern*	75	100	85
Model 33, .22 L.R.R.F., Plastic Stock, *Modern*	50	75	80
Model 33A, .22 L.R.R.F., Wood Stock, *Modern*	75	100	85

SHOTGUN, DOUBLE BARREL, SIDE-BY-SIDE

	V.G.	Exc.	Prior Edition Exc. Value
Model 420, Various Gauges, Hammerless, Checkered Stock, Recoil Pad, *Modern*	125	150	175

	V.G.	Exc.	Prior Edition Exc. Value
Model 420EK, Various Gauges, Hammerless, Checkered Stock, Recoil Pad, Fancy Wood, *Modern*	*$150*	*$175*	*$200*
Model 450E, Various Gauges, Hammerless, Checkered Stock, Recoil Pad, *Modern*	*200*	*250*	*290*

SHOTGUN, SEMI-AUTOMATIC

Model 80, .410 Ga., *Modern*	*100*	*150*	*155*

SHOTGUN, SLIDE ACTION

	V.G.	Exc.	Prior Ed.
Model 160 Deergun, 12 and 20 Gauges, Peep Sights, *Modern*	*75*	*125*	*150*
Model 166L Deergun, 12 and 16 Gauges, Peep Sights, *Modern*	*75*	*125*	*150*
Model 166LP Deergun, 12 and 16 Gauges, Peep Sights, *Modern*	*75*	*125*	*150*
Model 200, 20 Ga., Vent Rib, Adjustable Choke, *Modern*	*75*	*125*	*145*
Model 200, 20 Ga., Adjustable Choke, *Modern*	*75*	*125*	*145*
Model 200, 20 Ga., *Modern*	*75*	*125*	*140*
Model 200, 20 Ga., Trap Grade, *Modern*	*75*	*125*	*150*
Model 300, 12 Ga., Vent Rib, Adjustable Choke, *Modern*	*125*	*150*	*160*
Model 300, 12 Ga., Adjustable Choke, *Modern*	*75*	*125*	*145*
Model 300, 12 Ga., *Modern*	*75*	*125*	*145*
Model 300, 12 Ga., Trap Grade, *Modern*	*100*	*150*	*165*
Model 390, 12 Ga., Peep Sights, *Modern*	*75*	*125*	*145*
Model 40, 12 Ga., Hammerless, Solid Frame, Adjustable Choke, *Modern*	*75*	*125*	*135*
Model 400, .410 Ga., Skeet Grade, *Modern*	*75*	*125*	*140*
Model 400, .410 Ga., Adjustable Choke, *Modern*	*75*	*125*	*140*
Model 400, .410 Ga., Skeet Grade, Adjustable Choke, *Modern*	*100*	*150*	*155*
Model 400, .410 Ga., *Modern*	*75*	*125*	*140*
Model 50, 12 Ga., Hammerless, Solid Frame, *Modern*	*50*	*100*	*125*
Model 60, 12 and 16 Gauges, Hammerless, Solid Frame, Adjustable Choke, *Modern*	*75*	*125*	*130*
Model 602, 20 Ga., *Modern*	*75*	*125*	*140*
Model 602CLP, 20 Ga., Adjustable Choke, *Modern*	*75*	*125*	*145*
Model 602RCLP, 20 Ga., Adjustable Choke, Vent Rib, *Modern*	*100*	*150*	*155*
Model 602 RLP, 20 Ga., Vent Rib, *Modern*	*75*	*125*	*140*
Model 60ACP, 12 and 16 Gauges, Hammerless, Solid Frame, Adjustable Choke, Vent Rib, *Modern*	*75*	*125*	*130*
Model 60AF, 12 and 16 Gauges, Hammerless, Solid Frame, Vent Rib, Adjustable Choke, *Modern*	*75*	*125*	*135*
Model 60 RCLP, 12 and 16 Gauges, Hammerless, Solid Frame, Vent Rib, Adjustable Choke, Checkered Stock, *Modern*	*75*	*125*	*140*
Model 65, 12 and 16 Gauges, Hammerless, Solid Frame, *Modern*	*50*	*100*	*125*
Model 662CR, 20 Ga., Vent Rib, *Modern*	*75*	*125*	*150*
Model 66CLP, 12 and 16 Gauges, Adjustable Choke, *Modern*	*75*	*125*	*155*
Model 66RCLP, 12 and 16 Gauges, Hammerless, Solid Frame, Adjustable Choke, Vent Rib, *Modern*	*75*	*125*	*155*

	V.G.	Exc.	Prior Edition Exc. Value
Model 66RLP, 12 and 16 Gauges, Hammerless, Solid Frame, Vent Rib, *Modern*	$75	$125	$150
Model 66XLP, 12 and 16 Gauges, Hammerless, Solid Frame, *Modern*	75	125	140
Model 70, .410 Ga., *Modern*	50	100	110
Model 70CLP, .410 Ga., Hammerless, Solid Frame, Adjustable Choke, *Modern*	75	125	140
Model 70RL, .410 Ga., *Modern*	75	125	130
Model 70X, .410 Ga., *Modern*	50	100	125
Model 70XL, .410 Ga., *Modern*	50	100	130
Model 757, 20 Ga., Adjustable Choke, Lightweight, *Modern*	100	150	160

NOCK, HENRY London & Birmingham, England 1760–1810.
RIFLE, FLINTLOCK
.65, Ellett Carbine, Musket, Military, *Antique*	1,750	2,000	1,700

SHOTGUN, PERCUSSION
Fowler, Converted from Flintlock, Patent Breech, *Antique*	600	750	725

NONPAREIL Made by Norwich Falls Pistols Co., c. 1880.
HANDGUN, REVOLVER
.32 Short R.F., 5 Shot, Spur Trigger, Solid Frame, Single Action, *Antique*	150	175	165

NORTH AMERICAN ARMS CO. Freedom, Wyo.
HANDGUN, REVOLVER
.454 Casull Magnum, Single Action, Western Style, Stainless Steel, 5 Shot, *Modern*	650	950	450
Mini, .22 Short, 5 Shot, Single Action, Spur Trigger, 1" Barrel, Derringer, *Modern*	75	100	85
Mini, .22 L.R.R.F., 5 Shot, Single Action, Spur Trigger, 1" Barrel, Derringer, *Modern*	75	100	85
Mini, .22 L.R.R.F., 5 Shot, Single Action, Spur Trigger, 1½" Barrel, Derringer, *Modern*	75	100	90
Mini, .22 W.M.R., 5 Shot, Single Action, Spur Trigger, 1" Barrel, Derringer, *Modern*	100	125	100

NORTHWESTERNER Made by Stevens Arms.
RIFLE, BOLT ACTION
Model 52, .22 L.R.R.F., Single Action, Takedown, *Modern*	25	50	50

SHOTGUN, SINGLESHOT
Model 94, Various Gauges, Takedown, Automatic Ejector, Plain, Hammer, *Modern*	50	75	60

Prior
Edition
Exc.
V.G.   Exc.   Value

NORTON See Budischowsky and American Arms & Ammunition Co.

NORWEGIAN MILITARY
HANDGUN, SEMI-AUTOMATIC

	V.G.	Exc.	Prior Edition Exc. Value
Mauser Model 1914, .32 ACP, Blue, Clip Fed, *Modern*	$500	$575	$550
Model 1914, .45 ACP, Military, Clip Fed, *Modern*	300	350	340
Model 1914, .45 ACP, Military, Clip Fed, Nazi-Proofed, *Modern*	450	500	480

RIFLE, BOLT ACTION

Model 1894 Krag, 6.5 × 55mm, Military, Curio	150	175	155
Model 1925 Krag Sniper, 6.5 × 55mm, Military, *Curio*	150	175	165

NORWICH ARMS CO. Probably made by Norwich Falls Pistols Co.
HANDGUN, REVOLVER

.22 Short R.F., 7 Shot, Spur Trigger, Solid Frame, Single Action, Antique	150	175	165
.32 Short R.F., 5 Shot, Spur Trigger, Solid Frame, Single Action, Antique	125	150	170

NORWICH ARMS CO. Made by Crescent, c. 1900.
SHOTGUN, DOUBLE BARREL, SIDE-BY-SIDE

Various Gauges, Outside Hammers, Damascus Barrel, *Modern*	150	175	170
Various Gauges, Hammerless, Steel Barrel, *Modern*	175	200	190
Various Gauges, Hammerless, Damascus Barrel, *Modern*	150	175	170
Various Gauges, Outside Hammers, Steel Barrel, *Modern*	150	175	185

SHOTGUN, SINGLESHOT

Various Gauges, Hammer, Steel Barrel, *Modern*	50	75	85

NOT-NAC MFG. CO. Made by Crescent for Belknap Hardware Co., Louisville, Ky.
SHOTGUN, DOUBLE BARREL, SIDE-BY-SIDE

Various Gauges, Outside Hammers, Damascus Barrel, *Modern*	150	175	170
Various Gauges, Hammerless, Steel Barrel, *Modern*	150	200	190
Various Gauges, Hammerless, Damascus Barrel, *Modern*	150	175	170
Various Gauges, Outside Hammers, Steel Barrel, *Modern*	150	175	185

SHOTGUN, SINGLESHOT

Various Gauges, Hammer, Steel Barrel, *Modern*	50	75	85

	V.G.	Exc.	Prior Edition Exc. Value

NOVA La France Specialties, San Diego, Calif.

HANDGUN, SEMI-AUTOMATIC ·

Nova, 9mm Luger, Clip Fed, "Electrofilm" Finish, Reduced M1911 Style, *Modern* $400 $500 $495

NOYS, R. Wiltshire, England 1800–1830.

HANDGUN, FLINTLOCK

Pocket Pistol, Screw Barrel, Box Lock, Steel Barrel and Frame, Plain, *Antique* 550 700 657

NUMRICH ARMS CO. West Hurley, N.Y. Also see Auto Ordnance, Thompson, Hopkins & Allen.

HANDGUN, SEMI-AUTOMATIC

M1911A1, .45 ACP, Clip Fed, Blue, Military Style, *Modern* 200 250 250

Model 27A5, .45 ACP, Clip Fed, Finned Barrel, Adjustable Sights, with Compensator, (Numrich), *Modern* 300 350 350

RIFLE, SEMI-AUTOMATIC

Model 27A1, .45 ACP, Clip Fed, without Compensator, *Modern* 300 350 350

Model 27A1, .45 ACP, Clip Fed, without Compensator, Cased with Accessories, *Modern* 425 475 475

Model 27A1 Deluxe, .45 ACP, Clip Fed, Finned Barrel, Adjustable Sights, with Compensator, *Modern* 300 375 370

Model 27A3, .22 L.R.R.F., Clip Fed, Finned Barrel, Adjustable Sights, with Compensator, *Modern* 300 350 350

NUNNEMACHER, ABRAHAM York, Pa. 1779–1783. See Kentucky Rifles.

O

OAK LEAF Made by Stevens Arms.

SHOTGUN, SINGLESHOT

Model 90, Various Gauges, Takedown, Automatic Ejector, Plain, Hammer, *Modern* $25 $50 $60

OCCIDENTAL Belgium, c. 1880.

SHOTGUN, DOUBLE BARREL, SIDE-BY-SIDE

Various Gauges, Outside Hammers, Damascus Barrel, *Modern* 100 150 155

OLD TIMER Made by Stevens Arms.

SHOTGUN, SINGLESHOT

Model 94, Various Gauges, Takedown, Automatic Ejector, Plain, Hammer, *Modern* 25 50 60

OLYMPIC Made by Stevens Arms.

SHOTGUN, DOUBLE BARREL, SIDE-BY-SIDE

M 315, Various Gauges, Hammerless, Steel Barrel, *Modern* 150 175 180
Model 311, Various Gauges, Hammerless, Steel Barrel, *Modern* 150 175 180

SHOTGUN, SINGLESHOT

Model 94, Various Gauges, Takedown, Automatic Ejector, Plain, Hammer, *Modern* 25 50 60

O.M. Ojanguren y Marcaido, Eibar, Spain, c. 1920.

HANDGUN, REVOLVER

S & W Type, Various Calibers, Double Action, Swing-Out Cylinder, Blue, *Curio* 75 100 100

OMEGA Armero Especialistas Reunidas, Eibar, Spain, c. 1925.

HANDGUN, SEMI-AUTOMATIC

.25 ACP, Clip Fed, *Modern* 100 125 125
.32 ACP, Clip Fed, Grip Safety, *Modern* 125 150 140

	V.G.	Exc.	Prior Edition Exc. Value

OMEGA Torrance, Calif. Made by Hi-Shear Corp. Current.

RIFLE, BOLT ACTION

Omega III, Various Calibers, no Sights, Fancy Wood, Adjustable
Trigger, *Modern* $375 $425 $420

ORBEA HERMANOS Orbea Hermanos and Orbea y Cia., Eibar, Spain, c. 1860–1935.

HANDGUN, REVOLVER

S & W Type, .44 Russian, Double Action, Top-Break, *Antique* 100   125   130

OREA Orechowsky, Graz, Austria, c. 1930.

RIFLE, SINGLESHOT

Heeren Rifle, Various Calibers, Checkered Stock, Engraved,
Fancy Wood, *Modern* 1,250   1,750   1,650

Orbea Hermanos .44

Ortgies H O Vest Pocket   *Ortgies D Pocket*

	V.G.	Exc.	Prior Edition Exc. Value

ORTGIES Germany, 1918–1921, 1921 Taken over by Deutsche-Werke, Erfurt, Germany.

HANDGUN, SEMI-AUTOMATIC

	V.G.	Exc.	Prior Edition Exc. Value
D Pocket, .380 ACP, Clip Fed, *Modern*	$225	$275	$195
H O Pocket, .380 ACP, Clip Fed, *Modern*	200	250	185
D Pocket, .32 ACP, Clip Fed, *Modern*	175	225	170
D Vest Pocket, .25 ACP, Clip Fed, *Modern*	175	225	190
H O Vest Pocket, .25 ACP, Clip Fed, *Modern*	175	225	180

OSGOOD GUN WORKS Norwich, Conn., c. 1880.

HANDGUN, REVOLVER

	V.G.	Exc.	Prior Edition Exc. Value
Duplex, .22/.32 R.F., 8 Shot .22, Singleshot .32, Two Barrels, Spur Trigger, *Antique*	425	500	350

OUR JAKE

HANDGUN, REVOLVER

	V.G.	Exc.	Prior Edition Exc. Value
.32 R.F., Spur Trigger, Solid Frame, Hammer, *Antique*	125	150	145

OWA Oesterreichische Werke Anstalt, Vienna, Austria, c. 1920–1925.

HANDGUN, SEMI-AUTOMATIC

	V.G.	Exc.	Prior Edition Exc. Value
Model 1921 Standard, .25 ACP, Clip Fed, *Modern*	200	250	175

OXFORD ARMS Made by Stevens Arms.

SHOTGUN, DOUBLE BARREL, SIDE-BY-SIDE

	V.G.	Exc.	Prior Edition Exc. Value
Model 311, Various Gauges, Hammerless, Steel Barrel, *Modern*	150	175	180

OXFORD ARMS CO. Made by Crescent for Belknap Hdw. Co., Louisville, Ky.

SHOTGUN, DOUBLE BARREL, SIDE-BY-SIDE

	V.G.	Exc.	Prior Edition Exc. Value
Various Gauges, Outside Hammers, Damascus Barrel, *Modern*	125	175	170
Various Gauges, Hammerless, Steel Barrel, *Modern*	150	200	190
Various Gauges, Hammerless, Damascus Barrel, *Modern*	125	175	170
Various Gauges, Outside Hammers, Steel Barrel, *Modern*	125	175	185

SHOTGUN, SINGLESHOT

	V.G.	Exc.	Prior Edition Exc. Value
Various Gauges, Hammer, Steel Barrel, *Modern*	50	75	85

P

			Prior Edition Exc.
	V.G.	Exc.	Value

P.A.F. Pretoria Arms Factory, Pretoria, South Africa, c. 1955.

HANDGUN, SEMI-AUTOMATIC
Junior, For Cocking Indicator *Add* **10%–15%**

Junior, .25 ACP, High Slide, Clip Fed, Blue, *Curio*	$250	$300	$145
Junior, .25 ACP, Sight Rib, Clip Fed, Blue, *Curio*	300	350	170
Junior, .25 ACP, Low Slide, Clip Fed, Blue, *Curio*	275	325	150

PAGE, T. Norwich, England, 1766–1776.

HANDGUN, FLINTLOCK
.60, Queen Anne Style, Pocket Pistol, Screw Barrel, Box Lock,
Brass Furniture, Engraved, *Antique* 1,200   1,600   1,550

PAGE-LEWIS ARMS CO. See Stevens, J. Arms & Tool Co. for similar listings.

PALMER, THOMAS Philadelphia, Pa. 1772–1776. See Kentucky Rifles and U.S. Military.

PALMETTO Made by Stevens Arms.

SHOTGUN, SINGLESHOT
Model 90, Various Gauges, Takedown, Automatic Ejector, Plain,
Hammer, *Modern* 25   50   55

P.A.F. Junior

	V.G.	Exc.	Prior Edition Exc. Value
Model 94, Various Gauges, Takedown, Automatic Ejector, Plain, Hammer, *Modern*	$50	$75	$60

PANNABECKER, JEFFERSON Lancaster, Pa. 1790–1810. See Kentucky Rifles.

PANNABECKER, JESSE Lancaster, Pa. 1833–1860. See Kentucky Rifles.

PANTAX Tradename used by E. Woerther, Buenos Aires, Argentina.
HANDGUN, SEMI-AUTOMATIC

	V.G.	Exc.	Value
.22 R.F., Clip Fed, Blue, *Modern*	100	125	130

PANZER G.M.F. Corp., Watertown, Ct.
HANDGUN, DOUBLE BARREL, OVER-UNDER

	V.G.	Exc.	Value
Panzer, .22 L.R.R.F., Twist Barrel, Spur Trigger, *Modern*	25	50	40

PARAGON Made by Stevens Arms.
SHOTGUN, DOUBLE BARREL, SIDE-BY-SIDE

	V.G.	Exc.	Value
Model 311, Various Gauges, Hammerless, Steel Barrel, *Modern*	150	175	180

PARAGON Possibly made by Hopkins & Allen, c. 1880.
HANDGUN, REVOLVER

	V.G.	Exc.	Value
.32 Short R.F., 5 Shot, Spur Trigger, Solid Frame, Single Action, *Antique*	150	175	165

PARAMOUNT Retolaza Hermanos, Eibar, Spain, c. 1920.
HANDGUN, SEMI-AUTOMATIC

	V.G.	Exc.	Value
.32 ACP, Clip Fed, *Modern*	100	125	130
M 1914, .32 ACP, Clip Fed, Long Grip, *Modern*	125	150	135
Vest Pocket, .25 ACP, Clip Fed, *Modern*	100	125	125

PARKER BROTHERS Meriden, Conn. 1868–1934. In 1934 Parker Bros. was taken over by Remington Arms Co.
SHOTGUN, DOUBLE BARREL, SIDE-BY-SIDE
For Upgrades, *Deduct 25%–30%*
For Plain Extractor, *Deduct 30%–45%*
For Damascus Barrel, *Deduct 60%–75%*
Single Selective Trigger, *Add* **$200.00–$325.00**
Beavertail Forend, for BHE through A-1, *Add* **$250.00–$350.00**

	V.G.	Exc.	Prior Edition Exc. Value

Beavertail Forend, VHE through CHE, *Add* **$200.00–$300.00**

Extra Barrel, *Add* **30%–40%**

Vent Rib, *Add* **$275.00–$350.00**

Trap Grade, *Add* **15%–25%**

Skeet Grade, *Add* **15%–25%**

Outside Hammers with Steel Barrels, *Deduct* **20%–30%**

	V.G.	Exc.	Prior Ed. Exc. Value
A-1 Special, 12 Ga., Hammerless, Double Trigger, Automatic Ejector, *Modern*	$55,000	$65,000	$25,000
A-1 Special, 16 Ga., Hammerless, Double Trigger, Automatic Ejector, *Modern*	55,000	65,000	18,250
A-1 Special, 20 Ga., Hammerless, Double Trigger, Automatic Ejector, *Modern*	85,000	100,000	30,000
A-1 Special, 28 Ga., Hammerless, Double Trigger, Automatic Ejector, *Modern*		*RARE*	
A-1 Upgrade, .410 Ga., Hammerless, Double Trigger, Automatic Ejector, *Modern*	12,000	16,000	15,000
A-1 Upgrade, 12 and 16 Gauges, Hammerless, Double Trigger, Automatic Ejector, *Modern*	10,000	12,000	10,000
A-1 Upgrade, 20 Ga., Hammerless, Double Trigger, Automatic Ejector, *Modern*	7,500	9,500	9,250
A-1 Upgrade, 28 Ga., Hammerless, Double Trigger, Automatic Ejector, *Modern*	12,000	16,000	15,000
AAHE, 10 Ga., Hammerless, Double Trigger, Automatic Ejector, *Modern*	70,000	85,000	28,500
AAHE, 12 Ga., Hammerless, Double Trigger, Automatic Ejector, *Modern*	25,000	30,000	15,000
AAHE, 16 Ga., Hammerless, Double Trigger, Automatic Ejector, *Modern*	27,000	32,000	15,000
AAHE, 20 Ga., Hammerless, Double Trigger, Automatic Ejector, *Modern*	45,000	55,000	18,500
AAHE, 28 Ga., Hammerless, Double Trigger, Automatic Ejector, *Modern*	50,000	75,000	30,000
AHE, .410 Ga., Hammerless, Double Trigger, Automatic Ejector, *Modern*		*RARE*	
AHE, 10 Ga., Hammerless, Double Trigger, Automatic Ejector, *Modern*		*RARE*	
AHE, 12 Ga., Hammerless, Double Trigger, Automatic Ejector, *Modern*	15,000	18,000	13,000
AHE, 16 Ga., Hammerless, Double Trigger, Automatic Ejector, *Modern*	16,000	19,000	12,000
AHE, 20 Ga., Hammerless, Double Trigger, Automatic Ejector, *Modern*	20,000	25,000	17,500
AHE, 28 Ga., Hammerless, Double Trigger, Automatic Ejector, *Modern*	40,000	45,000	21,450
BHE, .410 Ga., Hammerless, Double Trigger, Automatic Ejector, *Modern*	40,000	45,000	19,500

	V.G.	Exc.	Prior Edition Exc. Value
BHE, 10 Ga., Hammerless, Double Trigger, Automatic Ejector, *Modern*		*RARE*	
BHE, 12 Ga., Hammerless, Double Trigger, Automatic Ejector, *Modern*	$4,500	$6,000	$11,000
BHE, 16 Ga., Hammerless, Double Trigger, Automatic Ejector, *Modern*	5,000	6,500	10,000
BHE, 20 Ga., Hammerless, Double Trigger, Automatic Ejector, *Modern*	7,500	9,000	15,000
BHE, 28 Ga., Hammerless, Double Trigger, Automatic Ejector, *Modern*	20,000	25,000	22,500
CHE, .410 Ga., Hammerless, Double Trigger, Automatic Ejector, *Modern*	35,000	37,500	13,500
CHE, 10 Ga., Hammerless, Double Trigger, Automatic Ejector, *Modern*		*RARE*	
CHE, 12 Ga., Hammerless, Double Trigger, Automatic Ejector, *Modern*	4,000	5,000	9,250
CHE, 26 Ga., Hammerless, Double Trigger, Automatic Ejector, *Modern*	5,000	5,700	8,500
CHE, 20 Ga., Hammerless, Double Trigger, Automatic Ejector, *Modern*	6,000	7,000	11,250
CHE, 28 Ga., Hammerless, Double Trigger, Automatic Ejector, *Modern*	12,500	15,000	14,500
DHE, .410 Ga., Hammerless, Double Trigger, Automatic Ejector, *Modern*	25,000	30,000	10,000
DHE, 10 Ga., Hammerless, Double Trigger, Automatic Ejector, *Modern*		*RARE*	
DHE, 12 Ga., Hammerless, Double Trigger, Automatic Ejector, *Modern*	5,000	5,500	8,750
DHE, 16 Ga., Hammerless, Double Trigger, Automatic Ejector, *Modern*	5,500	6,000	8,000
DHE, 20 Ga., Hammerless, Double Trigger, Automatic Ejector, *Modern*	6,000	7,000	10,500
DHE, 28 Ga., Hammerless, Double Trigger, Automatic Ejector, *Modern*	10,000	12,000	14,500
Early Model, Various Gauges, Outside Hammers, Damascus Barrel, Under-Lever, *Antique*	1,200	1,800	1,200
GHE, .410 Ga., Hammerless, Double Trigger, Automatic Ejector, *Modern*	20,000	24,000	8,500
GHE, 10 Ga. 3½", Hammerless, Double Trigger, Automatic Ejector, *Modern*		*RARE*	
GHE, 12 Ga., Hammerless, Double Trigger, Automatic Ejector, *Modern*	4,500	5,000	4,500
GHE, 16 Ga., Hammerless, Double Trigger, Automatic Ejector, *Modern*	5,000	5,500	4,000
GHE, 20 Ga., Hammerless, Double Trigger, Automatic Ejector, *Modern*	5,500	6,000	9,500
GHE, .28 Ga., Hammerless, Double Trigger, Automatic Ejector, *Modern*	8,000	9,000	9,500

	V.G.	Exc.	Prior Edition Exc. Value
Invincible, 12 Ga., Hammerless, Double Trigger, Automatic Ejector, *Modern*		*RARE*	
Invincible, 16 Ga., Hammerless, Double Trigger, Automatic Ejector, *Modern*		*RARE*	
Trojan, 12 and 16 Gauges, Hammerless, Double Trigger, *Modern*	*$1,200*	*$1,500*	*$995*
Trojan, 20 Ga., Hammerless, Double Trigger, *Modern*	*2,000*	*2,250*	*1,550*
Trojan, 16 Ga., Hammerless, Double Trigger, *Modern*	*2,000*	*2,250*	*20,000+*
VHE, .410 Ga., Hammerless, Double Trigger, Automatic Ejector, *Modern*	*17,000*	*20,000*	*8,250*
VHE, 10 Ga. 3¹/₂", Hammerless, Double Trigger, Automatic Ejector, *Modern*		*RARE*	
VHE, 12 Ga., Hammerless, Double Trigger, Automatic Ejector, *Modern*	*3,000*	*3,500*	*2,350*
VHE, 16 Ga., Hammerless, Double Trigger, Automatic Ejector, *Modern*	*3,500*	*4,000*	*2,250*
VHE, 20 Ga., Hammerless, Double Trigger, Automatic Ejector, *Modern*	*4,500*	*5,000*	*8,250*
VHE, 28 Ga., Hammerless, Double Trigger, Automatic Ejector, *Modern*	*8,000*	*9,000*	*8,750*

SHOTGUN, SINGLESHOT

	V.G.	Exc.	Prior Edition Exc. Value
S.A., 12 Ga., Hammerless, Vent Rib, Automatic Ejector, *Modern*	*3,000*	*3,500*	*7,750*
S.A.-1 Special, 12 Ga., Hammerless, Vent Rib, Automatic Ejector, *Modern*	*14,000*	*17,000*	*12,500*
S.A.A., 12 Ga., Hammerless, Vent Rib, Automatic Ejector, *Modern*	*4,500*	*5,000*	*9,250*
S.B., 12 Ga., Hammerless, Vent Rib, Automatic Ejector, *Modern*	*2,500*	*2,800*	*6,750*
S.C., 12 Ga., Hammerless, Vent Rib, Automatic Ejector, *Modern*	*1,500*	*1,700*	*5,750*

PARKER BROTHERS Imported from Italy by Jana International.
SHOTGUN, DOUBLE BARREL, OVER-UNDER

	V.G.	Exc.	Prior Edition Exc. Value
Field Model, 12 Ga. 3", Single Selective Trigger, Automatic Ejectors, Checkered Stock, Engraved, Vent Rib, *Modern*	*300*	*350*	*325*
Field Model, 12 Ga., Single Selective Trigger, Automatic Ejectors, Checkered Stock, Engraved, Vent Rib, *Modern*	*275*	*325*	*300*
Skeet Model, 12 Ga., Single Selective Trigger, Automatic Ejectors, Checkered Stock, Engraved, Vent Rib, *Modern*	*300*	*350*	*345*
Monte Carlo Trap Model, 12 Ga., Single Selective Trigger, Automatic Ejectors, Checkered Stock, Engraved, Vent Rib, *Modern*	*300*	*375*	*375*
California Trap Model, 12 Ga., Single Selective Trigger, Automatic Ejectors, Checkered Stock, Engraved, Double Vent Ribs, *Modern*	*475*	*550*	*525*

			Prior Edition Exc.
	V.G.	Exc.	Value

PARKER-HALE Birmingham, England.

HANDGUN, REVOLVER

	V.G.	Exc.	Value
S & W Victory, 22 L.R.R.F., Conversion, Adjustable Sights, *Modern*	$225	$250	$130

RIFLE, BOLT ACTION

	V.G.	Exc.	Value
Model 1200, Various Calibers, Checkered Stock, Open Rear Sight, Monte Carlo Stock, *Modern*	450	650	210
Model 1200M, Various Calibers, Magnum, Checkered Stock, Open Rear Sight, Monte Carlo Stock, *Modern*	600	700	225
Model 1200V, Various Calibers, Heavy Barrel, Checkered Stock, no Sights, Monte Carlo Stock, *Modern*	625	675	225

RIFLE, PERCUSSION

	V.G.	Exc.	Value
.54 Gallagher, Breech Loader, Carbine, Brass Furniture, Reproduction, *Antique*	150	175	175
.58 M1853 Enfield, Musket, Rifled, 2 Bands, Brass Furniture, Reproduction, *Antique*	175	200	190
.58 M1858 Enfield Rifle, Rifled, Brass Furniture, Reproduction, *Antique*	175	200	190
.58 M1861 Enfield, Musketoon, Rifled, 2 Bands, Brass Furniture, Reproduction, *Antique*	150	175	170
.451, Whitworth Military Target Rifle, 3 Bands, Target Sights, Checkered Stock, Reproduction, *Antique*	325	350	350

SHOTGUN, SEMI-AUTOMATIC

	V.G.	Exc.	Value
Model 900, 12 Ga., Checkered Stock, Vent Rib, *Modern*	400	450	200
Model 900, 12 Ga. 3", Checkered Stock, Vent Rib, *Modern*	450	500	220

PARKER SAFETY HAMMERLESS Made by Columbia Armory, Tenn., c. 1890.

HANDGUN, REVOLVER

	V.G.	Exc.	Value
.32 S & W, 5 Shot, Top Break, Hammerless, Double Action, *Modern*	75	100	100

PARKER, WILLIAM London, England 1790–1840.

SHOTGUN, FLINTLOCK

	V.G.	Exc.	Value
16 Ga., Double Barrel, Side by Side, Engraved, High Quality, *Antique*	3,500	4,000	4,000

SHOTGUN, PERCUSSION

	V.G.	Exc.	Value
14 Ga., Single Barrel, Smoothbore, High Quality, Cased with Accessories, *Antique*	1,250	1,500	1,500

PARKHILL, ANDREW Phila., Pa. 1778–1785. See Kentucky Rifles and Pistols.

	V.G.	Exc.	Prior Edition Exc. Value

PAROLE Made by Hopkins & Allen, c. 1880.

HANDGUN, REVOLVER

.22 Short R.F., 7 Shot, Spur Trigger, Solid Frame, Single Action,
Antique $150 $175 $165

PARR, J. Liverpool, England, c. 1810.

RIFLE, FLINTLOCK

.75, 3rd Model Brown Bess, Musket, Military, *Antique* 1,200 1,500 1,500

PARSONS, HIRAM Baltimore, Md., c. 1819. See Kentucky Rifles.

PATRIOT Made by Norwich Falls Pistol Co., c. 1880.

HANDGUN, REVOLVER

.32 Short R.F., 5 Shot, Spur Trigger, Solid Frame, Single Action,
Antique 150 175 165

PECK, ABIJAH Hartford, Conn. See U. S. Military.

PEERLESS Made by Stevens.

RIFLE, BOLT ACTION

Model 056 Buckhorn, .22 L.R.R.F., 5 Shot Clip, Peep Sights,
Modern 50 75 70

Model 066 Buckhorn, .22 L.R.R.F., Tube Feed, Peep Sights,
Modern 50 75 70

Model 53, .22 L.R.R.F., Singleshot, Takedown, *Modern* 25 50 50

PEERLESS Made by Crescent H. & D. Folsom, c. 1900.

SHOTGUN, DOUBLE BARREL, SIDE-BY-SIDE

Various Gauges, Outside Hammers, Damascus Barrel, *Modern* 150 175 170

Various Gauges, Hammerless, Steel Barrel, *Modern* 150 200 190

Various Gauges, Hammerless, Damascus Barrel, *Modern* 125 175 170

Various Gauges, Outside Hammers, Steel Barrel, *Modern* 150 200 185

SHOTGUN, SINGLESHOT

Various Gauges, Hammer, Steel Barrel, *Modern* 50 75 85

PENCE, JACOB Lancaster, Pa. 1771. See Kentucky Rifles and Pistols.

PENETRATOR Made by Norwich Falls Pistol Co., c. 1880.

HANDGUN, REVOLVER

.32 Short R.F., 5 Shot, Spur Trigger, Solid Frame, Single Action,
Modern 125 175 165

PENNYPACKER, DANIEL Berks County, Pa. 1773–1808. See Kentucky Rifles and Pistols.

PENNYPACKER, WM. Berks County, Pa. 1808–1858. See Kentucky Rifles and Pistols.

PERCUSSION ARMS, UNKNOWN MAKER
HANDGUN, PERCUSSION

	V.G.	Exc.	Prior Edition Exc. Value
.40 English, 6 Shot, Pepperbox, Pocket Pistol, Light Engraving, German Silver Frame, Steel Barrel, *Antique*	$350	$500	$395
.45, Pair French, Target Pistol, Octagon Barrel, Single Set Trigger, Brass Furniture, Cased with Accessories, *Antique*	2,500	3,000	2,500
.70, French Sotiau, Belt Pistol, Steel Furniture, Rifled, Octagon Barrel, *Antique*	450	600	575
Boot Pistol, Bar Hammer, Screw Barrel, *Antique*	200	250	150
Boot Pistol, Boxlock, Screw Barrel, *Antique*	250	300	165
Boot Pistol, Sidelock, Derringer Style, *Antique*	200	250	190
Pair, Duelling Pistols, Octagon Barrel, Single Set Trigger, German Silver Furniture, Medium Quality, Cased with Accessories, *Antique*	2,000	2,500	2,000

HANDGUN, REVOLVER

	V.G.	Exc.	Prior Edition Exc. Value
.36, Navy Colt Type, Belgian Make, Medium Quality, *Antique*	200	250	185
.45, Adams Type, Double Action, Octagon Barrel, Plain, Cased with Accessories, *Antique*	850	1,000	900

Percussion Arms, Unknown Maker Bench Rest Rifle

Percussion Holster Pistol

Percussion, Unknown Maker Military Style

	V.G.	Exc.	Prior Edition Exc. Value

RIFLE, PERCUSSION

American Indian Trade Gun, Belgian, Converted from Flintlock, Brass Furniture, *Antique* .... $1,000 / $1,200 / $900

Benchrest, Various Calibers, Heavy Barrel, Set Triggers, Target Sights, Light Decoration, *Antique* .... 700 / 850 / 765

Benchrest, Various Calibers, Heavy Barrel, Set Triggers, Target Sights, Medium Decoration, *Antique* .... 800 / 1,000 / 950

German, Schutzen Rifle, Rifled, Ivory Inlays, Gold Inlays, Ornate, *Antique* .... 5,000 / 6,000 / 5,550

SHOTGUN, PERCUSSION

English, 12 Ga., Double Barrel, Side by Side, Light Ornamentation, Medium Quality, *Antique* .... 350 / 500 / 465

English, 12 Ga., Double Barrel, Side by Side, Light Ornamentation, High Quality, Cased with Accessories, *Antique* .... 700 / 950 / 850

PERFECT Made by Foehl & Weeks. Phila., Pa., c. 1890.

HANDGUN, REVOLVER
.38 S & W, 5 Shot, Double Action, Top Break, *Modern* .... 75 / 100 / 100

PERFECTION Made by Crescent for H. & G. Lipscomb & Co., Nashville, Tenn.

SHOTGUN, DOUBLE BARREL, SIDE-BY-SIDE
Various Gauges, Outside Hammers, Damascus Barrel, *Modern* .... 125 / 175 / 170
Various Gauges, Hammerless, Steel Barrel, *Modern* .... 150 / 200 / 190
Various Gauges, Hammerless, Damascus Barrel, *Modern* .... 150 / 175 / 170
Various Gauges, Outside Hammers, Steel Barrel, *Modern* .... 150 / 200 / 185

SHOTGUN, SINGLESHOT
Various Gauges, Hammer, Steel Barrel, *Modern* .... 50 / 75 / 85

PERFECTION AUTOMATIC REVOLVER Made by Forehand Arms Co.

HANDGUN, REVOLVER
.32 S & W, 5 Shot, Double Action, Top Break, *Antique* .... 75 / 100 / 90
.32 S & W, 5 Shot, Double Action, Top Break, Hammerless, *Antique* .... 100 / 125 / 100

PERLA Frantisek Dusek, Opocno, Czechoslovakia, c. 1935.

HANDGUN, SEMI-AUTOMATIC
.25 ACP, Clip Fed, Blue, *Modern* .... 175 / 225 / 220

PETTIBONE, DANIEL Philadelphia, Pa. 1799–1814.

	V.G.	Exc.	Prior Edition Exc. Value

PHILLIPINE MILITARY
SHOTGUN, SINGLESHOT

	V.G.	Exc.	Prior Ed.
WW 2 Guerrilla Weapon, 12 Ga., *Modern*	$50	$75	$65

PHOENIX   Spain, Tomas de Urizar y Cia., c. 1920.
HANDGUN, SEMI-AUTOMATIC

Vest Pocket, .25 ACP, Clip Fed, *Modern*	125	150	135

PHOENIX ARMS CO.   Lowell Arms Co., Lowell, Mass., c. 1920.
HANDGUN, SEMI-AUTOMATIC

Vest Pocket, .25 ACP, Clip Fed, *Curio*	425	475	425

PIC   Made in West Germany for Precise Imports Corp., Suffern, N.Y.
HANDGUN, SEMI-AUTOMATIC

Vest Pocket, .25 ACP, Clip Fed, *Modern*	50	100	80
Vest Pocket, .22 Short R.F., Clip Fed, *Modern*	50	100	80

HANDGUN, REVOLVER

.22 L.R.R.F., Double Action, Blue, *Modern*	25	50	35

PICKFATT, HUMPHREY   London, England 1714–1730.
HANDGUN, FLINTLOCK

Pair, Queen Anne Style, Box Lock, Pocket Pistol, Silver Furniture, *Antique*	2,500	3,000	2,850
Pair, Holster Pistol, Engraved, Brass Furniture, High Quality, *Antique*	7,500	8,500	8,500

PIEDMONT   Made by Crescent for Piedmont Hdw. Danville, Pa.
SHOTGUN, DOUBLE BARREL, SIDE-BY-SIDE

Various Gauges, Outside Hammers, Damascus Barrel, *Modern*	150	175	170
Various Gauges, Hammerless, Steel Barrel, *Modern*	175	200	190
Various Gauges, Hammerless, Damascus Barrel, *Modern*	125	175	170
Various Gauges, Outside Hammers, Steel Barrel, *Modern*	150	200	185

SHOTGUN, SINGLESHOT

Various Gauges, Hammer, Steel Barrel, *Modern*	50	75	85

PIEPER   Henri Pieper, Harstal, Belgium 1884. Became Nicolas Pieper in 1898, and in 1905 became Anciens Etablissments Pieper.
COMBINATION WEAPON, SIDE-BY-SIDE

Various Calibers, Hammer, Open Rear Sight, Checkered Stock, Plain, *Modern*	375	450	395

Phoenix Arms Co. .25

Pieper Legia

PIC .25

Pieper Model D

	V.G.	Exc.	Prior Edition Exc. Value

HANDGUN, SEMI-AUTOMATIC

	V.G.	Exc.	Prior Edition Exc. Value
Bayard Model 1908 Pocket, .25 ACP, Blue, Clip Fed, *Modern*..........	$175	$200	$190
Bayard Model 1908 Pocket, .380 ACP, Blue, Clip Fed, *Modern*	150	175	165
Bayard Model 1923 Pocket, .25 ACP, Blue, Clip Fed, *Modern*......	150	175	170
Bayard Model 1923 Pocket, .32 ACP, Blue, Clip Fed, *Modern*......	200	225	210
Bayard Model 1930 Pocket, .25 ACP, Blue, Clip Fed, *Modern*......	200	225	210
Model A (Army), .32 ACP, Clip Fed, 7 Shot, *Modern*	150	175	150
Model B, .32 ACP, Clip Fed, 6 Shot, *Modern*	125	150	125
Model C, .25 ACP, Clip Fed, Long Grip, *Modern*...........................	150	175	170
Model C, .25 ACP, Clip Fed, *Modern*	125	150	140
Model D (1920), .25 ACP, Clip Fed, Tip-Up, *Modern*.....................	150	175	165
Model Legia, .25 ACP, Clip Fed, *Modern*......................................	125	150	130
Model Legia, .25 ACP, Clip Fed, Long Grip, *Modern*.....................	150	175	145
Model N, .32 ACP, Clip Fed, Tip-Up, 7 Shot, *Modern*	125	150	145

	V.G.	Exc.	Prior Edition Exc. Value
Model O, .32 ACP, Clip Fed, Tip-Up, 6 Shot, *Modern*	$125	$150	$130
Model P, .25 ACP, Clip Fed, Tip-Up, *Modern*	150	175	170

RIFLE, BOLT ACTION
Singleshot, .22 L.R.R.F., Plain, *Curio*	50	75	60

RIFLE, SEMI-AUTOMATIC
Pieper/Bayard Carbine, .22 Short, Checkered Stock, Pistol Grip, *Curio*	75	100	80
Pieper/Bayard Carbine, .22 Long, Checkered Stock, Pistol Grip, *Curio*	100	125	95
Pieper Carbine, .22 L.R.R.F., Checkered Stock, English Grip, *Curio*	100	125	95
Pieper Musket, .22 L.R.R.F., Military Style Stock, *Curio*	100	125	100
Pieper Musket, .22 L.R.R.F., Military Style Stock, with Bayonet, *Curio*	125	150	125

SHOTGUN, DOUBLE BARREL, SIDE-BY-SIDE
Bayard, Various Gauges, Hammerless, Boxlock, Light Engraving, Checkered Stock, *Modern*	175	200	185
Hammer Gun, Various Gauges, Plain, Steel Barrels, *Modern*	150	175	150
Hammer Gun, Various Gauges, Plain, Damascus Barrels, *Modern*	125	150	140
Hammer Gun, Various Gauges, Light Engraving, Steel Barrels, *Modern*	150	200	175

PIEPER, ABRAHAM Lancaster, Pa. 1801–1803. See Kentucky Rifles and Pistols.

PIEPER, HENRI Also see Pieper
COMBINATION WEAPON, SIDE-BY-SIDE
Various Calibers, Double Trigger, Outside Hammers, Side Lever, *Antique*	375	450	395

PINAFORE Made by Norwich Falls Pistol Co., c. 1880.
HANDGUN, REVOLVER
.22 Short R.F., 7 Shot, Spur Trigger, Solid Frame, Single Action, *Antique*	125	175	165

Pinafore

	V.G.	Exc.	Prior Edition Exc. Value

PINKERTON Gaspar Arizaga, Eibar, Spain, c. 1930.
HANDGUN, SEMI-AUTOMATIC
| Browning Type, .25 ACP, Clip Fed, Blue, *Modern* | $125 | $150 | $135 |
| Mondial Type, .25 ACP, Clip Fed, Blue, *Modern* | 175 | 200 | 180 |

PIONEER Made by Stevens Arms.
RIFLE, SEMI-AUTOMATIC
| Model 87, .22 L.R.R.F., Tube Feed, Open Rear Sight, *Modern* | 50 | 75 | 75 |

PIONEER Maker unknown, c. 1880.
HANDGUN, REVOLVER
| .38 Short R.F., 5 Shot, Spur Trigger, Solid Frame, Single Action, *Antique* | 150 | 175 | 170 |

PIONEER ARMS CO. Made by Crescent for Kruse Hardware Co. Cincinnati, Ohio.
SHOTGUN, DOUBLE BARREL, SIDE-BY-SIDE
Various Gauges, Outside Hammers, Damascus Barrel, *Modern*	150	175	170
Various Gauges, Hammerless, Steel Barrel, *Modern*	150	175	190
Various Gauges, Hammerless, Damascus Barrel, *Modern*	150	175	170
Various Gauges, Outside Hammers, Steel Barrel, *Modern*	150	175	185
SHOTGUN, SINGLESHOT
| Various Gauges, Hammer, Steel Barrel, *Modern* | 50 | 75 | 85 |

PIOTTI Brescia, Italy. Currently Imported by Ventura Imports.
SHOTGUN, DOUBLE BARREL, SIDE-BY-SIDE
| Westlake, 12 and 20 Gauges, Sidelock, Automatic Ejector, Double Trigger, Fancy Checkering, Fancy Engraving, *Modern* | 6,000 | 7,000 | 1,775 |
| Monte Carlo, 12 and 20 Gauges, Sidelock, Automatic Ejector, Single Selective Trigger, Fancy Checkering, Fancy Engraving, *Modern* | 7,000 | 8,500 | 3,850 |

PJK Bradbury, Calif.
RIFLE, SEMI-AUTOMATIC
| M-68, 9mm Luger, Clip Fed, Carbine, Flash Hider, *Modern* | 150 | 200 | 185 |

PLAINFIELD MACHINE CO. Dunellen, N.J., Also see Iver Johnson.
HANDGUN, SEMI-AUTOMATIC
| Super Enforcer, .30 Carbine, Clip Fed, *Modern* | 175 | 225 | 175 |

	V.G.	Exc.	Prior Edition Exc. Value

RIFLE, SEMI-AUTOMATIC

M-1, .30 Carbine, Carbine, *Modern*	*$150*	*$200*	*$175*
M-1, .30 Carbine, Carbine, Sporting Rifle, *Modern*...........................	*150*	*175*	*170*
M-1, 5.7mm Carbine, Carbine, *Modern*	*125*	*175*	*165*
M-1 Deluxe, .30 Carbine, Carbine, Sporting Rifle, Monte Carlo Stock, Checkered Stock, *Modern*..	*150*	*200*	*190*
M-1 Paratrooper, .30 Carbine, Carbine, Folding Stock, *Modern*........	*200*	*225*	*190*
M-1 Presentation, .30 Carbine, Carbine, Sporting Rifle, Monte Carlo Stock, Fancy Wood, *Modern*	*200*	*225*	*195*

PLAINFIELD ORDNANCE CO. Middlesex, N.J.

HANDGUN, SEMI-AUTOMATIC

Model 71, .22 L.R.R.F., Clip Fed, Stainless Steel, *Modern*..............	*100*	*125*	*105*
Model 71, .22 L.R.R.F. and .25 ACP, Clip Fed, Stainless Steel, with Conversion Kit, *Modern*	*125*	*150*	*125*
Model 71, .25 ACP, Clip Fed, Stainless Steel, *Modern*	*125*	*150*	*115*
Model 72, .22 L.R.R.F., Clip Fed, Lightweight, *Modern*..................	*125*	*150*	*115*
Model 72, .22 L.R.R.F. and .25 ACP, Clip Fed, Lightweight, with Conversion Kit, *Modern*	*150*	*175*	*140*
Model 72, .25 ACP, Clip Fed, Lightweight, *Modern*........................	*125*	*150*	*105*

PLANT'S MFG. CO. New Haven, Conn. 1860–1866.

HANDGUN, REVOLVER

.28 Cup Primed Cartridge, 6 Shot, Single Action, Spur Trigger, Solid Frame, *Antique*	*325*	*375*	*225*
.30 Cup Primed Cartridge, 6 Shot, Single Action, Spur Trigger, Solid Frame, *Antique*	*400*	*450*	*230*
.31 R.F., 6 Shot, Single Action, Solid Frame, Spur Trigger, *Antique*	*300*	*350*	*200*
.32 Short R.F., 6 Shot, Single Action, Solid Frame, Spur Trigger, *Antique*	*300*	*350*	*200*
.42 Cup Primed Cartridge, 6 Shot, Single Action, Spur Trigger, Solid Frame, *Antique*	*400*	*475*	*265*

Plant's .42 C.P.   *Plant's .28 C.P.*

	V.G.	Exc.	Prior Edition Exc. Value
.42 Cup Primed Cartridge, 6 Shot, Single Action, Spur Trigger, Solid Frame, 6" Barrel, *Antique*	$575	$650	$425
"Original", .28 Cup Primed Cartridge, 6 Shot, Single Action, Spur Trigger, Tip-Up, *Antique*	700	750	675
"Original", .30 Cup Primed Cartridge, 6 Shot, Single Action, Spur Trigger, Tip-Up, *Antique*	725	775	695
"Original", .42 Cup Primed Cartridge, 6 Shot, SIngle Action, Spur Trigger, Tip-Up, *Antique*	700	750	695
"Original", Various Cup-Primed Calibers, Extra Cylinder, Percussion, *Add* **$110.00–$185.00**			
Reynolds, .25 Short R.F., 5 Shot, Single Action, Spur Trigger, 3" Barrel, *Antique*	200	250	190

PLUS ULTRA Gabilondo y Cia., Eibar, Spain, c. 1930.
HANDGUN, SEMI-AUTOMATIC

.32 ACP, Extra Long Grip, Military, *Modern*	425	500	550

POND, LUCIUS Worcester, Mass., c. 1863–72.
HANDGUN, REVOLVER

Front Loader, .22, 7 Shot, 3¹/₂" bbl., *Antique*	500	600	300

PORTER, PATRICK W. New York City, c. 1851–54.
HANDGUN, PERCUSSION

Patent Turret Pistol, .41, 9 Shot, *Antique*	8,000	8,750	7,850

PORTUGUESE MILITARY
RIFLE, BOLT ACTION

Kropatchek M1886, 8mm, Tube Feed, *Antique*	100	125	120
Mauser-Vergueiro, 6.5mm, Rifle, *Curio*	75	100	100

POUS, EUDAL Spain, c. 1790.
HANDGUN, MIQUELET-LOCK

Pair, Holster Pistol, Low Quality, Light Brass Furniture, *Antique*	2,750	3,000	2,850

PRAGA Zbrojovka Praga, Prague, Czechoslovakia 1918–1926.
HANDGUN, SEMI-AUTOMATIC

Praga, .25 ACP, Clip Fed, Folding Trigger, *Curio*	200	225	195
Praha, .32 ACP, Clip Fed, *Curio*	225	275	265

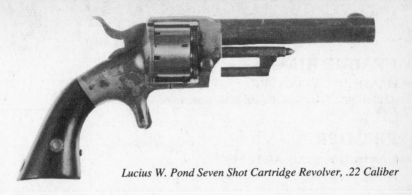

Lucius W. Pond Seven Shot Cartridge Revolver, .22 Caliber

Patrick W. Porter Patent Turret Pistol, .41 Caliber

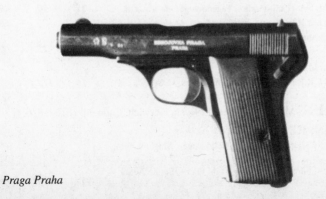

Praga Praha

	V.G.	Exc.	Prior Edition Exc. Value

PRAIRIE KING Made by Norwich Falls Pistol Co., c. 1880.

HANDGUN, REVOLVER

	V.G.	Exc.	Prior Ed.
.22 Short R.F., 7 Shot, Spur Trigger, Solid Frame, Single Action, Antique	$125	$150	$145

PREMIER Tomas de Urizar y Cia., Eibar, Spain, c. 1920.

HANDGUN, SEMI-AUTOMATIC

.25 ACP, Clip Fed, Blue, *Modern*	100	125	125

PREMIER Brooklyn, N.Y.

SHOTGUN, DOUBLE BARREL, SIDE-BY-SIDE

Ambassador, Various Calibers, Checkered Stock, Hammerless, Double Trigger, *Modern*	325	375	225
Brush King, 12 and 20 Gauges, Checkered Stock, Hammerless, Double Trigger, *Modern*	225	275	175
Continental, Various Calibers, Checkered Stock, Outside Hammers, Double Trigger, *Modern*	200	250	190
Magnum, 10 Ga. 3½", Checkered Stock, Hammerless, Double Trigger, *Modern*	275	350	210
Monarch, Various Calibers, Hammerless, Double Trigger, Checkered Stock, Engraved, Adjustable Choke, *Modern*	375	450	365
Presentation, Various Calibers, Adjustable Choke, Double Trigger, Fancy Engraving, Fancy Checkering, Extra Shotgun Barrel, *Modern*	850	1,000	900
Regent, Various Calibers, Checkered Stock, Hammerless, Double Trigger, *Modern*	225	250	165
Regent, Various Calibers, Checkered Stock, Hammerless, Double Trigger, Extra Shotgun Barrel, *Modern*	300	350	315

PREMIER Made by Stevens Arms.

RIFLE, BOLT ACTION

Model 52, .22 L.R.R.F., Singleshot, Takedown, *Modern*	25	50	45
Model 53, .22 L.R.R.F., Singleshot, Takedown, *Modern*	50	75	50
Model 66 Buckhorn, .22 L.R.R.F., Tube Feed, Open Rear Sight, *Modern*	50	75	60

RIFLE, SLIDE ACTION

Model 75, .22 L.R.R.F., Tube Feed, Hammerless, *Modern*	125	175	165

PREMIER Made by Thomas E. Ryan, Norwich, Conn., c. 1870–1876.

HANDGUN, REVOLVER

.22 Short R.F., 7 Shot, Spur Trigger, Solid Frame, Single Action, Antique	125	175	165
.38 Long R.F., 6 Shot, Spur Trigger, Solid Frame, Single Action, Antique	125	175	165

	V.G.	Exc.	Prior Edition Exc. Value

PREMIER TRAIL BLAZER Made by Stevens Arms.

RIFLE, SLIDE ACTION

Model 75, .22 L.R.R.F., Tube Feed, Hammerless, *Modern*	$125	$175	$165

PRESCOTT, E.A. Worcester, Mass. 1860–1874.

HANDGUN, REVOLVER

.22 Short R.F., 7 Shot, Spur Trigger, Solid Frame, Single Action, *Antique*	375	425	160
.30 R.F., 6 Shot, Spur Trigger, Solid Frame, Single Action, *Antique*	400	450	165
.32 Short R.F., 6 Shot, Spur Trigger, Solid Frame, Single Action, *Antique*	400	450	165
"Navy" .32 Short R.F., 6 Shot, Single Action, Solid Frame, Finger-Rest Trigger Guard, *Antique*	500	575	325
"Navy" .38 Short R.F., 6 Shot, Single Action, Solid Frame, Finger-Rest Trigger Guard, *Antique*	500	600	350

PRICE, J.W. Made by Stevens Arms.

SHOTGUN, SINGLESHOT

Model 90, Various Gauges, Takedown, Automatic Ejector, Plain, Hammer, *Modern*	50	75	60

PRIMA Mre. d'Armes des Pyrenees, Hendaye, France.

HANDGUN, SEMI-AUTOMATIC

.25 ACP, Clip Fed, *Modern*	125	150	140

PRINCEPS Tomas de Urizar, Eibar, Spain, c. 1920.

HANDGUN, SEMI-AUTOMATIC

.32 ACP, Clip Fed, Modern	125	150	135

Prima   *Princeps*

	V.G.	Exc.	Prior Edition Exc. Value

PRINCESS Unknown maker, c. 1880.
HANDGUN, REVOLVER
.22 Short R.F., 7 Shot, Spur Trigger, Solid Frame, Single Action, *Antique* $150 $175 $165

PROTECTOR Made by Norwich Falls Pistol Co., c. 1880.
HANDGUN, REVOLVER
.32 Short R.F., 5 Shot, Spur Trigger, Solid Frame, Single Action, *Antique* 150 175 170

PROTECTOR ARMS CO. Spain, c. 1900.
HANDGUN, SEMI-AUTOMATIC
M 1918, .25 ACP, Clip Fed, *Modern* 125 150 130

PURDEY, JAMES
RIFLE, DOUBLE BARREL, SIDE-BY-SIDE
.500 #2 Express, Damascus Barrel, Outside Hammers, Under-Lever, Engraved, Ornate, *Antique* 4,000 5,000 3,600

RIFLE, PERCUSSION
.52, Double Barrel, Side by Side, Damascus Barrel, Engraved, Fancy Wood, Gold Inlays, ... 6,500 7,500 6,000

PURDEY, JAS. & SONS London, England, 1816 to Date.
RIFLE, DOUBLE BARREL, SIDE-BY-SIDE
Various Calibers, Sidelock, Fancy Engraving, Fancy Checkering, Fancy Wood, *Modern* 45,000 50,000 14,500

RIFLE, BOLT ACTION
Sporting Rifle, Various Calibers, Fancy Wood, Checkered Stock, Express Sights, *Modern* 5,500 6,000 2,300

SHOTGUN, DOUBLE BARREL, OVER-UNDER
12 Ga., Vent Rib, Single Selective Trigger, Pistol-Grip Stock, *Modern* 25,000 30,000 16,250

Various Gauges, Extra Barrels Only **$3,000.00–$5,000.00**

Purdy, Various Gauges, Sidelock, Automatic Ejector, Double Trigger, Fancy Engraving, Fancy Checkering, *Modern* 20,000 25,000 12,500

Purdy, Various Gauges, Sidelock, Automatic Ejector, Single Trigger, Fancy Engraving, Fancy Checkering, *Modern* 20,000 25,000 14,500

Woodward, Various Gauges, Sidelock, Automatic Ejector, Double Trigger, Fancy Engraving, Fancy Checkering, *Modern* 15,000 20,000 10,500

Woodward, Various Gauges, Sidelock, Automatic Ejector, Single Trigger, Fancy Engraving, Fancy Checkering, *Modern* 25,000 30,000 17,500

	V.G.	Exc.	Prior Edition Exc. Value

SHOTGUN, DOUBLE BARREL, SIDE-BY-SIDE

12 Ga., Extra Barrel, Vent Rib, Single Selective Trigger, Engraved, Cased with Accessories, *Modern* $20,000 $25,000 $18,500

12 Ga., Extra Barrels, 10 Ga., Pistol-Grip Stock, Cased with Accessories, *Modern* 20,000 25,000 18,500

Various Gauges, Extra Barrels Only **$2,600.00–$3,750.00**

Featherweight, Various Gauges, Sidelock, Automatic Ejector, Double Trigger, Fancy Engraving, Fancy Checkering, *Modern* 15,000 20,000 12,500

Featherweight, Various Gauges, Sidelock, Automatic Ejector, Single Trigger, Fancy Engraving, Fancy Checkering, *Modern* 17,500 22,500 15,500

Game Gun, Various Gauges, Sidelock, Automatic Ejector, Double Trigger, Fancy Engraving, Fancy Checkering, *Modern* 15,000 20,000 13,500

Game Gun, Various Gauges, Sidelock, Automatic Ejector, Single Trigger, Fancy Engraving, Fancy Checkering, *Modern* 17,500 22,750 15,500

Pigeon Gun, 12 Ga., Single Selective Trigger, Vent Rib, Cased Straight Grip, *Modern* 17,500 22,750 15,500

Pigeon Gun, Various Gauges, Sidelock, Automatic Ejector, Double Trigger, Fancy Engraving, Fancy Checkering, *Modern* 15,000 20,000 12,500

Pigeon Gun, Various Gauges, Sidelock, Automatic Ejector, Single Trigger, Fancy Engraving, Fancy Checkering, *Modern* 15,000 20,000 13,500

Two-Inch, 12 Ga. 2", Sidelock, Automatic Ejector, Double Trigger, Fancy Engraving, Fancy Checkering, *Modern* 12,500 15,000 10,500

Two-Inch, 12 Ga. 2", Sidelock, Automatic Ejector, Single Trigger, Fancy Engraving, Fancy Checkering, *Modern* 15,000 20,000 12,750

SHOTGUN, SINGLESHOT

12 Ga., Vent Rig, Plain, Trap Grade, *Modern* 12,500 15,000 10,000

PZK Kohout & Spolecnost, Kydne, Czechoslovakia.

HANDGUN, SEMI-AUTOMATIC

PZK, .25 ACP, Clip Fed, *Modern* 150 200 190

Q

	V.G.	Exc.	Prior Edition Exc. Value

QUACKENBUSH Herkimer, N.Y., c. 1880.

RIFLE, SINGLESHOT

	V.G.	Exc.	Prior Edition Exc. Value
.22 R.F., Side Swing Breech, Nickel Plated, Takedown, *Modern*	$125	$175	$165

QUAIL Made by Crescent, c. 1900.

SHOTGUN, DOUBLE BARREL, SIDE-BY-SIDE

	V.G.	Exc.	Prior Edition Exc. Value
Various Gauges, Outside Hammers, Damascus Barrel, *Modern*	150	175	170
Various Gauges, Hammerless, Steel Barrel, *Modern*	150	200	190
Various Gauges, Hammerless, Damascus Barrel, *Modern*	150	175	170
Various Gauges, Outside Hammers, Steel Barrel, *Modern*	150	175	185

SHOTGUN, SINGLESHOT

	V.G.	Exc.	Prior Edition Exc. Value
Various Gauges, Hammer, Steel Barrel, *Modern*	50	75	85

QUAIL'S FARGO Tradename used by Dakin Gun Co. and Simmons Specialties.

SHOTGUN, DOUBLE BARREL, SIDE-BY-SIDE

	V.G.	Exc.	Prior Edition Exc. Value
12 Ga., Checkered Stock, Plain, *Modern*	150	175	175

QUEEN CITY Made by Crescent for Elmira Arms Co., c. 1900.

SHOTGUN, DOUBLE BARREL, SIDE-BY-SIDE

	V.G.	Exc.	Prior Edition Exc. Value
Various Gauges, Outside Hammers, Damascus Barrel, *Modern*	150	175	170
Various Gauges, Hammerless, Steel Barrel, *Modern*	150	200	190
Various Gauges, Hammerless, Damascus Barrel, *Modern*	150	175	170
Various Gauges, Outside Hammers, Steel Barrel, *Modern*	150	175	185

SHOTGUN, SINGLESHOT

	V.G.	Exc.	Prior Edition Exc. Value
Various Gauges, Hammer, Steel Barrel, *Modern*	50	75	85

R

	V.G.	Exc.	Prior Edition Exc. Value

RADIUM Gabilondo y Urresti, Guernica, Spain, c. 1910

HANDGUN, SEMI-AUTOMATIC
.25 ACP, Fixed Magazine, Side Loading, Blue, *Curio* $225 $275 $285

RADOM Fabryka Broni w Radomu, Radom, Poland, c. 1930 through WWII.

HANDGUN, REVOLVER
Ng 30, 7.62mm Nagant, Gas Seal, Double Action, *Curio* 225 275 215

HANDGUN, SEMI-AUTOMATIC
VIS 1935, 9mm Luger, Clip Fed, Military, Nazi-Proofed, Early
Type, *Modern* 750 850 285

VIS 1935, 9mm Luger, Clip Fed, Military, Nazi-Proofed, Late
Type, *Modern* 400 450 240

VIS 1935 Navy, 9mm Luger, Clip Fed, Military, Nazi-Proofed,
Modern 750 850 700

VIS 1935 Polish, 9mm Luger, Clip Fed, Military, *Modern* 725 800 650

Radom, Polish   *Radom, Early Nazi*   *Radom, Late Nazi*

	V.G.	Exc.	Prior Edition Exc. Value

RANGER Made by E.L. Dickinson, Springfield, Mass.

HANDGUN, REVOLVER

#2, .32 Short R.F., 5 Shot, Spur Trigger, Solid Frame, Single Action, *Antique* ... $125 / $175 / $155

RANGER Made by Stevens Arms.

RIFLE, SLIDE ACTION

Model 70, .22 L.R.R.F., Solid Frame, Hammer, *Modern* ... 125 / 175 / 160
Model 75, .22 L.R.R.F., Tube Feed, Hammerless, *Modern* ... 150 / 175 / 175

SHOTGUN, DOUBLE BARREL, SIDE-BY-SIDE

Model 315, Various Gauges, Steel Barrels, Hammerless, *Modern* ... 150 / 175 / 170
Model 215, 12 and 16 Gauges, Steel Barrels, Outside Hammers, *Modern* ... 125 / 175 / 170

SHOTGUN, SINGLESHOT

Model 89 Dreadnaught, Various Gauges, Hammer, *Modern* ... 50 / 75 / 60

RANGER Made by Hopkins & Allen, c. 1880.

HANDGUN, REVOLVER

.22 Short R.F., 7 Shot, Spur Trigger, Solid Frame, Single Action, *Antique* ... 150 / 175 / 155
.32 Short R.F., 6 Shot, Spur Trigger, Solid Frame, Single Action, *Antique* ... 150 / 175 / 165

RANGER ARMS, INC. Gainesville, Tex., c. 1972.

RIFLE, BOLT ACTION

Bench Rest/Varminter, Various Calibers, Singleshot, Target Rifle, Thumbhole Stock, Heavy Barrel, Recoil Pad, *Modern* ... 425 / 500 / 465
Governor Grade, Various Calibers, Sporting Rifle, Fancy Checkering, Fancy Wood, Recoil Pad, Sling Swivels, *Modern* ... 375 / 450 / 420
Governor Grade Magnum, Various Calibers, Sporting Rifle, Fancy Checkering, Fancy Wood, Recoil Pad, Sling Swivels, *Modern* ... 400 / 475 / 470
Senator Grade, Various Calibers, Sporting Rifle, Fancy Checkering, Recoil Pad, Sling Swivels, *Modern* ... 325 / 400 / 365
Senator Grade Magnum, Various Calibers, Sporting Rifle, Fancy Checkering, Recoil Pad, Sling Swivels, *Modern* ... 350 / 425 / 370
Statesman Grade, Various Calibers, Sporting Rifle, Checkered Stock, Recoil Pad, Sling Swivels, *Modern* ... 250 / 325 / 260
Statesman Grade Magnum, Various Calibers, Sporting Rifle, Checkered Stock, Recoil Pad, Sling Swivels, *Modern* ... 300 / 350 / 285

	V.G.	Exc.	Prior Edition Exc. Value

RANDALL Randall Firearms Mfg. Corp., Sun Valley, Calif.

HANDGUN, SEMI-AUTOMATIC

	V.G.	Exc.	Prior Edition Exc. Value
Compact Model, Various Calibers, Stainless Steel, M1911A1 Style, Herritt Grips, Adjustable Sights, *Modern*	$300	$350	$300
Service Model, Various Calibers, Stainless Steel, M1911A1 Style, Herritt Grips, Adjustable Sights, *Modern*	350	400	350
Target Model, Various Calibers, Stainless Steel, M1911A1 Style, Herritt Grips, Adjustable Sights with Rib, *Modern*	375	425	375

RASCH Brunswick, Germany 1790–1810.

RIFLE, FLINTLOCK

	V.G.	Exc.	Prior Edition Exc. Value
Yaeger, Octagon Barrel, Brass Furniture, Engraved, Carved, Target Sights, *Antique*	3,000	3,500	3,500

RATHFONG, GEORGE Lancaster, Pa. 1774–1809. See U.S. Military, Kentucky Rifles.

RATHFONG, JACOB Lancaster, Pa. 1810–1839. See Kentucky Rifles and Pistols.

RAVEN Raven Arms, Industry, Calif.

HANDGUN, SEMI-AUTOMATIC

	V.G.	Exc.	Prior Edition Exc. Value
P-25, .25 ACP, Clip Fed, Blue, *Modern*	50	75	40
P-25, .25 ACP, Clip Fed, Nickel, *Modern*	50	75	40
P-25, .25 ACP, Clip Fed, Chrome, *Modern*	50	75	40
MP-25, .25 ACP, Clip Fed, Teflon, *Modern*	50	75	50
MP-25, .25 ACP, Clip Fed, Nickel, *Modern*	50	75	50
MP-25, .25 ACP, Clip Fed, Chrome, *Modern*	50	75	50

REASOR, DAVID Lancaster, Pa. 1749–1780. See Kentucky Rifles and Pistols.

Raven MP-25

	V.G.	Exc.	Prior Edition Exc. Value

RECK Reck Sportwaffenfabrik, Arnsberg, West Germany.

HANDGUN, REVOLVER

.22 L.R.R.F., Double Action, Blue, *Modern*	$25	$50	$30

HANDGUN, SEMI-AUTOMATIC

P-8, .25 ACP, Clip Fed, Blue, *Modern*	50	75	65

RED CLOUD

HANDGUN, REVOLVER

.32 Long R.F., 5 Shot, Single Action, Solid Frame, Spur Trigger, *Antique*	150	175	165

RED JACKET Made by Lee Arms, Wilkes-Barre, Pa., c. 1870.

HANDGUN, REVOLVER

.22 Long R.F., 7 Shot, Single Action, Solid Frame, Spur Trigger, *Antique*	150	175	165
.32 Short R.F., 5 Shot, Single Action, Solid Frame, Spur Trigger, *Antique*	150	175	170

REED, JAMES Lancaster, Pa. 1778–1780. See Kentucky Rifles.

REFORM August Schueler, Suhl, Germany, c. 1910.

HANDGUN, MANUAL REPEATER

6mm R.F., 1 Barrel, Spur Trigger, Hammer, *Curio*	350	400	350
.25 ACP, 4 Barrels, Spur Trigger, Hammer, *Curio*	350	400	325
.25 ACP & 6mm R.F., 2 Sets of Barrels, Spur Trigger, Hammer, *Curio*	375	550	425

REFORM Spain, unknown maker, c. 1920.

HANDGUN, SEMI-AUTOMATIC

.25 ACP, Clip Fed, Blue, *Curio*	100	125	125

REGENT Gregorio Bolumburu, Eibar, Spain, c. 1925.

HANDGUN, SEMI-AUTOMATIC

.25 ACP, Clip Fed, Blue, *Modern*	100	125	130

REGENT Karl Burgsmuller, Kreiensen, West Germany.

HANDGUN, REVOLVER

.22 L.R.R.F., Double Action, Blue, *Modern*	25	50	40

Regnum   *Regina Vest Pocket*

	V.G.	Exc.	Prior Edition Exc. Value

REGINA Gregorio Bolumburu, Eibar, Spain, c. 1920.
HANDGUN, SEMI-AUTOMATIC

	V.G.	Exc.	Prior Edition Exc. Value
Pocket, .32 ACP, Clip Fed, Blue, *Modern*	$125	$150	$135
Vest Pocket, .25 ACP, Clip Fed, Blue, *Modern*	100	125	120

REGNUM Tradename used by August Menz, Suhl, Germany.
HANDGUN, MANUAL REPEATER

.25 ACP, 4 Barrels, Spur Trigger, Hammer, *Modern*	200	250	225

REID PATENT REVOLVERS Made by W. Irving for James Reid, N.Y. 1862–1884.
HANDGUN, REVOLVER

.22 Short R.F., 7 Shot, Spur Trigger, Solid Frame, Single Action, *Antique*	750	1,000	275
.32 Short R.F., 7 Shot, Spur Trigger, Solid Frame, Single Action, *Antique*	950	1,200	355
.41 Short R.F., 5 Shot, Spur Trigger, Solid Frame, Single Action, *Antique*	1,750	2,000	575
My Friend, .22 R.F., Knuckleduster, 7 Shot, *Antique*	600	675	400
My Friend, .32 R.F., Knuckleduster, 7 Shot, *Antique*	625	725	475

REIMS Azanza y Arrizabalaga, Eibar, Spain, c. 1914.
HANDGUN, SEMI-AUTOMATIC

1914 Model, .25 ACP, Clip Fed, *Modern*	100	125	125
1914 Model, .32 ACP, Clip Fed, *Modern*	125	150	140

	V.G.	Exc.	Prior Edition Exc. Value

REINA Mre. d'Armes des Pyrenees, Hendaye, France, c. 1930.
HANDGUN, SEMI-AUTOMATIC
.32 ACP, Clip Fed, Blue, *Modern* $125 $150 $145

REISING Hartford, Conn. 1916–1924.
HANDGUN, SEMI-AUTOMATIC
Target (Hartford), .22 L.R.R.F., Clip Fed, Hammer, *Modern* 300 375 350
Target (N.Y.), .22 L.R.R.F., Clip Fed, Hammer, *Modern* 400 450 495

REMINGTON ARMS CO. Eliphalet Remington, Herkimer County, N.Y. 1816–1831. Ilion, N.Y. 1831 to Date. 1856- E. Remington & Sons; 1888- Remington Arms Co.; 1910- Remington Arms U.M.C. Co.; 1925 to Date Remington Arms Co., Ilion, N.Y.

HANDGUN, DOUBLE BARREL, OVER-UNDER
Elliot Derringer, 1st. Model, .41 Short R.F., Spur Trigger, Tip-Up, no Extractor, Markings on Sides of Barrel, E. Remington & Sons, *Antique* 1,200 1,500 700
Elliot Derringer, 2nd. Model, .41 Short R.F., Spur Trigger, Tip-Up, with Extractor, Markings on Sides of Barrel, E. Remington & Sons, *Antique* 1,500 1,750 650
Elliot Derringer, 3rd. Model, .41 Short R.F., Spur Trigger, Tip-Up, with Extractor, Markings on Top of Barrel, E. Remington & Sons, *Antique* 650 750 450
Elliot Derringer, 4th Model, .41 Short R.F., Spur Trigger, Tip-Up, with Extractor, Markings on Top of Barrel, Remington Arms Co., *Curio* 550 600 400
Elliot Derringer, 5th Model, .41 Short R.F., Spur Trigger, Tip-Up, with Extractor, Markings on Top of Barrel, *Modern* 550 600 370
Elliot Derringer, 6th Model, .41 Short R.F., Spur Trigger, Tip-Up, with Extractor, Remington Arms Co. #'s L75925-L99941, *Modern* 500 550 315

HANDGUN, MANUAL REPEATER
Elliot Derringer, .22 Short R.F., 5 Shot, Double Action, Ring Trigger, Rotating Firing Block, *Antique* 950 1,200 475
Elliot Derringer, .32 Short R.F., 4 Shot, Double Action, Ring Trigger, Rotating Firing Block, *Antique* 1,000 1,150 450
Rider Magazine Pistol, .32 Extra Short R.F., Tube Feed, Spur Trigger, 5 Shot, *Antique* 4,000 5,000 585

HANDGUN, PERCUSSION
.31, Beals #1, Revolver, Pocket Pistol, 5 Shot, Octagon Barrel, 3" Barrel, *Antique* 750 900 475
.31, Beals #2, Revolver, Pocket Pistol, 5 Shot, Octagon Barrel, 3" Barrel, Spur Trigger, *Antique* 4,000 4,500 1,925

	V.G.	Exc.	Prior Edition Exc. Value
.31, Beals #3, Revolver, Octagon Barrel, 4" Barrel, Spur Trigger, with Loading Lever, *Antique*	$1,000	$1,250	$1,200
.31, New Model Pocket, Revolver, Safety Notches on Cylinder, Spur Trigger, 5 Shot, Octagon Barrel, *Antique*	1,250	1,500	575
.31, Rider Pocket, Revolver, Double Action, 5 Shot, Octagon Barrel, 3" Barrel, *Antique*	625	700	495
.36, Beals Navy, Revolver, Single Action, Octagon Barrel, 7½" Barrel, *Antique*	950	1,100	700
.36, Belt Model, Revolver, Safety Notches on Cylinder, Single Action, Octagon Barrel, 6½" Barrel, *Antique*	1,000	1,200	620
.36, Belt Model, Revolver, Safety Notches on Cylinder, Double Action, Octagon Barrel, 6½" Barrel, *Antique*	2,000	2,500	960
.36, Model 1861 Navy, Revolver, Channeled Loading Lever, Single Action, Octagon Barrel, 7½" Barrel, *Antique*	1,250	1,600	700
.36, New Model Navy, Revolver, Safety Notches on Cylinder, Single Action, Octagon Barrel, 7½" Barrel, *Antique*	1,050	1,300	760
.36, Police Model, Revolver, Single Action, Octagon Barrel, Various Barrel Lengths, 5 Shot, *Antique*	900	975	575
.44, Beals Army, Revolver, Single Action, Octagon Barrel, 8" Barrel, *Antique*	2,500	2,750	975
.44, Model 1861 Army, Revolver, Channeled Loading Lever, Single Action, Octagon Barrel, 8" Barrel, *Antique*	1,500	1,800	700
.44, New Model Army, Revolver, Safety Notches on Cylinder, Single Action, Octagon Barrel, 7½" Barrel, *Antique*	1,250	1,500	675

HANDGUN, REVOLVER

	V.G.	Exc.	Prior Edition Exc. Value
Iroquois, .22 L.R.R.F., 7 Shot, Solid Frame, Spur Trigger, Single Action, Fluted Cylinder, *Antique*	350	400	350
Iroquois, .22 L.R.R.F., 7 Shot, Solid Frame, Spur Trigger, Single Action, Unfluted Cylinder, *Antique*	400	450	450
Model 1875, .44-40 WCF, Single Action, Western Style, Solid Frame, *Antique*	3,250	3,750	1,150
Model 1875, .45 Colt, Single Action, Western Style, Solid Frame, *Antique*	3,000	3,500	1,100
Model 1890, .44-40 WCF, Single Action, Western Style, Solid Frame, *Antique*	3,500	4,000	1,750
Smoot #1, .30 Short R.F., 5 Shot, Solid Frame, Spur Trigger, Single Action, *Antique*	350	400	255
Smoot #2, .32 Short R.F., 5 Shot, Solid Frame, Spur Trigger, Single Action, *Antique*	325	375	235
Smoot #3, .38 Long R.F., 5 Shot, Solid Frame, Spur Trigger, Single Action, Birdhead Grip, *Antique*	400	450	325
Smoot #3, .38 Long R.F., 5 Shot, Solid Frame, Spur Trigger, Single Action, Saw Handle Grip, *Antique*	450	500	350
Smoot #4, .38 S & W, 5 Shot, Solid Frame, Spur Trigger, Single Action, no Ejector Housing, *Antique*	325	375	235
Smoot #4, .41 Short R.F., 5 Shot, Solid Frame, Spur Trigger, Single Action, no Ejector Housing, *Antique*	350	400	210

Remington Smoot #1

Remington .44 Model 1861 Army

Remington Model 51

Remington Smoot #3

Remington Elliot Repeater

Remington Elliot Derringer

	V.G.	Exc.	Prior Edition Exc. Value
Zig-Zag Derringer, .22 Short R.F., Pepperbox, Double Action, 6 Shot, Ring Trigger, *Antique*......	$2,000	$2,500	$1,450

HANDGUN, SEMI-AUTOMATIC

	V.G.	Exc.	Prior Edition Exc. Value
Model 51, .32 ACP, Early, Clip Fed, Grip Safety, *Modern*......	350	400	350
Model 51, .380 ACP, Early, Clip Fed, Grip Safety, *Modern*......	400	450	430
Model 51, .32 ACP, Late, Clip Fed, Grip Safety, *Modern*......	325	375	315
Model 51, .380 ACP, Late, Clip Fed, Grip Safety, *Modern*......	375	425	365

HANDGUN, SINGLESHOT

	V.G.	Exc.	Prior Edition Exc. Value
#1 Vest Pocket, .22 Short R.F., Iron Frame, no Breech Bolt, Spur Trigger, *Antique*......	625	700	400
#2 Vest Pocket, .30 Short R.F., Iron Frame, "Split Breech" Model, Spur Trigger, *Antique*......	775	850	515
#2 Vest Pocket, .41 Short R.F., Iron Frame, "Split Breech" Model, Spur Trigger, *Antique*......	850	1,200	465
Elliot Derringer, .41 Short R.F., Iron Frame, Birdhead Grip, no Breech Bolt, *Antique*......	1,175	1,400	600
Mark III, 10 Gauge, Signal Pistol, 9" Barrel, Spur Trigger, Brass Frame, *Curio*......	300	350	155
Model 1865 Navy, .50 Rem. Navy R.F., Rolling Block, Spur Trigger, 8½" Barrel, *Antique*......	2,000	2,500	1,400
Model 1867 Navy, .50 Rem. Rolling Block, 7" Barrel, *Antique*......	1,500	1,850	750
Model 1871 Army, .50 Rem., Rolling Block, 8" Barrel, *Antique*	1,500	1,650	550
Model 1891 Target, Rolling Block, 12" Barrel, *Add* **15%–20%**			
Model 1891 Target, Rolling Block, 10" Barrel, *Add* **15%–20%**			
Model 1891 Target, .22 L.R.R.F., Rolling Block, 8" Barrel, Half-Octagon Barrel, Plain Barrel, *Antique*......	1,750	2,000	1,200
Model 1891 Target, .25 Short R.F. Rolling Block, 8" Barrel, Half-Octagon Barrel, Plain Barrel, *Antique*......	1,250	1,500	715
Model 1891 Target, .32 Long R.F., Rolling Block, 8" Barrel, Half-Octagon Barrel, Plain Barrel, *Antique*......	1,400	1,600	870
Model 1891 Target, .32 S & W, Rolling Block, 8" Barrel, Half-Octagon Barrel, Plain Barrel, *Antique*......	1,650	1,800	1,100
Model 1891 Target, .32-20 WCF, Rolling Block, 8" Barrel, Half-Octagon Barrel, Plain Barrel, *Antique*......	2,000	2,250	1,300
Model 1901 Target, .22 L.R.R.F., Rolling Block, 10" Barrel, Checkered Stock, Half-Octagon Barrel, *Modern*......	1,450	1,650	1,050
Model 1901 Target, .44 Russian, Rolling Block, 10" Barrel, Checkered Stock, Half-Octagon Barrel, *Modern*......	1,800	2,050	1,225
XP-100, .221 Rem. Fireball, Bolt Action, Target Nylon Stock, 10½" Barrel, Vent Rib, Open Sights, Cased, *Modern*......	225	275	225
XP-100 Silhouette, 7mm BR Rem., Bolt Action, Target Nylon Stock, 15" Barrel, Vent Rib, Open Sights, Cased, *Modern*......	375	425	245

RIFLE, BOLT ACTION

	V.G.	Exc.	Prior Edition Exc. Value
Enfield 1914, .303 British, Full-Stocked, Military, *Curio*......	250	300	215

	V.G.	Exc.	Prior Edition Exc. Value
International (1961), Various Calibers, Singleshot, Target Stock, no Sights, with Accessories, *Modern*	$400	$450	$410
Model 1907/15 French, 8 × 50R Lebel, Military, *Curio*	175	225	170
Model 1907/15 French, 8 × 50R Lebel, Carbine, Military, *Curio*	150	200	155
Model 1917 U.S., .30-06 Springfield, Full-Stocked, Military, *Curio*	300	350	250
Model 30A, Various Calibers, Sporting Rifle, Plain, Open Rear Sight, *Modern*	375	425	265
Model 30F Premier, Various Calibers, Sporting Rifle, Fancy Checkering, Fancy Engraving, Fancy Wood, *Modern*	650	725	675
Model 30R, Various Calibers, Sporting Rifle, Plain, Carbine, Open Rear Sight, *Modern*	425	475	250
Model 30S, Various Calibers, Sporting Rifle, Checkered Stock, Peep Sights, *Modern*	450	525	345
Model 33A, .22 L.R.R.F., Plain, Singleshot, Open Rear Sight, *Modern*	75	100	65
Model 33A, .22 L.R.R.F., Plain, Singleshot, Peep Sights, *Modern*	75	100	65
Model 33NRA, .22 L.R.R.F., Plain, Singleshot, Peep Sights, Sling Swivels, *Modern*	100	125	75
Model 341A, .22 L.R.R.F., Tube Feed, Takedown, Open Rear Sight, *Modern*	100	125	95
Model 341P, .22 L.R.R.F., Tube Feed, Takedown, Peep Sights, *Modern*	150	175	110
Model 341SB, .22 L.R.R.F., Tube Feed, Takedown, Smoothbore, *Modern*	100	125	85
Model 34A, .22 L.R.R.F., Tube Feed, Takedown, Open Rear Sight, *Modern*	100	125	95
Model 34A, .22 L.R.R.F., Tube Feed, Takedown, Lyman Sights, *Modern*	100	125	95
Model 34NRA, .22 L.R.R.F., Tube Feed, Takedown, Lyman Sights, Target, *Modern*	125	175	110

Remington XP-100

Remington 40-XB-BR

	V.G.	Exc.	Prior Edition Exc. Value
Model 37A, .22 L.R.R.F., 5 Shot Clip, Target Stock, Target Sights, Target Barrel, *Modern*	$325	$400	$350
Model 37A, .22 L.R.R.F., 5 Shot Clip, Target Stock, Target Sights, Target Barrel, Fancy Wood, *Modern*	375	425	365
Model 37AX, .22 L.R.R.F., 5 Shot Clip, Target Stock, no Sights, Target Barrels, *Modern*	325	375	265
Model 40-XB CF-H2, Various Calibers, Stainless Steel Barrel, Heavy Barrel, Target Stock, no Sights, *Modern*	725	850	450
Model 40-XB CF-S2, Various Calibers, Stainless Steel Barrel, Target Stock, no Sights, *Modern*	700	875	475
Model 40-XB RF-H2, .22 L.R.R.F., Heavy Barrel, Target Stock, no Sights, *Modern*	500	575	285
Model 40-XB RF-S2, .22 L.R.R.F., Target Stock, no Sights, *Modern*	225	275	290
Model 40-XB-BR, For 2 oz. Trigger, *Add* **$40.00–$65.00**			
Model 40-XB-BR, Various Calibers, Stainless Steel Barrel, Heavy Barrel, Target Stock, no Sights, *Modern*	850	975	550
Model 40-XB-CF, For Repeater, *Add* **$25.00**			
Model 40X-CFH2, Various Calibers, Singleshot, Target Stock, no Sights, Heavy Barrel, *Modern*	500	575	295
Model 40X-CFS2, Various Calibers, Singleshot, Target Stock, no Sights, *Modern*	475	550	265
Model 40X-H1, .22 L.R.R.F., Singleshot, Target Stock, Target Sights, Heavy Barrel, *Modern*	475	550	245
Model 40X-H2, .22 L.R.R.F., Singleshot, Target Stock, no Sights, Heavy Barrel, *Modern*	425	525	220
Model 40X-S1, .22 L.R.R.F., Singleshot, Target Stock, Target Sights, *Modern*	400	500	225
Model 40X-S2, .22 L.R.R.F., Singleshot, Target Stock, no Sights, *Modern*	400	475	205
Model 40XB Sporter, .22 L.R.R.F., *Modern*	750	875	450
Model 40XC National Match, .308 Winchester, Target Stock, Target Sights, *Modern*	875	1,050	565
Model 40XR Position, .22 L.R.R.F., Target Stock, no Sights, *Modern*	675	750	375
Model 41A, .22 L.R.R.F., Takedown, Singleshot, Plain, Open Rear Sight, *Modern*	50	75	65
Model 41AS, .22 WRF, Takedown, Singleshot, Plain, Open Rear Sight, *Modern*	125	150	70
Model 41P, .22 L.R.R.F., Takedown, Singleshot, Plain, Target Sights, *Modern*	50	75	70
Model 41SB, .22 L.R.R.F., Takedown, Singleshot, Plain, Smoothbore, *Modern*	150	175	65
Model 510A, .22 L.R.R.F., Singleshot, Open Rear Sight, Plain, Takedown, *Modern*	50	75	70
Model 510C, .22 L.R.R.F., Singleshot, Carbine, Plain, Takedown, *Modern*	50	75	70

	V.G.	Exc.	Prior Edition Exc. Value
Model 510P, .22 L.R.R.F., Singleshot, Peep Sights, Plain, Takedown, *Modern*	$50	$75	$70
Model 510SB, .22 L.R.R.F., Singleshot, Smoothbore, Plain, Takedown, *Modern*	100	125	55
Model 510X, .22 L.R.R.F., Singleshot, Plain, *Modern*	75	100	48
Model 510X, .22 L.R.R.F., Singleshot, Plain, Smoothbore, *Modern*	75	100	48
Model 511 A, .22 L.R.R.F., Clip Fed, Open Rear Sight, Plain, Takedown, *Modern*	75	100	65
Model 511P, .22 L.R.R.F., Clip Fed, Peep Sights, Plain, Takedown, *Modern*	75	100	70
Model 511SB, .22 L.R.R.F., Clip Fed, Smoothbore, Plain, Takedown, *Modern*	75	100	70
Model 511X, .22 L.R.R.F., Clip Fed, Plain, *Modern*	75	100	70
Model 512A, .22 L.R.R.F., Tube Feed, Plain, Open Rear Sight, *Modern*	75	100	70
Model 512P, .22 L.R.R.F., Tube Feed, Plain, Peep Sights, *Modern*	75	100	75
Model 512SB, .22 L.R.R.F., Tube Feed, Plain, Smoothbore, *Modern*	75	100	75
Model 512X, .22 L.R.R.F., Tube Feed, Plain, *Modern*	75	100	75
Model 513SA, .22 L.R.R.F., Clip Fed, Sporting Rifle, Open Rear Sight, Takedown, Checkered Stock, *Modern*	150	200	135
Model 513SP, .22 L.R.R.F., Clip Fed, Sporting Rifle, Peep Sights, Takedown, Checkered Stock, *Modern*	175	200	140
Model 513TR, .22 L.R.R.F., Clip Fed, Target Stock, Target Sights, Takedown, *Modern*	200	225	150
Model 513TX, .22 L.R.R.F., Clip Fed, Target Stock, no Sights, Takedown, *Modern*	125	175	130
Model 514, .22 L.R.R.F., Singleshot, Plain, Open Rear Sight, *Modern*	50	75	48
Model 514BR (Youth), .22 L.R.R.F., Singleshot, Plain, Open Rear Sight, *Modern*	50	75	48
Model 514P, .22 L.R.R.F., Singleshot, Plain, Peep Sights, *Modern*	125	150	55
Model 521TL, .22 L.R.R.F., Takedown, Clip Fed, Target Stock, Lyman Sights, *Modern*	150	175	100
Model 540XR Position, .22 L.R.R.F., Target Stock, no Sights, *Modern*	225	275	245
Model 540XRJR Position, .22 L.R.R.F., Target Stock, no Sights, *Modern*	200	250	225
Model 541-S, .22 L.R.R.F., Clip Fed, Checkered Stock, Fancy Wood, *Modern*	275	325	210
Model 580, .22 L.R.R.F., Singleshot, Plain, *Modern*	75	100	65
Model 580 BR (Youth), .22 L.R.R.F., Singleshot, Plain, *Modern*	75	100	60
Model 580 SB, .22 L.R.R.F., Singleshot, Plain, Smoothbore, *Modern*	50	75	60

	V.G.	Exc.	Prior Edition Exc. Value
Model 581, .22 L.R.R.F., Clip Fed, Plain, *Modern*	$75	$100	$90
Model 581, .22 L.R.R.F., Clip Fed, Plain, Left-Hand, *Modern*	100	125	95
Model 582, .22 L.R.R.F., Tube Feed, Plain, *Modern*	75	100	105
Model 591, 5mm Rem. RFM, Clip Fed, Monte Carlo Stock, Plain, *Modern*	125	150	145
Model 592, 5mm Rem. RFM, Tube Feed, Monte Carlo Stock, Plain, *Modern*	125	150	145
Model 600, Various Calibers, Vent Rib, Carbine, Checkered Stock, *Modern*	225	275	220
Model 600, Various Calibers, Vent Rib, Carbine, Magnum, Recoil Pad, Checkered Stock, *Modern*	300	350	265
Model 600 Montana Centennial, Trap Grade, Carbine, Checkered Stock, Commemorative, *Curio*	300	425	295
Model 660, Various Calibers, Carbine, Checkered Stock, *Modern*	475	525	215
Model 660, Various Calibers, Carbine, Magnum, Recoil Pad, Checkered Stock, *Modern*	500	550	270
Model 700 Safari, Various Calibers, Magnum, Checkered Stock, Fancy Wood, *Modern*	675	750	475
Model 700ADL, Various Calibers, Checkered Stock, *Modern*	300	375	230
Model 700ADL, Various Calibers, Magnum, Checkered Stock, *Modern*	325	400	250
Model 700BDL, Various Calibers, Checkered Stock, Fancy Wood, *Modern*	350	400	285
Model 700BDL, Various Calibers, Magnum, Checkered Stock, Fancy Wood, *Modern*	375	425	295
Model 700BDL, Various Calibers, Heavy Barrel, Varmint, Checkered Stock, Fancy Wood, *Modern*	400	450	325
Model 700BDL, Various Calibers, Checkered Stock, Fancy Wood, Magnum, Left-Hand, *Modern*	400	450	325
Model 700BDL, Various Calibers, Checkered Stock, Fancy Wood, Left-Hand, *Modern*	325	400	310
Model 700C Custom, Various Calibers, Checkered Stock, Fancy Wood, *Modern*	775	850	510
Model 700D Peerless, Various Calibers, Fancy Checkering, Fancy Wood, Engraved, *Modern*	1,175	1,300	800
Model 700F Premier, Various Calibers, Fancy Checkering, Fancy Wood, Fancy Engraving, *Modern*	2,000	2,500	1,550
Model 720A, Various Calibers, Sporting Rifle, Open Rear Sight, *Modern*	950	1,200	225
Model 720A, Various Calibers, Sporting Rifle, Target Sights, *Modern*	1,050	1,300	270
Model 720R, Various Calibers, Sporting Rifle, Open Rear Sight, Carbine, *Modern*	1,000	1,250	250
Model 720R, Various Calibers, Sporting Rifle, Target Sights, Carbine, *Modern*	1,050	1,300	270
Model 720S, Various Calibers, Sporting Rifle, Target Sights, *Modern*	1,050	1,300	270

	V.G.	Exc.	Prior Edition Exc. Value
Model 721, For .300 H & H Magnum, *Add* **$20.00–$35.00**			
Model 721 Peerless, Various Calibers, Long Action, Sporting Rifle, Fancy Wood, Engraved, Fancy Checkering, *Modern*	$575	$750	$715
Model 721 Premier, Various Calibers, Long Action, Sporting Rifle, Fancy Wood, Fancy Engraving, Fancy Checkering, *Modern*	1,250	1,400	1,300
Model 721 Special, Various Calibers, Long Action, Sporting Rifle, Checkered Stock, Fancy Wood, *Modern*	200	250	200
Model 721A, Various Calibers, Long Action, Sporting Rifle, Plain, *Modern*	200	225	175
Model 721ADL, Various Calibers, Long Action, Sporting Rifle, Checkered Stock, *Modern*	300	350	195
Model 721BDL, Various Calibers, Long Action, Sporting Rifle, Monte Carlo Stock, Checkered Stock, Fancy Wood, *Modern*	375	450	195
Model 722, For .222 Rem. *Add* **$25.00–$35.00**			
Model 722A, Various Calibers, Short Action, Sporting Rifle, Plain, *Modern*	200	225	165
Model 722ADL, Various Calibers, Short Action, Sporting Rifle, Checkered Stock, *Modern*	300	350	185
Model 722BDL, Various Calibers, Short Action, Sporting Rifle, Checkered Stock, Fancy Wood, *Modern*	325	400	225
Model 722D Peerless, Various Calibers, Short Action, Sporting Rifle, Fancy Wood, Fancy Checkering, Engraved, *Modern*	950	1,200	700
Model 722F Premier, Various Calibers, Short Action, Sporting Rifle, Fancy Wood, Fancy Engraving, Fancy Checkering, *Modern*	1,250	1,650	1,025
Model 725ADL, Various Calibers, Long Action, Sporting Rifle, Checkered Stock, Fancy Wood, *Modern*	350	400	260
Model 725ADL, Various Calibers, Long Action, Magnum, Sporting Rifle, Checkered Stock, Fancy Wood, *Modern*	450	500	490
Model 725D Peerless, Various Calibers, Long Action, Sporting Rifle, Engraved, Fancy Checkering, Fancy Wood, *Modern*	1,000	1,225	710
Model 725F Premier, Various Calibers, Long Action, Sporting Rifle, Fancy Engraving, Fancy Checkering, Fancy Wood, *Modern*	2,150	2,600	1,350
Model 788, Various Calibers, Clip Fed, Plain, *Modern*	200	225	185
Model 788, Various Calibers, Clip Fed, Left-Hand, Plain, *Modern*	225	250	195
Nylon 10, .22 L.R.R.F., Singleshot, Plastic Stock, *Modern*	50	75	58
Nylon 10-SB, .22 L.R.R.F., Singleshot, Plastic Stock, Smoothbore, *Modern*	200	225	53
Nylon 12, .22 L.R.R.F., Tube Feed, Plastic, *Modern*	75	100	85

RIFLE, LEVER ACTION
Nylon 76, .22 L.R.R.F., Tube Feed, Plastic Stock, *Modern*	100	125	105

RIFLE, SEMI-AUTOMATIC
Model Four, Various Calibers, Clip Fed, Sporting Rifle, Open Rear Sight, Checkered Stock, Fancy Wood, *Modern*	300	350	325

	V.G.	Exc.	Prior Edition Exc. Value
Model 10C Mohawk, .22 L.R.R.F., Clip Fed, Plastic Stock, *Modern*	$75	$100	$75
Model 16, .22 Rem. Automatic R.F., Takedown, Tube Feed, *Modern*	175	225	205
Model 16D, .22 Rem. Automatic R.F., Takedown, Tube Feed, Checkered Stock, Engraved, *Modern*	400	450	400
Model 16F, .22 Rem. Automatic R.F., Takedown, Tube Feed, Fancy Checkering, Fancy Engraving, *Modern*	950	1,200	800
Model 241A, .22 L.R.R.F., Tube Feed, Takedown, Open Rear Sight, *Modern*	225	275	255
Model 241A, .22 Short R.F., Tube Feed, Takedown, Open Rear Sight, *Modern*	200	250	230
Model 241D, .22 L.R.R.F., Takedown, Tube Feed, Fancy Checkering, Engraved, *Modern*	400	475	400
Model 241F, .22 L.R.R.F., Takedown, Tube Feed, Fancy Checkering, Fancy Engraving, *Modern*	750	850	810
Model 24A, .22 L.R.R.F., Takedown, Plain, *Modern*	150	175	170
Model 24A, .22 Short R.F., Takedown, Plain, *Modern*	150	175	150
Model 24C, .22 L.R.R.F., Takedown, Checkered Stock, *Modern*	175	200	175
Model 24D Peerless, .22 L.R.R.F., Takedown, Fancy Checkering, Engraved, *Modern*	500	550	480
Model 24F Premier, .22 L.R.R.F., Takedown, Fancy Checkering, Fancy Engraving, *Modern*	900	1,050	910
Model 550-2G, .22 Short R.F., Takedown, Open Rear Sight, Plain, *Modern*	125	150	95
Model 550A, .22 L.R.R.F., Takedown, Open Rear Sight, Plain, *Modern*	100	125	90
Model 550P, .22 L.R.R.F., Takedown, Peep Sights, Plain, *Modern*	100	125	100
Model 552A, .22 L.R.R.F., Tube Feed, Plain, *Modern*	100	125	100
Model 552BDL, .22 L.R.R.F., Tube Feed, Checkered Stock, *Modern*	125	150	120
Model 552C, .22 L.R.R.F., Tube Feed, Carbine, Plain, *Modern*	100	125	100
Model 552GS, .22 Short R.F., Tube Feed, Plain, *Modern*	125	150	115
Model 740A, Various Calibers, Clip Fed, Sporting Rifle, Open Rear Sight, Plain, *Modern*	200	250	235
Model 740ADL, Various Calibers, Clip Fed, Sporting Rifle, Open Rear Sight, Checkered Stock, *Modern*	225	275	240
Model 740BDL, Various Calibers, Clip Fed, Sportint Rifle, Open Rear Sight, Checkered Stock, Fancy Wood, *Modern*	275	325	260
Model 740D Peerless, Various Calibers, Clip Fed, Sporting Rifle, Open Rear Sight, Fancy Checkering, Engraved, *Modern*	1,550	1,800	910
Model 740F Premier, Various Calibers, Clip Fed, Sporting Rifle, Open Rear Sight, Fancy Checkering, Fancy Engraving, *Modern*	3,000	3,500	1,500
Model 7400, Various Calibers, Clip Fed, Sporting Rifle, Open Rear Sight, Checkered Stock, *Modern*	325	350	280
Model 742, .30-06 Springfield, Bicentennial, Clip Fed, *Modern*	300	325	305

	V.G.	Exc.	Prior Edition Exc. Value
Model 742, Various Calibers, Clip Fed, Sporting Rifle, Open Rear Sight, Checkered Stock, *Modern*	$275	$300	$275
Model 742 Canadian Centennial, Clip Fed, Sporting Rifle, Open Rear Sight, Checkered Stock, Commemorative, *Curio*	325	350	305
Model 742ADL, Various Calibers, Clip Fed, Sporting Rifle, Open Rear Sight, Checkered Stock, *Modern*	250	275	250
Model 742BDL, Various Calibers, Clip Fed, Sporting Rifle, Open Rear Sight, Checkered Stock, Fancy Wood, *Modern*	325	300	295
Model 742C, Various Calibers, Clip Fed, Sporting Rifle, Open Rear Sight, Carbine, Checkered Stock, *Modern*	250	300	275
Model 742CDL, Various Calibers, Clip Fed, Sporting Rifle, Open Rear Sight, Carbine, Fancy Wood, *Modern*	275	325	290
Model 742D Peerless, Various Calibers, Clip Fed, Sporting Rifle, Open Rear Sight, Fancy Checkering, Engraved, *Modern*	1,700	1,900	910
Model 742F Premier, Various Calibers, Clip Fed, Sporting Rifle, Open Rear Sights, Fancy Checkering, Engraved, *Modern*	3,500	4,000	1,800
Model 81A, Various Calibers, Plain, Takedown, *Modern*	275	325	305
Model 81D Peerless, Various Calibers, Takedown, Fancy Checkering, Engraved, *Modern*	625	700	680
Model 81F Premier, Various Calibers, Takedown, Fancy Checkering, Fancy Engraving, Fancy Wood, *Modern*	1,150	1,400	1,300
Model 8A Standard, Various Calibers, Plain, *Modern*	275	325	280
Model 8C Special, Various Calibers, Checkered Stock, *Modern*	325	375	350
Model 8D Peerless, Various Calibers, Fancy Checkering, Light Engraving, *Modern*	600	675	650
Model 8E Expert, Various Calibers, Fancy Checkering, Engraved, *Modern*	875	950	900
Model 8F Premier, Various Calibers, Fancy Checkering, Fancy Engraving, Fancy Wood, *Modern*	950	1,250	1,225
Nylon 11, .22 L.R.R.F., Clip Fed, Plastic Stock, *Modern*	50	75	70
Nylon 66, .22 L.R.R.F., Tube Feed, Plastic Stock, *Modern*	75	100	85
Nylon 66, .22 L.R.R.F., Tube Feed, Bicentennial, Plastic Stock, *Modern*	150	175	95
Nylon 66 GS, .22 Short R.F., Tube Feed, Plastic Stock, *Modern*	100	125	90
Model 77, .22 L.R.R.F., Clip Fed, Plastic Stock, *Modern*	75	100	85

RIFLE, SINGLESHOT

	V.G.	Exc.	Prior Edition Exc. Value
Beals, .32 R.F., Sliding Barrel, Plain, *Antique*	625	700	400
Hepburn #3, Various Calibers, Sporting Rifle, Checkered Stock, Hammer, *Curio*	1,200	1,450	600
Model 1, Various Calibers, Rolling Block, Sporting Rifle, Adjustable Sights, Plain Stock, *Curio*	750	1,000	375
Model 1, Various Calibers, Rolling Block, Target, Adjustable Sights, Checkered Stock, *Curio*	2,100	2,500	670
Model 4, .22 L.R.R.F., Rolling Block, Takedown, *Modern*	425	500	180

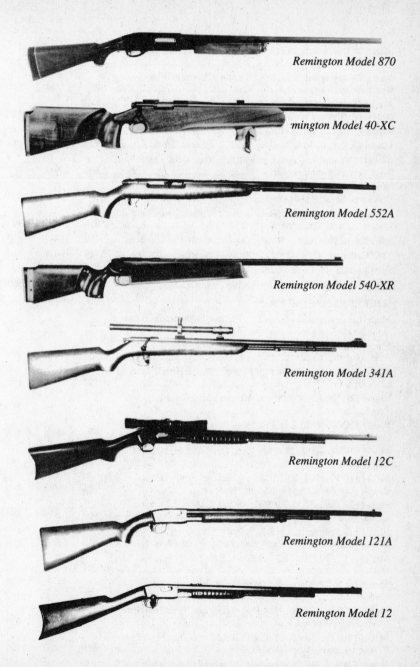

Remington Model 870

mington Model 40-XC

Remington Model 552A

Remington Model 540-XR

Remington Model 341A

Remington Model 12C

Remington Model 121A

Remington Model 12

	V.G.	Exc.	Prior Edition Exc. Value
Model 4S Boy Scout, .22 L.R.R.F., Rolling Block, Full-Stocked, *Curio*	$725	$800	$405
Model 4S Boy Scout, .22 L.R.R.F., Rolling Block, Full-Stocked, with Bayonet, *Curio*	775	900	535
Model 5, Various Calibers, Rolling Block, Sporting Rifle, Adjustable Sights, Plain Stock, *Curio*	750	875	460
Model 6, .22 L.R.R.F., Rolling Block, Takedown, *Modern*	300	350	150
Model 6, .32 Long Rifle, Rolling Block, Takedown, *Modern*	325	400	140
Model 7, Various Rimfires, Rolling Block, Target, Adjustable Sights, Checkered Stock, *Curio*	2,100	2,500	975
Model 7, Various Rimfires, Rolling Block, Target, Swiss Buttplate, Checkered Stock, Adjustable Sights, *Curio*	2,500	3,000	1,300
Model 7, Various Rimfires, Rolling Block, Target, Swiss Buttplate, Checkered Stock, Peep Sights, *Curio*	2,750	3,250	1,390
1867 Navy, .50/70 C.F., Military, Carbine, *Antique*	1,150	1,200	650
1867 Cadet Navy, .50/45 C.F., Military, *Antique*	1,450	1,700	750
Split Breech, .46 R.F., Military, Carbine, *Antique*	575	650	600
Split Breech, .50 R.F., Military, Carbine, *Antique*	750	850	800

RIFLE, SLIDE ACTION

	V.G.	Exc.	Prior Edition Exc. Value
Model Six, Various Calibers, Clip Fed, Sporting Rifle, Open Rear Sight, Monte Carlo Stock, Checkered Stock, *Modern*	275	325	290
Model 12A Standard, .22 L.R.R.F., Plain, Round Barrel, Tube Feed, *Modern*	150	175	170
Model 12B Gallery, .22 Short R.F., Plain, Round Barrel, Tube Feed, *Modern*	150	175	160
Model 12C, .22 L.R.R.F., Plain, Octagon Barrel, Tube Feed, Target, *Modern*	200	225	210
Model 12C-NRA, .22 L.R.R.F., Plain, Octagon Barrel, Tube Feed, Peep Sights, *Modern*	225	275	260
Model 12CS Special, .22 WRF, Plain, Octagon Barrel, Tube Feed, *Modern*	225	250	245
Model 12D Peerless, .22 L.R.R.F., Checkered Stock, Octagon Barrel, Tube Feed, Light Engraving, *Modern*	425	475	440
Model 12E Expert, .22 L.R.R.F., Fancy Checkering, Octagon Barrel, Tube Feed, Engraved, *Modern*	600	675	650
Model 12F Premier, .22 L.R.R.F., Fancy Checkering, Octagon Barrel, Tube Feed, Fancy Engraving, Fancy Wood, *Modern*	850	950	900
Model 121A, .22 L.R.R.F., Takedown, Tube Feed, Plain, *Modern*	225	250	230
Model 121A, .22 Short R.F., Takedown, Tube Feed, Plain, *Modern*	175	200	190
Model 121D Peerless, .22 L.R.R.F., Takedown, Tube Feed, Fancy Checkering, Engraved, *Modern*	550	625	615
Model 121F Premier, .22 L.R.R.F., Takedown, Tube Feed, Fancy Checkering, Fancy Engraving, *Modern*	850	950	925
Model 121S, .22 WRF, Takedown, Tube Feed, Plain, *Modern*	200	225	200

	V.G.	Exc.	Prior Edition Exc. Value
Model 121SB, .22 L.R.R.F., Takedown, Tube Feed, Plain, Smoothbore, *Modern*	$150	$200	$185
Model 14½ A, Various Calibers, Tube Feed, Short Action, Plain, *Modern*	250	300	280
Model 14½ R, Various Calibers, Tube Feed, Short Action, Carbine, Plain Barrel, *Modern*	275	350	330
Model 141A, Various Calibers, Takedown, Tube Feed, Plain, *Modern*	225	275	270
Model 141D Peerless, Various Calibers, Takedown, Tube Feed, Fancy Checkering, Engraved, *Modern*	550	650	630
Model 141F Premier, Various Calibers, Takedown, Tube Feed, Fancy Checkering, Fancy Engraving, *Modern*	1,000	1,150	1,100
Model 141R, Various Calibers, Takedown, Tube Feed, Plain, Carbine, *Modern*	200	275	255
Model 14A, Various Calibers, Tube Feed, Plain, *Modern*	200	250	230
Model 14C Special, Various Calibers, Tube Feed, Checkered Stock, *Modern*	225	275	270
Model 14D Peerless, Various Calibers, Tube Feed, Fancy Checkering, Engraved, *Modern*	525	600	580
Model 14F Premier, Various Calibers, Tube Feed, Fancy Checkering, Fancy Wood, Fancy Engraving, *Modern*	950	1,200	1,050
Model 14R, Various Calibers, Tube Feed, Carbine, Plain, *Modern*	475	550	300
Model 25A, Various Calibers, Takedown, Plain, *Modern*	225	275	240
Model 25D Peerless, Various Calibers, Takedown, Checkered Stock, Engraved, *Modern*	700	775	645
Model 25F Premier, Various Calibers, Takedown, Fancy Checkering, Fancy Engraving, *Modern*	950	1,150	1,100
Model 25R, Various Calibers, Takedown, Plain, Carbine, *Modern*	325	375	265
Model 572, .22 L.R.R.F., Tube Feed, Open Rear Sight, Lightweight, Fancy Checkering, Chrome, *Modern*	100	125	115
Model 572A, .22 L.R.R.F., Tube Feed, Open Rear Sight, Plain, *Modern*	125	150	120
Model 572BDL, .22 L.R.R.F., Tube Feed, Open Rear Sight, Checkered Stock, *Modern*	125	150	135
Model 572SB, .22 L.R.R.F., Tube Feed, Plain, Smoothbore, *Modern*	125	150	120
Model 760, .30-06 Springfield, Bicentennial, Clip Fed, *Modern*	250	300	260
Model 760A, Various Calibers, Clip Fed, Sporting Rifle, Open Rear Sight, Plain, *Modern*	225	275	220
Model 760ADL, Various Calibers, Clip Fed, Sporting Rifle, Open Rear Sight, Monte Carlo Stock, Checkered Stock, *Modern*	275	325	255
Model 760BDL, Various Calibers, Clip Fed, Sporting Rifle, Open Rear Sight, Monte Carlo Stock, Checkered Stock, *Modern*	200	275	280
Model 760C, Various Calibers, Clip Fed, Sporting Rifle, Open Rear Sight, Carbine, Plain, *Modern*	250	325	245

	V.G.	Exc.	Prior Edition Exc. Value
Model 760CDL, Various Calibers, Clip Fed, Sporting Rifle, Open Rear Sight, Carbine, Checkered Stock, *Modern*	$300	$375	$285
Model 760D Peerless, Various Calibers, Clip Fed, Sporting Rifle, Open Rear Sight, Fancy Checkering, Engraved, *Modern*	750	900	875
Model 760F Premier, Various Calibers, Clip Fed, Sporting Rifle, Open Rear Sight, Fancy Checkering, Fancy Engraving, *Modern*	1,650	1,850	1,800
Model 7600, Various Calibers, Clip Fed, Sporting Rifle, Open Rear Sight, Monte Carlo Stock, Checkered Stock, *Modern*	300	375	260

SHOTGUN, DOUBLE BARREL, OVER-UNDER

Model 32, Raised Solid Rib, *Add* **$55.00–$80.00**

Model 32, for Vent Rib, *Add* **$95.00–$135.00**

	V.G.	Exc.	Prior Edition Exc. Value
Model 32, 12 Ga., Skeet Grade, Engraved, Fancy Checkering, *Modern*	1,200	1,500	1,250
Model 32A, 12 Ga., Double Trigger, Automatic, Ejector, Plain Barrel, Engraved, Checkered Stock, *Modern*	800	950	650
Model 32A, 12 Ga., Single Selective Trigger, Automatic Ejector, Plain Barrel, Engraved, Checkered Stock, *Modern*	1,250	1,500	1,025
Model 32D, 12 Ga., Fancy Checkering, Fancy Wood, Fancy Engraving, *Modern*	2,250	2,700	2,350
Model 32E, 12 Ga., Fancy Checkering, Fancy Wood, Fancy Engraving, *Modern*	3,500	4,000	3,000
Model 32F, 12 Ga., Fancy Checkering, Fancy Wood, Fancy Engraving, *Modern*	5,000	5,500	4,350
Model 32TC, 12 Ga., Trap Grade, Single Selective Trigger, Engraved, Fancy Checkering, *Modern*	2,500	2,750	1,750
Model 3200, 12 Ga., Field Grade, Automatic Ejector, Single Selective Trigger, Vent Rib, Checkered Stock, *Modern*	775	850	925
Model 3200, 12 Ga., Skeet Grade, Automatic Ejector, Single Selective Trigger, Vent Rib, Checkered Stock, *Modern*	875	950	1,150
Model 3200, 12 Ga., Trap Grade, Automatic Ejector, Single Selective Trigger, Vent Rib, Checkered Stock, *Modern*	750	900	1,150
Model 3200, 12 Ga. Mag. 3", Field Grade, Automatic Ejector, Single Selective Trigger, Vent Rib, Checkered Stock, *Modern*	800	950	1,000
Model 3200 Competition, 12 Ga., Skeet Grade, Automatic Ejector, Single Selective Trigger, Vent Rib, Engraved, *Modern*	750	1,000	1,300
Model 3200 Competition, 12 Ga., Skeet Grade, Automatic Ejector, Single Selective Trigger, Vent Rib, Engraved, Extra Barrels, *Modern*	3,500	3,800	4,175
Model 3200 Competition, 12 Ga., Trap Grade, Automatic Ejector, Single Selective Trigger, Vent Rib, Engraved, *Modern*	1,050	1,350	1,300

SHOTGUN, DOUBLE BARREL, SIDE-BY-SIDE

	V.G.	Exc.	Prior Edition Exc. Value
Model 1882, Various Gauges, Hammer, Damascus Barrel, Checkered Stock, Double Trigger, *Antique*	900	975	440
Model 1883, Various Gauges, Hammer, Damascus Barrel, Checkered Stock, Double Trigger, *Antique*	625	700	440
Model 1883, Various Gauges, Hammer, Steel Barrel, Checkered Stock, Double Trigger, *Antique*	750	900	475

	V.G.	Exc.	Prior Edition Exc. Value
Model 1894 AE, Various Gauges, Hammerless, Damascus Barrel, Automatic Ejector, Checkered Stock, Double Trigger, *Curio*	$600	$750	$350
Model 1894 AEO, Various Gauges, Hammerless, Steel Barrel, Automatic Ejector, Checkered Stock, Double Trigger, *Curio*	775	850	575
Model 1894 AO, Various Gauges, Hammerless, Steel Barrel, Plain, Checkered Stock, Double Trigger, *Curio*	650	725	510
Model 1894 B, Various Gauges, Hammerless, Damascus Barrel, Light Engraving, Checkered Stock, Double Trigger, *Curio*	700	775	275
Model 1894 BE, Various Gauges, Hammerless, Damascus Barrel, Automatic Ejector, Light Engraving, Checkered Stock, *Curio*	775	875	425
Model 1894 BEO, Various Gauges, Hammerless, Steel Barrel, Automatic Ejector, Light Engraving, Checkered Stock, *Curio*	775	900	775
Model 1894 BO, Various Gauges, Hammerless, Steel Barrel, Light Engraving, Checkered Stock, Double Trigger, *Curio*	725	775	550
Model 1894 C, Various Gauges, Hammerless, Damascus Barrel, Engraved, Checkered Stock, Double Trigger, *Curio*	750	850	450
Model 1894 CE, Various Gauges, Hammerless, Damascus Barrel, Automatic Ejector, Engraved, Checkered Stock, *Curio*	850	950	525
Model 1894 CEO, Various Gauges, Hammerless, Steel Barrel, Automatic Ejector, Engraved, Checkered Stock, *Curio*	900	975	1,075
Model 1894 CO, Various Gauges, Hammerless, Steel Barrel, Engraved, Checkered Stock, Double Trigger, *Curio*	775	875	800
Model 1894 D, Various Gauges, Hammerless, Damascus Barrel, Fancy Engraving, Fancy Checkering, Fancy Wood, *Curio*	1,000	1,250	700
Model 1894 DE, Various Gauges, Hammerless, Damascus Barrel, Automatic Ejector, Fancy Engraving, Fancy Checkering, *Curio*	1,150	1,350	800
Model 1894 DEO, Various Gauges, Hammerless, Steel Barrel, Automatic Ejector, Fancy Engraving, Fancy Checkering, *Curio*	1,200	1,400	1,500
Model 1894 DO, Various Gauges, Hammerless, Steel Barrel, Fancy Engraving, Fancy Checkering, Fancy Wood, *Curio*	1,250	1,450	1,350
Model 1894 E, Various Gauges, Hammerless, Damascus Barrel, Fancy Engraving, Fancy Checkering, Fancy Wood, *Curio*	1,500	1,800	1,025
Model 1894 EE, Various Gauges, Hammerless, Damascus Barrel, Automatic Ejector, Fancy Engraving, Fancy Checkering, *Curio*	1,750	1,900	1,200
Model 1894 EEO, Various Gauges, Hammerless, Steel Barrel, Automatic Ejector, Fancy Engraving, Fancy Checkering, *Curio*	2,250	2,500	2,700
Model 1894 EO, Various Gauges, Hammerless, Steel Barrel, Fancy Engraving, Fancy Checkering, Fancy Wood, *Curio*	2,000	2,250	2,500
Model 1894 Special, Various Gauges, Hammerless, Steel Barrel, Automatic Ejector, Fancy Engraving, Fancy Checkering, *Curio*	6,000	7,000	6,650
Model 1894-A, Various Gauges, Hammerless, Damascus Barrel, Plain, Checkered Stock, Double Trigger, *Curio*	600	700	195
Model 1900 K, 12 and 16 Gauges, Hammerless, Steel Barrel, Plain, Checkered Stock, *Curio*	625	675	350
Model 1900 K D, 12 and 16 Gauges, Hammerless, Damascus Barrel, Plain, Checkered Stock, *Curio*	425	500	235
Model 1900 K E D, 12 and 16 Gauges, Hammerless, Damascus Barrel, Automatic Ejector, Palm Rest, Checkered Stock, *Curio*	475	550	280

	V.G.	Exc.	Prior Edition Exc. Value
Model 1900 KE, 12 and 16 Gauges, Hammerless, Steel Barrel, Automatic Ejector, Plain, Checkered Stock, *Curio*	$650	$750	$410
Model Parker 920, 12 Ga., Double Trigger, Checkered Stock, *Modern*		N/A	

SHOTGUN, SEMI-AUTOMATIC

Autoloading, 12 Ga., for Solid Rib, *Add* $25.00–$35.00

	V.G.	Exc.	Prior Edition Exc. Value
Autoloading-0, 12 Ga., Takedown, Riot Gun, Plain, *Modern*	200	250	185
Autoloading-1, 12 Ga., Takedown, Plain, *Modern*	200	250	190
Autoloading-2, 12 Ga., Takedown, Checkered Stock, *Modern*	275	325	250
Autoloading-4, 12 Ga., Takedown, Fancy Checkering, Fancy Wood, Engraved, *Modern*	750	850	625
Autoloading-6, 12 Ga., Takedown, Fancy Checkering, Fancy Wood, Fancy Engraving, *Modern*	1,000	1,250	1,025

Model 11, for Vent Rib, *Add* $35.00–$45.00

Model 11, Raised Solid Rib, *Add* $20.00–$30.00

	V.G.	Exc.	Prior Edition Exc. Value
Model 11 Sportsman, Various Gauges, Skeet Grade, Vent Rib, Light Engraving, Checkered Stock, *Modern*	225	275	350
Model 11-48 D Tournament, Various Gauges, Vent Rib, Fancy Wood, Fancy Engraving, Fancy Checkering, *Modern*	700	800	575
Model 11-48 Duck, Various Gauges, Vent Rib, Checkered Stock, *Modern*	225	275	205
Model 11-48 R, 12 Ga., Riot Gun, Plain Barrel, *Modern*	175	225	150
Model 11-48 RSS, 12 Ga., Open Rear Sight, Slug, Checkered Stock, *Modern*	225	275	205
Model 11-48 SA, Various Gauges, Skeet Grade, Vent Rib, Checkered Stock, *Modern*	250	325	225
Model 11-48A, Various Gauges, Plain Barrel, *Modern*	200	250	175
Model 11-48B, Various Gauges, Vent Rib, Checkered Stock, Fancy Wood, *Modern*	225	275	190
Model 11-48F Premier, Various Gauges, Vent Rib, Fancy Wood, Fancy Engraving, Fancy Checkering, *Modern*	1,200	1,450	1,200

Model 1100, for Left Hand, *Add* $25.00–$35.00

Model 1100, 12 Ga. Lightweight, *Add* $15.00–$25.00

Model 1100, for .28 Ga. or .410 Ga., *Add* $15.00–$25.00

	V.G.	Exc.	Prior Edition Exc. Value
Model 1100, 12 Ga., Bicentennial, Skeet Grade, Vent Rib, Checkered Stock, *Modern*	350	400	375
Model 1100, Various Gauges, Plain Barrel, Checkered Stock, *Modern*	250	275	325
Model 1100, Various Gauges, Vent Rib, Checkered Stock, *Modern*	275	325	360
Model 1100, Various Gauges, Plain Barrel, Magnum, Checkered Stock, *Modern*	300	350	310
Model 1100, Various Gauges, Vent Rib, Magnum, Checkered Stock, *Modern*	350	400	360
Model 1100, Various Gauges, Skeet Grade, Vent Rib, Checkered Stock, *Modern*	300	350	355

	V.G.	Exc.	Prior Edition Exc. Value
Model 1100 Cutts, Various Gauges, Skeet Grade, Vent Rib, Checkered Stock, *Modern*	$325	$375	$370
Model 1100 D Tournament, Various Gauges, Vent Rib, Fancy Checkering, Fancy Wood, Fancy Engraving, *Modern*	1,500	1,800	1,050
Model 1100 Deer Gun, Various Gauges, Open Rear Sight, Checkered Stock, *Modern*	250	300	375
Model 1100 F Premier, Various Gauges, Vent Rib, Fancy Checkering, Fancy Wood, Fancy Engraving, *Modern*	3,250	3,500	2,100
Model 1100 TA, 12 Ga., Bicentennial, Trap Grade, Vent Rib, Checkered Stock, *Modern*	275	325	410
Model 1100 TA, 12 Ga., Bicentennial, Trap Grade, Vent Rib, Monte Carlo Stock, Checkered Stock, *Modern*	300	350	425
Model 1100 TA, 12 Ga., Trap Grade, Vent Rib, Checkered Stock, *Modern*	250	300	400
Model 1100 TA, 12 Ga., Trap Grade, Vent Rib, Checkered Stock, Monte Carlo Stock, *Modern*	300	350	435
Model 11A, 12 Ga., Plain Barrel, *Modern*	175	225	195
Model 11A Sportsman, Various Gauges, Plain Barrel, Light Engraving, *Modern*	175	225	195
Model 11A, 12 Gauge, Plain Barrel, Fancy Wood, Checkered Stock, *Modern*	200	250	230
Model 11A Sportsman, 12 Gauge, Plain Barrel, Fancy Wood, Light Engraving, Checkered Stock, *Modern*	225	275	265
Model 11C, 12 Ga., Plain Barrel, Trap Grade, Fancy Checkering, Fancy Wood, *Modern*	325	375	350
Model 11D, 12 Ga., Plain Barrel, Fancy Checkering, Fancy Wood, Fancy Engraving, *Modern*	575	650	600
Model 11D Sportsman, Various Gauges, Plain Barrel, Engraved, Fancy Checkering, *Modern*	550	625	615
Model 11E, 12 Ga., Plain Barrel, Fancy Checkering, Fancy Wood, Fancy Engraving, *Modern*	750	900	750
Model 11E Sportsman, Various Gauges, Plain Barrel, Fancy Checkering, Fancy Wood, Fancy Engraving, *Modern*	800	950	775
Model 11F, 12 Ga., Plain Barrel, Fancy Checkering, Fancy Wood, Fancy Engraving, *Modern*	1,000	1,150	1,050
Model 11F Sportsman, Various Gauges, Plain Barrel, Fancy Checkering, Fancy Wood, Fancy Engraving, *Modern*	1,000	1,125	1,030
Model 11R, 12 Ga., Riot Gun, Military, *Modern*	200	250	170
Model 11R, 12 Ga., Riot Gun, Commercial, *Modern*	150	200	165
Model 48-D Sportsman, Various Gauges, Vent Rib, Fancy Checkering, Fancy Wood, Fancy Engraving, *Modern*	700	775	640
Model 48-F Sportsman, Various Gauges, Vent Rib, Fancy Checkering, Fancy Wood, Fancy Engraving, *Modern*	1,600	1,800	1,200
Model 48-SA Sportsman, Various Gauges, Skeet Grade, Vent Rib, Checkered Stock, *Modern*	200	250	210
Model 48A Sportsman, Various Gauges, Plain Barrel, *Modern*	175	200	165

	V.G.	Exc.	Prior Edition Exc. Value
Model 48B Sportsman, Various Gauges, Vent Rib, Checkered Stock, *Modern*	$225	$275	$185
Model 58 ADL, 12 and 20 Gauges, Vent Rib, Recoil Pad, Checkered Stock, Magnum, *Modern*	250	300	230
Model 58 ADL, Various Gauges, Plain Barrel, Checkered Stock, *Modern*	200	250	190
Model 58 ADL, Various Gauges, Vent Rib, Checkered Stock, *Modern*	250	300	230
Model 58 ADX, Various Gauges, Vent Rib, Checkered Stock, Fancy Wood, *Modern*	200	250	225
Model 58 BDL, Various Gauges, Plain Barrel, Checkered Stock, Fancy Wood, *Modern*	250	300	225
Model 58 BDL, Various Gauges, Vent Rib, Checkered Stock, Fancy Wood, *Modern*	300	350	230
Model 58 D Tournament, Various Gauges, Vent Rib, Fancy Checkering, Fancy Wood, Fancy Engraving, *Modern*	600	700	675
Model 58 F Premier, Various Gauges, Vent Rib, Fancy Checkering, Fancy Wood, Fancy Engraving, *Modern*	1,100	1,300	1,350
Model 58 RSS, 12 Ga. Slug, Open Rear Sight, Checkered Stock, *Modern*	200	250	215
Model 58 SA, Various Gauges, Skeet Grade, Vent Rib, Checkered Stock, *Modern*	275	325	270
Model 58 TB, 12 Ga., Trap Grade, Vent Rib, Checkered Stock, *Modern*	275	325	270
Model 878 A, 12 Ga., Plain Barrel, *Modern*	150	200	160
Model 878 A, 12 Ga., Vent Rib, *Modern*	175	225	170
Model 878 ADL, 12 Ga., Plain Barrel, Checkered Stock, *Modern*	175	225	170
Model 878 ADL, 12 Ga., Vent Rib, Checkered Stock, *Modern*	200	250	190
Model 878 D, 12 Ga., Vent Rib, Fancy Checkering, Fancy Wood, Fancy Engraving, *Modern*	575	650	580
Model 878 F, 12 Ga., Vent Rib, Fancy Checkering, Fancy Wood, Fancy Engraving, *Modern*	1,050	1,200	1,050
Model 878 SA, 12 Ga., Skeet Grade, Vent Rib, Checkered Stock, *Modern*	200	250	220

SHOTGUN, SINGLESHOT

	V.G.	Exc.	Prior Edition Exc. Value
Model 3 (M1893), 12 Ga., 24 Ga., 28 Ga., *Add* **$35.00**			
Model 3 (M1893), Various Gauges, Takedown, Plain, *Curio*	125	150	135
Model 9 (M1902), Various Gauges, Automatic Ejector, Plain, *Curio*	100	150	130
Model Parker 930, 12 Ga., Trap Grade, Vent Rib, Automatic Ejector, Fancy Checkering, *Modern*		N/A	
Model Parker 930, 12 Ga., Trap Grade, Vent Rib, Automatic Ejector, Fancy Checkering, Fancy Engraving, *Modern*		N/A	

SHOTGUN, SLIDE ACTION

	V.G.	Exc.	Prior Edition Exc. Value
Model 10A, 12 Ga., Takedown, Plain, *Modern*	175	225	200
Model 108, 12 Ga., Takedown, Checkered Stock, Fancy Wood, *Modern*	175	250	245

	V.G.	Exc.	Prior Edition Exc. Value
Model 10C, 12 Ga., Takedown, Fancy Wood, Checkered Stock, *Modern*	$250	$300	$280
Model 10D, 12 Ga., Takedown, Fancy Checkering, Fancy Wood, Engraved, *Modern*	550	625	615
Model 10E, 12 Ga., Takedown, Fancy Checkering, Fancy Wood, Fancy Engraving, *Modern*	750	825	800
Model 10F, 12 Ga., Takedown, Fancy Checkering, Fancy Engraving, Fancy Wood, *Modern*	950	1,100	1,050
Model 10R, 12 Ga., Takedown, Riot Gun, Plain, *Modern*	125	175	170
Model 10S, 12 Ga., Takedown, Trap Grade, Checkered Stock, *Modern*	200	250	245
Model 17, 20 Ga., for Solid Rib, *Add* **$25.00–$40.00**			
Model 17A, 20 Ga., Takedown, Plain, *Modern*	175	225	230
Model 17B, 20 Ga., Takedown, Checkered Stock, *Modern*	225	275	270
Model 17C, 20 Ga., Takedown, Fancy Wood, Checkered Stock, *Modern*	300	350	345
Model 17D, 20 Ga., Takedown, Fancy Wood, Fancy Checkering, Engraved, *Modern*	525	600	595
Model 17E, 20 Ga., Takedown, Fancy Wood, Fancy Checkering, Fancy Engraving, *Modern*	750	850	825
Model 17F, 20 Ga., Takedown, Fancy Wood, Fancy Checkering, Fancy Engraving, *Modern*	950	1,075	1,050
Model 17R, 20 Ga., Takedown, Riot Gun, Plain, *Modern*	175	225	205
Model 1908-0, 12 Ga., Takedown, Riot Gun, Plain, *Modern*	175	225	205
Model 1908-1, 12 Ga., Takedown, Plain, *Modern*	175	225	205
Model 1908-3, 12 Ga., Takedown, Checkered Stock, Fancy Wood, *Modern*	225	275	250
Model 1908-4, 12 Ga., Takedown, Fancy Checkering, Fancy Wood, Engraved, *Modern*	525	600	575
Model 1908-6, 12 Ga., Takedown, Fancy Checkering, Fancy Wood, Fancy Engraving, *Modern*	950	1,075	1,050
Model 29, for Solid Rib, *Add* **$25.00–$35.00**			
Model 29, for Vent Rib, *Add* **$35.00–$55.00**			
Model 29A Sportsman, 12 Ga., Plain Barrel, Takedown, *Modern*	175	225	235
Model 29B, 12 Ga., Checkered Stock, Takedown, *Modern*	175	225	240
Model 29C, 12 Ga., Trap Grade, Takedown, *Modern*	225	275	280
Model 29R, 12 Ga., Riot Gun, Plain Barrel, *Modern*	150	200	175
Model 29S, 12 Ga., Trap Grade, Plain Barrel, Checkered Stock, *Modern*	200	250	240
Model 29TA, 12 Ga., Trap Grade, Vent Rib, Checkered Stock, *Modern*	275	325	300
Model 29TC, 12 Ga., Trap Grade, Vent Rib, Checkered Stock, Fancy Wood, *Modern*	300	375	350
Model 29TD, 12 Ga., Trap Grade, Vent Rib, Fancy Checkering, Fancy Wood, Engraved, *Modern*	475	575	570

	V.G.	Exc.	Prior Edition Exc. Value
Model 29TE, 12 Ga., Trap Grade, Vent Rib, Fancy Checkering, Fancy Wood, Fancy Engraving, *Modern*	$700	$775	$750
Model 29TF, 12 Ga., Trap Grade, Vent Rib, Fancy Checkering, Fancy Wood, Fancy Engraving, *Modern*	950	1,050	1,025
Model 31, for Vent Rib, *Add* $45.00–$60.00			
Model 31, for Solid Rib, *Add* $15.00–$30.00			
Model 31, Various Gauges, Skeet Grade, Vent Rib, Checkered Stock, Fancy Wood, *Modern*	400	475	480
Model 31A, Various Gauges, Plain Barrel, *Modern*	375	325	200
Model 31B, Various Gauges, Plain Barrel, Checkered Stock, Fancy Wood, *Modern*	375	450	350
Model 31D Tournament, Various Gauges, Plain Barrel, Checkered Stock, Fancy Wood, Engraved, *Modern*	775	800	725
Model 31E Expert, Various Gauges, Plain Barrel, Fancy Checkering, Fancy Wood, Fancy Engraving, *Modern*	875	975	875
Model 31F Premier, Various Gauges, Plain Barrel, Fancy Checkering, Fancy Wood, Fancy Engraving, *Modern*	1,500	1,800	1,375
Model 31H Hunter, Various Gauges, Checkered Stock, Fancy Wood, Plain Barrel, *Modern*	300	375	370
Model 31R, 12 Ga., Plain Barrel, Riot Gun, *Modern*	175	225	215
Model 31S, 12 Ga., Raised Matted Rib, Checkered Stock, Fancy Wood, *Modern*	425	500	465
Model 31TC, 12 Ga., Trap Grade, Vent Rib, Recoil Pad, *Modern*	450	525	480
Model 870, For Lightweight 20, *Add* $20.00–$25.00			
Model 870, for .28 Ga. or .410 Ga., *Add* $20.00–$25.00			
Model 870, for Left-Hand, *Add* $10.00–$15.00			
Model 870, Various Gauges, Plain Barrel, Checkered Stock, *Modern*	175	225	230
Model 870, Various Gauges, Vent Rib, Checkered Stock, *Modern*	225	275	260
Model 870, Various Gauges, Plain Barrel, Magnum, Checkered Stock, *Modern*	200	250	245
Model 870, Various Gauges, Vent Rib, Magnum, Checkered Stock, *Modern*	225	300	280
Model 870 All American, 12 Ga., Trap Grade, Vent Rib, Fancy Checkering, Engraved, *Modern*	600	675	615
Model 870 Brushmaster, 12 and 20 Gauges, Open Rear Sight, Recoil Pad, Checkered Stock, *Modern*	225	275	255
Model 870 Competition, 12 Ga., Trap Grade, Vent Rib, Checkered Stock, Singleshot, *Modern*	325	400	360
Model 870 D Tournament, Various Gauges, Vent Rib, Fancy Checkering, Fancy Wood, Fancy Engraving, *Modern*	1,600	1,800	935
Model 870 Deergun, 12 Ga., Open Rear Sight, Checkered Stock, *Modern*	225	275	260
Model 870 F Premier, Various Gauges, Vent Rib, Fancy Checkering, Fancy Wood, Fancy Engraving, *Modern*	3,500	3,900	2,100
Model 870 Police, 12 Ga., Open Rear Sight, *Modern*	200	250	235

	V.G.	Exc.	Prior Edition Exc. Value
Model 870 Police, 12 Ga., Plain Barrel, *Modern*	$175	$225	$225
Model 870SA, 12 Ga., Bicentennial, Skeet Grade, Vent Rib, Checkered Stock, *Modern*	250	300	285
Model 870SA, Various Gauges, Skeet Grade, Vent Rib, Checkered Stock, *Modern*	250	300	285
Model 870SA Cutts, Various Gauges, Skeet Grade, Vent Rib, Checkered Stock, *Modern*	225	275	280
Model 870SC, Various Gauges, Skeet Grade, Vent Rib, Checkered Stock, *Modern*	250	300	285
Model 870TB, 12 Ga., Trap Grade, Vent Rib, Checkered Stock, *Modern*	225	275	270
Model 870TB, 12 Ga., Trap Grade, Vent Rib, Checkered Stock, Monte Carlo Stock, *Modern*	250	300	280
Model 870TB, 12 Ga., Bicentennial, Trap Grade, Vent Rib, Checkered Stock, *Modern*	250	300	280
Model 870TB, 12 Ga., Bicentennial, Trap Grade, Vent Rib, Checkered Stock, Monte Carlo Stock, *Modern*	250	300	280
Model 870TC, 12 Ga., Trap Grade, Vent Rib, Checkered Stock, *Modern*	325	375	350
Model 870TC, 12 Ga., Trap Grade, Vent Rib, Checkered Stock, Monte Carlo Stock, *Modern*	350	400	360

REPUBLIC Spain, unknown maker.
HANDGUN, SEMI-AUTOMATIC
.32 ACP, Clip Fed, Long Grip, *Modern*	125	150	150

RETRIEVER Made by Thomas Ryan, Norwich, Conn. 1870–1876.
HANDGUN, REVOLVER
.32 Short R.F., 5 Shot, Spur Trigger, Solid Frame, Single Action, *Antique*	150	175	165

REVELATION Trade name used by Western Auto.
RIFLE, BOLT ACTION
Model 107, .22 WMR, Clip Fed, *Modern*	50	75	70
Model 210B, 7mm Rem. Mag., Checkered Stock, Monte Carlo Stock, *Modern*	150	175	185
Model 220A, .308 Win., Checkered Stock, Monte Carlo Stock, *Modern*	150	175	170
Model 220AD, .308 Win., Checkered Stock, Monte Carlo Stock, Fancy Wood, *Modern*	175	200	195
Model 220B, .243 Win., Checkered Stock, Monte Carlo Stock, *Modern*	150	175	165
Model 220BD, .243 Win., Checkered Stock, Monte Carlo Stock, Fancy Wood, *Modern*	150	200	195

	V.G.	Exc.	Prior Edition Exc. Value
Model 220C, .22-250, Checkered Stock, Monte Carlo Stock, *Modern*	$150	$175	$165
Model 220CD, .22-250, Checkered Stock, Monte Carlo Stock, Fancy Wood, *Modern*	150	200	195

RIFLE, LEVER ACTION
Model 117, .22 L.R.R.F., Tube Feed, *Modern*	50	75	70

RIFLE, SEMI-AUTOMATIC
Model 125, .22 L.R.R.F., Clip Fed, *Modern*	25	50	60

RIFLE, SINGLESHOT
Model 100, .22 L.R.R.F., *Modern*	25	50	35

SHOTGUN, BOLT ACTION
Model 312B, 12 Ga., Clip Fed, *Modern*	25	50	55
Model 312BK, 12 Ga., Clip Fed, Adjustable Choke, *Modern*	50	75	65
Model 316B, 16 Ga., Clip Fed, *Modern*	25	50	50
Model 316BK, 16 Ga., Clip Fed, Adjustable Choke, *Modern*	25	50	55
Model 325B, 20 Ga., Clip Fed, *Modern*	25	50	55
Model 325BK, 20 Ga., Clip Fed, Adjustable Choke, *Modern*	25	50	55
Model 330, .410 Ga., Clip Fed, *Modern*	25	50	50

SHOTGUN, SLIDE ACTION
Model 310, Various Gauges, Plain Barrel, Takedown, *Modern*	125	150	135
Model 31OR, Various Gauges, Vent Rib, Takedown, *Modern*	125	150	140

REV-O-NOC Made by Crescent for Hibbard-Spencer-Bartlett Co., Chicago.

SHOTGUN, DOUBLE BARREL, SIDE-BY-SIDE
Various Gauges, Outside Hammers, Damascus Barrel, *Modern*	150	175	170
Various Gauges, Hammerless, Steel Barrel, *Modern*	175	200	190
Various Gauges, Hammerless, Damascus Barrel, *Modern*	150	175	170
Various Gauges, Outside Hammers, Steel Barrel, *Modern*	175	200	185

SHOTGUN, SINGLESHOT
Various Gauges, Hammer, Steel Barrel, *Modern*	75	100	85

REYNOLDS, PLANT & HOTCHKISS Also see Plant's Mfg. Co.

HANDGUN, REVOLVER
.25 Short R.F., 5 Shot, Single Action, Spur Trigger, 3" Barrel, *Antique*	150	200	190

R.G. INDUSTRIES R.G. tradename belongs to Rohm GmbH, Sontheim/ Brenz, W. Germany, and after 1968 also made in Miami, Fla. for American consumption.

	V.G.	Exc.	Prior Edition Exc. Value
HANDGUN, DOUBLE BARREL, OVER-UNDER			
RG-16, .22 WMR, 2 Shot, Derringer, *Modern*.................................	$25	$50	$35
RG-17, .38 Special, 2 Shot, Derringer, *Modern*..............................	25	50	35
HANDGUN, REVOLVER			
Partner RG-40P, .38 Special, 6 Shot, Double Action, Swing-Out Cylinder, *Modern*..	75	100	65
RG-14, .22 L.R.R.F., 6 Shot, Double Action, *Modern*......................	25	50	35
RG-23, .22 L.R.R.F., 6 Shot, Double Action, *Modern*......................	25	50	45
RG-30, .22 LR/.22 WMR Combo, 6 Shot, Double Action, Swing-Out Cylinder, *Modern*..	50	75	50
RG-30, .22 L.R.R.F., 6 Shot, Double Action, Swing-Out Cylinder, *Modern*..	25	50	35
RG-30, .22 WMR, 6 Shot, Double Action, Swing-Out Cylinder, *Modern*..	25	50	40
RG-30, .32 S & W Long, 6 Shot, Double Action, Swing-Out Cylinder, *Modern*..	25	50	40
RG-31, .32 S & W Long, 6 Shot, Double Action, *Modern*..............	50	75	45
RG-31, .38 Special, 5 Shot, Double Action, *Modern*.......................	50	75	45
RG-38S, .38 Special, 6 Shot, Double Action, Blue, *Modern*...........	75	100	60
RG-38S, .38 Special, 6 Shot, Double Action, Nickel Plated, *Modern*...	50	75	60
RG-40, .38 Special, 6 Shot, Double Action, Swing-Out Cylinder, *Modern*..	100	125	60
RG-57, .357 Magnum, 6 Shot, Double Action, Swing-Out Cylinder, *Modern*..	75	100	80
RG-57, .44 Magnum, 6 Shot, Double Action, Swing-Out Cylinder, *Modern*..	125	150	100
RG-63, .22 L.R.R.F., 6 Shot, Double Action, Western Style, *Modern*..	25	50	35

RG-38S

Rheinmetall

	V.G.	Exc.	Prior Edition Exc. Value
RG-66, .22LR/.22 WMR Combo, 6 Shot, Single Action, Western Style, *Modern*	$25	$50	$40
RG-66T, .22LR/.22 WMR Combo, 6 Shot, Single Action, Western Style, Adjustable sights, *Modern*	50	75	45
RG-74, .22 L.R.R.F., 6 Shot, Double Action, Swing-Out Cylinder, *Modern*	100	125	55
RG-88, .357 Magnum, 6 shot, Double Action, Swing-Out Cylinder, *Modren*	100	125	85

HANDGUN, SEMI-AUTOMATIC
RG-25, .25 ACP, *Modern*	25	50	45
RG-26, .25 ACP, *Modern*	25	50	45

RHEINMETALL Rheinsche Metallwaren u. Maschinenfabrik, Sommerda, Germany 1922–1927.

HANDGUN, SEMI-AUTOMATIC
.32 ACP, Clip Fed, Blue, *Curio*	250	300	350

RICHARDS, JOHN London & Birmingham, England 1745–1810.

SHOTGUN, FLINTLOCK
Blunderbuss, Half-Octagon, Cannon, Steel Barrel, Folding Bayonet, *Antique*	775	1,000	975

RICHARDS, W. Belgium, c. 1900

SHOTGUN, DOUBLE BARREL, SIDE-BY-SIDE
Various Gauges, Outside Hammers, Damascus Barrel, *Modern*	150	175	170
Various Gauges, Hammerless, Steel Barrel, *Modern*	150	175	190
Various Gauges, Hammerless, Damascus Barrel, *Modern*	150	175	170
Various Gauges, Outside Hammers, Steel Barrel, *Modern*	150	175	185

SHOTGUN, SINGLESHOT
Various Gauges, Hammer, Steel Barrel, *Modern*	50	75	85

RICHARDSON INDUSTRIES New Haven, Conn.

SHOTGUN, SINGLESHOT
Model R-5, 12 Ga., 24" Barrel, *Modern*	25	50	35

RICHLAND ARMS CO. Bussfield, Mich.

SHOTGUN, DOUBLE BARREL, OVER-UNDER
Model 808, 12 Ga., Single Trigger, Checkered Stock, Vent Rib, *Modern*	375	425	350
Model 810, 10 Ga. 3½", Double Trigger, Checkered Stock, Vent Rib, *Modern*	450	525	450

	V.G.	Exc.	Prior Edition Exc. Value
Model 828, 28 Ga., Single Trigger, Checkered Stock, *Modern*	$300	$375	$320
Model 844, 12 Ga., Single Trigger, Checkered Stock, *Modern*	275	350	240

SHOTGUN, DOUBLE BARREL, SIDE-BY-SIDE

	V.G.	Exc.	Prior Edition Exc. Value
Model 200, Various Gauges, Double Trigger, Checkered Stock, *Modern*	275	325	250
Model 202, Various Gauges, Double Trigger, Extra Shotgun Barrel, *Modern*	225	300	335
Model 707 Deluxe, 12 and 20 Gauges, Double Trigger, *Modern*	275	350	290
Model 707 Deluxe, 12 and 20 Gauges, Double Trigger, Checkered Stock, Extra Shotgun Barrel, *Modern*	350	400	370
Model 711, 10 Ga. 3½", Double Trigger, *Modern*	275	325	275
Model 711, 12 Ga. Mag. 3", Double Trigger, *Modern*	300	350	235

RIFLE, PERCUSSION

	V.G.	Exc.	Prior Edition Exc. Value
Wesson Rifle, .50, Set Triggers, Target Sights, Reproduction, *Antique*	200	250	200

RICHTER, CHARLES Made by Crescent for New York Sporting Goods Co. c. 1900.

SHOTGUN, DOUBLE BARREL, SIDE-BY-SIDE

	V.G.	Exc.	Prior Edition Exc. Value
Various Gauges, Outside Hammers, Damascus Barrel, *Modern*	125	150	170
Various Gauges, Hammerless, Steel Barrel, *Modern*	150	175	190
Various Gauges, Hammerless, Damascus Barrel, *Modern*	125	150	170
Various Gauges, Outside Hammers, Steel Barrel, *Modern*	150	175	185

SHOTGUN, SINGLESHOT

	V.G.	Exc.	Prior Edition Exc. Value
Various Gauges, Hammer, Steel Barrel, *Modern*	50	75	85

RICKARD ARMS Made by Crescent for J.A. Rickard Co. Schenectady, N.Y.

SHOTGUN, DOUBLE BARREL, SIDE-BY-SIDE

	V.G.	Exc.	Prior Edition Exc. Value
Various Gauges, Outside Hammers, Damascus Barrel, *Modern*	150	175	170
Various Gauges, Hammerless, Steel Barrel, *Modern*	150	200	190
Various Gauges, Hammerless, Damascus Barrel, *Modern*	150	175	170
Various Gauges, Outside Hammers, Steel Barrel, *Modern*	150	200	185

SHOTGUN, SINGLESHOT

	V.G.	Exc.	Prior Edition Exc. Value
Various Gauges, Hammer, Steel Barrel, *Modern*	75	100	85

RIGARMI Industria Galesi, Brescia, Italy.

HANDGUN, SEMI-AUTOMATIC

	V.G.	Exc.	Prior Edition Exc. Value
Militar, .22 L.R.R.F., Clip Fed, Hammer, Double Action, *Modern*	150	175	160
Pocket, .32 ACP, Clip Fed, Hammer, Double Action, *Modern*	125	150	155
RG-217, .22 Long R.F., Clip Fed, *Modern*	75	100	100

	V.G.	Exc.	Prior Edition Exc. Value
RG-218, .22 L.R.R.F., Clip Fed, *Modern*..	*$100*	*$125*	*$125*
RG-219, .25 ACP, Clip Fed, *Modern*..	*75*	*100*	*100*

RIGBY, JOHN & CO. Dublin, Ireland & London, England from 1867.

RIFLE, BOLT ACTION

.275 Rigby, Sporting Rifle, Express Sights, Checkered Stock, *Modern*...	*3,250*	*3,750*	*2,350*
.275 Rigby, Sporting Rifle, Lightweight, Express Sights, Checkered Stock, *Modern*...	*3,200*	*3,700*	*2,300*
.350 Rigby, Sporting Rifle, Express Sights, Checkered Stock, *Modren*...	*3,250*	*3,750*	*2,350*
Big Game, .416 Rigby, Sporting Rifle, Express Sights, Checkered Stock, *Modern*..	*3,450*	*3,950*	*2,350*

RIFLE, DOUBLE BARREL, SIDE-BY-SIDE

Best Grade, Various Calibers, Sidelock, Double Trigger, Express Sights, Fancy Engraving, Fancy Checkering, *Modern*	*40,000*	*45,000*	*13,250*
Second Grade, Various Calibers, Box Lock, Double Trigger, Express Sights, Fancy Engraving, Fancy Checkering, *Modern*.........	*20,000*	*25,000*	*8,750*
Third Grade, Various Calibers, Box Lock, Double Trigger, Express Sights, Engraved, Checkered Stock, *Modern*......................	*7,000*	*10,000*	*5,650*

SHOTGUN, DOUBLE BARREL, SIDE-BY-SIDE

Chatsworth, Various Gauges, Box Lock, Automatic Ejector, Double Trigger, Fancy Engraving, Fancy Checkering, *Modern*	*3,000*	*3,500*	*2,575*
Regal, Various Gauges, Sidelock, Automatic Ejector, Double Trigger, Fancy Engraving, Fancy Checkering, *Modern*	*10,000*	*12,000*	*9,250*
Sackville, Various Gauges, Box Lock, Automatic Ejector, Double Trigger, Fancy Engraving, Fancy Checkering, *Modern*	*4,000*	*5,000*	*3,150*
Sandringham, Various Gauges, Sidelock, Automatic Ejector, Double Trigger, Fancy Engraving, Fancy Checkering, *Modern*	*6,500*	*8,000*	*6,700*

RINO GALESI Industria Galesi, Brescia, Italy.

HANDGUN, SEMI-AUTOMATIC

Model 9, .25 ACP, Clip Fed, Blue, *Modern*.......................................	*100*	*125*	*120*

RIOT Made by Stevens Arms.

SHOTGUN, PUMP

Model 520, 12 Ga., Takedown, *Modern*	*125*	*150*	*145*
Model 620, Various Gauges, Takedown, *Modern*	*150*	*175*	*160*

RIPOLI

HANDGUN, MIQUELOT-LOCK

Ball Butt, Brass Inlay, Light Ornamentation, *Antique*.....................	*2,250*	*2,500*	*2,550*

			Prior Edition Exc.
	V.G.	Exc.	Value

Pair, Fluted Barrel, Pocket Pistol, Engraved, Silver Furniture,
Antique $7,000 $7,500 $7,300

RITTER, JACOB Phil., Pa. 1775–1783. See Kentucky Rifles and Pistols.

RIVERSIDE ARMS CO. Made by Stevens Arms & Tool Co.
SHOTGUN, DOUBLE BARREL, SIDE-BY-SIDE
Model 215, 12 and 16 Gauges, Outside Hammers, Steel Barrel,
Modern.. 150 175 175

ROB ROY Made by Hood Firearms Norwich, Conn., c. 1880.
HANDGUN, REVOLVER
.22 Short R.F., 7 Shot, Spur Trigger, Solid Frame, Single Action,
Antique 150 175 165

ROBBINS & LAWRENCE Robbins, Kendall & Lawrence, Windsor, Vt. 1844–1857. Became Robbins & Lawrence about 1846. Also see Sharps, U.S. Military.
HANDGUN, PERCUSSION
Pepperbox, Various Calibers, Ring Trigger, *Antique*...................... 550 700 575

ROBIN HOOD Made by Hood Firearms Norwich, Conn., c. 1875.
HANDGUN, REVOLVER
.22 Short R.F., 7 Shot, Spur Trigger, Solid Frame, Single Action,
Antique 125 150 165
.32 Short R.F., 5 Shot, Spur Trigger, Solid Frame, Single Action,
Antique 150 175 170

ROESSER, PETER Lancaster, Pa. 1741–1782. See Kentucky Rifles and Pistols.

ROGERS & SPENCER Willowvale, N.Y., c. 1862.
HANDGUN, PERCUSSION
.44 Army, Single Action, *Antique*.. 1,000 1,250 825

ROLAND Francisco Arizmendi, Eibar, Spain, c. 1922.
HANDGUN, SEMI-AUTOMATIC
.25 ACP, Clip Fed, Blue, *Curio*.. 100 125 125
.32 ACP, Clip Fed, Blue, *Curio*.. 125 150 135

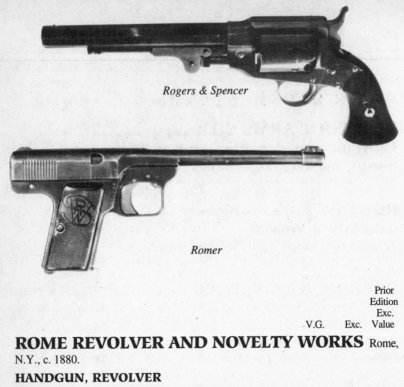

Rogers & Spencer

Romer

	V.G.	Exc.	Prior Edition Exc. Value

ROME REVOLVER AND NOVELTY WORKS Rome, N.Y., c. 1880.

HANDGUN, REVOLVER

.32 Short R.F., 5 Shot, Spur Trigger, Solid Frame, Single Action, *Antique* $125 $150 $165

ROMER Romerwerke AG, Suhl, Germany, c. 1925.

HANDGUN, SEMI-AUTOMATIC

.22 L.R.R.F., Clip Fed, 2¹/₂" and 6¹/₂" Barrels, Blue, *Curio* 750 900 995
.22 L.R.R.F., Clip Fed, One Barrel, Blue, *Curio* 600 750 850

ROOP, JOHN Allentown, Pa., c. 1775. See Kentucky Rifles.

ROSSI Amadeo Rossi S.A., Sao Leopoldo, Brazil. Also see Garrucha.

HANDGUN, REVOLVER

Model 31, .38 Special, Solid Frame, Swing-Out Cylinder, 5 Shot, 4" Barrel, *Modern* 100 125 110
Model 51, .22 L.R.R.F., Solid Frame, Swing-Out Cylinder, Adjustable Sights, 5 Shot, 6" Barrel, *Modern*.................................... 75 100 100
Model 68/2, .38 Special, Solid Frame, Swing-Out Cylinder, Adjustable Sights, 5 Shot, 2" Barrel, *Modern*.................................... 150 175 160
Model 68, .38 Special, Solid Frame, Swing-Out Cylinder, Adjustable Sights, 5 Shot, 3" Barrel, *Modern*.................................... 100 125 110

Rossi Model 68/2

Rossi M94

	V.G.	Exc.	Prior Edition Exc. Value
Model 69, .32 S & W Long, Solid Frame, Swing-Out Cylinder, Adjustable Sights, 5 Shot, 3" Barrel, *Modern*	$75	$100	$95
Model 70, .22 Short R.F., Solid Frame, Swing-Out Cylinder, Adjustable Sights, 5 Shot, 3" Barrel, *Modern*	75	100	95
Model 88, .38 Special, Solid Frame, Swing-Out Cylinder, Adjustable Sights, Stainless Steel, 5 Shot, 3" Barrel, *Modern*	150	175	140
Model 89, The Stainless Lady, .38 Special, Stainless, 3" Barrel, *Modern*	150	200	180
Model 94, .38 Special, Medium Frame, Shrouded Ejector Rod, *Modern*		N/A	

HANDGUN, SINGLESHOT

.22 Short R.F., Derringer, *Modern*	25	50	55

RIFLE, SLIDE ACTION

Saddle Ring, .357 Mag., Tube Feed, Hammer, Carbine, *Modern*	175	225	165
Saddle Ring, .357 Mag., Tube Feed, Hammer, Carbine, Engraved, *Modern*	200	250	215
Gallery, .22 L.R.R.F., Tube Feed, Takedown, Hammer, *Modern*	150	175	125
Gallery, .22 L.R.R.F., Tube Feed, Takedown, Hammer, Carbine, *Modern*	150	175	125

SHOTGUN, DOUBLE BARREL, SIDE-BY-SIDE

12 Ga. Mag. 3", Checkered Stock, Hammerless, Double Trigger, *Modern*	$175	$225	$195

Rossi Gallery Rifle

Rossi Overland Shotgun

Rossi Saddle Ring Carbine Rifle

	V.G.	Exc.	Prior Edition Exc. Value
12 Ga. Mag. 3", Hammerless, Double Trigger, *Modern*	200	200	185
Overland, 12 and 20 Gauges, Checkered Stock, Outside Hammers, Double Trigger, *Modern*	200	225	180
Overland, 12 and 20 Gauges, Outside Hammers, Double Trigger, *Modern*	200	225	180
Overland II, Various Gauges, Checkered Stock, Outside Hammers, Double Trigger, *Modern*	225	250	200
Squire Model 14, Various Gauges, Hammerless, Double Trigger, *Modern*	250	300	185

ROSS RIFLE CO. Quebec, Canada. Also see Canadian Military.

RIFLE, BOLT ACTION

	V.G.	Exc.	Prior Edition Exc. Value
Canadian Issue, .303 British, Military, *Modern*	225	275	225
Model 1903 MK I, .303 British, Sporting Rifle, Open Rear Sight, *Modern*	250	300	365
Model 1905 MK II, Various Calibers, Sporting Rifle, Open Rear Sight, *Modern*	250	300	335
Model 1910 MK III, Various Calibers, Sporting Rifle, Open Rear Sight, Checkered Stock, *Modern*	275	325	320

ROTTWEIL Germany, Imported by Eastern Sports Milford, N.H.

RIFLE, DOUBLE BARREL, OVER-UNDER

Standard Grade, Various Calibers, Engraved, Fancy Checkering, Open Rear Sight, *Modern* $2,000 $2,150 $2,300

SHOTGUN, DOUBLE BARREL, OVER-UNDER

Montreal, 12 Ga., Trap Grade, Vent Rib, Single Selective Trigger, Checkered Stock, *Modern* 1,350 1,600 1,850

Olympia, 12 Ga., Skeet Grade, Single Selective Trigger, Automatic Ejector, Vent Rib, Engraved, *Modern* 1,500 1,850 2,150

Olympia, 12 Ga., Trap Grade, Single Selective Trigger, Automatic Ejector, Vent Rib, Engraved, *Modern* 1,500 1,850 2,150

Olympia 72, 12 Ga., Skeet Grade, Trap Grade, Single Selective Trigger, Checkered Stock, *Modern* 1,450 1,650 1,850

Supreme, 12 Ga., Vent Rib, Single Selective Trigger, Checkered Stock, *Modern* 1,200 1,550 1,750

Supreme, 12 Ga., Field Grade, Single Selective Trigger, Automatic Ejector, Vent Rib, Engraved, *Modern* 1,500 1,950 2,150

American, 12 Ga., Trap Grade, Single Selective Trigger, Automatic Ejector, Vent Rib, Engraved, *Modern* 1,500 1,950 2,150

ROVIRO, ANTONIO Iqualada, Spain, c. 1790.

HANDGUN, MIQUELET-LOCK

Pair, Belt Pistol, Belt Hook, Engraved, Light Ornamentation, *Antique* 4,500 5,500 5,250

ROYAL Possibly Hopkins & Allen, c. 1880.

HANDGUN, REVOLVER

.22 Short R.F., 7 Shot, Spur Trigger, Solid Frame, Single Action, *Antique* 150 175 165

.32 Short R.F., 5 Shot, Spur Trigger, Solid Frame, Single Action, *Antique* 150 175 175

ROYAL M. Zulaika y Cia., Eibar, Spain

HANDGUN, SEMI-AUTOMATIC

Mauser M1896 Type, 7.63mm, Blue, *Modern* 325 375 395

Novelty, .25 ACP, Clip Fed, Blue, *Curio* 175 200 210

Novelty, .32 ACP, Clip Fed, Blue, *Curio* 200 225 225

.32 ACP, Clip Fed, Long Grip, *Modern* 175 200 185

12 Shot, .32 ACP, Clip Fed, Long Grip, *Modern* 225 250 255

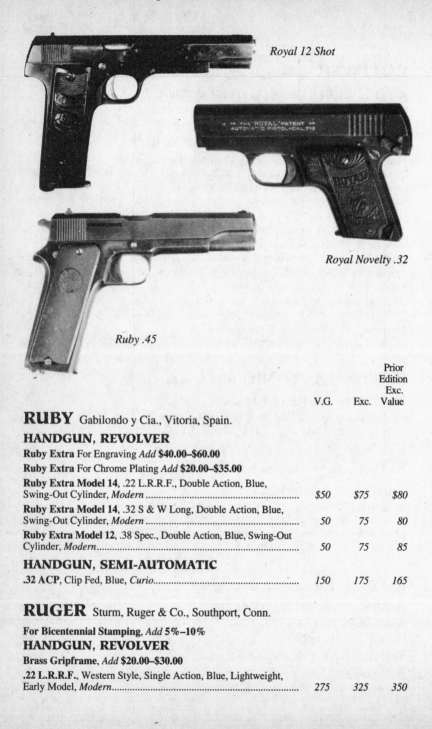

Royal 12 Shot

Royal Novelty .32

Ruby .45

	V.G.	Exc.	Prior Edition Exc. Value
RUBY Gabilondo y Cia., Vitoria, Spain.			
HANDGUN, REVOLVER			
Ruby Extra For Engraving *Add* **$40.00–$60.00**			
Ruby Extra For Chrome Plating *Add* **$20.00–$35.00**			
Ruby Extra Model 14, .22 L.R.R.F., Double Action, Blue, Swing-Out Cylinder, *Modern*	$50	$75	$80
Ruby Extra Model 14, .32 S & W Long, Double Action, Blue, Swing-Out Cylinder, *Modern*	50	75	80
Ruby Extra Model 12, .38 Spec., Double Action, Blue, Swing-Out Cylinder, *Modern*	50	75	85
HANDGUN, SEMI-AUTOMATIC			
.32 ACP, Clip Fed, Blue, *Curio*	150	175	165
RUGER Sturm, Ruger & Co., Southport, Conn.			
For Bicentennial Stamping, *Add* **5%–10%**			
HANDGUN, REVOLVER			
Brass Gripframe, *Add* **$20.00–$30.00**			
.22 L.R.R.F., Western Style, Single Action, Blue, Lightweight, Early Model, *Modern*	275	325	350

	V.G.	Exc.	Prior Edition Exc. Value
BP-7 Old Army Cap and Ball Revolver, .44 Black Powder, Blue, Walnut Grip, Reproduction, *Antique*	$200	$225	$235
KBP-7 Old Army Cap and Ball Revolver, .44 Black Powder, Stainless, Walnut Grip, Reproduction, *Antique*	225	275	300
KRH-35 Redhawk Double Action Revolver, .357 Magnum, Stainless, 7½" Barrel, *Modern*	300	350	395
KRH-355 Redhawk Double Action, Revolver, .357 Magnum, Stainless, 5½" Barrel, *Modern*	300	350	395
KRH-41 Redhawk Double Action Revolver, .41 Magnum, Stainless, 7½" Barrel, *Modern*	300	350	395
KRH-415 Redhawk Double Action Revolver, .41 Magnum, Stainless, 5½" Barrel, *Modern*	300	350	395
Bearcat, .22 L.R.R.F., Western Style, Single Action, Blue, Brass Gripframe, *Modern*	200	250	240
Bearcat, .22 L.R.R.F., Western Style, Single Action, Blue, Aluminum Gripframe, Early Model, *Modern*	225	275	290
Blackhawk, .30 Carbine, Western Style, Single Action, Blue, New Model, *Modern*	250	300	175
Blackhawk, .30 Carbine, Western Style, Single Action, Blue, *Modern*	275	325	225
Blackhawk, .357 Magnum, Western Style, Single Action, Blue, New Model, *Modern*	250	300	170
Blackhawk, .357 Magnum, Western Style, Single Action, Blue, *Modern*	275	325	225
Blackhawk, .357 Magnum, Western Style, Single Action, Blue, Flat-Top Frame, Early Model, *Modern*	300	350	450
Blackhawk, .357 Magnum, Western Style, Single Action, Blue, 10" Barrel, *Modern*	350	400	700
Blackhawk, .357 Maximum, Western Style, Single Action, Blue, New Model, *Modern*	300	350	250
Blackhawk, .357 Magnum, Western Style, Single Action, Stainless Steel, New Model, *Modern*	275	325	195
Blackhawk, .357 Magnum/9mm Combo, Western Style, Single Action, Blue, New Model, *Modern*	275	325	215
Blackhawk, .357 Magnum/9mm Combo, Western Style, Single Action, Blue, *Modern*	275	325	240
Blackhawk, .41 Magnum, Western Style, Single Action, Blue, New Model, *Modern*	250	300	185
Blackhawk, .41 Magnum, Western Style, Single Action, Blue, *Modern*	275	325	215
Blackhawk, .45 Colt, Western Style, Single Action, Blue, *Modern*	325	375	235
Blackhawk, .45 Colt, Western Style, Single Action, Blue, New Model, *Modern*	275	325	190
Blackhawk, .45 Colt/.45 ACP Combo, Western Style, Single Action, New Model, Blue, *Modern*	300	350	220
Blackhawk, .45 Colt/.45 ACP Combo, Western Style, Single Action, Blue, *Modern*	300	350	265

	V.G.	Exc.	Prior Edition Exc. Value
Security-Six, .357 Magnum, Double Action, Swing-Out Cylinder, Stainless Steel, Adjustable Sights, *Modern*	$200	$250	$200
Security-Six, .357 Magnum, Double Action, Swing-Out Cylinder, Blue, Adjustable Sights, *Modern*	175	225	185
Service-Six, .357 Magnum, Double Action, Swing-Out Cylinder, Blue, *Modern*	175	200	165
Service-Six, .357 Magnum, Double Action, Swing-Out Cylinder, Stainless Steel, *Modern*	200	225	190
Service-Six, 9mm Luger, Double Action, Swing-Out Cylinder, Blue, *Modern*	175	200	160
Service-Six, 9mm Luger, Double Action, Swing-Out Cylinder, Stainless Steel, *Modern*	200	225	190
Service-Six, .38 Special, Double Action, Swing-Out Cylinder, Blue, *Modern*	175	200	160
Service-Six, .38 Special, Double Action, Swing-Out Cylinder, Stainless Steel, *Modern*	175	225	185
Single-Six, .22 L.R.R.F., Western Style, Single Action, Blue, Engraved, Cased, *Modern*	2,500	3,500	850
Single-Six, .22 L.R.R.F., Western Style, Single Action, Blue, Flat Loading Gate, Early Model, *Modern*	300	350	310
Single-Six Colorado Centennial, .22 L.R.R.F., Commemorative, Cased, *Curio*	225	250	250
Speed-Six, .357 Magnum, Double Action, Swing-Out Cylinder, Blue, *Modern*	175	200	135
Speed-Six, .357 Magnum, Double Action, Swing-Out Cylinder, Stainless Steel, *Modern*	200	250	185
Speed-Six, .38 Special, Double Action, Swing-Out Cylinder, Blue, *Modern*	200	225	150
Speed-Six, .38 Special, Double Action, Swing-Out Cylinder, Stainless Steel, *Modern*	225	250	185
Speed-Six, 9mm Luger, Double Action, Swing-Out Cylinder, Blue, *Modern*	175	200	150
Super Blackhawk, .44 Magnum, Western Style, Single Action, Blue, New Model, 10½" Barrel, *Modern*	275	325	195
Super Blackhawk, .44 Magnum, Western Style, Single Action, Blue, New Model, *Modern*	275	325	190
Super Blackhawk, .44 Magnum, Western Style, Single Action, Stainless, New Model, *Modern*	325	375	235
Super Blackhawk, .44 Magnum, Western Style, Single Action, Stainless, New Model, 10½" Bull Barrel, *Modern*	350	400	230
Super Blackhawk, .44 Magnum, Western Style, Single Action, Stainless, 10½" Barrel, New Model, *Modern*	350	400	230
Super Blackhawk, .44 Magnum, Western Style, Single Action, Blue, *Modern*	300	350	300
Super Blackhawk, .44 Magnum, Western Style, Single Action, Blue, Flat-Top Frame, Early Model, *Modern*	600	650	715
Super Blackhawk, .44 Magnum, Western Style, Single Action, Blue, 10" Barrel, *Modern*	625	675	745

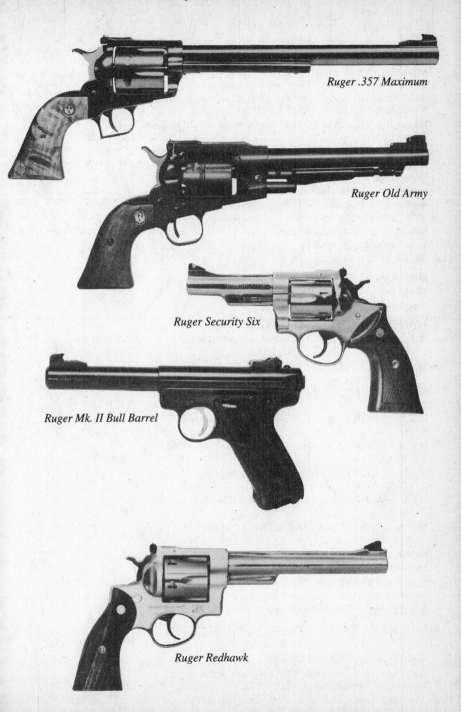

Ruger .357 Maximum

Ruger Old Army

Ruger Security Six

Ruger Mk. II Bull Barrel

Ruger Redhawk

	V.G.	Exc.	Prior Edition Exc. Value
Super Single Six, .22 LR/.22 WMR Combo, Western Style, Single Action, Blue, New Model, *Modern*	*$150*	*$200*	*$145*
Super Single Six, .22LR/.22 WMR Combo, Western Style, Single Action, Blue, New Model, 9½" Barrel, *Modern*	*150*	*200*	*145*
Super Single Six, .22LR/.22 WMR Combo, Western Style, Single Action, Blue, *Modern*	*175*	*225*	*185*
Super Single Six, .22LR/.22 WMR Combo, Western Style, Single Action, Blue, 9½" Barrel, *Model*	*200*	*250*	*195*
Super Single Six, .22LR/.22 WMR Combo, Western Style, Single Action, Stainless Steel, New Model, *Modern*	*175*	*225*	*170*
Redhawk, .44 Magnum, Double Action, Stainless, Interchangeable Sights, Swing-Out Cylinder, *Modern*	*275*	*325*	*280*
Bisley Single Six, .22 L.R., *Modern*	*250*	*275*	*258*
Bisley Single Six, .32 H&R Magnum, *Modern*	*250*	*275*	*258*
Blackhawk, .357 Magnum, *Modern*	*225*	*250*	*307*
Blackhawk, .41 Magnum, *Modern*	*225*	*250*	*307*
Blackhawk, .44 Magnum, *Modern*	*225*	*250*	*307*
Blackhawk, .45 Colt, *Modern*	*225*	*250*	*307*

HANDGUN, SEMI-AUTOMATIC

	V.G.	Exc.	Prior Edition Exc. Value
MK I, .22 L.R.R.F., Clip Fed, Adjustable Sights, Target Pistol, *Modern*	*125*	*175*	*150*
MK I, .22 L.R.R.F., Clip Fed, Adjustable Sights, Target Pistol, Wood Grips, *Modern*	*150*	*175*	*160*
MK II, .22 L.R.R.F., Clip Fed, Adjustable Sights, Target Pistol, *Modern*	*125*	*175*	*145*
MK II, .22 L.R.R.F., Clip Fed, Adjustable Sights, Stainless, *Modern*	*200*	*250*	*255*
MK II, .22 L.R.R.F., Clip Fed, Adjustable Sights, Target Pistol, Bull Barrel, *Modern*	*175*	*225*	*145*
MK II, .22 L.R.R.F., Clip Fed, Adjustable Sights, Target Pistol, Bull Barrel, Stainless, *Modern*	*225*	*275*	*255*
MK II Standard, .22 L.R.R.F., Clip Fed, Fixed Sights, Stainless, *Modern*	*200*	*250*	*225*
Signature RST-4, .22 L.R.R.F., Clip Fed, Commemorative, Stainless, *Modern*	*450*	*500*	*490*
Standard, .22 L.R.R.F., Clip Fed, *Modern*	*125*	*150*	*135*
Standard MK II, .22 L.R.R.F., Clip Fed, *Modern*	*125*	*150*	*130*
Standard (Under #25600), .22 L.R.R.F., Clip Fed, Early Model, Blue, *Modern*	*250*	*500*	*300*

HANDGUN, SINGLESHOT

	V.G.	Exc.	Prior Edition Exc. Value
Hawkeye, .256 Win. Mag., Western Style, Single Action, Blue, *Modern*	*950*	*1,200*	*650*

HANDGUN, PERCUSSION

	V.G.	Exc.	Prior Edition Exc. Value
Old Army, .44, Single Action, Blue, Adjustable Sights, Reproduction, *Antique*	*150*	*175*	*160*

Ruger Mark II Target Model Pistol

Ruger .22 Rimfire Bolt-Action Rifle

Ruger Mark II Standard Model, .22 Caliber Long Rifle

	V.G.	Exc.	Prior Edition Exc. Value
Old Army, .44, Single Action, Stainless, Adjustable Sights, Reproduction, *Antique*	*$225*	*$250*	*$210*

RIFLE, BOLT ACTION

M-77, for .338 Win. Mag., *Add* **$10.00–$15.00**

M-77, for .458 Win. Mag., *Add* **$40.00–$50.00**

M-77R, Various Calibers, Checkered Stock, Scope Mounts, no Sights, *Modern*	275	325	270
M-77RL, Various Calibers, Checkered Stock, Scope Mounts, Ultra Light, no Sights, *Modern*	275	325	315

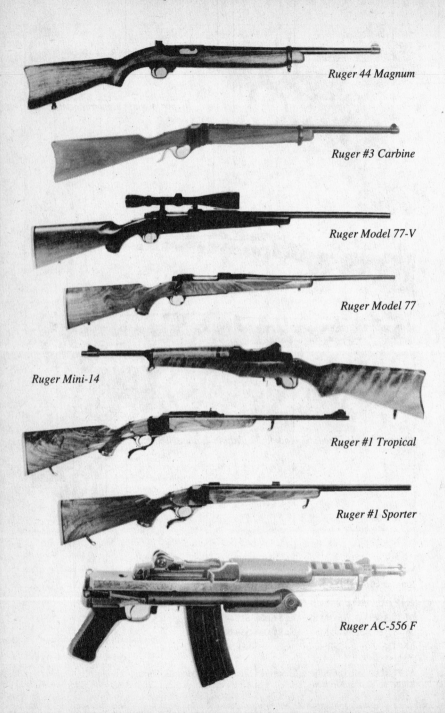

Ruger 44 Magnum

Ruger #3 Carbine

Ruger Model 77-V

Ruger Model 77

Ruger Mini-14

Ruger #1 Tropical

Ruger #1 Sporter

Ruger AC-556 F

	V.G.	Exc.	Prior Edition Exc. Value
M-77RS, Various Calibers, Checkered Stock, Open Rear Sight, Scope Mounts, *Modern*	$300	$350	$290
M-77RS Tropical, .458 Win. Mag., Checkered Stock, Open Rear Sight, Scope Mounts, *Modern*	375	450	340
M-77RSI, Various Calibers, Checkered Stock, Open Rear Sight, Mannlicher Stock, Scope Mounts, *Modern*	325	375	345
M-77ST, Various Calibers, Checkered Stock, Open Rear Sight, *Modern*	275	325	270
M-77V, Various Calibers, Heavy Barrel, Varmint, no Sights, Scope Mounts, Checkered Stock, *Modern*	275	325	270
M-77/22S, .22 Caliber Rimfire, Detachable Ten Shot Magazine, Blue, *Modern*	300	350	300
M-77/22R, .22 Caliber Rimfire, Detachable Ten Shot Magazine, Blue, *Modern*	300	350	300

RIFLE, SEMI-AUTOMATIC

	V.G.	Exc.	Prior
10/22, .22 L.R.R.F., Clip Fed, Plain, *Modern*	100	125	95
10/22 Canadian Centennial, .22 L.R.R.F., Commemorative, *Curio*	200	250	110
10/22 International, .22 L.R.R.F., Clip Fed, Full-Stocked, *Modern*	325	375	150
10/22 Sporter I, .22 L.R.R.F., Clip Fed, Monte Carlo Stock, *Modern*	125	150	115
10/22 Sporter II, .22 L.R.R.F., Clip Fed, Checkered Stock, *Modern*	125	150	120
10/22 Deluxe, .22 L.R.R.F., Clip Fed, Checkered Stock, *Modern*	150	175	120
Mini-14, .223 Rem., Clip Fed, Carbine, *Modern*	300	350	230
Mini-14, .223 Rem., Clip Fed, Carbine, Stainless, *Modern*	325	375	270
Mini-14/20 GB, .223 Rem., Clip Fed, Carbine, with Flash Hider and Bayonet Stud, *Modern*	300	350	230
Mini-14/20 GB-F, .223 Rem., Clip Fed, Carbine, Stainless, with Flash Hider and Bayonet Stud, *Modern*	325	375	265
K Mini-14/20 GB, .223 Rem., Clip Fed, Carbine, with Flash Hider and Bayonet Stud, Folding Stock, *Modern*	400	450	295
K Mini-14/20 GB-F, .223 Rem., Clip Fed, Carbine, Stainless, with Flash Hider and Bayonet Stud, Folding Stock, *Modern*	425	475	325
Model 44 Deluxe, .44 Magnum, Tube Feed, Plain, Peep Sights, Sling Swivels, *Modern*	350	400	235
Model 44 International, .44 Magnum, Tube Feed, Full-Stocked, *Modern*	500	550	245
Model 44 Sporter, .44 Magnum, Tube Feed, Monte Carlo Stock, *Modern*	300	350	245
Model 44 Standard, .44 Magnum, Tube Feed, Plain, Open Rear Sight, *Modern*	275	325	220
XGI, .308, *Modern*	350	400	425

RIFLE, SINGLESHOT

	V.G.	Exc.	Prior
#1 Canadian Centennial Deluxe, Commemorative, *Curio*	400	650	650

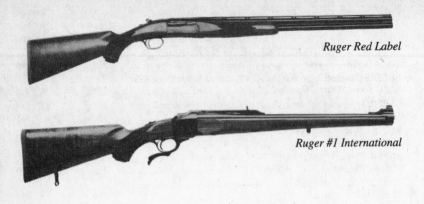

Ruger Red Label

Ruger #1 International

	V.G.	Exc.	Prior Edition Exc. Value
#1 Light Sporter, Various Calibers, Open Rear Sight, Checkered Stock, *Modern*	$375	$425	$295
#1 Medium Sporter, Various Calibers, Open Rear Sight, Checkered Stock, *Modern*	300	350	295
#1 Standard Sporter, Various Calibers, no Sights, Scope Mounts, Checkered Stock, *Modern*	300	350	285
#1 International, Various Calibers, Open Rear Sight, Checkered Mannlicher Stock, *Modern*	425	475	305
#1 Tropical, Various Calibers, Open Rear Sight, Checkered Stock, *Modern*	350	400	300
#1 Varminter, Various Calibers, Heavy Barrel, no Sights, Checkered Stock, *Modern*	325	375	300
#2 Canadian Centennial Set, Commemorative, *Curio*	400	450	420
#3 Canadian Centennial Set, Commemorative, *Curio*	275	325	310
#3 Carbine, Various Calibers, Open Rear Sight, *Modern*	175	200	200

SHOTGUN, DOUBLE BARREL, OVER-UNDER

	V.G.	Exc.	Prior Edition Exc. Value
Red Label, 12 or 20 Gauges, Checkered Stock, Single Trigger, *Modern*	600	675	650

RUMMEL Made by Crescent for A.J. Rummel Arms Co., Toledo, Ohio.

SHOTGUN, DOUBLE BARREL, SIDE-BY-SIDE

	V.G.	Exc.	Prior Edition Exc. Value
Various Gauges, Outside Hammers, Damascus Barrel, *Modern*	150	175	170
Various Gauges, Hammerless, Steel Barrel, *Modern*	150	200	190
Various Gauges, Hammerless, Damascus Barrel, *Modern*	150	175	170
Various Gauges, Outside Hammers, Steel Barrel, *Modern*	150	175	185

SHOTGUN, SINGLESHOT

	V.G.	Exc.	Prior Edition Exc. Value
Various Gauges, Hammer, Steel Barrel, *Modern*	50	75	85

Jacob Rupertus Patent Navy Six Shot, .36 Caliber

RUPERTUS, JACOB Philadelphia, Pa. 1858–1899.

	V.G.	Exc.	Prior Edition Exc. Value

HANDGUN, DOUBLE BARREL, SIDE-BY-SIDE

	V.G.	Exc.	Prior Edition Exc. Value
.22 Short R.F., Derringer, Side-Swing Barrel, Iron Frame, Spur Trigger, *Antique*	$650	$800	$425

HANDGUN, REVOLVER

	V.G.	Exc.	Prior Edition Exc. Value
.22 Short R.F., Pepperbox, 8 Shot, Iron Frame, Spur Trigger, *Antique*	500	575	395
.22 Short R.F., 7 Shot, Spur Trigger, Solid Frame, Single Action, *Antique*	150	200	170
.32 Short R.F., 5 Shot, Spur Trigger, Solid Frame, Single Action, *Antique*	175	225	190
.36 Patent Navy, Percussion, 6 Shot, *Antique*	5,500	7,000	4,650
.38 Short R.F., 5 Shot, Spur Trigger, Solid Frame, Single Action, *Antique*	200	250	195
.41 Short R.F., 5 Shot, Spur Trigger, Solid Frame, Single Action, *Antique*	250	300	220

HANDGUN, SINGLESHOT

	V.G.	Exc.	Prior Edition Exc. Value
.22 Short R.F., Derringer, Side-Swing Barrel, Iron Frame, Spur Trigger, *Antique*	250	300	230
.32 Short R.F., Derringer, Side-Swing Barrel, Iron Frame, Spur Trigger, *Antique*	200	250	190
.38 Short R.F., Derringer, Side-Swing Barrel, Iron Frame, Spur Trigger, *Antique*	225	275	195

RUPP, HERMAN Pa. 1784. See Kentucky Rifles.

RUPP, JOHN Allentown, Pa. See U.S. Military, Kentucky Rifles and Pistols.

RUPPERT, WILLIAM Lancaster, Pa., c. 1776. See U.S. Military, Kentucky Rifles and Pistols.

RUSH, JOHN Philadelphia, Pa. 1740–1750. See Kentucky Rifles and Pistols.

	V.G.	Exc.	Prior Edition Exc. Value

RUSSIAN MILITARY

HANDGUN, FREE PISTOL

	V.G.	Exc.	Prior Edition Exc. Value
MC, .22 L.R.R.F., Clip Fed, *Modern*	$200	$225	$200
MCU, .22 Short, Clip Fed, *Modern*	225	275	260
Vostok M-T0Z-35, .22 L.R.R.F., *Modern*	500	575	550
Vostok M-T0Z-35, .22 L.R.R.F., Cased with Accessories, *Modern*	775	875	850

HANDGUN, REVOLVER

	V.G.	Exc.	Prior Edition Exc. Value
M1890, 7.62mm Nagant, Gas-Seal Cylinder, Imperial, *Curio*	200	250	170
M1890, 7.62mm Nagant, Gas-Seal Cylinder, Police, *Curio*	175	225	230
M1890, 7.62mm Nagant, Gas-Seal Cylinder, Communist, *Curio*	175	200	140

HANDGUN, SEMI-AUTOMATIC

	V.G.	Exc.	Prior Edition Exc. Value
Makarov, 9mm Makarov, Clip Fed, Double Action, *Modern*	750	900	750
Tokarev TT-30, 7.62mm Tokarev, Clip Fed, *Modern*	250	300	430
Tokarev TT-33 Early, 7.62mm Tokarev, Clip Fed, *Modern*	200	250	260

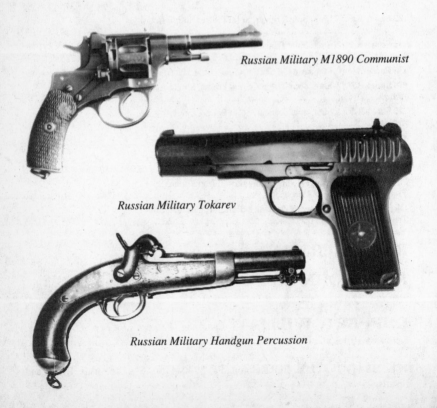

Russian Military M1890 Communist

Russian Military Tokarev

Russian Military Handgun Percussion

Russian Military Makarov

Czarist and Communist plants include: Tula, Izshevsky, and many others. Foreign manufacturers for Czarist Russia include: S.I.G. Neuhasen, Switzerland; St. Etienne, France, and Remington Arms U.S.A. Foreign manufacturers for Moisin-Nagant only. Tokarev and SKS Communist Russia produced.

NOTE: Russian ammo either 7.62 × 54R or 7.62 × 39M43 will not interchange with American 7.62 N.A.T.O. ammunition.

	V.G.	Exc.	Prior Edition Exc. Value
RIFLE, BOLT ACTION			
KK M, CM 2, .22 L.R.R.F., Match Rifle, Target Sights, *Modern*	$300	$375	$360
1891 Moisin-Nagant, 7.62 Cal, 31-Inch Barrel, Bolt Action. (The rear sight of these early rifles are graduated not in meters but in arshins. An arshin is equivalent to .78 yards. After the revolution, Russia adopted the metric system and the sights for the Model 1891/30 and later rifles and carbines are graduated in meters.)	75	100	90
1891/38 Carbine, 7.62.54 Cal., 20-Inch Barrel, Hooded Front Sight, Rear Sight Graduated From 100 - 1000 Meters, No Bayonet Mounting	100	125	100
1891 Remington, Same as Russian Nagant, Except Made in U.S.A., By Remington For Export To Czarist Russia. (Few were ever delivered. Much higher quality than Russian produced models)	125	150	115
1891/30 Sniper Rifle, Especially Selected For Accuracy, Bolt Handle Turned Down and Fitted with Either 4 × P.E. or 3.5 × P.U. Telescopic Sight, (Still in use in Russia.) *Very Rare*	575	650	220
M1910, 7.62 × 54R Russian, Military, Carbine, *Modern*	200	250	115
1938 Russian Tokarev, Semi-Automatic Gas Operated Rifle, Two Piece Stock, 10 Shot Magazine, Fitted with Muzzlebreak, Cleaning Rod On Right Side Of Stock, First of Tokarev Series	275	350	220
1940 Tokarev Model, 24-Inch Barrel, Semi-Automatic Gas Operated Rifle, (Similar to Model 1938 but much more rugged, was very successful action similar to that of Belgian FN Rifle.)	250	300	140
Russian SKS, 7.62.39M43 Cal., 20-Inch Barrel, (A Russian attempt to develop a gas operated carbine) 10 Shot Magazine, Folding Bayonet, Very Well Made	200	250	175

	V.G.	Exc.	Prior Edition Exc. Value

RWS Rheinische-Westfalische Sprengstoff, since 1931. Now Dynamit Nobel AG, Troisdorf-Oberlar, West Germany.

RIFLE, BOLT ACTION

Repeater, Various Calibers, Checkered Stock, Set Triggers, Open Sights, *Modern*.. $400 $475 $335

RYAN, THOMAS Norwich, Conn., c. 1870.

HANDGUN, REVOLVER

.22 Short R.F., 7 Shot, Spur Trigger, Solid Frame, Single Action, *Antique*.. 150 175 165

.32 Short R.F., 5 Shot, Spur Trigger, Solid Frame, Single Action, *Antique*.. 150 175 170

S

	V.G.	Exc.	Prior Edition Exc. Value

SABLE Belgium, unknown maker.

HANDGUN, REVOLVER

	V.G.	Exc.	Prior Edition Exc. Value
Baby Hammerless, .22 Short R.F., Folding Trigger, *Modern*	$100	$125	$100

SAKO O. Y. Sako AB, Riihmaki, Finland.

RIFLE, BOLT ACTION

	V.G.	Exc.	Prior Edition Exc. Value
Deluxe (Garcia), Various Calibers, Sporting Rifle, Monte Carlo Stock, Fancy Checkering, Long Action, *Modern*	650	725	435
Deluxe (Garcia), Various Calibers, Sporting Rifle, Monte Carlo Stock, Fancy Checkering, Medium Action, *Modern*	650	725	435
Deluxe (Garcia), Various Calibers, Sporting Rifle, Monte Carlo Stock, Fancy Checkering, Short Action, *Modern*	650	725	435
Finnbear, Various Calibers, Sporting Rifle, Monte Carlo Stock, Checkered Stock, Long Action, *Modern*	625	700	435
Finnbear Carbine, Various Calibers, Sporting Rifle, Monte Carlo Stock, Checkered Stock, Long Action, Full-Stocked, *Modern*	675	750	465
Forester, Various Calibers, Sporting Rifle, Monte Carlo Stock, Checkered Stock, Medium Action, *Modern*	600	675	420
Forester, Various Calibers, Sporting Rifle, Monte Carlo Stock, Checkered Stock, Medium Action, Heavy Barrel, *Modern*	600	675	420
Forester Carbine, Various Calibers, Sporting Rifle, Monte Carlo Stock, Checkered Stock, Medium Action, Full-Stocked, *Modern*	650	725	475
Hi-Power Mauser (FN), Various Calibers, Sporting Rifle, Monte Carlo Stock, Checkered Stock, *Modern*..	475	550	395
Magnum Mauser (FN), Various Calibers, Sporting Rifle, Monte Carlo Stock, Checkered Stock, *Modern*...	575	650	435
Model 74 (Garcia), Various Calibers, Sporting Rifle, Monte Carlo Stock, Checkered Stock, Long Action, *Modern*	400	475	375
Model 74 (Garcia), Various Calibers, Sporting Rifle, Monte Carlo Stock, Checkered Stock, Medium Action, *Modern*	400	475	375
Model 74 (Garcia), Various Calibers, Sporting Rifle, Monte Carlo Stock, Checkered Stock, Short Action, *Modern*................................	400	475	375
Model 74 (Garcia), Various Calibers, Sporting Rifle, Monte Carlo Stock, Checkered Stock, Heavy Barrel, Medium Action, *Modern*....	425	500	390
Model 74 (Garcia), Various Calibers, Sporting Rifle, Monte Carlo Stock, Checkered Stock, Heavy Barrel, Short Action, *Modern*.........	425	500	390

	V.G.	Exc.	Prior Edition Exc. Value
Model 78 (Stoeger), .22 L.R.R.F., Sporting Rifle, Monte Carlo Stock, Checkered Stock, *Modern*..............	$250	$325	$260
Model 78 (Stoeger), .22 Hornet, Sporting Rifle, Monte Carlo Stock, Checkered Stock, *Modern*..............	300	375	320
Model 78 (Stoeger), .22 W.M.R., Sporting Rifle, Monte Carlo Stock, Checkered Stock, *Modern*..............	375	450	290
Model 78 (Stoeger), .22 L.R.R.F., Sporting Rifle, Monte Carlo Stock, Checkered Stock, Heavy Barrel, *Modern*.............	400	475	295
Vixen, Various Calibers, Sporting Rifle, Monte Carlo Stock, Checkered Stock, Short Action, *Modern*............	650	750	350
Vixen, Various Calibers, Sporting Rifle, Monte Carlo Stock, Checkered Stock, Short Action, Heavy Barrel, *Modern*............	700	800	375
Vixen Carbine, Various Calibers, Sporting Rifle, Monte Carlo Stock, Checkered Stock, Short Action, Full-Stocked, *Modern*.........	750	850	395

RIFLE, LEVER ACTION

	V.G.	Exc.	
Finnwolf, Various Calibers, Sporting Rifle, Monte Carlo Stock, Checkered Stock, *Modern*..............	525	600	395

ST. LOUIS ARMS CO. Belgium for Shapleigh Hardware Co., c. 1900.

SHOTGUN, DOUBLE BARREL, SIDE-BY-SIDE

Various Gauges, Outside Hammers, Damascus Barrel, *Modern*.........	150	175	170
Various Gauges, Hammerless, Steel Barrel, *Modern*............	150	200	190
Various Gauges, Hammerless, Damascus Barrel, *Modern*..............	150	175	170
Various Gauges, Outside Hammers, Steel Barrel, *Modern*..............	125	175	185

SHOTGUN, SINGLESHOT

Various Gauges, Hammer, Steel Barrel, *Modern*............	50	75	85

SAMPLES, BETHUEL Urbana, Ohio. See Kentucky Rifles and Pistols.

SANDERSON Portage, Wisc.

SHOTGUN, DOUBLE BARREL, SIDE-BY-SIDE

M200-S 1, Various Gauges, Checkered Stock, Automatic Ejectors, Engraved, *Modern*..............	350	425	400
Neumann, Various Gauges, Checkered Stock, Automatic Ejectors, Engraved, *Modern*..............	225	275	250
Neumann, 10 Gauge Mag., Checkered Stock, Automatic Ejectors, Engraved, *Modern*..............	350	425	400

SARASQUETA, FELIX Eibar, Spain, imported by Sarasqueta of N.A., Coral Gables, Fla.

SHOTGUN, DOUBLE BARREL, OVER-UNDER "MERKE"

Model 500, 12 Gauge, Checkered Stock, Boxlock, Light Engraving, Double Triggers, *Modern*..............	175	275	240

	V.G.	Exc.	Prior Edition Exc. Value
Model 510, 20 Gauge, Checkered Stock, Boxlock with Sideplates, Light Engraving, Double Triggers, *Modern*	*$150*	*$225*	*$220*

SARASQUETA, VICTOR Victor Sarasqueta, Eibar, Spain from 1934.

RIFLE, DOUBLE BARREL, SIDE-BY-SIDE

	V.G.	Exc.	Prior Ed.
Various Calibers, Sidelock, Automatic Ejector, Fancy Engraving, Fancy Checkering, *Modern*	*1,750*	*2,500*	*2,500*

SHOTGUN, DOUBLE BARREL, SIDE-BY-SIDE

	V.G.	Exc.	Prior Ed.
#10E, Various Gauges, Sidelock, Fancy Checkering, Fancy Engraving, *Modern*	*1,500*	*1,650*	*975*
#11E, Various Gauges, Sidelock, Fancy Checkering, Fancy Engraving, *Modern*	*1,600*	*1,750*	*1,225*
#12E, Various Gauges, Sidelock, Fancy Checkering, Fancy Engraving, *Modern*	*1,750*	*2,000*	*1,450*
#3, Various Gauges, Double Trigger, Checkered Stock, Light Engraving, *Modern*	*500*	*600*	*295*
#4, Various Gauges, Sidelock, Checkered Stock, Light Engraving, *Modern*	*475*	*525*	*350*
#4E, Various Gauges, Sidelock, Checkered Stock, Light Engraving, *Modern*	*500*	*575*	*400*
203, Various Gauges, Sidelock, Fancy Checkering, Fancy Engraving, *Modern*	*525*	*600*	*700*
203E, Various Gauges, Sidelock, Fancy Checkering, Fancy Engraving, *Modern*	*600*	*700*	*825*
#6E, Various Gauges, Sidelock, Fancy Checkering, Engraved, *Modern*	*650*	*750*	*500*
#7E, Various Gauges, Sidelock, Fancy Checkering, Engraved, *Modern*	*700*	*800*	*595*

SATA Sabolti & Tantagiro Fabbrica o' Armi, Gardone Val Trompia, Italy.

HANDGUN, SEMI-AUTOMATIC

	V.G.	Exc.	Prior Ed.
.22 Short, Clip Fed, Blue, *Modern*	*125*	*150*	*155*
.25 ACP, Clip Fed, Blue, *Modern*	*150*	*175*	*160*

SAUER, J.P. & SOHN 1855 to date, first in Suftt, now in Eckernforde, West Germany. Also see Hawes.

COMBINATION WEAPON, OVER-UNDER

	V.G.	Exc.	Prior Ed.
BBF, Various Calibers, Double Trigger, Set Trigger Engraved, Checkered Stock, *Modern*	*1,700*	*1,900*	*1,475*
BBF Deluxe, Various Calibers, Double Trigger, Set Trigger, Fancy Engraving, Fancy Checkering, *Modern*	*1,900*	*2,100*	*1,735*

	V.G.	Exc.	Prior Edition Exc. Value

COMBINATION WEAPON, DRILLING

Model 3000E, Various Calibers, Double Trigger, Engraved, Checkered Stock, *Modern* .... $2,600 — $2,800 — $1,785

Model 3000E Deluxe, Various Calibers, Double Trigger, Fancy Engraving, Fancy Checkering, *Modern* .... 3,000 — 3,250 — 2,200

HANDGUN, MANUAL REPEATER

Bar Pistole, 7mm, Double Barrel, 4 Shot, Folding Trigger, *Curio* ...... 325 — 375 — 375

HANDGUN, SEMI-AUTOMATIC

Behorden, .32 ACP, Clip Fed, *Modern* .... 200 — 250 — 295

Behorden, .32 ACP, Clip Fed, Lightweight, *Modern* .... 350 — 400 — 450

Behorden 4mm, .32 ACP, Clip Fed, Extra Barrel, *Modern* .... 700 — 800 — 850

Behorden Dutch Navy, .32 ACP, Clip Fed, Military, *Modern* .... 350 — 400 — 425

Sauer Model H 38

Sauer Bar Pistole

Sauer Roth-Sauer

Sauer Model 1913 .25

	V.G.	Exc.	Prior Edition Exc. Value
Model 1913, .25 ACP, Clip Fed, *Modern*	$225	$275	$245
Model 1913, .32 ACP, Clip Fed, *Modern*	225	275	250
Model 28, .25 ACP, Clip Fed, *Modern*	250	300	275
Model H 38, .380 ACP, Double Action, Clip Fed, Hammer, *Modern*	750	1,000	495
Model H 38, .32 ACP, Double Action, Clip Fed, Hammer, Commercial, *Modern*	225	275	350
Model H 38, .32 ACP, Double Action, Clip Fed, Hammer, Nazi-Proofed, Military, *Modern*	225	325	325
Model H 38, .32 ACP, Double Action, Clip Fed, Hammer, Nazi-Proofed, No Safety, Military, *Modern*	275	325	300
Model H 38, .32 ACP, Double Action, Clip Fed, Hammer, Lightweight, *Modern*	475	550	675
Model H 38 Police, .32 ACP, Double Action, Clip Fed, Hammer, Nazi-Proofed, *Curio*	375	450	500
W.T.M. 1922, .25 ACP, Clip Fed, *Modern*	250	300	265
W.T.M. 1928, .25 ACP, Clip Fed, *Modern*	275	325	290
W.T.M. 1928/2, .25 ACP, Clip Fed, *Modern*	225	275	245
Roth-Sauer, 8mm, Clip Fed, *Curio*	900	1,200	900

RIFLE, BOLT ACTION

Mauser Custom, Various Calibers, Set Trigger, Checkered Stock, Octagon Barrel, *Modern*	450	550	500

SHOTGUN, DOUBLE BARREL, OVER-UNDER

Model 66 GR I, 12 Ga., Single Selective Trigger, Selective Ejector, Hammerless, Sidelock, Engraved, *Modern*	1,650	1,800	1,375
Model 66 GR I, 12 Ga., Skeet Grade, Selective Ejector, Hammerless, Sidelock, Engraved, *Modern*	1,450	1,600	1,200
Model 66 Gr II, 12 Ga., Single Selective Trigger, Selective Ejector, Hammerless, Sidelock, Fancy Engraving, *Modern*	2,500	2,800	1,625
Model 66 GR II, 12 Ga., Skeet Grade, Selective Ejector, Hammerless, Sidelock, Fancy Engraving, *Modern*	2,300	2,550	1,250
Model 66 GR II, 12 Ga., Trap Grade, Selective Ejector, Hammerless, Sidelock, Fancy Engraving, *Modern*	2,350	2,600	1,300
Model 66 GR III, 12 Ga., Single Selective Trigger, Selective Ejector, Hammerless, Sidelock, Fancy Engraving, *Modern*	3,000	3,500	2,350
Model 66 GR III, 12 Ga., Skeet Grade, Selective Ejector, Hammerless, Sidelock, Fancy Engraving, *Modern*	2,500	3,000	1,825
Model 66 GR III, 12 Ga., Trap Grade, Selective Ejector, Hammerless, Sidelock, Fancy Engraving, *Modern*	2,500	3,000	1,825

SHOTGUN, DOUBLE BARREL, SIDE-BY-SIDE

.410 Gauge, Double Trigger, Light Engraving, *Modern*	625	675	620
Artemis I, 12 Ga., Single Selective Trigger, Engraved, Checkered Stock, *Modern*	3,500	4,500	3,500
Artemis II, 12 Ga., Single Selective Trigger, Fancy Engraving, Fancy Checkering, *Modern*	4,500	5,500	4,000

	V.G.	Exc.	Prior Edition Exc. Value
Royal, 12 and 20 Gauges, Single Selective Trigger, Engraved, Checkered Stock, *Modern*	$1,250	$1,600	$865
Model Kim, Various Gauges, Double Triggers, Checkered Stock, Light Engraving, *Modern*	250	300	285
Model VIII, Various Gauges, Double Triggers, Checkered Stock, Light Engraving, *Modern*	250	300	285
Model VIII DES, Various Gauges, Single Selective Trigger, Selective Ejectors, Checkered Stock, Light Engraving, *Modern*	250	300	285
Model VIII DES-01, Various Gauges, Single Selective Trigger, Selective Ejectors, Checkered Stock, Engraved, *Modern*	325	375	365
Model VIII DES-07, Various Gauges, Single Selective Trigger, Selective Ejectors, Checkered Stock, Fancy Engraving, *Modern*	425	500	485
Model VIII DES-05, Various Gauges, Single Selective Trigger, Selective Ejectors, Checkered Stock, Fancy Engraving, Sideplates, *Modern*	700	800	795

SAVAGE ARMS CO. Utica, N.Y. 1893–1899, renamed Savage Arms Co. 1899. J. Stevens Arms Co. Springfield Arms Co. and A.H. Fox are all part of Savage. Also see U.S. Military.

COMBINATION WEAPON, OVER-UNDER

	V.G.	Exc.	Prior Edition Exc. Value
Model 24, Various Calibers, Hammer, *Modern*	100	125	130
Model 24-C, .22/20 Ga., Hammer, *Modern*	125	150	135
Model 24-D, Various Calibers, Hammer, *Modern*	175	200	150
Model 24-V, Various Calibers, Checkered Stock, Hammer, *Modern*	225	250	185
Model 2400, Various Calibers, Checkered Stock, Hammer, *Modern*	450	550	485

HANDGUN, SEMI-AUTOMATIC

Model 1907, Factory Nickel, *Add* **$35.00–$50.00**

Model 1907, Grade A Engraving (Light), *Add* **$75.00–$100.00**

Model 1907, Grade C Engraving (Fancy), *Add* **$225.00–$325.00**

	V.G.	Exc.	Prior Edition Exc. Value
Model 1907 (1908), .32 ACP, Clip Fed, Burr Cocking Piece, (under #10,899), *Curio*	300	350	255
Model 1907 (1909), .32 ACP, Clip Fed, Burr Cocking Piece, (#'s-10,900–70,499), *Curio*	275	325	195
Model 1907 (1912), .32 ACP, Clip Fed, Burr Cocking Piece, (Higher # than 70500), *Curio*	250	300	180
Model 1907 (1913), .380 ACP, Clip Fed, Burr Cocking Piece, *Curio*	325	375	255
Model 1907 (1914), .32 ACP, Spur Cocking Piece, *Curio*	250	300	175
Model 1907 (1914), .380 ACP, Spur Cocking Piece, *Curio*	275	325	205
Model 1907 (1918), .32 ACP, Clip Fed, no Cartridge Indicator, Burr Cocking Piece, (After # 175,000), *Curio*	225	275	165
Model 1907 (1918), .32 ACP, Clip Fed, Spur Cocking Piece, (After # 195000), *Curio*	250	300	185

	V.G.	Exc.	Prior Edition Exc. Value
Model 1907 (1918), .308 ACP, Clip Fed, Burr Cocking Piece, (After # 10000B), *Curio*	$325	$375	$280
Model 1907 Military, .32 ACP, Clip Fed, Burr Cocking Piece, *Curio*	225	275	155
Model 1907 Military, .32 ACP, Clip Fed, Burr Cocking Piece (Portuguese Contract), *Curio*	375	425	360
Model 1915, .32 ACP, Clip Fed, Hammerless, Grip Safety, *Curio*	250	300	245
Model 1915, .380 ACP, Clip Fed, Hammerless, Grip Safety, *Curio*	300	350	330
Model 1917, .32 ACP, Clip Fed, Spur Cocking Piece, Flared Grip, *Curio*	200	250	205
Model 1917, .380 ACP, Clip Fed, Spur Cocking Piece, Flared Grip, *Curio*	225	275	240
Military Model, .45 ACP, Clip Fed, Original, *Curio*	5,000	6,000	3,950
Military Model, .45 ACP, Clip Fed, Surplus, Reblue, *Curio*	3,500	4,000	2,925
.25 ACP, Clip Fed, Blue, *Curio*		RARE	

HANDGUN, SINGLESHOT

	V.G.	Exc.	Prior Edition Exc. Value
Model 101, .22 L.R.R.F., Western Style, Single Action, Swing-Out Cylinder, *Modern*	125	150	130

RIFLE, BOLT ACTION

	V.G.	Exc.	Prior Edition Exc. Value
Model 10, .22 L.R.R.F., Target Sights, (Anschutz), *Modern*	200	225	150
Model 110, Magnum Calibers, *Add* $15.00			
Model 110, Various Calibers, Open Rear Sight, Checkered Stock, *Modern*	175	200	180
Model 110-B, Various Calibers, Open Rear Sight, *Modern*	225	275	200
Model 110-BL, Various Calibers, Open Rear Sight, Left-Hand, *Modern*	250	300	225
Model 110-C, Various Calibers, Clip Fed, Open Rear Sight, *Modern*	200	250	260
Model 110-CL, Various Calibers, Clip Fed, Open Rear Sight, Left-Hand, *Modern*	225	275	275
Model 110-E, Various Calibers, Open Rear Sight, *Modern*	175	200	180
Model 110-EL, Various Calibers, Open Rear Sight, Left-Hand, *Modern*	175	225	185
Model 110-ES, Various Calibers, Internal Box Mag, Scope, *Modern*	250	300	300
Model 110-M, Various Calibers, Open Rear Sight, Monte Carlo Stock, Checkered Stock, Magnum Action, *Modern*	175	225	210
Model 110-MC, Various Calibers, Open Rear Sight, Monte Carlo Stock, Checkered Stock, *Modern*	150	175	180
Model 110-MCL, Various Calibers, Open Rear Sight, Monte Carlo Stock, Checkered Stock, Left-Hand, *Modern*	150	200	185
Model 110-ML, Various Calibers, Open Rear Sight, Monte Carlo Stock, Checkered Stock, Magnum Action, Left-Hand, *Modern*	175	225	220

	V.G.	Exc.	Prior Edition Exc. Value
Model 110-P, Various Calibers, Open Rear Sight, Fancy Wood, Monte Carlo Stock, Fancy Checkering, Sling Swivels, *Modern*	$300	$350	$345
Model 110-PE, Various Calibers, Engraved, Fancy Checkering, Fancy Wood, Sling Swivels, *Modern*	550	600	580
Model 110-PEL, Various Calibers, Engraved, Fancy Checkering, Fancy Wood, Sling Swivels, Left-Hand, *Modern*	550	600	580
Model 110-PL, Various Calibers, Fancy Wood, Monte Carlo Stock, Fancy Checkering, Sling Swivels, Left-Hand, *Modern*	350	400	390
Model 110-S Silhouette Rifle, .308 Winchester and 7mm-08 Remington, Free Floating Barrel, Monte Carlo Stock, *Modern*	275	325	360
Model 110-V Varmint, Various Calibers, 26" Heavy Barrel, *Modern*	300	350	360
Model 111, Various Calibers, Clip Fed, Monte Carlo Stock, Checkered Stock, *Modern*	200	250	235
Model 112-V, Various Calibers, Singleshot, no Sights, *Modern*	250	300	230
Model 1407, Sights Only, *Add* **$55.00–$85.00**			
Model 1407 "I.S.U.", .22 L.R.R.F., Heavy Barrel, no Sights, (Anschutz), *Modern*	425	475	460
Model 1407-L "I.S.U.", .22 L.R.R.F., Heavy Barrel, no Sights, Left-Hand, (Anschutz), *Modern*	450	500	480
Model 1408, .22 L.R.R.F., Heavy Barrel, no Sights, (Anschutz), *Modern*	350	400	380
Model 1408-ED, .22 L.R.R.F., Heavy Barrel, no Sights, (Anschutz), *Modern*	450	500	480
Model 1408-L, .22 L.R.R.F., Heavy Barrel, no Sights, Left-Hand, (Anschutz), *Modern*	325	375	375
Model 1411, Sights Only, *Add* **$55.00–$80.00**			
Model 1411 "Prone", .22 L.R.R.F., Heavy Barrel, no Sights, (Anschutz), *Modern*	425	500	500
Model 1411-L "Prone", .22 L.R.R.F., Heavy Barrel, no Sights, Left-Hand, (Anschutz), *Modern*	425	500	500
Model 1413, .22 L.R.R.F., Sights Only, *Add* **$55.00–$80.00**			
Model 1413 "Match", .22 L.R.R.F., Heavy Barrel, no Sights, (Anschutz), *Modern*	625	700	680
Model 1413-L "Match", .22 L.R.R.F., Heavy Barrel, No Sights, Left-Hand, (Anschutz), *Modern*	675	750	740
Model 1418, .22 L.R.R.F., Clip Fed, Mannlicher, Fancy Checkering, (Anschutz), *Modern*	300	350	345
Model 1432, .22 Hornet, Sporting Rifle, Clip Fed, Fancy Checkering, (Anschutz), *Modern*	425	500	480
Model 1433, .22 Hornet, Mannlicher, Clip Fed, Fancy Checkering, (Anschutz), *Modern*	450	550	535
Model 1518, .22 WMR, Clip Fed, Mannlicher, Fancy Checkering, (Anschutz), *Modern*	300	375	370
Model 1533, .222 Rem., Mannlicher, Clip Fed, Fancy Checkering, (Anschutz), *Modern*	450	525	510

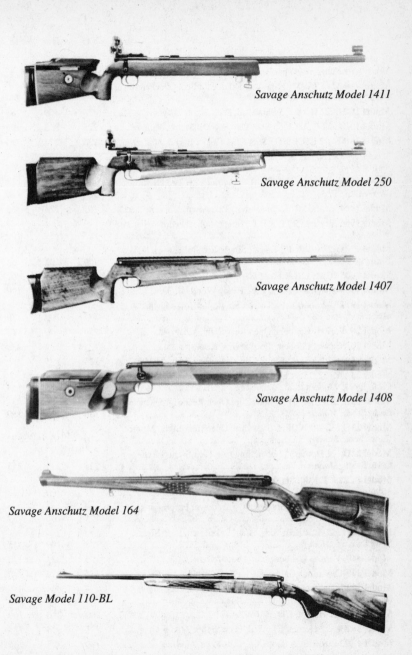

Savage Anschutz Model 1411

Savage Anschutz Model 250

Savage Anschutz Model 1407

Savage Anschutz Model 1408

Savage Anschutz Model 164

Savage Model 110-BL

	V.G.	Exc.	Prior Edition Exc. Value
Model 164, .22 L.R.R.F., Sporting Rifle, Clip Fed, Checkered Stock, (Anschutz), *Modern*	$225	$275	$260
Model 164-M, .22 WMR, Sporting Rifle, Clip Fed, Checkered Stock, (Anschutz), *Modern*	225	275	260
Model 19-H, .22 Hornet, 5 Shot Clip, Peep Sights, *Modern*	350	400	285
Model 19-L, .22 L.R.R.F., 5 Shot Clip, Lyman Sights, *Modern*	225	250	205
Model 19-M, .22 L.R.R.F., 5 Shot Clip, Heavy Barrel, *Modern*	225	275	215
Model 19-N.R.A., .22 L.R.R.F., 5 Shot Clip, Full-Stocked, Peep Sights, *Modern*	200	225	185
Model 19-Speed Lock, .22 L.R.R.F., 5 Shot Clip, Peep Sights, *Modern*	200	225	190
Model 1904, .22 L.R.R.F., Singleshot, Takedown, *Modern*	100	125	68
Model 1904-Special, .22 L.R.R.F., Singleshot, Takedown, Fancy Wood, *Modern*	125	150	100
Model 1905, .22 L.R.R.F., Target, Singleshot, Takedown, Swiss Buttplate, *Modern*	100	125	85
Model 1905-B, .22 L.R.R.F., *Modern*	125	150	62
Model 1905-Special, .22 L.R.R.F., Fancy Wood, *Modern*	150	175	140
Model 1911, .22 Short R.F., Target, Singleshot, Takedown, *Modern*	75	100	70
Model 20, Various Calibers, Open Rear Sight, *Modern*	250	300	245
Model 20, Various Calibers, Peep Sights, *Modern*	275	325	270
Model 23A, .22 L.R.R.F., 5 Shot Clip, Open Rear Sight, *Modern*	125	175	150
Model 23AA, .22 L.R.R.F., 5 Shot Clip, Open Rear Sight, Monte Carlo Stock, *Modern*	125	175	155
Model 23B, .25–20 WCF, 5 Shot Clip, Open Rear Sight, Monte Carlo Stock, *Modern*	150	200	180
Model 23C, .32–20 WCF, 5 Shot Clip, Open Rear Sight, Monte Carlo Stock, *Modern*	150	200	180
Model 23D, .22 Hornet, 5 Shot Clip, Open Rear Sight, Monte Carlo Stock, *Modern*	225	275	255
Model 3, .22 L.R.R.F., Singleshot, Takedown, Open Rear Sight, *Modern*	75	100	47
Model 3-S, .22 L.R.R.F., Singleshot, Takedown, Peep Sights, *Modern*	75	100	53
Model 3-ST, .22 L.R.R.F., Singleshot, Takedown, Peep Sights, Sling Swivels, *Modern*	75	100	58
Model 340, Various Calibers, Clip Fed, *Modern*	175	225	140
Model 340-C, Various Calibers, Clip Fed, Carbine, *Modern*	175	225	140
Model 340-S Deluxe, Various Calibers, Clip Fed, Peep Sights, *Modern*	225	275	145
Model 342, .22 Hornet, Clip Fed, *Modern*	200	250	160
Model 342-S, .22 Hornet, Clip Fed, Peep Sights, *Modern*	175	225	155
Model 4, .22 L.R.R.F., 5 Shot Clip, Takedown, *Modern*	100	125	65
Model 4-M, .22 WMR, 5 Shot Clip, Takedown, *Modern*	100	125	80
Model 35, .22 L.R.R.F., Clip Fed, *Modern*	75	100	60

	V.G.	Exc.	Prior Edition Exc. Value
Model 35-M, .22 W.R.M., Clip Fed, *Modern*	$75	$100	$65
Model 36, .22 L.R.R.F., Singleshot, *Modern*	75	100	55
Model 4-S, .22 L.R.R.F., 5 Shot Clip, Takedown, Peep Sights, *Modern*	75	100	70
Model 40, Various Calibers, Open Rear Sight, *Modern*	275	325	235
Model 45 Super, Various Calibers, Peep Sights, Checkered Stock, *Modern*	300	375	260
Model 5, .22 L.R.R.F., Tube Feed, Takedown, Open Rear Sight, *Modern*	100	125	75
Model 5-S, .22 L.R.R.F., Tube Feed, Takedown, Peep Sights, *Modern*	100	125	75
Model 54, .22 L.R.R.F., Sporting Rifle, Clip Fed, Fancy Checkering, (Anschutz), *Modern*	350	400	385
Model 54-M, .22 WMR, Sporting Rifle, Clip Fed, Fancy Checkering, (Anschutz), *Modern*	375	425	400
Model 63, .22 L.R.R.F., Singleshot, Open Rear Sight, *Modern*	50	75	47
Model 63-K, .22 L.R.R.F., Singleshot, Open Rear Sight, *Modern*	50	75	47
Model 63-M, .22 WMR, Singleshot, Open Rear Sight, *Modern*	75	100	60
Model 64, .22 L.R.R.F., Sights Only, *Add* **$30.00–$55.00**			
Model 64, .22 L.R.R.F., Heavy Barrel, no Sights, (Anschutz), *Modern*	200	250	225
Model 64-CS, .22 L.R.R.F., Heavy Barrel, no Sights, Lightweight, (Anschutz), *Modern*	200	275	255
Model 64-CSL, .22 L.R.R.F., Heavy Barrel, no Sights, Left-Hand, Lightweight, (Anschutz), *Modern*	225	275	270
Model 64-L, .22 L.R.R.F., Heavy Barrel, no Sights, Left-Hand, (Anschutz), *Modern*	200	250	230
Model 64-S, .22 L.R.R.F., Heavy Barrel, no Sights, (Anschutz), *Modern*	225	275	270
Model 64-SL, .22 L.R.R.F., Heavy Barrel, no Sights, Left-Hand, (Anschutz), *Modern*	250	300	280
Model 65-M, .22 WMR, Clip Fed, Open Rear Sight, *Modern*	75	100	80
Model 73, .22 L.R.R.F., Singleshot, *Modern*	50	75	48
Model 73-Y Boys, .22 L.R.R.F., Singleshot, *Modern*	50	75	48

RIFLE, LEVER ACTION

	V.G.	Exc.	Prior Edition Exc. Value
Model 1892, .30–40 Krag, Hammerless, Rotary Magazine, Military, *Antique*	1,250	1,500	1,475
Model 1895, .303 Savage, Hammerless, Rotary Magazine, Open Rear Sight, *Antique*	1,050	1,350	750
Model 1899, .30–30 Win., Hammerless, Rotary Magazine, Full-Stocked, Military, *Modern*	1,000	1,250	1,325
Model 1899, Various Calibers, Hammerless, Rotary Magazine, Open Rear Sight, *Modern*	450	600	275
Model 1899 A2, Various Calibers, Hammerless, Rotary Magazine, Checkered Stock, *Modern*	500	650	290

	V.G.	Exc.	Prior Edition Exc. Value
Model 1899 AB, Various Calibers, Light Engraving, Checkered Stock, Hammerless, Rotary Magazine, *Modern*	$500	$650	$465
Model 1899 BC, Various Calibers, Light Engraving, Checkered Stock, Hammerless, Rotary Magazine, *Modern*	450	600	415
Model 1899 Excelsior, Various Calibers, Light Engraving, Checkered Stock, Featherweight, Hammerless, Rotary Magazine, *Modern*	800	950	710
Model 1899 Leader, Various Calibers, Engraved, Checkered Stock, Hammerless, Rotary Magazine, *Modern*	750	900	695
Model 1899 Monarch, Various Calibers, Fancy Engraving, Fancy Checkering, Ornate, Hammerless, Rotary Magazine, *Modern*		RARE	
Model 1899 Premier, Various Calibers, Fancy Engraving, Fancy Checkering, Takedown, Hammerless, Rotary Magazine, *Modern*		RARE	
Model 1899 Rival, Various Calibers, Fancy Engraving, Fancy Checkering, Hammerless, Rotary Magazine, *Modern*		RARE	
Model 1899 Victor, Various Calibers, Engraved, Fancy Checkering, Hammerless, Rotary Magazine, *Modern*	950	1,200	975
Model 89, .22 L.R.R.F., Singleshot, Open Rear Sight, *Modern*	50	75	60
Model 99, for Extra Barrel, *Add* $75.00–$110.00			
Model 99 E, Various Calibers, Solid Frame, Carbine, Hammerless, Rotary Magazine, *Modern*	300	350	230
Model 99-1895 Anniversary, .308 Win., Octagon Barrel, Hammerless, Rotary Magazine, *Modern*	325	375	285
Model 99-358, .358 Win., Solid Frame, Hammerless, Rotary Magazine, *Modern*	350	400	250
Model 99-A, Various Calibers, Solid Frame, Hammerless, Rotary Magazine, *Modern*	425	500	240
Model 99-B, Various Calibers, Takedown, Hammerless, Rotary Magazine, *Modern*	675	750	295
Model 99-C, Various Calibers, Clip Fed, Solid Frame, Featherweight, Hammerless, *Modern*	400	475	250
Model 99-CD, Various Calibers, Hammerless, Clip Fed, Solid Frame, Monte Carlo Stock, *Modern*	375	425	275
Model 99-DE, Various Calibers, Solid Frame, Monte Carlo Stock, Light Engraving, Hammerless, Rotary Magazine, *Modern*	550	650	330
Model 99-DL, Various Calibers, Solid Frame, Monte Carlo Stock, Hammerless, Rotary Magazine, *Modern*	250	300	240
Model 99-D, Various Calibers, Solid Frame, Hammerless, Rotary Magazine, *Modern*	275	325	220
Model 99-EG, Various Calibers, Takedown, Checkered Stock, Hammerless, Rotary Magazine, *Modern*	375	425	230
Model 99-F, Various Calibers, Featherweight, Takedown, Hammerless, Rotary Magazine, *Modern*	275	325	280
Model 99-F, Various Calibers, Solid Frame, Featherweight, Hammerless, Rotary Magazine, *Modern*	250	300	230
Model 99-G, Various Calibers, Takedown, Checkered Stock, Hammerless, Rotary Magazine, *Modern*	475	525	250

	V.G.	Exc.	Prior Edition Exc. Value
Model 99-H, Various Calibers, Carbine, Solid Frame, Hammerless, Rotary Magazine, *Modern*	$250	$325	$230
Model 99-K, Various Calibers, Takedown, Light Engraving, Checkered Stock, Hammerless, Rotary Magazine, *Modern*	1,500	1,700	850
Model 99-PE, Various Calibers, Solid Frame, Monte Carlo Stock, Engraved, Hammerless, Rotary Magazine, *Modern*	750	900	750
Model 99-R, Various Calibers, Solid Frame, Checkered Stock, Pre-War, Hammerless, Rotary Magazine, *Modern*	400	450	445
Model 99-R, Various Calibers, Solid Frame, Checkered Stock, Hammerless, Rotary Magazine, *Modern*	250	300	235
Model 99-RS, Various Calibers, Solid Frame, Peep Sights, Pre-War, Hammerless, Rotary Magazine, *Modern*	475	525	355
Model 99-RS, Various Calibers, Solid Frame, Peep Sights, Hammerless, Rotary Magazine, *Modern*	275	325	250
Model 99-T, Various Calibers, Solid Frame, Featherweight, Hammerless, Rotary Magazine, *Modern*	275	325	320

RIFLE, SEMI-AUTOMATIC

	V.G.	Exc.	Prior Ed.
Model 1912, .22 L.R.R.F., Half-Octagon Barrel, Takedown, Clip Fed, *Curio*	200	250	225
Model 6, .22 L.R.R.F., Takedown, Tube Feed, Open Rear Sight, *Modern*	75	100	80
Model 6-S, .22 L.R.R.F., Takedown, Tube Feed, Peep Sights, *Modern*	100	125	85
Model 60, .22 L.R.R.F., Monte Carlo Stock, Checkered Stock, Tube Feed, *Modern*	75	100	90
Model 7, .22 L.R.R.F., 5 Shot Clip, Takedown, Open Rear Sight, *Modern*	75	100	70
Model 7-S, .22 L.R.R.F., 5 Shot Clip, Takedown, Open Rear Sight, *Modern*	100	125	80
Model 80, .22 L.R.R.F., Tube Feed, *Modern*	50	75	65
Model 88, .22 L.R.R.F., Tube Feed, *Modern*	50	75	75
Model 90, .22 L.R.R.F., Carbine, Tube Feed, *Modern*	75	100	80
Model 987 Stevens Rimfire, .22 Autoloader, Tubular Mag. 15 Rounds, Walnut Stock, *Modern*	100	125	115
Model 987-T Stevens Rimfire, .22 Autoloader, Tubular Mag. 15 Rounds, 4 × Scope and Mount, *Modern*	100	125	125

RIFLE, SINGLESHOT

	V.G.	Exc.	Prior Ed.
Model 219, Various Calibers, Hammerless, Top Break, Open Rear Sight, *Modern*	75	100	80
Model 219L, Various Calibers, Hammerless, Top Break, Open Rear Sight, Side Lever, *Modern*	75	100	80
Model 221, .30–30 Win., Hammerless, Top Break, Extra Shotgun Barrel, *Modern*	75	100	95
Model 222, .30–30 Win., Hammerless, Top Break, Extra Shotgun Barrel, *Modern*	100	125	100
Model 223, .30–30 Win., Hammerless, Top Break, Extra Shotgun Barrel, *Modern*	100	125	100

	V.G.	Exc.	Prior Edition Exc. Value
Model 227, .30–30 Win., Hammerless, Top Break, Extra Shotgun Barrel, *Modern*	$100	$125	$100
Model 228, .30–30 Win., Hammerless, Top Break, Extra Shotgun Barrel, *Modern*	100	125	100
Model 229, .30–30 Win., Hammerless, Top Break, Extra Shotgun Barrel, *Modern*	100	125	100
Model 71 Stevens Favorite, .22 L.R.R.F., Lever Action, Falling Block, Favorite, *Modern*	125	150	145
Model 72, .22 L.R.R.F., Lever Action, Falling Block, *Modern*	75	100	90
Model 89 Stevens Rimfire, .22 L.R.R.F., Lever Action, 18" Barrel, Sporting Sights, *Modern*	100	125	100

RIFLE, SLIDE ACTION

	V.G.	Exc.	Prior Edition Exc. Value
Model 170, Various Calibers, Open Rear Sight, *Modern*	150	175	155
Model 170-C, .30–30 Win., Carbine, Open Rear Sight, *Modern*	125	150	145
Model 1903, .22 L.R.R.F., Hammerless, Clip Fed, Octagon Barrel, *Modern*	175	200	130
Model 1903-EF, .22 L.R.R.F., Hammerless, Clip Fed, Octagon Barrel, Fancy Wood, Engraved, *Modern*	450	525	510
Model 1903-Expert, .22 L.R.R.F., Hammerless, Clip Fed, Octagon Barrel, Checkered Stock, Light Engraving, *Modern*	250	275	270
Model 1909, .22 L.R.R.F., Half-Octagon Barrel, Takedown, Clip Fed, *Modern*	125	150	135
Model 1914, .22 L.R.R.F., Half-Octagon Barrel, Takedown, Tube Feed, *Modern*	175	225	160
Model 1914-E.F., .22 L.R.R.F., Half-Octagon Barrel, Takedown, Tube Feed, Fancy Engraving, *Modern*	600	675	650
Model 1914-Expert, .22 L.R.R.F., Half-Octagon Barrel, Takedown, Tube Feed, Light Engraving, *Modern*	425	475	465
Model 1914-Gold Medal, .22 L.R.R.F., Half-Octagon Barrel, Takedown, Tube Feed, Checkered Stock, Light Engraving, *Modern*	250	300	295
Model 25, .22 L.R.R.F., Tube Feed, Octagon Barrel, Open Rear Sight, Monte Carlo Stock, *Modern*	200	250	135
Model 29, .22 L.R.R.F., Tube Feed, Octagon Barrel, Open Rear Sight, Monte Carlo Stock, *Modern*	175	225	195
Model 29, .22 L.R.R.F., Tube Feed, Round Barrel, Open Rear Sight, *Modern*	150	175	150
Model 29-G, .22 Short R.F., Tube Feed, *Modern*	150	175	160

SHOTGUN, BOLT ACTION

	V.G.	Exc.	Prior Edition Exc. Value
Model 58, .410 Ga., Singleshot, *Modern*	50	75	70

SHOTGUN, DOUBLE BARREL, OVER-UNDER

	V.G.	Exc.	Prior Edition Exc. Value
Model 242, .410 Ga., Hammer, Single Trigger, *Modern*	125	150	135
Model 330, 12 and 20 Gauges, Hammerless, Single Selective Trigger, *Modern*	350	400	380
Model 330, 12 and 20 Gauges, Hammerless, Extra Shotgun Barrel, Cased, *Modern*	425	475	460

Savage Model 99-C

Savage Model 24

Savage Model 30

Savage Model 170

Savage Model 30 Slug

Savage Fox Model B

Savage Model 94-Y

Savage Model 333

	V.G.	Exc.	Prior Edition Exc. Value
Model 333, 12 and 20 Gauges, Hammerless, Vent Rib, Single Selective Trigger, *Modern*	$450	$500	$460
Model 333-T, 12 Ga., Hammerless, Vent Rib, Trap Grade, Single Selective Trigger, *Modern*	425	475	445
Model 420, Various Gauges, Hammerless, Takedown, Double Trigger, *Modern*	250	300	260
Model 420, Various Gauges, Hammerless, Takedown, Single Trigger, *Modern*	300	350	320
Model 430, Various Gauges, Hammerless, Takedown, Checkered Stock, Recoil Pad, Double Trigger, *Modern*	300	350	300
Model 430, Various Gauges, Hammerless, Takedown, Checkered Stock, Recoil Pad, Single Trigger, *Modern*	375	425	360
Model 440, 12 Ga., Hammerless, Vent Rib, Single Selective Trigger, Checkered Stock, *Modern*	300	350	255
Model 440-B, 20 Ga., Hammerless, Vent Rib, Checkered Stock, *Modern*	350	400	300
Model 444, 12 Ga., Hammerless, Vent Rib, Single Selective Trigger, Checkered Stock, Selective Ejector, *Modern*	375	425	310
Model 444-T, 12 Ga., Hammerless, Trap Grade, *Modern*	400	450	310

RIFLE/SHOTGUN COMBINATION

	V.G.	Exc.	Prior Edition Exc. Value
Model 24 Field Combo, .22 L.R. Top Barrel, 4 10 Bore or 20 Gauge Bottom Barrel, Walnut Stock, *Modern*	125	175	180
Model 24-C Combo Gun, Camper's Break Action, .22 L.R. Top Barrel, 20 Gauge Bottom Barrel, *Modern*	150	200	215
Model 24-CS Camper/Survival Combo Gun, Break Action, .22 L.R. Top Barrel, 20 Gauge Bottom Barrel, Pistol Grip, Satin Nickel, *Modern*	175	225	230
Model 24-D Combo Gun, .22 L.R. Top Barrel, 20 Gauge Bottom Barrel, Folding Rear Sight, *Modern*	175	225	220
Model 24-V Combo Gun, Break Action, .22 Hornet Top Barrel, 20 Gauge Bottom Barrel, Monte Carlo Stock, *Modern*	175	225	250
Model 24-VS Camper/Survival Combo Gun, Break Action, .357 Magnum Top Barrel, 20 Gauge Bottom Barrel, Pistol Grip, Satin Nickel, *Modern*	200	250	270

SHOTGUN, DOUBLE BARREL, SIDE-BY-SIDE

	V.G.	Exc.	Prior Edition Exc. Value
Model B Fox, Various Gauges, Hammerless, Vent Rib, Double Trigger, *Modern*	175	225	230
Model B-SE Fox, Various Gauges, Hammerless, Vent Rib, Selective Ejector, Single Trigger, *Modern*	225	275	270

SHOTGUN, SEMI-AUTOMATIC

	V.G.	Exc.	Prior Edition Exc. Value
Model 720, 12 Ga., Tube Feed, Checkered Stock, Plain Barrel, *Modern*	125	175	150
Model 720-P, 12 Ga., Checkered Stock, Adjustable Choke, *Modern*	125	175	160
Model 720-R, 12 Ga., Riot Gun, *Modern*	100	150	150
Model 721, 12 Ga., Tube Feed, Checkered Stock, Raised Matted Rib, *Modern*	150	200	180

	V.G.	Exc.	Prior Edition Exc. Value
Model 722, 12 Ga., Tube Feed, Checkered Stock, Vent Rib, *Modern*	$150	$200	$200
Model 723, 16 Ga., Tube Feed, Checkered Stock, Plain Barrel, *Modern*	100	150	150
Model 724, 16 Ga., Tube Feed, Checkered Stock, Raised Matted Rib, *Modern*	125	175	155
Model 725, 16 Ga., Tube Feed, Checkered Stock, Vent Rib, *Modern*	125	175	155
Model 726, 12 and 16 Gauges, 3 Shot, Checkered Stock, Plain Barrel, *Modern*	125	175	150
Model 727, 12 and 16 Gauges, 3 Shot, Checkered Stock, Raised Matted Rib, *Modern*	125	175	160
Model 728, 12 and 16 Gauges, 3 Shot, Checkered Stock, Vent Rib, *Modern*	125	175	170
Model 740-C, 12 and 16 Gauges, Skeet Grade, *Modern*	175	225	200
Model 745, 12 Ga., Lightweight, *Modern*	150	200	180
Model 750, 12 Ga., *Modern*	175	225	200
Model 750-AC, 12 Ga., Adjustable Choke, *Modern*	175	225	200
Model 750-SC, 12 Ga., Adjustable Choke, *Modern*	175	225	205
Model 755, 12 and 16 Gauges, *Modern*	125	175	165
Model 755-SC, 12 and 16 Gauges, Adjustable Choke, *Modern*	150	200	180
Model 775, 12 and 16 Gauges, Lightweight, *Modern*	150	200	190
Model 775-SC, 12 and 16 Gauges, Adjustable Choke, Lightweight, *Modern*	150	200	190

SHOTGUN, SINGLESHOT

	V.G.	Exc.	Prior Edition Exc. Value
Model 220, Various Gauges, Hammerless, Takedown, *Modern*	50	75	52
Model 220-AC, Various Gauges, Hammerless, Takedown, Adjustable Choke, *Modern*	50	75	60
Model 220-P, Various Gauges, Hammerless, Takedown, Adjustable Choke, *Modern*	50	75	70
Model 94, Various Gauges, Hammer, Takedown, *Modern*	100	125	105
Model 94-C, Various Gauges, Hammer, Takedown, *Modern*	75	100	70
Model 94-Y Youth, Various Gauges, Hammer, Takedown, *Modern*	50	75	65
Model 9478, Various Gauges, Hammer, Auto Ejection, 42" to 52" Overall, *Modern*	100	125	100

SHOTGUN, SLIDE ACTION

	V.G.	Exc.	Prior Edition Exc. Value
Model 67, 12 or 20 Gauge, Tubular Mag, Hammerless, Walnut Stock, *Modern*	150	200	190
Model 67-T Stevens, 12 or 20 Gauge, Three Choke Tubes, 28" Barrel, *Modern*	175	225	200
Model 67-VR Stevens, 12 Gauge, 4 Shot Tubular, Vent Ribs, *Modern*	175	225	200
Model 69-N Guard Gun, 12 Gauge, 7 Shot Tubular Mag., 18¼" Cylinder Bore, Nickel, *Modern*	225	275	265

	V.G.	Exc.	Prior Edition Exc. Value
Model 69-R Guard Gun, 12 Gauge, 5 Shot Tubular Mag., 20" Cylinder Bore, *Modern*	$175	$225	$200
Model 69-RXL Guard Gun, 12 Gauge, 7 Shot Tubular Mag, 18¼" Cylinder Bore, *Modern*	175	225	200
Model 21-A, 12 Ga., Hammerless, Takedown, *Modern*	125	175	150
Model 21-B, 12 Ga., Hammerless, Takedown, Raised Matted Rib, *Modern*	125	175	155
Model 21-C, 12 Ga., Hammerless, Takedown, Riot Gun, *Modern*	100	150	140
Model 21-D, 12 Ga., Hammerless, Takedown, Trap Grade, *Modern*	200	250	235
Model 21-E, 12 Ga., Hammerless, Takedown, Fancy Wood, Fancy Checkering, Vent Rib, *Modern*	250	300	285
Model 28-A, 12 Ga., Hammerless, Takedown, *Modern*	125	175	150
Model 28-B, 12 Ga., Hammerless, Takedown, Raised Matted Rib, *Modern*	125	175	155
Model 28-C, 12 Ga., Hammerless, Takedown, Riot Gun, *Modern*	100	150	145
Model 28-D, 12 Ga., Hammerless, Takedown, Trap Grade, *Modern*	200	250	235
Model 28-S, 12 Ga., Hammerless, Takedown, Fancy Checkering, *Modern*	200	250	200
Model 30, For Vent Rib, *Add* **$15.00–$20.00**			
Model 30, Various Gauges, Hammerless, Solid Frame, *Modern*	100	150	130
Model 30-AC, Various Gauges, Hammerless, Solid Frame, Adjustable Choke, *Modern*	100	150	130
Model 30-ACL, Various Gauges, Hammerless, Solid Frame, Left-Hand, Adjustable Choke, *Modern*	100	150	140
Model 30-D, Various Gauges, Hammerless, Solid Frame, Light Engraving, Recoil Pad, *Modern*	125	175	155
Model 30-L, Various Gauges, Hammerless, Solid Frame, Left-Hand, *Modern*	100	150	135
Model 30-Slug, 12 Ga., Hammerless, Solid Frame, *Modern*	100	150	140
Model 30-T, 12 Ga., Hammerless, Solid Frame, Monte Carlo Stock, Recoil Pad, Vent Rib, *Modern*	125	175	160

SANTA BARBARA Santa Barbara of America, Inc. of Irving, Tx. on Mauser actions made in La Caruna, Spain.

RIFLE, BOLT ACTION

Sporter, Various Calibers, Custom Made, Medium Quality, *Modern*	125	150	135
Sporter, Various Calibers, Custom Made, High Quality, *Modern*	150	200	185

SCHALL & CO. Hartford, Conn.

HANDGUN, MANUAL REPEATER

.22 L.R.R.F., Target Pistol, Clip Fed, *Curio*	350	425	400

	V.G.	Exc.	Prior Edition Exc. Value

SCHEANER, WM. Reading, Pa. 1779–1790. See Kentucky Rifles.

SCHILLING, V. CHARLES Suhl, Germany. Also see Bergmann, German Military.

RIFLE, BOLT ACTION

Model 88 Sporter, Various Calibers, Checkered Stock, *Curio*	$300	$350	$325

SCHMIDT, ERNST Suhl, Germany.

RIFLE, SINGLESHOT

8mm Roth-Steyr, Schutzen Rifle, Engraved, Set Trigger, Takedown, Octagon Barrel, *Modern*	750	850	800

SCHMIDT, HERBERT Ostheim/Rhon, West Germany.

HANDGUN, REVOLVER

Liberty 11, .22 L.R.R.F., Double Action, Swing-Out Cylinder, Blue, *Modern*	50	75	40
Texas Scout, .22 L.R.R.F., Western Style, Blue, *Modern*	50	75	40

SCHMIDT & HABERMANN Suhl, Germany, 1920–1940.

COMBINATION WEAPON, OVER-UNDER

Various Calibers, Pre–WW2, Engraved, Checkered Stock, *Modern*	650	750	700

SCHOUBOE Dansk Rekylriffel Syndikat, Copenhagen, Denmark 1902–1917.

HANDGUN, SEMI-AUTOMATIC

Model 1903, .32 ACP, Clip Fed, Blue, *Curio*	3,250	4,000	3,650
Model 1902/07, 11.35mm Sch., *Curio*	4,000	5,000	4,750
Model 1902/10, 11.35mm Sch., *Curio*	4,000	5,000	4,750
Model 1902/10, 11.35mm Sch., with Holster Stock, *Curio*	5,500	6,500	6,200

SCHULTZ & LARSEN Otterup, Denmark.

HANDGUN, SINGLESHOT

Free Pistol, .22 L.R.R.F., Bolt Action, Target Trigger, Target Sights, *Modern*	275	350	295

RIFLE, BOLT ACTION

Model 47, .22 L.R.R.F., Target Rifle, Thumbhole Stock, Adjustable Trigger, Singleshot, *Modern*	550	650	485
M54, Various Calibers, *Modern*	725	800	665
M54J, Various Calibers, *Modern*	625	700	575

	V.G.	Exc.	Prior Edition Exc. Value
Model 61, .22 L.R.R.F., Target Rifle, Thumbhole Stock, Adjustable Trigger, Singleshot, *Modern*	$650	$750	$450
Model 62, Various Calibers, Target Rifle, Thumbhole Stock, Adjustable Trigger, Singleshot, *Modern*	800	950	525
Model 65DL, Various Calibers, Sporting Rifle, Checkered Stock, Adjustable Trigger, no Sights, Repeater, *Modern*	575	650	450
Model 68DL, .458 Win. Mag., Sporting Rifle, Checkered Stock, Adjustable Trigger, no Sights, Repeater, *Modern*	650	750	675
Model 68DL, Various Calibers, Sporting Rifle, Checkered Stock, Adjustable Trigger, no Sights, Repeater, *Modern*	575	650	550

SCHUTZEN RIFLES, UNKNOWN MAKER

RIFLE, SINGLESHOT

	V.G.	Exc.	
Aydt System, Various Calibers, Dropping Block, Plain Tyrol Stock, Light Engraving, Target Sights, *Modern*	750	900	600
Aydt System, Various Calibers, Dropping Block, Fancy Tyrol Stock, Fancy Engraving, Target Sights, *Modern*	1,000	1,200	900
Martini System, Various Calibers, Dropping Block, Fancy tyrol Stock, Fancy Engraving, Target Sights, *Modern*	750	1,000	835

SCHWARZLOSE   Andreas W. Schwarzlose, Berlin, Germany 1911–1927.

HANDGUN, SEMI-AUTOMATIC

	V.G.	Exc.	
Standardt, 7.63mm Mauser, Clip Fed, Blue, *Curio*	2,500	3,000	2,975
M 1908 Pocket, .32 ACP, Blow-Forward, Clip Fed, Grip Safety, *Curio*	400	475	475
M. 1908 W.A.C. Pocket, .32 ACP, Blow-Forward, Clip Fed, Grip Safety, *Curio*	375	450	450

SCOTT ARMS CO.   Probably Norwich Fall Pistol Co., c. 1880.

HANDGUN, REVOLVER

	V.G.	Exc.	
.32 Short R.F., 5 Shot, Spur Trigger, Solid Frame, Single Action, *Antique*	150	175	170

Schwarzlose M1908 WAC

	V.G.	Exc.	Prior Edition Exc. Value

SCOTT, D. Edinburgh, Scotland, 1727–1745.
HANDGUN, FLINTLOCK
Queen Anne Type, .59, Screw Barrel, Holster Pistol, Marked "Edinboro," *Antique* *$1,250* *$1,750* *$1,575*

SCOTT REVOLVER-RIFLE Hopkins & Allen, c. 1880.
HANDGUN, REVOLVER
24¹/²" Brass Barrel, .38 Short R.F., 5 Shot, Spur Trigger, Solid Frame, Single Action, *Antique* 225 275 275

SCOUT Made by Stevens.
SHOTGUN, DOUBLE BARREL, SIDE-BY-SIDE
Model 311, Various Gauges, Hammerless, Steel Barrel, *Modern* 175 200 175

SCOUT Made by Hood Firearms for Frankfurt Hardware of Milwaukee, Wisc., c. 1870.
HANDGUN, REVOLVER
.32 Short R.F., 5 Shot, Spur Trigger, Solid Frame, Single Action, *Antique* 150 175 165

S.E.A.M. Fab. d'Armes de Soc. Espanola de Armas y Municiones, Eibar, Spain.
HANDGUN, SEMI-AUTOMATIC
Eibar Type, .25 ACP, 13 Slide Grooves, Fair Quality, clip Fed, Blue, *Modern* 100 125 125
Eibar Type, .25 ACP, 11 Slide Grooves, Good Quality, Clip Fed, Blue, *Modern* 150 175 155
Walther Type, .25 ACP, Clip Fed, Blue, *Modern* 175 225 220

SEARS Sears, Roebuck & Co., Chicago, Ill. Also see Ted Williams.
RIFLE, BOLT ACTION
Semi-Sporterized Mauser, 8mm Mauser, Converted Military, *Modern* 100 125 125
Sporterized Mauser, 8mm Mauser, Converted Military, Recoil Pad, *Modern* 125 150 135
SHOTGUN, BOLT ACTION
.410 Gauge, Singleshot, Plain, *Modern* 25 50 40
.410 Gauge, Clip Fed, Blue, Plain, *Modern* 25 50 45
12 or 20 Gauges, Clip Fed, Blue, Plain, *Modern* 25 50 55
12 or 20 Gauges, Clip Fed, Adjustable Choke, Blue, Plain, *Modern* 50 75 60

Sears Youth

Sears 12 Ga. Bolt Action

	V.G.	Exc.	Prior Edition Exc. Value

SHOTGUN, SINGLESHOT

Various Gauges, Top Break, Plain, *Modern* $25 $50 $45
Youth, 20 or .410 Gauges, Plain, *Modern*.. 25 50 45

SECRET SERVICE SPECIAL Made for Fred Biffar, Chicago by Iver-Johnson and Meriden.

HANDGUN, REVOLVER

.32 S & W, 5 Shot, Top Break, Hammerless, Double Action, *Modern*.. 125 150 130
.38 S & W, 5 Shot, Top Break, Hammerless, Double Action, *Modern*.. 125 150 130

SECURITY INDUSTRIES OF AMERICA Little Ferry, N.J.

HANDGUN, REVOLVER

Police Pocket, .357 Magnum, Stainless Steel, 2" Barrel, Swing-Out Cylinder, Double Action, Spurless Hammer, *Modern*............... 175 225 170
Security Undercover, .357 Magnum, Stainless Steel, 2¹/₂" Barrel, Swing-Out Cylinder, Double Action, *Modern*................................... 175 225 165

SEDGLEY, R.F., INC. Philadelphia, Pa. 1911–1938. Successor to Henry Kolb.

HANDGUN, REVOLVER

Baby Hammerless, .22 L.R.R.F., Double Action, Folding Trigger, *Modern*.. 125 150 145

RIFLE, BOLT ACTION

Springfield, Various Calibers, Sporting Rifle, Lyman Sights, Checkered Stock, *Modern*.. 525 600 385
Springfield, Various Calibers, Sporting Rifle, Lyman Sights, Checkered Stock, Left-Hand, *Modern*.. 550 650 435
Springfield, Various Calibers, Sporting Rifle, Lyman Sights, Checkered Stock, Full-Stocked, *Modern*.. 600 700 500

Selecta Model 1919

	V.G.	Exc.	Prior Edition Exc. Value
SELECTA Echave y Arizmendi, Eibar, Spain.			
HANDGUN, SEMI-AUTOMATIC			
Model 1918, .25 ACP Double Safety, Clip Fed, *Modern*	$125	$150	$155
Model 1918, .25 ACP, Triple Safety, Clip Fed, *Modern*	150	175	175
Model 1919, .32 ACP, Double Safety, Clip Fed, *Modern*	150	175	170
Model 1919, .32 ACP, Triple Safety, Clip Fed, *Modern*	150	200	190
SEMMERLING Semmerling Corp., Newton, Mass.			
HANDGUN, MANUAL REPEATER			
LM-4, .45 ACP, Double Action, Clip Fed, *Modern*	1,000	1,200	560
SHAKANOOSA ARMS MFG. CO. 1862–1864. See Confederate Military.			
RIFLE, PERCUSSION			
.58, Military, Carbine, (C S A), *Antique*	1,750	2,000	1,800
.58, Military, (C S A), *Antique*	1,250	1,500	1,325
SHARPE English, 1670–1680.			
HANDGUN, FLINTLOCK			
Pair, Pocket Pistol, Screw Barrel, Octagon, High Quality, *Antique*	3,250	3,500	3,250
SHARPS Made by Shiloh Products, Farmingdale, N.Y.			
RIFLE, PERCUSSION			
Model 1859 New Model Cavalry Carbine, .54, Reproduction, *Antique*	300	350	350
Model 1863 Cavalry Carbine, .54, Reproduction, *Antique*	425	500	300
Model 1863 Sporting Rifle #3, .54, Reproduction, *Antique*	375	425	350
Model 1863 Sporting Rifle #2, .54, Reproduction, *Antique*	400	450	370
Model 1862 Robinson Confederate Cavalry Carbine, .54, Reproduction, *Antique*	525	600	325

	V.G.	Exc.	Prior Edition Exc. Value
Model 1863 New Model Military Rifle, .54, Reproduction, *Antique*	$525	$600	$350

RIFLE, SINGLESHOT

	V.G.	Exc.	Prior Edition Exc. Value
Model 1874 Military Rifle, Various Calibers, Reproduction, *Modern*	650	750	385
Model 1874 Military Carbine, Various Calibers, Reproduction, *Modern*	575	650	330
Model 1874 Hunter's Rifle, Various Calibers, Reproduction, *Modern*	375	425	360
Model 1874 Business Rifle, Various Calibers, Reproduction, *Modern*	550	625	360
Model 1874 Sporting Rifle #2, Various Calibers, Reproduction, *Modern*	450	500	460
Model 1874 Sporting Rifle #3, Various Calibers, Reproduction, *Modern*	550	625	380

SHARPS, CHRISTIAN Mill Creek, Pa. 1848; moved to Hartford, Conn. in 1851 and became Sharps Rifle Mfg. Co., changing it's name to Sharps Rifle Co. in 1874, continuing operations until 1881. In 1854 formed C. Sharps & Co. in Philadelphia, Pa., became Sharps & Hankins in 1862, C. Sharps & Co. again in 1866, and continued until 1874.

HANDGUN, MULTI-BARREL

	V.G.	Exc.	Prior Edition Exc. Value
.22 R.F., Model 1, 4 Barreled Pistol, Frame to Muzzle Distance 1/8", *Antique*	400	450	390
.22 R.F., Model 1, 4 Barreled Pistol, Frame to Muzzle Distance 1/2", *Antique*	375	425	285
.22 R.F., Model 1, 4 Barreled Pistol, Frame to Muzzle Distance 1/4", *Antique*	375	425	360
.22 R.F., Model 1, 4 Barreled Pistol, Frame to Muzzle Distance 1/4", Iron Frame, *Antique*	475	525	480
.30 R.F., Model 2, 4 Barreled Pistol, Frame to Muzzle Distance 5/8", *Antique*	400	450	340
.30 R.F., Model 2, 4 Barreled Pistol, Frame to Muzzle Distance 3/4", *Antique*	425	475	440
.32 R.F., Model 3, 4 Barreled Pistol, Mechanism in Frame, *Antique*	400	450	465

Christian Sharps Patent Single Shot, .36 Caliber

	V.G.	Exc.	Prior Edition Exc. Value
.32 R.F., Model 3, 4 Barreled Pistol, Mechanism on Hammer, *Antique*	$375	$425	$375
.32 R.F. Bulldog, Model 4, 4 Barreled Pistol, Screw Under Frame, *Antique*	400	450	375
.32 R.F. Bulldog, Model 4, 4 Barreled Pistol, Pin on Side of Frame, *Antique*	425	475	440

HANDGUN, PERCUSSION

	V.G.	Exc.	Prior Ed.
Revolver, .25, Tip-Up, 6 Shot, Blue, Spur Trigger, Single Action, *Antique*	1,000	1,150	895
Bryce Revolver, .25, Tip-Up, 6 Shot, Blue, Spur Trigger, Single Action, *Antique*	1,200	1,350	975

HANDGUN, SINGLESHOT

	V.G.	Exc.	Prior Ed.
Small Frame, Various Calibers, Single Action Dropping Block, Hammer, *Antique*	2,000	2,250	1,800
Medium Frame, Various Calibers, Single Action, Dropping Block, Hammer, *Antique*	2,250	2,750	1,975

RIFLE, PERCUSSION

	V.G.	Exc.	Prior Ed.
1851 Carbine, .52, Maynard Primer, *Antique*	4,000	4,500	2,650
1852 Carbine, .52, Pellet Primer, *Antique*	1,500	1,750	895
1853 Carbine, .52, Pellet Primer, *Antique*	1,250	1,500	975
1855 Carbine, .52, Maynard Primer, *Antique*	1,250	1,500	1,550
1855 Rifle, .52, Maynard Primer, *Antique*	2,000	2,500	1,975
1859 Carbine, .52, Pellet Primer, *Antique*	1,250	1,500	995
1863 Carbine, .52, Lawrence Cut-off, *Antique*	1,250	1,500	800
1863 Rifle, .52, Lawrence Cut-off, *Antique*	1,500	1,750	1,550

RIFLE, SINGLESHOT

	V.G.	Exc.	Prior Ed.
1874 Sporting Rifle, Various Calibers, Set Trigger, Target Sights, *Antique*	3,000	3,500	1,850
1874 Hunting Rifle, Various Calibers, Open Sights, *Antique*	2,500	3,000	1,350
Long Range Rifle, Various Calibers, Target Sights, *Antique*	5,250	6,000	2,900

SHARPSHOOTER Hijos de Calixto Arrizabalaga, Eibar, Spain, c. 1920.

HANDGUN, SEMI-AUTOMATIC

	V.G.	Exc.	Prior Ed.
"Sharp-Sooter", .25 ACP, Clip Fed, Hammer, Hinged Barrel, Blue, *Curio*	175	200	200
"Sharp-Sooter", .32 ACP, Clip Fed, Hammer, Hinged Barrel, Blue, *Curio*	200	225	230
"Sharp-Sooter", .380 ACP, Clip Fed, Hammer, Hinged Barrel, Blue, *Curio*	250	275	290

	V.G.	Exc.	Prior Edition Exc. Value

SHATTUCK, C.S. Hatfield, Mass. 1880–1890.

HANDGUN, REVOLVER
Lincoln/Garfield Grips, Hard Rubber, *Add* **20%–30%**

.22 R.F., Single Action, Spur Trigger, Swing-Out Cylinder, Antique ... $250 / $300 / $290

.32 R.F., Single Action, Spur Trigger, Swing-Out Cylinder, Antique ... 225 / 275 / 220

.38 R.F., Single Action, Spur Trigger, Swing-Out Cylinder, Antique ... 300 / 350 / 325

.41 R.F., Single Action, Spur Trigger, Swing-Out Cylinder, Antique ... 375 / 450 / 425

SHAW, JOHN London, England, c. 1688.

HANDGUN, FLINTLOCK
Holster Pistol, Engraved, Steel Mounts, High Quality, Antique ... 2,000 / 2,500 / 2,200

SHELL, JOHN Leslie County, Ky. 1810–1880. See Kentucky Rifles.

SHERIDEN Racine, Wisc. 1953–1960.

HANDGUN, SINGLESHOT
Knockabout, .22 L.R.R.F., Tip-Up Barrel, Single Action, Hammer, Blue, *Modern* ... 100 / 125 / 155

SHILEN Ennis, Tex.

RIFLE, BOLT ACTION
DGA Sporter, Various Calibers, Blind Magazine, Plain Stock, *Modern* ... 550 / 600 / 600

DGA Benchrest, Various Calibers, Target Rifle, *Modern* ... 625 / 700 / 675

DGA Silhouette, Various Calibers, Target Rifle, *Modern* ... 550 / 600 / 575

DGA Varmint, Various Calibers, Heavy Barrel, *Modern* ... 550 / 600 / 600

SHORER, ANDREW Northampton, Pa. 1775–1776. See Kentucky Rifles.

SICKEL'S ARMS CO. Belgium for Robert Sickels & Preston Co., Davenport, Iowa.

SHOTGUN, DOUBLE BARREL, SIDE-BY-SIDE
Various Gauges, Outside Hammers, Damascus Barrel, *Modern* ... 150 / 175 / 170

Various Gauges, Hammerless, Steel Barrel, *Modern* ... 175 / 200 / 190

Various Gauges, Hammerless, Damascus Barrel, *Modern* ... 150 / 175 / 170

Various Gauges, Outside Hammers, Steel Barrel, *Modern* ... 175 / 200 / 185

	V.G.	Exc.	Prior Edition Exc. Value

SHOTGUN, SINGLESHOT

Various Gauges, Hammer, Steel Barrel, *Modern*............................ $75 $100 $85

S.I.G. Schweizerische Industrie Gesellschaft, Neuhausen, Switzerland since 1857.

HANDGUN, SEMI-AUTOMATIC

P210 Luxus, Various Calibers, Clip Fed, Fancy Engraving, Gold
Inlay, High-Polish Blue Finish, Carved Wood Grips, *Modern*.......... 2,500 3,500 2,700

P210-1, .22 L.R.R.F., Clip Fed, Blue, High-Polish Finish, Wood
Grips, *Modern*.. 1,250 1,450 1,175

P210-1, .30 Luger, Clip Fed, Blue, High-Polish Finish, Wood
Grips, *Modern*.. 1,350 1,500 1,195

P210-1, 9mm Luger, Clip Fed, Blue, High-Polish Finish, Wood
Grips, *Modern*.. 1,400 1,550 1,195

P210-1, .22 L.R.R.F., Conversion Unit Only, *Modern*..................... 500 550 525

P210-1, Various Calibers, Clip Fed, High-Polish Finish, with
3 Caliber Conv. Units, Wood Grips, *Modern*.................................... 2,000 2,500 1,875

P210-2, .30 Luger, Clip Fed, Blue, Plastic Stock, *Modern* 950 1,200 975

P210-2, 9mm Luger, Clip Fed, Blue, Plastic Stock, *Modern*........... 1,000 1,150 925

P210-5, .30 Luger, Clip Fed, Blue, Plastic Stock, Target Pistol,
6" Barrel, *Modern* ....:.. 1,200 1,450 1,225

P210-5, 9mm Luger, Clip Fed, Blue, Plastic Stock, Target Pistol,
6" Barrel, *Modern* 1,250 1,400 1,175

P210-6, .30 Luger, Clip Fed, Blue, Plastic Stock, Target Pistol,
4³/₄" Barrel, *Modern* 1,050 1,250 1,025

P210-6, 9mm Luger, Clip Fed, Blue, Plastic Stock, Target Pistol,
4³/₄" Barrel, *Modern* 1,050 1,200 975

P 220 SIG-Sauer, Various Calibers, Clip Fed, Double Action,
Blue, *Modern* 500 550 425

P 225 SIG-Sauer, 9mm Luger, Clip Fed, Double Action, Blue,
Modern... 500 550 375

P 230 SIG-Sauer, 9mm Police, Clip Fed, Double Action, Blue,
Modern... 350 400 335

S.I.G. P 210-6

	V.G.	Exc.	Prior Edition Exc. Value
P 230 SIG-Sauer, Various Calibers, Clip Fed, Double Action, Blue, *Modern*	$300	$375	$300
SP 47/8, 9mm Luger, Clip Fed, German Border Patrol, *Modern*	1,750	2,000	1,825
SP 47/8, 9mm Luger, Clip Fed, Swiss Military, *Modern*	2,500	3,000	2,550

RIFLE, SEMI-AUTOMATIC

	V.G.	Exc.	Prior Ed.
SIG AMT, .308 Win., Clip Fed, Bipod, *Modern*	1,750	2,000	1,175
SIG STG-57, 7.5 Swiss, Clip Fed, Bipod, *Modern*	1,500	1,700	1,250

SILE Imported by Sile Distributers, N.Y.C., N.Y.

HANDGUN, SEMI-AUTOMATIC

	V.G.	Exc.	Prior Ed.
Seecamp, .25 ACP, Double Action, Clip Fed, Stainless Steel, *Modern*	250	300	135

SIMPLEX Made in Belgium. Also see Bergmann.

HANDGUN, SEMI-AUTOMATIC

	V.G.	Exc.	Prior Ed.
Simplex, 8mm Bergmann, Blue, *Curio*	650	750	675

SIMSON & CO. Waffenfabrik Simson & Co., Suhl, Germany 1910–1939. Also see Luger.

HANDGUN, SEMI-AUTOMATIC

	V.G.	Exc.	Prior Ed.
Vest Pocket, .25 ACP, Clip Fed, Blue, *Modern*	450	500	460

RIFLE, BOLT ACTION

	V.G.	Exc.	Prior Ed.
Precision Carbine, 6mm Shot, Singleshot, Plain, *Modern*	50	75	50
Precision Carbine, 9mm Shot, Singleshot, Plain, *Modern*	50	75	65
Model 1933, .22 Extra Long, Singleshot, Checkered Stock, Target Sights, *Modern*	100	125	100
Sportrifle #7, .22 Extra Long, Singleshot, Checkered Stock, Target Sights, *Modern*	75	100	85

SHOTGUN, DOUBLE BARREL, OVER-UNDER

	V.G.	Exc.	Prior Ed.
Trap Grade, 12 Ga., Automatic Ejectors, Checkered Stock, Engraved, Cocking Indicators, *Modern*	1,500	1,750	1,550

SHOTGUN, DOUBLE BARREL, SIDE-BY-SIDE

	V.G.	Exc.	Prior Ed.
Astora, Various Calibers, Checkered Stock, Plain, *Modern*	300	350	325
Magnum, 12 Gauge 3", Checkered Stock, Engraved, *Modern*	700	750	720
Monte Carlo, 12 Ga., Checkered Stock, Fancy Engraving, Automatic Ejectors, Sidelock, *Modern*	1,500	1,650	1,550

SINGER Arizmendi y Goenaga, Eibar, Spain.

HANDGUN, SEMI-AUTOMATIC

	V.G.	Exc.	Prior Ed.
.25 ACP, Clip Fed, Blue, *Modern*	100	125	130
.32 ACP, Clip Fed, Blue, *Modern*	125	150	140

	V.G.	Exc.	Prior Edition Exc. Value

SINGER Frantisek Dusek, Opocno, Czechoslovakia.
HANDGUN, SEMI-AUTOMATIC

	V.G.	Exc.	Prior Ed.
Duo, .25 ACP, Clip Fed, Blue, *Modern*	$100	$125	$120

SJOGREN Sweden.
SHOTGUN, SEMI-AUTOMATIC

12 Ga., 5 Shot, Checkered Stock, Recoil Operated, *Curio*	400	450	425

SKB Tokyo, Japan.
SHOTGUN, DOUBLE BARREL, OVER-UNDER

Model 500, 12 and 20 Gauges, Field Grade, Selective Ejector, Vent Rib, *Modern*	375	425	350
Model 500, 12 Ga. Mag. 3", Field Grade, Selective Ejector, Vent Rib, *Modern*	400	450	360
Model 600, 12 Ga., Trap Grade, Selective Ejector, Vent Rib, *Modern*	500	550	460
Model 600, 12 Ga., Trap Grade, Selective Ejector, Vent Rib, Monte Carlo Stock, *Modern*	475	525	460
Model 600, 12 and 20 Gauges, Field Grade, Selective Ejector, Vent Rib, *Modern*	400	475	440
Model 600, 12 and 20 Gauges, Skeet Grade, Selective Ejector, Vent Rib, *Modern*	475	525	460
Model 600, 20 and .410 Gauges, Skeet Grade, Selective Ejector, Vent Rib, *Modern*	500	550	470
Model 600 Combo Set, Various Gauges, Skeet Grade, Selective Ejector, Vent Rib, Cased, *Modern*	1,200	1,350	1,100
Model 680 English, 12 and 20 Gauges, Field Grade, Selective Ejector, Vent Rib, *Modern*	575	625	460
Model 700, 12 Ga., Trap Grade, Selective Ejector, Vent Rib, *Modern*	650	725	550
Model 700, 12 Ga., Trap Grade, Selective Ejector, Vent Rib, Monte Carlo Stock, *Modern*	675	750	550
Model 700, 12 and 20 Gauges, Skeet Grade, Selective Ejector, Vent Rib, *Modern*	675	750	550
Model 700 Combo Set, Various Gauges, Skeet Grade, Selective Ejector, Vent Rib, Cased, *Modern*	1,450	1,650	1,450

SHOTGUN, SEMI-AUTOMATIC

900 Deluxe, 12 and 20 Gauges, Vent Rib, *Modern*	225	275	180
900 XL, 12 Ga., Trap Grade, *Modern*	250	300	225
900 XL, 12 Ga., Trap Grade, Monte Carlo Stock, *Modern*	275	325	230
900 XL, 12 and 20 Gauges, Skeet Grade, *Modern*	250	300	215
900 XL Deluxe, 12 and 20 Gauges, Vent Rib, *Modern*	225	275	200
900 XL Slug, 12 and 20 Gauges, Open Rear Sight, *Modern*	250	300	200

	V.G.	Exc.	Prior Edition Exc. Value

SLOANS Importers, N.Y.C. Also see Charles Daly.

SHOTGUN, DOUBLE BARREL, SIDE-BY-SIDE

POS, .410 Ga., Checkered Stock, Hammerless, Double Trigger, *Modern* — $150 / $175 / $160

POS, 10 Ga., 3½", Checkered Stock, Hammerless, Double Trigger, *Modern* — 150 / 200 / 190

POS, 12 and 20 Gauges, Checkered Stock, Hammerless, Double Trigger, *Modern* — 150 / 175 / 155

POS Coach Gun, 12 and 20 Gauges, Checkered Stock, Outside Hammers, Double Trigger, *Modern* — 150 / 175 / 160

S-M CORP. Sydney Manson, Alexandria, Va., c. 1953.

HANDGUN, SEMI-AUTOMATIC

Sporter, .22 L.R.R.F., Blowback, *Modern* — 125 / 150 / 135

SMITH & WESSON Started in Norwich, Conn. in 1855 as Volcanic Repeating Arms Co. Reorganized at Springfield, Mass. as Smith & Wesson in 1857 (Volcanic Repeating Arms moved to New Haven, Conn. in 1856 and was purchased in 1857 by Winchester Repeating Arms Co.). Smith & Wesson at Springfield, Mass. to date. Also see U.S. Military.

HANDGUN, REVOLVER

.32 Double Action, .32 S & W, 1st Model, Top Break, 5 Shot, Straight-Cut Sideplate, Rocker Cylinder Stop, *Antique* — 3,500 / 4,000 / 1,450

.32 Double Action, .32 S & W, 2nd Model, Top Break, 5 Shot, Irregularly-Cut Sideplate, Rocker Cylinder Stop, *Antique* — 250 / 300 / 210

.32 Double Action, .32 S & W, 3rd Model, Top Break, 5 Shot, Irregularly-Cut Sideplate, *Antique* — 225 / 275 / 190

.32 Double Action, .32 S & W, 4th Model, Round-Back Trigger Guard, Top Break, 5 Shot, Irregularly-Cut Sideplate, *Modern* — 325 / 350 / 175

.32 Double Action, .32 S & W, 5th Model, Round-Back Trigger Guard, Top Break, 5 Shot, Irregularly-Cut Sideplate, Front Sight Forged on Barrel, *Modern* — 250 / 300 / 175

.32 Hand Ejector, .32 S & W Long, 1st Model, Solid Frame, Swing-Out Cylinder, Hammer Actuated Cylinder Stop, 6 Shot, *Modern* — 775 / 825 / 495

.32 Hand Ejector, .32 S & W Long, Solid Frame, Swing-Out Cylinder, 6 Shot, Target Sights, Double Action, *Modern* — 1,250 / 1,500 / 1,250

.32 Hand Ejector 1903, .32 S & W Long, Solid Frame, Swing-Out Cylinder, 6 Shot, Double Action, *Modern* — 500 / 550 / 195

.32 Regulation Police, .32 S & W Long, Solid Frame, Swing-Out Cylinder, 6 Shot, Double Action, *Modern* — 175 / 225 / 185

.32 Safety Hammerless, .32 S & W, 1st Model, Double Action, Top Break, 5 Shot, Push-Button Latch, *Modern* — 275 / 325 / 280

.32 Safety Hammerless, .32 S & W, 2nd Model, Double Action, Top Break, 5 Shot, T Latch, *Modern* — 175 / 225 / 165

	V.G.	Exc.	Prior Edition Exc. Value
.32 Safety Hammerless, .32 S & W, 3rd Model, Double Action, Top Break, 5 Shot, Over #170,000, *Modern*	$200	$250	$175
.32 Single Action, .32 S & W, Top Break, Spur Trigger, 5 Shot, *Antique*	400	450	395
.32 Single Action, .32 S & W, 6" or 8" Barrel, *Add 50%–75%*			
.32 Single Action, .32 S & W, 10" Barrel, *Add 75%–100%*			
.38 D A Perfected, .38 S & W, Solid Trigger Guard, Thumbpiece Hand-Ejector Action, Top Break, Double Action, *Modern*	325	375	330
.38 D A Perfected, .38 S & W, made without Thumbpiece, Hand-Ejector Action, Top Break, Double Action, *Modern*	500	550	485
.38 Double Action, .38 S & W, 1st Model, Straight-Cut Sideplate, Rocker Cylinder Stop, Double Action, Top Break, 5 Shot, *Antique*	700	775	700
.38 Double Action, .38 S & W, 2nd Model, Irregularly-Cut Sideplate, Rocker Cylinder Stop, Double Action, Top Break, 5 Shot, *Antique*	200	250	210
.38 Double Action, .38 S & W, 3rd Model, Irregularly-Cut Sideplate, Double Action, Top Break, 5 Shot, *Antique*	200	250	205
.38 Double Action, .38 S & W, 4th Model, #'s 322,701–539,000, Double Action, Top Break, 5 Shot, *Modern*	175	225	175
.38 Double Action, .38 S & W, 5th Model #'s 539,001–554,077. Double Action, Top Break, 5 Shot, *Modern*	150	200	165
.38 Double Action, .38 S & W, 4th Model, #;s 322,701–539,000, Double Action, Top Break, 5 Shot, Adjustable Sights, *Modern*	450	500	460
.38 Double Action, .38 S & W, 5th Model, #'s 539,001–554,077, Double Action, Top Break, 5 Shot, Adjustable Sights, *Modern*	425	475	400
.38 Hand Ejector, .38 Long Colt, 1st Model, Solid Frame, Swing-Out Cylinder, no Cylinder-Pin Front-Lock, U.S. Army Model, *Modern*	425	775	710
.38 Hand Ejector, .38 Long Colt, 1st Model, Solid Frame, Swing-Out Cylinder, no Cylinder-Pin Front-Lock, U.S. Navy Model, *Modern*	700	750	690
.38 Hand Ejector, .38 Long Colt, 2nd Model, Solid Frame, Swing-Out Cylinder, U.S. Navy Model, *Modern*	500	550	665
.38 Hand Ejector, .38 Special, 1st Model, Solid Frame, Swing-Out Cylinder, no Cylinder-Pin Front-Lock, *Modern*	350	400	360
.38 Hand Ejector, .38 Special, 1st Model, Solid Frame, Swing-Out Cylinder, no Cylinder-Pin Front-Lock, Adjustable Sights, *Modern*	625	675	590
.38 Hand Ejector, .38 Special, 2nd Model, Solid Frame, Swing-Out Cylinder, *Modern*	325	375	300
.38 Hand Ejector, .38 Special, 2nd Model, Solid Frame, Swing-Out Cylinder, Adjustable Sights, *Modern*	575	625	565
.38 Hand Ejector 1902, .38 Special, Military and Police, Solid Frame, Swing-Out Cylinder, Double Action, *Modern*	200	225	275
.38 Hand Ejector 1902, .38 Special, Military and Police, Solid Frame, Swing-Out Cylinder, Double Action, Adjustable Sights, *Modern*	450	500	465
.38 Hand Ejector 1905, .38 Special, Military and Police, Solid Frame, Swing-Out Cylinder, Double Action, *Modern*	275	300	260

S & W Model 28

S & W Model 39

S & W Straight Line

S & W .32 Hand Ejector

S & W .38 Double Action

S & W .38 Hand Ejector 1st Model

	V.G.	Exc.	Prior Edition Exc. Value
.38 Hand Ejector 1905, .38 Special, Military and Police, Solid Frame, Swing-Out Cylinder, Double Action, Adjustable Sights, *Modern*	$450	$500	$465
.38 Safety Hammerless, .38 S & W, 1st Model-Button Latch, Release on Left Topstrap, Top Break, Double Action, *Antique*	375	425	375
.38 Safety Hammerless, .38 S & W, 2nd Model-Button Latch, Release on Top of Frame, Top Break, Double Action, *Antique*	275	325	280
.38 Safety Hammerless, .38 S & W, 3rd Model-Button Latch, Release on Rear Topstrap, Top Break, Double Action, *Antique*	225	275	240
.38 Safety Hammerless, .38 S & W, 4th Model T-Shaped Latch, Top Break, Double Action, *Modern*	225	275	230
.38 Safety Hammerless, .38 S & W, 5th Model T-Shaped Latch, Top Break, Double Action, Front Sight Forged on Barrel, *Modern*	225	275	210
.38 Single Action, .38 S & W, 1st Model, Baby Russian, Top Break, Spur Trigger, *Antique*	375	425	360
.38 Single Action, .38 S & W, 2nd Model, Top Break, Spur Trigger, Short Ejector Housing, *Antique*	250	300	250
.38 Single Action, .38 S & W, 3rd Model, Top Break, with Trigger Guard, *Modern*	600	675	600
.38 Single Action, .38 S & W, 3rd Model, Top Break, with Trigger Guard, with Extra Single-Shot Barrel, *Modern*	950	1,050	900
.38 Single Action, .38 S & W, Mexican Model, Top Break, Spur Trigger, 5 Shot, *Modern*	1,700	1,950	1,700
.38 Win. Double Action, .38-40 WCF, Top Break, *Modern*	1,100	1,250	1,025
.44 Double Action, for Target Sights, *Add 20%–30%*			
.44 Double Action, .44 Russian, 1st Model, Top Break, 6 Shot, *Antique*	525	600	550
.44 Double Action, .44 Russian, Wesson Favorite, 6 Shot, Lightweight, Top Break, *Antique*	1,700	1,850	1,700
.44 Double Action Frontier, for Target Sights, *Add 20%–30%*			
.44 Double Action Frontier, .44-40 WCF, Top Break, 6 Shot, *Antique*	700	850	725
.44 Hand Ejector, Calibers other than .44 Spec., *Add 15%–25%*			
.44 Hand Ejector, 1st Model, for Target Sights, *Add 20%–30%*			
.44 Hand Ejector, Calibers other than .44 Spec., *Add 15%–25%*			
.44 Hand Ejector, 2nd Model, for Target Sights, *Add 20%–30%*			
.44 Hand Ejector, 3rd Model, for Target Sights, *Add 20%–30%*			
.44 Hand Ejector, .44 Special, 1st Model, Triple-Lock, Solid Frame, Swing-Out Cylinder, New Century, *Modern*	725	800	750
.44 Hand Ejector, .44 Special, 2nd Model, Un-Shrouded Ejector Rod, Solid Frame, Swing-Out Cylinder, *Modern*	500	550	490
.44 Hand Ejector, .44 Special, 3rd Model, Shrouded Ejector Rod, Solid Frame, Swing-Out Cylinder, *Modern*	450	500	440
.455 MK II Hand Ejector, Solid Frame, Swing-Out Cylinder, Double Action, Military, *Modern*	450	500	465
22/32 Bekeart Model, .22 L.R.R.F., #'s 138,220–139,275, Target Pistol, Double Action, Adjustable Sights, 6" Barrel, *Modern*	550	625	575

	V.G.	Exc.	Prior Edition Exc. Value
22/32 Kit Gun, .22 L.R.R.F., Early Model, Double Action, Adjustable Sights, 4" Barrel, *Modern*	$275	$325	$270
32/20 Hand Ejector, .32–20 WCF, 1st Model, Solid Frame, Swing-Out Cylinder, 6 Shot, no Cylinder-Pin Front-Lock, *Modern*	425	475	410
32/20 Hand Ejector 1902, .32–20 WCF, 2nd Model, Solid Frame, Swing-Out Cylinder, 6 Shot, *Modern*	325	375	340
32/20 Hand Ejector 1902, .32–20 WCF, 2nd Model, Solid Frame, Swing-Out Cylinder, 6 Shot, Adjustable Sights, *Modern*	500	550	490
32/20 Hand Ejector 1905, .32–20 WCF, Solid Frame, Swing-Out Cylinder, 6 Shot, Adjustable Sights, *Modern*	450	500	435
32/20 Hand Ejector 1905, .32–20 WCF, Solid Frame, Swing-Out Cylinder, 6 Shot, *Modern*	300	350	310
38/200 British, .38 S & W, Military & Police, Solid Frame, Swing-Out Cylinder, Double Action, Military, *Modern*	200	250	200
First Model Schofield, .45 S & W, Top Break, Single Action, Military, *Antique*	2,000	2,500	1,600
First Model Schofield, .45 S & W, Top Break, Single Action, Commercial, *Antique*	3,000	3,500	2,450
First Model Schofield, .45 S & W, Wells Fargo, Top Break, Single Action, *Antique*	2,500	3,000	1,425
K-22 Hand Ejector, .22 L.R.R.F., 1st Model, Double Action, Adjustable Sights, 6" Barrel, *Modern*	300	350	275
K-22 Masterpiece, .22 L.R.R.F., 2nd Model K-22 Hand Ejector, Speed Lock Action, Double Action, Adjustable Sights, 6" Barrel, *Modern*	475	525	440
K-32 Hand Ejector, .32 S & W Long, 1st Model, Pre-War, 6 Shot, Adjustable Sights, Target Pistol, *Modern*	600	675	595
K-32 Hand Ejector, .32 S & W Long, 2nd Model, Post-War, 6 Shot, Adjustable Sights, Target Pistol, *Modern*	275	325	250
Model #1, .22 Short R.F., 1st Issue, Tip-Up, Spur Trigger, 7 Shot, *Antique*	3,000	3,500	2,750
Model #1, .22 Short R.F., 2nd Issue, Tip-Up, Spur Trigger, 7 Shot, *Antique*	2,000	2,250	1,500
Model #1, .22 Short R.F., 3rd Issue, Tip-Up, Spur Trigger, 7 Shot, *Antique*	1,000	1,225	950
Model #1¹/₂, .32 Short R.F., 1st Issue, Tip-Up, Spur Trigger, 5 Shot, Non-Fluted Cylinder, *Antique*	400	450	375
Model #1¹/₂, .32 Short R.F., 2nd Issue, Tip-Up, Spur Trigger, 5 Shot, Fluted Cylinder, *Antique*	375	425	360
Model #2 Old Army, .32 Long R.F., Tip-Up, Spur Trigger, 6 Shot, *Antique*	500	550	475
Model #3 American, .44 Henry, 1st Model, Single Action, Top Break, 6 Shot, *Antique*	1,750	1,975	1,750
Model #3 American, .44 Henry, 2nd Model, #'s 8,000–32,800, Single Action, Top Break, 6 Shot, *Antique*	1,500	1,750	1,575
Model #3 American, .44 S & W, 1st Model, Single Action, Top Break, 6 Shot, *Antique*	1,000	1,275	985

	V.G.	Exc.	Prior Edition Exc. Value
Model #3 American, .44 S & W, 2nd Model, #'s 8,000–32,800, Single Action, Top Break, 6 Shot, *Antique*	$900	$1,050	$880
Model #3 Frontier, .44–40 WCF, Single Action, Top Break, 6 Shot, *Antique*	1,250	1,500	1,250
Model #3 New Model, Calibers other than .44 Russian, *Add* **40%–60%**			
Model #3 New Model, .44 Russian, Australian Police with Shoulder Stock, *Add* **200%–225%**			
Model #3 New Model, .44 Russian, Single Action, Top Break, 6 Shot, *Antique*	875	950	720
Model #3 New Model, .44 Russian Japanese Navy Issue, *Add* **30%–45%**			
Model #3 New Model, .44 Russian, Australian Police with Shoulder Stock, *Add* **200%–225%**			
Model #3 New Model, .44 Russian, Argentine Model, *Add* **25%–35%**			
Model #3 New Model, .44 S & W, Turkish Model, *Add* **15%–25%**			
Model #3 New Model, Various Calibers, Calibers other than .44 Russian, *Add* **40%–60%**			
Model # Russian, .44 Russian, 1st Model, Single Action, Top Break, 6 Shot, Military, *Antique*	925	1,050	900
Model #3 Russian, .44 Russian, 2nd Model, Finger-Rest Trigger Guard, Single Action, Top Break, 6 Shot, *Antique*	850	925	800
Model #3 Russian, .44 Russian, 2nd Model, Finger-Rest Trigger Guard, Single Action, Top Break, with Shoulder Stock, *Antique*	1,450	1,575	1,400
Model #3 Russian, .44 Russian, 3rd Model, Front Sight Forged on Barrel, Single Action, Top Break, 6 Shot, *Antique*	925	1,050	925
Model #3 Target, .32–44 S & W, .38–44 S & W, New Model #3, Single Action, Top Break, *Modern*	850	925	750
Target Models, For Target Hammer, Target Trigger, Target Stocks, *Add* **$30.00–$40.00**			
Target Models, For Target Hammer, Target Trigger, Target Stocks, *Add* **$30.00–$45.00**			
Model 10, .38 Special, Double Action, Blue, Various Barrel Lengths, Swing-Out Cylinder, *Modern*	200	250	175
Model 10, .38 Special, Double Action, Swing-Out Cylinder, 4" Barrel, Heavy Barrel, Blue, *Modern*	225	275	185

S & W Model 10

S & W Model 36

S & W Model 61

S & W .38 Single Action

S & W .35 Automatic

S & W Model 15

S & W Model 52

	V.G.	Exc.	Prior Edition Exc. Value
Model 10, .38 Special, Double Action, Swing-Out Cylinder, 4" Barrel, Heavy Barrel, Nickel Plated, *Modern*	$250	$300	$190
Model 10, .38 Special, Double Action, Swing-Out Cylinder, Various Barrel Lengths, Nickel Plated, *Modern*	225	275	180
Model 11, .38 S & W, Double Action, Swing-Out Cylinder, *Modern*	400	450	350
Model 12, .38 Special, Double Action, Swing-Out Cylinder, Various Barrel Lengths, Blue, *Modern*	300	350	220
Model 12, .38 Special, Double Action, Swing-Out Cylinder, Various Barrel Lengths, Nickel Plated, *Modern*	275	325	235
Model 12 USAF, .38 Special, Double Action, Swing-Out Cylinder, Lightweight, *Modern*	425	475	410
Model "13" Army, .38 Special, Double Action, Swing-Out Cylinder, Lightweight, *Modern*	500	575	500
Model 13, .357 Magnum, Double Action, Swing-Out Cylinder, 4" Barrel, Heavy Barrel, Blue, *Modern*	200	250	185
Model 13, .357 Magnum, Double Action, Swing-Out Cylinder, 4" Barrel, Nickel Plated, Heavy Barrel, *Modern*	225	275	195
Model 14, .38 Special, Double Action, Swing-Out Cylinder, 6" Barrel, Blue, Adjustable Sights, *Modern*	225	275	220
Model 14, .38 Special, Double Action, Swing-Out Cylinder, 8³/₈" Barrel, Blue, Adjustable Sights, *Modern*	250	300	225
Model 14 SA, .38 Special, Single Action, Swing-Out Cylinder, 6" Barrel, Blue, Adjustable Sights, *Modern*	275	325	245
Model 14 SA, .38 Special, Single Action, Swing-Out Cylinder, 8³/₈" Barrel, Blue, Adjustable Sights, *Modern*	275	325	260
Model 15, .38 Special, Double Action, Swing-Out Cylinder, Various Barrel Lengths, Blue, Adjustable Sights, *Modern*	225	275	190
Model 15, .38 Special, Double Action, Swing-Out Cylinder, Various Barrel Lengths, Nickel Plated, Adjustable Sights, *Modern*	250	300	200
Model 16, .32 S & W Long, Double Action, Swing-Out Cylinder, Adjustable Sights, Target Pistol, *Modern*	375	425	385
Model 17, .22 L.R.R.F., Double Action, Swing-Out Cylinder, 6" Barrel, Adjustable Sights, Blue, *Modern*	275	325	230
Model 17, .22 L.R.R.F., Double Action, Swing-Out Cylinder, 8³/₈" Barrel, Adjustable Sights, Blue, *Modern*	275	325	240
Model 18, .22 L.R.R.F., Double Action, Swing-Out Cylinder, 4" Barrel, Adjustable Sights, Blue, *Modern*	250	300	225
Model 19, .357 Magnum, Double Action, Swing-Out Cylinder, Various Barrel Lengths, Adjustable Sights, Blue, *Modern*	300	350	235
Model 19, .357 Magnum, Double Action, Swing-Out Cylinder, Various Barrel Lengths, Adjustable Sights, Nickel Plated, *Modern*	275	325	240
Model 19 Texas Ranger, .357 Magnum, Commemorative, Blue, Cased, with Knife, *Curio*	400	650	560
Model 1917, .45 Auto-Rim, Double Action, Swing-Out Cylinder, *Modern*	500	550	460

	V.G.	Exc.	Prior Edition Exc. Value
Model 1917, .45 Auto-Rim, Double Action, Swing-Out Cylinder, Military, *Modern*	$375	$425	$350
Model 20, .38 Special, Double Action, Swing-Out Cylinder, *Modern*	400	450	380
Model 21, .44 Special, Double Action, Swing-Out Cylinder, Various Barrel Lengths, *Modern*	500	575	515
Model 22, .45 Auto-Rim, Double Action, Swing-Out Cylinder, *Modern*	400	450	370
Model 23, .38 Special, Double Action, Swing-Out Cylinder, Adjustable Sights, Target Pistol, *Modern*	475	525	465
Model 24, .44 Special, Double Action, Swing-Out Cylinder, Various Barrel Lengths, Adjustable Sights, *Modern*	475	525	450
Model 25, .45 Auto-Rim, Double Action, Swing-Out Cylinder, Target Pistol, Blue, Cased with Accessories, *Modern*	375	425	350
Model 25, .45 Auto-Rim, Double Action, Swing-Out Cylinder, Target Pistol, Blue, *Modern*	325	375	300
Model 26, .45 Auto-Rim, Double Action, Swing-Out Cylinder, *Modern*	475	550	500
Model 27, .357 Magnum, Double Action, Swing-Out Cylinder, Pre-War, Adjustable Sights, *Modern*	575	625	550
Model 27, .357 Magnum, Double Action, Swing-Out Cylinder, Various Barrel Lengths, Adjustable Sights, Blue, *Modern*	325	375	305
Model 27, .357 Magnum, Double Action, Swing-Out Cylinder, Nickel Plated, *Modern*	325	375	315
Model 27, .357 Magnum, Double Action, Swing-Out Cylinder, 8⅜" Barrel, Blue, *Modern*	325	375	310
Model 27, .357 Magnum, Double Action, Swing-Out Cylinder, 8⅜" Barrel, Nickel Plated, *Modern*	325	375	310
Model 27, .357 Magnum, Double Action, Various Barrel Lengths, Adjustable Sights, Cased with Accessories, Blue, *Modern*	350	400	340
Model 27, .357 Magnum, Double Action, 8⅜" Barrel, Adjustable Sights, Cased with Accessories, Nickel Plated, *Modern*	350	400	345
Model 27, .357 Magnum, Double Action, Various Barrel Lengths, Adjustable Sights, Cased with Accessories, Nickel Plated, *Modern*	350	400	340
Model 27, .357 Magnum, Double Action, 8⅜" Barrel, Adjustable Sights, Cased with Accessories, Blue, *Modern*	350	400	350
Model 27 with Registration, .357 Magnum, Double Action, Swing-Out Cylinder, Pre-War, Adjustable Sights, *Modern*	1,000	1,250	875
Model 28, .357 Magnum, Double Action, Various Barrel Lengths, Adjustable Sights, Blue, *Modern*	250	300	225
Model 28, .357 Magnum, Double Action, Various Barrel Lengths, Target Grips, Adjustable Sights, Blue, *Modern*	250	300	225
Model 29, .44 Magnum, Double Action, Various Barrel Lengths, Adjustable Sights, Swing-Out Cylinder, Blue, *Modern*	375	425	355
Model 29, .44 Magnum, Double Action, Various Barrel Lengths, Adjustable Sights, Swing-Out Cylinder, Nickel Plated, *Modern*	375	425	365

S & W .32 Safety
Hammerless

S & W Model 27

S & W Model 38

S & W .38 Safety
Hammerless

S & W Model 25

S & W Model #3 Frontier

	V.G.	Exc.	Prior Edition Exc. Value
Model 29, .44 Magnum, Double Action, 8³/₈" Barrel, Adjustable Sights, Swing-Out Cylinder, Blue, *Modern*	$425	$475	$380
Model 29, .44 Magnum, Double Action, 8³/₈" Barrel, Adjustable Sights, Swing-Out Cylinder, Nickel Plated, *Modern*	400	450	370
Model 29, .44 Magnum, Double Action, Various Barrel Lengths, Adjustable Sights, Cased with Accessories, Blue, *Modern*	400	450	365
Model 29, .44 Magnum, Double Action, Various Barrel Lengths, Adjustable Sights, Cased with Accessories, Nickel Plated, *Modern*	400	450	375
Model 29, .44 Magnum, Double Action, 8³/₈" Barrel, Adjustable Sights, Cased with Accessories, Blue, *Modern*	425	475	385
Model 29, .44 Magnum, Double Action, 8³/₈" Barrel, Adjustable Sights, Cased with Accessories, Nickel Plated, *Modern*	400	450	375
Model 30, .32 S & W Long, Double Action, Swing-Out Cylinder, *Modern*	300	350	270
Model 31, .32 S & W Long, Double Action, Swing-Out Cylinder, Various Barrel Lengths, Nickel Plated, *Modern*	325	375	200
Model 31, .32 S & W Long, Double Action, Swing-Out Cylinder, Various Barrel Lengths, Blue, *Modern*	225	275	195
Model 32, .38 S & W, Double Action, Swing-Out Cylinder, 2" Barrel, *Modern*	275	325	245
Model 33, .38 S & W, Double Action, Swing-Out Cylinder, *Modern*	325	375	255
Model 34, .22 L.R.R.F., Double Action, Swing-Out Cylinder, Various Barrel Lengths, Adjustable Sights, Blue, *Modern*	275	325	205
Model 34, .22 L.R.R.F., Double Action, Swing-Out Cylinder, Various Barrel Lengths, Adjustable Sights, Nickel Plated, *Modern*	225	275	210
Model 35, .22 L.R.R.F., Double Action, Swing-Out Cylinder, Target Pistol, Adjustable Sights, *Modern*	325	375	330
Model 36, .38 Special, Double Action, Swing-Out Cylinder, Various Barrel Lengths, Blue, *Modern*	225	275	190
Model 36, .38 Special, Double Action, Swing-Out Cylinder, Various Barrel Lengths, Nickel Plated, *Modern*	250	300	210
Model 36, .38 Special, Double Action, Swing-Out Cylinder 3" Barrel, Heavy Barrel, Blue, *Modern*	225	275	195
Model 36, .38 Special, Double Action, Swing-Out Cylinder, 3" Barrel, Heavy Barrel, Nickel Plated, *Modern*	225	275	205
Model 37, .38 Special, Double Action, Swing-Out Cylinder, Various Barrel Lengths, Lightweight, Blue, *Modern*	225	275	205
Model 37, .38 Special, Double Action, Swing-Out Cylinder, Various Barrel Lengths, Lightweight, Nickel Plated, *Modern*	225	275	215
Model 38, .38 Special, Swing-Out Cylinder, 2" Barrel, Hammer Shroud, Nickel Plated, Double Action, *Modern*	275	325	230
Model 38, .38 Special, Double Action, Swing-Out cylinder, 2" Barrel, Hammer Shroud, Blue, *Modern*	300	350	225
Model 40, .38 Special, Double Action, Swing-Out Cylinder, Hammerless, *Modern*	375	425	385

	V.G.	Exc.	Prior Edition Exc. Value
Model 42, .38 Special, Double Action, Swing-Out Cylinder, Hammerless, Lightweight, *Modern*	$500	$550	$495
Model 43, .22 L.R.R.F., Double Action, Swing-Out Cylinder, Adjustable Sights, Lightweight, *Modern*	400	450	440
Model 45, .22 L.R.R.F., Double-Action, Swing-Out Cylinder, Commercial, *Modern*	775	850	800
Model 45 USPO, .22 L.R.R.F., Double Action, Swing-Out Cylinder, *Modern*	575	650	600
Model 48, .22 WMR, Double Action, Swing-Out Cylinder, Various Barrel Lengths, Blue, Adjustable Sights, *Modern*	225	250	230
Model 48, .22 WMR, Double Action, Swing-Out Cylinder, 8³/₈" Barrel, Blue, Adjustable Sights, *Modern*	225	275	230
Model 49, .38 Special, Double Action, Swing-Out Cylinder, 2" Barrel, Hammer Shroud, Nickel Plated, *Modern*	200	250	235
Model 49, .38 Special, Double Action, Swing-Out Cylinder, 2" Barrel, Hammer Shroud, Blue, *Modern*	175	225	215
Model 50, .38 Special, Double Action, Swing-Out Cylinder, Adjustable Sights, *Modern*	700	775	765
Model 51, .22LR/.22 WMR Combo, Double Action, Swing-Out Cylinder, Adjustable Sights, *Modern*	475	525	515
Model 51, .22 WMR, Double Action, Swing-Out Cylinder, Adjustable Sights, *Modern*	425	475	450
Model 53, .22 Rem. Jet, Double Action, Swing-Out Cylinder, Adjustable Sights, *Modern*	625	675	650
Model 53, .22 Rem. Jet, Double Action, Swing-Out Cylinder, Adjustable Sights, Extra Cylinder, *Modern*	650	725	700
Model 56, .38 Special, Double Action, Swing-Out Cylinder, 2" Barrel, Adjustable Sights, *Modern*	875	925	875
Model 57, .41 Magnum, Double Action, Swing-Out Cylinder, Various Barrel Lengths, Blue, Adjustable Sights, *Modern*	275	325	295
Model 57, .41 Magnum, Double Action, Swing-Out Cylinder, Various Barrel Lengths, Nickel Plated, Adjustable Sights, *Modern*	300	350	295
Model 57, .41 Magnum, Double Action, Swing-Out Cylinder, 8³/₈" Barrel, Blue, Adjustable Sights, *Modern*	300	350	305
Model 57, .41 Magnum, Double Action, Swing-Out Cylinder, 8³/₈" Barrel, Nickel Plated, Adjustable Sights, *Modern*	325	375	305
Model 57, .41 Magnum, Double Action, Swing-Out Cylinder, Various Barrel Lengths, Blue, Cased with Accessories, *Modern*	300	350	320
Model 57, .41 Magnum, Double Action, Swing-Out Cylinder, Various Barrel Lengths, Nickel Plated, Cased with Accessories, *Modern*	325	375	340
Model 57, .41 Magnum, Double Action, Swing-Out Cylinder, 8³/₈" Barrel, Blue, Cased with Accessories, *Modern*	325	375	340
Model 57, .41 Magnum, Double Action, Swing-Out Cylinder, 8³/₈" Barrel, Blue, Cased with Accessories, *Modern*	325	375	340
Model 58, .41 Magnum, Double Action, Swing-Out Cylinder, 4" Barrel, Blue, *Modern*	250	300	310

	V.G.	Exc.	Prior Edition Exc. Value
Model 58, .41 Magnum, Double Action, Swing-Out Cylinder, 4" Barrel, Nickel Plated, *Modern*	$275	$325	$335
Model 60, .38 Special, Double Action, Swing-Out Cylinder, Stainless Steel, Adjustable Sights, *Modern*	850	950	925
Model 60, .38 Special, Double Action, Swing-Out Cylinder, Stainless Steel, 2" Barrel, *Modern*	250	300	260
Model 60, .38 Special, Double Action, Swing-Out Cylinder, Early High Polish Stainless Steel, 2" Barrel, *Modern*	325	375	365
Model 63, .22 L.R.R.F., Double Action, Swing-Out Cylinder, Stainless Steel, 4" Barrel, Adjustable Sights, *Modern*	250	300	235
Model 64, .38 Special, Double Action, Swing-Out Cylinder, Stainless Steel, Various Barrel Lengths, *Modern*	225	275	195
Model 65, .357 Magnum, Double Action, Swing-Out Cylinder, Stainless Steel, 4" Barrel, Heavy Barrel, *Modern*	225	275	225
Model 66, .357 Magnum, Double Action, Swing-Out Cylinder, Stainless Steel, 2¹/₂" Barrel, *Modern*	300	350	240
Model 66, .357 Magnum, Double Action, Swing-Out Cylinder, Stainless Steel, Various Barrel Lengths, *Modern*	300	350	230
Model 67, .38 Special, Double Action, Swing-Out Cylinder, Stainless Steel, 4" Barrel, *Modern*	275	325	220
Model 547, 9mm Luger, Double Action, Swing-Out Cylinder, Blue, *Modern*	200	250	215
Model 581, .357 Magnum, Double Action, Swing-Out Cylinder, Blue, *Modern*	175	225	185
Model 581, .357 Magnum, Double Action, Swing-Out Cylinder, Nickel, *Modern*	175	225	190
Model 586, .357 Magnum, Double Action, Swing-Out Cylinder, Blue, Adjustable Sights, *Modern*	225	275	235
Model 586, .357 Magnum, Double Action, Swing-Out Cylinder, Nickel, Adjustable Sights, *Modern*	225	275	245
Model 629, .44 Magnum, Double Action, Swing-Out Cylinder, Stainless Steel, Adjustable Sights, *Modern*	400	475	430
Model 629, .44 Magnum, Double Action, Swing-Out Cylinder, 8³/₈" Barrel, Stainless Steel, Adjustable Sights, *Modern*	400	475	440
Model 649 Bodyguard, .38 Special, J Frame, 5 Shot, Stainless Steel, *Modern*	325	375	326
Model 650, .22 W.M.R., Double Action, Swing-Out Cylinder, Stainless Steel, *Modern*	200	250	225
Model 651, .22 W.M.R., Double Action, Swing-Out Cylinder, Stainless Steel, Adjustable Sights, *Modern*	275	325	240
Model 681, .357 Magnum, Double Action, Swing-Out Cylinder, Stainless Steel, *Modern*	200	250	205
Model 686, .357 Magnum, Double Action, Swing-Out Cylinder, Stainless Steel, Adjustable Sights, *Modern*	225	275	250
Model M Hand Ejector, .22 Long R.F., 1st Model Ladysmith, Solid Frame, Swing-Out Cylinder, Double Action, *Curio*	800	875	810
Model M Hand Ejector, .22 Long R.F., 2nd Model Ladysmith, Solid Frame, Swing-Out Cylinder, Double Action, *Curio*	700	750	675

S & W Model 66

S & W Model 586

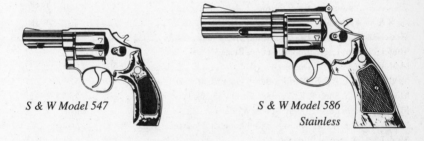

S & W Model 547

S & W Model 586
Stainless

S & W Model 34

S & W Model 41

	V.G.	Exc.	Prior Edition Exc. Value
Model M Hand Ejector, .22 Long R.F., 3rd Model Ladysmith, Solid Frame, Swing-Out Cylinder, Double Action, *Curio*	$675	$725	$640
Model M Hand Ejector, .22 Long R.F., 3rd Model Ladysmith, Solid Frame, Swing-Out Cylinder, Double Action, Adjustable Sights, *Curio*	900	975	915
Second Model Schofield, .45 S & W, Knurled Latch, Top Break, Single Action, Military, *Antique*	1,250	1,450	1,350
Second Model Schofield, .45 S & W. Knurled Latch, Top Break, Single Action, Commercial, *Antique*	1,650	1,850	1,750
Second Model Schofield, .45 S & W, Wells Fargo, Knurled Latch, Top Break, Single Action, *Antique*	1,200	1,375	1,285
Victory, .38 Special Military & Police, Solid Frame, Swing-Out Cylinder, Double Action, Military, *Modern*	200	250	200

HANDGUN, SEMI-AUTOMATIC

	V.G.	Exc.	Prior Edition Exc. Value
.32 ACP, Blue, *Curio*	2,500	2,750	1,200
.32 ACP, Nickel Plated, *Curio*		N/A	
.35 S & W Automatic, Blue, *Curio*	525	600	550
.35 S & W Automatic, Nickel Plated, *Curio*	550	700	650
Model 39, 9mm Luger, Double Action, Steel Frame, *Curio*	850	950	1,250
Model 39, 9mm Luger, Double Action, Blue, *Modern*	275	325	270
Model 39-1, .38 AMU, Double Action, *Curio*	2,500	2,750	2,500
Model 41, .22 L.R.R.F., Various Barrel Lengths, *Modern*	500	550	285
Model 41-1, .22 Short R.F., Various Barrel Lengths, *Modern*	675	750	350
Model 44, 9mm Luger, Single Action, *Modern*		RARE	
Model 46, .22 L.R.R.F., Various Barrel Lengths, *Modern*	425	500	345
Model 52, .38 Special, Blue, *Modern*	575	650	425
Model 59, 9mm Luger, Double Action, Blue, *Modern*	325	375	290
Model 59, 9mm Luger, Double Action, Nickel Plated, *Modern*	325	425	330
Model 61-1, .22 L.R.R.F., Clip Fed, Nickel Plated, *Modern*	250	300	260
Model 61-1, .22 L.R.R.F., Clip Fed, Blue, *Modern*	225	275	230
Model 61-2, .22 L.R.R.F., Clip Fed, Nickel Plated, *Modern*	250	300	260
Model 61-2, .22 L.R.R.F., Clip Fed, Blue, *Modern*	250	300	250
Model 61-3, .22 L.R.R.F., Clip Fed, Nickel Plated, *Modern*	250	300	260
Model 61-3, .22 L.R.R.F., Clip Fed, Blue, *Modern*	225	275	235
Model 439, 9mm Luger, Double Action, Blue, *Modern*	300	350	270
Model 439, 9mm Luger, Double Action, Nickel Plated, *Modern*	325	375	290
Model 459, 9mm Luger, Double Action, Blue, *Modern*	325	375	330
Model 459, 9mm Luger, Double Action, Nickel Plated, *Modern*	350	400	380
Model 469, (12 Shot), 9mm Luger, Double Action, Blue, *Modern*	325	375	400
Model 539, 9mm Luger, Double Action, Blue, *Modern*	325	375	285
Model 539, 9mm Luger, Double Action, Nickel Plated, *Modern*	350	400	300
Model 559, 9mm Luger, Double Action, Blue, *Modern*	375	425	325
Model 559, 9mm Luger, Double Action, Nickel Plated, *Modern*	400	450	350
Model 639, 9mm Luger, Double Action, Stainless, *Modern*	375	425	300

	V.G.	Exc.	Prior Edition Exc. Value
Model 659, 9mm Luger, Double Action, Stainless, *Modern*	$400	$450	$325
Model 669 (12 Shot), 9mm Luger, Double Action, Stainless Steel, *Modern*..	375	425	439

HANDGUN, SINGLESHOT

	V.G.	Exc.	Prior Ed.
Model 1891, .22 L.R.R.F., Target Pistol, Single Action, 1st Model, Various Barrel Lengths, *Antique*......................	375	425	385
Model 1891, .22 L.R.R.F., Target Pistol, Single Action, 2nd Model, no Hand or Cylinder Stop, *Modern*......................	350	400	350
Model 1891 Set, Various Calibers, Extra Cylinder, Extra Barrel, Target Pistol, Single Action, 1st Model, *Antique*	750	825	770
Perfected, .22 L.R.R.F., Double Action, Top Break, Target Pistol, *Modern*..	375	425	375
Perfected Olympic, .22 L.R.R.F., Double Action, Top Break, Tight Bore and Chamber, Target Pistol, *Modern*	700	750	660
Straight Line, .22 L.R.R.F., Cased, *Curio*.........................	1,100	1,250	1,175

RIFLE, BOLT ACTION

	V.G.	Exc.	Prior Ed.
Model 125 Deluxe, Various Calibers, Monte Carlo Stock, *Modern*..	150	175	200
Model 125 STD, Various Calibers, Monte Carlo Stock, *Modern*.........	125	150	175
Model 1500, Various Calibers, Monte Carlo Stock, Checkered Stock, *Modern*..	200	250	235
Model 1500 Deluxe, Various Calibers, Monte Carlo Stock, Checkered Stock, *Modern*..................................	225	275	265
Model 1500 Magnum, Various Calibers, Monte Carlo Stock, Checkered Stock, *Modern*..................................	200	250	255
Model 1500 Varmint, Various Calibers, Monte Carlo Stock, Checkered Stock, Heavy Barrel, *Modern*	225	275	280
Model 1700 Classic, Various Calibers, Monte Carlo Stock, Checkered Stock, Clip Fed, *Modern*..................................	275	325	300
Model A, Various Calibers, Monte Carlo Stock, Checkered Stock, *Modern*..	275	325	280
Model B, Various Calibers, Monte Carlo Stock, Checkered Stock, *Modern*..	225	275	250
Model C, Various Calibers, Sporting Rifle, Checkered Stock, *Modern*..	225	275	250
Model D, Various Calibers, Mannlicher, Checkered Stock, *Modern*..	325	375	280
Model E, Various Calibers, Monte Carlo Stock, Mannlicher, *Modern*..	325	375	295

RIFLE, REVOLVER

	V.G.	Exc.	Prior Ed.
Model 320, .320 S & W Rifle, Single Action, Top Break, 6 Shot, Adjustable Sights, Cased with Accessories, *Antique*.........................	5,000	6,000	3,875

RIFLE, SEMI-AUTOMATIC

	V.G.	Exc.	Prior Ed.
Light Rifle, MK I, 9mm Luger, Clip Fed, Carbine, *Curio*	1,250	1,500	1,800
Light Rifle MK II, 9mm Luger, Clip Fed, Carbine, *Curio*...............	1,500	2,000	2,500

S & W Model 1000

	V.G.	Exc.	Prior Edition Exc. Value
SHOTGUN, SEMI-AUTOMATIC			
Model 1000 Field, 12 Ga., Vent Rib, *Modern*	$250	$300	$360
Model 1000 Field, 12 Ga., 3", Vent Rib, *Modern*	275	325	385
Model 1000 Slug, 12 Ga., Open Sights, *Modern*	275	325	385
Model 1000 Skeet, 12 Ga., Vent Rib, *Modern*	300	350	390
SHOTGUN, SLIDE ACTION			
Model 916 Eastfield, Various Gauges, Plain Barrel, *Modern*	125	150	140
Model 916 Eastfield, Various Gauges, Plain Barrel, Recoil Pad, *Modern*	100	125	130
Model 3000 Field, 12 Ga. 3", Vent Rib, *Modern*	250	275	235
Model 3000 Slug, 12 Ga. 3", Open Sights, *Modern*	225	275	235
Model 3000 Police, 12 Ga., Open Sights, *Modern*	225	250	215
Model 3000 Police, 12 Ga., Open Sights, Folding Stock, *Modern*	250	300	255

SMITH, ANTHONY Northampton, Pa., 1770–1779. See Kentucky Rifles and Pistols.

SMITH, L.C. GUN CO. Syracuse, N.Y., 1877–1890, in 1890 became Hunter Arms, and in 1948 became a division of Marlin.

SHOTGUN, DOUBLE BARREL, SIDE-BY-SIDE

	V.G.	Exc.	Prior Edition Exc. Value
Crown Grade, Various Calibers, Sidelock, Single Selective Trigger, Automatic Ejector, Fancy Engraving, Fancy Checkering, *Modern*	5,500	6,250	3,800
Crown Grade, Various Calibers, Sidelock, Double Trigger, Automatic Ejector, Fancy Engraving, Fancy Checkering, *Modern*	5,000	5,850	3,500
Field Grade, Various Calibers, Sidelock, Double Trigger, Checkered Stock, Light Engraving, *Modern*	950	1,275	745
Field Grade, Various Calibers, Sidelock, Double Trigger, Automatic Ejector, Checkered Stock, Light Engraving, *Modern*	900	1,200	690
Field Grade, Various Calibers, Sidelock, Single Trigger, Checkered Stock, Light Engraving, *Modern*	925	1,250	725
Field Grade, Various Calibers, Sidelock, Single Trigger, Automatic Ejector, Checkered Stock, Light Engraving, *Modern*	900	1,200	695
Ideal Grade, Various Calibers, Sidelock, Double Trigger, Checkered Stock, Engraved, *Modern*	900	1,200	695
Ideal Grade, Various Calibers, Sidelock, Double Trigger, Automatic Ejector, Checkered Stock, Engraved, *Modern*	1,200	1,400	845

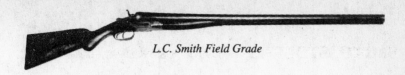

L.C. Smith Field Grade

	V.G.	Exc.	Prior Edition Exc. Value
Ideal Grade, Various Calibers, Sidelock, Single Selective Trigger, Checkered Stock, Engraved, *Modern*	$1,250	$1,500	$1,200
Ideal Grade, Various Calibers, Sidelock, Single Selective Trigger, Automatic Ejector, Engraved, Checkered Stock, *Modern*	1,400	1,550	1,250
Marlin Deluxe, 12 Ga., Double Trigger, Checkered Stock, Vent Rib, *Modern*	575	650	545
Marlin Field, 12 Ga., Double Trigger, Checkered Stock, *Modern*	500	550	440
Olympic Grade, Various Calibers, Sidelock, Single Selective Trigger, Automatic Ejector, Engraved, Checkered Stock, *Modern*	750	975	975
Skeet Grade, Various Calibers, Sidelock, Single Selective Trigger, Automatic Ejector, Engraved, Checkered Stock, *Modern*	2,000	2,500	1,175
Skeet Grade, Various Calibers, Sidelock, Single Trigger, Automatic Ejector, Engraved, Checkered Stock, *Modern*	1,500	1,750	995
Specialty Grade, Various Calibers, Sidelock, Double Trigger, Engraved, Checkered Stock, *Modern*	2,250	2,500	1,250
Specialty Grade, Various Calibers, Sidelock, Single Selective Trigger, Automatic Ejector, Engraved, Checkered Stock, *Modern*	2,500	2,750	1,265
Trap Grade, 12 Ga., Sidelock, Single Selective Trigger, Automatic Ejector, Engraved, Checkered Stock, *Modern*	1,250	1,500	1,185

SHOTGUN, SINGLESHOT

	V.G.	Exc.	Prior Edition Exc. Value
Crown Grade, 12 Ga., Trap Grade, Vent Rib, Automatic Ejector, Fancy Engraving, Fancy Checkering, *Modern*	2,500	3,000	2,800
Olympic Grade, 12 Ga., Trap Grade, Vent Rib, Automatic Ejector, Engraved, Fancy Checkering, *Modern*	1,250	1,500	1,250
Specialty Grade, 12 Ga., Trap Grade, Vent Rib, Automatic Ejector, Engraved, Fancy Checkering, *Modern*	1,500	1,800	1,700

SMITH, OTIS A. Middlefield & Rockfall, Conn. 1873–1890.

HANDGUN, REVOLVER

	V.G.	Exc.	Prior Edition Exc. Value
.22 Short R.F., 7 Shot, Spur Trigger, Solid Frame, Single Action, *Antique*	200	250	165
.32 S & W, 5 Shot, Single Action, Top Break, Spur Trigger, *Antique*	175	225	140
.32 Short R.F., 5 Shot, Spur Trigger, Solid Frame, Single Action, *Antique*	200	250	165
.38 Short R.F., 5 Shot, Spur Trigger, Solid Frame, Single Action, *Antique*	200	250	175
.41 Short R.F., 5 Shot, Spur Trigger, Solid Frame, Single Action, *Antique*	225	275	200

	V.G.	Exc.	Prior Edition Exc. Value

SMITH, STOEFFEL Pa. 1790–1800. See Kentucky Rifles and Pistols.

SMITH, THOMAS London, England, c. 1850.
RIFLE, PERCUSSION

	V.G.	Exc.	Prior Edition Exc. Value
16 Ga., Smoothbore, Anson-Deeley Lock, Octagon Barrel, Fancy Wood, Cased with Accessories, *Antique*	$2,500	$3,250	$3,000

SMITH, WM. England.
HANDGUN, SEMI-AUTOMATIC

	V.G.	Exc.	Prior Edition Exc. Value
Pocket, .25 ACP, Clip Fed, 1906 Browning Type, *Modern*	375	450	435

SMOKER Made by Johnson Bye & Co. 1875–1884.
HANDGUN, REVOLVER

	V.G.	Exc.	Prior Edition Exc. Value
#1, .22 Short R.F., 7 Shot, Spur Trigger, Solid Frame, Single Action, *Antique*	150	175	165
#2, .32 Short R.F., 5 Shot, Spur Trigger, Solid Frame, Single Action, *Antique*	150	175	170
#3, .38 Short R.F., 5 Shot, Spur Trigger, Solid Frame, Single Action, *Antique*	150	175	170
#4, .41 Short R.F., 5 Shot, Spur Trigger, Solid Frame, Single Action, *Antique*	150	200	200

SNAPHAUNCE, UNKNOWN MAKER
HANDGUN, SNAPHAUNCE

	V.G.	Exc.	Prior Edition Exc. Value
.45 Italian Early 1700's, Holster Pistol, Half-Octagon Barrel, Engraved, Carved, High Quality, Furniture, *Antique*	2,000	2,500	2,500
Early 1800's Small, Plain, *Antique*	750	1,000	1,000
English Late 1500's, Ovoid Pommel, Engraved, Gold Damascened, High Quality, *Antique*	15,000	20,000	20,000
Italian Early 1700's, Medium Quality, Brass Furniture, Plain, *Antique*	750	1,000	1,000
Italian 1700's, High Quality, Belt Pistol, Light Ornamentation, *Antique*	2,500	3,000	2,800

RIFLE, SNAPHAUNCE

	V.G.	Exc.	Prior Edition Exc. Value
Arabian, .59, Ornate, Inlaid with Silver, Ivory buttstock Inlays, *Antique*	450	600	600
Italian Mid-1600's, Half-Octagon Barrel, Carved, Engraved, Silver Inlay, Steel Furniture, Ornate, *Antique*	7,500	10,000	10,000

SODIA, FRANZ Ferlach, Austria
COMBINATION WEAPON, MULTI-BARREL

	V.G.	Exc.	Prior Edition Exc. Value
Bochdrilling, Various Calibers, Fancy Wood, Fancy Checkering, Fancy Engraving, *Antique*	5,500	6,500	3,750

	V.G.	Exc.	Prior Edition Exc. Value
Doppelbuchse, Various Calibers, Fancy Wood, Fancy Checkering, Fancy Engraving, *Antique*	*$3,750*	*$4,500*	*$2,800*
Over-Under Rifle, Various Calibers, Fancy Wood, Fancy Checkering, Fancy Engraving, *Antique*	*3,250*	*4,000*	*2,450*

SOLER Ripoll, Spain, c. 1625.
HANDGUN, WHEEL-LOCK

	V.G.	Exc.	Prior Edition Exc. Value
Enclosed Mid-1600's, Ball Pommel, Ornate, *Antique*	*10,000*	*12,500*	*12,500*

SOUTHERN ARMS CO. Made by Crescent for H. & D. Folsom, N.Y.C.
SHOTGUN, DOUBLE BARREL, SIDE-BY-SIDE

	V.G.	Exc.	Prior Edition Exc. Value
Various Gauges, Outside Hammers, Damascus Barrel, *Modern*	*150*	*175*	*170*
Various Gauges, Hammerless, Steel Barrel, *Modern*	*150*	*200*	*190*
Various Gauges, Hammerless, Damascus Barrel, *Modern*	*150*	*175*	*170*
Various Gauges, Outside Hammers, Steel Barrel, *Modern*	*175*	*200*	*185*

SHOTGUN, SINGLESHOT

	V.G.	Exc.	Prior Edition Exc. Value
Various Gauges, Hammer, Steel Barrel, *Modern*	*75*	*100*	*85*

SPAARMAN, ANDREAS Berlin, Germany, c. 1680.
RIFLE, FLINTLOCK

	V.G.	Exc.	Prior Edition Exc. Value
.72, Jaeger, Octagon Barrel, Swamped, Rifled, Iron Mounts, Ornate, Set Trigger, *Antique*	*3,500*	*4,000*	*4,000*

SPANISH MILITARY Also see Astra, Star.
HANDGUN, SEMI-AUTOMATIC

	V.G.	Exc.	Prior Edition Exc. Value
Jo-Lo-Ar, 9mm Bergmann, Clip Fed, Military, Hammer, *Curio*	*150*	*175*	*150*
M1913–16 Campo-Giro, 9mm Bergmann, Clip Fed, Military, *Curio*	*150*	*175*	*170*

RIFLE, BOLT ACTION

	V.G.	Exc.	Prior Edition Exc. Value
Destroyer, 9mm Bayard Long, Clip Fed, Carbine, *Modern*	*75*	*100*	*95*
M98 La Caruna, 8mm Mauser, Military, *Curio*	*50*	*75*	*75*

RIFLE, SEMI-AUTOMATIC

	V.G.	Exc.	Prior Edition Exc. Value
CETME Sport, .308 Win., Clip Fed, *Modern*	*325*	*400*	*380*

SPENCER ARMS CO. Windsor, Conn. 1886–1888.
SHOTGUN, SLIDE ACTION

	V.G.	Exc.	Prior Edition Exc. Value
Spencer, Roper, 12 Ga., Tube Feed, *Antique*	*350*	*400*	*395*

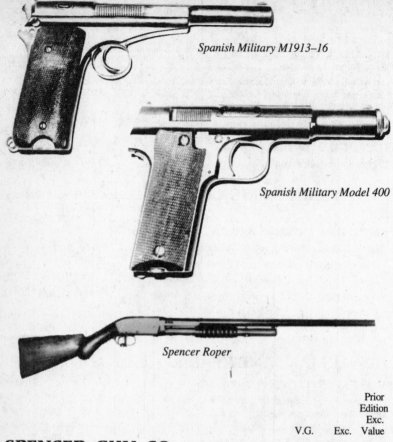

Spanish Military M1913–16

Spanish Military Model 400

Spencer Roper

	V.G.	Exc.	Prior Edition Exc. Value

SPENCER GUN CO. Made by Crescent for Hibbard & Spencer Bartlett, c. 1900.

SHOTGUN, DOUBLE BARREL, SIDE-BY-SIDE

	V.G.	Exc.	Prior Edition Exc. Value
Various Gauges, Outside Hammers, Damascus Barrel, *Modern*	$150	$175	$170
Various Gauges, Hammerless, Steel Barrel, *Modern*......................	175	200	190
Various Gauges, Hammerless, Damascus Barrel, *Modern*	150	175	170
Various Gauges, Outside Hammers, Steel Barrel, *Modern*..............	175	200	185

SHOTGUN, SINGLESHOT

	V.G.	Exc.	Prior Edition Exc. Value
Various Gauges, Hammer, Steel Barrel, *Modern*.............................	75	100	85

SPENCER SAFETY HAMMERLESS Made by Columbia Armory, Tenn., c. 1892.

HANDGUN, REVOLVER

	V.G.	Exc.	Prior Edition Exc. Value
.38 S & W, 5 Shot, Top Break, Hammerless, Double Action, *Antique*	100	125	100

	V.G.	Exc.	Prior Edition Exc. Value

SPORTSMAN Made by Steven Arms.
SHOTGUN, DOUBLE BARREL, SIDE-BY-SIDE
M 315, Various Gauges, Hammerless, Steel Barrel, *Antique*............ $150 | $175 | $170

SHOTGUN, SINGLESHOT
Model 90, Various Gauges, Takedown, Automatic Ejector, Plain, Hammer, *Antique* .... 50 | 75 | 55

SPORTSMAN Made by Crescent for W. Bingham Co. Cleveland, Ohio, c. 1900.
SHOTGUN, DOUBLE BARREL, SIDE-BY-SIDE
Various Gauges, Outside Hammers, Damascus Barrel, *Modern* .... 125 | 150 | 170
Various Gauges, Hammerless, Steel Barrel, *Modern*...................... 150 | 175 | 190
Various Gauges, Hammerless, Damascus Barrel, *Modern* .... 125 | 150 | 170
Various Gauges, Outside Hammers, Steel Barrel, *Modern*.............. 150 | 175 | 185

SHOTGUN, SINGLESHOT
Various Gauges, Hammer, Steel Barrel, *Modern*............................ 50 | 75 | 85

SPRINGFIELD ARMORY Geneseo, Ill.
RIFLE, SEMI-AUTOMATIC
M1A Super Match, .308 Win., Clip Fed, Version of M-14, Heavy Barrel, *Modern*................ 1,250 | 1,450 | 675
M1A Match, .308 Win., Clip Fed, Version of M-14, *Modern* .... 1,050 | 1,250 | 600
M1A Standard, .308 Win., Clip Fed, Version of M-14, *Modern*........ 850 | 1,000 | 545
M1A Standard, .308 Win., Clip Fed, Version of M-14, Folding Stock, *Modern*................. 950 | 1,100 | 585

SPRINGFIELD ARMS Made by Crescent, c. 1900.
SHOTGUN, DOUBLE BARREL, SIDE-BY-SIDE
Various Gauges, Outside Hammers, Damascus Barrel, *Modern* .... 150 | 175 | 170
Various Gauges, Hammerless, Steel Barrel, *Modern*...................... 175 | 200 | 190
Various Gauges, Hammerless, Damascus Barrel, *Modern* .... 150 | 175 | 170
Various Gauges, Outside Hammers, Steel Barrel, *Modern*.............. 175 | 200 | 185

SHOTGUN, SINGLESHOT
Various Gauges, Hammer, Steel Barrel, *Modern*............................ 75 | 100 | 85

SPY Made by Norwich Falls Pistol Co., c. 1880.
HANDGUN, REVOLVER
.22 Short R.F., 7 Shot, Spur Trigger, Solid Frame, Single Action, *Antique* .... 150 | 175 | 165

	V.G.	Exc.	Prior Edition Exc. Value

SQUARE DEAL Made by Crescent for Stratton-Warren Hdw. Co., Memphis, Tenn.

SHOTGUN, DOUBLE BARREL, SIDE-BY-SIDE

	V.G.	Exc.	Prior Edition Exc. Value
Various Gauges, Outside Hammers, Damascus Barrel, *Modern*	$150	$175	$170
Various Gauges, Hammerless, Steel Barrel, *Modern*	175	200	190
Various Gauges, Hammerless, Damascus Barrel, *Modern*	150	175	170
Various Gauges, Outside Hammers, Steel Barrel, *Modern*	175	200	185

SHOTGUN, SINGLESHOT

	V.G.	Exc.	Prior Edition Exc. Value
Various Gauges, Hammer, Steel Barrel, *Modern*	75	100	85

SQUIBMAN Made by Squires, Bingham, Makati, Phillipines.

HANDGUN, REVOLVER

	V.G.	Exc.	Prior Edition Exc. Value
Model 100 D, .38 Spec., Double Action, Blue, Swing-Out Cylinder, Vent Rib, *Modern*	100	125	140
Model 100 DC, .38 Spec., Double Action, Blue, Swing-Out Cylinder, *Modern*	100	125	125
Thunder Chief, .38 Spec., Double Action, Blue, Swing-Out Cylinder, Vent Rib, Heavy Barrel, *Modern*	125	150	160

RIFLE, SEMI-AUTOMATIC

	V.G.	Exc.	Prior Edition Exc. Value
Auto, .22 L.R.R.F., Clip Fed, Shell Deflector, Flash Hider, *Modern*	50	75	60

SQUIRES BINGHAM Makati, Phillipines.

HANDGUN, REVOLVER

	V.G.	Exc.	Prior Edition Exc. Value
M 100-D, .22LR/.22 WMR Combo, Double Action, Solid Frame, Swing-Out Cylinder, Adjustable Sights, *Modern*	50	75	80

RIFLE, BOLT ACTION

	V.G.	Exc.	Prior Edition Exc. Value
M 14D, .22 L.R.R.F., Clip Fed, Checkered Stock, *Modern*	25	50	55
M 15, .22 WMR, Clip Fed, Checkered Stock, *Modern*	50	75	75

RIFLE, SEMI-AUTOMATIC

	V.G.	Exc.	Prior Edition Exc. Value
M-16, .22 L.R.R.F., Clip Fed, Flash Hider, *Modern*	50	75	70
M20D, .22 L.R.R.F., Clip Fed, Checkered Stock, *Modern*	50	75	65

SHOTGUN, SLIDE ACTION

	V.G.	Exc.	Prior Edition Exc. Value
M 30/28, 12 Ga., Plain, *Modern*	75	100	120

STAGGS-BILT Staggs Enterprises, Phoenix, Ariz., c. 1970.

COMBINATION WEAPON, OVER-UNDER

	V.G.	Exc.	Prior Edition Exc. Value
20 Ga./.30–30, Top Break, Hammerless, Double Triggers, Top Break, *Modern*	100	125	115

	V.G.	Exc.	Prior Edition Exc. Value

STANDARD ARMS CO. Wilmington, Del., 1909–1911.

RIFLE, SEMI-AUTOMATIC

Model G, Various Calibers, Takedown, Tube Feed, Hammerless, *Curio* $400 $450 $350

RIFLE, SLIDE ACTION

Model M, Various Calibers, Takedown, Tube Feed, Hammerless, *Curio* 275 325 265

STANLEY Belgium, c. 1900.

SHOTGUN, DOUBLE BARREL, SIDE-BY-SIDE

Various Gauges, Outside Hammers, Damascus Barrel, *Modern* 150 175 170
Various Gauges, Hammerless, Steel Barrel, *Modern* 175 200 190
Various Gauges, Hammerless, Damascus Barrel, *Modern* 150 175 170
Various Gauges, Outside Hammers, Steel Barrel, *Modern* 175 200 185

SHOTGUN, SINGLESHOT

Various Gauges, Hammer, Steel Barrel, *Modern* 75 100 85

STANTON London, England, c. 1778.

HANDGUN, FLINTLOCK

.55 Officers, Belt Pistol, Screw Barrel, Box Lock, Brass, *Antique* 1,750 2,000 1,750

STAR Made by Bonifacio Echeverria, Eibar, Spain 1911 to date.

HANDGUN, SEMI-AUTOMATIC

Model A, .25 ACP, Clip Fed, *Modern* 200 250 195
Model A, .38 ACP, Clip Fed, *Modern* 200 250 140
Model A, .45 ACP, Clip Fed, Early Model, Adjustable Sights, Various Barrel Lengths, *Modern* 225 275 195
Model A, Carbine 7.63 Mauser, Clip Fed, Early Model, Adjustable Sights, Various Barrel Lengths, Stock Lug, *Modern* 1,250 1,500 1,350
Model A, 9mm Bergmann, Clip Fed, Early Model, Adjustable Sights, Various Barrel Lengths, *Modern* 175 225 160
Model A, Various Calibers, Holster Stock, *Add* **$150.00–$250.00**
Model AS, .38 Super, Clip Fed, *Modern* 200 250 160
Model B, 9mm Luger, Clip Fed, *Modern* 200 250 160
Model B, 9mm Luger, Clip Fed, Early Model, Various Barrel Lengths, *Modern* 225 275 160
Model BKM, 9mm Luger, Clip Fed, Lightweight, *Modern* 225 275 200
Model BKS-Starlight, 9mm Luger, Clip Fed, Lightweight, *Modern* 250 300 225
Model BM, 9mm Luger, Clip Fed, Steel Frame, *Modern* 225 275 200

Star Model A   *Star Model 1 .32*

	V.G.	Exc.	Prior Edition Exc. Value
Model C, 9mm Bayard Long, Clip Fed, 8 Shot, *Modern*..................	*$175*	*$225*	*$160*
Model C O, .25 ACP, Clip Fed, *Modern*	*150*	*200*	*150*
Model C U, .25 ACP, Clip Fed, Lightweight, *Modern*....................	*125*	*175*	*125*
Model D, .380 ACP, Clip Fed, 6 Shot, *Modern*.............................	*150*	*200*	*150*
Model D, .380 ACP, Clip Fed, 15 Shot Clip, *Modern*	*175*	*225*	*170*
Model DK, .380 ACP, Clip Fed, Lightweight, *Modern*...................	*150*	*200*	*145*
Model E Vest Pocket, .25 ACP, Clip Fed, *Modern*......................	*150*	*200*	*145*
Model F, .22 L.R.R.F., Clip Fed, *Modern*.....................................	*125*	*175*	*135*
Model F R S, .22 L.R.R.F., Clip Fed, Target Pistol, Adjustable Sights, *Modern*..	*175*	*225*	*130*
Model F T B, .22 L.R.R.F., Clip Fed, Target Pistol, *Modern*...........	*150*	*200*	*115*
Model F-Olympic, .22 Short R.F., Clip Fed, Target Pistol, *Modern*..	*200*	*250*	*175*
Model F-Sport, .22 L.R.R.F., Clip Fed, 6" Barrel, *Modern*	*150*	*200*	*120*
Model FR, .22 L.R.R.F., Clip Fed, *Modern*....................................	*125*	*175*	*135*
Model H, .32 ACP, Clip Fed, 7 Shot, *Modern*...............................	*125*	*175*	*135*
Model HF, .22 L.R.R.F., Clip Fed, *Modern*....................................	*150*	*200*	*180*
Model HN, .380 ACP, Clip Fed, *Modern*	*150*	*175*	*145*
Model I, .32 ACP, Clip Fed, 9 Shot, *Modern*	*125*	*150*	*135*
Model Lancer, .22 L.R.R.F., Clip Fed, Lightweight, *Modern*	*125*	*150*	*145*
Model M, .38 ACP, Clip Fed, *Modern*..	*125*	*175*	*135*
Model MMS, 7.63 Mauser, Clip Fed, Stock Lug, *Modern*...............	*750*	*1,000*	*1,000*
Model NZ, .25 ACP, Clip Fed, *Modern*	*375*	*450*	*435*
Model 1, .25 ACP, Clip Fed, *Modern*	*225*	*275*	*250*
Model 1, .32 ACP, Clip Fed, *Mo, .380 ACP, Clip Fed, Modern*	*225*	*275*	*250*
Model P, .45 ACP, Clip Fed, *Modern*..	*250*	*300*	*160*
Model PD, .45 ACP, Clip Fed, *Modern*..	*250*	*300*	*240*

	V.G.	Exc.	Prior Edition Exc. Value
Model S, .380 ACP, Clip Fed, *Modern*	$200	$250	$135
Model S I, *Modern*	200	250	145
Model Military, 9mm, Clip Fed, *Modern*	225	275	175
Model NZ, .25 ACP, Clip Fed, *Modern*	400	450	425
Model 28, .9mm Luger, Clip Fed, *Modern*	300	350	365
Model SM, .380 ACP, Clip Fed, *Modern*	200	250	130
Model Starfire, .380 ACP, Clip Fed, Lightweight, *Modern*	325	375	135
Model Starlet, .25 ACP, Clip Fed, Lightweight, *Modern*	225	275	120
Model Super A, .38 ACP, Clip Fed, *Modern*	250	300	165
Model Super B, 9mm Luger, Clip Fed, *Modern*	250	300	160
Model Super P, .45 ACP, Clip Fed, *Modern*	275	325	185

RIFLE, SINGLESHOT

	V.G.	Exc.	Prior
Rolling Block, Various Calibers, Carbine, *Modern*	125	175	155

STAR GAUGE Spain, Imported by Interarms.

SHOTGUN, DOUBLE BARREL, SIDE-BY-SIDE

	V.G.	Exc.	Prior
12 and 20 Gauges, Checkered Stock, Adjustable Choke, Double Trigger, *Modern*	175	225	220

STARR ARMS CO. Yonkers and Binghamton, N.Y. 1860–1868.

HANDGUN, PERCUSSION

	V.G.	Exc.	Prior
1858 Navy, .36, Revolver, 6 Shot, 6" Barrel, Double Action, *Antique*	650	750	675
1858 Army, .44, Revolver, 6 Shot, 6" Barrel, Double Action, *Antique*	550	650	500
1863 Army, .44, Revolver, 6 Shot, 6" Barrel, Double Action, *Antique*	550	650	600

RIFLE, PERCUSSION

	V.G.	Exc.	Prior
Carbine, :54, Underlever, *Antique*	700	850	695

RIFLE, SINGLESHOT

	V.G.	Exc.	Prior
Carbine, .52 R.F., Underlever, *Antique*	800	950	825

STATE ARMS CO. Made by Crescent for J.H. Lau & Co., c. 1900.

SHOTGUN, DOUBLE BARREL, SIDE-BY-SIDE

	V.G.	Exc.	Prior
Various Gauges, Outside Hammers, Damascus Barrel, *Modern*	150	175	170
Various Gauges, Hammerless, Steel Barrel, *Modern*	150	200	190
Various Gauges, Hammerless, Damascus Barrel, *Modern*	125	175	170
Various Gauges, Outside Hammers, Steel Barrel, *Modern*	150	200	185

SHOTGUN, SINGLESHOT

	V.G.	Exc.	Prior
Various Gauges, Hammer, Steel Barrel, *Modern*	75	100	85

	V.G.	Exc.	Prior Edition Exc. Value

STEIGLEDER, ERNST Suhl & Berlin, Germany 1921–1935.
RIFLE, DOUBLE BARREL, SIDE-BY-SIDE
Various Calibers, Box Lock, Engraved, Checkered Stock, Color Case Hardened Frame, *Modern* $2,250 $2,750 $2,650

STENDA Stenda Werke Waffenfabrik, Suhl, Germany, c. 1920.
HANDGUN, SEMI-AUTOMATIC
.32 ACP, Blue, Clip Fed, *Modern* 175 225 210

STERLING ARMS CORP. Gasport and Lockport, N.Y.
HANDGUN, SEMI-AUTOMATIC

	V.G.	Exc.	Prior Edition
#283 Target 300, .22 L.R.R.F., Hammer, Adjustable Sights, Various Barrel Lengths, *Modern* .:...	125	150	130
#284 Target 300 L, .22 L.r.R.F., Hammer, Adjustable Sights, Tapered Barrel, *Modern*..	125	150	130
#285 Huskey, .22 L.R.R.F., Hammer, Heavy Barrel, *Modern*..........	100	125	120
#286 Trapper, .22 L.R.R.F., Hammer, Tapered Barrel, *Modern*	100	125	120
Model 300B, .25 ACP, Blue, *Modern*...	75	100	80
Model 300N, .25 ACP, Nickel Plated, *Modern*..................................	75	100	85
Model 300S, .25 ACP, Stainless Steel, *Modern*................................	75	100	95
Model 302B, .22 L.R.R.F., Blue, *Modern*..	75	100	80
Model 302N, .22 L.R.R.F., Nickel Plated, *Modern*	75	100	85
Model 302S, .22 L.R.R.F., Stainless Steel, *Modern*........................	75	100	95
Model 400B, .380 ACP, Blue, Clip Fed, *Modern*	125	150	145
Model 400N, .380 ACP, Nickel Plated, Clip Fed, *Modern*...............	125	150	150
Model 400S, .380 ACP, Stainless Steel, Clip Fed, *Modern*.............	150	175	175
Model 402, .22 L.R.R.F., Blue, Clip Fed, *Modern*............................	100	125	110
Model 402, .22 L.R.R.F., Nickel Plated, Clip Fed, *Modern*	100	125	110
Model 402 MkII, .32 ACP, Blue, Clip Fed, *Modern*.........................	125	150	145
Model 402 MkIIS, .32 ACP, Stainless Steel, Clip Fed, *Modern*......	150	175	175
Model 450, .45 ACP, Clip Fed, Double Action, Adjustable Sights, Blue, *Modern*	225	275	265
Model PPL, .380 ACP, Short Barrel, Clip Fed, *Modern*	125	150	150

Sterling PPL

	V.G.	Exc.	Prior Edition Exc. Value

RIFLE, SINGLESHOT
Backpacker, .22 L.R.R.F., Takedown, *Modern*................................ $25 $50 $35

STERLING ARMS CORP. Made by Crescent for H. & D. Folsom, C. 1900.

SHOTGUN, DOUBLE BARREL, SIDE-BY-SIDE

	V.G.	Exc.	Prior
Various Gauges, Outside Hammers, Damascus Barrel, *Modern*.........	150	175	170
Various Gauges, Hammerless, Steel Barrel, *Modern*.......................	175	200	190
Various Gauges, Hammerless, Damascus Barrel, *Modern*	150	175	170
Various Gauges, Outside Hammers, Steel Barrel, *Modern*...............	175	200	185

SHOTGUN, SINGLESHOT

Various Gauges, Hammer, Steel Barrel, *Modern*............................	75	100	85

STERLING REVOLVERS Maker unknown, c. 1880.

HANDGUN, REVOLVER

.22 Short R.F., 7 Shot, Spur Trigger, Solid Frame, Single Action, *Antique*..	150	175	165
.32 Short R.F., 5 Shot, Spur Trigger, Solid Frame, Single Action, *Antique*..	150	175	170

STEVENS, J. ARMS & TOOL CO. Chicopee Falls, Mass. 1864–1886. Became J. Stevens Arms & Tools Co. in 1886, absorbed Page-Lewis Arms Co., Davis-Warner Arms Co., and Crescent Firearms Co. in 1926. Became a subsidiary of Savage in 1936.

COMBINATION WEAPON, OVER-UNDER

Model 22-410, .22–.410 Ga., Hammer, Plastic Stock, *Modern*........	75	100	85
Model 22-410, .22–.410 Ga., Hammer, Wood Stock, *Modern*.........	100	125	95

HANDGUN, SINGLESHOT

1888 #1, Various Calibers, Tip-Up, Octagon Barrel, Open Rear Sight, *Antique*..	150	175	155
1888 #2 "Gallery", .22 L.R.R.F., Tip-Up, Octagon Barrel, Open Rear Sight, *Antique*	150	175	150
1888 #3 "Combined Sight", Various Calibers, Tip-Up, Octagon Barrel, *Antique*	150	175	165
1888 #4 "Combined Sight", .22 L.R.R.F., Tip-Up, Octagon Barrel, *Antique*	150	175	155
1888 #5 "Expert", Various Calibers, Tip-Up, Half Octagon Barrel, *Antique*	150	175	165
1894 "New Ideal", Various Calibers, Level Action, Falling Block, Vernier Sights, *Antique*...	275	325	315
Model 23 "Sure-Shot", .22 L.R.R.F., Side-Swing Barrel, Hammer, *Antique*	100	125	120

	V.G.	Exc.	Prior Edition Exc. Value
Model 34 "Hunters Pet", Various Rimfires, Tip-Up, Octagon Barrel, with Shoulder Stock, *Curio*	$400	$450	$440
Model 39 New Model Pocket Shotgun, Various Calibers, Tip-Up, Smoothbore, with Shoulder Stock, *Class 3*	125	175	160
Model 40 New Model Pocket Rifle, Various Calibers, Tip-Up, with Shoulder Stock, *Curio*	400	450	405
Model 42 Reliable Pocket Rifle, .22 L.R.R.F., Tip-Up, with Shoulder Stock, *Curio*	250	300	275
Model "Offhand", .410 Ga., Tip-Up, *Class 3*	250	300	275
Model 10, .22 L.R.R.F., Tip-Up, Target, Various Barrel Lengths, *Modern*	150	175	150
Model 34 "Hunters Pet", Various Rimfires, Tip-Up, Half-Octagon Barrel, with Shoulder Stock, Vernier Sights, *Curio*	450	500	450
Model 35 "Offhand", .22 L.R.R.F., Tip-Up, Target, Various Barrel Lengths, *Modern*	300	350	310
Model 35 "Offhand", .22 L.R.R.F., Tip-Up, Target, Ivory Grips, Various Barrel Lengths, *Modern*	350	400	365
Model 35 Autoshot, .410 Ga., Tip-Up, Various Barrel Lengths, *Class 3*	250	300	260
Model 37 "Gould", Various Calibers, Tip-Up, *Modern*	250	300	285
Model 38 "Conlin", .22 L.R.R.F., Tip-Up, *Modern*	325	375	350
Model 41, .22 L.R.R.F., Tip-Up, Pocket Pistol, *Modern*	150	175	155
Model 43 "Diamond", .22 L.R.R.F., Tip-Up, Spur Trigger, 6" Barrel, Octagon Barrel, *Modern*	175	200	180
Model 43 "Diamond", .22 L.R.R.F., Tip-Up, Spur Trigger, 10" Barrel, Octagon Barrel, *Modern*	200	225	190
Model 43 "Diamond", .22 L.R.R.F., Tip-Up, Spur Trigger, 6" Barrel, Globe Sights, *Modern*	200	225	200
Model 43 "Diamond", .22 L.R.R.F., Tip-Up, Spur Trigger, 10" Barrel, Globe Sights, *Modern*	225	275	245

RIFLE, BOLT ACTION

	V.G.	Exc.	Prior Edition Exc. Value
Model 053 Buckhorn, Various Rimfires, Singleshot, Peep Sights, *Modern*	50	75	55
Model 056 Buckhorn, .22 L.R.R.F., 5 Shot Clip, Peep Sights, *Modern*	75	100	80
Model 066 Buckhorn, .22 L.R.R.F., Tube Feed, Peep Sights, *Modern*	75	100	80
Model 083, .22 L.R.R.F., Singleshot, Peep Sights, Takedown, *Modern*	50	75	60
Model 084, .22 L.R.R.F., 5 Shot Clip, Peep Sights, Takedown, *Modern*	50	75	65
Model 086, .22 L.R.R.F., Tube Feed, Takedown, Peep Sights, *Modern*	75	100	75
Model 15, .22 L.R.R.F., Singleshot, (Springfield), *Modern*	50	75	48
Model 15Y, .22 L.R.R.F., Singleshot, *Modern*	50	75	48
Model 322, .22 Hornet, Clip Fed, Carbine, Open Rear Sight, *Modern*	125	150	130

	V.G.	Exc.	Prior Edition Exc. Value
Model 322-S, .22 Hornet, Clip Fed, Carbine, Peep Sights, *Modern*	$125	$150	$135
Model 325, .30–30 Win., Clip Fed, Carbine, Open Rear Sight, *Modern*	125	150	130
Model 325-S, .30–30 Win., Clip Fed, Carbine, Peep Sights, *Modern*	125	150	135
Model 416, .22 L.R.R.F., 5 Shot Clip, Peep Sights, Target Stock, *Modern*	200	225	195
Model 419, .22 L.R.R.F., Singleshot, Peep Sights, *Modern*	75	100	85
Model 48, .22 L.R.R.F., Singleshot, Takedown, *Modern*	50	75	48
Model 49, .22 L.R.R.F., Singleshot, Takedown, *Modern*	50	75	48
Model 50, .22 L.R.R.F., Singleshot, Takedown, *Modern*	50	75	48
Model 51, .22 L.R.R.F., Singleshot, Takedown, *Modern*	50	75	48
Model 52, .22 L.R.R.F., Singleshot, Takedown, *Modern*	50	75	55
Model 53, .22 L.R.R.F., Singleshot, Takedown, *Modern*	50	75	55
Model 56 Buckhorn, .22 L.R.R.F., 5 Shot Clip, Open Rear Sight, *Modern*	50	75	65
Model 65 "Little Krag", .22 L.R.R.F., Singleshot, Takedown, *Modern*	150	175	165
Model 66 Buckhorn, .22 L.R.R.F., Tube Feed, Open Rear Sight, *Modern*	50	75	60
Model 82, .22 L.R.R.F., Singleshot, Peep Sights, (Springfield), *Modern*	50	75	48
Model 83, .22 L.R.R.F., Singleshot, Open Rear Sight, Takedown, *Modern*	25	50	42
Model 84, .22 L.R.R.F., 5 Shot Clip, Open Rear Sight, Takedown, *Modern*	50	75	60
Model 86, .22 L.R.R.F., Tube Feed, Takedown, Open Rear Sight, *Modern*	50	75	70

RIFLE, LEVER ACTION

	V.G.	Exc.	Prior Edition Exc. Value
Model 425, Various Calibers, Hammer, *Curio*	225	250	230
Model 430, Various Calibers, Hammer, Checkered Stock, *Curio*	250	300	280
Model 435, Various Calibers, Hammer, Light Engraving, Fancy Checkering, *Curio*	375	425	395
Model 440, Various Calibers, Hammer, Fancy Checkering, Fancy Engraving, Fancy Wood, *Curio*	800	950	885

RIFLE, SEMI-AUTOMATIC

	V.G.	Exc.	Prior Edition Exc. Value
Model 057 Buckhorn, .22 L.R.R.F., 5 Shot Clip, Peep Sights, *Modern*	75	100	85
Model 076 Buckhorn, .22 L.R.R.F., Peep Sights, Tube Feed, *Modern*	75	100	85
Model 085 Springfield, .22 L.R.R.F., 5 Shot Clip, Peep Sights, *Modern*	75	100	85
Model 57 Buckhorn, .22 L.R.R.F., 5 Shot Clip, Open Rear Sight, *Modern*	75	100	80

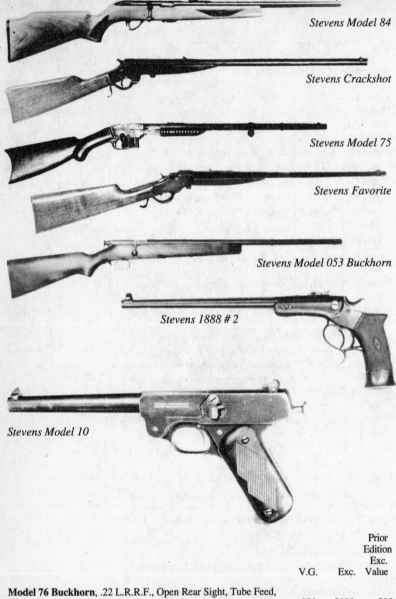

Stevens Model 84

Stevens Crackshot

Stevens Model 75

Stevens Favorite

Stevens Model 053 Buckhorn

Stevens 1888 # 2

Stevens Model 10

	V.G.	Exc.	Prior Edition Exc. Value
Model 76 Buckhorn, .22 L.R.R.F., Open Rear Sight, Tube Feed, *Modern*	$75	$100	$85
Model 85 Springfield, .22 L.R.R.F., 5 Shot Clip, Open Rear Sight, *Modern*	75	100	85
Model 87, .22 L.R.R.F., Tube Feed, Open Rear Sight, *Modern*	75	100	85
Model 87-S, .22 L.R.R.F., Peep Sights, Rube Feed, *Modern*	75	100	85

	V.G.	Exc.	Prior Edition Exc. Value
Model 87K Scout, .22 L.R.R.F., Tube Feed, Open Rear Sight, Carbine, *Modern*	$75	$100	$85

RIFLE, SINGLESHOT

	V.G.	Exc.	Prior Edition Exc. Value
1888 #10 "Range", Various Calibers, Tip-Up, Half-Octagon Barrel, Fancy Wood, Vernier Sights, *Antique*	250	275	245
1888 #22 "Ladies", Various Calibers, Tip-Up, Half-Octagon Barrel, Open Rear Sight, *Antique*	200	225	180
1888 #12 "Ladies", Various Calibers, Tip-Up, Half-Octagon Barrel, Open Rear Sight, Fancy Wood, *Antique*	375	325	275
1888 #13 "Ladies", Various Calibers, Tip-Up, Half-Octagon Barrel, Vernier Sights, *Antique*	225	275	245
1888 #14 "Ladies", Various Calibers, Tip-Up, Half-Octagon Barrel, Vernier Sights, Fancy Wood, *Antique*	275	325	300
1888 #15 "Crack Shot", Various Calibers, Tip-Up, Half-Octagon Barrel, Peep Sights, *Antique*	225	250	230
1888 #16 "Crack Shot", Various Calibers, Tip-Up, Half-Octagon Barrel, Peep Sights, Fancy Wood, *Antique*	250	275	245
1888 #6 "Expert", Various Calibers, Tip-Up, Half-Octagon Barrel, Fancy Wood, *Antique*	200	225	205
1888 #7 "Premier", Various Calibers, Tip-Up, Half-Octagon Barrel, Globe Sights, *Antique*	175	225	185
1888 #8 "Premier", Various Calibers, Tip-Up, Half-Octagon Barrel, Fancy Wood, Globe Sights, *Antique*	225	275	230
1888 #9 "Range", Various Calibers, Tip-Up, Half-Octagon Barrel, Vernier Sights, *Antique*	175	225	195
Model 101 Featherweight, .44–40 WCF, Lever Action, Tip-Up, Smoothbore, Takedown, Half-Octagon Barrel, *Modern*	150	175	160
Model 101, with Extra 22 Barrel, .44–40 WCF, Lever Action, Tip-Up, Smoothbore, Takedown, Half-Octagon Barrel, *Modern*	225	250	230
Model 11 "Ladies", Various Rimfires, Tip-Up, Open Rear Sight, *Modern*	175	200	180
Model 12 "Marksman", Various Rimfires, Hammer, Lever Action, Tip-Up, *Modern*	150	175	145
Model 13 "Ladies", Various Rimfires, Tip-Up Vernier Sights, *Modern*	175	200	185
Model 14 "Little Scout", .22 L.R.R.F., Hammer, Rolling Block, *Curio*	175	200	165
Model 14¹/² "Little Scout", .22 L.R.R.F., Hammer, Rolling Block, *Modern*	150	175	130
Model 15 "Maynard Jr.", .22 L.R.R.F., Lever Action, Tip-Up, *Modern*	125	150	130
Model 15¹/² "Maynard Jr.", .22 L.R.R.F., Lever Action, Tip-Up, *Modern*	125	150	135
Model 17, Various Rimfires, Lever Action, Takedown, Favorite, Open Rear Sight, *Modern*	150	175	150
Model 18, Various Rimfires, Lever Action, Takedown, Favorite, Vernier Sights, *Modern*	175	200	165

557 ANTIQUE AND MODERN FIREARMS

	V.G.	Exc.	Prior Edition Exc. Value
Model 19, Various Rimfires, Lever Action, Takedown, Favorite, Lyman Sights, *Modern*	$150	$175	$160
Model 2, Various Rimfires, Tip-Up, Open Rear Sight, *Modern*	250	275	240
Model 20, Various Rimfires, Lever Action, Takedown, Favorite, Smoothbore, *Curio*	150	175	130
Model 26, Crack-Shot, Various Rimfires, Lever Action, Takedown, Open Rear Sight, *Curio*	150	175	140
Model 26¹/₂, Various Rimfires, Lever Action, Takedown, Smoothbore, *Modern*	150	175	140
Model 27, Various Rimfires, Lever Action, Takedown, Favorite, Octagon Barrel, Open Rear Sight, *Modern*	175	200	160
Model 28, Various Rimfires, Lever Action, Takedown, Favorite, Octagon Barrel, Vernier Sights, *Modern*	175	200	170
Model 29, Various Rimfires, Lever Action, Takedown, Favorite, Octagon Barrel, Lyman Sights, *Modern*	175	200	170
Model 404, .22 L.R.R.F., Hammer, Falling Block, Target Sights, Full-Stocked, *Modern*	475	525	480
Model 414 "Armory", .22 L.R.R.F., Lever Action, Lyman Sights, *Modern*	325	350	330
Model 417¹/₂, Various Calibers, Lever Action, Walnut Hill, *Modern*	400	450	430
Model 417-0, Various Calibers, Lever Action, Walnut Hill, *Modern*	400	450	430
Model 417-1, Various Calibers, Lever Action, Lyman Sights, Walnut Hill, *Modern*	400	450	430
Model 417-2, Various Calibers, Lever Action, Vernier Sights, Walnut Hill, *Modern*	450	500	460
Model 417-3, Various Calibers, Lever Action, no Sights, Walnut Hill, *Modern*	425	475	430
Model 418, .22 L.R.R.F., Lever Action, Takedown, Walnut Hill, *Modern*	300	325	285
Model 418¹/₂, Various Rimfires, Lever Action, Takedown, Walnut Hill, *Modern*	275	300	275
Model 44 "Ideal", Various Calibers, Lever Action, Rolling Block, *Modern*	325	350	330
Model 44¹/₂ "Ideal", Various Calibers, Lever Action, Falling Block, *Modern*	375	425	405
Model 49 "Ideal", Various Calibers, Walnut Hill, Lever Action, Falling Block, Engraved, Fancy Checkering, *Modern*	825	900	865
Model 5, Various Rimfires, Tip-Up, Vernier Sights, *Modern*	225	250	230
Model 51 "Pope", Various Calibers, Schutzen Rifle, Lever Action, Falling Block, Engraved, Fancy Checkering, *Modern*	775	825	810
Model 52 "Pope, Jr.", Various Calibers, Schutzen Rifle, Lever Action, Falling Block, Engraved, Fancy Checkering, *Modern*	750	825	785
Model 54 "Pope", Various Calibers, Schutzen Rifle, Lever Action, Falling Block, Fancy Engraving, Fancy Checkering, *Modern*	850	950	915
Model 56 "Pope Ladies", Various Calibers, Schutzen Rifle, Lever Action, Falling Block, Fancy Checkering, *Modern*	425	450	430

	V.G.	Exc.	Prior Edition Exc. Value
Model 7 "Swiss Butt", Various Rimfires, Tip-Up, Vernier Sights, *Modern*	$250	$275	$250

RIFLE, SLIDE ACTION

	V.G.	Exc.	Prior Edition Exc. Value
Model 70, .22 L.R.R.F., Hammer, Solid Frame, *Modern*	175	200	175
Model 71, .22 L.R.R.F., Hammer, Solid Frame, *Modern*	200	225	190
Model 75, .22 L.R.R.F., Tube Feed, Hammerless, *Modern*	200	225	205
Model 80, Various Rimfires, Tube Feed, Takedown, *Modern*	150	175	160

SHOTGUN, BOLT ACTION

	V.G.	Exc.	Prior Edition Exc. Value
Model 237, 20 Ga., Takedown, Singleshot, (Springfield), *Modern*	25	50	48
Model 258, 20 Ga., Takedown, Clip Fed, *Modern*	50	75	70
Model 37, .410 Ga., Takedown, Singleshot, (Springfield), *Modern*	50	75	55
Model 38, .410 Ga., Takedown, Clip Fed, (Springfield), *Modern*	50	75	60
Model 39, .410 Ga., Takedown, Tube Feed, (Springfield), *Modern*	50	75	60
Model 58, .410 Ga., Takedown, Clip Fed, *Modern*	50	75	60
Model 59, .410 Ga., Takedown, Tube Feed, *Modern*	50	75	70

SHOTGUN, DOUBLE BARREL, OVER-UNDER

	V.G.	Exc.	Prior Edition Exc. Value
Model 240, .410 Ga., Hammer, Plastic Stock, *Modern*	175	200	175
Model 240, .410 Ga., Hammer, Wood Stock, *Modern*	200	225	180

SHOTGUN, DOUBLE BARREL, SIDE-BY-SIDE

	V.G.	Exc.	Prior Edition Exc. Value
M 315, Various Gauges, Hammerless, Steel Barrel, *Modern*	175	200	185
Model 215, 12 and 16 Gauges, Outside Hammers, Steel Barrel, *Modern*	175	200	175
Model 235, Various Gauges, Outside Hammers, Checkered Stock, Steel Barrel, *Modern*	150	175	170
Model 250, Various Gauges, Outside Hammers, Checkered Stock, Steel Barrel, *Modern*	150	175	170
Model 255, 12 and 16 Gauges, Outside Hammers, Checkered Stock, Steel Barrel, *Modern*	150	175	170
Model 260 "Twist", Various Gauges, Outside Hammers, Checkered Stock, Damascus Barrel, *Modern*	150	175	155
Model 265 "Krupp", 12 and 16 Gauges, Outside Hammers, Checkered Stock, Steel Barrel, *Modern*	175	200	170
Model 270 "Nitro", Various Gauges, Outside Hammers, Checkered Stock, Damascus Barrel, *Modern*	175	200	175
Model 311, Various Gauges, Hammerless, Steel Barrel, *Modern*	200	225	200
Model 311-R Guard Gun, 12 or 20 Gauge, Double Trigger, 18½" Cylinder Bore, Solid Rib, *Modern*	250	300	280
Model 311 ST, Various Gauges, Hammerless, Steel Barrel, Single Trigger, *Modern*	200	225	205
Model 3151, Various Gauges, Hammerless, Recoil Pad, Front and Rear Bead Sights, *Modern*	200	225	190

	V.G.	Exc.	Prior Edition Exc. Value
Model 330, Various Gauges, Hammerless, Checkered Stock, *Modern*	$175	$200	$170
Model 335, 12 and 16 Gauges, Hammerless, Steel Barrel, Checkered Stock, Double Trigger, *Modern*	175	200	175
Model 345, 20 Ga., Hammerless, Checkered Stock, Steel Barrel, Double Trigger, *Modern*	175	200	175
Model 355, 12 and 16 Gauges, Hammerless, Steel Barrel, Checkered Stock, Double Trigger, *Modern*	175	200	170
Model 365 "Krupp", 12 and 16 Gauges, Hammerless, Checkered Stock, Steel Barrel, Double Trigger, *Modern*	175	200	185
Model 375 "Krupp", 12 and 16 Gauges, Hammerless, Light Engraving, Fancy Checkering, Double Trigger, Steel Barrel, *Modern*	200	225	195
Model 385 "Krupp", 12 and 16 Gauges, Hammerless, Fancy Checkering, Fancy Engraving, Double Trigger, Steel Barrel, *Modern*	225	250	230
Model 515, Various Gauges, Hammerless, *Modern*	150	175	150
Model 5151, Various Gauges, Hammerless, Steel Barrel, *Modern*	175	200	170
Model 530, Various Gauges, Hammerless, Steel Barrel, Double Trigger, *Modern*	175	200	165
Model 530 ST, Various Gauges, Hammerless, Steel Barrel, Single Trigger, *Modern*	200	225	200
Model 530M, Various Gauges, Hammerless, Plastic Stock, *Modern*	150	175	140

SHOTGUN, PUMP

	V.G.	Exc.	
Model 520, 12 Ga., Takedown, *Modern*	150	175	150
Model 620, Various Gauges, Takedown, *Modern*	150	175	145

SHOTGUN, SEMI-AUTOMATIC

Model 124, 12 Ga., Plastic Stock, *Modern*	125	150	125

SHOTGUN, SINGLESHOT

Various Gauges, Hammer, Automatic Ejector, *Modern*	50	75	70
Various Gauges, Hammer, Automatic Ejector, Raised Matted Rib, *Modern*	75	100	80
1888 "New Style", Various Gauges, Tip-Up, Hammer, Damascus Barrel, *Antique*	250	275	240
Model 100, Various Gauges, Selective Ejector, Hammer, *Modern*	50	75	60
Model 102, .410 Ga., Hammer, Featherweight, *Modern*	50	75	47
Model 102, 24, 28 and 32 Gauges, Hammer, Featherweight, *Modern*	50	75	53
Model 104, .410 Ga., Hammer, Featherweight, Automatic Ejector, *Modern*	50	75	53
Model 104, 24, 28 and 32 Gauges, Hammer, Automatic Ejector, Featherweight, *Modern*	50	75	67
Model 105, 20 Ga., Hammer, *Modern*	50	75	50

	V.G.	Exc.	Prior Edition Exc. Value
Model 105, 28 Ga., Hammer, *Modern*	$50	$75	$55
Model 106, .410 Ga. 2½", Hammer, *Modern*	50	75	45
Model 106, .44-40 WCF, Hammer, Smoothbore, *Modern*	50	75	60
Model 106, .32 Ga., Hammer, *Modern*	50	75	50
Model 107, Various Gauges, Hammer, Automatic Ejector, *Modern*	50	75	60
Model 108, .410 Ga. 2½", Hammer, Automatic Ejector, *Modern*	50	75	50
Model 108, .44-40 WCF, Hammer, Automatic Ejector, Smoothbore, *Modern*	50	75	70
Model 108, 32 Ga., Hammer, Automatic Ejector, *Modern*	50	75	55
Model 110, Various Gauges, Selective Ejector, Checkered Stock, Hammer, *Modern*	50	75	55
Model 120, Various Gauges, Selective Ejector, Fancy Checkering, Hammer, *Modern*	50	75	60
Model 125 Ladies, 20 Ga., Automatic Ejector, Hammer, *Modern*	50	75	60
Model 125 Ladies, .28 Ga., Automatic Ejector, Hammer, *Modern*	50	75	70
Model 140, Various Gauges, Selective Ejector, Hammerless, Checkered Stock, *Modern*	50	75	70
Model 160, Various Gauges, Hammer, *Modern*	50	75	48
Model 165, Various Gauges, Automatic Ejector, Hammer, *Modern*	50	75	48
Model 170, Various Gauges, Automatic Ejector, Hammer, Checkered Stock, *Modern*	50	75	48
Model 180, Various Gauges, Hammerless, Automatic Ejector, Checkered Stock, Round Barrel, *Modern*	75	100	90
Model 182, 12 Ga., Hammerless, Automatic Ejector, Light Engraving, Checkered Stock, Trap Grade, *Modern*	125	150	125
Model 185, For Damascus Barrel, *Deduct 25%*			
Model 185, For 16 or 20 Gauge, *Add 20%*			
Model 185, 12 Ga., Hammerless, Automatic Ejector, Checkered Stock, Half-Octagon Barrel, *Modern*	125	150	140
Model 190, For Damascus Barrel, *Deduct 25%*			
Model 190, For 16 or 20 Gauge, *Add 20%*			
Model 190, 12 Ga., Hammerless, Automatic Ejector, Fancy Checkering, Light Engraving, Half-Octagon Barrel, *Modern*	175	200	170
Model 195, For Damascus Barrel, *Deduct 25%*			
Model 195, For 16 or 20 Gauge, *Add 20%*			
Model 195, 12 Ga., Hammerless, Automatic Ejector, Fancy Checkering, Fancy Engraving, Half-Octagon Barrel, *Modern*	300	325	285
Model 89 Dreadnaught, Various Gauges, Hammer, *Modern*	50	75	67
Model 90, Various Gauges, Takedown, Automatic Ejector Plain, Hammer, *Modern*	50	75	58
Model 93, 12 and 16 Gauges, Hammer, *Modern*	50	75	52

	V.G.	Exc.	Prior Edition Exc. Value
Model 94, Various Gauges, Takedown, Automatic Ejector Plain, Hammer, *Modern*	$50	$75	$52
Model 944, .410 Ga., Hammer, Automatic Ejector, (Springfield), *Modern*	50	75	52
Model 94A, Various Gauges, Hammer, Automatic Ejector, *Modern*	50	75	52
Model 94C, Various Gauges, Hammer, Automatic Ejector, *Modern*	50	75	52
Model 95, 12 and 16 Gauges, *Modern*	50	75	57
Model 958, .410 Ga., Automatic Ejector, Hammer, *Modern*	50	75	52
Model 958, 32 Ga., Automatic Ejector, Hammer, *Modern*	50	75	68
Model 97, 12 and 16 Gauges, Hammer, Automatic Ejector, *Modern*	25	50	47
Model 970, 12 Ga., Hammer, Automatic Ejector, Checkered Stock, Half-Octagon Barrel, *Modern*	50	75	58

SHOTGUN, SLIDE ACTION

	V.G.	Exc.	Prior Edition Exc. Value
Model 520, 12 Ga., Takedown, *Modern*	150	175	160
Model 522, 12 Ga., Trap Grade, Takedown, Raised Matted Rib, *Modern*	150	175	155
Model 621, Various Gauges, Hammerless, Checkered Stock, Raised Matted Rib, Takedown, *Modern*	150	175	160
Model 620, Various Gauges, Takedown, *Modern*	150	175	150
Model 67, Various Gauges, Hammerless, Solid Frame, (Springfield), *Modern*	125	150	125
Model 67-VR, Various Gauges, Hammerless, Solid Frame, Vent Rib (Springfield), *Modern*	125	150	140
Model 77, For Vent Rib, *Add* **$10.00–$15.00**			
Model 77, 12 and 16 Gauges, Hammerless, Solid Frame, *Modern*	150	175	160
Model 77, Various Gauges, Hammerless, Solid Frame, *Modern*	125	150	140
Model 77 S C, 12 and 16 Gauges, Hammerless, Solid Frame, Recoil Pad, Adjustable Choke, *Modern*	150	175	170
Model 77-AC, Various Gauges, Hammerless, Solid Frame, Adjustable Choke, *Modern*	125	150	135
Model 77-M, 12 Ga., Hammerless, Solid Frame, Adjustable Choke, *Modern*	125	150	140
Model 820, 12 Ga., Hammerless, Solid Frame, *Modern*	125	150	130

STEVENS, JAMES
SHOTGUN, PERCUSSION

	V.G.	Exc.	Prior Edition Exc. Value
14 Ga., Double Barrel, Side by Side, Engraved, Light Ornamentation, *Antique*	450	550	550

STEYR Since 1963 in Steyr, Austria as Werndl Co.; in 1869 became Oesterreichische Waffenfabrik Gesellschaft; after WW I became Steyr Werke; in 1934 became

	V.G.	Exc.	Prior Edition Exc. Value

Steyr-Daimler-Puch. Also see German Military, Austrian Military, Mannlicher-Schoenauer.

HANDGUN, SEMI-AUTOMATIC

	V.G.	Exc.	Prior Edition Exc. Value
Model 1901 Mannlicher, 7.63mm Mannlicher, Commercial, *Curio*	$700	$750	$675
Model 1905 Mannlicher, 7.63mm Mannlicher, Military, *Curio*	375	425	390
Model 1908, .32 ACP, Clip Fed, Tip-Up, *Modern*	225	250	175
Model 1909, .25 ACP, Clip Fed, Tip-Up, *Modern*	225	275	155
Model 1909, .32 ACP, Clip Fed, Tip-Up, *Modern*	250	300	165
Model 1911, 9mm Steyr, Commercial, *Curio*	350	400	435
Model 1912, 9mm Luger, Nazi-Proofed, Military, *Curio*	400	450	320
Model 1912, 9mm Steyr, Military, *Curio*	200	225	210
Model 1912 Roumanian, 9mm Steyr, Military, *Curio*	250	275	270
Model GB, 9mm Luger, Clip Fed, Double Action, *Modern*	400	450	365
Model SP, .32 ACP, Clip Fed, Double Action, *Modern*	300	350	300
Solothurn, .32 ACP, Clip Fed, *Modern*	200	225	190

Steyr Model 1909

Franz Stock .25

Franz Stock .22

	V.G.	Exc.	Prior Edition Exc. Value

STOCK, FRANZ Franz Stock Maschinen u. Werkbaufabrik, Berlin, Germany 1920–1940.

HANDGUN, SEMI-AUTOMATIC

	V.G.	Exc.	Prior Edition Exc. Value
.22 L.R.R.F., Clip Fed, *Modern*	$300	$325	$235
.25 ACP, Clip Fed, *Modern*	275	300	220
.32 ACP, Clip Fed, *Modern*	275	300	230

STOCKMAN, HANS Dresden, Germany 1590–1621.

HANDGUN, WHEEL-LOCK

	V.G.	Exc.	Prior Edition Exc. Value
Pair, Holster Pistol, Pear Pommel, Horn Inlays, Light Ornamentation, *Antique*	12,500	15,000	15,000

STOEGER, A.F. Stoeger Arms Corp., N.Y.C., now in South Hackensack, N.J. Also see Luger.

COMBINATION WEAPON, OVER-UNDER

	V.G.	Exc.	Prior Edition Exc. Value
Model 290, Various Calibers, Blitz System, Box Lock, Double Triggers, Engraved, Checkered Stock, *Modern*	1,250	1,500	1,200

COMBINATION WEAPON, DRILLING

	V.G.	Exc.	Prior Edition Exc. Value
Model 259, 3 Calibers, Side Barrel, Box Lock, Double Triggers, Checkered Stock, *Modern*	1,500	1,750	1,500
Model 297, Various Calibers, 2 Rifle Barrels, Box Lock, Double Triggers, Engraved, Checkered Stock, *Modern*	1,500	1,750	1,600
Model 300, Vierling, 4 Barrels, Box Lock, Double Triggers, Checkered Stock, *Modern*	1,500	2,000	2,000

SHOTGUN, DOUBLE BARREL, SIDE-BY-SIDE

	V.G.	Exc.	Prior Edition Exc. Value
Victor Special, 12 Ga., Checkered Stock, Double Triggers, *Modern*	175	200	180

SHOTGUN, SINGLESHOT

	V.G.	Exc.	Prior Edition Exc. Value
Model 27 Trap, 12 Ga., Engraved, Vent Rib, Checkered Stock, Recoil Pad, *Modern*	700	750	725

STOSEL Retolaza Hermanos, Eibar, Spain.

HANDGUN, SEMI-AUTOMATIC

	V.G.	Exc.	Prior Edition Exc. Value
Model 1913, .25 ACP, Clip Fed, *Modern*	125	150	140

STUART, JOHAN Edinburgh, Scotland 1701–1750.

HANDGUN, SNAPHAUNCE

	V.G.	Exc.	Prior Edition Exc. Value
All Steel Highland, Engraved, Scroll Butt, Ball Trigger, *Antique*	7,500	10,000	10,000

	V.G.	Exc.	Prior Edition Exc. Value

SULLIVAN ARMS CO. Made by Crescent for Sullivan Hardware, Anderson, S.C., c. 1900.

SHOTGUN, DOUBLE BARREL, SIDE-BY-SIDE

	V.G.	Exc.	Prior
Various Gauges, Outside Hammers, Damascus Barrel, *Modern*	$150	$175	$170
Various Gauges, Hammerless, Steel Barrel, *Modern*	175	200	190
Various Gauges, Hammerless, Damascus Barrel, *Modern*	150	175	170
Various Gauges, Outside Hammers, Steel Barrel, *Modern*	175	200	185

SHOTGUN, SINGLESHOT

Various Gauges, Hammer, Steel Barrel, *Modern*	75	100	85

SUPER DREADNAUGHT Made by Stevens Arms.

SHOTGUN, SINGLESHOT

Model 89 Dreadnaught, Various Gauges, Hammer, *Modern*	50	75	65

SUPER RANGE GOOSE Made by Stevens Arms.

RIFLE, SEMI-AUTOMATIC

Model 85 Springfield, .22 L.R.R.F., 5 Shot Clip, Open Rear Sight, *Modern*	50	75	65

SUTHERLAND, JAMES Edinburgh, Scotland, c. 1790.

HANDGUN, FLINTLOCK

.50, all Steel, Engraved, Ram's Horn Butt, *Antique*	2,500	2,750	2,600

SUTHERLAND, RAMSEY London and Birmingham, England, 1790–1827.

HANDGUN, FLINTLOCK

.67, George III, Cavalry Pistol, Military, Tapered Round Barrel, Brass Furniture, *Antique*	1,000	1,200	1,200

RIFLE, FLINTLOCK

.75, 3rd Model Brown Bess, Musket, Military, *Antique*	1,250	1,500	1,500

SVENDSON E. Svendson, Itasca, Ill., c. 1965.

HANDGUN, MANUAL REPEATER

Four Aces, .22 Short, Four Barrels, Derringer, Spur Trigger, *Modern*	50	75	65

	V.G.	Exc.	Prior Edition Exc. Value

SWAMP ANGEL Made by Forehand & Wadsworth, Worcester, Mass., c. 1871.

HANDGUN, REVOLVER

.41 Short R.F., 5 Shot, Spur Trigger, Solid Frame, Single Action,
Antique $175 $200 $195

SWEDISH MILITARY

HANDGUN, REVOLVER

M1887 Husqvarna, 7.5mm, Double Action, Blue, *Antique*   200   250   220

RIFLE, SINGLESHOT

M1867/89 Remington, 8mm, Full Stock, *Antique*...........................   300   350   325

RIFLE, BOLT ACTION

M1896 Mauser, 6.5 × 55mm, Gustav, *Curio*   200   225   200

SWEITZER, DANIEL & CO. Lancaster, Pa. 1808–1814. See Kentucky Rifles.

SWIFT Made by Iver Johnson, Fitchburg, Mass. 1890–1900.

HANDGUN, REVOLVER

.38 S & W, 5 Shot, top Break, Hammerless, Double Action,
Curio   75   100   95
.38 S & W, 5 Shot, Double Action, Top Break, *Curio*......................   75   100   95

SWISS MILITARY

HANDGUN, REVOLVER

M1872 Swiss Ordnance, 10.4mm R.F., Double Action, Blue,
Military, *Antique*..   800   850   800

M1872/78 Swiss Ordnance, 10.4mm C.F., Double Action, Blue,
Military, *Antique*..   400   475   450

M1882 Swiss Ordnance, 7.5mm, Double Action, Blue, Military,
Antique..   150   200   185

M1882 Swiss Ordnance, 7.5mm, Double Action, Blue, Military,
with Holster Stock and All Leather, *Antique*.................................... 1,250 1,500 1,500

RIFLE, BOLT ACTION

Vetterli, Carbine, .41 Swiss R.F., Tube Feed, Military, *Antique*......   400   450   400
Vetterli, Bern 1878, .41 Swiss R.F., Tube Feed, Military, *Antique*......   150   175   170
Vetterli, Bern 1878/81, .41 Swiss R.F., Tube Feed, Military,
Antique..   175   200   180
M 1889, 7.5 × 55 Swiss, Military, *Modern*   175   200   175

pow# po# po

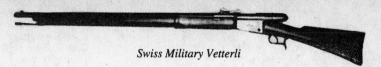

Swiss Military Vetterli

	V.G.	Exc.	Prior Edition Exc. Value
M 1889/1900, 7.5 × 55 Swiss, Short Rifle, *Curio*	$400	$450	$420
M 1893, 7.5 × 55 Swiss, Military, *Curio*	400	450	420
M1911 Schmidt Rubin, 7.5 × 55 Swiss, Clip Fed, Military, *Curio*	100	125	110
M1911 Schmidt Rubin, 7.5 × 55 Swiss, Clip Fed, Carbine, Military, *Curio*	125	150	125

RIFLE, PERCUSSION

	V.G.	Exc.	Prior Edition Exc. Value
Federal Rifle, .41 Caliber, Full Stocked, *Antique*	750	850	795

T

	V.G.	Exc.	Prior Edition Exc. Value

T.A.C. Trocaola, Aranzabal y Cia., Eibar, Spain.

HANDGUN, REVOLVER

Modelo Militar, .44 Spec., S & W Triple Lock Copy, Double Action, Blue *Modern* ... $175 | $225 | $225

OP No. 2 Mk. I, .455 Eley, British Military, Double Action, Top Break, *Curio* ... 150 | 175 | 160

S & W Frontier Copy, .44 American, Double Action, Break Top, Blue, *Modern* ... 125 | 150 | 135

S & W M&P Copy, .38 Spec., Double Action, Blue, *Modern* ... 75 | 100 | 90

TALLARES Tallares Armas Livianas Argentinas, Punta Alta, Argentina.

HANDGUN, SEMI-AUTOMATIC

T.A.L.A., .22 L.R.R.F., Clip Fed, *Modern* ... 125 | 150 | 130

TANARMI Made in Italy, Imported by Excam.

HANDGUN, REVOLVER

E-15, For Chrome, *Add* **$5.00**

E-15, .22LR/.22 WMR Combo, Single Action, Western Style, *Modern* ... 25 | 50 | 40

E-15, .22 L.R.R.F., Single Action, Western Style, *Modern* ... 25 | 50 | 30

TA-22, For Chrome, *Add* **$5.00**

TA-22, .22LR/.22 WMR Combo, Single Action, Western Style, Brass Grip Frame, *Modern* ... 50 | 75 | 60

TA-22, .22 L.R.R.F., Single Action, Western Style, Brass Grip Frame, *Modern* ... 25 | 50 | 45

TA-76, For Chrome, *Add* **$5.00**

TA-76, .22LR/.22WMR Combo, Single Action, Western Style, *Modern* ... 25 | 50 | 45

TA-76, .22 L.R.R.F., Single Action, Western Style, *Modern* ... 25 | 50 | 35

TANKE Maker unknown.

HANDGUN, SEMI-AUTOMATIC

.25 ACP, Clip Fed, *Modern* ... 125 | 150 | 125

	V.G.	Exc.	Prior Edition Exc. Value

TANNER Andrae Tanner, Werkstatte fur Praszisionswaffen, Fulenbach, Switzerland.

RIFLE, BOLT ACTION

	V.G.	Exc.	Prior Ed.
Standard UIT, .308 Win., Singleshot, Target Rifle, Monte Carlo Target Stock, *Modern*	$3,500	$3,900	$1,300
Standard UIT, .308 Win., Repeater, Target Rifle, Monte Carlo Target Stock, *Modern*	3,250	3,500	1,350
300m Match, .308 Win., Offhand Target Rifle, Target Stock, Palm Rest, *Modern*	3,500	4,000	1,500
50m Match, .22 L.R.R.F., Offhand Target Rifle, Target Stock, Palm Rest, *Modern*	2,250	2,500	1,000
Hunting Match, Various Calibers, Checkered Monte Carlo Stock, Singleshot, *Modern*	2,500	2,750	1,200

TANQUE Ojanguran y Vidosa, Eibar, Spain, c. 1930.

HANDGUN, SEMI-AUTOMATIC

	V.G.	Exc.	Prior Ed.
.25 ACP, Clip Fed, *Modern*	150	175	160

TARGA Guiseppi Tanfoglio, Gardone Val Trompia, Italy, imported by Excam.

HANDGUN, SEMI-AUTOMATIC

Chrome Plating, For All Models *Add* $5.00

	V.G.	Exc.	Prior Ed.
GT22B, .22 L.R.R.F., Clip Fed, Blue, *Modern*	75	100	90
GT32C, .22 L.R.R.F., Clip Fed, Blue, *Modern*	75	100	95
GT27, .25 ACP, Clip Fed, Blue, *Modern*	25	50	40
GT380B, .380 ACP, Clip Fed, Blue, *Modern*	100	125	110
GT380BE, .380 ACP, Clip Fed, Engraved, Blue, *Modern*	125	150	140
GT380XE, .380 ACP, Clip Fed, *Modern*	125	150	140
GT32XEB, .32 ACP, Clip Fed, *Modern*	125	150	125

T.A.R.N. Swift Rifle Co., London, England, c. 1943.

HANDGUN, SEMI-AUTOMATIC

	V.G.	Exc.	Prior Ed.
Polish Air Force, 9mm Luger, Clip Fed, Blue, *Curio*	3,500	4,000	3,800

TAURUS Forjas Taurus S.A., Porto Alegre, Brazil.

HANDGUN, REVOLVER

	V.G.	Exc.	Prior Ed.
Model 65, .38 Special, Solid Frame, Swing-Out Cylinder, Double Action, *Modern*	175	225	125
Model 66, .38 Special, Solid Frame, Swing-Out Cylinder, Double Action, Adjustable Sights, *Modern*	200	250	135
Model 73, .32 S & W Long, Solid Frame, Swing-Out Cylinder, Double Action, Fixed Sights, *Modern*	150	200	95

	V.G.	Exc.	Prior Edition Exc. Value
Model 74, .32 S & W Long, Solid Frame, Swing-Out Cylinder, Double Action, Adjustable Sights, *Modern*......................................	$125	$175	$95
Model 80, .38 Special, Solid Frame, Swing-Out Cylinder, Double Action, *Modern*..	125	175	115
Model 82, .38 Special, Solid Frame, Swing-Out Cylinder, Double Action, Heavy Barrel, *Modern*..	150	175	110
Model 83, .38 Special, Solid Frame, Swing-Out Cylinder, Double Action, Adjustable Sights, *Modern*..	150	175	120
Model 84, .38 Special, Solid Frame, Swing-Out Cylinder, Double Action, Adjustable Sights, *Modern*..	150	175	120
Model 85, .38 Special, Solid Frame, Swing-Out Cylinder, Double Action, 3" Barrel, *Modern*	175	200	110
Model 86, .38 Special, Solid Frame, Swing-Out Cylinder, Double Action, Adjustable Sights, 6" Barrel, *Modern*..................................	200	225	130
Model 94, .22 L.R.R.F., Solid Frame, Swing-Out Cylinder, Double Action, Adjustable Sights, *Modern*..	150	175	135
Model 96, .22 L.R.R.F., Solid Frame, Swing-Out Cylinder, Double Action, Adjustable Sights, 6" Barrel, *Modern*..................................	225	250	125

HANDGUN, SEMI-AUTOMATIC

	V.G.	Exc.	Prior Edition Exc. Value
PT-92, 9mm Luger, Clip Fed, Blue, Double Action, *Modern*...........	350	400	225
PT-99, 9mm Luger, Clip Fed, Blue, Double Action, *Modern*...........	375	425	285

T.D.E. El Monte, Calif. Also see Auto-Mag.

HANDGUN, SEMI-AUTOMATIC

	V.G.	Exc.	Prior Edition Exc. Value
Backup, .380 ACP, Stainless Steel, *Modern*.....................................	225	250	175

TED WILLIAMS Trade name of Sears Roebuck, also see Sears.

RIFLE, BOLT ACTION

	V.G.	Exc.	Prior Edition Exc. Value
Model 52703, .22 L.R.R.F., Singleshot, Plain, *Modern*....................	25	50	40
Model 52774, .22 L.R.R.F., Clip Fed, Plain, *Modern*......................	50	75	55
Model 53, Various Calibers, Checkered Stock, *Modern*...................	150	175	155

RIFLE, LEVER ACTION

	V.G.	Exc.	Prior Edition Exc. Value
Model 120, .30-30 Win., Carbine, *Modern*.....................................	75	100	80

RIFLE, SEMI-AUTOMATIC

	V.G.	Exc.	Prior Edition Exc. Value
model 34, .22 L.R.R.F., *Modern*	50	75	55
Model 34, .22 L.R.R.F., Carbine, *Modern*	50	75	55
Model 3T, .22 L.R.R.F., Checkered Stock, *Modern*	75	100	85
Model 52811, .22 L.R.R.F., Plain, Tube Feed, Takedown, *Modern*...	50	75	60
Model 52814, .22 L.R.R.F., Checkered Stock, Clip Fed, Takedown, *Modern*...	100	125	115

	V.G.	Exc.	Prior Edition Exc. Value

SHOTGUN, BOLT ACTION

	V.G.	Exc.	Prior Edition Exc. Value
Model 51106, 12 or 20 Gauges, Clip Fed, Adjustable Choke, *Modern*	$50	$75	$60
Model 51142, .410 Gauge, Clip Fed, *Modern*	25	50	50

SHOTGUN, DOUBLE BARREL, OVER-UNDER

	V.G.	Exc.	Prior Edition Exc. Value
Model Laurona, 12 Ga., Checkered Stock, Light Engraving, Double Trigger, Vent Rib, *Modern*	325	350	325
Model Zoli, 12 Ga., Checkered Stock, Light Engraving, Double Trigger, Vent Rib, Automatic Ejector, *Modern*	275	300	275
Model Zoli, 12 and 20 Gauges, Checkered Stock, Light Engraving, Double Trigger, Vent Rib, *Modern*	275	300	280

SHOTGUN, DOUBLE BARREL, SIDE-BY-SIDE

	V.G.	Exc.	Prior Edition Exc. Value
Model 51226, 12 and 20 Gauges, Plain, Double Trigger, *Modern*	125	150	125
Model Laurona, 12 and 20 Gauges, Checkered Stock, Light Engraving, Hammerless, *Modern*	150	175	155

SHOTGUN, SEMI-AUTOMATIC

	V.G.	Exc.	Prior Edition Exc. Value
Model 300, 12 Ga., Plain, *Modern*	150	175	155
Model 300, 12 and 20 Gauges, Checkered Stock, Vent Rib, Adjustable Choke, *Modern*	175	200	175
Model 300, 12 and 20 Gauges, Checkered Stock, Vent Rib, *Modern*	175	200	170

SHOTGUN, SINGLESHOT

	V.G.	Exc.	Prior Edition Exc. Value
Model 5108, Various Gauges, Plain, *Modern*	25	50	45

SHOTGUN, SLIDE ACTION

	V.G.	Exc.	Prior Edition Exc. Value
Model 200, 12 and 20 Gauges, Checkered Stock, Vent Rib, Adjustable Choke, *Modern*	150	175	155
Model 200, 12 and 20 Gauges, Checkered Stock, Vent Rib, *Modern*	125	150	140
Model 200, 12 and 20 Gauges, Plain, *Modern*	100	125	115
Model 200, 12 and 20 Gauges, Checkered Stock, Plain Barrel, *Modern*	125	150	125
Model 51454, .410 Ga., Plain, *Modern*	100	125	100

TEN STAR Belgium, c. 1900.

SHOTGUN, DOUBLE BARREL, SIDE-BY-SIDE

	V.G.	Exc.	Prior Edition Exc. Value
Various Gauges, Outside Hammers, Damascus Barrel, *Modern*	150	175	170
Various Gauges, Hammerless, Steel Barrel, *Modern*	175	200	190
Various Gauges, Hammerless, Damascus Barrel, *Modern*	150	175	170
Various Gauges, Outside Hammers, Steel Barrel, *Modern*	175	200	185

SHOTGUN, SINGLESHOT

	V.G.	Exc.	Prior Edition Exc. Value
Various Gauges, Hammer, Steel Barrel, *Modern*	75	100	85

	V.G.	Exc.	Prior Edition Exc. Value

TERRIBLE Hijos de Calixto Arrizabalaga, Eibar, Spain, c. 1930.

HANDGUN, SEMI-AUTOMATIC

.25 ACP, Clip Fed, Blue, *Modern* $125 $150 $130

TERRIER Made by J. Rupertus, Philadelphia, Pa. Sold by Tryon Bros., c. 1880.

HANDGUN, REVOLVER

.22 Short R.F., 7 Shot, Spur Trigger, Solid Frame, Single Action,
Antique 150 175 165

.32 Short R.F., 5 Shot, Spur Trigger, Solid Frame, Single Action,
Antique 150 175 170

.38 Short R.F., 5 Shot, Spur Trigger, Solid Frame, Single Action,
Antique 150 175 170

.41 Short R.F., 5 Shot, Spur Trigger, Solid Frame, Single Action,
Antique 175 200 195

TERROR Made by Forehand & Wadsworth, c. 1870.

HANDGUN, REVOLVER

.32 Short R.F., 5 or 6 Shot, Spur Trigger, Solid Frame, Single
Action, *Antique* 150 175 165

TEUF-TEUF Arizmendi y Goenaga, Eibar, Spain, c. 1912.

HANDGUN, SEMI-AUTOMATIC

.25 ACP, Clip Fed, Blue, *Curio* 125 150 130

TEUF-TEUF Unknown Belgian maker, c. 1907.

HANDGUN, SEMI-AUTOMATIC

.25 ACP, Clip Fed, Blue, *Curio* 150 175 160

TEXAS RANGER Made by Stevens Arms.

SHOTGUN, SINGLESHOT

Model 95, 12 and 16 Gauges, *Modern* 25 50 50

THAMES ARMS CO. Norwich, Conn., c. 1907.

HANDGUN, REVOLVER

.22 L.R.R.F., 7 Shot, Double Action, Top Break, *Curio* 100 125 110

.32 S & W, 5 Shot, Double Action, Top Break, *Curio* 75 100 100

.38 S & W, 5 Shot, Double Action, Top Break, *Curio* 75 100 100

	V.G.	Exc.	Prior Edition Exc. Value

THAYER, ROBERTSON & CARY Norwich, Conn., c. 1907.

HANDGUN, REVOLVER

	V.G.	Exc.	Prior Edition Exc. Value
.32 S & W, 5 Shot, Double Action, Top Break, *Curio*	$75	$100	$95
.38 S & W, 5 Shot, Double Action, Top Break, *Curio*	75	100	95

THOMPSON Developed by Auto-Ordnance, invented by Gen. John T. Thompson, made by various companies. Also see Numrich Arms.

HANDGUN, SEMI-AUTOMATIC

	V.G.	Exc.	Prior Edition Exc. Value
Model 27A5, .45 ACP, Clip Fed, Finned Barrel, Adjustable Sights, with Compensator, (Numrich), *Modern*	275	325	275

RIFLE, SEMI-AUTOMATIC

	V.G.	Exc.	Prior Edition Exc. Value
Model 27A1, .45 ACP, Clip Fed, without Compensator, (Numrich), *Modern*	325	375	350
Model 27A1, .45 ACP, Clip Fed, without Compensator, Cased with Accessories, (Numrich), *Modern*	300	350	325
Model 27A1 Deluxe, .45 ACP, Clip Fed, Finned Barrel, Adjustable Sights, with Compensator, (Numrich), *Modern*	300	350	315
Model 27A3, .22 L.R.R.F., Clip Fed, Finned Barrel, Adjustable Sights, with Compensator (Numrich), *Modern*	325	375	350

THOMPSON, SAMUEL Columbus, Ohio 1820–1822. See Kentucky Rifles.

THOMPSON/CENTER Rochester, N.H.

HANDGUN, SINGLESHOT

	V.G.	Exc.	Prior Edition Exc. Value
Contender, Various Calibers, Adjustable Sights, *Modern*	225	275	190
Contender, Various Calibers, Adjustable Sights, Vent Rib, *Modern*	250	300	200

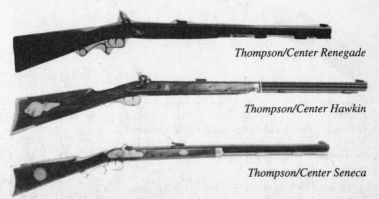

Thompson/Center Renegade

Thompson/Center Hawkin

Thompson/Center Seneca

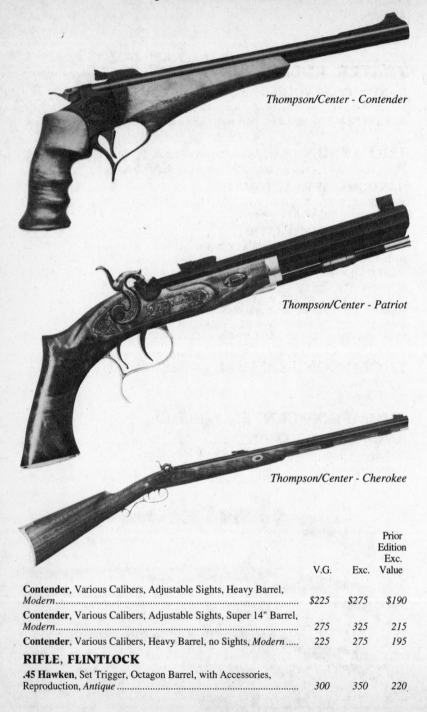

Thompson/Center - Contender

Thompson/Center - Patriot

Thompson/Center - Cherokee

	V.G.	Exc.	Prior Edition Exc. Value
Contender, Various Calibers, Adjustable Sights, Heavy Barrel, *Modern*	$225	$275	$190
Contender, Various Calibers, Adjustable Sights, Super 14" Barrel, *Modern*	275	325	215
Contender, Various Calibers, Heavy Barrel, no Sights, *Modern*	225	275	195

RIFLE, FLINTLOCK
	V.G.	Exc.	Prior Edition Exc. Value
.45 Hawken, Set Trigger, Octagon Barrel, with Accessories, Reproduction, *Antique*	300	350	220

	V.G.	Exc.	Prior Edition Exc. Value
.45 Hawken, Set Trigger, Octagon Barrel, Reproduction, *Antique*	$275	$325	$210
.50 Hawken, Set Trigger, Octagon Barrel, with Accessories, Reproduction, *Antique*	300	350	220
.50 Hawken, Set Trigger, Octagon Barrel, Reproduction, *Antique*	275	325	210
Hawken Cougar, .45 and .50 Caliber Caplock, Stainless Furniture, Reproduction, *Antique*	375	425	300

HANDGUN, PERCUSSION

	V.G.	Exc.	Value
.45 Patriot, Set Trigger, Octagon Barrel, Reproduction, *Antique*	200	250	130
.45 Patriot, Set Trigger, Octagon Barrel, with Accessories, Reproduction, *Antique*	225	275	145

RIFLE, PERCUSSION

Cherokee, .32 or .45 Caliber, Brass Furniture, 24" Barrel, *Modern*	300	350	250
.36 Seneca, Set Trigger, Octagon Barrel, with Accessories, Reproduction, *Antique*	275	325	210
.36 Seneca, Set Trigger, Octagon Barrel, Reproduction, *Antique*	250	300	200
.45 Hawken, Set Trigger, Octagon Barrel, with Accessories, Reproduction, *Antique*	275	325	210
.45 Hawken, Set Trigger, Octagon Barrel, Reproduction, *Antique*	250	300	200
.45 Seneca, Set Trigger, Octagon Barrel, with Accessories, Reproduction, *Antique*	275	325	210
.45 Seneca, Set Trigger, Octagon Barrel, Reproduction, *Antique*	250	300	200
.50 Hawken, Set Trigger, Octagon Barrel, with Accessories, Reproduction, *Antique*	275	325	210
.50 Hawken, Set Trigger, Octagon Barrel, Reproduction, *Antique*	250	300	200
.54 Renegade, Set Trigger, Octagon Barrel, with Accessories, Reproduction, *Antique*	200	250	165
.54 Renegade, Set Trigger, Octagon Barrel, Reproduction, *Antique*	175	225	150

RIFLE, SINGLESHOT

TCR83 Sports Rifle, Various Calibers, Interchangeable Barrels, Adjustable Double Set Triggers, *Modern*	500	550	475

THREE-BARREL GUN CO. Moundsville, W. Va., 1906–1908, also at Wheeling, W. Va. as Royal Gun Co. and as Hollenbeck Gun Co.

COMBINATION WEAPON, DRILLING

Various Calibers, Damascus Barrel, *Antique*	950	1,200	1,100

THUNDER Martin Bascaran, Eibar, Spain, made for Alberdi, Teleria y Cia. 1912–1919.

HANDGUN, SEMI-AUTOMATIC

M1919, .25 ACP, Clip Fed, *Curio*	100	125	125

	V.G.	Exc.	Prior Edition Exc. Value

TIGER Maker Unknown, c. 1880.

HANDGUN, REVOLVER

#2, .32 Short R.F., 5 Shot, Spur Trigger, Solid Frame, Single Action, *Antique* $150 $175 $165

TIGER Made by Crescent for J.H. Hill Co. Nashville, Tenn., c. 1900.

SHOTGUN, DOUBLE BARREL, SIDE-BY-SIDE

Various Gauges, Outside Hammers, Damascus Barrel, *Modern* 150 175 170
Various Gauges, Outside Hammers, Steel Barrel, *Modern* 175 200 185

SHOTGUN, SINGLESHOT

Various Gauges, Hammer, Steel Barrel, *Modern* 75 100 85

TIKKA Oy Tikkakoski AB, Tikkakoski, Finland.

RIFLE, BOLT ACTION

Model 55 Standard, Various Calibers, Clip Fed, Checkered Stock, *Modern* 450 525 280
Model 55 Sporter, Various Calibers, Clip Fed, Checkered Stock, Heavy Barrel, *Modern* 475 550 300
Model 55 Deluxe, Various Calibers, Clip Fed, Checkered Stock, *Modern* 475 550 300
Model 65 Standard, Various Calibers, Clip Fed, Checkered Stock, *Modern* 450 525 280
Model 65 Sporter, Various Calibers, Clip Fed, Checkered Stock, Target Rifle, Heavy Barrel, *Modern* 550 650 400
Model 65 Deluxe, Various Calibers, Clip Fed, Checkered Stock, *Modern* 475 550 300

TINDALL & DUTTON London, England 1790–1820.

HANDGUN, FLINTLOCK

Pocket Pistol, Various Calibers, Boxlock, *Antique* 350 450 450

TINGLE MFG. CO. Shelbyville, Ind.

HANDGUN, PERCUSSION

Model 1960 Target, Octagon Barrel, Rifled, Reproduction, *Antique* 125 150 140

RIFLE, PERCUSSION

Model 1962 Target, Octagon Barrel, Brass Furniture, Rifled, Reproduction, *Antique* 175 200 200

SHOTGUN, PERCUSSION

Model 1960, 10 or 12 Gauges, Vent Rib, Double Barrel, Over-Under, Reproduction, *Antique* 200 225 215

	V.G.	Exc.	Prior Edition Exc. Value

TIPPING & LAWDEN Birmingham, England, c. 1875.
HANDGUN, REVOLVER
Thomas Patent, .450, Solid Frame, Double Action, *Antique* .... | $500 | $575 | $425

HANDGUN, MANUAL REPEATER
Sharps Derringer, Various Calibers, 4 Barrels, Spur Trigger, Cased with Accessories, *Antique* .... | 625 | 700 | 675

TITAN Guiseppi Tanfoglio, Gardone Val Trompia, Italy. Also see F.I.E.
HANDGUN, SEMI-AUTOMATIC
Vest Pocket, .25 ACP, Clip Fed, Hammer, *Modern* .... | 50 | 75 | 60

TITAN Retoloza Hermanos, Eibar, Spain, c. 1900.
HANDGUN, SEMI-AUTOMATIC
M 1913, .25 ACP, Clip Fed, *Curio* .... | 100 | 125 | 125

TITANIC Retoloza Hermanos, Eibar, Spain, c. 1900.
HANDGUN, SEMI-AUTOMATIC
M 1913, .25 ACP, Clip Fed, *Curio* .... | 100 | 125 | 125
M 1914, .32 ACP, Clip Fed, *Curio* .... | 125 | 150 | 140

TOMPKINS Varsity Mfg. Co., Springfield, Mass., c. 1947.
HANDGUN, SINGLESHOT
Target, .22 L.R.R.F., Full Stock, *Modern* .... | 200 | 225 | 220

TOWER'S POLICE SAFETY Made by Hopkins & Allen, Norwich, Conn. c. 1875
HANDGUN, REVOLVER
.38 Short R.F., 5 Shot, Spur Trigger, Solid Frame, Single Action, *Antique* .... | 150 | 175 | 170

TRADEWINDS, INC. Tacoma, Wash., also see HVA.
RIFLE, BOLT ACTION
Husky (Early), Various Calibers, Checkered Stock, Monte Carlo Stock, *Modern* .... | 400 | 450 | 325
Husky M-5000, Various Calibers, Checkered Stock, Clip Fed, *Modern* .... | 300 | 350 | 195
Husqvarna, Various Calibers, Checkered Stock, Monte Carlo Stock, Lightweight, *Modern* .... | 525 | 575 | 425
Husqvarna, Various Calibers, Checkered Stock, Monte Carlo Stock, Lightweight, Full-Stocked, *Modern* .... | 525 | 600 | 450

	V.G.	Exc.	Prior Edition Exc. Value
Husqvarna Crown Grade, Various Calibers, Checkered Stock, Monte Carlo Stock, *Modern*	$575	$625	$475
Husqvarna Imperial, Various Calibers, Checkered Stock, Monte Carlo Stock, Lightweight, *Modern*	500	550	425
Husqvarna Imperial Custom, Various Calibers, Checkered Stock, Monte Carlo Stock, *Modern*	475	525	425
Husqvarna Presentation, Various Calibers, Checkered Stock, Monte Carlo Stock, *Modern*	700	750	600
Model 1998, .222 Rem., no Sights, Heavy Barrel, Target Stock, *Modern*	475	525	375
Model 600K, Various Calibers, Clip Fed, no Sights, Heavy Barrel, Set Trigger, *Modern*	300	350	250
Model 600S, Various Calibers, Clip Fed, Heavy Barrel, Octagon Barrel, *Modern*	475	525	220

RIFLE, SEMI-AUTOMATIC

	V.G.	Exc.	Prior Edition Exc. Value
Model 260A, .22 L.R.R.F., 5 Shot Clip, Checkered Stock, *Modern*	150	200	140

SHOTGUN, DOUBLE BARREL, OVER-UNDER

	V.G.	Exc.	Prior Edition Exc. Value
Gold Shadow Indy, 12 Ga., Field Grade, Engraved, Fancy Checkering, Automatic Ejector, Vent Rib, *Modern*	1,200	1,550	1,400
Gold Shadow Indy, 12 Ga., Skeet Grade, Engraved, Fancy Checkering, Automatic Ejector, Vent Rib, *Modern*	1,250	1,500	1,400
Gold Shadow Indy, 12 Ga., Trap Grade, Engraved, Fancy Checkering, Automatic Ejector, Vent Rib, *Modern*	1,450	1,600	1,400
Shadow Indy, 12 Ga., Field Grade, Automatic Ejector, Vent Rib, Checkered Stock, *Modern*	475	525	425
Shadow Indy, 12 Ga., Skeet Grade, Automatic Ejector, Vent Rib, Checkered Stock, *Modern*	500	550	425
Shadow Indy, 12 Ga., Trap Grade, Automatic Ejector, Vent Rib, Checkered Stock, *Modern*	525	575	425
Shadow-7, 12 Ga., Field Grade, Automatic Ejector, Vent Rib, *Modern*	325	350	300
Shadow-7, 12 Ga., Skeet Grade, Automatic Ejector, Vent Rib, *Modern*	350	375	300
Shadow-7, 12 Ga., Trap Grade, Automatic Ejector, Vent Rib, *Modern*	375	400	300

SHOTGUN, DOUBLE BARREL, SIDE-BY-SIDE

	V.G.	Exc.	Prior Edition Exc. Value
Model G-1032, 10 Ga. 3½", Checkered Stock, *Modern*	225	250	165
Model G-1228, 12 Ga. Mag. 3", Checkered Stock, *Modern*	250	275	170
Model G-2028, 20 Ga. Mag., Checkered Stock, *Modern*	250	275	170

SHOTGUN, SEMI-AUTOMATIC

	V.G.	Exc.	Prior Edition Exc. Value
Model D-200, 12 Ga., Field Grade, Vent Rib, Engraved, *Modern*	250	300	200
Model H-150, 12 Ga., Field Grade, *Modern*	200	225	160
Model H-170, 12 Ga., Field Grade, Vent Rib, *Modern*	250	300	180
Model T-220, 12 Ga., Trap Grade, Vent Rib, Engraved, *Modern*	250	300	200

	V.G.	Exc.	Prior Edition Exc. Value

SHOTGUN, SINGLESHOT
Model M50, 10 Ga., 3½" Barrel, Checkered Stock, *Modern*............ *$125* *$175* *$120*

TRAMPS TERROR Made by Hoods Firearms Co. Norwich, Conn., c. 1870.

HANDGUN, REVOLVER
.22 Short R.F., 7 Shot, Spur Trigger, Solid Frame, Single Action,
Antique... *150* *175* *160*

TRIOMPH Apaolozo Hermanos, Eibar, Spain.

HANDGUN, SEMI-AUTOMATIC
.25 ACP, Clip Fed, Blue, *Modern*... *100* *125* *125*

TRIUMPH Made by Stevens Arms.

SHOTGUN, DOUBLE BARREL, SIDE-BY-SIDE
Model 311, Various Gauges, Hammerless, Steel Barrel, *Modern*........ *150* *175* *170*

TRUE BLUE Made by Norwich Falls Pistols Co., c. 1880.

HANDGUN, REVOLVER
.32 Short R.F., 5 Shot, Spur Trigger, Solid Frame, Single Action,
Antique... *125* *175* *170*

TRUST Fab. d'Armes de Guerre de Grande Precision, Eibar, Spain.

HANDGUN, SEMI-AUTOMATIC
.25 ACP, Clip Fed, Blue, *Modern*... *100* *125* *125*
.32 ACP, Clip Fed, Blue, *Modern*... *125* *150* *140*

TRUST SUPRA Fab. d'Armes de Guerre de Grande Precision, Eibar, Spain.

HANDGUN, SEMI-AUTOMATIC
.25 ACP, Clip Fed, Blue, *Modern*... *100* *125* *125*

TUE-TUE C.F. Galand, Liege, Belgium and Paris, France.

HANDGUN, REVOLVER
Velo Dog, Various Calibers, Double Action, Hammerless, *Curio*....... *125* *150* *135*

TURBIAUX J.E. Turbiaux, Paris, France, c. 1885.

HANDGUN, MANUAL REPEATER
Le Protector, Various Calibers, Palm Pistol, *Antique*...................... *600* *750* *550*

	V.G.	Exc.	Prior Edition Exc. Value

TURNER Dublin, C. 1820.

HANDGUN, FLINTLOCK

.62, Double Barrel, Pocket Pistol, Platinum Furniture, Plain,
Antique $1,000 $1,500 $1,500

TURNER & ROSS Made by Hood Firearms, Norwich, Conn., c. 1875.

HANDGUN, REVOLVER

.22 Short R.F., 7 Shot, Spur Trigger, Solid Frame, Single Action,
Antique 150   175   165

TWIGG London, England 1760–1813.

HANDGUN, FLINTLOCK

.58, Pair, Belt Pistol, Flared, Octagon Barrel, Cased with
Accessories, Plain, *Antique*.. 3,000 3,500 3,400

TYCOON Made by Johnson-Bye, Worcester, Mass. 1873–1887.

HANDGUN, REVOLVER

#1, .22 Short R.F., 7 Shot, Spur Trigger, Solid Frame, Single
Action, *Antique*... 150   175   165

#2, .32 Short R.F., 5 Shot, Spur Trigger, Solid Frame, Single
Action, *Antique*... 150   200   195

#3, .38 Short R.F., 5 Shot, Spur Trigger, Solid Frame, Single
Action, *Antique*... 150   175   165

#4, .41 Short R.F., 5 Shot, Spur Trigger, Solid Frame, Single
Action, *Antique*... 125   150   145

#5, Short R.F., 5 Shot, Spur Trigger, Solid Frame, Single Action,
Antique 200   250   225

TYROL Made in Belgium for Tyrol Sport Arms, Englewood, Colo., c. 1963.

RIFLE, BOLT ACTION

Model DCM, Various Calibers, Mannlicher Style, Checkered
Stock, Recoil Pad, *Modern* 225   250   225

Model DC, Various Calibers, Mannlicher Style, Checkered Stock,
Modern.. 275   200   200

Model DM, Various Calibers, Checkered Stock, *Modern*............... 150   175   180

u

UHLINGER, W.L. & CO. Philadelphia, Pa., c. 1880.

HANDGUN, REVOLVER

.22 R.F., 7 Shot, Spur Trigger, Solid Frame, Single Action,
Antique $200 $225 $225
.32 Short R.F., 6 Shot, Spur Trigger, Solid Frame, Single Action,
Antique 225   275   275

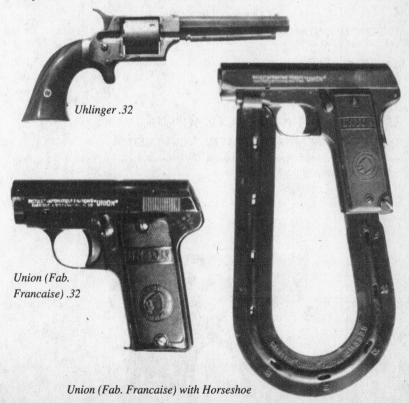

Uhlinger .32

*Union (Fab.
Francaise) .32*

Union (Fab. Francaise) with Horseshoe

	V.G.	Exc.	Prior Edition Exc. Value

U.M.C. ARMS CO. Probably Norwich Arms Co., c. 1880.

HANDGUN, REVOLVER

.32 Short R.F., 5 Shot, Spur Trigger, Solid Frame, Single Action, *Antique* .... | $95 | $175 | $165

UNION Fab. Francaise.

HANDGUN, SEMI-AUTOMATIC

| **.32 ACP**, Ruby Style, Clip Fed, *Modern* .... | 150 | 200 | 190 |
| **.32 ACP**, Ruby Style, with Horseshoe Magazine, *Modern* .... | 650 | 750 | 850 |

UNION France, M. Seytres.

HANDGUN, SEMI-AUTOMATIC

| **.25 ACP**, Clip Fed, Long Grip, *Modern* .... | 100 | 125 | 125 |
| **.32 ACP**, Clip Fed, Long Grip, *Modern* .... | 125 | 150 | 125 |

UNION Unceta y Cia., Guernica, Spain 1924–1931.

HANDGUN, SEMI-AUTOMATIC

Model I, .25 ACP, Clip Fed, *Modern*	100	150	145
Model II, .25 ACP, Clip Fed, *Modern*	125	150	140
Model III, .32 ACP, Clip Fed, *Modern*	150	175	160
Model IV, .32 ACP, Clip Fed, *Modern*	150	175	160

UNION FIREARMS CO. Toledo, Ohio, c. 1910.

HANDGUN, SEMI-AUTOMATIC, REVOLVER

| **Lefever Patent**, .32 S & W, 5 Shot, Top Break, *Curio* .... | 800 | 875 | 875 |
| **Reifgraber Patent**, .32 S & W, 8 Shot, *Curio* .... | 850 | 950 | 950 |

Union Model I .25

	V.G.	Exc.	Prior Edition Exc. Value

UNION JACK Made by Hood Firearms Norwich, Conn., c. 1880.

HANDGUN, REVOLVER

.22 Short R.F., 7 Shot, Spur Trigger, Solid Frame, Single Action, Antique — $125 / $150 / $165

.32 Short R.F., 5 Shot, Spur Trigger, Solid Frame, Single Action, Antique — 150 / 175 / 170

UNION REVOLVER Maker unknown, c. 1880.

HANDGUN, REVOLVER

.22 Short R.F., 7 Shot, Spur Trigger, Solid Frame, Single Action, Antique — 125 / 150 / 165

.32 Short R.F., 5 Shot, Spur Trigger, Solid Frame, Single Action, Antique — 150 / 175 / 170

UNIQUE Made by C.S. Shattuck, c. 1880.

HANDGUN, REVOLVER

.32 Short R.F., 5 Shot, Spur Trigger, Solid Frame, Single Action, Antique — 150 / 200 / 190

.38 Short R.F., 5 Shot, Spur Trigger, Solid Frame, Single Action, Antique — 150 / 200 / 190

HANDGUN, REPEATER

Shattuck Palm Pistol, Various Calibers, 4 Shot, *Curio* — 575 / 650 / 600

UNIQUE Mre. d'Armes de Pyrenees, Hendaye, France, 1923 to date.

HANDGUN, SEMI-AUTOMATIC

Kriegsmodell, .32 ACP, Clip Fed, Magazine Disconnect, 9 Shot, Nazi-Proofed, Hammer, *Curio* — 250 / 300 / 245

Model 10, .25 ACP, Clip Fed, Magazine Disconnect, *Modern* — 150 / 200 / 125

Model 11, .25 ACP, Clip Fed, Magazine Disconnect, Grip Safety, Cartridge Indicator, *Modern* — 200 / 250 / 150

Model 12, .25 ACP, Clip Fed, Magazine Disconnect, Grip Safety, *Modern* — 200 / 225 / 135

Model 13, .25 ACP, Clip Fed, Magazine Disconnect, Grip Safety, 7 Shot, *Modern* — 200 / 225 / 130

Model 14, .25 ACP, Clip Fed, Magazine Disconnect, Grip Safety, 9 Shot, *Modern* — 175 / 225 / 135

Model 15, .32 ACP, Clip Fed, Magazine Disconnect, 6 Shot, *Modern* — 200 / 250 / 125

Model 16, .32 ACP, Clip Fed, Magazine Disconnect, 7 Shot, *Modern* — 200 / 250 / 125

Model 17, .32 ACP, Clip Fed, Magazine Disconnect, 9 Shot, Nazi-Proofed, *Curio* — 300 / 350 / 200

	V.G.	Exc.	Prior Edition Exc. Value
Model 17, .32 ACP, Clip Fed, Magazine Disconnect, 9 Shot, *Modern*	$225	$275	$135
Model 18, .32 ACP, Clip Fed, Magazine Disconnect, 6 Shot, *Modern*	200	250	135
Model 19, .32 ACP, Clip Fed, Magazine Disconnect, 7 Shot, *Modern*	200	250	130
Model 20, .32 ACP, Clip Fed, Magazine Disconnect, 9 Shot, *Modern*	225	275	145
Model 21, .380 ACP, Clip Fed, Magazine Disconnect, 6 Shot, *Modern*	225	275	145
Model 51, .32 ACP, Clip Fed, Magazine Disconnect, 9 Shot, *Modern*	200	250	125
Model 51, .380 ACP, Clip Fed, Magazine Disconnect, 6 Shot, *Modern*	200	250	130
Model 52, .22 L.R.R.F., Clip Fed, Hammer, Various Barrel Lengths, *Modern*	175	225	120
Model 540, .32 ACP, Clip Fed, Magazine Disconnect, 9 Shot, *Modern*	200	250	125
Model 550, .380 ACP, Clip Fed, Magazine Disconnect, 6 Shot, *Modern*	200	250	125
Model C, .32 ACP, Clip Fed, 9 Shot, Hammer, *Modern*	200	250	115
Model D-1, .22 L.R.R.F., Clip Fed, Hammer, 3" Barrel, *Modern*	200	250	110
Model D-2, .22 L.R.R.F., Clip Fed, Hammer, Adjustable Sights, 4" Barrel, *Modern*	225	275	125
Model D-3, .22 L.R.R.F., Clip Fed, Hammer, Adjustable Sights, 8" Barrel, *Modern*	200	250	135
Model D-4, .22 L.R.R.F., Clip Fed, Hammer, Muzzle Brake, Adjustable Sights, 9½" Barrel, *Modern*	225	275	155
Model D-6, .22 L.R.R.F., Clip Fed, Hammer, Adjustable Sights, 6" Barrel, *Modern*	225	275	125
Model E-1, .22 Short R.F., Clip Fed, Hammer, 3" Barrel, *Modern*	100	125	90
Model E-2, .22 Short R.F., Clip Fed, Hammer, Adjustable Sights, 4" Barrel, *Modern*	125	150	125
Model E-3, .22 Short R.F., Clip Fed, Hammer, Adjustable Sights, 8" Barrel, *Modern*	125	150	125
Model E-4, .22 Short R.F., Clip Fed, Hammer, Muzzle Brake, Adjustable Sights, 9½" Barrel, *Modern*	150	200	150
Model F, .380 ACP, Clip Fed, 8 Shot, Hammer, *Modern*	225	275	130
Model L (Corsair), .22 L.R.R.F., Clip Fed, Hammer, Lightweight, *Modern*	175	225	120
Model L (Corsair), .22 L.R.R.F., Clip Fed, Hammer, *Modern*	175	225	120
Model L (Corsair), .32 ACP, Clip Fed, Hammer, Lightweight, *Modern*	125	150	120
Model L (Corsair), .32 ACP, Clip Fed, Hammer, *Modern*	125	150	120
Model L (Corsair), .380 ACP, Clip Fed, Hammer, Lightweight, *Modern*	125	150	125

Unique Model L

	V.G.	Exc.	Prior Edition Exc. Value
Model L (Corsair), .380 ACP, Clip Fed, Hammer, *Modern*	$150	$175	$135
Model Mikros, .25 ACP, Clip Fed, Magazine Disconnect, 6 Shot, *Modern*	150	175	125
Model RD (Ranger), .22 L.R.R.F., Clip Fed, Hammer, *Modern*	75	100	75
Model RD (Ranger), .22 L.R.R.F., Clip Fed, Muzzle Brake, Hammer, *Modern*	100	125	90
Model DES/69, .22 L.R.R.F., Clip Fed, Target Pistol, *Modern*	500	550	325
Model DES/VO, .22 L.R.R.F., Clip Fed, Rapid Fire Target Pistol, *Modern*	525	600	350
Model DES/VO 79, .22 L.R.R.F., Clip Fed, Rapid Fire Target Pistol, Gas Ports, *Modern*	650	750	400

RIFLE, BOLT ACTION

	V.G.	Exc.	Prior Edition Exc. Value
Dioptra 4131, .22 W.M.R., Checkered Stock, Open Sights, *Modern*	575	650	300
Dioptra 3121, .22 L.R.R.F., Checkered Stock, Open Sights, *Modern*	450	500	225
Dioptra 3121, .22 L.R.R.F., Checkered Stock, Target Sights, *Modern*	575	650	300
Model T-66, .22 L.R.R.F., Target Stock, Target Sights, Singleshot, *Modern*	375	425	400
Audax, .22 L.R.R.F., Checkered Stock, Open Sights, *Modern*	150	175	150

UNITED STATES ARMS Riverhead, N.Y., distributed by Mossberg.

HANDGUN, REVOLVER

	V.G.	Exc.	Prior Edition Exc. Value
Abilene, .44 Magnum, Single Action, Western Style, Adjustable Sights, *Modern*	300	350	190
Abilene, .44 Magnum, Stainless Steel, Single Action, Western Style, Adjustable Sights, *Modern*	325	375	200
Abilene, .44 Magnum, Stainless Steel, Single Action, Western Style, 10" Barrel, Adjustable Sights, *Modern*	350	400	225
Abilene, Various Calibers, Single Action, Western Style, Adjustable Sights, *Modern*	300	350	180
Abilene, Various Calibers, Single Action, Western Style, Adjustable Sights, Stainless Steel, *Modern*	325	375	200

	V.G.	Exc.	Prior Edition Exc. Value

UNIVERSAL Made by Hopkins & Allen, Norwich, Conn., c. 1890.

HANDGUN, REVOLVER

.32 S & W, 5 Shot, Double Action, Solid Frame, *Curio*	$75	$100	$80

UNIVERSAL Hialeah, Fla., Now owned by Iver Johnson-Jax

HANDGUN, SEMI-AUTOMATIC

Model 3000 Enforcer, .30 Carbine, Clip Fed, *Modern*	200	250	170
Model 3005 Enforcer, .30 Carbine, Clip Fed, Nickel Plated, *Modern*	225	275	180
Model 3010 Enforcer, .30 Carbine, Clip Fed, Gold Plated, *Modern*	225	275	185

RIFLE, SEMI-AUTOMATIC

Model 1001, .30 Carbine, Carbine, Clip Fed, *Modern*	150	200	130
Model 1002, .30 Carbine, Carbine, Clip Fed, Bayonet Lug, *Modern*	200	250	135
Model 1003, .30 Carbine, Carbine, Clip Fed, Walnut Stock, *Modern*	125	175	125
Model 1004, .30 Carbine, Carbine, Clip Fed, Scope Mounted, *Modern*	200	250	135
Model 1010, .30 Carbine, Carbine, Clip Fed, Nickel Plated, *Modern*	225	275	135
Model 1011 Deluxe, .30 Carbine, Carbine, Clip Fed, Nickel Plated, Monte Carlo Stock, *Modern*	250	300	170
Model 1015, .30 Carbine, Carbine, Clip Fed, Gold Plated, *Modern*	250	300	170
Model 1016 Deluxe, .30 Carbine, Carbine, Clip Fed, Gold Plated, Monte Carlo Stock, *Modern*	300	350	180
Model 1025 Ferret, .256 Win. Mag., Carbine, Clip Fed, Sporting Rifle, *Modern*	175	225	150
Model 1025 Ferret, .30 Carbine, Carbine, Clip Fed, Sporting Rifle, *Modern*	175	225	145
Model 1941 Field Commander, .30 Carbine, Carbine, Clip Fed, Fancy Wood, *Modern*	175	225	150

RIFLE, SLIDE ACTION

Vulcan 440, .44 Magnum, Clip Fed, Sporting Rifle, Open Rear Sight, *Modern*	150	200	160

SHOTGUN, DOUBLE BARREL, OVER-UNDER

Baikal 1J-27, 12 Ga., Double Trigger, Vent Rib, Engraved, Checkered Stock, *Modern*	200	250	200
Baikal 1J-27, 12 Ga., Double Trigger, Vent Rib, Engraved, Checkered Stock, Automatic Ejector, *Modern*	225	275	220

	V.G.	Exc.	Prior Edition Exc. Value

SHOTGUN, SINGLESHOT

Model 7212, 12 Ga., Trap Grade, Vent Rib, Engraved, Checkered Stock, Monte Carlo Stock, *Modern* $850 $950 $600

Model IJ18, 12 Ga., Hammerless, *Modern*........................ 50 75 45

UNWIN & ROGERS Yorkshire, England, c. 1850.

HANDGUN, PERCUSSION

Knife Pistol with Ramrod and Mould, Cased with Accessories, *Antique* 1,000 1,250 1,100

U.S. ARMS CO. Brooklyn, N.Y. 1874–1878.

HANDGUN, REVOLVER

.22 Short R.F., 7 Shot, Spur Trigger, Solid Frame, Single Action, *Antique* 125 175 165

.32 Short R.F., 5 Shot, Spur Trigger, Solid Frame, Single Action, *Antique* 150 175 170

.38 Short R.F., 5 Shot, Spur Trigger, Solid Frame, Single Action, *Antique* 150 175 170

.41 Short R.F., 5 Shot, Spur Trigger, Solid Frame, Single Action, *Antique* 150 200 195

U.S. ARMS CO. Made by Crescent for H & D Folsom, c. 1900.

SHOTGUN, DOUBLE BARREL, SIDE-BY-SIDE

Various Gauges, Outside Hammers, Damascus Barrel, *Modern* 150 175 170

Various Gauges, Hammerless, Steel Barrel, *Modern*....................... 150 200 190

Various Gauges, Hammerless, Damascus Barrel, *Modern* 150 200 170

Various Gauges, Outside Hammers, Steel Barrel, *Modern*.............. 150 200 185

SHOTGUN, SINGLESHOT

Various Gauges, Hammer, Steel Barrel, *Modern*............................ 75 100 85

U.S. MILITARY

HANDGUN, FLINTLOCK

.54 M1805 (06), Singleshot, Smoothbore, Brass Mounts, Dated 1806, *Antique* 7,500 10,500 7,600

U.S. Arms Co. .41

	V.G.	Exc.	Prior Edition Exc. Value
.54 M1805 (06), Singleshot, Smoothbore, Brass Mounts, Dated 1807, *Antique*	$5,000	$5,500	$2,300
.54 M1805 (06), Singleshot, Smoothbore, Brass Mounts, Dated 1808, *Antique*	5,500	6,500	2,000
.54 M1807-8, Singleshot, Smoothbore, Brass Mounts, Various Contractors, *Antique*	6,500	7,500	3,500
.54 M1816, Singleshot, Smoothbore, S North Army, Brass Furniture, *Antique*	1,250	1,500	750
.54 M1819, Singleshot, Smoothbore, S North Army, Iron Mounts, *Antique*	1,500	1,750	·975
.54 M1826, Singleshot, Smoothbore, S North Army, Iron Mounts, *Antique*	3,000	3,500	1,250
.54 M1836, Singleshot, Smoothbore R Johnson Army, Iron Mounts, *Antique*	1,000	1,200	840
.64 M1808, Singleshot, Smoothbore, S North Army, Brass Furniture, *Antique*	5,750	6,500	1,850
.69 M1799, Singleshot, North & Cheney, Brass Furniture, Brass Frame, *Antique*	25,000	30,000	18,000
.69 M1811, Singleshot, Smoothbore, S North Army, Brass Furniture, *Antique*	4,000	4,500	2,200
.69 M1817 (18), Singleshot, Smoothbore, Springfield, Iron Mounts, *Antique*	6,750	7,500	2,550

HANDGUN, PERCUSSION

	V.G.	Exc.	Prior Edition Exc. Value
.54 M1836, Singleshot, Smoothbore, Gedney Conversion from Flintlock, Iron Mounts, *Antique*	1,250	1,500	995
.54 M1842 Aston, Singleshot, Smoothbore, Brass Mounts, *Antique*	850	950	575
.54 M1842 Johnson, Singleshot, Smoothbore, Brass Mounts, *Antique*	800	900	575
.54 M1843 Deringer Army, Singleshot, Smoothbore, Brass Mounts, *Antique*	1,000	1,200	750
.54 M1843 Deringer Army, Singleshot, Rifled, Brass Mounts, *Antique*	1,500	1,750	995
.54 M1843 Deringer Navy, Singleshot, Smoothbore, Brass Mounts, *Antique*	1,250	1,500	875

HANDGUN, SINGLESHOT

	V.G.	Exc.	Prior Edition Exc. Value
Liberator, .45 ACP, Military, *Curio*	550	600	200

RIFLE, BOLT ACTION

	V.G.	Exc.	Prior Edition Exc. Value
M1871 Ward-Burton, .50 C.F., Iron Mountings, Rifle, *Antique*	1,750	2,000	835
M1871 Ward-Burton, .50 C.F., Iron Mountings, Carbine, *Antique*	2,000	2,500	975
M1882 Chaffee-Reese, 45–70, Rifle, *Antique*	1,250	1,500	825
M1892/6 Krag, .30–40 Krag, Rifle, *Antique*	475	550	375
M1895 Lee Straight Pull, 6mm Lee Navy, Musket, *Antique*	1,000	1,200	800
M1896 Krag, .30–40 Krag, Rifle, *Antique*	500	650	400
M1896 Krag, .30–40 Krag, Cadet, *Antique*	12,500	15,000	2,000

	V.G.	Exc.	Prior Edition Exc. Value
M1896 Krag, .30–40 Krag, Carbine, *Antique*	$850	$1,000	$550
M1898 Krag, .30–40 Krag, Carbine, *Curio*	1,300	1,450	775
M1898 Krag, .30–40 Krag, Rifle, *Curio*	400	450	350
M1899 Krag, .30–40 Krag, Carbine, *Curio*	600	700	400
M1903, .30–06 Springfield, Machined Parts, *Modern*	675	750	325
M1903/5, 30–03 Springfield, *Curio*	5,000	6,000	1,100
M1903/5, 30–06 Springfield, *Curio*	1,500	2,000	350
M1903/7, 30–06 Springfield, Early Receivers, *Curio*	1,250	1,500	600
M1903/WWI, 30–06 Springfield, *Curio*	750	1,000	450
M1903/Postwar, 30–06 Springfield, *Curio*	1,000	1,250	375
M1903 National Match, .30–06 Springfield, Target Rifle, *Curio*	2,000	2,500	725
M1903A1, .30–06 Springfield, Parkerized, Checkered Butt, Machined Parts, *Curio*	1,250	1,500	270
M1903A1 National Match, .30–06 Springfield, Target Rifle, *Curio*	1,750	2,000	675
M1903A3, .30–06 Springfield, Stamped Parts, *Curio*	500	550	240
M1903A4 Sniper, .30–06 Springfield, Scope Mounts, *Curio*	3,000	3,500	995
M1917 Eddystone, .30–06 Springfield, *Curio*	500	550	220
M1917 Remington, .30–06 Springfield, *Curio*	525	575	235
M1917 Winchester, .30–06 Springfield, *Curio*	550	600	250
M1922 Trainer, .22 L.R.R.F., Target Rifle, *Curio*	2,000	2,500	975
M1922M2 Trainer, .22 L.R.R.F., Target Rifle, *Curio*	750	1,000	595

RIFLE, FLINTLOCK

	V.G.	Exc.	Prior Edition Exc. Value
.52, M1819 Hall, Rifled, Breech Loader, 32½" Barrel, 3 Bands, *Antique*	4,500	5,000	2,650
.52, M1819 Hall Whitney, Rifled, Breech Loader, 32½" Barrel, 3 Bands, *Antique*	3,500	4,000	2,550
.54, M1803 Harper's Ferry, Rifled, 32½" Barrel, *Antique*	5,500	6,500	2,300
.54, M1807 Springfield, Indian, Carbine, 27¾" Barrel, *Antique*	10,000	12,000	2,300
.54, M1814 Ghriskey, Rifled, 36" Barrel, *Antique*	3,000	3,500	2,500

RIFLE, PERCUSSION

	V.G.	Exc.	Prior Edition Exc. Value
.57, M1841 U.S., Cadet Musket, 40" Barrel, 2 Bands, *Antique*	8,000	9,000	1,150
.57, M1851 U.S., Cadet Musket, Rifled, 40" Barrel, 2 Bands, *Antique*	1,000	1,200	1,200
.57, M1851 U.S., Cadet Musket, Smoothbore, 40" Barrel, 2 Bands, *Antique*	950	1,100	1,100
.58 Lindner, Breech Loader, Carbine, Rising Block, *Antique*	1,500	1,750	1,150
.58, M1841 Contract, Rifled, 33" Barrel, 2 Bands, (Mississippi Rifle), *Antique*	2,000	2,500	965
.58, M1855 U.S., Rifled, 40" Barrel, 3 Bands, with Tape Priming System, *Antique*	2,500	3,000	1,500
.58, M1855 U.S., Carbine, Rifled, 22" Barrel, 1 Band, with Tape Priming System, *Antique*	7,000	7,500	1,700

	V.G.	Exc.	Prior Edition Exc. Value
.64, M1833 Hall-North, Rifled, Breech Loader, Carbine, 26¹/₈" Barrel, 2 Bands, *Antique*	$2,500	$3,000	$1,475
.69, M1842 U.S., Musket, 42" Barrel, 3 Bands, *Antique*	1,250	1,500	765
.69, M1842 U.S., Rifled, Musket, 42" Barrel, 3 Bands, *Antique*	1,000	1,250	800
.69, M1847 Artillery, Musketoon, 26" Barrel, 2 Bands, Steel Furniture, *Antique*	2,500	3,000	950
.69, M1847 Cavalry, Musketoon, 26" Barrel, 2 Bands, Brass Furniture, *Antique*	2,000	2,500	800
.69, M1847 Sappers, Musketoon, 26" Barrel, 2 Bands, Bayonet Stud on Right Side, *Antique*	3,000	3,500	1,400
M 1864 Training Rifle, Military, Wood Barrel, *Antique*	200	250	135

RIFLE, SEMI-AUTOMATIC

	V.G.	Exc.	Prior Edition Exc. Value
M1941 Johnson, 30–06 Springfield, Military, *Curio*	775	850	500
M-1 Carbine Inland, .30 Carbine, Clip Fed, *Curio*	525	600	300
M-1 Carbine Nat. Postal Meter, .30 Carbine, Clip Fed, *Curio*	600	650	725
M-1 Carbine Rockola, .30 Carbine, Clip Fed, *Curio*	750	850	1,550
M-1 Carbine Underwood, .30 Carbine, Clip Fed, *Curio*	550	600	1,600
M-1 Carbine Irwin-Pedersen, .30 Carbine, Clip Fed, *Curio*	1,000	1,200	725
M-1 Carbine IBM, .30 Carbine, Clip Fed, *Curio*	625	700	725
M-1 Carbine Quality Hdw., .30 Carbine, Clip Fed, *Curio*	550	600	835
M-1 Carbine Winchester, .30 Carbine, Clip Fed, *Curio*	800	850	385
M-1 Garand, .30–06 Springfield, Military, *Curio*	725	800	850
M-1 Garand National Match, .30–06 Springfield, Military, Target Sights, Target Trigger, Target Barrel, *Curio*	1,000	1,200	1,050
M-1 Garand Winchester, .30–06 Springfield, *Curio*	1,000	1,250	950
M-180, .22 L.R.R.F., Carbine, 177 Round Drum Magazine, *Modern*	450	500	325
M-1A1 Carbine, .30 Carbine, Clip Fed, Folding Stock, *Modern*	600	650	500

U.S. REVOLVER CO.
MADE BY IVER JOHNSON

	V.G.	Exc.	Prior Edition Exc. Value
.32 S & W, 5 Shot, Double Action, Solid Frame, *Modern*	75	100	85
.32 S & W, 5 Shot, Top Break, Hammerless, Double Action, *Modern*	75	100	95
.32 S & W, 5 Shot, Double Action, Top Break, *Modern*	75	100	95
.32 Short R.F., 5 Shot, Spur Trigger, Solid Frame, Single Action, *Antique*	150	175	165
.38 S & W, 5 Shot, Double Action, Solid Frame, *Modern*	50	75	75
.38 S & W, 5 Shot, Top Break, Hammerless, Double Action, *Modern*	75	100	100
.38 S & W, 5 Shot, Double Action, Top Break, *Modern*	75	100	100

V

	V.G.	Exc.	Prior Edition Exc. Value

VALIANT Made by Stevens Arms for Spear & Co., Pittsburgh, Pa.

RIFLE, BOLT ACTION

	V.G.	Exc.	Prior Ed.
Model 51, .22 L.R.R.F., Singleshot, Takedown, *Modern*	$25	$50	$45

VALMET Valmet Oy, Tourula Works, Jyvaskyla, Finland.

RIFLE, SEMI-AUTOMATIC

	V.G.	Exc.	Prior Ed.
M78 HV, .223 Rem., Clip Fed, Bipod, *Modern*	1,000	1,200	1,100
M78 Standard, .308 Win., Clip Fed, Bipod, *Modern*	1,000	1,200	1,100
M-62S, 7.62 × 39 Russian, Clip Fed, AK-47 Type, Sporting Version of Military Rifle, *Modern*	800	850	795
M-72S, .223 Rem., Clip Fed, AK-47 Type, Sporting Version of Military Rifle, *Modern*	700	750	700

VALOR ARMS Importers Miami, Fla.

HANDGUN, REVOLVER

	V.G.	Exc.	Prior Ed.
.22 L.R.R.F., Double Action, Lightweight, *Modern*	25	50	25
.32 S & W, Double Action, Lightweight, *Modern*	25	50	25

VANDERFRIFT, ISAAC AND JEREMIAH Philadelphia, Pa. 1809–1815. See Kentucky Rifles and Pistols.

VEGA Sacramento, Calif.

HANDGUN, SEMI-AUTOMATIC

	V.G.	Exc.	Prior Ed.
Vega 1911a1, .45 ACP, Stainless Steel, Clip Fed, *Modern*	300	350	325

VELO DOG Various makers, c. 1900.

HANDGUN, REVOLVER

	V.G.	Exc.	Prior Ed.
5mm Velo Dog, Hammerless, Folding Trigger, *Curio*	75	100	100
5mm Velo Dog, Hammer, Folding Trigger, *Curio*	75	100	95
5mm Velo Dog, Hammerless, Trigger Guard, *Curio*	75	100	95

	V.G.	Exc.	Prior Edition Exc. Value
.25 ACP, Hammerless, Folding Trigger, *Curio*..................................	$100	$125	$110
.25 ACP, Hammer, Folding Trigger, *Curio*.......................................	100	125	110

VENCEDOR San Martin y Cia., Eibar, Spain.
HANDGUN, SEMI-AUTOMATIC
.25 ACP, Clip Fed, Blue, *Modern*.....................................	100	125	125
.35 ACP, Clip Fed, Blue, *Modern*..	125	150	140

VENTURA IMPORTS (CONTENTO) Seal Beach, Calif.
Also see Bertuzzi and Piotti.

SHOTGUN, DOUBLE BARREL, OVER-UNDER
MK-1 Contento, 12 Ga., Field Grade, Automatic Ejector, Single Selective Trigger, Engraved, Checkered Stock, *Modern*....................	850	1,000	465
MK-2 Contento, 12 Ga., Field Grade, Automatic Ejector, Single Selective Trigger, Engraved, Checkered Stock, *Modern*....................	1,100	1,300	675
MK-2 Contento, 12 Ga., Trap Grade, with Extra Single Trap Barrel, Engraved, Checkered Stock, *Modern*	1,400	1,600	1,150
MK-2 Luxe Contento, 12 Ga., Field Grade, Automatic Ejector, Single Selective Trigger, Engraved, Checkered Stock, *Modern*	1,000	1,200	825
MK-2 Luxe Contento, 12 Ga., Trap Grade, with Extra Single Trap Barrel, Engraved, Checkered Stock, *Modern*............................	1,500	1,800	1,350
MK-3 Contento, 12 Ga., Field Grade, Automatic Ejector, Single Selective Trigger, Engraved, Checkered Stock, *Modern*....................	1,250	1,500	1,050
MK-3 Contento, 12 Ga., Trap Grade, with Extra Single Trap Barrel, Engraved, Checkered Stock, *Modern*	2,000	2,500	1,750
MK-3 Luxe Contento, 12 Ga., Field Grade, Automatic Ejector, Single Selective Trigger, Engraved, Checkered Stock, *Modern*	1,500	1,800	1,350
MK-3 Luxe Contento, 12 Ga., Trap Grade, with Extra Single Trap Barrel, Engraved, Checkered Stock, *Modern*	2,500	3,000	2,100
Nettuno Contento, 12 Ga., Field Grade, Automatic Ejector, Single Selective Trigger, Engraved, Checkered Stock, *Modern*....................	400	450	395

SHOTGUN, DOUBLE BARREL, SIDE-BY-SIDE
Ventura Model 51, 12 and 20 Gauges, Boxlock, Checkered Stock, *Modern*..	350	400	395
Ventura Model 62 Standard, 12 and 20 Gauges, Sidelock, Checkered Stock, Engraved, *Modern*	800	900	725
Ventura Model 64 Standard, 12 and 20 Gauges, Sidelock, Checkered Stock, Engraved, *Modern*	775	850	725

VENUS Tomas de Urizar y Cia., Eibar, Spain.
HANDGUN, SEMI-AUTOMATIC
.32 ACP, Clip Fed, *Modern*...	100	150	135

	V.G.	Exc.	Prior Edition Exc. Value

VENUS Venus Waffenwerk Oskar Will, Zella Mehlis, Germany, c. 1912.
HANDGUN, SEMI-AUTOMATIC
.32 ACP, Target Pistol, Hammerless, Blue, *Curio* .... *$500* | *$600* | *$565*

VERNEY-CARRON St. Etienne, France.
HANDGUN, SEMI-AUTOMATIC
.25 ACP, Clip Fed, Blue, *Modern* .... *150* | *175* | *165*
SHOTGUN, DOUBLE BARREL, OVER-UNDER
Field Grade, 12 Ga., Automatic Ejectors, Checkered Stock,
Engraved, *Modern* .... *800* | *950* | *695*

VESTA Hijos de A. Echeverra, Eibar, Spain.
HANDGUN, SEMI-AUTOMATIC
Pocket, .32 ACP, Clip Fed, Long Grip, *Modern* .... *125* | *150* | *130*
Vest Pocket, .25 ACP, Clip Fed, *Modern* .... *100* | *125* | *125*

VETERAN Made by Norwich Falls Pistol Co., c. 1880.
HANDGUN, REVOLVER
.32 Short R.F., 5 Shot, Spur Trigger, Solid Frame, Single Action,
Antique .... *125* | *175* | *165*

VETO Unknown maker, c. 1880.
HANDGUN, REVOLVER
.32 Short R.F., 5 Shot, Spur Trigger, Solid Frame, Single Action,
Antique .... *150* | *175* | *165*

Vesta

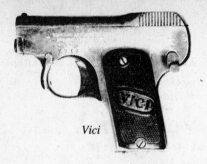

Vici

	V.G.	Exc.	Prior Edition Exc. Value

VICI Unknown Belgian maker.

HANDGUN, SEMI-AUTOMATIC

	V.G.	Exc.	Prior Edition Exc. Value
.25 ACP, Clip Fed, *Modern*	$100	$125	$130

VICTOR Made by Crescent, c. 1900.

SHOTGUN, DOUBLE BARREL, SIDE-BY-SIDE

	V.G.	Exc.	Prior Edition Exc. Value
Various Gauges, Outside Hammers, Damascus Barrel, *Modern*	150	175	170
Various Gauges, Hammerless, Steel Barrel, *Modern*	175	200	190
Various Gauges, Hammerless, Damascus Barrel, *Modern*	150	175	170
Various Gauges, Outside Hammers, Steel Barrel, *Modern*	150	200	185

SHOTGUN, SINGLESHOT

	V.G.	Exc.	Prior Edition Exc. Value
Various Gauges, Hammer, Steel Barrel, *Modern*	75	100	85

VICTOR Francisco Arizmendi, Eibar, Spain, c. 1916.

HANDGUN, SEMI-AUTOMATIC

	V.G.	Exc.	Prior Edition Exc. Value
.25 ACP, Clip Fed, Blue, *Curio*	100	125	125
.32 ACP, Clip Fed, Blue, *Curio*	125	150	140

VICTOR #1 Made by Harrington & Richardson, c. 1876.

HANDGUN, REVOLVER

	V.G.	Exc.	Prior Edition Exc. Value
.32 S & W, 5 Shot, Single Action, Solid Frame, *Antique*	75	100	95
#1, .22 Short R.F., 7 Shot, Spur Trigger, Solid Frame, Single Action, *Antique*	150	175	165
#2, .32 Short R.F., 5 Shot, Spur Trigger, Solid Frame, Single Action, *Antique*	150	175	165

VICTOR SPECIAL Made by Crescent for Hibbard-Spencer-Bartlett Co., c. 1900.

SHOTGUN, DOUBLE BARREL, SIDE-BY-SIDE

	V.G.	Exc.	Prior Edition Exc. Value
Various Gauges, Hammerless, Damascus Barrel, *Modern*	150	175	170
Various Gauges, Outside Hammers, Steel Barrel, *Modern*	150	200	185

	V.G.	Exc.	Prior Edition Exc. Value

SHOTGUN, SINGLESHOT
Various Gauges, Hammer, Steel Barrel, *Modern*.............. $75 $100 $85

VICTORIA Made by Hood Firearms, c. 1875.
HANDGUN, REVOLVER
.32 Short R.F., 5 Shot, Spur Trigger, Solid Frame, Single Action,
Antique 150 175 165

VICTORIA Spain, Esperanza y Unceta, c. 1900.
HANDGUN, SEMI-AUTOMATIC
M1911, .32 ACP, Clip Fed, *Modern* 125 150 145
.25 ACP, Clip Fed, *Modern*.............. 100 125 125

VICTORY M. Zulaica y Cia., Eibar, Spain.
HANDGUN, SEMI-AUTOMATIC
.25 ACP, Clip Fed, *Modern*.............. 100 150 150

VILAR Spain, unknown maker 1920–1938.
HANDGUN, SEMI-AUTOMATIC
Pocket, .32 ACP, Clip Fed, Long Grip, *Modern*.............. 100 125 125

VINCITOR M. Zulaica y Cia., Eibar, Spain.
HANDGUN, SEMI-AUTOMATIC
Model 1914, .25 ACP, Clip Fed, Blue, *Curio*.............. 125 150 150
Model 14 No. 2, .32 ACP, Clip Fed, Blue, *Curio*.............. 150 175 160

VINDEX Mre. d'Armes des Pyrenees, Hendaye, France.
HANDGUN, SEMI-AUTOMATIC
.32 ACP, Clip Fed, Blue, *Modern*.............. 100 125 120

Victoria

	V.G.	Exc.	Prior Edition Exc. Value

VIRGINIA ARMS CO. Made by Crescent for Virginia-Caroline Co., c. 1900.

SHOTGUN, DOUBLE BARREL, SIDE-BY-SIDE

	V.G.	Exc.	Prior Edition Exc. Value
Various Gauges, Outside Hammers, Damascus Barrel, *Modern*	$150	$175	$170
Various Gauges, Hammerless, Steel Barrel, *Modern*......................	175	200	190
Various Gauges, Hammerless, Damascus Barrel, *Modern*	150	175	170
Various Gauges, Outside Hammers, Steel Barrel, *Modern*..............	175	200	185

SHOTGUN, SINGLESHOT

	V.G.	Exc.	Prior Edition Exc. Value
Various Gauges, Hammer, Steel Barrel, *Modern*............................	75	100	85

VIRGINIAN Made by Interarms, Alexandria, Va.

HANDGUN, REVOLVER

	V.G.	Exc.	Prior Edition Exc. Value
Dragoon, Buntline, Various Calibers, Single Action, Western Style, Target Sights, Blue, *Modern*...,	200	250	190
Dragoon, Deputy, Various Calibers, Single Action, Western Style, Fixed Sights, Blue, *Modern*	175	225	180
Dragoon, Deputy, Various Calibers, Single Action, Western Style, Fixed Sights, Stainless Steel, *Modern*......................................	175	225	180
Dragoon, Silhouette, .44 Magnum, Single Action, Western Style, Target Sights, Stainless Steel, *Modern*	225	275	235
Dragoon, Standard, Various Calibers, Single Action, Western Style, Target Sights, Blue, *Modern*......................................	200	250	190
Dragoon, Standard, Various Calibers, Single Action, Western Style, Target Sights, Stainless Steel, *Modern*	200	250	200
Dragoon, Engraved, Various Calibers, Single Action, Western Style, Target Sights, Blue, *Modern*......................................	350	425	360
Dragoon, Engraved, Various Calibers, Single Action, Western Style, Target Sights, Stainless Steel, *Modern*....................................	375	450	385

VOERE Voere GmbH, Vohrenbach, West Germany.

RIFLE, BOLT ACTION

	V.G.	Exc.	Prior Edition Exc. Value
Model 3145 DJV, .223 Rem., Match Rifle, Target Stock, *Modern*..	500	550	465
Model 2145, .308 Win., Match Rifle, Target Stock, *Modern*............	700	800	665
Premier Mauser, Various Calibers, Sporting Rifle, Checkered Stock, Recoil Pad, Open Rear Sight, *Modern*....................................	300	350	200
Shikar, Various Calibers, Sporting Rifle, Fancy Checkering, Fancy Wood, Recoil Pad, no Sights, *Modern*....................................	450	500	385
Titan-Menor, Various Calibers, Sporting Rifle, Checkered Stock, Recoil Pad, Open Rear Sight, *Modern*...	350	400	285

	Prior Edition

	V.G.	Exc.	Exc. Value

VOERE Voere Tiroler Jagd u. Sportwaffenfabrik, Kufstein, Austria.

RIFLE, BOLT ACTION

Model 2155, Various Calibers, Sporting Rifle, Checkered Stock, Open Rear Sight, *Modern* $325 $375 $235

Model 2165/1, Various Calibers, Sporting Rifle, Checkered Stock, Recoil Pad, Open Rear Sight, *Modern* 475 525 425

VITE Echave y Arizmendi, Eibar, Spain, c. 1913.

HANDGUN, SEMI-AUTOMATIC

Model 1912, .25 ACP, Clip Fed, Blue, *Curio* 100 125 125
Model 1915, .32 ACP, Clip Fed, Blue, *Curio* 125 150 130

VOLUNTEER Made by Stevens Arms for Belknap Hardware Co., Louisville, Ky.

SHOTGUN, SINGLESHOT

Model 94, Various Gauges, Takedown, Automatic Ejector, Plain, Hammer, *Modern* 50 75 65

VULCAN ARMS CO. Made by Crescent, c. 1900.

SHOTGUN, DOUBLE BARREL, SIDE-BY-SIDE

Various Gauges, Outside Hammers, Damascus Barrel, *Modern* 150 175 170
Various Gauges, Hammerless, Steel Barrel, *Modern* 175 200 190
Various Gauges, Hammerless, Damascus Barrel, *Modern* 150 175 170
Various Gauges, Outside Hammers, Steel Barrel, *Modern* 175 200 185

SHOTGUN, SINGLESHOT

Various Gauges, Hammer, Steel Barrel, *Modern* 75 100 85

W

	V.G.	Exc.	Prior Edition Exc. Value

WAFFENFABRIK BERN Eidgenosssische Wallenfabrik, Bern, Switzerland. Also see Swiss Military.

RIFLE, BOLT ACTION

	V.G.	Exc.	Prior Edition Exc. Value
Model 31, 7.5mm Swiss, Military Style, *Modern*	$575	$650	$650
Model 31 Target, 7.5mm Swiss, Military Style, Match Rifle, Target Sights, *Modern*	775	850	825

WALDMAN Arizmendi Y Goenaga, Eibar, Spain.

HANDGUN, SEMI-AUTOMATIC

.25 ACP, Clip Fed, *Curio*	100	125	130
.32 ACP, Clip Fed, *Curio*	125	150	145

WALMAN F. Arizmendi Y Goenaga, Eibar, Spain.

HANDGUN, SEMI-AUTOMATIC

.25 ACP, Clip Fed, *Curio*	100	125	130
.32 ACP, Clip Fed, *Curio*	125	150	145
.380 ACP, Clip Fed, *Curio*	175	225	220

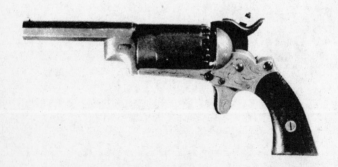

Walsh Pocket .31

	V.G.	Exc.	Prior Edition Exc. Value

WALSH FIREARMS CO. N.Y.C., c. 1860.
HANDGUN, PERCUSSION
Navy, .36, Revolver, 12 Shot, Double-Charge Cylinder, *Antique*	$3,000	$3,500	$2,000
Pocket, .31, Revolver, 12 Shot, Double-Charge Cylinder, *Antique*	1,000	1,250	650

WALSH, JAMES Philadelphia, Pa. 1775–1779. See Kentucky Rifles and Pistols and U.S. Military.

WALTHER First started in 1886 by Carl Walther in Zella Mehlis, Germany. After his death in 1915 the firm was operated by his sons Fritz, George, and Erich, and after WWII moved to Ulm/Donau, West Germany. Also see German Military, Manurhin.

AIRGUNS
	V.G.	Exc.	Prior
Model CP-2 C02, .177 Caliber, Blue, Single Shot, *Modern*	600	650	700
Model LP-3, .177 Caliber, Blue, Single Shot, *Modern*	450	500	400

HANDGUN, SEMI-AUTOMATIC
	V.G.	Exc.	Prior
Model 1, .25 ACP, Blue, *Curio*	400	450	300
Model 2, .25 ACP, Pop-Up Rear Sight, Blue, *Curio*	375	425	725
Model 3, .32 ACP, Blue, *Curio*	1,250	1,500	675
Model 4, .32 ACP, Blue, *Curio*	350	400	230
Model 5, .25 ACP, Solid Rib, Blue, *Curio*	300	350	230
Model 6, 9mm Luger, Blue, *Curio*	4,500	5,000	1,400
Model 7, .25 ACP, Blue, *Curio*	450	500	350
Model 8, .25 ACP, Blue, *Modern*	350	400	275
Model 9, .25 ACP, Blue, *Modern*	375	425	280
Model GSP, .22 L.R.R.F., 5 Shot Clip, Target Pistol, *Modern*	1,250	1,500	675
Model GSP C, .22 Short, 5 Shot Clip, Target Pistol, *Modern*	1,500	1,650	750
Model GSP C, .22 Short, 5 Shot Clip, Target Pistol, with .22 L.R. Converstion Kit, *Modern*	2,500	3,000	1,300
Model HP, .30 Luger, Single Action, *Modern*	4,000	5,000	5,000
Model HP, .30 Luger, Single Action, Wood Grips, *Modern*	5,000	5,500	5,500
Model HP, Commercial Finish, 9mm Luger, Double Action, Lightweight, *Modern*	3,500	4,000	3,650
Olympia Rapid Fire, .22 L.R.R.F., Target Pistol, *Modern*	750	900	750
Olympia Sport, .22 L.R.R.F., Target Pistol, *Modern*	800	850	625
Model OSP, .22 Short, Blue, Five Rounds Capacity, *Modern*	1,500	1,800	1,050
P .38, 9mm Luger, Double Action, Military, *Modern*	675	750	525
P .38 (Current), .22 L.R.R.F., Double Action, *Modern*	775	850	525
P-38 (Current), .30 Luger, Double Action, Blue, *Modern*	500	550	475
P .38 (Current), 9mm Luger, Double Action, *Modern*	550	600	450
P. 38 "480", 9mm Luger, Double Action, Military, *Curio*	1,450	1,600	650

	V.G.	Exc.	Prior Edition Exc. Value
P. 38 1st, Model Zero Series, 9mm Luger, Double Action, *Modern*	$2,750	$3,250	$1,400
P .38 2nd, Model Zero Series, 9mm Luger, Double Action, Military, *Curio*	2,000	2,500	950
P .38 3rd, Model Zero Series, 9mm Luger, Double Action, Military, *Curio*	1,400	1,600	630
P .38 ac No Date, 9mm Luger, Double Action, Military, *Curio*	850	1,000	775
P .38 ac-45 Zero Series, 9mm Luger, Double Action, Military, *Curio*	450	500	450
P .38 ac-40, 9mm Luger, Double Action, Military, *Curio*	525	600	490
P .38 ac-41, 9mm Luger, Double Action, Military, *Curio*	525	600	480
P .38 ac-41 Military Finish, 9mm Luger, Double Action, Military, *Curio*	500	550	360
P .38 ac-42, 9mm Luger, Double Action, Military, *Curio*	450	500	295
P .38 ac-43 Double Line, 9mm Luger, Double Action, Military, *Modern*	450	500	425
P .38 ac-43 Police, 9mm Luger, Double Action, Military, *Modern*	1,000	1,200	1,100
P .38 ac-43 Single Line, 9mm Luger, Double Action, Military, *Curio*	350	400	300
P .38 ac-43 WaA 135, 9mm Luger, Double Action, Military, *Curio*	375	425	310
P .38 ac-44, 9mm Luger, Double Action, Military, *Curio*	325	375	290
P .38 ac-44 Police, 9mm Luger, Double Action, Military, *Curio*	675	750	800
P .38 ac-44 WaA140, 9mm Luger, Double Action, Military, *Curio*	425	475	385
P .38 ac-45, 9mm Luger, Double Action, Military, *Curio*	425	475	305
P .38 ac-45 Mismatch, 9mm Luger, Double Action, Military, *Curio*	375	425	315
P .38 byf-42, 9mm Luger, Double Action, Military, *Curio*	400	450	400
P .38 byf-43, 9mm Luger, Double Action, Military, *Curio*	400	450	320
P .38 byf-43 Police, 9mm Luger, Double Action, Military, *Modern*	675	750	770
P .38 byf-44, 9mm Luger, Double Action, Military, *Curio*	400	450	340
P .38 byf-44 Police F Dual T, 9mm Luger, Double Action, Military, *Modern*	775	850	850
P .38 byf-44 Police L Dual T, 9mm Luger, Double Action, Military, *Modern*	1,250	1,500	1,500
P .38 byf-44 Police L, 9mm Luger, Double Action, Military, *Modern*	850	1,000	1,000
P .38 cyq, 9mm Luger, Double Action, Military, *Curio*	325	375	320
P .38 cyq 1945, 9mm Luger, Double Action, Military, *Curio*	350	400	375
P .38 cyq Zero Series, 9mm Luger, Double Action, Military, *Curio*	625	700	360
P .38 svw-45, 9mm Luger, Double Action, Military, *Curio*	325	350	305

	V.G.	Exc.	Prior Edition Exc. Value
P .38 svw-45 French, 9mm Luger, Double Action, Military, *Modern*	$600	$650	$620
P .38 svw-45 Police, 9mm Luger, Double Action, Military, *Modern*	1,250	1,500	1,300
P .38 svw-46, 9mm Luger, Double Action, Military, *Modern*	675	750	750
P .38k, 9mm Luger, Double Action, Short Barrel, *Modern*	550	600	475
P .38-IV (P .4), 9mm Luger, Double Action, *Modern*	550	600	475
P .5, 9mm Luger, Interarms, Double Action, Blue, *Modern*	775	800	700
PP, .22 L.R.R.F., Double Action, Pre-War, Commercial, Nickel Plated, *Curio*		RARE	
PP, .22 L.R.R.F., Double Action, Pre-War, Commercial, Nickel Plated, Nazi-Proofed, *Curio*		RARE	
PP, .22 L.R.R.F., Double Action, Pre-War, Commercial, High-Polish Finish, *Modern*	750	850	400
PP, .22 L.R.R.F., Double Action, Pre-War, Commercial, High-Polish Finish, Nazi-Proofed, *Modern*	725	800	410
PP, .22 L.R.R.F., Double Action, Lightweight, *Modern*	850	1,000	500
PP, .25 ACP, Double Action, Pre-War, Commercial, High-Polish Finish, *Curio*	3,000	3,250	1,175
PP, .32 ACP, Double Action, Pre-War, Commercial, Lightweight, High-Polish Finish, *Curio*	500	550	510
PP, .32 ACP, Double Action, Pre-War, Nazi-Proofed, Lightweight, High-Polish Finish, *Curio*	475	525	510
PP, .32 ACP, Double Action, Pre-War, Nazi-Proofed, Lightweight, *Curio*	400	450	400
PP, .32 ACP, Double Action, Pre-War, Commercial, Nickel Plated, *Curio*		RARE	
PP, .32 ACP, Double Action, Pre-War, Commercial, Nickel Plated, Nazi-Proofed, *Curio*		RARE	
PP, .32 ACP, Double Action, Pre-War, Commercial, High-Polish Finish, *Modern*	375	400	320
PP, .32 ACP, Double Action, Pre-War, Commercial, High-Polish Finish, Nazi-Proofed, *Modern*	375	400	335
PP, .32 ACP, Double Action, Pre-War, Commercial, Nazi-Proofed, *Modern*	325	375	340
PP, .32 ACP Double Action, Lightweight, *Curio*	400	450	430
PP, .380 ACP, Double Action, Pre-War, Commercial, High-Polish Finish, *Modern*	775	850	440
PP, .380 ACP, Double Action, Pre-War, Commercial, High-Polish Finish, Nazi-Proofed, *Modern*	800	875	450
PP, .380 ACP, Double Action, Pre-War, Commercial, Nickel Plated, *Curio*		RARE	
PP, .380 ACP, Double Action, Pre-War, Commercial, Nickel Plated, Nazi-Proofed, *Curio*		RARE	
PP "Nairobi", .32 ACP, Double Action, Pre-War, High-Polish Finish, *Curio*	1,250	1,500	700
PP (Current), .22 L.R.R.F., Double Action, *Modern*	425	475	415

	V.G.	Exc.	Prior Edition Exc. Value
PP (Current), .32 ACP, Double Action, Blue, *Modern*	$375	$425	$385
PP (Current), .380 ACP, Double Action, Blue, *Modern*	400	450	410
PP (Early) 90 Degree Safety, .32 ACP, Double Action, Pre-War, Commercial, High-Polish Finish, *Modern*	700	775	410
PP (Early) Bottom Magazine Release, .380 ACP, Double Action, Pre-War, Commercial, High-Polish Finish, *Curio*	775	850	1,175
PP AC, .32 ACP, Double Action, Nazi-Proofed, *Modern*	275	300	675
PP AC Police F, .32 ACP, Double Action, Pre-War, Nazi-Proofed, *Curio*	700	775	380
PP AC Waffenamt, .32 ACP, Double Action, Pre-War, Nazi-Proofed, *Curio*	300	350	400
PP Bottom Magazine Release, .32 ACP, Double Action, Pre-War, Commercial, High-Polish Finish, *Curio*	775	850	480
PP Bottom Magazine Release, .32 ACP, Double Action, Pre-War, Commercial, High-Polish Finish, Lightweight, *Curio*	850	950	480
PP Czech, .32 ACP, Double Action, Pre-War, Commercial, High-Polish Finish, *Curio*	800	900	700
PP Mark II "Manurhin", .22 L.R.R.F., Double Action, High-Polish Finish, Blue, *Curio*	350	425	435
PP Mark II "Manurhin", .32 ACP, Double Action, High-Polish Finish, Blue, *Curio*	300	375	365
PP Mark II "Manurhin", .380 ACP, Double Action, High-Polish Finish, Blue, *Curio*	300	400	390
PP NSKK, .32 ACP, Double Action, Pre-War, High-Polish Finish, Nazi-Proofed, *Curio*	1,500	2,000	950
PP PDM, .32 ACP, Double Action, Pre-War, High-Polish Finish, *Curio*	650	800	495
PP Persian, .380 ACP, Double Action, Pre-War, Commercial, High-Polish Finish, *Curio*	1,500	1,750	1,700
PP Police C, .32 ACP, Double Action, Pre-War, High-Polish Finish, Nazi-Proofed, *Curio*	750	900	440
PP Police C, .32 ACP, Double Action, Pre-War, Nazi-Proofed, *Curio*	725	800	365
PP Police F, .32 ACP, Double Action, Pre-War, Nazi-Proofed, *Curio*	600	650	330
PP RFV, .32 ACP, Double Action, Pre-War, High-Polish, *Curio*	600	650	520
PP RJ, .32 ACP, Double Action, Pre-War, High-Polish Finish, *Curio*	650	700	470
PP SA, .32 ACP, Double Action, Pre-War, High-Polish Finish, *Curio*	1,250	1,500	620
PP Stoeger, .32 ACP, Double Action, Pre-War, High-Polish Finish, *Curio*	1,250	1,500	510
PP Super, 9 × 18mm, Clip Fed, Blue, *Modern*	450	500	475
PP Verchromt, .32 ACP, Double Action, Pre-War, Commercial, *Curio*	1,250	1,500	675
PP Verchromt, .380 ACP, Double Action, Pre-War, Commercial, *Curio*	1,500	2,000	725

	V.G.	Exc.	Prior Edition Exc. Value
PP with Lanyard Loop, .32 ACP, Double Action, Pre-War, Commercial, High-Polish Finish, Nazi-Proofed, *Modern*	$450	$500	$465
PP Waffenamt, .32 ACP, Double Action, Pre-War, High-Polish Finish, Nazi-Proofed, *Curio*	450	500	380
PP Waffenamt, .32 ACP, Double Action, Pre-War, Nazi-Proofed, *Curio*	400	450	360
PP Waffenamt, .380 ACP, Double Action, Pre-War, High-Polish Finish, Nazi-Proofed, *Curio*	675	750	535
PPK, .22 L.R.R.F., Double Action, Pre-War, Commercial, High-Polish Finish, *Modern*	850	1,000	470
PPK, .22 L.R.R.F., Double Action, Pre-War, Commercial, High-Polish Finish, Nazi-Proofed, *Modern*	900	1,050	515
PPK, .22 L.R.R.F., Double Action, Post-War, *Modern*	625	700	395
PPK, .22 L.R.R.F., Double Action, Lightweight, Post-War, *Modern*	425	475	565
PPK, .25 ACP, Double Action, Pre-War, Commercial, High-Polish Finish, *Curio*	4,500	5,500	1,475
PPK, .32 ACP, Double Action, Pre-War, Commercial, Lightweight, High-Polish Finish, *Curio*	550	600	540
PPK, .32 ACP, Double Action, Pre-War, Nazi-Proofed, Lightweight, High-Polish Finish, *Curio*	500	550	540
PPK, .32 ACP, Double Action, Pre-War, Nazi-Proofed, Lightweight, *Curio*	550	600	415
PPK, .32 ACP, Double Action, Pre-War, Commercial, High-Polish Finish, *Modern*	475	525	390
PPK, .32 ACP, Double Action, Pre-War, Commercial, High-Polish Finish, Nazi-Proofed, *Modern*	450	500	415
PPK, .32 ACP, Double Action, Pre-War, Commercial, Nazi-Proofed, *Modern*	400	450	375
PPK, .32 ACP, Double Action, Post-War, *Modern*	400	450	325
PPK, .32 ACP, Double Action, Lightweight, Post-War, *Modern*	350	400	575
PPK, .380 ACP, Double Action, Pre-War, Commercial, Nickel Plated, *Curio*	1,750	2,000	1,000
PPK, .380 ACP, Double Action, Pre-War, Commercial, Nickel Plated, Nazi-Proofed, *Curio*	1,250	1,500	1,250
PPK, .380 ACP, Double Action, Pre-War, Commercial, High-Polish Finish, *Modern*	1,600	1,800	720
PPK, .380 ACP, Double Action, Pre-War, Commercial, High-Polish Finish, Nazi-Proofed, *Modern*	900	1,000	925
PPK, .380 ACP, Double Action, Post-War, *Modern*	550	600	485
PPK "Nairobi", .32 ACP, Double Action, Pre-War, High-Polish Finish, *Curio*	1,250	1,500	815
PPK (Early) 90 Degree Safety, .32 ACP, Double Action, Pre-War, Commercial, High-Polish Finish, *Modern*	550	600	410
PPK (Early) Bottom Magazine Release, .32 ACP, Double Action, Pre-War, Commercial, High-Polish Finish, *Curio*	675	750	1,150

	V.G.	Exc.	Prior Edition Exc. Value
PPK Czech, .32 ACP, Double Action, Pre-War, Commercial, High-Polish Finish, *Curio*	$775	$900	$950
PPK DRP, .32 ACP, Double Action, Pre-War, High-Polish Finish, *Curio*	750	800	590
PPK Mark II "Manurhin", .22 L.R.R.F., Double Action, High-Polish Finish, Blue, *Curio*	450	500	620
PPK Mark II "Manurhin", .22 L.R.R.F., Double Action, High-Polish Finish, Blue, Lightweight, *Curio*	500	550	715
PPK Mark II "Manurhin", .32 ACP, Double Action, High-Polish Finish, Blue, *Curio*	350	400	530
PPK Mark II "Manurhin", .32 ACP, Double Action, High-Polish Finish, Blue, Lightweight, *Curio*	400	450	650
PPK Mark II "Manurhin, .380 ACP, Double Action, High-Polish Finish, Blue, *Curio*	400	450	625
PPK Party Leader, .32 ACP, Double Action, Pre-War, High-Polish Finish, *Curio*	1,750	2,250	1,375
PPK PDM, .32 ACP, Double Action, Pre-War, High-Polish Finish, Lightweight, *Curio*	850	950	975
PPK Police C, .32 ACP, Double Action, Pre-War, High-Polish Finish, Nazi-Proofed, *Curio*	675	750	490
PPK Police C, .32 ACP, Double Action, Pre-War, Nazi-Proofed, *Curio*	550	600	450
PPK Police F, .32 ACP, Double Action, Pre-War, Nazi-Proofed, *Curio*	675	750	430
PPK RFV, .32 ACP, Double Action, Pre-War, High-Polish Finish, *Curio*	850	950	680
PPK RZM, .32 ACP, Double Action, Pre-War, High-Polish Finish, *Curio*	775	850	565
PPK Stoeger, .32 ACP, Double Action, Pre-War, High-Polish Finish, *Curio*	950	1,100	650
PPK Verchromt, .32 ACP, Double Action, Pre-War, Commercial, *Curio*	1,650	1,800	825
PPK Verchromt, .380 ACP, Double Action, Pre-War, Commercial, *Curio*	2,000	2,250	1,085
PPK Waffenamt, .32 ACP, Double Action, Pre-War, High-Polish Finish, Nazi-Proofed, *Curio*	725	800	585
PPK Waffenamt, .32 ACP, Double Action, Pre-War, Nazi-Proofed, *Curio*	700	750	465
PPKS (Current), .22 L.R.R.F., Double Action, *Modern*	550	600	365
PPKS (Current), .32 ACP, Double Action, Blue, *Modern*	425	475	410
PPKS (Current), .380 ACP, Double Action, Blue, *Modern*	500	550	410
TPH, .22 L.R.R.F., Double Action, Clip Fed, *Modern*	500	550	475
PPK/S Double Action, .380 ACP, Stainless Steel, Seven Rounds Capacity, *Modern*	400	450	515
PPK/S Double Action, .380 ACP, Blue, Seven Rounds Capacity, *Modern*	400	450	470

	V.G.	Exc.	Prior Edition Exc. Value

RIFLE, BOLT ACTION

Model B, Various Calibers, Checkered Stock, Mauser Action, Set Triggers, *Modern* ... $400 — $450 — $350

GX-1 Match, .22 L.R.R.F., Singleshot, Target Stock, with Accessories, *Modern* ... 1,250 — 1,500 — 900

KKJ, .22 Hornet, 5 Shot Clip, Open Rear Sight, Checkered Stock, *Modern* ... 675 — 750 — 450

KKJ, .22 Hornet, 5 Shot Clip, Open Rear Sight, Checkered Stock, Set Trigger, *Modern* ... 700 — 775 — 465

KKJ, .22 L.R.R.F., 5 Shot Clip, Open Rear Sight, Checkered Stock, *Modern* ... 500 — 550 — 385

KKJ, .22 L.R.R.F., 5 Shot Clip, Open Rear Sight, Checkered Stock, Set Trigger, *Modern* ... 500 — 575 — 495

KKJ, .22 WMR, 5 Shot Clip, Open Rear Sight, Checkered Stock, *Modern* ... 500 — 550 — 375

KKJ, .22 WMR, 5 Shot Clip, Open Rear Sight, Checkered Stock, Set Trigger, *Modern* ... 525 — 575 — 400

KKM International Match, .22 L.R.R.F., Singleshot, Target Stock, with Accessories, *Modern* ... 800 — 900 — 695

Model GX-1, .22 L.R., Singleshot, Blue, *Modern* ... 1,750 — 2,000 — 1,200

KKM-S Silhouette, .22 L.R., Singleshot, Blue, *Modern* ... 875 — 950 — 725

Model KKW, .22 L.R.R.F., Pre-WW2, Singleshot, Tangent Sights, Military Style Stock, *Modern* ... 500 — 550 — 460

Model LGR, .177 Caliber, Singleshot, Blue, *Modern* ... 675 — 725 — 650

Model LGR Match, .177 Caliber, Singleshot, Blue, *Modern* ... 725 — 800 — 725

Model LGR Running Boar, .177 Caliber, Singleshot, Blue, *Modern* ... 800 — 900 — 675

Running Boar, .22 L.R., Singleshot, Blue, *Modern* ... 825 — 825 — 775

U.I.T.-E. Universal Match, .22 L.R., Singleshot, Blue, *Modern* ... 1,250 — 1,500 — 1,200

Model V, Singleshot, Sporting Rifle, Open Rear Sight, *Modern* ... 325 — 375 — 365

Model V "Meisterbushse", Singleshot, Pistol-Grip Stock, Target Sights, *Modern* ... 350 — 400 — 385

Moving Target, .22 L.R.R.F., Singleshot, Target Stock, with Accessories, *Modern* ... 700 — 750 — 690

Olympic, .22 L.R.R.F., Singleshot, Target Stock, with Accessories, *Modern* ... 850 — 950 — 565

Prone "400", .22 L.R.R.F., Singleshot, Target Stock, with Accessories, *Modern* ... 575 — 650 — 485

UIT Match, .22 L.R.R.F., Singleshot, Target Stock, with Accessories, *Modern* ... 850 — 1,000 — 750

UIT Super, .22 L.R.R.F., Singleshot, Target Stock, with Accessories, *Modern* ... 750 — 900 — 665

RIFLE, SEMI-AUTOMATIC

Model 1, Clip Fed, Carbine, *Modern* ... 325 — 375 — 285

Model 2, .22 L.R.R.F., Clip Fed, *Modern* ... 425 — 475 — 285

	V.G.	Exc.	Prior Edition Exc. Value

SHOTGUN, DOUBLE BARREL, SIDE-BY-SIDE

	V.G.	Exc.	Prior Edition Exc. Value
Model S.F., 12 or 16 Gauges, Checkered Stock, Cheekpiece, Double Triggers, Sling Swivels, *Modern*	$425	$475	$400
Model S.F.D., 12 or 16 Gauges, Checkered Stock, Cheekpiece, Double Triggers, Sling Swivels, *Modern*	550	600	500

WAMO Wamo Mfg. Co., San Gabriel, Calif.

HANDGUN, SINGLESHOT

	V.G.	Exc.	Prior
Powermaster, .22 L.R.R.F., Target Pistol, *Modern*	100	125	120

WARNANT L. & J. Warnant Freres, Hognee, Belgium.

HANDGUN, SEMI-AUTOMATIC

.25 ACP, Clip Fed, Blue, *Curio*	175	225	200

HANDGUN, REVOLVER

.32 S & W, Double Action, Folding Trigger, Break Top, *Curio*	75	100	85
.38 S & W, Double Action, Folding Trigger, Break Top, *Curio*	75	100	85

HANDGUN, SINGLESHOT

Traff, 6mm R.F., Spur Trigger, Parlor Pistol, *Curio*	50	75	55
Traff, 9mm R.F., Spur Trigger, Parlor Pistol, *Curio*	50	75	60

RIFLE, SINGLESHOT

Amelung, Various Rimfires, Plain, Parlor Rifle, *Curio*	50	75	50
Amelung, Various Rimfires, Checkered Stock, Set Triggers, Parlor Rifle, *Curio*	75	100	85

WARNER Warner Arms Corp., Brooklyn, N.Y., formed about 1912, moved to Norwich, Mass. in 1913, and in 1917 merged and became Davis-Warner Arms Corp., Assonet, Mass., out of business about 1919. Also see Schwarzlose.

SEMI-AUTOMATIC

Revolver, .32 CAL., 5-Shot, *Modern*	125	150	215
Infallable, .32 ACP, Clip Fed, *Modern*	275	325	235

WARREN ARMS CORP. Belgium, c. 1900.

SHOTGUN, DOUBLE BARREL, SIDE-BY-SIDE

Various Gauges, Outside Hammers, Damascus Barrel, *Modern*	150	175	170
Various Gauges, Hammerless, Steel Barrel, *Modern*	175	200	190
Various Gauges, Hammerless, Damascus Barrel, *Modern*	150	175	170
Various Gauges, Outside Hammers, Steel Barrel, *Modern*	175	200	185

SHOTGUN, SINGLESHOT

Various Gauges, Hammer, Steel Barrel, *Modern*	75	100	85

	V.G.	Exc.	Prior Edition Exc. Value

WATSON BROS. London, England 1885–1931.

RIFLE, BOLT ACTION

.303 British, Express Sights, Sporting Rifle, Checkered Stock,
Modern $625 $700 $675

RIFLE, DOUBLE BARREL, SIDE-BY-SIDE

.450/.400 N.E. 3", Double Trigger, Recoil Pad, Plain, Cased,
Modern 3,500 4,000 3,800

WATTERS, JOHN Carlisle, Pa. 1778–1785. See Kentucky Rifles.

WEATHERBY'S, INC. South Gate, Calif.

HANDGUN, SINGLESHOT

Mk. V. Silhouette, Various Calibers, Thumbhole Target Stock,
Target Sights, *Modern* 850 1,000 600

RIFLE, BOLT ACTION

For German Manufacture *Add* **30%–50%**

Deluxe, .378 Wby. Mag., Magnum, Checkered Stock, *Modern* 850 950 400

Deluxe, Various Calibers, Checkered Stock, *Modern* 800 900 285

Deluxe, Various Calibers, Magnum, Checkered Stock, *Modern* 825 925 365

Mark V, .378 Wby. Mag., Checkered Stock, *Modern* 900 1,100 490

Mark V, .460 Wby. Mag., Checkered Stock, *Modern* 1,000 1,250 590

Mark V, Various Calibers, Varmint, Checkered Stock, *Modern* 850 950 415

Mark V, Various Calibers, Checkered Stock, *Modern* 750 850 415

Mark V Crown Custom, Various Calibers, 24" or 26" Barrel,
Right Hand Only, *Modern* 3,000 3,500 2,600

Mark V Fibermark, Various Calibers, Fiberglass, Right Hand
Only, *Modern* 850 1,000 880

Mark V Lazermark, Various Calibers, Carved Stock (Carved
With Laser Beam), *Modern* 850 1,100 1,208

Vanguard, Various Calibers, Checkered Stock, *Modern* 425 500 320

RIFLE, SEMI-AUTOMATIC

Mark XXII, .22 L.R.R.F., Clip Fed, Checkered Stock, *Modern* 300 325 210

Mark XXII, .22 L.R.R.F., Tube Feed, Checkered Stock, *Modern* 325 350 250

Model M-82, Various Gauges, Gas Operated, Various Barrel
Lengths, *Modern* 400 450 440

Weatherby, Mk.V

Weatherby Athens O/U Shotgun

	V.G.	Exc.	Prior Edition Exc. Value

SHOTGUN, DOUBLE BARREL, OVER-UNDER

Athena Skeet Grade, 12 Gauge, Single Selective Trigger, 26" Barrels, *Modern*.. $1,000 $1,250 $1,200

Athena Trap Grade, 12 Gauge, Single Selective Trigger, 30" Barrels, *Modern*.. 1,000 1,250 1,200

Orion Field Grade, 12 Gauge, Single Selective Trigger, 26" or 28" Barrel, *Modern* 775 800 790

Orion 20 Field Grade, 20 Gauge, Single Selective Trigger, 26" or 28" Barrel, *Modern* 775 850 700

Orion Skeet Grade, 12 Gauge, Single Selective Trigger, 26" Barrel, *Modern* 800 875 825

Orion Trap Grade, 12 Gauge, Single Selective Trigger, 30" or 32" Barrel, *Modern* 800 875 825

Regency, 12 Gauge, Trap Grade, Vent Rib, Checkered Stock, Engraved, Single Selective Trigger, *Modern*..................................... 725 800 700

Regency, Field Grade, 12 and 20 Gauges, Vent Rib, Checkered Stock, Engraved, Single Selective Trigger, *Modern*.......................... 725 775 675

SHOTGUN, SEMI-AUTOMATIC

Centurion, 12 Gauge, Field Grade, Vent Rib, Checkered Stock, *Modern*.. 225 275 225

Centurion, 12 Gauge Trap Grade, Checkered Stock, Vent Rib, *Modern*.. 250 300 250

Centurion Deluxe, 12 Gauge, Checkered Stock, Vent Rib, Light Engraving, Fancy Wood, *Modern*... 325 375 270

SHOTGUN, SLIDE ACTION

Model M-92, 12 Gauge, Vent Rib, Three Shell Mag, *Modern* 225 275 350

Patrician, 12 Gauge, Field Grade, Checkerked Stock, Vent Rib, *Modern*.. 200 225 195

Patrician, 12 Gauge, Trap Grade, Checkered Stock, Vent Rib, *Modern*.. 225 250 225

Patrician, Deluxe, 12 Gauge, Checkered Stock, Light Engraving, Fancy Wood, Vent Rib, *Modern*... 225 275 235

WEAVER, CRYPRET Pa., c. 1818. See Kentucky Rifles.

WEBLEY & SCOTT Located in Birmingham, England operating as P. Webley & Son, 1860–1897; Webley & Scott Revolver & Arms Co., 1898–1906; Webley & Scott since 1906.

	V.G.	Exc.	Prior Edition Exc. Value

HANDGUN, REVOLVER

	V.G.	Exc.	Prior Edition Exc. Value
#1, .577 Eley, Solid Frame, Double Action, Blue, *Curio*	$150	$200	$170
British Bulldog, Various Calibers, Solid Frame, Double Action, *Curio*	300	350	140
Tower Bulldog, Various Calibers, Solid Frame, Double Action, *Curio*	275	325	130
Webley Kaufmann, .45 Colt, Top Break, Square-Butt, Commercial, *Antique*	400	475	475
Webley Mk 1, .455 Revolver Mk 1, Top Break, Round Butt, Military, *Antique*	225	250	235
Webley Mk 1*, .455 Revolver Mk 1, Top Break, Round Butt, Military, *Antique*	200	225	225
Webley Mk 1 Navy**, .455 Revolver Mk 1, Top Break, Round Butt, Military, *Modern*	200	225	210
Webley Mk 2, .455 Revolver Mk 1, Top Break, Round Butt, Military, *Antique*	225	250	225
Webley Mk 2*, .455 Revolver Mk 1, Top Break, Round Butt, Military, *Curio*	225	250	230
Webley Mk 2**, .455 Revolver Mk 1, Top Break, Round Butt, Military, *Curio*	225	250	230
Webley Mk 3, .455 Revolver Mk 1, Top Break, Round Butt, Military, *Curio*	250	275	255
Webley Mk 4, .455 Revolver Mk 1, Top Break, Round Butt, Military, *Curio*	200	250	230
Webley Mk 5, .455 Revolver Mk 1, Top Break, Round Butt, Military, *Curio*	225	275	250
Webley Mk 6, .455 Revolver Mk 1, Top Break, Square-Butt, Military, *Curio*	300	350	220
Webley Mk 6, Detachable Buttstock Only	300	350	275
Webley Mk III M & P, .38 S & W, Top Break, Square-Butt, Commercial, *Modern*	250	300	170
Webley Mk VI, .22 L.R.R.F., Top Break, Square-Butt, Commercial, *Modern*	400	475	235
Webley Mk IV, .38 S & W, Top Break, Square-Butt, Military, *Curio*	175	200	175
Webley R I C, .455 Revolver Mk 1, Solid Frame, Square-Butt, Commercial, *Antique*	225	250	155
Webley-Green, .455 Revolver Mk 1, Top Break, Square-Butt, Commercial, Target Pistol, *Antique*	425	475	390
Webley-Green, .476 Enfield Mk 3, Top Break, Square-Butt, Commercial, Target Pistol, *Antique*	425	475	465

HANDGUN, SEMI-AUTOMATIC

	V.G.	Exc.	Prior Edition Exc. Value
Model 1904, .455 Webley Auto., Clip Fed, Grip Safety, Hammer, *Curio*	650	750	800
Model 1906, .25 ACP, Clip Fed, Hammer, *Modern*	225	250	200
Model 1909, .32 ACP, Clip Fed, Hammerless, *Modern*	225	250	325
Model 1909, .25 ACP, Clip Fed, Hammerless, *Modern*	175	200	275

	V.G.	Exc.	Prior Edition Exc. Value
Model 1909 M & P, 9mm Browning Long, Clip Fed, Hammer, *Curio*	$400	$450	$450
Model 1909 M & P, 9mm Browning Long, South African Police, Clip Fed, Hammer, *Curio*	500	550	650
Model 1910, .38 ACP, Clip Fed, Hammerless, *Curio*	400	450	425
Model 1911 Metro Police, .32 ACP, Clip Fed, Hammer, *Modern*	625	700	255
Model 1911 Metro Police, .380 ACP, Clip Fed, Hammer, *Modern*	700	800	325
Model 1913, .38 ACP, Clip Fed, Hammerless, *Curio*	1,000	1,250	420
Model 1913 Mk 1, .455 Webley Auto., Clip Fed, Grip Safety, Military, Hammer, *Curio*	2,000	2,250	445
Model 1913 Mk 1 #2, .455 Webley Auto., Clip Fed, Grip Safety, Adjustable Sights, Hammer, *Curio*	950	1,200	875

SHOTGUN, DOUBLE BARREL, SIDE-BY-SIDE

	V.G.	Exc.	
Model 700, 12 and 20 Gauges, Box Lock, Hammerless, Checkered Stock, Light Engraving, Single Trigger, *Modern*	1,450	1,600	500
Model 701, 12 and 20 Gauges, Box Lock, Hammerless, Checkered Stock, Fancy Engraving, Double Trigger, *Modern*	2,000	2,500	800
Model 701, 12 and 20 Gauges, Box Lock, Hammerless, Checkered Stock, Fancy Engraving, Single Trigger, *Modern*	2,200	2,600	850
Model 702, 12 and 20 Gauges, Box Lock, Hammerless, Checkered Stock, Engraved, Double Trigger, *Modern*	1,750	2,200	600
Model 702, 12 and 20 Gauges, Box Lock, Hammerless, Checkered Stock, Engraved, Single Trigger, *Modern*	1,750	2,250	650

WELSHANTZ, DAVID York, Pa. 1780–1783. See Kentucky Rifles, U.S. Military.

WELSHANTZ, JACOB York, Pa. 1777–1792. See Kentucky Rifles, U.S. Military.

WELSHANTZ, JOSEPH York, Pa. 1779–1783. See Kentucky Rifles, U.S. Military.

WESSON & HARRINGTON Worcester, Mass. 1871–1874.
Succeeded by Harrington and Richardson.

HANDGUN, REVOLVER

	V.G.	Exc.	
.22 Short R.F., 7 Shot, Spur Trigger, Solid Frame, Single Action, *Antique*	150	175	170
.32 Short R.F., 5 Shot, Spur Trigger, Solid Frame, Single Action, *Antique*	150	175	170
.38 Short R.F., 5 Shot, Spur Trigger, Solid Frame, Single Action, *Antique*	175	200	185

	V.G.	Exc.	Prior Edition Exc. Value

WESSON, FRANK Worcester, Mass. 1854 to 1865. 1865–1875 at Springfield, Mass. Also see U.S. Military, Wesson & Harrington, Harrington & Richardson.

HANDGUN, SINGLESHOT

	V.G.	Exc.	Prior Value
Model 1859, .22 Short, Tip-Up Barrel, Spur Trigger, *Antique*	$600	$650	$215
Model 1862, .22 Short, Tip-Up Barrel, Spur Trigger, *Antique*	500	550	180
Model 1859, .39 R.F., Tip-Up Barrel, Spur Trigger, *Antique*	450	500	215
Model 1862, .30 R.F., Tip-Up Barrel, Spur Trigger, *Antique*	450	500	215
Model 1859, .32 R.F., Tip-Up Barrel, Spur Trigger, *Antique*	450	500	215
Model 1862, .32 R.F., Tip-Up Barrel, Spur Trigger, *Antique*	450	500	215
Model 1862 Pocket Rifle, Various Calibers, Medium Frame, Spur Trigger, Target Sights, Detachable Stock, *Antique*	500	550	320
Model 1870 Pocket Rifle, .22 Short, Small Frame, Spur Trigger, Target Sights, Detachable Stock, *Antique*	400	450	370
Model 1870 Pocket Rifle, Various Calibers, Medium Frame, Spur Trigger, Target Sights, Detachable Stock, *Antique*	350	400	315
Model 1870 Pocket Rifle, Various Calibers, Large Frame, Spur Trigger, Target Sights, Detachable Stock, *Antique*	725	775	575

HANDGUN, DOUBLE BARREL, OVER-UNDER

	V.G.	Exc.	Prior Value
Vest Pocket, .22 Short, Twist Barrel, Spur Trigger, *Antique*	700	800	525
Vest Pocket, .32 Short, Twist Barrel, Spur Trigger, *Antique*	500	550	365
Vest Pocket, .41 Short, Twist Barrel, Spur Trigger, with Knife, *Antique*	750	850	675

RIFLE, SINGLESHOT

	V.G.	Exc.	Prior Value
.32 Long R.F., Double Trigger, Tip-Up, *Antique*	500	550	500

WESTERN ARMS CO.

HANDGUN, REVOLVER

	V.G.	Exc.	Prior Value
.32 Long R.F., 5 Shot, Folding Trigger, Double Action, *Antique*	75	100	95

WESTERN FIELD Trade name for Montgomery Ward.

RIFLE, BOLT ACTION

	V.G.	Exc.	Prior Value
Model 56 Buckhorn, .22 L.R.R.F., 5 Shot Clip, Open Rear Sight, *Modern*	50	75	55
Model 724, .30-06 Springfield, Checkered Stock, Full-Stocked, *Modern*	125	175	175
Model 732, .30-06 Springfield, Checkered Stock, Recoil Pad, *Modern*	125	175	180
Model 734, 7mm Rem. Mag., Checkered Stock, Recoil Pad, *Modern*	125	175	190
Model 765, .30-06 Springfield, Checkered Stock, *Modern*	100	150	150
Model 770, Various Calibers, Checkered Stock, Sling Swivels, *Modern*	125	175	175

	V.G.	Exc.	Prior Edition Exc. Value
Model 78, Various Calibers, Checkered Stock, Sling Swivels, *Modern*	$125	$175	$175
Model 780, Various Calibers, Checkered Stock, Sling Swivels, *Modern*	150	175	160
Model 815, .22 L.R.R.F., Singleshot, *Modern*	25	50	30
Model 822, .22 WMR, Clip Fed, *Modern*	25	50	55
Model 83, .22 L.R.R.F., Singleshot, Open Rear Sight, Takedown, *Modern*	25	50	40
Model 830, .22 L.R.R.F., Clip Fed, *Modern*	25	50	45
Model 832, .22 L.R.R.F., Clip Fed, Checkered Stock, *Modern*	25	50	45
Model 84, .22 L.R.R.F., 5 Shot Clip, Open Rear Sight, Takedown, *Modern*	25	50	45
Model 840, .22 W.M.R., Clip Fed, *Modern*	50	75	55
Model 842, .22 L.R.R.F., Tube Feed, *Modern*	25	50	45
Model 852, .22 L.R.R.F., Clip Fed, *Modern*	25	50	45
Model 86, .22 L.R.R.F., Tube Feed, Takedown, Open Rear Sight, *Modern*	25	50	55

RIFLE, LEVER ACTION

	V.G.	Exc.	
Model 72, .30-30 Win., Pistol-Grip Stock, Plain, Tube Feed, *Modern*	100	125	120
Model 72C, .30-30 Win., Straight Grip, Plain, Tube Feed, *Modern*	100	125	120
Model 79, .30-30 Win., Pistol-Grip Stock, Plain, Tube Feed, *Modern*	100	125	125
Model 865, .22 L.R.R.F., Tube Feed, Sling Swivels, *Modern*	50	75	70
Model 895, .22 L.R.R.F., Tube Feed, Carbine, *Modern*	50	75	70

RIFLE, SEMI-AUTOMATIC

	V.G.	Exc.	
Model 808, .22 L.R.R.F., Tube Feed, *Modern*	25	50	55
Model 828, .22 L.R.R.F., Clip Fed, Checkered Stock, *Modern*	50	75	60
Model 836, .22 L.R.R.F., Tube Feed, *Modern*	50	75	60
Model 846, .22 L.R.R.F., Tube Feed, *Modern*	50	75	60
Model 850, .22 L.R.R.F., Clip Fed, *Modern*	50	75	60
Model 880, .22 L.R.R.F., Tube Feed, *Modern*	50	50	55
Model M-1, .30 Carbine, Clip Fed, *Modern*	125	150	145

SHOTGUN, BOLT ACTION

	V.G.	Exc.	
Model 150, .410 Ga., Clip Fed, *Modern*	25	50	55
Model 172-5, 12 and 20 Gauges, Magnum, Clip Fed, Adjustable Choke, *Modern*	50	75	60

SHOTGUN, DOUBLE BARREL, SIDE-BY-SIDE

	V.G.	Exc.	
12 and 20 Gauges, Single Trigger, Hammerless, Checkered Stock, *Modern*	125	150	155
Various Gauges, Hammerless, Plain, *Modern*	100	125	130
Long-Range, Various Gauges, Double Trigger, Hammerless, *Modern*	150	175	170

	V.G.	Exc.	Prior Edition Exc. Value
Long-Range, Various Gauges, Single Trigger, Hammerless, *Modern*	$175	$200	$195
Model 330, Various Gauges, Hammerless, Checkered Stock, *Modern*	125	150	155
Model 5151, Various Gauges, Hammerless, Steel Barrel, *Modern*	125	150	155

SHOTGUN, SEMI-AUTOMATIC

	V.G.	Exc.	Value
Model 60, 12 Ga., Takedown, Plain Barrel, Checkered Stock, *Modern*	125	150	140
Model 600, 12 Ga., Takedown, Vent Rib, Checkered Stock, *Modern*	125	150	155

SHOTGUN, SINGLESHOT

	V.G.	Exc.	Value
Model 100, Various Gauges, Hammerless, Adjustable Choke, *Modern*	25	50	50
Trap, 12 Ga., Hammer, Solid Rib, Checkered Stock, *Modern*	75	100	85

SHOTGUN, SLIDE ACTION

	V.G.	Exc.	Value
Model 500, .410 Ga., Plain, Takedown, *Modern*	100	125	130
Modern 502, .410 Ga., Checkered Stock, Light Engraving, Takedown, Vent Rib, *Modern*	100	125	135
Model 520, 12 Ga., Takedown, *Modern*	100	125	135
Model 550, 12 and 20 Gauges, Checkered Stock, Light Engraving, Vent Rib, Takedown, *Modern*	100	125	135
Model 550, 12 and 20 Gauges, Checkered Stock, Light Engraving, Vent Rib, Takedown, Adjustable Choke, *Modern*	125	150	150
Model 550, 12 and 20 Gauges, Plain, Takedown, *Modern*	100	125	130
Model 620, Various Gauges, Takedown, *Modern*	125	150	145

WESTLEY RICHARDS London, England, Since 1812.

RIFLE, BOLT ACTION

	V.G.	Exc.	Value
Best Quality, Various Calibers, Express Sights, Fancy Wood, Fancy Checkering, Repeater, *Modern*	2,500	2,750	2,400

RIFLE, DOUBLE BARREL, SIDE-BY-SIDE

	V.G.	Exc.	Value
Best Quality, Various Calibers, Sidelock, Double Trigger, Fancy Engraving, Fancy Checkering, Express Sights, *Modern*	30,000	35,000	13,500

SHOTGUN, DOUBLE BARREL, OVER-UNDER

	V.G.	Exc.	Value
Owundo, 12 Ga., Sidelock, Single Selective Trigger, Selective Ejector, Fancy Engraving, Fancy Checkering, *Moder*	15,000	17,500	17,500

SHOTGUN, DOUBLE BARREL, SIDE-BY-SIDE

	V.G.	Exc.	Value
10 Ga. Pinfire, Engraved, Carbine, *Antique*	850	950	700
Best Quality, Various Gauges, Sidelock, Hammerless, Fancy Engraving, Fancy Checkering, Double Trigger, *Modern*	17,500	20,000	11,500
Best Quality, Various Gauges, Sidelock, Hammerless, Fancy Engraving, Fancy Checkering, Single Selective Trigger, *Modern*	20,000	22,500	13,500
Best Quality, Various Gauges, Box Lock, Hammerless, Fancy Engraving, Fancy Checkering, Double Trigger, *Modern*	10,000	12,000	8,900

	V.G.	Exc.	Prior Edition Exc. Value
Best Quality, Various Gauges, Box Lock, Hammerless, Fancy Engraving, Fancy Checkering, Single Selective Trigger, *Modern*	$11,000	$13,000	$10,000
Best, Pigeon, 12 Ga. Mag. 3", Sidelock, Hammerless, Fancy Engraving, Fancy Checkering, Double Trigger, *Modern*	17,500	20,000	18,000
Best, Pigeon, 12 Ga. Mag. 3", Sidelock, Hammerless, Fancy Engraving, Fancy Checkering, Single Selective Trigger, *Modern*	18,500	21,000	19,000
Deluxe Quality, Various Gauges, Sidelock, Hammerless, Fancy Engraving, Fancy Checkering, Double Trigger, *Modern*	12,500	15,000	12,000
Deluxe Quality, Various Gauges, Sidelock, Hammerless, Fancy Engraving, Fancy Checkering, Single Selective Trigger, *Modern*	13,500	16,000	13,000
Deluxe Quality, Various Gauges, Box Lock, Hammerless, Fancy Engraving, Fancy Checkering, Double Trigger, *Modern*	9,000	10,500	7,800
Deluxe Quality, Various Gauges, Box Lock, Hammerless, Fancy Engraving, Fancy Checkering, Single Selective Trigger, *Modern*	9,500	11,500	8,600
Model E, Various Gauges, Box Lock, Hammerless, Engraved, Double Trigger, Selective Ejector, *Modern*	5,000	5,500	5,000
Model E, Various Gauges, Box Lock, Hammerless, Engraved, Double Trigger, *Modern*	4,000	4,250	3,800
Model E Pigeon, 12 Ga. Mag. 3", Box Lock, Hammerless, Engraved, Double Trigger, Selective Ejector, *Modern*	6,000	6,000	5,500
Model E Pigeon, 12 Ga. Mag 3", Box Lock, Hammerless, Engraved, Double Trigger, *Modern*	4,250	4,750	4,300
SHOTGUN, SINGLESHOT			
12 Ga., Trap Grade, Vent Rib, Fancy Engraving, Fancy Checkering, Hammerless, *Modern*	7,500	8,500	8,000
12 Ga., Vent Rib, Plain, Monte Carlo Stock, Trap Grade, *Modern*	2,500	3,000	2,700

WESTON, EDWARD Sussex, England 1800–1835.

HANDGUN, FLINTLOCK

	V.G.	Exc.	Prior Edition Exc. Value
.67, Pair, Duelling Pistols, Octagon Barrel, Silver Furniture, Plain, *Antique*	2,500	2,750	2,600

WHEEL-LOCK, UNKNOWN MAKER

COMBINATION WEAPON, PISTOL

	V.G.	Exc.	Prior Edition Exc. Value
German, 1500's War-Hammer, All Metal, *Antique*	9,000	15,000	15,000

HANDGUN, WHEEL-LOCK

	V.G.	Exc.	Prior Edition Exc. Value
Augsburg, Late 1500's, Ball Pommel, Engraved, Ornate, *Antique*	14,000	20,000	20,000
Brescian, Mid-1600's, Military, Fish-Tail Butt, Plain, *Antique*	1,500	2,600	2,600
Embellished Original, Ornate, *Antique*	2,500	3,550	3,550
Enclosed Lock German, Mid-1600's, Engraved, Holster Pistol, *Antique*	3,000	3,800	3,800
Enclosed Lock, Late 1600's, Military, Plain, *Antique*	1,500	2,500	2,500
English, Mid-1600's, Ornate, *Antique*	14,000	20,000	20,000

	V.G.	Exc.	Prior Edition Exc. Value
English, Mid-1600's, Military, Holster Pistol, Plain, *Antique*	$1,500	$2,500	$2,500
French, Early 1600's, Military, Silver Inlay, *Antique*	2,500	3,600	3,600
German, 1600, Dagger-Handle Butt, Military, Plain, *Antique*	2,000	2,800	2,800
German, Late 1500's, Carved, Horn Inlays, Ball Pommel, Flattened, *Antique*	12,500	18,000	18,000
German, Mid-1500's, Horn Inlays, Dagger-Handle Butt, Gold and Silver Damascened, Ornate, *Antique*	35,000	55,000	55,000
German, Mid-1600's, Military, Fish-Tail Butt, Plain, *Antique*	1,250	2,000	2,000
German Puffer, Late 1500's, Horn Inlays, Ball Pommel, *Antique*	6,000	10,000	10,000
German Style, Reproduciton, Engraved, Inlays, High Quality, *Antique*	1,400	2,000	2,000
Italian, 1500's, Dagger-Handle, External Mechanism, *Antique*	9,000	16,500	16,500
Late 1500's Odd Butt, all Metal, Engraved, Ornate, *Antique*	7,000	10,000	10,000
Old Reproduction, High Quality, *Antique*	1,200	1,800	1,800
Pair Brescian, Mid-1600's, Inlays, Engraved, Ornate, Fish-Tail Butt, *Antique*	18,000	25,000	25,000
Pair Dutch, Mid-1600's, Holster Pistol, Gold Damascened, Inlays, Ornate, *Antique*	18,000	25,000	25,000
Pair Saxon, Late 1500's, Ball Pommel, Medium Ornamentation, *Anitque*	14,000	20,000	20,000
Pair Saxon, Late 1500's, Ball Pommel, Light Ornamentation, *Antique*	9,000	15,000	15,000
Pair Saxon, Late 1500's, Ball Pommel, Inlays, Engraved, *Antique*	2,4000	30,000	30,000
Saxon, Double Barrel, Over-Under, Inlays, Ornate, Ball Pommel, *Antique*	24,000	30,000	30,000
Saxon, Dated 1579, Horn Inlays, Engraved, Ball Pommel, *Antique*	6,000	10,000	10,000
Saxon, Late 1500's, Ball Pommel, Checkered Stock, Military, Plain, *Antique*	4,000	6,000	6,000

RIFLE, WHEEL-LOCK
Brandenburg 1620, Cavalry Rifle, Military, *Antique*	5,500	8,000	8,000

WHIPPET Made by Stevens Arms.
SHOTGUN, SINGLESHOT
Model 94A, Various Gauges, Hammer, Automatic Ejector, *Modern*	50	75	55

WHITE POWDER WONDER Made by Stevens Arms.
SHOTGUN, SINGLESHOT
Model 90, Various Gauges, Takedown, Automatic Ejector, Plain, Hammer, *Modern*	50	75	55

	V.G.	Exc.	Prior Edition Exc. Value

WHITE, ROLLIN, ARMS CO. Hartford, Conn. 1849–1858; Lowell, Mass. 1864–1892.

HANDGUN, REVOLVER

.22 Short R.F., 7 Shot, Spur Trigger, Tip-Up, *Antique*	$425	$500	$290

HANDGUN, SINGLESHOT

SS Pocket, .32 Cal., no Trigger Guard, *Antique*	500	650	260

WHITE STAR Maker unknown, c. 1880.

HANDGUN, REVOLVER

.32 Short R.F., 5 Shot, Spur Trigger, Solid Frame, Single Action, *Antique*	150	175	165

HANDGUN, REVOLVER

.32 Short R.F., 5 Shot, Spur Trigger, Solid Frame, Single Action, *Antique*	150	175	170

WHITNEY ARMS CO. New Haven, Conn. 1866–1876, also see U.S. Military.

HANDGUN, PERCUSSION

Hooded Cylinder, .28, 6 Shot, Hammer, *Antique*	1,750	2,000	1,450
Whitney-Beals, .31, Ring Trigger, 7 Shot, *Antique*	800	950	525
Whitney-Beals Walking Beam Pocket Revolver, .31, 6 Shot, *Antique*	1,650	1,800	1,600
Navy, .36, 6 Shot, Colt 1851 Type, *Antique*	900	1,000	800
Whitney Navy, .36, 6 Shot, Single Action, Hammer, *Antique*	1,500	1,650	425
Pocket Model, .31, 5 Shot, Single Action, *Antique*	675	750	285
New Pocket Model, .28, 6 Shot, Single Action, *Antique*	625	700	420

HANDGUN, REVOLVER

.22 Short R.F., 7 Shot, Spur Trigger, Solid Frame, Single Action, *Antique*	275	325	165
.38 Short R.F., 5 Shot, Spur Trigger, Solid Frame, Single Action, *Antique*	275	325	165
.32 Short R.F., 5 or 6 Shots, Spur Trigger, Solid Frame, Single Action, *Antique*	300	350	170

RIFLE, SINGLESHOT

Whitney-Howard, .44 R.F., Carbine, Lever Action, *Antique*	1,250	1,500	395
Whitney-Howard, .44 R.F., RIfle, Lever Action, *Antique*	1,000	1,250	465
Phoenix, Various Calibers, Carbine, Hammer, *Antique*	1,750	2,000	725
Phoenix, Various Calibers, Rifle, Hammer, *Antique*	1,000	1,250	365
Rolling Block, Various Calibers, Carbine, *Antique*	1,000	1,250	500
Rolling Block, Various Calibers, Rifle, *Antique*	900	1,000	350

Rollin White Single Shot Pocket Pistol, .32 Caliber

Whitney Beals Standard Revolver, .31 Caliber

Whitney Beals Walking Beam Pocket Revolver, .31 Caliber

	V.G.	Exc.	Prior Edition Exc. Value

RIFLE, LEVER ACTION

	V.G.	Exc.	Prior Edition Exc. Value
Kennedy, Various Calibers, Tube Feed, Plain, *Antique*....................	$1,250	$1,500	$575
Model 1886, Various Calibers, Tube Feed, Plain, *Antique*..............	1,500	1,750	875

SHOTGUN, DOUBLE BARREL, SIDE-BY-SIDE

12 Ga., Damascus Barrel, Outside Hammers, *Antique*......................	650	750	320

WHITNEY FIREARMS CO. Harford, Conn. 1955–1962

HANDGUN, SINGLESHOT

Wolverine, .22 L.R.R.F., Blue, *Modern*..	400	475	135

WHITENEYVILLE ARMORY See Whitney Arms Co.

WHITWORTH Made in England, imported by Interarms.

RIFLE, BOLT ACTION

Express, Various Calibers, Checkered Stock, *Modern*.....................	650	750	400

WICHITA ENGINEERING & SUPPLY Wichita, Kans.

HANDGUN, SINGLESHOT

Classic, Various Calibers, Singleshot, Target, *Modern*.....................	2,500	2,750	900
Silhouette Pistol, Various Calibers, Bolt Action, *Modern*	750	1,000	500

RIFLE, BOLT ACTION

Varmint, Various Calibers, Repeater, Target, *Modern*.....................	1,500	1,800	700
Classic, Various Calibers, Singleshot, Target, *Modern*....................	2,250	2,500	900
Classic, Various Calibers, Repeater, *Modern*....................................	2,500	2,750	975

WICKLIFFE Triple-S Development, Wickliffe, Ohio.

RIFLE, SINGLESHOT

Stinger Standard, Various Calibers, Falling Block, *Modern*...........	350	400	260
Stinger Deluxe, Various Calibers, Falling Block, *Modern*...............	425	475	310
'76 Standard, Various Calibers, Falling Block, *Modern*..................	350	400	260
'76 Deluxe, Various Calibers, Falling Block, *Modern*......................	400	450	310
Traditional, Various Calibers, Falling Block, *Modern*	350	400	260

WIDE AWAKE Made by Hood Fire Arms, Norwich, Conn., c. 1875.

HANDGUN, REVOLVER

.32 Short R.F., 5 Shot, Spur Trigger, Solid Frame, Single Action, *Antique*	150	175	165

	V.G.	Exc.	Prior Edition Exc. Value

WILKINSON ARMS South El Monte, Calif., c. 1976.
HANDGUN, SEMI-AUTOMATIC
Diane, .25 ACP, Clip Fed, Blue, *Modern*... $125 $150 $160

WILKINSON ARMS Parma, Ind.
HANDGUN, SEMI-AUTOMATIC
Linda, 9mm Luger, Clip Fed, Blue, *Modern* 275 325 300

WILKINSON ARMS CO. Made in Belgium for Richmond Hardware Co. Richmond, Va., c. 1900.
SHOTGUN, DOUBLE BARREL, SIDE-BY-SIDE
Various Gauges, Outside Hammers, Damascus Barrel, *Modern* 150 175 170
Various Gauges, Hammerless, Steel Barrel, *Modern*....................... 175 200 190
Various Gauges, Hammerless, Damascus Barrel, *Modern* 150 175 170
Various Gauges, Outside Hammers, Steel Barrel, *Modern*.............. 175 200 185
SHOTGUN, SINGLESHOT
Various Gauges, Hammer, Steel Barrel, *Modern*............................. 75 100 85

WILLIAMS, FREDERICK Birmingham, England 1893–1929.
SHOTGUN, DOUBLE BARREL, SIDE-BY-SIDE
12 Ga., Damascus Barrel, Outside Hammers, Checkered Stock,
Engraved, *Antique*.. 400 450 465

WILLIAMSON, DAVID Brooklyn, N.Y. and Greenville, N.J. 1864–1874. Also see Moore's Patent Firearms Co.
HANDGUN, SINGLESHOT
.41 Short R.F., Derringer, Nickel Plated, *Antique*............................ 275 325 300

WILLIS, RICHARD Lancaster, Pa., c. 1776. See Kentucky Rifles and Pistols.

WILMONT ARMS CO. Belgium, c. 1900.
SHOTGUN, DOUBLE BARREL, SIDE-BY-SIDE
Various Gauges, Outside Hammers, Damascus Barrel, *Modern* 150 175 170
Various Gauges, Hammerless, Steel Barrel, *Modern*....................... 175 200 190
Various Gauges, Hammerless, Damascus Barrel, *Modern* 150 175 170
Various Gauges, Outside Hammers, Steel Barrel, *Modern*.............. 175 200 185
SHOTGUN, SINGLESHOT
Various Gauges, Hammer, Steel Barrel, *Modern*............................. 75 100 85

		Prior Edition
		Exc.
V.G.	Exc.	Value

WILSON, R. London, England 1720–1750.

SHOTGUN, FLINTLOCK

	V.G.	Exc.	Value
Fowling, 9 Ga., Queen Anne Style, Half-Stock, *Antique*	$1,250	$1,500	$1,600

WILTSHIRE ARMS CO. Belgium, c. 1900.

SHOTGUN, DOUBLE BARREL, SIDE-BY-SIDE

	V.G.	Exc.	Value
Various Gauges, Outside Hammers, Damascus Barrel, *Modern*	150	175	170
Various Gauges, Hammerless, Steel Barrel, *Modern*	175	200	190
Various Gauges, Hammerless, Damascus Barrel, *Modern*	150	175	170
Various Gauges, Outside Hammers, Steel Barrel, *Modern*	175	200	185

SHOTGUN, SINGLESHOT

	V.G.	Exc.	Value
Various Gauges, Hammer, Steel Barrel, *Modern*	75	100	85

WINCHESTER REPEATING ARMS CO. New Haven, Conn. 1866 to date. In 1857 Oliver Winchester reorganized the Volcanic Repeating Arms Co. into the New Haven Arms Co., and it became Winchester Repeating Arms Co. in 1866. In 1869 Winchester absorbed Fogerty Repeating Rifle Co., and the American Rifle Co. In 1870 it acquired The Spencer Repeating Arms Co. and Adirondack Arms Co. in 1874. In 1881 was purchased by U.S. Repeating Arms Co. Also see U.S. Military.

For Custom Features, Add **50%–100%**
For Special Sights, Add **25%–50%**

AUTOMATIC WEAPON, ASSAULT RIFLE

RIFLE, BOLT ACTION

	V.G.	Exc.	Value
Hotchkiss, .40-65 Win., Sporting Rifle, *Antique*	800	1,000	1,150
Hotchkiss 1st Model Fancy, .45-70 Government, Sporting Rifle, *Antique*	575	750	900
Hotchkiss 1st Model, .45-70 Government, Military, Rifle, *Antique*	410	2,500	650
Hotchkiss 1st Model, .45-70 Government, Military, Carbine, *Antique*	430	1,000	695
Hotchkiss 1st Model, .45-70 Government, Sporting Rifle, *Antique*	475	700	750
Hotchkiss 2nd Model, .45-70 Government, Military, Rifle, *Antique*	475	900	750
Hotchkiss 2nd Model, .45-70 Government, Sporting Rifle, *Antique*	575	700	850
Hotchkiss 3rd Model, .45-70 Government, Military Rifle, *Antique*	375	900	725
Hotchkiss 3rd Model, .45-70 Government, Military, Carbine, *Antique*	500	900	840
Hotchkiss 3rd Model, .45-70 Government Military Rifle, *Antique*	565	850	935

	V.G.	Exc.	Prior Edition Exc. Value
Lee Straight-Pull, 6mm Lee Navy, Musket, *Antique*	$485	$850	$650
Lee Straight-Pull, 6mm Lee Navy, Sporting Rifle, *Antique*	825	900	760
M121, .22 L.R.R.F., Singleshot, *Modern*	50	75	58
M121-Y, .22 L.R.R.F., Singleshot, *Modern*	50	75	58
M121 Deluxe, .22 L.R.R.F., Singleshot, *Modern*	50	75	70
M131, .22 L.R.R.F., Clip Fed, Open Rear Sight, *Modern*	100	125	85
M135, .22 WMR, Clip Fed, *Modern*	100	125	95
M141, .22 WMR, Tube Feed, *Modern*	125	150	80
M145, .22 WMR, Tube Feed, *Modern*	125	150	90
M1900, .22 Long R.F., Singleshot, *Modern*	300	350	125
M1902, Various Rimfires, Singleshot, *Curio*	150	175	160
M1904, Various Rimfires, Singleshot, *Curio*	175	200	160
Thumb Trigger, .22 L.R.R.F., Singleshot, *Curio*	225	275	240
M43, Various Calibers, Sporting Rifle, *Modern*	475	550	275
M43 Special Grade, Various Calibers, *Modern*	525	600	330
M47, .22 L.R.R.F., Singleshot, *Modern*	250	300	100
M52, .22 L.R.R.F., Heavy Barrel, *Modern*	350	400	400
M52 Slow-Lock, .22 L.R.R.F., *Modern*	300	350	290
M52 Speed-Lock, .22 L.R.R.F., *Modern*	400	450	330
M52 Sporting, .22 L.R.R.F., Rifle, *Modern*	1,500	1,800	860
M52-B, .22 L.R.R.F., *Modern*	1,350	1,600	350
M52-B, .22 L.R.R.F., Heavy Barrel, *Modern*	550	600	400
M52-B, .22 L.R.R.F., Bull Gun, *Modern*	575	625	450
M52-B, .22 L.R.R.F., Sporting Rifle, *Modern*	1,350	1,600	825
M52-C, .22 L.R.R.F., *Modern*	550	600	330
M52-C, .22 L.R.R.F., Standard Barrel, *Modern*	475	525	350
M52-C, .22 L.R.R.F., Bull Gun, *Modern*	575	650	470
M52-D, .22 L.R.R.F., *Modern*	475	525	470
M52 International, .22 L.R.R.F., *Modern*	625	700	750
M52 Internatinal Prone, .22 L.R.R.F., *Modern*	600	650	565
M54, .270 Win., Carbine, *Curio*	600	650	750
M54, .30-06 Springfield, Sniper Rifle, *Modern*	750	850	600
M54, Various Calibers, Carbine, *Modern*	575	650	550
M54, Various Calibers, Sporting Rifle, *Modern*	500	575	550
M54 Match, Various Calibers, Sniper Rifle, *Modern*	675	750	700
M54 National Match, Various Calibers, *Modern*	750	850	525
M54 Super Grade, Various Calibers, *Modern*	725	825	580
M54 Target, Various Calibers, *Modern*	550	600	565
M56, .22 L.R.R.F., Sporting Rifle, Clip Fed, *Modern*	450	500	165
M57, Various Rimfires, Target, *Modern*	450	500	430
M58, .22 L.R.R.F., Singleshot, *Modern*	250	275	135
M59, .22 L.R.R.F., Singleshot, *Modern*	375	425	160

	V.G.	Exc.	Prior Edition Exc. Value
M60, .22 L.R.R.F., Singleshot, *Modern*	$275	$350	$135
M60-A, .22 L.R.R.F., Target, Singleshot, *Modern*	400	475	170
M67, Various Rimfires, Singleshot, *Modern*	100	125	110
M67 Boy's Rifle, Various Rimfires, Singleshot, *Modern*	100	125	100
M68, Various Rimfires, Singleshot, *Modern*	125	150	125
M69, .22 L.R.R.F., Clip Fed, *Modern*	150	175	150
M69 Match, .22 L.R.R.F., Clip Fed, *Modern*	150	200	175
M69 Target, .22 L.R.R.F., Clip Fed, *Modern*	125	175	160
M70 Action Only, Various Calibers, Pre '64, *Modern*	300	350	275
M70 Barreled Action Only, Various Calibers, Pre '64, Checkered Stock, *Modern*	475	550	435
M70, For Pre-War, *Add 25%–50%*			
M70, For Mint Unfired, Pre '64, *Add 50%–100%*			
M70 African, .458 Win. Mag., Pre '64, *Modern*	1,400	1,600	950
M70 Alaskan, Various Calibers, Pre '64, Checkered Stock, *Modern*	1,500	1,700	700
M70 Bull Gun, Various Calibers, Pre '64, Checkered Stock, *Modern*	1,250	1,500	825
M70 Carbine, Various Calibers, Pre '64, Checkered Stock, *Modern*	1,250	1,500	800
M70 Featherweight Sporter Grade, Various Calibers, Pre '64, Checkered Stock, *Modern*	1,500	1,750	800
M70 Featherweight, Various Calibers, Pre '64, Checkered Stock, *Modern*	775	850	690
M70 National Match, .30-06 Springfield, Pre '64, *Modern*	1,000	1,200	825
M70 Target, Various Calibers, Pre '64, Checkered Stock, *Modern*	750	1,000	900
M70 Varmint, Various Calibers, Pre '64, Checkered Stock, *Modern*	650	800	715
M70 Westerner, Various Calibers Pre '64, Checkered Stock, *Modern*	650	800	690
Model 70, Various Calibers, Post '64, Checkered Stock, Open Rear Sight, Magnum Action, *Modern*	250	300	250
Model 70 African, .458 Win. Mag., Post '64, Checkered Stock, Open Rear Sight, Magnum Action, *Modern*	600	675	365
Model 70 International Match, .308 Win., Post '64, Checkered Stock, Target Stock, *Modern*	575	650	475
Model 70 Standard, Various Calibers, Post '64, Checkered Stock, Open Rear Sight, *Modern*	275	325	210
Model 70 Target, Various Calibers, Post '64, Checkered Stock, Target Stock, *Modern*	475	525	350
Model 70 Varmint, Various Calibers, Post '64, Checkered Stock, Heavy Barrel, *Modern*	300	350	225
Model 70A, Various Calibers, Post '64, Magnum Action, *Modern*	300	350	250
Model 70A Police, Various Calibers, Post '64, *Modern*	250	300	210

	V.G.	Exc.	Prior Edition Exc. Value
Model 70A Standard, Various Calibers, Post '64, *Modern*	$225	$275	$190
M70 Super Grade, Various Calibers, Pre '64, *Modern*	775	850	835
Model 70XTR Featherweight, Various Calibers, No Sights, *Modern*	350	400	365
Model 70XTR Featherweight, Various Calibers, with Sights, *Modern*	400	450	400
Model 70XTR Sporter, Various Calibers, *Modern*	325	375	325
Model 70XTR Super Express Magnum, .375 H&H, *Modern*	500	575	500
Model 70XTR Super Express Magnum, .458 Win., *Modern*	525	600	525
Model 70XTR Varmint, Various Calibers, *Modern*	325	375	320
Model 70XTR Westerner, Various Calibers, No Scope, *Modern*	275	325	275
M72, .22 L.R.R.F., Tube Feed, *Modern*	125	150	140
M75, .22 L.R.R.F., Sporting Rifle, Clip Fed, *Modern*	625	700	290
M75 Target, .22 L.R.R.F., Clip Fed, *Modern*	450	500	260
M99 Thumb Trigger, Various Rimfires, Singleshot, *Modern*	325	375	350
Model 52 I.M., .22 L.R.R.F., Post '64, Heavy Barrel, Target Stock, *Modern*	425	475	580
Model 52 I.M.I.S.U., .22 L.R.R.F., Post '64, Heavy Barrel, Target Stock, *Modern*	525	575	635
Model 52 I.M. Kenyon, .22 L.R.R.F., Post '64, Heavy Barrel, Target Stock, *Modern*	450	500	575
Model 52 International Prone, .22 L.R.R.F., Post '64, Heavy Barrel, Target Stock, *Modern*	425	475	440
Model 52D, .22 L.R.R.F., Post '64, Heavy Barrel, Target Stock, *Modern*	375	425	290
Model 670, Various Calibers, Post '64, Scope Mounted, *Modern*	200	250	180

RIFLE, LEVER ACTION

	V.G.	Exc.	Prior Edition Exc. Value
Henry, .44 Henry, Iron Frame, Rifle, *Antique*	20,000	25,000	8,500
Henry, .44 Henry, Brass Frame, Rifle, *Antique*	10,000	15,000	6,575
Henry, .44 Henry, Brass Frame, Military, Rifle, *Antique*	15,000	20,000	7,000
M1866, .44 Henry, Musket, *Antique*	6,500	8,000	1,850
M1866, .44 Henry, Rifle, *Antique*	10,000	12,000	2,075
M1866, .44 Henry, Carbine, *Antique*	7,500	10,000	1,700
M1866 Improved Henry, .44 Henry, Carbine, *Antique*	7,500	9,000	1,850
M1866 Improved Henry, .44 Henry, Rifle, *Antique*	5,500	7,000	2,250
M1873, Various Calibers, Rifle, *Modern*	1,750	2,000	1,300
M1873, Various Calibers, Musket, *Modern*	1,500	1,800	1,500
M1873, Various Calibers, Carbine, *Modern*	2,000	2,500	1,150
M1873 1 of 1,000, Various Calibers, Rifle, *Antique*	50,000	75,000	12,000
M1873, For Deluxe, *Add* **$350.00–$500.00**			
M1873, For Extra Fancy Deluxe, *Add* **$2,000.00–$5,000.00**			
M1873, under #525,299, Various Calibers, Musket, *Antique*	1,750	2,000	1,500
M1873, under #525,299, Various Calibers, Carbine, *Antique*	2,500	2,750	1,290

Winchester M21 Grand American

Winchester M1866

Winchester M1873

	V.G.	Exc.	Prior Edition Exc. Value
M1873, under #525,299, Various Calibers, Rifle, *Antique*	$2,000	$2,200	$1,475
M1876, Various Calibers, Carbine, *Antique*	2,000	2,250	1,575
M1876, Various Calibers, Octagon Barrel, Rifle, *Antique*	1,450	1,600	1,485
M1876, Various Calibers, Round Barrel, Rifle, *Antique*	1,250	1,400	1,250
M1876, Varoius Calibers, Musket, *Antique*	4,250	5,000	2,400
M1876, For Deluxe, *Add* **$400.00–$550.00**			
M1876, For Extra Fancy Deluxe, *Add* **$2,000.00–$5,000.00**			
M1876 RCMP, Various Calibers, Carbine, *Antique*	3,000	3,500	1,650
M1886, Various Calibers, Rifle, *Modern*	3,000	3,500	700
M1886, Various Calibers, Carbine, *Modern*	4,500	5,000	925
M1886, Various Calibers, Musket, *Modern*	6,000	7,000	1,000
M1886, For Deluxe, *Add* **$200.00–$400.00**			
M1886, For Extra Fancy Deluxe, *Add* **$1,500.00–$3,500.00**			
M1886, under #118,433, Various Calibers, Musket, *Antique*	7,000	8,000	1,250
M1886, under #118,443, Various Calibers, Rifle, *Antique*	3,500	4,000	825
M1886, under #118,443, Various Calibers, Carbine, *Antique*	5,500	6,000	1,200
M150, .22 L.R.R.F., Tube Feed, *Modern*	100	125	95
M250, .22 L.R.R.F., Tube Feed, *Modern*	100	125	100
M250 Deluxe, .22 L.R.R.F., Tube Feed, *Modern*	125	150	115
M255, .22 WMR, Tube Feed, *Modern*	125	150	105
M255 Deluxe, .22 WMR, Tube Feed, *Modern*	150	175	130

	V.G.	Exc.	Prior Edition Exc. Value
M53, Various Calibers, *Modern*	$1,000	$1,250	$750
M55, Various Calibers, *Modern*	650	750	700
M64, .219 Zipper, Pre '64. *Modern*	600	650	590
M64, .30-30 Win., Late Model, *Modern*	200	250	220
M64, Various Calibers, Pre '64, *Modern*	500	550	470
M64 Deer Rifle, Various Calibers, Pre '64, *Modern*	675	750	510
M65, .218 Bee, *Modern*	2,000	2,500	900
M65, Various Calibers, *Modern*	1,750	2,000	590
M71, .348 Win., Tube Feed, *Modern*	725	800	535
M71 Special, .348 Win., Tube Feed, *Modern*	750	950	680
M92, Various Calibers, Rifle, *Modern*	1,000	1,250	500
M92, Various Calibers, Carbine, *Modern*	1,250	1,500	610
M92, Various Calibers, Musket, *Modern*	1,500	1,750	750
M92, For Takedown, *Add* **$150.00–$275.00**			
M92, under #103316, Various Calibers, Rifle, *Antique*	1,500	1,750	600
M92, under #103316, Various Calibers, Carbine, *Antique*	1,750	2,000	690
M92, under #103316, Various Calibers, Musket, *Antique*	4,000	5,000	850
M94, .30-30 Win., Carbine, Late Model, *Modern*	200	250	150
M94, .44 Magnum, Carbine, *Modern*	225	275	300
M94, Various Calibers, Carbine, Pre '64, *Modern*	375	450	460
M94, Various Calibers, Carbine, Pre-War, *Modern*	750	850	530
M94, Various Calibers, Rifle, Pre-War, *Modern*	600	750	590
M94, Various Calibers, Rifle, Takedown, Pre-War, *Modern*	800	900	685
M94 Alaska Centennial, .30-30 Win., Commemorative, Carbine, *Curio*	1,000	1,500	1,475
Antlered Game, .30-30 Win., Commemorative, *Modern*	350	450	430
M94 Bicentennial, .30-30 Win., Commemorative, *Curio*	450	600	700
M94 Buffalo Bill 1 of 300, .30-30 Win., Commemorative, Rifle, *Curio*	1,750	2,000	1,400
M94 Buffalo Bill, .30-30 Win., Commemorative, Rifle, *Curio*	300	400	270
M94 Buffalo Bill, .30-30 Win., Commemorative, Carbine, *Curio*	275	375	270
M94 Canadian Centennial, .30-30 Win., Commemorative, Rifle, *Curio*	250	350	275
M94 Canadian Centennial, .30-30 Win., Commemorative, Carbine, *Curio*	250	350	275
M94 Centennial 66, .30-30 Win., Commemorative, Rifle, *Curio*	300	400	340
M94 Centennial 66, .30-30 Win., Commemorative, Carbine, *Curio*	300	400	330
M94 Classic, .30-30 Win., Rifle, *Modern*	150	200	185
M94 Cowboy 1 of 300, .30-30 Win., Commemorative, Carbine, *Curio*	1,500	2,500	1,700
M94 Cowboy, .30-30 Win., Commemorative, Carbine, *Curio*	275	400	400
Duke, .32-40 Win., Commemorative, *Modern*	2,000	3,000	2,000

	V.G.	Exc.	Prior Edition Exc. Value
M94 Golden Spike, .30-30 Win., Commemorative, Carbine, *Curio*	$250	$350	$300
M94 Illinois, .30-30 Win., Commemorative, Carbine, *Curio*	250	350	265
John Wayne, .32-40 Win., Commemorative, *Modern*	650	800	580
M94 Klondike, .30-30 Win., Commemorative, *Curio*	550	700	400
Legendary Frontiersman, .38-55 Win., Commemorative, *Modern*	375	450	400
Legendary Lawman, .30-30 Win., Commemorative, *Modern*	375	450	400
Limited Edition I, .30-30 Win., Commemorative, *Modern*	950	1,400	1,675
Limited Edition II, .30-30 Win., Commemorative, *Modern*	950	1,400	1,675
M94 Lone Star, .30-30 Win., Commemorative, Rifle, *Curio*	325	425	330
M94 Lone Star, .30-30 Win., Commemorative, Carbine, *Curio*	325	425	330
M94 Lone Star Set, .30-30 Win., Commemorative, *Curio*	600	750	725
M94 Nebraska Centennial, .30-30 Win., Commemorative, Carbine, *Curio*	900	1,300	1,200
M94 NRA, .30-30 Win., Commemorative, Musket, *Curio*	275	350	280
M94 NRA, .30-30 Win., Commemorative, Rifle, *Curio*	275	350	270
M94 NRA Set, .30-30 Win., Commemorative, *Curio*	450	650	600
Oliver Winchester, .38-55 Win., Commemorative, *Modern*	400	550	500
M94, RCMP, .30-30 Win., Commemorative, *Curio*	600	750	615
M94 Texas Ranger, .30-30 Win., Commemorative, *Curio*	550	700	500
M94 Theodore Roosevelt, .30-30 Win., Commemorative, Rifle, *Curio*	325	400	310
M94 Theodore Roosevelt, .30-30 Win., Commemorative, Carbine, *Curio*	325	400	310
M94 Theodore Roosevelt Set, .30-30 Win., Commemorative, *Curio*	600	750	675
U.S. Border Patrol, .30-30 Win., Commemorative, *Modern*	450	600	900
Wells Fargo, .30-30 Win., Commerative, *Modern*	400	500	580
M94 Wyoming Diamond Jubilee, .30-30 Win., Commemorative, Carbine, *Curio*	900	1,300	1,375
M94, under #50,000 Various Calibers, Carbine, *Antique*	1,750	2,000	600
M94, under #50,000, Various Calibers, Rifle, *Antique*	1,250	1,500	675
M94XTR, .30-30 Win., *Modern*	175	250	185
M94 Standard, .30-30 Win., *Modern*	175	250	175
M94 Trapper, .30-30 Win., *Modern*	200	275	170
M94XTR Big Bore, .375 Win., *Modern*	200	275	210
M95, Various Calibers, Rifle, *Modern*	1,500	2,000	700
M95, Various Calibers, Carbine, *Modern*	1,250	1,500	820
M95, Various Calibers, Musket, *Modern*	1,000	1,250	900
M95, For Takedown, *Add* **$100.00–$200.00**			
M95, under #19,477, Various Calibers, Rifle, *Antique*	2,000	2,500	900
M95, under #19,477, Various Calibers, Carbine, *Antique*	1,500	2,000	1,050
Model 9422, .22 L.R.R.F., Tube Feed, *Modern*	200	250	170

	V.G.	Exc.	Prior Edition Exc. Value
Model 9422M, .22 WMR, Tube Feed, *Modern*	$250	$275	$185
Model 9422XTR, .22 L.R.R.F., Tube Feed, *Modern*	275	300	210
Model 9422MXTR, .22 WMR, Tube Feed, *Modern*	300	325	230

RIFLE, SEMI-AUTOMATIC

	V.G.	Exc.	Prior
M100, Various Calibers, Clip Fed, *Modern*	275	325	395
M100, Various Calibers, Clip Fed, Carbine, *Modern*	325	375	380
M1903, .22 Win. Auto R.F., Tube Feed, *Modern*	325	375	330
M1905, Various Calibers, Clip Fed, *Modern*	350	400	560
M1907, .351 Win. Self-Loading, Clip Fed, *Modern*	550	600	460
M1907 Police, .351 Win. Self-Loading, Clip Fed, *Modern*	475	525	515
M1910, .401 Win. Self-Loading, Clip Fed, *Modern*	475	550	465
M190, .22 L.R.R.F., Tube Feed, *Modern*	100	125	70
M290 Deluxe, .22 L.R.R.F., Tube Feed, *Modern*	125	150	80
M490 Deluxe, .22 L.R.R.F., Clip Fed, Monte Carlo Stock, *Modern*	200	225	265
M55 Automatic, .22 L.R.R.F., *Modern*	150	175	150
M63, .22 L.R.R.F., Tube Feed, *Modern*	400	475	450
M74, .22 L.R.R.F., Clip Fed, *Modern*	150	175	190
M77, .22 L.R.R.F., Clip Fed, *Modern*	125	150	125
M77, .22 L.R.R.F., Tube Feed, *Modern*	150	175	125

RIFLE, SINGLESHOT

	V.G.	Exc.	Prior
Model 310, .22 L.R.R.F., Bolt Action, *Modern*	75	100	80
High-Wall, Various Calibers, Sporting Rifle, *Curio*	1,250	1,500	590
High-Wall, Various Calibers, Sporting Rifle, Takedown, *Curio*	1,500	1,750	750
High-Wall, Various Calibers, Schutzen Rifle, Takedown, *Curio*	4,000	4,500	1,700
High-Wall, Various Calibers, Schutzen Rifle, *Curio*	3,500	4,000	1,300
Low-Wall, .22 Long R.F., Musket, *Curio*	700	750	390
Low-Wall, Various Calibers, Sporting Rifle, *Curio*	600	650	410
Winder, .22 Long R.F., Musket, Takedown, *Curio*	625	700	525
Winder, .22 Long R.F., Musket, *Curio*	600	650	450

RIFLE, SLIDE ACTION

	V.G.	Exc.	Prior
M1890, Various Rimfires, *Modern*	575	625	360
M1890, Various Rimfires, Solid Frame, *Curio*	600	650	375
M1890, under #64,521, Various Rimfires, *Antique*	625	675	450
M1906, .22 L.R.R.F., Tube Feed, Hammer, *Modern*	600	650	400
M270, .22 L.R.R.F., Tube Feed, *Modern*	75	100	95
M270 Deluxe, .22 L.R.R.F., Tube Feed, *Modern*	100	125	120
M275, .22 WMR, Tube Feed, *Modern*	100	125	105
M275 Deluxe, .22 WMR, Tube Feed, *Modern*	125	150	135
M61, .22 L.R.R.F., Tube Feed, *Modern*	425	475	400
M61, Various Rimfires, Tube Feed, Octagon Barrel, *Modern*	850	1,000	465
M61 Magnum, .22 WMR, Tube Feed, *Modern*	550	600	485
M62, .22 L.R.R.F., Tube Feed, Hammer, *Modern*	350	400	400

	V.G.	Exc.	Prior Edition Exc. Value
M62 Gallery, .22 Short R.F., Tube Feed, Hammer, *Modern*............	*$400*	*$425*	*$435*

SHOTGUN, BOLT ACTION

Model 36, 9mm Shotshell, Takedown, Singleshot, *Curio*	*550*	*600*	*235*
Model 41, .410Ga., Takedown, Singleshot, *Modern*.........................	*425*	*475*	*225*
Model 41, .410 Ga., Takedown, Singleshot, Checkered Stock, *Modern*...	*450*	*500*	*260*

SHOTGUN, DOUBLE BARREL, OVER-UNDER

Model 101, 12 Ga., Trap Grade, Monte Carlo Stock, Single Trigger, Automatic Ejector, Engraved, *Modern*................................	*1,000*	*1,200*	*790*
Model 101, 12 Ga., Trap Grade, Single Trigger, Automatic Ejector, Checkered Stock, Engraved, *Modern*..................................	*1,000*	*1,200*	*790*
Model 101, 12 Ga. Mag. 3", Vent Rib, Single Trigger, Automatic Ejector, Checkered Stock, Engraved, *Modern*..................................	*675*	*750*	*775*
Model 101, Various Gauges, Skeet Grade, Single Trigger, Automatic Ejector, Checkered Stock, Engraved, *Modern*.................	*900*	*975*	*790*
Model 101, Various Gauges, Featherweight, Single Trigger, Automatic Ejector, Checkered Stock, Engraved, *Modern*.................	*850*	*950*	*790*
Model 101 3 Ga. Set, Various Gauges, Skeet Grade, Single Trigger, Automatic Ejector, Checkered Stock, Engraved, *Modern*.......	*2,500*	*3,000*	*1,750*
Model 101, 12 Ga., Field Grade, Single Trigger, Automatic Ejector, Engraved, *Modern*...	*675*	*725*	*775*
Model 101 Pigeon, 12 Ga., Trap Grade, Single Trigger, Automatic Ejector, Engraved, *Modern*...	*1,000*	*1,200*	*775*
Model 101 Pigeon, 12 Ga., Trap Grade, Monte Carlo Stock, Single Trigger, Automatic Ejector, Engraved, *Modern*......................	*1,050*	*1,250*	*775*
Model 101 Pigeon, 12 and 20 Gauges, Skeet Grade, Checkered Stock, Single Trigger, Automatic Ejector, Engraved, *Modern*..........	*1,000*	*1,200*	*850*
Model 101 Magnum, 12 Ga. 3", Single Trigger, Automatic Ejector, Engraved, *Modern*...	*700*	*800*	*795*
Model 96, 12 Ga., Trap Grade, Checkered Stock, Vent Rib, *Modern*...	*600*	*650*	*610*
Model 96, 12 Ga., Trap Grade, Monte Carlo Stock, Vent Rib, *Modern*...	*600*	*650*	*610*
Model 96, 12 and 20 Gauges, Field Grade, Checkered Stock, Vent Rib, *Modern*...	*575*	*625*	*595*
Model 96, 12 and 20 Gauges, Skeet Grade, Checkered Stock, Vent Rib, *Modern*	*600*	*650*	*610*

SHOTGUN, DOUBLE BARREL, SIDE-BY-SIDE

Model 21, For Extra Barrels, *Add* **25%–30%**			
Model 21, For Vent Rib, *Add* **$350.00–$400.00**			
Model 21, 410 Ga., Checkered Stock, Fancy Wood, *Modern*...........	*20,000*	*25,000*	*7,500*
Model 21, 12 Ga., Trap Grade, Hammerless, Single Selective Trigger, Selective Ejector, Vent Rib, *Modern*....................................	*3,500*	*3,750*	*4,250*
Model 21, 12 Ga., Trap Grade, Hammerless, Single Selective Trigger, Selective Ejector, Raised Matted Rib, *Modern*...................	*3,000*	*3,250*	*4,000*

	V.G.	Exc.	Prior Edition Exc. Value
Model 21, 12 and 16 Gauges, Skeet Grade, Hammerless, Single Selective Trigger, Selective Ejector, Vent Rib, *Modern*	$2,750	$3,000	$4,000
Model 21, 12 and 16 Gauges, Field Grade, Double Trigger, Automatic Ejector, Hammerless, *Modern*	3,000	3,500	3,400
Model 21, 12 and 16 Gauges, Field Grade, Double Trigger, Automatic Ejector, Hammerless, *Modern*	3,200	3,600	3,550
Model 21, 12 and 16 Gauges, Field Grade, Single Selective Trigger, Automatic Ejector, Hammerless, *Modern*	3,300	3,800	3,700
Model 21, 12 and 16 Gauges, Field Grade, Single Selective Trigger, Selective Ejector, Hammerless, *Modern*	3,350	3,850	3,700
Model 21, 20 Ga., Skeet Grade, Hammerless, Single Selective Trigger, Selective Ejector, Vent Rib, *Modern*	4,500	5,000	4,550
Model 21, 20 Ga., Skeet Grade, Hammerless, Single Selective Trigger, Selective Ejector, Raised Matted Rib, *Modern*	4,250	4,750	4,300
Model 21, 20 Ga., Field Grade, Double Trigger, Automatic Ejector, Hammerless, *Modern*	3,250	3,750	3,700
Mode 21, 20 Ga., Field Grade, Double Trigger, Selective Ejector, Hammerless, *Modern*	3,500	4,000	3,900
Model 21, 20 Ga., Field Grade, Single Selective Trigger, Automatic Ejector, Hammerless, *Modern*	3,750	4,250	4,000
Model 21, 20 Ga., Field Grade, Single Selective Trigger, Selective Ejector, Hammerless, *Modern*	4,000	4,500	4,100
Model 21 Custom, 12 Ga., Hammerless, Single Selective Trigger, Selective Ejector, Fancy Engraving, Fancy Checkering, *Modern*	6,750	7,500	6,000
Model 21 Custom, 20 Ga., Hammerless, Single Selective Trigger, Selective Ejector, Fancy Checkering, Fancy Engraving, *Modern*	7,500	8,500	6,750
Model 21 Duck, 12 Ga. Mag. 3", Hammerless, Single Selective Trigger, Selective Ejector, Raised Matted Rib, *Modern*	3,250	3,750	3,900
Model 21 Duck, 12 Ga. Mag. 3", Hammerless, Single Selective Trigger, Selective Ejector, Vent Rib, *Modern*	3,750	4,250	3,950
Model 21 Grand American, 12 Ga., Hammerless, Single Selective Trigger, Selective Ejector, Fancy Engraving, Fancy Checkering, *Modern*	10,500	12,500	9,750
Model 21 Grand American, 20 Ga., Hammerless, Single Selective Trigger, Selective Ejector, Fancy Checkering, Fancy Engraving, *Modern*	12,500	15,000	10,500
Model 21 Pigeon, 12 Ga., Hammerless, Single Selective Trigger, Selective Ejector, Fancy Engraving, Fancy Checkering, *Modern*	7,500	10,000	6,250
Model 21 Pigeon, 20 Ga., Hammerless, Single Selective Trigger, Selective Ejector, Fancy Engraving, Fancy Checkering, *Modern*	15,000	17,500	7,000
Model 23 English, 12 or 20 Gauges, Hammerless, Single Trigger, Selective Ejector, Fancy Checkering, Engraved, *Modern*	850	1,000	865
Model 23 Pigeon, 12 or 20 Gauges, Hammerless, Single Trigger, Selective Ejector, Engraved, Fancy Checkering, *Modern*	900	1,050	825
Model 23 Grand European, 12 Ga., Hammerless, Single Selective Trigger, Selective Ejector, Fancy Engraving, Fancy Checkering, *Modern*	1,250	1,450	1,250

Winchester Big Bore 94XTR

Winchester Model 23 Pigeon Grade XTR Field Gun

Winchester M1400

	V.G.	Exc.	Prior Edition Exc. Value
Model 24, Various Gauges, Double Trigger, Automatic Ejector, *Modern*	*$450*	*$500*	*$350*
SHOTGUN, LEVER ACTION			
M 1887, Various Gauges, *Antique*	*1,500*	*1,750*	*565*
M 1887, Deluxe Grade, Various Gauges, *Antique*	*2,250*	*2,500*	*615*
M 1887, Deluxe Grade, 10 Ga., 2⅛, Tube Feed, Checkered Stock, Damascus Barrel, *Curio*	*2,500*	*2,750*	*535*
M 1887, 10 Ga., 2⅛, Tube Feed, Plain, *Curio*	*1,650*	*1,850*	*460*
1901, 10 Ga., 2⅛, Tube Feed, Plain, *Curio*	*1,000*	*1,250*	*580*
SHOTGUN, SEMI-AUTOMATIC			
Model 1400 Trap, 12 Ga., Vent Rib, *Modern*	*300*	*350*	*270*
Model 1400 Trap, 12 Ga., Monte Carlo Stock, Vent Rib, *Modern*	*325*	*375*	*295*
Model 1400 Trap, 12 Ga., Vent Rib, Recoil Reducer, *Modern*	*375*	*425*	*325*
Model 1400 Skeet, 12 and 20 Gauges, Vent Rib, *Modern*	*300*	*350*	*270*
Model 1400 Deer, 12 Ga., Open Sights, Slug Gun, *Modern*	*225*	*250*	*235*
Model 1400 Field, 12 and 20 Gauges, Winchoke, *Modern*	*275*	*325*	*220*
Model 1400 Field, 12 and 20 Gauges, Winchoke, Vent Rib, *Modern*	*300*	*350*	*235*
Model 1500, 12 or 20 Gauges, Field Grade, Plain, *Modern*	*225*	*275*	*295*
Model 1500, 12 or 20 Gauges, Field Grade, Vent Rib, *Modern*	*250*	*300*	*320*
Model 1911, 12 Ga., Takedown, Plain, *Modern*	*350*	*400*	*340*
Model 1911, 12 Ga., Takedown, Checkered Stock, *Modern*	*375*	*425*	*410*

	V.G.	Exc.	Prior Edition Exc. Value
Model 40, 12 Ga., Takedown, Field Grade, *Modern*	$375	$425	$350
Model 40, 12 Ga., Takedown, Skeet Grade, Adjustable Choke, *Modern*	425	475	400
Model 50, 12 Ga., Trap Grade, Vent Rib, Monte Carlo Stock, *Modern*	350	400	485
Model 50, 12 and 20 Gauges, Field Grade, Plain Barrel, Checkered Stock, *Modern*	300	350	300
Model 50, 12 and 20 Gauges, Field Grade, Vent Rib, Checkered Stock, *Modern*	350	400	335
Model 50, 12 and 20 Gauges, Skeet Grade, Vent Rib, Checkered Stock, *Modern*	350	400	450

SHOTGUN, SINGLESHOT

	V.G.	Exc.	Prior
Model 101, 12 Ga., Trap Grade, Vent Rib, *Modern*	575	650	490
Model 20, .410 Ga., 2¹/₈", Takedown, Hammer, Checkered Stock, *Modern*	225	275	270
Model 37, For Red Letter, *Add* **25%–40%**			
Model 37, .410 Ga., Takedown, Automatic Ejector, Plain Barrel, *Modern*	150	175	140
Model 37, 12 Ga., Takedown, Automatic Ejector, Plain Barrel, *Modern*	125	150	125
Model 37, 16 Ga., Takedown, Automatic Ejector, Plain Barrel, *Modern*	125	150	115
Model 37, 20 Ga., Takedown, Automatic Ejector, Plain Barrel, *Modern*	125	150	135
Model 37, 28 Ga., Takedown, Automatic Ejector, Plain Barrel, *Modern*	400	500	165

SHOTGUN, SLIDE ACTION

	V.G.	Exc.	Prior
Model 12, 12 Ga., Pre '64, Takedown, Trap Grade, Raised Matted Rib, *Modern*	675	750	750
Model 12, 12 Ga., Pre '64, Takedown, Trap Grade, Vent Rib, *Modern*	725	800	830
Model 12, 12 Ga., Pre '64, Takedown, Trap Grade, Vent Rib, Monte Carlo Stock, *Modern*	775	850	875
Model 12, 12 Ga., Pre-War, Takedown, Vent Rib, *Modern*	600	650	575
Model 12, 12 Ga., Pre-War, Takedown, Riot Gun, *Modern*	650	700	420
Model 12, 12 Ga., Post '64, Trap Grade, Checkered Stock, *Modern*	550	600	575
Model 12, 12 Ga., Post '64, Trap Gun, Monte Carlo Stock, *Modern*	575	625	575
Model 12, Various Gauges, Pre '64, Takedown, Skeet Grade, Raised Matted Rib, *Modern*	600	650	700
Model 12, Various Gauges, Pre '64, Takedown, Skeet Grade, Vent Rib, *Modern*	650	700	750
Model 12, Various Gauges, Pre '64, Takedown, Skeet Grade, Plain Barrel, *Modern*	575	625	675
Model 12, Various Gauges, Pre '64, Takedown, Skeet Grade, Plain Barrel, Adjustable Choke, *Modern*	600	650	710

	V.G.	Exc.	Prior Edition Exc. Value
Model 12, Various Gauges, Pre '64, Takedown, Raised Matted Rib, *Modern*	$550	$600	$645
Model 12, Featherweight, Various Gauges, Pre '64, Takedown, *Modern*	500	550	625
Model 12, Heavy Duck, 12 Ga. Mag. 3", Pre '64, Takedown, Vent Rib, *Modern*	600	650	675
Model 12, Heavy Duck, 12 Ga. Mag. 3", Pre '64, Takedown, Raised Matted Rib, *Modern*	575	625	650
Model 12, Pigeon Grade, 12 Ga., Pre '64, Takedown, Trap Grade, Vent Rib, *Modern*	1,600	1,800	1,350
Model 12, Pigeon Grade, 12 Ga., Pre '64, Takedown, Trap Grade, Raised Matted Rib, *Modern*	1,450	1,650	1,200
Model 12, Pigeon Grade, 12 Ga., Various Gauges, Pre '64, Takedown, Skeet Choke, Raised Matted Rib, *Modern*	1,400	1,550	1,075
Model 12, Pigeon Grade, Various Gauges, Pre '64, Takedown, Skeet Choke, Vent Rib, *Modern*	1,400	1,600	1,175
Model 12, Pigeon Grade, Various Gauges, Pre '64, Takedown, Skeet Choke, Plain Barrel, Adjustable Choke, *Modern*	800	900	975
Model 12, Pigeon Grade, Various Gauges, Pre '64, Takedown, Plain Barrel, *Modern*	1,250	1,500	920
Model 12, Pigeon Grade, Various Gauges, Pre '64, Takedown, Vent Rib, *Modern*	1,500	1,750	1,000
Model 12, Standard, Various Gauges, Pre '64, Takedown, *Modern*	550	600	565
Model 12, Super Pigeon, 12 Ga., Post '64, Takedown, Vent Rib, Engraved, Checkered Stock, *Modern*	2,000	2,500	2,100
Model 1200, For Recoil Reducer, *Add* **$35.00–$50.00**			
Model 1200 Field, 12 and 20 Gauges, Adjustable Choke, *Modern*	200	250	170
Model 1200 Field, 12 and 20 Gauges, Adjustable Choke, Vent Rib, *Modern*	225	275	175
Model 1200 Field, 12 and 20 Gauges, *Modern*	150	200	150
Model 1200 Field, 12 and 20 Gauges, Vent Rib, *Modern*	175	225	160
Model 1200 Field, 12 Ga. Mag. 3", *Modern*	175	200	170
Model 1200 Field, 12 Ga. Mag. 3", Vent Rib, *Modern*	175	225	180
Model 1200 Deer, 12 Ga., Open Sights, *Modern*	150	200	175
Model 1200 Defender, 12 Ga., *Modern*	125	250	165
Model 1200 Police Stainless, 12 Ga., *Modern*	200	250	270
Model 1300, 12 or 20 Gauges, Plain Barrel, *Modern*	250	300	195
Model 1300, 12 or 20 Gauges, Vent Rib, *Modern*	275	325	215
Model 1300, 12 or 20 Gauges, Plain Barrel, Winchoke, *Modern*	300	350	230
Model 1300, 12 or 20 Gauges, Vent Rib, Winchoke, *Modern*	325	375	265
Model 1300 Deer, 12 Ga., Open Sights, *Modern*	275	325	240
Model 25, 12 Ga., Solid Frame, Plain Barrel, *Modern*	300	350	265
Model 42, .410 Ga., Field Grade, Takedown, *Modern*	750	850	685

	V.G.	Exc.	Prior Edition Exc. Value
Model 42, .410 Ga., Field Grade, Takedown, Raised Matted Rib, *Modern*	$750	$1,000	$735
Model 42, .420 Ga., Skeet Grade, Takedown, Raised Matted Rib, *Modern*	1,350	1,550	865
Model 42 Deluxe, .410 Ga., Takedown, Vent Rib, Fancy Checkering, Fancy Wood, *Modern*	1,500	1,750	975
Model 97, 12 Ga., Solid Frame, Plain, *Modern*	500	550	260
Model 97, 12 Ga., Takedown, Plain, *Modern*	550	600	330
Model 97, 12 Ga., Takedown, Riot Gun, *Modern*	375	425	365
Model 97, 12 Ga., Solid Frame, Riot Gun, *Modern*	425	475	320
Model 97, 16 Ga., Solid Frame, Plain, *Modern*	450	500	235
Model 97, 16 Ga., Takedown, Plain, *Modern*	500	550	265
Model 97 Pigeon, 12 Ga., Takedown, Checkered, *Modern*	2,000	2,500	1,175
Model 97 Tournament, 12 Ga., Takedown, Checkered Stock, *Modern*	800	900	735
Model 97 Trap, 12 Ga., Takedown, Checkered Stock, *Modern*	750	850	580
Model 97 Trench, 12 Ga., Solid Frame, Riot Gun, Military, *Curio*	650	750	460
Model 97 Trench, 12 Ga., Solid Frame, Riot Gun, Military, with Bayonet, *Curio*	650	800	535

WINFIELD ARMS CO. Made by Norwich Falls Pistol Co., c. 1880.

HANDGUN, REVOLVER

.32 Short R.F., 5 Shot, Spur Trigger, Solid Frame, Single Action, *Antique* 150 175 165

WINFIELD ARMS CO. Made by Crescent, c. 1900.

SHOTGUN, DOUBLE BARREL, SIDE-BY-SIDE

Various Gauges, Outside Hammers, Damascus Barrel, *Modern* 150 175 170
Various Gauges, Hammerless, Steel Barrel, *Modern* 175 200 190
Various Gauges, Hammerless, Damascus Barrel, *Modern* 150 175 170
Various Gauges, Outside Hammers, Steel Barrel, *Modern* 175 200 185

SHOTGUN, SINGLESHOT

Various Gauges, Hammer, Steel Barrel, *Modern* 75 100 85

WINGERT, RICHARD Lancaster, Pa. 1775–1777. See Kentucky Rifles, U.S. Military.

WINOCA ARMS CO. Made by Crescent for Jacobi Hardware Co., Philadelphia, Pa.

SHOTGUN, DOUBLE BARREL, SIDE-BY-SIDE

Various Gauges, Outside Hammers, Damascus Barrel, *Modern* 150 175 170
Various Gauges, Hammerless, Steel Barrel, *Modern* 175 200 190

	V.G.	Exc.	Prior Edition Exc. Value
Various Gauges, Hammerless, Damascus Barrel, *Modern*	$150	$175	$170
Various Gauges, Outside Hammers, Steel Barrel, *Modern*..............	175	200	185
SHOTGUN, SINGLESHOT			
Various Gauges, Hammer, Steel Barrel, *Modern*............,..............	75	100	85

WINSLOW ARMS CO. Established in Venice, Fla. about 1962, moved to Osprey, Fla. about 1976, and is now in Camden, S.C.

RIFLE, BOLT ACTION

For Left-Hand Act, Add $50.00–$70.00

	V.G.	Exc.	
Crown, Various Calibers, Carved, Fancy Wood, Inlays, *Modern*........	1,000	1,250	1,125
Emperor, Various Calibers, Carved, Fancy Engraving, Ornate, Fancy Wood, Inlays, *Modern*..............	4,500	5,500	5,000
Imperial, Various Calibers, Carved, Engraved, Fancy Wood, Inlays, *Modern*..............	3,000	3,250	2,800
Regal, Various Calibers, Fancy Checkering, Inlays, *Modern*...........	550	600	550
Regent, Various Calibers, Inlays, Carved, Fancy Wood, *Modern*........	650	725	675
Regimental, Various Calibers, Carved, Inlays, *Modern*..................	750	900	850
Royal, Various Calibers, Carved, Fancy Wood, Inlays, *Modern*......	1,250	1,500	1,450
Commander, Various Calibers, Fancy Checkering, Inlays, *Modern*..............	450	500	695

WITHERS, MICHAEL Lancaster, Pa. 1774–1805. See Kentucky Rifles, U.S. Military.

WITTES HDW. CO. Made by Stevens Arms.

SHOTGUN, DOUBLE BARREL, SIDE-BY-SIDE

Model 311, Various Gauges, Hammerless, Steel Barrel, *Modern*	150	175	175

SHOTGUN, SINGLESHOT

Model 90, Various Gauges, Takedown, Automatic Ejector, Plain, Hammer, *Modern*..............	50	75	60
Model 94, Various Gauges, Takedown, Automatic Ejector, Plain, Hammer, *Modern*..............	50	75	60

WOGDON London, England & Dublin, Ireland 1760–1797.

HANDGUN, FLINTLOCK

.56, Officers, Holster Pistol, Flared, Octagon Barrel, Steel Furniture, Engraved, High Quality, *Antique*..............	2,500	3,000	2,900

WOLF Spain, c. 1900.

HANDGUN, SEMI-AUTOMATIC

.25 ACP, Clip Fed, *Modern*..............	125	150	135

			Prior Edition
	V.G.	Exc.	Exc. Value

WOLF, A.W. Suhl, German, c. 1930.
SHOTGUN, DOUBLE BARREL, SIDE-BY-SIDE
12 Ga., Engraved, Platinium Inlays, Ivory Inlays, Ornate, Cased,
Modern $6,000 $7,000 $6,800

WOLFHEIMER, PHILIP Lancaster, Pa., c. 1774. See Kentucky
Rifles.

WOLVERINE ARMS CO. Made by Crescent for Fletcher Hardware Co., c. 1900.
SHOTGUN, DOUBLE BARREL, SIDE-BY-SIDE
Various Gauges, Outside Hammers, Damascus Barrel,
Modern 150 175 170
Various Gauges, Hammerless, Steel Barrel, *Modern* 175 200 190
Various Gauges, Hammerless, Damascus Barrel, *Modern* 150 175 170
Various Gauges, Outside Hammers, Steel Barrel, *Modern* 175 200 185
SHOTGUN, SINGLESHOT
Various Gauges, Hammer, Steel Barrel, *Modern* 75 100 85

WOODWARD, JAMES & SONS London, England.
SHOTGUN, DOUBLE BARREL, OVER-UNDER
Best Quality, Various Gauges, Sidelock, Automatic Ejector,
Double Trigger, Fancy Engraving, Fancy Checkering, *Modern* 20,000 25,000 15,000
Best Quality, Various Gauges, Sidelock, Automatic Ejector,
Single Trigger, Fancy Engraving, Fancy Checkering, *Modern* 22,000 27,000 17,000
SHOTGUN, DOUBLE BARREL, SIDE-BY-SIDE
Best Quality, Various Gauges, Sidelock, Automatic Ejector,
Double Trigger, Fancy Engraving, Fancy Checkering, *Modern* 15,000 20,000 12,000
Best Quality, Various Gauges, Sidelock, Automatic Ejector,
Single Trigger, Fancy Engraving, Fancy Checkering, *Modern* 17,000 22,000 13,500
SHOTGUN, SINGLESHOT
12 Ga., Trap Grade, Vent Rib, Hammerless, Fancy Engraving,
Fancy Checkering, *Modern* 7,000 9,500 14,000

WORTHINGTON ARMS Made by Stevens Arms.
SHOTGUN, DOUBLE BARREL, SIDE-BY-SIDE
M 315, Various Gauges, Hammerless, Steel Barrel, *Modern* 150 175 175
Model 215, 12 and 16 Gauges, Outside Hammers, Steel Barrel,
Modern 150 175 165

	V.G.	Exc.	Prior Edition Exc. Value

WORTHINGTON ARMS CO. Made by Crescent for Geo.
Worthington Co., Cleveland, Ohio.

SHOTGUN, DOUBLE BARREL, SIDE-BY-SIDE

	V.G.	Exc.	Prior Edition Exc. Value
Various Gauges, Outside Hammers, Damascus Barrel, *Modern*	$150	$175	$170
Various Gauges, Hammerless, Steel Barrel, *Modern*	175	200	190
Various Gauges, Hammerless, Damascus Barrel, *Modern*	150	175	170
Various Gauges, Outside Hammers, Steel Barrel, *Modern*	175	200	185

SHOTGUN, SINGLESHOT

	V.G.	Exc.	Prior Edition Exc. Value
Various Gauges, Hammer, Steel Barrel, *Modern*	75	100	85

WORTHINGTON, GEORGE Made by Stevens Arms.

SHOTGUN, DOUBLE BARREL, SIDE-BY-SIDE

	V.G.	Exc.	Prior Edition Exc. Value
M 315, Various Gauges, Hammerless, Steel Barrel, *Modern*	150	175	165
Model 215, 12 and 16 Gauges, Outside Hammers, Steel Barrel, *Modern*	125	150	160
Model 311, Various Gauges, Hammerless, Steel Barrel, *Modern*	150	175	170

WUETHRICH W. Wuethrich, Werkzeugbau, Lutzelfluh, Switzerland.

RIFLE, SINGLESHOT

	V.G.	Exc.	Prior Edition Exc. Value
Falling Block, Various Calibers, Engraved, Fancy Wood, Scope Mounted, *Modern*	1,000	1,250	1,250

Y

YATO Hamada Arsenal, Japan.

HANDGUN, SEMI-AUTOMATIC

	V.G.	Exc.	Prior Edition Exc. Value
Yato, .32 ACP, Clip Fed, Pre-War, *Curio*	$2,500	$3,000	$3,000
Yato, .32 ACP, Clip Fed, Military, *Curio*	2,000	2,200	2,200

YDEAL Made by Francisco Arizmendi, Eibar, Spain.

HANDGUN, SEMI-AUTOMATIC

	V.G.	Exc.	Prior Edition Exc. Value
.25 ACP, Clip Fed, Blue, *Modern*	100	125	135
.32 ACP, Clip Fed, Blue, *Modern*	125	150	145

YOU BET Made by Hopkins & Allen, c. 1880.

HANDGUN, REVOLVER

	V.G.	Exc.	Prior Edition Exc. Value
.22 Short R.F., 7 Shot, Spur Trigger, Solid Frame, Single Action, *Antique*	150	175	165

YOUNG AMERICA See Harrington & Richardson Arms Co.

YOUNG, HENRY Easton, Pa. 1774–1780. See Kentucky Rifles.

YOUNG, JOHN Easton, Pa. 1775–1788. See Kentucky Rifles, U.S. Military.

Z

Z Ceska Zbrojovka, Prague, Czechoslovakia.

HANDGUN, SEMI-AUTOMATIC

	V.G.	Exc.	Prior Edition Exc. Value
Vest Pocket, .25 ACP, Clip Fed, *Modern*	$100	$125	$125

ZABALA Zabala Hermanos, Eibar, Spain.

SHOTGUN, DOUBLE BARREL, SIDE-BY-SIDE

12 Ga., Boxlock, Chackered Stock, Double Triggers, *Modern*	150	175	170

ZANOTTI Ravenna, Italy.

HANDGUN, FLINTLOCK

Brescia Style, .50, Carved Stock, Engraved, Reproduction, *Antique*	125	150	130

ZARAGOZA Zaragoza, Mexico.

HANDGUN, SEMI-AUTOMATIC

Corla, Type 1, .22 L.R.R.F., Colt System, Clip Fed, Blue, *Modern*	575	650	650
Corla, Type 2, .22 L.R.R.F., Clip Fed, Blue, *Modern*	400	450	450

ZASTAVA Zavodi Crvena Zastava, Kragujevac, Yugoslavia. Also see Mark X.

HANDGUN, SEMI-AUTOMATIC

Model 65, 9mm Luger, Clip Fed, Blue, *Modern*	200	250	250
Model 67, .32 ACP, Clip Fed, Blue, *Modern*	125	150	140

ZEHNA Made by E. Zehner Waffenfabrik, Suhl, Germany 1919–1928.

HANDGUN, SEMI-AUTOMATIC

Vest Pocket, .25 ACP, Under #5,000, Clip Fed, Blue, *Curio*	250	300	265
Vest Pocket, .25 ACP, Clip Fed, Blue, *Curio*	300	350	300

	V.G.	Exc.	Prior Edition Exc. Value

ZEPHYR Tradename of A.F. Stoeger.

SHOTGUN, DOUBLE BARREL, SIDE-BY-SIDE

Woodlander II, Various Gauges, Checkered Stock, Boxlock, Double Triggers, Light Engraving, *Modern* .... $425 | $475 | $220

Sterlingworth II, Various Gauges, Checkered Stock, Sidelock, Double Triggers, Light Engraving, *Modern* .... 575 | 650 | 320

ZOLI, ANGELO Brescia, Italy.

RIFLE, PERCUSSION

.50 Hawkin, Brass Furniture, Reproduction, *Antique* .... 150 | 175 | 155

SHOTGUN, DOUBLE BARREL, OVER-UNDER

Angel, 12 Ga., Trap Grade, Single Selective Trigger, Engraved, Checkered Stock, *Modern* .... 700 | 775 | 465

Angel, 12 and 20 Gauges, Field Grade, Single Selective Trigger, Engraved, Checkered Stock, *Modern* .... 675 | 750 | 420

Condor, 12 Ga., Trap Grade, Single Selective Trigger, Engraved, Checkered Stock, *Modern* .... 625 | 700 | 390

Condor, 12 and 20 Gauges, Single Selective Trigger, Field Grade, Checkered Stock, Engraved, *Modern* .... 600 | 675 | 365

Monte Carlo, 12 Ga., Trap Grade, Single Selective Trigger, Engraved, Checkered Stock, *Modern* .... 775 | 875 | 545

Monte Carlo, 12 and 20 Gauges, Field Grade, Single Selective Trigger, Engraved, Checkered Stock, *Modern* .... 750 | 850 | 520

ZOLI, ANTONIO Gardone, V.T., Italy.

SHOTGUN, DOUBLE BARREL, OVER-UNDER

Golden Snipe, 12 Ga., Trap Grade, Single Trigger, Automatic Ejector, Engraved, Checkered Stock, *Modern* .... 450 | 500 | 445

Golden Snipe, 12 and 20 Gauges, Vent Rib, Single Trigger, Automatic Ejector, Engraved, Checkered Stock, *Modern* .... 500 | 550 | 385

Golden Snipe, 12 and 20 Gauges, Skeet Grade, Single Trigger, Automatic Ejector, Engraved, Checkered Stock, *Modern* .... 550 | 600 | 450

Silver Snipe, 12 Ga., Trap Grade, Single Trigger, Vent Rib, Engraved, Checkered Stock, *Modern* .... 450 | 500 | 365

Silver Snipe, 12 and 20 Gauges, Vent Rib, Single Trigger, Engraved, Checkered Stock, *Modern* .... 425 | 475 | 335

Silver Snipe, 12 and 20 Gauges, Skeet Grade, Single Trigger, Vent Rib, Engraved, Checkered Stock, *Modern* .... 450 | 500 | 365

SHOTGUN, DOUBLE BARREL, SIDE-BY-SIDE

Silver Hawk, 12 and 20 Gauges, Double Trigger, Engraved, Checkered Stock, *Modern* .... 400 | 450 | 345

	V.G.	Exc.	Prior Edition Exc. Value

ZONDA Hispano Argentina Fab. de Automiviles, Buenos Aires, Argentina.

HANDGUN, SINGLESHOT

.22 L.R.R.F., Blue, *Modern* $225 $275 $275

ZULAICA M. Zulaica y Cia., Eibar, Spain.

HANDGUN, SEMI-AUTOMATIC

.32 ACP, Clip Fed, Blue, Military, *Curio* 150 175 160

AUTOMATIC REVOLVER

.22 L.R.R.F., Zig-Zag Cylinder, Blue, *Curio*.................................... 650 750 900

CARTRIDGE PRICES

The newcomers joining the swelling ranks of cartridge collectors have made prices in this specialized field quite volatile because of increased demand. This trend will continue for the foreseeable future.

The prices shown are based on the average value of a single cartridge with (unless otherwise noted) a common headstamp ranging from very good to excellent condition. Rare headstamps, unusual bullets, scarce case construction, will add to the value of the item. On common cartridges, empty cases are worth about **20%** to **25%** of the value shown; with rare calibers the empties should bring about **75%** to **80%** of the price of the loaded round. Dummies and blanks are worth about the same as the value shown. Full boxes of ammunition of common type should earn a discount of **15%** to **20%** per cartridge, whereas full boxes of rare ammo will command a premium because of the collectibility of the box itself.

	V.G.	Exc.	Prior Edition Exc. Value
.145 Alton Jones, *Modern*	$4.50	$6.00	$4.00
.17 Alton Jones, *Modern*	2.50	3.25	2.25
.17 Rem., Jacketed Bullet, *Modern*	.75	1.15	.80
.218 Bee, Various Makers, *Modern*	.75	1.15	.80
.219 Zipper, Various Makers, *Modern*	.95	1.60	1.20
.22 BB Cap R.F., Lead Bullet, *Antique*	.20	.30	.25
.22 CB Cap R.F., Lead Bullet, *Antique*	.20	.30	.25
.22 CB Cap R.F., Two Piece Case, *Antique*	.25	.45	.35
.22 Extra Long R.F., Various Makers, *Curio*	1.25	1.65	1.35
.22 Hi-Power, Various Makers, *Modern*	1.15	1.75	1.25
.22 Hornet, Various Makers, *Modern*	.75	1.05	.75
.22 L.R.R.F., Various Makers, *Modern*	.10	.15	.10
.22 L.R.R.F., Shotshell, Various Makers, *Modern*	.15	.20	.15
.22 L.R.R.F., Brass Case Russian, *Antique*	.45	.60	.50
.22 L.R.R.F., Brass Case Austrian, *Antique*	.35	.55	.45
.22 L.R.R.F., British Raised K, *Antique*	2.50	3.75	3.25
.22 L.R.R.F., Wadcutter, *Modern*	.35	.60	.50
.22 L.R.R.F., Tracer, U.M.C., *Modern*	.75	1.15	.85
.22 L.R.R.F., Tracer, Gevelot, *Modern*	.25	.40	.30
.22 L.R.R.F., Devastator, *Modern*	.20	.30	.25
.22 L.R.R.F., U.M.C., "S & W Long", *Modern*	3.50	5.55	4.85
.22 Long R.F., Various Makers, *Modern*	.09	.11	.09
.22 Long R.F., Lead Bullet, *Antique*	.20	.30	.25

	V.G.	Exc.	Prior Edition Exc. Value
.22 Maynard Extra Long, Various Makers, *Curio*	$1.75	$2.25	$1.75
.22 Newton, Soft Point Bullet, *Modern*	12.00	17.00	15.00
.22 Rem. Auto. R.F., Various Makers, *Modern*	.35	.50	.45
.22 Rem. Jet, Jacketed Bullet, *Modern*	.65	.95	.65
.22 Short R.F., Various Makers, *Modern*	.06	.10	.05
.22 Short R.F., Blank, Various Makers, *Modern*	.10	.15	.10
.22 Short R.F., Copper Case Raised "U", *Antique*	2.25	3.85	3.45
.22 Short R.F., Copper Case Raised "H", *Antique*	2.00	3.35	2.95
.22 Short R.F., Lead Bullet, *Antique*	.20	.30	.25
.22 WCF, Various Makers, *Modern*	.65	.80	.75
.22 Win. Auto. R.F., Various Makers, *Modern*	.25	.40	.35
.22 WMR, Various Makers, *Modern*	.15	.25	.17
.22 WMR, Shotshell, Various Makers, *Modern*	.20	.35	.25
.22 WRF, Various Makers, *Modern*	.15	.20	.17
.22-15-60 Stevens, Lead Bullet *Curio*	3.00	5.00	4.00
.22-3000 G & H, Soft Point Bullet, *Modern*	1.50	3.05	2.35
.220 Swift, Various Makers, *Modern*	.85	1.70	1.20
.221 Rem. Fireball, Various Makers, *Modern*	.45	.85	.65
.222 Rem., Various Makers, *Modern*	.45	.85	.65
.222 Rem. Mag., Various Makers, *Modern*	.40	.65	.55
.22-250, Various Makers, *Modern*	.50	.90	.70
.223 Rem., Various Makers, *Modern*	.65	.80	.60
.223 Rem., Military, Various Makers, *Modern*	.55	.70	.50
.223 Armalite, Experimental, *Modern*	4.00	6.25	5.25
.224 Wby., Varmintmaster, *Modern*	1.00	1.75	1.25
.224 Win., Experimental, *Modern*	3.75	5.50	4.50
.224 Win., E2 Ball WCC 58, *Modern*	5.00	6.75	6.25
.225 Win., Various Makers, *Modern*	.50	.85	.65
.230 Long, Various Makers, *Modern*	1.25	1.95	1.65
.230 Short, Various Makers, *Modern*	.75	1.20	1.00
.236 U.S. Navy Rimless, *Modern*	7.50	10.00	8.00
.236 U.S. Navy Rimmed, *Modern*	4.00	6.50	5.50
.240 Belted N.E., Jacketed Bullet, *Modern*	1.50	2.00	1.50
.240 Flanged N.E., Various Makers, *Modern*	2.00	3.50	3.00
.240 Wby. Mag., *Modern*	1.00	1.65	1.35
.242 Rimless N.E., Various Makers, *Modern*	4.00	5.50	5.00
.243 Win., Various Makers, *Modern*	.65	.95	.75
.244 H &H Mag., Jacketed Bullet, *Modern*	4.00	5.40	4.80
.244 Halger Mag., Various Makers, *Modern*	20.00	31.00	27.00
.244 Rem., Various Makers, *Modern*	1.10	1.40	1.10
.246 Purdey, Soft Point Bullet, *Modern*	3.00	4.50	4.00
.247 Wby. Mag., *Modern*	1.10	1.75	1.45
.25 ACP, Various Makers, *Modern*	.35	.45	.35

	V.G.	Exc.	Prior Edition Exc. Value
.25 L.F., Various Makers, #50 Allen, *Curio*	$3.50	$5.25	$4.75
.25 Rem., Various Makers, *Modern*	.80	1.45	1.25
.25 Short R.F., Lead Bullet, *Antique*	.25	.55	.45
.25 Stevens R.F., Wood Shotshell Bullet, *Modern*	1.25	1.75	1.25
.25 Stevens Short R.F., Various Makers, *Modern*	.25	.55	.45
.25 Stevens Long R.F., Various Makers, *Modern*	.40	.50	.40
.25-06 Rem., Various Makers, *Modern*	.75	.95	.75
.25-20 WCF, Lead Bullet, Various Makers, *Modern*	.40	.55	.45
.25-20 WCF, Jacketed Bullet, Various Makers, *Modern*	.45	.60	.50
.25-21, Jacketed Bullet, *Curio*	3.25	4.75	4.25
.25-25, Various Makers, *Modern*	3.00	4.50	4.00
.25-35 WCF, Various Makers, *Modern*	.60	1.05	.85
.25-36, Jacketed Bullet, *Curio*	1.90	2.85	2.45
.250 Savage, Various Makers, *Modern*	.65	1.00	.80
.255 Rook, Various Makers, *Curio*	.90	1.65	1.35
.256 Gibbs Mag., Various Makers, *Modern*	4.25	5.50	5.00
.256 Newton, Soft Point Bullet, *Modern*	1.75	2.75	2.25
.256 Win. Mag., Various Makers, *Modern*	.60	.85	.65
.257 Roberts, Various Makers, *Modern*	.75	.95	.75
.257 Wby. Mag., *Modern*	1.00	1.60	1.40
.26 BSA, Soft Point Bullet, *Modern*	3.25	4.75	4.25
.264 Win. Mag., Various Makers, *Modern*	.65	1.00	.80
.267 Rem. R.F., Experimental, *Curio*	8.50	11.25	10.25
.270 Wby. Mag., *Modern*	1.10	1.50	1.30
.270 Win., Various Makers, *Modern*	.80	1.00	.80
.270 Win., Flare Cartridge, Various Makers, *Modern*	1.85	2.70	2.40
.275 Flanged Mag., Various Makers, *Modern*	1.85	2.75	2.25
.275 H & H Mag., Various Makers, *Modern*	3.50	4.75	4.25
.275 Rigby, Various Makers, *Modern*	3.00	4.25	3.75
.276 Pederson, Various Makers, Military, *Curio*	3.00	3.75	3.25
.276 Garand, Military, Experimental, *Curio*	3.00	3.75	3.25
.276 Enfield, Various Makers, Military, *Modern*	6.50	8.75	8.25
.28 Cup Primed Cartridge, Various Makers, *Curio*	9.50	11.25	10.25
.28-30-120 Stevens, Lead Bullet, *Curio*	4.25	5.00	4.50
.280 Flanged N.E., Various Makers, *Modern*	4.00	4.75	4.25
.280 Halgar Mag., Various Makers, *Modern*	4.10	4.95	4.65
.280 Jeffery, Various Makers, *Modern*	4.75	6.50	6.00
.280 Rem., Various Makers, *Modern*	.75	1.05	.75
.280 Ross, Various Makers, *Modern*	3.25	3.95	3.65
.280/30 Experimental, Various Makers, Military, *Modern*	8.75	10.50	9.50
.284 Win., Various Makers, *Modern*	.75	1.05	.75
.295 Rook, Various Makers, *Modern*	1.10	1.55	1.15
.297/.230 Morris, Various Makers, *Modern*	1.05	1.40	1.10

	V.G.	Exc.	Prior Edition Exc. Value
.297/.230 Morris Short, Various Makers, *Modern*	$1.00	$1.20	$1.00
.297/.250 Rook, Various Makers, *Modern*	1.10	1.55	1.15
.297 R. F. Revolver, Various Makers, *Modern*	4.00	4.75	4.25
.30 Carbine, Various Makers, *Modern*	.50	.75	.55
.30 Carbine, Various Makers, Military, *Modern*	.55	.65	.45
.30 Cup Primed Cartridge, Various Makers, *Curio*	1.55	2.25	7.75
.30 H & H Super Mag. Flanged, Various Makers, *Modern*	2.75	4.25	3.75
.30 Long R.F., Merwin Cone Base, *Antique*	25.00	32.00	29.00
.30 Long R.F., Various Makers, *Antique*	1.90	2.75	2.25
.30 Luger, Various Makers, *Modern*	.50	.75	.55
.30 Newton, Soft Point Bullet, *Modern*	2.75	3.50	3.00
.30 Pederson, Various Makers, Military, *Modern*	3.00	3.75	3.25
.30 Rem., Various Makers, *Modern*	.65	.95	.75
.30 Short R.F., Various Makers, *Curio*	3.25	4.95	4.25
.30-03 Springfield, Various Makers, *Curio*	1.50	2.75	2.25
.30-06 Springfield, Various Makers, *Modern*	.75	1.10	.80
.30-06 Springfield, Various Makers, Military, *Modern*	.45	.65	.45
.30-06 Springfield, Accelerator, *Modern*	.75	1.20	.90
.30-06 Springfield, Flare Cartridge, Various Makers, *Modern*	2.25	2.75	2.50
.30-30 Wesson, Lead Bullet, *Curio*	26.00	29.75	27.25
.30-30 Win., Various Makers, *Modern*	.75	.95	.65
.30-30 Win., Bicentennial, Various Makers, *Modern*	.75	.95	.75
.30-30 Win., Flare Cartridge, Various Makers, *Modern*	2.25	3.00	2.50
.30-40 Krag, Various Makers, *Modern*	.80	1.10	.80
.300 AMU Mag., Various Makers, Military, *Modern*	2.75	3.50	3.00
.300 Hoffman Mag., Soft Point Bullet, *Modern*	3.50	4.25	3.75
.300 H & H Mag., Various Makers, *Modern*	.85	1.40	1.10
.300 Rook, Various Makers, *Modern*	1.35	1.65	1.35
.300 Savage, Various Makers, *Modern*	.90	1.10	.80
.300 Sherwood, Various Makers, *Modern*	2.75	3.50	3.00
.300 Wby. Mag., *Modern*	1.25	1.80	1.40
.300 Win. Mag., Various Makers, *Modern*	1.10	1.50	1.10
.303/.22, Soft Point Bullet, *Modern*	7.50	10.00	9.00
.303 British, Various Makers, *Modern*	.90	1.10	.80
.303 Lewis Rimless, Various Makers, Military, *Modern*	3.90	4.40	4.80
.303 Mag., Various Makers, *Modern*	4.25	4.75	4.25
.303 Savage, Various Makers, *Modern*	.90	1.10	.80
.305 Rook, Various Makers, *Modern*	2.00	2.50	2.00
.308 Norma Mag., Various Makers, *Modern*	1.65	1.85	1.55
.308 Win., Various Makers, *Modern*	.90	1.10	.80
.308 Win., Various Makers, Military, *Modern*	.55	.70	.50
.308 Win., Flare Cartridge, Various Makers, *Modern*	2.25	2.75	2.50

	V.G.	Exc.	Prior Edition Exc. Value
.31 Eley R.F., Lead Bullet, Dished Base, *Modern*	$12.00	$17.00	$15.00
.31 Crispin, Patent Ignition, *Antique*	165.00	195.00	165.00
.31 Milbank, Patent Ignition, *Antique*	57.50	62.50	57.50
.31 Theur, Patent Ignition, *Antique*	15.00	16.90	14.30
.31 Volcanic, Patent Ignition, *Antique*	17.50	19.50	16.50
.310 Cadet, Various Makers, *Modern*	1.75	2.25	1.75
.318 Rimless N.E., Various Makers, *Modern*	2.00	2.35	1.95
.32 ACP, Various Makers, *Modern*	.45	.65	.45
.32 Ballard Extra Long, Lead Bullet, *Curio*	1.60	1.80	1.50
.32 Colt New Police, Various Makers, *Modern*	.50	.65	.45
.32 Extra Long R.F., Various Makers, *Curio*	6.00	8.00	7.00
.32 Extra Short R.F., Lead Bullet, *Antique*	1.20	1.40	1.10
.32 Ideal, Lead Bullet, *Curio*	1.65	2.00	1.50
.32 Teat-Fire Cartridge, Various Makers, *Curio*	3.80	4.25	3.75
.32 L.F., Various Makers, #52 Allen, *Curio*	7.90	8.55	7.85
.32 Long Colt, Various Makers, *Modern*	.45	.60	.40
.32 Long R.F., Various Makers, *Modern*	7.25	9.00	8.00
.32 Long R.F., Shotshell, *Curio*	.65	.75	.55
.32 Long Rifle, Lead Bullet, *Antique*	4.50	5.25	4.75
.32 Rem., Various Makers, *Modern*	.90	1.10	.80
.32 Rem. Rimless, Various Makers, *Modern*	1.05	1.20	.90
.32 S & W, Various Makers, *Modern*	.35	.45	.35
.32 S & W, Shotshell, Various Makers, *Modern*	.45	.55	.35
.32 S & W, Blank Cartridge, Various Makers, *Modern*	.25	.30	.25
.32 S & W Long, Various Makers, *Modern*	.35	.45	.35
.32 Short Colt, Various Makers, *Modern*	.45	.45	.35
.32 Short R.F., Various Makers, *Modern*	.40	.50	.40
.32 Win. Self-Loading, Various Makers, *Modern*	.90	1.10	.80
.32 Win. Special, Various Makers, *Modern*	.90	1.10	.80
.32-20 WCF, Lead Bullet, Various Makers, *Modern*	.90	1.10	.90
.32-20 WCF, Jacketed Bullet, Various Makers, *Modern*	1.65	1.70	1.30
.32-20 Rem., Lead Bullet, *Curio*	4.75	5.35	4.65
.32-35 Stevens & Maynard, Lead Bullet, *Curio*	4.25	4.75	4.50
.32-40 Bullard, Lead Bullet, *Curio*	3.00	3.50	3.00
.32-40 Rem., Lead Bullet, *Curio*	3.25	3.70	3.00
.32-40 WCF, Various Makers, *Modern*	.90	1.05	.80
.320 Rook, Various Makers, *Modern*	1.05	1.40	1.10
.320 Extra Long Rifle, Various Makers, *Modern*	2.75	3.25	2.75
.322 Swift, Various Makers, *Modern*	6.25	7.00	6.00
.33 BSA, Soft Point Bullet, *Modern*	3.75	4.50	4.00
.33 Win., Soft Point Bullet, *Modern*	1.95	2.15	1.75
.333 Flanged N.E., Various Makers, *Modern*	4.75	5.40	4.80

	V.G.	Exc.	Prior Edition Exc. Value
.333 Rimless N.E., Various Makers, *Modern*	$5.25	$5.70	$4.90
.338 Win. Mag., Various Makers, *Modern*	1.35	1.60	1.20
.340 Wby. Mag., *Modern*	1.50	1.75	1.45
.340 R.F. Revolver, Various Makers, *Modern*	2.75	3.25	2.75
.348 Win., Various Makers, *Modern*	1.50	1.80	1.40
.35 Allen R.F., Lead Bullet, *Curio*	14.50	17.00	15.00
.35 Newton, Soft Point Bullet, *Modern*	4.25	4.75	4.25
.35 Rem., Various Makers, *Modern*	.80	1.10	.80
.35 S & W Auto., Jacketed Bullet, *Curio*	1.35	1.60	1.20
.35 Win., Various Makers, *Modern*	3.25	3.75	3.25
.35 Win. Self-Loading, Various Makers, *Modern*	.85	1.10	.80
.35-30 Maynard, Lead Bullet, with Riveted Head, *Curio*	12.50	15.00	13.00
.35-30 Maynard, Lead Bullet, without Riveted Head, *Curio*	7.25	8.00	7.00
.35-40 Maynard, Various Makers, *Curio*	15.00	16.50	13.50
.350 Rem. Mag., Various Makers, *Modern*	1.45	1.70	1.30
.350 Rigby, Various Makers, *Modern*	3.75	4.50	4.00
.351 Win. Self-Loading, Various Makers, *Modern*	2.35	2.70	2.10
.357 Magnum, Lead Bullet, Various Makers, *Modern*	.55	.70	.50
.357 Magnum, Jacketed Bullet, Various Makers, *Modern*	.55	.70	.50
.358 Norma Mag., Various Makers, *Modern*	1.40	1.70	1.40
.358 Win., Various Makers, *Modern*	1.35	1.65	1.15
.36 L.F., #56 Allen, Various Makers, *Curio*	6.00	8.50	7.50
.36 Crispin, Patent Ignition, *Antique*	190.00	210.00	200.00
.36 Theur Navy, Patent Ignition, *Antique*	14.50	16.50	15.50
.360 #5 Rook, Various Makers, *Modern*	14.50	16.50	13.50
.360 N.E., Various Makers, *Modern*	2.25	2.50	2.00
.360 N.E. #2, Various Makers, *Curio*	3.00	3.50	3.00
.369 Purdey, Soft Point Bullet, *Curio*	6.75	7.50	7.00
.370 Flanged, Various Makers, *Modern*	2.10	2.30	2.00
.375 Flanged Mag. N.E., Various Makers, *Modern*	3.00	3.50	3.00
.375 Flanged N.E., Various Makers, *Modern*	4.25	4.45	3.65
.375 H & H Mag., Various Makers, *Modern*	1.75	2.00	1.60
.375 Rimless N.E. 2¼", Various Makers, *Curio*	1.50	1.70	1.50
.375/.303 Axite, Various Makers, *Curio*	3.25	3.55	2.85
.378 Wby. Mag., *Modern*	3.35	3.75	3.25
.38 ACP, Various Makers, *Modern*	.25	.50	.40
.38 AMU, Various Makers, Military, *Modern*	.80	1.00	.70
.38 Ballard Extra Long, Lead Bullet, *Curio*	2.15	2.50	2.00
.38 Extra Long R.F., Lead Bullet, *Curio*	6.00	6.50	5.50
.38 Long CF, Lead Bullet, *Curio*	.95	1.10	.80
.38 Long Colt, Various Makers, *Modern*	.50	.70	.50
.38 Long R.F., Various Makers, *Curio*	4.75	5.25	4.25

	V.G.	Exc.	Prior Edition Exc. Value
.38 S & W, Various Makers, *Modern*	$.45	$.65	$.45
.38 S & W, Blank Cartridge, Various Makers, *Modern*	.35	.50	.30
.38 Short R.F., Various Makers, *Modern*	3.75	4.25	3.75
.38 Short R.F., Shotshell, *Curio*	.65	.80	.60
.38 Short Colt, Various Makers, *Modern*	.35	.50	.30
.38 Special, Lead Bullet, Various Makers, *Modern*	.35	.50	.40
.38 Special, Flare Cartridge, Various Makers, *Modern*	2.25	2.75	2.25
.38 Special, Sub-Velocity Ammo, Various Makers, *Modern*	.35	.50	.30
.38 Special, Shotshell, Various Makers, *Modern*	.35	.50	.40
.38 Special, Blank Cartridge, Various Makers, *Modern*	.25	.30	.25
.38 Special, Tracer, Military, *Modern*	.50	.75	.55
.38 Super, Various Makers, *Modern*	.45	.65	.45
.38-40 Rem. Hepburn, Various Makers, *Curio*	3.70	4.40	3.80
.38-40 WCF, Various Makers, *Modern*	.80	.95	.75
.38-44, Various Makers, *Modern*	.50	.65	.45
.38-45 Bullard, Lead Bullets, *Curio*	6.00	6.75	5.75
.38-50 Ballard, Lead Bullet, *Curio*	5.75	6.40	5.80
.38-50 Maynard, Various Makers, *Curio*	14.50	16.50	13.50
.38-50 Rem. Hepburn, Lead Bullet, *Curio*	4.00	4.45	3.65
.38-55 Win. & Ballard, Various Makers, *Modern*	1.65	2.00	1.60
.38-56 Win., Lead Bullet, *Curio*	2.75	3.50	3.00
.38-72 Win., Lead Bullet, *Curio*	4.75	5.10	4.20
.38-90 Win. Express, Lead Bullet, *Curio*	6.75	7.75	7.25
.380 ACP, Various Makers, *Modern*	.45	.65	.45
.380 Revolver, Various Makers, Military, *Modern*	.50	.80	.60
.380 Revolver, Shotshell, *Modern*	1.25	1.55	1.15
.40-40 Maynard, Lead Bullet, *Curio*	12.50	16.00	13.00
.40-50 Sharps (Necked), Lead Bullet, *Curio*	6.50	7.25	5.75
.40-50 Sharps (Straight), Lead Bullet, *Curio*	5.50	6.05	4.65
.40-60 Marlin, Various Makers, *Curio*	15.00	18.00	14.00
.40-69 Maynard, Lead Bullet, *Curio*	17.00	23.00	19.00
.40-60 Win., Various Makers, *Modern*	4.75	5.00	4.00
.40-63 Ballard, Lead Bullet, *Antique*	8.50	9.50	8.00
.40-65 Win., Lead Bullet, *Curio*	4.75	5.40	2.80
.40-70 Ballard, Lead Bullet, *Curio*	6.10	6.95	4.65
.40-70 Maynard, Lead Bullet, *Curio*	20.00	25.50	20.50
.40-70 Peabody "What Cheer", Lead Bullet, *Curio*	37.00	41.00	33.00
.40-70 Rem., Lead Bullet, *Curio*	5.25	6.00	5.00
.40-70 Sharps (Necked), Various Makers, *Curio*	6.25	7.00	6.00
.40-70 Sharps (Straight), Various Makers, *Curio*	5.75	6.50	5.50
.40-70 Win., Lead Bullet, *Antique*	4.75	5.50	4.50
.40-72 Win., Various Makers, *Modern*	4.80	5.55	2.85

	V.G.	Exc.	Prior Edition Exc. Value
.40-75 Bullard, Lead Bullet, *Curio*	$7.25	$8.00	$7.00
.40-82 Win., Various Makers, *Modern*	3.75	4.25	3.25
.40-82 Win., Shotshell, Various Makers, *Modern*	5.25	6.00	5.00
.40-85 Ballard, Lead Bullet, *Curio*	6.50	7.25	6.75
.40-90 Ballard, Lead Bullet, *Curio*	7.50	10.00	8.00
.40-90 Peabody "What Cheer", Lead Bullet, *Curio*	57.00	62.00	60.00
.40-90 Sharps (Necked), Various Makers, *Curio*	7.50	8.25	7.25
.40-90 Sharps (Straight), Lead Bullet, *Curio*	14.50	16.00	13.00
.40-110 Win., Lead Bullet, *Curio*	27.00	32.00	25.00
.400 Nitro 3", Various Makers, *Modern*	7.50	8.25	7.25
.40/.350 Rigby Flanged, Various Makers, *Modern*	4.50	5.25	4.25
.400/.360 Purdey Flanged, Various Makers, *Curio*	4.50	5.25	4.25
.400/.375 H & H, Various Makers, *Modern*	4.50	5.25	4.25
.401 Herter Mag., Various Makers, *Modern*	1.25	1.70	1.30
.401 Win. Self-Loading, Various Makers, *Modern*	1.50	1.90	1.50
.404 N.E., Various Makers, *Modern*	4.50	5.00	4.00
.405 Win., Jacketed Bullet, *Modern*	1.75	2.25	1.75
.41 Long Colt, Wood Shotshell Bullet, *Modern*	2.00	2.30	1.80
.41 Long Colt, Various Makers, *Modern*	1.05	1.20	.80
.41 Long R.F., Various Makers, *Curio*	5.00	6.00	5.00
.41 Short C.F., Lead Bullet, *Modern*	.70	.85	.55
.41 Magnum, Jacketed Bullet, Various Makers, *Modern*	.50	.65	.55
.41 Magnum, Lead Bullet, Various Makers, *Modern*	.50	.70	.50
.41 Short R.F., Various Makers, *Modern*	3.75	4.20	3.25
.41 Swiss R.F., Various Makers, *Modern*	2.75	3.45	2.65
.41 Swiss R.F., Kynoch with Raised "C", *Antique*	5.50	6.00	5.00
.41 Volcanic, Patent Ignition, *Antique*	22.50	25.00	21.00
416 Ribgy, Soft Point Bullet, *Modern*	5.50	6.25	5.25
.42 Allen R.F., Lead Bullet, *Antique*	4.75	5.25	4.25
.42 Cup Primed Cartridge, Various Makers, *Curio*	9.75	10.75	9.25
.425 Westley Richards Mag., Various Makers, *Modern*	4.75	5.45	4.65
.44 AMP, Various Makers, *Modern*	1.25	1.60	1.20
.44 Bulldog, Lead Bullet, *Antiquet*	.95	1.20	.80
.44 Colt, Various Makers, *Modern*	1.25	1.60	1.10
.44 Crispin, Patent Ignition, *Antique*	150.00	180.00	175.00
.44 Evans Short, Various Makers, *Curio*	6.75	7.50	6.50
.44 Extra Long Ballard, Lead Bullet, *Curio*	10.00	12.50	10.50
.44 Henry R.F., Blank Cartridge, *Curio*	5.00	6.00	5.00
.44 Henry R.F., Lead Bullet, *Curio*	3.75	4.25	3.25
.44 L.F., #58 Allen, Various Makers, *Curio*	22.00	24.00	20.00
.44 Long R.F., Various Makers, *Curio*	5.50	7.00	6.00
.44 Russian, Lead Bullet, *Modern*	1.25	1.60	1.10
.44 S & W, Various Makers, *Modern*	.50	.65	.45

	V.G.	Exc.	Prior Edition Exc. Value
.44 S & W, Sub-Velocity Ammo, Various Makers, *Modern*	$.30	$.40	$.30
.44 Magnum, Various Makers, *Modern*	.80	1.05	.75
.44 Magnum, Shotshell, Various Makers, *Modern*	.75	.95	.75
.44 Short R.F., Lead Bullet, *Curio*	1.75	2.25	1.45
.44 Short R.F., Blank Cartridge, *Antique*	.60	.85	.55
.44 Theur, Patent Ignition, *Antique*	25.00	28.00	24.00
.44 Webley, Blank Cartridge, *Curio*	.90	1.10	.70
.44-100 Ballard, Lead Bullet, *Curio*	15.00	18.50	15.50
.44-100 Wesson, Lead Bullet, *Curio*	4.50	5.00	4.00
.44-40 WCF, Various Makers, *Modern*	.95	1.10	.80
.44-40 WCF, Shotshell, Various Makers, *Modern*	1.10	1.40	1.10
.44-60 Sharps, Lead Bullet, *Curio*	5.75	6.25	5.25
.44-60 Win., Lead Bullet, *Curio*	4.05	4.45	3.65
.44-70 Maynard, Lead Bullet, *Curio*	45.00	48.00	46.00
.44-75 Ballard Everlasting, Lead Bullet, *Curio*	4.50	5.00	4.00
.44-77 Sharps & Rem., Lead Bullet, *Curio*	5.50	6.25	6.25
.44-90 Rem., Lead Bullet, *Curio*	12.00	13.75	10.75
.44-90 Rem. Special, Various Makers, *Curio*	25.00	27.50	22.50
.44-90 Sharps, Various Makers, *Curio*	10.00	12.00	10.00
.44-95 Peabody "What Cheer", Lead Bullet, *Curio*	37.50	42.50	37.50
.440 Eley R.F., Lead Bullet, no Headstamp, *Modern*	.55	1.20	.90
.442 Eley R.F., Lead Bullet, no Headstamp, *Modern*	1.50	1.65	1.15
.444 Marlin, Various Makers, *Modern*	1.05	1.30	.90
.45 ACP, Various Makers, *Modern*	.55	.70	.50
.45 ACP, Military, Tracer, *Modern*	1.10	1.30	.90
.45 Auto-Rim, Various Makers, *Modern*	.55	.70	.50
.45 Colt, Various Makers, *Modern*	.55	.70	.50
.45 Colt, Wood Shotshell Bullet, *Modern*	2.25	2.75	2.25
.45 Danish R.F., Lead Bullet, no Headstamp, *Modern*	22.50	25.00	21.00
.45 S & W, Various Makers, *Modern*	3.75	4.50	3.25
.45 Teat-Fire Cartridge, Various Makers, *Curio*	57.50	62.50	57.50
.45 Webley, Lead Bullet, *Modern*	1.50	1.70	1.20
.45-100 Ballard, Various Makers, *Curio*	15.00	17.00	13.00
.45-100 Sharps, Lead Bullet, *Curio*	24.50	26.00	20.00
.45-125 Win., Lead Bullet, *Curio*	27.50	31.50	26.50
.45-50 Peabody, Lead Bullet, *Curio*	22.00	24.50	19.50
.45-60 Win., Lead Bullet, *Curio*	4.00	4.50	3.00
.45-70 Marlin, Various Makers, *Modern*	5.50	6.50	5.50
.45-70 Government, Various Makers, *Modern*	.85	1.10	.80
.45-70 Van Choate, Lead Bullet, *Curio*	31.00	36.50	35.00
.45-75 Sharps, Lead Bullet, (Rigby), *Curio*	15.00	18.00	14.00
.45-75 Sharps, Lead Bullet, *Curio*	10.00	12.00	10.00

	V.G.	Exc.	Prior Edition Exc. Value
.45-75 Win., Various Makers, *Modern*	$3.25	$3.70	$2.90
.45-80 Sharpshooter, Various Makers, *Curio*	3.50	4.00	3.00
.45-85 Marlin, Various Makers, *Modern*	6.25	7.00	6.00
.45-85 Win., Lead Bullet, *Curio*	5.75	6.50	5.50
.45-90 Win., Lead Bullet, *Curio*	4.00	4.45	3.65
.45-90 Win., Jacketed Bullet, *Curio*	4.75	5.15	4.25
.450 Gatling, Various Makers, *Modern*	6.50	7.00	6.00
.450 #2 N.E. 3½", Various Makers, *Modern*	10.75	12.25	10.75
.450 Long Revolver, Various Makers, *Curio*	2.75	3.25	2.25
.450 N.E. 3¼", Various Makers, New Make, *Modern*	5.50	6.00	5.00
.450 N.E. 3¼", Various Makers, *Curio*	6.00	6.50	6.50
.450 Revolver, Various Makers, *Curio*	1.50	1.75	1.25
.450 #1 Carbine, Various Makers, *Modern*	5.50	6.05	5.65
.450 Rigby Match 2.4", Soft Point Bullet, *Modern*	5.00	5.50	4.50
.450/.400 BPE, Various Makers, *Modern*	4.75	5.25	4.25
.450/.400 Mag. N.E. 3¼", Various Makers, *Modern*	6.25	6.70	5.90
.450/.400 N.E. 3", Various Makers, *Modern*	5.50	6.00	5.00
.454 Casull Mag., Various Makers, *Modern*	1.20	1.40	.90
.455 Revolver Mk 1, Jacketed Bullet, Military, *Modern*	.95	1.10	.80
.455 Webley Mk 2, Various Makers, *Modern*	1.25	1.60	1.10
.458 Win. Mag., Various Makers, Full Jacketed Bullet, *Modern*	2.25	2.75	2.25
.458 Win. Mag., Soft Point Bullet, Various Makers, *Modern*	1.50	1.80	1.50
.46 Extra Long R.F., Various Makers, *Curio*	22.50	26.00	22.00
.46 Extra Short R.F., Lead Bullet, *Curio*	27.50	32.50	27.50
.46 Long R.F., Lead Bullet, *Antique*	4.25	4.70	3.90
.46 Remington & Ballard, Lead Bullet, *Curio*	7.50	8.25	7.25
.46 Short R.F., Various Makers, *Curio*	7.25	8.00	7.00
.460 Wby. Mag., *Modern*	2.75	3.45	2.65
.470 N.E., Various Makers, *Modern*	5.75	6.50	5.50
.475 #2 N.E., Various Makers, *Modern*	8.25	9.00	8.00
.475 N.E., Various Makers, *Modern*	8.00	9.25	7.75
.476 N.E., Soft Point Bullet, *Modern*	8.50	9.25	7.75
5-in-One, Blank Cartridge, Various Makers, *Modern*	.70	.90	.70
.50 BMG, Various Makers, Military, *Modern*	2.10	2.40	1.80
.50 Rem., Various Makers, *Curio*	4.15	4.55	3.85
.50 Rem. Navy R.F., Various Makers, *Curio*	30.00	34.00	28.00
.50 U.S. Carbine, Various Makers, *Curio*	5.50	6.25	5.75
.50-100 Win., Various Makers, *Curio*	7.50	8.50	7.50
.50-110 Win., Lead Bullet, *Curio*	5.00	5.75	5.25
.50-115 Bullard, Lead Bullet, *Curio*	7.00	7.75	7.25
.50-140 Sharps, Lead Bullet, *Curio*	47.50	53.50	48.50
.50-140 Win. Express, Lead Bullet, *Curio*	115.00	135.00	125.00

	V.G.	Exc.	Prior Edition Exc. Value
.50-50 Maynard, Lead Bullet, *Curio*	$7.50	$8.25	$7.25
.50-70 Government R.F., Various Makers, *Curio*	35.00	44.00	38.00
.50-70 Musket, New Make, Various Makers, *Modern*	2.75	3.25	2.25
.50-70 Musket, Various Makers, *Curio*	16.50	19.00	15.00
.50-70 Musket, Shotshell, Various Makers, *Modern*	6.00	8.50	7.50
.50-90 Sharps, Lead Bullet, *Curio*	22.00	27.50	22.50
.50-90 Win., Various Makers, *Curio*	3.25	4.00	4.00
.500 #2 Express, Soft Point Blue, *Modern*	5.50	7.00	6.00
.500 Jeffery, Various Makers, *Modern*	20.00	24.00	20.00
.500 Irish Constabulary Revolver, Various Makers, *Modern*	25.00	29.50	24.50
.500 N.E. 3", Various Makers, *Modern*	5.50	6.25	5.25
.500 Nitro BPE, Various Makers, *Curio*	8.75	10.75	9.25
.500/.450 #1 Express, Various Makers, *Modern*	5.75	6.50	5.50
.500/.450 #2 Musket, Various Makers, *Modern*	4.00	4.75	4.25
.500/.450 Mag. N.E. 3¼", Various Makers, *Modern*	7.75	9.25	9.25
.500/.465 N.E., Various Makers, *Modern*	6.25	7.00	6.00
.505 Gibbs, Lead Bullet, *Modern*	8.25	9.50	8.50
.52-70 Sharps R.F., Lead Bullet, *Curio*	38.00	44.00	40.00
.54 Ballard R.F., Lead Bullet, *Curio*	52.50	55.50	48.50
.55-100 Maynard, Lead Bullet, *Curio*	45.00	51.00	45.00
.56-46 Spencer R.F., Various Makers, *Curio*	30.00	35.00	30.00
.56-50 Spencer R.F., WRA, Commercial, *Antique*	3.50	4.00	3.00
.56-52 Spencer R.F., Various Makers, *Curio*	4.50	5.35	4.45
.56-52 Spencer R.F., Shotshell, Various Makers, *Curio*	20.00	22.25	23.75
.56-56 Spencer R.F., Various Makers, *Antique*	7.50	8.25	7.25
.577 N.E. 2¾", Various Makers, *Modern*	8.75	10.25	9.25
.577 N.E. 3", Various Makers, *Modern*	10.50	11.25	10.25
.577 Snyder, Various Makers, *Modern*	5.25	6.50	6.00
.577 Snyder, Shotshell, Various Makers, *Modern*	7.50	8.25	7.25
.577/.450 Martini-Henry, Various Makers, *Modern*	6.25	7.00	6.00
.577/.500 3⅛", Various Makers, *Modern*	7.50	8.00	7.50
.58 Berdan, Various Makers, *Curio*	6.50	7.70	6.90
.58 Gatling R.F., Lead Bullet, *Curio*	30.00	35.00	30.00
.58 Joslyn Carbine R.F., Various Makers, *Curio*	37.50	42.50	37.50
.58 Mont Storm R.F., Various Makers, *Curio*	45.00	51.00	45.00
.58 U.S. Musket, Lead Bullet, *Curio*	20.00	24.00	20.00
.600 N.E., Lead Bullet, *Curio*	32.00	37.00	31.00
.70-150 Win., Cartridge Board Dummy, *Curio*	145.00	170.00	150.00
2mm Rimfire, Blank Cartridge, *Modern*	.25	.30	.20
2mm Rimfire, Lead Bullet, *Modern*	.40	.55	.45
2.8mm Kolibri, Jacketed Bullet, *Curio*	16.50	19.50	16.50
3mm Kolibri, Various Makers, *Curio*	18.00	23.50	18.50

	V.G.	Exc.	Prior Edition Exc. Value
4mm R.F., Lead Bullet, *Antique*	$.25	$.35	$.25
4.25mm Liliput, Jacketed Bullet, *Curio*	6.50	8.00	7.00
5.5mm Soemmerda, Various Makers, *Modern*	3.75	5.00	4.00
5.5mm Velo Dog, Lead Bullet, *Curio*	.90	1.10	.80
5.6 × 33 Rook, Various Makers, *Modern*	1.75	2.15	1.85
5.6 × 35R Vierling, Various Makers, *Modern*	1.60	1.70	1.10
5.6 × 50R Mag., Various Makers, *Modern*	1.50	2.05	1.45
5.6 × 50 Mag., Various Makers, *Modern*	1.25	1.75	1.45
5.6 × 52R, Various Makers, *Modern*	1.00	1.40	1.10
5.6 × 57, Various Makers, *Modern*	1.25	1.75	1.45
5.6 × 61 Vom Hofe Express, Soft Point Bullet, *Modern*	4.75	5.50	5.00
5.6 × 57R, Various Makers, *Modern*	1.25	1.85	1.55
5.6 × 61R Vom Hofe Express, Various Makers, *Modern*	5.25	6.00	5.00
5.7mm Target Pistol, Various Makers, *Modern*	4.75	5.45	4.65
5.75mm Velo-Dog, Various Makers, *Modern*	1.25	2.00	1.40
5.75mm Vel-Dog Short, Various Makers, *Modern*	3.00	3.85	2.95
5mm Bergmann, Various Makers, *Curio*	8.25	10.50	9.50
5mm Bergmann, Grooved, Various Makers, *Curio*	7.50	8.00	7.00
5mm Brun, Various Makers, *Modern*	20.00	24.00	18.00
5mm Clement, Soft Point Bullet, *Curio*	4.25	5.25	4.75
5mm French Revolver, Various Makers, *Modern*	1.15	1.40	1.00
5mm Pickert, Various Makers, *Modern*	18.00	23.00	19.00
5mm Rem. RFM, Jacketed Bullet, Modern	.20	.30	.25
6 × 58 Forster, Various Makers, *Curio*	8.75	9.50	9.00
6 × 58R Forster, Various Makers, *Curio*	4.25	4.95	4.45
6.35mm Pickert, Various Makers, *Modern*	5.50	6.25	5.75
6.5 × 48R Sauer, Various Makers, *Curio*	2.75	3.50	3.00
6.5 × 52 Mannlicher-Carcano, Various Makers, *Modern*	.90	1.10	.90
6.5 × 54 M.S., Various Makers, *Modern*	1.50	2.15	1.65
6.5 × 54 Mauser, Soft Point Bullet, *Modern*	2.75	3.50	3.00
6.5 × 55 Swedish, Various Makers, *Modern*	1.05	1.40	1.00
6.5 × 57, Various Makers, *Modern*	1.20	1.80	1.50
6.5 × 57R, Various Makers, *Modern*	1.20	1.80	1.50
6.5 × 58 Vergueiro, Various Makers, Military, *Modern*	5.00	6.25	5.75
6.5mm Dutch, Various Makers, Military, *Modern*	.20	.35	.25
6.5 × 58R Sauer, Jacketed Bullet, *Modern*	2.35	3.50	3.00
6.5mm Jap, Various Makers, *Modern*	.75	1.25	.95
6.5 × 68 Schuler, Various Makers, *Modern*	1.50	2.30	1.90
6.5 × 68R, Various Makers, *Modern*	2.25	3.00	2.50
6.5mm Bergmann, Various Makers, *Curio*	11.75	14.00	12.00
6.5mm Bergmann Grooved, Various Makers, *Curio*	7.50	9.05	7.35
6.50mm Mannlicher, Various Makers, *Modern*	6.50	7.25	6.75

	V.G.	Exc.	Prior Edition Exc. Value
6.8mm Gasser, Various Makers, *Modern*	$5.75	$6.50	$6.00
6.8mm Schulhof, Various Makers, *Modern*	3.50	4.35	3.95
6mm Lee Navy, Various Makers, Military, *Modern*	3.25	3.75	3.25
6mm Loron, Patent Ignition, *Antique*	4.25	4.75	4.50
6mm Flobert, 2 Piece Case, *Antique*	.70	1.00	.70
6mm Merveilleux, Various Makers, *Modern*	2.50	3.25	2.75
6mm Protector, Various Makers, *Modern*	1.85	2.40	2.00
6mm Rem., Various Makers, *Modern*	.85	1.10	.80
6.5mm Reg. Mag., Various Makers, *Modern*	1.20	1.60	1.20
7 × 57R, Various Makers, *Modern*	1.25	1.65	1.35
7 × 61 Norma, Various Makers, *Modern*	1.30	1.70	1.40
7 × 64 Brenneke, Various Makers, *Modern*	1.40	1.90	1.60
7 × 64, Various Makers, *Modern*	1.50	2.00	1.60
7 × 65R, Various Makers, *Modern*	1.75	2.05	1.65
7 × 72R, Various Makers, *Modern*	3.50	4.25	3.75
7 × 72R, Dummy Cartridge, *Curio*	3.25	4.00	3.50
7 × 73 Vom Hofe, Soft Point Bullet, *Modern*	9.50	11.75	9.95
7.25mm Adler, Various Makers, *Modern*	85.00	105.00	95.00
7.35mm Carcano, Various Makers, Military, *Modern*	.25	.35	.25
7.5 × 54 MAS, Various Makers, Military, *Modern*	.25	.30	.25
7.5 × 55 Swiss, Military, *Modern*	1.00	1.20	1.00
7.5mm Swedish Nagent, Various Makers, *Modern*	1.05	1.30	1.00
7.5mm Swiss Nagent, *Modern*	1.20	1.55	1.15
7.66mm Mauser Revolver, Various Makers, *Modern*	7.50	10.00	9.00
7.62 × 39 Russian, Various Makers, Military, *Modern*	.75	.90	.60
7.62 × 39 Russian, Various Makers, *Modern*	1.10	1.35	.85
7.62 × 54R Russian, Various Makers, *Modern*	.90	1.25	.95
7.62mm Nagent, Various Makers, Military, *Modern*	2.25	2.85	2.25
7.62mm Tokarev, Various Makers, Military, *Modern*	.95	1.20	.80
7.63 Mannlicher, Various Makers, Military, *Modern*	.25	.30	.25
7.63 Mauser, Various Makers, *Modern*	.30	.45	.35
7.65 Borchardt, Various Makers, *Modern*	3.25	3.75	3.50
7.65mm Francotte, Various Makers, *Modern*	28.00	32.50	27.50
7.65mm Glisenti, Various Makers, *Modern*	95.00	110.00	100.00
7.65mm Pickert, Various Makers, *Modern*	4.50	5.25	4.75
7.65 Roth-Sauer, Various Makers, *Curio*	3.50	4.00	4.00
7.65 × 53 Mauser, Military, *Modern*	.90	1.20	.90
7.65 Argentine, Various Makers, *Modern*	.95	1.25	.95
7.65 Argentine Navy Match, Military, *Curio*	37.50	42.00	38.00
7.7mm Jap, Various Makers, *Modern*	1.05	1.25	.95
7.7mm Bittner, Various Makers, *Modern*	35.00	39.00	34.00
7.8mm Bergmann #5, Various Makers, *Modern*	7.50	8.40	7.80

	V.G.	Exc.	Prior Edition Exc. Value
7.92 × 33 Kurz, Various Makers, Military, *Modern*	$1.25	$1.70	$1.40
7mm Baer, Various Makers, *Modern*	2.50	3.25	2.75
7mm Charola, Various Makers, *Modern*	6.50	7.25	6.75
7mm Flobert, Lead Bullet, *Antique*	.70	.95	.65
7mm French Revolver, Various Makers, *Modern*	1.75	2.10	1.70
7mm H & H, Soft Point Bullet, *Modern*	2.50	3.25	2.75
7mm Mauser, Various Makers, *Modern*	.85	1.20	.80
7mm Mauser, Various Makers, Military, *Modern*	.30	.50	.40
7mm Nambu, Various Makers, *Curio*	8.35	9.55	8.85
7mm Rem. Mag., Various Makers, *Modern*	.95	1.30	1.10
7mm Rem. Mag., Various Makers, Flare Cartridge, *Modern*	2.20	2.70	2.40
7mm Rigby Mag., Soft Point Bullet, *Modern*	3.10	3.75	3.25
7mm Target Pistol, Various Makers, *Modern*	2.25	2.95	2.65
7mm Vom Hofe S.E., Various Makers, *Modern*	7.50	9.25	8.75
7mm Wby. Mag., *Modern*	1.25	1.80	1.40
8 × 48R Sauer, Various Makers, *Curio*	4.50	5.25	4.75
8 × 50R Lebel, Various Makers, Military, *Modern*	.30	.50	.40
8 × 50R Mannlicher, Various Makers, *Modern*	2.25	2.95	2.65
8 × 51 Mauser, Various Makers, *Curio*	1.25	1.95	1.55
8 × 51R Mauser, Various Makers, *Curio*	6.50	7.40	6.80
8 × 56R Mannlicher, Various Makers, Military, *Modern*	4.95	6.75	6.25
8 × 56R Kropatschek, Various Makers, Military, *Curio*	.55	.70	.50
8 × 57 Jrs, Various Makers, *Modern*	1.25	1.70	1.40
8 × 57S, Various Makers, *Modern*	.95	1.15	.95
8 × 58R Krag, Jacketed Bullet, Military, *Modern*	3.50	4.15	3.55
8 × 58R Saver, Various Makers, *Curio*	3.75	4.75	4.25
8 × 60 Mauser, Various Makers, *Modern*	2.75	3.25	2.75
8 × 60S, Various Makers, *Modern*	1.75	2.30	1.90
8 × 64 Brenneke, Various Makers, *Modern*	2.25	2.75	2.25
8 × 68S, Various Makers, *Modern*	1.65	2.15	1.75
8 × 75, Various Makers, *Curio*	4.50	5.00	4.50
8 × 75R, Various Makers, *Curio*	3.75	4.50	4.00
8.1 × 72R, Lead Bullet, *Modern*	3.85	4.40	3.70
8.15 × 46R, Lead Bullet, *Modern*	1.25	1.65	1.35
8.15 × 46R, Soft Point Bullet, *Modern*	2.50	2.75	2.25
8mm Bergmann #4, Various Makers, *Modern*	17.50	20.00	16.00
8mm Bergmann-Simplex, Various Makers, *Modern*	2.50	3.25	2.75
8mm Dormus, Various Makers, *Modern*	27.50	32.50	21.50
8mm Gaulois, Various Makers, *Curio*	1.25	1.75	1.45
8mm Lebel Revolver, Various Makers, Military, *Modern*	.85	1.20	.80
8mm Lebel Revolver, Various Makers, *Modern*	1.65	2.10	1.70
8mm Kromar, Various Makers, *Modern*	44.75	49.50	46.50
8mm Mauser, Various Makers, *Modern*	.95	1.20	.80

	V.G.	Exc.	Prior Edition Exc. Value
8mm Mitrailleuse, Various Makers, *Modern*	$1.55	$1.95	$1.55
8mm Nambu, Various Makers, Military, *Modern*	3.75	4.40	3.80
8mm Pieper Revolver, Lead Bullet, *Modern*	1.75	2.10	1.70
8mm Protector, Various Makers, *Modern*	1.45	1.70	1.40
8mm Rast-Gasser, Various Makers, *Modern*	1.75	2.10	1.70
8mm Schulhof, Various Makers, *Modern*	6.50	7.20	6.80
8mm Steyr Revolver, Various Makers, *Modern*	58.00	65.00	65.00
8mm Roth-Steyr, Various Makers, *Modern*	1.75	2.10	1.70
9 × 56 M.S., Soft Point Bullet, *Modern*	1.35	1.65	1.35
9 × 63, Various Makers, *Modern*	3.50	4.25	3.75
9.3 × 53R Swiss, Lead Bullet, *Curio*	1.25	1.70	1.40
9.3 × 57, Various Makers, *Modern*	1.30	1.75	1.45
9.3 × 57R, Various Makers, *Modern*	4.50	5.25	4.75
9.3 × 62 Mauser, Various Makers, *Modern*	1.75	2.10	1.80
9.3 × 64 Brenneke, Various Makers, *Modern*	2.25	2.75	2.25
9.3 × 72R, Various Makers, *Modern*	2.25	2.75	2.25
9.3 × 74R, Various Makers, *Modern*	2.40	2.85	2.35
9.3 × 82R, Lead Bullet, *Modern*	2.75	3.50	3.00
9.3 × 82R, Soft Point Bullet, *Modern*	3.50	3.85	3.45
9.4mm Dutch Rev., Various Makers, *Modern*	3.75	4.25	3.75
9.5 × 57 M.S., Various Makers, *Modern*	2.25	2.75	2.25
9.5 × 60R Turkish, Lead Bullet, *Modern*	28.50	34.00	30.00
9mm Bayard Long, Various Makers, Military, *Modern*	.55	.70	.50
9mm Borchardt, Various Makers, *Modern*	72.50	80.00	75.00
9mm Browning Long, Various Makers, *Modern*	1.25	1.95	1.65
9mm Devisme, Patent Ignition, *Antique*	15.00	18.00	14.00
9mm Devisme, *Modern*	2.50	2.85	2.25
9mm Danish Ronge, Lead Bullet, *Modern*	.95	1.20	.90
9mm Flobert, Lead Bullet, *Antique*	.45	.60	.55
9mm Campo Giro, Various Makers, *Modern*	17.00	20.00	18.00
9mm Gasser-Kropatschek Rev., Various Makers, *Modern*	4.50	5.25	4.75
9mm Glisenti, Various Makers, *Modern*	1.25	1.95	1.65
9mm Bergmann, Jacketed Bullet, Military, *Modern*	.30	.55	.45
9mm Luger, Various Makers, *Modern*	.55	.70	.50
9mm Luger, Various Makers, Military, *Modern*	.35	.50	.40
9mm, Lead Bullet, *Modern*	5.25	5.95	5.65
9mm Makarov, Jacketed Bullet, Military, *Modern*	15.00	19.50	16.50
9mm Mauser, Various Makers, *Modern*	1.25	1.65	1.35
9mm Nagent, Various Makers, *Modern*	2.25	2.85	2.45
9mm Salvo Squeeze Bore, Various Makers, *Curio*	22.50	26.00	24.00
9mm Steyr, Various Makers, Military, *Modern*	1.05	1.30	1.00
10mm Hirst Auto Pistol, Various Makers, *Modern*	25.00	29.00	25.00

	V.G.	Exc.	Prior Edition Exc. Value
10mm Soerabaja, Lead Bullet, *Antique*	$4.00	$4.75	$4.25
10,15 × 61R Jarmann, Paper-Patched, Lead Bullet, *Curio*	5.50	6.40	5.80
10.3 × 65R Baenziger, Soft Point Bullet, *Modern*	4.75	5.50	5.00
10.4 Italian Revolver, Military, *Modern*	1.75	2.60	2.00
10.4mm Swiss Ordnance Rev., Various Makers, *Modern*	3.75	4.50	4.00
10.4 × 47R Italian Vetterli, Jacketed Bullet, *Modern*	1.25	1.70	1.30
10.6mm Schulhof, Various Makers, *Modern*	2.25	2.80	2.45
10.6mm Spanish Ordnance Rev., Various Makers, *Modern*	2.00	2.50	2.00
10.75 × 58R Berdan, Military, Various Makers, *Curio*	2.00	2.50	2.00
10.75 × 68 Mauser, Various Makers, *Modern*	2.25	2.75	2.25
10.75 × 73, Various Makers, *Modern*	2.50	2.85	2.45
19.8mm Montenegrin Rev., Various Makers, *Modern*	17.50	23.50	18.50
11 × 59R Gras, Jacketed Bullet, *Curio*	1.75	2.25	1.75
11 × 59R Gras, Lead Bullet, *Curio*	2.25	2.70	2.10
11.15 × 58R Werndl, Lead Bullet, *Modern*	5.75	6.50	6.00
11.15 × 60R Mauser, Lead Bullet, *Modern*	5.00	5.75	5.25
11.15 × 65R, Lead Bullet, *Modern*	3.75	4.25	3.75
11.2mm Gasser, Various Makers, *Modern*	7.50	10.00	9.00
11.43 × 50R Egyptian, Various Makers, *Modern*	2.75	3.50	3.00
11.43 × 50R Egyptian, Wood Shotshell Bullet, *Modern*	3.75	4.50	4.00
11.5 × 57R Spanish, Various Makers, *Modern*	3.75	4.50	4.00
11.5mm Montenegrin-Gasser, Various Makers, *Modern*	8.75	10.25	9.25
11.5mm Werder, Various Makers, *Modern*	7.25	8.75	8.25
11mm Danish Ordnance Rev., Various Makers, *Modern*	35.00	39.00	33.00
11mm Chassepot, Patent Ignition, *Antique*	6.00	6.75	6.25
11mm Devisme, Patent Ignition, *Antique*	15.00	18.00	14.00
11mm French Ordnance, Various Makers, *Curio*	1.25	1.55	1.25
11mm German Service, Various Makers, *Curio*	1.75	2.40	1.90
11mm Loran, Patent Ignition, *Antique*	3.50	4.25	3.75
11mm Mannlicher, Military, Paper-Patched Lead Bullet, *Curio*	.55	.75	.55
11mm Rapnael, Patent Ignition, Outside Primed, *Antique*	35.00	40.00	30.00
11mm Rapnael, Patent Ignition, Inside Primed, *Antique*	42.00	47.00	39.00
12.7 Russian M.G., Various Makers, Military, *Modern*	1.25	1.50	1.00
15mm French Rev., Various Makers, *Modern*	17.00	20.50	17.50
4 Ga., Various Makers, Paper Case, Shotshell, *Modern*	3.50	4.75	4.25
8 Ga., Various Makers, Paper Case, Shotshell, *Modern*	3.25	4.50	4.00